Praise for Upgrading and Repairing PCs, Tenth Anniversary Edition and Scott Mueller from current and future readers like you...

"**Scott Mueller's classic book just got better!** I've used earlier editions for over six years and have found this book to be the most useful hardware reference available for aiding in the solution of difficult PC computer problems. I highly recommend this book!"

RICHARD L. GABRIEL, SR. ENGINEER, RETIRED, General Electric Co.

"Scott Mueller's *Upgrading and Repairing PCs* is my **#1 resource tool**. I received my A+ Certification by studying his book. Without a doubt, the *Tenth Anniversary Edition* will lie on my computer work bench!"

BAUTE LANHAM, JR.

"**Scott's book has saved my life many times over!** My copy is dogeared from countless page turning. I still consider *Upgrading and Repairing PCs* the Bible of computer hardware. It's the only book I've ever needed for computer maintenance and the only manual of its kind I will ever buy."

RUSSELL CLARK

"**Accuracy, detail, and simplicity all in one!** This is one of few books I recommend to anyone—beginners and advanced alike."

EDMUND S.W. KIM

"This is the book I reach for whenever I need information on hardware or its interaction with software. It is clear, concise, accurate, up-to-date, and **a gold mine of information**... invaluable to everyone who works with personal computers, from the full-time professional to the hobbyist who wants to learn about the inner workings of the computer."

ALAN M. FOWLER, FIEAust CPEng, Melbourne, Australia

"Scott Mueller has done an incredible job to amass diverse info into a how-to manual for the experienced PC Guru as well as the aspiring student and curiosity seeker. Whether you have done many upgrades and repairs or are starting your first, this book gives you the technology, techniques, hints, and traps so you can ask the right question, the one that solves your roadblock."

PHIL LEE, PC SYSTEMS ENGINEER, Lee & Assoc.

"Scott Mueller's *Upgrading and Repairing PCs, Tenth Anniversary Edition* is a most valuable resource for finding answers to my PC questions. **It is the most exceptional book of its type**, and it covers about everything one might need to know about PCs. Every time I refer to the book, I easily find whatever I need along with in-depth coverage of the topic."

TYRONE DAVOODIAN

"*Upgrading and Repairing PCs* is **one of the best computer books I have ever used**. Scott Mueller's *Tenth Anniversary Edition* maintains the high quality of content that made the previous editions invaluable assets. The information on the newest CPUs and motherboards alone is easily worth the price of the book. It belongs on the desktop of every computer user, whether a beginner or expert."

WAYNE TOBA

"**BIGGER IS BETTER!** The several hundred new pages that were added dealing with microprocessors and motherboards are worth the admission. If you're a dedicated propeller head, grab this book and get up-to-date!"

PAUL F. PESCE

"This is the most concise and yet exhaustive upgrade book I have ever laid my eyes on. I could not put it down. I was overwhelmed by how up-to-date the information is for everyday practical use. The terms are easy to use for anyone just getting starting in the PC world. PC books for dummies, look out...this new edition is a knockout."

MARK BARBOUR, FINANCIAL SYSTEMS CONSULTANT

"There are approximately 12 lineal feet of bookshelf in the den devoted to computer technology. They are generally nice and clean and properly arranged. There is one tattered book handy on the workbench, and that is the **Gospel according to St. Scott**. This one is the motherload. You realize of course that it is roughly analogous to giving the keys to a new Lamborgini to one of my grandkids! I wonder if you have any idea how many thousands of us out here really depend on you?"

JACK WILLIAMS

"Once again, Scott has produced **THE definitive book on computers**. It is not only the most comprehensive and informative computer book that I have come across, but it also is written in a style that it is easy to understand. This is a must-read for anyone interested in this subject."

RICHARD DRAKE, PRESIDENT, Compucycle

"I haven't found a computing book more thorough and precise than *Upgrading and Repairing PCs*. Many hours of frustration have been saved through this book!"

PHILLIP DAVIS

"Scott Mueller has an uncanny ability to take very complex and wide-ranging material and make it VERY understandable. His newest book is yet another example of his thoroughness, being up-to-date, and hitting the mark for those of us involved with PCs. Scott's books always answer my questions. **I wouldn't touch, buy, open, or use a PC without having Scott's newest edition at my side.**"

JOHN P. COWAN, INTERNET FACILITATOR, Business Insurance Group

"If I'd had the book as a reference in the field, there is no doubt in my mind that I would have saved many hours of time. For me, this would more than justify three times the books price in saved time for my small, one-man operation."

BRETT HAVENER, COMPUTER TECH/BUSINESS OWNER

"Never have I felt compelled to send anyone a thank you until I touched Upgrading and Repairing PCs. If you're like me and your company depends on this information, you'll appreciate the value of having all this knowledge in just one place."

NELSON G. COE, PRESIDENT, Nelco Distribution Inc.

"With the new information, this is one book that will not be gathering dust on a bookshelf."

JAY BRATCHER, SYSTEM TECHNICIAN, Strategic Supply, Inc.

"Scott's book is simply the best on the market. It's clear and to the point, the most comprehensive volume to date. My business couldn't get by without it! It's the only true computer Bible I own."

RUSSELL ALLEN CLARK, Artistic Endeavors

UPGRADING
AND
REPAIRING PCs

Tenth Anniversary Edition

Scott Mueller

with Craig Zacker

Contents at a Glance

Upgrading and Repairing PCs Tenth Anniversary Edition

International Standard Book Number: 0-7897-1636-4

Library of Congress Catalog Card Number: 98-84282

Printed in the United States of America

First Printing: September 1998

00 99 98   4 3 2 1

Trademarks

Executive Editor
Jim Minatel

Acquisitions Editor
Jill Byus

Development Editor
Rick Kughen

Technical Reviewers
Kent Easley
Deb Fogle
Tyson Heyn
Russ Jacobs
Doug Klippert
Kevin Langston
Carl Larson
Pete Lenges
Bob Pierson
Pat Regan
John Rourke
Jeff Sloan

Managing Editor
Thomas F. Hayes

Project Editor
Gina Brown

Copy Editor
Julie McNamee

Indexer
Chris Wilcox

Software Development Specialist
John Warriner

Production
Maribeth Echard
John Etchison
Christy M. Lemasters

Contents

9 Audio Hardware   549

10 I/O Interfaces   583

19 File Systems and Data Recovery   1065

20 IBM Personal Computer Family Hardware   1099

If you have questions about PC hardware, suggestions for the next version of this book, or any comments in general, send them to Scott via e-mail at **scottmueller@compuserve.com**. Correspondence through standard mail takes him much longer to answer!

When he is not working on PC-related books or teaching seminars, Scott can usually be found in the garage working on his LT4-powered 1994 Impala SS, LT4-powered 1995 Caprice 9C1 (police package), or Buick Turbo V6-powered 1989 Trans Am, as well as various other performance car-related projects. He can also be found testing the vehicles at the local drag strip, or showing them off at car shows or the local cruise/drive-in scene.

About the Contributing Author:

Craig Zacker is a writer and editor and has worked as an administrator of Novell NetWare networks and as a PC support technician while operating a freelance desktop publishing business. Craig worked extensively on the integration of Windows NT into existing NetWare internetworks, and was employed as a technical writer, content provider, and Webmaster for the online services group of a large software company. Craig has authored or contributed to many books on operating systems and networking topics, and has published articles in top industry publications including *Windows NT Magazine*, for which he is a contributing editor. He can be contacted through his Web site at **http://www.zacker.com**, or at **craig@zacker.com**. Que and Scott would like to thank Craig for updating several chapters for this edition, and for writing Chapter 14, "Printers."

Acknowledgments

This *Tenth Anniversary Edition* is the product of a great deal of additional research and development over the previous editions. Several people have helped me with both the research and production of this book. I would like to thank the following people:

First, a very special thanks to my wife and partner, Lynn. This book continues to be an incredible burden on both our business and family life, and she has put up with a lot! Lynn is excellent at dealing with the many companies we have to contact for product information and research. She is the backbone of MTR.

Thanks to Lisa Carlson of Mueller Technical Research for helping with product research and office management. She has fantastic organizational skills that have been a tremendous help in managing all the information that comes into and goes out of this office. Thanks to John Rourke, who not only teaches many of the MTR seminars, but is also the designer and creator of the Discovery card—which is the first card on the market for troubleshooting IRQ and DMA conflicts.

Thanks to all the companies who have provided hardware, software, and research information that has been helpful in developing this book. Thanks to David Means for feedback from the trenches about various products and especially data-recovery information.

I would like to offer a special thanks to the people at Que who have made this book possible. Thanks also to all the editors and staff who work so hard to get these books out!

Thanks to all the readers who have e-mailed me with suggestions concerning this book; I welcome all your comments. A special thanks to Paul Reid who always has many suggestions to offer for improving the book and making it more accurate.

Finally, I would like to thank the more than ten thousand people who have attended my seminars; you may not realize how much I learn from each of you and your questions! Thanks also to those of you on the Internet and CompuServe forums with both questions and answers, from which I have also learned a great deal.

Scott Mueller, July 1998

About the Technical Reviewers

Kent Easley is a lecturer in computer science and mathematics at Sul Ross State University. He teaches introductory computer science, networking, and programming with Visual Basic. Kent is the network administrator for the department's Windows NT network. He also teaches mathematics.

Kent has two Masters' degrees: Library and Information Science, and Mathematics and Computer Science. He has experience as a reference and systems librarian. Kent began teaching at Sul Ross in 1996 after earning his second Master's degree in Computer Science and Mathematics. He is also a Microsoft Certified Professional.

Tyson Heyn is manager of product and technology communications for Seagate Technology, Inc. He dedicates most of his time to high-end storage products and technologies, including Seagate's Cheetah and Barracuda disc drives. Prior to Seagate, Tyson served within an industry sales function and freelanced his writings.

A resident of Santa Cruz, CA, and based at the company's Scotts Valley headquarters, Heyn has an extensive history with personal computing, and with published industry works dating back as far as 1989. He has studied Computer Engineering and Business Economics at University of California, Santa Cruz, and Church Leadership at Bethany Bible College. He can be contacted at **tysonheyn@aol.com**.

Doug Klippert is an independent contract trainer living in Tacoma, Washington. He is a Microsoft Certified Solutions Engineer and an expert Microsoft Office User Specialist in Word 97, Excel 97, and PowerPoint 97. Doug is the Credit Manager for a Public Utility and has a B.A. in Accounting and an MBA.

Carl Larson is a product line manager for the P6 family of microprocessors in Intel's Mircroprocessor Products Group. Carl joined Intel in 1990n as the Product Marketing Engineer for the Intel386 DX microprocessor. Since then Larson has held a variety of product marketing positions, including performance marketing, pricing and demand forecasting, and Intel 486 family product management. In 1994 Carl became the manager of Intel's pricing department. Since 1996 Carla has been a product line manager for the P6 family of microprocessors including the Pentium II Xeon, Pentium II, and

Celeron processors. Larson graduated from the University of Illinois in 1985 with a B.S. in Electrical Engineering and received a Master of Management degree from the Kellogg School of Management at Northwestern University.

Pete Lenges is a Technical Software Instructor for New Horizons Computer Learning Centers, one of the world's largest software training integrators. He is an A+ Certified Technician with a specialty in Microsoft Operating Systems as well as an MCT (Microsoft Certified Trainer) and MCP (Microsoft Certified Professional). He currently conducts both hardware and software classes at the Indianapolis facility and also assists in the everyday management of his company's LAN/WAN.

John P. Rourke is president of Allied Computer Products, Inc., a manufacturer of computer diagnostic hardware and software, and also serves on the board of directors of several other PC technology companies. With over 18 years in the PC industry, he currently travels across North America and Europe giving seminars in PC troubleshooting, data recovery, and internetworking. He is also involved with writing and delivering coursework in A+ Certification and ISO-9000 curricula.

John can be reached via e-mail at **john@allied-computer.com**.

Jeff Sloan manages the BIOS for Dimension desktop line of business for Dell Computers. Prior to his move to Dell, he worked at IBM for 15 1/2 years. He spent eight of those 15 years in PS/2 BIOS development and problem determination swat team. Jeff has a BS in computer science from the University of Pittsburgh in 1979. Jeff is currently working on an MS degree in computer science at Southwest Texas State University. Jeff has technically edited four MCP books, including two Peter Norton hardware books.

Tell Us What You Think!

As the reader of this book, *you* are our most important critic and commentator. We value your opinion and want to know what we're doing right, what we could do better, what areas you'd like to see us publish in, and any other words of wisdom you're willing to pass our way.

As the Executive Editor for the General Desktop Applications team at Macmillan Computer Publishing, I welcome your comments. You can fax, e-mail, or write me directly to let me know what you did or didn't like about this book—as well as what we can do to make our books stronger.

Please note that I cannot help you with technical problems related to the topic of this book, and that due to the high volume of mail I receive, I might not be able to reply to every message.

When you write, please be sure to include this book's title and author as well as your name and phone or fax number. I will carefully review your comments and share them with the author and editors who worked on the book.

Fax: 317-817-7070

E-mail: **hardware@mcp.com**

Mail: General Desktop Applications
           Macmillan Computer Publishing
           201 West 103rd Street
           Indianapolis, IN 46290 USA

- Special bus architectures and devices, including high-speed PCI (Peripheral Component Interconnect), AGP (Accelerated Graphics Port), and the 100MHz processor bus.

- Bus resources that often conflict such as Interrupt ReQuest (IRQ) lines, Direct Memory Access (DMA) channels, and Input Output (I/O) port addresses.

- Plug-and-Play architecture.

- Larger, faster hard drives and hard drive interfaces and technologies, including new IDE specifications such as ATA-3 and ATA-4 and the latest on all the variations of SCSI.

- Floppy drives and other removable storage devices such as Zip and LS-120 drives, tape drives, and recordable CDs.

- Increasing system memory capacity with SIMM and DIMM modules and increasing system reliability with ECC RAM.

- New types of memory, including Synchronous Pipeline Burst cache, EDO RAM, Burst EDO, Synchronous DRAM, and RAMBUS.

- Large-screen Super VGA monitors, high-speed graphics adapters, and 3D graphics accelerators.

- Peripheral devices such as sound cards, modems, DVD drives, and network interface cards.

- PC-Card and Cardbus devices for laptops.

- Laser and dot matrix printer features, maintenance, and repair.

- How all these components interact with today's popular operating systems.

This book also shows you how to troubleshoot the kind of hardware problems that can make PC upgrading and repairing difficult. Troubleshooting coverage includes IRQ, DMA channel, and I/O port addressees, as well as memory address conflicts. This book tells you how to avoid problems with these system resources, and how to make installing a new adapter board in your computer a simple Plug-and-Play operation. This book also focuses on software problems, starting with the basics of how DOS or Windows works with your system hardware to start up your system. You also learn how to troubleshoot and avoid problems involving system hardware, the operating system, and applications software.

This book is the result of years of research and development in the production of my PC hardware, operating system, and data recovery seminars. Since 1982, I have personally taught (and still teach) thousands of people about PC troubleshooting, upgrading, maintenance, repair, and data recovery. This book represents the culmination of many years of field experience and knowledge culled from the experiences of thousands of others. What originally started out as a simple course workbook has over the years grown into a complete reference on the subject. Now you can benefit from this experience and research.

What Are the Main Objectives of This Book?

Upgrading and Repairing PCs focuses on several objectives. The primary objective is to help you learn how to maintain, upgrade, and repair your PC system. To that end, *Upgrading and Repairing PCs* helps you fully understand the family of computers that has grown from the original IBM PC, including all PC-compatible systems. This book discusses all areas of system improvement such as floppy disks, hard disks, central processing units, and power-supply improvements. The book discusses proper system and component care; it specifies the most failure-prone items in different PC systems, and tells you how to locate and identify a failing component. You'll learn about powerful diagnostics hardware and software that enable a system to help you determine the cause of a problem and how to repair it.

The PC-compatible microcomputer family is moving forward rapidly in power and capabilities. Processor performance increases with every new chip design. *Upgrading and Repairing PCs* helps you gain an understanding of each of the CPU chips used in PC-compatible computer systems.

This book covers the important differences between major system architectures from the original Industry Standard Architecture (ISA) to the latest in PCI and AGP systems. *Upgrading and Repairing PCs* covers each of these system architectures and their adapter boards to help you make decisions about which kind of system you may want to buy in the future, and to help you upgrade and troubleshoot such systems.

The amount of storage space available to modern PCs is increasing geometrically. *Upgrading and Repairing PCs* covers storage options ranging from larger, faster hard drives to state-of-the-art storage devices. In addition, this book provides detailed information on upgrading and troubleshooting system RAM.

When you finish reading this book, you should have the knowledge to upgrade, troubleshoot, and repair almost all systems and components.

Who Should Use This Book?

Upgrading and Repairing PCs is designed for people who want a thorough understanding of how their PC systems work. Each section fully explains common and not-so common problems, what causes problems, and how to handle problems when they arise. You will gain an understanding of disk configuration and interfacing, for example, that can improve your diagnostics and troubleshooting skills. You'll develop a feel for what goes on in a system so that you can rely on your own judgment and observations and not some table of canned troubleshooting steps. This book is for people who are truly interested in their systems and how they operate.

Upgrading and Repairing PCs is written for people who will select, install, configure, maintain, and repair systems they or their companies use. To accomplish these tasks, you need a level of knowledge much higher than that of an average system user. You must subtlety throughout the rest of the book as any remaining references to specific IBM models and compatibility have been updated to refer to system types and families that are common to all PC vendors.

- The updating of Chapter 3, "Microprocessor Types and Specifications," involved a major reorganization of the chapter and adding some 50 pages of new coverage. The new organization looks at all the relevant processors (and coprocessors and processor upgrades) in terms of the family of processor they belong to. The coverage of Intel Pentium, Pentium Pro, and Pentium II processors has been strengthened with up-to-date listings of steppings, processors from AMD, Cyrix, and other vendors have been given more coverage, and cutting-edge features such as Dual Independent Bus (DIB) Architecture are explained in more detail. I hope that you will like the substantial additions of illustrations and photographs to better show items such as socket types, processor features, and markings.

- Chapter 4, "Motherboards and Buses," takes the new approach of covering the motherboards and the buses found on the motherboards together as one topic. In addition, you will find extensive new coverage of Pentium, Pentium Pro, and Pentium II chipsets, which form the basis of all modern motherboards. This chapter includes coverage of the features, capabilities, and limitations of the chipsets in common use today.

- Chapter 5, "Memory," has been reorganized to begin by looking at types of memory and how they are installed first. All of the more recent types of memory including EDO RAM and SDRAM are explained in more detail in this edition. You'll also find answers to often asked questions relating memory speed to processor speed and a more thorough explanation of why error checking is still an important memory feature. This chapter also features many new illustrations to make it easier to identify SIMM and SIMM types and how to insert them.

- Chapter 10, "I/O Interfaces," represents a major reorganization for the book. In this chapter, you will now find information about any standard input and output interface on the PC. This includes everything from standard serial and parallel ports to ATA (IDE), SCSI, USB, and FireWire.

- Chapter 12, "Magnetic Storage," takes what used to be three separate chapters about floppy drives, hard disk drives, and drive installation and treats this as part of the larger topic of magnetic storage. Everything about magnetic storage is covered here.

- Chapter 14, "Printers," is new to this edition. I thank the many readers who have suggested this recently (as well as their many other suggestions) helping to make this a reality.

- Chapters 17, "Diagnostics, Testing, and Maintenance," and 18, "Operating Systems Software and Troubleshooting," both have much new and different coverage. Much of this is a reflection of newer operating systems such as Windows 98. The fact that troubleshooting and configuration tools are less dependent on hardware system vendors (such as IBM or Compaq) and more generally are third-party software tools necessitates a new way to look at setup and testing.

- Chapter 19, "File Systems and Data Recovery," is substantially new for this edition.

- Chapter 21, "A Final Word," looks at the new A+ certification exam and how the various objectives of the exam are covered by the book.

Although those are the major changes to the core of the book, every chapter has seen substantial updates. I can say without hesitation that this edition represents the most major overhaul of this book since the original edition. In addition to those updates to the core chapters, you may also be interested in these major changes to the appendixes:

- Although there will always be some vendor with a new phone number or address, we have checked every vendor's contact information for Appendix A, "Vendor List." As always, if you notice any of these that have changed, contact me at the e-mail address listed in my biography and let me know the change.

- Appendix B, "Useful Hardware Web Sites," is new to this addition, listing Web sites that are of interest that aren't related to any of the specific vendors listed in Appendix A.

- Appendix C, "Glossary," has been greatly expanded. Over 100 new terms are listed in this edition to make it easier to look up and understand the ever-growing technical language of the PC field.

- By popular demand, the technical reference that was cut from the previous edition has been added back. You'll find all new tables of modern hard drive parameters, updated BIOS error codes, and much more to make this a valuable reference.

- If you have trouble keeping track of the meanings of abbreviations and acronyms, I hope you'll make extensive use of the new listing of these along with their expanded meaning.

- We've added a new index of vendors to make it easy to find references to products and technologies by vendor.

- The main index of the book is substantially improved. Although I'm sure most of you don't "read" the index, you can tell a good one from a bad one based on whether you can find what you are looking for in the book from the index. Thanks to a new indexing process at Que, this index is more detailed and comprehensive than any of the editions that preceded it.

The Tenth Anniversary Edition CD-ROMs

As if everything included in the printed book isn't enough, this edition contains two all-new CD-ROMs. Whether or not you have ever purchased a previous edition of this book with a CD-ROM, you'll find the new content on these CDs to be a valuable treat to supplement the book. Here is an overview of the content of the CDs:

- One of the hardest things to do in supporting hardware is finding documentation for legacy systems. Thanks to Micro House, that doesn't have to stop you any more. The CDs with this book contain a portion of Micro House's Support Source Hardware module. This fully searchable electronic database includes technical documentation showing configuration, and diagrams for today's most popular PC products. The portion included with this book includes drive parameters for over 3,600 hard drives and configuration and setup information for over 100 models each of modems, NICs, hard drive, drive controllers, and motherboards. The Support Source engine also links you to their Tech Crawler, which is a Web-based search engine tuned to index and search 1,200 hardware-related Web sites and their FCC ID locator, which helps you locate the company who manufactured any PC product by entering the FCC ID number found on the product.

■ Are you thinking about taking A+ certification classes or testing to improve your professional standing? The CD contains a tutorial preparing you for the new A+ core exam module. As A+ certification is rapidly becoming a criterion for employment in this industry, those of you looking at a career working with PCs will find this essential. Note that *Upgrading and Repairing PCs* has always been the most widely used and recommended reference in preparing for the A+ certification tests, and now it will be even more useful!

■ Are you an instructor or student using this book in a PC hardware class? If so, you don't have to buy a separate CD to get the workbook anymore. It's now included on the CDs with the book at no extra charge.

■ A new collection of digital videos showing key excerpts from my seminars and demonstrations of hardware procedures that just can't be shown in the printed book.

■ A collection of utilities from Micro House highlighted by their Image Cast LE. This program makes it a snap to duplicate entire hard drives (making up to three simultaneous copies) and is a must-have for anyone configuring PCs for end-user use.

A Personal Note

I am so excited about all the new changes in this edition, I can hardly wait for everybody to see it. I and everybody else at Que have worked hard to make this the best edition ever. I am so grateful to everybody who has helped me with this book over the last 10 years as well as all of the loyal readers who have been reading this book, many of you since the first edition came out. I have had personal contact with many thousands of you in the seminars I have been teaching since 1982, and all I can say is I enjoy your comments and even criticisms tremendously. Using this book in a teaching environment has been a major factor in its development. Some of you may be interested to know that I originally began writing this book all the way back in 1985; back then it was used exclusively in my PC hardware seminars before being published by Que in 1988. I just realized that I have been writing and rewriting this book almost continuously for more than 13 years! In the more than 10 years since it was first published, *Upgrading and Repairing PCs* has proven to be not only the *first* but absolutely the *best* book of its kind on the market, and now with the new *Tenth Anniversary Edition*, it is even better than ever. Your comments, suggestions, and support have helped this book to become the best PC hardware book on the market. I look forward to hearing your comments after you see this exciting new edition.

Scott

Chapter 1

Personal Computer Background

Many discoveries and inventions have directly and indirectly contributed to the development of the personal computer. Examining a few important developmental landmarks can help bring the entire picture into focus.

Personal Computing History

A modern digital computer is largely a collection of electronic switches. These switches are used to represent and control the routing of data elements called *binary digits* (or *bits*). Because of the on or off nature of the binary information and signal routing used by the computer, an efficient electronic switch was required. The first electronic computers used vacuum tubes as switches, and although the tubes worked, they had many problems.

The tube was inefficient as a switch. It consumed a great deal of electrical power and gave off enormous heat—a significant problem in the earlier systems. Primarily because of the heat they generated, tubes were notoriously unreliable—one failed every couple of hours or so in the larger systems.

The invention of the transistor, or semiconductor, was one of the most important developments leading to the personal computer revolution. The transistor was invented in 1948 by Bell Laboratories engineers John Bardeen, Walter Brattain, and William Shockley. The transistor, which essentially functions as a solid-state electronic switch, replaced the much less suitable vacuum tube. Because the transistor was so much smaller and consumed significantly less power, a computer system built with transistors was much smaller, faster, and more efficient than a computer system built with vacuum tubes.

The conversion to transistors began the trend toward miniaturization that continues to this day. Today's small laptop (or palmtop) PC systems, which run on batteries, have more computing power than many earlier systems that filled rooms and consumed huge amounts of electrical power.

In 1959, engineers at Texas Instruments invented the *integrated circuit (IC)*, a semiconductor circuit that contains more than one transistor on the same base (or substrate material) and connects the transistors without wires. The first IC contained only six transistors. By comparison, the Intel Pentium Pro microprocessor used in many of today's high-end systems has more than 5.5 million transistors, and the integral cache built into some of these chips contains as many as an additional 32 million transistors! Today, many ICs have transistor counts in the multimillion range.

In 1969, Intel introduced a 1Kbit memory chip, which was much larger than anything else available at the time. (1Kbit equals 1,024 bits, and a byte equals 8 bits. This chip, therefore, stored only 128 bytes—not much by today's standards.) Because of Intel's success in chip manufacturing and design, Busicomp, a Japanese calculator manufacturing company, asked Intel to produce 12 different logic chips for one of its calculator designs. Rather than produce 12 separate chips, Intel engineers included all the functions in a single chip.

In addition to incorporating all the functions and capabilities of the 12-chip design into one multipurpose chip, the engineers designed the chip to be controlled by a program that could alter the function of the chip. The chip was generic in nature, meaning it could function in designs other than calculators. Previous designs were hard-wired for one purpose, with built-in instructions; this chip would read from memory a variable set of instructions that would control the function of the chip. The idea was to design almost an entire computing device on a single chip that could perform different functions, depending on what instructions it was given.

The first microprocessor—the Intel 4004, a 4-bit processor—was introduced in 1971. The chip operated on 4 bits of data at a time. The successor to the 4004 chip was the 8008 8-bit microprocessor, introduced in 1972.

In 1973, some of the first microcomputer kits based on the 8008 chip were developed. These kits were little more than demonstration tools and did little except blink lights. In late 1973, Intel introduced the 8080 microprocessor, which was 10 times faster than the earlier 8008 chip and addressed 64K of memory. This was the breakthrough the personal computer industry had been seeking.

MITS introduced the Altair kit in a cover story in the January 1975 issue of *Popular Electronics* magazine. The Altair kit, considered to be the first personal computer, included an 8080 processor, a power supply, a front panel with a large number of lights, and 256 bytes (not kilobytes) of memory. The kit sold for $395 and had to be assembled. The computer included an open architecture bus (slots) that prompted various add-ons and peripherals from aftermarket companies. The new processor inspired other companies to write programs, including the CP/M (Control Program for Microprocessors) operating system and the first version of the Microsoft BASIC (Beginners All-purpose Symbolic Instruction Code) programming language.

IBM introduced what can be called its first *personal computer* in 1975. The Model 5100 had 16K of memory, a built-in 16-line by 64-character display, a built-in BASIC language interpreter, and a built-in DC-300 cartridge tape drive for storage. The system's $9,000 price placed it out of the mainstream personal computer marketplace, which was dominated by experimenters (affectionately referred to as *hackers*) who built low-cost kits ($500 or so) as a hobby. Obviously, the IBM system was not in competition for this low-cost market and did not sell well.

The Model 5100 was succeeded by the 5110 and 5120 before IBM introduced what we know as the IBM Personal Computer (Model 5150). Although the 5100 series preceded the IBM PC, the older systems and the 5150 IBM PC had nothing in common. The PC IBM turned out was more closely related to the IBM System/23 DataMaster, an office computer system introduced in 1980. In fact, many of the engineers who developed the PC at IBM had originally worked on the DataMaster.

In 1976, a new company called Apple Computer introduced the Apple I, which sold for $695. This system consisted of a main circuit board screwed to a piece of plywood. A case and power supply were not included. Only a few of these computers were made, and they reportedly have sold to collectors for more than $20,000. The Apple II, introduced in 1977, helped set the standard for nearly all the important microcomputers to follow, including the IBM PC.

The microcomputer world was dominated in 1980 by two types of computer systems. One type, the Apple II, claimed a large following of loyal users and a gigantic software base that was growing at a fantastic rate. The other type, CP/M systems, consisted not of a single system but of all the many systems that evolved from the original MITS Altair. These systems were compatible with one another and were distinguished by their use of the CP/M operating system and expansion slots, which followed the S-100 (for slots with 100 pins) standard. All these systems were built by a variety of companies and sold under various names. For the most part, however, these companies used the same software and plug-in hardware. It is interesting to note that none of these systems were PC-compatible, or Mac-compatible, the two primary standards in place today.

The IBM Personal Computer

At the end of 1980, IBM decided to truly compete in the rapidly growing low-cost personal computer market. The company established what was called the Entry Systems Division, located in Boca Raton, Florida, to develop the new system. This small group consisted of 12 engineers and designers under the direction of Don Estridge. The team's chief designer was Lewis Eggebrecht. The division developed IBM's first real PC (IBM considered the 5100 system, developed in 1975, to be an intelligent programmable terminal rather than a genuine computer, even though it truly was a computer). Nearly all these engineers had been moved to the new division from the System/23 DataMaster project, which in 1980 introduced a small office computer system that was the closest predecessor to the IBM PC.

Much of the PC's design was influenced by the DataMaster's design. In the DataMaster's single-piece design, the display and keyboard were integrated into the unit. Because these features were limiting, they became external units on the PC, although the PC keyboard layout and electrical designs were copied from the DataMaster.

Several other parts of the IBM PC system also were copied from the DataMaster, including the expansion bus (or input/output slots), which included not only the same physical 62-pin connector, but also almost identical pin specifications. This copying was possible because the PC used the same interrupt controller as the DataMaster and a similar direct memory access (DMA) controller. Also, expansion cards already designed for the DataMaster could easily be redesigned to function in the PC.

The DataMaster used an Intel 8085 CPU, which had a 64K address limit, and an 8-bit internal and external data bus. This arrangement prompted the PC design team to use the Intel 8088 CPU, which offered a much larger (1M) memory address limit, and an internal 16-bit data bus, but only an 8-bit external data bus. The 8-bit external data bus and similar instruction set allowed the 8088 to be easily interfaced into the earlier DataMaster designs.

Estridge and the design team rapidly developed the design and specifications for the new system. In addition to borrowing from the System/23 DataMaster, the team studied the marketplace, which also had enormous influence on the IBM PC's design. The designers looked at the prevailing standards, learned from the success of those systems, and incorporated into the new PC all the features of the popular systems—and more. With the parameters for design made obvious by the market, IBM produced a system that filled its niche in the market.

IBM brought its system from idea to delivery in one year by using existing designs and purchasing as many components as possible from outside vendors. The Entry Systems Division was granted autonomy from IBM's other divisions and could tap resources outside the company, rather than go through the bureaucratic procedures that required exclusive use of IBM resources. IBM contracted out the PC's languages and operating system to a small company named Microsoft. That decision was the major factor in establishing Microsoft as the dominant force in PC software today.

> **Note**
>
> It is interesting to note that IBM had originally contacted Digital Research (the company that created CP/M, then the most popular personal computer operating system) to have them develop an operating system for the new IBM PC, but they were leery of working with IBM, and especially balked at the nondisclosure agreement IBM wanted them to sign. Microsoft jumped on the opportunity left open by Digital Research, and as a result has become one of the largest software companies in the world. IBM's use of outside vendors in developing the PC was an open invitation for the aftermarket to jump in and support the system—and it did.

On Wednesday, August 12, 1981, a new standard was established in the microcomputer industry with the debut of the IBM PC. Since then, hundreds of millions of PC-compatible systems have been sold, as the original PC has grown into an enormous family of computers and peripherals. More software has been written for this computer family than for any other system on the market.

The IBM-Compatible Marketplace 17 Years Later

In the more than 17 years since the original IBM PC was introduced, many changes have occurred. The IBM-compatible computer, for example, advanced from a 4.77MHz 8088-based system to 300MHz or faster Pentium II-based systems—nearly *2,000 times faster* than the original IBM PC (in actual processing speed, not just clock speed). The original PC had only one or two single-sided floppy drives that stored 160K each using DOS 1.0, whereas modern systems easily can have 10G (10 billion bytes) or more of hard disk storage. A rule of thumb in the computer industry is that available processor performance and disk-storage capacity at least double every two to three years. Since the beginning of the PC industry, this pattern has shown no sign of changing.

In addition to performance and storage capacity, another major change since the original IBM PC was introduced is that IBM is not the only manufacturer of "PC-compatible" systems. IBM originated the PC-compatible standard, of course, and it continues to set standards that compatible systems follow, but the company does not dominate the PC market as it once did. More often than not, new standards in the PC industry are developed by companies and organizations other than IBM. Today, it is Intel and Microsoft who are primarily responsible for developing and extending the PC hardware and software standards, respectively. Some have even taken to calling PCs "Wintel" systems, owing to the dominance of those two companies.

▶▶　See "Who Controls PC Software," p. 16

▶▶　See "Who Controls PC Hardware," p. 18

Even so, there are literally hundreds of system manufacturers producing computers that are fully PC-compatible, not to mention the thousands of peripheral manufacturers whose components expand and enhance PC-compatible systems.

PC-compatible systems have thrived, not only because compatible hardware can be assembled easily, but also because the primary operating system was available not from IBM but from a third party (Microsoft). The core of the system software is the BIOS (Basic Input/Output System), and this was also available from third-party companies such as AMI, Award, Phoenix, and others. This situation allowed other manufacturers to license the operating system and BIOS software and to sell their own compatible systems. The fact that DOS borrowed the functionality and user interface from both CP/M and UNIX probably had a lot to do with the amount of software that became available. Later, with the success of Windows, there would be even more reasons for software developers to write programs for PC-compatible systems.

One of the reasons why Apple Macintosh systems will likely never enjoy the success of PC-compatibles is that Apple controls all the software (BIOS and OS), and until recently had not licensed any of it to other companies for use in compatible systems. Apple now seems to recognize this flawed stance because they have begun to license this software. However, it seems too late for them to effectively compete with the PC-compatible juggernaut. It is fortunate for the computing public as a whole that IBM created a more open and extendible standard. The competition among manufacturers and vendors of PC-compatible systems is the reason why such systems offer so much performance and so many capabilities for the money.

The IBM-compatible market continues to thrive and prosper. New technology continues to be integrated into these systems, enabling them to grow with the times. These systems offer a high value for the money and have plenty of software available to run on them. It's a safe bet that PC-compatible systems will dominate the personal computer marketplace for the next 15 to 20 years.

Chapter 2

PC Components, Features, and System Design

This chapter defines what a "PC" really is and then continues by defining the types of PCs on the market. In addition, the chapter gives an overview of the components found in a modern PC.

What Is a PC?

I normally ask the question, "What is a PC?" when I begin one of my PC hardware seminars. Of course, most people immediately answer that PC stands for personal computer, which in fact it does. Most would define a personal computer as any small computer system purchased and used by an individual. Unfortunately, that definition is not nearly precise or accurate enough for our purposes. I would agree that a PC is a personal computer, but certainly not all personal computers are PCs. For example, an Apple Macintosh system is clearly a personal computer, but nobody I know would call a Mac a PC, least of all Mac users! For the true definition of what a PC is, you must look deeper.

Calling something a PC implies that it is something much more specific than just any personal computer. One thing it implies is an origin in the first IBM PC from 1981. In fact, I'll go so far as to say IBM literally *invented* the PC; that is, they designed and created the first one. However, it is also clear that IBM did not invent the personal computer. (The historical origins of the personal computer are in the MITS Altair introduced in 1975.) Some people would take this further and define a PC as any personal computer that is "IBM compatible." In fact, many years back we used to call PCs either IBM compatibles or IBM clones, in essence paying homage to the origins of the PC at IBM.

The reality is that although IBM clearly designed and created the first PC in 1981, and controlled the development and evolution of the PC standard for several years thereafter, IBM is no longer in control of the PC standard. IBM lost control of the PC standard in 1987 when they introduced their PS/2 line

In retrospect, this is exactly why there are no clones or compatibles of the Apple Macintosh system. It is not that Mac systems cannot be duplicated; in fact, the Mac hardware is fairly simple and easy to produce using off-the-shelf parts. The real problem is that Apple owns the MAC OS, and because they have seen fit not to license it, no other company can sell an Apple-compatible system. Also, the Mac BIOS and OS are very tightly integrated; their BIOS is very large, complex, and is essentially a part of the OS. This has allowed both their BIOS and OS to escape any clean room duplication efforts, so without their blessing (licensing), no Mac clones are likely to ever exist.

Because IBM did not own DOS (or Windows) but licensed it non-exclusively from Microsoft, anybody else who wanted to put MS-DOS or Windows on their system could license the code from Microsoft. This allowed any company who wanted to develop an IBM-compatible system to circumvent IBM completely, and produce a functionally identical machine whether IBM liked it or not. Because people desire backward compatibility, when one company controls the operating system, they naturally control all the software that goes around it, including everything from drivers to application programs. As long as we use PCs with Microsoft operating systems, they will have the upper hand in controlling PC software.

Who Controls PC Hardware?

Although it is clear that Microsoft has always controlled PC software by virtue of their control over the PC operating system, what about hardware? It is easy to see that IBM controlled the PC hardware standard up through 1987. After all, IBM invented the core PC motherboard design, expansion bus slot architecture (8/16-bit ISA bus), serial and parallel port design, video card design through VGA and XGA standards, floppy and hard disk interface and controller designs, power supply design, keyboard interface and design, mouse interface, and even the physical shapes (form factors) of everything from the motherboard to the expansion cards, power supplies, and system chassis. All these pre-1987 IBM design features are still influencing modern systems today.

But the real question is what company has been responsible for creating and inventing new PC hardware designs, interfaces, and standards? When I ask that question, I normally see some hesitation in the response—some people say Microsoft (but they control the software not the hardware), some say Compaq or name a few other big name system manufacturers, and a few surmise the correct answer—Intel.

I can see why many people don't immediately realize this, I mean how many people actually own an Intel PC? No, not just one that says "intel inside" on it (which refers only to the system having an Intel processor), but I mean a system that was designed and built by Intel or even purchased through them. Believe it or not, I would say that most people today *do* have Intel PCs!

Certainly that does not mean that they purchased their systems from Intel, because it is well known that Intel does not sell complete PCs. You cannot currently order a system from Intel, nor purchase an Intel brand system from somebody else. What I am talking about is the motherboard. In my opinion, the single most important part in a system is the motherboard, and I'd say that whoever made your motherboard should be considered the legitimate manufacturer of your system.

▶▶ See "Motherboards" p. 167

The top tier system manufacturers do make their own motherboards. According to *Computer Reseller News* magazine, the top three desktop systems manufacturers for the last several years have consistently been Compaq, Packard Bell, and IBM. These companies do design and manufacture their own motherboards, and many other system components. In some cases they even design their own chips and chipset components for their own boards. Although sales are high for these individual companies, there is a larger overall segment of the market that can be called the second tier.

In the second tier we find companies who do not really manufacture systems but assemble them. That is, they purchase motherboards, cases, power supplies, disk drives, peripherals, and so on, and assemble and market the components together as complete systems. Dell, Gateway, and Micron are some of the larger system assemblers today, but there are hundreds more who can be listed. In overall total volume, this ends up being the largest segment of the PC marketplace today. What is interesting about the second tier systems is that with very few exceptions, you and I can purchase the same motherboards and other components any of the second tier manufacturers can (although we will pay more than they do). We can also assemble a virtually identical system from scratch ourselves, but that is a story for another chapter, and is covered in Chapter 16, "Building or Upgrading Systems."

If Gateway, Dell, Micron, and others do not manufacture their own motherboards, then who does? You guessed it—Intel. Not only do those specific companies use pretty much exclusively Intel motherboards, if you check around you'll find today that *most* of the systems on the market in the second tier come with Intel motherboards. I just checked a review of 10 Pentium II systems in the current *Computer Shopper* magazine, and I'm not kidding, eight out of the 10 systems they evaluated had Intel motherboards. In fact, those eight used the exact *same* Intel motherboard. That means that these systems differ only in the cosmetics of the exterior case assembly and by what video card, disk drives, keyboards, and so on the assembler used that week.

The other two systems in the review had boards from manufacturers other than Intel, but even those boards used Intel Pentium II processors and Intel motherboard chipsets, which together comprise more than 90% of the motherboard cost.

▶▶ See "Pentium II," p. 140
▶▶ See "Chipsets," p. 183

How and when did this happen? Of course, Intel has always been the dominant PC processor supplier since IBM chose the Intel 8088 CPU in the original IBM PC in 1981. By controlling the processor they naturally had control of the chips needed to integrate host bus on the motherboard. The processor data bus or host bus is also sometimes referred to as the local bus because it is local to the processor that is connected directly to it. Any other devices connected to the host bus essentially appear as if they are directly connected to the processor as well. If the processor has a 32-bit data bus, then the motherboard must be wired to have a 32-bit processor host bus. This would mean that the system could move 32-bits worth of data into or out of the processor in a single cycle.

Different processors have different data bus widths, and the motherboards designed to accept them would require a processor host bus with a matching width. Table 2.1 lists all the Intel processors and their data bus widths.

Table 2.1 Intel Processors and Their Data Bus Widths

Processor	Data Bus Width
8088	8-bit
8086	16-bit
286	16-bit
386SX	16-bit
386SL	16-bit
386DX	32-bit
486SX	32-bit
486SX2	32-bit
487SX	32-bit
486DX	32-bit
486DX2	32-bit
486DX4	32-bit
486Pentium OD	32-bit
Pentium 60/66	64-bit
Pentium 75-200	64-bit
Pentium MMX	64-bit
Pentium Pro	64-bit
Pentium II	64-bit

A common misconception arises when discussing processor widths. Although the Pentium processors all have 64-bit data bus widths, their internal registers are only 32 bits wide and they process 32-bit commands and instructions. Thus, from a software point-of-view, all chips from the 386 to the Pentium II have 32-bit registers and execute 32-bit instructions. From the electronic or physical perspective, these 32-bit software capable processors have been available in physical forms with 16-bit (386SX), 32-bit (386DX, 486), and 64-bit (Pentium) data bus widths. The data bus width is the major factor in motherboard and memory system design as that dictates how many bits move in and out of the chip in one cycle.

The future P7 processor, code-named Merced, will have a new 64-bit instruction set but will also process the same 32-bit instructions as 386 through Pentium processors do. It is not known whether Merced will have a 64-bit data bus like the Pentium or whether it will include a 128-bit data bus as some suspect.

▶▶ See "Processor Specifications," p. 31

From Table 2.1 you can see that 486 systems have a 32-bit processor bus, which would mean that any 486 motherboard would have a 32-bit processor host bus. Pentium processors, whether they are the original Pentium, Pentium MMX, Pentium Pro, or even the Pentium II, all have 64-bit data busses, which means that Pentium motherboards have a 64-bit processor host bus. You cannot put a 64-bit processor on a 32-bit motherboard, which is one reason that 486 motherboards cannot accept true Pentium processors.

As you can see from this table we can break systems down into the following hardware categories:

- 8-bit
- 16-bit
- 32-bit
- 64-bit

What is interesting is that besides the bus width, the 16-bit through 64-bit systems are remarkably similar in basic design and architecture. The older 8-bit systems are very different, however. This gives us two basic system types, or *classes*, of hardware:

- 8-bit (PC/XT-class) systems
- 16/32/64-bit (AT-class) systems

PC stands for *personal computer*, *XT* stands for an *eXTended PC*, and *AT* stands for an *advanced technology PC*. The terms *PC*, *XT*, and *AT* as used here are taken from the original IBM systems of those names. The XT basically was a PC system that included a hard disk for storage in addition to the floppy drive(s) found in the basic PC system. These systems had an 8-bit 8088 processor and an 8-bit Industry Standard Architecture (ISA) Bus for system expansion. The *bus* is the name given to expansion slots in which additional plug-in circuit boards can be installed. The 8-bit designation comes from the fact that the ISA Bus found in the PC/XT class systems can send or receive only 8 bits of data in a single cycle. The data in an 8-bit bus is sent along eight wires simultaneously, in parallel.

▶▶ See "The ISA Bus," p. 233

16-bit and greater systems are said to be *AT-class*, which indicates that they follow certain standards and follow the basic design first set forth in the original IBM AT system.

AT is the designation IBM applied to systems that first included more advanced 16-bit (and later, 32- and 64-bit) processors and expansion slots. AT-class systems must have any processor that is compatible with Intel 286 or higher processors (including the 386, 486, Pentium, Pentium Pro, and Pentium II processors) and must have a 16-bit or greater system bus. The system bus architecture is central to the AT system design along with the basic memory architecture, Interrupt ReQuest (IRQ), DMA (Direct Memory Access), and I/O port address design. All AT-class systems are similar in the way these resources are allocated and how they function.

The first AT-class systems had a 16-bit version of the ISA Bus, which is an extension of the original 8-bit ISA Bus found in the PC/XT-class systems. Eventually, several expansion slot or bus designs were developed for AT-class systems, including those in the following list:

- 16-bit ISA bus

- 16/32-bit Extended ISA (EISA) bus

- 16/32-bit PS/2 Micro Channel Architecture (MCA) bus

- 16-bit PC-Card (PCMCIA) bus

- 32-bit Cardbus (PCMCIA) bus

- 32-bit VESA Local (VL) bus

- 32/64-bit Peripheral Component Interconnect (PCI) bus

- 32-bit Accelerated Graphics Port (AGP)

A system with any of these types of expansion slots is by definition an AT-class system, regardless of the actual Intel or Intel-compatible processor used. AT-type systems with 386 or higher processors have special capabilities not found in the first generation of 286-based ATs. The 386 and higher systems have distinct capabilities regarding memory addressing, memory management, and possible 32- or 64-bit wide access to data. Most systems with 386DX or higher chips also have 32-bit bus architectures to take full advantage of the 32-bit data transfer capabilities of the processor.

Most PC systems today incorporate 16-bit ISA slots for backward compatibility and lower function adapters, and PCI slots for truly high performance adapters. Most portable systems use PC-Card and Cardbus slots in the portable unit, and ISA and PCI slots in optional docking stations.

Chapter 4, "Motherboards and Buses," contains a great deal of in-depth information on these and other PC system buses, including technical information such as pinouts, performance specifications, and bus operation and theory.

Table 2.2 summarizes the primary differences between the older 8-bit (PC/XT) systems and a modern AT system. This information distinguishes between these systems and includes all IBM and compatible models.

Table 2.2 Differences Between PC/XT and AT Systems		
System Attributes	**(8-bit) PC/XT Type**	**(16/32/64-bit) AT Type**
Supported processors	All x86 or x88	286 or higher
Processor modes	Real	Real/Protected/Virtual Real
Software supported	16-bit only	16- or 32-bit
Bus slot width	8-bit	16/32/64-bit
Slot type	ISA only	ISA, EISA, MCA, PC-Card, Cardbus, VL-Bus, PCI
Hardware interrupts	8 (6 usable)	16 (11 usable)
DMA channels	4 (3 usable)	8 (7 usable)
Maximum RAM	1M	16M/4G or more
Floppy controller speed	250 Kbit/sec	250/300/500/ 1,000 Kbit/sec
Standard boot drive	360K or 720K	1.2M/1.44M/2.88M
Keyboard interface	Unidirectional	Bidirectional
CMOS memory/clock	None standard	MC146818-compatible
Serial-port UART	8250B	16450/16550A

The easiest way to identify a PC/XT (8-bit) system is by the 8-bit ISA expansion slots. No matter what processor or other features the system has, if all the slots are 8-bit ISA, then the system is a PC/XT. AT (16-bit plus) systems can be similarly identified by having 16-bit or greater slots of any type. These could be ISA, EISA, MCA, PC-Card (formerly PCMCIA), Cardbus, VL-Bus, or PCI. Using this information, you can properly categorize virtually any system as a PC/XT type or an AT type. There really have been no PC/XT type (8-bit) systems manufactured for many years. Unless you are in a computer museum, virtually every system you would encounter today is based on the AT type design.

System Components

A modern PC is both simple and complicated. It is simple in the sense that over the years many of the components used to construct a system have become integrated with other components into fewer and fewer actual parts. It is complicated in the sense that each part in a modern system performs many more functions than the same types of parts in older systems.

In this section, we briefly examine all the components in a modern PC system. Each of these components will be expanded on in later chapters.

Here are the components needed to assemble a basic modern PC system:

- Motherboard
- Processor
- Memory (RAM)

- Case (chassis)
- Power supply
- Floppy drive
- Hard disk
- CD-ROM drive
- Keyboard
- Mouse
- Video card
- Monitor (display)
- Sound card
- Speakers

Motherboard

The motherboard is the core of the system. It really *is* the PC, everything else is connected to it, and it controls everything in the system. Motherboards are available in several different shapes or form factors. The motherboard usually contains the following individual components:

- Processor socket (or slot)
- Processor voltage regulators
- Motherboard chipset
- Level 2 cache
- Memory SIMM or DIMM sockets
- Bus slots
- ROM BIOS
- Clock/CMOS battery
- Super I/O chip

The chipset is the main component of the motherboard and it essentially is the motherboard circuit. The chipset controls the processor host bus interface, the L2 cache and main memory, system bus slots, system resources and more. The chipset plays a big role in determining what sorts of features a system can support. For example, which processors you can use, which types of memory, what speeds you can run the machine, and what types of system buses your system can support are all tied in to the motherboard chipset. The ROM BIOS contains the initial POST (Power-On Self Test) program, bootstrap loader (which loads the operating system), drivers for items built-in to the board (the actual BIOS code), and usually a system setup program (often called

CMOS setup) for configuring the system. Motherboards are covered in detail in Chapter 4.

Processor

The processor is often thought of as the "engine" of the computer. A sophisticated piece of miniaturized electronics with millions of transistors, the processor (often called the CPU or Central Processing Unit) is like the conductor in an orchestra. The processor reads program instructions (commands) from memory that tell it what it needs to do to accomplish the work that the user wants, and then executes them. The processor has the distinction of being one of the most expensive parts of most computers, even though it is also one of the smallest parts.

Microprocessors are covered in detail in Chapter 3, "Microprocessor Types and Specifications."

Memory (RAM)

The system memory is often called RAM for Random Access Memory. This is the primary memory that holds all the programs and data the processor is using at a given time. RAM requires power to maintain storage, so when you turn off the computer everything in RAM is cleared, and when you turn it back on the memory must be reloaded with programs for the processor to run. The initial programs for the processor come from a special type of memory called ROM (Read Only Memory), which cannot normally be erased. This contains instructions to get the system to load an operating system and other programs from one of the disk drives into the main memory so that the system can be running normally and perform useful work. Newer operating systems allow several programs to run at one time, with each program or data file loaded using some of the memory. Generally, the more memory your system has, the more programs you can run simultaneously.

Memory is normally purchased and installed in a modern system in SIMM (Single Inline Memory Module) or DIMM (Dual Inline Memory Module) form. Formerly very expensive, more recently memory prices have dropped, significantly reducing the cost of memory as compared to other parts of the system. Even so, the cost of the recommended amount of memory for a given system is usually equal or greater than that of the motherboard.

Memory is covered in detail in Chapter 5, "Memory."

Case (Chassis)

The box or outer shell that houses most of the computer, the case is one of the least emphasized and most overlooked parts of the PC. Although it may seem only cosmetic, the case actually performs several important functions for your PC, including protection for the system components, directing cooling airflow, and allowing installation of and access to the system components. The case often includes a matching power supply, and must also be designed with the form factor of the motherboard and other system components in mind.

The case is covered in detail in Chapter 6, "Power Supply and Case."

Power Supply

The power supply is what feeds electrical power to every single part in the PC. As such it has a very important job, yet it is one of the least glamorous parts of the system, so it receives little attention. Unfortunately, this often means it is one of the components that is most skimped on when constructing a system. The main function of the supply is to convert the 110v AC wall current into the 3.3v, 5v, and 12fv power that the system requires for operation.

The power supply is covered in detail in Chapter 6.

Floppy Disk Drive

Floppy disks are the smallest and slowest form of offline storage. Floppy disks provide a simple, convenient way to transfer information, install new software, and back up small amounts of files. With the advent of CD-ROM discs as the primary method of installing or loading new software in a system, the floppy drive component is not as important as it was years ago. Even so, virtually all PCs made in the last 10 years use a standard 3 1/2-inch, 1.44M capacity floppy drive. Recently some advancements have created floppy drives with up to 120M or more of storage, but these have yet to fully catch on as a standard PC component.

Floppy disk drives are covered in detail in Chapter 12, "Magnetic Storage."

Hard Disk Drive

The hard disk is the primary archival storage memory for the system. It is used to contain copies of all programs and data not currently active in main memory. A hard drive is so named because it consists of spinning platters of aluminum or ceramic that are coated with a magnetic media. The platters come in various sizes, and by the density, size, and number of platters, hard drives can be created with many different storage capacities. Most desktop systems today use drives with 3 1/2-inch platters, while most laptop or notebook computers use 2 1/2-inch platter drives.

Hard disk drives are also covered in detail in Chapter 12.

CD-ROM Drive

CD-ROM stands for Compact Disk-Read Only Memory. As the name implies, CD-ROM drives use small discs, identical to the ones that hold music, to hold computer information. Also as the name implies, they are a read-only medium. You can read information from them but not write to them (except for some special exceptions). CD-ROMs are currently the most popular way that computer companies distribute applications and games, and are ideal for multimedia information such as videos, music, and large graphics files.

CD-ROM drives are covered in detail in Chapter 13, "Optical Storage."

Keyboard

The keyboard is the main input device for most computers. It is used to input text or enter commands into the PC. Keyboards are pretty much standard affairs these days, although they can vary greatly in quality and some may have additional features.

Keyboards are covered in detail in Chapter 7, "Input Devices."

Mouse

Until the invention of the Graphical User Interface (GUI), the keyboard was the only way that most people input information into their PCs. The mouse is used in graphical environments to let users provide simple "point and click" instructions to the computer. The main advantage of a mouse over the keyboard is simplicity. There are many operations that are much easier to perform with a mouse than a keyboard (such as picking an item on a screen or choosing from a list of options).

The mouse is covered in detail in Chapter 7.

Video Card

The video card controls the information you see on the monitor. All video cards have four basic parts—a video chip or chipset, Video RAM, a DAC (Digital to Analog Converter), and a BIOS. The video chip is what actually controls the information on the screen by writing data to the video RAM. The DAC reads the video RAM and converts the digital data there into analog signals to drive the monitor. The BIOS holds the primary video driver that allows the display to function during boot time and at a DOS prompt in basic text mode. More enhanced drivers are then usually loaded from disk to enable advanced video modes for Windows or applications software.

Video cards are covered in detail in Chapter 8, "Video Hardware."

Monitor (Display)

The monitor is a specialized, high-resolution screen, similar to a high-quality television. The video card sends the contents of its video memory out to your monitor normally at a rate of 60 or more times per second. The actual display screen is made up of red, green, and blue dots that are illuminated by an electron beam from behind. The video card DAC chip controls the sweep of the electron beam, which then controls what dots are lit up and how bright they are, which then determines the picture you see on the screen.

Monitors are covered in detail in Chapter 8.

Chapter 3

Microprocessor Types and Specifications

The brain or engine of the PC is the processor (sometimes called microprocessor), or *Central Processing Unit* (CPU). The CPU performs the system's calculating and processing. The processor is easily the most expensive single component in the system, costing up to four or more times greater than the motherboard it plugs into. Intel is generally credited with inventing the microprocessor in 1971 and they have almost total control over that market today, at least for PC systems. This means that all PC-compatible systems use either Intel processors or processors from a handful of competitors (such as AMD or Cyrix).

The following sections cover the different types of processor chips that have been used in personal computers since the first PC was introduced almost two decades ago. These sections provide a great deal of technical detail about these chips and explain why one type of CPU chip can do more work than another in a given period of time.

Processor Specifications

Many confusing specifications often are quoted in discussions of processors. The following sections discuss some of these specifications, including the data bus, address bus, and speed. The next section includes a table that lists the specifications of virtually all PC processors.

Processors can be identified by two main parameters: how *wide* they are and how *fast* they are. The speed of a processor is a fairly simple concept. Speed is counted in megahertz (MHz), which means millions of cycles per second, and faster *is* better! The width of a processor is a little more complicated to discuss because there are three main specifications in a processor that are expressed in width. They are

- Data input and output bus
- Internal registers
- Memory address bus

Table 3.1 lists the primary specifications for the Intel family of processors used in IBM and compatible PCs. The following sections explain these specifications in detail.

Note that the Pentium II processor includes 512K of 1/2-core speed L2 cache on the processor card.

The transistor count figures do not include the standard 256K or 512K Level 2 cache built in to the Pentium Pro and Pentium II CPU packages. The L2 cache contains an additional 15.5 (256K), 31 (512K), or optionally 62 million (1M) transistors!

Table 3.1 Intel Processor Specifications

Processor	CPU Clock	Voltage	Internal Register Size	Data I/O Bus Width	Memory Address Bus Width	Maximum Memory
8088	1x	5v	16-bit	8-bit	20-bit	1M
8086	1x	5v	16-bit	16-bit	20-bit	1M
286	1x	5v	16-bit	16-bit	24-bit	16M
386SX	1x	5v	32-bit	16-bit	24-bit	16M
386SL	1x	3.3v	32-bit	16-bit	24-bit	16M
386DX	1x	5v	32-bit	32-bit	32-bit	4G
486SX	1x	5v	32-bit	32-bit	32-bit	4G
486SX2	2x	5v	32-bit	32-bit	32-bit	4G
487SX	1x	5v	32-bit	32-bit	32-bit	4G
486DX	1x	5v	32-bit	32-bit	32-bit	4G
486SL[2]	1x	3.3v	32-bit	32-bit	32-bit	4G
486DX2	2x	5v	32-bit	32-bit	32-bit	4G
486DX4	2-3x	3.3v	32-bit	32-bit	32-bit	4G
486Pentium OD	2.5x	5v	32-bit	32-bit	32-bit	4G
Pentium 60/66	1x	5v	32-bit	64-bit	32-bit	4G
Pentium 75-200	1.5-3x	3.3v[3]	32-bit	64-bit	32-bit	4G
Pentium MMX	1.5-3x	1.8-2.8v	32-bit	64-bit	32-bit	4G
Pentium Pro	2-3x	3.3v	32-bit	64-bit	36-bit	64G
Pentium II MMX	3.5-5x	1.8-2.8v	32-bit	64-bit	36-bit	64G
Pentium II Celeron	3.5-5x	1.8-2.8v	32-bit	64-bit	36-bit	64G
Pentium II Xeon	3.5-5x	1.8-2.8v	32-bit	64-bit	36-bit	64G

FPU = Floating-Point Unit (internal math coprocessor)
WT = Write-Through cache (caches reads only)
WB = Write-Back cache (caches both reads and writes)
[1] The 386SL contains an integral-cache controller, but the cache memory must be provided outside the chip.
[2] Intel later marketed SL Enhanced versions of the SX, DX, and DX2 processors. These processors were available in both 5v and 3.3v versions and included power-management capabilities.

Processor Speed Ratings

A common misunderstanding about processors is their different speed ratings. This section covers processor speed in general and then provides more specific information about Intel processors.

Level 1 Cache	L1 Cache Type	Level 2 Cache	L2 Cache Speed	Integral FPU	No. of Transistors	Date Introduced
-	-	-	-	-	29,000	June '79
-	-	-	-	-	29,000	June '78
-	-	-	-	-	134,000	Feb. '82
-	-	-	-	-	275,000	June '88
0K[1]	WT	-	-	-	855,000	Oct. '90
-	-	-	-	-	275,000	Oct. '85
8K	WT	-	-	-	1,185,000	April '91
8K	WT	-	-	-	1,185,000	April '94
8K	WT	-	-	Yes	1,200,000	April '91
8K	WT	-	-	Yes	1,200,000	April '89
8K	WT	-	-	Opt.	1,400,000	Nov. '92
8K	WT	-	-	Yes	1,100,000	March '92
16K	WT	-	-	Yes	1,600,000	Feb. '94
2x16K	WB	-	-	Yes	3,100,000	Jan. '95
2x8K	WB	-	-	Yes	3,100,000	March '93
2x8K	WB	-	-	Yes	3,300,000	Oct. '94
2x16K	WB	-	-	Yes	4,100,000	Jan. '97
2x8K	WB	256K[4]	Core	Yes	5,500,000	Nov. '95
2x16K	WB	512K	Core	Yes	7,500,000	May '97
2x16K	WB	0K	-	Yes	7,500,000	April '98
2x16K	WB	1M/ 2M	Core	Yes	7,500,000	April '98

[3] *There are several different voltage variations of Pentium processors, including what Intel calls VRE (3.5v), STD (3.3v), and newer 3.1v, 2.8v, 2.5v, 2.1v, and 1.8v versions.*
[4] *There are versions of the Pentium Pro processor with 256K, 512K, or 1M of full core speed L2 cache in a separate die within the chip.*

A computer system's clock speed is measured as a frequency, usually expressed as a number of cycles per second. A crystal oscillator controls clock speeds, using a sliver of quartz in a small tin container. As voltage is applied to the quartz, it begins to vibrate (oscillate) at a harmonic rate dictated by the shape and size of the crystal (sliver). The oscillations emanate from the crystal in the form of a current that alternates at the harmonic rate of the crystal. This alternating current is the clock signal. A typical computer system runs millions of these cycles per second, so speed is measured in megahertz. (One hertz is equal to one cycle per second.)

Note

The hertz was named for the German physicist Heinrich Rudolf Hertz. In 1885, Hertz confirmed the electromagnetic theory, which states that light is a form of electromagnetic radiation and is propagated as waves.

A single cycle is the smallest element of time for the processor. Every action requires at least one cycle and usually multiple cycles. To transfer data to and from memory, for example, a modern processor such as the Pentium II needs a minimum of three cycles to set up the first memory transfer, and then only a single cycle per transfer for the next three to six consecutive transfers. The extra cycles on the first transfer are normally called wait states. A *wait state* is a clock tick in which nothing happens. This ensures that the processor isn't getting ahead of the rest of the computer.

▶▶ See "SIMMs and DIMMs," p. 324

The time required to execute instructions also varies. The original 8086 and 8088 processors take an average of 12 cycles to execute a single instruction. The 286 and 386 processors improve this rate to about 4.5 cycles per instruction; the 486 drops the rate further to about two cycles per instruction. The Pentium architecture includes twin instruction pipelines and other improvements that provide for operation at one or two instructions per cycle, while the Pentium Pro and Pentium II can execute as many as three or more instructions per cycle.

Different instruction execution times (in cycles) make it difficult to compare systems based purely on clock speed, or number of cycles per second. How can two processors that run at the same clock rate perform differently, with one running "faster" than the other? The answer is simple: efficiency.

The main reason why the 486 is fast compared to a 386 is that it executes twice as many instructions in the same number of cycles. The same thing is true for a Pentium; it executes about twice as many instructions in a given number of cycles as a 486. Thus, a 133MHz 486 (such as the AMD 5x86-133) is not even as fast as a 75MHz Pentium! That is because Pentium megahertz are worth about double what 486 megahertz are worth. The Pentium II is about 50% faster than an equivalent Pentium at a given clock speed because it can execute about that many more instructions in the same number of cycles.

Comparing relative processor performance, you can see that a 500MHz Pentium II is about equal to a (theoretical) 750MHz Pentium, which is about equal to a 1400MHz 486, which is about equal to a 2800MHz 386 or 286, which is about equal to a 5600MHz 8088. Considering that the original PC's 8088 ran at only 4.77MHz, we have systems today that are comparatively more than 1,000 times faster. As you can see, you have to be careful in comparing systems based on pure MHz alone; many other factors affect system performance.

Evaluating CPU performance can be tricky. CPUs with different internal architectures do things differently and may be relatively faster at certain things, slower at others. To fairly compare different CPUs at different clock speeds, Intel has devised a specific series of benchmarks that can be run against Intel chips to produce a relative gauge of performance. It has recently been updated to reflect performance on 32-bit systems, and is called the iCOMP 2.0 (intel COmparative Microprocessor Performance) index. Table 3.2 shows the relative power, or iCOMP 2.0 index, for several processors.

Table 3.2 Intel iCOMP 2.0 Index Ratings	
Processor	**iCOMP 2.0 Index**
Pentium 75	67
Pentium 100	90
Pentium 120	100
Pentium 133	111
Pentium 150	114
Pentium 166	127
Pentium 200	142
Pentium-MMX 166	160
Pentium-MMX 200	182
Pentium-MMX 233	203
Pentium Pro 180	197
Pentium Pro 200	220
Pentium II 233	267
Pentium II 266	303
Pentium II 300	332
Pentium II 333	366
Pentium II 350	386
Pentium II 400	440

The iCOMP 2.0 index is derived from several independent benchmarks and is a stable indication of relative processor performance. The benchmarks balance integer with floating point and multimedia performance.

Processor Speeds and Markings Versus Motherboard Speed. Another confusing factor when comparing processor performance is that virtually all modern processors since the 486DX2 run at some multiple of the motherboard speed. For example, a Pentium II 333 runs at a multiple of five times the motherboard speed of 66MHz, while a Pentium II 400 runs at four times the motherboard speed of 100MHz. Most motherboards run at 66MHz because that is all Intel supported with their processors until early '98 or they then released processors and chipsets designed to run on 100MHz motherboards. Cyrix has a few processors designed to run on 75MHz motherboards, and many Pentium motherboards are capable of running that speed as well. Normally, you can set the motherboard speed and multiplier setting via jumpers or other configuration mechanism (such as CMOS setup) on the motherboard.

Modern systems use a variable-frequency synthesizer circuit usually found in the main motherboard chipset to control the motherboard and CPU speed. Most Pentium motherboards will have three or four speed settings. The processors used today are available in a variety of versions that run at different frequencies based on a given motherboard speed. For example, most of the Pentium chips run at a speed that is some multiple of the true motherboard speed. For example, Pentium processors and motherboards run at the speeds shown in Table 3.3.

Table 3.3 Intel Processor and Motherboard Speeds		
CPU Type/Speed	**CPU Clock**	**Motherboard Speed**
Pentium 60	1x	60
Pentium 66	1x	66
Pentium 75	1.5x	50
Pentium 90	1.5x	60
Pentium 100	1.5x	66
Pentium 120	2x	60
Pentium 133	2x	66
Pentium 150	2.5x	60
Pentium/Pentium Pro/MMX 166	2.5x	66
Pentium/Pentium Pro 180	3x	60
Pentium/Pentium Pro/MMX 200	3x	66
Pentium-MMX/Pentium II 233	3.5x	66
Pentium-MMX(Mobile)/Pentium-II	266 4x	66
Pentium II 300	4.5x	66
Pentium II 333	5x	66
Pentium II 350	3.5x	100
Pentium II 400	4x	100
Pentium II 450	4.5x	100

If all other variables are equal—including the type of processor, the number of wait states (empty cycles) added to different types of memory accesses, and the width of the data bus—you can compare two systems by their respective clock rates. However, the construction and design of the memory subsystem can have an enormous effect on a system's final execution speed.

In building a processor, a manufacturer tests it at different speeds, temperatures, and pressures. After the processor is tested, it receives a stamp indicating the maximum safe speed at which the unit will operate under the wide variation of temperatures and pressures encountered in normal operation. The rating system usually is simple. For example, the top of the processor in one of my systems is marked like this:

A80486DX2–66

The A is Intel's indicator that this chip has a Ceramic Pin Grid Array form factor, or an indication of the physical packaging of the chip. The 80486DX2 is the part number, which identifies this processor as a clock-doubled 486DX processor. The –66 at the end indicates that this chip is rated to run at a maximum speed of 66MHz. Because of the clock doubling, the maximum motherboard speed is 33MHz. This chip would be acceptable for any application in which the chip runs at 66MHz or slower. For example, you could use this processor in a system with a 25MHz motherboard, in which case the processor would happily run at 50MHz.

Most 486 motherboards also have a 40MHz setting, in which case the DX2 would run at 80MHz internally. Because this is 14MHz beyond its rated speed, many would not work; or if they worked at all, it would be only for a short time. On the other hand, I have found that most of the newer chips marked with –66 ratings seem to run fine (albeit somewhat hotter) at the 40/80MHz settings. This is called *overclocking* and can end up being a simple, cost-effective way to speed up your system. However, I would not recommend this for mission-critical applications where the system reliability is of the utmost importance; a system pushed beyond specification like this can often exhibit erratic behavior under stress.

> **Note**
>
> One good source of online overclocking information is located at **http://www.sysopt.com**. It includes, among other things, fairly thorough overclocking FAQs, and an ongoing survey of users who have successfully (and sometimes unsuccessfully) overclocked their CPUs.

Sometimes, however, the markings don't seem to indicate the speed directly. In the older 8086, for example, –3 translates to 6MHz operation. This marking scheme is more common in some of the older chips, which were manufactured before some of the marking standards used today were standardized.

A more modern example would be the Cyrix/IBM 6x86 processors, which use a PR (Performance Rating) scale that is not equal to the true clock speed in megahertz. For example, the Cyrix/IBM 6x86MX-PR200 actually runs at 166MHz (2.5 × 66MHz). This is a little misleading—you must set up the motherboard as if a 166MHz processor were being installed, not the 200MHz you might suspect.

A manufacturer sometimes places the CPU under a heat sink, which can prevent you from reading the rating printed on the chip. (A *heat sink* is a metal device that draws heat away from an electronic device.) Fortunately, most CPU manufacturers are placing marks on the top and bottom of the processor. If the heat sink is difficult to remove from the chip, you can take the heat sink and chip out of the socket together and read the markings on the bottom of the processor to determine what you have. Most processors running at 50MHz and later should have a heat sink installed to prevent the processor from overheating.

Data Bus

Perhaps the most common way to describe a processor is by the width of the processor's external data bus. This defines the number of data bits that can be moved into or out of the processor in one cycle. A *bus* is simply a series of connections that carry common signals. Imagine running a pair of wires from one end of a building to another. If you connect a 110v AC power generator to the two wires at any point and place outlets at convenient locations along the wires, you have constructed a power bus. No matter which outlet you plug the wires into, you have access to the same signal, which in this example is 110v AC power. Any transmission medium that has more than one outlet at each end can be called a bus. A typical computer system has several internal and external buses.

The processor bus discussed most often is the external *data bus*–the bundle of wires (or pins) used to send and receive data. The more signals that can be sent at the same time, the more data can be transmitted in a specified interval and, therefore, the faster the bus. A wider data bus is like having a highway with more lanes, which allows for greater throughput.

Data in a computer is sent as digital information consisting of a time interval in which a single wire carries 5v to signal a 1 data bit, or 0v to signal a 0 data bit. The more wires you have, the more individual bits you can send in the same time interval. A chip such as the 286 or 386SX, which has 16 wires for transmitting and receiving such data, has a 16-bit data bus. A 32-bit chip, such as the 386DX and 486, has twice as many wires dedicated to simultaneous data transmission as a 16-bit chip; a 32-bit chip can send twice as much information in the same time interval as a 16-bit chip. Modern processors such as the Pentium series have 64-bit external data buses. This means that Pentium processors including the original Pentium, Pentium Pro, and Pentium II can all transfer 64 bits of data at a time to and from the system memory.

A good way to understand this flow of information is to consider a highway and the traffic it carries. If a highway has only one lane for each direction of travel, only one car at a time can move in a certain direction. If you want to increase traffic flow, you can add another lane so that twice as many cars pass in a specified time. You can think of an 8-bit chip as being a single-lane highway because one byte flows through at a time. (One byte equals eight individual bits.) The 16-bit chip, with two bytes flowing at a time, resembles a two-lane highway. You may have four lanes in each direction to move a large number of automobiles. This structure corresponds to a 32-bit data bus, which has the capability to move four bytes of information at a time. Taking this further, a 64-bit data bus is like having an 8-lane highway moving data in and out of the chip!

Just as you can describe a highway by its lane width, you can describe a chip by the width of its data bus. When you read an advertisement that describes a 32-bit or 64-bit computer system, the ad usually refers to the CPU's data bus. This number provides a rough idea of the chip's performance potential (and, therefore, the system).

Perhaps the most important ramification of the data bus in a chip is that the width of the data bus also defines the size of a bank of memory. This means that a 32-bit processor, such as the 486 class chips, reads and writes memory 32 bits at a time. Pentium class processors, including the Pentium II, read and write memory 64 bits at a time. Because standard 72-pin SIMMs (Single Inline Memory Modules) are only 32 bits wide, they must be installed one at a time in most 486 class systems they're installed two at a time in most Pentium class systems. Newer DIMMs (Dual Inline Memory Modules) are 64 bits wide, so they are installed one at a time in Pentium class systems. Each DIMM is equal to a complete bank of memory in Pentium systems, which makes system configuration easy—they can then be installed or removed one at a time. This information is discussed in more detail in Chapter 5, "Memory."

▶▶ See "Memory Banks," p. 338

Internal Registers

The size of the internal registers indicate how much information the processor can *operate* on at one time, and how it moves data around internally within the chip. The register size is essentially the internal data bus size. A *register* is a holding cell within the processor; for example, the processor can add numbers in two different registers, storing the result in a third register. The register size determines the size of data the processor can operate on. The register size also describes the type of software or commands and instructions a chip can run. That is, processors with 32-bit internal registers can run 32-bit instructions that are processing 32-bit chunks of data, but processors with 16-bit registers cannot. Most advanced processors today—chips from the 386 to the Pentium II—use 32-bit internal registers and can therefore run the same 32-bit operating systems and software.

Some processors have an internal data bus (made up of data paths and storage units called *registers*) that is larger than the external data bus. The 8088 and 386SX are examples of this structure. Each chip has an internal data bus twice the width of the external bus. These designs, which sometimes are called *hybrid designs*, usually are low-cost versions of a "pure" chip. The 386SX, for example, can pass data around internally with a full 32-bit register size; for communications with the outside world, however, the chip is restricted to a 16-bit–wide data path. This design enables a systems designer to build a lower-cost motherboard with a 16-bit bus design and still maintain software and instruction set compatibility with the full 32-bit 386.

Internal registers often are larger than the data bus, which means that the chip requires two cycles to fill a register before the register can be operated on. For example, both the 386SX and 386DX have internal 32-bit registers, but the 386SX has to "inhale" twice (figuratively) to fill them, whereas the 386DX can do the job in one "breath." The same thing would happen when the data is passed from the registers back out to the system bus.

The Pentium is an example of this type of design. All Pentiums have a 64-bit data bus and 32-bit registers—a structure that may seem to be a problem until you understand that the Pentium has two internal 32-bit pipelines for processing information. In many ways, the Pentium is like two 32-bit chips in one. The 64-bit data bus provides for very efficient filling of these multiple registers. Multiple pipelines are called *superscalar architecture*. See the section on the Pentium processor for more information on superscalar architecture.

More advanced sixth-generation processors such as the Pentium Pro and Pentium II have as many as six internal pipelines for executing instructions. Although some of these internal pipes are dedicated to special functions, these processors can still execute as many as three instructions in one clock cycle.

Address Bus

The *address bus* is the set of wires that carry the addressing information used to describe the memory location to which the data is being sent, or from which the data is being retrieved. As with the data bus, each wire in an address bus carries a single bit of information. This single bit is a single digit in the address. The more wires (digits) used in calculating these addresses, the greater the total number of address locations. The size (or width) of the address bus indicates the maximum amount of RAM that a chip can address.

The highway analogy can be used to show how the address bus fits in. If the data bus is the highway and the size of the data bus is equivalent to the number of lanes, the address bus relates to the house number or street address. The size of the address bus is equivalent to the number of digits in the house address number. For example, if you live on a street in which the address is limited to a two-digit (base 10) number, no more than 100 distinct addresses (00 to 99) can exist for that street (10 to the power of 2). Add another digit, and the number of available addresses increases to 1,000 (000 to 999), or 10 to the third power.

Computers use the binary (base 2) numbering system, so a two-digit number provides only four unique addresses (00, 01, 10, and 11) calculated as 2 to the power of 2; a three-digit number provides only eight addresses (000 to 111), which is 2 to the 3rd power. For example, the 8086 and 8088 processors use a 20-bit address bus that calculates as a maximum of 2 to the 20th power or 1,048,576 bytes (1M) of address locations. Table 3.4 describes the memory-addressing capabilities of Intel processors.

Table 3.4 Intel Processor Memory-Addressing Capabilities					
Processor Family	**Address Bus**	**Bytes**	**Kilobytes**	**Megabytes**	**Gigabytes**
8088/8086	20-bit	1,048,576	1,024	1	-
286/386SX	24-bit	16,777,216	16,384	16	-
386DX/486/Pentium	32-bit	4,294,967,296	4,194,304	4,096	4
Pentium Pro/II	36-bit	68,719,476,736	67,108,864	65,536	64

The data bus and address bus are independent, and chip designers can use whatever size they want for each. Usually, however, chips with larger data buses have larger address buses. The sizes of the buses can provide important information about a chip's relative power, measured in two important ways. The size of the data bus is an indication of the chip's information-moving capability, and the size of the address bus tells you how much memory the chip can handle.

Internal (Level 1) Cache

All modern processors starting with the 486 family include an integrated (Level 1) cache controller. That controller has 8K (or more) built-in full core-speed cache memory. This cache basically is an area of very fast memory built into the processor and is used to hold some of the current working set of code and data. Cache memory can be accessed with no wait states because it can fully keep up with the speed of the processor core.

Using cache memory reduces a traditional system bottleneck because system RAM often is much slower than the CPU. This prevents the processor from having to wait for code and data from much slower main memory, therefore improving performance. Without the Level 1 (L1) cache, a processor frequently would be forced to wait until system memory caught up.

L1 cache is even more important in modern processors because it is often the only memory in the entire system that can truly keep up with the chip. Most modern processors are clock multiplied, which means they are running at a speed that is really a multiple of the motherboard they are plugged into. The Pentium II 333MHz, for example, runs at a very high multiple of five times the true motherboard speed of 66MHz. Because the main memory is plugged into the motherboard, it can also run at only 66MHz maximum. The only 333MHz memory in such a system is the L1 cache built in to the processor core. In this example, the Pentium II 333MHz processor has 32K of integrated L1 cache in two separate 16K blocks.

▶▶ See "Memory Speeds," p. 312

If the data that the processor wants is already in the internal cache, the CPU does not have to wait. If the data is not in the cache, the CPU must fetch it from the Level 2 cache or (in less sophisticated system designs) from the system bus, meaning main memory directly.

The organization of the cache memory in the 486 and Pentium family is called a *four-way set associative cache*, which means that the cache memory is split into four blocks. Each block also is organized as 128 or 256 lines of 16 bytes each.

To understand how a four-way set associative cache works, consider a simple example. In the simplest cache design, the cache is set up as a single block into which you can load the contents of a corresponding block of main memory. This procedure is similar to using a bookmark to locate the current page of a book that you are reading. If main memory equates to all the pages in the book, the bookmark indicates which pages are held in cache memory. This procedure works if the required data is located within the pages marked with the bookmark, but it does not work if you need to refer to a previously read page. In that case, the bookmark is of no use.

An alternative approach is to maintain multiple bookmarks to mark several parts of the book simultaneously. Additional hardware overhead is associated with having multiple bookmarks, and you also have to take time to check all the bookmarks to see which one marks the pages of data you need. Each additional bookmark adds to the overhead, but also increases your chance of finding the desired pages.

If you settle on marking four areas in the book, you have essentially constructed a four-way set associative cache. This technique splits the available cache memory into four blocks, each of which stores different lines of main memory. Multitasking environments, such as Windows, are good examples of environments in which the processor needs to operate on different areas of memory simultaneously and in which a four-way cache would improve performance greatly.

The contents of the cache must always be in sync with the contents of main memory to ensure that the processor is working with current data. For this reason, the internal cache in the 486 family is a *Write-Through cache*. Write-Through means that when the processor writes information out to the cache, that information is automatically written through to main memory as well.

By comparison, the Pentium and later chips have an internal *Write-Back cache*, which means that both reads and writes are cached, further improving performance. Even though the internal 486 cache is Write-Through, the system can employ an external Write-Back cache for increased performance. In addition, the 486 can buffer up to four bytes before actually storing the data in RAM, improving efficiency in case the memory bus is busy.

The cache controller built into the processor also is responsible for watching the memory bus when alternate processors, known as *busmasters*, are in control of the system. This process of watching the bus is referred to as *Bus Snooping*. If a busmaster device writes to an area of memory that also is stored in the processor cache currently, the cache contents and memory no longer agree. The cache controller then marks this data as invalid and reloads the cache during the next memory access, preserving the integrity of the system.

A secondary external L2 cache of extremely fast static RAM (SRAM) chips also is used in most 486 and Pentium-based systems. It further reduces the amount of time that the CPU must spend waiting for data from system memory. The function of the secondary processor cache is similar to that of the onboard cache. The secondary processor cache holds information that is moving to the CPU, thereby reducing the time that the CPU spends waiting and increasing the time that the CPU spends performing calculations. Fetching information from the secondary processor cache rather than from system memory is much faster because of the SRAM chips' extremely fast speed—15 nanoseconds (ns) or less.

Pentium systems incorporate the secondary cache on the motherboard, while Pentium Pro and Pentium II systems have the secondary cache inside the processor package. By moving the L2 cache into the processor, they are able to run it at speeds higher than the motherboard—up to as fast as the processor core.

As clock speeds increase, cycle time decreases. Most SIMM memory used today in Pentium and earlier systems was 60ns, which works out to be only about 16MHz! Standard motherboard speed today is 66MHz or 100MHz, and processors are available at 450MHz or more. Newer systems don't use cache on the motherboard any longer, as the faster SDRAM used in modern Pentium II systems can keep up with the motherboard speed. Table 3.5 illustrates the need for and function of Level 1 (internal) and Level 2 (external) cache in modern systems.

Table 3.5 CPU Speeds Relative to Cache, SIMM/DIMM, and Motherboard					
CPU Type:	**486 DX4**	**Pentium**	**Pentium Pro**	**Pentium II ('97)**	**Pentium II ('98)**
CPU speed:	100MHz	233MHz	200MHz	333MHz	450MHz
L1 cache speed:	10ns (100MHz)	4ns (233MHz)	5ns (200MHz)	3ns (333MHz)	2ns (450MHz)
L2 cache speed:	30ns (33MHz)	15ns (66MHz)	5ns (200MHz)	6ns (167MHz)	4ns (225MHz)
Motherboard speed:	33MHz	66MHz	66MHz	66MHz	100MHz
SIMM/DIMM speed:	60ns (16MHz)	60ns (16MHz)	60ns (16MHz)	15ns (66MHz)	10ns (100MHz)
SIMM/DIMM type:	FPM	FPM/EDO	FPM/EDO	SDRAM	SDRAM

As you can see, having two levels of cache between the very fast CPU and the much slower main memory helps minimize any wait states the processor might have to endure. This allows the processor to keep working closer to its true speed.

Processor Modes

All Intel 32-bit and later processors, from the 386 on up, can run in several modes. Processor modes refer to the various operating environments and affect the instructions and capabilities of the chip. The processor mode controls how the processor sees and manages the system memory and the tasks that use it.

Three different modes of operation possible are

- Real mode
- Protected mode
- Virtual Real mode (Real within Protected)

The original IBM PC included an 8088 processor that could execute 16-bit instructions using 16-bit internal registers, and could address only 1M of memory using 20 address lines. All original PC software was created to work with this chip, and was designed around the 16-bit instruction set and 1M memory model. For example, DOS and all DOS software, Windows 1.x through 3.x, and all Windows 1.x through 3.x applications are written using 16-bit instructions. These 16-bit operating systems and applications are designed to run on an original 8088 processor.

◀◀ See "Internal Registers," p. 39
◀◀ See "Address Bus," p. 40

Later processors like the 286 could also run the same 16-bit instructions as the original 8088, but much faster. In other words, the 286 was fully compatible with the original 8088 and could run all 16-bit software just the same as an 8088, but, of course, that software would run faster. The 16-bit instruction mode of the 8088 and 286 processors has become known as *real mode*. All software running in real mode must use only 16-bit instructions and live within the 20-bit (1M) memory architecture it supports. Software of this type is normally single-tasking, which means that only one program can run at a time. There is no built-in protection to keep one program from overwriting another program or even the operating system in memory, which means that if more than one program is running, it is possible for one of them to bring the entire system to a crashing halt.

Then came the 386, which was the PC industry's first 32-bit processor. This chip could run an entirely new 32-bit instruction set. To fully take advantage of the 32-bit instruction set you need a 32-bit operating system and a 32-bit application. This new 32-bit mode was referred to as *protected mode*, which alludes to the fact that software programs running in that mode are protected from overwriting one another in memory. Such protection helps make the system much more crashproof, as an errant program cannot very easily damage other programs or the operating system. In addition, a crashed program can simply be terminated, while the rest of the system continues to run unaffected.

Knowing that new operating systems and applications to take advantage of the 32-bit protected mode would take some time to develop, Intel wisely built in a backward-compatible real mode into the 386. That allowed it to run unmodified 16-bit operating systems and applications. It ran them quite well, much faster than any previous chip. For most people, that was enough; they did not necessarily want any new 32-bit software—they just wanted their existing 16-bit software to run faster. Unfortunately, that meant that the chip was never running in the 32-bit protected mode, and all the features of that capability were being ignored.

When a high-powered processor like a Pentium II is running in real mode, it acts like a "Turbo 8088." Turbo 8088 means that the processor has the advantage of speed in running any 16-bit programs; it otherwise can use only the 16-bit instructions and access memory within the same 1M memory map of the original 8088. This means if you have a 64M Pentium II system running Windows 3.x or DOS, you are effectively using only the first megabyte of memory, leaving the other 63M largely unused!

New operating systems and applications that ran in the 32-bit protected mode of the modern processors were needed. Being stubborn, we resisted all the initial attempts at getting us switched over to a 32-bit environment. It seems that as a user community, we are very resistant to change and would be content with our older software running faster rather than adopting new software with new features. I'll be the first one to admit that I was one of those stubborn users myself!

Due to this resistance, 32-bit operating systems such as UNIX, OS/2, and even Windows NT have had a very hard time getting any market share in the PC marketplace. Out of those, Windows NT is the only one that will likely be close to mainstream, and that is only because Microsoft has coerced us in that direction with Windows 95 and 98. Windows 3.x was the last full 16-bit operating system. In fact, it was not a complete operating system because it ran on top of DOS.

Microsoft realized how stubborn the installed base of PC users was, so it developed Windows 95 as a bridge to a full 32-bit world. Windows 95 is a mostly 32-bit operating system, but it retains enough 16-bit capability to fully run our old 16-bit applications. Windows 95 came out in August of '95, a full 10 years later than the introduction of the first 32-bit PC processor! It has taken us only 10 years to migrate to software that can fully use the processors we have in front of us.

The key to the backward compatibility of the Windows 95 32-bit environment is the third mode in the processor: *virtual real* mode. Virtual real is essentially a virtual real mode 16-bit environment that runs inside 32-bit protected mode. When you run a DOS prompt window inside Windows 95/98, you have created a virtual real mode session. Because protected mode allows true multitasking, you can actually have several real mode sessions running, each with its own software running on a virtual PC. This can all run simultaneously, even while other 32-bit applications are running.

Note that any program running in a virtual real mode window can access up to only 1M of memory, which that program will believe is the first and only megabyte of memory in the system. In other words, if you run a DOS application in a virtual real window, it will have a 640K limitation on memory usage. That is because there is only 1M of total RAM in a 16-bit environment, and the upper 384K is reserved for system use. The virtual real window fully emulates an 8088 environment, so that aside from speed, the software runs as if it were on an original real-mode-only PC. Each virtual machine gets its own 1M address space, an image of the real hardware BIOS routines, and emulation of all other registers and features found in real mode.

Virtual real mode is used when you use a DOS window or run a DOS or Windows 3.x 16-bit program in Windows 95/98. When you start a DOS application, Windows 95 creates a virtual DOS machine under which it can run.

One interesting thing to note is that all Intel processors power up in real mode. If you load a 32-bit operating system, it will automatically switch the processor into 32-bit mode and take control from there.

Some DOS and Windows 3.x applications misbehave, which means they do things that even virtual real mode will not support. Diagnostics software is a perfect example of this. Such software will not run properly in a real-mode (virtual real) window under Windows 95/98 or NT. In that case, you can still run your Pentium II in the original no-frills real mode by interrupting the boot process and commanding the system to boot plain DOS. This is accomplished on most Windows 95/98/NT systems by pressing the F8 key when you see the prompt "Starting Windows..." on the screen. You will then see the Startup menu; you can select one of the Command Prompt choices, which tell the system to boot plain 16-bit real-mode DOS. The choice of "Safe mode command prompt" is best if you are going to run true hardware diagnostics, which do not normally run in protected mode and should be run with a minimum of drivers and other software loaded.

Although real mode is used by DOS and "standard" DOS applications, there are special programs available that "extend" DOS and allow access to extended memory (over 1M). These are sometimes called *DOS extenders* and are usually included as a part of any DOS or Windows 3.x software that uses them. The protocol that describes how to make DOS work in protected mode is called DPMI (DOS protected mode interface). DPMI was used by Windows 3.x to access extended memory for use with Windows 3.x applications. It allowed them to use more memory even though they were still 16-bit programs. DOS extenders are especially popular in DOS games, because it allows them to access much more of the system memory than the standard 1M most real-mode programs can address. These DOS extenders work by switching the processor in and out of real mode, or in the case of those that run under Windows, they use the DPMI interface built in to Windows, allowing them to share a portion of the system's extended memory.

Another exception in real mode is that the first 64K of extended memory is actually accessible to the PC in real mode, despite the fact that it's not supposed to be possible. This is the result of a bug in the original IBM AT with respect to the 21st memory address line, known as A20 (A0 is the first address line). By manipulating the A20 line, real-mode software can gain access to the first 64K of extended memory—the first 64K of memory past the first megabyte. This area of memory is called the *high memory area* (HMA).

▶▶ See "High Memory Area (HMA) and the A20 Line," p. 378

Processor Features

Modern PC processors have several different features that are described in the following sections. The most notable are:

- SMM (power management)
- Superscalar execution
- MMX technology
- Dynamic execution
- Dual Independent bus (DIB) architecture

SMM (Power Management). Spurred on primarily by the goal of putting faster and more powerful processors in laptop computers, Intel has created power management circuitry. This circuitry enables processors to conserve energy use and lengthen battery life. This was introduced initially in the Intel 486SL processor, which is an enhanced version of the 486DX processor. Subsequently, the power-management features were universalized and incorporated into all Pentium and later processors. This feature set is called SMM, which stands for System Management Mode.

SMM circuitry is integrated into the physical chip but operates independently to control the processor's power use based on its activity level. It allows the user to specify time intervals after which the CPU will be partially or fully powered down. It also supports the suspend/resume feature that allows for instant power on and power off, used mostly with laptop PCs. These settings are normally controlled via system BIOS settings.

Superscalar Execution. The fifth-generation Pentium and newer processors feature multiple internal instruction execution pipelines, which enable them to execute multiple instructions at the same time. The 486 and all preceding chips can perform only a single instruction at a time. Intel calls the capability to execute more than one instruction at a time *superscalar technology*. This technology provides additional performance compared with the 486.

Superscalar architecture usually is associated with high-output RISC (Reduced Instruction Set Computer) chips. The Pentium is one of the first CISC (Complex Instruction Set Computer) chips to be considered superscalar. This is now a standard feature of all fifth-generation and newer PC processors.

MMX Technology. MMX technology is named for Multi-Media eXtensions, or Matrix Math eXtensions, depending on whom you ask. Intel states that it is actually not an acronym and stands for nothing special; however, the internal origins are probably one of the preceding. MMX technology was introduced in the later fifth-generation Pentium processors (see Figure 3.1) as a kind of add-on that improves video compression/decompression, image manipulation, encryption, and I/O processing—all of which are used in a variety of today's software.

FIG. 3.1 An Intel Pentium MMX chip shown from the top and bottom (exposing the die). *Photograph used by permission of Intel Corporation.*

MMX consists of two main processor architectural improvements. The first is very basic; all MMX chips have a larger internal L1 cache than their non-MMX counterparts. This improves the performance of any and all software running on the chip, regardless of whether it actually uses the MMX-specific instructions.

The other part of MMX is that it extends the processor instructions set with 57 new commands or instructions, as well as a new instruction capability called Single Instruction, Multiple Data (SIMD).

Modern multimedia and communication applications often use repetitive loops that, while occupying 10% or less of the overall application code, can account for up to 90% of the execution time. SIMD enables one instruction to perform the same function on multiple pieces of data, similar to a teacher telling an entire class to "sit down," rather than addressing each student one at a time. SIMD allows the chip to reduce processor-intensive loops common with video, audio, graphics, and animation.

Intel also added 57 new instructions specifically designed to manipulate and process video, audio, and graphical data more efficiently. These instructions are oriented to the highly parallel and often repetitive sequences often found in multimedia operations. *Highly parallel* refers to the fact that the same processing is done on many different data points, such as when modifying a graphic image.

Intel has licensed the MMX capabilities to competitors such as AMD and Cyrix, who were then able to upgrade their own Intel-compatible processors with MMX technology.

Dynamic Execution. First used in the P6 or sixth-generation processors, Dynamic Execution is an innovative combination of three processing techniques designed to help the processor manipulate data more efficiently. Those techniques are multiple branch prediction, data flow analysis, and speculative execution. Dynamic execution enables the processor to be more efficient by manipulating data in a more logically ordered fashion rather than simply processing a list of instructions.

The way software is written can dramatically influence a processor's performance. For example, performance will be adversely affected if the processor is frequently required to stop what it is doing and jump or branch to a point elsewhere in the program. Delays also occur when the processor cannot process a new instruction until the current instruction is completed. Dynamic execution allows the processor to not only dynamically predict the order of instructions, but execute them out of order internally, if necessary, for an improvement in speed.

Dynamic execution consists of the following:

Multiple Branch Prediction. Predicts the flow of the program through several branches. Using a special algorithm, the processor can anticipate jumps or branches in the instruction flow. It uses this to predict where the next instructions can be found in memory with an accuracy of 90% or greater. This is possible because while the processor is fetching instructions, it is also looking at instructions further ahead in the program.

Data Flow Analysis. Analyzes and schedules instructions to be executed in an optimal sequence, independent of the original program order. The processor looks at decoded software instructions and determines whether they are available for processing or are instead dependent on other instructions to be executed first. The processor then determines the optimal sequence for processing and executes the instructions in the most efficient manner.

Speculative Execution. Increases performance by looking ahead of the program counter and executing instructions that are likely to be needed later. Because the software instructions being processed are based on predicted branches, the results are stored in a pool for later referral. If they are to be executed by the resultant program flow, the already completed instructions are retired and the results are committed to the processor's main registers in the original program execution order. This technique essentially allows the processor to complete instructions in advance and then grab the already completed results when necessary.

Dynamic execution is one of the hallmarks of all sixth-generation processors.

Dual Independent Bus (DIB) Architecture. The Dual Independent Bus (DIB) architecture was first implemented in the first sixth-generation processor. DIB was created to improve processor bus bandwidth and performance. Having two (dual) independent data I/O buses enables the processor to access data from either of its buses simultaneously and in parallel, rather than in a singular sequential manner (as in a single-bus system). The second or backside bus in a processor with DIB is used for the L2 cache, allowing it to run at much greater speeds than if it were to share the main processor bus.

Two buses make up the Dual Independent Bus architecture: the L2 cache bus and the processor-to-main-memory, or system, bus. The P6 Pentium Pro and Pentium II processors can use both buses simultaneously, eliminating a bottleneck there. The Dual Independent Bus architecture enables the L2 cache of the 400MHz Pentium II processor, for example, to run more than three times as fast as the L2 cache of older Pentium processors. Because the backside or L2 cache bus is coupled to the speed of the processor core, as the frequency of future Pentium II processors increases, so will the speed of the L2 cache.

The key to implementing DIB is to move the L2 cache memory off of the motherboard and into the processor package. This allows the L2 cache to run at speeds more like the L1 cache, much faster than the motherboard memory. To move the cache into the processor, modifications had to be made to the CPU socket. The only socket-based processor that supports DIB is the Pentium Pro, which plugs into Socket 8. In the Pentium Pro, the L1 cache is directly on the processor die (as with all 486 and higher processors), and the L2 cache is contained within the chip package but on separate die(s). This, unfortunately, made the chip expensive and difficult to produce, although it did mean that the L2 cache ran at full processor speed.

The Pentium II adopted a less expensive and easier-to-manufacture approach. By placing the processor and L2 cache as separate chips inside a cartridge, they now have a CPU module that is easier and less expensive to make. The Single Edge Contact (SEC) cartridge is an innovative—if a bit unwieldy—package design that incorporates the backside bus and L2 cache internally. Using the SEC design, the core and L2 cache are fully enclosed in a plastic and metal cartridge. These subcomponents are surface mounted directly to a substrate (or base) inside the cartridge to enable high-frequency operation. The SEC cartridge technology allows the use of widely available, high-performance industry standard Burst Static RAMs (BSRAMs) for the dedicated L2 cache. This greatly reduces the cost compared to the proprietary cache chips used inside the CPU package in the Pentium Pro.

Most Pentium IIs run the L2 cache at exactly 1/2-core speed, but that can easily be scaled up or down in future Pentium II processors. Also, most have 512K of L2 cache internally, but that can be easily changed in the future because Intel is now using off-the-shelf cache chips in the processor cartridge. Intel will make Pentium IIs with anywhere from no L2 caches to multiple megabytes.

The Pentium II SEC processor connects to a motherboard via a single-edge connector instead of the multiple pins used in existing Pin Grid Array socket packages.

DIB also allows the system bus to perform multiple simultaneous transactions (instead of singular sequential transactions), accelerating the flow of information within the system and boosting performance. Overall Dual Independent Bus architecture offers up to three times the bandwidth performance over a single-bus architecture processor.

Processor Manufacturing

Processors are manufactured primarily from silicon, the most common element on earth. Silicon is the primary ingredient in beach sand (silicon dioxide); however, in that form it isn't pure enough to be used in chips.

To be made into chips, raw silicon is purified, melted down, and then allowed to solidify into large cylindrical crystals called *boules*. Each boule is currently about 8 inches in diameter and over 50 inches long and weighs hundreds of pounds. The boule is then ground into a perfect 200-mm-diameter cylinder (the current standard), often with a flat cut on one side for positioning accuracy and handling. Each boule is then cut with a high-precision diamond saw into over a thousand circular wafers less than a millimeter thick each. Each wafer is polished to a mirror-smooth surface.

Chips are manufactured using a process called *photolithography*. Through this photographic process, transistors and circuit and signal pathways are created in semiconductors by depositing different layers of various materials on the chip, one after the other. Where two specific circuits intersect, a transistor or switch can be formed.

The photolithographic process starts by coating the wafer with a layer of specially doped semiconductor material, covering that layer with a photoresist chemical, and then projecting the image of the chip onto the now light-sensitive surface. *Doping* is the term used to describe chemical impurities added to silicon (which is naturally a non-conductor), creating a material with semiconductor properties. The projector uses a specially created mask, which is essentially a map of that particular layer of the chip. The Pentium II currently has four individual layers, although other modern processors may have six or more layers. Each processor design requires as many masks as layers to produce the chips.

As the light passes through the first mask, it is focused on the wafer surface, imprinting it with the image of that layer of the chip. Each chip image is called a *die*. A device called a *stepper* then moves the wafer over a small amount and the same mask is used to imprint another chip die immediately next to the previous one. After the entire wafer is imprinted with chips, a caustic solution washes away the areas where the light struck the photoresist, leaving the mask imprints of the individual chip *vias* (interconnections between layers) and circuit pathways. Then, another layer of semiconductor material is deposited on the wafer with more photoresist on top, and the next mask is used to produce the next layer of circuitry. Using this method, the layers of each chip are built one on top of the other, until the chips are completed.

A completed circular wafer will have as many chips imprinted on it as can possibly fit. Because each chip is normally square or rectangular, there are some unused portions at the edges of the wafer, but every attempt is made to use every square millimeter of surface.

The standard wafer size used in the industry today is 200mm in diameter, or just under 8 inches. This results in a wafer of about 31,416 square millimeters. The current Pentium II 300MHz processor is made up of 7.5 million transistors using a 0.35 micron (millionth of a meter) process. This process results in a die of exactly 14.2mm on each side, which is 202 square millimeters of area. This means that about 150 total Pentium II 300MHz chips on the .35 micron process can be made from a single 200mm-diameter wafer.

The trend in the industry is to go to both larger wafers and a smaller chip die process. *Process* refers to the size of the individual circuits and transistors on the chip. For example, the Pentium II 333MHz is made on a newer and smaller .25 micron process, which reduces the total chip die size to only 10.2mm on each side, or a total chip area of 104 square millimeters. On the same 200mm (8-inch) wafer as before, Intel can make about 300 Pentium II chips using this process, or double the amount over the larger .35 micron process 300MHz version.

The trend in wafers is to move from the current 200mm (8-inch) diameter to a bigger, 300mm (12-inch) diameter wafer. This will increase surface area dramatically over the smaller 200mm design, and boost chip production to about 675 chips per wafer. Intel and other manufacturers expect to have 300mm wafer production in place just after the year 2000. After that happens, chip prices should drop dramatically as the supply increases.

Note that all the chips on each wafer will not be good, especially as a new production line starts. As the manufacturing process for a given chip or production line is perfected, more and more of the chips will be good. The ratio of good to bad chips on a wafer is called the *yield*. Yields well under 50% are common when a new chip starts production; however, by the end of a given chip's life, the yields are normally in the 90% range. Most chip manufacturers guard their yield figures and are very secretive about them, as knowledge of yield problems can give their competitors an edge. A low yield causes problems both in the cost per chip and in delivery delays to their customers. If a company has specific knowledge of competitors' improving yields, they can set prices or schedule production to get higher market share at a critical point. For example, AMD was plagued by low-yield problems during '97 and '98, which cost them significant market share and was rumored to cause the departure of their primary chip designer, Vinhod Dahm. They have been solving the problems, but they also signed up with IBM Microelectronics to manufacture some of their processors for them. IBM is well-known as a leader in chip manufacturing technologies, with chip production plants (called *fabs*) that are second to none in terms of quality and production capability.

After a wafer is complete, a special fixture tests each of the chips on the wafer and marks the bad ones to be separated out later. The chips are then cut from the wafer using either a high-powered laser or diamond saw.

After being cut from the wafers, the individual die are then retested, packaged, and retested again. The packaging process is also referred to as *bonding*, because the die is placed into a chip housing where a special machine bonds fine gold wires between the die and the pins on the chip. The package is the container for the chip die, and it essentially seals it from the environment.

After the chips are bonded and packaged, final testing is done to determine both proper function and rated speed. Different chips in the same batch will often run at different speeds. Special test fixtures run each chip at different pressures, temperatures, and speeds, looking for the point at which the chip stops working. At this point, the maximum successful speed is noted and the final chips are sorted into bins with those that tested at a similar speed. For example, the Pentium II 233, 266, and 300 are all exactly the same chip made using the same die. They were sorted at the end of the manufacturing cycle by speed.

One interesting thing about this is that as a manufacturer gains more experience and perfects a particular chip assembly line, the yield of the higher-speed versions goes way up. This means that out of a wafer of 150 total chips, perhaps more than 100 of them check out at 300MHz, while only a few won't run at that speed. The paradox is that Intel sells a lot more of the lower-priced 233 and 266 chips, so they will just dip into the bin of 300MHz processors and label them as 233 or 266 chips and sell them that way. People began discovering that many of the lower-rated chips would actually run at speeds much higher than they were rated, and the business of overclocking was born. Overclocking describes the operation of a chip at a speed higher than it was rated for. In many cases, people have successfully accomplished this because, in essence, they had a higher-speed processor already—it was marked with a lower rating only because it was sold as the slower version.

Intel has seen fit to put a stop to this by building overclock protection into most of their newer chips. This is usually done in the bonding process, where the chips are intentionally altered so they won't run at any speeds higher than they are rated. Normally this involves changing the Bus Frequency (BF) pins on the chip, which control the internal multipliers the chip uses. Even so, enterprising individuals have found ways to run their motherboards at bus speeds higher than normal, so even though the chip won't allow a higher multiplier, you can still run it at a speed higher than it was designed.

I recently installed a 200MHz Pentium processor in a system, which is supposed to run at a 3x multiplier based off a 66MHz motherboard speed. I tried changing the multiplier to 3.5x but the chip refused to go any faster; in fact, it ran at the same or lower speed than before. This is a sure sign of overclock protection inside. My motherboard included a jumper setting for an unauthorized speed of 75MHz, which when multiplied by 3x resulted in an actual processor speed of 225MHz. This worked like a charm and the system is now running fast and clean. Note that I am not necessarily recommending overclocking for everybody; in fact, I normally don't recommend it at all for any important systems. If you have a system you want to fool around with, it is interesting to try. Like my cars, I always seem to want to hotrod my computers!

Physical Packaging

Processors come in many physical packages, but the most common are Pin Grid Array (PGA), Tape Carrier Package (TCP), and Single Edge Cartridge (SEC) designs. The following sections explain the PGA and SEC packages, which are used in desktop systems. TCP is covered in Chapter 15, along with the other coverage of technologies specific to mobile computing.

▶▶ See "Tape Carrier Packaging," p. 923, and "Mobile Module," p. 926

PGA. PGA packaging has been the most common chip package used until recently. It was used starting with the 286 processor all the way back in the '80s and is still used today for Pentium and Pentium Pro processors. PGA takes its name from the fact that the chip has a grid-like array of pins on the bottom of the package. PGA chips are inserted into sockets, which are often of a ZIF (Zero Insertion Force) design. A ZIF socket has a lever to allow for easy installation and removal of the chip.

Most Pentium processors use a variation on the regular PGA called SPGA (Staggered Pin Grid Array), where the pins are staggered on the underside of the chip rather than in standard rows and columns. This was done to move the pins closer together and decrease the overall size of the chip when a large number of pins is required. Figure 3.2 shows a Pentium Pro that uses the SPGA (on the left) next to an older Pentium 66 that uses the regular PGA. Note that the right half of the Pentium Pro shown here has additional pins staggered among the other rows and columns.

FIG. 3.2   PGA on Pentium 66 (left) and SPGA on Pentium Pro (right).

Single Edge Cartridge (SEC). Abandoning the chip-in-a-socket approach used by virtually all processors until this point, the Pentium II chip is characterized by its Single Edge Contact (SEC) cartridge design. The processor, along with several L2 cache chips, is mounted on a small circuit board (much like an oversized memory SIMM), which is then sealed in a metal and plastic cartridge. The cartridge is then plugged into the motherboard through an edge connector called Slot 1, which looks very much like an adapter card slot.

Slot 1 is the connection to the motherboard, and has 242 pins. The Slot 1 dimensions are shown in Figure 3.3. The SEC cartridge processor is plugged into slot 1 and secured with a processor-retention mechanism, which is a bracket that holds it in place. There may also be a retention mechanism or support for the processor heat sink. Figure 3.4 shows the parts of the cover that make up the SEC package. Note the large thermal plate used to aid in dissipating the heat from this processor.

The main reason for going to this package was to be able to move the L2 cache memory off of the motherboard and onto the processor in an economical and scalable way. Using the SEC design, Intel can easily offer Pentium II processors with more or less cache and faster or slower cache.

Processor Sockets

Intel has created a set of socket designs—Socket 1 through Socket 8—used for their chips from the 486 through the Pentium Pro. Each socket is designed to support a different range of original and upgrade processors. Table 3.6 shows the specifications of these sockets.

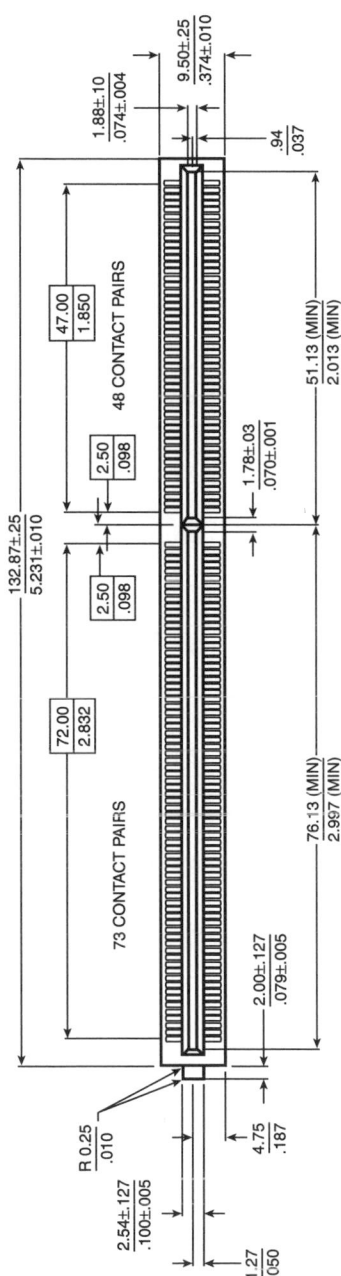

FIG. 3.3 Pentium II Processor Slot 1 dimensions (metric/English).

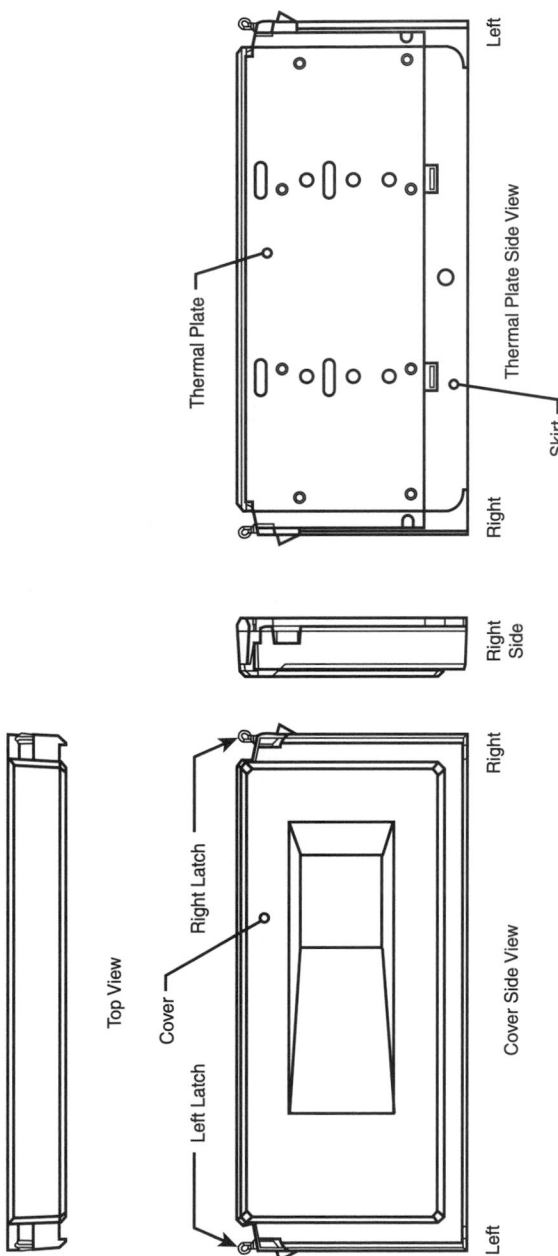

FIG. 3.4 Pentium II Processor SEC package parts.

Table 3.6	Intel 486/Pentium CPU Socket Types and Specifications			
Socket Number	**No. of Pins**	**Pin Layout**	**Voltage**	**Supported Processors**
Socket 1	169	17×17 PGA	5v	SX/SX2, DX/DX2*, DX4 OverDrive
Socket 2	238	19×19 PGA	5v	SX/SX2, DX/DX2*, DX4 OverDrive, 486 Pentium OverDrive
Socket 3	237	19×19 PGA	5v/3.3v	SX/SX2, DX/DX2, DX4, 486 Pentium OverDrive
Socket 4	273	21×21 PGA	5v	Pentium 60/66, Pentium 60/66 OverDrive
Socket 5	320	37×37 SPGA	3.3v	Pentium 75-133, Pentium 75+ OverDrive
Socket 6**	235	19×19 PGA	3.3v	DX4, 486 Pentium OverDrive
Socket 7	321	37×37 SPGA	VRM	Pentium 75-300, Pentium 75+ OverDrive
Socket 8	387	Dual pattern SPGA	VRM	Pentium Pro
Slot 1	242	Slot	VRM	Pentium II

DX4 also can be supported with the addition of an aftermarket 3.3v voltage-regulator adapter.
**Socket 6 was a paper standard only and was never actually implemented in any systems.*
PGA = Pin Grid Array
SPGA = Staggered Pin Grid Array
VRM = Voltage Regulator Module

Sockets 1, 2, 3, and 6 are 486 processor sockets and are shown together in Figure 3.5 so you can see the overall size comparisons and pin arrangements between these sockets. Sockets 4, 5, 7, and 8 are Pentium and Pentium Pro processor sockets and are also shown together in Figure 3.6 so you can see the overall size comparisons and pin arrangements between these sockets. More detailed drawings of each socket are included throughout the remainder of this section with the detailed descriptions of the sockets.

The original OverDrive socket, now officially called Socket 1, is a 169-pin PGA socket. Motherboards that have this socket can support any of the 486SX, DX, and DX2 processors, and the DX2/OverDrive versions. This type of socket is found on most 486 systems that originally were designed for OverDrive upgrades. Figure 3.7 shows the pinout of Socket 1.

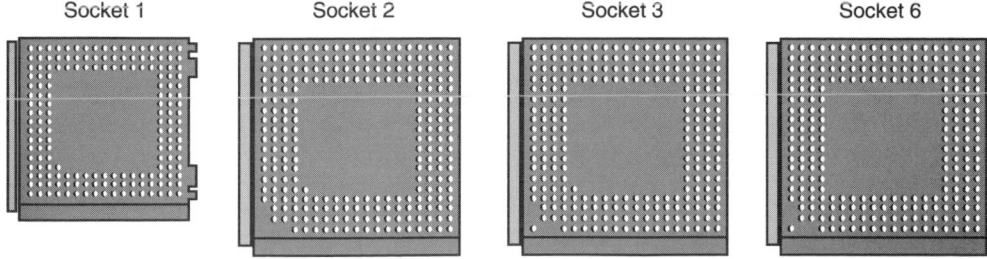

FIG. 3.5   486 Processor Sockets.

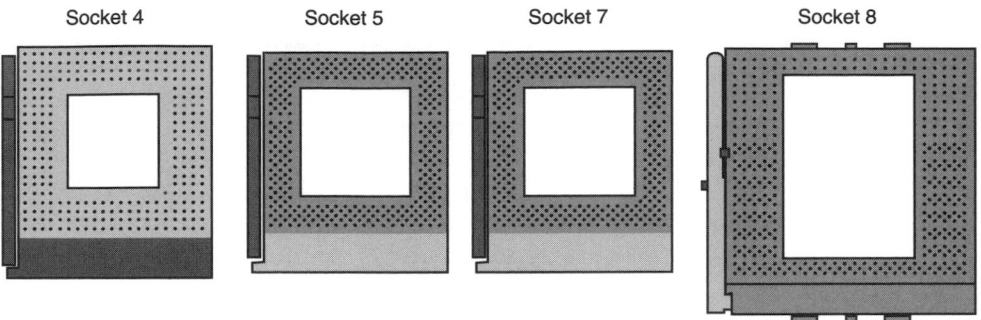

FIG. 3.6 Pentium and Pentium Pro Processor Sockets.

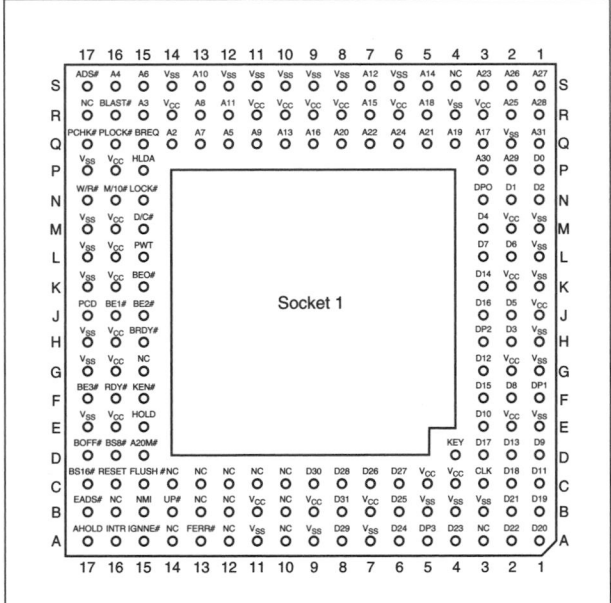

FIG. 3.7 Intel Socket 1 pinout.

The original DX processor draws a maximum 0.9 amps of 5v power in 33MHz form (4.5 watts) and a maximum 1 amp in 50MHz form (5 watts). The DX2 processor or OverDrive processor draws a maximum 1.2 amps at 66MHz (6 watts). This minor increase in power requires only a passive heat sink consisting of aluminum fins that are glued to the processor with thermal transfer epoxy. Passive heat sinks don't have any mechanical components like fans. Heat sinks with fans or other devices that use power are called *active* heat sinks. OverDrive processors rated at 40MHz or less do not have heat sinks.

When the DX2 processor was released, Intel already was working on the new Pentium processor. The company wanted to offer a 32-bit, scaled-down version of the Pentium as an upgrade for systems that originally came with a DX2 processor. Rather than just increasing the clock rate, Intel created an all new chip with enhanced capabilities derived from the Pentium.

The chip, called the Pentium OverDrive Processor, plugs into a processor socket with the Socket 2 or Socket 3 design. These sockets will hold any 486 SX, DX, or DX2 processor, as well as the Pentium OverDrive. Because this chip is essentially a 32-bit version of the (normally 64-bit) Pentium chip, many have taken to calling it a *Pentium-SX*. It is available in 25/63MHz and 33/83MHz versions. The first number indicates the base motherboard speed, while the second number indicates the actual operating speed of the Pentium OverDrive chip. As you can see, it is a clock-multiplied chip that runs at 2.5 times the motherboard speed. Figure 3.8 shows the pinout configuration of the official Socket 2 design.

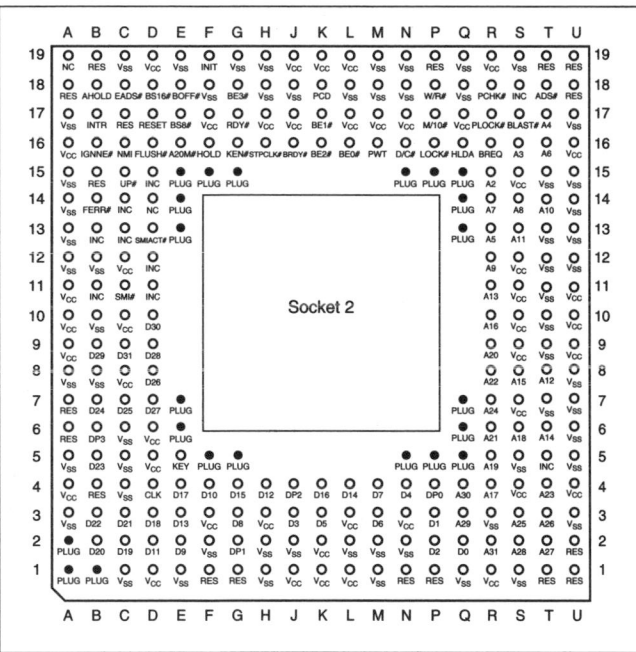

FIG. 3.8 238-pin Intel Socket 2 configuration.

Notice that although the new chip for Socket 2 is called Pentium OverDrive, it is not a full-scale (64-bit) Pentium. Intel released the design of Socket 2 a little prematurely and found that the chip ran too hot for many systems. The company solved this problem by adding a special active heat sink to the Pentium OverDrive processor. This active heat sink is a combination of a standard heat sink and a built-in electric fan. Unlike the aftermarket glue-on or clip-on fans for processors that you may have seen, this one actually draws 5v power directly from the socket to drive the fan. No external connection to disk drive cables or the power supply is required. The fan/heat sink assembly clips and plugs directly into the processor, providing for easy replacement should the fan ever fail.

Another requirement of the active heat sink is additional clearance—no obstructions for an area about 1.4 inches off the base of the existing socket to allow for heat-sink clearance. The Pentium OverDrive upgrade will be difficult or impossible in systems that were not designed with this feature.

Another problem with this particular upgrade is power consumption. The 5v Pentium OverDrive processor will draw up to 2.5 amps at 5v (including the fan) or 12.5 watts, which is more than double the 1.2 amps (6 watts) drawn by the DX2 66 processor. Intel did not provide this information when it established the socket design, so the company set up a testing facility to certify systems for thermal and mechanical compatibility with the Pentium OverDrive upgrade. For the greatest peace of mind, ensure that your system is certified compatible before you attempt this upgrade.

> **Note**
>
> See Intel's Web site at **http://www.intel.com** for a comprehensive list of certified OverDrive-compatible systems.

Figure 3.9 shows the dimensions of the Pentium OverDrive processor and the active heat sink/fan assembly.

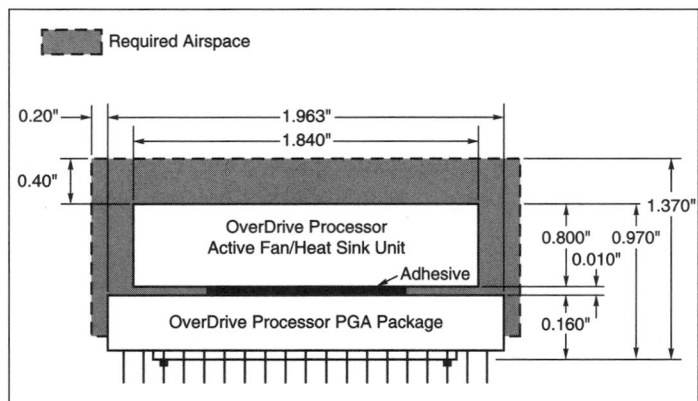

FIG. 3.9 The physical dimensions of the Intel Pentium OverDrive processor and active heat sink.

Because of problems with the original Socket 2 specification and the enormous heat the 5v version of the Pentium OverDrive processor generates, Intel came up with an improved design. The new processor is the same as the previous Pentium OverDrive processor, with the exception that it runs on 3.3v and draws a maximum 3.0 amps of 3.3v (9.9 watts) and 0.2 amp of 5v (1 watt) to run the fan, for a total 10.9 watts. This configuration provides a slight margin over the 5v version of this processor. The fan will be easy to remove from the OverDrive processor for replacement, should it ever fail.

Intel had to create a new socket to support both the DX4 processor, which runs on 3.3v, and the 3.3v Pentium OverDrive processor. In addition to the new 3.3v chips, this new socket supports the older 5v SX, DX, DX2, and even the 5v Pentium OverDrive chip. The design, called Socket 3, is the most flexible upgradable 486 design. Figure 3.10 shows the pinout specification of Socket 3.

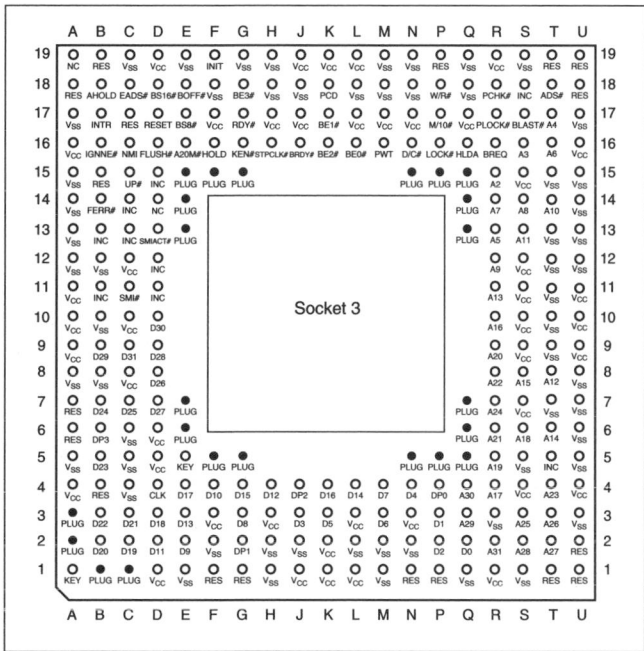

FIG. 3.10 237-pin Intel Socket 3 configuration.

Notice that Socket 3 has one additional pin and several others plugged compared with Socket 2. Socket 3 provides for better keying, which prevents an end user from accidentally installing the processor in an improper orientation. One serious problem exists, however: This socket cannot automatically determine the type of voltage that will be provided to it. A jumper is likely to be added on the motherboard near the socket to enable the user to select 5v or 3.3v operation.

Caution

Because this jumper must be manually set, however, a user could install a 3.3v processor in this socket when it is configured for 5v operation. This installation will instantly destroy a very expensive chip when the system is powered on. It will be up to the end user to make sure that this socket is properly configured for voltage, depending on which type of processor is installed. If the jumper is set in 3.3v configuration and a 5v processor is installed, no harm will occur, but the system will not operate properly unless the jumper is reset for 5v.

The original Pentium processor 60MHz and 66MHz versions had 273 pins and would plug into a 273-pin Pentium processor socket—a 5v-only socket, because all the original Pentium processors run on 5v. This socket will accept the original Pentium 60MHz or 66MHz processor, and the OverDrive processor. Figure 3.11 shows the pinout specification of Socket 4.

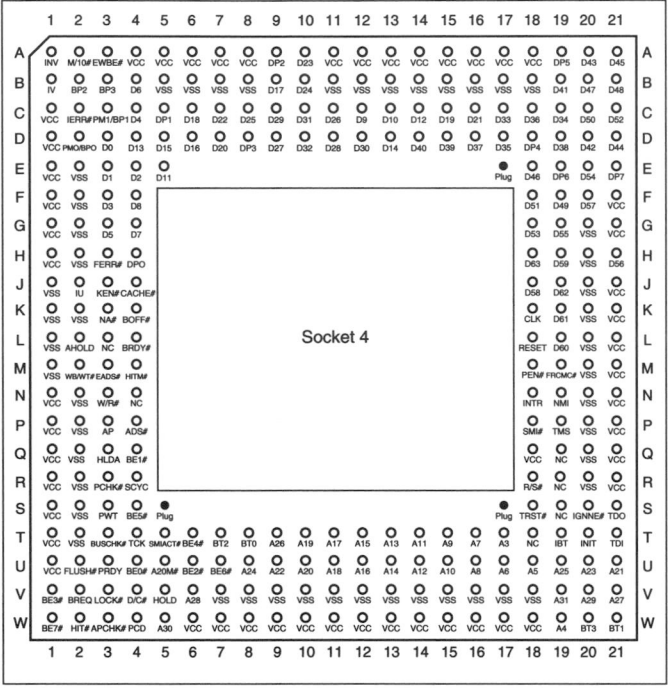

FIG. 3.11   273-pin Intel Socket 4 configuration.

Somewhat amazingly, the original Pentium 66MHz processor consumes up to 3.2 amps of 5v power (16 watts), not including power for a standard active heat sink (fan), whereas the 66MHz OverDrive processor that replaced it consumes a maximum 2.7 amps (13.5 watts), including about 1 watt to drive the fan. Even the original 60MHz Pentium processor consumes up to 2.91 amps at 5v (14.55 watts). It may seem strange that the replacement processor, which is twice as fast, consumes less power than the original, but this has to do with the manufacturing processes used for the original and OverDrive processors.

Although both processors will run on 5v, the original Pentium processor was created with a circuit size of 0.8 micron, making that processor much more power-hungry than the newer 0.6-micron circuits used in the OverDrive and the other Pentium processors. Shrinking the circuit size is one of the best ways to decrease power consumption. Although the OverDrive processor for Pentium-based systems will draw less power than the original processor, additional clearance may have to be allowed for the active heat sink assembly that is mounted on top. As in other OverDrive processors with built-in fans, the power to run the fan will be drawn directly from the chip socket, so no separate power-supply connection is required. Also, the fan will be easy to replace should it ever fail.

When Intel redesigned the Pentium processor to run at 75, 90, and 100MHz, the company went to a 0.6-micron manufacturing process and 3.3v operation. This change resulted in lower power consumption: only 3.25 amps at 3.3v (10.725 watts). Therefore, the 100MHz Pentium processor can use far less power than even the original 60MHz version. The newest 120 and higher Pentium, Pentium Pro, and Pentium II chips use an even smaller die 0.35-micron process. This results in even lower power consumption and allows the extremely high clock rates without overheating.

The Pentium 75 and higher processors actually have 296 pins, although they plug into the official Intel Socket 5 design, which calls for a total 320 pins. The additional pins are used by the Pentium OverDrive for Pentium processors. This socket has the 320 pins configured in a Staggered Pin Grid Array, in which the individual pins are staggered for tighter clearance.

Several OverDrive processors for existing Pentiums are currently available. If you have a first-generation Pentium 60 or 66 with a Socket 4, you can purchase a standard Pentium OverDrive chip that effectively doubles the speed of your old processor. An OverDrive chip with MMX technology is available for second-generation 75MHz, 90MHz, and 100MHz Pentiums using Socket 5 or Socket 7. Processor speeds after upgrade are 125MHz for the Pentium 75, 150MHz for the Pentium 90, and 166MHz for the Pentium 100. MMX greatly enhances processor performance, particularly under multimedia applications, and is discussed in the section "Pentium-MMX Processors" in this chapter. Figure 3.12 shows the standard pinout for Socket 5.

The Pentium OverDrive for Pentium Processors has an active heat sink (fan) assembly that draws power directly from the chip socket. The chip requires a maximum 4.33 amps of 3.3v to run the chip (14.289 watts) and 0.2 amp of 5v power to run the fan (1 watt), which means total power consumption of 15.289 watts. This is less power than the original 66MHz Pentium processor requires, yet it runs a chip that is as much as four times faster!

The last 486 socket was created especially for the DX4 and the 486 Pentium OverDrive Processor. Socket 6 is a slightly redesigned version of Socket 3, which has an additional two pins plugged for proper chip keying. Socket 6 has 235 pins and will accept only 3.3v 486 or OverDrive processors. This means that Socket 6 will accept only the DX4 and the 486 Pentium OverDrive Processor. Because this socket provides only 3.3v, and because the only processors that plug into it are designed to operate on 3.3v, there's no chance that damaging problems will occur, like those with the Socket 3 design. In practice, Socket 6 has seen very limited use. Figure 3.13 shows the Socket 6 pinout.

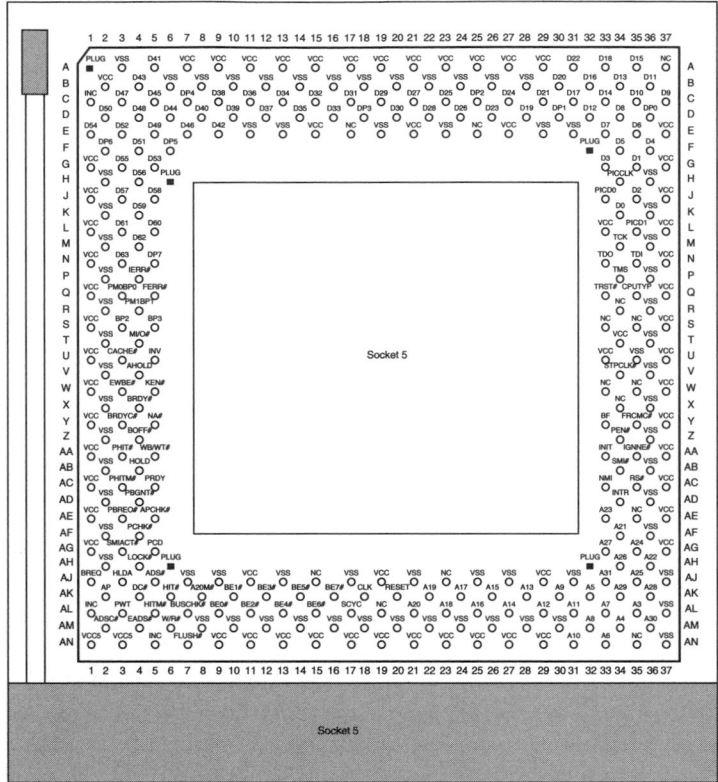

FIG. 3.12   320-pin Intel Socket 5 configuration.

Socket 7 is essentially the same as Socket 5 with one additional key pin in the opposite inside corner of the existing key pin. Socket 7, therefore, has 321 pins total in a 21×21 SPGA arrangement. The real difference with Socket 7 is not the socket, but with the companion VRM (Voltage Regulator Module) that must accompany it.

The VRM is a small circuit board. The VRM contains all the voltage regulation circuitry used to drop the 5v power supply signal to the correct voltage for the processor. The VRM was implemented for several good reasons. One is that voltage regulators tend to run hot and are very failure-prone. Soldering these circuits on the motherboard, as has been done with the Pentium Socket 5 design, makes it very likely that a failure of the regulator will require a complete motherboard replacement. Although technically the regulator could be replaced, many are surface-mount soldered, which would make the whole procedure very time-consuming and expensive. Besides, in this day and age, when the top-of-the-line motherboards are worth only $250 (less the processor and any memory), it is just not cost-effective to service them. Having a replaceable VRM plugged into a socket will make it easy to replace the regulators should they ever fail.

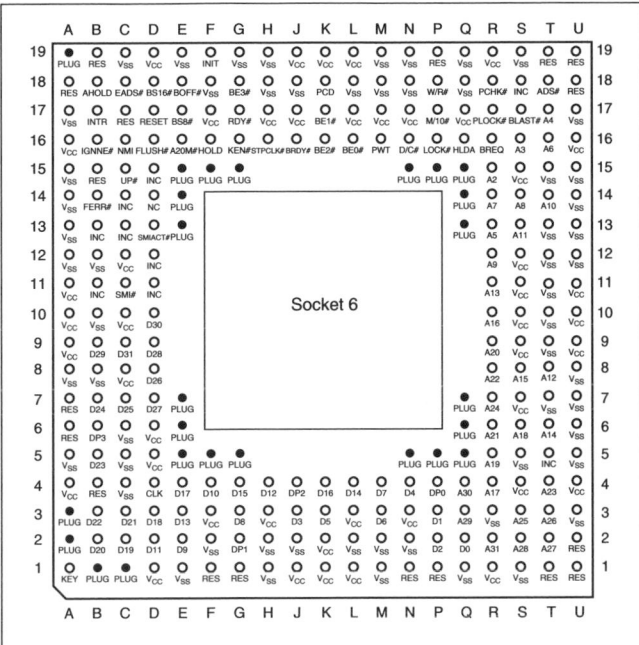

FIG. 3.13   235-pin Intel Socket 6 configuration.

Although replaceability is nice, the main reason behind the VRM design is that Intel is building new Pentium processors to run on a variety of voltages. Intel has several different versions of the Pentium, Pentium-MMX, Pentium Pro, and Pentium II processors that run on 3.3v (called *VR*), 3.465v (called *VRE*), and 3.1v, 2.8v, and 2.45v. Because of this, most newer motherboards are either including VRM sockets or building adaptable VRMs right into the motherboard.

In other words, if you want to purchase a Pentium board that can be upgraded to the next generation of even higher-speed Pentium processors, look for a system with a Socket 7 and an integrated VRM supporting different voltage selections. Figure 3.14 shows the Socket 7 pinout.

Socket 8 is a special SPGA socket featuring a whopping 387 pins! This was specifically designed for the Pentium Pro processor with the integrated L2 cache. The additional pins are to allow the chipset to control the L2 cache that is integrated in the same package as the processor. Figure 3.15 shows the Socket 8 pinout.

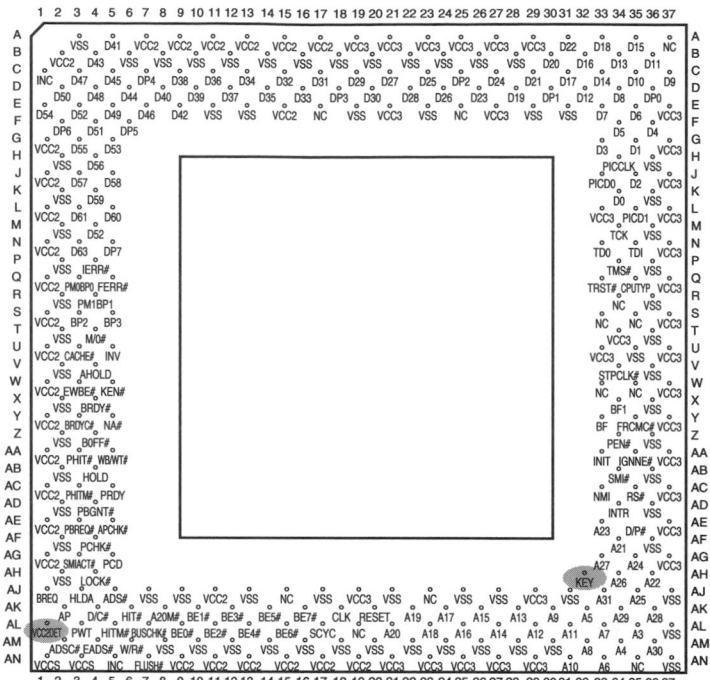

FIG. 3.14   Socket 7 (Pentium) Pinout—top view.

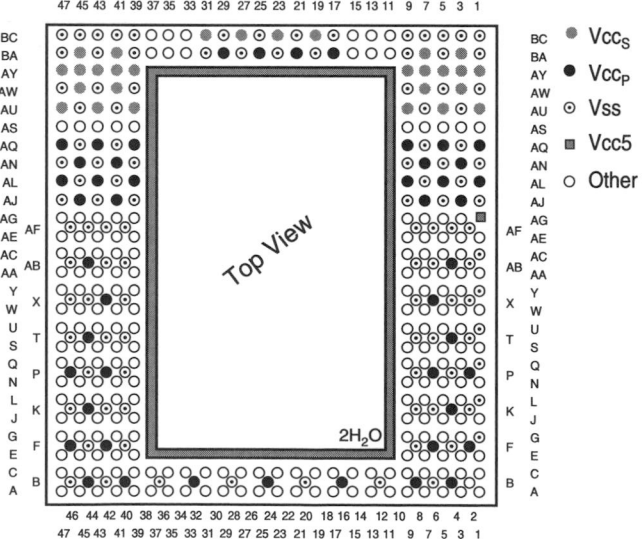

FIG. 3.15   Socket 8 (Pentium Pro) Pinout showing power pin locations.

Zero Insertion Force (ZIF) Sockets. When Intel created the Socket 1 specification, they realized that if users were going to upgrade processors, they had to make the process easier. They found that it typically takes 100 pounds of insertion force to install a chip in a standard 169-pin screw machine socket 1. With this much force involved, you easily could damage either the chip or socket during removal or reinstallation. Because of this, some motherboard manufacturers began using Low Insertion Force (LIF) sockets, which typically required only 60 pounds of insertion force for a 169-pin chip. With the LIF or standard socket, I usually advise removing the motherboard—that way you can support the board from behind when you insert the chip. Pressing down on the motherboard with 60 to 100 pounds of force can crack the board if it is not supported properly. A special tool is also required to remove a chip from one of these sockets. As you can imagine, even the *low* insertion force was relative, and a better solution was needed if the average person was going to ever replace their CPU.

Manufacturers began inserting special Zero Insertion Force (ZIF) sockets in their later Socket 1 motherboard designs. Since then, virtually all processor sockets have been of the ZIF design. Note, however, that a given Socket X specification has nothing to do with whether it is ZIF, LIF, or standard; the socket specification covers only the pin arrangement. These days, nearly all motherboard manufacturers are using ZIF sockets. These sockets almost eliminate the risk involved in upgrading because no insertion force is necessary to install the chip. Most ZIF sockets are handle-actuated; you simply lift the handle, drop the chip into the socket, and then close the handle. This design makes replacing the original processor with the upgrade processor an easy task.

Slot 1. Slot 1 is used by the SEC (Single Edge Cartridge) design used with the Pentium II processors. Inside the cartridge is a substrate card that includes the processor and L2 cache. Unlike the Pentium Pro, the L2 cache is mounted on the circuit board and not within the same chip package as the processor. This allows Intel to use aftermarket SRAM chips instead of making them internally, and also allows them to make Pentium II processors with different amounts of cache easily. For example, the Celeron versions of the Pentium II have no L2 cache, while other future versions will have more than the standard 512K included in most Pentium II processors. Figure 3.16 shows the Slot 1 connector dimensions and pin layout.

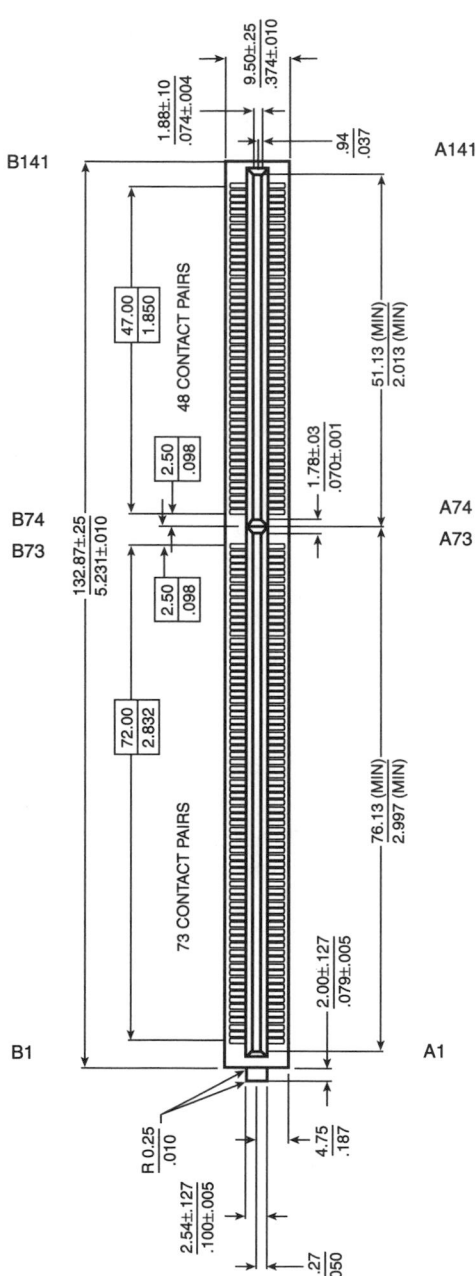

FIG. 3.16 Slot 1 connector dimensions and pin layout.

Table 3.7 lists the names of each of the pins in the Slot 1 connector.

Table 3.7	Signal Listing in Order by Pin Number		
Pin No.	**Pin Name**	**Pin No.**	**Pin Name**
A1	VCC_VTT	B1	EMI
A2	GND	B2	FLUSH#
A3	VCC_VTT	B3	SMI#
A4	IERR#	B4	INIT#
A5	A20M#	B5	VCC_VTT
A6	GND	B6	STPCLK#
A7	FERR#	B7	TCK
A8	IGNNE#	B8	SLP#
A9	TDI	B9	VCC_VTT
A10	GND	B10	TMS
A11	TDO	B11	TRST#
A12	PWRGOOD	B12	Reserved
A13	TESTHI	B13	VCC_CORE
A14	GND	B14	Reserved
A15	THERMTRIP#	B15	Reserved
A16	Reserved	B16	LINT[1]/NMI
A17	LINT[0]/INTR	B17	VCC_CORE
A18	GND	B18	PICCLK
A19	PICD[0]	B19	BP#[2]
A20	PREQ#	B20	Reserved
A21	BP#[3]	B21	BSEL#
A22	GND	B22	PICD[1]
A23	BPM#[0]	B23	PRDY#
A24	BINIT#	B24	BPM#[1]
A25	DEP#[0]	B25	VCC_CORE
A26	GND	B26	DEP#[2]
A27	DEP#[1]	B27	DEP#[4]
A28	DEP#[3]	B28	DEP#[7]
A29	DEP#[5]	B29	VCC_CORE
A30	GND	B30	D#[62]
A31	DEP#[6]	B31	D#[58]
A32	D#[61]	B32	D#[63]
A33	D#[55]	B33	VCC_CORE
A34	GND	B34	D#[56]
A35	D#[60]	B35	D#[50]
A36	D#[53]	B36	D#[54]

(continues)

Pin No.	Pin Name	Pin No.	Pin Name
A37	D#[57]	B37	VCC_CORE
A38	GND	B38	D#[59]
A39	D#[46]	B39	D#[48]
A40	D#[49]	B40	D#[52]
A41	D#[51]	B41	EMI
A42	GND	B42	D#[41]
A43	D#[42]	B43	D#[47]
A44	D#[45]	B44	D#[44]
A45	D#[39]	B45	VCC_CORE
A46	GND	B46	D#[36]
A47	Reserved	B47	D#[40]
A48	D#[43]	B48	D#[34]
A49	D#[37]	B49	VCC_CORE
A50	GND	B50	D#[38]
A51	D#[33]	B51	D#[32]
A52	D#[35]	B52	D#[28]
A53	D#[31]	B53	VCC_CORE
A54	GND	B54	D#[29]
A55	D#[30]	B55	D#[26]
A56	D#[27]	B56	D#[25]
A57	D#[24]	B57	VCC_CORE
A58	GND	B58	D#[22]
A59	D#[23]	B59	D#[19]
A60	D#[21]	B60	D#[18]
A61	D#[16]	B61	EMI
A62	GND	B62	D#[20]
A63	D#[13]	B63	D#[17]
A64	D#[11]	B64	D#[15]
A65	D#[10]	B65	VCC_CORE
A66	GND	B66	D#[12]
A67	D#[14]	B67	D#[7]
A68	D#[9]	B68	D#[6]
A69	D#[8]	B69	VCC_CORE
A70	GND	B70	D#[4]
A71	D#[5]	B71	D#[2]
A72	D#[3]	B72	D#[0]
A73	D#[1]	B73	VCC_CORE
A74	GND	B74	RESET#

Table 3.7   Signal Listing in Order by Pin Number Continued

Pin No.	Pin Name	Pin No.	Pin Name
A75	BCLK	B75	BR1#
A76	BR0#	B76	FRCERR
A77	BERR#	B77	VCC_CORE
A78	GND	B78	A#[35]
A79	A#[33]	B79	A#[32]
A80	A#[34]	B80	A#[29]
A81	A#[30]	B81	EMI
A82	GND	B82	A#[26]
A83	A#[31]	B83	A#[24]
A84	A#[27]	B84	A#[28]
A85	A#[22]	B85	VCC_CORE
A86	GND	B86	A#[20]
A87	A#[23]	B87	A#[21]
A88	Reserved	B88	A#[25]
A89	A#[19]	B89	VCC_CORE
A90	GND	B90	A#[15]
A91	A#[18]	B91	A#[17]
A92	A#[16]	B92	A#[11]
A93	A#[13]	B93	VCC_CORE
A94	GND	B94	A#[12]
A95	A#[14]	B95	A#[8]
A96	A#[10]	B96	A#[7]
A97	A#[5]	B97	VCC_CORE
A98	GND	B98	A#[3]
A99	A#[9]	B99	A#[6]
A100	A#[4]	B100	EMI
A101	BNR#	B101	SLOTOCC#
A102	GND	B102	REQ#[0]
A103	BPRI#	B103	REQ#[1]
A104	TRDY#	B104	REQ#[4]
A105	DEFER#	B105	VCC_CORE
A106	GND	B106	LOCK#
A107	REQ#[2]	B107	DRDY#
A108	REQ#[3]	B108	RS#[0]
A109	HITM#	B109	VCC5
A110	GND	B110	HIT#
A111	DBSY#	B111	RS#[2]
A112	RS#[1]	B112	Reserved

(continues)

Table 3.7   Signal Listing in Order by Pin Number Continued

Pin No.	Pin Name	Pin No.	Pin Name
A113	Reserved	B113	VCC_L2
A114	GND	B114	RP#
A115	ADS#	B115	RSP#
A116	Reserved	B116	AP#[1]
A117	AP#[0]	B117	VCC_L2
A118	GND	B118	AERR#
A119	VID[2]	B119	VID[3]
A120	VID[1]	B120	VID[0]
A121	VID[4]	B121	VCC_L2

CPU Operating Voltages

Until the Pentium MMX, most processors had a single voltage level that was used by the motherboard and the processor together, typically 5, 3.5, or 3.3 volts. As processors have increased in speed and size, the desire to use less overall power (which also produces less heat) has led designers to use lower voltage levels. The first step was to reduce the voltage level to 3.5 or 3.3 volts. Newer processors reduce voltage levels even more by using what is called a *dual voltage*, or *split rail design*.

A split rail processor uses two different voltages. The external data or I/O voltage is higher, typically 3.3v for compatibility with the other chips on the motherboard. The internal or core voltage is lower: from 1.8 to 2.9 volts in most examples. This design allows these lower-voltage CPUs to be used without requiring wholesale changes to motherboards, chipsets, and so on. The voltage regulator on the motherboard is what must be changed to supply the correct voltages to the processor socket.

Pentium processors have run on a number of voltages, but the latest MMX versions are all 2.8v, except for mobile Pentium processors, which are as low as 1.8v. Table 3.8 lists the voltage settings used by Intel Pentium (non-MMX) processors that use a single power plane. This means that both the CPU core and the I/O pins run at the same voltage.

Table 3.8   Pentium Voltage Settings

Name	Comment	Nominal Voltage	Acceptable Range
+5v	Power supply	5.000v	4.750v– to 5.250v
STD (3.3v)	Standard	3.300v	3.135v– to 3.600v
VR (3.3v)	Voltage reduced	3.380v	3.300v– to 3.465v
VRE (3.5v)	VR extended	3.500v	3.400v– to 3.600v

Table 3.9 shows the voltage settings required by processors that use a dual plane (split voltage) where the voltage indicated is the core requirement. All I/O pins on dual-plane processors are 3.3v.

Table 3.9   Dual-Plane Processor Voltages

Name	Comment	Nominal Voltage	Acceptable Range
MMX (2.8v)	Intel MMX	2.800v	2.700v– to 2.900v
2.9v	AMD K6 Model 6	2.800v	2.700v– to 2.900v
3.2v	AMD K6 Model 6	2.800v	2.700v– to 2.900v
2.2v	AMD K6 Model 7	2.800v	2.700v– to 2.900v
MMX (2.8v)	Cyrix 6x86MX	2.800v	2.700v– to 2.900v
MMX (2.8v)	Cyrix 6x86L	2.800v	2.700v– to 2.900v
STD (3.3v)	Cyrix 6x86	3.300v	3.135v– to 3.600v
VRE (3.5v)	Cyrix 6x86	3.500v	3.400v– to 3.600v

Normally, the acceptable range is plus or minus 5% from the nominal intended setting.

Most Socket 7 and later Pentium motherboards supply several voltages (such as 2.5V, 2.7V, 2.8V, and 2.9V) for compatibility with future devices. A voltage regulator built into the motherboard converts the power supply voltage into the different levels required by the processor core. Check the documentation for your motherboard and processor to find the appropriate settings.

The Pentium Pro and Pentium II processors automatically determine their voltage settings by controlling the motherboard-based voltage regulator. That's done through built-in Voltage ID (VID) pins. Those are explained in more detail in the Pentium Pro and Pentium II sections.

Heat and Cooling Problems

Heat can be a problem in any high-performance system. The higher-speed processors normally consume more power and therefore generate more heat. If your system is based on any of the 66MHz or faster processors, you must dissipate the extra thermal energy; the fan inside your computer case may not be able to handle the load.

To cool a system in which processor heat is a problem, you can buy (for less than $5 in most cases) a special attachment for the CPU chip called a *heat sink,* which draws heat away from the CPU chip. Many applications may need only a larger standard heat sink with additional or longer fins for a larger cooling area. Several heat-sink manufacturers are listed in Appendix A, "Vendor List."

Two main types of heat sinks on the market are active and passive. Active heat sinks use a fan or other electric cooling device, which require power to run. The fan type is most common but some use a peltier cooling device, which is basically a solid-state refrigerator. Active heat sinks require power and normally plug into a disk drive-power connector or special 12v fan power connectors on the motherboard. If you do get a fan type heat sink, be aware that there are some of very poor quality on the market. The bad ones have motors that use sleeve bearings, that freeze up after a very short life. I only recommend fans with ball-bearing motors which will last about 10 times longer than the sleeve-bearing types. Of course, they cost more, but only about twice as much, which means you'll save money in the long run.

The passive-type heat sinks are 100% reliable, as they have no mechanical components to fail. They are basically an aluminum-finned radiator that dissipates heat through convection. Passive types don't work well unless there is some airflow across the fins, normally provided by the power supply fan or an extra fan in the case. If your case or power supply is properly designed, you can use a less expensive passive heat sink instead of an active one.

Most of the newer systems on the market use an improved motherboard form factor (shape) design called *ATX*. Systems made from this type of motherboard and case allow for improved cooling of the processor due to its being repositioned in the case near the power supply. Also, the power supply fan in most ATX systems is designed to blow cool air directly on the chip, allowing for a passive (no fan) heat sink to be used.

▶▶ See "ATX Style," p. 398
▶▶ See "ATX," p. 173

Math Coprocessors

The next several sections cover the floating-point unit contained in the processor, which was formerly a separate external math coprocessor in the 386 and older chips. Older central processing units designed by Intel (and cloned by other companies) used an external math-coprocessor chip. However, when Intel introduced the 486DX, they included a built-in math coprocessor, and every processor built by Intel (and AMD and Cyrix, for that matter) since then includes a math coprocessor. Coprocessors provide hardware for floating-point math, which otherwise would create an excessive drain on the main CPU. Math chips speed your computer's operation only when you are running software designed to take advantage of the coprocessor.

Math chips (as coprocessors sometimes are called) can perform high-level mathematical operations—long division, trigonometric functions, roots, and logarithms, for example—at 10 to 100 times the speed of the corresponding main processor. The operations performed by the math chip are all operations that make use of noninteger numbers (numbers that contain digits after the decimal point). The need to process numbers in which the decimal is not always the last character leads to the term *floating point* because the decimal (point) can move (float), depending on the operation. The integer units in the primary CPU work with integer numbers, so they perform addition, subtraction, and multiplication operations. The primary CPU is designed to handle such computations; these operations are not offloaded to the math chip.

The instruction set of the math chip is different from that of the primary CPU. A program must detect the existence of the coprocessor and then execute instructions written explicitly for that coprocessor; otherwise, the math coprocessor draws power and does nothing else. Fortunately, most modern programs that can benefit from the use of the coprocessor correctly detect and use the coprocessor. These programs usually are math-intensive: spreadsheet programs, database applications, statistical programs, and graphics programs, such as computer-aided design (CAD) software. Word processing programs do not benefit from a math chip and therefore are not designed to use one. Table 3.10 summarizes the coprocessors available for the Intel family of processors.

Table 3.10 Math Coprocessor Summary	
Processor	**Coprocessor**
8086	8087
8088	8087
80286	80287
80386SX	80387SX
80386SL	80387SX
80386SLC	80387SX
80486SLC	80387SX
80486SLC2	80387SX
80386DX	80387DX
80486SX	80487SX, DX2/OverDrive*
80487SX*	Built-in FPU
80486SX2	DX2/OverDrive**
80486DX	Built-in FPU
80486DX2	Built-in FPU
80486DX4	Built-in FPU
Pentium/Pentium-MMX	Built-in FPU
Pentium Pro	Built-in FPU
Pentium II	Built-in FPU

FPU = Floating-Point Unit
*The 487SX chip is a modified pinout 486DX chip with the math coprocessor enabled. When you plug in a 487SX chip, it disables the 486SX main processor and takes over all processing.
**The DX2/OverDrive is equivalent to the SX2 with the addition of a functional FPU.

Within each 8087 group, the maximum speed of the math chips varies. A suffix digit after the main number, as shown in Table 3.11, indicates the maximum speed at which a system can run a math chip.

Table 3.11 Maximum Math Chip Speeds	
Part	**Speed**
8087	5MHz
8087-3	5MHz
8087-2	8MHz
8087-1	10MHz

(continues)

Table 3.11 Maximum Math Chip Speeds Continued	
Part	**Speed**
80287	6MHz
80287-6	6MHz
80287-8	8MHz
80287-10	10MHz

The 387 math coprocessors, and the 486 or 487 and Pentium processors, always indicate their maximum speed rating in MHz in the part-number suffix. A 486DX2-66, for example, is rated to run at 66MHz. Some processors incorporate clock multiplication, which means that they may run at different speeds compared with the rest of the system.

> **Tip**
>
> The performance increase in programs that use the math chip can be dramatic—usually, a geometric increase in speed occurs. If the primary applications that you use can take advantage of a math coprocessor, you should upgrade your system to include one.

Most systems that use the 386 or earlier processors are socketed for a math coprocessor as an option, but they do not include a coprocessor as standard equipment. A few systems on the market don't even have a socket for the coprocessor because of cost and size considerations. These systems are usually low-cost or portable systems, such as older laptops, the IBM PS/1, and the PCjr. For more specific information about math coprocessors, see the discussions of the specific chips—8087, 287, 387, and 487SX—in the later sections. Table 3.12 shows some of the specifications of the various math coprocessors.

Table 3.12 Intel Math Coprocessor Specifications					
Name	**Power Consumption**	**Case Minimum Temperature**	**Case Maximum Temperature**	**No. of Transistors**	**Date Introduced**
8087	3 watts	0°C, 32°F	85°C, 185°F	45,000	1980
287	3 watts	0°C, 32°F	85°C, 185°F	45,000	1982
287XL	1.5 watts	0°C, 32°F	85°C, 185°F	40,000	1990
387SX	1.5 watts	0°C, 32°F	85°C, 185°F	120,000	1988
387DX	1.5 watts	0°C, 32°F	85°C, 185°F	120,000	1987

Most often, you can learn what CPU and math coprocessor are installed in a particular system by checking the markings on the chip.

Processor Bugs

Processor manufacturers use specialized equipment to test their own processors, but you have to settle for a little less. The best processor-testing device to which you have access is a system that you know is functional; you then can use the diagnostics available from various utility software companies or your system manufacturer to test the motherboard and processor functions.

Companies such as Diagsoft, Symantec, Micro 2000, Trinitech, Data Depot, and others offer specialized diagnostics software that can test the system, including the processor. If you don't want to purchase this kind of software, you can perform a quick-and-dirty processor evaluation by using the diagnostics program supplied with your system.

Because the processor is the brain of a system, most systems don't function with a defective one. If a system seems to have a dead motherboard, try replacing the processor with one from a functioning motherboard that uses the same CPU chip. You may find that the processor in the original board is the culprit. If the system continues to play dead, however, the problem is elsewhere.

A few system problems are built in at the factory, although these bugs or design defects are rare. By learning to recognize these problems, you may avoid unnecessary repairs or replacements. Each processor section describes several known defects in that generation of processors. For more information on these bugs and defects, contact the processor manufacturer.

Processor Update Feature

All processors can contain design defects or errors. Many times, the effects of any given bug can be avoided by implementing hardware or software workarounds. Intel documents these bugs and workarounds well for their processors in their processor Specification Update manuals; this manual is available from their Web site. Most of the other processor manufacturers also have bulletins or tips on their Web sites listing any problems or special fixes or patches for their chips.

Previously, the only way to fix a processor bug was to work around it or replace the chip with one that had the bug fixed. Now, a new feature built into the Intel P6 processors, including the Pentium Pro and Pentium II, can allow many bugs to be fixed by altering the microcode in the processor. These processors incorporate a new feature called *reprogrammable microcode*, which allows certain types of bugs to be worked around via microcode updates. The microcode updates reside in the system ROM BIOS and are loaded into the processor by the system BIOS during the Power-On Self Test, or POST. Each time the system is rebooted, the fix code is reloaded ensuring that it will have the bug fix installed anytime the processor is operating.

The easiest method for checking the microcode update is to use the Pentium Pro and Pentium II Processor Update Utility, which is developed and supplied by Intel. This utility can verify whether the correct update is present for all Pentium Pro processor-based motherboards. The utility displays the processor stepping and version of the microcode update. To install a new microcode update, however, the motherboard BIOS must contain the routines to support the microcode update, which virtually all Pentium Pro and Pentium II BIOSs do have. The Intel Processor Update Utility determines whether the code is present in the BIOS, compares the processor stepping with the microcode update currently loaded, and installs the new update, if needed. Use of this utility with motherboards containing the BIOS microcode update routine allows just the microcode update data to be changed; the rest of the BIOS is unchanged. A version of the update utility is provided with all Intel boxed processors. The term *boxed processors* refers to processors packaged for use by system integrators, that is, people who build systems. If you want the most current version of this utility, you have to contact an Intel processor dealer to download it. Intel only supplies it to their dealers.

Note that if the BIOS in your motherboard does not include the processor microcode update routine, you should get a complete system BIOS upgrade from the motherboard vendor.

When you are building a system with a Pentium Pro or Pentium II processor, you must use the Processor Update Utility to check that the System BIOS contains microcode updates that are specific to particular silicon stepping of the processor you are installing. In other words, you must ensure that the update matches the processor stepping being used.

Table 3.13 contains the current microcode update revision for each processor stepping. These update revisions are contained in the microcode update database file that comes with the Pentium Pro processor and Pentium II processor update utility. Processor steppings are listed in the sections on the Pentium, Pentium Pro, and Pentium II processors later in this chapter.

Table 3.13   Processor Steppings (Revisions) and Microcode Update Revisions Supported by the Update Database File PEP6.PDB

Processor	Stepping	Stepping Signature	Microcode Update Revision Required
Pentium Pro Processor	C0	0x612	0xC6
Pentium Pro Processor	sA0	0x616	0xC6
Pentium Pro Processor	sA1	0x617	0xC6
Pentium Pro Processor	sB1	0x619	0xD1
Pentium II Processor	C0	0x633	0x32
Pentium II Processor	C1	0x634	0x33
Pentium II Processor	dA0	0x650	0x15

Using the processor update utility (CHECKUP3.EXE), a system builder can easily verify that the correct microcode update is present in all systems based on the Pentium Pro and Pentium II processors. For example, if a system contains a processor with stepping C1 and stepping signature 0x634, the BIOS should contain the microcode update revision 0x33. The processor update utility identifies the processor stepping, signature, and microcode update revision that is currently in use.

If a new microcode update needs to be installed in the system BIOS, the system BIOS must contain the Intel-defined processor update routines so the processor update utility can permanently install the latest update. Otherwise, a complete system BIOS upgrade is required from the motherboard manufacturer. It is recommended that the Processor Update Utility be run after upgrading a motherboard BIOS and before installing the operating system when building a system based on the Pentium Pro processor or Pentium II processor. The utility is easy to use and executes in just a few seconds. Because the update utility may need to load new code into your BIOS, ensure that any jumper settings on the motherboard are placed in the "enable flash upgrade" position. This enables writing to the flash memory.

After running the utility, turn off power to the system and reboot—do not warm boot—to ensure that the new update is correctly initialized in the processor. Also ensure that all jumpers, such as any flash upgrade jumpers and so on, are returned to their normal position.

Intel Processor Codenames

Intel has always used codenames when talking about future processors. The codenames are normally not supposed to become public, but often they do. They can be often found in magazine articles talking about future generation processors. Sometimes, they even appear in motherboard manuals because the manuals are written before the processors are officially introduced. Table 3.14 lists Intel processor codenames for reference.

Table 3.14   Intel Processors and Codenames

Codename	Processor
P4	486DX
P4S	486SX
P23	486SX
P23S	487SX
P23N	487SX
P23T	486 OverDrive for the 80486 (169-pin PGA)
P4T	486 OverDrive for the 486 (168-pin PGA)
P24	486DX2
P24S	486DX2
P24D	486DX2WB (Write Back)
P24C	486DX4
P24CT	486DX4WB (Write Back)
P5	Pentium 60 or 66MHz, Socket 4, 5v
P24T	486 Pentium OverDrive, 63 or 83MHz, Socket 3
P54C	Classic Pentium 75-200MHz, Socket 5/7, 3.3v
P55C	Pentium MMX 166-266MHz, Socket 7, 2.8v
P54CTB	Pentium MMX OverDrive 125+, Socket 5/7, 3.3v
Tillamook	Mobile Pentium MMX 0.25 micron, 166-266MHz, 1.8v
P6	Pentium Pro, Socket 8
Klamath	Pentium II, slot 1
Deschutes	Pentium II, 0.25 micron, slot 1 or 2
Covington	Pentium II, low-end Deschutes, no L2 cache
Mendocino	Pentium II, low-end Deschutes, 300 MHz, 128K L2 cache
Katmai	Pentium II, MMX2
Willamette	Pentium II, improved Katmai
Merced	P7, First IA-64 processor

Intel-Compatible Processors

Several companies—mainly AMD and Cyrix—have developed processors that are compatible with Intel processors. These chips are fully Intel-compatible, which means that they emulate every processor instruction in the Intel chips. Most of the chips are pin-compatible, which means that they can be used in any system designed to accept an Intel processor; others require a custom motherboard design. Any hardware or software that works on Intel-based PCs will work on PCs made with these third-party CPU chips. A number of companies currently offer Intel-compatible chips, and I will discuss some of the most popular ones here.

AMD Processors

Advanced Micro Devices (AMD) has become a major player in the Pentium-compatible chip market with their own line of Intel-compatible processors. AMD ran into trouble with Intel several years ago because their 486-clone chips used actual Intel microcode. These differences have been settled and AMD now has a five-year cross-license agreement with Intel. In 1996, AMD finalized a deal to absorb NexGen, another maker of Intel-compatible CPUs. AMD currently offers a wide variety of CPUs, from 486 upgrades to the MMX-capable K6. The following table lists the basic processors offered by AMD and their Intel socket.

CPU	Clock Speed	Socket
Am486DX4-100	100	Socket 1,2,3
Am486DX4-120	120	Socket 1,2,3
Am5x86	133	Socket 1,2,3
K5 PR75	75	Socket 5,7
K5 PR90	90	Socket 5,7
K5 PR100	100	Socket 5,7
K5 PR120	90	Socket 5,7
K5 PR133	100	Socket 5,7
K5 PR166	116.66	Socket 5,7
K6-166 MMX	166	Socket 7
K6-200 MMX	200	Socket 7
K6-233 MMX	233	Socket 7
K6-266 MMX	266	Socket 7
K6-300 MMX	300	Socket 7

Notice in the table that for the K5 PR120 through PR166 the model designation does not match the CPU clock speed. This is called a PR rating instead and is further described later in the chapter. The later K5 chips benefit from improved design, so they run faster at a given clock speed. The model designations are meant to represent performance comparable with an equivalent Pentium-based system. AMD chips, particularly the new K6, have typically fared well in performance comparisons, and usually have a much lower cost. There is more information on the respective AMD chips in the sections for each different type of processor.

Cyrix

Cyrix has become an even larger player in the market since being purchased by National Semiconductor in November of 1997. Prior to that, they had been a fabless company, meaning they have no chip-manufacturing capability. All the Cyrix chips are manufactured for them by IBM. Currently, IBM still manufactures the bulk of Cyrix processors; however, National Semiconductor will likely be assuming some, if not all, this production eventually.

Like Intel, Cyrix has begun to limit its selection of available CPUs to only the latest technology. Cyrix is currently focusing on the Pentium market with the M1 (6x86) and M2 (6x86MX) processors. The 6x86 has dual internal pipelines and a single, unified 16K internal cache. It offers speculative and out-of-order instruction execution, much like the Intel Pentium Pro processor. The 6x86MX adds MMX technology to the CPU. The chip is Socket 7 compatible, but some require modified chipsets and new motherboard designs. Table 3.15 lists Cyrix M1 processors and bus speeds.

Table 3.15	Cyrix Processor Ratings Versus Actual Speeds		
CPU Type/Speed	**Clock Speed**	**CPU Clock**	**Motherboard Speed**
6x86-PR120	100	2x	50
6x86-PR133	110	2x	55*
6x86-PR150	120	2x	60
6x86-PR166	133	2x	66
6x86-PR200	150	2x	75**
6x86MX-PR166	150	2.5x	60
6x86MX-PR200	166	2.5x	66
6x86MX-PR233	188	2.5x	75**

Not all motherboards support a 55MHz bus speed.
**This 75MHz bus speed requires a special motherboard and chipset.*

The 6x86MX features 64K of unified L1 cache and more than double the performance of the previous 6x86 CPUs. The 6x86MX is offered in clock speeds ranging from 180 to 225MHz, and like the 6x86, it is Socket 7-compatible. All Cyrix chips are manufactured by IBM, who also markets the clone chips under its own name.

Note that later versions of the 6x86MX chip have been renamed the MII to deliberately invoke comparisons with the Pentium II, instead of the regular Pentium processor. The MII chips are not redesigned; they are, in fact, the same 6x86MX chips as before, only running at higher clock rates. The first renamed 6x86MX chip is the MII 300, which actually runs at only 233MHz on a 66MHz Socket 7 motherboard. There is also an MII 333, which will run at a 250MHz clock speed on newer 100MHz Socket 7 mother-boards.

Cyrix also has made an attempt at capturing even more of the low-end market than they already have by introducing a processor called the MediaGX. This is a low-performance cross between a 486 and a Pentium combined with a custom motherboard chipset in a two-chip package. These two chips contain everything necessary for a motherboard except the Super I/O chip, and make very low-cost PCs possible. Expect to see the MediaGX processors on the lowest-end, virtually disposable-type PCs. Later versions of these chips will include more multimedia and even network support.

IDT Winchip

Another recent offering in the chip market is from Integrated Device Technology (IDT). A longtime chip manufacturer who was more well-known for making SRAM (cache memory) chips, IDT acquired Centaur Technology, who had designed a chip called the C6 Winchip. Now with IDT's manufacturing capability, the C6 processor became a reality.

Featuring a very simple design, the C6 Winchip is more like a 486 than a Pentium. It does not have the superscalar (multiple instruction pipelines) of a Pentium, opting for a single high-speed pipeline, instead. Internally, it seems the C6 has little in common with other fifth- and sixth-generation x86 processors. Even so, according to Centaur, it closely matches the performance of a Pentium MMX when running the Winstone 97 business benchmark, although that benchmark does not focus on multimedia performance. It also has a much smaller die (88 mm2) than a typical Pentium, which means it should cost significantly less to manufacture.

The C6 has two large internal caches (32K each for instructions and data), and will run at 180, 200, 225, and 240MHz. The power consumption is very low—14W maximum at 200MHz for the desktop chip, and 7.1 to 10.6W for the mobile chips. This processor will likely have some success in the low-end market.

P-Ratings

To make it easier to understand processor performance, the P-rating system was jointly developed by Cyrix, IBM Microelectronics, SGS-Thomson Microelectronics, and Advanced Micro Devices. This new rating, titled the P (Performance) rating, equates delivered performance of microprocessor to that of an Intel Pentium. To determine a specific P-rating, Cyrix and AMD use benchmarks such as Winstone 9x. Winstone 9x is a widely used, industry-standard benchmark that runs a number of Windows-based software applications.

The idea is fine, but in some cases it can be misleading. A single or even a group of benchmarks cannot tell the whole story on system or processor performance. In most cases, the companies selling PR-rated processors have people believing that they are really running at the speed indicated on the chip. For example, a Cyrix/IBM 6x86MX-PR200 does not really run at 200MHz; instead, it runs at 166MHz. I guess the idea is that it "feels" like 200MHz, or compares to some Intel processor running at 200MHz (which one?). I am not in favor of the P- or PR-rating system and prefer to just report the processor's true speed in MHz. If it happens to be 166 but runs faster than most other 166 processors, so be it—but I don't like to number it based on some comparison like that.

The Ziff-Davis Winstone benchmark is used because it is a real-world, application-based benchmark that contains the most popular software applications (based on market share) that run on a Pentium processor. Winstone also is a widely used benchmark, and is freely distributed and available.

Processor Types

Knowing the processors used in a system can be very helpful in understanding the capabilities of the system, and in servicing it. To fully understand the capabilities of a system and perform any type of servicing, you must know at least the type of processor that the system uses.

P1 (086) First-Generation Processors

8088 and 8086 Processors. Intel introduced a revolutionary new processor called the 8086 back in June of 1978. The 8086 was one of the first 16-bit processor chips on the market; at the time virtually all other processors were 8-bit designs. The 8086 had 16-bit internal registers and could run a new class of software using 16-bit instructions. It also had a 16-bit external data path, which meant it could transfer data to memory 16 bits at a time.

The address bus was 20 bits wide, which meant that the 8086 could address a full 1M (2 to the 20th power) of memory. This was in stark contrast to most other chips of that time that had 8-bit internal registers, an 8-bit external data bus, and a 16-bit address bus allowing a maximum of only 64K of RAM (2 to the 16th power).

Unfortunately, most of the personal computer world at the time was using 8-bit processors, which ran 8-bit CP/M (Control Program for Microprocessors) operating systems and software. The board and circuit designs at the time were largely 8-bit as well. Building a full 16-bit motherboard and memory system would be costly, pricing such a computer out of the market.

The cost was high because the 8086 needed a 16-bit data bus rather than a less expensive 8-bit bus. Systems available at that time were 8-bit, and slow sales of the 8086 indicated to Intel that people weren't willing to pay for the extra performance of the full 16-bit design. In response, Intel introduced a kind of crippled version of the 8086, called the 8088. The 8088 essentially deleted 8 of the 16 bits on the data bus, making the 8088 an 8-bit chip as far as data input and output were concerned. However, because it retained the full 16-bit internal registers and the 20-bit address bus, the 8088 ran 16-bit software and was able to address a full 1M of RAM.

For these reasons, IBM selected the 8-bit 8088 chip for the original IBM PC. Years later, they were criticized for using the 8-bit 8088 instead of the 16-bit 8086. In retrospect, it was a very wise decision. IBM even covered up the physical design in their ads, which at the time indicated their new PC had a "high-speed 16-bit microprocessor." They could say that because the 8088 still ran the same powerful 16-bit software the 8086 ran, just a little more slowly. In fact, programmers universally thought of the 8088 as a 16-bit chip because there was virtually no way a program could distinguish an 8088 from an 8086. This allowed IBM to deliver a PC capable of running a new generation of 16-bit software, while retaining a much less expensive 8-bit design for the hardware. Because of this, the

IBM PC was actually priced less at its introduction than the most popular PC of the time, the Apple II. For the trivia buffs out there, the IBM PC listed for $1,265 and included only 16K of RAM, while a similarly configured Apple II cost $1,355.

The original IBM PC used the Intel 8088. The 8088 was introduced in June of 1979 but the IBM PC did not appear until August of 1981. Back then, there was often a significant lag time between the introduction of a new processor and systems which incorporated it. That is unlike today, when new processors and systems using them are often released on the same day.

The 8088 in the IBM PC ran at 4.77MHz, or 4,770,000 cycles (essentially computer heart-beats) per second. Each cycle represents a unit of time to the system, with different in-structions or operations requiring one or more cycles to complete. The average instruction on the 8088 took 12 cycles to complete.

Computer users sometimes wonder why a 640K conventional-memory barrier exists if the 8088 chip can address 1M of memory. The conventional-memory barrier exists be-cause IBM reserved 384K of the upper portion of the 1,024K (1M) address space of the 8088 for use by adapter cards and system BIOS. The lower 640K is the conventional memory in which DOS and software applications execute.

80186 and 80188 Processors. After Intel produced the 8086 and 8088 chips, it turned its sights toward producing a more powerful chip with an increased instruction set. The company's first efforts along this line—the 80186 and 80188—were unsuccessful. But incorporating system components into the CPU chip was an important idea for Intel because it led to faster, better chips, such as the 286.

The relationship between the 80186 and 80188 is the same as that of the 8086 and 8088; one is a slightly more advanced version of the other. Compared CPU to CPU, the 80186 is almost the same as the 8088 and has a full 16-bit design. The 80188 (like the 8088) is a hybrid chip that compromises the 16-bit design with an 8-bit external communications interface. The advantage of the 80186 and 80188 is that they combine on a single chip 15 to 20 of the 8086–8088 series system components, a fact that can greatly reduce the number of components in a computer design. The 80186 and 80188 chips were used for highly intelligent peripheral adapter cards of that age, such as network adapters.

8087 Coprocessor. Intel introduced the 8086 processor in 1976. The math coprocessor that was paired with the chip—the 8087—often was called the numeric data processor (NDP), the math coprocessor, or simply the math chip. The 8087 is designed to perform high-level math operations at many times the speed of the main processor. The primary advantage of using this chip is the increased execution speed in number-crunching pro-grams, such as spreadsheet applications.

P2 (286) Second-Generation Processors
286 Processors. The Intel 80286 (normally abbreviated as 286) processor did not suffer from the compatibility problems that damned the 80186 and 80188. The 286 chip, first introduced in 1981, is the CPU behind the original IBM AT. Other computer makers

manufactured what came to be known as IBM clones, many of these manufacturers calling their systems AT-compatible or AT-class computers.

When IBM developed the AT, it selected the 286 as the basis for the new system because the chip provided compatibility with the 8088 used in the PC and the XT. That means that software written for those chips should run on the 286. The 286 chip is many times faster than the 8088 used in the XT, and it offered a major performance boost to PCs used in businesses. The processing speed, or throughput, of the original AT (which ran at 6MHz) was five times greater than that of the PC running at 4.77MHz. The die for the 286 is shown in Figure 3.17.

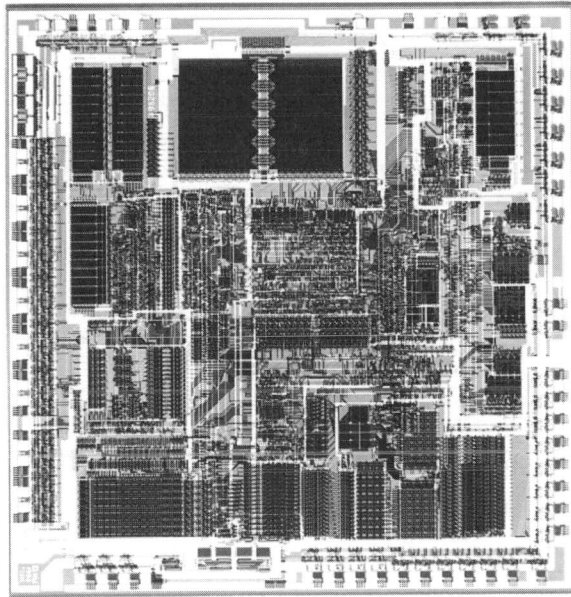

FIG. 3.17 286 Processor die. *Photograph used by permission of Intel Corporation.*

286 systems are faster than their predecessors for several reasons. The main reason is that 286 processors are much more efficient in executing instructions. An average instruction takes 12 clock cycles on the 8086 or 8088, but an average 4.5 cycles on the 286 processor. Additionally, the 286 chip can handle up to 16 bits of data at a time through an external data bus twice the size of the 8088.

The 286 chip has two modes of operation: real mode and protected mode. The two modes are distinct enough to make the 286 resemble two chips in one. In real mode, a 286 acts essentially the same as an 8086 chip and is fully object-code compatible with the 8086 and 8088. (A processor with object-code compatibility can run programs written for another processor without modification and execute every system instruction in the same manner.)

In the protected mode of operation, the 286 was truly something new. In this mode, a program designed to take advantage of the chip's capabilities believes that it has access to 1G of memory (including virtual memory). The 286 chip, however, can address only 16M of hardware memory. A significant failing of the 286 chip is that it cannot switch from protected mode to real mode without a hardware reset (a warm reboot) of the system. (It can, however, switch from real mode to protected mode without a reset.) A major improvement of the 386 over the 286 is that software can switch the 386 from real mode to protected mode, and vice versa. See the Processor Modes section earlier in this chapter for more information.

Only a small amount of software that took advantage of the 286 chip was sold until Windows 3.0 offered Standard Mode for 286 compatibility; by that time, the hottest-selling chip was the 386. Still, the 286 was Intel's first attempt to produce a CPU chip that supported multitasking, in which multiple programs run at the same time. The 286 was designed so that if one program locked up or failed, the entire system didn't need a warm boot (reset) or cold boot (power off or on). Theoretically, what happened in one area of memory didn't affect other programs. Before multitasked programs could be "safe" from one another, however, the 286 chip (and subsequent chips) needed an operating system that works cooperatively with the chip to provide such protection.

80287 Coprocessor. The 80287, internally, is the same math chip as the 8087, although the pins used to plug them into the motherboard are different. Both the 80287 and the 8087 operate as though they were identical.

In most systems, the 80286 internally divides the system clock by two to derive the processor clock. The 80287 internally divides the system-clock frequency by three. For this reason, most AT-type computers run the 80287 at one third the system clock rate, which also is two thirds the clock speed of the 80286. Because the 286 and 287 chips are asynchronous, the interface between the 286 and 287 chips is not as efficient as with the 8088 and 8087.

In summary, the 80287 and the 8087 chips perform about the same at equal clock rates. The original 80287 is not better than the 8087 in any real way—unlike the 80286, which is superior to the 8086 and 8088. In most AT systems, the performance gain that you realize by adding the coprocessor is much less substantial than the same type of upgrade for PC- or XT-type systems, or for the 80386.

286 Processor Problems. After you remove a math coprocessor from an AT-type system, you must rerun your computer's Setup program. Some AT-compatible SETUP programs do not properly unset the math-coprocessor bit. If you receive a POST error message because the computer cannot find the math chip, you may have to unplug the battery from the system board temporarily. All SETUP information will be lost, so be sure to write down the hard drive type, floppy drive type, and memory and video configurations before unplugging the battery. This information is critical in reconfiguring your computer correctly.

P3 (386) Third-Generation Processors

386 Processors. The Intel 80386 (normally abbreviated as 386) caused quite a stir in the PC industry because of the vastly improved performance it brought to the personal computer. Compared with 8088 and 286 systems, the 386 chip offered greater performance in almost all areas of operation.

The 386 is a full 32-bit processor optimized for high-speed operation and multitasking operating systems. Intel introduced the chip in 1985, but the 386 appeared in the first systems in late 1986 and early 1987. The Compaq Deskpro 386 and systems made by several other manufacturers introduced the chip; somewhat later, IBM used the chip in its PS/2 Model 80. The 386 chip rose in popularity for several years, which peaked around 1991. Obsolete 386 processor systems are mostly retired or scrapped, having been passed down the user chain. If they are in operating condition, they can be useful for running old DOS or Windows 3.x-based applications, which they can do quite nicely.

The 386 can execute the real-mode instructions of an 8086 or 8088, but in fewer clock cycles. The 386 was as efficient as the 286 in executing instructions, which means that the average instruction took about 4.5 clock cycles. In raw performance, therefore, the 286 and 386 actually seemed to be at almost equal clock rates. Many 286 system manufacturers were touting their 16MHz and 20MHz 286 systems as being just as fast as 16MHz and 20MHz 386 systems, and they were right! The 386 offered greater performance in other ways, mainly due to additional software capability (modes) and a greatly enhanced Memory Management Unit (MMU). The die for the 386 is shown in Figure 3.18.

The 386 can switch to and from protected mode under software control without a system reset, a capability that makes using protected mode more practical. In addition, the 386 has a new mode, called virtual real mode, which enables several real-mode sessions to run simultaneously under protected mode.

The protected mode of the 386 is fully compatible with the protected mode of the 286. The protected mode for both chips often is called their *native mode of operation*, because these chips are designed for advanced operating systems such as OS/2 and Windows NT, which run only in protected mode. Intel extended the memory-addressing capabilities of 386 protected mode with a new MMU that provided advanced memory paging and program switching. These features were extensions of the 286 type of MMU, so the 386 remained fully compatible with the 286 at the system-code level.

The 386 chip's virtual real mode was new. In virtual real mode, the processor could run with hardware memory protection while simulating an 8086's real-mode operation. Multiple copies of DOS and other operating systems, therefore, could run simultaneously on this processor, each in a protected area of memory. If the programs in one segment crashed, the rest of the system was protected. Software commands could reboot the blown partition.

Numerous variations of the 386 chip exist, some of which are less powerful and some of which are less power-hungry. The following sections cover the members of the 386-chip family and their differences.

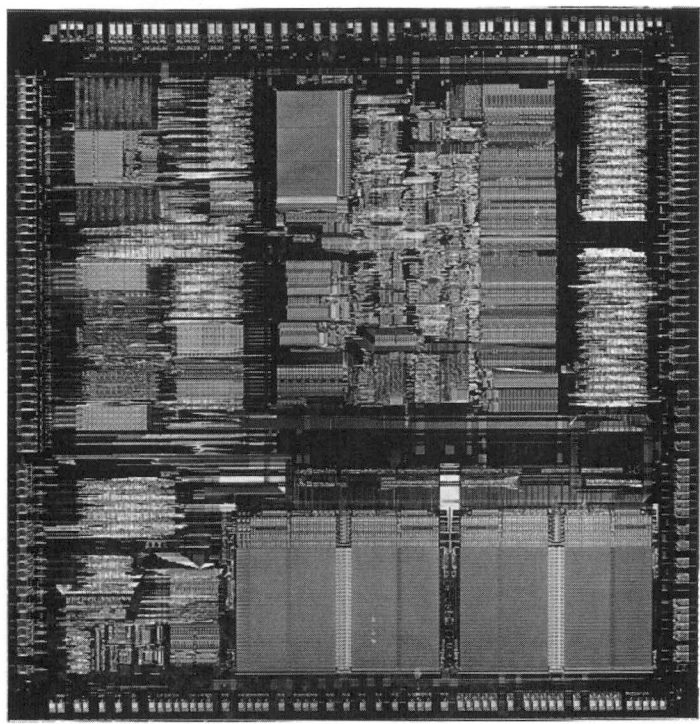

FIG. 3.18   386 Processor die. *Photograph used by permission of Intel Corporation.*

386DX Processors. The 386DX chip was the first of the 386-family members that Intel introduced. The 386 is a full 32-bit processor with 32-bit internal registers, a 32-bit internal data bus, and a 32-bit external data bus. The 386 contains 275,000 transistors in a VLSI (Very Large Scale Integration) circuit. The chip comes in a 132-pin package and draws approximately 400 milliamperes (ma), which is less power than even the 8086 requires. The 386 has a smaller power requirement because it is made of CMOS (Complementary Metal Oxide Semiconductor) materials. The CMOS design enables devices to consume extremely low levels of power.

The Intel 386 chip was available in clock speeds ranging from 16MHz to 33MHz; other manufacturers, primarily AMD and Cyrix, offered comparable versions with speeds up to 40MHz.

The 386DX can address 4G of physical memory. Its built-in virtual memory manager enables software designed to take advantage of enormous amounts of memory to act as though a system has 64T of memory. (A *terabyte—T—*is 1,099,511,627,776 bytes of memory.)

386SX Processors. The 386SX was designed for systems designers who were looking for 386 capabilities at 286-system prices. Like the 286, the 386SX is restricted to only 16 bits when communicating with other system components, such as memory. Internally, however, the 386SX is identical to the DX chip; the 386SX has 32-bit internal registers, and can therefore run 32-bit software. The 386SX uses a 24-bit memory-addressing scheme like that of the 286, rather than the full 32-bit memory address bus of the standard 386. The 386SX, therefore, can address a maximum 16M of physical memory rather than the 4G of physical memory that the 386DX can address. Before it was discontinued, the 386SX was available in clock speeds ranging from 16 to 33MHz.

The 386SX signaled the end of the 286 because of the 386SX chip's superior MMU and the addition of the virtual real mode. Under a software manager such as Windows or OS/2, the 386SX can run numerous DOS programs at the same time. The capability to run 386-specific software is another important advantage of the 386SX over any 286 or older design. For example, Windows 3.1 runs nearly as well on a 386SX as it does on a 386DX.

Note

One common fallacy about the 386SX is that you can plug one into a 286 system and give the system 386 capabilities. This is not true; the 386SX chip is not pin-compatible with the 286 and does not plug into the same socket. Several upgrade products, however, have been designed to adapt the chip to a 286 system. In terms of raw speed, converting a 286 system to a 386 CPU chip results in little performance gain—286 motherboards are built with a restricted 16-bit interface to memory and peripherals. A 16MHz 386SX is not markedly faster than a 16MHz 286, but it does offer improved memory-management capabilities on a motherboard designed for it, and the capability to run 386-specific software.

386SL Processors. The 386SL is another variation on the 386 chip. This low-power CPU had the same capabilities as the 386SX, but it was designed for laptop systems in which low power consumption was needed. The SL chips offer special power-management features that were important to systems that ran on batteries. The SL chip offered several sleep modes to conserve power.

The chip included an extended architecture that contained a *System Management Interrupt* (*SMI*), which provided access to the power-management features. Also included in the SL chip was special support for LIM (Lotus Intel Microsoft) expanded memory functions and a cache controller. The cache controller was designed to control a 16–64K external processor cache.

These extra functions account for the higher transistor count in the SL chips (855,000) compared with even the 386DX processor (275,000). The 386SL was available in 25MHz clock speed.

Intel offered a companion to the 386SL chip for laptops called the 82360SL I/O subsystem. The 82360SL provided many common peripheral functions, such as serial and parallel ports, a direct memory access (DMA) controller, an interrupt controller, and power-management logic for the 386SL processor. This chip subsystem worked with the processor to provide an ideal solution for the small size and low power-consumption requirements of portable and laptop systems.

80387 Coprocessor. Although the 80387 chips ran asynchronously, 386 systems were designed so that the math chip runs at the same clock speed as the main CPU. Unlike the 80287 coprocessor, which was merely an 8087 with different pins to plug into the AT motherboard, the 80387 coprocessor was a high-performance math chip designed specifically to work with the 386.

All 387 chips used a low power-consumption CMOS design. The 387 coprocessor had two basic designs: the 387DX coprocessor, which was designed to work with the 386DX processor, and the 387SX coprocessor, which was designed to work with the 386SX, SL, or SLC processors.

Intel originally offered several speeds for the 387DX coprocessor. But when the company designed the 33MHz version, a smaller mask was required to reduce the lengths of the signal pathways in the chip. This increased the performance of the chip by roughly 20%.

> **Note**
>
> Because Intel lagged in developing the 387 coprocessor, some early 386 systems were designed with a socket for a 287 coprocessor. Performance levels associated with that union, however, leave much to be desired.

Installing a 387DX is easy, but you must be careful to orient the chip in its socket properly; otherwise, the chip will be destroyed. The most common cause of burned pins on the 387DX is incorrect installation. In many systems, the 387DX was oriented differently from other large chips. Follow the manufacturer's installation instructions carefully to avoid damaging the 387DX; Intel's warranty does not cover chips that are installed incorrectly.

Several manufacturers developed their own versions of the Intel 387 coprocessors, some of which were touted as being faster than the original Intel chips. The general compatibility record of these chips was very good.

Weitek Coprocessors. In 1981, several Intel engineers formed the Weitek Corporation. Weitek developed math coprocessors for several systems, including those based on Motorola processor designs. Intel originally contracted Weitek to develop a math coprocessor for the Intel 386 CPU, because Intel was behind in its own development of the 387 math coprocessor. The result was the Weitek 1167, a custom math coprocessor that uses a proprietary Weitek instruction set, which is incompatible with the Intel 387.

To use the Weitek coprocessor, your system must have the required additional socket, which was different from the standard Intel coprocessor sockets.

80386 Bugs. Some early 16MHz Intel 386DX processors had a small bug that appeared as a software problem. The bug, which apparently was in the chip's 32-bit multiply routine, manifested itself only when you ran true 32-bit code in a program such as OS/2 2.x, UNIX/386, or Windows in Enhanced mode. Some specialized 386 memory-management software systems also may invoke this subtle bug, but 16-bit operating systems (such as DOS and OS/2 1.x) probably will not.

The bug usually causes the system to lock up. Diagnosing this problem can be difficult because the problem generally is intermittent and software-related. Running tests to find the bug is difficult; only Intel, with proper test equipment, can determine whether your chip has a bug. Some programs can diagnose the problem and identify a defective chip, but they cannot identify all defective chips. If a program indicates a bad chip, you certainly have a defective one; if the program passes the chip, you still may have a defective one.

Intel requested that its 386 customers return possibly defective chips for screening, but many vendors did not return them. Intel tested returned chips and replaced defective ones. The defective chips later were sold to bargain liquidators or systems houses that wanted chips that would not run 32-bit code. The defective chips were stamped with a 16-bit SW Only logo, indicating that they were authorized to run only 16-bit software.

Chips that passed the test, and all subsequent chips produced as bug-free, were marked with a double-sigma code (ΣΣ). 386DX chips that are not marked with either of these designations have not been tested by Intel and may be defective.

The following marking indicates that a chip has not yet been screened for the defect; it may be either good or bad.

> 80386-16

The following marking indicates that the chip has been tested and has the 32-bit multiply bug. The chip works with 16-bit software (such as DOS) but not with 32-bit, 386-specific software (such as Windows or OS/2).

> 80386-16
>
> 16-bit SW Only

The following mark on a chip indicates that it has been tested as defect-free. This chip fulfills all the capabilities promised for the 80386.

> 80386-16
>
> ΣΣ

This problem was discovered and corrected before Intel officially added DX to the part number. So if you have a chip labeled as 80386DX or 386DX, it does not have this problem.

Another problem with the 386DX can be stated more specifically. When 386-based versions of XENIX or other UNIX implementations are run on a computer that contains a 387DX math coprocessor, the computer locks up under certain conditions. The problem does not occur in the DOS environment, however. For the lockup to occur, all the following conditions must be in effect:

- Demand page virtual memory must be active.

- A 387DX must be installed and in use.

- DMA (direct memory access) must occur.

- The 386 must be in a wait state.

When all these conditions are true at the same instant, the 386DX ends up waiting for the 387DX, and vice versa. Both processors will continue to wait for each other indefinitely. The problem is in certain versions of the 386DX, not in the 387DX math coprocessor.

Intel published this problem (Errata 21) immediately after it was discovered to inform its OEM customers. At that point, it became the responsibility of each manufacturer to implement a fix in its hardware or software product. Some manufacturers, such as Compaq and IBM, responded by modifying their motherboards to prevent these lockups from occurring.

The Errata 21 problem occurs only in the B Stepping version of the 386DX and not in the later, D Stepping version. You can identify the D Stepping version of the 386DX by the letters DX in the part number (for example, 386DX-20). If DX is part of the chip's part number, the chip does not have this problem.

P4 (486) Fourth-Generation Processors
486 Processors. In the race for more speed, the Intel 80486 (normally abbreviated as 486) was another major leap forward. The additional power available in the 486 fueled tremendous growth in the software industry. Tens of millions of copies of Windows, and millions of copies of OS/2, have been sold largely because the 486 finally made the GUI of Windows and OS/2 a realistic option for people who work on their computers every day.

Four main features make a given 486 processor roughly twice as fast as an equivalent MHz 386 chip. These features are

- *Reduced instruction-execution time.* A single instruction in the 486 takes an average of only two clock cycles to complete, compared with an average of more than four cycles on the 386. Clock-multiplied versions such as the DX2 and DX4 further reduced this to about two cycles per instruction.

- *Internal (Level 1) cache.* The built-in cache has a hit ratio of 90–95%, which describes how often zero-wait-state read operations will occur. External caches can improve this ratio further.

- *Burst-mode memory cycles.* A standard 32-bit (4-byte) memory transfer takes two clock cycles. After a standard 32-bit transfer, more data up to the next 12 bytes (or three transfers) can be transferred with only one cycle used for each 32-bit (4-byte) transfer. Thus, up to 16 bytes of contiguous, sequential memory data can be transferred in as little as five cycles instead of eight cycles or more. This effect can be even greater when the transfers are only 8 bits or 16 bits each.

▶▶ See "Burst EDO," p. 316

■ *Built-in (synchronous) enhanced math coprocessor (some versions).* The math coprocessor runs synchronously with the main processor and executes math instructions in fewer cycles than previous designs did. On average, the math coprocessor built in to the DX-series chips provides two to three times greater math performance than an external 387 chip.

The 486 chip is about twice as fast as the 386, which means that a 386DX-40 is about as fast as a 486SX-20. This made the 486 a much more desirable option, primarily because it could more easily be upgraded to a DX2 or DX4 processor at a later time. You can see why the arrival of the 486 rapidly killed off the 386 in the marketplace.

Before the 486, many people avoided GUIs because they didn't have time to sit around waiting for the hourglass, which indicates that the system is performing behind-the-scenes operations that the user cannot interrupt. The 486 changed that situation. Many people believe that the 486 CPU chip spawned the widespread acceptance of GUIs.

With the release of its faster Pentium CPU chip, Intel began to cut the price of the 486 line to entice the industry to shift over to the 486 as the mainstream system. Intel later did the same thing with its Pentium chips, spelling the end of the 486 line. The 486 is now offered by Intel only for use in embedded microprocessor applications, used primarily in expansion cards.

Most of the 486 chips were offered in a variety of maximum speed ratings, varying from 16MHz all the way up to 120MHz. Additionally, 486 processors have slight differences in overall pin configurations. The DX, DX2, and SX processors have a virtually identical 168-pin configuration, whereas the OverDrive chips have either the standard 168-pin configuration or a specially modified 169-pin OverDrive (sometimes also called 487SX) configuration. If your motherboard has two sockets, the primary one likely supports the standard 168-pin configuration, and the secondary (OverDrive) socket supports the 169-pin OverDrive configuration. Most newer motherboards with a single ZIF socket support any of the 486 processors except the DX4. The DX4 is different because it requires 3.3v to operate instead of 5v, like most other chips up to that time.

A processor rated for a given speed always functions at any of the lower speeds. A 100MHz-rated 486DX4 chip, for example, runs at 75MHz if it is plugged into a 25MHz motherboard. Note that the DX2/OverDrive processors operate internally at two times the motherboard clock rate, whereas the DX4 processors operate at two, two-and-a-half, or three times the motherboard clock rate. Table 3.16 shows the different speed combinations that can result from using the DX2 or DX4 processors with different motherboard clock speeds.

Table 3.16   Intel DX2 and DX4 Operating Speeds Versus Motherboard Clock Speeds

	DX2 Processor speed	DX4 (2×mode) Speed	DX4 (2.5×mode) Speed	DX4 (3×mode) Speed
16MHz Motherboard	32MHz	32MHz	40MHz	48MHz
40MHz Motherboard	80MHz	80MHz	100MHz	120MHz
20MHz Motherboard	40MHz	40MHz	50MHz	60MHz
50MHz Motherboard	N/A	100MHz	N/A	N/A
25MHz Motherboard	50MHz	50MHz	63MHz	75MHz
33MHz Motherboard	66MHz	66MHz	83MHz	100MHz

The internal core speed of the DX4 processor is controlled by the CLKMUL (Clock Multiplier) signal at pin R-17 (Socket 1) or S-18 (Socket 2, 3, or 6). The CLKMUL input is sampled only during a reset of the CPU, and defines the ratio of the internal clock to the external bus frequency CLK signal at pin C-3 (Socket 1) or D-4 (Socket 2, 3, or 6). If CLKMUL is sampled low, the internal core speed will be two times the external bus frequency. If driven high or left floating (most motherboards would leave it floating), triple speed mode is selected. If the CLKMUL signal is connected to the BREQ (Bus Request) output signal at pin Q-15 (Socket 1) or R-16 (Socket 2, 3, or 6), the CPU internal core speed will be 2.5 times the CLK speed. To summarize, here is how the socket has to be wired for each DX4 speed selection:

CPU Speed	CLKMUL (Sampled Only at CPU Reset)
2x	Low
2.5x	Connected to BREQ
3x	High or Floating

You will have to determine how your particular motherboard is wired and whether it can be changed to alter the CPU core speed in relation to the CLK signal. In most cases, there would be one or two jumpers on the board near the processor socket. The motherboard documentation should cover these settings if they can be changed.

One interesting capability here is to run the DX4-100 chip in a doubled mode with a 50MHz motherboard speed. This would give you a very fast memory bus, along with the same 100MHz processor speed, as if you were running the chip in a 33/100MHz tripled mode.

> **Note**
>
> One caveat is that if your motherboard has VL-Bus slots, they will have to be slowed down to 33 or 40MHz to operate properly.

Many VL-Bus motherboards can run the VL-Bus slots in a buffered mode, add wait states, or even selectively change the clock only for the VL-Bus slots to keep them compatible. In most cases, they will not run properly at 50MHz. Consult your motherboard—or even better, your chipset documentation—to see how your board is set up.

> **Caution**
>
> If you are upgrading an existing system, be sure that your socket will support the chip that you are installing. In particular, if you are putting a DX4 processor in an older system, you need some type of adapter to regulate the voltage down to 3.3v. If you put the DX4 in a 5v socket, you will destroy the chip! See the earlier section on processor sockets for more information.

The 486-processor family is designed for greater performance than previous processors because it integrates formerly external devices, such as cache controllers, cache memory, and math coprocessors. Also, 486 systems were the first designed for true processor upgradability. Most 486 systems can be upgraded by simple processor additions or swaps that can effectively double the speed of the system.

486DX Processors. The original Intel 486DX processor was introduced on April 10, 1989, and systems using this chip first appeared during 1990. The first chips had a maximum speed rating of 25MHz; later versions of the 486DX were available in 33MHz- and 50MHz-rated versions. The 486DX originally was available only in a 5v, 168-pin PGA version, but now is also available in 5v, 196-pin PQFP (Plastic Quad Flat Pack) and 3.3v, 208-pin SQFP (Small Quad Flat Pack). These latter form factors are available in SL Enhanced versions, which are intended primarily for portable or laptop applications in which saving power is important.

Two main features separate the 486 processor from older processors:

- The 486DX integrates functions such as the math coprocessor, cache controller, and cache memory into the chip.

- The 486 also was designed with upgradability in mind; double-speed OverDrive are upgrades available for most systems.

The 486DX processor is fabricated with low-power CMOS (Complementary Metal Oxide Semiconductor) technology. The chip has a 32-bit internal register size, a 32-bit external data bus, and a 32-bit address bus. These dimensions are equal to those of the 386DX processor. The internal register size is where the "32-bit" designation used in advertisements comes from. The 486DX chip contains 1.2 million transistors on a piece of silicon no larger than your thumbnail. This figure is more than four times the number of components on 386 processors and should give you a good indication of the 486 chip's relative power. The die for the 486 is shown in Figure 3.19.

FIG. 3.19 486 Processor die. *Photograph used by permission of Intel Corporation.*

The standard 486DX contains a processing unit, a Floating-Point Unit (math coprocessor), a memory-management unit, and a cache controller with 8K of internal-cache RAM. Due to the internal cache and a more efficient internal processing unit, the 486 family of processors can execute individual instructions in an average of only two processor cycles. Compare this figure with the 286 and 386 families, both of which execute an average 4.5 cycles per instruction. Compare it also with the original 8086 and 8088 processors, which execute an average 12 cycles per instruction. At a given clock rate (MHz), therefore, a 486 processor is roughly twice as efficient as a 386 processor; a 16MHz 486SX is roughly equal to a 33MHz 386DX system; and a 20MHz 486SX is equal to a 40MHz 386DX system. Any of the faster 486s are way beyond the 386 in performance.

The 486 is fully instruction-set–compatible with previous Intel processors, such as the 386, but offers several additional instructions (most of which have to do with controlling the internal cache).

Like the 386DX, the 486 can address 4G of physical memory and manage as much as 64T of virtual memory. The 486 fully supports the three operating modes introduced in the 386: real mode, protected mode, and virtual real mode.

- In real mode, the 486 (like the 386) runs unmodified 8086-type software.

- In protected mode, the 486 (like the 386) offers sophisticated memory paging and program switching.

- In virtual real mode, the 486 (like the 386) can run multiple copies of DOS or other operating systems while simulating an 8086's real-mode operation. Under an operating system such as Windows or OS/2, therefore, both 16-bit and 32-bit programs can run simultaneously on this processor with hardware memory protection. If one program crashes, the rest of the system is protected, and you can reboot the blown portion through various means, depending on the operating software.

The 486DX series has a built-in math coprocessor that sometimes is called an MCP (math coprocessor) or FPU (Floating-Point Unit). This series is unlike previous Intel CPU chips, which required you to add a math coprocessor if you needed faster calculations for complex mathematics. The FPU in the 486DX series is 100% software-compatible with the external 387 math coprocessor used with the 386—but it delivers more than twice the performance. It runs in synchronization with the main processor and executes most instructions in half as many cycles as the 386.

486SL. The 486SL was a short-lived, standalone chip. The SL enhancements and features became available in virtually all the 486 processors (SX, DX, and DX2) in what are called SL Enhanced versions. SL Enhancement refers to a special design that incorporates special power-saving features.

The SL Enhanced chips originally were designed to be installed in laptop or notebook systems that run on batteries, but they found their way into desktop systems, as well. The SL Enhanced chips featured special power-management techniques, such as sleep mode and clock throttling, to reduce power consumption when necessary. These chips were available in 3.3v versions, as well.

Intel designed a power-management architecture called *System Management Mode (SMM)*. This mode of operation is totally isolated and independent from other CPU hardware and software. SMM provides hardware resources such as timers, registers, and other I/O logic that can control and power down mobile-computer components without interfering with any of the other system resources. SMM executes in a dedicated memory space called System Management Memory, which is not visible and does not interfere with operating-system and application software. SMM has an interrupt called *System Management Interrupt (SMI)*, which services power-management events and is independent from, and higher priority than, any of the other interrupts.

SMM provides power management with flexibility and security that were not available previously. For example, an SMI occurs when an application program tries to access a peripheral device that is powered down for battery savings, which powers up the peripheral device and re-executes the I/O instruction automatically.

Intel also designed a feature called suspend/resume in the SL processor. The system manufacturer can use this feature to provide the portable-computer user with instant-on-and-off capability. An SL system typically can resume (instant on) in one second from the suspend state (instant off) to exactly where it left off. You do not need to reboot, load the operating system, load the application program, and then load the application data. Simply push the suspend/resume button and the system is ready to go.

The SL CPU was designed to consume almost no power in the suspend state. This feature means that the system can stay in the suspend state possibly for weeks and yet start up instantly right where it left off. An SL system can keep working data in normal RAM memory safe for a long time while it is in the suspend state, but saving to a disk still is prudent.

486SX. The 486SX, introduced in April 1991, was designed to be sold as a lower-cost version of the 486. The 486SX is virtually identical to the full DX processor, but the chip does not incorporate the FPU or math coprocessor portion.

As you read earlier in this chapter, the 386SX was a scaled-down (some people would say crippled) 16-bit version of the full-blown 32-bit 386DX. The 386SX even had a completely different pinout and was not interchangeable with the more powerful DX version. The 486SX, however, is a different story. The 486SX is, in fact, a full-blown 32-bit 486 processor that is basically pin-compatible with the DX. A few pin functions are different or rearranged, but each pin fits into the same socket.

The 486SX chip is more a marketing quirk than new technology. Early versions of the 486SX chip actually were DX chips that showed defects in the math-coprocessor section. Instead of being scrapped, the chips simply were packaged with the FPU section disabled and sold as SX chips. This arrangement lasted for only a short time; thereafter, SX chips got their own mask, which is different from the DX mask. (A *mask* is the photographic blueprint of the processor and is used to etch the intricate signal pathways into a silicon chip.) The transistor count dropped to 1.185 million (from 1.2 million) to reflect this new mask.

The 486SX chip is twice as fast as a 386DX with the same clock speed. Intel marketed the 486SX as being the ideal chip for new computer buyers, because fewer entry-level programs of that day used math-coprocessor functions.

The 486SX was normally available in 16, 20, 25, and 33MHz-rated speeds, and there was also a 486 SX/2 that ran at up to 50 or 66MHz. The 486SX normally comes in a 168-pin version, although other surface-mount versions are available in SL Enhanced models.

Despite what Intel's marketing and sales information implies, no technical provision exists for adding a separate math coprocessor to a 486SX system; neither is a separate math coprocessor chip available to plug in. Instead, Intel wanted you to add a new 486 processor with a built-in math unit and disable the SX CPU that already was on the motherboard. If this situation sounds confusing, read on, because this topic brings you to the most important aspect of 486 design: upgradability.

487SX. The 487SX math coprocessor, as Intel calls it, really is a complete 25MHz 486DX CPU with an extra pin added and some other pins rearranged. When the 487SX is installed in the extra socket provided in a 486SX-CPU-based system, the 487SX turns off the existing 486SX via a new signal on one of the pins. The extra key pin actually carries no signal itself and exists only to prevent improper orientation when the chip is installed in a socket.

The 487SX takes over all CPU functions from the 486SX and also provides math coprocessor functionality in the system. At first glance, this setup seems rather strange and wasteful, so perhaps further explanation is in order. Fortunately, the 487SX turned out simply to be a stopgap measure while Intel prepared its real surprise: the OverDrive processor. The DX2/OverDrive speed-doubling chips, which are designed for the 487SX 169-pin socket, have the same pinout as the 487SX. These upgrade chips are installed in exactly the same way as the 487SX; therefore, any system that supports the 487SX also supports the DX2/OverDrive chips.

Although in most cases you can upgrade a system by removing the 486SX CPU and replacing it with a 487SX (or even a DX or DX2/OverDrive), Intel originally discouraged this procedure. Instead, Intel recommended that PC manufacturers include a dedicated upgrade (OverDrive) socket in their systems, because several risks were involved in removing the original CPU from a standard socket. (The following section elaborates on those risks.) Now Intel recommends—or even insists on—the use of a single processor socket of a ZIF design, which makes upgrading an easy task physically.

Very few early 486 systems had a socket for the Weitek 4167 coprocessor chip for 486 systems that existed in November 1989.

DX2/OverDrive and DX4 Processors. On March 3, 1992, Intel introduced the DX2 speed-doubling processors. On May 26, 1992, Intel announced that the DX2 processors also would be available in a retail version called OverDrive. Originally, the OverDrive versions of the DX2 were available only in 169-pin versions, which meant that they could be used only with 486SX systems that had sockets configured to support the rearranged pin configuration.

On September 14, 1992, Intel introduced 168-pin OverDrive versions for upgrading 486DX systems. These processors could be added to existing 486 (SX or DX) systems as an upgrade, even if those systems did not support the 169-pin configuration. When you use this processor as an upgrade, you simply install the new chip in your system, which subsequently runs twice as fast.

The DX2/OverDrive processors run internally at twice the clock rate of the host system. If the motherboard clock is 25MHz, for example, the DX2/OverDrive chip runs internally at 50MHz; likewise, if the motherboard is a 33MHz design, the DX2/OverDrive runs at 66MHz. The DX2/OverDrive speed doubling has no effect on the rest of the system; all components on the motherboard run the same as they do with a standard 486 processor. Therefore, you do not have to change other components (such as memory) to accommodate the double-speed chip. The DX2/OverDrive chips have been available in several speeds. Three different speed-rated versions have been offered:

■ 40MHz DX2/OverDrive for 16MHz or 20MHz systems

■ 50MHz DX2/OverDrive for 25MHz systems

■ 66MHz DX2/OverDrive for 33MHz systems

Notice that these ratings indicate the maximum speed at which the chip is capable of running. You could use a 66MHz-rated chip in place of the 50MHz- or 40MHz-rated parts with no problem, although the chip will run only at the slower speeds. The actual speed of the chip is double the motherboard clock frequency. When the 40MHz DX2/OverDrive chip is installed in a 16MHz 486SX system, for example, the chip will function only at 32MHz—exactly double the motherboard speed. Intel originally stated that no 100MHz DX2/OverDrive chip would be available for 50MHz systems—which technically has not been true, because the DX4 could be set to run in a clock-doubled mode and used in a 50MHz motherboard (see the discussion of the DX4 processor in this section).

The only part of the DX2 chip that doesn't run at double speed is the bus interface unit, a region of the chip that handles I/O between the CPU and the outside world. By translating between the differing internal and external clock speeds, the bus interface unit makes speed doubling transparent to the rest of the system. The DX2 appears to the rest of the system to be a regular 486DX chip, but one that seems to execute instructions twice as fast.

DX2/OverDrive chips are based on the 0.8-micron circuit technology that was first used in the 50MHz 486DX. The DX2 contains 1.1 million transistors in a three-layer form. The internal 8K cache, integer, and Floating-Point Units all run at double speed. External communication with the PC runs at normal speed to maintain compatibility.

Besides upgrading existing systems, one of the best parts of the DX2 concept was the fact that system designers could introduce very fast systems by using cheaper motherboard designs, rather than the more costly designs that would support a straight high-speed clock. This means that a 50MHz 486DX2 system was much less expensive than a straight 50MHz 486DX system. The system board in a 486DX-50 system operates at a true 50MHz. The 486DX2 CPU in a 486DX2-50 system operates internally at 50MHz, but the motherboard operates at only 25MHz.

You may be thinking that a true 50MHz DX-processor–based system still would be faster than a speed-doubled 25MHz system, and this generally is true, but the differences in speed actually are very slight—a real testament to the integration of the 486 processor and especially to the cache design.

When the processor has to go to system memory for data or instructions, for example, it has to do so at the slower motherboard operating frequency (such as 25MHz). Because the 8K internal cache of the 486DX2 has a hit rate of 90–95%, however, the CPU has to access system memory only 5–10% of the time for memory reads. Therefore, the performance of the DX2 system can come very close to that of a true 50MHz DX system and cost much less. Even though the motherboard runs only at 33.33MHz, a system with a DX2 66MHz processor ends up being faster than a true 50MHz DX system, especially if the DX2 system has a good Level 2 cache.

Many 486 motherboard designs also include a secondary cache that is external to the cache integrated into the 486 chip. This external cache allows for much faster access when the 486 chip calls for external-memory access. The size of this external cache can vary anywhere from 16K to 512K or more. When you add a DX2 processor, an external cache is even more important for achieving the greatest performance gain. This cache greatly reduces the wait states that the processor will have to add when writing to system memory or when a read causes an internal-cache miss. For this reason, some systems perform better with the DX2/OverDrive processors than others, usually depending on the size and efficiency of the external-memory cache system on the motherboard. Systems that have no external cache will still enjoy a near-doubling of CPU performance, but operations that involve a great deal of memory access will be slower.

This brings us to the DX4 processor. Although the standard DX4 technically was not sold as a retail part, it could be purchased from several vendors, along with the 3.3v voltage adapter needed to install the chip in a 5v socket. These adapters have jumpers that enable you to select the DX4 clock multiplier and set it to 2x, 2.5x, or 3x mode. In a 50MHz DX system, you could install a DX4/voltage-regulator combination set in 2x mode for a motherboard speed of 50MHz and a processor speed of 100MHz! Although you may not be able to take advantage of certain VL-Bus adapter cards, you will have one of the fastest 486-class PCs available.

Intel also sold a special DX4 OverDrive processor that included a built-in voltage regulator and heat sink that are specifically designed for the retail market. The DX4 OverDrive chip is essentially the same as the standard 3.3v DX4 with the main exception that it runs on 5v because it includes an on-chip regulator. Also, the DX4 OverDrive chip will run only in the tripled speed mode, and not the 2x or 2.5x modes of the standard DX4 processor.

> **Note**
>
> As of this writing, Intel has discontinued all 486 and DX2/DX4/OverDrive processors, including the so-called Pentium OverDrive Processor.

Pentium OverDrive for 486SX2 and DX2 Systems. The Pentium OverDrive Processor became available in 1995. An OverDrive chip for 486DX4 systems had been planned, but poor marketplace performance of the SX2/DX2 chip meant that it never saw the light of day. One thing to keep in mind about the 486 Pentium OverDrive chip is that although it is intended primarily for SX2 and DX2 systems, it should work in any upgradable 486SX or DX system that has a Socket 2 or Socket 3. If in doubt, check Intel's online upgrade guide for compatibility.

The Pentium OverDrive Processor is designed for systems that have a processor socket that follows the Intel Socket 2 specification. This processor also will work in systems that have a Socket 3 design, although you should ensure that the voltage is set for 5v rather than 3.3v. The Pentium OverDrive chip includes a 32K internal Level 1 cache, and the same superscalar (multiple instruction path) architecture of the real Pentium chip.

Besides a 32-bit Pentium core, these processors feature increased clock-speed operation due to internal clock multiplication, and incorporate an internal Write-Back cache (standard with the Pentium). If the motherboard supports the Write-Back cache function, increased performance will be realized. Unfortunately, most motherboards, especially older ones with the Socket 2 design, only support Write-Through cache.

Most tests of these OverDrive chips show them to be only slightly ahead of the DX4-100, and behind the DX4-120 and true Pentium 60, 66, or 75. Unfortunately, these are the only solutions still offered by Intel for upgrading the 486. Based on the relative affordability today of low-end "real" Pentiums, it seems hard not to justify making the step up to a more modern system. I would not recommend the 486 Pentium OverDrive chips as a viable solution for the future.

"Vacancy"—Secondary OverDrive Sockets. Perhaps you saw the Intel advertisements—both print and television—that featured a 486SX system with a neon Vacancy sign pointing to an empty socket next to the CPU chip. Unfortunately, these ads were not very informative, and they made it seem that only systems with the extra socket could be upgraded. I was worried when I first saw these ads because I had just purchased a 486DX system, and the advertisements implied that only 486SX systems with the empty OverDrive socket were upgradable. This, of course, was not true, but the Intel advertisements surely did not communicate that fact very well.

I later found that upgradability does not depend on having an extra OverDrive socket in the system and that virtually any 486SX or DX system can be upgraded. The secondary OverDrive socket was designed simply to make upgrading easier and more convenient. Even in systems that have the second socket, you can actually remove the primary SX or DX CPU and plug the OverDrive processor directly into the main CPU socket, rather than into the secondary OverDrive socket.

In that case, you would have an upgraded system with a single functioning CPU installed; you could remove the old CPU from the system and sell it or trade it in for a refund. Unfortunately, Intel does not offer a trade-in or core-charge policy; it simply does not want your old chip. For this reason, some people saw the OverDrive socket as being a way for Intel to sell more CPUs. Some valid reasons exist, however, to use the OverDrive socket and leave the original CPU installed.

One reason is that many PC manufacturers void the system warranty if the CPU has been removed from the system. Also, most manufacturers require that the system be returned with only the original parts when systems are serviced; you must remove all add-in cards, memory modules, upgrade chips, and similar items before sending the system in for servicing. If you replace the original CPU when you install the upgrade, returning the system to its original condition will be much more difficult.

Another reason for using the upgrade socket is that the system will not function if the main CPU socket is damaged when you remove the original CPU or install the upgrade processor. By contrast, if a secondary upgrade socket is damaged, the system still should work with the original CPU.

80487 Upgrade. The Intel 80486 processor was introduced in late 1989, and systems using this chip appeared during 1990. The 486DX integrated the math coprocessor into the chip.

The 486SX began life as a full-fledged 486DX chip, but Intel actually disabled the built-in math coprocessor before shipping the chip. As part of this marketing scheme, Intel marketed what it called a 487SX math coprocessor. Motherboard manufacturers installed an Intel-designed socket for this so-called 487 chip. In reality, however, the 487SX math chip was a special 486DX chip with the math coprocessor enabled. When you plugged this chip into your motherboard, it disabled the 486SX chip and gave you the functional equivalent of a full-fledged 486DX system.

AMD 486 (5x86). AMD makes a line of 486-compatible chips that install into standard 486 motherboards. In fact, AMD makes the fastest 486 processor available, which they call the Am5x86(TM)-P75. The name is a little misleading, as the 5x86 part makes some people think that this is a fifth-generation Pentium-type processor. In reality, it is a fast clock-multiplied (4x clock) 486 that runs at four times the speed of the 33MHz 486 motherboard you plug it into.

The 5x85 offers high-performance features such as a unified 16K write-back cache and 133MHz core clock speed, and is approximately comparable to a Pentium 75, which is why it is denoted with a P-75 in the part number. It is the ideal choice for cost-effective 486 upgrades, where changing the motherboard is difficult or impossible.

Not all motherboards support the 5x86. The best way to verify that your motherboard supports the chip is by checking with the documentation that came with the board. Look for key words such as "Am5X86," "AMD-X5," "clock-quadrupled," "133MHz," or other similar wording. Another good way to determine whether your motherboard supports the AMD 5x86 is to look for it in the listed models on AMD's Web site.

There are a few things to note when installing a 5x86 processor into a 486 motherboard:

■ The operating voltage for the 5x86 is 3.45v +/- 0.15v. Not all motherboards may have this setting, but most that incorporate a Socket 3 design should. If your 486 motherboard is a Socket 1 or 2 design, you cannot use the 5x86 processor directly. The 3.45 volt processor will not operate in a 5-volt socket and may be damaged. To convert a 5-volt motherboard to 3.45 volts, adapters can be purchased from several vendors including Kingston, Evergreen, and AMP. In fact, Kingston and Evergreen sell the 5x86 complete with a voltage regulator adapter attached in an easy-to-install package. These versions are ideal for older 486 motherboards that don't have a Socket 3 design.

■ It is generally better to purchase a new motherboard with Socket 3 than to buy one of these adapters; however, 486 motherboards are hard to find these days, and your old board may be in a proprietary form factor for which it is impossible to find a replacement. Buying a new motherboard is also better than using an adapter because the older BIOS may not understand the requirements of the processor as far as speed is concerned. BIOS updates are often required with older boards.

■ Most Socket 3 motherboards have jumpers, allowing you to set the voltage manually. Some boards don't have jumpers, but have voltage autodetect instead. These systems check the VOLDET pin (pin S4) on the microprocessor when the system is powered on.

■ The VOLDET pin is tied to ground (Vss) internally to the microprocessor. If you cannot find any jumpers for setting voltage, you can check the motherboard as follows: Switch the PC off, remove the microprocessor, connect pin S4 to a Vss pin on the ZIF socket, power on, and check any Vcc pin with a voltmeter. This should read 3.45 (± 0.15) volts. See the previous section on CPU sockets for the pinout.

■ The 5x86 requires a 33MHz motherboard speed, so be sure the board is set to that frequency. The 5x86 operates at an internal speed of 133MHz. Therefore, the jumpers must be set for "clock-quadrupled" or "4X Clock" mode. By setting the jumpers correctly on the motherboard, the CLKMUL pin (pin R17) on the processor will be connected to ground (Vss). If there is no 4x clock setting, the standard DX2 2x clock setting should work.

■ Some motherboards have jumpers that configure the internal cache in either Write-Back (WB) or Write-Through (WT) mode. They do this by pulling the WB/WT pin (pin B13) on the microprocessor to logic High (Vcc) for WB, or to ground (Vss) for WT. For best performance, configure your system in WB mode; however, reset the cache to WT mode if there are problems running applications or the floppy drive doesn't work right (DMA conflicts).

■ The 5x86 runs hot, so a heat sink is required; it normally must have a fan.

In addition to the 5x86, the AMD Enhanced 486 product line includes 80MHz, 100MHz, and 120MHz CPUs. These are the A80486DX2-80SV8B (40MHz x 2), A80486DX4-100SV8B (33MHz x 3), and the A80486DX4-120SV8B (40MHz x 3).

Cyrix/TI 486. The Cyrix 486DX2/DX4 processors were available in 100MHz, 80MHz, 75MHz, 66MHz, and 50MHz versions. Like the AMD 486 chips, the Cyrix versions are fully compatible with Intel's 486 processors and work in most 486 motherboards.

The Cx486DX2/DX4 incorporates an 8K write-back cache, an integrated Floating-Point Unit, advanced power management, and SMM, and was available in 3.3v versions.

> **Note**
>
> TI originally made all the Cyrix-designed 486 processors, and under their agreement they also sold them under the TI name. Eventually, TI and Cyrix had a falling out, and now IBM makes most of the Cyrix chips, although that may change since National Semiconductor has purchased Cyrix.

P5 (586) Fifth-Generation Processors

Pentium. On October 19, 1992, Intel announced that the fifth generation of its compatible microprocessor line (code-named P5) would be named the Pentium processor rather than the 586, as everybody had been assuming. Calling the new chip the 586 would have been natural, but Intel discovered that it could not trademark a number designation, and the company wanted to prevent other manufacturers from using the same name for any clone chips that they might develop. The actual Pentium chip shipped on March 22, 1993. Systems that use these chips were only a few months behind.

The Pentium is fully compatible with previous Intel processors, but it also differs from them in many ways. At least one of these differences is revolutionary: The Pentium features twin data pipelines, which enable it to execute two instructions at the same time. The 486 and all preceding chips can perform only a single instruction at a time. Intel calls the capability to execute two instructions at the same time *superscalar technology*. This technology provides additional performance compared with the 486.

The standard 486 chip can execute a single instruction in an average of two clock cycles—cut to an average of one clock cycle with the advent of internal clock multiplication used in the DX2 and DX4 processors. With superscalar technology, the Pentium can execute many instructions at a rate of two instructions per cycle. Superscalar architecture usually is associated with high-output RISC (Reduced Instruction Set Computer) chips. The Pentium is one of the first CISC (Complex Instruction Set Computer) chips to be considered superscalar. The Pentium is almost like having two 486 chips under the hood. Table 3.17 shows the Pentium processor specifications.

Table 3.17 Pentium Processor Specifications

Introduced:	March 22, 1993 (first generation); March 7, 1994 (second generation)
Maximum rated speeds:	60, 66MHz (first generation); 75, 90, 100, 120, 133, 150, 166, 200MHz (second generation)
CPU clock multiplier:	1x (first generation), 1.5x–3x (second generation)
Register size:	32-bit
External data bus:	64-bit
Memory address bus:	32-bit
Maximum memory:	4G
Integral-cache size:	8K code, 8K data
Integral-cache type:	2-Way Set Associative, Write-Back Data
Burst-mode transfers:	Yes
Number of transistors:	3.1 million
Circuit size:	0.8 micron (60/66MHz), 0.6 micron (75–100MHz), 0.35 micron (120MHz and up)
External package:	273-pin PGA, 296-pin SPGA, Tape Carrier
Math coprocessor:	Built-in FPU (Floating-Point Unit)

(continues)

Table 3.17 Pentium Processor Specifications Continued	
Power management:	SMM (System Management Mode), enhanced in second generation
Operating voltage:	5v (first generation), 3.465v, 3.3v, 3.1v, 2.9v (second generation)

PGA = Pin Grid Array
SPGA = Staggered Pin Grid Array

The two instruction pipelines within the chip are called the u- and v-pipes. The *u-pipe*, which is the primary pipe, can execute all integer and floating-point instructions. The *v-pipe* is a secondary pipe that can execute only simple integer instructions and certain floating-point instructions. The process of operating on two instructions simultaneously in the different pipes is called *pairing*. Not all sequentially executing instructions can be paired, and when pairing is not possible, only the u-pipe is used. To optimize the Pentium's efficiency, you can recompile software to allow more instructions to be paired.

The Pentium is 100% software-compatible with the 386 and 486, and although all current software will run much faster on the Pentium, many software manufacturers want to recompile their applications to exploit even more of the Pentium's true power. Intel has developed new compilers that will take full advantage of the chip; the company will license the technology to compiler firms so that software developers can take advantage of the Pentium's superscalar (parallel processing) capability. This optimization rapidly started to appear in the software on the market. Optimized software improved performance by allowing more instructions to execute simultaneously in both pipes.

The Pentium processor has a Branch Target Buffer (BTB), which employs a technique called *branch prediction*. It minimizes stalls in one or more of the pipes caused by delays in fetching instructions that branch to nonlinear memory locations. The BTB attempts to predict whether a program branch will be taken and then fetches the appropriate instructions. The use of branch prediction enables the Pentium to keep both pipelines operating at full speed. Figure 3.20 shows the internal architecture of the Pentium processor.

The Pentium has a 32-bit address bus width, giving it the same 4G memory-addressing capabilities as the 386DX and 486 processors. But the Pentium expands the data bus to 64 bits, which means that it can move twice as much data into or out of the CPU, compared with a 486 of the same clock speed. The 64-bit data bus requires that system memory be accessed 64 bits wide, which means that each bank of memory is 64 bits.

On most motherboards, memory is installed via SIMMs (Single Inline Memory Modules) or DIMMs (Dual Inline Memory Modules). SIMMs are available in 8-bit-wide and 32-bit-wide versions, while DIMMs are 64 bits wide. There are also versions with additional bits for parity or ECC (Error Correcting Code) data. Most Pentium systems use the 32-bit-wide SIMMs—two of these SIMMs per bank of memory. Most Pentium motherboards have at least four of these 32-bit SIMM sockets, providing for a total of two banks of memory. The newest Pentium systems and most Pentium II systems today use DIMMs, which are 64 bits wide—just like the processor's external data bus so only one DIMM is used per bank. This makes installing or upgrading memory much easier because DIMMs can go in one at a time and don't have to be matched up in pairs.

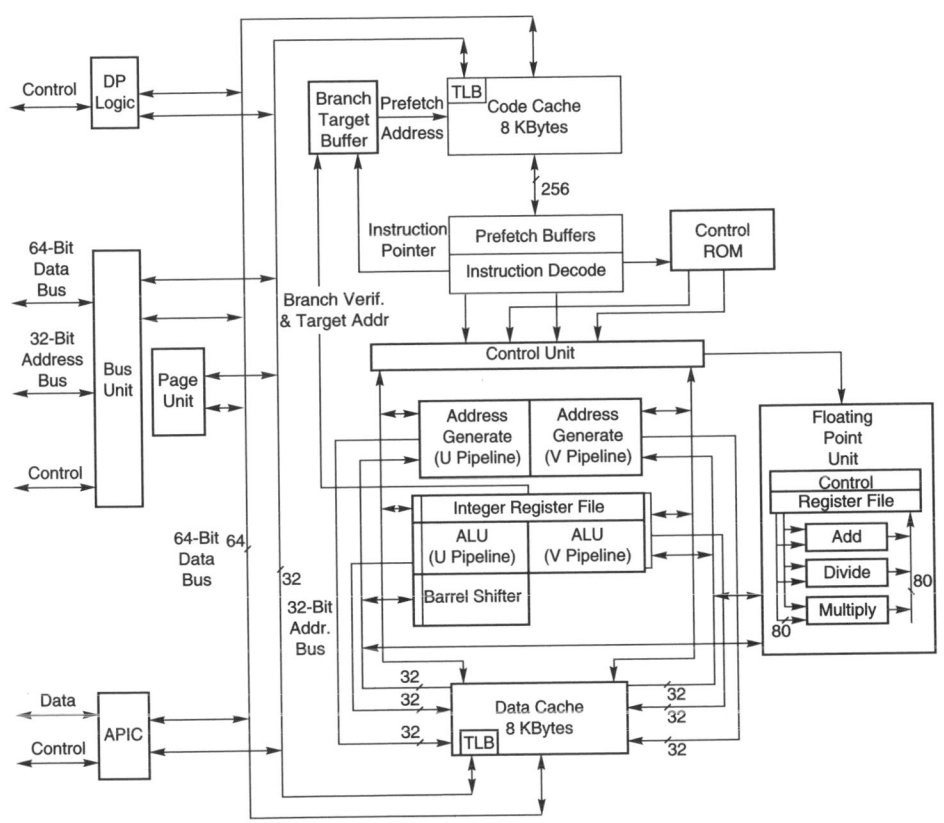

FIG. 3.20 Pentium processor internal architecture.

▶▶ See "SIMMs and DIMMs," p. 324, and "Memory Banks," p. 338

Even though the Pentium has a 64-bit data bus that transfers information 64 bits at a time into and out of the processor, the Pentium has only 32-bit internal registers. As instructions are being processed internally, they are broken down into 32-bit instructions and data elements, and processed in much the same way as in the 486. Some people thought that Intel was misleading them by calling the Pentium a 64-bit processor, but 64-bit transfers do indeed take place. Internally, however, the Pentium has 32-bit registers that are fully compatible with the 486.

The Pentium has two separate internal 8K caches, compared with a single 8K or 16K cache in the 486. The cache-controller circuitry and the cache memory are embedded in the CPU chip. The cache mirrors the information in normal RAM by keeping a copy of the data and code from different memory locations. The Pentium cache also can hold information to be written to memory when the load on the CPU and other system components is less. (The 486 makes all memory writes immediately.)

The separate code and data caches are organized in a two-way set associative fashion, with each set split into lines of 32 bytes each. Each cache has a dedicated Translation Lookaside Buffer (TLB), which translates linear addresses to physical addresses. You can configure the data cache as Write-Back or Write-Through on a line-by-line basis. When you use the Write-Back capability, the cache can store write operations and reads, further improving performance over read-only Write-Through mode. Using Write-Back mode results in less activity between the CPU and system memory—an important improvement, because CPU access to system memory is a bottleneck on fast systems. The code cache is an inherently write-protected cache because it contains only execution instructions and not data, which is updated. Because burst cycles are used, the cache data can be read or written very quickly.

Systems based on the Pentium can benefit greatly from secondary processor caches (Level 2), which usually consist of up to 512K or more of extremely fast (15ns or less) Static RAM (SRAM) chips. When the CPU fetches data that is not already available in its internal processor (Level 1) cache, wait states slow the CPU. If the data already is in the secondary processor cache, however, the CPU can go ahead with its work without pausing for wait states.

The Pentium uses a BiCMOS (Bipolar Complementary Metal Oxide Semiconductor) process and superscalar architecture to achieve the high level of performance expected from the chip. BiCMOS adds about 10% to the complexity of the chip design, but adds about 30–35% better performance without a size or power penalty.

All Pentium processors are SL Enhanced, meaning that they incorporate the SMM to provide full control of power-management features, which helps reduce power consumption. The second-generation Pentium processors (75MHz and faster) incorporate a more advanced form of SMM that includes processor clock control. This allows you to throttle the processor up or down to control power use. You can even stop the clock with these more advanced Pentium processors, putting the processor in a state of suspension that requires very little power. The second-generation Pentium processors run on 3.3v power (instead of 5v), reducing power requirements and heat generation even further.

Many current motherboards supply either 3.465v or 3.3v. The 3.465v setting is called *VRE (Voltage Reduced Extended)* by Intel and is required by some versions of the Pentium, particularly some of the 100MHz versions. The standard 3.3v setting is called *STD (Standard)*, which most of the second-generation Pentiums use. STD voltage means anything in a range from 3.135v to 3.465v with 3.3v nominal. There is also a special 3.3v setting called *VR (Voltage Reduced)*, which reduces the range from 3.300v to 3.465v with 3.38v nominal. Some of the processors require this narrower specification, which most motherboards provide. Here is a summary:

Voltage Specification	Nominal	Tolerance	Minimum	Maximum
STD (Standard)	3.30v	±0.165	3.135v	3.465v
VR (Voltage Reduced)	3.38v	±0.083	3.300v	3.465v
VRE (VR Extended)	3.50v	±0.100	3.400v	3.600v

For even lower power consumption, Intel has introduced special Pentium processors with Voltage Reduction Technology in the 75 to 266MHz family; the processors are intended for mobile computer applications. They do not use a conventional chip package and are instead mounted using a new format called *Tape Carrier Packaging* (*TCP*). The tape carrier packaging does not encase the chip in ceramic or plastic as with a conventional chip package, but instead covers the actual processor die directly with a thin, protective plastic coating. The entire processor is less than 1mm thick, or about half the thickness of a dime, and weighs less than 1 gram. They are sold to system manufacturers in a roll that looks very much like a filmstrip. The TCP processor is directly affixed (soldered) to the motherboard by a special machine, resulting in a smaller package, lower height, better thermal transfer, and lower power consumption. Special solder plugs on the circuit board located directly under the processor draw heat away and provide better cooling in the tight confines of a typical notebook or laptop system—no cooling fans are required. For more information on mobile processors and systems, see Chapter 15, "Portable PCs."

The Pentium, like the 486, contains an internal math coprocessor or FPU. The FPU in the Pentium has been rewritten and performs significantly better than the FPU in the 486, yet it is fully compatible with the 486 and 387 math coprocessor. The Pentium FPU is estimated at 2 to as much as 10 times faster than the FPU in the 486. In addition, the two standard instruction pipelines in the Pentium provide two units to handle standard integer math. (The math coprocessor handles only more complex calculations.) Other processors, such as the 486, have only a single-standard execution pipe and one integer-math unit. Interestingly, the Pentium FPU contains a flaw that received widespread publicity. See the discussion in the section "Pentium Defects" later in this chapter.

First-Generation Pentium Processor. The Pentium has been offered in three basic designs, each with several versions. The first-generation design, which is no longer available, came in 60 and 66MHz processor speeds. This design used a 273-pin PGA form factor and ran on 5v power. In this design, the processor ran at the same speed as the motherboard—in other words, a 1x clock is used.

The first-generation Pentium was created through an 0.8-micron BiCMOS process. Unfortunately, this process, combined with the 3.1 million transistor count, resulted in a die that was overly large and complicated to manufacture. As a result, reduced yields kept the chip in short supply; Intel could not make them fast enough. The 0.8-micron process was criticized by other manufacturers, including Motorola and IBM, which had been using 0.6-micron technology for their most advanced chips. The huge die and 5v operating voltage caused the 66MHz versions to consume up to an incredible 3.2 amps or 16 watts of power, resulting in a tremendous amount of heat—and problems in some systems that did not employ conservative design techniques. Fortunately, adding a fan to the processor would solve most cooling problems, as long as the fan kept running.

Much of the criticism leveled at Intel for the first-generation Pentium was justified. Some people realized that the first-generation design was just that; they knew that new Pentium versions, made in a more advanced manufacturing process, were coming. Many of those people advised against purchasing any Pentium system until the second-generation version became available.

> **Tip**
>
> A cardinal rule of computing is never to buy the first generation of any processor. Although you can wait forever because something better always will be on the horizon, a little waiting is worthwhile in some cases.

If you do have one of these first-generation Pentiums, do not despair. As with previous 486 systems, Intel offers OverDrive upgrade chips that effectively double the processor speed of your Pentium 60 or 66. These are a single-chip upgrade, meaning they replace your existing CPU. Because subsequent Pentiums are incompatible with the Pentium 60/66 Socket 4 arrangement, these OverDrive chips were the only way to upgrade an existing first-generation Pentium without replacing the motherboard.

Rather than upgrading the processor with one only twice as fast, you should really consider a complete motherboard replacement, which would accept a newer design processor that would potentially be many times faster.

Second-Generation Pentium Processor. Intel announced the second-generation Pentium on March 7, 1994. This new processor was introduced in 90 and 100MHz versions, with a 75MHz version not far behind. Eventually, 120, 133, 150, 166, and 200MHz versions were also introduced. The second-generation Pentium uses 0.6-micron (75/90/100MHz) BiCMOS technology to shrink the die and reduce power consumption. The newer, faster 120 MHz (and higher) second-generation versions incorporate an even smaller die built on a 0.35-micron BiCMOS process. These smaller dies are not changed from the 0.6-micron versions; they are basically a photographic reduction of the P54C die. The die for the Pentium is shown in Figure 3.21. Additionally, these new processors run on 3.3v power. The 100MHz version consumes a maximum 3.25 amps of 3.3v power, which equals only 10.725 watts. Further up the scale, the 150MHz chip uses 3.5 amps of 3.3v power (11.6 watts); the 166MHz unit draws 4.4 amps (14.5 watts); and the 200MHz processor uses 4.7 amps (15.5 watts).

The second-generation Pentium processors come in a 296-pin SPGA form factor that is physically incompatible with the first-generation versions. The only way to upgrade from the first generation to the second is to replace the motherboard. The second-generation

Pentium processors also have 3.3 million transistors—more than the earlier chips. The extra transistors exist because additional clock-control SL enhancements were added, as were an on-chip Advanced Programmable Interrupt Controller (APIC) and dual-processor interface.

The APIC and dual-processor interface are responsible for orchestrating dual-processor configurations in which two second-generation Pentium chips can process on the same motherboard simultaneously. Many of the Pentium motherboards designed for file servers come with dual Socket 7 specification sockets, which fully support the multiprocessing capability of the new chips. Software support for what usually is called Symmetric Multi-Processing (SMP) is being integrated into operating systems such as Windows NT and OS/2.

FIG. 3.21   Pentium Processor die. *Photograph used by permission of Intel Corporation.*

The second-generation Pentium processors use clock-multiplier circuitry to run the processor at speeds faster than the bus. The 150MHz Pentium processor, for example, can run at 2.5 times the bus frequency, which normally is 60MHz. The 200MHz Pentium processor can run at a 3x clock in a system using a 66MHz bus speed.

Note

Some Pentium systems support 75MHz or even up to 100MHz with newer motherboard and chipset designs.

Virtually all Pentium motherboards have three speed settings: 50, 60, and 66MHz. Pentium chips are available with a variety of internal clock multipliers that cause the processor to operate at various multiples of these motherboard speeds. Table 3.18 lists the speeds of currently available Pentium processors and motherboards.

Table 3.18 Pentium CPU and Motherboard Speeds		
CPU Type/Speed	**CPU Clock**	**Motherboard Speed**
Pentium 75	1.5x	50
Pentium 90	1.5x	60
Pentium 100	1.5x	66
Pentium 120	2x	60
Pentium 133	2x	66
Pentium 150	2.5x	60
Pentium 166	2.5x	66
Pentium 200	3x	66
Pentium 233	3.5x	66
Pentium 266	4x	66

The Core-to-Bus frequency ratio or clock multiplier is controlled in a Pentium processor by two pins on the chip labeled BF1 and BF2. Table 3.19 shows how the state of the BFx pins will affect the clock multiplication in the Pentium processor.

Table 3.19 Pentium BFx Pins and Clock Multipliers				
BF1	**BF2**	**Clock Multiplier**	**Bus Speed (MHz)**	**Core Speed (MHz)**
0	1	3x	66	200
0	1	3x	60	180
0	1	3x	50	150
0	0	2.5x	66	166
0	0	2.5x	60	150
0	0	2.5x	50	125
1	0	2x/4x	66	133/266*
1	0	2x	60	120
1	0	2x	50	100
1	1	1.5x/3.5x	66	100/233*
1	1	1.5x	60	90
1	1	1.5x	50	75

The 233 and 266MHz processors have modified the 1.5x and 2x multipliers to 3.5x and 4x, respectively.

Not all chips support all the Bus Frequency (BF) pins or combinations of settings. In other words, some of the Pentium processors will operate only at specific combinations of these settings, or may even be fixed at one particular setting. Many of the newer motherboards have jumpers or switches that allow you to control the BF pins and there-fore alter the clock multiplier ratio within the chip. In theory, you could run a 75MHz-rated Pentium chip at 133MHz by changing jumpers on the motherboard. This is called *overclocking*, and is discussed in the "Processor Speed Ratings" section of this chapter. What Intel has done to discourage overclockers in its most recent Pentiums is discussed near the end of the "Processor Manufacturing" section of this chapter.

A single-chip OverDrive upgrade is currently offered for second-generation Pentiums. These OverDrive chips are fixed at a 3x multiplier; they replace the existing Socket 5 or 7 CPU, increase processor speed up to 200MHz (with a 66MHz motherboard speed), and add MMX capability, as well. Simply stated, this means that a Pentium 100, 133, or 166 system equipped with the OverDrive chip will have a processor speed of 200MHz. Per-haps the best feature of these Pentium OverDrive chips is that they incorporate MMX technology. MMX provides greatly enhanced performance while running the multi-media applications that are becoming so popular today.

If you have a Socket 7 motherboard, then you may not need the special OverDrive ver-sions of the Pentium processor that have built-in voltage regulators. Instead, you can purchase a standard Pentium or Pentium-compatible chip and simply replace the exist-ing processor with it. You will have to be sure to set the multiplier and voltage settings so that they are correct for the new processor.

Pentium-MMX Processors. A third generation of Pentium processors (code-named P55C) was released in January 1997, which incorporates what Intel calls *MMX technology* into the second-generation Pentium design. These Pentium-MMX processors are avail-able in clock rates of 66/166MHz, 66/200MHz, and 66/233MHz, and a mobile-only ver-sion, which is 66/266MHz. The MMX processors share much in common with other second-generation Pentiums, including superscalar architecture, multiprocessor support, on-chip local APIC controller, and power-management features. New features include a pipelined MMX unit, 16K code, Write-Back cache (versus 8K in earlier Pentiums), and 4.5 million transistors. Pentium-MMX chips are produced on an enhanced 0.35-micron CMOS silicon process that allows for a lower 2.8v voltage level. The newer mobile 233MHz and 266MHz processors are built on a 0.25 micron process and run on only 1.8 volts. With this newer technology, the 266 processor actually uses less power than the non-MMX 133.

To use the Pentium-MMX, the motherboard must be able to supply the lower (2.8v or less) voltage these processors use. To allow a more universal motherboard solution with respect to these changing voltages, Intel has come up with the Socket 7 with VRM. The VRM is a socketed module that plugs in next to the processor and supplies the correct voltage. Because the module is easily replaced, it is easy to reconfigure a motherboard to support any of the voltages required by the newer Pentium processors.

Of course, lower voltage is nice, but MMX is what this chip is really all about. MMX technology was developed by Intel as a direct response to the growing importance and increasing demands of multimedia and communication applications. Many such applica-tions run repetitive loops of instructions that take vast amounts of time to execute. As a result, MMX incorporates a process Intel calls *Single Instruction Multiple Data* (*SIMD*), which allows one instruction to perform the same function on many pieces of data. Furthermore, 57 new instructions that are designed specifically to handle video, audio, and graphics data have been added to the chip.

If you want maximum future upgradability to the MMX Pentiums, make sure that your Pentium motherboard includes 321-pin processor sockets that fully meet the Intel Socket 7 specification. These would also include the VRM (Voltage Regulator Module) socket. If you have dual sockets, you can add a second Pentium processor to take advantage of SMP (Symmetric Multi-Processing) support in some newer operating systems.

Also make sure that any Pentium motherboard you buy can be jumpered or recon-figured for both 60 and 66MHz operation. This will enable you to take advantage of future Pentium OverDrive processors that will support the higher motherboard clock speeds. These simple recommendations will enable you to perform several dramatic up-grades without changing the entire motherboard.

Pentium Defects. Probably the most famous processor bug in history is the now legend-ary flaw in the Pentium FPU. It has often been called the FDIV bug, because it affects primarily the FDIV (Floating-Point Divide) instruction, although several other instruc-tions that use division are also affected. Intel officially refers to this problem as Errata No. 23, titled "Slight precision loss for floating-point divides on specific operand pairs." The bug has been fixed in the D1 or later steppings of the 60/66MHz Pentium processors, as well as the B5 and later steppings of the 75/90/100MHz processors. The 120MHz and higher processors are manufactured from later steppings, which do not include this prob-lem. There are tables listing all the different variations of Pentium processors and steppings and how to identify them later in this chapter.

This bug caused a tremendous fervor when it first was reported on the Internet by a mathematician in October, 1994. Within a few days, news of the defect had spread na-tionwide, and even people who did not have computers had heard about it. The Pentium would incorrectly perform floating-point division calculations with certain number com-binations, with errors anywhere from the third digit on up.

By the time the bug was publicly discovered outside of Intel, they had already incorpo-rated the fix into the next stepping of both the 60/66MHz and the 75/90/100MHz Pentium processor, along with the other corrections they had made.

After the bug was made public and Intel admitted to already knowing about it, a fury erupted. As people began checking their spreadsheets and other math calculations, many discovered that they had also encountered this problem and did not know it. Others who had not encountered the problem had their faith in the core of their PCs very shaken. People had come to put so much trust in the PC that they had a hard time com-ing to terms with the fact that it might not even be able to do math correctly!

One interesting result of the fervor surrounding this defect is that people are less likely to implicitly trust their PCs, and are therefore doing more testing and evaluating of impor-tant results. The bottom line is that if your information and calculations are important enough, you should implement some results tests. In looking for problems with math, several programs were found to have problems. For example, a bug was discovered in the yield function of Excel 5.0 that some were attributing to the Pentium processor. In this case, the problem turned out to be the software, which has been corrected in later versions (5.0c and later).

Intel finally decided that in the best interest of the consumer and their public image, they would begin a lifetime replacement warranty on the affected processors. This means that if you ever encounter one of the Pentium processors with the Errata 23 Floating-Point bug, they will replace the processor with an equivalent one without this problem. Normally, all you have to do is call Intel and ask for the replacement. They will ship you a new part matching the ratings of the one you are replacing in an overnight shipping box. The replacement is free, including all shipping charges. You merely remove your old processor, replace it with the new one, and put the old one back in the box. Then you call the overnight service who will pick it up and send it back. Intel will take a credit card number when you first call for the replacement only to ensure that the original defective chip is returned. As long as they get the original CPU back within a specified amount of time, there will be no charges to you. Intel has indicated that these defective processors will be destroyed and will not be remarketed or resold in another form.

Testing for the FPU Bug. Testing a Pentium for this bug is relatively easy. All you have to do is execute one of the test division cases cited here and see if your answer compares to the correct result.

The division calculation can be done in a spreadsheet (such as Lotus 123, Microsoft Excel, or any other), in the Microsoft Windows built-in calculator, or in any other calculating program that uses the FPU. Make sure that for the purposes of this test the FPU has not been disabled. That would normally require some special command or setting specific to the application, and would, of course, ensure that the test came out correct, no matter whether the chip is flawed or not.

The most severe Pentium floating-point errors occur as early as the third significant digit of the result. Here is an example of one of the more severe instances of the problem:

962,306,957,033 / 11,010,046 = 87,402.6282027341 (correct answer)

962,306,957,033 / 11,010,046 = 87,399.5805831329 (flawed Pentium)

Note that your particular calculator program may not show the answer to the number of digits shown here. Most spreadsheet programs limit displayed results to 13 or 15 significant digits.

As you can see, in the previous case the error turns up in the third most significant digit of the result. In an examination of over 5,000 integer pairs in the 5- to 15-digit range found to produce Pentium floating-point division errors, errors beginning in the sixth significant digit were the most likely to occur.

Here is another division problem that will come out incorrectly on a Pentium with this flaw:

4,195,835 / 3,145,727 = 1.33382044913624100 (correct answer)

4,195,835 / 3,145,727 = 1.33373906890203759 (flawed Pentium)

This one shows an error in the fifth significant digit. A variation on the previous calculation can be performed as follows:

x = 4,195,835

y = 3,145,727

z = x – (x/y)*y

4,195,835 – (4,195,835 / 3,145,727) * 3,145,727 = 0 (correct answer)

4,195,835 – (4,195,835 / 3,145,727) * 3,145,727 = 256 (flawed Pentium)

With an exact computation, the answer here should be zero. In fact, you will get zero on most machines, including those using Intel 286, 386, and 486 chips. But, on the Pentium, the answer is 256!

Here is one more calculation you can try:

5,505,001 / 294,911 = 18.66665197 (correct answer)

5,505,001 / 294,911 = 18.66600093 (flawed Pentium)

This one represents an error in the sixth significant digit.

There are several workarounds for this bug, but they extract a performance penalty. Because Intel has agreed to replace any Pentium processor with this flaw under a lifetime warranty replacement program, the best workaround is a free replacement!

Power Management Bugs. Starting with the second-generation Pentium processors, Intel added functions that allow these CPUs to be installed in energy-efficient systems. These are usually called Energy Star systems because they meet the specifications imposed by the EPA Energy Star program, but they are also unofficially called "Green PCs" by many users.

Unfortunately, there have been several bugs with respect to these functions, causing them to either fail or be disabled. These bugs are in some of the functions in the power-management capabilities accessed through SMM. These problems are applicable only to the second-generation 75/90/100MHz processors. That's because the first-generation 60/66MHz processors do not have SMM or power-management capabilities, and all higher-speed (120MHz and up) processors have the bugs fixed.

Most of the problems are related to the STPCLK# pin and the HALT instruction. If this condition is invoked by the chipset, the system will hang. For most systems, the only workaround for this problem is to simply disable the power-saving modes, such as suspend or sleep. Unfortunately, this means that your green PC won't be so green anymore! The best way to repair the problem is to replace the processor with a later stepping version that does not have the bug. These bugs affect the B1 stepping version of the 75/

90/100MHz Pentiums, and were fixed in the B3 and later stepping versions.

Pentium Processor Models and Steppings. We know that like software, no processor is truly ever perfect. From time to time, the manufacturers will gather up what problems they have found and put into production a new *stepping*, which consists of a new set of masks that incorporate the corrections. Each subsequent stepping is better and more refined than the previous ones. Although no microprocessor is ever perfect, they come closer to perfection with each stepping. In the life of a typical microprocessor, a manufacturer may go through half a dozen or more such steppings.

Table 3.20 shows all the versions of the Pentium processor Model 1 (60/66MHz version) indicating the various steppings that have been available.

Table 3.20	Pentium Processor Model 1 (60/66MHz Version) Steppings						
Type	**Family**	**Model**	**Stepping**	**Mfg. Stepping**	**Speed**	**Specification**	**Comments Number**
0	5	1	3	B1	50	Q0399	ES
0	5	1	3	B1	60	Q0352	
0	5	1	3	B1	60	Q0400	ES
0	5	1	3	B1	60	Q0394	ES,HS
0	5	1	3	B1	66	Q0353	5v1
0	5	1	3	B1	66	Q0395	ES,HS,5v1
0	5	1	3	B1	60	Q0412	
0	5	1	3	B1	60	SX753	
0	5	1	3	B1	66	Q0413	5v2
0	5	1	3	B1	66	SX754	5v2
0	5	1	5	C1	60	Q0466	HS
0	5	1	5	C1	60	SX835	HS
0	5	1	5	C1	60	SZ949	HS,BOX
0	5	1	5	C1	66	Q0467	HS,5v2
0	5	1	5	C1	66	SX837	HS,5v2
0	5	1	5	C1	66	SZ950	HS,BOX,5v2
0	5	1	7	D1	60	Q0625	HS
0	5	1	7	D1	60	SX948	HS
0	5	1	7	D1	60	SX974	HS,5v3
0	5	1	7	D1	60	-*	HS,BOX
0	5	1	7	D1	66	Q0626	HS,5v2
0	5	1	7	D1	66	SX950	HS,5v2
0	5	1	7	D1	66	Q0627	HS,5v3
0	5	1	7	D1	66	SX949	HS,5v3
0	5	1	7	D1	66	-*	HS,BOX,5v2

Tables 3.21, 3.22, 3.23, and 3.24 show all the different variations of Pentium 75/90/100/ 120/133/150/166/200/233/266MHz, classic, and MMX processors. Table 3.21 lists classic (non-MMX) desktop models. Table 3.22 lists MMX desktop models. Explanations of all the specifications and the comments in the comments column follow Table 3.23, the listing of Pentium OverDrive models.

Table 3.21 Pentium Processor Versions and Steppings

Type	Family	Model	Stepping	Core Stepping	Speed (MHz) Core-Bus	S-Spec	Comments
0	5	2	1	B1	75-50	Q0540	ES
2	5	2	1	B1	75-50	Q0541	ES
0	5	2	1	B1	90-60	Q0542	STD
0	5	2	1	B1	90-60	Q0613	VR
2	5	2	1	B1	90-60	Q0543	DP
0	5	2	1	B1	100-66	Q0563	STD
0	5	2	1	B1	100-66	Q0587	VR
0	5	2	1	B1	100-66	Q0614	VR
0	5	2	1	B1	90-60	SX879	STD
0	5	2	1	B1	90-60	SX885	STD, MD
0	5	2	1	B1	90-60	SX909	VR
2	5	2	1	B1	90-60	SX874	DP,STD
0	5	2	1	B1	100-66	SX886	STD, MD
0	5	2	1	B1	100-66	SX910	VR, MD
0	5	2	2	B3	90-60	Q0628	STD
0/2	5	2	2	B3	90-60	Q0611	STD
0/2	5	2	2	B3	90-60	Q0612	VR
0	5	2	2	B3	100-66	Q0677	VRE
0	5	2	2	B3	90-60	SX923	STD
0	5	2	2	B3	90-60	SX922	VR
0	5	2	2	B3	90-60	SX921	STD
2	5	2	2	B3	90-60	SX942	DP,STD
2	5	2	2	B3	90-60	SX943	DP,VR
2	5	2	2	B3	90-60	SX944	DP,MD
0	5	2	2	B3	90-60	SZ951	BOX,STD
0	5	2	2	B3	100-66	SX960	VRE, MD
0/2	5	2	4	B5	75-50	Q0666	STD
0/2	5	2	4	B5	90-60	Q0653	STD
0/2	5	2	4	B5	90-60	Q0654	VR
0/2	5	2	4	B5	90-60	Q0655	STD, MD
0/2	5	2	4	B5	100-66	Q0656	STD, MD
0/2	5	2	4	B5	100-66	Q0657	VR, MD

Type	Family	Model	Stepping	Core Stepping	Speed (MHz) Core-Bus	S-Spec	Comments
0/2	5	2	4	B5	100-66	Q0658	VRE, MD
0	5	2	4	B5	120-60	Q0707	VRE
0	5	2	4	B5	120-60	Q0708	STD
0/2	5	2	4	B5	75-50	SX961	STD
0/2	5	2	4	B5	75-50	SZ977	BOX,STD
0/2	5	2	4	B5	90-60	SX957	STD
0/2	5	2	4	B5	90-60	SX958	VR
0/2	5	2	4	B5	90-60	SX959	STD, MD
0/2	5	2	4	B5	90-60	SZ978	BOX,STD
0/2	5	2	4	B5	100-66	SX962	VRE, MD
0/2	5	2	5	C2	75-50	Q0700	STD
0/2	5	2	5	C2	75-50	Q0749	STD, MD
0/2	5	2	5	C2	90-60	Q0699	STD
0/2	5	2	5	C2	100-50/66	Q0698	VRE, MD
0/2	5	2	5	C2	100-50/66	Q0697	STD
0	5	2	5	C2	120-60	Q0711	VRE, MD
0	5	2	5	C2	120-60	Q0732	VRE, MD
0	5	2	5	C2	133-66	Q0733	STD, MD
0	5	2	5	C2	133-66	Q0751	STD, MD
0	5	2	5	C2	133-66	Q0775	VRE, MD
0/2	5	2	5	C2	75-50	SX969	STD
0/2	5	2	5	C2	75-50	SX998	STD, MD
0/2	5	2	5	C2	75-50	SZ994	BOX,STD
0/2	5	2	5	C2	75-50	SU070	BOXF,STD
0/2	5	2	5	C2	90-60	SX968	STD
0/2	5	2	5	C2	90-60	SZ995	BOX,STD
0/2	5	2	5	C2	90-60	SU031	BOXF,STD
0/2	5	2	5	C2	100-50/66	SX970	VRE, MD
0/2	5	2	5	C2	100-50/66	SX963	STD
0/2	5	2	5	C2	100-50/66	SZ996	BOX,STD
0/2	5	2	5	C2	100-50/66	SU032	BOXF,STD
0	5	2	5	C2	120-60	SK086	VRE, MD
0	5	2	5	C2	120-60	SX994	VRE, MD
0	5	2	5	C2	120-60	SU033	BOXF,VRE, MD
0	5	2	5	C2	133-66	SK098	STD, MD
0/2	5	2	B	cB1	120-60	Q0776	STD,No,STP
0/2	5	2	B	cB1	133-66	Q0772	STD,No,STP
0/2	5	2	B	cB1	133-66	Q0773	STD,STP

(continues)

Table 3.21   Pentium Processor Versions and Steppings Continued

Type	Family	Model	Stepping	Core Stepping	Speed (MHz) Core-Bus	S-Spec	Comments
0/2	5	2	B	cB1	133-66	Q0774	VRE,No,STP, MD
0/2	5	2	B	cB1	120-60	SK110	STD,No,STP
0/2	5	2	B	cB1	133-66	SK106	STD,No,STP
0/2	5	2	B	cB1	133-66	S106J	STD,No,STP
0/2	5	2	B	cB1	133-66	SK107	STD,STP
0/2	5	2	B	cB1	133-66	SU038	BOXF,STD, No,STP
0/2	5	2	C	cC0	133-66	Q0843	STD,No
0/2	5	2	C	cC0	133-66	Q0844	STD
0/2	5	2	C	cC0	150-60	Q0835	STD
0/2	5	2	C	cC0	150-60	Q0878	STD,PPGA
0/2	5	2	C	cC0	150-60	SU122	BOXF,STD
0/2	5	2	C	cC0	166-66	Q0836	VRE,No
0/2	5	2	C	cC0	166-66	Q0841	VRE
0/2	5	2	C	cC0	166-66	Q0886	VRE,PPGA
0/2	5	2	C	cC0	166-66	Q0890	VRE,PPGA
0	5	2	C	cC0	166-66	Q0949	VRE,PPGA
0/2	5	2	C	cC0	200-66	Q0951F	VRE,PPGA
0	5	2	C	cC0	200-66	Q0951	VRE,PPGA
0	5	2	C	cC0	200-66	SL25H	BOXF,VRE, PPGA
0/2	5	2	C	cC0	120-60	SL22M	BOXF,STD
0/2	5	2	C	cC0	120-60	SL25J	BOX,STD
0/2	5	2	C	cC0	120-60	SY062	STD
0/2	5	2	C	cC0	133-66	SL22Q	BOXF,STD
0/2	5	2	C	cC0	133-66	SL25L	BOX,STD
0/2	5	2	C	cC0	133-66	SY022	STD
0/2	5	2	C	cC0	133-66	SY023	STD,No
0/2	5	2	C	cC0	133-66	SU073	BOXF,STD,No
0/2	5	2	C	cC0	150-60	SY015	STD
0/2	5	2	C	cC0	150-60	SU071	BOXF,STD
0/2	5	2	C	cC0	166-66	SL24R	VRE,No,MAXF
0/2	5	2	C	cC0	166-66	SY016	VRE,No
0/2	5	2	C	cC0	166-66	SY017	VRE
0/2	5	2	C	cC0	166-66	SU072	BOXF,VRE,No
0	5	2	C	cC0	166-66	SY037	VRE,PPGA
0/2	5	2	C	cC0	200-66	SY044	VRE,PPGA

Type	Family	Model	Stepping	Core Stepping	Speed (MHz) Core-Bus	S-Spec	Comments
0	5	2	C	cC0	200-66	SY045	BOXUF,VRE, PPGA
0	5	2	C	cC0	200-66	SU114	BOX,VRE, PPGA
0	5	2	C	cC0	200-66	SL24Q	VRE,PPGA,No, MAXF
0/2	5	2	6	E0	75-50	Q0837	STD
0/2	5	2	6	E0	90-60	Q0783	STD
0/2	5	2	6	E0	100-50/66	Q0784	STD
0/2	5	2	6	E0	120-60	Q0785	VRE
0/2	5	2	6	E0	75-50	SY005	STD
0/2	5	2	6	E0	75-50	SU097	BOX,STD
0/2	5	2	6	E0	75-50	SU098	BOXF,STD
0/2	5	2	6	E0	90-60	SY006	STD
0/2	5	2	6	E0	100-50/66	SY007	STD
0/2	5	2	6	E0	100-50/66	SU110	BOX,STD
0/2	5	2	6	E0	100-50/66	SU099	BOXF,STD
0/2	5	2	6	E0	120-60	SY033	STD
0/2	5	2	6	E0	120-60	SU100	BOXF,STD

Table 3.22 Pentium MMX Processor Versions and Steppings

Type	Family	Model	Stepping	Core Stepping	Core Speed (MHz)	S-Spec	Comments
0/2	5	4	4	xA3	150	Q020	ES,PPGA
0/2	5	4	4	xA3	166	Q019	ES,PPGA
0/2	5	4	4	xA3	200	Q018	ES,PPGA
0/2	5	4	4	xA3	166	SL23T	BOXF,SPGA
0/2	5	4	4	xA3	166	SL23R	BOX,PPGA
0/2	5	4	4	xA3	166	SL25M	BOXF,PPGA
0/2	5	4	4	xA3	166	SY059	PPGA
0/2	5	4	4	xA3	166	SL2HU	BOX,SPGA
0/2	5	4	4	xA3	166	SL239	SPGA
0/2	5	4	4	xA3	166	SL26V	SPGA,MAXF
0/2	5	4	4	xA3	166	SL26H	PPGA,MAXF
0/2	5	4	4	xA3	200	SL26J	BOXUF,PPGA, MAXF
0/2	5	4	4	xA3	200	SY060	PPGA

(continues)

Table 3.22   Pentium MMX Processor Versions and Steppings Continued

Type	Family	Model	Stepping	Core Stepping	Core Speed (MHz)	S-Spec	Comments
0/2	5	4	4	xA3	200	SL26Q	BOX,PPGA, MAXF
0/2	5	4	4	xA3	200	SL274	BOXF,PPGA, MAXF
0/2	5	4	4	xA3	200	SL23S	BOX,PPGA
0/2	5	4	4	xA3	200	SL25N	BOXF,PPGA
0/2	5	4	3	xB1	166	Q125	ES,PPGA
0/2	5	4	3	xB1	166	Q126	ES,SPGA
0/2	5	4	3	xB1	200	Q124	ES,PPGA
0/2	5	4	3	xB1	233	Q140	ES,PPGA
0/2	5	4	3	xB1	166	SL27H	PPGA
0/2	5	4	3	xB1	166	SL27K	SPGA
0/2	5	4	3	xB1	166	SL2HX	BOX,SPGA
0/2	5	4	3	xB1	166	SL23X	BOXF,SPGA
0/2	5	4	3	xB1	166	SL2FP	BOX,PPGA
0/2	5	4	3	xB1	166	SL23V	BOXF,PPGA
0/2	5	4	3	xB1	200	SL27J	PPGA
0/2	5	4	3	xB1	200	SL2FQ	BOX,PPGA
0/2	5	4	3	xB1	200	SL23W	BOXF,PPGA
0/2	5	4	3	xB1	233	SL27S	PPGA
0/2	5	4	3	xB1	233	SL2BM	BOX,PPGA
0/2	5	4	3	xB1	233	SL293	BOXF,PPGA

All the Pentium MMX Processors listed in the table run on a 66MHz bus except for model that runs on a 60MHz bus.

Table 3.23 shows all the versions of the Pentium OverDrive processors, indicating the various steppings that have been available. Note that the Type 1 chips in this table are 486 Pentium OverDrive processors, which are designed to replace 486 chips in systems with Socket 2 or 3. The other OverDrive processors are designed to replace existing Pentium processors in Socket 4 or 5/7.

Table 3.23   Pentium OverDrive Steppings

Type	Family	Model	Stepping	Mfg. Stepping	Speed	Spec. Number	Product	Version
1	5	3	1	B1	63	SZ953	PODP5v63	1.0
1	5	3	1	B2	63	SZ990	PODP5v63	1.1
1	5	3	2	C0	83	SU014	PODP5v83	2.1
0	5	1	A	tA0	133	SU082	PODP5v133	1.0

Type	Family	Model	Stepping	Mfg. Stepping	Speed	Spec. Number	Product	Version
0	5	2	C	aC0	125	SU081	PODP3v125	1.0
0	5	2	C	aC0	150	SU083	PODP3v150	1.0
0	5	2	C	aC0	166	SU084	PODP3v166	1.0
1	5	4	4	oxA3	125/50, 150/60	SL24V	PODPMT60X150	1.0
1	5	4	4	oxA3	166/66	SL24W	PODPMT66X166	1.0
1	5	4	3	oxB1	180/60	SL2FE	PODPMT60X180	2.0
1	5	4	3	oxB1	200/66	SL2FF	PODPMT66X200	2.0

The following list explains all the entries in the Comments columns of these tables.

ES = Engineering Sample. These chips were not sold through normal channels but were designed for development and testing purposes.

HS = Heat Spreader Package. This indicates a chip with a metal plate on the top, which is used to spread heat away from the center part of the chip. The heat spreader helps the chip run cooler; however, most later chips use a smaller, more powerful, more efficient die, and Intel has been able to eliminate the heat spreader from these.

DP = Dual Processor version where Type 0 is Primary only, Type 2 is Secondary only, and Type 0 or 2 is either.

MD = Minimum Delay timing restrictions on several processor signals.

STD = Standard voltage range. The range for the C2 and subsequent steppings of the Pentium processor is 3.135V to 3.6V. The voltage range for B-step parts remains at 3.135V–3.465V. Note that all E0-step production parts are standard voltage.

VR = Voltage Reduced (3.300v to 3.465v).

VRE = VR and Extended (3.45v to 3.60v).

VRT = Voltage Reduction Technology.

TCP = Tape Carrier Package.

BOX = A retail boxed processor with a standard passive heat sink.

BOXF = A retail boxed processor with an active (fan-cooled) heat sink.

The absence of a package type in the comments column means the processor is SPGA by default.

2.285v = This is a mobile Pentium processor with MMX technology with a core operating voltage of 2.285v – 2.665v.

MAXF = The part may run only at the maximum specified frequency. Specifically, a 200-MHz may be run at 200MHz +0/–5 MHz (195 – 200MHz) and a 166-MHz may be run at 166MHz +0/–5MHz (161 – 166MHz).

BOXUF = This part also ships as a boxed processor with an unattached fan heat sink.

1.8v = This is a mobile Pentium processor with MMX technology with a core operating voltage of 1.665v – 1.935v and an I/O operating voltage of 2.375v – 2.625v.

2.2v = This is a mobile Pentium processor with MMX technology with a core operating voltage of 2.10v – 2.34v.

2.0v = This is a mobile Pentium Processor with MMX technology with a core operating voltage of 1.850v – 2.150v and an I/O operating voltage of 2.375v – 2.625v.

STP = The cB1 stepping is logically equivalent to the C2-step, but on a different manufacturing process. The mcB1 step is logically equivalent to the cB1 step (except it does not support DP, APIC, or FRC). The mcB1, mA1, mA4, and mcC0-steps also use Intel's VRT (Voltage Reduction Technology), and are available in the TCP and/or SPGA package, primarily to support mobile applications. The mxA3 is logically equivalent to the xA3 stepping (except it does not support DP or APIC).

NO = Means that part meets the specifications but is not tested to support 82498/82493 and 82497/82492 cache timings.

* = These chips have no Specification number.

In these tables, the processor Type heading refers to the dual processor capabilities of the Pentium. Versions indicated with a Type 0 can be used only as a primary processor, while those marked as Type 2 can be used only as the secondary processor in a pair. If the processor is marked as Type 0/2, it can serve as the primary or secondary processor, or both.

The Family designation for all Pentiums is 5 (for 586), while the model indicates the particular revision. Model 1 indicates the first-generation 60/66MHz version, while Model 2 or later indicates the second-generation 75+MHz version. The stepping number is the actual revision of the particular model. The family, model, and stepping number can be read by software such as the Intel CPUID program. These also correspond to a particular Manufacturer Stepping code, which is how Intel designates the chips in-house. These are usually an alphanumeric code. For example, stepping 5 of the Model 2 Pentium is also known as the C2 stepping inside Intel.

Manufacturing stepping codes that begin with an m indicate a mobile processor. Most Pentium processors come in a standard Ceramic Pin Grid Array (CPGA) package; however, the mobile processors also use the Tape Carrier Package (TCP). Now there is also a Plastic Pin Grid Array (PPGA) package being used to reduce cost.

To determine the specifications of a given processor, you need to look up the S-spec number in the table of processor specifications. To find your S-spec number, you have to read it off of the chip directly. It can be found printed on both the top and bottom of the chip. If your heat sink is glued on, remove the chip and heat sink from the socket as a unit and read the numbers from the bottom of the chip. Then you can look up the S-spec number in the table; it will tell you the specifications of that particular processor.

Intel is introducing new chips all the time, so visit their Web site and search for the Pentium processor "Quick Reference Guide" in the developer portion of their site. There you will find a complete listing of all current processor specifications by S-spec number.

One interesting item to note is that there are several subtly different voltages required by different Pentium processors. Table 3.24 summarizes the different processors and their required voltages:

Table 3.24	Pentium Processor Voltages		
Model	**Stepping**	**Voltage spec.**	**Voltage range**
1	-	Std.	4.75–5.25v
1	-	5v1	4.90–5.25v
1	-	5v2	4.90–5.40v
1	-	5v3	5.15–5.40v
2+	B1-B5	Std.	3.135–3.465v
2+	C2+	Std.	3.135–3.600v
2+	-	VR	3.300–3.465v
2+	B1-B5	VRE	3.45–3.60v
2+	C2+	VRE	3.40–3.60v
4+	-	MMX	2.70–2.90v
4	3	Mobile	2.285–2.665v
4	3	Mobile	2.10–2.34v
8	1	Mobile	1.850–2.150v
8	1	Mobile	1.665–1.935v

Many of the newer Pentium motherboards have jumpers that allow for adjustments to the different voltage ranges. If you are having problems with a particular processor, it may not be matched correctly to your motherboard voltage output.

If you are purchasing an older, used Pentium system today, I would recommend using only Model 2 (second generation) or later version processors that are available in 75MHz or faster speeds. I would definitely want stepping C2 or later. Virtually all the important bugs and problems were fixed in the C2 and later releases. The newer Pentium processors have no serious bugs to worry about.

AMD-K5. The AMD-K5 is a Pentium-compatible processor developed by AMD and available as the PR75, PR90, PR100, PR120, PR133, and PR-166. Because it is designed to be physically and functionally compatible, any motherboard that properly supports the Intel Pentium should support the AMD-K5. However, a BIOS upgrade may be required to properly recognize the AMD-K5. AMD keeps a list of motherboards that have been tested for compatibility.

The K5 has the following advanced features:

■ 16K instruction cache, 8K write-back data cache

- Dynamic execution—branch prediction with speculative execution

- 5-stage RISC-like pipeline with 6 parallel functional units

- High-performance Floating-Point Unit

- Pin-selectable clock multiples of 1.5x and 2x

The K5 is sold under the P-rating system, which means that the number on the chip does not indicate true clock speed, only apparent speed when running certain applications.

The actual bus speed and clock multiplier breakdowns are as follows:

P-Rating	Clock	Multiplier	True CPU speed
PR-75	50MHz	1.5x	75MHz
PR-90	60MHz	1.5x	90MHz
PR-100	66MHz	1.5x	100MHz
PR-120	60MHz	1.5x	90MHz
PR-133	66MHz	1.5x	100MHz
PR-166	66MHz	1.75x	117MHz

Note

The 1.75 multiplier setting is achieved by setting the motherboard for 2.5.

Note that several of these processors do not run at their apparent rated speed. For example, the PR-166 version actually runs at only 117 true MHz. Sometimes this can confuse the system BIOS, which may report the true speed rather than the P-rating, which compares the chip against an Intel Pentium of that speed. AMD claims that due to architecture enhancements over the Pentium, they do not need to run the same clock frequency to achieve that same performance. Even with such improvements, AMD markets the K5 as a fifth-generation processor, just like the Pentium.

The AMD-K5 operates at 3.52 volts (VRE Setting). Some older motherboards default to 3.3 volts, which is below specification for the K5 and could cause erratic operation.

Pseudo-Fifth-Generation Processors

There is at least one processor that, while generally regarded as a fifth-generation processor, lacks many of the functions of that class of chip—the IDT Centaur C6 Winchip. True fifth-generation chips would have multiple internal pipelines, which is called *superscalar architecture*, allowing more than one instruction to be processed at one time. They would also feature branch prediction, another fifth-generation chip feature. As it lacks these features, the C6 is more closely related to a 486; however, the performance levels and the pinout put it firmly in the class with Pentium processors. It has turned out to be an ideal Pentium Socket 7-compatible processor for low-end systems.

IDT Centaur C6 Winchip. The C6 processor is a recent offering from Centaur, a subsidiary of IDT (Integrated Device Technologies). It is Socket 7-compatible with Intel's

Pentium, includes MMX extensions, and is available at clock speeds of 180, 200, 225, and 240MHz. Pricing is below Intel on the Pentium MMX.

Centaur is led by Glenn Henry, who spent more than two decades as a computer architect at IBM and six years as chief technology officer at Dell Computer Corp. The company is a wholly owned subsidiary of Integrated Device Technology (IDT), a well-established semiconductor manufacturer well-known for SRAM and other components.

As a manufacturer, IDT owns its own fabs (semiconductor manufacturing plants), which will help keep costs low on the C6 Winchip. Their expertise in SRAM manufacturing may be applied in new versions of the C6, which integrate onboard L2 cache in the same package as the core processor, similar to the Pentium Pro.

The C6 has 32K each of instruction and data cache, just like AMD's K6 and Cyrix's 6x86MX, yet it has only 5.4 million transistors, compared with the AMD chip's 8.8 million and the Cyrix chip's 6.5 million. This allows for a very small processor die, which also reduces power consumption. Centaur achieved this small size with a streamlined design. Unlike competitor chips, the C6 is not superscalar—it issues only one instruction per clock cycle like the 486. However, with large caches, an efficient memory-management unit, and careful performance optimization of commonly used instructions, the C6 achieves performance that's comparable to a Pentium. Another benefit of the C6's simple design is low power consumption—low enough for notebook PCs. Neither AMD nor Cyrix has a processor with power consumption low enough for most laptop designs.

To keep the design simple, Centaur compromised on floating-point and MMX speed and focused instead on typical application performance. As a result, the chip's performance trails the other competitors' on some multimedia applications and games. IDT indicates that faster floating-point and MMX performance will be available in an enhanced version due out in mid-'98.

P6 (686) Sixth-Generation Processors

The P6 (686) processors represent a new generation with features not found in the previous generation units. The two main processors in the P6 class are the Pentium Pro and Pentium II. Despite their conservative names, they are more than just enhanced P5 Pentium processors.

The main new feature in the fifth-generation Pentium processors was the superscalar architecture, where two instruction execution units could execute instructions simultaneously in parallel. Later fifth-generation chips also added MMX technology to the mix, as well. So then what did Intel add in the sixth-generation to justify calling it a whole new generation of chip? Besides many minor improvements, the real key features of all sixth-generation processors are Dynamic Execution and the Dual Independent Bus (DIB) architecture, plus a greatly improved superscalar design.

Dynamic Execution enables the processor to execute more instructions on parallel, so that tasks are completed more quickly. This technology innovation is comprised of three main elements:

■ Multiple branch prediction, to predict the flow of the program through several branches

■ Dataflow analysis, which schedules instructions to be executed when ready, independent of their order in the original program

■ Speculative execution, which increases the rate of execution by looking ahead of the program counter and executing instructions that are likely to be needed

Branch prediction is a feature formerly found only in high-end mainframe processors. It allows the processor to keep the instruction pipeline full while running at a high rate of speed. A special fetch/decode unit in the processor uses a highly optimized branch prediction algorithm to predict the direction and outcome of the instructions being executed through multiple levels of branches, calls, and returns. It is like a chess player working out multiple strategies in advance of game play by predicting the opponent's strategy several moves into the future. By predicting the instruction outcome in advance, the instructions can be executed with no waiting.

Dataflow analysis studies the flow of data through the processor to detect any opportunities for out-of-order instruction execution. A special dispatch/execute unit in the processor monitors many instructions and can execute these instructions in an order that optimizes the use of the multiple superscalar execution units. The resulting out-of-order execution of instructions can keep the execution units busy even when cache misses and other data dependent instructions might otherwise hold things up.

Speculative execution is the processor's capability to execute instructions in advance of the actual program counter. The processor's dispatch/execute unit uses dataflow analysis to execute all available instructions in the instruction pool and store the results in temporary registers. A retirement unit then searches the instruction pool for completed instructions that are no longer data dependent on other instructions to run or which have unresolved branch predictions. If any such completed instructions are found, the results are committed to memory by the retirement unit or the appropriate standard Intel Architecture in the order they were originally issued. They are then retired from the pool.

Dynamic Execution essentially removes the constraint and dependency on linear instruction sequencing. By promoting out-of-order instruction execution, it can keep the instruction units working rather than waiting for data from memory. Even though instructions can be predicted and executed out of order, the results are committed in the original order so as not to disrupt or change program flow. This allows the P6 to run existing Intel Architecture software exactly as the P5 (Pentium) and previous processors did, just a whole lot more quickly!

The other main P6 architecture feature is known as the Dual Independent Bus. This refers to the fact that the processor has two data buses, one for the system (motherboard) and the other just for cache. This allows the cache memory to run at speeds previously not possible.

Previous P5 generation processors have only a single motherboard host processor bus, and all data, including cache transfers, must flow through it. The main problem with that is the cache memory was restricted to running at motherboard bus speed, which was 66MHz until recently and has now moved to 100MHz. We have cache memory today that can run 500MHz or more, and main memory (SDRAM) that runs at 66 and 100MHz, so a method was needed to get faster memory closer to the processor. The solution was to essentially build in what is called a backside bus to the processor, otherwise known as a dedicated cache bus. The L2 cache would then be connected to this bus and could run at any speed. The first implementation of this was in the Pentium Pro, where the L2 cache was built right into the processor package and ran at the full core processor speed. Later, that proved to be too costly, so the L2 cache was moved outside of the processor package and onto a cartridge module, which we now know as the Pentium II. With that design, the cache bus could run at any speed, with the first units running the cache at half-processor speed.

By having the cache on a backside bus directly connected to the processor, the speed of the cache is scalable to the processor. In current PC architecture—66MHz Pentiums all the way through the 333MHz Pentium IIs—the motherboard runs at a speed of 66MHz. Newer Pentium II systems run a 100MHz motherboard bus and have clock speeds of 350MHz and higher. If the cache were restricted to the motherboard as is the case with Socket 7 (P5 processor) designs, then the cache memory would have to remain at 66MHz even though the processor was running as fast as 333MHz; with newer boards the cache would be stuck at 100MHz, while the processor ran as fast as 500MHz or more. With the Dual Independent Bus (DIB) design in the P6 processors, as the processor runs faster, at higher multiples of the motherboard speed, the cache would increase by the same amount that the processor speed increases. The cache on the DIB is coupled to processor speed, so that doubling the speed of the processor also doubles the speed of the cache.

The Dual Independent Bus architecture is necessary to have decent processor performance in the 300MHz and beyond range. Older Socket 7 (P5 processor) designs will not be able to move up to these higher speeds without suffering a tremendous performance penalty due to the slow motherboard-bound L2 cache. That is why Intel is not developing any Pentium (P5 class) processors beyond 266MHz; however, the P6 processors will be available in speeds of up to 500MHz or more.

Finally, the P6 architecture upgrades the superscalar architecture of the P5 processors by adding more instruction execution units, and by breaking down the instructions into special micro-ops. This is where the CISC (Complex Instruction Set Computer) instructions are broken down into more RISC (Reduced Instruction Set Computer) commands. The RISC-level commands are smaller and easier for the parallel instruction units to execute more efficiently. With this design, Intel has brought the benefits of a RISC processor—high-speed dedicated instruction execution—to the CISC world. Note that the P5 had only two instruction units, while the P6 has at least six separate dedicated instruction units. It is said to be three-way superscalar, because the multiple instruction units can execute up to three instructions in one cycle.

Other improvements in efficiency also are included in the P6 architecture: built-in multiprocessor support, enhanced error detection and correction circuitry, and optimization for 32-bit software.

Rather than just being a faster Pentium, the Pentium Pro, Pentium II, and other sixth-generation processors have many feature and architectural improvements. The core of the chip is very RISC (Reduced Instruction Set Computer)-like, while the external instruction interface is classic Intel CISC (Complex Instruction Set Computer). By breaking down the CISC instructions into several different RISC instructions and running them down parallel execution pipelines, the overall performance is increased.

Compared to a Pentium at the same clock speed, the P6 processors are faster—as long as you're running 32-bit software. The P6 Dynamic Execution is optimized for performance primarily when running 32-bit software such as Windows NT. If you are using 16-bit software, such as Windows 95 or 98 (which operate part time in a 16-bit environment) and most older applications, the P6 will not provide as marked a performance improvement over similarly speed-rated Pentium and Pentium-MMX processors. That's because the dynamic execution capability will not be fully exploited. Because of this, Windows NT is often regarded as the most desirable operating system for use with Pentium Pro/II processors. While this is not exactly true (a Pentium Pro/II will run just fine under Windows 95/98), Windows NT does take better advantage of the P6's capabilities. Note that it is really not so much the operating system, but which applications you use. Software developers can take steps to gain the full advantages of the sixth-generation processors. This includes using modern compilers that can improve performance for all current Intel processors, writing 32-bit code where possible and making code as predictable as possible to take advantage of the processor's "Dynamic Execution" multiple branch prediction capabilities.

Pentium Pro Processor. Intel's successor to the Pentium is called the *Pentium Pro*. The Pentium Pro was the first chip in the P6 or sixth-generation processor family. It was introduced in September of 1995, and became widely available in 1996. The chip is a 387-pin unit that resides in Socket 8, so it is not pin-compatible with earlier Pentiums. The new chip is unique among processors as it is constructed in a Multi-Chip Module (MCM) physical format, which Intel is calling a *Dual Cavity PGA* (*Pin Grid Array*) package. Inside the 387-pin chip carrier are two dies. One contains the actual Pentium Pro processor (shown in Figure 3.22), and the other a 256K (the Pentium Pro with 256K cache is shown in Figure 3.23), 512K, or 1M (the Pentium Pro with 1M cache is shown in Figure 3.24) L2 cache. The processor die contains 5.5 million transistors, the 256K cache die contains 15.5 million transistors, and the 512K cache die(s) have 31 million transistors each, for a potential total of nearly 68 million transistors in a Pentium Pro with 1M of internal cache! A Pentium Pro with 1M cache has two 512K cache die and a standard P6 processor die.

The main processor die includes a 16K split L1 cache with an 8K two-way set associative cache for primary instructions, and an 8K four-way set associative cache for data.

Another sixth-generation processor feature found in the Pentium Pro is the Dual Independent Bus (DIB) architecture, which addresses the memory bandwidth limitations of previous-generation processor architectures. Two buses make up the Dual Independent Bus architecture: the L2 cache bus (contained entirely within the processor package) and the processor-to-main-memory system bus. The speed of the dedicated L2 cache bus on the Pentium Pro is equal to the full core speed of the processor. This was accomplished by embedding the cache chips directly into the Pentium Pro package. The DIB processor bus architecture addresses processor-to-memory bus bandwidth limitations. It offers up to three times the performance bandwidth of the single-bus, "Socket 7" generation processors, such as the Pentium.

FIG. 3.22   Pentium Pro Processor die. *Photograph used by permission of Intel Corporation.*

FIG. 3.23   Pentium Pro Processor with 256K L2 cache (left). *Photograph used by permission of Intel Corporation.*

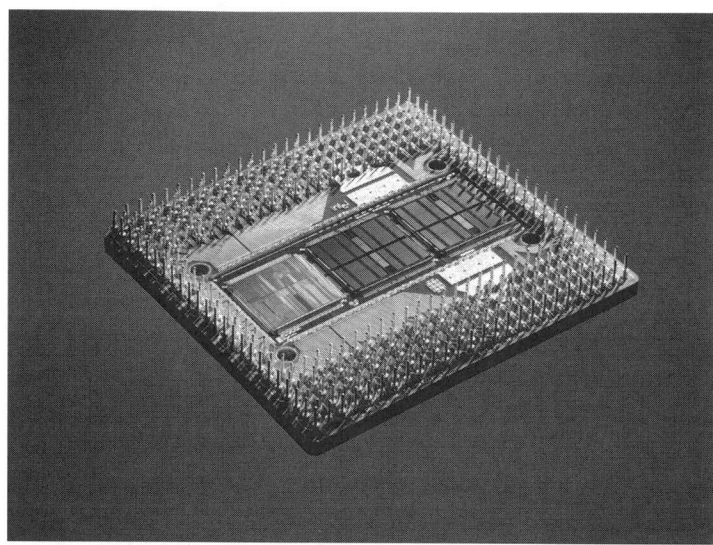

FIG. 3.24 Pentium Pro Processor with 1M L2 cache (center and right). *Photograph used by permission of Intel Corporation.*

Table 3.25 shows Pentium Pro processor specifications. Table 3.26 shows the specifications for each model within the Pentium Pro family, as there are many variations from model to model.

Table 3.25 Pentium Pro Family Processor Specifications	
Introduced:	**September 1995**
Maximum rated speeds:	150, 166, 180, 200MHz
CPU clock multiplier:	2.5x, 3x
Internal Registers:	32-bit
External Data Bus:	64-bit
Memory Address Bus:	36-bit
Addressable memory:	64G
Virtual memory:	64T
Integral L1-cache size:	8K code, 8K data (16K total)
Integrated L2-cache bus:	64-bit, full core-speed
Socket/Slot:	Socket 8
Physical Package:	387-pin Dual Cavity Pin Grid Array
Package dimensions:	2.46 (6.25cm) x 2.66 (6.76cm)
Math coprocessor:	Built-in FPU (Floating-Point Unit)
Power management:	SMM (System Management Mode)
Operating voltage:	3.1v or 3.3v

Table 3.26   Pentium Pro Processor Specifications by Processor Model

Pentium Pro Processor (200MHz) with 1M Integrated Level 2 Cache

Introduction date:	August 18, 1997
Clock speeds:	200MHz (66MHz x 3)
Number of transistors:	5.5 million (0.35 micron process), plus 62 million in 1M L2 cache (0.35 micron)
Cache Memory:	8Kx2 (16K) L1, 1M core-speed L2
Die Size:	0.552 inches per side (14.0mm)

Pentium Pro Processor (200MHz)

Introduction date:	November 1, 1995
Clock speeds:	200MHz (66MHz x 3)
iCOMP Index 2.0 rating:	220
Number of transistors:	5.5 million (0.35 micron process), plus 15.5 million in 256K L2 cache (0.6 micron), or 31 million in 512K L2 cache (0.35 micron)
Cache Memory:	8Kx2 (16K) L1, 256K or 512K core-speed L2
Die Size:	0.552 inches per side (14.0mm)

Pentium Pro Processor (180MHz)

Introduction date:	November 1, 1995
Clock speeds:	180MHz (60MHz x 3)
iCOMP Index 2.0 rating:	197
Number of transistors:	5.5 million (0.35 micron process), plus 15.5 million in 256K L2 cache (0.6 micron)
Cache Memory:	8Kx2 (16K) L1, 256K core-speed L2
Die Size:	0.552 inches per side (14.0mm)

Pentium Pro Processor (166MHz)

Introduction date:	November 1, 1995
Clock speeds:	166MHz (66MHz x 2.5)
Number of transistors:	5.5 million (0.35 micron process), plus 31 million in 512K L2 cache (0.35 micron)
Cache Memory:	8Kx2 (16K) L1, 512K core-speed L2
Die Size:	0.552 inches per side (14.0mm)

Pentium Pro Processor (150MHz)

Introduction date:	November 1, 1995
Clock speeds:	150MHz (60MHz x 2.5)
Number of transistors:	5.5 million (0.6 micron process), plus 15.5 million in 256K L2 cache (0.6 micron)
Cache Memory:	8Kx2 (16K) L1, 256K core-speed L2
Die Size:	0.691 inches per side (17.6mm)

As you saw in Table 3.2, performance comparisons on the iCOMP 2.0 Index rate a classic Pentium 200MHz at 142, whereas a Pentium Pro 200MHz scores an impressive 220. Just for comparison, note that a Pentium MMX 200MHz falls right about in the middle in regards to performance at 182. Keep in mind that using a Pentium Pro with any 16-bit software applications will nullify much of the performance gain shown by the iCOMP 2.0 rating.

Like the Pentium before it, the Pentium Pro runs clock multiplied on a 66MHz motherboard. The following table lists speeds for Pentium Pro processors and motherboards.

CPU Type/Speed	CPU Clock	Motherboard Speed
Pentium Pro 150	2.5x	60
Pentium Pro 166	2.5x	66
Pentium Pro 180	3x	60
Pentium Pro 200	3x	66

The integrated L2 cache is one of the really outstanding features of the Pentium Pro. By building the L2 cache into the CPU and getting it off the motherboard, they can now run the cache at full processor speed rather than the slower 60 or 66MHz motherboard bus speeds. In fact, the L2 cache features its own internal 64-bit backside bus, which does not share time with the external 64-bit frontside bus used by the CPU. The internal registers and data paths are still 32-bit, as with the Pentium. By building the L2 cache into the system, motherboards can be cheaper because they no longer require separate cache memory. Some boards may still try to include cache memory in their design, but the general consensus is that Level 3 cache (as it would be called) would offer less improvement with the Pentium Pro than with the Pentium.

One of the features of the built-in L2 cache is that multiprocessing is greatly improved. Rather than just SMP, as with the Pentium, the Pentium Pro supports a new type of multiprocessor configuration called the *Multi-Processor Specification* (*MPS 1.1*). The Pentium Pro with MPS allows configurations of up to four processors running together. Unlike other multiprocessor configurations, the Pentium Pro avoids cache coherency problems because each chip maintains a separate L1 and L2 cache internally.

Pentium Pro-based motherboards are pretty much exclusively PCI and ISA bus-based, and Intel is producing their own chipsets for these motherboards. The first chipset was the 450KX/GX (code-named Orion), while the most recent chipset for use with the Pentium Pro is the 440LX (Natoma). Due to the greater cooling and space requirements, Intel designed the new ATX motherboard form factor to better support the Pentium Pro and other future processors, like the Pentium II. Even so, the Pentium Pro can be found in all types of motherboard designs; ATX is not mandatory.

▶▶   See "Motherboard Form Factors," p. 167, and "Sixth-Generation (P6 Pentium Pro / Pentium II Class) Chipsets," p. 199

Some Pentium Pro system manufacturers have been tempted to stick with the Baby-AT form factor. The big problem with the standard Baby-AT form factor is keeping the CPU properly cooled. The massive Pentium Pro processor consumes more than 25 watts and generates an appreciable amount of heat.

Four special Voltage Identification (VID) Pins are on the Pentium Pro processor. These pins can be used to support automatic selection of power supply voltage. This means that a Pentium Pro motherboard does not have voltage regulator jumper settings like most Pentium boards, which greatly eases the setup and integration of a Pentium Pro system. These pins are not actually signals, but are either an open circuit in the package or a short circuit to voltage. The sequence of opens and shorts define the voltage required by the processor. In addition to allowing for automatic voltage settings, this feature has been designed to support voltage specification variations on future Pentium Pro processors. The VID pins are named VID0 through VID3 and the definition of these pins is shown in Table 3.27. A 1 in this table refers to an open pin and 0 refers to a short to ground. The voltage regulators on the motherboard should supply the voltage that is requested or disable itself.

Table 3.27 Pentium Pro Voltage Identification Definition			
VID[3:0]	**Voltage Setting**	**VID[3:0]**	**Voltage Setting**
0000	3.5	1000	2.7
0001	3.4	1001	2.6
0010	3.3	1010	2.5
0011	3.2	1011	2.4
0100	3.1	1100	2.3
0101	3.0	1101	2.2
0110	2.9	1110	2.1
0111	2.8	1111	No CPU Present

Most Pentium Pro processors run at 3.3v, but a few run at 3.1v. Although those are the only versions available now, support for a wider range of VID settings will benefit the system in meeting the power requirements of future Pentium Pro processors. Note that the 1111 (or all opens) ID can be used to detect the absence of a processor in a given socket.

The Pentium Pro never did become very popular on the desktop, but has found a niche in file server applications due primarily to the full core-speed high-capacity internal L2 cache. It is expected that Intel will introduce only one or two more variations of the Pentium Pro, primarily as upgrade processors for those who want to install a faster CPU in their existing Pentium Pro motherboard. In most cases, it would be wiser to install a new Pentium II motherboard instead.

The following tables list the unique specifications of the different models of the Pentium Pro.

As with other processors, the Pentium Pro has been available in a number of different revisions and steppings. The following table shows all the versions of the Pentium Pro. They can be identified by the Specification number printed on the top and bottom of the chip.

Type	Family	Model	Stepping	Mfg. Stepping
0	6	1	1	B0
0	6	1	1	B0
0	6	1	1	B0
0	6	1	1	B0
0	6	1	1	B0
0	6	1	1	B0
0	6	1	1	B0
0	6	1	2	C0
0	6	1	2	C0
0	6	1	2	C0
0	6	1	2	C0
0	6	1	6	sA0 2
0	6	1	6	sA0 2
0	6	1	6	sA0 2
0	6	1	6	sA0 2
0	6	1	6	sA0 2
0	6	1	6	sA0 2
0	6	1	6	sA0 2
0	6	1	6	sA0 2
0	6	1	6	sA0 2
0	6	1	6	sA0 2
0	6	1	7	sA1
0	6	1	7	sA1
0	6	1	7	sA1
0	6	1	7	sA1
0	6	1	7	sA1
0	6	1	7	sA1
0	6	1	7	sA1
0	6	1	7	sA1
0	6	1	7	sA1
0	6	1	7	sA1
0	6	1	7	sA1
0	6	1	7	sA1
0	6	1	7	sA1
0	6	1	7	sA1
0	6	1	7	sA1
0	6	1	7	sA1

L2 Size/ Stepping	Speed Core/ Bus	Spec.	Voltage (+/-5%)	Notes
256/a	133/66	Q0812	3.1V	3,4
256/a	150/60	Q0813	3.1V	3,4
256/a	133/66	Q0815	3.1V	3,4
256/a	150/60	Q0816	3.1V	3,4
256/a	150/60	SY002	3.1V	3
256/a	150/60	SY011	3.1V	
256/a	150/60	SY014	3.1V	
256/a	150/60	Q0822	3.1V	3,4
256/a	150/60	Q0825	3.1V	4
256/a	150/60	Q0826	3.1V	4
256/a	150/60	SY010	3.1V	
256/a	180/60	Q0858	3.3V	4
256/a	200/66	Q0859	3.3V	4
256/a	180/60	Q0860	3.3V	4,5
256/a	200/66	Q0861	3.3V	4,5
512/Pre 6	166/66	Q0864	3.3V	4
512/Pre 6	200/66	Q0865	3.3V	4
256/a	180/60	Q0873	3.3V	4
256/a	200/66	Q0874	3.3V	4
256/a	180/60	Q0910	3.3V	
256/a	180/60	SY012	3.3V	
256/a	200/66	SY013	3.3V	
256/a	200/66	Q076	3.3V	7
256/a	180/60	Q0871	3.3V	4
256/a	200/66	Q0872	3.3V	4
256/a	180/60	Q0907	3.3V	4
256/a	200/66	Q0908	3.3V	4
256/b	200/66	Q0909	3.3V	4
512/Pre 6	166/66	Q0918	3.3V	4
512/Pre 6	200/66	Q0920	3.3V	4
512/Pre 6	200/66	Q0924	3.3V	4
512/a	166/66	Q0929	3.3V	4
512/a	200/66	Q932	3.3V	4
512/b	166/66	Q935	3.3V	4
512/b	200/66	Q936	3.3V	4
256/a	200/66	SL245	3.5V	7
256/a	200/66	SL247	3.5V	7
256/b	180/60	SU103	3.3V	8

(continues)

Type	Family	Model	Stepping	Mfg. Stepping
0	6	1	7	sA1
0	6	1	7	sA1
0	6	1	7	sA1
0	6	1	7	sA1
0	6	1	7	sA1
0	6	1	7	sA1
0	6	1	7	sA1
0	6	1	7	sA1
0	6	1	9	sB1
0	6	1	9	sB1
0	6	1	9	sB1
0	6	1	9	sB1
0	6	1	9	sB1
0	6	1	9	sB1
0	6	1	9	sB1
0	6	1	9	sB1
0	6	1	9	sB1
0	6	1	9	sB1
0	6	1	9	sB1
0	6	1	9	sB1
0	6	1	9	sB1
0	6	1	9	sB1
0	6	1	9	sB1
0	6	1	9	sB1
0	6	1	9	sB1
0	6	1	9	sB1
0	6	1	9	sB1
0	6	1	9	sB1
0	6	1	9	sB1

NOTES:

1. *L2 Cache Stepping refers to the silicon revision of the 256-K, 512-K, or 1M on-chip L2 cache. The a designation refers to the first production steppings, the b to the second production steppings, and so on.*
2. *The sA0 stepping is logically equivalent to the C0 stepping, but on a different manufacturing process.*
3. *The VID pins are not supported on these parts.*
4. *These are engineering samples only, provided under a Pentium Pro processor nondisclosure loan agreement.*
5. *The VID pins are functional but not tested on these parts.*
6. *These sample parts are equipped with a preproduction 512-K L2 cache.*

L2 Size/ Stepping	Speed Core/ Bus	Spec.	Voltage (+/-5%)	Notes
256/b	200/66	SU104	3.3V	8
256/b	180/60	SY031	3.3V	
256/b	200/66	SY032	3.3V	
512/a	166/66	SY034	3.3V	
256/a	180/60	SY039	3.3V	
256/b	200/66	SY040	3.3V	
512/b	166/66	SY047	3.3V	
512/b	200/66	SY048	3.3V	
512/b	166/66	Q008	3.3V	4
512/b	166/66	Q009	3.3V	4
512/b	200/66	Q010	3.3V	4
512/b	200/66	Q011	3.3V	4
256/b	180/60	Q033	3.3V	4
256/b	200/66	Q034	3.3V	4
256/b	180/60	Q035	3.3V	4
256/b	200/66	Q036	3.3V	4
256/b	200/66	Q083	3.5V	7
256/b	200/66	Q084	3.5V	7
256/b	180/60	SL22S	3.3V	
256/b	200/66	SL22T	3.3V	
256/b	180/60	SL22U	3.3V	
256/b	200/66	SL22V	3.3V	9
512/b	166/66	SL22X	3.3V	
512/b	200/66	SL22Z	3.3V	
256/b	180/60	SL23L	3.3V	8
256/b	200/66	SL23M	3.3V	8
256/b	200/66	SL254	3.5V	7
256/b	200/66	SL255	3.5V	7
512/b	166/66	SL2FJ	3.3V	8
1024/g	200/66	SL259	3.3V	
1024/g	200/66	SL25A	3.3V	

7. These components have additional specification changes associated with them:
   a. Primary Voltage = 3.5V
   b. Max Thermal Design Power = 39.4W @ 200MHz, 256K L2
   c. Max Current = 11.9A
   d. The VID pins are not supported on these parts.
8. This is a boxed Pentium Pro processor with an unattached fan heat sink.
9. This part also ships as a boxed processor with an unattached fan heat sink.

Pentium II. Intel revealed its latest P6 family processor in May 1997, when it pulled the wraps off the Pentium II. Prior to its official unveiling, the Pentium II processor was popularly referred to by its code name "Klamath," and was surrounded by much speculation throughout the industry. The Pentium II is essentially the same sixth-generation processor as the Pentium Pro with MMX technology added (double the L1 cache and 57 new MMX instructions); however, there are a few twists to the design. The Pentium II processor die is shown in Figure 3.25.

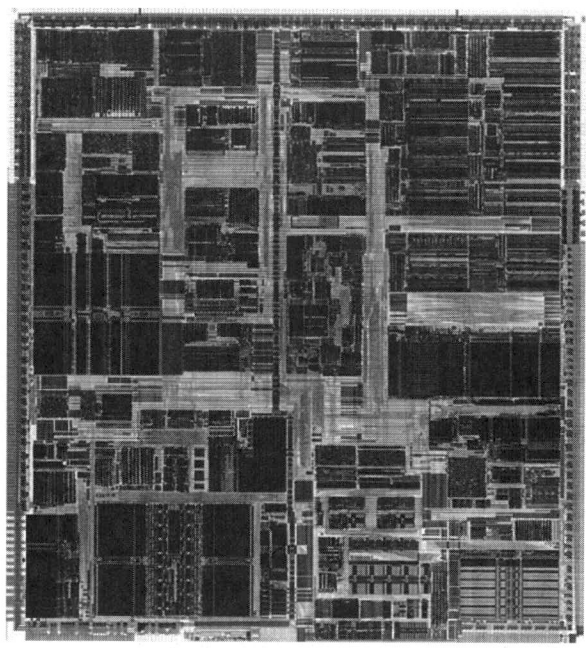

FIG. 3.25 Pentium II Processor die. *Photograph used by permission of Intel Corporation.*

From a physical standpoint, it is truly something new. Abandoning the chip in a socket approach used by virtually all processors up until this point, the Pentium II chip is characterized by its Single Edge Contact (SEC) cartridge design. The processor, along with several L2 cache chips, is mounted on a small circuit board (much like an oversized-memory SIMM) as shown in Figure 3.26, which is then sealed in a metal and plastic cartridge. The cartridge is then plugged into the motherboard through an edge connector called Slot 1, which looks very much like an adapter card slot.

By using separate chips mounted on a circuit board, Intel can build the Pentium II much less expensively than the multiple die within a package used in the Pentium Pro. They can also use cache chips from other manufacturers, and more easily vary the amount of cache in future processors compared to the Pentium Pro design.

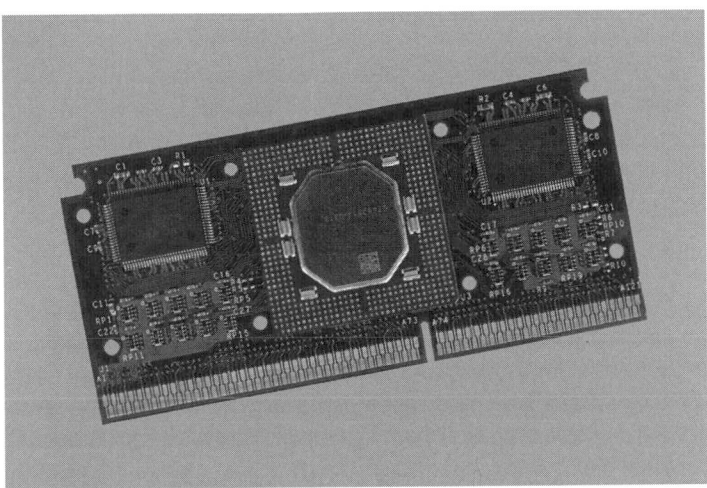

FIG. 3.26   Pentium II Processor Board (inside SEC cartridge). *Photograph used by permission of Intel Corporation.*

At present, Intel is offering Pentium II processors with the following speeds:

CPU Type/Speed	CPU Clock	Motherboard Speed
Pentium II 233MHz	3.5x	66MHz
Pentium II 266MHz	4x	66MHz
Pentium II 300MHz	4.5x	66MHz
Pentium II 333MHz	5x	66MHz
Pentium II 350MHz	3.5x	100MHz
Pentium II 400MHz	4x	100MHz
Pentium II 450MHz	4.5x	100MHz

The Pentium II processor core has 7.5 million transistors and is based on Intel's advanced P6 architecture. The Pentium II started out using .35-micron process technology, although the 333MHz and faster Pentium IIs are based on 0.25-micron technology. This enables a smaller die, allowing increased core frequencies and reduced power consumption. At 333MHz, the Pentium II processor delivers a 75–150% performance boost, compared to the 233MHz Pentium processor with MMX technology, and approximately 50% more performance on multimedia benchmarks. These are very fast processors, at least for now. As shown in Table 3.2, the iCOMP 2.0 Index rating for the Pentium II 266MHz chip is more than twice as fast as a classic Pentium 200MHz.

Aside from speed, the best way to think of the Pentium II is as a Pentium Pro with MMX technology instructions and a slightly modified cache design. It has the same multi-processor scalability as the Pentium Pro, as well as the integrated L2 cache. The 57 new multimedia-related instructions carried over from the MMX processors and the capability to process repetitive loop commands more efficiently are also included. Also included as a part of the MMX upgrade is double the internal L1 cache from the Pentium Pro (from 16K total to 32K total in the Pentium II).

The original Pentium II processors were manufactured using a 0.35-micron process. More recent models, starting with the 333MHz version, have been manufactured using a newer 0.25 micron process. Intel is considering going to a 0.18-micron process in the future. By going to the smaller process, power draw is greatly reduced.

Maximum power usage for the Pentium II is shown in the following table.

Core Speed	Power Draw	Process	Voltage
400MHz	27.9w	0.25 micron	2.0v
350MHz	24.5w	0.25 micron	2.0v
333MHz	23.7w	0.25 micron	2.0v
300MHz	43.0w	0.35 micron	2.8v
266MHz	38.2w	0.35 micron	2.8v
233MHz	34.8w	0.35 micron	2.8v

You can see that the newer 400MHz version of the Pentium II actually uses less power than the original 233MHz version! This was accomplished by using the smaller 0.25-micron process and running the processor on a lower voltage of only 2.0v. Future Pentium II processors will use the 0.25 and 0.18-micron processes and 2.0v and lower voltages to continue this trend.

The Pentium II includes Dynamic Execution, which describes unique performance-enhancing developments by Intel, first introduced in the Pentium Pro processor. Major features of Dynamic Execution include Multiple Branch Prediction, which speeds execution by predicting the flow of the program through several branches; Dataflow Analysis, which analyzes and modifies the program order to execute instructions when ready; and Speculative Execution, which looks ahead of the program counter and executes instruction which are likely to be needed. The Pentium II processor expands on these capabilities in sophisticated and powerful new ways to deliver even greater performance gains.

Like the Pentium Pro, the Pentium II also includes DIB architecture. The term *Dual Independent Bus* comes from the existence of two independent buses on the Pentium II processor—the L2 cache bus and the processor-to-main-memory system bus. The Pentium II processor can use both buses simultaneously, thus getting as much as 2X more data in and out of the Pentium II processor than a single-bus architecture processor. The DIB architecture enables the L2 cache of the 333MHz Pentium II processor to run 2.5 times as fast as the L2 cache of Pentium processors. As the frequency of future Pentium II processors increases, so will the speed of the L2 cache. Also, the pipelined system bus enables simultaneous parallel transactions instead of singular sequential transactions. Together, these Dual Independent Bus architecture improvements offer up to three times the bandwidth performance over a single-bus architecture as with the regular Pentium.

Table 3.28 shows the general Pentium II processor specifications. Table 3.29 shows the specifications that vary by model for the models that have been introduced to date.

Table 3.28 Pentium II General Processor Specifications

Bus Speeds:	66MHz, 100MHz
CPU clock multiplier:	3.5x,4x,4.5x,5x
CPU Speeds:	233MHz, 266MHz, 300MHz, 333MHz, 350MHz, 400MHz, 450MHz
Cache Memory:	16Kx2 (32K) L1, 512K 1/2-speed L2
Internal Registers:	32-bit
External Data Bus:	64-bit System Bus w/ECC; 64-bit Cache Bus w/optional ECC
Memory Address Bus:	36-bit
Addressable Memory:	64G
Virtual Memory:	64T
Physical package:	Single Edge Contact Cartridge (S.E.C.), 242 pins
Package Dimensions:	5.505-inches (12.82cm)×2.473 inches (6.28cm)×0.647 inches (1.64cm)
Math coprocessor:	Built-in FPU (Floating-Point Unit)
Power management:	SMM (System Management Mode)

Table 3.29 Pentium II Specifications by Model

Pentium II MMX Processor (350 and 400MHz)

Introduction date:	April 15, 1998
Clock speeds:	350MHz (100MHz x 3.5) and 400MHz (100MHz x 4)
iCOMP Index 2.0 rating:	86 (350MHz) and 440 (400MHz)
Number of transistors:	7.5 million (0.25 micron process), plus 31 million in 512K L2 cache
Cacheable RAM:	4GB
Operating voltage:	2.0v
Slot:	Slot 2
Die Size:	0.400 inches per side (10.2mm)

Pentium II MMX Processor (333MHz)

Introduction date:	January 26, 1998
Clock speeds:	333MHz (66MHz x 5)
iCOMP Index 2.0 rating:	366
Number of transistors:	7.5 million (0.25 micron process), plus 31 million in 512K L2 cache
Cacheable RAM:	512MB
Operating voltage:	2.0v
Slot:	Slot 1
Die Size:	0. 400 inches per side (10.2mm)

(continues)

Table 3.29 Pentium II Specifications by Model Continued	
Pentium II MMX Processor (300MHz)	
Introduction date:	May 7, 1997
Clock speeds:	300MHz (66MHz x 4.5)
iCOMP Index 2.0 rating:	332
Number of transistors:	7.5 million (0.35 micron process), plus 31 million in 512K L2 cache
Cacheable RAM:	512MB
Die Size:	0. 560 inches per side (14.2mm)
Pentium II MMX Processor (266MHz)	
Introduction date:	May 7, 1997
Clock speeds:	266MHz (66MHz x 4)
iCOMP Index 2.0 rating:	303
Number of transistors:	7. 5 million (0.35 micron process), plus 31 million in 512K L2 cache
Cacheable RAM:	512MB
Slot:	Slot 1
Die Size:	0.560 inches per side (14.2mm)
Pentium II MMX Processor (233MHz)	
Introduction date:	May 7, 1997
Clock speeds:	233MHz (66MHz x 3.5)
iCOMP Index 2.0 rating:	267
Number of transistors:	7.5 million (0.35 micron process), plus 31 million in 512K L2 cache
Cacheable RAM:	512MB
Slot:	Slot 1
Die Size:	0.560 inches per side (14.2mm)

As you can see from the table, the Pentium II can handle up to 64G of physical memory. Like the Pentium Pro, the CPU incorporates Dual Independent Bus architecture. This means the chip has two independent buses: one for accessing the L2 cache, the other for accessing main memory. These dual buses can operate simultaneously, greatly accelerating the flow of data within the system. The L1 cache always runs at full core speeds because it is mounted directly on the processor die. The L2 cache in the Pentium II normally runs at 1/2-core speed, which saves money and allows for less expensive cache chips to be utilized. For example, in a 333MHz Pentium II, the L1 cache runs at a full 333MHz, while the L2 cache runs at 167MHz. Even though the L2 cache is not at full core speed as it was with the Pentium Pro, this is still far superior to having cache memory on the motherboard running at the 66MHz motherboard speed of most Socket 7 Pentium designs. Intel claims that the Dual Independent Bus architecture in the Pentium II allows up to three times the bandwidth of normal single-bus processors like the original Pentium.

By removing the cache from the processor's internal package and using external chips mounted on a substrate and encased in the cartridge design, Intel can now use more cost-effective cache chips and more easily scale the processor up to higher speeds. The Pentium Pro was limited in speed to 200MHz, largely due to the inability to find affordable cache memory that runs any faster. By running the cache memory at 1/2-core speed, the Pentium II can run up to 400MHz while still using 200MHz rated cache chips. To offset the 1/2-core speed cache used in the Pentium II, Intel doubled the basic amount of integrated L2 cache from 256K standard in the Pro to 512K standard in the Pentium II.

Note that the tag-RAM included in the L2 cache will allow up to 512MB of main memory to be cacheable in PII processors from 233MHz to 333MHz. The 350MHz, 400MHz, and faster versions include an enhanced tag-RAM that allows up to 4G of main memory to be cacheable. This is very important if you ever plan on adding more than 512M of memory. In that case, you would definitely want the 350MHz or faster version; otherwise, memory performance would suffer.

The system bus of the Pentium II provides "glueless" support for up to two processors. This enables low-cost, two-way symmetric multiprocessing without extra external chips, providing a significant performance boost for multitasking operating systems and multi-threaded applications. Future chipsets will be able to "glue" four or more PII processors into a unified multiprocessor system, primarily for file server use.

Versions of the Pentium II are available with ECC (Error Correction Code) functionality on the L2 cache bus. These are designed especially for servers or other mission-critical system use where reliability and data integrity are important. All Pentium IIs also include parity-protected address/request and response system bus signals with a retry mechanism for high data integrity and reliability.

To install the Pentium II in a system, a special processor-retention mechanism is required. This consists of a mechanical support that attaches to the motherboard and secures the Pentium II processor in slot 1 to prevent shock and vibration damage. Retention mechanisms should be provided by the motherboard manufacturer. (For example, the Intel Boxed AL440FX and DK440LX motherboards include a retention mechanism, plus other important system integration components.)

The Pentium II can generate a significant amount of heat that must be dissipated. This is accomplished by installing a heat sink on the processor. Many of the Pentium II processors will use an active heat sink that incorporates a fan. Unlike heat sink fans for previous Intel boxed processors, the Pentium II fans draw power from a three-pin power header on the motherboard. Most motherboards provide several fan connectors to supply this power.

Special heat sink supports are needed to furnish mechanical support between the fan heat sink and support holes on the motherboard. Normally, a plastic support is inserted into the heat sink holes in the motherboard next to the CPU, before installing the CPU/heat sink package. Most fan heat sinks have two components: a fan in a plastic shroud and a metal heat sink. The heat sink is attached to the processor's thermal plate and should not be removed. The fan can be removed and replaced if necessary, for example, if it has failed. Figure 3.27 shows the SEC assembly with fan, power connectors, mechanical supports, and the slot and support holes on the motherboard.

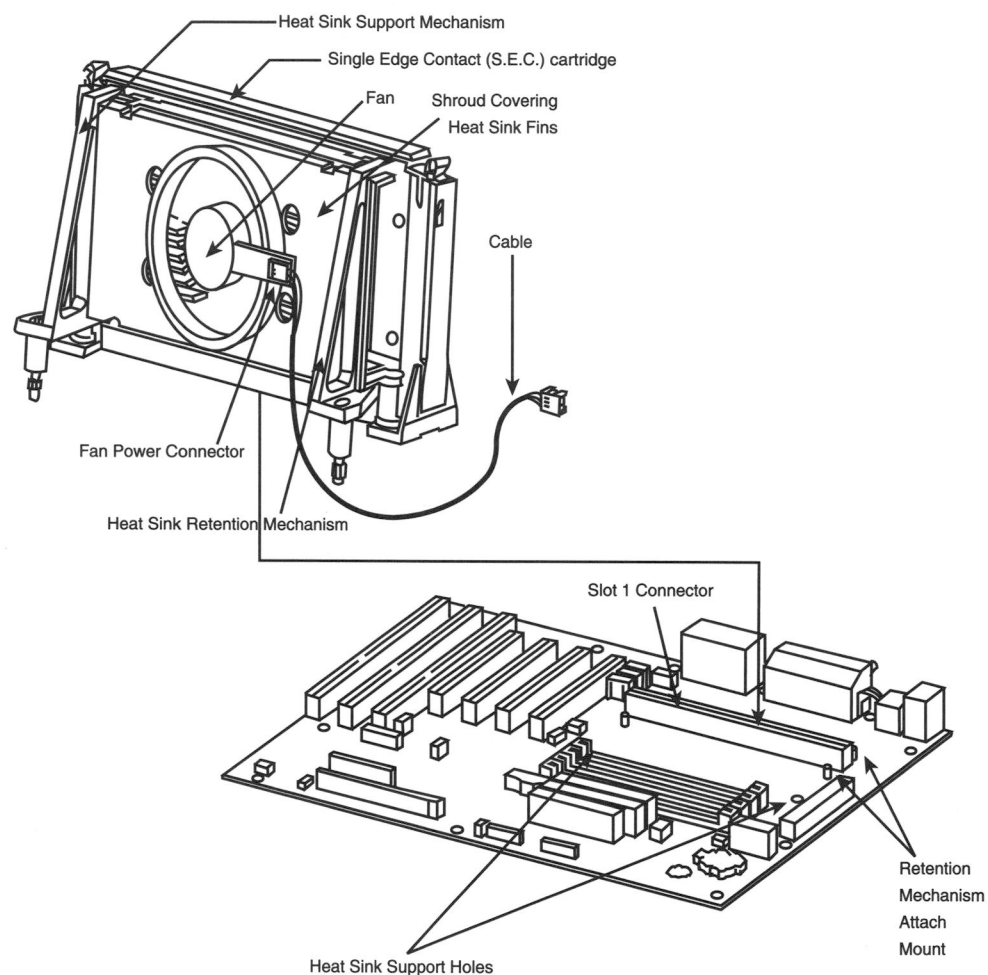

FIG. 3.27 Pentium II Processor and Heat Sink Assembly.

The following tables show the specifications unique to certain versions of the Pentium II processor.

To identify exactly which Pentium II processor you have and what its capabilities are, just look at the specification number printed on the SEC cartridge. You will find the specification number in the dynamic mark area on the top of the processor module. See Figure 3.28 to locate these markings.

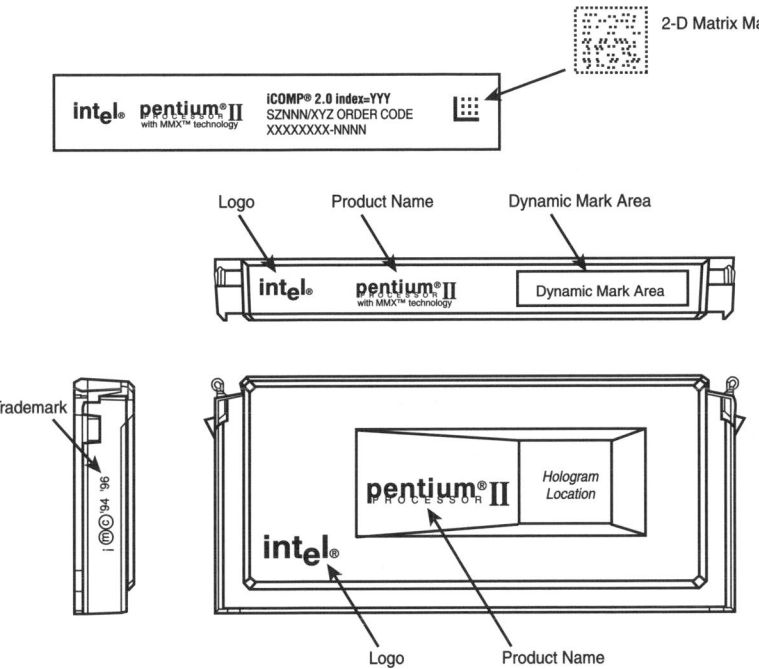

FIG. 3.28 Pentium II Single Edge Contact Cartridge.

After you have located the specification number (actually, it is an alphanumeric code), then you can look it up in Table 3.30 to see exactly which processor you have.

For example, a specification number of SL2KA identifies the processor as a Pentium II 333MHz running on a 66MHz system bus, with an ECC L2 cache, and that this processor runs on only 2.0 volts. The stepping is also identified, and by looking in the *Pentium II Specification Update Manual* published by Intel, you could figure out exactly which bugs were fixed in that revision.

Table 3.30 Basic Pentium II Processor Identification Information

Type	Family	Model	Stepping	Core Stepping	L1 Size (K)
0	6	3	3	C0	512
0	6	3	3	C0	512
0	6	3	3	C0	512
0	6	3	3	C0	512
0	6	3	3	C0	512
0	6	3	3	C0	512
0	6	3	3	C0	512
0	6	3	3	C0	512
0	6	3	3	C0	512
0	6	3	4	C1	512
0	6	3	4	C1	512
0	6	3	4	C1	512
0	6	3	4	C1	512
0	6	3	4	C1	512
0	6	3	4	C1	512
0	6	3	4	C1	512
0	6	3	4	C1	512
0	6	3	4	C1	512
0	6	5	0	dA0	512
0	6	5	0	dA0	512
0	6	5	1	dA1	512
0	6	5	1	dA1	512
0	6	5	1	dA1	512
0	6	5	1	dA1	512
0	6	5	1	dA1	512
0	6	5	1	dA1	512

Core processor voltage is 2.8v +100/-70mv for all Pentium II processors unless indicated otherwise.
2.0v = Core processor voltage (Vcc_CORE) is 2.0v +100/-70mv for these Pentium II processors.
The allowed processor temperature range for all Pentium II processors is 5°C–75°C unless indicated otherwise.
72°C = Allowed processor temperature range 5°C–72°C.

TagRAM/ stepping	S-Spec	ECC/ Non-ECC	Speed(MHz) Core/Bus	Notes
T6/B0	SL264	non-ECC	233/66	
T6/B0	SL265	non-ECC	266/66	
T6/B0	SL268	ECC	233/66	
T6/B0	SL269	ECC	266/66	
T6/B0	SL28K	non-ECC	233/66	2.0v
T6/B0	SL28L	non-ECC	266/66	2.0v
T6/B0	SL28R	ECC	300/66	72°C
T6/B0	SL2MZ	ECC	300/66	72°C, 2.0v
T6/B0	SL2PV	ECC	266/66	2.0v
T6/B0	SL2HA	ECC	300/66	72°C
T6/B0	SL2HC	non-ECC	266/66	
T6/B0	SL2HD	non-ECC	233/66	
T6/B0	SL2HE	ECC	266/66	
T6/B0	SL2HF	ECC	233/66	
T6/B0	SL2QA	non-ECC	233/66	BOXF
T6/B0	SL2QB	non-ECC	266/66	BOXF
T6/B0	SL2QC	ECC	300/66	72°C, BOXF
T6/B0	SL2QD	ECC	266/66	BOXF
T6P/A3	SL2KA	ECC	333/66	2.0v, 65°C
T6P/A3	SL2QF	ECC	333/66	BOXF,2.0v,65°C
T6P-e/A0	SL2QH	ECC	333/66	BOXF,2.0v,4GB
T6P-e/A0	SL2S5	ECC	333/66	2.0v,4GB
T6P-e/A0	SL2S6	ECC	350/100	2.0v,4GB
T6P-e/A0	SL2S7	ECC	400/100	2.0v,4GB
T6P-e/A0	SL2SF	ECC	350/100	BOXF,2.0v,4GB
T6P-e/A0	SL2SH	ECC	400/100	BOXF,2.0v,4GB

65°C = Allowed processor temperature range 5°C–65°C.
BOXF = This is a boxed Pentium II processor with an attached fan heat sink.
4G = These processors have an enhanced L2 cache, which can cache up to 4G of main memory standard PII processors can only cache up to 512MB of main memory.

Pentium II motherboards have an onboard voltage regulator circuit that is designed to power the CPU. Currently, there are Pentium II processors that run at several different voltages, so the regulator must be set to supply the correct voltage for the specific processor you are installing. As with the Pentium Pro and unlike the older Pentium, there are no jumpers or switches to set; the voltage setting is handled completely automatically through the Voltage ID (VID) pins on the processor cartridge. Table 3.31 shows the relationship between the pins and the selected voltage.

Table 3.31   Pentium II Voltage ID Definition

Processor Pins

VID4	VID3	VID2	VID1	VID0	Voltage
0	1	1	1	1	Reserved
0	1	1	1	0	Reserved
0	1	1	0	1	Reserved
0	1	1	0	0	Reserved
0	1	0	1	1	Reserved
0	1	0	1	0	Reserved
0	1	0	0	1	Reserved
0	1	0	0	0	Reserved
0	0	1	1	1	Reserved
0	0	1	1	0	Reserved
0	0	1	0	1	**1.80**
0	0	1	0	0	**1.85**
0	0	0	1	1	**1.90**
0	0	0	1	0	**1.95**
0	0	0	0	1	**2.00**
0	0	0	0	0	**2.05**
1	1	1	1	1	**No CPU**
1	1	1	1	0	**2.1**
1	1	1	0	1	**2.2**
1	1	1	0	0	**2.3**
1	1	0	1	1	**2.4**
1	1	0	1	0	**2.5**
1	1	0	0	1	**2.6**
1	1	0	0	0	**2.7**
1	0	1	1	1	**2.8**
1	0	1	1	0	2.9
1	0	1	0	1	3.0
1	0	1	0	0	3.1
1	0	0	1	1	3.2

VID4	VID3	VID2	VID1	VID0	Voltage
1	0	0	1	0	3.3
1	0	0	0	1	3.4
1	0	0	0	0	3.5

0 = Processor pin connected to Vss.
1 = Open on processor.

To ensure the system is ready for all Pentium II processor variations, the values in **BOLD** must be supported. Most Pentium II processors run at 2.8v, with some newer ones at 2.0v.

The Pentium II Mobile Module is a Pentium II for notebooks that includes the North Bridge of the high-performance 440BX chipset. This is the first chipset on the market that allows 100MHz processor bus operation, although that is currently not supported in the mobile versions. The 440BX chipset was released at the same time as the 350 and 400MHz versions of the Pentium II; it is the recommended minimum chipset for any new Pentium II motherboard purchases.

▶▶ See "Mobile Pentium II," p. 919

Pentium II Future. There are several new developments on target for the Pentium II processors. There will be higher-end, faster versions and "SX" type low-end versions coming out (Celeron). Intel's goal is to spread the Pentium II line to cover everything from the least expensive home systems to the most expensive top-of-the-line server systems, and everything in between, including laptops, notebooks, and portables. '98 will be known as the year the Pentium died, as Intel stops production and moves the Pentium II in to fill the role of the lower-end systems.

Pentium II processors at 333MHz and up were the first members of the Pentium II processor family to be based on the "Deschutes" core (0.25-micron technology). Deschutes is the internal code name for Pentium II processors using the 0.25-micron process technology first seen on the mobile Pentium processors. The name comes from a river in Oregon.

Pentium II processors for Slot 1 running at 450 and 500MHz with a 100MHz system bus for desktops and entry-level servers and workstations will also be announced in the latter part of '98. All Pentium II processors for Slot 1 are capable of one- and two-way processing.

For the Basic PC market segment (PCs priced at under $1,000), the Pentium II processor family includes a version with no L2 cache, a 66MHz system bus, and operating frequencies of at least 266MHz. These are the Celeron processors, which were released in early '98, and are based on the Slot 1 form factor. Versions of the Celeron PC that incorporate up to a 256K L2 cache resident on the processor (also referred to as "on-die") will be available in the second half of '98.

New Pentium II Xeon processors are coming during mid-'98 for mid-range to high-end servers, and workstations are designed with larger L2 cache sizes, a full-speed L2 cache bus, and increased cacheable address space. The first Pentium II Xeon processor family members for Slot 2 will offer a clock speed of 400MHz and a 100MHz system bus. A Pentium II Xeon processor for Slot 2 will also be available at 450MHz by the end of the year. L2 cache sizes will start at 512KB and are planned for up to 1M and 2M for the Slot 2 versions. Pentium II processors for Slot 2 will offer glueless (meaning no external custom chips) support for up to four-way multiprocessing.

Note that the Slot 2 Xeon processors do not replace the Slot 1 processors. Pentium II Xeon processors for Slot 2 will be targeted at the mid-range to high-end server and workstation market segments, offering larger, full-speed L2 caches and four-way multiprocessor support. Pentium II processors for Slot 1 will continue to be the processor used in the business and home desktop market segments, and for entry-level servers and workstations (single and dual processor systems).

Notebook PCs got their first mobile versions of the Pentium II in the first half of '98. The Pentium II processor for mobile PCs comes in both Mobile module and Mobile cartridge form factors. The power consumption of the new Pentium II processors for mobile use is comparable to today's mobile Pentium processor with MMX technology. Expect Mobile PII processors at 300MHz and beyond by the end of '98.

Pseudo-Sixth-Generation Processors

These are a class of processor, that feature many sixth-generation capabilities, but are instead designed for fifth-generation systems. These processors are not quite full P6 level, because they lack the DIB architecture, which is one of the key elements of a true sixth-generation processor. The lack of DIB capability is tied to their backward compatibility with the Pentium processor. Designed primarily as Pentium replacements, these pseudo-P6 processors plug into a P5 (Pentium) processor socket and as such are limited to Pentium-class motherboards. This limits cache and memory performance to that of the fifth-generation processors.

Nexgen Nx586. Nexgen was founded by Vinod Dahm, who was one of the original architects of the Pentium processor at Intel. At Nexgen, he created the Nx586, a processor that was functionally the same as the Pentium but not pin compatible. As such, it was always supplied with a motherboard; in fact, it was normally soldered in. Nexgen did not manufacture the chips or the motherboards they came in; for that they hired IBM Microelectronics. Later Nexgen was bought by AMD, and the design of the Nx586 was combined with the AMD K5 to create the more powerful AMD K6 processor.

The Nx586 had all the standard fifth-generation processor features, such as superscalar execution with two internal pipelines and a high performance integral Level 1 cache with separate code and data caches. One advantage was that the Nx586 includes separate 16K instruction and 16K data caches compared to 8K each for the Pentium. These caches keep key instruction and data close to the processing engines to increase overall system performance.

The Nx586 also included branch prediction capabilities, which are one of the hallmarks of a sixth-generation processor. Branch prediction means the processor has internal functions to predict program flow to optimize the instruction execution.

The Nx586 processor also featured a RISC (Reduced Instruction Set Computer) core. A translation unit dynamically translates x86 instructions into RISC86 instructions. These RISC86 instructions were specifically designed with direct support for the x86 architecture while obeying RISC performance principles. They are thus simpler and easier to execute than the complex x86 instructions. This type of capability is another feature normally found only in P6 class processors.

The Nx586 was discontinued after the merger with AMD and the features in it were merged with the AMD-K5 to create the AMD-K6.

AMD-K6. The AMD-K6 processor is a high-performance pseudo-sixth-generation processor that is physically installable in a P5 (Pentium) motherboard. It delivers performance levels somewhere between the Pentium and Pentium II processor due to its unique hybrid design. Because it is designed to install in Socket 7, which is a fifth-generation processor socket and motherboard design, it cannot perform quite as a true sixth-generation chip because the Socket 7 architecture severely limits cache and memory performance. However, with this processor, AMD is giving Intel a lot of competition in the low- to mid-range market, where the Pentium is still popular.

The K6 processor contains an industry-standard, high-performance implementation of the new multimedia instruction set (MMX), enabling a high level of multimedia performance. AMD designed the K6 processor to fit the low-cost, high-volume Socket 7 infrastructure. This enables PC manufacturers and resellers to speed time to market and deliver systems with an easy upgrade path for the future. AMD's state-of-the-art manufacturing facility in Austin, Texas (Fab 25), makes the AMD-K6 processor using AMD's 0.35-micron, five-metal layer process technology. Newer versions are being migrated to 0.25 micron to increase production quantities due to reduced die size, as well as to reduce power consumption.

AMD-K6 Processor technical features include:

- Sixth-generation internal design, fifth-generation external interface

- Internal RISC core, translates x86 to RISC instructions

- Superscalar parallel execution units (seven)

- Dynamic execution

- Branch prediction

- Speculative execution

- Large 64K L1 cache (32K instruction cache plus 32K writeback dual-ported data cache)

- Built-in floating-point unit (FPU)

- Industry-standard MMX instruction support
- System Management Mode (SMM)
- Ceramic Pin Grid Array (CPGA) Socket 7 design
- Manufactured using a 0.35-micron and 0.25-micron, five-layer design

The AMD-K6 processor architecture is fully x86 binary code compatible, which means it runs all Intel software, including MMX instructions. To make up for the lower L2 cache performance of the Socket 7 design, AMD has beefed up the internal L1 cache to 64K total, twice the size of the Pentium II. This, plus the dynamic execution capability, allows the K6 to outperform the Pentium and come close to the Pentium II in performance for a given clock rate.

Both the AMD-K5 and AMD-K6 processors are Socket 7 bus-compatible. However, certain modifications may be necessary for proper voltage setting and BIOS revisions. To ensure reliable operation of the AMD-K6 processor, the motherboard must meet specific voltage requirements.

The AMD-K6-166, 200MHz operates at 2.9v Core/ 3.3v I/O, while the AMD-K6-233MHz at 3.2v Core/ 3.3v I/O. Most older split-voltage motherboards default to 2.8v Core/3.3v I/O, which is below specification for the AMD-K6 and could cause erratic operation. To work properly, the motherboard must have Socket 7 with a dual-plane voltage regulator supplying 2.9v or 3.2v (233MHz) to the CPU core voltage (Vcc2) and 3.3v for the I/O (Vcc3). The voltage regulator must be capable of supplying up to 7.5A (9.5A for the 233MHz) to the processor. When used with a 200MHz or slower processor, the voltage regulator must maintain the core voltage within 145 mV of nominal (2.9V+/-145 mV). When used with a 233MHz processor, the voltage regulator must maintain the core voltage within 100 mV of nominal (3.2V+/-100 mV).

If the motherboard has a poorly designed voltage regulator that cannot maintain this performance, unreliable operation may result. If the CPU voltage exceeds the absolute maximum voltage range, the processor may be permanently damaged. Also note that the K6 can run hot. Ensure your heat sink is securely fitted to the processor and the thermally conductive grease or pad is properly applied.

The motherboard must have an AMD-K6 processor-ready BIOS with support for the K6 built in. Award has that support in their March 1, 1997 or later BIOS, AMI had K6 support in any of their BIOS with CPU Module 3.31 or later, and Phoenix supports the K6 in version 4.0, release 6.0, or release 5.1 with build dates of 4/7/97 or later.

Because these specifications can be fairly complicated, AMD keeps a list of motherboards that have been verified to work with the AMD-K6 processor on their Web site. All the motherboards on that list have been tested to work properly with the AMD K6, so unless these requirements can be verified elsewhere, it is recommended that you only use a motherboard from that list with the AMD-K6 processor.

The multiplier, bus speed, and voltage settings for the K6 are shown in Table 3.32. You can identify which AMD K6 you have by looking at the markings on this chip as shown in Figure 3.29.

Table 3.32	AMD K6 Speeds and Voltages		
CPU Speed	**Multiplier**	**Bus Speed**	**Voltage**
166MHz	2.5x	66MHz	2.9v Core/3.3v I/O
200MHz	3.0x	66MHz	2.9v Core/3.3v I/O
233MHz	3.5x	66MHz	3.2v Core/3.3v I/O
266MHz	4.0x	66MHz	2.2v Core/3.3v I/O
320303MHz	43.5x	66MHz	23.2v Core/3.435vv I/O

Older motherboards achieve the 3.5x setting by setting jumpers for 1.5x. The 1.5x setting for older motherboards equates to a 3.5x setting for the AMD-K6 and newer Intel parts.

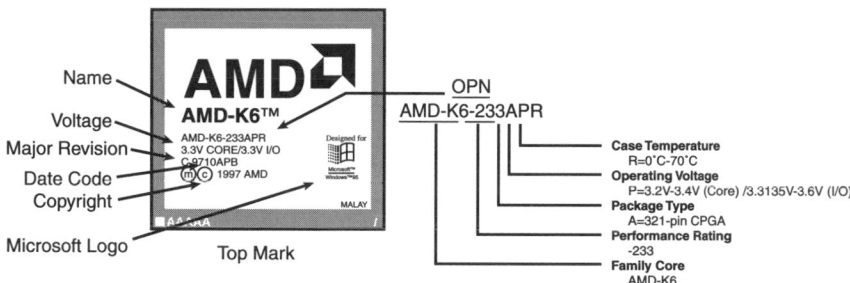

FIG. 3.29   AMD K6 processor markings.

Unlike Cyrix and some of the other Intel competitors, AMD is a manufacturer and a designer. This means they design and build their chips in their own fabs. The K6 has 8.8 million transistors and is built on a 0.35-micron, five-layer process. The die is 12.7mm on each side or about 162 square mm. Like Intel, AMD is migrating to 0.25-micron process technology and beyond. This will enable even higher yields and greater numbers of processors. AMD has recently won contracts with Intel and other high-end system suppliers, which will give them an edge on the other Intel competitors. AMD has delivered more than 50 million Windows-compatible CPUs in the last five years.

Cyrix MediaGX. The Cyrix MediaGX is designed for low-end sub-$1,000 retail store systems that must be highly integrated and low priced. The MediaGX integrates the sound, graphics, and memory control by putting these functions directly within the processor. With all these functions pulled "on chip," MediaGX-based PCs are priced lower than other systems with similar features.

The MediaGX processor integrates the PCI interface, coupled with audio, graphics, and memory control functions, right into the processor unit. As such, a system with the MediaGX doesn't require a costly graphics or sound card. Not only that, but on the motherboard level, the MediaGX and its companion chip replace the processor, North and South Bridge chips, the memory control hardware, and L2 cache found on competitive Pentium boards. Finally, the simplified PC design of the MediaGX, along with its low-power and low-heat characteristics, allow the OEM PC manufacturer to design a system in a smaller form factor with a reduced power-supply requirement.

The MediaGX processor is not a Socket 7 processor; in fact, it does not go in a socket at all—it is permanently soldered into its motherboard. Because of the processor's high level of integration, motherboards supporting MediaGX processors and its companion chip (Cx5510) are of a different design than conventional Pentium boards. As such, a system with the MediaGX processor is more of a disposable system than an upgradable. One will not be able to easily upgrade most components in the system, but that is often not important in the very low-end market. If upgradability is important, then look elsewhere. On the other hand, if you need the lowest-priced system possible, one with the MediaGX might fill the bill.

The MediaGX is fully Windows-compatible and will run the same software as an equivalent Pentium. A user can expect a MediaGX system to provide equivalent performance as a given Pentium system at the same megahertz. The difference with the MediaGX is that this performance level is achieved at a much lower cost. Because the MediaGX processor is soldered into the motherboard and requires a custom chipset, it is only sold in a complete motherboard form.

There is also an improved MMX-enhanced MediaGX processor that features MPEG1 support, Microsoft PC97 compliance for Plug-and-Play access, integrated game port control, and AC97 audio compliance. It supports Windows 95 and DOS-based games, and MMX software as well. Such systems will also include two universal serial bus (USB) ports, which will accommodate the new generation of USB peripherals such as printers, scanners, joysticks, cameras, and more.

The MediaGX processor is offered at 166 and 180MHz, while the MMX-enhanced MediaGX processor is available at 200MHz with higher megahertz speeds available later in '98. Compaq is using the MMX-enhanced MediaGX processor in its Presario 1220 notebook PCs, which is a major contract win for Cyrix. Other retailers and resellers are offering low-end, low-cost systems in retail stores nationwide.

Cyrix/IBM 6x86 and 6x86MX. The Cyrix 6x86 processor family consists of the now-discontinued 6x86 and the newer 6x86MX processors. They are similar to the AMD-K5 and K6 in that they offer sixth-generation internal designs in a fifth-generation P5 Pentium compatible Socket 7 exterior.

The Cyrix 6x86 and 6x86MX (renamed MII) processors incorporate two optimized superpipelined integer units and an on-chip Floating-Point Unit. These processors include the dynamic execution capability that is the hallmark of a sixth-generation CPU design. This includes branch prediction and speculative execution.

The 6x86MX/MII processor is compatible with MMX technology to run the latest MMX games and multimedia software. With its enhanced memory-management unit, a 64K internal cache, and other advanced architectural features, the 6x86MX processor achieves higher performance and offers better value than competitive processors.

Features and benefits of the 6x86 processors include:

- *Superscalar Architecture.* Two pipelines to execute multiple instructions in parallel.

- *Branch Prediction.* Predicts with high accuracy the next instructions needed.

- *Speculative Execution.* Allows the pipelines to continuously execute instructions following a branch without stalling the pipelines.

- *Out-of-Order Completion.* Lets the faster instruction exit the pipeline out of order, saving processing time without disrupting program flow.

The 6x86 incorporates two caches: a 16-K dual-ported unified cache and a 256-byte instruction line cache. The unified cache is supplemented with a small quarter-K sized high-speed, fully associative instruction line cache. The improved 6x86MX design quadruples the internal cache size to 64K, which significantly improves performance.

The 6x86MX also includes the 57 MMX instructions that speed up the processing of certain computing-intensive loops found in multimedia and communication applications.

All 6x86 processors feature support for System Management Mode (SMM). This provides an interrupt that can be used for system power management or software transparent emulation of I/O peripherals. Additionally, the 6x86 supports a hardware interface that allows the CPU to be placed into a low-power suspend mode.

The 6x86 is compatible with x86 software and all popular x86 operating systems, including Windows 95/98, Windows, Windows NT, OS/2, DOS, Solaris, and UNIX. Additionally, the 6x86 processor has been certified Windows 95 compatible by Microsoft.

As with the AMD-K6, there are some unique motherboard requirements for the 6x86 processors. Cyrix maintains a list of recommended motherboards on their Web site that should be consulted if you are considering installing one of these chips in a board.

When installing or configuring a system with the 6x86 processors, you have to set the correct motherboard bus speed and multiplier settings. The Cyrix processors are numbered based on a P-rating scale, which is not the same as the true megahertz clock speed of the processor.

The following table shows the correct and true speed settings for the Cyrix 6x86 processors:

Processor/P-rating	Bus Speed	Multiplier	Actual Speed
6x86-PR120+	50MHz	2x	100MHz
6x86-PR133+	55MHz	2x	110MHz
6x86-PR150+	60MHz	2x	120MHz
6x86-PR166+	66MHz	2x	133MHz
6x86-PR200+	75MHz	2x	150MHz
6x86MX-PR166	60MHz	2.5x	150MHz
6x86MX-PR200	66MHz	2.5x	166MHz
6x86MX-PR233	75MHz	2.5x	188MHz
6x86MX-PR233	66MHz	3.0x	200MHz
6x86MX-PR266166	75MHz	32.05x	212858MHz
6x86MX-PR266	66MHz	3.5x	233MHz
6x86MX-PR300	75MHz	3.5x	263MHz
6x86MX-PR300	66MHz	4.0x	266MHz

Note that due to the use of the P-rating system, the actual speed of the chip is not the same number at which it is advertised. For example, the 6x86MX-PR300 is not a 300MHz chip; it actually runs at only 263MHz or 266MHz, depending on exactly how the motherboard bus speed and CPU clock multipliers are set. Cyrix says it runs as fast as a 300MHz Pentium, hence the P-rating. Personally, I wish they would just label the chips at the correct speed, and then say that it runs faster than a Pentium at the same speed.

To install the 6x86 processors in a motherboard, you also have to set the correct voltage. Normally, the markings on top of the chip indicate which voltage setting is appropriate. Various versions of the 6x86 run at 3.52v (use VRE setting), 3.3v (VR setting), or 2.8v (MMX) settings. The MMX versions use the standard split-plane 2.8v core 3.3v I/O settings.

P7 (786) Seventh-Generation Processors

What is coming after the Pentium II? The next processor is code-named either P7 or Merced.

Intel has indicated that the new 64-bit Merced processor will be available in sample volumes in 1999, with planned production volumes moving from 1999 to mid-2000. The Merced processor will be the first processor in Intel's IA-64 (Intel Architecture 64-bit) product family, and will incorporate innovative performance-enhancing architecture techniques, such as predication and speculation.

Merced. The most current generation of processor is the P6, which was first seen in the Pentium Pro introduced in November of 1995, and most recently found in the latest Pentium II processors. Obviously, then, the next generation processor from Intel will be called the P7.

Although the Merced processor program is still far from being released, the program has made considerable progress to date according to Intel, including:

- Definition of the 64-bit instruction set architecture with Hewlett-Packard.

- Completion of the fundamental microarchitecture design.

- Completion of functional model and initial physical layout.

- Completion of mechanical and thermal design and validation with system vendors.

- Specifications complete and designs underway for chipset and other system components.

- Progress on 64-bit compiler development and IA-64 software development kits.

- Real-time software emulation capability to speed the development of IA-64 optimized software.

- Multiple operating systems running in Merced simulation environment.

- All required platform components planned for alignment with 1999 Merced processor samples for initial system assembly and testing.

Intel's IA-64 product family is expected to expand the capabilities of the Intel architecture to address the high-performance server and workstation market segments. A variety of industry players—among them leading workstation and server-system manufacturers, leading operating system vendors, and dozens of independent software vendors—have already publicly committed their support for the Merced processor and the IA-64 product family.

As with previous new processor introductions, the P7 will not replace the P6 or P5, at least not at first. It will feature an all-new design that will be initially expensive and will be found only in the highest end systems such as file servers or workstations. Intel expects the P7 will become the mainstream processor by the year 2004 and that the P6 will likely be found in low-end systems only. Intel is already developing an even more advanced P7 processor, due to ship in 2001, that will be significantly faster than Merced.

Intel and Hewlett-Packard began jointly working on the P7 processor in 1994. It was then that they began a collaboration on what will eventually become Intel's next-generation CPU. Although we don't know exactly what the new CPU will be like, Intel has begun slowly releasing information about the new processor to prepare the industry for its eventual release. In October of 1997, more than three years after they first disclosed their plan to work together on a new microprocessor architecture, Intel and HP officially announced some of the new processor's technical details.

The first chip to implement the P7 architecture won't ship until 1999. Merced will be the first microprocessor that will be based on the 64-bit, next-generation Intel Architecture-64 (IA-64) specification. IA-64 is a completely different processor design, which will use a concept called Very Long Instruction Words (VLIW), instruction prediction, branch elimination, speculative loading, and other advanced processes for enhancing parallelism from program code. The new chip will feature elements of both CISC and RISC design.

There is also a new architecture Intel calls Explicitly Parallel Instruction Computing (EPIC), which will let the processor execute parallel instructions—several instructions at the same time. In the P7, three instructions will be encoded in one 128-bit word, so that each instruction has a few more bits than today's 32-bit instructions. The extra bits let the chip address more registers and tell the processor which instructions to execute in parallel. This approach simplifies the design of processors with many parallel-execution units and should let them run at higher clock rates. In other words, besides being able to execute several instructions in parallel within the chip, the P7 will have the capability to be linked to other P7 chips in a parallel processing environment.

Besides having new features and running a completely new 64-bit instruction set, Intel and HP promise full backward compatibility between the Merced, the current 32-bit Intel x86 software, and even HP's own PA-RISC software. The P7 will incorporate three different kinds of processors in one and therefore be able to run advanced IA-64 parallel-processing software and IA-32 Windows and HP-RISC UNIX programs at the same time. In this way, Merced will support 64-bit instructions while retaining compatibility with today's 32-bit applications. This backward compatibility will be a powerful selling point.

To use the IA-64 instructions, programs will have to be recompiled for the new instruction set. This is similar to what happened in 1985, when Intel introduced the 80386, the first 32-bit PC processor. The 386 was to give IBM and Microsoft a platform for an advanced 32-bit operating system that tapped this new power. To ensure immediate acceptance, the 386 and future 32-bit processors still ran 16-bit code. To take advantage of the 32-bit capability first found in the 386, new software would have to be written. Unfortunately, software evolves much more slowly than hardware. It took Microsoft a full 10 years after the 386 debuted to release Windows 95, the first mainstream 32-bit operating system for Intel processors.

Intel claims that won't happen with the P7: Microsoft has already begun working on a 64-bit version of Windows NT for Merced. Despite that, it will likely take several years before the software market shifts to 64-bit operating systems and software. The installed base of 32-bit processors is simply too great, and the backward-compatible 32-bit mode of the P7 will allow it to run 32-bit software very well, because it will be done in the hardware rather than through software emulation.

Merced will use 0.18-micron technology, which is one generation beyond the 0.25-micron process used today. This will allow them to pack many more transistors in the same space. Early predictions have the Merced sporting between 10 and 12 million transistors!

Intel's initial goal with IA-64 is to dominate the workstation and server markets, competing with chips such as the Digital Alpha, Sun Sparc, and Motorola PowerPC. Microsoft will provide a version of Windows NT that runs on the P7, and Sun plans to provide a version of Solaris, its UNIX operating-system software, to support Merced as well. NCR has already announced that it will build Merced-powered systems that use Solaris.

Processor Upgrades

Since the 486, processor upgrades have been relatively easy for most systems. With the 486 and later processors, Intel designed in the capability to upgrade by designing standard sockets that would take a variety of processors. Thus, if you have a motherboard with Socket 3, you can put virtually any 486 processor in it; if you have a Socket 7 motherboard, it should be able to accept virtually any Pentium processor.

To maximize your motherboard, you can almost always upgrade to the fastest processor your particular board will support. Normally, that can be determined by the type of socket on the motherboard. Table 3.33 lists the fastest processor upgrade solution for a given processor socket.

Table 3.33 Maximum Processor Speeds by Socket	
Socket Type	**Fastest Processor Supported**
Socket 1	5x86-133MHz with 3.3v adapter
Socket 2	5x86-133MHz with 3.3v adapter
Socket 3	5x86-133MHz
Socket 4	Pentium OverDrive 133MHz
Socket 5	Pentium MMX 233MHz or AMD K6 with 2.8v adapter
Socket 7	Pentium MMX 233MHz, AMD K6
Socket 8	Pentium Pro OverDrive
Slot 1	Pentium II 333MHz (66MHz bus)
Slot 1	Pentium II 450MHz (100MHz bus)
Slot 2	Pentium II Xeon 450MHz (100MHz bus)

For example, if your motherboard has a Pentium Socket 5, then you can install a Pentium MMX 233MHz processor with a 2.8v voltage regulator adapter, or optionally an AMD K6, also with a voltage regulator adapter. If you are lucky enough to have Socket 7, then your motherboard should be able to support the lower voltage Pentium MMX or AMD K6 directly without any adapters.

Rather than purchasing processors and adapters separately, I normally recommend you purchase them together in a module from companies such as Kingston or Evergreen (see Appendix A).

Upgrading the processor can in some cases double the performance of a system, such as if you were going from a Pentium 100 to an MMX 233. However, if you already have a Pentium 233, then you already have the fastest processor that goes in that socket. In that case, you really should look into a complete motherboard change, which would let you upgrade to a Pentium II processor at the same time. If your chassis design is not proprietary and your system uses an industry standard Baby AT or ATX motherboard design, I normally recommend changing the motherboard and processor rather than trying to find an upgrade processor that will work with your existing board.

OverDrive Processors

Intel has stated that all its future processors will have OverDrive versions available for upgrading at a later date. Often these are repackaged versions of the standard processors, sometimes including necessary voltage regulators and fans. Usually they are more expensive than other solutions, but they are worth a look.

OverDrive Processor Installation

You can upgrade many systems with an OverDrive processor. The most difficult aspect of the installation is simply having the correct OverDrive processor for your system. Currently, 486 Pentium OverDrive processors are available for replacing 486SX and 486DX processors. Pentium and Pentium-MMX OverDrive processors are also available for some Pentium processors. Unfortunately, Intel no longer offers upgrade chips for 168-pin socket boards. The following table lists the current OverDrive processors offered by Intel.

Processor Designation	Replaces	Socket	Heat Sink
486 Pentium OverDrive	486SX/DX/SX2/DX2	Socket 2 or 3	Active
120/133 Pentium OverDrive	Pentium 60/66	Socket 4	Active
200MHz Pentium OverDrive with MMX	Pentium 75/90/100	Socket 5/7	Active

Upgrades that use the newer OverDrive chips for Sockets 2–7 are likely to be much easier because these chips almost always go into a ZIF socket and therefore require no tools. In most cases, special configuration pins in the socket and on the new OverDrive chips take care of any jumper settings for you. In some cases, however, you may have to set some jumpers on the motherboard to configure the socket for the new processor. If you have an SX system, you also will have to run your system's Setup program because you must inform the CMOS memory that a math coprocessor is present. (Some DX systems also require you to run the setup program.) Intel provides a utility disk that includes a test program to verify that the new chip is installed and functioning correctly.

After verifying that the installation functions correctly, you have nothing more to do. You do not need to reconfigure any of the software on your system for the new chip. The only difference that you should notice is that everything works nearly twice as fast as it did before the upgrade.

OverDrive Compatibility Problems

Although you can upgrade many older 486SX or 486DX systems with the OverDrive processors, some exceptions exist. Four factors can make an OverDrive upgrade difficult or impossible:

- BIOS routines that use CPU-dependent timing loops

- Lack of clearance for the OverDrive heat sink (25MHz and faster)

- Inadequate system cooling

- A 486 CPU that is soldered in rather than socketed

In some rare cases, problems may occur in systems that should be upgradable but are not. One of these problems is related to the ROM BIOS. A few 486 systems have a BIOS that regulates hardware operations by using timing loops based on how long it takes the CPU to execute a series of instructions. When the CPU suddenly is running twice as fast, the prescribed timing interval is too short, resulting in improper system operation or even hardware lockups. Fortunately, you usually can solve this problem by upgrading the system's BIOS. Intel offers BIOS updates with the OverDrive processors it sells.

Another problem is related to physical clearance. All OverDrive chips have heat sinks glued or fastened to the top of the chip. The heat sink can add 0.25 to 1.2 inches to the top of the chip. This extra height can interfere with other components in the system, especially in small desktop systems and portables. Solutions to this problem must be determined on a case-by-case basis. You can sometimes relocate an expansion card or disk drive, or even modify the chassis slightly to increase clearance. In some cases, the interference cannot be resolved, leaving you only the option of running the chip without the heat sink. Needless to say, removing the glued-on heat sink will at best void the warranty provided by Intel and will at worst damage the chip or the system due to overheating. I do not recommend removing the heat sink.

The OverDrive chips can generate up to twice the heat of the chips that they replace. Even with the active heat sink/fan built into the faster OverDrive chips, some systems do not have enough airflow or cooling capability to keep the OverDrive chip within the prescribed safe operating-temperature range. Small desktop systems or portables are most likely to have cooling problems. Unfortunately, only proper testing can indicate whether a system will have a heat problem. For this reason, Intel has been running an extensive test program to certify systems that are properly designed to handle an OverDrive upgrade.

Finally, some systems have a proprietary design that precludes the use of the OverDrive processor. This would, for example, include virtually all portable, laptop, or notebook computers that have their processor soldered in to the motherboard. Some of the newer ones use the Intel Mobile Module, which is potentially upgradable.

To clarify which systems are tested to be upgradable without problems, Intel has compiled an extensive list of compatible systems. To determine whether a PC is upgradable with an OverDrive processor, contact Intel via its FaxBack system (see the vendor list in Appendix A) and ask for the OverDrive Processor Compatibility Data documents. The information is also available on Intel's Web site. These documents list the systems that have been tested with the OverDrive processors and indicate which other changes you may have to make for the upgrade to work (for example, a newer ROM BIOS or Setup program).

> **Note**
>
> If your system is not on the list, the warranty on the OverDrive processor is void. Intel recommends OverDrive upgrades only for systems that are in the compatibility list. The list also includes notes about systems that may require a ROM upgrade, a jumper change, or perhaps a new setup disk.

After upgrading your system, I suggest running a diagnostic program such as the Norton Utilities to verify that the new processor is running correctly.

▶▶ See "Norton Utilities Diagnostics," p. 993

Processor Benchmarks

People love to know how fast (or slow) their computers are. We have always been interested in speed; it is human nature. To help us with this quest, various benchmark test programs can be used to measure different aspects of processor and/or system performance. Although no single numerical measurement can completely describe the performance of a complex device like a processor or a complete PC, benchmarks can be useful tools for comparing different components and systems.

However, the only truly accurate way to measure your system's performance is to test the system using the actual software applications you use. Though you think you may be testing one component of a system, often other parts of the system can have an effect. It is inaccurate to compare systems with different processors, for example, if they also have different amounts or types of memory, different hard disks, video cards, and so on. All these things and more will skew the test results.

Benchmarks can normally be divided into two kinds: component or system tests. Component benchmarks measure the performance of specific parts of a computer system, such as a processor, hard disk, video card, or CD-ROM drive, while system benchmarks typically measure the performance of the entire computer system running a given application or test suite.

Benchmarks are, at most, only one kind of information that you may use during the upgrading or purchasing process. You are best served by testing the system using your own set of software operating systems and applications, and in the configuration you will be running.

There are several companies that specialize in benchmark tests and software. The following table lists the company and the benchmarks they are known for. You can contact these companies via the information in the vendor list in Appendix A.

Company	Benchmarks Published	Benchmark Type
Intel	iCOMP index 2.0	Processor
Intel	iCOMP index 2.0 Intel Media Benchmark	System
Business Applications Performance Corporation (BAPCo)	SYSmark/NT	System
Business Applications Performance Corporation for Windows (BAPCo)	SYSmark/NT, SYSmark95	System
Standard Performance Evaluation Corporation (SPEC)	SPECint95	Processor
Standard Performance Evaluation Corporation (SPEC)	SPECint95, SPECfp95	Processor
Ziff-Davis Benchmark Operation	CPUmark32	Processor
Ziff-Davis Benchmark Operation	Winstone 98	System
Ziff-Davis Benchmark Operation	WinBench 98	System
Ziff-Davis Benchmark Operation	CPUmark32, Winstone 98, WinBench 98, 3D WinBench 98	System
Symantec Corporation	Norton SI32	Processor
Symantec Corporation	Norton SI32, Norton Multimedia Benchmark	System

Chapter 4

Motherboards and Buses

Without a doubt, the most important component in a PC system is the main board or motherboard. Some companies refer to the motherboard as a system board or planar. The terms *motherboard*, *main board*, *system board*, and *planar* are interchangeable. In this chapter, we will examine the different types of motherboards available and those components usually contained on the motherboard and motherboard interface connectors.

Motherboard Form Factors

There are several common form factors used for PC motherboards. The form factor refers to the physical dimensions and size of the board, and dictates what type of case the board will fit into. Some are true standards (meaning that all boards with that form factor are interchangeable), while others are not standardized enough to allow for interchangeability. Unfortunately these nonstandard form factors preclude any easy upgrade, which generally means they should be avoided. The PC motherboard form factors generally available include the following:

- Baby-AT
- Full-size AT
- LPX
- ATX
- NLX
- Backplane Systems
- Proprietary Designs

Baby-AT

The first popular PC motherboard was, of course, the original IBM PC released in 1981. Figure 20.3 shows how this board looked. IBM followed the PC with the XT motherboard in 1983, which had the same basic shape as the PC board, but it had eight slots instead of only five, and the slots were spaced 0.8 inch apart instead of 1 inch apart as in the PC (see Figure 20.6). The XT also deleted the weird cassette port in the back, which was supposed to be used to save BASIC programs on cassette tape instead of the much more expensive (at the time) floppy drive.

▶▶ See "An Introduction to the PC (5150)," p. 1101

▶▶ See "An Introduction to the XT (5160)," p. 1115

The minor differences in the slot positions and the now lonesome keyboard connector on the back required a minor redesign of the case. This motherboard became very popular and many other PC motherboard manufacturers of the day copied IBM's XT design and produced similar boards. By the time most of these clones or compatible systems came out, IBM had released their AT system, which initially used a larger form factor motherboard. Due to the advances in circuit miniaturization, these companies found they could fit all the additional circuits found on the 16-bit AT motherboard into the XT motherboard form factor. Rather than call these boards XT-sized, which may have made people think they were 8-bit designs, they referred to them as Baby-AT, which ended up meaning an XT-sized board with AT motherboard design features (16-bit or greater).

Thus, the Baby-AT form factor is essentially the same as the original IBM XT motherboard. The only difference is a slight modification in one of the screw hole positions to fit into an AT-style case (see Figure 4.1). These motherboards also have specific placement of the keyboard and slot connectors to match the holes in the case. Note that virtually all full-size AT and Baby-AT motherboards use the standard 5-pin DIN type connector for the keyboard. Baby-AT motherboards can be used to replace full-sized AT motherboards and will fit into a number of different case designs. Because of their flexibility, from 1983 into early 1996 the Baby-AT form factor was the most popular motherboard type. Starting in mid-1996, Baby-AT has been replaced by the superior ATX motherboard design, which is not directly interchangeable. Most new systems sold since 1996 have used the improved ATX design and Baby-AT is getting harder and harder to come by. Figure 4.1 shows the dimensions and layout of a Baby-AT motherboard.

▶▶ See "Power Supply Form Factors," p. 393

Any case that accepts a full-sized AT motherboard will also accept a Baby-AT design. Since its debut in the IBM XT motherboard in 1983 lasting well into 1996, the Baby-AT motherboard form factor has been by far the most popular design. I can get a PC motherboard with virtually any processor from the original 8088 to the fastest Pentium II in this design. As such, systems with Baby-AT motherboards are virtually by definition upgradable systems. Because any Baby-AT motherboard can be replaced with any other Baby-AT motherboard, this is an interchangeable design.

Until 1996 I had recommended to most people that they make sure any PC system they purchased had a Baby-AT motherboard. They would sometimes say, "I've never heard of that brand before." "Of course," I'd tell them, "that's not a brand, but a shape!" The point being that if they had a Baby-AT board in their system, when a year or so goes by and they longed for something faster, it would be easy and inexpensive to purchase a newer board with a faster processor and simply swap it in. If they purchased a system with a proprietary or semi-proprietary board, they would be out of luck when it came time to upgrade, because they had a disposable PC. Disposable PCs may be cheaper initially, but they are usually much more expensive in the long run because they can't easily or inexpensively be upgraded or repaired.

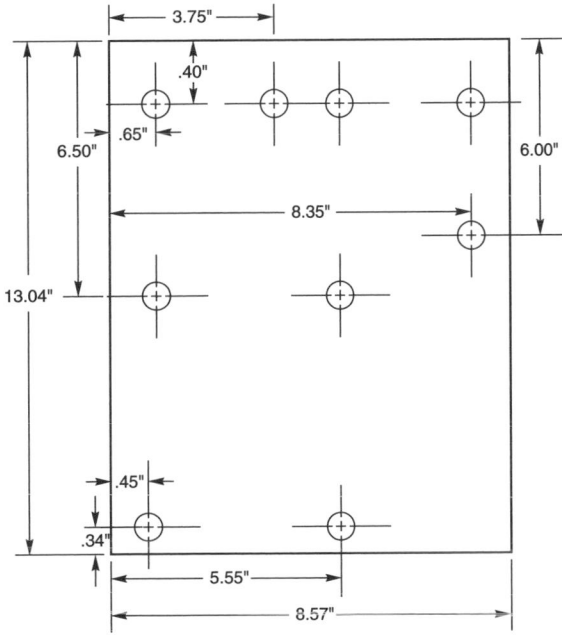

FIG. 4.1 Baby-AT motherboard form factor.

The easiest way to identify a Baby-AT form factor system without opening it is to look at the rear of the case. In a Baby-AT motherboard, the cards plug directly into the board at a 90-degree angle; in other words, the slots in the case for the cards are perpendicular to the motherboard. Also, the Baby-AT motherboard has only one visible connector directly attached to the board, which is the keyboard connector. Normally this connector is the full-sized 5-pin DIN type connector, although some Baby-AT systems will use the smaller 6-pin min-DIN connector (sometimes called a PS/2 type connector) and may even have a mouse connector. All other connectors will be mounted on the case or on card edge brackets and attached to the motherboard via cables.

▶▶ See "Keyboard/Mouse Interface Connectors," p. 470

Full-Size AT

The full-size AT motherboard matches the original IBM AT motherboard design. This allows for a very large board of up to 12 inches wide by 13.8 inches deep. IBM needed more room for additional circuits when they migrated from the 8-bit architecture of the PC/XT to the 16-bit architecture of the AT, so they basically took an XT board and extended it in two directions (see Figures 20.11 and 20.12).

The board was redesigned slightly a year after introduction by making it slightly smaller. Then it was redesigned again as IBM shrank it down to XT-size in a system they called the XT-286 (see Figure 20.14). The XT-286 board size was adopted by most PC-compatible manufacturers and became known as Baby-AT.

▶▶ See "An Introduction to the AT," p. 1129
▶▶ See "An Introduction to the XT Model 286," p. 1145

The keyboard connector and slot connectors in the full-sized AT boards still conformed to the same specific placement requirements to fit the holes in the XT cases already in use, but a larger case was still required to fit the larger board. Due to the larger size of the board, a full-size AT motherboard will fit into full-size AT desktop or Tower cases only. Because these motherboards will not fit into the smaller Baby-AT or Mini-Tower cases, and because of advances in component miniaturization, they are no longer being produced by most motherboard manufacturers, except in some cases for dual processor server applications.

Note that you can always replace a full-size AT motherboard with a Baby-AT board, but the opposite is not true unless the case is large enough to accommodate the full-size AT design.

LPX

The LPX and Mini-LPX form factor boards are a semi-proprietary design originally developed by Western Digital for some of their motherboards back in 1987. Although they no longer produce PC motherboards, the form factor lives on and has been duplicated by many other motherboard manufacturers. Unfortunately, because the specifications were never laid out in exact detail—especially with regard to the bus-riser portion of the design—these boards are termed semi-proprietary and are *not* interchangeable between manufacturers. This means that if you have a system with an LPX board, you have a system that you cannot upgrade or replace the motherboard with something better. In other words, you have a disposable PC, something I would never recommend anybody purchase.

Most people are not aware of the semi-proprietary nature of the design of these boards, and they are extremely popular in what I call "retail store" PCs. This would include primarily the Compaq and Packard Bell systems, and any others who use this form factor. These boards are most often used in the Low Profile or Slimline case systems, but can also be found in tower cases, too. These are often lower-cost systems such as those sold at retail electronics superstores. Due to their proprietary nature, I recommend staying away from any system that uses an LPX motherboard.

The LPX boards are characterized by several distinctive features. The most noticeable is that the expansion slots are mounted on a bus riser card that plugs into the motherboard. Expansion cards must plug sideways into the riser card. This sideways placement allows for the low profile case design. Slots will be located on one or both sides of the riser card depending on the system and case design.

Another distinguishing feature of the LPX design is the standard placement of connectors on the back of the board. An LPX board will have a row of connectors for video (VGA 15-pin), parallel (25-pin), two serial ports (9-pin each), and mini-DIN PS/2 style mouse and keyboard connectors. All of these connectors are mounted across the rear of the motherboard and protrude through a slot in the case. Some LPX motherboards may have additional connectors for other internal ports such as Network or SCSI adapters. Figure 4.2 shows the standard form factors for the LPX and Mini-LPX motherboards used in many systems today.

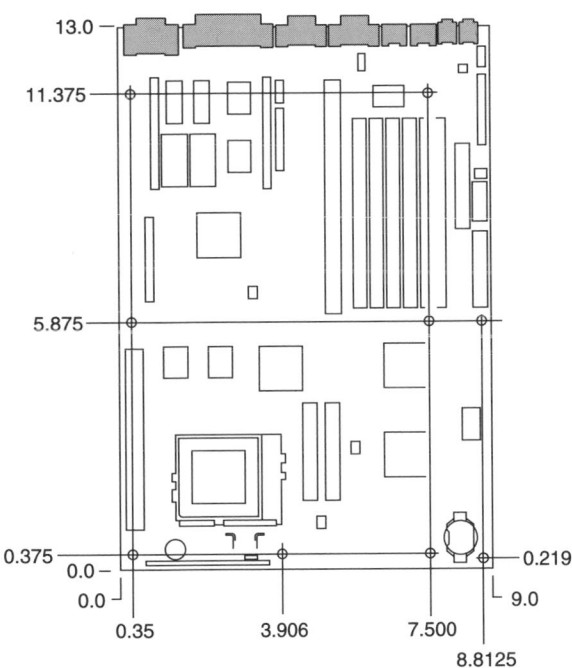

FIG. 4.2 LPX motherboard dimension.

I am often asked, "How can I tell if a system has an LPX board before I purchase it?" Fortunately, this is easy and you don't even have to open the system up or remove the cover. LPX motherboards have a very distinctive design with the bus slots on a riser card that plugs into the motherboard. This means that any card slots will be parallel to the motherboard, because the cards stick out sideways from the riser. Looking at the back of a system, you should be able to tell whether the card slots are parallel to the motherboard. This implies a bus riser card is used, which also normally implies that the system is an LPX design. Another riser card design is called NLX—the differentiating factors are that LPX puts the riser in the middle of the motherboard while NLX has the riser to the side (the motherboard actually plugs into the riser in NLX). Also, the LPX design has only a single row of connectors along the bottom of the board, while the NLX design has half single-row and half double-row connectors. See the section on NLX motherboards later in this chapter for more information on NLX.

That is not the only feature you should look for; the other is that LPX boards have a unique connector arrangement. They have a row of built-in connectors along the back of the board, which clearly distinguishes them from other motherboard designs. See Figure 4.3 for an example of the connectors on the back of an LPX board.

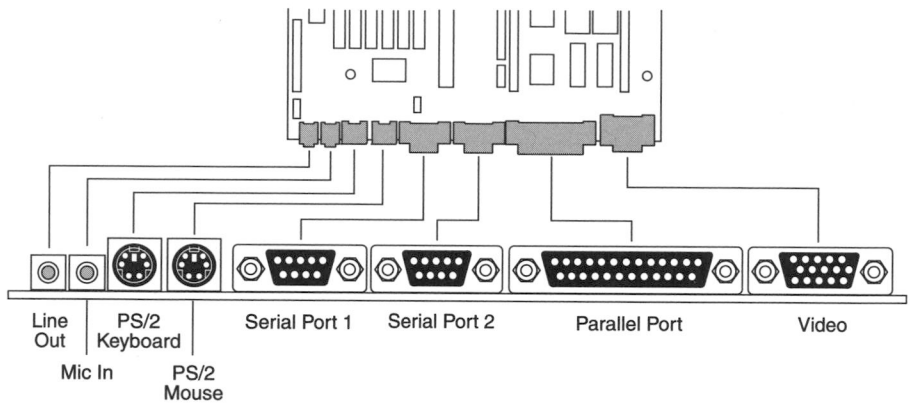

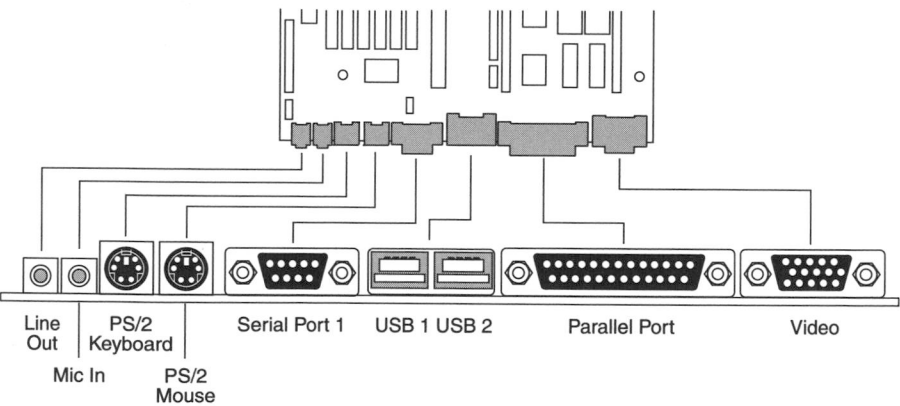

FIG. 4.3 LPX motherboard back panel connectors.

Having connectors along the rear of the board prevents expansion cards from being plugged into the motherboard; that is why a riser card design was employed for expansion. The built-in connectors were the one good idea from LPX that was useful but was not found in the Baby-AT design. What we needed was a standard and fully interchangeable (non-proprietary) motherboard design that fixed the shortcomings of the Baby-AT design, such as having connectors in the rear for the built-in motherboard features. We finally got what we wanted in 1996 with the advent of the ATX motherboard form factor.

ATX

The ATX form factor is a recent evolution in motherboard form factors. ATX is a combination of the best features of the Baby-AT and LPX motherboard designs, with many new enhancements and features thrown in. The ATX form factor is essentially a Baby-AT motherboard turned sideways in the chassis, along with a modified power supply location and connector. The most important thing to know initially about the ATX form factor is that it is physically incompatible with either the previous Baby-AT or LPX designs. In other words, a different case and power supply are required to match the ATX motherboard. These new case and power supply designs have become common, and can be found in many new systems.

The official ATX specification was initially released by Intel in July 1995, and has been written as an open specification for the industry. These boards didn't hit the market in force until mid-1996 when they rapidly began replacing Baby-AT boards in new systems. The latest revision of the specification is Version 2.01, published in February 1997. Intel has published detailed specifications so other manufacturers can use the ATX design in their systems. Currently, ATX is by far the most popular motherboard form factor, and it is the one I recommend most people get in their systems today. An ATX system will be upgradable for many years to come, exactly like Baby-AT was in the past.

ATX improves on the Baby-AT and LPX motherboard designs in several major areas:

- *Built-in double high external I/O connector panel.* The rear portion of the motherboard includes a stacked I/O connector area that is 6.25 inches wide by 1.75 inches tall. This allows external connectors to be located directly on the board and negates the need for cables running from internal connectors to the back of the case as with Baby-AT designs.

- *Single keyed internal power supply connector.* This is a boon for the average end user, who always had to worry about interchanging the Baby-AT power supply connectors and subsequently blowing the motherboard! The ATX specification includes a single keyed and shrouded power connector that is easy to plug in, and which cannot be installed incorrectly. This connector also features pins for supplying 3.3v to the motherboard, which means that ATX motherboards will not require built-in voltage regulators that are susceptible to failure.

▶▶ See "Power Supply Connectors," p. 403

- *Relocated CPU and memory.* The CPU and memory modules are relocated so they cannot interfere with any bus expansion cards, and they can easily be accessed for upgrade without removing any of the installed bus adapters. The CPU and memory are relocated next to the power supply, which has a single fan blowing air across them, thus eliminating the need for often inefficient and failure-prone CPU cooling fans. There is room for a large passive heat sink above the CPU, as well.

> **Note**
>
> Note that systems from smaller vendors may still include CPU fans even in ATX systems, as Intel supplies processors with attached high-quality (ball bearing) fans for CPUs sold to smaller vendors. These are so-called "boxed" processors as they are sold in single-unit box quantities instead of pallets of 100 or more raw CPUs that are sold to the larger vendors. Intel includes the fan as insurance because smaller vendors and system assemblers lack the engineering knowledge necessary to perform thermal analysis, temperature measurements, and the testing required to select the properly sized passive heat sink. By putting a fan on these "boxed" processors, Intel is covering their bases as the fan will ensure adequate CPU cooling. Larger vendors have the engineering talent to select the proper passive heat sink, thus reducing the cost of the system as well as increasing reliability.

- *Relocated internal I/O connectors.* The internal I/O connectors for the floppy and hard disk drives are relocated to be near the drive bays and out from under the expansion board slot and drive bay areas. This means that internal cables to the drives can be much shorter, and accessing the connectors will not require card or drive removal.

- *Improved cooling.* The CPU and main memory are positioned so they can be cooled directly by the power supply fan, eliminating the need for separate case or CPU cooling fans. Also as recommended (but not required) in the ATX specification, ATX power supply fans blow *into* the system chassis, thus pressurizing the system which greatly minimizes dust and dirt intrusion. If desired, an air filter can be easily added to the air intake vents on the power supply, creating a system that is even more immune to dirt or dust in the environment.

- *Lower cost to manufacture.* The ATX specifications eliminates the need for the rat's nest of cables to external port connectors found on Baby-AT motherboards, additional CPU or chassis cooling fans, or onboard 3.3v voltage regulators; uses a single power supply connector; and allows for shorter internal drive cables. These all conspire to greatly reduce not only the cost of the motherboard, but also significantly reduce the cost of a complete system—including the case and power supply.

Figure 4.4 shows the new ATX system layout and chassis features. Notice how virtually the entire motherboard is clear of the drive bays, and how the devices such as CPU, memory, and internal drive connectors are easy to access and do not interfere with the bus slots. Also notice the power supply orientation and the single power supply fan that blows into the case directly over the high heat, cooling items such as the CPU and memory.

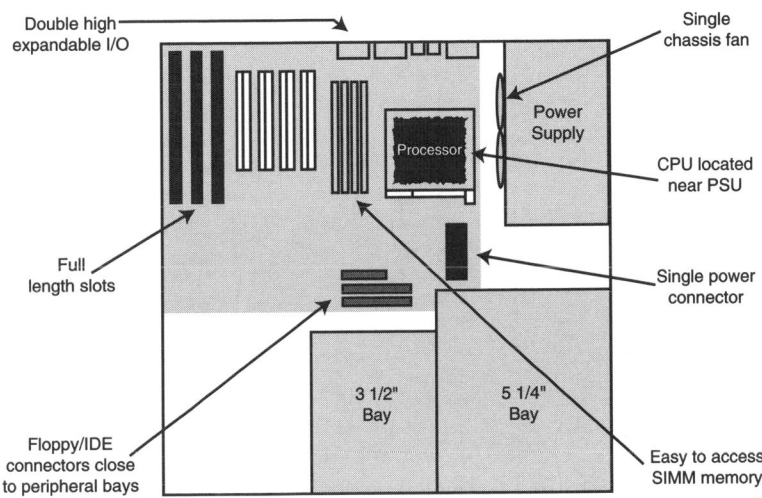

FIG. 4.4 ATX system chassis layout and features.

The ATX motherboard is basically a Baby-AT design rotated sideways. The expansion slots are now parallel to the shorter side dimension and do not interfere with the CPU, memory, or I/O connector sockets. In addition to a full-sized ATX layout, Intel also has specified a mini-ATX design which will fit into the same case. Although the case holes are similar to the Baby-AT case, cases for the two formats are generally not compatible. The power supplies would require a connector adapter to be interchangeable, but the basic ATX power supply design is similar to the standard Slimline power supply. The ATX and mini-ATX motherboard dimensions are shown in Figure 4.5.

Clearly, the advantages of the ATX form factor make it the best choice for new systems. For backward compatibility, you can still find Baby-AT boards for use in upgrading older systems, but the choices are becoming slimmer every day. I would never recommend building or purchasing a new system with a Baby-AT motherboard, as you will severely limit your future upgrade possibilities. In fact, I have been recommending only ATX systems for new system purchases since late '96 and will probably continue to do so for the next several years.

The best way to tell whether your system has an ATX-board design without removing the lid is to look at the back of the system. There are two distinguishing features that identify ATX. One is that the expansion boards plug directly into the motherboard; there is no riser card like with LPX or NLX. Thus, the slots will be perpendicular to the plane of the motherboard. Also, ATX boards have a unique double-high connector area for all the built-in connectors on the motherboard (see Figure 4.6). This will be found just to the side of the bus slot area, and can be used to easily identify an ATX board.

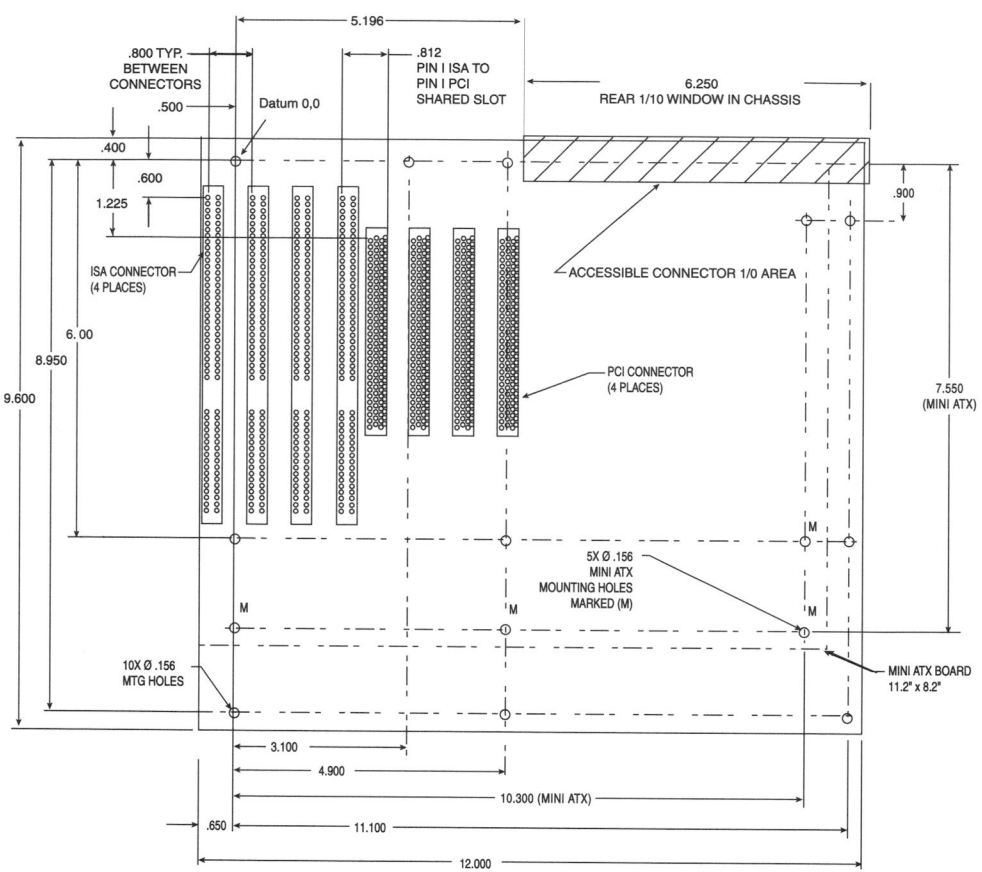

FIG. 4.5 ATX specification version 2.01.

NLX

NLX is the latest development in desktop motherboard technology, and may prove to be the form factor of choice for low-cost, low-end systems, or even Slimline corporate desktop systems in the future. It is a low-profile form factor similar in appearance to LPX, but with a number of improvements designed to allow full integration of the latest technologies. NLX is basically an improved version of the proprietary LPX design. Besides design improvements, it is fully standardized, which means you should be able to replace one NLX board with another from a different manufacturer, something that was not possible with LPX.

Another limitation of LPX boards includes difficulties in handling the physical size of the newer Pentium II processors and their higher output thermal characteristics. The NLX form factor has been designed specifically to address these problems.

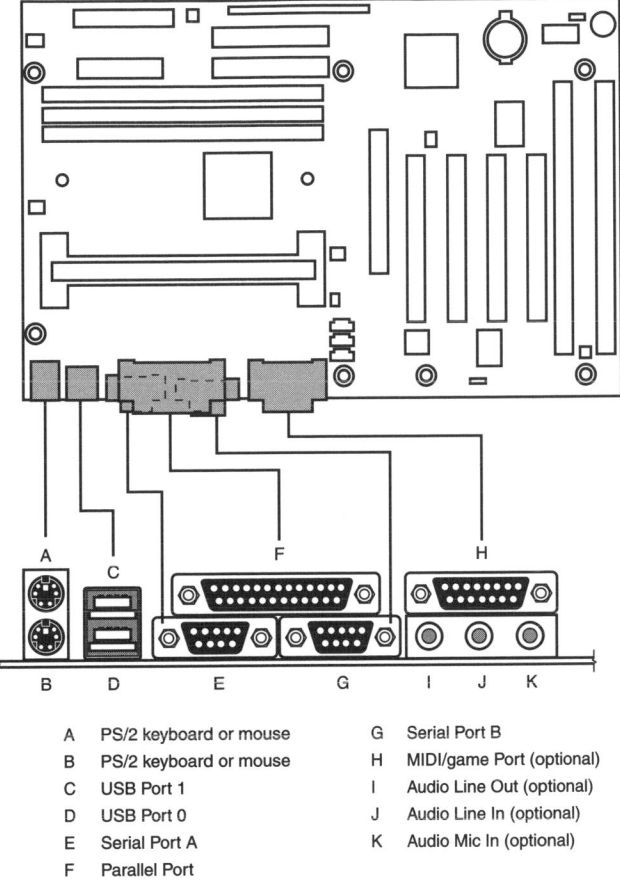

A	PS/2 keyboard or mouse	G Serial Port B
B	PS/2 keyboard or mouse	H MIDI/game Port (optional)
C	USB Port 1	I Audio Line Out (optional)
D	USB Port 0	J Audio Line In (optional)
E	Serial Port A	K Audio Mic In (optional)
F	Parallel Port	

FIG. 4.6 Typical ATX motherboard rear panel connectors.

Specific advantages of the NLX form factor include:

■ *Support for current processor technologies.* This is especially important in Pentium II systems, because the size of the Single Edge Contact cartridge this processor uses can limit its use on existing Baby-AT and LPX motherboards.

■ *Flexibility in the face of rapidly changing processor technologies.* Backplane-like flexibility has been built into the form by allowing a new motherboard to be easily and quickly installed without tearing your entire system to pieces. But unlike traditional backplane systems, many industry leaders are putting their support behind NLX, including AST, Digital, Gateway, Hewlett-Packard, IBM, Micron, NEC, and others.

■ *Support for other emerging technologies.* This includes Accelerated Graphics Port (AGP) high-performance graphic solutions, Universal Serial Bus (USB), and tall memory modules and DIMM technology. Furthermore, with the emerging importance of multimedia applications, connectivity support for such things as video playback, enhanced graphics, and extended audio have been built into the motherboard. This should represent a good cost savings over expensive daughterboard arrangements that have been necessary for many advanced multimedia uses in the past. Although ATX also has this support, LPX and Baby-AT don't have the room for these additional connectors.

Figure 4.7 shows the basic NLX system layout, while the NLX motherboard dimensions are shown in Figure 4.8. Notice that, like ATX, the system is clear of the drive bays and other chassis-mounted components. Also, the motherboard and I/O cards (which, like the LPX form factor, are mounted parallel to the motherboard) can easily be slid in and out of the side of the chassis, leaving the riser card and other cards in place. The processor can be easily accessed and enjoys greater cooling than in a more closed-in layout.

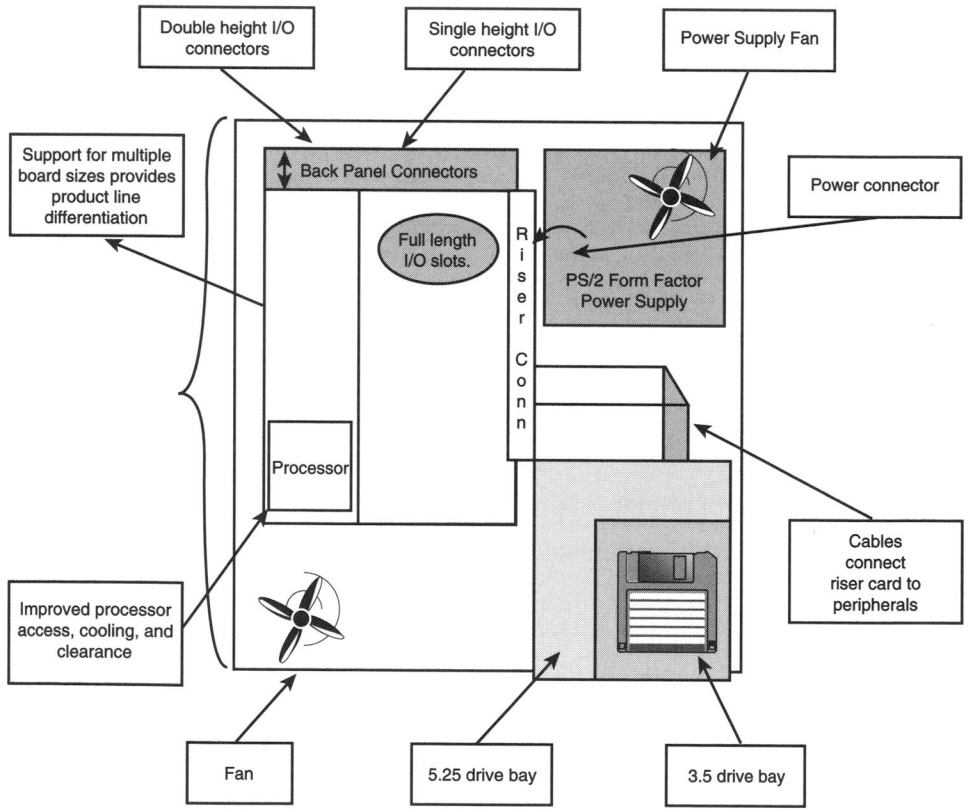

FIG. 4.7 NLX system chassis layout and features.

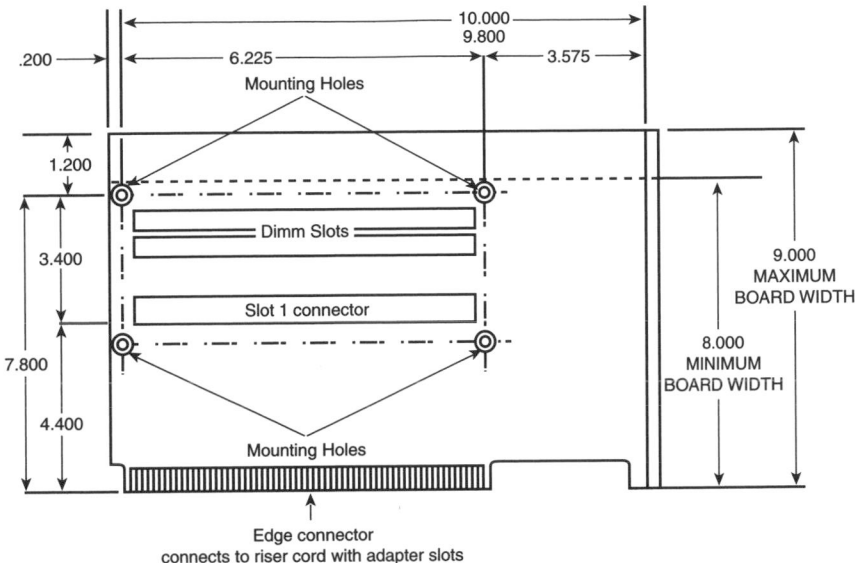

FIG. 4.8 NLX form factor. This shows a 10-inch long NLX board. The NLX specification also allows 11.2-inch and 13.6-inch long versions.

As you can see, the NLX form factor has been designed for maximum flexibility and space efficiency. Even extremely long I/O cards will fit easily, without getting in the way of other system components—a problem with Baby-AT form factor systems.

ATX and NLX form factors will probably be used in most future systems. I usually do not recommend LPX style systems if upgradability is a factor because it is not only difficult to locate a new motherboard that will fit, but LPX systems are also limited in expansion slots and drive bays. ATX is still the absolute best choice for new systems where expandability, upgradability, low cost, and ease of service are of prime importance.

Proprietary Designs

Motherboards that are not one of the standard form factors such as Full-sized AT, Baby-AT, ATX, or NLX are deemed proprietary. Most people purchasing PCs should avoid proprietary designs because they do not allow for a future motherboard, power supply, or case upgrade, which greatly limits future use of the system. To me, proprietary systems are disposable PCs, because you can neither upgrade them, nor can you easily repair them. The problem is that the proprietary parts can only come from the original system manufacturer, and they usually cost many times more than non-proprietary parts. This means that after your proprietary system goes out of warranty, it is essentially no longer worth repairing. If the motherboard goes bad, you will be better off purchasing a whole new standard system than paying five times the normal price for a new motherboard. In addition, a new motherboard in a standard form-factor system would be a generation newer and faster than the one you are replacing. In a proprietary system, the replacement board would be the same as the one that failed.

The popular LPX motherboard design is at the heart of most proprietary systems. These systems are sold primarily in the retail store channel. This class of system is dominated by Compaq and Packard Bell, and, as such, virtually all their systems have the problems inherent with their proprietary designs.

Some of these manufacturers seem to go out of their way to make their systems as physically incompatible as possible with any other system. Then, replacement parts, repairs, and upgrades are virtually impossible to find—except, of course, from the original system manufacturer and at a significantly higher price than the equivalent part would cost to fit a standard PC-compatible system.

For example, if the motherboard in my current ATX form factor system (and any system using a Baby-AT motherboard and case) dies, I can find any number of replacement boards that will bolt directly in—with my choice of processors and clock speeds—at very good (no, make that great) prices. If the motherboard dies in a newer Compaq, Packard Bell, Hewlett-Packard, or other proprietary-shaped system, you'll pay for a replacement available only from the original manufacturer, and you have little or no opportunity to select a board with a faster or better processor than the one that failed. In other words, upgrading or repairing one of these systems via a motherboard replacement is difficult and usually not cost effective.

Systems sold by the leading mail order suppliers such as Dell, Gateway, Micron, and others are available in standard ATX form factors, which allow for easy upgrading and system expansion in the future. The ATX form factor also means that you can replace your own motherboards, power supplies, and other components easily and select components from any number of suppliers other than where you originally bought the system.

Backplane Systems

One type of proprietary design is the backplane system. These systems do not have a motherboard in the true sense of the word. In a backplane system, the components normally found on a motherboard are located instead on an expansion adapter card plugged into a slot. In these systems, the board with the slots is called a *backplane*, rather than a motherboard. Systems using this type of construction are called *backplane systems*.

Backplane systems come in two main types—*passive* and *active*. A passive backplane means the main backplane board does not contain any circuitry at all except for the bus connectors and maybe some buffer and driver circuits. All the circuitry found on a conventional motherboard is contained on one or more expansion cards installed in slots on the backplane. Some backplane systems use a passive design that incorporates the entire system circuitry into a single mothercard. The mothercard is essentially a complete motherboard that is designed to plug into a slot in the passive backplane. The passive backplane/mothercard concept allows the entire system to be easily upgraded by changing one or more cards. Because of the expense of the high-function mothercard, this type of system design is rarely found in PC systems. The passive backplane design does enjoy popularity in industrial systems, which are often rack-mounted. Some high-end file servers also feature this design.

An active backplane means the main backplane board contains bus control and usually other circuitry as well. Most active backplane systems contain all the circuitry found on a typical motherboard except for the processor complex. The *processor complex* is the name of the circuit board that contains the main system processor and any other circuitry directly related to it, such as clock control, cache, and so forth. The processor complex design allows the user to easily upgrade the system later to a new processor type by changing one card. In effect, it amounts to a modular motherboard with a replaceable processor section. Most modern PC systems that use a backplane design use an active backplane/processor complex. Both IBM and Compaq, for example, have used this type of design in some of their high-end (server class) systems. This allows an easier and generally more affordable upgrade than the passive backplane/mothercard design because the processor complex board is usually much cheaper than a mothercard. Unfortunately, because there are no standards for the processor complex interface to the system, these boards are proprietary and can only be purchased from the system manufacturer. This limited market and availability causes the prices of these boards to be higher than most complete motherboards from other manufacturers.

The motherboard system design and the backplane system design have both advantages and disadvantages. Most original personal computers were designed as backplanes in the late 1970s. Apple and IBM shifted the market to the now traditional motherboard with a slot-type design because this type of system generally is cheaper to mass-produce than one with the backplane design. The theoretical advantage of a backplane system, however, is that you can upgrade it easily to a new processor and new level of performance by changing a single card. For example, you can upgrade a system's processor just by changing the card. In a motherboard-design system, you often must change the motherboard, a seemingly more formidable task. Unfortunately, the reality of the situation is that a backplane design is often much more expensive to upgrade. For example, because the bus remains fixed on the backplane, the backplane design precludes more comprehensive upgrades that involve adding local bus slots.

Another nail in the coffin of backplane designs is the upgradable processor. Intel has designed all 486, Pentium, Pentium Pro, and Pentium II processors to be upgradable to faster (sometimes called *OverDrive*) processors in the future by simply swapping (or adding) the new processor chip. Changing only the processor chip for a faster one is the easiest and generally most cost-effective way to upgrade without changing the entire motherboard. To allow processor upgrades, Intel has standardized on a number of different types of CPU sockets and slots that allow for upgrading to any faster processors designed to fit the same common socket or slot.

Because of the limited availability of the processor complex boards or mothercards, they usually end up being more expensive than a complete new motherboard that uses an industry-standard form factor.

Motherboard Components

A modern motherboard has several components built in, including various sockets, slots, connectors, chips, and other components. This section examines the components found on a typical motherboard.

Most modern motherboards have the following components on them:

- Processor Socket/Slot

- Chipset

- Super I/O chip

- BIOS

- SIMM/DIMM sockets

- Bus Slots

- CPU Voltage Regulator

- Battery

These components are discussed in the following sections.

Processor Sockets/Slots

The CPU is installed in a socket for all systems up to and including the Pentium Pro processor. The Pentium II processors and beyond use a slot where the processor card or cartridge plugs in.

Starting with the 486 processors, Intel designed the processor to be a user installable and replaceable part, and developed standards for CPU sockets that would allow different models of the same basic processor to plug in. These socket specifications were numbered and based on the socket or slot number you have on your motherboard. This means that you will know exactly what types of processors can be installed.

◀◀ See "Processor Sockets," p. 54

Sockets for processors prior to the 486 were not numbered, and interchangeability was limited. Table 4.1 shows the relationship between the various processor sockets/slots and the chips designed to go into them.

Table 4.1	CPU Socket Specifications			
Socket Number	**Pins**	**Pin Layout**	**Voltage**	**Supported Processors**
Socket 1	169	17×17 PGA	5v	486 SX/SX2, DX/DX2*, DX4 OverDrive
Socket 2	238	19×19 PGA	5v	486 SX/SX2, DX/DX2*, DX4 OverDrive, 486 Pentium OverDrive

Socket Number	Pins	Pin Layout	Voltage	Supported Processors
Socket 3	237	19×19 PGA	5v/3.3v	486 SX/SX2, DX/DX2, DX4, 486 Pentium OverDrive, 5x86
Socket 4	273	21×21 PGA	5v	Pentium 60/66, OverDrive
Socket 5	320	37×37 SPGA	3.3v/3.5v	Pentium 75-133, OverDrive
Socket 6**	235	19×19 PGA	3.3v	486 DX4, 486 Pentium OverDrive
Socket 7	321	37×37 SPGA	VRM	Pentium 75-266+, MMX, OverDrive, 6x86, K6
Socket 8	387	dual pattern SPGA	Auto VRM	Pentium Pro
Slot 1	242	SEC/SEPP Slot	Auto VRM	Pentium II MMX, Pentium II Celeron
Slot 2	n/a	SEC Slot	Auto VRM	Pentium II Xeon

Non-OverDrive DX4 also can be supported with the addition of an aftermarket 3.3v voltage-regulator adapter.
**Socket 6 was a proposed standard only and was never actually implemented in any systems.*
PGA = Pin Grid Array
SPGA = Staggered Pin Grid Array
VRM = Voltage Regulator Module
SEC = Single Edge Contact cartridge
SEPP = Single Edge Processor Package (Pentium II without the plastic cartridge)

Chipsets

When the first PC motherboards were created by IBM, they used many discrete chips to complete the design. Besides the processor, there were many other components required to complete the system. These other components included things such as the clock generator, bus controller, system timer, interrupt and DMA controllers, CMOS RAM and clock, and the keyboard controller. There were also a number of other simple logic chips used to complete the entire motherboard circuit, plus, of course, things such as the actual processor, math coprocessor (floating-point unit), memory, and other parts. Table 4.2 lists all the primary chip components used on the original PC/XT and AT motherboards.

Table 4.2 Primary Chip Components on Motherboards		
Chip Function	**PC/XT Version**	**AT Version**
Processor	8088	80286
Math Coprocessor (Floating-Point Unit	8087	80287
Clock Generator	8284	82284
Bus Controller	8288	82288
System Timer	8253	8254
Low-order Interrupt Controller	8259	8259
High-order Interrupt Controller	-	8259
Low-order DMA Controller	8237	8237

(continues)

Table 4.2 Primary Chip Components on Motherboards Continued		
Chip Function	**PC/XT Version**	**AT Version**
High-order DMA Controller	-	8237
CMOS RAM/Clock	-	MC146818
Keyboard Controller	8255	8042

All these components came from Intel or an Intel-licensed manufacturer except the CMOS/Clock chip, which came from Motorola. To build a clone or copy of one of these IBM systems back then would require all these chips plus many smaller discrete logic chips, totaling up to 100 or more individual chips. This kept the price of a motherboard high, and left little room on the board to integrate other functions.

In 1986, a company called Chips and Technologies introduced a revolutionary component called the 82C206, the main part of the first PC motherboard chipset. This was a single chip that integrated into it all the functions of the main motherboard chips in an AT-compatible system. This chip included the functions of the 82284 Clock Generator, 82288 Bus Controller, 8254 System Timer, dual 8259 Interrupt Controllers, dual 8237 DMA Controllers, and even the MC146818 CMOS/Clock chip. Besides the processor, virtually all the major chip components on a PC motherboard could now be replaced by a single chip. Four other chips augmented the 82C206 acting as buffers and memory controllers, thus completing virtually the entire motherboard circuit with five total chips. This first chipset was called the CS8220 chipset by Chips and Technologies. Needless to say, this was a revolutionary concept in PC motherboard manufacturing. Not only did it greatly reduce the cost to build a PC motherboard, but it also made it much easier to design a motherboard and the reduced component count meant the boards had more room for integrating other items formerly found on expansion cards. Later the four chips augmenting the 82C206 were replaced by a new set of only three chips, and the entire set was called the New Enhanced AT (NEAT) CS8221 chipset. This was later followed by the 82C836 Single Chip AT (SCAT) chipset, which finally condensed all the chips in the set down to a single chip.

The chipset idea was rapidly copied by other chip manufacturers. Companies such as Acer, Erso, Opti, Suntac, Symphony, UMC, and VLSI each gained an important share of this market. Unfortunately for many of them, the chipset market has been a volatile one, and many of them have long since gone out of business. In 1993 VLSI had become the dominant force in the chipset market and had the vast majority of the market share; by the next year, they, along with virtually everybody else in the chipset market, would be fighting to stay alive. This is because a new chipset manufacturer had come on the scene, and within a year or so of getting serious they were totally dominating the chipset market. That company is Intel, and since 1994 they have had a virtual lock on the chipset market. If you have a motherboard built since 1994, chances are far better than not that it has an Intel chipset on it along with an Intel processor. There are very few chipset competitors left, and the ones that are left are scratching for the lower end of the market. Today, that would include primarily ALi (Acer Laboratories, Inc.), VIA Technologies, and SiS (Silicon integrated Systems). It is interesting to note that Chips and Technologies survived by changing course to design and manufacture video chips, and found a niche in that market specifically for laptop and notebook video chipsets. They were bought out by Intel in 1998 as a way for Intel to get into the video chipset business.

Intel Chipsets

You cannot talk about chipsets today without primarily discussing Intel. They currently own well over 90% of the chipset market, and virtually 100% of the higher-end Pentium II chipset market. It is interesting to note that we probably have Compaq to thank for forcing Intel into the chipset business in the first place. The thing that really started it all was the introduction of the EISA bus designed by Compaq in 1989. At that time, they had shared the bus with other manufacturers in an attempt to make it a market standard. However, they refused to share their EISA bus chipset, a set of custom chips needed to implement this bus on a motherboard. Enter Intel, who decided to supply the chipset void for the rest of the PC manufacturers wanting to build EISA bus motherboards. The EISA bus failed to become a market success except for the niche server business, but Intel now had a taste of the chipset business and this they apparently wouldn't forget. With the introduction of the 486 processor, Intel became impatient with how long it was taking the other chipset companies to create chipsets around their new processor designs, which then delayed the introduction of motherboards that supported the new processors. Intel couldn't sell their processors in volume until there were ready-made motherboards that would support them, so they thought that by developing motherboard chipsets for a new processor in parallel with the new processor, they could jumpstart the motherboard business by providing ready-made chipsets. By the time the first Pentium processor debuted in 1993, Intel had their first Pentium motherboard chipset ready to go at the same time. Now it took only scant months before the first Pentium motherboards were available, rather than the year or more it had historically taken.

Since then, Intel has thrived in the chipset market, always introducing new chipsets to go with their new processors. Their success in chipsets prompted them to take the final step—making complete PC motherboards using their own processors and chipsets. Now as they develop new processors, they develop chipsets and even complete motherboards simultaneously, which means they can be announced and shipped in unison. This eliminates the delay between introducing new processors and having motherboards and systems be able to use them, which was common in the industry's early days. This delay is virtually eliminated today. It was amazing to me that on the day they introduced the first Pentium II processor, not only was there a new chipset available to support it, but complete motherboards, as well. That very day, you could call Gateway or Dell and order a complete Intel system using the new Intel PII processor, chipset, and motherboard. This has not made companies such as Compaq (who still like to make their own motherboards rather than purchase somebody else's off-the-shelf product) happy, to say the least.

First with the advent of the Pentium, then the Pentium Pro, and now the Pentium II processor, not only do more than 90% of the systems sold use Intel processors, but their motherboards also most likely have an Intel chipset on them and, in fact, their entire motherboard was most likely made by Intel. In my seminars, I ask how many people in the class have Intel brand PCs. Of course, Intel does not sell or market a PC under their own name, so nobody thinks they have an Intel brand PC. But I say if your motherboard was made by Intel, then you have an Intel brand PC, as far as I am concerned. Does it really matter whether Dell, Gateway, or Micron put that same Intel motherboard into a slightly different looking case with their name on it?

Intel Chipset Model Numbers. Intel started a pattern of numbering their chipsets as follows:

Chipset Number	Processor Family
420xx	P4 (486)
430xx	P5 (Pentium)
440xx	P6 (Pentium Pro/Pentium II)
450xx	P6 Server (Pentium Pro/Pentium II Xeon)

The chipset numbers listed here are an abbreviation of the actual chipset numbers stamped on the individual chips. For example, one of the current popular Pentium II chipsets is the 440BX chipset, which really consists of two components, the 82443BX North Bridge and the 82371EX South Bridge. By reading the number and letter combinations on the larger chips on your motherboard, you can usually quickly identify the chipset your motherboard uses.

Most all of Intel's chipsets (and those of Intel's competitors) are broken into a two-tiered architecture incorporating a North Bridge and South Bridge section. The North Bridge is the main portion of the chipset and incorporates the interface between the processor and the rest of the motherboard. The North Bridge components are what the chipset is named after, meaning that, for example, what we call the 440BX chipset is actually derived from the fact that the actual North Bridge chip part number for that set is 82443BX.

The North Bridge contains the cache and main memory controllers and the interface between the high-speed (33MHz, 50MHz, 66MHz or 100MHz) processor bus and the 33MHz PCI (Peripheral Component Interconnect) and or 66MHz AGP (Accelerated Graphics Port) buses. Intel often refers to the North Bridge of their more recent chipsets as the PAC (PCI/AGP Controller). The North Bridge is essentially the main component of the motherboard and is the only motherboard circuit besides the processor that normally runs at full motherboard (processor bus) speed. Most modern chipsets use a single-chip North Bridge; however, some of the older ones actually consisted of up to three individual chips to make up the complete North Bridge circuit.

The South Bridge is the lower speed component in the chipset and has always been a single individual chip. The South Bridge is a somewhat interchangeable component in that different North Bridge chipsets often are designed to use the same South Bridge component. This modular design of the chipset allows for lower cost and greater flexibility for motherboard manufacturers. The South Bridge connects to the 33MHz PCI bus and contains the interface to the 8MHz ISA bus. It also normally contains the dual IDE hard disk controller interfaces, and the USB (Universal Serial Bus) interface—and even the CMOS RAM and clock functions. The South Bridge contains all the components that make up the ISA bus, including the interrupt and DMA controllers.

Let's start by examining the Intel 486 motherboard chipsets and then work our way through the latest Pentium II sets.

Intel's Early 386/486 Chipsets

Intel's first real PC motherboard chipset was the 82350 chipset for the 386DX and 486 processors. This chipset was not very successful, mainly because the EISA bus was not very popular, and because there were many other manufacturers making standard 386 and 486 motherboard chipsets at the time. The market changed very quickly, and Intel dropped the EISA bus support and introduced follow-up 486 chipsets that were much more successful.

Table 4.3 shows the Intel 486 chipsets.

Table 4.3 Intel 486 Motherboard Chipsets			
Chipset	**420TX**	**420EX**	**420ZX**
Codename	Saturn	Aries	Saturn II
Date Introduced	Nov. '92	March '94	March '94
Processor	5v 486	5v/3.3v 486	5v/3.3v 486
Bus Speed	up to 33 MHz	up to 50 MHz	up to 333 MHz
SMP (dual CPUs)	No	No	No
Memory Types	FPM	FPM	FPM
Parity/ECC	Parity	Parity	Parity
Max. Memory	128MMB	128MMB	160MMB
L2 Cache Type	Async	Async	Async
PCI Support	2.0	2.0	2.1
AGP Support	No	No	No

SMP = Symmetric Multi-processing (Dual Processors)
FPM = Fast Page Mode
PCI = Peripheral Component Interconnect
AGP = Accelerated Graphics Port
Note: PCI 2.1 supports concurrent PCI operations.

Intel had pretty good success with their 486 chipsets. They had developed their current two-tiered approach to system design even back then. This design is such that all Intel 486, Pentium, Pentium Pro, and Pentium II have been designed using two main components, which are commonly called the *North Bridge* and the *South Bridge*.

Fifth-Generation (P5 Pentium Class) Chipsets

With the advent of the Pentium processor in March of '93, Intel also introduced their first Pentium chipset, the 430LX (code-named Mercury) chipset. This was the first Pentium chipset on the market and set the stage as Intel took this lead and ran with it. Other manufacturers took months to a year or more to get their Pentium chipsets out the door. Since the debut of their Pentium chipsets, Intel has dominated the chipset market with nobody even coming close. Table 4.4 shows the Intel Pentium motherboard chipsets.

Table 4.4 Intel Pentium Motherboard Chipsets

Chipset	430LX	430NX	430FX
Codename	Mercury	Neptune	Triton
Date Introduced	Mar. '93	Mar. '94	Jan. '95
Bus Speed	66 MHz	66 MHz	66 MHz
CPUs Supported	P60/66	P75+	P75+
SMP (dual CPUs)	No	Yes	No
Memory Types	FPM	FPM	FPM/EDO
Parity/ECC	Parity	Parity	Neither
Max. Memory	192M	512M	128M
Max. Cacheable	192M	512M	64M
L2 Cache Type	Async	Async	Async/Pburst
PCI Support	2.0	2.0	2.0
AGP Support	No	No	No
South Bridge	SIO	SIO	PIIX

SMP = Symmetric Multi-processing (Dual Processors)
FPM = Fast Page Mode
EDO = Extended Data Out
BEDO = Burst EDO
SDRAM = Synchronous Dynamic RAM

Pburst = Pipeline Burst (Synchronous)
PCI = Peripheral Component Interconnect
AGP = Accelerated Graphics Port
SIO = System I/O
PIIX = PCI ISA IDE Xcelerator

> **Note**
>
> PCI 2.1 supports concurrent PCI operations.

Table 4.5 shows all the applicable Intel South Bridge chips, which are the second part of the modern Intel motherboard chipsets.

Table 4.5 Intel South Bridge Chips

Chip Name	SIO	PIIX	PIIX3	PIIX4	PIIX4E
Part Number	82378IB/ZB	82371FB	82371SB	82371AB	82371EB
IDE Support	None	BMIDE	BMIDE	UDMA	UDMA
USB Support	None	None	Yes	Yes	Yes
CMOS/Clock	No	No	No	Yes	Yes
Power Management	SMM	SMM	SMM	SMM	ACPI 1.0

SIO = System I/O
PIIX = PCI ISA IDE Xcelerator
USB = Universal Serial Bus
IDE = Integrated Drive Electronics (AT Attachment)
BMIDE = Bus Master IDE
UDMA = Ultra-DMA IDE
SMM = System Management Mode
ACPI = Advanced Configuration and Power Interface specification

430MX	430HX	430VX	430TX
Mobile Triton	Triton II	Triton III	n/a
Oct. '95	Feb. '96	Feb. '96	Feb. '97
66 MHz	66 MHz	66 MHz	66 MHz
P75+	P75+	P75+	P75+
No	Yes	No	No
FPM/EDO	FPM/EDO	FPM/EDO/SDRAM	FPM/EDO/SDRAM
Neither	Both	Neither	Neither
128M	512M	128M	256M
64M	512M	64M	64M
Async/Pburst	Async/Pburst	Async/Pburst	Async/Pburst
2.0	2.1	2.1	2.1
No	No	No	No
MPIIX	PIIX3	PIIX3	PIIX4

The following sections detail all the Pentium motherboard chipsets and their specifications.

Intel 430LX (Mercury). The 430LX was introduced in March of 1993 concurrent with the introduction of the first Pentium processors. This chipset was only used with the original Pentiums, which came in 60MHz and 66MHz versions. These were 5v chips and were used on motherboards with Socket 4 processor sockets.

◀◀ See "Processor Sockets," p. 54
◀◀ See "First-Generation Pentium Processor," p. 109

The 430LX chipset consisted of three total chips for the North Bridge portion. The main chip was the 82434LX system controller. This main chip contained the processor-to-memory interface, cache controller, and PCI bus controller. There was also a pair of PCI bus interface accelerator chips, which were identical 82433LX chips.

The 430LX chipset was noted for the following:

- Single processor
- Support for up to 512K of L2 cache
- Support for up to 192M of standard DRAM

This chipset died off along with the 5v 60/66MHz Pentium processors.

Intel 430NX (Neptune). Introduced in March of '94, the 430NX was the first chipset designed to run the new 3.3v second generation Pentium processor. These were noted by having Socket 5 processor sockets, and an onboard 3.3v/3.5v voltage regulator for both the processor and chipset. This chipset was primarily designed for Pentiums with speeds from 75MHz to 133MHz, although mostly it was used with 75MHz to 100MHz systems. Along with the lower-voltage processor, this chipset ran faster, cooler, and more reliably than the first-generation Pentium processor and the corresponding 5v chipsets.

◀◀ See "CPU Operating Voltages," p. 72
◀◀ See "Second-Generation Pentium Processor," p. 110

The 430NX chipset consisted of three chips for the North Bridge component. The primary chip was the 82434NX, which included the cache and main memory (DRAM) controller and the control interface to the PCI bus. The actual PCI data was managed by a pair of 82433NX chips called *local bus accelerators*. Together, these two chips plus the main 82434NX chip constituted the North Bridge.

The South Bridge used with the 430NX chipset was the 82378ZB System I/O (SIO) chip. This component connected to the PCI bus and generated the lower-speed ISA bus.

The 430NX chipset introduced the following improvements over the Mercury (430LX) chipset:

- Dual processor support

- Support for 512M of system memory (up from 192M for the LX Mercury chipset)

This chipset rapidly became the most popular chipset for the early 75MHz to 100MHz systems, overshadowing the older 60MHz and 66MHz systems that used the 430LX chipset.

Intel 430FX (Triton). The 430FX (Triton) chipset rapidly became the most popular chipset ever after it was introduced in January of '95. This chipset is noted for being the first to support EDO (Extended Data Out) memory, which also became popular at the time. EDO was slightly faster than the standard FPM (Fast Page Mode) memory that had been used up until that time, but cost no more than the slower FPM. Unfortunately, while being known for faster memory support, the Triton chipset was also known as the first Pentium chipset without support for parity checking for memory. This was a major blow to PC reliability, although many did not know it at the time.

▶▶ See "EDO RAM," p. 315
▶▶ See "Parity Checking," p. 347

The Triton chipset lacked not only parity support from the previous 430NX chipset, but it also would only support a single CPU. The 430FX was designed as a low-end chipset, for home or non-mission-critical systems. As such, it did not replace the 430NX, which carried on in higher-end network file servers and other more mission-critical systems.

The 430FX consisted of a three-chip North Bridge. The main chip was the 82437FX system controller that included the memory and cache controllers, CPU interface, and PCI bus controller, along with dual 82438FX data path chips for the PCI bus. The South Bridge was the first PIIX (PCI ISA IDE Xcelerator) chip that was the 82371FB. This chip acted not only as the bridge between the 33MHz PCI bus and the slower 8MHz ISA bus, but it also incorporated for the first time a dual-channel IDE interface. By moving the IDE interface off of the ISA bus and into the PIIX chip, it was now effectively connected to the PCI bus, allowing for much faster Bus Master IDE transfers. This was key in supporting the ATA-2 or Enhanced IDE interface for better hard disk performance.

The major points on the 430FX are

- Support for EDO memory

- Support for higher-speed—pipelined burst cache

- PIIX South Bridge with high-speed Bus Master IDE

- Lack of support for parity-checked memory

- Only single CPU support

- Supported only 128M of RAM, of which only 64M could be cached

That last issue is one that many people are not aware of. The 430FX chipset can only cache up to 64M of main memory. This means that if you install more than 64M of RAM in your system, performance will suffer greatly. Now, many think this won't be that much of a problem—after all, they don't normally run enough software to load past the first 64M anyway. That is another misunderstanding, because Windows 95 and NT load from the top down. This means, for example, that if you install 96M of RAM (one 64M and one 32M bank), then virtually all of your software, including the main operating system, will be loading into the non-cached region above 64M. Only if you use more than 32M would you begin to see an improvement in performance. Try disabling the L2 cache via your CMOS setup to see how slow your system will run without it. That is the performance you can expect if you install more than 64M of RAM in a 430FX-based system.

This lack of cacheable memory plus the lack of support for parity or ECC (error correcting code) memory make this a non-recommended chipset in my book. Fortunately, this chipset became obsolete when the more powerful 430HX was introduced.

Intel 430HX (Triton II). The Triton II 430HX chipset was created by Intel as a true replacement for the powerful 430NX chip. It added some of the high-speed memory features from the low-end 430FX, such as support for EDO memory and pipeline burst L2 cache. It also retained dual-processor support and in addition to supporting parity checking to detect memory errors, it also added support for ECC (error-correcting code) memory to not only detect, but to correct, single bit error on-the-fly. And the great thing was that this was implemented using plain parity memory.

This was a chipset suitable for high-end or mission-critical system use such as file servers, while also working well for lower-end systems. Parity or ECC memory was not required—the chipset could easily be configured to use less expensive nonparity, noncorrecting memory as well.

The HX chipset's primary advantages over the FX are

- Support for parity and ECC memory

- Dual-processor support

- Support for a full 512M of system memory instead of just 128M

- Support for 512M of cached system memory instead of just 64M (if the optional larger tag RAM is installed)

- Improved performance, due to faster memory timing and more I/O buffers

- PCI level 2.1 compliance, which allowed concurrent PCI operations

- USB support

- Independent device timing for IDE/ATA drives.

The memory problems with caching in the 430FX were corrected in the 430HX. This chipset allowed for the possibility of caching the full 512M of possible RAM as long as the correct amount of cache tag was installed. Tag is a small cache memory chip used to store the index to the data in the cache. Most 430HX systems shipped with a tag chip that could only manage 64M of cached main memory, while you could optionally upgrade it to a larger-capacity tag chip that would allow for caching the full 512M of RAM.

The 430HX chipset was a true one-chip North Bridge. It was also one of the first chips out in a ball-grid array package, where the chip leads were configured as balls on the bottom of the chip. This allowed for a smaller chip package than the previous PQFP (Plastic Quad Flat Pack) packaging used on the older chips, and, because there was only one chip for the North Bridge, a very compact motherboard was possible. The South Bridge was the PIIX3 (82371SB) chip, which allowed for independent timing of the dual IDE channels. This meant that you could install two different speed devices on the same channel and configure their transfer speeds independently. Previous PIIX chips allowed both devices to work at the lowest common denominator speed supported by both. The PIIX3 also incorporated the USB (Universal Serial Bus) for the first time on a PC motherboard. Unfortunately at the time, there were no devices available to attach to USB, nor was there any operating systems or driver support for the bus. USB ports were a curiosity at the time, and nobody had a use for them.

The 430HX supports the newer PCI 2.1 standard, which allowed for concurrent PCI operations and greater performance. Combined with the support for EDO and pipelined burst cache, this was perhaps the best Pentium chipset for the power user's system. It offered not only excellent performance, but with ECC memory it offered a truly reliable and stable system design.

The 430HX was the only modern Intel Pentium-class chipset to offer parity and error-corrected memory support. This made it the recommended Intel chipset for mission-critical applications such as file servers, database servers, business systems, and so on. Of course, today few would recommend using any type of Pentium system as a file server in lieu of a more powerful, and yet not much more expensive, Pentium II system.

As this chipset and most of the Pentium processors are being phased out, you should look toward Pentium II systems for this kind of support.

Intel 430VX (Triton III). The 430VX chipset never had an official code-name, although many in the industry began calling it the Triton III. The 430VX was designed to be a replacement for the low-end 430FX chipset. It was not a replacement for the higher-powered 430HX chipset. As such, the VX has only one significant technical advantage over the HX, but in almost all other respects is more like the 430FX than the HX.

The VX has the following features:

- Support for 66MHz SDRAM (synchronous DRAM)
- No parity or ECC memory support
- Single processor only
- Supports only 128M RAM
- Supports only 64M of cached RAM

Although the support for SDRAM is a nice bonus, the actual speed derived from such memory is limited. This is because with a good L2 cache, there will only be a cache miss about 5% of the time the system is reading or writing memory, which means that the cache performance is actually more important than main memory performance. This is why most 430HX systems are faster than 430VX systems even though the VX can use faster SDRAM memory. Also, note that because the VX was designed as a low-end chipset for low-cost retail systems, most of them would never see any SDRAM memory anyway.

Like with the 430FX, the VX has the limitation of being able to cache only 64M of main memory. With the memory price crash of 1996 bringing memory prices down to where more than 64M is actually affordable for most people, and with Windows software using more and more memory, this is really becoming a limitation.

The 430VX chipset was rapidly made obsolete in the market by the 430TX chipset that followed.

Intel 430TX. The 430TX chipset never had a code-name that I am aware of; however, some persisted in calling it the Triton IV. The 430TX was Intel's last Pentium chipset. It was designed not only to be used in desktop systems, but it was designed to replace the 430MX mobile Pentium chipset for laptop and notebook systems.

The 430TX has some refinements over the 430VX, but, unfortunately, it still lacks support for parity or ECC memory, and retains the 64M cacheable RAM limitation of the older FX and VX chipsets. The 430TX was not designed to replace the high-end 430HX chipset, which still remained the chipset of choice for mission-critical systems. This is probably due to Intel's de-emphasizing of the Pentium; they are trying to wean us from Pentium processors and force the market, especially for higher-end mission-critical systems, to the more powerful Pentium II.

The TX chipset features include:

- 66MHz SDRAM support

- Cacheable memory still limited to 64M

- Support for Ultra-ATA, or Ultra-DMA IDE transfers

- Lower power consumption for mobile use

- No parity or ECC memory support

- Single processor only

Because the Pentium processor has been relegated to low-end system use only, the fact that it lacks parity or ECC memory support, as well as the lack of support for cacheable memory over 64M, has not been that much of a problem for the market for which this chipset is intended. You should not use it for business-class systems, especially those that are mission-critical.

Those seeking a true high-performance chipset and a system that is robust—and which has support for mission-critical features such as ECC memory or for caching more than 64M of memory—should be looking at Pentium II systems and not the lowly Pentium. Intel has recently stopped all further Pentium processor manufacturing and is only continuing to sell what they have in inventory.

Third-Party (Non-Intel) P5 Pentium Class Chipsets

VIA Technologies. VIA Technologies, Inc. was founded in 1987, and has become a major designer of PC motherboard chipsets. VIA employs state-of-the-art manufacturing capability through foundry relationships with leading silicon manufacturers, such as Toshiba and Taiwan Semiconductor Manufacturing Corporation.

Apollo VP-1. The VT82C580VP Apollo VP-1 is a 4-chip set released in October of 1995 and used in older Socket 5 and Socket 7 systems. The Apollo VP-1 is an equivalent alternative to the Intel 430VX chipset, and features support for SDRAM, EDO, or Fast Page Mode memory as well as pipeline-burst SRAM cache. The VP-1 consists of the VT82C585VP 208-pin PQFP (Plastic Quad Flat Pack) and two VT82C587VP 100-pin PQFP chips acting as the North Bridge, and the VT82C586 208-pin PQFP South Bridge chip.

Apollo VP2. The two-chip Apollo VP2 chipset was released in May of 1996. The VP2 is a high-performance Socket-7 chipset including several features over the previous VP-1 chipset. The VP2 adds support for ECC (Error Correcting Code) memory over the VPX.

The VP2 has also been licensed by AMD as their AMD 640 chipset. Motherboards using the Apollo VP2 can support P5 class processors, including the Intel Pentium and Pentium MMX, AMD K5 and K6, and Cyrix/IBM 6x86 and 6x86MX (MII) processors.

The VP2 chipset consists of the VT82C595 328 pin BGA (Ball Grid Array) package North Bridge chip, which supports up to 2M of L2 cache and up to 512M DRAM. Additional performance-related features include a fast DRAM controller with support for SDRAM, EDO, BEDO, and FPM DRAM types in mixed combinations with 32/64-bit data bus widths and row and column addressing, a deeper buffer with enhanced performance, and an intelligent PCI bus controller with Concurrent PCI master/CPU/IDE (PCI 2.1) operations. For data integrity and server use, the VP2/97 incorporates support for Error Checking and Correcting (ECC) or parity memory.

The Apollo VP2 features the VIA VT82C586B PCI-IDE South Bridge controller chip, which complies with the Microsoft PC97 industry specification by supporting ACPI/OnNow, Ultra DMA/33, and USB technologies.

Apollo VPX. The VT82C580VPX Apollo VPX is a 4-chip set for Socket-7 motherboards released in December of 1996. The Apollo VPX is functionally equivalent to the Intel 430TX chipset, but also has specific performance enhancements relative to the 430TX. The VPX was designed as a replacement for the VP-1 chipset, and is an upgrade of that set designed to add support for the newer AMD and Cyrix P5 processors.

The Apollo VPX consists of the VT82C585VPX North Bridge and VT82C586B South Bridge chips. There are also two 208-pin PQFP frame buffers that go with the North Bridge memory interface. The Apollo VPX/97 features the VIA VT82C586B PCI-IDE South Bridge controller chip that complies with the Microsoft PC97 industry standard by supporting ACPI/OnNow, Ultra-DMA/33, and USB technologies. VIA also offers a non-PC97 version of the Apollo VPX that includes the older VT82C586A South Bridge and which was used in more entry-level PC designs.

Motherboards using the Apollo VPX can support P5 class processors, including the Intel Pentium and Pentium MMX, AMD K5 and K6, and Cyrix/IBM 6x86 and 6x86MX (MII) processors. To enable proper implementation of the Cyrix/IBM 6x86 200+ processor, the chipset features an asynchronous CPU bus that operates at either 66 or 75 MHz speeds. The Apollo VPX is an upgrade over the Apollo VP-1 with the additional feature of Concurrent PCI master/CPU/IDE operations (PCI 2.1). The VPX also supports up to 2M of L2 cache and up to 512M DRAM.

Apollo VP3. The Apollo VP3 is one of the first P5 class chipsets to implement the Intel AGP (Advanced Graphics Port) specification. Intel offers that interface with their Pentium II (P6) class chipsets. This allows a higher performance Socket 7 motherboard to be built that can accept the faster AGP video cards. The Socket 7 interface allows P5 class processors such as the Intel Pentium and Pentium MMX, AMD K5 and K6, and Cyrix/IBM 6x86 and 6x86MX (MII) to be utilized.

The Apollo VP3 chipset consists of the VT82C597 North Bridge system controller (472-pin BGA) and the VT82C586B South Bridge (208-pin PQFP). The VT82C597 North Bridge provides superior performance between the CPU, optional synchronous cache, DRAM, AGP bus, and the PCI bus with pipelined, burst, and concurrent operation. The VT82C597 complies with the Accelerated Graphics Port Specification 1.0 and features a 66 MHz master system bus.

Apollo MVP3. The Apollo MVP3 adds to the VP3 chip by supporting the new Super-7 100MHz Socket 7 specification. This allows the newer high-speed P5 processors such as the AMD K6 and Cyrix/IBM MII processors to be supported. The Apollo MVP3 chipset is a 2-chip chipset that consists of the VT82C598AT North Bridge system controller and the VT82C586B South Bridge. The VT82C598AT chip is a 476-pin BGA (Ball Grid Array) package while the VT82C586B chip is a 208-pin PQFP (Plastic Quad Flat Pack) package.

The VT82C598AT North Bridge chip includes the CPU-to-PCI bridge, the L2 cache and buffer controller, the DRAM controller, the AGP interface, and the PCI IDE controller. The VT82C598AT North Bridge provides superior performance between the CPU, optional synchronous cache, DRAM, AGP bus, and the PCI bus with pipelined, burst, and concurrent operation. The DRAM controller supports standard Fast page Mode (FPM), EDO, SDRAM, and DDR (Double Data Rate) SDRAM. The VT82C598AT complies with the Accelerated Graphics Port Specification 1.0 and features support for 66/75/83/100 MHz CPU bus frequencies and the 66MHz AGP bus frequency.

The VT82C586B South Bridge includes the PCI-to-ISA bridge, ACPI support, SMBus, the USB host/hub interface, the Ultra-33 IDE Master controller, PS/2 Keyboard/Mouse controller, and the I/O controller. The chip also contains the keyboard and PS/2 mouse controller.

This chipset is closest to the Intel 430TX in that it supports Socket 7 chips (Pentium and P5-compatible processors), SDRAM DIMM memory, and is physically a two-chip set. It differs mainly in that it allows operation at speeds up to 100MHz and supports AGP, features only available with the Pentium II boards and chipsets from Intel. This is an attempt to make the Socket 7 motherboards and processors more competitive with the lower-end Pentium II chips such as the Celeron. The South Bridge is compatible with the newer Intel PIIX4e in that it includes UDMA IDE, USB, CMOS RAM, plus ACPI 1.0 power management.

One big benefit over the Intel 430TX is support for ECC (Error Correcting Code) memory or parity checking can be selected on a bank-by-bank basis, which allows mixing of parity and ECC modules. The 430TX from Intel doesn't support any ECC or parity functions at all. Memory timing for FPM is X-3-3-3, while EDO is X-2-2-2, and SDRAM is X-1-1-1, which is similar to the Intel 430TX.

Another benefit over the 430TX is in memory cacheability. The 430TX allows caching up to only 64M of main memory, a significant limitation in higher-end systems. The maximum cacheable range is determined by a combination of cache memory size and the number of cache tag bits used. The most common L2 cache sizes will be 512K or 1M of

L2 cache on the motherboard, allowing either 128M or 256M of main memory to be cached. The maximum configuration of 2M of L2 cache will allow up to 512M of main memory to be cacheable. Intel solves this in the Pentium II by including sufficient cache tag RAM in the L2 cache built in to the Pentium II processors to allow either 512M of main memory or 4G of main memory to be cached.

The MVP3 seems to be the chipset of choice in the higher-end Socket 7 motherboards from DFI, FIC, Tyan, Acer, and others.

Acer Laboratories, Inc (ALi). Acer Laboratories, Inc. (ALi) was originally founded in 1987 as an independent research and development center for the Acer Group. In 1993, ALi separated financially and legally from Acer Inc. and became a member company of the Acer Group. ALi has rapidly claimed a prominent position among PC chipset manufacturers.

Aladdin IV. The Aladdin IV from Acer Labs is a two-chip set for P5 class processors consisting of the M1531 North Bridge and either an M1533 or M1543 South Bridge chip. The Aladdin IV supports all Intel, AMD, Cyrix/IBM and other P5-class CPUs including the Intel Pentium and Pentium MMX, AMD K5 and K6, and the Cyrix/IBM 6x86 and 6x86MX (MII) processors. The Aladdin IV is equivalent to the Intel 430TX chipset, with the addition of error-correcting memory support and higher-speed 75MHz and 83.3MHz operation. Also, when using the M1543 South Bridge, an additional Super I/O chip is not necessary as those functions are included in the M1543 South Bridge.

The M1531 North Bridge is a 328-pin BGA (Ball Grid Array) chip that supports CPU bus speeds of 83.3 MHz, 75 MHz, 66 MHz, 60 MHz, and 50MHz. The M1531 also supports Pipelined-Burst SRAM cache in sizes of up to 1M, allowing either 64M (with 8-bit Tag SRAM) or up to 512M (with 11-bit Tag SRAM) of cacheable main memory. Either FPM, EDO, or SDRAM main memory modules are supported for a total capacity of 1GB in up to 4 total banks. Memory timing is 6-3-3-3 for back-to-back FPM reads, 5-2-2-2 for back-to-back EDO reads, and 6-1-1-1 for back-to-back SDRAM reads. For reliability and integrity in mission-critical or server applications, ECC (Error Correcting Code) or parity is supported. PCI spec. 2.1 is also supported, allowing concurrent PCI operations.

The M1533 South Bridge integrates ACPI support, 2-channel Ultra-DMA 33 IDE master controller, 2-port USB controller, and a standard Keyboard/Mouse controller. A more full-function M1543 South Bridge is also available that has everything in the M1533 South Bridge plus all the functions of a normally separate Super I/O controller. The M1543 integrates ACPI support, 2-channel Ultra-DMA 33 IDE controller, 2-port USB controller, and a standard keyboard/mouse controller. Also included is an integrated Super I/O including a 2.88M floppy disk controller, two high-performance serial ports, and a multi-mode parallel port. The serial ports incorporate 16550-compatible UARTs (Universal Asynchronous Receiver Transmitters) with 16-byte FIFO (First In First Out) buffers and Serial Infra Red (SIR) capability. The multimode Parallel Port includes support for Standard Parallel Port (SPP) mode, PS/2 bidirectional mode, Enhanced Parallel Port (EPP) mode, and the Microsoft and Hewlett Packard Extended Capabilities Port (ECP) mode.

Aladdin V. The Acer Labs (ALi) Aladdin V Chipset is a two-chip set that consists of the M1541 North Bridge chip and the M1543 South Bridge/Super I/O controller combo chip. The M1541 North Bridge is a 456-pin BGA package chip while the M1543 South Bridge is a 328-pin BGA package chip. The M1541 chipset is similar to the previous M1532 chipset with the addition of higher speed (up to 100MHz) operation and AGP (Accelerated Graphics Port) support.

The M1541 North Bridge includes the CPU-to-PCI bridge, the L2 cache and buffer controller, the DRAM controller, the AGP interface, and the PCI controller. The M1541 supports the Super-7 high-speed 100MHz Socket 7 processor interface used by some of the newer AMD and Cyrix/IBM P5 processors. It will also run the processor bus at 83.3MHz, 75MHz, 66 MHz, 60 MHz, and 50MHz for backward compatibility. When running the CPU bus at 75MHz, the PCI bus only runs at 30MHz; however, when the CPU bus is running at 83.3MHz or 100MHz, the PCI bus will run at full 33MHz PCI standard speed.

The M1541 also integrates enough cache Tag RAM (16K×10) internally to support 512KB of L2 cache, simplifying the L2 cache design and further reducing the number of chips on the motherboard. Cacheable memory is up to 512M of RAM when using 512KB L2 cache and 1GB of RAM when using 1M of L2 cache. Either FPM, EDO, or SDRAM memory is supported, in up to four banks and up to 1GB total RAM. ECC/Parity is also supported for mission-critical or fileserver applications to improve reliability. Memory timing is 6-3-3-3-3-3-3-3 for back-to-back FPM reads, 5-2-2-2-2-2-2-2 for back-to-back EDO reads, and 6-1-1-1-2-1-1-1 for back-to-back SDRAM reads. Finally, Accelerated Graphics Port (AGP) Interface specification V1.0 is supported, along with 1x and 2x modes, allowing the latest graphics cards to be utilized.

The M1543 South Bridge and Super I/O combo chip includes ACPI support, the USB host/hub interface, dual channel Ultra-DMA/33 IDE host interface, keyboard and mouse controller, and the Super I/O controller. The built-in Super I/O consists of an integrated floppy disk controller, two serial ports with infrared support, and a multimode parallel port.

Silicon integrated Systems (SiS). Silicon integrated Systems (SiS) was formerly known as Symphony Labs and is one of the three largest non-Intel PC motherboard chipset manufacturers.

5581 and 5582. The SiS5581 and 5582 chips are both 553-pin BGA package single-chip sets incorporating both North and South Bridge functions. The SiS5582 is targeted for AT/ATX form factor motherboards while the SiS5581 is intended to be used on LPX/NLX form factor boards. In all other ways, the two North Bridge chips are identical. The SiS 5581/5582 is a single-chip set designed to be a high-performance, low-cost alternative that is functionally equivalent to Intel's 430TX chipset. By having everything in a single chip, a low-cost motherboard can be produced.

The 5581/5582 consists of both North and South Bridge functions, including PCI to ISA bridge function, PCI IDE function, Universal Serial Bus host/hub function, Integrated RTC, and Integrated Keyboard Controller. These chips support a CPU bus speed of 50, 55, 60, 66, and 75MHz.

A maximum of 512KB of L2 cache is supported, with a maximum cacheable range of 128M of main memory. The maximum cacheable range is determined by a combination of cache memory size, and the number of Tag bits used. The most common cache size that will allow caching of up to 128M of RAM will be 512k, although up to 384M of RAM can technically be installed in up to three total banks. Because this is designed for low-cost systems, ECC (Error Correcting Code) or parity functions are not supported. Main memory timing is x-3-3-3 for FPM, while EDO timing is x-2-2-2, and SDRAM timing is x-1-1-1.

The 5581/5582 chipset also includes Advanced Configuration and Power Interface (ACPI) power management, a dual channel Ultra-DMA/33 IDE interface, USB controller, and even the CMOS RAM and Real Time Clock (RTC). PCI v2.1 is supported that allows con-current PCI operation; however, AGP is not supported in this chipset.

5591 and 5592. The SiS 5591/5592 is a three-chip set consisting of either a 5591 or 5592 North Bridge chip along with a SiS5595 South Bridge. The 5591/5592 North Bridge chips are both 3.3v 553-pin BGA package chips, while the 5595 South Bridge chip is a 5v 208-pin PQFP (Plastic Quad Flat Pack) package chip. The SiS5591 North Bridge is targeted for ATX form factor motherboards while the SiS5592 version is intended to be used on the NLX form factor. In all other ways, the two North Bridge chips are identical.

The 5591/5592 North Bridge chips include the Host-to-PCI bridge, the L2 cache control-ler, the DRAM controller, the Accelerated Graphics Port interface, and the PCI IDE con-troller. The SiS5595 South Bridge includes the PCI-to-ISA bridge, the ACPI/APM power management unit, the Universal Serial Bus host/hub interface, and the ISA bus interface that contains the ISA bus controller, the DMA controllers, the interrupt controllers, and the Timers. It also integrates the Keyboard controller and the Real Time Clock (RTC).

The 5591/5592 North Bridge chips support CPU bus speeds of up to 75MHz. They also support up to 1M of L2 cache allowing up to 256M of main memory to be cacheable. The maximum cacheable main memory amount is determined by a combination of cache memory size and the number of Tag bits used. Most common cache sizes will be 512K and 1M. The 512K cache with 7 Tag bits will allow only 64M of memory to be cached, while 8 Tag bits will allow caching of up to 128M. With 1M of cache onboard, the cacheable range is doubled to a maximum of 256M.

A maximum of 256M of total RAM is allowed in up to three banks. Both ECC and parity are supported for mission-critical or file server applications. Main memory timing for FPM memory is x-3-3-3, EDO timing is x-2-2-2, and SDRAM is x-1-1-1.

PCI specification 2.1 is supported at up to 33MHz, and AGP specification 1.0 is supported in both 1x and 2x modes. The separate 5595 South Bridge includes a dual-channel Ultra-DMA/33 interface and support for USB.

Sixth-Generation (P6 Pentium Pro/Pentium II Class) Chipsets

Although Intel clearly dominated the Pentium chipset world, they are virtually the only game in town for the Pentium Pro and Pentium II chipsets. The biggest reason for this is that since the Pentium first came out in 1993, Intel has been introducing new chipsets (and even complete ready-to-go motherboards) simultaneously with their new processors. This makes it hard for anybody else to catch up. Another problem for other chipset manufacturers is that Intel has yet to license the Slot 1 interface used by the Pentium II processor, while the Socket 7 interface used by the Pentium has been freely available for license. Clearly, Intel wants the Pentium II market to themselves.

Even though Intel has refused to license the Slot 1 interface, several of the third-party chipset manufacturers such as VIA Technologies, Acer Laboratories, Inc (ALi), and Silicon integrated Systems (SiS) have recently introduced Pentium II chipsets for Slot 1 motherboards. Without direct licensing, these companies have had to reverse engineer the Slot 1 design, which is perhaps the biggest reason why it has taken so long for third-party Pentium Pro and Pentium II chipsets to come out.

Note that because the Pentium Pro and Pentium II are essentially the same processor with slightly different cache designs, the same chipset can be used for both Socket 8 (Pentium Pro) and Slot 1 (Pentium II) designs. At least that was true for the some of the older P6 class chipsets such as the Intel 440FX. Newer chipsets starting with the 440LX are optimized for the Slot 1 architecture and probably won't be used on Socket 8 designs. This is also true for the Pentium Pro, which is essentially obsolete compared to the Pentium II and is currently being used only in limited file server applications.

Although there are a few newcomers to the P6 chipset market, virtually all Pentium Pro and Pentium II motherboards use Intel chipsets; their market share here is for all practical purposes near 100%.

The sixth-generation P6 (Pentium Pro/II) chipsets continue with the North Bridge/South Bridge design first debuted in the Pentium processor chipsets. In fact, the South Bridge portion of the chipset is the same as that used in many of the Pentium chipsets.

Table 4.6 shows the processors used on Pentium Pro motherboards.

Table 4.6 Pentium Pro Chipsets			
Chipset	**450KX**	**450GX**	**440FX**
Codename	Orion Workstation	Orion Server	Natoma
Date Introduced	Nov. '95	Nov. '95	May '96
Bus Speed	66 MHz	66 MHz	66 MHz
SMP (dual CPUs)	Yes	Yes (4 CPUs)	Yes
Memory Types	FPM	FPM	FPM/EDO/BEDO
Parity/ECC	Both	Both	Both
Maximum Memory	8GGB	1GB	1GB
L2 Cache Type	In CPU	In CPU	In CPU
Maximum Cacheable	1GB	1GB	1GB
PCI Support	2.0	2.0	2.1
AGP Support	No	No	No

Chipset	450KX	450GX	440FX
AGP Speed	n/a	n/a	n/a
South Bridge	various	various	PIIX3

SMP = Symmetric Multi-processing (Dual Processors)
FPM = Fast Page Mode
EDO = Extended Data Out
BEDO = Burst EDO
SDRAM = Synchronous Dynamic RAM
Pburst = Pipeline Burst (Synchronous)
PCI = Peripheral Component Interconnect
AGP = Accelerated Graphics Port
SIO = System I/O
PIIX = PCI ISA IDE Xcelerator

> **Note**
>
> PCI 2.1 supports concurrent PCI operations.

For Pentium II chipsets, Intel offers the chipsets in Table 4.7.

Table 4.7   Pentium II Chipsets

Chipset	440FX	440LX	440EX	440BX
Codename	Natoma	none	none	none
Date Introduced	May '96	Aug. '97	April '98	April '98
Bus Speed	66 MHz	66 MHz	66 MHz	66/100 MHz
SMP (dual CPUs)	Yes	Yes	No	Yes
Memory Types	FPM/EDO/ BEDO	FPM/EDO/ SDRAM	FPM/EDO/ SDRAM	FPM/EDO/ SDRAM
Parity/ECC	Both	Both	Neither	Both
Maximum Memory	1G	1GB EDO/ 512MM SDRAM	256MM	1G
L2 Cache Type	In CPU	In CPU	In CPU	In CPU
Max. Cacheable	1G	1G	1G	1G
PCI Support	2.1	2.1	2.1	2.1
AGP Support	No	AGP-1x	AGP-1x	AGP-2x
AGP Speed	n/a	266M M/sec	266M M/sec	533M M/sec
South Bridge	PIIX3	PIIX4	PIIX4E	PIIX4E

SMP = Symmetric Multi-processing (Dual Processors)
FPM = Fast Page Mode
EDO = Extended Data Out
BEDO = Burst EDO
SDRAM = Synchronous Dynamic RAM
Pburst = Pipeline Burst (Synchronous)
PCI = Peripheral Component Interconnect
AGP = Accelerated Graphics Port
SIO = System I/O
PIIX = PCI ISA IDE Xcelerator

> **Note**
>
> Pentium Pro and Pentium II CPUs have their secondary cache integrated into the CPU package. Therefore, cache characteristics for these machines are not dependent on the chipset but are quite dependent on the Pentium Pro or Pentium II processor instead. Note also that the Pentium II Celeron has no L2 (secondary) cache.

Each Intel chipset is designed as a two-part system, using a North Bridge and a South Bridge component. Often the same South Bridge component can be used with several different North Bridge chipsets. Table 4.8 shows a list of all the current Intel South Bridge components and their capabilities.

Table 4.8   Intel South Bridge Chips

Chip Name	SIO	PIIX	PIIX3	PIIX4	PIIX4E
Part Number	82378IB/ZB	82371FB	82371SB	82371AB	82371EB
IDE Support	None	BMIDE	BMIDE	UDMA	UDMA
USB Support	None	None	Yes	Yes	Yes
CMOS/Clock	No	No	No	Yes	Yes
Power Management	SMM	SMM	SMM	SMM	ACPI 1.0

SIO = System I/O
PIIX = PCI ISA IDE Xcelerator
USB = Universal Serial Bus
IDE = Integrated Drive Electronics (AT Attachment)
BMIDE = Bus Master IDE
UDMA = Ultra-DMA IDE
SMM = System Management Mode
ACPI = Advanced Configuration and Power Interface specification

The following sections examine the P6 chipsets for both the Pentium Pro and Pentium II processors.

Intel 450KX/GX (Orion Workstation/Server). The first chipsets to support the Pentium Pro were actually a pair code-named Orion. The 450KX was designed for workstations while the more powerful 450GX was designed for file servers. The GX server chipset is particularly powerful, as it supports up to 8G of 4-way interleaved memory, quad Pentium Pro processors, and even two separate PCI buses. The 450KX is the workstation or user version of Orion and as such it supports fewer processors (only two) and less memory (1G). Both chipsets support parity or ECC memory.

The 450GX and 450KX North Bridge is comprised of four individual chip components—an 82454KX/GX PCI Bridge, an 82452KX/GX Data Path (DP), an 82453KX/GX Data Controller (DC), and an 82451KX/GX Memory Interface Controller (MIC). Options for

QFP (Quad Flat Pack) or BGA (Ball Grid Array) packaging were available on the PCI Bridge and the DP. BGA uses less space on a board.

The 450's high reliability is obtained through ECC from the Pentium Pro processor data bus to memory. Reliability is also enhanced by parity protection on the processor bus, control bus, and on all PCI signals. In addition, single-bit error correction is provided, thereby avoiding server downtime due to spurious memory errors caused by cosmic rays.

▶▶ See "Memory Reliability," p. 344

Until the introduction of the following 440FX chipset, these were used almost exclusively in file servers. After the debut of the 440FX, the expensive Orion chips all but disappeared due to their complexity and high cost.

Intel 440FX (Natoma). The first mainstream Pentium Pro chipset was the 440FX (code-named Natoma). It is very similar to the 430HX Triton II Pentium chipset, offering improved performance over the Orion at a much lower cost. Even so, the 440FX does not quite match the multiprocessing power of the 450GX chipset, making the latter still preferred for very high-end applications until recently.

The 440FX uses half the number of components than the previous Intel chipset. It offers additional features such as support for the PCI 2.1 (Concurrent PCI) standard, Universal Serial Bus (USB) support, and reliability through Error Checking and Correction (ECC).

The Concurrent PCI processing architecture maximizes system performance with simultaneous activity on the CPU, PCI, and ISA buses. Concurrent PCI provides increased bandwidth to better support 2D/3D graphics, video and audio, and processing for host-based applications. ECC memory support delivers improved reliability to business system users.

The main features of this chipset include:

- Support for up to 1G of EDO memory
- Full 1G cacheability (based on the processor because the L2 cache and tag are in the CPU)
- Support for USB
- Support for BusMaster IDE
- Full parity/ECC support

The 440FX consists of a two-chip North Bridge. The main component is the 82441FX PCI Bridge and Memory controller, along with the 82442FX Data Bus accelerator for the PCI bus. This chipset uses the PIIX3 82371SB South Bridge chip that supports high-speed busmaster DMA IDE interfaces and USB, and it acts as the bridge between the PCI and ISA buses.

Note that this was the first P6 chipset to support EDO memory, but it lacked support for the faster SDRAM. Also, the PIIX3 used with this chipset does not support the faster Ultra DMA IDE hard drives.

The 440FX was the chipset used on the first Pentium II motherboards, which have the same basic architecture as the Pentium Pro. The Pentium II was released several months before the chipset that was supposedly designed for it was ready, and so early PII motherboards used the older 440FX chipset. This chipset was never designed with the Pentium II in mind, while the newer 440LX was optimized specifically to take advantage of the Pentium II architecture. For that reason, I normally recommended that people stay away from the original 440FX-based PII motherboards and wait for Pentium II systems that used the forthcoming 440LX chipset. When the new chipset was introduced, the 440FX was quickly superseded by the improved 440LX design.

Intel 440LX. The 440LX quickly took over in the marketplace after it debuted in August of '97. This was the first chipset to really take full advantage of the Pentium II processor. Compared to the 440FX, the 440LX chipset offers several improvements:

- Support for the new Advanced Graphics Port (AGP) video card bus

- Support for 66MHz SDRAM memory

- Support for the Ultra DMA IDE interface

- Support for Universal Serial Bus (USB)

The 440LX rapidly became the most popular chip for all new Pentium II systems from the end of '97 through the beginning of '98.

Intel 440EX. The 440EX is designed to be a low-cost lower performance alternative to the 440LX chipset. It was introduced in April '98 along with the Intel Celeron low-end Pentium II processor. The 440EX lacks several features in the more powerful 440LX, including dual processor and ECC or parity memory support. This chipset is basically designed for low-end 66MHz bus-based systems that use the new Intel Celeron low-end Pentium II processor. Note that boards with the 440EX will fully support a full blown Pentium II but lack some of the features of the more powerful 440LX or 440BX chipsets.

The main things to note about the 440EX are:

- Designed with a feature set tuned for the low-end PC market

- Primarily for the Intel Celeron processor

- Supports AGP

- Does not support ECC or parity memory

- Single processor support only

Although it is based on the core technology of the Intel 440LX, the 440EX is basically considered a lower-feature, lower-reliability version of that chipset designed for non-mission-critical systems.

The 440EX consists of a 82443EX PCI AGP Controller (PAC) North Bridge component and the new 82371EB (PIIX4E) South Bridge chip. Although this chipset is fine for most low-end use, I would normally recommend the faster, more powerful, and more reliable (with ECC memory) 440BX instead.

Intel 440BX. The Intel 440BX chipset was introduced in April of '98 and is the first chipset to run the processor host bus (and basically the motherboard) at 100MHz. This is designed specifically to support the newer Pentium II processors at 350MHz, 400MHz, or 450MHz. A mobile version of this chipset also is the first Pentium II chipset for notebook or laptop systems.

The main change from the 440LX to the BX is that the 440BX chipset improves performance by increasing the bandwidth of the system bus from 66MHz to 100MHz. The chipset can run at either 66- or 100MHz, allowing one basic motherboard design to support all Pentium II processor speeds from 233MHz to 450MHz and beyond.

Intel 440BX Highlights:

- Supports 100MHz SDRAM

- Supports both 100MHz or 66MHz system and memory bus designs

- Supports ACPI (Advanced Configuration and Power Interface specification)

- The first chipset to support the Mobile Intel Pentium II processor.

▶▶ See "Mobile Pentium II," p. 919

The Intel 440BX consists of a single North Bridge chip called the 82443BX Host Bridge/ Controller, which is paired with a new 82371EB PCI-ISA/IDE Xcelerator (PIIX4E) South Bridge chip. The new South Bridge adds support for the ACPI specification version 1.0.

The 440BX is currently the highest-end chipset in the Intel arsenal for standard desktop users. It offers superior performance and high reliability through the use of ECC (Error Correcting Code), SDRAM (Synchronous DRAM), and DIMMs (Dual Inline Memory Modules).

If you are in the market for a new Pentium II-based system, I would recommend a motherboard with this chipset.

Third-Party (Non-Intel) P6 Class Chipsets

Acer Laboratories, Inc. (ALi)

Aladdin Pro II. The Acer Labs (ALi) Aladdin Pro II M1621 is a two-chip set for P6 (Pentium Pro and Pentium II) processors consisting of two BGA package chips, the 456-pin BGA package M1621 North Bridge, and either the M1533 or M1543 South Bridge. This is one of the first Slot 1 P6 processor chipsets from a company other than Intel.

The M1621 North Bridge includes an AGP, memory and I/O controller, and a data path with multiport buffers for data acceleration. It can support multiple Pentium II processors with bus speeds of 60, 66, and 100MHz. This chipset is equivalent to the 440BX chipset from Intel.

The integrated memory controller supports FPM, EDO, and SDRAM with a total capacity of up to 1G (SDRAM) or 2G (EDO). ECC (Error Correcting Code) memory is supported, allowing use in mission-critical or fileserver applications. Memory timing is x-1-1-1-1-1-1-1 in back-to-back SDRAM reads, or x-2-2-2-2-2-2-2 in back-to-back EDO reads.

The M1621 supports AGP v1.0, in both 1x and 2x modes, and is fully compliant with PCI Rev. 2.1, allowing for concurrent PCI operations. The M1621 can be used with either the M1533 South Bridge or M1543 South Bridge/Super I/O combo chips.

The M1533 South Bridge includes the following features:

- PCI-to-ISA Bridge

- Built-in keyboard/mouse controller

- Enhanced Power Management featuring ACPI (Advanced Configuration and Power Interface)

- Two-port USB interface

- Dual channel Ultra-DMA/33 IDE host adapter

- 328-pin BGA package

M1543 includes all features in the 1533 plus fully integrated Super I/O, including a Floppy Disk Controller, two high-speed serial ports, and one multimode parallel port.

VIA Technologies

Apollo P6/97. The VT82C680 Apollo P6 is a high-performance, cost-effective, and energy-efficient chipset for the implementation of PCI/ISA desktop and notebook personal computer systems based on 64-bit Intel P6 processors. This was one of the first non-Intel P6 chipsets of any kind available and is functionally equivalent to the Intel 440FX chipset. The Apollo P6 chipset supports dual processor configurations with up to 66MHz external CPU bus speed. The DRAM and PCI bus are also independently powered so that each of the buses can be run at 3.3v or 5v. The ISA bus always runs at 5v. The Apollo P6 supports up to 1G of DRAM. This chipset never really achieved much popularity in the market.

Apollo Pro. The Apollo Pro is a high-performance chipset for Slot 1 mobile and desktop PC systems. The Apollo Pro includes support for advanced system power management capability for both desktop and mobile PC applications, PC100 SDRAM, AGP 2x mode, and multiple CPU/DRAM timing configurations. The Apollo Pro chipset is comparable in features to the 440BX and PIIX4e chipset from Intel, and represents one of the first non-Intel chipsets to support the Socket 1 architecture.

The VIA Apollo Pro consists of two devices—the VT82C691 North Bridge chip and the VT82C596, a BGA-packaged South Bridge with a full set of mobile, power-management features. For cost-effective desktop designs, the VT82C691 can also be configured with the VT82C586B South Bridge.

The VT82C691 Apollo Pro North Bridge supports all Slot-1 (Intel Pentium II) and Socket-8 (Intel Pentium Pro) processors. The Apollo Pro also supports the 66MHz and the newer 100 MHz CPU external bus speed required by the 350MHz and faster Pentium II processors. AGP v1.0 and PCI 2.1 are also supported, as are FPM, EDO, and SDRAM. Different DRAM types may be used in mixed combinations in up to eight banks and up to 1G of DRAM. EDO memory timing is 5-2-2-2-2-2-2-2 for back-to-back accesses, and SDRAM timing is 6-1-1-1-2-1-1-1 for back-to-back accesses.

The VT82C596 South Bridge supports both ACPI (Advanced Configuration and Power Interface) and APM (Advanced Power Management), and includes an integrated USB Controller, and dual UltraDMA-66 EIDE ports.

Silicon integrated Systems (SiS)

SiS5600/5595. The 5600/5595 chipset was introduced in June of 1998 and is designed for low-cost Celeron CPUs with a 66MHz or 100MHz host bus. SiS intends to use this low-cost chipset to help push the Pentium II PC technology toward the sub-$1,000 PC market.

Super I/O Chips

The third major chip seen on most PC motherboards is called the Super I/O chip. This is a chip that normally integrates devices formerly found on separate expansion cards in older systems.

Most Super I/O chips contain at a minimum the following components:

- Floppy controller
- Dual serial port controllers
- Parallel port controller

The floppy controllers on most Super I/O chips will handle two drives, but some of them can only handle one. Older systems often required a separate floppy controller card.

The dual serial port is another item that was formerly on one or more cards. Most of the better Super I/O chips implement a buffered serial port design known as a UART (Universal Asynchronous Receiver Transmitter), one for each port. Most mimic the standalone NS16550A high-speed UART, which was created by National Semiconductor. By putting the function of two of these chips into the Super I/O chip, we essentially have these ports built into the motherboard.

Virtually all Super I/O chips also include a high-speed multimode parallel port. The better ones allow three modes, called standard (bidirectional), Enhanced Parallel Port (EPP), and the Enhanced Capabilities Port (ECP) modes. The ECP mode is the fastest and most powerful, but selecting it also means your port will use an ISA bus 8-bit DMA channel, usually DMA channel 3. As long as you account for this and don't set anything else to that channel (such as a sound card, and so on), then the EPC mode parallel port should work fine. Some of the newer printers and scanners that connect to the system via the parallel port will use ECP mode, which was initially invented by Hewlett Packard.

The Super I/O chip may contain other components, as well. For example, currently the most popular Pentium II motherboard on the market—the Intel SE440BX ATX motherboard—uses an SMC (Standard Microsystems Corp.) FDC37C777 Super I/O chip. This chip incorporates the following functions:

- Single floppy drive interface

- Two high-speed serial ports

- One ECP/EPP multimode parallel port

- 8042-style keyboard and mouse controller

Only the keyboard and mouse controller are surprising here; all the other components are in most Super I/O chips. The integrated keyboard and mouse controller saves the need to have this chip as a separate part on the board.

One thing I've noticed over the years is that the role of the Super I/O chip has decreased more and more in the newer motherboards. This is primarily due to Intel moving Super I/O functions such as IDE directly into the chipset South Bridge component, where these devices can attach to the PCI bus rather than the ISA bus. One of the shortcomings of the Super I/O chip is that it is interfaced to the system via the ISA bus, and shares all the speed and performance limitations of that 8MHz bus. Moving the IDE over to the PCI bus allowed higher-speed IDE drives to be developed that could transfer at the faster 33MHz PCI bus speed.

As Intel combines more and more functions into their main chipset, and as USB-based peripherals replace standard serial, parallel, and floppy controller-based devices, we will probably see the Super I/O chip fade away on some future motherboard designs. At least one of the third-party chipsets has already combined the South Bridge and Super I/O chip into a single component, saving space and reducing parts count on the motherboard.

BIOS

All motherboards must have a special chip containing software we call the BIOS or ROM BIOS. ROM stands for Read Only Memory, and BIOS stands for Basic Input/Output System. This chip contains the startup programs and drivers that are used to get the system running and act as the interface to the basic hardware in the system. There is also a POST (Power-On Self Test) in the BIOS that tests the major components in the system when you turn it on, and normally a SETUP program used to store system configuration data in the CMOS (Complementary Metal-Oxide Semiconductor) memory powered by a battery on the motherboard.

The BIOS is a collection of programs embedded in an *EPROM* (Erasable Programmable Read-Only Memory) or *EEPROM* (Electrically Erasable PROM)—otherwise called a Flash

ROM chip or chips, depending on the design of your computer. That collection of programs is the first thing loaded when you start your computer, even before the operating system. Simply put, the BIOS in most PCs has four main functions:

- *POST—Power-On Self Test.* The POST tests your computer's processor, memory, chipset, video adapter, disk controllers, disk drives, keyboard, and other crucial components.

- *Bootstrap loader.* A routine that finds the operating system and loads, or boots, it. If an operating system is found, it is loaded and given control of your computer.

- *BIOS—Basic Input Output System.* This refers to the collection of actual drivers used to act as a basic interface between the operating system and your hardware. When running DOS or Windows in Safe Mode, you are running solely on BIOS drivers.

- *CMOS setup.* System configuration and setup program. This is a normally menu-driven program that allows you to configure the motherboard and chipset settings, along with the date and time, passwords, disk drives, and other basic system settings. Some older systems did not have the Setup program in ROM and required that you boot from a special Setup disk.

The following section discusses the motherboard BIOS.

▶▶ See "ROM," p. 304

ROM BIOS Compatibility. The issue of ROM BIOS compatibility is important. If the BIOS is not compatible with the PC standard IBM originally created, any number of problems can result. The BIOS is the interface between the system hardware and the operating system, so compatibility with popular operating systems like Windows is important. By including drivers in the BIOS for any unique or custom components, a system manufacturer can ensure that any of these components will work with the popular operating systems and software on the market.

OEMs. Many OEMs (Original Equipment Manufacturers) have developed their own compatible ROMs independently. Companies such as Compaq and AT&T have developed their own BIOS products that are comparable to those offered by AMI, Phoenix, and others. These companies also offer upgrades to newer versions that often can offer more features and improvements or fix problems with the older versions. If you use a system with a proprietary ROM, make sure that it is from a larger company with a track record and one that will provide updates and fixes as necessary. Ideally, upgrades should be available for download from the Internet.

Other OEMs have their BIOS written for them by a third-party company. For example, Hewlett Packard systems have a custom proprietary design, and, as such, need a unique BIOS. Rather than write their own, they contract with Phoenix, a well-known BIOS supplier, to develop the motherboard BIOSs used in all the HP Vectra PCs. Note that even though Phoenix may have done the development, you still have to get any upgrades or fixes from Hewlett Packard.

Several companies have specialized in the development of a compatible ROM BIOS product. The three major companies that come to mind in discussing ROM BIOS software are American Megatrends, Inc. (AMI), Award Software, and Phoenix Software. Each company licenses its ROM BIOS to a motherboard manufacturer so that the manufacturer can worry about the hardware rather than the software. To obtain one of these ROMs for a motherboard, the OEM must answer many questions about the design of the system so that the proper BIOS can be either developed or selected from those already designed. Combining a ROM BIOS and a motherboard is not a haphazard task. No single, generic, compatible ROM exists, either. AMI, Award, Microid Research, and Phoenix ship many variations of their BIOS code to different board manufacturers, each one custom-tailored to that specific motherboard.

Recently, there have been some big changes in the BIOS industry. Phoenix landed a contract with Intel, and now provides all of Intel's motherboard BIOSes, replacing AMI who previously had the contract. This is a big deal because Intel sells about 80% or more of all PC motherboards. What that basically means is that if you purchase a PC today, you will probably be getting an Intel-made motherboard with the new Phoenix BIOS.

Another development is that in mid-'98, Phoenix bought Award, and all of their new products will be under the Phoenix name. Thus the big-3 BIOS developers are now reduced to the big-2—Phoenix and AMI. Most of the offshore motherboard manufacturers still continue to use the AMI BIOS. However, Phoenix is currently the leading BIOS company. They are not only developing the BIOS for most newer systems on the market, but they also are the primary BIOS developer responsible for new BIOS development and new BIOS standards.

AMI. Although AMI customizes the ROM code for a particular system, it does not sell the ROM source code to the OEM. An OEM must obtain each new release as it becomes available. Because many OEMs don't need or want every new version developed, they might skip several version changes before licensing a new one. The AMI BIOS is currently the most popular BIOS in PC systems. Newer versions of the AMI BIOS are called Hi-Flex due to the high flexibility found in the BIOS configuration program. The AMI Hi-Flex BIOS is used in Intel, AMI, and many other manufacturers' motherboards. One special AMI feature is that it is the only third-party BIOS manufacturer to make its own motherboard.

During powerup, the BIOS ID string is displayed on the lower left of the screen. This string tells you valuable information about which BIOS version you have, and certain settings that are determined by the built-in setup program.

> **Tip**
>
> A good trick to help you view the BIOS ID string is to shut down and either unplug your keyboard, or hold down a key as you power back on. This will cause a keyboard error, and the string will remained displayed.

The primary BIOS Identification string (ID String 1) is displayed by any AMI BIOS during the POST (Power-On Self Test) at the bottom-left corner of the screen, below the copyright message. Two additional BIOS ID strings (ID String 2 and 3) can be displayed by the AMI Hi-Flex BIOS by pressing the Insert key during POST. These additional ID strings display the options that are installed in the BIOS.

The general BIOS ID String 1 format for older AMI BIOS versions is shown in Table 4.9.

Table 4.9   ABBB-NNNN-mmddyy-KK

Position	Description
A	BIOS Options: D = Diagnostics built-in. S = Setup built-in. E = Extended Setup built-in.
BBB	Chipset or Motherboard Identifier: C&T = Chips & Technologies chipset. NET = C&T NEAT 286 chipset. 286 = Standard 286 motherboard. SUN = Suntac chipset. PAQ = Compaq motherboard. INT = Intel motherboard. AMI = AMI motherboard. G23 = G2 chipset 386 motherboard.
NNNN	The manufacturer license code reference number.
mmddyy	The BIOS release date, mm/dd/yy.
KK	The AMI keyboard BIOS version number.

The BIOS ID String 1 format for AMI Hi-Flex BIOS versions is shown in Table 4.10.

Table 4.10   AB-CCcc-DDDDDD-EFGHIJKL-mmddyy-MMMMMMMM-N

Position	Description
A	Processor Type: 0 = 8086 or 8088. 2 = 286. 3 = 386. 4 = 486. 5 = Pentium. 6 = Pentium Pro/II.
B	Size of BIOS: 0 = 64K BIOS. 1 = 128K BIOS.

(continues)

Table 4.10 AB-CCcc-DDDDDD-EFGHIJKL-mmddyy-MMMMMMMM-N Continued

Position	Description
CCcc	Major and Minor BIOS version number.
DDDDDD	Manufacturer license code reference number.
	0036xx = AMI 386 motherboard, xx = Series #.
	0046xx = AMI 486 motherboard, xx = Series #.
	0056xx = AMI Pentium motherboard, xx = Series #.
	0066xx = AMI Pentium Pro motherboard, xx = Series #.
E	1 = Halt on Post Error.
F	1 = Initialize CMOS every boot.
G	1 = Block pins 22 and 23 of the keyboard controller.
H	1 = Mouse support in BIOS/keyboard controller.
I	1 = Wait for <F1> key on POST errors.
J	1 = Display floppy error during POST.
K	1 = Display video error during POST.
L	1 = Display keyboard error during POST.
mmddyy	BIOS Date, mm/dd/yy.
MMMMMMMM	Chipset identifier or BIOS name.
N	Keyboard controller version number.

AMI Hi-Flex BIOS ID String 2 is shown in Table 4.11.

Table 4.11 AAB-C-DDDD-EE-FF-GGGG-HH-II-JJJ

Position	Description
AA	Keyboard controller pin number for clock switching.
B	Keyboard controller clock switching pin function: H = High signal switches clock to high speed. L = High signal switches clock to low speed.
C	Clock switching through chipset registers: 0 = Disable. 1 = Enable.
DDDD	Port address to switch clock high.
EE	Data value to switch clock high.
FF	Mask value to switch clock high.
GGGG	Port Address to switch clock low.
HH	Data value to switch clock low.
II	Mask value to switch clock low.
JJJ	Pin number for Turbo Switch Input.

AMI Hi-Flex BIOS ID String 3 is shown in Table 4.12.

Table 4.12   AAB-C-DDD-EE-FF-GGGG-HH-II-JJ-K-L

Position	Description
AA	Keyboard controller pin number for cache control.
B	Keyboard controller cache control pin function: H = High signal enables the cache. L = High signal disables the cache.
C	1 = High signal is used on the keyboard controller pin.
DDD	Cache control through chipset registers: 0 = Cache control off. 1 = Cache control on.
EE	Port address to enable cache.
FF	Data value to enable cache.
GGGG	Mask value to enable cache.
HH	Port address to disable cache.
II	Data value to disable cache.
JJ	Mask value to disable cache.
K	Pin number for resetting the 82335 memory controller.
L	BIOS Modification Flag: 0 = The BIOS has not been modified. 1–9, A–Z = Number of times the BIOS has been modified.

The AMI BIOS has many features, including a built-in setup program activated by pressing the Delete or Esc key in the first few seconds of booting up your computer. The BIOS will prompt you briefly as to which key to press and when to press it. The AMI BIOS offers user-definable hard disk types, essential for optimal use of many IDE or ESDI drives. The 1995 and newer BIOS versions also support Enhanced IDE drives and will auto-configure the drive parameters.

A unique feature of some of the AMI BIOS versions was, in addition to the setup, they had a built-in, menu-driven diagnostics package, essentially a very limited version of the standalone AMIDIAG product. The internal diagnostics are not a replacement for more comprehensive disk-based programs, but they can help in a pinch. The menu-driven diagnostics do not do extensive memory testing, for example, and the hard disk low-level formatter works only at the BIOS level rather than at the controller register level. These limitations often have prevented it from being capable of formatting severely damaged disks. Most newer AMI BIOS versions no longer include the full diagnostics.

AMI doesn't produce BIOS documentation; they leave that up to the motherboard manufacturers who include their BIOS on the motherboard. However, AMI has published a detailed version of their documentation called the *Programmer's Guide to the AMIBIOS*, published by Windcrest/McGraw-Hill and available under the ISBN 0-07-001561-9. This is a book written by AMI engineers that describes all the BIOS functions, features, error codes, and more. I would recommend this book to anybody with an AMI BIOS in their system, as this provides a complete version of the documentation for which they may have been looking.

The AMI BIOS is sold through distributors, a list of which is available at **http://www.ami.com/distributor.html**. However, keep in mind that you cannot buy upgrades and replacements directly from AMI.

Award. Award is unique among BIOS manufacturers because it sells its BIOS code to the OEM and allows the OEM to customize the BIOS. Of course, then the BIOS no longer is Award BIOS, but rather a highly customized version. AST uses this approach on its systems, as do other manufacturers, for total control over the BIOS code without having to write it from scratch. Although AMI and Phoenix customize the ROM code for a particular system, they do not sell the ROM's source code to the OEM. Some OEMs that seem to have developed their own ROM code started with a base of source code licensed to them by Award or some other company.

The Award BIOS has all the normal features you expect, including a built-in setup program activated by pressing Ctrl+Alt+Esc or a particular key on startup (normally prompted on the screen). This setup offers user-definable drive types, required in order to fully use IDE or ESDI hard disks. The POST is good, and Award runs technical support on its Web site at **http://www.award.com**.

Award was purchased by Phoenix in mid-1998 and no longer produces a BIOS under the Award name. However, they will continue to support their past BIOS versions and develop updates if necessary.

Phoenix. The Phoenix BIOS for many years has been a standard of compatibility by which others are judged. It was one of the first third-party companies to legally reverse-engineer the IBM BIOS using a "clean room" approach. In this approach, a group of engineers studied the IBM BIOS and wrote a specification for how that BIOS should work and what features should be incorporated. This information then was passed to a second group of engineers who had never seen the IBM BIOS. They could then legally write a new BIOS to the specifications set forth by the first group. This work would then be unique and not a copy of IBM's BIOS; however, it would function the same way.

The Phoenix BIOS excels in two areas that put it high on my list of recommendations. One is that the POST is excellent. The BIOS outputs an extensive set of beep codes that can be used to diagnose severe motherboard problems that would prevent normal operation of the system. In fact, this POST can isolate memory failures in Bank 0 right down to the individual SIMM or DIMM module with beep codes alone. The Phoenix BIOS also has an excellent setup program free from unnecessary frills, but that offers all the features one would expect, such as user-definable drive types, and so on. The built-in setup is activated by pressing either Ctrl+Alt+S, Ctrl+Alt+Esc, or a particular key on startup such as F2, depending on the version of BIOS you have.

The second area in which Phoenix excels is the documentation. Not only are the manuals that you get with the system detailed, but also Phoenix has written a set of BIOS technical-reference manuals that are a standard in the industry. The set consists of three books, titled *System BIOS for IBM PC/XT/AT Computers and Compatibles, CBIOS for IBM PS/2 Computers and Compatibles*, and *ABIOS for IBM PS/2 Computers and Compatibles*. In addition to being an excellent reference for the Phoenix BIOS, these books serve as an outstanding overall reference to the BIOS in general.

Phoenix has extensive technical support and documentation on their Web site at **http://www.phoenix.com**, as does their largest nationwide distributor, Micro Firmware, Inc. at **http://www.firmware.com**, or check the phone numbers listed in the vendor list in Appendix A. Micro Firmware offers upgrades to many older systems with a Phoenix BIOS, including many Packard Bell, Gateway 2000 (with Micronics motherboards), Micron Technologies, and other systems.

These companies' products are established as ROM BIOS standards in the industry, and frequent updates and improvements ensure that a system containing these ROMs will have a long life of upgrades and service.

Upgrading the ROM BIOS

In this section, you learn that ROM BIOS upgrades can improve a system in many ways. You also learn that the upgrades can be difficult and may require much more than plugging in a generic set of ROM chips.

The *ROM BIOS*, or read-only memory basic input/output system, provides the crude brains that get your computer's components working together. A simple BIOS upgrade can often give your computer better performance and more features.

The BIOS is the reason why different operating systems can operate on virtually any PC-compatible system despite hardware differences. Because the BIOS communicates with the hardware, the BIOS must be specific to the hardware and match it completely. Instead of creating their own BIOSs, many computer makers buy a BIOS from specialists such as American Megatrends, Inc. (AMI), Award Software (now part of Phoenix), Microid Research, or Phoenix Technologies Ltd. A motherboard manufacturer that wants to license a BIOS must undergo a lengthy process of working with the BIOS company to tailor the BIOS code to the hardware. This process is what makes upgrading a BIOS somewhat problematic; the BIOS usually resides on ROM chips on the motherboard and is specific to that motherboard model or revision. In other words, you must get your BIOS upgrades from your motherboard manufacturer.

▶▶ See "ROM," p. 304

In older systems, you often must upgrade the BIOS to take advantage of some other upgrade. To install some of the larger and faster IDE (Integrated Drive Electronics) hard drives and LS-120 (120 megabyte) floppy drives in older machines, for example, you may need a BIOS upgrade. Some machines are still being sold with older BIOSs that do not support hard drives larger than 8GB, for example.

The following list shows the primary functions of a ROM BIOS upgrade:

- Adding LS-120 (120M) floppy drive support
- Adding support for hard drives greater than 8G
- Adding support for Ultra-DMA/33 IDE hard drives
- Adding support for bootable ATAPI CD-ROM drives
- Adding or improving Plug-and-Play support and compatibility
- Correcting year-2000 and leap-year bugs
- Correcting known bugs or compatibility problems with certain hardware and software
- Upgrading the CPU

For most BIOS upgrades, you must contact the motherboard manufacturer by phone or download the upgrade from their Web site. You will need to know the following information:

- The make and model of the motherboard or system unit
- The type of CPU (for example, Pentium MMX, AMD K6, Cyrix/IBM 6x86MX, MII, Pentium II, and so on)
- The version of the existing BIOS

You can normally identify the BIOS you have by watching the screen when the system is first powered up. It helps to turn the monitor on first as some take a few seconds to warm up and often the BIOS information is displayed for only a few seconds. You can also often find the BIOS ID information in the CMOS Setup.

After you have this information, you should be able to contact the motherboard manufacturer to see if there is a new BIOS for your system. If you go to their Web site, check to see whether there is a version newer than the one you have. If so, you can download it and install it in your system.

Keyboard-Controller Chips. Besides the main system ROM, AT-class (286 and higher) computers also have a keyboard controller or keyboard ROM, which is a keyboard-controller microprocessor with its own built-in ROM. This is often found in the South Bridge of the chipset or even the Super I/O chip on some boards. The keyboard controller usually is an Intel 8042 microcontroller, which incorporates a microprocessor, RAM, ROM, and I/O ports. The keyboard controller was originally a 40-pin chip that often had a copyright notice identifying the BIOS code programmed into the chip. Modern boards have this function integrated into the chipset.

The keyboard controller controls the reset and A20 lines and also deciphers the keyboard scan codes. The A20 line is used in extended memory and other protected-mode operations. In many systems, one of the unused ports is used to select the CPU clock speed. Because of the tie-in with the keyboard controller and protected-mode operation, many problems with keyboard controllers became evident when upgrading from DOS to either Windows or OS/2 on these older systems. If you experience lockups or keyboard problems with either Windows or OS/2 software—or with any software that runs in protected mode, such as Lotus 1-2-3 Release 3.x—get a replacement from your BIOS vendor or system-board vendor.

Problems with the keyboard controller were solved in most systems in the early 1990s, so you shouldn't have to deal with this issue in systems newer than that. With older systems, when you upgraded the BIOS in the system, the BIOS vendor often included a new keyboard controller.

Using a Flash BIOS. Virtually all PCs built since 1996 include a Flash ROM to store the BIOS. A Flash ROM is a type of *EEPROM* (Electrically Erasable Programmable Read-Only Memory) chip that you can erase and reprogram directly in the system without special equipment. Older EPROMs required a special ultraviolet light source and an EPROM programmer device to erase and reprogram them, while Flash ROMs can be erased and rewritten without even removing them from the system.

Using Flash ROM enables a user to download ROM upgrades from a Web site or receive them on disk; you then can load the upgrade into the Flash ROM chip on the motherboard without removing and replacing the chip. Normally, these upgrades are downloaded from the manufacturer's Web site, and then an included utility is used to create a bootable floppy with the new BIOS image and the update program. It is important to run this procedure from a boot floppy so there is no other software or drivers in the way that might interfere with the update. This method saves time and money for both the system manufacturer and the end user.

Sometimes the Flash ROM in a system is write-protected, and you must disable the protection before performing an update, usually by means of a jumper or switch that controls the lock on the ROM update. Without the lock, any program that knows the right instructions can rewrite the ROM in your system—not a comforting thought. Without the write protection, it is conceivable that virus programs could be written that copy themselves directly into the ROM BIOS code in your system. Even without a physical write-protect lock, modern Flash ROM BIOSs have a security algorithm that helps to prevent unauthorized updates. This is the technique that Intel uses on their motherboards.

Note that motherboard manufacturers will not notify you when they upgrade the BIOS for a particular board. You must periodically log into their Web site to check for updates. Normally, any Flash updates are free.

Before proceeding with a BIOS upgrade, you must first locate and download the updated BIOS from your motherboard manufacturer. Consult Appendix A, "Vendor List," to find the Web site address or other contact information for your motherboard manufacturer. Log in to their Web site and follow the menus to the BIOS updates page, and then select and download the new BIOS for your motherboard.

The BIOS upgrade utility is contained in a self-extracting archive file that can be initially downloaded to your hard drive, but it must be extracted and copied to a floppy before the upgrade can proceed. Different motherboard manufacturers have slightly different procedures and programs to accomplish a Flash ROM upgrade, so it is best if you read the directions normally included with the update. I will include instructions here for Intel motherboards because they are by far the most common.

The Intel BIOS upgrade utility will fit on a floppy disk and provides the capability to save, verify, and update the system BIOS. The upgrade utility also provides the capability to install alternate languages for BIOS messages and the SETUP utility.

The first step in the upgrade after downloading the new BIOS file is to enter CMOS setup and write down your existing CMOS settings because they will be erased during the upgrade. Then you will create a DOS boot floppy, and uncompress or extract the BIOS upgrade files to the floppy from the file you downloaded. Then you reboot on the newly created upgrade disk and follow the menus for the actual reflash procedure.

Here is a step-by-step procedure for the process:

1. Save your CMOS RAM setup configuration. You can do so by pressing the appropriate key during boot (F1 with an AMI BIOS, F2 with a Phoenix BIOS) and write down all your current CMOS settings. You will need to reset these settings after you have upgraded to the latest BIOS. Write down all settings that are unique to the system. These settings will be needed later to reconfigure the system. Pay special attention to any hard drive settings: These are very important. If you fail to restore these properly, you may not be able to boot from the drive or access the data on it.

2. Exit the BIOS Setup and restart the system. Allow the system to fully start Windows and bring up a DOS prompt window or boot directly to a DOS prompt via the Windows Start menu (for example, press F8 when you see "Starting Windows," and select Command Prompt).

3. Place a floppy disk in the A: floppy drive and format the floppy using the /S option on the FORMAT command as follows:

   ```
   C:\>FORMAT A: /S
   ```

4. Alternatively, if you have an otherwise blank preformatted floppy in the floppy drive use the SYS command to make it bootable as follows:

   ```
   C:\>SYS A:
   ```

5. The file you originally downloaded from the Intel Web site will be a self-extracting compressed archive that includes other files that need to be extracted. Put the file in a temporary directory, then from within this directory, double-click the BIOS file you downloaded or type the file name of the file and press Enter. This will cause

the file to self-extract. For example, if the file you downloaded was called SEBIOS04.EXE (for the Intel SE440BX motherboard), you would enter the following command:

```
C:\TEMP>SEBIOS04 <enter>
```

6. The extracted files resulting from this should contain a file named BIOS.EXE and a software license text file. You then do another extract on the BIOS.EXE file to the bootable floppy you created using the following command:

```
C:\TEMP>BIOS A:
```

7. Now you can restart the system with the bootable floppy in drive A: containing the new BIOS files you just extracted. Upon booting from this disk, the IFLASH program will automatically start; press Enter when prompted.

8. Highlight `Save flash memory area to a file` and press Enter. Follow the prompts to enter a filename. This will create a backup of your existing BIOS. This will be valuable should the new BIOS cause unexpected problems.

9. Highlight `Update Flash Memory From a File` and press Enter. Follow the prompts to select the name of the BIOS image file you will use to update the Flash ROM. Press the Tab key to highlight the filename and press Enter.

10. The system will now give a warning stating that continuing will destroy the current contents of the flash memory area. Press Enter to continue—the update should take about three minutes. Do not interrupt this procedure or the Flash BIOS will be corrupted.

11. When you're told that the BIOS has been successfully loaded, remove the bootable floppy from the drive and press Enter to reboot the system.

12. Press F1 or F2 to enter Setup. On the first screen within SETUP, check the BIOS version to ensure that it is the new version.

13. In Setup, load the default values. If you have an AMI BIOS, press the F5 key; with a Phoenix BIOS go to the Exit submenu and highlight `Load Setup Defaults` and press Enter. If you do not set the values back to default, the system may function erratically.

14. If the system had unique settings, re-enter those settings now. Press F10 to save the values, exit Setup, and restart the system. Your system should now be fully functional with the new BIOS.

Note

If you encounter a CMOS checksum error or other problems after rebooting, try rebooting the system again. CMOS checksum errors require that you enter Setup, check and save your settings, and exit Setup a second time.

Flash BIOS Recovery. When you performed the Flash reprogramming, you should have seen a warning message on the screen similar to the following:

> "The BIOS is currently being updated. DO NOT REBOOT OR POWER DOWN until the update is completed (typically within three minutes)..."

If you fail to heed this warning or something interrupts the update procedure, you will be left with a system that has a corrupted BIOS. This means you will not be able to restart the system and redo the procedure, at least not easily. Depending on the mother-board, you may have to replace the Flash ROM chip with one that was preprogrammed by the motherboard manufacturer because your board will be nonfunctional until a non-corrupted ROM is present. This is why I still keep my trusty ROM burner around; it is very useful for those motherboards with socketed Flash ROM chips. In minutes, I can use the ROM burner to reprogram the chip and reinstall it in the board. If you need a ROM programmer, I recommend either Andromeda Research or Bytek (see Appendix A, "Vendor List").

In most systems today, the Flash ROM is soldered into the motherboard so it cannot be replaced, rendering the reprogramming idea moot. However, this doesn't mean that the only way out is a complete motherboard replacement: Most motherboards with soldered-in Flash ROMs have a special BIOS Recovery procedure that can be performed. This hinges on a special unerasable part of the Flash ROM that is reserved for this purpose.

In the unlikely event that a Flash upgrade is interrupted catastrophically, the BIOS may be left in an unusable state. Recovering from this condition requires the following steps. A minimum of a power supply, speaker, and a floppy drive configured as drive A: should be attached to the motherboard for this procedure to work.

1. Change the Flash Recovery jumper to the recovery mode position. Virtually all Intel motherboards and many third-party motherboards have a jumper or switch for BIOS recovery, which is normally labeled "Recover/Normal." Figure 4.9 shows this jumper on the Intel SE440BX, a typical motherboard.

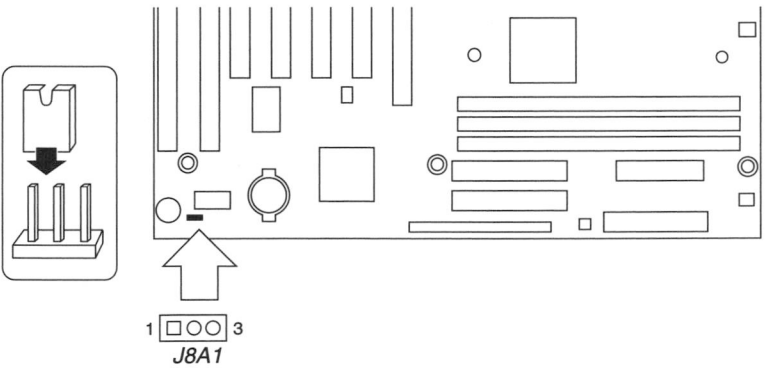

FIG. 4.9 Typical Intel motherboard BIOS recovery jumper.

2. Install the bootable BIOS upgrade disk you previously created to do the Flash upgrade into drive A: and reboot the system.

Because of the small amount of code available in the nonerasable Flash boot block area, no video prompts are available to direct the procedure. In other words, you will see nothing on the screen. In fact, it is not even necessary for a video card to be connected for this procedure to work. The procedure can be monitored by listening to the speaker and looking at the floppy drive LED. When the system beeps and the floppy drive LED is lit, the system is copying the BIOS recovery code into the Flash device.

3. As soon as the drive LED goes off, the recovery should be complete. Power the system off.

4. Change the Flash recovery jumper back to the default position for normal operation.

When you power the system back on, the new BIOS should be installed and functional. However, you might want to leave the BIOS upgrade floppy in drive A: and check to see that the proper BIOS version was installed. Note that this BIOS recovery procedure is often the fastest way to update a large number of machines, especially if you are performing other upgrades at the same time. This is how it is normally done in a system assembly or production environment.

Using IML System Partition BIOS. IBM and Compaq used a scheme similar to a Flash ROM in some of their older Pentium and 486 systems called *Initial Microcode Load (IML)*. IML is a technique in which the BIOS code is installed on the hard disk in a special hidden system partition and is loaded every time the system is powered up. Of course, the system still has a core BIOS on the motherboard, but all that BIOS does is locate and load updated BIOS code from the system partition. This technique enabled Compaq and IBM to distribute ROM updates on disk for installation in the system partition. The IML BIOS is loaded every time the system is reset or powered on.

Along with the system BIOS code, the system partition contains a complete copy of the Setup and Diagnostics or Reference Disk, which provides the option of running the setup and system-configuration software at any time during a reboot operation. This option eliminates the need to boot from this disk to reconfigure the system, and gives the impression that the entire Setup and Diagnostics or Reference Disk is contained in ROM.

One drawback to this technique is that the BIOS code is installed on the hard disk; the system cannot function properly without the correctly set-up hard disk connected. You always can boot from the Reference Disk floppy should the hard disk fail or become disconnected, but you cannot boot from a standard floppy disk.

This scheme makes hard drive updates problematic, and causes all kinds of support nightmares. I recommend avoiding any system with an IML BIOS, especially if you are buying it used, as support for these types of configurations is hard to come by and not many people know how to deal with them.

BIOS Error Messages

The ROM maps of most PCs are similar to the original IBM systems with which they are compatible—with the exception of the Cassette BASIC portion (also called *ROM BASIC*). It may come as a surprise to some PC users, but the original IBM PC actually had a jack on the rear of the system for connecting a cassette tape recorder. This was to be used for loading programs and data to or from a cassette tape. Tapes were used at the time because floppy drives were very costly, and hard disks were not even an option yet. Floppy drives came down in price quickly at the time, and the cassette port never appeared on any subsequent IBM systems. The cassette port also never appeared on any compatible system.

The original PC came standard with only 16K of memory in the base configuration. No floppy drives were included, so you could not load or save files from disks. Most computer users at the time would either write their own programs in the BASIC (Beginner's All-Purpose Symbolic Instruction Code) language or run programs written by others. A BASIC language interpreter was built in to the ROM BIOS of these early IBMs, and was designed to access the cassette port on the back of the system.

What is really strange is that IBM kept this ROM BASIC relationship all the way into the early '90s! I liken this to humans having an appendix. The ROM BASIC in those IBM systems is a sort of vestigial organ—a leftover that had some use in prehistoric ancestors, but that has no function today.

You can catch a glimpse of this ROM BASIC on older IBM systems that have it by disabling all the disk drives in the system. In that case, with nothing to boot from, most IBM systems unceremoniously dump you into the strange (vintage 1981) ROM BASIC screen. When this occurs, the message looks like this:

```
The IBM Personal Computer Basic
Version C1.10 Copyright IBM Corp 1981
62940 Bytes free
Ok
```

Many people used to dread seeing this because it usually meant that your hard disk had failed to be recognized! Because no compatible systems ever had the Cassette BASIC interpreter in ROM, they had to come up with different messages to display for the same situations in which an IBM system would invoke this BASIC. Compatibles that have an AMI BIOS in fact display a confusing message as follows:

```
NO ROM BASIC - SYSTEM HALTED
```

This message is a BIOS error message that is displayed by the AMI BIOS when the same situations occur that would cause an IBM system to dump into Cassette BASIC, which, of course, is not present in an AMI BIOS (or any other compatible BIOS, for that matter). Other BIOS versions display different messages. For example, under the same circumstances, a Compaq BIOS displays the following:

```
Non-System disk or disk error
replace and strike any key when ready
```

This is somewhat confusing on Compaq's part because this very same (or similar) error message is contained in the DOS Boot Sector, and would normally be displayed if the system files were missing or corrupted.

In the same situations that you would see Cassette BASIC on an IBM system, a system with an Award BIOS would display the following:

```
DISK BOOT FAILURE, INSERT SYSTEM DISK AND PRESS ENTER
```

Phoenix BIOS systems will display either:

```
No boot device available -
strike F1 to retry boot, F2 for setup utility
```

or

```
No boot sector on fixed disk -
strike F1 to retry boot, F2 for setup utility
```

The first or second Phoenix message displays depending on which error actually occurred.

Although the message displayed varies from BIOS to BIOS, the cause is the same for all of them. Two things can generally cause any of these messages to be displayed, and they both relate to specific bytes in the Master Boot Record, which is the first sector of a hard disk at the physical location Cylinder 0, Head 0, Sector 1.

The first problem relates to a disk that has either never been partitioned, or has had the Master Boot Sector corrupted. During the boot process, the BIOS checks the last two bytes in the Master Boot Record (the first sector of the drive) for a "signature" value of 55AAh. If the last two bytes are not 55AAh, an Interrupt 18h is invoked. This calls the subroutine that displays the message you received, and the others indicated, or on an IBM system invokes Cassette (ROM) BASIC.

The Master Boot Sector (including the signature bytes) is written to the hard disk by the DOS FDISK program. Immediately after you low-level format a hard disk, all the sectors are initialized with a pattern of bytes, and the first sector does *not* contain the 55AAh signature. In other words, these ROM error messages are exactly what you see if you attempt to boot from a hard disk that has been low-level formatted, but has not yet been partitioned.

Now consider the second situation that can cause these messages. If the signature bytes are correct, the BIOS executes the Master Partition Boot Record code, which performs a test of the Boot Indicator Bytes in each of the four partition table entries. These bytes are at offset 446 (1BEh), 462 (1CEh), 478 (1DEh), and 494 (1EEh), respectively. They are used to indicate which of the four possible partition table entries contain an active (bootable) partition. A value of 80h in any of these byte offsets indicates that table contains the active partition, whereas all other values must be 00h. If more than one of these bytes is 80h (indicating multiple active partitions), or any of the byte values is anything other than 80h or 00h, you see the following error message:

```
Invalid partition table
```

If all these four Boot Indicator Bytes are 00h, indicating no active (bootable) partitions, then you also see Cassette BASIC on an IBM system or the other messages indicated earlier depending on which BIOS you have. This is exactly what occurs if you were to remove the existing partitions from a drive using FDISK, but had not created new partitions on the drive, or had failed to make one of the partitions Active (bootable) with FDISK before rebooting your system.

Unfortunately, there is no easy way to clear out the partition table on a system where it is damaged. You can try to use FDISK to remove damaged partitions, but FDISK will not always allow it. In that case, you have to resort to something more powerful such as the DISKEDIT command found in the Norton Utilities package by Symantec.

Motherboard CMOS RAM Addresses

In the original AT system, a Motorola 146818 chip was used as the RTC (Real Time Clock) and CMOS (Complementary Metal-Oxide Semiconductor) RAM chip. This is a special chip that had a simple digital clock that used 10 bytes of RAM, and an additional 54 more bytes of leftover RAM in which you could store anything you wanted. The designers of the IBM AT used these extra 54 bytes to store the system configuration.

Modern PC systems don't use the Motorola chip; instead, they incorporate the functions of this chip into the motherboard chipset (South Bridge), Super I/O chip, or they use a special battery and NVRAM (Non-Volatile RAM) module from companies such as Dallas or Benchmarq.

Table 4.13 shows the standard format of the information stored in the 64-byte standard CMOS RAM module. This information controls the configuration of the system and is read and written by the system Setup program.

Table 4.13   AT CMOS RAM Addresses

Offset Hex	Offset Dec	Field Size	Function
00h	0	1 byte	Current second in binary coded decimal (BCD)
01h	1	1 byte	Alarm second in BCD
02h	2	1 byte	Current minute in BCD
03h	3	1 byte	Alarm minute in BCD
04h	4	1 byte	Current hour in BCD
05h	5	1 byte	Alarm hour in BCD
06h	6	1 byte	Current day of week in BCD
07h	7	1 byte	Current day in BCD
08h	8	1 byte	Current month in BCD
09h	9	1 byte	Current year in BCD

0Ah	10	1 byte	Status register A
			  Bit 7 = Update in progress
			    0 = Date and time can be read
			    1 = Time update in progress

Offset Hex	Offset Dec	Field Size	Function
			Bits 6–4 = Time frequency divider 010 = 32.768KHz Bits 3–0 = Rate selection frequency 0110 = 1.024KHz square wave frequency
0Bh	11	1 byte	Status register B Bit 7 = Clock update cycle 0 = Update normally 1 = Abort update in progress Bit 6 = Periodic interrupt 0 = Disable interrupt (default) 1 = Enable interrupt Bit 5 = Alarm interrupt 0 = Disable interrupt (default) 0 = Disable interrupt (default) 1 = Enable interrupt Bit 4 = Update-ended interrupt 0 = Disable interrupt (default) 1 = Enable interrupt Bit 3 = Status register A square wave frequency 0 = Disable square wave (default) 1 = Enable square wave Bit 2 = Date format 0 = Calendar in BCD format (default) 1 = Calendar in binary format Bit 1 = 24-hour clock 0 = 24-hour mode (default) 1 = 12-hour mode Bit 0 = Daylight Savings Time 0 = Disable Daylight Savings (default) 1 = Enable Daylight Savings
0Ch	12	1 byte	Status register C Bit 7 = IRQF flag Bit 6 = PF flag Bit 5 = AF flag Bit 4 = UF flag Bits 3-0 = Reserved
0Dh	13	1 byte	Status register D Bit 7 = Valid CMOS RAM bit 0 = CMOS battery dead 1 = CMOS battery power good Bits 6–0 = Reserved
0Eh	14	1 byte	Diagnostic status Bit 7 = Real-time clock power status 0 = CMOS *has not* lost power 1 = CMOS *has* lost power Bit 6 = CMOS checksum status 0 = Checksum is good 1 = Checksum is bad Bit 5 = POST configuration information status 0 = Configuration information is valid 1 = Configuration information is invalid

(continues)

Table 4.13   AT CMOS RAM Addresses Continued

Offset Hex	Offset Dec	Field Size	Function

			Bit 4 = Memory size compare during POST
			  0 = POST memory equals configuration
			  1 = POST memory *not equal* to configuration
			Bit 3 = Fixed disk/adapter initialization
			  0 = Initialization good
			  1 = Initialization failed
			Bit 2 = CMOS time status indicator
			  0 = Time is valid
			  1 = Time is Invalid
			Bits 1-0 = Reserved

0Fh	15	1 byte	Shutdown code
			  00h = Power on or soft reset
			  01h = Memory size pass
			  02h = Memory test pass
			  03h = Memory test fail
			  04h = POST end; boot system
			  05h = JMP double word pointer with EOI
			  06h = Protected mode tests pass
			  07h = Protected mode tests fail
			  07h = Protected mode tests fail
			  08h = Memory size fail
			  09h = Int 15h block move
			  0Ah = JMP double word pointer without EOI
			  0Bh = used by 80386

10h	16	1 byte	Floppy disk drive types
			  Bits 7-4 = Drive 0 type
			  Bits 3-0 = Drive 1 type
			    0000 = None
			    0001 = 360K
			    0010 = 1.2M
			    0011 = 720K
			    0100 = 1.44M

11h	17	1 byte	Reserved

12h	18	1 byte	Hard disk types
			  Bits 7–4 = Hard disk 0 type (0–15)
			  Bits 3–0 = Hard disk 1 type (0–15)

13h	19	1 byte	Reserved

14h	20	1 byte	Installed equipment
			  Bits 7–6 = Number of floppy disk drives
			    00 = 1 floppy disk drive
			    01 = 2 floppy disk drives
			  Bits 5–4 = Primary display
			    00 = Use display adapter BIOS
			    01 = CGA 40-column
			    10 = CGA 80-column
			    11 = Monochrome Display Adapter
			  Bits 3–2 = Reserved
			  Bit 1 = Math coprocessor present
			  Bit 0 = Floppy disk drive present

15h	21	1 byte	Base memory low-order byte
16h	22	1 byte	Base memory high-order byte

Offset Hex	Offset Dec	Field Size	Function
17h	23	1 byte	Extended memory low-order byte
18h	24	1 byte	Extended memory high-order byte
19h	25	1 byte	Hard Disk 0 Extended Type (0–255)
1Ah	26	1 byte	Hard Disk 1 Extended Type (0–255)
1Bh	27	9 bytes	Reserved
2Eh	46	1 byte	CMOS checksum high-order byte
2Fh	47	1 byte	CMOS checksum low-order byte
30h	48	1 byte	Actual extended memory low-order byte
31h	49	1 byte	Actual extended memory high-order byte
32h	50	1 byte	Date century in BCD
33h	51	1 byte	POST information flag 　　Bit 7 = Top 128K base memory status 　　　　0 = Top 128K base memory not installed 　　　　1 = Top 128K base memory installed 　　Bit 6 = Setup program flag 　　　　0 = Normal (default) 　　　　1 = Put out first user message 　　Bits 5–0 = Reserved
34h	52	2 bytes	Reserved

Note that many newer systems have more than 64 bytes of CMOS RAM; in fact, in some systems they may have 2K or 4K. The extra room is used to store the Plug-and-Play information detailing the configuration of adapter cards and other options in the system. As such, there is no 100% standard for how CMOS information is stored in all systems. Table 4.13 only shows how the original systems did it; newer BIOS versions and motherboard designs can do things differently. You should consult the BIOS manufacturer for more information if you want the full details of how CMOS is stored as the CMOS configuration and Setup program is normally a part of the BIOS. This is another example of how close the relationship is between the BIOS and the motherboard hardware.

There are backup programs and utilities in the public domain for CMOS RAM information, which can be useful for saving and later restoring a configuration. Unfortunately, these programs would be BIOS specific and would only function on a BIOS they are designed for. As such, I don't normally rely on these programs as they are too motherboard and BIOS specific and will not work on all my systems seamlessly.

Table 4.14 shows the values that may be stored by your system BIOS in a special CMOS byte called the *diagnostics status byte*. By examining this location with a diagnostics program, you can determine whether your system has set *trouble codes*, which indicate that a problem previously has occurred.

Table 4.14 CMOS RAM Diagnostic Status Byte Codes		
Bit Number **7 6 5 4 3 2 1 0**	**Hex**	**Function**
1 • • • • • • •	80	Real-time clock (RTC) chip lost power
• 1 • • • • • •	40	CMOS RAM checksum is bad
• • 1 • • • • •	20	Invalid configuration information found at POST
• • • 1 • • • •	10	Memory size compare error at POST
• • • • 1 • • •	08	Fixed disk or adapter failed initialization
• • • • • 1 • •	04	Real-time clock (RTC) time found invalid
• • • • • • 1 •	02	Adapters do not match configuration
• • • • • • • 1	01	Time-out reading an adapter ID
• • • • • • • •	00	No errors found (Normal)

If the Diagnostic status byte is any value other than zero, you will normally get a CMOS configuration error on bootup. These types of errors can be cleared by rerunning the Setup program.

Motherboard Interface Connectors

There are a variety of different connectors on a modern motherboard. Figure 4.10 shows the location of these connectors on a typical motherboard (using the Intel SE440BX model as the example). Several of these connectors such as power supply connectors, serial and parallel ports, and keyboard/mouse connectors are covered in other chapters. Tables 4.15–4.19 contain the pinouts of most of the other different interface and I/O connectors you will find.

▶▶ See "Power Supply Connectors," p. 403

▶▶ See "Serial Ports," p. 583, and "Parallel Ports," p. 593

▶▶ See "Keyboard/Mouse Interface Connectors," p. 470

▶▶ See "USB (Universal Serial Bus)," p. 601

▶▶ See "ATA I/O Connector," p. 615

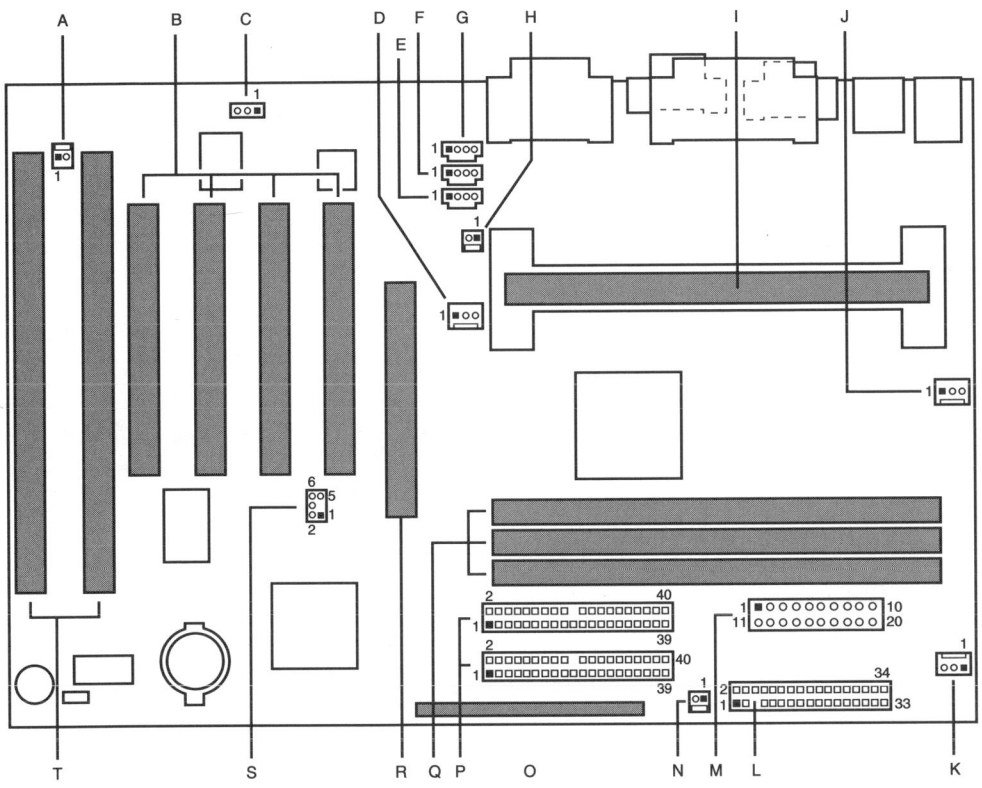

FIG. 4.10 Typical motherboard connectors (Intel SE440BX shown).

A	Wake on Ring (J1A1)	K	Fan 1 (J8M1)
B	PCI slots (J4D2, J4D1, J4C1, J4B1)	L	Diskette drive (J8K1)
C	Optional Wake on LAN technology (J1C1)	M	Power supply (J7L1)
D	Fan 3 (J3F2)	N	Optional SCSI LED (J8J1)
E	Optional Auxiliary Line In (J2F2)	O	Front panel (J8G2)
F	Optional telephony (J2F1)	P	Primary and secondary IDE (J7G1, J8G1)
G	Optional CD-ROM audio (J1F1)	Q	DIMMs (J6J1, J6J2, J7J1)
H	Optional chassis intrusion (J3F1)	R	A.G.P. (J4E1)
I	Slot 1 (J4J1)	S	PC/PCI (J6D1)
J	Fan 2 (J4M1)	T	ISA slots (J4B2, J4A1)

Table 4.15   Infrared Data (IrDA) Pin-Header Connector

Pin	Signal Name	Pin	Signal Name
1	+5 V	4	Ground
2	Key	5	IrTX
3	IrRX	6	CONIR (Consumer IR)

Table 4.16   Battery Connector

Pin	Signal	Pin	Signal
1	Gnd	3	KEY
2	Unused	4	+6v

Table 4.17   LED and Keylock Connector

Pin	Signal	Pin	Signal
1	LED Power (+5v)	4	Keyboard Inhibit
2	KEY	5	Gnd
3	Gnd		

Table 4.18   Speaker Connector

Pin	Signal	Pin	Signal
1	Ground	3	Board-Mounted Speaker
2	KEY	4	Speaker Output

Table 4.19   Microprocessor Fan Power Connector

Pin	Signal Name
1	Ground
2	+12V
3	Sense tachometer

Caution

Do not place a jumper on this connector; serious board damage will result if the 12v is shorted to ground.

Note that some boards have a board mounted piezo speaker. It is enabled by placing a jumper over pins 3 and 4, which routes the speaker output to the board-mounted speaker. Removing the jumper allows a conventional speaker to be plugged in.

Some other connectors that you may find on some newer motherboards are listed in Tables 4.20–4.25.

Table 4.20   Chassis Intrusion (Security) Pin-Header

Pin	Signal Name
1	Ground
2	CHS_SEC

Table 4.21   Wake on LAN Pin-Header

Pin	Signal Name
1	+5 VSB
2	Ground
3	WOL

Table 4.22   CD Audio Connector

Pin	Signal Name	Pin	Signal Name
1	CD_IN-Left	3	Ground
2	Ground	4	CD_IN-Right

Table 4.23   Telephony Connector

Pin	Signal Name	Pin	Signal Name
1	Audio Out (monaural)	3	Ground
2	Ground	4	Audio In (monaural)

Table 4.24   ATAPI-Style Line In Connector

Pin	Signal Name	Pin	Signal Name
1	Left Line In	3	Ground
2	Ground	4	Right Line In (monaural)

Table 4.25   Wake on Ring Pin-Header

Pin	Signal Name
1	Ground
2	RINGA

Intel and several other motherboard manufacturers like to place all the front-panel motherboard connectors in a single row as shown in Figure 4.11.

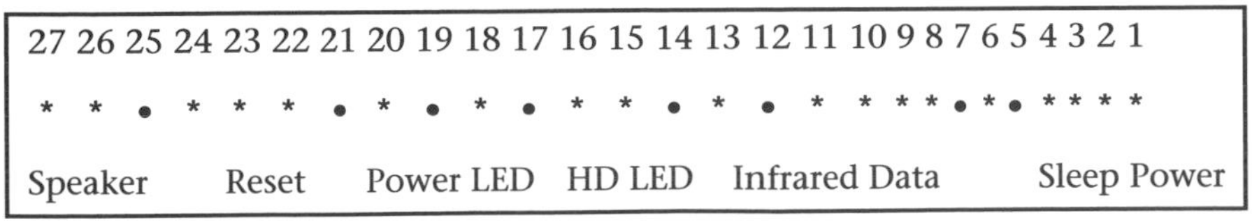

Figure 4.11 Typical ATX motherboard front panel connectors (Intel motherboard shown).

Table 4.26 shows the designations for the front-panel motherboard connectors commonly used on Intel ATX motherboards.

Table 4.26   Typical ATX Motherboard Front Panel Connectors (Intel Motherboard shown)

Connector	Pin	Signal Name
Speaker	27	SPKR_HDR
	26	PIEZO_IN
	25	Key
	24	Ground
Reset	23	SW_RST
	22	Ground
none	21	No connect/Key
Sleep/Power LED	20	PWR_LED
	19	Key
	18	Ground
none	17	No connect/Key
Hard Drive LED	16	HD_PWR
	15	HD Active#
	14	Key
	13	HD_PWR +5 V
none	12	No connect
IrDA	11	CONIR (Consumer IR)
	10	IrTX
	9	Ground
	8	IrRX
	7	Key
	6	+5V
none	5	No connect
Sleep/Resume	4	SLEEP_PU (pullup)
	3	SLEEP
Power On	2	Ground
	1	SW_ON#

System Bus Functions and Features

At the heart of every motherboard are the buses that make it up. A *bus* is nothing but a common pathway across which data can travel within a computer. This pathway is used for communication and can be established between two or more computer elements.

The PC has a hierarchy of different buses. Most modern PCs have at least three different buses; some have four or more. They are hierarchical because each slower bus is connected to the faster one above it. Each device in the system is connected to one of the buses, and some devices (primarily the chipset) act as bridges between the various buses.

The main buses in a modern system are as follows:

- *The Processor Bus.* This is the highest-speed bus in the system and is at the core of the chipset and motherboard. This bus is used primarily by the processor to pass information to and from cache or main memory, and the North Bridge of the chipset. The processor bus in Pentium II systems runs at either 66 or 100MHz and has the full 64-bit data path width of the processor.

- *The AGP (Accelerated Graphics Port) Bus.* This is a high-speed 66MHz, 32-bit bus specifically for a video card. It is connected to the North Bridge of the chipset and is manifested as a single AGP slot in systems that support it.

- *The PCI (Peripheral Component Interconnect) Bus.* This is a 33Mhz, 32-bit bus found in virtually all newer 486 systems and virtually all Pentium and higher processor systems. This bus is generated by the chipset North Bridge, which acts as the PCI controller. This bus is manifested in the system as a collection of 32-bit slots, normally about four on most motherboards. High-speed peripherals such as SCSI adapters, network cards, video cards, and more can be plugged into PCI bus slots. The chipset South Bridge is plugged into the PCI bus, and from there generates the IDE and USB ports.

- *The ISA (Industry Standard Architecture) Bus.* This is an 8MHz, 16-bit bus that remains in systems today after first appearing in the original PC in 8-bit, 5MHz form, and in the 1984 IBM AT in full 16-bit form. It is a very slow-speed bus, but still ideal for certain slow-speed or older peripherals. The PC industry has been loath to give up this bus, despite pressure from Microsoft and Intel to do away with it in future PC designs. Most people have used it in recent times for plug-in modems, sound cards, and various other low-speed peripherals. The ISA bus is generated by the South Bridge part of the motherboard chipset, which acts as the ISA bus controller and the interface between the ISA bus and the faster PCI bus above it. The motherboard's Super I/O chip is normally connected to this bus.

The system chipset is the conductor that controls the orchestra of system components, allowing each to have their turn on their respective buses.

Bus Type	Width (bits)	Speed (MHz)	Bandwidth (M M/sec)
8-bit ISA	8	4.77	2.39
16-bit ISA	16	8.33	8.33
EISA*	32	8.33	33.3
VLB*	32	33.33	133.33
PCI	32	33.33	133.33

(continues)

(continued)

Bus Type	Width (bits)	Speed (MHz)	Bandwidth (M M/sec)
PCI-2x**	32	66.66	266.66
PCI 64-bit**	64	33.33	266.66
PCI-2x 64-bit**	64	66.66	533.33
AGP	32	66.66	266.66
AGP-2x	32	66.66	533.33
AGP-4x*	32	66.66	1,066.66

* EISA and VLB are no longer used in current motherboard designs.
** Note that these bus types are proposed and have not yet been implemented in PC systems.

The PCI bus has two proposed extensions. One is to go from 32 bits to 64 bits. The other is to double the clock speed of the bus to 66MHz. So far, neither of these has been implemented in PC systems, and it doesn't seem likely they will in the near future. More likely is that we will see the future implementations of AGP sooner; that is, a 2x mode and a 4x mode. Interestingly enough, these faster modes will be achieved at the same clock rate; the only difference is that 2 or 4 bits will be transferred for every hertz (cycle) rather than the 1 bit per cycle standard today. This will allow the AGP bus to keep pace with future video needs, all the way to over 1,066M/sec!

The following sections discuss the processor and other subset buses in the system, and the main I/O buses mentioned in the previous chart.

The Processor Bus

The *processor bus* is the communication pathway between the CPU and motherboard chipset, more specifically the North Bridge. This bus runs at the full motherboard speed, which is normally 66MHz, 75MHz, or 100MHz, and is used to transfer data between the CPU and the chipset North Bridge, and between the CPU and an external memory cache on Pentium (P5 class) systems. Figure 4.12 shows how this bus fits into a typical Pentium (P5 class) PC system.

In Figure 4.12 you can see where and how the other main buses, such as the PCI and IDE buses, fit into the system. As you can see there is clearly a three-tier architecture with the fastest CPU bus on top, the PCI bus next, and the ISA bus at the bottom. Different components in the system are connected to one of these three main buses.

Pentium (P5) class systems have an external cache for the CPU; these caches are connected to the processor bus that runs at the motherboard speed (normally 66MHz). Thus, as the Pentium processors have been getting faster and faster, the L2 cache has unfortunately remained at the relatively slow motherboard speed. This was solved in the Pentium Pro and Pentium II systems. They have moved the L2 cache off of the motherboard and directly onto the CPU. By incorporating the L2 cache in the CPU, they can run it at a speed closer to the true CPU speed. In the Pentium Pro, the L2 cache actually does run at full CPU speed, but in the Pentium II it runs at one half of the processor speed. This is still much faster than the motherboard-bound cache on the Socket 7 P5 class systems. The built-in L2 CPU cache is one of the main reasons the Socket 8 and Slot 1 architecture is superior to the Socket 7 designs.

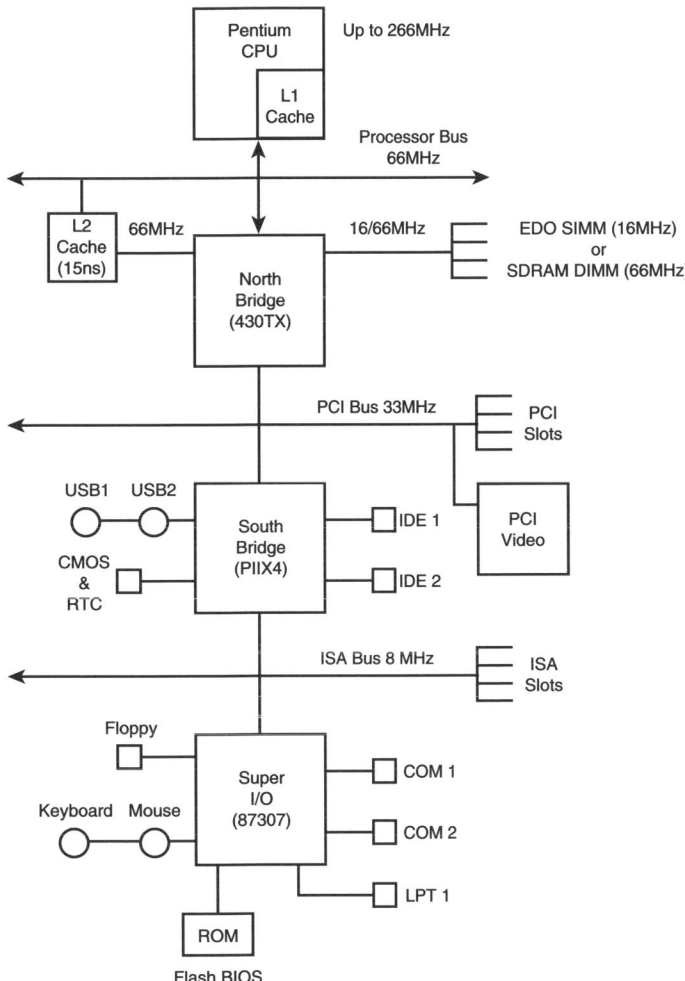

FIG. 4.12 Typical Pentium (P5 Class) system architecture showing the different bus levels in the system.

Note that recently there is a new version of the Socket 7 architecture called "Super-7" designed primarily by AMD and Cyrix for their new Socket 7 P5 class processors that run at motherboard speeds up to 100MHz. This is definitely better than 66MHz, but still not quite up to the Slot-1 architecture where the L2 cache automatically scales up in speed along with the processor. By moving the L2 cache off the motherboard, the Slot-1 designs offer greater performance.

Figure 4.13 shows the typical Pentium II system design. You can see the two main changes: One is the L2 cache now runs at half processor core speed rather than motherboard speed. Also note that the motherboard speed has been increased to 100MHz, which dramatically improves main memory performance combined with 100MHz SDRAM memory. The other main change is the addition of a new single slot bus called AGP (Accelerated Graphics Port). This allows the video card to be on its own dedicated high-speed bus, which runs at twice the speed of PCI. Actually, the speed is misleading as AGP has 2x and 4x modes that allow a further doubling or quadrupling of the speed over the base of 66MHz. This results in incredible video bandwidth, necessary for full-motion video capture and display.

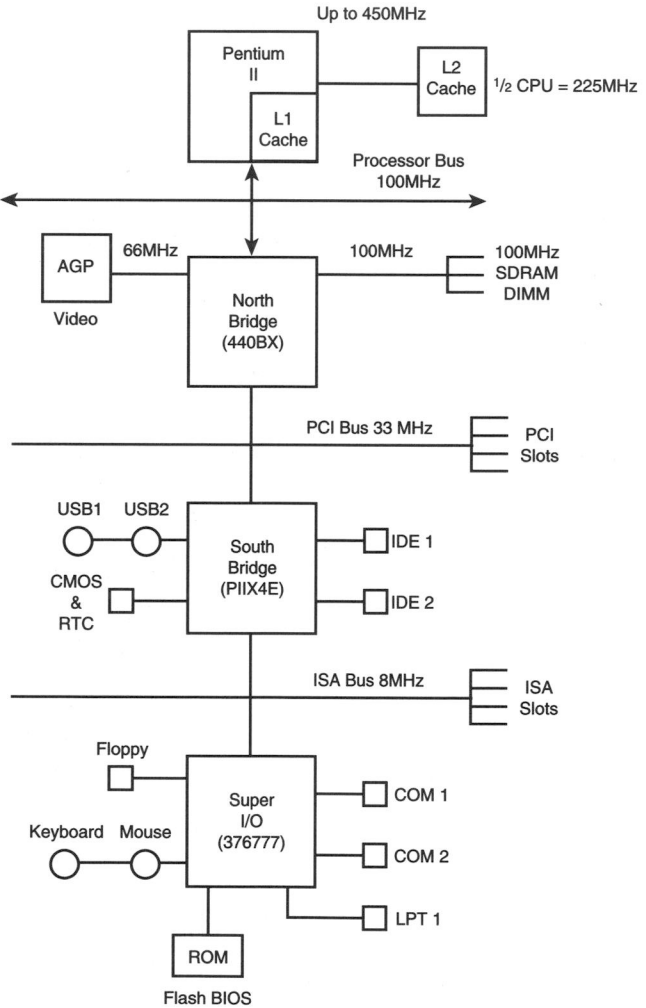

FIG. 4.13 Typical Pentium II (P6 Class) system architecture showing the different bus levels in the system.

Because the purpose of the processor bus is to get information to and from the CPU at the fastest possible speed, this bus operates at a much faster rate than any other bus in your system; no bottleneck exists here. The bus consists of electrical circuits for data, for addresses (the address bus, which is discussed in the following section), and for control purposes. In a Pentium-based system, the processor bus has 64 data lines, 32 address lines, and associated control lines. The Pentium Pro and Pentium II have 36 address lines, but otherwise are the same as the Pentium and Pentium MMX.

The processor bus operates at the same base clock rate as the CPU does externally. This can be misleading as most CPUs these days run internally at a higher clock rate than they do externally. For example, a Pentium 266 system has a Pentium CPU running at 266MHz internally, but only 66.6MHz externally, while a Pentium II 450 runs at 450MHz internally but only 100MHz externally. A Pentium 133, 166, 200, and even a Pentium 233 also run the processor external bus at 66.6MHz. In most newer systems, the actual processor speed is some multiple (1.5x, 2x, 2.5x, 3x, and so on) of the processor bus.

◀◀ See "Processor Speed Ratings," p. 33

The processor bus is tied to the external processor pin connections and can transfer one bit of data per data line every one or two clock cycles. Thus, a Pentium, Pentium Pro, or Pentium II can transfer 64 bits of data at a time.

To determine the transfer rate for the processor bus, you multiply the data width (64 bits for a Pentium, Pentium Pro, or Pentium II) by the clock speed of the bus (the same as the base or unmultiplied clock speed of the CPU). If you are using a Pentium, Pentium MMX, Pentium Pro, or Pentium II chip that runs at a 66MHz motherboard speed, and it can transfer a bit of data each clock cycle on each data line, you have a maximum instantaneous transfer rate of roughly 528M/sec. You get this result by using the following formula:

66MHz×64 bits = 4,224Mbit/sec

4,224Mbit/sec÷8 = 528M/sec

This transfer rate, often called the *bandwidth* of the bus, represents a maximum. Like all maximums, this rate does not represent the normal operating bandwidth; you should expect much lower average throughput. Other limiting factors such as chipset design, memory design and speed, and so on conspire to lower the effective average throughput.

The Memory Bus

The *memory bus* is used to transfer information between the CPU and main memory—the RAM in your system. This bus is connected to the motherboard chipset North Bridge chip. Depending on the type of memory your chipset (and therefore motherboard) is designed to handle, the North Bridge will run the memory bus at different speeds. Systems that use FPM (Fast Page Mode) or EDO (Extended Data Out) memory with a 60ns access time run the memory bus at only 16MHz. That is because 16MHz results in about 60ns cycling speed. Newer chipsets and motherboards that support SDRAM can run the memory bus at 66MHz (15ns) or up to 100MHz (10ns). This obviously results in faster memory performance and virtually negates the need for having cache memory on the motherboard. That is why the Pentium II processor was designed to include a higher speed L2 cache built in, as the SDRAM memory on the motherboard already runs at the same speed as the motherboard cache found in older Pentium systems. Figure 4.12 and Figure 4.13 show how the memory bus fits into your PC.

> **Note**
>
> Notice that the main memory bus is always the same width as the processor bus. This will define the size of what is called a "bank" of memory. Memory banks and their width relative to processor buses are discussed in the "Memory Banks" section in Chapter 5.

The Need for Expansion Slots

The I/O bus or expansion slots are what enables your CPU to communicate with peripheral devices. The bus and its associated expansion slots are needed because basic systems cannot possibly satisfy all the needs of all the people who buy them. The I/O bus enables you to add devices to your computer to expand its capabilities. The most basic computer components, such as sound cards and video cards, can be plugged into expansion slots; you also can plug in more specialized devices, such as network interface cards, SCSI host adapters, and others.

> **Note**
>
> In most modern PC systems, a variety of basic peripheral devices are built into the motherboard. Most systems today have at least dual (primary and secondary) IDE interfaces, dual USB (Universal Serial Bus) ports, a floppy controller, two serial ports, a parallel port, keyboard, and mouse controller built directly into the motherboard. These devices are normally distributed between the motherboard chipset South Bridge and the *Super I/O chip*. (Super I/O chips are discussed earlier in this chapter.)
>
> Many will even add more items such as a built-in sound card, video adapter, SCSI host adapter, or network interface also built into the motherboard. Those items are not built into the motherboard chipset or Super I/O chip, but would be configured as additional chips installed on the board. Nevertheless, these built-in controllers and ports still use the I/O bus to communicate with the CPU. In essence, even though they are built in, they act as if there are cards plugged into the system's bus slots, including using system resources in the same manner.

Types of I/O Buses

Since the introduction of the first PC, many I/O buses have been introduced. The reason is quite simple—faster I/O speeds are necessary for better system performance. This need for higher performance involves three main areas:

- Faster CPUs
- Increasing software demands
- Greater multimedia requirements

Each of these areas requires the I/O bus to be as fast as possible. Surprisingly, virtually all PC systems shipped today still incorporate the same basic bus architecture as the 1984 vintage IBM PC/AT. However, most of these systems now also include a second high-speed local I/O bus such as VL-Bus or PCI, which offer much greater performance for adapters that need it. Many of the newest systems also include a third high-speed bus called AGP for improved video performance beyond what PCI offers.

One of the primary reasons why new I/O-bus structures have been slow in coming is compatibility—that old Catch-22 that anchors much of the PC industry to the past. One of the hallmarks of the PC's success is its standardization. This standardization spawned thousands of third-party I/O cards, each originally built for the early bus specifications of the PC. If a new high-performance bus system is introduced, it often had to be compatible with the older bus systems so that the older I/O cards would not be obsolete. Therefore, bus technologies seem to evolve rather than make quantum leaps forward.

You can identify different types of I/O buses by their architecture. The main types of I/O architecture are:

- ISA
- Micro Channel Architecture (MCA)
- EISA
- VESA Local Bus (VL-Bus)
- PCI Local Bus
- AGP
- PC-Card (formerly PCMCIA)
- FireWire (IEEE-1394)
- Universal Serial Bus (USB)

▶▶ See "PC Cards," p. 932
▶▶ See "Firewire (IEEE 1394)," p. 604
▶▶ See "USB (Universal Serial Bus)," p. 601

The differences among these buses consist primarily of the amount of data that they can transfer at one time and the speed at which they can do it. Each bus architecture is implemented by a chipset that is connected to the processor bus. Typically, this chipset also controls the memory bus. The following sections describe the different types of PC buses.

The ISA Bus

ISA, which is an acronym for *Industry Standard Architecture*, is the bus architecture that was introduced as an 8-bit bus with the original IBM PC in 1981 and later expanded to 16 bits with the IBM PC/AT in 1984. ISA is the basis of the modern personal computer and the primary architecture used in the vast majority of PC systems on the market today. It may seem amazing that such a seemingly antiquated architecture is used in today's high-performance systems, but this is true for reasons of reliability, affordability, and compatibility, plus this old bus is still faster than many of the peripherals that we connect to it!

Two versions of the ISA bus exist, based on the number of data bits that can be transferred on the bus at a time. The older version is an 8-bit bus; the newer version is a 16-bit bus. The original 8-bit version ran at 4.77MHz in the PC and XT. The 16-bit version used in the AT ran at 6MHz and then 8MHz. Later, the industry agreed on an 8.33MHz maximum standard speed for 8/16-bit versions of the ISA bus for backward compatibility. Some systems have the capability to run the ISA bus faster than this, but some adapter cards will not function properly at higher speeds. ISA data transfers require anywhere from two to eight cycles. Therefore, the theoretical maximum data rate of the ISA bus is about 8M/sec, as the following formula shows:

8MHz×16 bits = 128Mbit/sec

128Mbit/sec÷2 cycles = 64Mbit/sec

64Mbit/sec÷8 = 8M/sec

The bandwidth of the 8-bit bus would be half this figure (4M/sec). Remember, however, that these figures are theoretical maximums; because of I/O bus protocols, the effective bandwidth is much lower—typically by almost half. Even so, at 8M/sec, the ISA bus is still faster than many of the peripherals we connect to it.

The 8-Bit ISA Bus. This bus architecture is used in the original IBM PC computers. Although virtually nonexistent in new systems today, this architecture still exists in hundreds of thousands of PC systems in the field.

Physically, the 8-bit ISA expansion slot resembles the tongue-and-groove system that furniture makers once used to hold two pieces of wood together. It is specifically called a *Card/Edge connector*. An adapter card with 62 contacts on its bottom edge plugs into a slot on the motherboard that has 62 matching contacts. Electronically, this slot provides eight data lines and 20 addressing lines, enabling the slot to handle 1M of memory. Figure 4.14 describes the pinouts for the 8-bit ISA bus. Figure 4.15 shows how these pins are oriented in the expansion slot.

Although the design of the bus is simple, IBM waited until 1987 to publish full specifications for the timings of the data and address lines. In the early days of PC compatibles, manufacturers had to do their best to figure out how to make adapter boards. This problem was solved, however, as PC-compatible personal computers became more widely accepted as the industry standard and manufacturers had more time and incentive to build adapter boards that worked correctly with the bus.

The dimensions of 8-bit ISA adapter cards are as follows:

4.2 inches (106.68mm) high

13.13 inches (333.5mm) long

0.5 inch (12.7mm) wide

Signal	Pin	Pin	Signal
Ground	B1	A1	-I/O CH CHK
RESET DRV	B2	A2	Data Bit 7
+5 Vdc	B3	A3	Data Bit 6
IRQ 2	B4	A4	Data Bit 5
-5 Vdc	B5	A5	Data Bit 4
DRQ 2	B6	A6	Data Bit 3
-12 Vdc	B7	A7	Data Bit 2
-CARD SLCTD	B8	A8	Data Bit 1
+12 Vdc	B9	A9	Data Bit 0
Ground	B10	A10	-I/O CH RDY
-SMEMW	B11	A11	AEN
-SMEMR	B12	A12	Address 19
-IOW	B13	A13	Address 18
-IOR	B14	A14	Address 17
-DACK 3	B15	A15	Address 16
DRQ 3	B16	A16	Address 15
-DACK 1	B17	A17	Address 14
DRQ 1	B18	A18	Address 13
-Refresh	B19	A19	Address 12
CLK(4.77MHz)	B20	A20	Address 11
IRQ 7	B21	A21	Address 10
IRQ 6	B22	A22	Address 9
IRQ 5	B23	A23	Address 8
IRQ 4	B24	A24	Address 7
IRQ 3	B25	A25	Address 6
-DACK 2	B26	A26	Address 5
T/C	B27	A27	Address 4
BALE	B28	A28	Address 3
+5 Vdc	B29	A29	Address 2
OSC(14.3MHz)	B30	A30	Address 1
Ground	B31	A31	Address 0

FIG. 4.14   Pinouts for the 8-bit ISA bus.

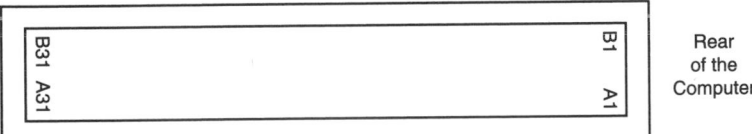

FIG. 4.15   The 8-bit ISA bus connector.

The 16-Bit ISA Bus. IBM threw a bombshell on the PC world when it introduced the AT with the 286 processor in 1984. This processor had a 16-bit data bus, which meant that communications between the processor, the motherboard, and memory would now be 16 bits wide instead of only 8 bits wide. Although this processor could have been installed on a motherboard with only an 8-bit I/O bus, that would have meant a huge sacrifice in the performance of any adapter cards or other devices installed on the bus.

The introduction of the 286 chip posed a problem for IBM in relation to its next generation of PCs. Should the company create a new I/O bus and associated expansion slots, or should it try to come up with a system that could support both 8- and 16-bit cards? IBM opted for the latter solution, and the PC/AT was introduced with a set of expansion slots with 16-bit extension connectors. You can plug an 8-bit card into the forward part of the slot or a 16-bit card into both parts of the slot.

> **Note**
>
> The expansion slots for the 16-bit ISA bus also introduced access keys to the PC environment. An *access key* is a cutout or notch in an adapter card that fits over a corresponding tab in the connector into which the adapter card is inserted. Access keys typically are used to keep adapter cards from being inserted into a connector improperly.

The extension connector in each 16-bit expansion slot adds 36 connector pins to carry the extra signals necessary to implement the wider data path. In addition, two of the pins in the 8-bit portion of the connector were changed. These two minor changes do not alter the function of 8-bit cards. Figure 4.16 describes the pinouts for the full 16-bit ISA expansion slot. Figure 4.17 shows the orientation and relation of 8-bit and 16-bit ISA bus slots.

The extended 16-bit slots physically interfere with some 8-bit adapter cards that have a *skirt*—an extended area of the card that drops down toward the motherboard just after the connector. To handle these cards, IBM left two expansion ports in the PC/AT without the 16-bit extensions. These slots, which are identical to the expansion slots in earlier systems, can handle any skirted PC or XT expansion card. This is not a problem today, as no skirted 8-bit cards have been manufactured for years.

> **Note**
>
> 16-bit ISA expansion slots were introduced in 1984. Since then, virtually every manufacturer of 8-bit expansion cards have designed them without drop-down skirts so that they fit properly in 16-bit slots. Most new systems do not have any 8-bit-only slots, because a properly designed 8-bit card will work in any 16-bit slot.
>
> Note that some poorly designed motherboards or adapter cards may have fitting problems. It is not uncommon to find that a full-length card will not work in a particular slot due to interference with the processor heat sink, SIMM or DIMM memory, voltage regulators, or other components on the board. Systems using the LPX motherboard and even the Baby-AT motherboard form factors are especially prone to these problems. This is another reason I recommend ATX form factor systems because things fit so much better.

The dimensions of a typical AT expansion board are as follows:

> 4.8 inches (121.92mm) high
>
> 13.13 inches (333.5mm) long
>
> 0.5 inch (12.7mm) wide

Two heights actually are available for cards that are commonly used in AT systems—4.8 inches and 4.2 inches (the height of older PC-XT cards). The shorter cards became an issue when IBM introduced the XT Model 286. Because this model has an AT motherboard in an XT case, it needs AT-type boards with the 4.2-inch maximum height. Most board makers trimmed the height of their boards; many manufacturers now make only 4.2-inch tall (or less) boards so that they will work in systems with either profile.

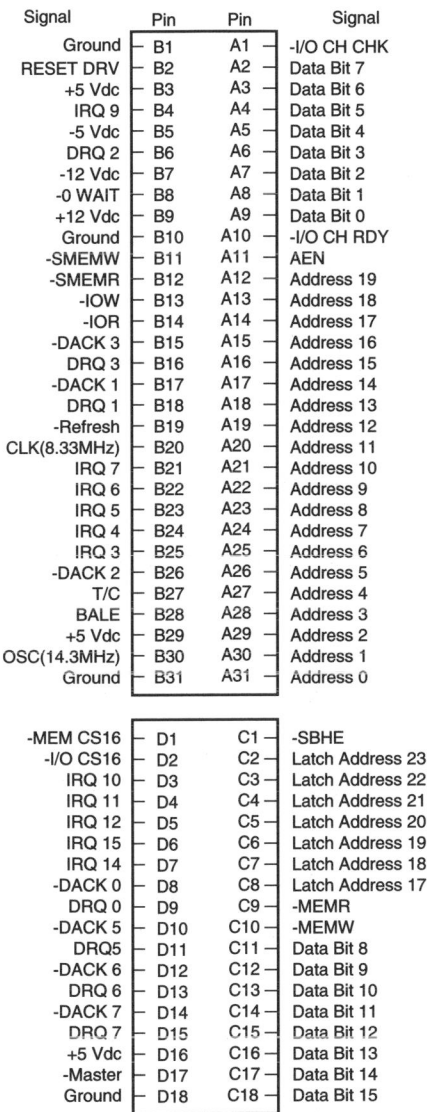

Signal	Pin	Pin	Signal
Ground	B1	A1	-I/O CH CHK
RESET DRV	B2	A2	Data Bit 7
+5 Vdc	B3	A3	Data Bit 6
IRQ 9	B4	A4	Data Bit 5
-5 Vdc	B5	A5	Data Bit 4
DRQ 2	B6	A6	Data Bit 3
-12 Vdc	B7	A7	Data Bit 2
-0 WAIT	B8	A8	Data Bit 1
+12 Vdc	B9	A9	Data Bit 0
Ground	B10	A10	-I/O CH RDY
-SMEMW	B11	A11	AEN
-SMEMR	B12	A12	Address 19
-IOW	B13	A13	Address 18
-IOR	B14	A14	Address 17
-DACK 3	B15	A15	Address 16
DRQ 3	B16	A16	Address 15
-DACK 1	B17	A17	Address 14
DRQ 1	B18	A18	Address 13
-Refresh	B19	A19	Address 12
CLK(8.33MHz)	B20	A20	Address 11
IRQ 7	B21	A21	Address 10
IRQ 6	B22	A22	Address 9
IRQ 5	B23	A23	Address 8
IRQ 4	B24	A24	Address 7
IRQ 3	B25	A25	Address 6
-DACK 2	B26	A26	Address 5
T/C	B27	A27	Address 4
BALE	B28	A28	Address 3
+5 Vdc	B29	A29	Address 2
OSC(14.3MHz)	B30	A30	Address 1
Ground	B31	A31	Address 0

Signal	Pin	Pin	Signal
-MEM CS16	D1	C1	-SBHE
-I/O CS16	D2	C2	Latch Address 23
IRQ 10	D3	C3	Latch Address 22
IRQ 11	D4	C4	Latch Address 21
IRQ 12	D5	C5	Latch Address 20
IRQ 15	D6	C6	Latch Address 19
IRQ 14	D7	C7	Latch Address 18
-DACK 0	D8	C8	Latch Address 17
DRQ 0	D9	C9	-MEMR
-DACK 5	D10	C10	-MEMW
DRQ5	D11	C11	Data Bit 8
-DACK 6	D12	C12	Data Bit 9
DRQ 6	D13	C13	Data Bit 10
-DACK 7	D14	C14	Data Bit 11
DRQ 7	D15	C15	Data Bit 12
+5 Vdc	D16	C16	Data Bit 13
-Master	D17	C17	Data Bit 14
Ground	D18	C18	Data Bit 15

FIG. 4.16 Pinouts for the 16-bit ISA bus.

8/16-bit ISA Bus Pinouts.

8-bit PC/XT Connector: 16-bit AT Connector:

Signal	Pin Numbers		Signal
GROUND	B1	A1	-I/O CHK
RESET DRV	B2	A2	DATA 7
+5 Vdc	B3	A3	DATA 6
IRQ 2	B4	A4	DATA 5
-5 Vdc	B5	A5	DATA 4
DRQ 2	B6	A6	DATA 3
-12 Vdc	B7	A7	DATA 2
-CARD SLCT	B8	A8	DATA 1
+12 Vdc	B9	A9	DATA 0
GROUND	B10	A10	-I/O RDY
-SMEMW	B11	A11	AEN
-SMEMR	B12	A12	ADDR 19
-IOW	B13	A13	ADDR 18
-IOR	B14	A14	ADDR 17
-DACK 3	B15	A15	ADDR 16
DRQ 3	B16	A16	ADDR 15
-DACK 1	B17	A17	ADDR 14
DRQ 1	B18	A18	ADDR 13
-REFRESH	B19	A19	ADDR 12
CLK (4.77MHz)	B20	A20	ADDR 11
IRQ 7	B21	A21	ADDR 10
IRQ 6	B22	A22	ADDR 9
IRQ 5	B23	A23	ADDR 8
IRQ 4	B24	A24	ADDR 7
IRQ 3	B25	A25	ADDR 6
-DACK 2	B26	A26	ADDR 5
T/C	B27	A27	ADDR 4
BALE	B28	A28	ADDR 3
+5 Vdc	B29	A29	ADDR 2
OSC (14.3MHz)	B30	A30	ADDR 1
GROUND	B31	A31	ADDR 0

Signal	Pin Numbers		Signal
GROUND	B1	A1	-I/O CHK
RESET DRV	B2	A2	DATA 7
+5 Vdc	B3	A3	DATA 6
IRQ 9	B4	A4	DATA 5
-5 Vdc	B5	A5	DATA 4
DRQ 2	B6	A6	DATA 3
-12 Vdc	B7	A7	DATA 2
-OWS	B8	A8	DATA 1
+12 Vdc	B9	A9	DATA 0
GROUND	B10	A10	-I/O RDY
-SMEMW	B11	A11	AEN
-SMEMR	B12	A12	ADDR 19
-IOW	B13	A13	ADDR 18
-IOR	B14	A14	ADDR 17
-DACK 3	B15	A15	ADDR 16
DRQ 3	B16	A16	ADDR 15
-DACK 1	B17	A17	ADDR 14
DRQ 1	B18	A18	ADDR 13
-REFRESH	B19	A19	ADDR 12
CLK (8.33MHz)	B20	A20	ADDR 11
IRQ 7	B21	A21	ADDR 10
IRQ 6	B22	A22	ADDR 9
IRQ 5	B23	A23	ADDR 8
IRQ 4	B24	A24	ADDR 7
IRQ 3	B25	A25	ADDR 6
-DACK 2	B26	A26	ADDR 5
T/C	B27	A27	ADDR 4
BALE	B28	A28	ADDR 3
+5 Vdc	B29	A29	ADDR 2
OSC (14.3MHz)	B30	A30	ADDR 1
GROUND	B31	A31	ADDR 0

Signal	Pin Numbers		Signal
-MEM CS16	D1	C1	-SBHE
-I/O CS16	D2	C2	LADDR 23
IRQ 10	D3	C3	LADDR 22
IRQ 11	D4	C4	LADDR 21
IRQ 12	D5	C5	LADDR 20
IRQ 15	D6	C6	LADDR 19
IRQ 14	D7	C7	LADDR 18
-DACK 0	D8	C8	LADDR 17
DRQ 0	D9	C9	-MEMR
-DACK 5	D10	C10	-MEMW
DRQ 5	D11	C11	DATA 8
-DACK 6	D12	C12	DATA 9
DRQ 6	D13	C13	DATA 10
-DACK 7	D14	C14	DATA 11
DRQ 7	D15	C15	DATA 12
+5 Vdc	D16	C16	DATA 13
-MASTER	D17	C17	DATA 14
GROUND	D18	C18	DATA 15

FIG. 4.17 The 8-bit and 16-bit ISA bus connectors.

32-Bit Buses. After 32-bit CPUs became available, it was some time before 32-bit bus standards became available. Before MCA and EISA specs were released, some vendors began creating their own proprietary 32-bit buses, which were extensions of the ISA bus. Although the proprietary buses were few and far between, they do still exist.

The expanded portions of the bus typically are used for proprietary memory expansion or video cards. Because the systems are proprietary (meaning that they are nonstandard), pinouts and specifications are not available.

The Micro Channel Bus

The introduction of 32-bit chips meant that the ISA bus could not handle the power of another new generation of CPUs. The 386DX chips can transfer 32 bits of data at a time, but the ISA bus can handle a maximum of 16 bits. Rather than extend the ISA bus again, IBM decided to build a new bus; the result was the MCA bus. *MCA (Micro Channel Architecture)* is completely different from the ISA bus and is technically superior in every way.

IBM not only wanted to replace the old ISA standard, but also to receive royalties on it; the company required vendors that licensed the new MCA bus to pay IBM royalties for using the ISA bus in all previous systems. This requirement led to the development of the competing EISA bus (see the next section on the EISA bus) and hindered acceptance of the MCA bus. Another reason why MCA has not been adopted universally for systems with 32-bit slots is that adapter cards designed for ISA systems do not work in MCA systems.

> **Note**
>
> The MCA bus is not compatible with the older ISA bus, so cards designed for the ISA bus do not work in an MCA system.

MCA runs asynchronously with the main processor, meaning that fewer possibilities exist for timing problems among adapter cards plugged into the bus.

MCA systems produced a new level of ease of use, as anyone who has set up one of these systems can tell you. An MCA system has no jumpers and switches—neither on the motherboard nor on any expansion adapter. You don't need an electrical engineering degree to plug a card into a PC.

The MCA bus also supports bus mastering. Through implementing bus mastering, the MCA bus provides significant performance improvements over the older ISA buses. (Bus mastering is also implemented in the EISA bus. General information related to bus mastering is discussed in the "Bus Mastering" section later in this chapter.) In the MCA bus mastering implementation, any bus mastering devices can request unobstructed use of the bus in order to communicate with another device on the bus. The request is made through a device known as the *Central Arbitration Control Point (CACP)*. This device arbitrates the competition for the bus, making sure all devices have access and that no single device monopolizes the bus.

Each device is given a priority code to ensure that order is preserved within the system. The main CPU is given the lowest priority code. Memory refresh has the highest priority, followed by the DMA channels, and then the bus masters installed in the I/O slots. One exception to this is when an NMI (nonmaskable interrupt) occurs. In this instance, control returns to the CPU immediately.

The MCA specification provides for four adapter sizes, which are described in Table 4.27.

Table 4.27 Physical Sizes of MCA Adapter Cards		
Adapter Type	**Height (in Inches)**	**Length (in Inches)**
Type 3	3.475	12.3
Type 3 half	3.475	6.35
Type 5	4.825	13.1
Type 9	9.0	13.1

Four types of slots are involved in the MCA design:

- 16-bit

- 16-bit with video extensions

- 16-bit with memory-matched extensions

- 32-bit

The sixth edition of this book, included on the CD-ROM, has detailed information about each of these cards and what systems they can be found in. IBM still has all of the technical reference manuals for MCA available; however, development has stopped for MCA devices due to the other faster and more feature-rich buses available today.

The EISA Bus

EISA (*Extended Industry Standard Architecture*) is a standard announced in September 1988 as a response to IBM's introduction of the MCA bus—more specifically, to the way that IBM wanted to handle licensing of the MCA bus. Vendors did not feel obligated to pay retroactive royalties on the ISA bus, so they turned their backs on IBM and created their own buses.

The EISA standard was developed primarily by Compaq, and was intended as being their way of taking over future development of the PC bus away from IBM. Compaq knew that nobody would clone their bus if they were the only company that had it, so they essentially gave the design away to other leading manufacturers. They formed the EISA committee, a nonprofit organization designed specifically to control development of the EISA bus. Very few EISA adapters were ever developed. Those that were developed centered mainly around disk array controllers and server-type network cards.

The EISA bus provides 32-bit slots for use with 386DX or higher systems. The EISA slot enables manufacturers to design adapter cards that have many of the capabilities of MCA adapters, but the bus also supports adapter cards created for the older ISA standard. EISA provides markedly faster hard drive throughput when used with devices such as SCSI bus-mastering hard drive controllers. Compared with 16-bit ISA system architecture, EISA permits greater system expansion with fewer adapter conflicts.

The EISA bus adds 90 new connections (55 new signals) without increasing the physical connector size of the 16-bit ISA bus. At first glance, the 32-bit EISA slot looks much like the 16-bit ISA slot. The EISA adapter, however, has two rows of connectors. The first row is the same kind used in 16-bit ISA cards; the other, thinner row extends from the 16-bit connectors. This means that ISA cards can still be used in EISA bus slots. Although this compatibility was not enough to ensure the popularity of EISA buses, it is a feature that was carried over into the newer VL-bus standard. The physical specifications of an EISA card are as follows:

5 inches (127mm) high

13.13 inches (333.5mm) long

0.5 inch (12.7mm) wide

The EISA bus can handle up to 32 bits of data at an 8.33MHz cycle rate. Most data transfers require a minimum of two cycles, although faster cycle rates are possible if an adapter card provides tight timing specifications. The maximum bandwidth on the bus is 33M/sec, as the following formula shows:

8.33MHz×32 bits = 266.56Mbit/sec

266.56Mbit/sec÷8 = 33.32M/sec

Data transfers through an 8- or 16-bit expansion card across the bus would be reduced appropriately. Remember, however, that these figures represent theoretical maximums. Wait states, interrupts, and other protocol factors can reduce the effective bandwidth— typically, by half. Figure 4.18 describes the pinouts for the EISA bus. Figure 4.19 shows the locations of the pins.

Automated Setup. EISA systems also use an automated setup to deal with adapter-board interrupts and addressing issues. These issues often cause problems when several different adapter boards are installed in an ISA system. EISA setup software recognizes potential conflicts and automatically configures the system to avoid them. EISA does, however, enable you to do your own troubleshooting, and to configure the boards through jumpers and switches. This concept was not new to EISA; IBM's MCA bus also supported configuration via software. Another new feature of EISA systems is IRQ sharing, meaning that multiple bus cards can share a single interrupt. This feature has also been implemented in PCI bus cards.

> **Note**
>
> Although automated setup traditionally has not been available in ISA systems, it is now available with Plug-and-Play (PnP) systems and components. PnP systems are discussed toward the end of this chapter in the section titled "Plug-and-Play Systems."

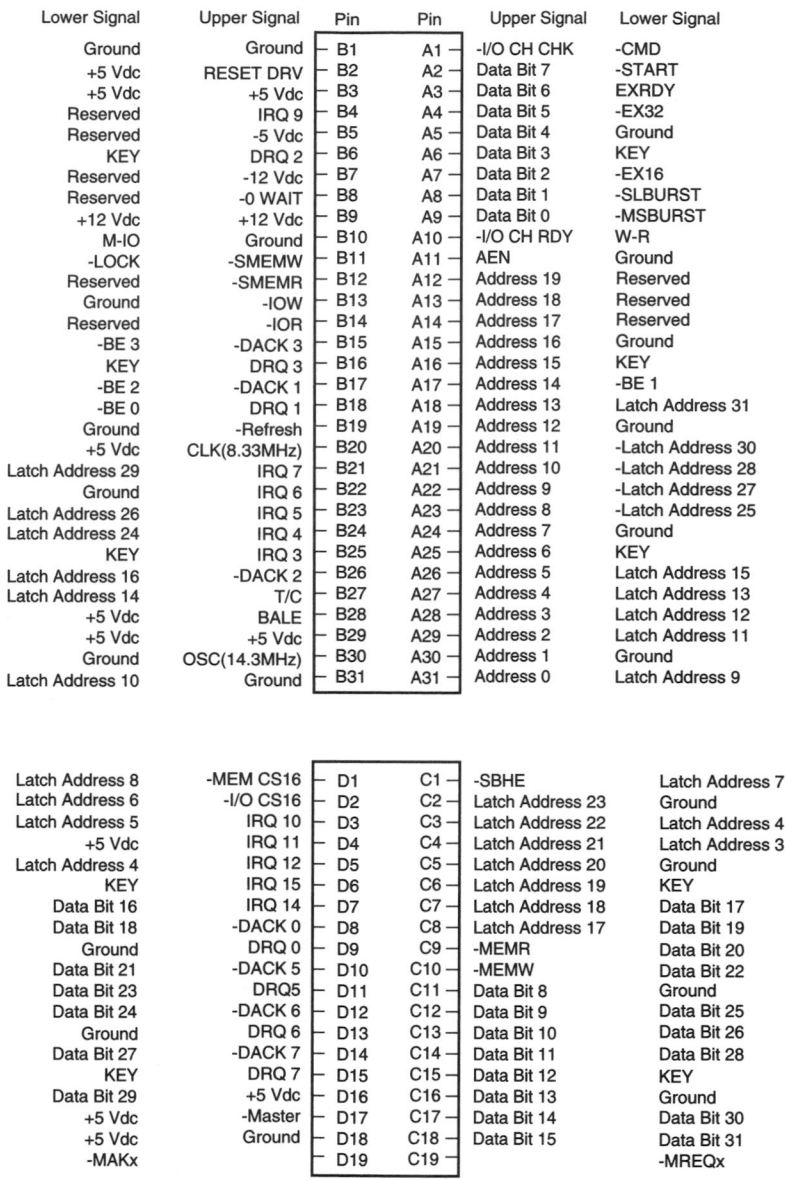

Lower Signal	Upper Signal	Pin	Pin	Upper Signal	Lower Signal
Ground	Ground	B1	A1	-I/O CH CHK	-CMD
+5 Vdc	RESET DRV	B2	A2	Data Bit 7	-START
+5 Vdc	+5 Vdc	B3	A3	Data Bit 6	EXRDY
Reserved	IRQ 9	B4	A4	Data Bit 5	-EX32
Reserved	-5 Vdc	B5	A5	Data Bit 4	Ground
KEY	DRQ 2	B6	A6	Data Bit 3	KEY
Reserved	-12 Vdc	B7	A7	Data Bit 2	-EX16
Reserved	-0 WAIT	B8	A8	Data Bit 1	-SLBURST
+12 Vdc	+12 Vdc	B9	A9	Data Bit 0	-MSBURST
M-IO	Ground	B10	A10	-I/O CH RDY	W-R
-LOCK	-SMEMW	B11	A11	AEN	Ground
Reserved	-SMEMR	B12	A12	Address 19	Reserved
Ground	-IOW	B13	A13	Address 18	Reserved
Reserved	-IOR	B14	A14	Address 17	Reserved
-BE 3	-DACK 3	B15	A15	Address 16	Ground
KEY	DRQ 3	B16	A16	Address 15	KEY
-BE 2	-DACK 1	B17	A17	Address 14	-BE 1
-BE 0	DRQ 1	B18	A18	Address 13	Latch Address 31
Ground	-Refresh	B19	A19	Address 12	Ground
+5 Vdc	CLK(8.33MHz)	B20	A20	Address 11	-Latch Address 30
Latch Address 29	IRQ 7	B21	A21	Address 10	-Latch Address 28
Ground	IRQ 6	B22	A22	Address 9	-Latch Address 27
Latch Address 26	IRQ 5	B23	A23	Address 8	-Latch Address 25
Latch Address 24	IRQ 4	B24	A24	Address 7	Ground
KEY	IRQ 3	B25	A25	Address 6	KEY
Latch Address 16	-DACK 2	B26	A26	Address 5	Latch Address 15
Latch Address 14	T/C	B27	A27	Address 4	Latch Address 13
+5 Vdc	BALE	B28	A28	Address 3	Latch Address 12
+5 Vdc	+5 Vdc	B29	A29	Address 2	Latch Address 11
Ground	OSC(14.3MHz)	B30	A30	Address 1	Ground
Latch Address 10	Ground	B31	A31	Address 0	Latch Address 9

Lower Signal	Upper Signal	Pin	Pin	Upper Signal	Lower Signal
Latch Address 8	-MEM CS16	D1	C1	-SBHE	Latch Address 7
Latch Address 6	-I/O CS16	D2	C2	Latch Address 23	Ground
Latch Address 5	IRQ 10	D3	C3	Latch Address 22	Latch Address 4
+5 Vdc	IRQ 11	D4	C4	Latch Address 21	Latch Address 3
Latch Address 4	IRQ 12	D5	C5	Latch Address 20	Ground
KEY	IRQ 15	D6	C6	Latch Address 19	KEY
Data Bit 16	IRQ 14	D7	C7	Latch Address 18	Data Bit 17
Data Bit 18	-DACK 0	D8	C8	Latch Address 17	Data Bit 19
Ground	DRQ 0	D9	C9	-MEMR	Data Bit 20
Data Bit 21	-DACK 5	D10	C10	-MEMW	Data Bit 22
Data Bit 23	DRQ5	D11	C11	Data Bit 8	Ground
Data Bit 24	-DACK 6	D12	C12	Data Bit 9	Data Bit 25
Ground	DRQ 6	D13	C13	Data Bit 10	Data Bit 26
Data Bit 27	-DACK 7	D14	C14	Data Bit 11	Data Bit 28
KEY	DRQ 7	D15	C15	Data Bit 12	KEY
Data Bit 29	+5 Vdc	D16	C16	Data Bit 13	Ground
+5 Vdc	-Master	D17	C17	Data Bit 14	Data Bit 30
+5 Vdc	Ground	D18	C18	Data Bit 15	Data Bit 31
-MAKx		D19	C19		-MREQx

FIG. 4.18   Pinouts for the EISA bus.

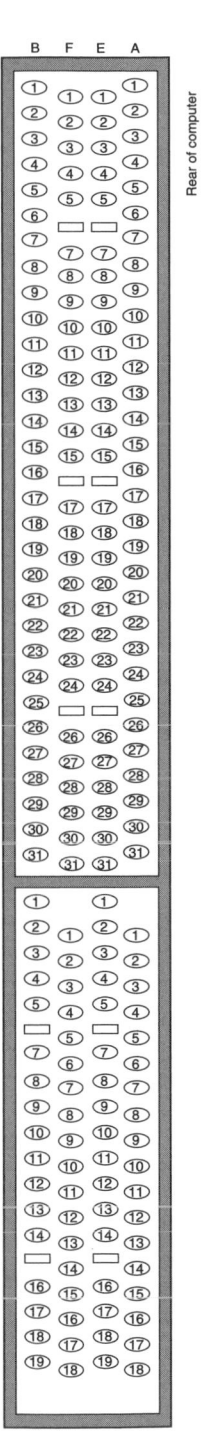

FIG. 4.19 The card connector for the EISA bus.

Local Buses

The I/O buses discussed so far (ISA, MCA, and EISA) have one thing in common—relatively slow speed. The three newer bus types that we will look at in the following few sections all use the *local bus* concept explained in this section to address the speed issue. The three main local buses found in PC systems are

■ VL-Bus (VESA Local Bus)

■ PCI (Peripheral Component Interconnect)

■ AGP (Accelerated Graphics Port)

The speed limitation of ISA, MCA, and EISA is a carryover from the days of the original PC, when the I/O bus operated at the same speed as the processor bus. As the speed of the processor bus increased, the I/O bus realized only nominal speed improvements, primarily from an increase in the bandwidth of the bus. The I/O bus had to remain at a slower speed, because the huge installed base of adapter cards could operate only at slower speeds.

Figure 4.20 shows a conceptual block diagram of the buses in a computer system.

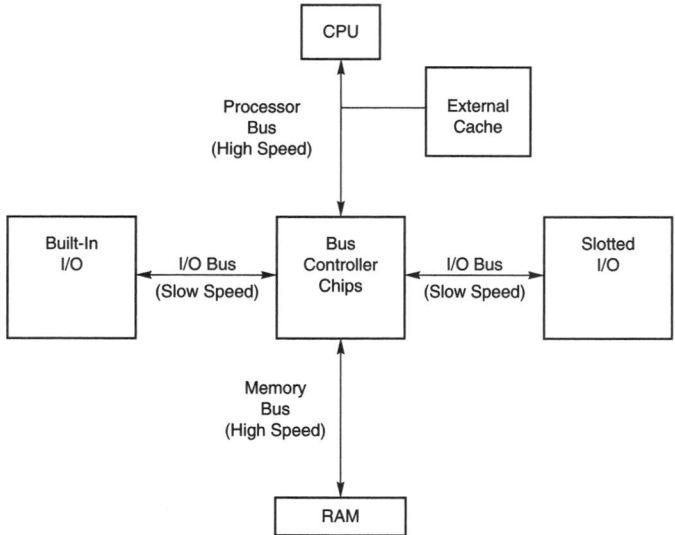

FIG. 4.20   Bus layout in a traditional PC.

The thought of a computer system running slower than it could bothers some computer users. Even so, the slow speed of the I/O bus is nothing more than a nuisance in most cases. You don't need blazing speed to communicate with a keyboard or a mouse because you gain nothing in performance. The real problem occurs in subsystems in which you need the speed, such as video and disk controllers.

The speed problem became acute when graphical user interfaces (such as Windows) became prevalent. These systems required the processing of so much video data that the I/O bus became a bottleneck for the entire computer system. In other words, it did little good to have a processor that was capable of 66MHz to 450MHz or faster if you could put data through the I/O bus at a rate of only 8MHz.

An obvious solution to this problem is to move some of the slotted I/O to an area where it could access the faster speeds of the processor bus—much the same way as the external cache. Figure 4.21 shows this arrangement.

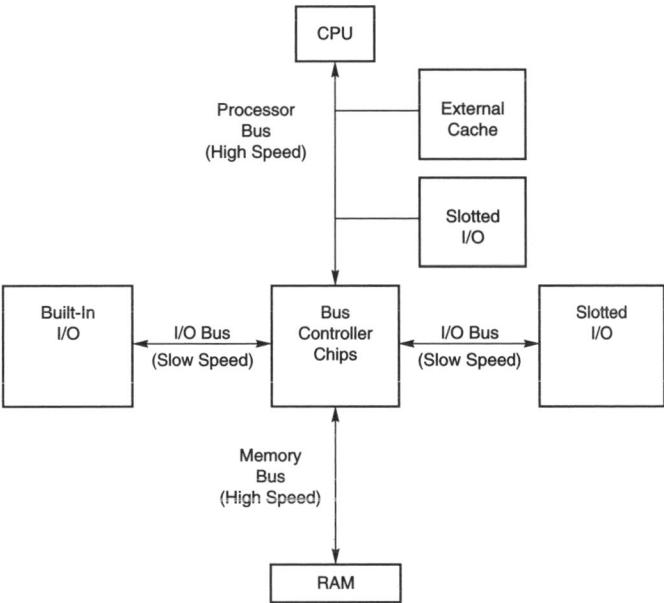

FIG. 4.21 How a local bus works.

This arrangement became known as *local bus*, because external devices (adapter cards) now could access the part of the bus that was local to the CPU—the processor bus. Physically, the slots provided to tap this new configuration would need to be different from existing bus slots, to prevent adapter cards designed for slower buses from being plugged into the higher bus speeds that this design made accessible.

It is interesting to note that the very first 8-bit and 16-bit ISA buses were a form of Local Bus architecture. These systems had the processor bus as the main bus, and everything ran at full processor speeds. When ISA systems ran faster than 8MHz, the main ISA bus had to be decoupled from the processor bus because expansion cards, memory, and so on could not keep up. In 1992, an extension to the ISA bus called the *VESA Local Bus* (VL-Bus) started showing up on PC systems, indicating a return to Local Bus architecture. Since then, the *Peripheral Component Interconnect* (PCI) local bus has supplanted VL-Bus and the Accelerated Graphics Port (AGP) bus has been introduced to complement PCI.

> **Note**
>
> A system does not have to have a local-bus expansion slot to incorporate local-bus technology; instead, the local-bus device can be built directly into the motherboard. (In such a case, the local-bus-slotted I/O shown in Figure 4.21 would be built-in I/O.) This built-in approach to local bus is the way the first local-bus systems were designed.

Local-bus solutions do not replace earlier standards, such as ISA; they are designed into the system as a bus that is closer to the processor in the system architecture. Older buses such as ISA have been kept around for backward compatibility with slower types of adapters that don't need any faster connection to the system (such as modems). Therefore, a typical system will have AGP, PCI, and ISA slots. Older cards still are compatible with the system, but high-speed adapter cards can take advantage of the AGP and PCI local-bus slots, as well.

The performance of graphical user interfaces such as Windows and OS/2 have been tremendously improved by moving the video cards off of the slow ISA bus and onto faster PCI and now AGP local buses.

VESA Local Bus

The VESA Local Bus was the most popular local bus design from its debut in August 1992 through 1994. It was created by the VESA committee, a nonprofit organization founded by NEC to further develop video display and bus standards. In a similar fashion to how EISA evolved, NEC had done most of the work on the VL-bus (as it would be called), and after founding the nonprofit VESA committee, they turned over future development to VESA. At first, the local-bus slot seemed primarily designed to be used for video cards. Improving video performance was a top priority at NEC to help sell their high-end displays and their own PC systems. By 1991, video performance had become a real bottleneck in most PC systems.

The *Video Electronics Standards Association* (*VESA*) developed a standardized local-bus specification known as *VESA Local Bus* or simply *VL-Bus*. As in earlier local-bus implementations, the VL-Bus slot offers direct access to system memory at the speed of the processor. The VL-Bus can move data 32 bits at a time, enabling data to flow between the CPU and a compatible video subsystem or hard drive at the full 32-bit data width of the 486 chip. The maximum rated throughput of the VL-Bus is 128M to 132M/sec. In other words, local bus went a long way toward removing the major bottlenecks that existed in earlier bus configurations.

Additionally, VL-Bus offers manufacturers of hard-drive interface cards an opportunity to overcome another traditional bottleneck—the rate at which data can flow between the hard drive and the CPU. The average 16-bit IDE drive and interface can achieve throughput of up to 5M/sec, whereas VL-Bus hard drive adapters for IDE drives are touted as providing throughput of as much as 8M/sec. In real-world situations, the true throughput of VL-Bus hard drive adapters is somewhat less than 8M/sec, but VL-Bus still provides a substantial boost in hard-drive performance.

Despite all the benefits of the VL-Bus (and, by extension, of all local buses), this technology has are a few drawbacks, which are described in the following list:

- *Dependence on a 486 CPU.* The VL-Bus inherently is tied to the 486 processor bus. This bus is quite different from that used by Pentium and later processors. A VL-Bus that operates at the full-rated speed of a Pentium has not been developed, although stopgap measures (such as stepping down speed or developing bus bridges) are available. Unfortunately, these result in poor performance. Some systems have been developed with both VL-Bus and PCI slots, but because of design compromises, performance often suffers.

- *Speed limitations.* The VL-Bus specification provides for speeds of up to 66MHz on the bus, but the electrical characteristics of the VL-Bus connector limit an adapter card to no more than 40 to 50MHz. In practice, running the VL-Bus at speeds over 33MHz causes many problems, so 33MHz has become the acceptable speed limit. Systems that use faster processor bus speeds must buffer and step down the clock on the VL-Bus or add wait states. Note that if the main CPU uses a clock modifier (such as the kind that doubles clock speeds), the VL-Bus uses the unmodified CPU clock speed as its bus speed.

- *Electrical limitations.* The processor bus has very tight timing rules, which may vary from CPU to CPU. These timing rules were designed for limited loading on the bus, meaning that the only elements originally intended to be connected to the local bus are elements such as the external cache and the bus controller chips. As you add more circuitry, you increase the electrical load. If the local bus is not implemented correctly, the additional load can lead to problems such as loss of data integrity and timing problems between the CPU and the VL-Bus cards.

- *Card limitations.* Depending on the electrical loading of a system, the number of VL-Bus cards is limited. Although the VL-Bus specification provides for as many as three cards, this can be achieved only at clock rates of up to 40MHz with an otherwise low system-board load. As the system-board load increases and the clock rate increases, the number of cards supported decreases. Only one VL-Bus card can be supported at 50MHz with a high system-board load. In practice, these limits can not usually be reached without problems.

The VL-Bus did not seem to be a well-engineered concept. The design was simple indeed—just take the pins from the 486 processor and run them out to a card connector socket. In other words, the VL-Bus is essentially the raw 486 processor bus. This allowed a very inexpensive design, because no additional chipsets or interface chips were required. A motherboard designer could add VL-Bus slots to their 486 motherboards very easily and at a very low cost. This is why these slots appeared on virtually all 486 system designs overnight.

Unfortunately, the 486 processor bus was not designed to have multiple devices (called *loads*) plugged into it at one time. Problems arose with timing glitches caused by the capacitance introduced into the circuit by different cards. Because the VL-Bus ran at the same speed as the processor bus, different processor speeds meant different bus speeds and full compatibility was difficult to achieve. Although the VL-Bus could be adapted to other processors, including the 386 or even the Pentium, it was designed for the 486, and worked best as a 486 solution only. Despite the low cost, after a new bus called *PCI (Peripheral Component Interconnect)* appeared, VL-Bus fell into disfavor very quickly. It never did catch on with Pentium systems, and there is little or no further development of the VL-Bus in the PC industry. I would not recommend purchasing VL-Bus cards or systems today.

For a used system, or as an inexpensive upgrade for an older system, VL-Bus might be appropriate and can provide an acceptable solution for high-speed computing.

Physically, the VL-Bus slot is an extension of the slots used for whatever type of base system you have. If you have an ISA system, the VL-Bus is positioned as an extension of your existing 16-bit ISA slots. Likewise, if you have an EISA system or MCA system, the VL-Bus slots are extensions of those existing slots. Figure 4.22 shows how the VL-Bus slots could be situated in an ISA system. The VESA extension has 112 contacts and uses the same physical connector as the MCA bus.

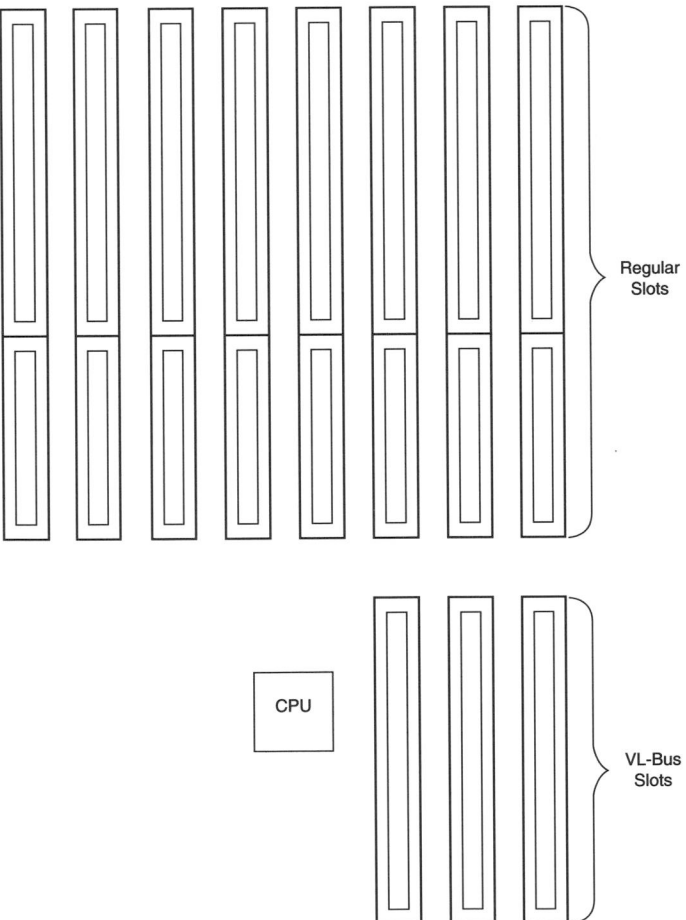

FIG. 4.22 An example of VL-Bus slots in an ISA system.

The VL-Bus adds 116 pin locations to the bus connectors that your system already has. Table 4.28 lists the pinouts for only the VL-Bus connector portion of the total connector. (For pins for which two purposes are listed, the second purpose applies when the card is in 64-bit transfer mode.)

Table 4.28   Pinouts for the VL-Bus

Pin	Signal Name	Pin	Signal Name
B1	Data 0	A1	Data 1
B2	Data 2	A2	Data 3
B3	Data 4	A3	Ground
B4	Data 6	A4	Data 5
B5	Data 8	A5	Data 7
B6	Ground	A6	Data 9
B7	Data 10	A7	Data 11
B8	Data 12	A8	Data 13
B9	VCC	A9	Data 15
B10	Data 14	A10	Ground
B11	Data 16	A11	Data 17
B12	Data 18	A12	VCC
B13	Data 20	A13	Data 19
B14	Ground	A14	Data 21
B15	Data 22	A15	Data 23
B16	Data 24	A16	Data 25
B17	Data 26	A17	Ground
B18	Data 28	A18	Data 27
B19	Data 30	A19	Data 29
B20	VCC	A20	Data 31
B21	Address 31 or Data 63	A21	Address 30 or Data 62
B22	Ground	A22	Address 28 or Data 60
B23	Address 29 or Data 61	A23	Address 26 or Data 58
B24	Address 27 or Data 59	A24	Ground
B25	Address 25 or Data 57	A25	Address 24 or Data 56
B26	Address 23 or Data 55	A26	Address 22 or Data 54
B27	Address 21 or Data 53	A27	VCC
B28	Address 19 or Data 51	A28	Address 20 or Data 52
B29	Ground	A29	Address 18 or Data 50
B30	Address 17 or Data 49	A30	Address 16 or Data 48
B31	Address 15 or Data 47	A31	Address 14 or Data 46
B32	VCC	A32	Address 12 or Data 44
B33	Address 13 or Data 45	A33	Address 10 or Data 42
B34	Address 11 or Data 43	A34	Address 8 or Data 40

(continues)

Table 4.28	Pinouts for the VL-Bus Continued		
Pin	**Signal Name**	**Pin**	**Signal Name**
B35	Address 9 or Data 41	A35	Ground
B36	Address 7 or Data 39	A36	Address 6 or Data 38
B37	Address 5 or Data 37	A37	Address 4 or Data 36
B38	Ground	A38	Write Back
B39	Address 3 or Data 35	A39	Byte Enable 0 or 4
B40	Address 2 or Data 34	A40	VCC
B41	Unused or LBS64#	A41	Byte Enable 1 or 5
B42	Reset	A42	Byte Enable 2 or 6
B43	Data/Code Status	A43	Ground
B44	Memory-I/O Status or Data 33	A44	Byte Enable 3 or 7
B45	Write/Read Status or Data 32	A45	Address Data Strobe
B46	Access key	A46	Access key
B47	Access key	A47	Access key
B48	Ready Return	A48	Local Ready
B49	Ground	A49	Local Device
B50	IRQ 9	A50	Local Request
B51	Burst Ready	A51	Ground
B52	Burst Last	A52	Local Bus Grant
B53	ID0	A53	VCC
B54	ID1	A54	ID2
B55	Ground	A55	ID3
B56	Local Clock	A56	ID4 or ACK64#
B57	VCC	A57	Unused
B58	Local Bus Size 16	A58	Loc/Ext Address Data Strobe

Figure 4.23 shows the locations of the pins.

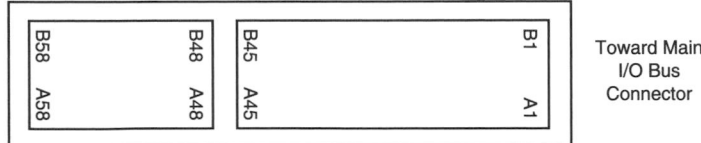

FIG. 4.23   The card connector for the VL-Bus.

The PCI Bus

In early 1992, Intel spearheaded the creation of another industry group. It was formed with the same goals as the VESA group in relation to the PC bus. Recognizing the need to overcome weaknesses in the ISA and EISA buses, the *PCI Special Interest Group* was formed.

The *Peripheral Component Interconnect* (PCI) bus specification, released in June 1992 as version 1.0, was later updated in April 1993 as version 2.0. The latest revision, version 2.1, appeared in early 1995. PCI redesigned the traditional PC bus by inserting another bus between the CPU and the native I/O bus by means of bridges. Rather than tap directly into the processor bus, with its delicate electrical timing (as was done in the VL-Bus), a new set of controller chips was developed to extend the bus, as shown in Figure 4.24.

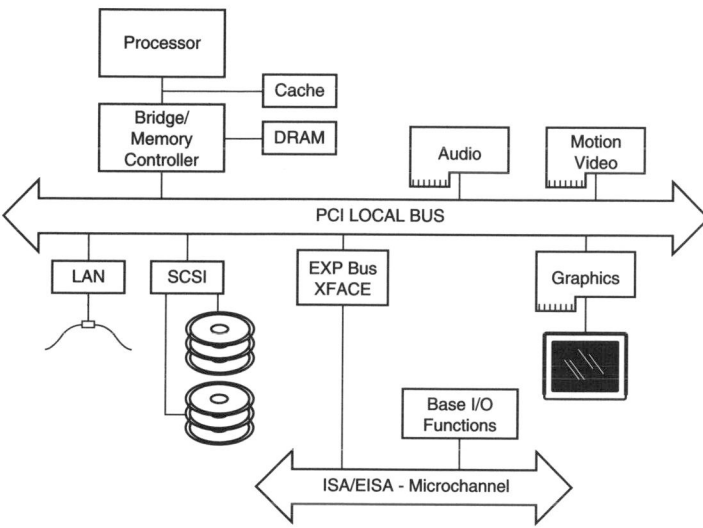

FIG. 4.24 Conceptual diagram of the PCI bus.

The PCI bus often is called a *mezzanine bus* because it adds another layer to the traditional bus configuration. PCI bypasses the standard I/O bus; it uses the system bus to increase the bus clock speed and take full advantage of the CPU's data path. Systems that integrate the PCI bus became available in mid-1993 and have since become the mainstay high-end systems.

Information is transferred across the PCI bus at 33MHz, at the full data width of the CPU. When the bus is used in conjunction with a 32-bit CPU, the bandwidth is 132M per second, as the following formula shows:

33MHz×32 bits = 1,056Mbit/sec

1,056Mbit/sec÷8 = 132M/sec

When the bus is used in future 64-bit implementations, the bandwidth doubles, meaning that you can transfer data at speeds up to 264M/sec. Real-life data transfer speeds necessarily will be lower, but still much faster than anything else that is currently available. Part of the reason for this faster real-life throughput is the fact that the PCI bus can operate concurrently with the processor bus; it does not supplant it. The CPU can be processing data in an external cache while the PCI bus is busy transferring information between other parts of the system—a major design benefit of the PCI bus.

A PCI adapter card uses its own unique connector. This connector can be identified within a computer system because it typically is offset from the normal ISA, MCA, or EISA connectors (see Figure 4.25). The size of a PCI card can be the same as that of the cards used in the system's normal I/O bus.

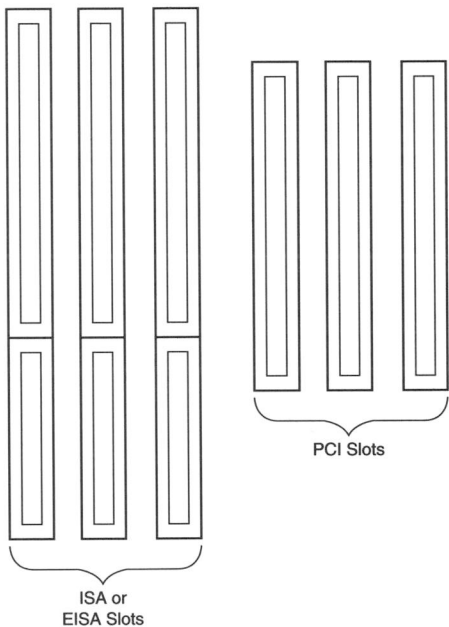

FIG. 4.25 Possible configuration of PCI slots in relation to ISA or EISA slots.

The PCI specification identifies three board configurations, each designed for a specific type of system with specific power requirements. The 5v specification is for stationary computer systems, the 3.3v specification is for portable machines, and the universal specification is for motherboards and cards that work in either type of system.

Table 4.29 shows the 5v PCI pinouts, and Figure 4.26 shows the pin locations. Table 4.30 shows the 3.3v PCI pinouts; the pin locations are indicated in Figure 4.27. Finally, Table 4.31 shows the pinouts, and Figure 4.28 shows the pin locations for a universal PCI slot and card. Notice that each figure shows both the 32-bit and 64-bit variations on the respective specifications.

Note

If the PCI card supports only 32 data bits, it needs only pins B1/A1 through B62/A62. Pins B63/A63 through B94/A94 are used only if the card supports 64 data bits.

Table 4.29   Pinouts for a 5v PCI Bus

Pin	Signal Name	Pin	Signal Name
B1	–12v	A1	Test Reset
B2	Test Clock	A2	+12v
B3	Ground	A3	Test Mode Select
B4	Test Data Output	A4	Test Data Input
B5	+5v	A5	+5v
B6	+5v	A6	Interrupt A
B7	Interrupt B	A7	Interrupt C
B8	Interrupt D	A8	+5v
B9	PRSNT1#	A9	Reserved
B10	Reserved	A10	+5v I/O
B11	PRSNT2#	A11	Reserved
B12	Ground	A12	Ground
B13	Ground	A13	Ground
B14	Reserved	A14	Reserved
B15	Ground	A15	Reset
B16	Clock	A16	+5v I/O
B17	Ground	A17	Grant
B18	Request	A18	Ground
B19	+5v I/O	A19	Reserved
B20	Address 31	A20	Address 30
B21	Address 29	A21	+3.3v
B22	Ground	A22	Address 28
B23	Address 27	A23	Address 26
B24	Address 25	A24	Ground
B25	+3.3v	A25	Address 24
B26	C/BE 3	A26	Init Device Select
B27	Address 23	A27	+3.3v
B28	Ground	A28	Address 22
B29	Address 21	A29	Address 20
B30	Address 19	A30	Ground
B31	+3.3v	A31	Address 18
B32	Address 17	A32	Address 16
B33	C/BE 2	A33	+3.3v
B34	Ground	A34	Cycle Frame
B35	Initiator Ready	A35	Ground
B36	+3.3v	A36	Target Ready
B37	Device Select	A37	Ground

(continues)

Table 4.29   Pinouts for a 5v PCI Bus Continued

Pin	Signal Name	Pin	Signal Name
B38	Ground	A38	Stop
B39	Lock	A39	+3.3v
B40	Parity Error	A40	Snoop Done
B41	+3.3v	A41	Snoop Backoff
B42	System Error	A42	Ground
B43	+3.3v	A43	PAR
B44	C/BE 1	A44	Address 15
B45	Address 14	A45	+3.3v
B46	Ground	A46	Address 13
B47	Address 12	A47	Address 11
B48	Address 10	A48	Ground
B49	Ground	A49	Address 9
B50	Access key	A50	Access key
B51	Access key	A51	Access key
B52	Address 8	A52	C/BE 0
B53	Address 7	A53	+3.3v
B54	+3.3v	A54	Address 6
B55	Address 5	A55	Address 4
B56	Address 3	A56	Ground
B57	Ground	A57	Address 2
B58	Address 1	A58	Address 0
B59	+5v I/O	A59	+5v I/O
B60	Acknowledge 64-bit	A60	Request 64-bit
B61	+5v	A61	+5v
B62	+5v Access key	A62	+5v Access key
B63	Reserved	A63	Ground
B64	Ground	A64	C/BE 7
B65	C/BE 6	A65	C/BE 5
B66	C/BE 4	A66	+5v I/O
B67	Ground	A67	Parity 64-bit
B68	Address 63	A68	Address 62
B69	Address 61	A69	Ground
B70	+5v I/O	A70	Address 60
B71	Address 59	A71	Address 58
B72	Address 57	A72	Ground
B73	Ground	A73	Address 56

Pin	Signal Name	Pin	Signal Name
B74	Address 55	A74	Address 54
B75	Address 53	A75	+5v I/O
B76	Ground	A76	Address 52
B77	Address 51	A77	Address 50
B78	Address 49	A78	Ground
B79	+5v I/O	A79	Address 48
B80	Address 47	A80	Address 46
B81	Address 45	A81	Ground
B82	Ground	A82	Address 44
B83	Address 43	A83	Address 42
B84	Address 41	A84	+5v I/O
B85	Ground	A85	Address 40
B86	Address 39	A86	Address 38
B87	Address 37	A87	Ground
B88	+5v I/O	A88	Address 36
B89	Address 35	A89	Address 34
B90	Address 33	A90	Ground
B91	Ground	A91	Address 32
B92	Reserved	A92	Reserved
B93	Reserved	A93	Ground
B94	Ground	A94	Reserved

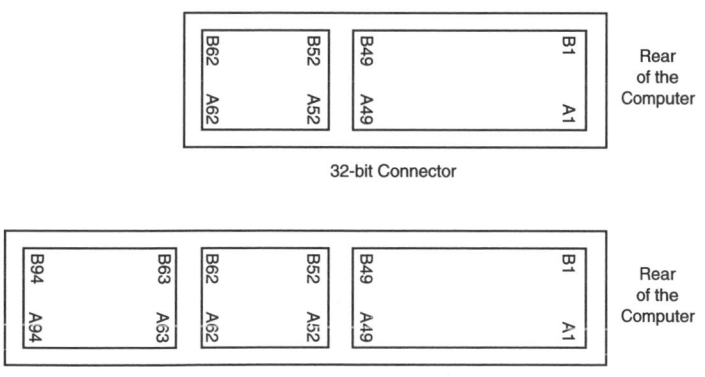

FIG. 4.26 The 5v PCI slot and card configuration.

Table 4.30   Pinouts for a 3.3v PCI Bus

Pin	Signal Name	Pin	Signal Name
B1	–12v	A1	Test Reset
B2	Test Clock	A2	+12v
B3	Ground	A3	Test Mode Select
B4	Test Data Output	A4	Test Data Input
B5	+5v	A5	+5v
B6	+5v	A6	Interrupt A
B7	Interrupt B	A7	Interrupt C
B8	Interrupt D	A8	+5v
B9	PRSNT1#	A9	Reserved
B10	Reserved	A10	+3.3v
B11	PRSNT2#	A11	Reserved
B12	Access key	A12	Access key
B13	Access key	A13	Access key
B14	Reserved	A14	Reserved
B15	Ground	A15	Reset
B16	Clock	A16	+3.3v
B17	Ground	A17	Grant
B18	Request	A18	Ground
B19	+3.3v	A19	Reserved
B20	Address 31	A20	Address 30
B21	Address 29	A21	+3.3v
B22	Ground	A22	Address 28
B23	Address 27	A23	Address 26
B24	Address 25	A24	Ground
B25	+3.3v	A25	Address 24
B26	C/BE 3	A26	Init Device Select
B27	Address 23	A27	+3.3v
B28	Ground	A28	Address 22
B29	Address 21	A29	Address 20
B30	Address 19	A30	Ground
B31	+3.3v	A31	Address 18
B32	Address 17	A32	Address 16
B33	C/BE 2	A33	+3.3v
B34	Ground	A34	Cycle Frame
B35	Initiator Ready	A35	Ground
B36	+3.3v	A36	Target Ready
B37	Device Select	A37	Ground
B38	Ground	A38	Stop
B39	Lock	A39	+3.3v

Pin	Signal Name	Pin	Signal Name
B40	Parity Error	A40	Snoop Done
B41	+3.3v	A41	Snoop Backoff
B42	System Error	A42	Ground
B43	+3.3v	A43	PAR
B44	C/BE 1	A44	Address 15
B45	Address 14	A45	+3.3v
B46	Ground	A46	Address 13
B47	Address 12	A47	Address 11
B48	Address 10	A48	Ground
B49	Ground	A49	Address 9
B50	Ground	A50	Ground
B51	Ground	A51	Ground
B52	Address 8	A52	C/BE 0
B53	Address 7	A53	+3.3v
B54	+3.3v	A54	Address 6
B55	Address 5	A55	Address 4
B56	Address 3	A56	Ground
B57	Ground	A57	Address 2
B58	Address 1	A58	Address 0
B59	+3.3v	A59	+3.3v
B60	Acknowledge 64-bit	A60	Request 64-bit
B61	+5v	A61	+5v
B62	+5v Access key	A62	+5v Access key
B63	Reserved	A63	Ground
B64	Ground	A64	C/BE 7
B65	C/BE 6	A65	C/BE 5
B66	C/BE 4	A66	+3.3v
B67	Ground	A67	Parity 64-bit
B68	Address 63	A68	Address 62
B69	Address 61	A69	Ground
B70	+3.3v	A70	Address 60
B71	Address 59	A71	Address 58
B72	Address 57	A72	Ground
B73	Ground	A73	Address 56
B74	Address 55	A74	Address 54
B75	Address 53	A75	+3.3v
B76	Ground	A76	Address 52
B77	Address 51	A77	Address 50

(continues)

Table 4.30 Pinouts for a 3.3v PCI Bus Continued			
Pin	**Signal Name**	**Pin**	**Signal Name**
B78	Address 49	A78	Ground
B79	+3.3v	A79	Address 48
B80	Address 47	A80	Address 46
B81	Address 45	A81	Ground
B82	Ground	A82	Address 44
B83	Address 43	A83	Address 42
B84	Address 41	A84	+3.3v
B85	Ground	A85	Address 40
B86	Address 39	A86	Address 38
B87	Address 37	A87	Ground
B88	+3.3v	A88	Address 36
B89	Address 35	A89	Address 34
B90	Address 33	A90	Ground
B91	Ground	A91	Address 32
B92	Reserved	A92	Reserved
B93	Reserved	A93	Ground
B94	Ground	A94	Reserved

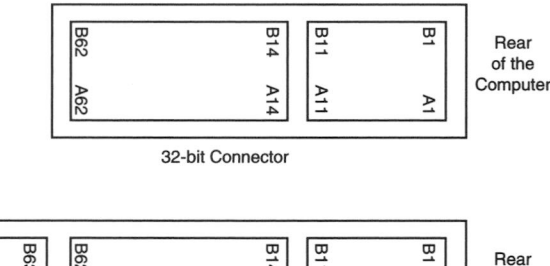

FIG. 4.27 The 3.3v PCI slot and card configuration.

Table 4.31 Pinouts for a Universal PCI Bus			
Pin	**Signal Name**	**Pin**	**Signal Name**
B1	−12v	A1	Test Reset
B2	Test Clock	A2	+12v
B3	Ground	A3	Test Mode Select
B4	Test Data Output	A4	Test Data Input
B5	+5v	A5	+5v

Pin	Signal Name	Pin	Signal Name
B6	+5v	A6	Interrupt A
B7	Interrupt B	A7	Interrupt C
B8	Interrupt D	A8	+5v
B9	PRSNT1#	A9	Reserved
B10	Reserved	A10	+v I/O
B11	PRSNT2#	A11	Reserved
B12	Access key	A12	Access key
B13	Access key	A13	Access key
B14	Reserved	A14	Reserved
B15	Ground	A15	Reset
B16	Clock	A16	+v I/O
B17	Ground	A17	Grant
B18	Request	A18	Ground
B19	+v I/O	A19	Reserved
B20	Address 31	A20	Address 30
B21	Address 29	A21	+3.3v
B22	Ground	A22	Address 28
B23	Address 27	A23	Address 26
B24	Address 25	A24	Ground
B25	+3.3v	A25	Address 24
B26	C/BE 3	A26	Init Device Select
B27	Address 23	A27	+3.3v
B28	Ground	A28	Address 22
B29	Address 21	A29	Address 20
B30	Address 19	A30	Ground
B31	+3.3v	A31	Address 18
B32	Address 17	A32	Address 16
B33	C/BE 2	A33	+3.3v
B34	Ground	A34	Cycle Frame
B35	Initiator Ready	A35	Ground
B36	+3.3v	A36	Target Ready
B37	Device Select	A37	Ground
B38	Ground	A38	Stop
B39	Lock	A39	+3.3v
B40	Parity Error	A40	Snoop Done
B41	+3.3v	A41	Snoop Backoff
B42	System Error	A42	Ground
B43	+3.3v	A43	PAR
B44	C/BE 1	A44	Address 15

(continues)

Table 4.31 Pinouts for a Universal PCI Bus Continued

Pin	Signal Name	Pin	Signal Name
B45	Address 14	A45	+3.3v
B46	Ground	A46	Address 13
B47	Address 12	A47	Address 11
B48	Address 10	A48	Ground
B49	Ground	A49	Address 9
B50	Access key	A50	Access key
B51	Access key	A51	Access key
B52	Address 8	A52	C/BE 0
B53	Address 7	A53	+3.3v
B54	+3.3v	A54	Address 6
B55	Address 5	A55	Address 4
B56	Address 3	A56	Ground
B57	Ground	A57	Address 2
B58	Address 1	A58	Address 0
B59	+5 I/O	A59	+v I/O
B60	Acknowledge 64-bit	A60	Request 64-bit
B61	+5v	A61	+5v
B62	+5v Access key	A62	+5v Access key
B63	Reserved	A63	Ground
B64	Ground	A64	C/BE 7
B65	C/BE 6	A65	C/BE 5
B66	C/BE 4	A66	+v I/O
B67	Ground	A67	Parity 64-bit
B68	Address 63	A68	Address 62
B69	Address 61	A69	Ground
B70	+v I/O	A70	Address 60
B71	Address 59	A71	Address 58
B72	Address 57	A72	Ground
B73	Ground	A73	Address 56
B74	Address 55	A74	Address 54
B75	Address 53	A75	+v I/O
B76	Ground	A76	Address 52
B77	Address 51	A77	Address 50
B78	Address 49	A78	Ground
B79	+v I/O	A79	Address 48
B80	Address 47	A80	Address 46
B81	Address 45	A81	Ground
B82	Ground	A82	Address 44

Pin	Signal Name	Pin	Signal Name
B83	Address 43	A83	Address 42
B84	Address 41	A84	+v I/O
B85	Ground	A85	Address 40
B86	Address 39	A86	Address 38
B87	Address 37	A87	Ground
B88	+v I/O	A88	Address 36
B89	Address 35	A89	Address 34
B90	Address 33	A90	Ground
B91	Ground	A91	Address 32
B92	Reserved	A92	Reserved
B93	Reserved	A93	Ground
B94	Ground	A94	Reserved

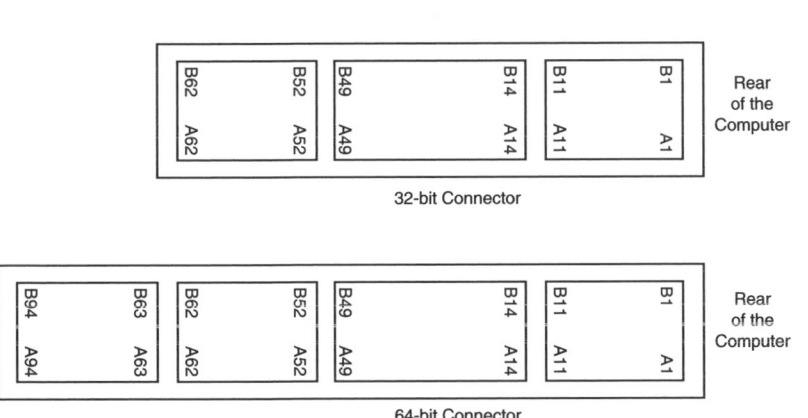

FIG. 4.28   The universal PCI slot and card configuration.

Notice that the universal PCI board specifications effectively combine the 5v and 3.3v specifications. For pins for which the voltage is different, the universal specification labels the pin simply V I/O. This type of pin represents a special power pin for defining and driving the PCI signaling rail.

Another important feature of PCI is the fact that it was the model for the Intel PnP specification. This means that PCI cards do not have jumpers and switches, and are instead configured through software. True PnP systems are able to automatically configure the adapters, while non-PnP systems with ISA slots have to configure the adapters through a program that is usually a part of the system CMOS configuration. Starting in late 1995, most PC-compatible systems have included a PnP BIOS that allows the automatic PnP configuration.

PCI Internal Interrupts.   The PCI bus uses its own internal interrupt system for dealing with requests from the cards on the bus. These interrupts are often called "#A", "#B",

"#C", and "#D" to avoid confusion with the normal numbered system IRQs, although they are sometimes called "#1" through "#4". These interrupt levels are not generally seen by the user except in the BIOS setup screen for PCI, where they can be used to control how PCI cards operate.

These interrupts, if needed by cards in the slots, are mapped to regular interrupts, normally IRQ9 through IRQ12. The PCI slots in most systems can be mapped to at most four regular IRQs. In systems that have more than four PCI slots, or that have four slots and a USB controller (which uses PCI), two or more of the PCI devices share an IRQ.

▶▶ See "USB (Universal Serial Bus)," p. 601

If you are using Windows 95 OEM SR2 (OEM Service Release 2) or Windows 98, you may see additional entries for your PCI devices under the Device Manager. Each device may have an additional entry entitled "IRQ Holder for PCI Steering." PCI steering is a feature that is part of the Plug-and-Play portions of the system, and enables the IRQ used for PCI devices to be controlled by the operating system to avoid resource problems. Having this listed in addition to another device under the IRQ list does not mean you have a resource conflict.

PCI supports full-device bus mastering, and provides bus arbitration facilities through the system chipset. PCI's design allows bus mastering of multiple devices on the bus simultaneously, with the arbitration circuitry working to ensure that no device on the bus (including the processor!) locks out any other device. At the same time, however, it allows any given device to use the full bus throughput if no other device needs to transfer anything. In a way, the PCI bus acts like a tiny local area network inside the computer, in which multiple devices can each talk to one another, sharing a communication channel that is managed by the chipset.

Accelerated Graphics Port (AGP)

Like the ISA bus before it, traffic on the PCI bus is starting to become heavy on high-end PCs, with video, hard disk, and peripheral data all competing for the same I/O bandwidth. To combat the eventual saturation of the PCI bus with video information, a new interface has been pioneered by Intel, designed specifically for the video subsystem. It is called the *Accelerated Graphics Port (AGP)*.

AGP was developed in response to the trend toward greater and greater performance requirements for video. As software evolves and computer use continues into previously unexplored areas, such as 3D acceleration and full-motion video playback, both the processor and the video chipset need to process more and more information. The PCI bus is reaching its performance limits in these applications, especially with hard disks and other peripherals also in there fighting for the same bandwidth.

The idea behind AGP is simple—Create a faster, dedicated interface between the video chipset and the system processor. The interface is only between these two devices; this has three major advantages: It makes it easier to implement the port, makes it easier to increase AGP in speed, and makes it possible to put enhancements into the design that are specific to video.

AGP is considered a port, and not a bus, because it only involves two devices (the processor and video card) and is not expandable. One of the great advantages of AGP is that it isolates the video subsystem from the rest of the PC so there isn't nearly as much contention over I/O bandwidth as there is with PCI. With the video card removed from the PCI bus, other PCI devices will also benefit from improved bandwidth.

AGP is a new technology and was just introduced to the market in the third quarter of 1997. The first support for this new technology was in the Intel 440LX Pentium II chipset. The AGP interface is in many ways still quite similar to PCI. The slot is similar physically in shape and size, but is offset further from the edge of the motherboard than PCI slots are. The AGP specification is based on the PCI 2.1 specification, which includes a high-bandwidth 66MHz speed that was never implemented on the PC. AGP motherboards have a single expansion card slot for the AGP video card, and usually one fewer PCI slot, and are otherwise quite similar to PCI motherboards.

The AGP bus is 32 bits wide, just the same as PCI is, but instead of running at equal or less than half of the system (memory) bus speed the way PCI does, it runs at twice the speed of PCI, or 66MHz. This, of course, immediately doubles the bandwidth of the port; instead of the limit of 133M/s as with PCI, AGP in its lowest speed mode has a bandwidth of 266M/s. Plus, of course, it includes the benefits of not having to share bandwidth with other PCI devices.

In addition to doubling the speed of the bus, AGP has defined a 2x mode (and a future 4x mode), which uses special signaling to allow twice as much data to be sent over the port at the same clock speed. What the hardware does is send information on both the rising and falling edges of the clock signal—normally, information is only sent once per clock cycle, but with this 2x mode, information can be sent twice. Think of the 1x mode as transferring information everytime a drummer's stick hits the drum. In 2x mode, an additional transfer would occur everytime the stick was raised. The result is that the performance doubles again, to 533M/s theoretical bandwidth. There is also a plan to implement a 4x mode, which will perform four transfers per clock cycle—a whopping 1.066G/s of bandwidth.

AGP will allow the speed of the video card to pace the requirements for high-speed, full-motion video on the PC in the future.

System Resources

System resources are the communications channels, addresses, and other signals used by hardware devices to communicate on the bus. At their lowest level, these resources typically include the following:

- Memory addresses
- IRQ (Interrupt Request) channels

- DMA (Direct Memory Access) channels

- I/O Port addresses

I have listed these roughly in the order you would experience problems with them. Memory conflicts are perhaps the most troublesome of these, certainly the most difficult to fully explain and overcome. These are discussed in Chapter 5, "Memory," which focuses on the others listed here in the order you will likely have problems with them. IRQs cause more problems than DMA because they are in much higher demand; therefore, virtually all cards will use IRQ channels. There are fewer problems with DMA channels because few cards use them, and there are usually more than enough channels to go around. I/O ports are used by all hardware devices on the bus, but there are technically 64K of them, which means plenty to go around. With all of these resources, you have to make sure that a unique card or hardware function uses each resource; they cannot or should not be shared.

These resources are required and used by many different components of your system. Adapter cards need these resources to communicate with your system and to perform their functions. Not all adapter cards have the same resource requirements. A serial communications port, for example, needs an IRQ channel and I/O port address; whereas a sound board needs these resources and at least one DMA channel as well. Most network cards use a 16K block of memory addresses, an IRQ channel, and an I/O port address.

As your system increases in complexity, the chance for resource conflicts increases dramatically. Modern systems with sound cards and network cards can really push the envelope and can become a configuration nightmare for the uninitiated. So that you can resolve conflicts, most adapter cards allow you to modify resource assignments by using the Plug-and-Play software that comes with the card or the Device Manager in Windows 95 and later. Even if the automatic configuration gets confused (which happens more often than it should), fortunately in almost all cases there is a logical way to configure the system—once you know the rules.

Interrupts (IRQs)

Interrupt request channels (IRQs), or hardware interrupts, are used by various hardware devices to signal the motherboard that a request must be fulfilled. This procedure is the same as a student raising his hand to indicate that he needs attention.

These interrupt channels are represented by wires on the motherboard and in the slot connectors. When a particular interrupt is invoked, a special routine takes over the system, which first saves all the CPU register contents in a stack and then directs the system to the interrupt vector table. This vector table contains a list of memory addresses that correspond to the interrupt channels. Depending on which interrupt was invoked, the program corresponding to that channel is run.

The pointers in the vector table point to the address of whatever software driver is used to service the card that generated the interrupt. For a network card, for example, the vector may point to the address of the network drivers that have been loaded to operate the card; for a hard disk controller, the vector may point to the BIOS code that operates the controller.

After the particular software routine finishes performing whatever function the card needed, the interrupt-control software returns the stack contents to the CPU registers, and the system then resumes whatever it was doing before the interrupt occurred.

Through the use of interrupts, your system can respond to external events in a timely fashion. Each time that a serial port presents a byte to your system, an interrupt is generated to ensure that the system reads that byte before another comes in. Keep in mind that in some cases a port device—in particular, a modem with a 16550 or higher UART chip—may incorporate a byte buffer that allows multiple characters to be stored before an interrupt is generated.

Hardware interrupts are generally prioritized by their numbers; with some exceptions, the highest-priority interrupts have the lowest numbers. Higher-priority interrupts take precedence over lower-priority interrupts. As a result, several interrupts can occur in your system concurrently, each interrupt nesting within another.

If you overload the system—in this case, by running out of stack resources (too many interrupts were generated too quickly)—an internal stack overflow error occurs and your system halts. The message usually appears as Internal stack overflow—system halted at a DOS prompt. If you experience this type of system error and run DOS, you can compensate for it by using the STACKS parameter in your CONFIG.SYS file to increase the available stack resources. Most people will not see this error in Windows 95 or Windows NT.

The ISA bus uses edge-triggered *interrupt sensing*, in which an interrupt is sensed by a signal sent on a particular wire located in the slot connector. A different wire corresponds to each possible hardware interrupt. Because the motherboard cannot recognize which slot contains the card that used an interrupt line and therefore generated the interrupt, confusion would result if more than one card were set to use a particular interrupt. Each interrupt, therefore, usually is designated for a single hardware device, and most of the time, interrupts cannot be shared.

A device can be designed to share interrupts, and a few devices allow this; most cannot, however, because of the way interrupts are signaled in the ISA bus. The PCI bus allows interrupt sharing; in fact, virtually all PCI cards are set to PCI interrupt A. The real problem is that for these cards to work in your system, they must be mapped to ISA interrupts, which are nonsharable. That is why your PCI cards still work the same way as before as far as interrupts are concerned. That is, you will have to assign a nonconflicting interrupt for each card.

External hardware interrupts often are referred to as *maskable interrupts*, which simply means that the interrupts can be masked or turned off for a short time while the CPU is used for other critical operations. It is up to the programmer to manage interrupts properly and efficiently for the best system performance.

Because interrupts usually cannot be shared in an ISA bus system, you often run into conflicts and can even run out of interrupts when you are adding boards to a system. If two boards use the same IRQ to signal the system, the resulting conflict prevents either board from operating properly. The following sections discuss the IRQs that any standard devices use, and what may be free in your system.

8-Bit ISA Bus Interrupts. The PC and XT (the systems based on the 8-bit 8086 CPU) provide for eight different external hardware interrupts. Table 4.32 shows the typical uses for these interrupts, which are numbered 0 through 7.

Table 4.32 8-Bit ISA Bus Default Interrupt Assignments		
IRQ	**Function**	**Bus Slot**
0	System Timer	No
1	Keyboard Controller	No
2	Available	Yes (8-bit)
3	Serial Port 2 (COM2:)	Yes (8-bit)
4	Serial Port 1 (COM1:)	Yes (8-bit)
5	Hard Disk Controller	Yes (8-bit)
6	Floppy Disk Controller	Yes (8-bit)
7	Parallel Port 1 (LPT1:)	Yes (8-bit)

If your system has one of the original 8-bit ISA buses, you will find that the IRQ resources provided by the system present a severe limitation. Installing several devices that need the services of system IRQs in a PC/XT-type system can be a study in frustration, because the only way to resolve the interrupt-shortage problem is to remove the adapter board that you need the least.

16-Bit ISA, EISA, and MCA Bus Interrupts. The introduction of the AT, based on the 286 processor, was accompanied by an increase in the number of external hardware interrupts that the bus would support. The number of interrupts was doubled to 16 by using two Intel 8259 interrupt controllers and piping the interrupts generated by the second one through the unused IRQ 2 in the first controller. This arrangement effectively means that 15 IRQ assignments are available, and IRQ 2 is effectively inaccessible.

By routing all of the interrupts from the second IRQ controller through IRQ 2 on the first, all of these new interrupts are assigned a nested priority level between IRQ 1 and IRQ 3. Thus, IRQ 15 ends up having a higher priority than IRQ 3. Figure 4.29 shows how the two 8259 chips were wired to create the cascade through IRQ 2 on the first chip.

To prevent problems with boards set to use IRQ 2, the AT system designers routed one of the new interrupts (IRQ 9) to fill the slot position left open after removing IRQ 2. This means that any card you install in a modern system that claims to use IRQ 2 is really using IRQ 9 instead. Some cards now label this selection as IRQ 2/9, while others may call it IRQ 2 or IRQ 9. No matter what the labeling says, you must never assign two cards to use that interrupt!

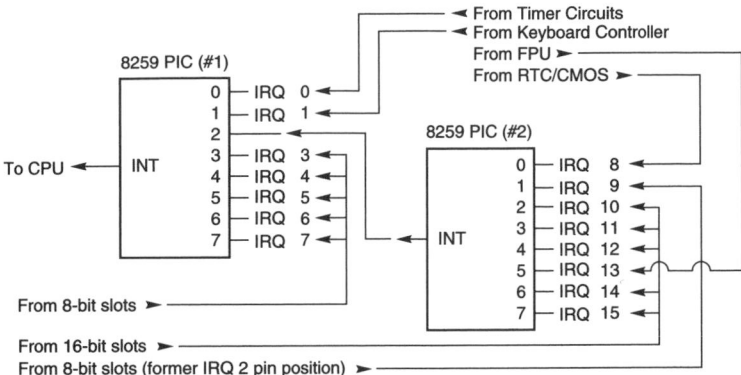

FIG. 4.29   Interrupt controller cascade wiring.

Table 4.33 shows the typical uses for interrupts in the 16-bit ISA, EISA, and MCA buses and lists them in priority order from highest to lowest.

Table 4.33 16/32-Bit ISA/PCI Default Interrupt Assignments				
IRQ	**Standard Function**	**Bus Slot**	**Card Type**	**Recommended Use**
0	System Timer	No	-	-
1	Keyboard Controller	No	-	-
2	2nd IRQ Controller Cascade	No	-	-
8	Real-Time Clock	No	-	-
9	Available (Appears as IRQ 2)	Yes	8/16-bit	Network Interface Card
10	Available	Yes	16-bit	USB
11	Available	Yes	16-bit	SCSI Host Adapter
12	Motherboard Mouse Port/Available	Yes	16-bit	Motherboard Mouse Port
13	Math Coprocessor	No	-	-
14	Primary IDE	Yes	16-bit	Primary IDE (Hard disks)
15	Secondary IDE/Available	Yes	16-bit	Secondary IDE (CDROM/Tape)
3	Serial Port 2 (COM2:)	Yes	8/16-bit	COM2:/Internal Modem
4	Serial Port 1 (COM1:)	Yes	8/16-bit	COM1:
5	Sound/Parallel Port 2 (LPT2:)	Yes	8/16-bit	Sound Card
6	Floppy Disk Controller	Yes	8/16-bit	Floppy Controller
7	Parallel Port 1 (LPT1:)	Yes	8/16-bit	LPT1:

Notice that interrupts 0, 1, 2, 8, and 13 are not on the bus connectors and are not accessible to adapter cards. Interrupts 8, 10, 11, 12, 13, 14, and 15 are from the second interrupt controller and are accessible only by boards that use the 16-bit extension connector, because this is where these wires are located. IRQ 9 is rewired to the 8-bit slot connector in place of IRQ 2, which means that IRQ 9 replaces IRQ 2 and therefore is available to 8-bit cards, which treat it as though it were IRQ 2.

> **Note**
>
> Although the 16-bit ISA bus has twice as many interrupts as systems that have the 8-bit ISA bus, you still may run out of available interrupts because only 16-bit adapters can use most of the newly available interrupts.

The extra IRQ lines in a 16-bit ISA system are of little help unless the adapter boards that you plan to use enable you to configure them for one of the unused IRQs. Some devices are hard-wired so that they can use only a particular IRQ. If you have a device that already uses that IRQ, you must resolve the conflict before installing the second adapter. If neither adapter enables you to reconfigure its IRQ use, you probably cannot use the two devices in the same system.

IRQ Conflicts. One of the most common areas of IRQ conflict involves serial (COM) ports. You may have noticed in the preceding two sections that two IRQs are set aside for two COM ports. IRQ 3 is used for COM2:, and IRQ 4 is used for COM1:. The problem occurs when you have more than two serial ports in a system. The problem is that when people add COM3: and COM4: ports, they often don't set them to nonconflicting interrupts, resulting in a conflict and nonfunctioning ports.

Contributing to the problem are poorly designed COM port boards that do not allow IRQ settings other than 3 or 4. What happens is that they end up setting COM3: to IRQ 4 (sharing it with COM1:), and COM4: to IRQ 3 (sharing it with COM2:). This is not acceptable, as it will prevent you from using the two COM ports on any one of the interrupt channels simultaneously. This was somewhat acceptable under plain DOS, because single-tasking (running only one program at a time) was the order of the day, but is totally unacceptable with Windows and OS/2. If you must share IRQs, you can usually get away with sharing devices on the same IRQ as long as they use different COM ports. For instance, a scanner and an internal modem could share an IRQ, although if the two devices are used simultaneously, a conflict will result.

The best solution is to purchase a multiport serial I/O card that will allow nonconflicting interrupt settings, or an intelligent card with its own processor that can handle the multiple ports onboard and only use one interrupt in the system.

▶▶ See "Serial Ports," p. 583

If a device listed in the table is not present, such as the motherboard mouse port (IRQ 12) or parallel port 2 (IRQ 5), then you can consider those interrupts as available. For example, a second parallel port is a rarity, and most systems will have a sound card installed and set for IRQ 5. Also, on most systems IRQ 15 is assigned to a secondary IDE controller. If you do not have a second IDE hard drive, you could disable the secondary IDE controller to free up that IRQ for another device.

Note that an easy way to check your interrupt settings is to use the Device Manager in Windows 95/98 or NT 5.0 or later. By double-clicking the computer properties icon in the Device Manager, you can get concise lists of all used system resources. Microsoft has also included a program called HWDIAG on Windows 95B and newer versions that does an excellent job of reporting system resource usage.

DMA Channels

DMA (Direct Memory Access) channels are used by high-speed communications devices that must send and receive information at high speed. A serial or parallel port does not use a DMA channel, but a sound card or SCSI adapter often does. DMA channels sometimes can be shared if the devices are not of the type that would need them simultaneously. For example, you can have a network adapter and a tape backup adapter sharing DMA channel 1, but you cannot back up while the network is running. To back up during network operation, you must ensure that each adapter uses a unique DMA channel.

8-Bit ISA Bus DMA Channels. In the 8-bit ISA bus, four DMA channels support high-speed data transfers between I/O devices and memory. Three of the channels are available to the expansion slots. Table 4.34 shows the typical uses of these DMA channels.

Table 4.34 8-Bit ISA Default DMA-Channel Assignments		
DMA	**Standard Function**	**Bus Slot**
0	Dynamic RAM Refresh	No
1	Available	Yes (8-bit)
2	Floppy disk controller	Yes (8-bit)
3	Hard disk controller	Yes (8-bit)

Because most systems typically have both a floppy and hard disk drive, only one DMA channel is available in 8-bit ISA systems.

16-Bit ISA DMA Channels. Since the introduction of the 286 CPU, the ISA bus has supported eight DMA channels, with seven channels available to the expansion slots. Like the expanded IRQ lines described earlier in this chapter, the added DMA channels were created by cascading a second DMA controller to the first one. DMA channel 4 is used to cascade channels 0 through 3 to the microprocessor. Channels 0 through 3 are available for 8-bit transfers, and channels 5 through 7 are for 16-bit transfers only. Table 4.35 shows the typical uses for the DMA channels.

Table 4.35 16/32-Bit ISA/PCI Default DMA-Channel Assignments

DMA	Standard Function	Bus Slot	Card Type	Transfer	Recommended Use
0	Available	Yes	16-bit	8-bit	None
1	Available	Yes	8/16-bit	8-bit	8-bit Sound
2	Floppy Disk Controller	Yes	8/16-bit	8-bit	Floppy Controller
3	Available	Yes	8/16-bit	8-bit	LPT1: in ECP Mode
4	1st DMA Controller Cascade	No	-	16-bit	-
5	Available	Yes	16-bit	16-bit	16-bit Sound
6	Available	Yes	16-bit	16-bit	ISA SCSI Adapter
7	Available	Yes	16-bit	16-bit	Available

The only standard DMA channel used in all systems is DMA 2, which is universally used by the floppy controller. DMA 4 is not usable, and does not appear in the bus slots. DMA channels 1 and 5 are most commonly used by sound cards such as the Sound Blaster 16. These cards use both an 8- and a 16-bit DMA channel for high-speed transfers.

> **Note**
>
> Although DMA channel 0 appears in a 16-bit slot connector extension and therefore can only be used by a 16-bit card, it only does 8-bit transfers! Because of this, you will generally not see DMA 0 as a choice on 16-bit cards. Most 16-bit cards (such as SCSI host adapters) that use DMA channels have their choices limited to DMA 5 through 7.

EISA. Realizing the shortcomings inherent in the way DMA channels are implemented in the ISA bus, the creators of the EISA specification created a specific DMA controller for their new bus. They increased the number of address lines to include the entire address bus, thus allowing transfers anywhere within the address space of the system. Each DMA channel can be set to run either 8-, 16-, or 32-bit transfers. In addition, each DMA channel can be separately programmed to run any of four types of bus cycles when transferring data:

- *Compatible.* This transfer method is included to match the same DMA timing as used in the ISA bus. This is done for compatibility reasons; all ISA cards can operate in an EISA system in this transfer mode.

- *Type A.* This transfer type compresses the DMA timing by 25 percent over the compatible method. It was designed to run with most (but not all) ISA cards and still yield a speed increase.

- *Type B.* This transfer type compresses timing by 50 percent over the compatible method. Using this method, most EISA cards function properly, but only a few ISA cards will be problem-free.

■ *Type C.* This transfer method compresses timing by 87.5 percent over the compatible method; it is the fastest DMA transfer method available under the EISA specification. No ISA cards will work using this transfer method.

EISA DMA also allows for special reading and writing operations referred to as *scatter write* and *gather read*. Scattered writes are done by reading a contiguous block of data and writing it to more than one area of memory at the same time. Gathered reads involve reading from more than one place in memory and writing to a device. These functions are often referred to as *Buffered Chaining*, and they increase the throughput of DMA operations.

MCA. It might be assumed that because MCA is a complete rebuilding of the PC bus structure that DMA in an MCA environment would be better constructed. This is not so. Quite the opposite is true; DMA in MCA systems were for the most part all designed around one DMA controller with the following issues:

■ It can only connect to two 8-bit data paths. This can only transfer one or two bytes per bus cycle.

■ It is only connected to AO:A23 on the address bus. This means it can only make use of the lower 16M of memory.

■ Runs at 10MHz.

The inability of the DMA controller to address more than two bytes per transfer severely cripples this otherwise powerful bus.

I/O Port Addresses

Your computer's I/O ports enable communications between devices and software in your system. They are equivalent to two-way radio channels. If you want to talk to your serial port, then you need to know what I/O port (radio channel) it is listening on. Similarly, if you want to receive data from the serial port, you need to listen on the same channel on which it is transmitting.

Unlike IRQs and DMA channels, we have an abundance of I/O ports in our systems. There are 65,535 ports, to be exact (numbered from 0000h to FFFFh), and this is an artifact of the Intel processor design more than anything else. Even though most devices use up to eight ports for themselves, with that many to spare, we aren't going to run out anytime soon. The biggest problem you have to worry about is setting two devices to use the same port.

Most modern Plug-and-Play systems will resolve any port conflicts and select alternate ports for one of the conflicting devices.

One confusing issue is that I/O ports are designated by hexadecimal addresses similar to memory addresses. They are not memory; they are ports. The difference is that when you send data to memory address 1000h, it gets stored in your SIMM or DIMM memory. If you send data to I/O port address 1000h, it gets sent out on the bus on that "channel" and anybody listening in would then "hear" it. If nobody was listening to that port address, then the data would reach the end of the bus and be absorbed by the bus terminating resistors.

Driver programs are primarily what interact with devices at the different port addresses. The driver must know which ports the device is using to work with it, and vice versa. That is not usually a problem because the driver and device both come from the same company.

Motherboard and chipset devices are normally set to use I/O port addresses from 0h to FFh, and all other devices use from 100h to FFFFh. Table 4.36 shows the commonly used motherboard and chipset based I/O port usage:

Table 4.36   Motherboard and Chipset-based Device Port Addresses

Address (hex)	Size	Description
000–000F	16 bytes	Chipset—8237 DMA 1
0020–0021	2 bytes	Chipset—8259 Interrupt Controller 1
002E–002F	2 bytes	Super I/O Controller Configuration Registers
0040–0043	4 bytes	Chipset—Counter/Timer 1
0048–004B	4 bytes	Chipset—Counter/Timer 2
0060	1 byte	Keyboard/Mouse Controller Byte—Reset IRQ
0061	1 byte	Chipset—NMI, Speaker Control
0064	1 byte	Keyboard/Mouse Controller, CMD/STAT Byte
0070, bit 7	1 bit	Chipset— Enable NMI
0070, bits 6:0	7 bits	MC146818— Real Time Clock, Address
0071	1 byte	MC146818— Real Time Clock, Data
0078	1 byte	Reserved— Board Configuration
0079	1 byte	Reserved— Board Configuration
0080–008F	16 bytes	Chipset— DMA Page Registers
00A0–00A1	2 bytes	Chipset—8259 Interrupt Controller 2
00B2	1 byte	APM control port
00B3	1 byte	APM status port
00C0–00DE	31 bytes	Chipset—8237 DMA 2
00F0	1 byte	Math Coprocessor Reset Numeric Error

To find out exactly what port addresses are being used on your motherboard, consult the motherboard documentation or look these settings up in the Windows Device Manager.

Bus-based devices normally use the addresses from 100h on up. Table 4.37 lists the commonly used bus-based device addresses and also lists some common adapter cards and their settings.

Table 4.37   Bus-Based Device Port Addresses

Address (hex)	Size	Description
0130–0133	4 bytes	Adaptec SCSI Adapter (alternate)
0134–0137	4 bytes	Adaptec SCSI Adapter (alternate)
0168–016F	8 bytes	Fourth IDE Interface
0170–0177	8 bytes	Secondary IDE Interface
01E8–01EF	8 bytes	Third IDE Interface
01F0–01F7	8 bytes	Primary IDE / AT (16-bit) Hard Disk Controller
0200–0207	8 bytes	Gameport or Joystick Adapter
0210–0217	8 bytes	IBM XT Expansion Chassis
0220–0233	20 bytes	Creative Labs Sound Blaster 16 Audio (default)
0230–0233	4 bytes	Adaptec SCSI Adapter (alternate)
0234–0237	4 bytes	Adaptec SCSI Adapter (alternate)
0238–023B	4 bytes	MS Bus Mouse (alternate)
023C–023F	4 bytes	MS Bus Mouse (default)
0240–024F	8 bytes	SMC Ethernet Adapter (default)
0240–0253	20 bytes	Creative Labs Sound Blaster 16 Audio (alternate)
0258–025F	8 bytes	Intel Above Board
0260–026F	8 bytes	SMC Ethernet Adapter (alternate)
0260–0273	20 bytes	Creative Labs Sound Blaster 16 Audio (alternate)
0270–0273	4 bytes	Plug and Play I/O read ports
0278–027F	8 bytes	Parallel Port 2 (LPT2)
0280–028F	8 bytes	SMC Ethernet Adapter (alternate)
0280–0293	19 bytes	Creative Labs Sound Blaster 16 Audio (alternate)
02A0–02AF	8 bytes	SMC Ethernet Adapter (alternate)
02C0–02CF	8 bytes	SMC Ethernet Adapter (alternate)
02E0–02EF	8 bytes	SMC Ethernet Adapter (alternate)
02E8–02EF	8 bytes	Serial Port 4 (COM4)
02EC–02EF	4 bytes	Video, 8514 or ATI standard ports
02F8–02FF	8 bytes	Serial Port 2 (COM2)
0300–0301	2 bytes	MPU-401 MIDI Port (secondary)
0300–030F	8 bytes	SMC Ethernet Adapter (alternate)
0320–0323	4 bytes	XT (8-bit) Hard Disk Controller
0320–032F	8 bytes	SMC Ethernet Adapter (alternate)
0330–0331	2 bytes	MPU-401 MIDI Port (default)
0330–0333	4 bytes	Adaptec SCSI Adapter (default)
0334–0337	4 bytes	Adaptec SCSI Adapter (alternate)
0340–034F	8 bytes	SMC Ethernet Adapter (alternate)
0360–036F	8 bytes	SMC Ethernet Adapter (alternate)

(continues)

Table 4.37 Bus-Based Device Port Addresses Continued

Address (hex)	Size	Description
0366	1 byte	Fourth IDE Command Port
0367, bits 6:0	7 bits	Fourth IDE Status Port
0370–0375	6 bytes	Secondary Floppy Controller
0376	1 byte	Secondary IDE Command Port
0377, bit 7	1 bit	Secondary Floppy Controller Disk Change
0377, bits 6:0	7 bits	Secondary IDE Status Port
0378–037F	8 bytes	Parallel Port 1 (LPT1)
0380–038F	8 bytes	SMC Ethernet Adapter (alternate)
0388–038B	4 bytes	Audio—FM Synthesizer
03B0–03BB	12 bytes	Video, Mono/EGA/VGA standard ports
03BC–03BF	4 bytes	Parallel Port 1 (LPT1) in some systems
03BC–03BF	4 bytes	Parallel Port 3 (LPT3)
03C0–03CF	16 bytes	Video, EGA/VGA standard ports
03D0–03DF	16 bytes	Video, CGA/EGA/VGA standard ports
03E6	1 byte	Third IDE Command Port
03E7, bits 6:0	7 bits	Third IDE Status Port
03E8–03EF	8 bytes	Serial Port 3 (COM3)
03F0–03F5	6 bytes	Primary Floppy Controller
03F6	1 byte	Primary IDE Command Port
03F7, bit 7	1 bit	Primary Floppy Controller Disk Change
03F7, bits 6:0	7 bits	Primary IDE Status Port
03F8–03FF	8 bytes	Serial Port 1 (COM1)
04D0–04D1	2 bytes	Edge/level triggered PCI Interrupt Controller
0530–0537	8 bytes	Windows Sound System (default)
0604–060B	8 bytes	Windows Sound System (alternate)
0678–067F	8 bytes	LPT2 in ECP mode
0778–077F	8 bytes	LPT1 in ECP mode
0A20–0A23	4 bytes	IBM Token Ring Adapter (default)
0A24–0A27	4 bytes	IBM Token Ring Adapter (alternate)
0CF8–0CFB	4 bytes	PCI Configuration Address Registers
0CF9	1 byte	Turbo and Reset Control Register
0CFC–0CFF	4 bytes	PCI Configuration Data Registers
FF00–FF07	8 bytes	IDE Bus Master Registers
FF80–FF9F	32 bytes	Universal Serial Bus (USB)
FFA0–FFA7	8 bytes	Primary Bus Master IDE Registers
FFA8–FFAF	8 bytes	Secondary Bus Master IDE Registers

To find out exactly what your devices are using, again I recommend consulting the documentation for the device or looking the device up in the Windows Device Manager.

Virtually all devices on your system buses use I/O port addresses. Most of these are fairly standardized, meaning you won't often have conflicts or problems with these settings. In the next section, you learn some of the techniques that you can use to solve this problem.

Resolving Resource Conflicts

The resources in a system are limited, while the demands on those resources seem to be unlimited. As you add more and more adapter cards to your system, you will find that the potential for resource conflicts increases. If your system is fully PnP-compatible, then potential conflicts should be resolved automatically.

How do you know whether you have a resource conflict? Typically, one of the devices in your system stops working. Resource conflicts can exhibit themselves in other ways, though. Any of the following events could be diagnosed as a resource conflict:

- A device transfers data inaccurately.
- Your system frequently locks up.
- Your sound card doesn't sound quite right.
- Your mouse doesn't work.
- Garbage appears on your video screen for no apparent reason.
- Your printer prints gibberish.
- You cannot format a floppy disk.
- The PC starts in Safe Mode (Windows 95).

Windows 95 and newer versions will also show conflicts by highlighting a device in yellow or red in the Device Manager representation. By using the Windows Device Manager, you can usually spot the conflicts quickly.

In the following sections, you learn some of the steps that you can take to head off resource conflicts or to track them down when they occur.

> **Caution**
>
> Be careful in diagnosing resource conflicts; a problem may not be a resource conflict at all, but a computer virus. Many computer viruses are designed to exhibit themselves as glitches or as periodic problems. If you suspect a resource conflict, it may be worthwhile to run a virus check first to ensure that the system is clean. This procedure could save you hours of work and frustration.

Resolving Conflicts Manually

Unfortunately, the only way to resolve conflicts manually is to take the cover off your system and start changing switches or jumper settings on your adapter cards. Each of these changes then must be accompanied by a system reboot, which implies that they take a great deal of time. This situation brings us to the first rule of resolving conflicts: When you set about ridding your system of resource conflicts, make sure that you allow a good deal of uninterrupted time.

Also make sure that you write down your current system settings before you start making changes. That way, you will know where you began and can go back to the original configuration (if necessary).

Finally, dig out the manuals for all your adapter boards; you will need them. If you cannot find the manuals, contact the manufacturers to determine what the various jumper positions and switch settings mean. Additionally, you could look for more current information online at the manufacturers' Web sites.

One of the greatest resources for product documentation is Micro House International. They produce several documentation support products including *Support Source for Hardware*. In it you will find information including resource settings for virtually every type of adapter card. Que also publishes a set of books, *The Micro House PC Hardware Library* (ISBN 0-7897-1662-3), based on this material. There is a selection of it included in the Support Source program on the CD with this book. I highly recommend you check this out. Once you see how much information is there, you will use it all the time. It's especially useful for older hardware where the original documentation has been lost or the company has gone out of business.

Now you are ready to begin your detective work. As you try various switch settings and jumper positions, keep the following questions in mind; the answers will help you narrow down the conflict areas:

■ *When did the conflict first become apparent?* If the conflict occurred after you installed a new adapter card, that new card probably is causing the conflict. If the conflict occurred after you started using new software, chances are good that the software uses a device that is taxing your system's resources in a new way.

■ *Are there two similar devices in your system that do not work?* For example, if your modem and mouse—devices that use a COM port—do not work, chances are good that these devices are conflicting with each other.

■ *Have other people had the same problem, and if so, how did they resolve it?* Public forums—such as those on CompuServe, Internet newsgroups, and America Online—are great places to find other users who may be able to help you solve the conflict.

Whenever you make changes in your system, reboot and see whether the problem persists. When you believe that you have solved the problem, make sure that you test all your software. Fixing one problem often seems to causes another to crop up. The only way to make sure that all problems are resolved is to test everything in your system.

One of the best pieces of advice I can give you here is to try changing one thing at a time and then retest. That is the most methodical and simplest way to isolate a problem quickly and efficiently.

As you attempt to resolve your resource conflicts, you should work with and update a system-configuration template, as discussed in the following section.

Using a System-Configuration Template

A *system-configuration template* is helpful, simply because it is easier to remember something that is written down than it is to keep it in your head. To create a configuration template, all you need to do is start writing down what resources are used by which parts of your system. Then, when you need to make a change or add an adapter, you can quickly determine where conflicts may arise. You can also use the Windows 95, 98, or NT 5.0+ device manager to list and print this information.

I like to use a worksheet split into three main areas—one for interrupts, another for DMA channels, and a middle area for devices that do not use interrupts. Each section lists the IRQ or DMA channel on the left and the I/O port device range on the right. This way, you get the clearest picture of what resources are used and which ones are available in a given system.

See the System Resource Map on page 284—it's the system-configuration template I have developed over the years and still use almost daily.

This type of configuration sheet is resource-based instead of component-based. Each row in the template represents a different resource, and lists the component using the resource and the resources used. The chart has pre-entered all of the fixed items in a modern PC, whose configuration cannot be changed.

To fill out this type of chart, you would perform the following steps:

1. Enter the default resources used by standard components, such as serial and parallel ports, disk controllers, and video. You can use the filled-out example I have provided to see how most standard devices are configured.

2. Enter the default resources used by additional add-on components such as sound cards, SCSI cards, network cards, proprietary cards, and so on.

3. Change any configuration items that are in conflict. Try to leave built-in devices at their default settings, and sound cards. Other installed adapters may have their settings changed, but be sure to document the changes.

Of course, a template such as this is best used when first installing components, not after. Once you have it completely filled out to match your system, you can label it and keep it with the system. When you add any more devices, the template will be your guide as to how any new devices should be configured.

The example on page 285 is the same template filled out for a typical modern PC system.

System Resource Map

PC Make and Model: _____

Serial Number: _____

Date: _____

Interrupts (IRQs):   I/O Port Addresses:

0 - Timer Circuits.......................   040-04B............

1 - Keyboard / Mouse Controller..........   060 & 064..........

2 - 2nd 8259 IRQ Controller..............   0A0-0A1............

8 - Real Time Clock / CMOS RAM..........   070-071............

9 - _____   _____

10 - _____   _____

11 - _____   _____

12 - _____   _____

13 - Math Coprocessor...................   0F0................

14 - _____   _____

15 - _____   _____

3 - _____   _____

4 - _____   _____

5 - _____   _____

6 - _____   _____

7 - _____   _____

Devices not using Interrupts: I/O Port Addresses:

Mono/EGA/VGA Standard Ports...............   3B0-3BB............

EGA/VGA Standard Ports....................   3C0-3CF............

CGA/EGA/VGA Standard Ports................   3D0-3DF............

_____   _____

_____   _____

_____   _____

_____   _____

_____   _____

DMA Channels:

0 - _____

1 - _____

2 - _____

3 - _____

4 - DMA Channel 0-3 Cascade..............

5 - _____

6 - _____

7 - _____

System Resource Map

PC Make and Model: Intel AL440LX_____

Serial Number: 100000 _____

Date: 06/09/98_____

Interrupts (IRQs):			I/O Port Addresses:
0	-	Timer Circuits......................	040-04B...........
1	-	Keyboard / Mouse Controller..........	060 & 064..........
2	-	2nd 8259 IRQ Controller..............	0A0-0A1...........
8	-	Real Time Clock / CMOS RAM..........	070-071...........
9	-	SMC EtherEZ Ethernet card_____	340-35F_____
10	-	_____	_____
11	-	Adaptec 1542CF SCSI Adapter (scanner)	334-337*_____
12	-	Motherboard Mouse Port_____	060 & 064_____
13	-	Math Coprocessor...................	0F0...............
14	-	Primary IDE (hard disk 1 and 2)_____	1F0-1F7, 3F6_____
15	-	Secondary IDE (CDROM/tape)_____	170-177, 376_____
3	-	Serial Port 2 (Modem)_____	3F8-3FF_____
4	-	Serial Port 1 (COM1)_____	2F8-2FF_____
5	-	Sound Blaster 16 Audio_____	220-233_____
6	-	Floppy Controller_____	3F0-3F5_____
7	-	Parallel Port 1 (Printer)_____	378-37F_____

Devices not using Interrupts:	I/O Port Addresses:
Mono/EGA/VGA Standard Ports...............	3B0-3BB...........
EGA/VGA Standard Ports....................	3C0-3CF...........
CGA/EGA/VGA Standard Ports................	3D0-3DF...........
ATI Mach 64 Video card additional ports___	102,1CE-1CF,2EC-2EF
Sound Blaster 16 MIDI port_____	330-331_____
Sound Blaster 16 Game port (joystick)_____	200-207_____
Sound Blaster 16 FM synthesizer (music)___	388-38B_____
_____	_____

DMA Channels:		
0	-	_____
1	-	Sound Blaster 16 (8-bit DMA)_____
2	-	Floppy Controller_____
3	-	Parallel Port 1 (in ECP mode)_____
4	-	DMA Channel 0-3 Cascade..............
5	-	Sound Blaster 16 (16-bit DMA)_____
6	-	Adaptec 1542CF SCSI adapter*_____
7	-	_____

*Represents a resource setting that had to be changed to resolve a conflict.

As you can see from this template, only one IRQ and two DMA channels remain available, and there would be no IRQs if I enabled the USB on the motherboard! This example also shows that interrupt shortages are a big problem in modern systems. In that case, I would probably find a way to recover one of the other interrupts. For example, I am not really using COM1: so I could disable that port and gain back IRQ 4. In this example configuration, the primary and secondary IDE connectors were built into the motherboard:

- Floppy controller

- Two serial ports

- One parallel port

Whether these devices are built into the motherboard or on a separate card makes no difference because the resource allocations are the same in either case. All default settings are normally used for these devices, and are indicated in the completed configuration. Next, the accessory cards were configured. In this example, the following cards were installed:

- SVGA video card (ATI Mach 64)

- Sound card (Creative Labs Sound Blaster 16)

- SCSI host adapter (Adaptec AHA-1542CF)

- Network interface card (SMC EtherEZ)

It helps to install the cards in this order. Start with the video card; next, add the sound card. Due to problems with software that must be configured to the sound card, it is best to install it early and make sure only default settings are used. It is better to change settings on other cards than the sound card.

After the sound card, the SCSI adapter was installed; however, the default I/O Port addresses (330-331) and DMA channel (DMA 5) used were in conflict with other cards (mainly the sound card). These settings were changed to their next logical settings which did not cause a conflict.

Finally, the network card was installed, which also had default settings that conflicted with other cards. In this case, the Ethernet card came preconfigured to IRQ 3, which was already in use by COM2:. The solution was to change the setting, and IRQ 9 was the next logical choice in the card's configuration settings.

Even though this is a fully loaded configuration, only three individual items among all of the cards had to be changed to achieve an optimum system configuration. Using a configuration template such as the one shown can make what would otherwise be a jumble of settings come together in an easy-to-follow manner. The only real problems you will run into once you work with these templates are cards that do not allow for enough adjustment in their settings, or cards that are lacking in documentation. As you can imagine, you will need the documentation for each adapter card, and the motherboard, in order to accurately complete a configuration table such as the one shown.

Tip

Do not rely too much on third-party software diagnostics such as MSD.EXE that claim to be able to show hardware settings such as IRQ and I/O port settings. While they can be helpful in certain situations, they are often wrong with respect to at least some of the information they are displaying about your system. One or two items shown incorrectly can be very troublesome if you believe the incorrect information and configure your system based on it!

A much better utility to view these settings is the Device Manager built in to Windows 95/98 and NT 5.0+. On a Plug-and-Play system, it will not only report settings, but also will allow you to change them. On older legacy hardware, you will be able to view the settings but not change them.

Heading Off Problems: Special Boards

A number of devices that you may want to install in a computer system require IRQ lines or DMA channels, which means that a world of conflict could be waiting in the box that the device comes in. As mentioned in the preceding section, you can save yourself problems if you use a system-configuration template to keep track of the way that your system is configured.

You also can save yourself trouble by carefully reading the documentation for a new adapter board before you attempt to install it. The documentation details the IRQ lines that the board can use, and its DMA-channel requirements. In addition, the documentation will detail the adapter's upper-memory needs for ROM and adapter.

The following sections describe some of the conflicts that you may encounter when you install today's most popular adapter boards. Although the list of adapter boards covered in these sections is far from comprehensive, the sections serve as a guide to installing complex hardware with minimum hassle. Included are tips on sound boards, SCSI host adapters, and network adapters.

Sound Boards. Sound cards are probably the biggest single resource hog in your system. They usually use at least one IRQ, two DMA channels, and multiple I/O port address ranges. This is because a sound card is actually several different pieces of hardware all on one board. Most sound cards are similar to the Sound Blaster 16 from Creative Labs.

Figure 4.30 shows the default resources used by the components on a typical Sound Blaster 16 card.

As you can see, these cards use quite a few resources. If you take the time to read your sound board's documentation and determine its communications-channel needs, compare those needs to the IRQ lines and DMA channels that already are in use in your system, and then change the settings of the other adapters to avoid conflicts with the sound card, your installation will go quickly and smoothly.

Device	Interrupt	I/O Ports	16-bit DMA	8-bit DMA
Audio	IRQ5	220h-233h	DMA 5	DMA 1

Device	Interrupt
MIDI Port	330h-331h
FM Synthesizer	388h-38Bh
Game Port	200h-207h

FIG. 4.30 Default resources for Sound Blaster 16 card.

> ### Tip
>
> The greatest single piece of advice I have for installing a sound card is to put the sound card in before all other cards except the video card. In other words, let the sound card retain all of its default settings; never change a resource setting to prevent a conflict. Instead, always change the settings of other adapters when a conflict with the sound card arises. The problem here is that many educational and game programs that use sound are very poorly written with respect to supporting alternate resource settings on sound cards. Save yourself some grief and let the sound card have its way!

One example of a potential sound-board conflict is the combination of a Sound Blaster 16 and an Adaptec SCSI adapter. The Sound and SCSI adapters will conflict on DMA 5 and on I/O ports 330-331. Rather than changing the settings of the sound card, it is best to alter the SCSI adapter to the next available settings that will not conflict with the sound card or anything else. The final settings were shown in the previous configuration template.

The cards in question (Sound Blaster 16 and AHA-1542CF) are not singled out here because there is something wrong with them, but instead because they happen to be the most popular cards of their respective types, and as such will often be paired together.

Most people would be using PCI versions of these cards today, but they will still require the same types of resource settings with the only exception being DMA channels. Unfortunately, it wasn't DMA channels that we were really running out of. The interrupt shortage continues even with PCI cards because they must be mapped to ISA IRQs. The real solution will be in a year or so when we start to see a new breed of PC that lacks any ISA slots and that breaks ties with that bus forever. When that happens, we will be free of the interrupt restrictions we have been on for so many years.

One tip worth mentioning is that the newer PCI sound cards are largely incompatible with older DOS-based software because they don't use DMA channels like their ISA counterparts. Either update your software to 32-bit Windows versions or you will not be able to use these newer PCI bus sound cards. Most of the newer PCI cards do include an emulation program that allows the card to work with older DMA-dependent software, but the results are often problematic.

SCSI Adapter Boards. SCSI adapter boards use more resources than just about any other type of add-in device except perhaps a sound card. They will often use resources that are in conflict with sound cards or network cards. A typical SCSI host adapter requires an IRQ line, a DMA channel, a range of I/O port addresses, plus a 16K range of unused upper memory for its ROM and possible scratch-pad RAM use. Fortunately, the typical SCSI adapter is also easy to reconfigure, and changing any of these settings should not affect performance or software operation.

Before installing a SCSI adapter, be sure to read the documentation for the card, and make sure that any IRQ lines, DMA channels, I/O ports, and upper memory that the card needs are available. If the system resources that the card needs are already in use, use your system-configuration template to determine how you can alter the settings on the SCSI card or other cards to prevent any resource conflicts before you attempt to plug in the adapter card.

Network Interface Cards (NICs). Networks are becoming more and more popular all the time. A typical network adapter does not require as many resources as some of the other cards discussed here, but will require at least a range of I/O port addresses and an interrupt. Most NICs will also require a 16K range of free upper memory to be used for the RAM transfer buffer on the network card. As with any other cards, make sure that all of these resources are unique to the card, and are not shared with any other devices.

Multiple-COM-Port Adapters. A serial port adapter usually has two or more ports on-board. These COM ports require an interrupt and a range of I/O ports each. There aren't too many problems with the I/O port addresses, because the ranges used by up to four COM ports in a system are fairly well-defined. The real problem is with the interrupts. Most older installations of more than two serial ports have any additional ones sharing the same interrupts as the first two. This is incorrect, and will cause nothing but problems with software that runs under Windows or OS/2. With these older boards, make sure that each serial port in your system has a unique I/O port address range, and more importantly, a unique interrupt setting.

Because COM ports are required for so many peripherals that connect to the modern PC, and because the number of COM ports that can be used is strictly limited by the IRQ setup in the basic IBM system design, special COM-port cards are available that enable you to assign a unique IRQ to each of the COM ports on the card. For example, you can use such a card to leave COM1: and COM2: configured for IRQ 4 and IRQ 3, respectively, but to configure COM3: for IRQ 10 and COM4: for IRQ 12 (provided you do not have a motherboard-based mouse port in your system).

Many newer multiport adapter cards—such as those offered by Byte Runner Technologies—allow "intelligent" interrupt sharing among ports. In some cases, you can have up to 12 COM port settings without conflict problems. Check with your adapter card's manufacturer to determine whether it allows for automatic or "intelligent" interrupt sharing.

Although most people have problems incorrectly trying to share interrupts when installing more than two serial ports in a system, there is a fairly common problem with the I/O port addressing that should be mentioned. Many of the high-performance video chipsets, such as those from S3 Inc. and ATI, use some additional I/O port addresses that will conflict with the standard I/O port addresses used by COM4:.

In the example system-configuration just covered, you can see that the ATI video card uses some additional I/O port addresses, specifically 2EC-2EF. This is a problem because COM4: is normally configured as 2E8-2EF, which overlaps with the video card. The video cards that use these addresses are not normally adjustable for this setting, so you will either have to change the address of COM4: to a nonstandard setting, or simply disable COM4:. This restricts yourself to using only three serial ports in the system. If you do have a serial adapter that supports nonstandard I/O address settings for the serial ports, you must ensure that those settings are not used by other cards, and you must inform any software or drivers, such as those in Windows, of your nonstandard settings.

With a multiple-COM-port adapter card installed and properly configured for your system, you can have devices hooked to numerous COM ports, and up to four devices can be functioning at the same time. For example, you can use a mouse, modem, plotter, and serial printer at the same time.

USB (Universal Serial Bus). USB ports are now found on most motherboards and with Windows 98 we finally have an operating system that will properly support it. The big problem is that USB will take another interrupt from your system and many either don't have any free or were down to their last one. In that case, you should look at what other devices you can disable (such as COM or LPT ports) to gain back a necessary interrupt for other devices.

If you aren't using any USB devices, you should turn off the port using your motherboard CMOS setup so that the IRQ it was using will be freed. In the future, as we move to USB-based keyboards, mice, modems, printers, and so on, the IRQ shortage will be less of a problem. Also, the elimination of the ISA bus in our systems will go a long way to solve this problem.

Miscellaneous Boards. Some video cards ship with advanced software that allows special video features such as oversized desktops, custom monitors, switch modes on-the-fly, and so on. Unfortunately, this software requires that the card be configured to use an interrupt. I suggest that you dispense with this unnecessary software and configure the card to free up the interrupt for other devices.

Also related to video is the use of an MPEG decoder add-on card that works in addition to your normal graphics adapter. These are used more in specialized video production, editing, and in playing DVD movies. However, they do use additional system resources that must be available.

Plug-and-Play Systems

Plug and Play (PnP) represents a major revolution in recent interface technology. PnP first came on the market in 1995, and most new systems come ready to take advantage of it. In the past, PC users were forced to muddle through a nightmare of dip switches and jumpers every time they wanted to add new devices to their systems. The results, all too often, were system resource conflicts and nonfunctioning cards.

PnP is not an entirely new concept. It was a key design feature of MCA and EISA interfaces, but the limited appeal of MCA and EISA meant that they never became industry standards. Therefore, mainstream PC users still worry about I/O addresses, DMA channels, and IRQ settings. But now that PnP specifications are available for ISA-, PCI-, SCSI-, IDE-, and PCMCIA-based systems, worry-free hardware setup is within the grasp of all new computer buyers.

Of course, PnP may well be within your grasp, but that does not necessarily mean you are ready to take advantage of it. For PnP to work, the following components are required:

- PnP hardware
- PnP BIOS
- PnP operating system (optional)

Each of these components needs to be PnP-compatible, meaning that it complies with the PnP specifications.

The Hardware Component. The *hardware component* refers to both computer systems and adapter cards. The term does not mean, however, that you cannot use your older ISA adapter cards (referred to as *legacy cards*) in a PnP system. You can use these cards; in fact, your PnP BIOS automatically reassigns PnP-compatible cards around existing legacy components.

PnP adapter cards communicate with the system BIOS and the operating system to convey information about what system resources are needed. The BIOS and operating system, in turn, resolve conflicts (wherever possible) and inform the adapter cards which specific resources it should use. The adapter card then can modify its configuration to use the specified resources.

The BIOS Component. The BIOS component means that most users of older PCs need to update their BIOSs or purchase new machines that have PnP BIOSs. For a BIOS to be compatible, it must support 13 additional system function calls, which can be used by the OS component of a PnP system. The PnP BIOS specification was developed jointly by Compaq, Intel, and Phoenix Technologies.

The PnP features of the BIOS are implemented through an expanded POST. The BIOS is responsible for identification, isolation, and possible configuration of PnP adapter cards. The BIOS accomplishes these tasks by performing the following steps:

1. Disable any configurable devices on the motherboard or on adapter cards.
2. Identify any PnP PCI or ISA devices.
3. Compile an initial resource-allocation map for ports, IRQs, DMAs, and memory.

4. Enable I/O devices.

5. Scan the ROMs of ISA devices.

6. Configure initial-program-load (IPL) devices, which are used later to boot the system.

7. Enable configurable devices by informing them which resources have been assigned to them.

8. Start the bootstrap loader.

9. Transfer control to the operating system.

The Operating-System Component. The operating-system component can be implemented by most newer systems, such as OS/2, Windows 95, Windows 98, or DOS extensions. Extensions of this type should be familiar to most DOS users; extensions have been used for years to provide support for CD-ROM drives. Extension software is available now for existing operating systems, and you can expect all new PC operating systems to have PnP support built in. If you are using Windows NT 4.0, PnP drivers may or may not have been loaded automatically. If not, the driver can be found on the Windows NT 4.0 CD in the DRVLIB\PNPISA\ directory. Open the correct subdirectory for your chipset and install the file PNPISA.INF. Windows NT 5.0 has full support for Plug and Play built in.

It is the responsibility of the operating system to inform users of conflicts that cannot be resolved by the BIOS. Depending on the sophistication of the operating system, the user then could configure the offending cards manually (onscreen) or turn the system off and set switches on the physical cards. When the system is restarted, the system is checked for remaining (or new) conflicts, any of which are brought to the user's attention. Through this repetitive process, all system conflicts are resolved.

> **Note**
>
> Plug and Play is still going through some revisions. Windows 95 requires at least version 1.0a of the ISA PnP BIOS. If your system does not have the most current BIOS, I suggest that you install a BIOS upgrade. With the Flash ROM used in most PnP systems, you can just download the new BIOS image from the system vendor or manufacturer and run the supplied BIOS update program.

Knowing What to Look For (Selection Criteria)

As a consultant, I am often asked to make a recommendation for purchases. Making these types of recommendations is one of the most frequent tasks a consultant performs. Many consultants charge a large fee for this advice. Without guidance, many individuals don't have any rhyme or reason to their selections and instead base their choices solely on magazine reviews or, even worse, on some personal bias. To help eliminate this haphazard selection process, I have developed a simple checklist that will help you select a system. This list takes into consideration several important system aspects overlooked by most checklists. The goal is to ensure that the selected system truly is compatible and has a long life of service and upgrades ahead.

It helps to think like an engineer when you make your selection. Consider every aspect and detail of the motherboards in question. For instance, you should consider any future uses and upgrades. Technical support at a professional (as opposed to a user) level is extremely important. What support will be provided? Is there documentation, and what does it cover?

In short, a checklist is a good idea. Here is one for you to use in evaluating any PC-compatible system. You might not have to meet every one of these criteria to consider a particular system, but if you miss more than a few of these checks, consider staying away from that system. The items at the top of the list are the most important, and the items at the bottom are perhaps of lesser importance (although I think each item is important). The rest of this chapter discusses in detail the criteria in this checklist:

- *Processor.* A Pentium motherboard should use as a minimum the Pentium MMX processor, which requires a Socket 7-type socket for the processor to plug into. A bonus would be one of the newer boards supporting the 100MHz "Super-7" standard developed by AMD and Cyrix for their newest Socket 7 processors. There should also be a built-in adjustable voltage regulator allowing for different voltage CPUs to be accommodated without purchasing an additional regulator module. I can barely recommend a Pentium system anymore; these days one should really consider a Pentium II machine as the minimum. The lowest cost PII processor is the Celeron introduced by Intel in mid-1998. This is a PII processor without the Level 2 cache, which makes it slower than a regular Pentium II but still faster than the Pentium. All Celeron systems can be upgraded to full PII status by merely plugging in a PII processor, because the motherboards are the same. All Pentium Pro motherboards use Socket 8, and all nonserver Pentium II systems use Slot 1 in which to install the processor.

- *Processor sockets.* A Pentium motherboard should have at least one ZIF socket that follows the Intel Socket 7 (321-pin) specification. The Socket 7 with a built-in VRM (Voltage Regulator Module) rather than a socket for one that plugs in is best. This is because if you change the processor later; the built-in VRM can be reconfigured with jumpers, while if you have only a VRM socket, you will have to purchase a new VRM to go with each new voltage processor you try.

Pentium Pro (P6) motherboards use Socket 8, and many are set up for multiple processors. Pentium II boards use either Slot 1 or Slot 2. The Slot 1 systems are for normal use, while Slot 2 systems are only for the higher-end Pentium II Xenon server processors. There are Slot 1 and Slot 2 boards available with multiple processor sockets. Before going to the expense of buying a multiprocessor board, ensure that your operating system is able to handle it. For instance, while Windows 95 or 98 cannot really benefit from more than one CPU, Windows NT, OS/2, and some others may run considerably faster.

■ *Motherboard speed.* A Pentium or Pentium Pro motherboard should run at 66MHz minimum; some can be set to an unauthorized (but often fully functional) speed of 75MHz. Pentium II motherboards are available to run at either 66MHz or 100MHz for the newer boards. Notice that all the Pentium processors sold today run at a multiple of the motherboard speed. For example, the Pentium II 350, 400 and higher megahertz processors run at a motherboard speed of 100MHz, and would therefore require a motherboard capable of 100MHz operation. Pentium 333MHz and lower-speed processors run at 66MHz maximum. All components on the motherboard (especially cache memory on Pentium boards) should be rated to run at the maximum allowable motherboard speed.

■ *Cache memory.* All classic Pentium motherboards should have 256–512K of Level 2 cache onboard, some will have 1M. Pentium Pro and Pentium II processors use a built-in L1/L2 cache, which means that there will be no cache on a Pentium Pro or Pentium II motherboard. The Pentium Pro can have either 256K, 512K, or 1M of Level 2 cache built-in while the Pentium II can have either 0K (Celeron) or 512K, and 1M or more in the Xenon processors. The Level 2 cache on a classic Pentium board should be populated with chips that are fast enough to support the maximum motherboard speed, which should be 15ns or faster for 66MHz maximum motherboard speeds, and 13ns or better for 75MHz operation. For Pentium boards, the cache should be a Synchronous SRAM (Static RAM) type, which is also called *Pipelined Burst SRAM.*

■ *SIMM/DIMM memory.* If the board is being used to upgrade an older system that used 72-pin SIMMs, then it may be desirable to get the type that has both SIMM and DIMM sockets. If you are getting all new memory for the board (recommended), then I highly recommend only using boards that take SDRAM (Synchronous DRAM) 168-pin DIMMs (Dual Inline Memory Modules). Due to the 64-bit design of these boards, the 72-pin SIMMs must be installed in matched pairs, while DIMMs are installed one at a time (one per 64-bit bank). Be sure that the memory is compatible with the chipset you are using, and more specifically is rated for the 66MHz or 100MHz speed it will be running. Carefully consider the total amount of memory you will need, and how much the board supports. Classic Pentium systems with the 430FX, VX, or TX chipset only support a maximum of 64M of cacheable memory, which effectively limits you to that amount. Pentium II systems will allow caching for all the memory you can fit into the board, and most will handle 384M or more of SDRAM DIMM memory. The 333MHz and lower Pentium II processors can cache up to 512M of RAM (note most motherboards won't handle that much) while the newer 350MHz and faster Pentium IIs will cache up to 4G of system RAM. Although 32M is regarded as a minimum for today's memory-hungry applications, you may actually require much more. I recommend installing 64M in most new systems. For maximum performance, look for systems that support 3.3v SDRAM (Synchronous DRAM) as a minimum. Future systems will use even faster RDRAM (Rambus DRAM) RIMMs (Rambus Inline Memory Modules) with speeds of 800MHz or more.

■ Mission-critical systems should use parity or ECC (Error Correcting Code) DIMMs and ensure that the motherboard fully supports ECC (Error Correcting Code) operation. Most Pentium (430 series) chipsets *do not* support ECC, while most Pentium II chipsets do. Note that the low-end 440EX boards normally used in Celeron processor-based systems do not support ECC and should not be used for mission-critical applications.

■ Finally, note that most Pentium and Pentium II motherboards support either 3 or 4 DIMM sockets. Be sure that you populate them wisely so you don't have to resort to removing memory later to add more, which is not very cost-effective.

■ *Bus type*. Pentium, Pentium Pro, and Pentium II motherboards should have one or more ISA bus slots and at least three or four PCI local bus slots. Make sure the PCI slots conform to the PCI 2.1 revision (primarily based on the chipset). Take a look at the layout of the slots to ensure that cards inserted in them will not block access to memory sockets, or be blocked by other components in the case. Newer systems should also feature one AGP (Accelerated Graphics Port) slot for a high-performance AGP video card.

■ *BIOS*. The motherboard should use an industry-standard BIOS such as those from AMI, Phoenix, or Award. The BIOS should be of a Flash ROM or EEPROM (Electrically Erasable Programmable Read Only Memory) design for easy updating. Look for a BIOS Recover jumper or mode setting, and possibly a Flash ROM write-protect jumper on some systems. The BIOS should support the Plug-and-Play (PnP) specification, and Enhanced IDE or Fast ATA hard drives. There should also be support for the newer LS-120 (120M) floppy drives and IDE CD-ROM drives as boot devices. APM (Advanced Power Management) support should be built into the BIOS, as well.

■ *Form factor*. For maximum flexibility, performance, reliability, and ease-of-use, the ATX form factor cannot be beat. ATX has several distinct performance and functional advantages over Baby-AT, and is vastly superior to any proprietary designs such as LPX. Additionally, the new NLX form factor may be a consideration for low-profile or low-cost desktop systems.

■ *Built-in interfaces*. Ideally, a motherboard should contain as many built-in standard controllers and interfaces as possible (except perhaps video). A motherboard should have a built-in floppy controller, built-in primary and secondary local bus (PCI or VL-Bus) Enhanced IDE (also called Fast ATA) connectors, two built-in high-speed serial ports (must use 16550A type buffered UARTs), two built-in USB (Universal Serial Bus) ports, and a built-in high-speed parallel port (must be EPP/ECP-compliant). A built-in PS/2 type (6-pin mini-DIN) mouse port should be included, as well.

The USB ports have taken a while to catch on, but they will become a "must-have" in the near future as more and more USB peripherals become available. A built-in SCSI port is a bonus as long as it conforms to ASPI (Advanced SCSI Programming Interface) standards. Built-in network adapters are also nice as long as they are the type that matches your network needs. A built-in sound card is a great feature; they usually offer full Sound Blaster compatibility and functions, and may offer additional features. If your sound needs are more demanding, then you may find the built-in solutions less desirable, and will want to have a separate sound card in your system. Built-in video adapters are also a bonus in some situations, but because there are many different video chipset and adapter designs to choose from, generally, there are better choices in external local bus video adapters. This is especially true if you need the highest performance video available.

Normally built-in devices can be disabled to allow future add-ons, but there can be problems.

- *Plug and Play (PnP)*. The motherboard and BIOS should fully support the Intel PnP specification. This will allow automatic configuration of PCI adapters and PnP ISA adapters.

> **Tip**
>
> Even if a motherboard doesn't list that it's PnP-compatible, it may be. PCI motherboards are required to be PnP-compatible, as it is a part of the PCI standard.

- *Power Management*. The motherboard should fully support SL Enhanced processors with APM (Advanced Power Management) and SMM (System Management Mode) protocols that allow for powering down various system components to different levels of readiness and power consumption. The latest standard for power management is called ACPI (Advanced Configuration & Power Interface) version 1.0; make sure any new board you purchase supports that as a minimum. An Energy-Star-compliant system is also a bonus as that means it will use less than 30 watts of electrical energy when in sleep mode, saving energy and your electric bill.

- *Motherboard chipset*. Pentium II motherboards should use a high-performance chipset that supports SDRAM DIMMs—preferably one that allows ECC memory, such as the Intel 440LX or 440BX. The 440EX that is designed for low-cost and low-end systems only, does not support ECC memory and should not be used in mission-critical systems. Note that for Classic Pentium systems, most of the available Intel chipsets do not support parity or ECC memory. In that case, boards with chipsets from ALi (Acer Laboratories, Inc.), VIA technologies, or SiS (Silicon Integrated Systems) should be considered. These companies have continued making high-performance classic Pentium chipsets, and many of their offerings do support SDRAM DIMMs with ECC.

- *Documentation*. Good technical documentation is a requirement. Documents should include information on any and all jumpers and switches found on the board, connector pinouts for all connectors, specifications for cache RAM chips, SIMMs, and other plug-in components, and any other applicable technical information. I would also acquire separate documentation from the BIOS manufacturer covering the specific BIOS used in the system, and the data books covering the specific chipset used in the motherboard. Additional data books for any other controller or I/O chips onboard are a bonus, and may be acquired from the respective chip manufacturers.

Another nice thing to have is available online support and documentation updates, although this should not be accepted in place of good hardcopy manuals.

You may notice that these selection criteria seem fairly strict, and may disqualify many motherboards on the market, including what you already have in your system! These criteria will, however, guarantee you the highest quality motherboard offering the latest in PC technology that will be upgradable, expandable, and provide good service for many years. Most of the time, I recommend purchasing boards from better-known motherboard manufacturers such as Intel, Acer, ABIT, AsusTek, Elitegroup, FIC (First International Computer), and others. These boards might cost a little more than others that you have never heard of, but there is some safety in the more well-known brands. That is, the more boards that they sell, the more likely that any problems will have been discovered by others and solved long before you get yours. Also, if service or support are needed, the larger vendors are more likely to be around in the long run.

Documentation

As mentioned, extensive documentation is an important factor to consider when you're planning to purchase a motherboard. Most motherboard manufacturers design their boards around a particular chipset, which actually counts as the bulk of the motherboard circuitry. There are a number of manufacturers offering chipsets, such as Intel, VIA, ALi, SiS, and others. I recommend obtaining the data book or other technical documentation on the chipset directly from the chipset manufacturer.

One of the more common questions I hear about a system relates to the BIOS Setup program. People want to know what the "Advanced Chipset Setup" features mean and what will the effects of changing them be. Often they go to the BIOS manufacturer thinking that the BIOS documentation will offer help. Usually, however, people find that there is no real coverage of what the chipset setup features are in the BIOS documentation. You will find this information in the data book provided by the chipset manufacturer. Although these books are meant to be read by the engineers who design the boards, they contain all the detailed information about the chipset's features, especially those that might be adjustable. With the chipset data book, you will have an explanation of all the controls in the Advanced Chipset Setup section of the BIOS Setup program.

Besides the main chipset data books, I also recommend collecting any data books on the other major chips in the system. This would include any floppy or IDE controller chips, Super I/O chips, and, of course, the main processor. You will find an incredible amount of information on these components in the data books.

Caution

Most chipset manufacturers only make a particular chip for a short time, rapidly superseding it with an improved or changed version. The data books are only available during the time the chip is being manufactured, so if you wait too long, you will find that such documents may no longer be available. The time to collect documentation on your motherboard is *now*!

Using Correct Speed-Rated Parts

Some compatible vendors use substandard parts in their systems to save money. Because the CPU is one of the most expensive components on the motherboard, and motherboards are sold to system assemblers without the CPU installed, it is tempting for the assembler to install a CPU rated for less than the actual operating speed. A system could be sold as a 266MHz system, for example, but when you look "under the hood," you may find a CPU rated for only 233MHz. This is called *overclocking*, and many vendors have practiced this over the last few years. Some even go so far as to remark the CPUs, so that even if you look, the part appears to have the correct rating. The only way to stop that is to purchase systems from known reliable vendors, and processors from distributors that are closely connected with the manufacturer. Overclocking is fine if you want to do it yourself and understand the risks, but when I purchase a system new, I expect that all the parts included be rated to run at the speed to which they are set.

◄◄ See "Processor Speed Ratings," p. 33

When a chip is run at a speed higher than it is rated for, it will run hotter than it would normally. This may cause the chip to overheat occasionally, which would appear as random lockups, glitches, and frustration. I highly recommend that you check to be sure you are getting the correct speed-rated parts for which you are paying.

Also make sure that you use the recommended heat sink compound (thermal grease). This can improve the efficiency of your heat sink by up to 30%.

This practice is easy to fall into because the faster-rated chips cost more money, and Intel and other chip manufacturers usually rate their chips very conservatively. Over the years, I have taken several 25MHz 486 processors and run them at 33MHz, and they seemed to work fine. The Pentium 166 and even some 133 chips I have seem to run fine at 200MHz. Although I might purchase a Pentium 166 system and make a decision to run it at 200MHz, if I were to experience lockups or glitches in operation, I would immediately return it to 166MHz and retest. If I purchase a 200MHz system from a vendor, I fully expect it to have 200MHz parts, not 166mHz parts running past their rated speed! These days, many chips will have some form of heat sink on them, which helps to prevent overheating, but which can also sometimes cover up for a "pushed" chip. Fortunately, since the Pentium processor, Intel has been marking all their chips on the bottom and the top.

The practice of overclocking may be all but over for Intel processor systems. Intel has recently begun building overclock protection into their CPUs, which prevents them from running at any speed higher than they are rated at. They will run at lower speeds, but not higher ones. This was done mainly to combat those re-marking CPUs and deceiving customers, although, unfortunately, it also prevents those who want to from hot-rodding their chips.

The AMD and Cyrix chips may not be marked on the bottom such as Intel's chips—and of special note is that the ink used on the AMD chips is very easy to wipe off. Because most AMD chips seem to be capable of running well over their rated speed, this has contributed to a great deal of remarking of those chips. If you purchase an AMD K6 processor or a system with that processor, verify that the markings are the original AMD markings and that the speed rating on the chip is what you really paid for.

The bottom line is if the price is too good to be true, ask before you buy: "Are the parts really manufacturer-rated for the system speed?"

To determine the rated speed of a CPU chip, look at the writing on the chip. Most of the time, the part number will end in a suffix of *–xxx* where the *xxx* is a number indicating the maximum speed. For example, –333 indicates that the chip is rated for 333MHz operation.

Caution

Be careful when running software to detect processor speed. Such programs can only tell you what speed the chip is currently running at, not what the true rating is. Also ignore the speed indicator lights on the front of some cases. These digital displays can literally be set via jumpers to read any speed you desire! They have no true relation to actual system speed.

Most of the better diagnostics on the market such as the Norton Utilities from Symantec will read the processor ID and stepping information. You can consult the processor manufacturer or Chapter 3 for tables listing the various processor steppings to see exactly how yours stacks up.

Chapter 5

Memory

This chapter looks at memory from both a physical and logical point of view. We will first look at what memory is, where it fits into the PC architecture, and how it works. We will discuss the different types of memory, speeds, and packaging of the chips and memory modules that you can purchase and install.

The chapter also looks at the logical layout of memory, defining the different areas and uses of these areas from the system's point of view. Because the logical layout and uses are within the "mind" of the processor, memory mapping and logical layout remain as perhaps the most difficult subjects to grasp in the PC universe. This chapter contains useful information that removes the mysteries associated with memory and enables you to get the most out of your system.

Memory Basics

Memory is the workspace for the computer's processor. It is a temporary storage area where the programs and data being operated on by the processor must reside. Memory storage is considered temporary because the data and programs will remain there only as long as the computer has electrical power or is not reset. Before being shut down or reset, any data that has been changed should be saved to a more permanent storage device of some type (usually a hard disk) so it can be reloaded into memory again in the future.

We often call memory RAM, for Random Access Memory. Main memory is called RAM because you can randomly (and quickly) access any location in memory. When we talk about a computer's *memory*, we usually mean the RAM in the system, meaning primarily the memory chips or modules that make up the primary active program and data storage used by the processor. This is often confused with the term "storage," which should be used when referring to things such as disk and tape drives (although some people do consider them a form of memory).

RAM can refer to both the physical chips that make up the memory in the system, and the logical mapping and layout of that memory. Logical mapping and layout refer to how the memory addresses are mapped to actual chips, and what address locations contain what types of system information.

People new to computers often confuse main memory with disk storage, as both have capacities that are expressed in similar megabyte or gigabyte terms. The best analogy to explain the relationship between memory and disk storage I've found is to think of a small office with a desk and a file cabinet.

In this popular analogy, the file cabinet represents the system's hard disk, where both programs and data are stored for long-term safekeeping. The desktop represents the system's main memory, which allows the person working at the desk (acting as the processor) direct access to any files placed on it. To work on a particular file, it first must be retrieved from the cabinet and placed on the desktop. If the desktop is large enough, you may be able to have several files open on it at one time; likewise, if your system has more memory, you can run more or larger programs.

Adding hard disk space to a system is like putting a bigger file cabinet in the office; more files can be permanently stored. Adding more memory to a system is like getting a bigger desk; you can work on more programs and data at the same time.

One difference between this analogy and the way things really work in a computer is that when a file is loaded into memory, it is a copy of the file that is actually loaded; the original still resides on the hard disk. Note that because of the temporary nature of memory, any files that have been changed after being loaded into memory must then be saved back to the hard disk before the system is powered off and the memory subsequently cleared. If the changed file is not saved, then the original copy of the file on the hard disk will remain unaltered. This is like saying that any changes made to any files left on the desktop will be discarded when the office is closed, although the original files themselves will still be present in the cabinet.

Memory temporarily stores programs when they are running, along with the data being used by those programs. RAM chips are sometimes termed *volatile storage* because when you turn off your computer or an electrical outage occurs, whatever is stored in RAM is lost unless you saved it to your hard drive. Because of the volatile nature of RAM, many computer users make it a habit to save their work frequently. (Some software applications can do timed backups automatically.)

Launching a computer program brings files into RAM, and as long as they are running, computer programs reside in RAM. The CPU executes programmed instructions in RAM, and also stores results in RAM. RAM stores your keystrokes when you use a word processor, and also stores numbers used in calculations. Telling a program to save your data instructs the program to store RAM contents on your hard drive as a file.

Physically, the main memory in a system is a collection of chips or modules containing chips that are normally plugged into the motherboard. These chips or modules vary in both their electrical and physical design and must be compatible with the system into which they are being installed in order to function properly. In this chapter, we will discuss the different types of chips and modules that may be installed in different systems.

Next to the processor, memory can be one of the more expensive components in a modern PC, although the total amount spent on memory for a typical system has declined over the last few years. Even after the price drops, you should still be spending more on the memory for your system than the cost of your motherboard; in fact, up to twice as much. Prior to the memory price crash in mid-'96, memory had maintained a fairly consistent price for many years of about $40 per megabyte. 16M (a typical configuration back then) cost more than $600. In fact, memory was so expensive at that time, it was worth more than its weight in gold. These high prices caught the attention of criminals as memory module manufacturers were robbed at gunpoint in several large heists. These robberies were partially induced by the fact that memory was so valuable, the demand was high, and stolen chips or modules were virtually impossible to trace. After the rash of armed robberies and other thefts, memory module manufacturers began posting armed guards and implementing beefed-up security procedures.

By the end of '96, memory prices had cooled considerably to about $4 a meg, a tenfold price drop in less than a year. Prices continued to fall after the major crash and recently have reached about a dollar and a half per meg, or about $100 for 64M, a typical configuration today. This means that out of all the money spent on a PC system today, we are now installing about four times more memory in a system compared to a few years ago and, at the same time, are spending about 1/6 of the total amount for it.

Memory may cost us less now than a few years ago, but its useful life has also become much shorter. New types of memory are being adopted more quickly than before, and it is now more likely that any new systems you purchase will not accept the same memory as your existing ones. This means that in an upgrade or repair situation, you will often have to change the memory if you change the motherboard. The chance that you can reuse the memory in an existing motherboard when upgrading to a new one is slim. This is likely to continue in the future, meaning that the system or upgrade motherboard you purchase next year will most likely not be able to use the memory in your current systems.

Because of this, it is important to understand all the different types of memory on the market today, so you can best determine which types are required by which systems, and thus more easily plan for future upgrades and repairs.

Types of Memory

To better understand physical memory in a system, it is necessary to see where and how it fits into the system. Three main types of physical memory used in modern PCs are

- *ROM*. Read Only Memory
- *DRAM*. Dynamic Random Access Memory
- *SRAM*. Static RAM

ROM

Read Only Memory, or ROM, is a type of memory that can permanently or semi-permanently hold data. It is called read-only because it is either impossible or difficult to write to. ROM is also often referred to as non-volatile memory because any data stored in ROM will remain, even if the power is turned off. As such, ROM is an ideal place to put the PC's startup instructions—that is, the software that boots the system.

Note that ROM and RAM are not opposites, as some people seem to believe. In fact, ROM is technically a subset of the system's RAM. In other words, a portion of the system's Random Access Memory address space is mapped into one or more ROM chips. This is necessary to contain the software that enables the PC to boot up; otherwise, the processor would have no program in memory to execute when it was powered on.

▶▶ See "The Boot Process," p. 1042

For example, when a PC is turned on, the processor automatically jumps to address FFFF0h, expecting to find instructions to tell the processor what to do. This location is exactly 16 bytes from the end of the first megabyte of RAM space, and the end of the ROM. If this location was mapped into regular memory chips, any data stored there would have disappeared when the power was turned off previously, and the processor would subsequently find no instructions to run the next time power was turned on. By placing a ROM chip at this address, a system startup program can be permanently loaded into the ROM and will be available every time the system is turned on.

▶▶ For more information about Dynamic RAM, see "DRAM," p. 311

Normally, the system ROM will start at address F0000h, which is 64K prior to the end of the first megabyte. Because the ROM chip is normally 64K in size, the ROM programs occupy the entire last 64K of the first megabyte, including the critical FFFF0h startup instruction address.

Some think it strange that the PC would start executing instructions 16 bytes from the end of the ROM, but this design was intentional. All the ROM programmer has to do is place a JMP (jump) instruction at that address, which instructs the processor to jump to the actual beginning of the ROM—in most cases close to F0000h, which is about 64K earlier in the memory map. It's kind of like deciding to read every book starting 16 pages from the end, and then having all book publishers agree to place an instruction there to jump back the necessary number of pages to get to page 1. By setting the startup location in this way, Intel allowed the ROM to grow to be any size, all the while keeping it at the upper end of addresses in the first megabyte of the memory address space.

The main ROM BIOS is contained in a ROM chip on the motherboard, but there are also adapter cards with ROMs on them as well. ROMs on adapter cards contain auxiliary BIOS routines and drivers needed by the particular card, especially for those cards that must be active early in the boot process, such as video cards. Cards that don't need drivers active at boot time will normally not have a ROM because those drivers can be loaded from the hard disk later in the boot process.

The motherboard ROM normally contains four main programs, including the following in most systems:

- *POST*. Power-On Self Test. A series of test routines that ensure the system components are operating properly.

- *CMOS Setup*. A menu-driven application that allows the user to set system configuration parameters, options, security settings, and preferences.

- *Bootstrap Loader*. The routine that first scans the floppy drive and then the hard disk, looking for an operating system to load.

- *BIOS*. Basic Input/Output System. A series of device driver programs designed to present a standard interface to the basic system hardware, especially hardware that must be active during the boot process.

Because the BIOS is the main portion of the code stored in ROM, we often call the ROM the ROM BIOS. In older PCs, the motherboard ROM BIOS could consist of up to five or six total chips, but most PCs have required only a single chip for many years now. For more information on the motherboard ROM, see Chapter 4, "Motherboards and Buses."

Adapter cards that require startup drivers also have ROMs on them. This includes cards such as video cards, most SCSI (Small Computer Systems Interface) cards, Enhanced IDE controller cards, and some Network cards. The ROM chip on these cards contains drivers and startup programs that will be executed by the motherboard ROM at boot time. This, for example, is how a video card can be recognized and initialized, even though your motherboard ROM does not contain specific drivers for it. You wouldn't want to load the initial VGA mode drivers from disk because the screen would remain dark until those drivers were loaded. What happens is the motherboard ROM scans a special adapter ROM area of RAM (addresses C0000-DFFFFh), looking for a 55AAh signature byte pair that indicates the start of a ROM. The motherboard BIOS automatically runs the programs in any adapter ROMs it finds during the scan. You see this in most systems when you turn your system on, and during the POST you see the video card BIOS initialize and announce its presence.

ROM chips are very slow by nature, with normal access times of 150ns (nanoseconds, or billionths of a second; for more information, see the Memory Speed section later in this chapter), compared to DRAM access times of 60ns or less. Due to this fact, in many systems the ROMs are *shadowed*, which means they are copied into DRAM chips at startup to allow faster access during normal operation. The shadowing procedure copies the ROM into RAM, and then assigns that RAM the same address as the ROM originally used, disabling the actual ROM in the process. This makes the system seem like it has 60ns (or whatever the RAM speed is) ROM. The performance gain from shadowing is often very slight, and it can cause problems if not set up properly, so in most cases it is wise to shadow only the motherboard and maybe video card BIOS, and leave the others alone.

Shadowing is mostly useful only if you are running 16-bit operating systems such as DOS or Windows 3.x. If you are running a 32-bit operating system such as Windows 95, Windows 98, or Windows NT, then shadowing is virtually useless because those operating systems do not use the 16-bit ROM code while running. Instead, those operating systems load 32-bit drivers into RAM, which replace the 16-bit BIOS code used only during system startup. Shadowing controls are found in the CMOS Setup program in the motherboard ROM, which is covered in more detail in Chapter 4.

Four different types of ROM chips are

- *ROM.* Read Only Memory

- *PROM.* Programmable ROM

- *EPROM.* Erasable PROM

- *EEPROM.* Electrically Erasable PROM, also called a flash ROM

No matter which type of ROM you use, the data stored in a ROM chip is non-volatile and will remain indefinitely unless intentionally erased or overwritten.

Table 5.1 lists the identifying part numbers typically used for each type of ROM chip along with any other identifying information.

Table 5.1 ROM Chip Part Numbers		
ROM Type	**Part Number**	**Other**
ROM	No longer in use	
PROM	27nnnn	
EPROM	27nnnn	Quartz window
EEPROM	28xxxx or 29xxxx	

Mask ROM

Originally, most ROMs were manufactured with the 0s and 1s already "cast in" or integrated into the die. The die represents the actual silicon chip. These are called mask ROMs, because the data is formed into the mask from which the ROM die is photolithographically produced. This type of manufacturing method is economical if you are making hundreds of thousands of ROMs with the exact same information. If you have to change a single bit, however, you must remake the mask, which is an expensive proposition. Due to costs and inflexibility, nobody uses mask ROMs anymore.

PROM

PROMs are a type of ROM that is blank when new and must be programmed with whatever data you want. The PROM was invented in the late '70s by Texas Instruments, and has been available in sizes from 1K (8K bits) to 2M (16M bits) or more. They can be identified by their part numbers, which are usually 27nnnn, where the 27 indicates the TI type PROM and the nnnn indicates the size of the chip in Kbits. For example, most PCs that used PROMs came with 27512 or 271000 chips, which indicate 512K bits (64K bytes) or 1M bits (128K bytes).

Although we say these chips are blank when new, they are technically preloaded with binary 1s. In other words, a 1Mbit ROM chip used in a modern PC would come with 1 million (actually 1,048,576) bit locations, each containing a binary 1. A blank PROM can then be programmed, which is the act of writing to it. This normally requires a special machine called a Device Programmer, ROM Programmer, or ROM burner (see Figure 5.1). We sometimes refer to programming the ROM as "burning" it because that is technically an apt description of the process. Each binary 1 bit can be thought of as a fuse that is intact. Most chips run on 5 volts, but when we program a PROM, we place a higher voltage (normally 12 volts) at the various addresses within the chip. This higher voltage actually blows or burns the fuses at the locations we desire, thus turning any given 1 into a 0. Although we can turn a 1 into a 0, you should note that the process is irreversible; that is, we cannot turn a 0 back into a 1. The programmer device examines the program you want to write into the chip, and then selectively changes only the 1s to 0s where necessary in the chip. PROM chips are often referred to as OTP (One Time Programmable) chips for this reason. They can be programmed once, and never erased. Most PROMs are very inexpensive, on the order of $3 for a typical PC motherboard PROM, so if you wanted to change the program in a PROM, you discard it and program a fresh one with the new data.

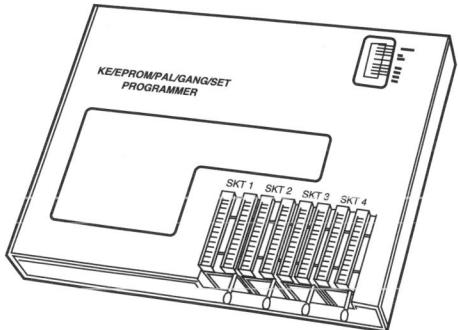

FIG. 5.1 Typical Gang (multi-socket) Device Programmer (PROM Burner).

The act of programming a PROM takes anywhere from a few seconds to a few minutes, depending on the size of the chip and the algorithm used by the programming device. Figure 5.1 shows a typical PROM programmer that has multiple sockets. This is called a gang-programmer and can program several chips at once, saving time if you have several chips to write with the same data. Less expensive programmers are available with only one socket, which is fine for most individual use.

I use and recommend a very inexpensive programmer from a company called Andromeda Research (see Appendix A, "Vendor List"). Besides being economical, their unit has the advantage of connecting to a PC via the parallel port for fast and easy data transfer of files between the PC and the programming unit. Their unit is also portable and comes built in to a convenient carrying case. It is operated by an included menu-driven program that you install on the connected PC. The program contains several features, including a function that allows you to read the data from a chip and save it in a file on your system; you can also write a chip from a data file, verify a chip matches a file, and verify a chip is blank before programming begins.

Chapter 4 shows how I used my PROM programmer to modify the BIOS in some of my older PCs. With today's systems primarily using flash ROMs, this capability is somewhat limited, but I include the information because I think it is very interesting.

> **Note**
>
> I even used my PROM programmer to reprogram the PROM in my '89 Turbo Trans Am, changing the factory preset speed and rpm limiters, turbocharger boost, torque converter lockup points, spark advance, fuel delivery, idle speed, and much more! I also incorporated a switch box under the dash that allows me to switch among four different chips even while the vehicle is running. One chip I created I call the "valet chip," which when engaged will cut off the fuel injectors at a preset speed of 36 miles per hour, and restart them when the vehicle coasts down to 35 mph. I imagine this type of modification would be useful for those with teenagers driving, as you could set the mph or engine rpm limit to whatever you want! Another chip I created cuts off all fuel to the engine altogether, which I engage when the vehicle is parked, for security purposes. No matter how clever, a thief will not be able to steal this car unless they tow it away. If you are interested in such a chip-switching device or custom chips for your Turbo Trans Am or Buick Grand National, contact Casper's Electronics (see the vendor list in Appendix A). For other vehicles with replaceable PROMs, companies such as Superchips, Hypertech, and Evergreen offer custom PROMs for improved performance (see Appendix A). I installed a Superchips chip in a Ford Explorer I had and it made a dramatic improvement in engine operation and vehicle performance.

EPROM

One variation of the PROM that has been very popular is the EPROM. An EPROM is a PROM that is erasable. An EPROM chip can be easily recognized by the clear quartz crystal window set in the chip package directly over the die. You can actually see the die through the window! EPROMs have the same 27xxxx part numbering scheme as the standard PROM, and are functionally and physically identical except for the clear quartz window above the die.

The purpose of the window is to allow ultraviolet light to reach the chip die, because the EPROM is erased by exposure to intense UV light. The window is quartz crystal because regular glass will block UV light. You can't get a suntan through a window! The quartz window makes the EPROMS more expensive than the OTP PROMs. This extra expense is needless if erasability is not important.

The UV light erases the chip by causing a chemical reaction that essentially melts the fuses back together! Thus, any binary 0s in the chip become 1s, and the chip is restored to new condition with binary 1s in all locations. To work, the UV exposure must be at a specific wavelength (2,537 angstroms), at a fairly high intensity (12,000 uw/cm2), in close proximity (2–3cm or about 1 inch), and last for between 5 and 15 minutes duration. An EPROM eraser (see Figure 5.2) is a device that contains a UV light source (usually a sunlamp-type bulb) above a sealed compartment drawer where you place the chip or chips.

FIG. 5.2   A professional EPROM eraser.

Figure 5.2 shows a professional-type EPROM eraser that can handle up to 50 chips at a time. I use a much smaller and less expensive one called the DataRase by Walling Co. (see the vendor list). This device erases up to four chips at a time and is both economical and portable.

The quartz crystal window on an EPROM is normally covered by tape, which prevents accidental exposure to UV light. There is UV light in sunlight, of course, and even in standard room lighting, such that over time a chip exposed to the light may begin to degrade. For this reason, after a chip is programmed, it is a good idea to put a sticker over the window to protect it.

EEPROM/Flash ROM

A newer type of ROM is the EEPROM, which stands for Electrically Erasable PROM. These chips are also called flash ROMs, and are characterized by their capability to be erased and reprogrammed directly in the circuit board in which they are installed, with no special equipment required. By using an EEPROM or flash ROM, it is possible to erase and reprogram the motherboard ROM in a PC without removing the chip from the system, or even opening up the system chassis! With a flash ROM or EEPROM, you don't need a UV eraser or device programmer to program or erase chips. Not only do virtually all PC motherboards built since 1994 use flash ROMs or EEPROMs, most automobiles built since then also use them as well. For example, my '94 Chevy Impala SS has a PCM (Powertrain Control Module) with an integral flash ROM.

The EEPROM or flash ROM can be identified by a 28xxxx or 29xxxx part number, and the lack of a window on the chip. Having an EEPROM or flash ROM in your PC motherboard means you can now easily upgrade the motherboard ROM without having to swap chips. In most cases, you will download the updated ROM from the motherboard manufacturer's Web site, and then run a special program they provide to update the ROM. This procedure is described in more detail in Chapter 4.

◄◄ See "Upgrading the ROM BIOS," p. 215

It is recommended that you periodically check with your motherboard manufacturer to see whether an updated BIOS is available for your system. An updated BIOS may contain bug fixes or enable new features not originally found in your system. For example, you might find fixes for a potential Year 2000 date problem or new drivers to support booting from LS-120 (120M floppy) drives.

►► See "LS-120 (120M) Floptical Drives," p. 798

Note

For the auto enthusiasts out there, you might want to do the same for your car; that is, check to see if ROM upgrades are available for your vehicle's computer. Now that updates are so easy and inexpensive, vehicle manufacturers are releasing bug-fix ROM upgrades for cars that correct operational problems or improve vehicle performance. In most cases, you will have to check with your dealer to see whether any new vehicle ROMs are available. If you have a GM car, GM has a site on the Web where you can get information about the BIOS revisions available for your car, which they call Vehicle Calibrations. The GM Vehicle Calibration Information site address is as follows:

http://207.74.147.14/vci/

When you enter your VIN (Vehicle Identification Number), this page displays the calibration history for the vehicle, which is a list of all the different flash ROM upgrades (calibrations) developed since the vehicle was new. For example, when I entered the VIN on my '94 Impala, I found that there have been five different flash ROM calibrations over the years, and my car had only the second revision installed originally, meaning there had been three newer ROMs than the one I had! The fixes in the various calibration updates are listed also. A trip to the dealer with this information allowed them to use their diagnostic computer to connect to my car and reflash the PCM with the latest software, which, in my case, fixed several problems including engine surging under specific conditions, shift clunks, erroneous "check engine" light warnings, and several other minor problems.

With the flash ROM capability, I began experimenting with running calibrations originally intended for other vehicles and now, in fact, run a modified Camaro calibration loaded into the flash ROM in my Impala. The spark advance curve and fuel delivery parameters are much more aggressive in the Camaro calibration, as are the transmission shift points and other features. If you are interested in having a custom program installed in your flash ROM-equipped vehicle, I recommend you contact Wright Automotive or Evergreen Performance (see the vendor list).

These days, many objects with embedded computers controlling them are using flash ROMs. Pretty soon you'll be taking your toaster in for flash ROM upgrades! The method for locating and updating your PC motherboard flash ROMs is shown in Chapter 4. Other devices may have flash ROMs, as well—for example, I have updated the flash ROMs in my Motorola ISDN modem and in my Kodak digital camera. Both of these items had minor quirks that were fixed by updating their internal ROM code, which was as easy as downloading a file from their respective Web sites and running the update program included in the file. Flash ROMs are also frequently used to add new capabilities to peripherals or update peripherals such as modems to the latest standards, such as updating a modem from X2 or Kflex to v.90.

DRAM

Dynamic RAM is the type of memory chip used for most of the main memory in a modern PC. The main advantages of DRAM is that it is very dense, meaning you can pack a lot of bits into a very small chip, and it is very inexpensive, which makes it affordable for large amounts of memory.

The memory cells in a DRAM chip are tiny capacitors that retain a charge to indicate a bit. The problem with DRAM is that it is dynamic, and because of the design must be constantly *refreshed* or the electrical charges in the individual memory capacitors will drain and the data will be lost. Refresh occurs when the system memory controller takes a tiny break and accesses all the rows of data in the memory chips. Most systems have a memory controller (normally built in to the motherboard chipset), which is set for an industry-standard refresh rate of 15µs (microseconds). The memory is accessed in such a way that all rows of data will be accessed after exactly 128 of these special refresh cycles. This means that every 1.92ms (milliseconds or 128×15µsec), all the rows in the memory are read to refresh the data.

◄◄ See "Chipsets," p. 183

Refreshing the memory unfortunately takes processor time away from other tasks because each refresh cycle takes several CPU cycles to complete. In older systems, the refresh cycling could take up to 10% or more of the total CPU time, but with modern systems running in the hundreds of megahertz, refresh overhead is now on the order of

1% or less of the total CPU time. Some systems allow you to alter the refresh timing parameters via the CMOS Setup, but be aware that increasing the time between refresh cycles to speed up your system can allow some of the memory cells to begin draining, which can cause random soft memory errors to appear. A soft error is a data error that is not caused by a defective chip. It is safer to stick with the recommended or default refresh timing in most cases. Because refresh consumes less than 1% of modern system overall bandwidth, altering the refresh rate has little effect on performance.

DRAMs use only one transistor and capacitor pair per bit, which makes them very dense, offering a lot of memory capacity per chip than other types of memory. There are currently DRAM chips available with densities of up to 256Mbits or more. This means that there are DRAM chips with 256 million or more transistors! Compare this to a Pentium II, which has 7.5 million transistors, and it makes the processor look wimpy by comparison. The difference is that in a memory chip, the transistors and capacitors are all consistently arranged in a (normally square) grid of very simple repetitive structures, unlike the processor, which is a much more complex circuit of different structures and elements interconnected in a highly irregular fashion. At least one manufacturer is working on chips, intended for the 2001-2002 timeframe, with 256-gigabit densities using circuit line widths of 0.05 micron, indicating that memory densities will continue to rise as they have been for years.

The transistor for each DRAM bit cell is used to read the charge state of the adjacent capacitor. If the capacitor is charged, the cell is read to contain a 1; no charge indicates a 0. The charge in the tiny capacitors is constantly draining, which is why the memory must be refreshed constantly. Even a momentary power interruption, or anything that interferes with the refresh cycles, will cause a DRAM memory cell to lose the charge and therefore the data.

DRAM is used in PC systems because it is inexpensive and the chips can be densely packed, meaning that a lot of memory capacity can fit in a small space. Unfortunately, DRAM is also slow, normally much slower than the processor. For this reason, there have been many different types of DRAM architectures developed to improve performance.

Memory Speeds

The speed and performance issue with memory is confusing to some because memory speed is usually expressed in ns (nanoseconds), while processor speed is expressed in MHz (megahertz).

A nanosecond is defined as one billionth of a second—a very short time indeed. To put some perspective on that, note that the speed of light is 186,282 miles (299,792 kilometers) per second in a vacuum. In one billionth of a second, a beam of light would travel a mere 11.80 inches or 29.98 centimeters, less than the length of a typical ruler!

Chip and system speed has been expressed in megahertz (MHz), which is millions of cycles per second. There are systems today with processors running 500MHz or faster, and we should see gigahertz (GHz or billions of cycles per second) speeds within a few years.

Because it is confusing to speak in these different terms for speeds, I thought it would be interesting to see how they compare. Table 5.2 shows the relationship between nanoseconds (ns) and megahertz (MHz) for the speeds associated with PCs today.

Table 5.2   The Relationship Between Clock Speeds in Megahertz (MHz) to Cycle Times in Nanoseconds (ns)

Clock Speed	Cycle Time	Clock Speed	Cycle Time
6MHz	166ns	120MHz	8.3ns
8MHz	125ns	133MHz	7.5ns
10MHz	100ns	150MHz	6.6ns
12MHz	83ns	166MHz	6.0ns
16MHz	62ns	180MHz	5.5ns
20MHz	50ns	200MHz	5.0ns
25MHz	40ns	233MHz	4.2ns
33MHz	30ns	250MHz	4.0ns
40MHz	25ns	300MHz	3.3ns
50MHz	20ns	333MHz	3.0ns
60MHz	16ns	350MHz	2.8ns
66MHz	15ns	400MHz	2.5ns
75MHz	13ns	450MHz	2.2ns
80MHz	12ns	500MHz	2.0ns
100MHz	10ns	550MHz	1.8ns

As you can see from this table, as clock speeds increase, cycle time decreases. If you examine this table, you can clearly see that the DRAM memory used in the typical PC for many years is totally inadequate when compared to processor speeds of 400MHz and higher. Note that until recently, most DRAM memory used in PCs has been rated at an access time of 60ns, which works out to be only about 16.7MHz! Consider that this super slow memory has been installed in systems running up to 300MHz or faster; you can see what a mismatch there is between processor and main memory performance.

System memory timing is a little more involved than converting nanoseconds to megahertz. Because the transistors for each bit in a memory chip are most efficiently arranged in a grid, each transistor is accessed by using a row and column scheme. All memory accesses involve first selecting a row address, then a column address, and then transferring the data. The initial setup for a memory transfer where the row and column addresses are selected is a necessary overhead normally referred to as *latency*. The access time for memory is the cycle time plus latency for selecting the row and column addresses. For example, memory rated at 60ns normally has a latency of about 25ns (to select the row and column address) and a cycle time of about 35ns to actually transfer the data. Thus, the true memory clock rate in a system with 60ns memory would be on the order of 28.5MHz (35ns = 28.5MHz). Even so, a single memory transfer will still require a full 60ns, so consecutive transfers will happen at a rate of only 16.7MHz (60ns) because of the added latency.

What happens when a 300MHz processor is trying to read multiple bytes of data from 16MHz memory? The answer is a lot of wait states! A *wait state* is an additional "do-nothing" cycle that the processor must execute while waiting for the data to become ready. In the case with memory cycling every 60ns (16MHz) and a processor cycling every 3ns (300MHz), the processor would have to execute approximately 19 wait states before the data would be ready on the 20th cycle. Adding wait states in this fashion effectively slows the processing speed to that of the memory, or 16MHz in this example. To reduce the number of wait states required, there are several types of faster memory and cache available, all of which are discussed in this chapter.

Fast Page Mode (FPM) DRAM
Standard DRAM is accessed via a technique called *paging*. Normal memory access requires that a row and column address be selected, which takes time. Paging allows for faster access to all the data within a given row of memory by keeping the row address the same and changing only the column. Memory that uses this technique is called *Page Mode* or *Fast Page Mode* memory. Other variations on Page Mode were called Static Column or Nibble Mode memory.

Paged memory is a simple scheme for improving memory performance that divides memory into pages ranging from 512 bytes to a few kilobytes long. The paging circuitry then enables memory locations within a page to be accessed with fewer wait states. If the desired memory location is outside the current page, one or more wait states are added while the system selects the new page.

To improve further on memory access speeds, systems have evolved to allow for faster access to DRAM. One of the more significant changes was the implementation of burst mode access in the 486 and later processors. Burst mode cycling takes advantage of the fact that most memory accesses are consecutive in nature. After setting up the row and column addresses for a given access, using burst mode, one can then access the next three adjacent addresses with no additional latency or wait states. A burst access is normally limited to four total accesses. To describe this, we often refer to the timing in the number of cycles for each access. A typical burst mode access of standard DRAM would be expressed as x-y-y-y, where x is the time for the first access (latency plus cycle time) and y represents the number of cycles required for each consecutive access.

Standard 60ns DRAM normally runs 5-3-3-3 burst mode timing. This means the first access takes a total of five cycles (on a 66MHz system bus, this would be about 75ns total or 5×15ns cycles), while the consecutive cycles take three cycles each (3×15ns = 45ns). As you can see, the actual system timing is somewhat less than the memory is technically rated for. Note that without the bursting technique, memory access would be 5-5-5-5 because the full latency would be needed for each memory transfer.

DRAM memory that supports paging and this bursting technique is called *Fast Page Mode (FPM) memory*. The term comes from the fact that memory accesses to data on the same page can be done with less latency. Most 486 and newer systems use FPM memory, while older systems used conventional DRAM.

Another technique for speeding up FPM memory was a technique called *interleaving*. This is a design where two separate banks of memory are used together, alternating access from one to the other as even and odd bytes. While one is being accessed, the other is being precharged, where the row and column addresses are being selected. Then, by the time the first bank in the pair is finished returning data, the second bank in the pair is finished with the latency part of the cycle and is now ready to return data. While the second bank is returning data, the first bank is being precharged, selecting the row and column address of the next access. This overlapping of accesses in two banks reduces the effect of the latency or precharge cycles and allows for faster overall data retrieval. The only problem is that to utilize interleaving, you must install identical pairs of banks together, doubling the amount of SIMMs or DIMMs required. This was popular on 32-bit wide memory systems on 486 processors, but fell out of favor on Pentiums due to the 64-bit wide memory width on those systems. To do interleaving on a Pentium machine, you would need to install memory 128 bits at a time, meaning four 72-pin SIMMs or two DIMMs at a time.

EDO RAM

Starting in 1995, a new type of memory became available for Pentium systems called *EDO (Extended Data Out) RAM*. EDO is a modified form of FPM memory and is also referred to as *Hyper Page Mode*. EDO was invented and patented by Micron Technology, although they have licensed production to numerous other memory manufacturers. EDO memory consists of specially manufactured chips that allow for a timing overlap between successive accesses. The name Extended Data Out refers specifically to the fact that unlike FPM, the data output drivers on the chip are not turned off when the memory controller removes the column address to begin the next cycle. This allows the next cycle to overlap the previous one, saving approximately 10ns per cycle.

The effect of EDO is that cycle times are improved by allowing the memory controller to begin a new column address instruction while it is reading data at the current address. This is almost identical to what was achieved in older systems by interleaving banks of memory, but unlike interleaving, you don't need to install two identical banks of memory in the system at a time.

EDO RAM allows for burst mode cycling of 5-2-2-2, as compared to the 5-3-3-3 of standard Fast Page Mode memory. This means that to do four memory transfers, EDO would require 11 total system cycles as compared to 14 total cycles for FPM. This is a 22% improvement in overall cycling time, but in actual testing EDO normally increases overall system benchmark speed by about 5%. Even though the overall system improvement may seem small, the important thing about EDO is that it uses the same basic DRAM chip design as FPM, meaning that there is virtually no additional cost over FPM. As such, EDO costs about the same as FPM and offers higher performance.

To actually use EDO memory, your motherboard chipset must support it. Most motherboard chipsets since the Intel 430FX (Triton), which debuted in 1995, have offered support for EDO. Because EDO memory chips cost the same to manufacture as standard chips, combined with the fact that Intel began to support EDO in all their chipsets, the PC market jumped on the EDO bandwagon full force.

◀◀ See "Fifth-Generation (P5 Pentium Class) Chipsets," p. 187, and "Sixth-Generation (P6 Pentium Pro / Pentium II Class) Chipsets," p. 199

EDO RAM is ideal for systems with bus speeds of up to 66MHz, which fit perfectly with the PC market up through 1997; however, for 1998 and beyond, the market for EDO will rapidly decline as the newer and faster SDRAM (Synchronous DRAM) architecture becomes the standard for new PC system memory.

Burst EDO

A variation of EDO is *Burst Extended-Data-Out Dynamic Random Access Memory (BEDO DRAM)*. BEDO is basically EDO memory with special burst features for even speedier data transfers than standard EDO. Unfortunately, only one chipset (Intel 440FX Natoma) supported it, and it was quickly overshadowed by SDRAM, which seemed to be favored among PC system chipset and system designers. As such, you won't see BEDO being used in systems today, and it is no longer in production.

SDRAM

SDRAM stands for Synchronous DRAM, a type of DRAM that runs in synchronization with the memory bus. SDRAM delivers information in very high-speed bursts using a high-speed, clocked interface. SDRAM removes most of the latency involved in asynchronous DRAM because the signals are already in synchronization with the motherboard clock.

Like EDO RAM, your chipset must support this type of memory for it to be usable in your system. Starting in 1997 with the 430VX and 430TX, all of Intel's subsequent chipsets fully support SDRAM, making it the most popular type of memory for new systems. SDRAM is especially suited to the Pentium II architecture, and the new high-performance motherboards that run it.

Performance of SDRAM is dramatically improved over FPM or EDO RAM. Because SDRAM is still a type of DRAM, the initial latency is the same, but overall cycle times are much faster than with FPM or EDO. SDRAM timing for a burst access would be 5-1-1-1, meaning that four memory reads would complete in only eight system bus cycles, as compared to 11 cycles for EDO and 14 cycles for FPM.

Besides the fact that SDRAM can work in fewer cycles, it is also capable of supporting 100MHz (10ns) or faster system bus cycling, which has become the new standard for system speed starting in 1998. As such, virtually all new PC systems sold in 1998 and for probably two years thereafter will include SDRAM memory.

It is anticipated that in the near future, this figure will be pushed to 200MHz in order to keep up with faster systems of the future. SDRAM is sold in DIMM form, and is often rated by megahertz speed rather than nanosecond cycling time. As such, you will see SDRAM sold as 66MHz or 15ns, 83MHz or 12ns, or 100MHz or 10ns. Due to the extreme timing at the 100MHz level, Intel has created a PC/100 standard that defines the performance criteria a 100MHz memory module must meet to be reliable in a 100MHz system. To meet the criteria with enough overhead to spare, most PC/100-certified memory will be 8ns, or 125MHz. Even though they are technically capable of 125MHz, they will be PC/100 or 100MHz "certified." Although 10ns memory might work, Intel feels that it will not be reliable enough because the margins are too close.

Although SDRAM is significantly faster than previous types of memory, prices are not appreciably higher, which has made the acceptance of SDRAM even more rapid.

▶▶ See "SIMMs and DIMMs," p. 324

Future DRAM Memory Technologies

RDRAM

The RDRAM, or Rambus DRAM, is a radical new memory design that will be used in high-end PC systems starting in the 1999-2000 timeframe. It is endorsed by Intel and will be directly supported in the future chipsets released during that timeframe.

RDRAMs boost raw memory bandwidth by doubling the on-chip data bus to 16 bits and increasing the clock to 800MHz, for a peak bandwidth of 1.6 Gbytes/second. Rambus made improvements to the bus protocol so that it no longer multiplexes or shares control information on the data bus. Instead, it creates an independent control and address bus split into two groups of pins for row and column commands, while data is transferred across the 2-byte-wide data bus. Synchronization is achieved by sending packets on the falling edge of the clock.

The architecture supports multiple, simultaneous interleaved transactions. Internally, the 64-Mbit device uses a total 128-bit-wide data path operating at 100MHz, allowing 16-byte transfers to or from the core every 10ns. Because RDRAMs have four power-down modes and automatically transition into standby at the end of a transaction, total module power is slightly lower than an SDRAM's at the desktop and similar to EDO for mobile systems.

RDRAM chips will be installed in modules called RIMMs (Rambus Inline Memory Modules). A RIMM (shown in Figure 5.3) is similar in size and form to current DIMMs, but they are not interchangeable.

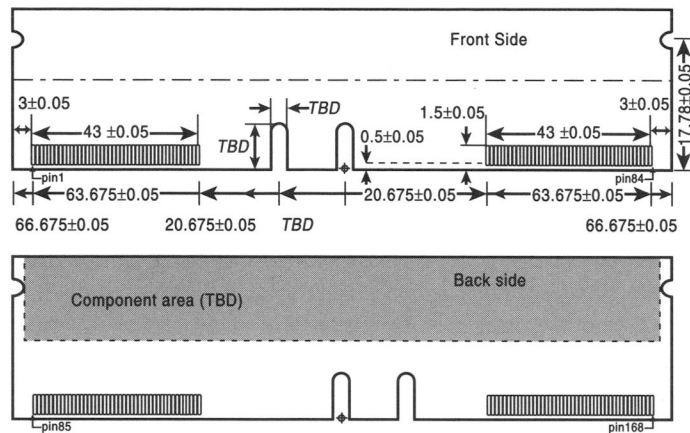

FIG. 5.3 168-pin RIMM module.

An RDRAM memory controller with a single Rambus channel supports up to three RIMM modules, which at the 64Mbit chip density level supports 256M per RIMM. Future RIMM versions will be available in higher capacities, up to 1G or more, and it will be possible to develop chipsets (with integral Rambus memory controllers), which can support more Rambus channels, allowing for more RIMM sockets per board.

Interestingly Rambus does not manufacture either the RDRAM chips or the RIMMs; that is left to other companies. Rambus is merely a design company, and they have no chip fabs or manufacturing facilities of their own. They license their technology to other companies who then manufacture the devices and modules. There are at least 13 RDRAM licensees, such as Fujitsu Ltd., Hitachi Ltd., Hyundai Electronics Industry Co. Ltd., IBM Microelectronics, LG Semiconductor Co. Ltd., Micron Technology Inc., Mitsubishi Electric Corp., NEC Corp., Oki Electric Industry Co. Ltd., Samsung Electronics Corp., Siemens AG, and Toshiba Corp. All these companies will be manufacturing both the RDRAM devices and the RIMMs that contain them.

DDR SDRAM

Double Data Rate (DDR) SDRAM memory is an evolutionary design of standard SDRAM where data is transferred twice as fast. Instead of doubling the actual clock rate, DDR memory achieves the doubling in performance by transferring two times per transfer cycle, once at the leading and once at the trailing edge of the cycle. This effectively doubles the transfer rate, even though the same overall clock and timing signals are used.

DDR is being proposed by processor companies such as AMD and Cyrix, and chipset manufacturers such as VIA Technologies, ALi (Acer Labs, Inc.), and SiS (Silicon integrated Systems) as a low-cost license-free alternative to RDRAMs. Intel is officially supporting only RDRAMs for new high-end systems in 1999 and beyond, while DDR seems destined for the lower-end commodity PCs as an alternative. Official standardization of DDR was undertaken by the DDR Consortium, an industry panel consisting of Fujitsu, Ltd., Hitachi, Ltd., Hyundai Electronics Industries Co., Mitsubishi Electric Corp., NEC Corp., Samsung Electronics Co., Texas Instruments, Inc., and Toshiba Corp.

Expect DDR SDRAM to make an appearance during 1999, primarily in non-Intel processor-based systems.

Cache Memory—SRAM

There is another distinctly different type of memory that is significantly faster than most types of DRAM. SRAM stands for Static RAM, which is so named because it does not need the periodic refresh rates like DRAM (Dynamic RAM). Due to the design of SRAM, not only are refresh rates unnecessary, but SRAM is much faster than DRAM and is fully able to keep pace with modern processors.

SRAM memory is available in access times of 2ns or less, which means it can keep pace with processors running 500MHz or faster! This is due to the SRAM design, which calls for a cluster of six transistors for each bit of storage. The use of transistors but no capacitors means that refresh rates are not necessary because there are no capacitors to lose their charges over time. As long as there is power, SRAM will remember what is stored. With these attributes, then why don't we use SRAM for all system memory? The answers are simple:

Type	Speed	Density	Cost
DRAM	Slow	High	Low
SRAM	Fast	Low	High

Compared to DRAM, SRAM is much faster, but also much lower in density and much more expensive. The lower density means that SRAM chips are physically larger and store many less bits overall. The high number of transistors and the clustered design means that SRAM chips are both physically larger and much more expensive to produce than DRAM chips. For example, a DRAM module might contain 64M of RAM or more, while SRAM modules of the same approximate physical size would have room for only 2M or so of data and would cost the same as the 64M DRAM module. Basically, SRAM is up to 30 times larger physically and up to 30 times more expensive than DRAM. The high cost and physical constraints have prevented SRAM from being used as the main memory for PC systems.

Even though SRAM is too expensive for PC use as main memory, PC designers have found a way to use SRAM to dramatically improve PC performance. Rather than spend the money for all RAM to be SRAM memory, which can run fast enough to match the CPU, it is much more cost-effective to design in a small amount of high-speed SRAM memory, called *cache memory*. The cache runs at speeds close to or even equal to the processor, and is the memory from which the processor normally directly reads from and writes to. During read operations, the data in the high-speed cache memory is resupplied from the lower-speed main memory or DRAM in advance.

Up until recently, DRAM was limited to about 60ns (16MHz) in speed. When PC systems were running 16MHz and less, it was possible for the DRAM to fully keep pace with the motherboard and system processor, and there was no need for cache. However, as soon as processors crossed the 16MHz barrier, it was no longer possible for DRAM to keep pace, and that is exactly when SRAM began to enter PC system designs. This occurred back in 1986–1987 with the debut of systems with the 386 processor running at 16- and 20MHz. These were among the first PC systems to employ what we call *cache memory*, a high-speed buffer made up of SRAM that directly feeds the processor. Because the cache can run at the speed of the processor, the system is designed so the cache controller will anticipate the processor's memory needs, and preload the high-speed cache memory with that data. Then, as the processor calls for a memory address, the data can be retrieved from the high-speed cache rather than the much lower speed main memory.

Cache effectiveness is expressed as a *hit ratio*. This is the ratio of cache hits to total memory accesses. A *hit* is when the data the processor needs has been preloaded into the cache from the main memory, meaning that the processor can read it from the cache. A *cache miss* is when the cache controller did not anticipate the need for a specific address; the desired data was not preloaded into the cache; therefore, the processor must retrieve the data from the slower main memory, instead of the faster cache. Anytime the processor reads data from main memory, the processor will have to wait because the main memory cycles at a much slower rate than the processor. If the processor is running at 233MHz, then it is cycling at nearly 4ns, while the main memory might be 60ns, which means it is running at only 16MHz. Thus, every time the processor reads from main memory, it would effectively slow down to 16MHz! The slowdown is accomplished by having the processor execute what are called *wait states*, which are cycles where nothing is done; the processor essentially cools its heels while waiting for the slower main memory to return the desired data. Obviously, we don't want our processors slowing down, so cache function and design become very important as system speeds increase.

To minimize the situation where the processor is forced to read data from the slow main memory, there are normally two stages of cache in a modern system, called Level 1 (L1) and Level 2 (L2). The Level 1 cache is also called integral or internal cache because it is directly built in to the processor, and is actually a part of the processor die (raw chip). Because of this, L1 cache always runs at the full speed of the processor core, and is the fastest cache in any system. All 486 and higher processors incorporate integral L1 cache, making them significantly faster than their predecessors. Level 2 cache is also called external cache because it is external to the processor chip. Originally, this meant that it was installed on the motherboard, as was the case with all 386, 486, and Pentium systems. In those systems, the L2 cache runs at motherboard speed because it is installed on the motherboard. You can normally find the L2 cache directly adjacent to the processor socket in Pentium and earlier systems.

In the interest of improved performance, later processor designs from Intel, including the Pentium Pro and Pentium II, have included the L2 cache as a part of the processor. It is still external to the actual CPU die, and is instead a separate die or chip mounted inside the processor package or module. As such, Pentium Pro or Pentium II systems will not have any cache on the motherboard; it is all contained within the processor module, instead.

The key to understanding both cache and main memory is to see where they fit in the overall system architecture.

Figure 5.4 shows a typical Pentium MMX system with the Intel 430TX chipset.

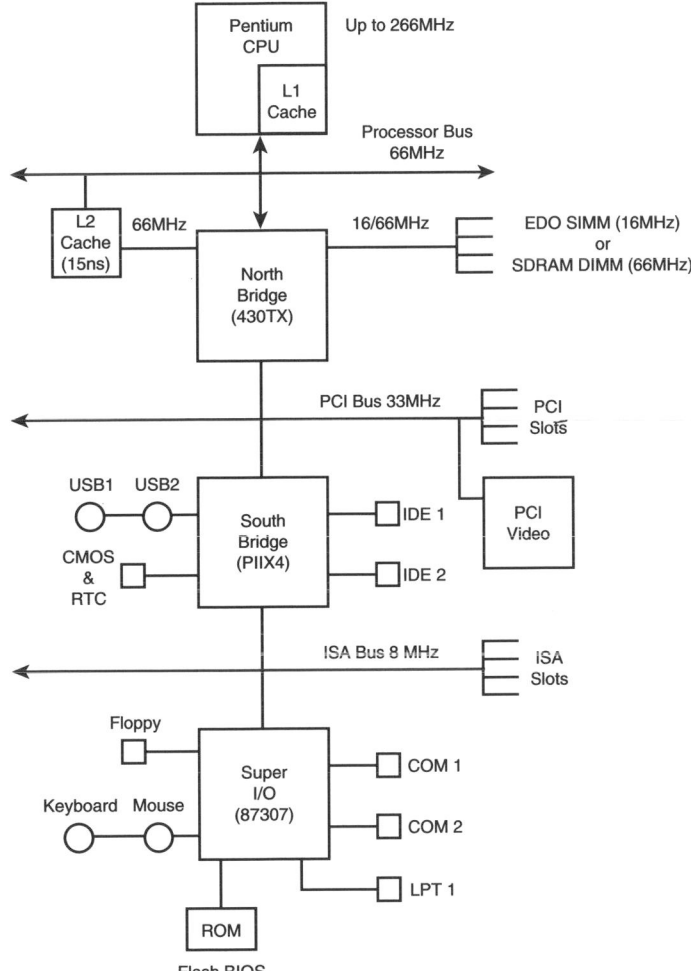

FIG. 5.4 System Architecture, Pentium MMX system with an Intel 430TX chipset.

Table 5.3 illustrates the need for and function of Level 1 (internal) and Level 2 (external) cache in modern systems.

Table 5.3   The Relationship Between Level 1 (Internal) and Level 2 (External) Cache in Modern Systems

CPU Type	486 DX4	Pentium	Pentium Pro	Pentium II (1997)	Pentium II (1998)
Typical CPU Speed:	100MHz	233MHz	200MHz	300MHz	400MHz
L1 Cache Speed:	10ns (100MHz)	4ns (233MHz)	5ns (200MHz)	3ns (300MHz)	2ns (400MHz)
L2 Cache Speed:	30ns (33MHz)	15ns (66MHz)	5ns (200MHz)	6ns (150MHz)	5ns (200MHz)
Motherboard Speed:	33MHz	66MHz	66MHz	66MHz	100MHz
SIMM/DIMM Speed:	60ns (16MHz)	60ns (16MHz)	60ns (16MHz)	15ns (66MHz)	10ns (100MHz)

Cache designs were originally asynchronous, meaning they ran at a clock speed that was not identical or in sync with the processor bus. Starting with the 430FX chipset released in early '95, a new type of synchronous cache design was supported. This required that the chips now run in sync or at the same identical clock timing as the processor bus, further improving speed and performance. Also added at that time was a feature called Pipeline Burst mode, which reduced overall cache latency (wait states) by allowing for single-cycle accesses for multiple transfers after the first one. Because both synchronous and pipeline burst capability came at the same time in new modules, usually specifying one implies the other. Overall synchronous pipeline burst cache allowed for about a 20% improvement in overall system performance, which was a very significant jump.

The cache controller for a modern system is contained within either the North Bridge of the chipset as with Pentium and lesser systems, or within the processor as with the Pentium Pro/II and newer systems. The capabilities of the cache controller dictate the performance and capabilities of the cache. One important thing to note is that most cache controllers have a limitation of the amount of memory that may be cached. Often, this limit can be quite low, as with the 430TX chipset-based Pentium systems. The 430TX chipset can cache data only within the first 64M of system RAM. If you have more memory than that, you will experience a noticeable slowdown in system performance because all data outside the first 64M will never be cached, and would always be accessed with all the wait states required by the slower DRAM. Depending on what software you use and where data is stored in memory, this can be very significant. For example, 32-bit operating systems such as Win95/98 and NT load from the top down, so if you had 96M of RAM, the operating system and applications would be loading directly into the upper 32M (past 64M), which is not cached. This would result in a dramatic slowdown in overall system use. Removing the additional memory to bring the system total down to the cacheable limit of 64M would be the solution. In short, it is unwise to install more main RAM memory than your system (chipset) can cache. Consult your system documentation or the chipset section in Chapter 4, "Motherboards and Buses," for more information.

Physical Memory

The CPU and motherboard architecture (chipset) dictates a particular computer's physical memory capacity, and the types and forms of memory that can be installed. Over the years, there have been two main changes occurring with computer memory—it has gradually become faster and wider! The speed and width requirements are indicated by the CPU and the memory controller circuitry. The memory controller in a modern PC resides in the motherboard chipset. Even though a system may physically support a given amount of memory, the type of software you run may dictate whether or not all the memory can be used.

The 8088 and 8086, with 20 address lines, can use as much as 1M (1024K) of RAM. The 286 and 386SX CPUs have 24 address lines; they can keep track of as much as 16M of memory. The 386DX, 486, Pentium, Pentium-MMX, and Pentium Pro CPUs have a full set of 32 address lines; they can keep track of 4G of memory, while the Pentium II with 36 address lines can manage an impressive 64G!

◄◄ See "Processor Specifications," p. 31

When the 286 and higher chips emulate the 8088 chip (as they do when running 16-bit software such as DOS or Windows 3.x), they implement a hardware operating mode called *real mode*. Real mode is the only mode available on the 8086 and 8088 chips used in PC and XT systems. In real mode, all Intel processors—even the mighty Pentium—are restricted to using only 1M of memory, just as their 8086 and 8088 ancestors were, and the system design reserves 384K of that amount. Only in protected mode can the 286 or better chips use their maximum potential for memory addressing.

◄◄ See "Processor Modes," p. 43

Pentium-based systems can address as much as 4G of memory, and Pentium Pro/II systems can address 64G. To put these memory-addressing capabilities into perspective, 64G (65,536M) of memory would cost about $100,000! Even if you could afford all this memory, some of the largest memory modules available today are 168-pin DIMMs with 256M capacity. To install 64G of RAM would require 256 of the largest 256M DIMMs available, and most systems today can support up to only four or maybe eight DIMM sockets.

Most Pentium II motherboards have a maximum of only three to six DIMM sockets, which allows a maximum of .75–1.5G if all the sockets are filled. These limitations are from the chipset, not the processor. Technically, a Pentium can address 4G of memory and a Pentium II can address 64G, but there isn't a chipset on the market that will allow that! Most of the PII chipsets today are limited to 1G of memory.

Pentium systems have even further limitations. Pentium systems have been available since '93, but only those built in '97 or later use a motherboard chipset that will support SDRAM DIMMs. Even those using the newest 430TX chipset from Intel will not support more than 256M of total memory, and should not have more than 64M actually in-stalled due to memory-caching limitations. Don't install more than 64M of RAM in your Pentium system unless you are sure the motherboard and chipset will allow the L2 cache to function with the additional memory. See the chipset section in Chapter 4 for the maximum cacheable limits on all the Intel and other motherboard chipsets.

Older 386 and 486 motherboards may have problems addressing memory past 16M due to DMA (Direct Memory Access) controller problems. If you install an ISA adapter that uses a DMA channel (such as a busmaster SCSI adapter) and you have more than 16M of memory, you have the potential for problems because the ISA bus allows only DMA access to 16M. Attempted transfers beyond 16M cause the system to crash. This should not be an issue with newer 32-bit operating systems, and 32-bit slots such as PCI. The 32-bit operating systems will automatically remap ISA bus DMA transfers beyond 16M prop-erly, and PCI simply doesn't have any such limitations.

SIMMs and DIMMs

Originally, systems had memory installed via individual chips. These are often referred to as DIP (Dual Inline Package) chips because of their design. The original IBM XT and AT had 36 sockets on the motherboard for these individual chips, and then more of them would be installed on various memory cards plugged into the bus slots. I remember spending hours populating boards with these chips, which was a tedious job.

Besides being a time-consuming and labor-intensive way to deal with memory, DIP chips had one notorious problem—they would creep out of their sockets over time as the sys-tem would go through thermal cycles. Every day when you powered the system on and off, it would heat and cool, and the chips would gradually walk their way out of the sockets. Eventually, good contact would be lost and memory errors would result. Fortu-nately, reseating all the chips back in their sockets would usually rectify the problem, but that was labor-intensive if you had a lot of systems to support.

The alternative to this at the time was to have the memory soldered into either the motherboard or an expansion card. This prevented the chips from creeping and made the connections more permanent, but that caused another problem. If a chip did go bad, you would either have to attempt desoldering and resoldering a new one, or resort to scrapping the motherboard or memory card in which the chip was installed. This was expensive, and it made memory troubleshooting very difficult.

What was needed was a chip that was both soldered yet removable, and that is exactly what was found in the chip that we call a SIMM. For memory storage, most modern systems have adopted the single inline memory module (SIMM) or dual inline memory module (DIMM) as an alternative to individual memory chips. These small boards plug into special connectors on a motherboard or memory card. The individual memory chips are soldered to the SIMM/DIMM, so removing and replacing individual memory chips is impossible. Instead, you must replace the entire module if any part of it fails. The SIMM/DIMM is treated as though it were one large memory chip.

PC systems use two main physical types of SIMMs—30-pin (8 bits plus one optional parity bit) and 72-pin (32 bits plus four optional parity bits)—with various capacities and other specifications. The 30-pin SIMMs are smaller than the 72-pin versions, and may have chips on either one or both sides. 30-pin SIMMs are basically obsolete, and they are being followed rapidly by the 72-pin versions. This is true primarily because the 64-bit systems, which are now the industry standard, would require eight 30-pin SIMMs or two 72-pin SIMMs per bank. DIMMs, which have become popular on Pentium-MMX and Pentium Pro-based systems, are 168-pin units with 64-bit (non-parity) or 72-bit (parity or ECC) data paths.

Figures 5.5, 5.6, and 5.7 show typical 30-pin (8-bit) and 72-pin (32-bit) SIMMs, and a 168-pin (64-bit) DIMM, respectively. The pins are numbered from left to right and are connected through to both sides of the module on the SIMMs. The pins on the DIMM are different on each side. Note that all dimensions are in both inches and millimeters (in parentheses).

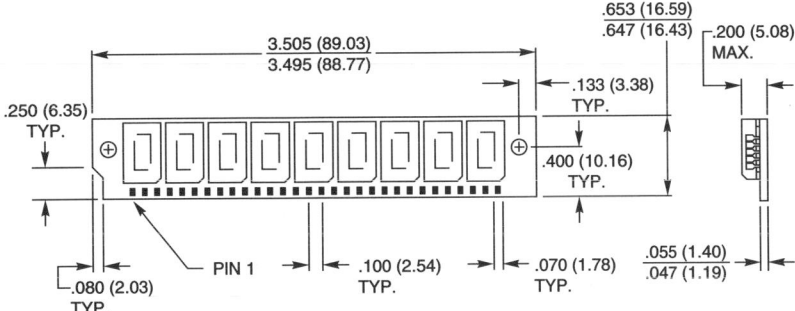

FIG. 5.5 A typical 30-pin SIMM. The one shown here is 9-bit, although the dimensions would be the same for 8-bit as well.

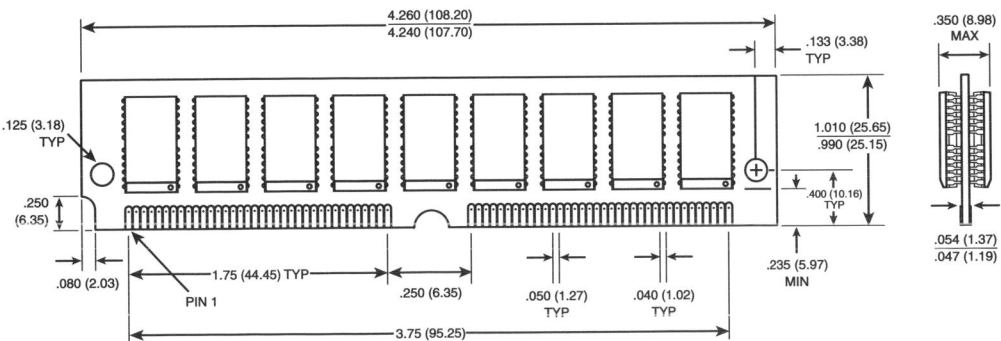

FIG. 5.6 A typical 72-pin SIMM. The one shown here is 36-bit, although the dimensions would be the same for 32-bit as well.

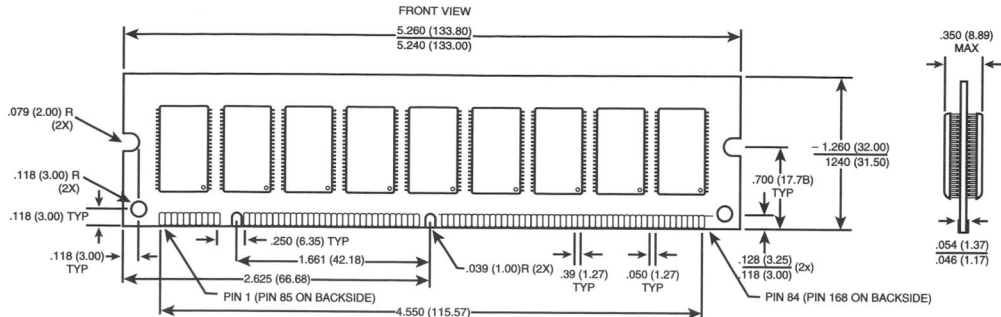

FIG. 5.7 A typical 168-pin DIMM. The one shown here is 72-bit, although the dimensions would be the same for 64-bit as well.

Single inline pinned packages, sometimes called SIPPs, really are SIMMs with pins, not contacts. The pins are designed to be installed in a long connector socket that is much cheaper than the standard SIMM socket. SIPPs are inferior to SIMMs because they lack the positive latching mechanism that retains the module, and the connector lacks the high-force wiping contacts that resist corrosion. SIPPs are rarely used today.

> **Note**
>
> It would be possible to convert a SIPP to a SIMM by cutting off the pins, or to convert a SIMM to a SIPP by soldering pins on. Also, some companies have made SIPP-to-SIMM converters that allow the SIPPs to be plugged into 30-pin SIMM sockets.

These memory modules are extremely compact considering the amount of memory they hold. SIMMs and DIMMs are available in several capacities and speeds. Table 5.4 lists the different capacities available for both the 30-pin and 72-pin SIMMs, and 168-pin DIMMs.

Table 5.4   SIMM and DIMM Capacities

30-Pin SIMM Capacities

Capacity	Parity SIMM	Non-Parity SIMM
256K	256K×9	256K×8
1M	1M×9	1M×8
4M	4M×9	4M×8
16M	16M×9	16M×8

72-Pin SIMM Capacities

Capacity	Parity SIMM	Non-Parity SIMM
1M	256K×36	256K×32
2M	512K×36	512K×32
4M	1M×36	1M×32
8M	2M×36	2M×32

Capacity	Parity SIMM	Non-Parity SIMM
16M	4M×36	4M×32
32M	8M×36	8M×32
64M	16M×36	16M×32
128M	32M×36	32M×32

168-Pin DIMM Capacities

Capacity	Parity DIMM	Non-Parity DIMM
8M	1M×72	1M×64
16M	2M×72	2M×64
32M	4M×72	4M×64
64M	8M×72	8M×64
128M	16M×72	16M×64
256M	32M×72	32M×64

Dynamic RAM (DRAM) SIMMs and DIMMs of each type and capacity are available in different speed ratings. SIMMs have been available in many different speed ratings, ranging from 120ns for some of the slowest, to 50ns for some of the fastest available. DIMMs are available in speeds from 60ns to 10ns or faster. Many of the first systems to use SIMMs used versions rated at 120ns. These were quickly replaced in the market by 100ns and even faster versions. Today, you generally purchase EDO SIMMs rated at 60ns, and SDRAM DIMMs rated at 10ns. Both faster and slower ones are available, but they are not frequently required and are difficult to obtain.

If a system requires a specific speed, you can almost always substitute faster speeds if the one specified is not available. There are no problems in mixing SIMM speeds, as long as you use SIMMs equal to or faster than what the system requires. Because very little price difference exists between the different speed versions, I usually buy faster SIMMs than are needed for a particular application. This may make them more usable in a future system that may require the faster speed.

> **Note**
>
> Most DIMMs are Synchronous DRAM (SDRAM) memory, which means they deliver data in very high-speed bursts using a clocked interface. SDRAM supports bus speeds of up to 100MHz, with data transfer rates of up to 200MHz possible in the future.

Several variations on the 30-pin SIMMs can affect how they work (if at all) in a particular system. First, there are actually two variations on the pinout configurations. Most systems use a *generic* type of SIMM, which has an industry-standard pin configuration. Many older IBM systems used a slightly modified 30-pin SIMM, starting with the XT-286 introduced in 1986 through the PS/2 Model 25, 30, 50, and 60. These systems require a SIMM with different signals on five of the pins. These are known as *IBM-style* 30-pin SIMMs. You can modify a generic 30-pin SIMM to work in the IBM systems and vice versa, but purchasing a SIMM with the correct pinouts is much easier. Be sure you tell the SIMM vendor if you need the specific IBM-style versions.

Another issue with respect to the 30-pin SIMMs relates to the chip count. The SIMM acts as if it were a single chip of 8 bits wide (with optional parity), and it really does not matter how this total is derived. Older SIMMs were constructed with eight or nine individual 1-bit-wide chips to make up the module, whereas many newer SIMMs use two 4-bit-wide chips and optionally one 1-bit-wide chip for parity, making a total of two or three chips on the SIMM. Accessing the two- or three-chip SIMMs can require adjustments to the refresh timing circuits on the motherboard, and many older 386 and 486 motherboards could not cope. Most newer motherboards automatically handle the slightly different refresh timing of both the 2/3-chip or 8/9-chip SIMMs, and in this case the 2/3-chip versions are more reliable, use less power, and generally cost less as well. If you have an older system, most likely it will also work with the 2/3-chip SIMMs, but some do not. Unfortunately, the only way to know is to try them. To prevent the additional time required to change them for 8/9-chip versions should the 2/3-chip versions not work in an older system, it seems wise to stick with the 8/9-chip variety in any older system.

The 72-pin SIMMs do not have different pinouts and are differentiated only by capacity and speed. These SIMMs are not affected by the number of chips on them. The 72-pin SIMMs are ideal for 32-bit systems such as 486 machines because they comprise an entire bank of memory (32 data bits plus 4 parity bits). When you configure a 32-bit (486) system that uses 72-pin SIMMs, you can usually add or remove memory as single SIMM modules (except on systems that use interleaved memory schemes to reduce wait states). This is because a 32-bit chip such as a 486 reads and writes banks of memory 32 bits wide, and a 72-pin SIMM is exactly 32 bits wide (36 bits with optional parity).

In 64-bit systems—which includes any Pentium or newer processor—72-pin SIMMs must be used in pairs to fill a single bank. A few motherboard manufacturers offer so-called "SIMM-saver" motherboards that are designed for newer Pentium processors, but have both 72- and 30-pin SIMM sockets. Although this is not the most desirable arrangement, it allowed users on a budget to reuse their old 30-pin SIMMs. In this situation, eight 30-pin SIMMs can be used at a time to fill one bank. Alternatively, you could pair four 30-pin SIMMs with one 72-pin SIMM to create one bank. This really is not a very efficient setup because it consumes large amounts of space on the motherboard.

Other options available are SIMM stackers and converters. These items allow you to use 30-pin SIMMs in 72-pin sockets, thereby saving you the expense of having to scrap all those old 30-pin SIMMs you have lying around. Again, such adapters can cause problems—especially if overhead clearance is tight—so investigate carefully before you buy. With the falling prices of SIMMs today, you are probably better off staying with 72-pin SIMMs and 168-pin DIMMs.

Remember that some older high-performance 486 systems use interleaved memory to reduce wait states. This requires a multiple of two 72-pin 36-bit (32-bit) SIMMs because interleaved memory access is alternated between the SIMMs to improve performance. Thus, a 32-bit processor ends up using two 32-bit banks together in an alternating fashion.

> **Note**
>
> A *bank* is the smallest amount of memory that can be addressed by the processor at one time and usually corresponds to the data bus width of the processor. If the memory is interleaved, a virtual bank may be twice the absolute data bus width of the processor.

You cannot always replace a SIMM with a greater-capacity unit and expect it to work. Systems may have specific design limitations as to the maximum capacity of SIMM they will take. A larger-capacity SIMM works only if the motherboard is designed to accept it in the first place. Consult your system documentation to determine the correct capacity and speed to use.

All systems on the market today use SIMMs, and many use DIMMs. The SIMM/DIMM is not a proprietary memory system, but an industry-standard device. As mentioned, some SIMMs have slightly different pinouts and specifications other than speed and capacity, so be sure that you obtain the correct SIMMs for your system.

SIMM Pinouts

Tables 5.5 and 5.6 show the interface connector pinouts for both 30-pin SIMM varieties and the standard 72-pin version. Also included is a special presence detect table that shows the configuration of the presence detect pins on various 72-pin SIMMs. The presence detect pins are used by the motherboard to detect exactly what size and speed SIMM is installed. Industry-standard 30-pin SIMMs do not have a presence detect feature, but IBM did add this capability to their modified 30-pin configuration.

Table 5.5   Industry-Standard and IBM 30-Pin SIMM Pinouts

Pin	Standard SIMM Signal Names	IBM SIMM Signal Names
1	+5 Vdc	+5 Vdc
2	Column Address Strobe	Column Address Strobe
3	Data Bit 0	Data Bit 0
4	Address Bit 0	Address Bit 0
5	Address Bit 1	Address Bit 1
6	Data Bit 1	Data Bit 1
7	Address Bit 2	Address Bit 2
8	Address Bit 3	Address Bit 3
9	Ground	Ground
10	Data Bit 2	Data Bit 2
11	Address Bit 4	Address Bit 4
12	Address Bit 5	Address Bit 5
13	Data Bit 3	Data Bit 3
14	Address Bit 6	Address Bit 6
15	Address Bit 7	Address Bit 7
16	Data Bit 4	Data Bit 4

(continues)

Pin	Standard SIMM Signal Names	IBM SIMM Signal Names
Table 5.5	**Industry-Standard and IBM 30-Pin SIMM Pinouts Continued**	
17	Address Bit 8	Address Bit 8
18	Address Bit 9	Address Bit 9
19	Address Bit 10	Row Address Strobe 1
20	Data Bit 5	Data Bit 5
21	Write Enable	Write Enable
22	Ground	Ground
23	Data Bit 6	Data Bit 6
24	No Connection	Presence Detect (Ground)
25	Data Bit 7	Data Bit 7
26	Data Bit 8 (Parity) Out	Presence Detect (1M = Ground)
27	Row Address Strobe	Row Address Strobe
28	Column Address Strobe Parity	No Connection
29	Data Bit 8 (Parity) In	Data Bit 8 (Parity) I/O
30	+5 Vdc	+5 Vdc

Pin	SIMM Signal Name	Pin	SIMM Signal Name
Table 5.6	**Standard 72-Pin SIMM Pinout**		
1	Ground	22	Data Bit 5
2	Data Bit 0	23	Data Bit 21
3	Data Bit 16	24	Data Bit 6
4	Data Bit 1	25	Data Bit 22
5	Data Bit 17	26	Data Bit 7
6	Data Bit 2	27	Data Bit 23
7	Data Bit 18	28	Address Bit 7
8	Data Bit 3	29	Address Bit 11
9	Data Bit 18	30	+5 Vdc
10	+5 Vdc	31	Address Bit 8
11	Presence Detect 5	32	Address Bit 9
12	Address Bit 0	33	Row Address Strobe 3
13	Address Bit 1	34	Row Address Strobe 2
14	Address Bit 2	35	Parity Data Bit 2
15	Address Bit 3	36	Parity Data Bit 0
16	Address Bit 4	37	Parity Data Bit 1
17	Address Bit 5	38	Parity Data Bit 3
18	Address Bit 6	39	Ground
19	Address Bit 10	40	Column Address Strobe 0
20	Data Bit 4	41	Column Address Strobe 2
21	Data Bit 20	42	Column Address Strobe 3

Pin	SIMM Signal Name	Pin	SIMM Signal Name
43	Column Address Strobe 1	58	Data Bit 28
44	Row Address Strobe 0	59	+5 Vdc
45	Row Address Strobe 1	60	Data Bit 29
46	Reserved	61	Data Bit 13
47	Write Enable	62	Data Bit 30
48	ECC Optimized	63	Data Bit 14
49	Data Bit 8	64	Data Bit 31
50	Data Bit 24	65	Data Bit 15
51	Data Bit 9	66	Reserved
52	Data Bit 25	67	Presence Detect 1
53	Data Bit 10	68	Presence Detect 2
54	Data Bit 26	69	Presence Detect 3
55	Data Bit 11	70	Presence Detect 4
56	Data Bit 27	71	Reserved
57	Data Bit 12	72	Ground

Notice that the 72-pin SIMMs employ a set of four or five pins to indicate the type of SIMM to the motherboard. These presence detect pins are either grounded or not connected to indicate the type of SIMM to the motherboard. Presence detect outputs must be tied to the ground through a zero-ohm resistor on the SIMM—to generate a high logic level when the pin is open or low logic level when the pin is grounded by the motherboard. This produces signals that are decodable by the memory interface logic. If presence detect signals are employed by the motherboard, then a Power-On Self Test procedure can determine the size and speed of the installed SIMMs and adjust control and addressing signals automatically. This allows the memory size and speed to be autodetected.

Note

In many ways, this is similar to the industry-standard DX code used on modern 35mm film rolls to indicate the ASA (speed) rating of the film to the camera. When you drop the film into the camera, electrical contacts can read the film's speed rating via an industry standard configuration.

Table 5.7 shows the JEDEC industry standard presence detect configuration listing for the 72-pin SIMM family. JEDEC is the Joint Electronic Devices Engineering Council, an organization of the U.S. semiconductor manufacturers and users that sets package outline dimension and other standards for chip and module packages.

Table 5.7 Presence Detect Pin Configurations for 72-Pin SIMMs

Size	Speed	Pin 67	Pin 68	Pin 69	Pin 70	Pin 11
1M	100ns	Gnd	-	Gnd	Gnd	-
1M	80ns	Gnd	-	-	Gnd	-

(continues)

Table 5.7	Presence Detect Pin Configurations for 72-Pin SIMMs Continued					
Size	**Speed**	**Pin 67**	**Pin 68**	**Pin 69**	**Pin 70**	**Pin 11**
1M	70ns	Gnd	-	Gnd	-	-
1M	60ns	Gnd	-	-	-	-
2M	100ns	-	Gnd	Gnd	Gnd	-
2M	80ns	-	Gnd	-	Gnd	-
2M	70ns	-	Gnd	Gnd	-	-
2M	60ns	-	Gnd	-	-	-
4M	100ns	Gnd	Gnd	Gnd	Gnd	-
4M	80ns	Gnd	Gnd	-	Gnd	-
4M	70ns	Gnd	Gnd	Gnd	-	-
4M	60ns	Gnd	Gnd	-	-	-
8M	100ns	-	-	Gnd	Gnd	-
8M	80ns	-	-	-	Gnd	-
8M	70ns	-	-	Gnd	-	-
8M	60ns	-	-	-	-	-
16M	80ns	Gnd	-	-	Gnd	Gnd
16M	70ns	Gnd	-	Gnd	-	Gnd
16M	60ns	Gnd	-	-	-	Gnd
16M	50ns	Gnd	-	Gnd	Gnd	Gnd
32M	80ns	-	Gnd	-	Gnd	Gnd
32M	70ns	-	Gnd	Gnd	-	Gnd
32M	60ns	-	Gnd	-	-	Gnd
32M	50ns	-	Gnd	Gnd	Gnd	Gnd

- = No Connection (open)
Gnd = Ground
Pin 67 = Presence detect 1
Pin 68 = Presence detect 2
Pin 69 = Presence detect 3
Pin 70 = Presence detect 4
Pin 11 = Presence detect 5

Unfortunately, unlike the film industry, not everybody in the computer industry follows established standards. As such, presence detect signaling is not a standard throughout the PC industry. Different system manufacturers sometimes use different configurations for what is expected on these four pins. Compaq, IBM (mainly PS/2 systems), and Hewlett-Packard are notorious for this type of behavior; many of their systems require special SIMMs that are basically the same as standard 72-pin SIMMs, except for special presence detect requirements. Table 5.8 shows how IBM defines these pins.

Table 5.8   72-Pin SIMM Presence Detect Pins

67	68	69	70	SIMM Type	IBM Part Number
-	-	-	-	Not a valid SIMM	N/A
Gnd	-	-	-	1M 120ns	N/A
-	Gnd	-	-	2M 120ns	N/A
Gnd	Gnd	-	-	2M 70ns	92F0102
-	-	Gnd	-	8M 70ns	64F3606
Gnd	-	Gnd	-	Reserved	N/A
-	Gnd	Gnd	-	2M 80ns	92F0103
Gnd	Gnd	Gnd	-	8M 80ns	64F3607
-	-	-	Gnd	Reserved	N/A
Gnd	-	-	Gnd	1M 85ns	90X8624
-	Gnd	-	Gnd	2M 85ns	92F0104
Gnd	Gnd	-	Gnd	4M 70ns	92F0105
-	-	Gnd	Gnd	4M 85ns	79F1003 (square notch) L40-SX
Gnd	-	Gnd	Gnd	1M 100ns	N/A
Gnd	-	Gnd	Gnd	8M 80ns	79F1004 (square notch) L40-SX
-	Gnd	Gnd	Gnd	2M 100ns	N/A
Gnd	Gnd	Gnd	Gnd	4M 80ns	87F9980
Gnd	Gnd	Gnd	Gnd	2M 85ns	79F1003 (square notch) L40SX

- = No Connection (open)
Gnd = Ground
Pin 67 = Presence detect 1
Pin 68 = Presence detect 2
Pin 69 = Presence detect 3
Pin 70 = Presence detect 4

Custom variations on these pins are why you must often specify IBM, Compaq, HP, or generic SIMMs when you order memory.

Table 5.9 shows the pinout configuration of a 168-pin standard unbuffered SDRAM DIMM.

Table 5.9   168-Pin SDRAM DIMM Pinouts

Pin	x64 Non-Parity	x72 Parity/ECC	Pin	x64 Non-Parity	x72 Parity/ECC
1	Gnd	Gnd	85	Gnd	Gnd
2	Data Bit 0	Data Bit 0	86	Data Bit 32	Data Bit 32
3	Data Bit 1	Data Bit 1	87	Data Bit 33	Data Bit 33
4	Data Bit 2	Data Bit 2	88	Data Bit 34	Data Bit 34
5	Data Bit 3	Data Bit 3	89	Data Bit 35	Data Bit 35
6	+5V	+5V	90	+5V	+5V

(continues)

Table 5.9   168-Pin SDRAM DIMM Pinouts Continued

Pin	x64 Non-Parity	x72 Parity/ECC	Pin	x64 Non-Parity	x72 Parity/ECC
7	Data Bit 4	Data Bit 4	91	Data Bit 36	Data Bit 36
8	Data Bit 5	Data Bit 5	92	Data Bit 37	Data Bit 37
9	Data Bit 6	Data Bit 6	93	Data Bit 38	Data Bit 38
10	Data Bit 7	Data Bit 7	94	Data Bit 39	Data Bit 39
11	Data Bit 8	Data Bit 8	95	Data Bit 40	Data Bit 40
12	Gnd	Gnd	96	Gnd	Gnd
13	Data Bit 9	Data Bit 9	97	Data Bit 41	Data Bit 41
14	Data Bit 10	Data Bit 10	98	Data Bit 42	Data Bit 42
15	Data Bit 11	Data Bit 11	99	Data Bit 43	Data Bit 43
16	Data Bit 12	Data Bit 12	100	Data Bit 44	Data Bit 44
17	Data Bit 13	Data Bit 13	101	Data Bit 45	Data Bit 45
18	+5V	+5V	102	+5V	+5V
19	Data Bit 14	Data Bit 14	103	Data Bit 46	Data Bit 46
20	Data Bit 15	Data Bit 15	104	Data Bit 47	Data Bit 47
21	-	Check Bit 0	105	-	Check Bit 4
22	-	Check Bit 1	106	-	Check Bit 5
23	Gnd	Gnd	107	Gnd	Gnd
24	-	-	108	-	-
25	-	-	109	-	-
26	+5V	+5V	110	+5V	+5V
27	Write Enable	Write Enable	111	Column Address Strobe	Column Address Strobe
28	Byte Mask 0	Byte Mask 0	112	Byte Mask 4	Byte Mask 4
29	Byte Mask 1	Byte Mask 1	113	Byte Mask 5	Byte Mask 5
30	S0	S0	114	S1	S1
31	Reserved	Reserved	115	Row Address Strobe	Row Address Strobe
32	Gnd	Gnd	116	Gnd	Gnd
33	Address Bit 0	Address Bit 0	117	Address Bit 1	Address Bit 1
34	Address Bit 2	Address Bit 2	118	Address Bit 3	Address Bit 3
35	Address Bit 4	Address Bit 4	119	Address Bit 5	Address Bit 5
36	Address Bit 6	Address Bit 6	120	Address Bit 7	Address Bit 7
37	Address Bit 8	Address Bit 8	121	Address Bit 9	Address Bit 9
38	Address Bit 10	Address Bit 10	122	Bank Address 0	Bank Address 0
39	Bank Address 1	Bank Address 1	123	Address Bit 11	Address Bit 11
40	+5V	+5V	124	+5V	+5V
41	+5V	+5V	125	Clock 1	Clock 1
42	Clock 0	Clock 0	126	Address Bit 12	Address Bit 12

Pin	x64 Non-Parity	x72 Parity/ECC	Pin	x64 Non-Parity	x72 Parity/ECC
43	Gnd	Gnd	**127**	Gnd	Gnd
44	Reserved	Reserved	**128**	Clock Enable 0	Clock Enable 0
45	S2	S2	**129**	S3	S3
46	Byte Mask 2	Byte Mask 2	**130**	Byte Mask 6	Byte Mask 6
47	Byte Mask 3	Byte Mask 3	**131**	Byte Mask 7	Byte Mask 7
48	Reserved	Reserved	**132**	Address Bit 13	Address Bit 13
49	+5V	+5V	**133**	+5V	+5V
50	-	-	**134**	-	-
51	-	-	**135**	-	-
52	-	Check Bit 2	**136**	-	Check Bit 6
53	-	Check Bit 3	**137**	-	Check Bit 7
54	Gnd	Gnd	**138**	Gnd	Gnd
55	Data Bit 16	Data Bit 16	**139**	Data Bit 48	Data Bit 48
56	Data Bit 17	Data Bit 17	**140**	Data Bit 49	Data Bit 49
57	Data Bit 18	Data Bit 18	**141**	Data Bit 50	Data Bit 50
58	Data Bit 19	Data Bit 19	**142**	Data Bit 51	Data Bit 51
59	+5V	+5V	**143**	+5V	+5V
60	Data Bit 20	Data Bit 20	**144**	Data Bit 52	Data Bit 52
61	-	-	**145**	-	-
62	Voltage Reference	Voltage Reference	**146**	Voltage Reference	Voltage Reference
63	Clock Enable 1	Clock Enable 1	**147**	-	-
64	Gnd	Gnd	**148**	Gnd	Gnd
65	Data Bit 21	Data Bit 21	**149**	Data Bit 53	Data Bit 53
66	Data Bit 22	Data Bit 22	**150**	Data Bit 54	Data Bit 54
67	Data Bit 23	Data Bit 23	**151**	Data Bit 55	Data Bit 55
68	Gnd	Gnd	**152**	Gnd	Gnd
69	Data Bit 24	Data Bit 24	**153**	Data Bit 56	Data Bit 56
70	Data Bit 25	Data Bit 25	**154**	Data Bit 57	Data Bit 57
71	Data Bit 26	Data Bit 26	**155**	Data Bit 58	Data Bit 58
72	Data Bit 27	Data Bit 27	**156**	Data Bit 59	Data Bit 59
73	+5V	+5V	**157**	+5V	+5V
74	Data Bit 28	Data Bit 28	**158**	Data Bit 60	Data Bit 60
75	Data Bit 29	Data Bit 29	**159**	Data Bit 61	Data Bit 61
76	Data Bit 30	Data Bit 30	**160**	Data Bit 62	Data Bit 62
77	Data Bit 31	Data Bit 31	**161**	Data Bit 63	Data Bit 63
78	Gnd	Gnd	**162**	Gnd	Gnd
79	Clock 2	Clock 2	**163**	Clock 3	Clock 3
80	-	-	**164**	-	-

(continues)

Table 5.9 168-Pin SDRAM DIMM Pinouts Continued					
Pin	**x64 Non-Parity**	**x72 Parity/ECC**	**Pin**	**x64 Non-Parity**	**x72 Parity/ECC**
81	-	-	**165**	Serial PD Address 0	Serial PD Address 0
82	Serial Data I/O	Serial Data I/O	**166**	Serial PD Address 1	Serial PD Address 1
83	Serial Clock Input	Serial Clock Input	**167**	Serial PD Address 2	Serial PD Address 2
84	+5V	+5V	**168**	+5V	+5V

- = No Connection (open)
Gnd = Ground

The DIMM uses a completely different type of Presence Detect called Serial Presence Detect. This consists of a small EEPROM (Electrically Erasable Programmable Read Only Memory) or even a flash memory chip on the DIMM that contains specially formatted data indicating the features of the DIMM. This serial data can be read via the serial data pins on the DIMM, and allows the motherboard to autoconfigure to the exact type of DIMM installed.

Physical RAM Capacity and Organization

Several types of memory chips have been used in PC system motherboards. Most of these chips are single-bit-wide chips, available in several capacities. The following table lists available RAM chips and their capacities:

RAM Chip	**Capacity**
16K by 1 bit	These devices were used in the original IBM PC with a Type 1 motherboard.
64K by 1 bit	These chips were used in the standard IBM PC Type 2 motherboard and in the XT Type 1 and 2 motherboards. Many memory adapters of the era, such as the popular vintage AST six-pack boards, also used these chips.
128K by 1 bit	These chips, used in the IBM AT Type 1 motherboard, often were a strange physical combination of two 64K chips stacked one on top of the other and soldered together. Single-chip versions were used also for storing the parity bits in the IBM XT 286.
256K by 1 bit (or 64K by 4 bits)	These chips once were very popular in motherboards and memory cards. The IBM XT Type 2 and IBM AT Type 2 motherboards, and most compatible systems of that era used these chips.
1M by 1 bit (or 256K by 4 bits)	1M chips were very popular for a number of years and were most often used in 256K to 8M SIMMs.
4M by 1 bit (or 1M by 4 bits)	4M chips are used primarily in SIMMs from 1M to 16M in capacity. They are used primarily in 4M and 8M SIMMs and generally are not sold as individual chips.
16M by 1 bit (or 4M by 4 bits)	16M chips are often used in 72-pin SIMMs of 16M to 32M capacity.

RAM Chip	Capacity
64M by 1 bit (or 16M by 4 bits)	64M chips are popular in high-capacity 16M or larger memory modules, especially for notebook systems.
256M by 1 bit (or 64M by 4 bits)	256M chips are the most recent on the market. These chips allow enormous SIMM capacities of 128M or larger! Because of the high expense and limited availability of these chips, you see them only in the most expensive and highest capacity modules on the market.

Note that chip capacity normally goes up by factors of 4 because the die that make up the chips are square. When they increase capacity, this normally results in 4 times more transistors and 4 times more capacity. Most modern SIMMs and DIMMs use 16M-bit to 256M-bit chips onboard.

Figure 5.8 shows the markings on a typical older memory chip. Many memory manufacturers use similar schemes for numbering their chips; however, if you are really trying to identify a particular chip, it is best to consult the manufacturer catalog for more information.

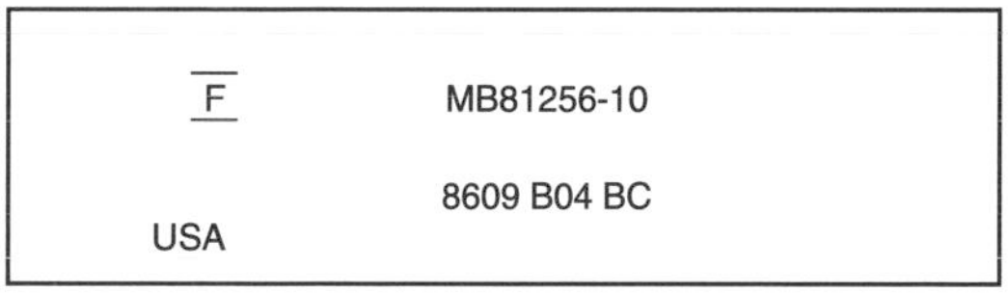

```
     ‾F‾            MB81256-10

                    8609 B04 BC
     USA
```

FIG. 5.8 The markings on a typical older memory chip.

The -10 on the chip corresponds to its speed in nanoseconds (a 100-nanosecond rating). MB81256 is the chip's part number, which usually contains a clue about the chip's capacity. The key digits are 1256, which indicate that this chip is 1 bit wide and has a depth of 256K. The 1 means that to make a full byte with parity, you need nine of these single-bit-wide chips. A chip with a part number KM4164B-10 indicates a 64K-by-1-bit chip at a speed of 100 nanoseconds. The following list matches common chips with their industry-standard part numbers:

Part Number	Chip
4164	64K by 1 bit
4464	64K by 4 bits
41128	128K by 1 bit
44128	128K by 4 bits
41256	256K by 1 bit
44256	256K by 4 bits
41000	1M by 1 bit
44000	1M by 4 bits

Chips wider than 1 bit are used to construct banks of less than 9, 18, or 36 chips (depending on the system architecture). For example, a 32-bit SIMM can be constructed of only eight 4-bit wide chips.

In Figure 5.8, the "F" symbol centered between two lines is the manufacturer's logo for Fujitsu Microelectronics. The 8609 indicates the date of manufacture (ninth week of 1986). Some manufacturers, however, use a Julian date code. To decode the chip further, contact the manufacturer or chip vendor.

SIMMs and DIMMs also have part numbers that can be difficult to decode. Unfortunately, there is no industry standard for numbering these modules, so you will have to contact the manufacturer if you want to decode the numbers. Figure 5.9 shows how Micron Technology (also Crucial Technology) SIMMs are encoded.

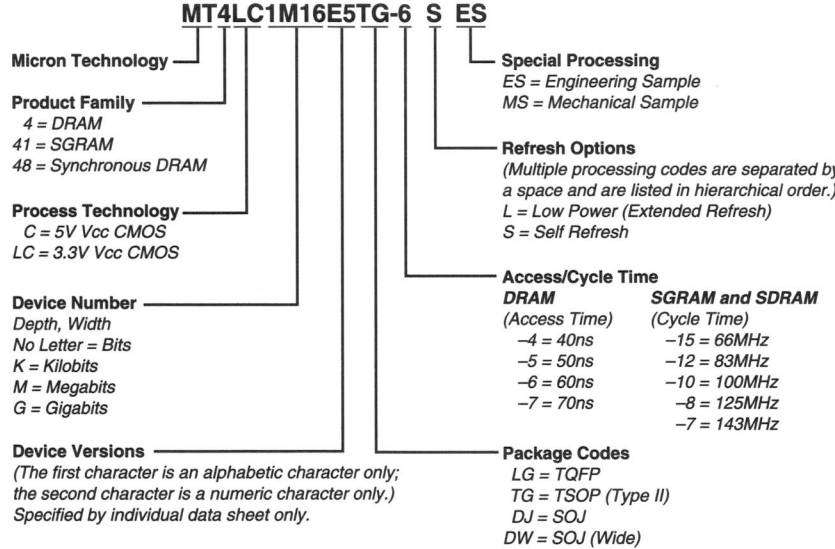

FIG. 5.9 Typical SIMM part numbers for Micron (Crucial Technology) SIMMs.

Memory Banks

Memory chips (DIPs, SIMMs, SIPPs, and DIMMs) are organized in *banks* on motherboards and memory cards. You should know the memory bank layout and position on the motherboard and memory cards.

You need to know the bank layout when adding memory to the system. In addition, memory diagnostics report error locations by byte and bit addresses, and you must use these numbers to locate which bank in your system contains the problem.

The banks usually correspond to the data bus capacity of the system's microprocessor. Table 5.10 shows the widths of individual banks based on the type of PC.

Table 5.10 Memory Bank Widths on Different Systems						
Processor	Data Bus	Memory Bank Size (No Parity)	Memory Bank Size (Parity)	30-Pin SIMMs per Bank	72-Pin SIMMs per Bank	168-Pin SIMMs per Bank
8088	8-bit	8-bits	9-bits	1	N/A	N/A
8086	16-bit	16-bits	18-bits	2	N/A	N/A
286	16-bit	16-bits	18-bits	2	N/A	N/A
386SX, SL, SLC	16-bit	16-bits	18-bits	2	N/A	N/A
386DX	32-bit	32-bits	36-bits	4	1	N/A
486SLC, SLC2	16-bit	16-bits	18-bits	2	N/A	N/A
486SX, DX, DX2,DX4	32-bit	32-bits	36-bits	4	1	N/A
Pentium	64-bit	64-bits	72-bits	8	2	1
Pentium Pro, PII	64-bit	64-bits	72-bits	8	2	1

The number of bits for each bank can be made up of single chips, SIMMs, or DIMMs. Modern systems don't use individual chips, but only SIMMs or DIMMs, instead. If the system has a 16-bit processor such as a 386SX, it would probably use 30-pin SIMMs and have two SIMMs per bank. All the SIMMs in a single bank must be the same size and type.

A 486 system would require four 30-pin SIMMs or one 72-pin SIMM to make up a bank. A single 72-pin SIMM is 32 bits wide or 36 bits wide if it supports parity. You can often tell whether or not a SIMM supports parity by counting its chips. To make a 32-bit SIMM, you could use 32 individual 1-bit-wide chips, or you could use eight individual 4-bit-wide chips to make up the data bits. If the system used parity, then four extra bits would be required (36 bits total), so you would see one more 4-bit-wide or four individual 1-bit-wide chips added to the bank for the parity bits.

As you might imagine, 30-pin SIMMs are less than ideal for 32-bit or 64-bit systems (i.e., 486 or Pentium) because you must use them in increments of four or eight per bank! Because these SIMMs are available in 1M, 4M, and 16M capacities today, this means that a single bank of 30-pin SIMMs in a 486 system would be 4M, 16M, or 64M; for a Pentium system, this would be 8M, 32M, or 128M of memory, with no in-between amounts. Using 30-pin SIMMs in 32- and 64-bit systems artificially constrains memory configurations and such systems are not recommended. If a 32-bit system (such as any PC with a 486 processor) uses 72-pin SIMMs, each SIMM represents a separate bank, and the SIMMs can be added or removed on an individual basis rather than in groups of four, as would be required with 30-pin SIMMs. This makes memory configuration much easier and more flexible. In modern 64-bit systems that use SIMMs, two 72-pin SIMMs are required per bank.

DIMMs are ideal for Pentium and higher systems, as the 64-bit width of the DIMM exactly matches the 64-bit width of the Pentium processor data bus. This means that each DIMM represents an individual bank, and they can be added or removed one at a time.

The physical orientation and numbering of the SIMMs or DIMMs used on a motherboard is arbitrary and determined by the board's designers. Documentation covering your system or card comes in very handy. You can determine the layout of a motherboard or adapter card through testing, but this takes time and may be difficult, particularly after you have a problem with a system.

RAM Chip Speed

PC memory speeds vary from about 10ns to 200ns. When you replace a failed memory module, you must install a module of the same type and speed as the failed module. You can substitute a chip with a different speed only if the speed of the replacement chip is equal to or faster than that of the failed chip.

Some people have had problems when "mixing" chips because they used a chip that did not meet the minimum required specifications (for example, refresh timing specifications) or was incompatible in pinout, depth, width, or design. Chip access time always can be less (that is, faster) as long as your chip is the correct type and meets all other specifications.

Substituting faster memory usually doesn't provide improved performance because the system still operates the memory at the same speed. In systems not engineered with a great deal of "forgiveness" in the timing between memory and system, however, substituting faster memory chips might improve reliability.

To place more emphasis on timing and reliability, Intel has created standards for the new high-speed 100MHz memory supported by their newer chipsets. This is called the PC/100 standard, and it is a standard by which memory modules can be certified to perform within Intel's timing and performance guidelines. At 100MHz, there is not very much "forgiveness" or slop allowable in memory timing.

The same common symptoms result when the system memory has failed or is simply not fast enough for the system's timing. The usual symptoms are frequent parity check errors or a system that does not operate at all. The POST also might report errors. If you're unsure of what chips to buy for your system, contact the system manufacturer or a reputable chip supplier.

▶▶ See "Parity Checking," p. 347

Gold Versus Tin

Many people don't understand the importance of the SIMM and DIMM electrical contacts in a computer system. Both SIMMs and DIMMs are available in gold or tin-plated contact form. I initially thought that gold contact SIMMs or DIMMs were the best way to go for reliability in all situations, but that is not true. To have the most reliable system, you must install SIMMs or DIMMs with gold-plated contacts into gold-plated sockets and SIMMs or DIMMs with tin-plated contacts into only tin-plated sockets.

If you don't heed this warning and install memory with gold-plated contacts into tin sockets or vice versa, you will experience memory errors at a future date. In my experiences, this will occur between six months to one year after installation. I have encountered this several times in my own systems and in several systems I have serviced. I have even been asked to assist one customer in a lawsuit, where the customer purchased several hundred machines from a vendor, and severe memory failures began appearing in most of the machines approximately a year after delivery. The cause was traced to dissimilar metals between the memory modules and sockets (gold SIMMs in tin sockets, in this case). The vendor refused to replace the SIMMs with tin-plated versions, hence the lawsuit.

Most Intel Pentium and 486 motherboards that were designed to accept 72-pin SIMMs have tin-plated sockets, so they must have tin-plated memory. Intel now specifically recommends *not* mixing dissimilar metals in a system's memory. Studies done by the connector manufacturers show that a type of corrosion called *fretting* occurs when tin comes in pressure contact with gold or any other metal. Fretting corrosion is where tin oxide transfers to the gold surface and hardens, eventually causing a high resistance connection. This occurs where gold comes into contact with tin, no matter how thick or thin the gold coating. Over time, depending on the environment fretting, corrosion can and will cause high resistance at the contact point and thus cause memory errors.

One would think that tin would make a poor connector material because it does readily oxidize. Even so, electrical contact is easily made between two tin surfaces under pressure because the oxides on both soft surfaces will bend and break, ensuring contact. This is especially true in SIMMs or DIMMs where a lot of pressure is placed on the contacts.

When tin and gold come into contact, because one surface is hard, the oxidation builds up and will not break easily under pressure. Increased contact resistance ultimately results in memory failures. The bottom line is that you should place only gold SIMMs into gold sockets, and only tin SIMMs into tin sockets.

The connector manufacturer AMP has published several documents from the AMP Contact Physics Research Department that discuss this issue, but there are two that are most applicable. One is titled *Golden Rules: Guidelines for the Use of Gold on Connector Contacts*, and the other is called *The Tin Commandments: Guidelines for the Use of Tin on Connector Contacts*. Both can be downloaded in .PDF form from the AMP Web site at **http// www.ampincorporated.com/**. Here is an excerpt from the *Tin Commandments*, specifically commandment Number Seven, which states "7. Mating of tin-coated contacts to gold-coated contacts is not recommended." For further technical details, you can contact Intel or AMP at the sites I have recommended.

Certainly, the best type of setup would be gold to gold, as in having gold-plated SIMMs or DIMMs and gold-plated sockets on the motherboard. Most high-end file servers or other high-reliability systems are designed this way. In fact, most systems that require SDRAM DIMMs use gold-plated sockets and therefore require SDRAM DIMMs with gold-plated contacts.

If you have mixed metals in your memory now, the correct response would be to replace the memory modules with the appropriate contact type to match the socket. Another much less desirable solution would be to wait until problems appear (about six months to a year in my experience), then remove the modules, clean the contacts, reinstall, and repeat the cycle. This is probably fine if you are an individual with one or two systems, but it is *not* fine if you are maintaining hundreds of systems. Note that if your system does not feature parity or ECC memory (most systems sold today do not), when the problems do occur, you may not be able to immediately identify them as memory related (Global Protection Faults, crashes, file and data corruption, and so on).

One problem with cleaning is that the hard tin oxide deposits that form on the gold surface are difficult to remove, and often require abrasive cleaning (such as by using an eraser or crocus cloth). This should never be done dry because this will generate static discharges that can damage the chips. Instead, use a contact cleaner to lubricate the contacts, which when wet will minimize the potential for static discharge damage when rubbing the eraser or other abrasive on the surface.

To further forestall this problem from occurring, I highly recommend using a liquid contact enhancer and lubricant called Stabilant 22 from DW Electrochemicals when installing SIMMs or DIMMs. They have a detailed application note on their Web site on this subject if you are interested in more technical details.

Some people have accused me of being too picky by insisting that the memory match the socket. On several occasions, I have either returned memory or motherboards because the vendor putting them together did not have a clue this was a problem. When I tell some people about this, they tell me they have a lot of PCs out there with mixed metal contacts that run fine and, in many cases, have been doing so for many years.

Of course, that is certainly a poor argument against doing the right thing. There are a lot of people running SCSI buses that are way too long, with improper termination, and they say it runs "fine." Parallel port cables are by the spec limited to 10 feet in length, yet I see many have longer cables, which they claim work "fine." The IDE cable limit is 18 inches; that spec is violated and people get away with it, saying their drive runs just "fine." I see cheap, crummy power supplies that put out noise, hash, and loosely regulated voltages, and I have even measured up to 69 volts AC of ground leakage, and yet the systems were running "fine." I have encountered *numerous* systems without proper CPU heat sinks, or where the active heat sink (fan) was stalled, and the system ran "fine." This reminds me of when Johnny Carson would interview 100-year-old people and would often get them to admit that they drank heavily and smoked cigarettes every day, as if those are good practices that will ensure longevity!

The truth is I am often amazed at how poorly designed or implemented some systems are, and yet they do seem to work... for the most part. The occasional lockup or crash is just written off by the user as "that's they way they all are." All except *my* systems, of course. In *my* systems, I adhere to proper design and engineering practices; in fact, I am often guilty of engineering or specifying overkill into things. Although it adds to the cost, they do seem to run better because of it.

In other words, what one individual can "get away" with does not change the laws of physics—this does not change the fact that for those supporting many systems or selling systems where the maximum in reliability and service life is desired, the gold/tin issue *does* matter.

Another issue that was brought to my attention was the thickness of the gold on the contacts; people are afraid that it is so thin, it will wear off after one or two insertions. Certainly, the choice of gold coating thickness depends on the durability required by the application; due to the high cost of gold, it is prudent to keep the gold coating thickness as low as is appropriate for the durability requirements.

An aid to durability is that the gold coatings are usually hardened by adding small amounts of cobalt or nickel to the gold. Such coatings are defined as "hard gold" and produce coatings with a low coefficient of friction and excellent durability characteristics. Hard gold-coated contacts can generally withstand hundreds to thousands of durability cycles without failing. The durability of hard gold coatings can be enhanced by using an underlayer having a hardness value that is greater than that of gold and which will provide mechanical support. Nickel is generally recommended as an underlayer for this purpose. Lubricants are also effective at increasing the durability of gold coatings. Generally, lubrication can increase the durability of a gold contact by an order of magnitude.

Increasing the thickness of a hard gold coating increases durability. The following laboratory results were obtained by AMP for the wear-through of a hard gold coating to the 1.3 micron (50 microinch) thick nickel underplate. The following data is for a 0.635 cm. (0.250 in.) diameter ball wiped a distance of 1.27 cm. (0.500 in.) under a normal force of 100 grams for each cycle.

Thickness Microns	Thickness Micro-in	Cycles to Failure
0.4	15	200
0.8	30	1000
1.3	50	2000

As you can see from this table, an 0.8 micron (30 microinch) coating of hard gold results in durability that is more than adequate for most connector applications, as it would allow 1,000 insertion and removal cycles before wearing through. I studied the specification sheets for DIMM and SIMM sockets produced by AMP and found that their gold-plated sockets come mostly as .000030 (30 microinches)-thick gold over .000050 (50 microinches)-thick nickel in the contact area. As far as I can determine, the coating on virtually all SIMM and DIMM contacts would be similar in thickness, allowing for the same durability.

AMP also has a few gold-plated sockets with specifications of .001020 (1,020 microinches)-thick gold over .001270 (1,270 microinches)-thick nickel. I'd guess that the latter sockets were for devices such as SIMM testers, where many insertions were expected over the life of the equipment. They could also be used in high vibration or very high humidity environments, as well.

For reference, all their tin-contact SIMM and DIMM sockets have the following connector plating specifications: .000030 (30 microinches) minimum thick tin on mating edge over .000050 (50 microinches) minimum thick nickel on entire contact.

The bottom line is that the thickness of the coating in current SIMM and DIMM sockets and modules is not an issue for the expected use of these devices. The thickness of the plating used in current SIMM and DIMM systems is also not relevant with regard to the tin versus gold matability issue. The only drawback to a thinner gold plating is that it will wear after fewer insertion/removal cycles, exposing the nickel underneath and allowing the onset of fretting corrosion to occur.

In my opinion, this tin/gold issue will be even *more important* for those using DIMMs. This will be for two reasons. With SIMMs, you really have two connections for each pin (one on each side of the module), so if one of them goes high resistance, it will not matter; there is a built-in redundancy. With DIMMs, you have many, many more connections (168 versus 72), and no redundant connections. The chance for failure will be much greater. Also, most DIMM applications will be SDRAM, where the timing is down in the 15–10ns range for 66MHz and 100MHz boards, respectively. At these speeds, the slightest additional resistance in the connection *will* cause problems.

Because of these issues, for the future I would specify only motherboards that have gold-plated SDRAM DIMM connectors, and then, of course, use only SDRAMs with gold-plated contacts. I noted that, for example, Micron produces only SDRAM DIMMs with gold-plated contacts, and all the DIMM sockets I've seen so far are gold plated, as well. I would not currently recommend any motherboards using tin-lead SDRAM DIMM connectors, nor would I recommend purchasing tin-lead SDRAM DIMMs.

Memory Reliability

A part of the nature of memory is that it will inevitably fail. These failures are usually classified as two basic types: hard fails and soft errors.

The most well understood are hard fails, in which the chip is working and then, due to some flaw, physical damage, or other event, becomes damaged and experiences a permanent failure. Fixing this type of failure normally requires replacement of some part of the memory hardware, such as the chip, SIMM, or DIMM. Hard error rates are known as HERs.

The other more insidious type of failure is the soft error. A *soft error* is a nonpermanent failure that may never reoccur, or occur at infrequent intervals. (Soft fails are effectively "fixed" by powering the system off and back on.) Soft error rates are known as SERs.

About 20 years ago, Intel made a discovery that shook the memory industry with respect to soft errors. They found that alpha-particles were causing an unacceptably high rate of soft errors or Single Event Upsets (SEUs, as they are sometimes called) in the 16K DRAMs that were available at the time. Because alpha-particles are low-energy particles that can be stopped by something as thin and light as a sheet of paper, it became clear that for alpha-particles to cause a DRAM soft error, they would have to be coming from within the semiconductor material. Testing showed that there were trace elements of thorium and uranium found in the plastic and ceramic chip packaging materials used at the time. This forced all the memory manufacturers to evaluate their manufacturing process to produce materials free from contamination.

Today, the memory manufacturers have all but totally eliminated the alpha-particle source of soft errors; due to this, many were believing that this was justification for the industry trend to drop parity checking. The argument is that, for example, a 16M memory subsystem built with 4M technology would experience a soft error due to alpha-particles only about once every 16 years! The real problem with this thinking is that it is seriously flawed, and many system manufacturers and vendors were coddled into removing parity and other memory fault-tolerant techniques from their systems even though soft errors continue to be an ongoing problem. There are more recent discoveries that prove that alpha-particles are now only a small fraction of the cause of DRAM soft errors!

As it turns out, the biggest cause of soft errors today are cosmic rays. IBM researchers began investigating the potential of terrestrial cosmic rays in causing soft errors similar to alpha-particles. The difference is that cosmic rays are very high-energy particles and cannot be stopped by sheets of paper or other more powerful types of shielding. The leader in this line of investigation was Dr. J. F. Ziegler of the IBM Watson Research Center in Yorktown Heights, New York. He has produced landmark research into the understanding of cosmic rays and their influence on soft errors in memory.

One example of the magnitude of the cosmic ray soft-error phenomenon demonstrated that with a certain sample of non-IBM DRAMs, the Soft Error Rate (SER)—as measured under real-life conditions, and with the benefit of millions of device hours of testing— at sea level was measured at 5950 FIT (Failures in Time, which is measured at 1 billion hours) per chip. In an average system with 36 memory chips among the SIMMs, this would result in a soft error occurring every six months! In power user or server systems with a larger amount of memory, this could mean an error per month or more. When the exact same test setup and DRAMs were moved to an underground vault shielded by over 50 feet of rock, thus eliminating all cosmic rays, there were absolutely no soft errors recorded! This not only demonstrates how problematic cosmic rays can be, but it also proves that the packaging contamination and alpha-particle problem has indeed been solved.

Cosmic ray-induced errors are even more of a problem in SRAMs than DRAMS. This is because the amount of charge required to flip a bit in an SRAM cell is less than is required to flip a DRAM cell capacitor. Cosmic rays are also more of a problem for higher-density memory. As chip density increases, it becomes easier for a stray particle to flip a bit. It has been predicted by some that the Soft Error Rate of a 64M DRAM will be double that of a 16M chip, and a 256M DRAM will have a rate four times higher.

Unfortunately, the PC industry has largely failed to recognize this new cause of memory errors. The random and intermittent nature of a soft error can be much more easily explained away by electrostatic discharge, power surges, or unstable software, especially right after a new release of an operating system or major application.

Studies have shown that the soft-error rate for ECC systems is on the order of 30 times greater than the hard-error rate. This is not surprising to those familiar with the full effects of cosmic ray-generated soft errors. Data now exists that suggests some 16M DRAM chip designs will actually experience soft errors numbering in the 24,000 FIT (Failures In Time - per 1 billion hours) range. This would result in a soft error about once a month for most systems today!

How can we deal with these errors? Just ignoring them is certainly not the best way to deal with them, but unfortunately that is what many system manufacturers and vendors are doing today. The best way to deal with this problem is to increase the system's fault tolerance. This means implementing ways of detecting and possibly correcting errors in PC systems. There are basically three levels and techniques for fault tolerance used in modern PCs:

- Non-parity

- Parity

- ECC (Error Correcting Code)

Non-parity systems have no fault tolerance at all. The reason they are even used is because they have the lowest inherent cost. No additional memory is necessary as is the case with parity or ECC techniques. Because a parity-type data byte has nine bits versus eight for non-parity, memory cost is 12.5 percent higher. Also the non-parity memory controller is simplified because it does not need the logic gates to calculate parity or ECC check bits. Portable systems that place a premium on minimizing power might benefit from the reduction in memory power due to fewer DRAM chips. Finally, the memory system data bus is narrower, which reduces the amount of data buffers. The statistical probability of memory failures in a modern office desktop computer is now estimated at about one error every few months, more or less depending on how much memory you have.

This error rate may be tolerable for low-end systems that are not used for mission-critical applications. In this case, their extreme market cost sensitivity probably can't justify the extra cost of parity or ECC memory, and such errors will then have to be tolerated.

At any rate, employing no fault tolerance in a system is simply gambling that memory errors are unlikely, and if they do occur, result in an inherent cost less than the additional hardware necessary for error detection. However, the disadvantage is that the errors can lead to a serious problem such as calculating the wrong value to go into a bank check, or in the case of a system being used as a server, a memory error forcing a system hang and bringing down all LAN-resident client systems with subsequent loss of productivity. Finally, with a non-parity or non-ECC memory system, problem traceability is difficult, which is not the case with parity or ECC. These techniques at least isolate to a memory source as the culprit, thus reducing both the time and cost of problem resolutions.

Parity Checking. One standard IBM set for the industry is that the memory chips in a bank of nine each handle one bit of data: eight bits per character plus one extra bit called the *parity bit*. The parity bit enables memory-control circuitry to keep tabs on the other eight bits—a built-in cross-check for the integrity of each byte in the system. If the circuitry detects an error, the computer stops and displays a message informing you of the malfunction. If you are running a newer operating system such as Windows or OS/2, a parity error will generally manifest itself as a locked system. When you reboot, the BIOS should detect the error and display the appropriate error message.

SIMMs and DIMMs are available both with and without parity bits. Originally, all PC systems used parity-checked memory to ensure accuracy. Starting in 1994, a disturbing trend developed in the PC-compatible marketplace. Most vendors began shipping systems without parity checking or any other means of detecting or correcting errors! These systems can use cheaper non-parity SIMMs, which saves about 10–15 percent on memory costs for a system. Parity memory results in increased initial system cost due primarily to the additional memory bits involved. Parity cannot correct system errors, but, because parity can detect errors, it can make the user aware of memory errors when they occur. This has two basic benefits:

■ Parity guards against the consequences of faulty calculations based on incorrect data.

■ Parity pinpoints the source of errors, which assists in problem resolution, thus improving system serviceability.

PC systems can easily be designed to function using either parity or non-parity memory. The cost of implementing parity as an option on a motherboard is virtually nothing; the only cost involved is in actually purchasing the parity SIMMs or DIMMs, which are about 10–15 percent more expensive than non-parity versions. This would enable a system manufacturer to offer their system purchasers the choice of parity if they feel the additional cost is justified for their particular application.

Unfortunately, several of the big names began selling systems without parity to reduce the price of their systems, and they did not make it well-known that the lower cost was due to parity memory no longer being included as standard. This began happening mostly in 1994-1995, and has continued until very recently with few people understanding the full implications. After one or two major vendors did this, most of the others were forced to follow to remain price-competitive.

Because nobody wanted to announce this information, it remained as a sort of dirty little secret within the industry. Originally, when this happened, you could still specify parity memory when you ordered a system, even though the default configurations no longer included it. There would be a 10–15 percent surcharge on the memory, but those who wanted reliable, trustworthy systems could at least get them, provided they knew to ask, of course. Then a major bomb hit the industry, in the form of the Intel Triton 430FX Pentium chipset, which was the first major chipset on the market that did not support parity checking at all! This also became the most popular chipset of its time, and was found in virtually all Pentium motherboards sold in the 1995 timeframe. This set a disturbing trend for the next few years. All but one of Intel's Pentium processor chipsets after the 430FX also did not support parity-checked memory; the only one that did was the 430HX Triton II. The good news is that this trend now seems to be over, and the system manufacturers and users are finally coming around to the importance of fault-tolerant memory. As such, all the Pentium Pro and Pentium II chipsets currently available do support parity and ECC, and more and more people are realizing that this type of memory is worthwhile. I do expect new low-end chipsets even for the Pentium II to emerge that will not support parity, but these are designed for the sub-$1,000 market, where price and not system integrity is the most important concern.

Let's look at how parity checking works, and then examine in more detail the successor to parity checking, called ECC (Error Correcting Code), which can not only detect but correct memory errors on-the-fly.

IBM originally established the *odd parity* standard for error checking. The following explanation may help you understand what is meant by odd parity. As the eight individual bits in a byte are stored in memory, a parity generator/checker, which is either part of the CPU or located in a special chip on the motherboard, evaluates the data bits by counting the number of 1s in the byte. If an even number of 1s is in the byte, the parity generator/checker creates a 1 and stores it as the ninth bit (parity bit) in the parity memory chip. That makes the total sum for all nine bits an odd number. If the original sum of the eight data bits is an odd number, the parity bit created is 0, keeping the 9-bit sum an odd number. The value of the parity bit is always chosen so that the sum of all nine bits (eight data bits plus one parity bit) is an odd number. Remember that the eight data bits in a byte are numbered 0 1 2 3 4 5 6 7. The following examples may make it easier to understand:

```
Data bit number:   0 1 2 3 4 5 6 7    Parity bit
Data bit value:    1 0 1 1 0 0 1 1    0
```

In this example, because the total number of data bits with a value of 1 is an odd number (5), the parity bit must have a value of 0 to ensure an odd sum for all nine bits.

The following is another example:

```
Data bit number:   0 1 2 3 4 5 6 7    Parity bit
Data bit value:    0 0 1 1 0 0 1 1    1
```

In this example, because the total number of data bits with a value of 1 is an even number (4), the parity bit must have a value of 1 to create an odd sum for all nine bits.

When the system reads memory back from storage, it checks the parity information. If a (9-bit) byte has an even number of bits with a parity bit value of 1, that byte must have an error. The system cannot tell which bit has changed, or if only a single bit has changed. If three bits changed, for example, the byte still flags a parity-check error; if two bits changed, however, the bad byte may pass unnoticed. The following examples show parity-check messages for three types of systems:

```
For the IBM PC:                    PARITY CHECK x
For the IBM XT:                    PARITY CHECK x    yyyyy (z)
For the IBM AT and late model XT:  PARITY CHECK x    yyyyy
```

Where *x* is 1 or 2:

1 = Error occurred on the motherboard

2 = Error occurred in an expansion slot

yyyyy represents a number from 00000 through FFFFF that indicates, in hexadecimal notation, the byte in which the error has occurred.

Where *(z)* is (S) or (*E*):

(S) = Parity error occurred in the system unit

(*E*) = Parity error occurred in the expansion chassis

> **Note**
>
> An expansion chassis was an option IBM sold for the original PC and XT systems to add more expansion slots. This unit consisted of a backplane motherboard with eight slots, one of which contained a special extender/receiver card cabled to a similar extender/receiver card placed in the main system. Due to the extender/receiver cards in the main system and the expansion chassis, the net gain was six slots.

When a parity-check error is detected, the motherboard parity-checking circuits generate a *non-maskable interrupt* (NMI), which halts processing and diverts the system's attention to the error. The NMI causes a routine in the ROM to be executed. The routine clears the screen and then displays a message in the upper-left corner of the screen. The message differs depending on the type of computer system. On some older IBM systems, the ROM parity-check routine halts the CPU. In such a case, the system locks up, and you must perform a hardware reset or a power-off/power-on cycle to restart the system. Unfortunately, all unsaved work is lost in the process.

Most systems do not halt the CPU when a parity error is detected; instead, they offer you a choice of either rebooting the system or continuing as though nothing happened. Additionally, these systems may display the parity error message in a different format from IBM, although the information presented is basically the same. For example, many systems with a Phoenix BIOS display these messages:

```
Memory parity interrupt at xxxx:xxxx
Type (S)hut off NMI, Type (R)eboot, other keys to continue
```

or

```
I/0 card parity interrupt at xxxx:xxxx
Type (S)hut off NMI, Type (R)eboot, other keys to continue
```

The first of these two messages indicates a motherboard parity error (Parity Check 1), and the second indicates an expansion-slot parity error (Parity Check 2). Notice that the address given in the form *xxxx:xxxx* for the memory error is in a segment:offset form rather than a straight linear address such as with IBM's error messages. The segment:offset address form still gives you the location of the error to a resolution of a single byte.

You have three ways to proceed after viewing this error message.

- You can press S, which shuts off parity checking and resumes system operation at the point where the parity check first occurred.

- Pressing R forces the system to reboot, losing any unsaved work.

- Pressing any other key causes the system to resume operation with parity checking still enabled.

If the problem occurs, it is likely to cause another parity-check interruption. In most cases, it is most prudent to press S, which disables the parity checking so that you can then save your work. It would be best in this case to save your work to a floppy disk to prevent the possible corruption of a hard disk. You should also avoid overwriting any previous (still good) versions of whatever file you are saving, because in fact you may be saving a bad file due to the memory corruption. Because parity checking is now disabled, your save operations will not be interrupted. Then you should power the system off, restart it, and run whatever memory diagnostics software you have to try and track down the error. In some cases, the POST finds the error on the next restart, but, in most cases, you need to run a more sophisticated diagnostics program, perhaps in a continuous mode, to locate the error.

The AMI BIOS displays the parity error messages in the following forms:

```
ON BOARD PARITY ERROR ADDR (HEX) = (xxxxx)
```

or

```
OFF BOARD PARITY ERROR ADDR (HEX) = (xxxxx)
```

These messages indicate that an error in memory has occurred during the POST, and the failure is located at the address indicated. The first one indicates the error occurred on the motherboard, whereas the second message indicates an error in an expansion slot adapter card. The AMI BIOS also can display memory errors in the following manner:

```
Memory Parity Error at xxxxx
```

or

```
I/O Card Parity Error at xxxxx
```

These messages indicate that an error in memory has occurred at the indicated address during normal operation. The first one indicates a motherboard memory error, and the second indicates an expansion slot adapter memory error.

Although many systems enable you to continue processing after a parity error, and even allow for the disabling of further parity checking, continuing to use your system after a parity error is detected can be dangerous. The idea behind letting you continue using either method is to give you time to save any unsaved work before you diagnose and service the computer, but be careful how you do this.

> **Caution**
>
> When you are notified of a memory parity error, remember the parity check is telling you that memory has been corrupted. Do you want to save potentially corrupted data over the good file from the *last* time you saved? Definitely not! Make sure that you save your work to a different file name. In addition, after a parity error, save only to a floppy disk if possible and avoid writing to the hard disk; there is a slight chance that the hard drive could become corrupted if you save the contents of corrupted memory.

After saving your work, determine the cause of the parity error and repair the system. You may be tempted to use an option to shut off further parity checking and simply continue using the system as if nothing were wrong. Doing so resembles unscrewing the oil pressure warning indicator bulb on a car with an oil leak so that the oil pressure light won't bother you anymore!

ECC (Error Correcting Code). ECC goes a big step beyond simple parity error detection. Rather than just detecting an error, ECC allows a single bit error to be corrected, which means the system can continue on without interruption and without corrupting data. ECC as implemented in most PCs can only detect and not correct double-bit errors. Because studies have indicated that approximately 98 percent of memory errors are single-bit variety, the most commonly used type of ECC is one in which the attendant memory controller detects and corrects single-bit errors in an accessed data word (double-bit errors can be detected, but not corrected). This type of ECC is known as SEC-DED and requires an additional seven check bits over 32 bits in a 4-byte system and eight check bits in an 8-byte system. ECC in a 4-byte system obviously costs more than non-parity or parity, but in an 8-byte system, ECC and parity costs are equal.

ECC entails the memory controller calculating the check bits on a memory-write operation, performing a compare between the read and calculated check-bits on a read operation and, if necessary, correcting bad bit(s). The additional ECC logic in the memory controller is not very significant in this age of inexpensive, high-performance VLSI logic, but ECC actually affects memory performance on writes. This is because the operation must be timed to wait for the calculation of check bits and, when the system waits for corrected data, reads. On a partial-word write, the entire word must first be read, the affected byte(s) rewritten, and then new check bits calculated. This turns partial-word write operations into slower read-modify writes.

Most memory errors are of a single-bit nature, which are correctable by ECC. Incorporating this fault-tolerant technique provides high system reliability and attendant availability. An ECC-based system is a good choice for servers, workstations, or mission-critical applications in which the cost of a potential memory error outweighs the additional memory and system cost to correct it, along with ensuring that it does not detract from system reliability. What I'm saying is that if you value your data and use your system for important (to you) tasks, then you'll want ECC memory.

By designing a system that allows the user to make the choice of ECC, parity, or non-parity, the user can choose the level of fault tolerance desired, as well as how much they want to gamble with their data.

Installing Memory Upgrades

Adding memory to a system is one of the most useful upgrades that you can perform, and also one of the least expensive, especially when you consider the increased capabilities of Windows 95/98, Windows NT, and OS/2 when you give them access to more memory. In some cases, doubling the memory can virtually double the speed of a computer.

This section discusses adding memory, including selecting memory chips, installing memory chips, and testing the installation.

Upgrade Options and Strategies

Adding memory can be an inexpensive solution; at this writing, the cost of memory has fallen to about $1.50 per megabyte. A small dose can give your computer's performance a big boost.

How do you add memory to your PC? You have three options, listed in order of convenience and cost:

- Adding memory in vacant slots on your motherboard.

- Replacing your current motherboard's memory with higher-capacity memory.

- Purchasing a memory expansion card (not a cost-effective or performance-effective solution for any system currently on the market).

Adding expanded memory to PC- or XT-type systems is not a good idea, mainly because an expanded memory board with a couple of megabytes of expanded memory installed can cost more than the entire system is worth. Also, this memory does not function for Windows, and a PC- or XT-class system cannot run OS/2. Instead, purchase a more powerful system—for example, an inexpensive Pentium II 266—with greater expansion capabilities.

If you decide to upgrade to a more powerful computer system, you normally cannot salvage the memory from a PC or XT system. The 8-bit memory boards are useless in 16-bit systems, and the speed of the memory chips usually is inadequate for newer systems. All new systems use high-speed SIMM or DIMM modules rather than chips. A pile of 150ns (nanoseconds), 64K, or 256K chips is useless if your next system is a high-speed system that uses SIMMs or memory devices faster than 70ns.

Be sure to weigh carefully your future needs for computing speed and for a multitasking operating system (OS/2, Windows 95/98, Windows NT, or Linux, for example) with the amount of money that you spend to upgrade current equipment.

Before you add RAM to a system (or replace defective RAM chips), you must determine the memory chips required for your system. Your system documentation contains this information.

If you need to replace a defective SIMM or DIMM and do not have the system documentation, you can determine the correct module for your system by inspecting the ones that are already installed. Each module has markings that indicate the module's capacity and speed. RAM capacity and speed are both discussed in detail earlier in this chapter.

If you do not have the documentation for your system and the manufacturer does not offer technical support, open your system case and carefully write down the markings that appear on your memory chips. Then, contact a local computer store or module vendor such as Kingston, Micron (Crucial), PNY, or others for help in determining the proper RAM chips for your system. Adding the wrong modules to a system can make it as unreliable as leaving a defective module installed and trying to use the system in that condition.

> **Note**
>
> Before upgrading a system beyond 64M of RAM, be sure that your chipset supports caching of more than 64M. Adding RAM beyond the amount that your system can cache will slow performance rather than increase it. See the section "Cache Memory—SRAM" earlier in this chapter and the discussion of chipsets in Chapter 4 for a more complete explanation of this common system limitation.

Selecting and Installing Motherboard Memory with Chips, SIMMs, or DIMMs

If you are upgrading a motherboard by adding memory, follow the manufacturer's guidelines on which memory chips or modules to purchase. As you learned earlier, memory comes in various form factors, including individual chips known as DIP memory chips, SIMMs (single inline memory modules), and DIMMs. Your computer may use one or possibly a mixture of these form factors.

No matter what type of memory chips you have, the chips are installed in memory banks. A *memory bank* is a collection of memory chips that make up a block of memory. Each bank of memory is read by your processor in one pass. A memory bank does not work unless it is filled with memory chips. (Banks are discussed in more detail earlier in this chapter in the section "Memory Banks.")

Pentium, Pentium Pro, and Pentium II computers also normally have between two and four banks of memory, but each bank usually requires two 72-pin (32- or 36-bit) SIMMs or one 168-pin DIMM.

Installing extra memory on your motherboard is an easy way to add memory to your computer. Most systems have at least one vacant memory bank in which you can install extra memory at a later time and speed your computer.

Replacing SIMMS and DIMMs with Higher Capacity

If all the SIMM or DIMM slots on your motherboard are occupied, your best option is to remove an existing bank of memory and replace it with higher memory. For example, if you have a 16M of RAM in a Pentium system with four SIMM slots filled with 4M 72-pin SIMMs, you may be able to replace all four SIMMs with 8M SIMMs and increase the system memory to 32M. Alternately, you could keep two of the existing 4M SIMMs and replace two with 8M SIMMs, increasing the total RAM to 24M. Remember that just as when you install SIMMs, they need to be replaced in a full bank and all the SIMMs in the bank need to be the same capacity. The multiple module requirement is not an issue with DIMMs as in all current systems; a DIMM constitutes at least one full bank of memory.

However, just because there are higher-capacity SIMMs or DIMMs available that are the correct pin count to plug into your motherboard, don't automatically assume the higher-capacity memory will work. The chipset and BIOS of your system will set limits on the capacity of the memory you can use. Check your system or motherboard documentation to see what size SIMMs or DIMMs will work with it before purchasing the new RAM.

Adding Adapter Boards

Memory expansion boards typically are a last-resort way to add memory. For many systems (such as older models from Compaq) with proprietary local bus memory-expansion connectors, you must purchase all memory-expansion boards from that company. Similarly, IBM used proprietary memory connectors in many of the PS/2 systems. For other industry-standard systems that use nonproprietary memory expansion, you can purchase from hundreds of vendors memory-expansion boards that plug into the standard bus slots.

Unfortunately, any memory expansion that plugs into a standard bus slot runs at bus speed rather than at full-system speed. For this reason, most systems today provide standard SIMM or DIMM connector sockets directly on the motherboard so that the memory can be plugged directly into the system's local bus. Using memory adapter cards in these systems only slows them down. Other systems use proprietary local bus connectors for memory-expansion adapters, which can cause additional problems and expense when you have to add or service memory. Upgrading a system by using a memory adapter card is no longer cost-effective, either. Because most systems and motherboards built on 486 or later processors can be upgraded with SIMMs or DIMMs, the only systems that would be upgraded with an adapter card are so old, it would be less expensive to replace the entire motherboard than to upgrade these old systems.

Installing Memory

This section discusses installing memory —specifically, new SIMM or DIMM modules. The section also covers the problems that you are most likely to encounter and how to avoid them. You will also get information on configuring your system to use new memory.

When you install or remove memory, you are most likely to encounter the following problems:

- Electrostatic discharge
- Broken or bent pins
- Incorrectly seated SIMMs and DIMMs
- Incorrect switch and jumper settings

To prevent electrostatic discharge (ESD) when you install sensitive memory chips or boards, do not wear synthetic-fiber clothing or leather-soled shoes. Remove any static charge that you are carrying by touching the system chassis before you begin, or better yet, wear a good commercial grounding strap on your wrist. You can order one from an electronics parts store or mail-order house. A grounding strap consists of a conductive wristband grounded at the other end by a wire clipped to the system chassis. Leave the system unit plugged in—but turned off—to keep it grounded.

Caution

Be sure to use a properly designed commercial grounding strap; *do not make one yourself*. Commercial units have a one-megohm resistor that serves as protection if you accidentally touch live power. The resistor ensures that you do not become the path of least resistance to the ground and therefore become electrocuted. An improperly designed strap can cause the power to conduct through you to the ground, possibly killing you.

Broken or bent leads are another potential problem associated with installing individual memory chips (DIPs) or SIPP modules. Fortunately, this is not a problem you will encounter installing a SIMM or DIMM. Sometimes, the pins on new chips are bent into a V, making them difficult to align with the socket holes. If you notice this problem on a DIP chip, place the chip on its side on a table, and press gently to bend the pins so that they are at a 90-degree angle to the chip. For a SIPP module, you may want to use needle-nose pliers to carefully straighten the pins so that they protrude directly down from the edge of the module, with equal amounts of space between pins. Then, you should install the chips in the sockets one at a time.

Caution

Straightening the pins on a DIP chip or SIPP module is not difficult work, but if you are not careful, you could easily break off one of the pins, rendering the chip or memory module useless. Use great care when you straighten the bent pins on any memory chip or module. You can use chip-insertion and pin-straightening devices to ensure that the pins are straight and aligned with the socket holes; these inexpensive tools can save you a great deal of time.

Each memory chip or module must be installed to point in a certain direction. Each device has a polarity marking on one end. This is normally a notch on SIMMs or DIMMs, and may be a notch, circular indentation, or mark on any individual chip. The chip socket may have a corresponding notch. Otherwise, the motherboard may have a printed legend that indicates the orientation of the chip. If the socket is not marked, you should use other chips as a guide. The orientation of the notch indicates the location of Pin 1 on the device. Aligning this notch correctly with the others on the board ensures that you do not install the chip backward. Gently set each chip into a socket, ensuring that every pin is properly aligned with the connector into which it fits. Then push the chip in firmly with both thumbs until the chip is fully seated.

SIMM memory is oriented by a notch on one side of the module that is not present on the other side, as shown in Figure 5.9. The socket has a protrusion that must fit into this notched area on one side of the module. This protrusion makes it impossible to install a SIMM backward unless you break the connector. Figure 5.10 shows a detailed blowup of the backside of the SIMM, showing the notch and the locking clip. Figure 5.11 shows a closeup of a DIMM (note that it, too, is keyed to ensure proper expansion socket installation).

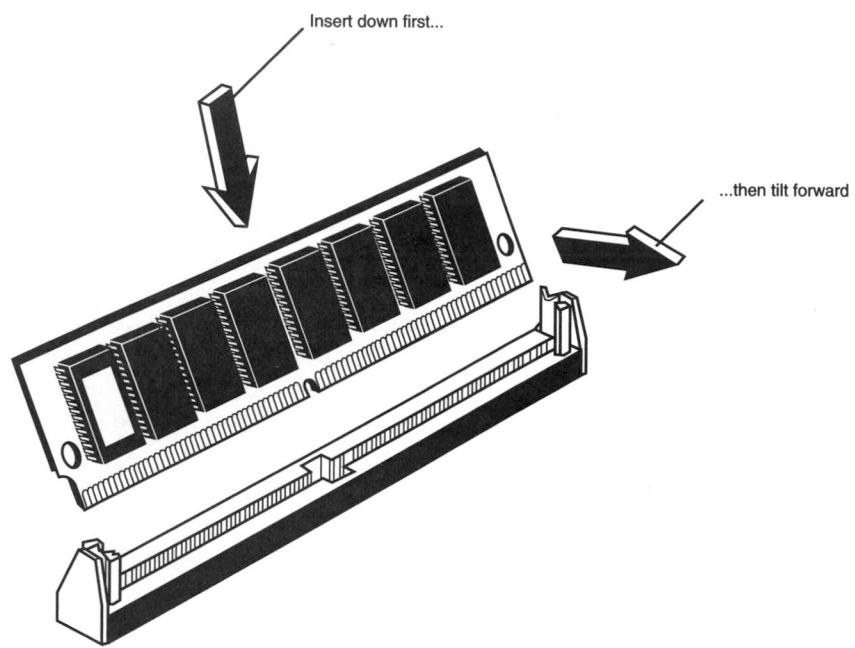

FIG. 5.10 The notch on this SIMM is shown on the left end. Insert the SIMM at an angle and then tilt it forward until the locking clips snap into place.

Similarly, DIMMs are keyed by notches along the bottom connector edge that are offset from center so that they can be inserted in only one direction, as shown in Figure 5.12. SIPP modules, however, do not plug into a keyed socket; you have to orient them properly. The system documentation can be helpful if the motherboard has no marks to guide you. You also can use existing SIPP modules as a guide.

The DIMM ejector tab locks into place in the notch on the side of the DIMM when it is fully inserted. Some DIMM sockets have ejector tabs on both ends. When installing SIMMs and DIMMs, take care not to force the module into the socket. If the module does not slip easily into the slot and then snap into place, there is a good chance the module is not oriented or aligned correctly. Forcing the module could break the module or the socket. If the retaining clips on the socket break, the memory will not be held firmly in place and there is a good chance you will experience random memory errors because the module will not make consistent electrical contact if it is loose.

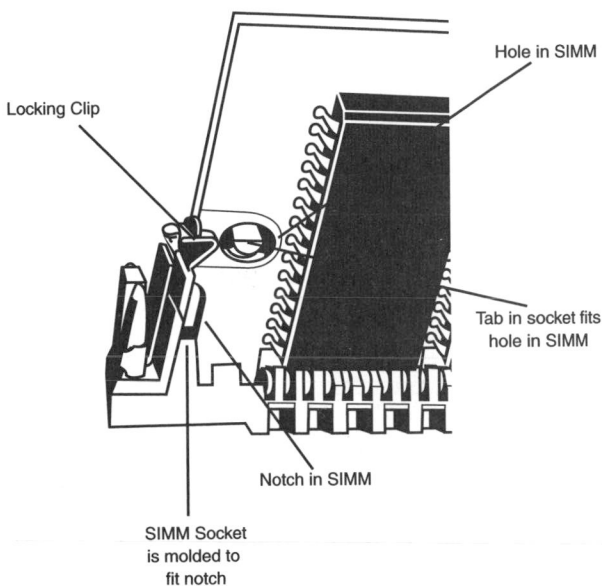

FIG. 5.11 This closeup shows the backside of a SIMM inserted in the SIMM socket with the notch aligned, the locking clip locked, and the hole in the SIMM aligned with the tab that sticks out from the socket.

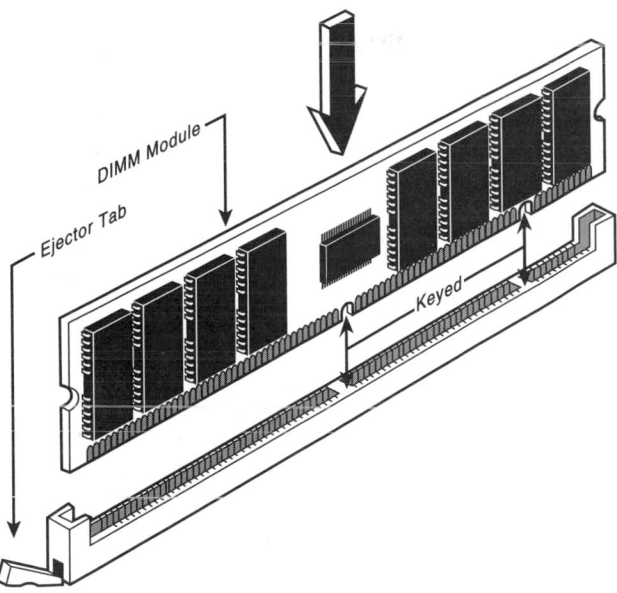

FIG. 5.12 DIMMs keys match the protrusions in the DIMM sockets.

As explained earlier in this chapter, DIMMs can come in several different varieties, including unbuffered or buffered and 3.3v or 5v. Buffered DIMMs have additional buffer chips on them to interface to the motherboard. Unfortunately, these buffer chips slow the DIMM down and are not effective at higher speeds. For this reason, all PC systems use unbuffered DIMMs. The voltage is simple—DIMM designs for PCs are almost universally 3.3v. If you install a 5v DIMM in a 3.3v socket, it would be damaged, but fortunately keying in the socket and on the DIMM will prevent that.

Modern PC systems only use unbuffered 3.3v DIMMs. Apple and other non-PC systems may use the buffered 5v versions. Fortunately, the key notches along the connector edge of a DIMM are spaced differently for RFU and buffered DIMMs and 5.0v DIMMs, as shown in Figure 5.13. This prevents inserting a DIMM of the wrong type into a socket.

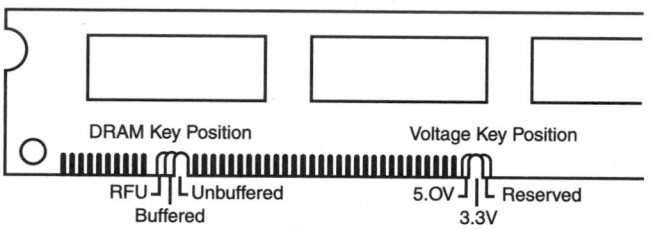

FIG. 5.13 168-pin DRAM DIMM notch key definitions.

Before installing memory, make sure that the system power is off. Then remove the PC cover and any installed cards. SIMMs and DIMMs snap easily into place, but chips can be more difficult to install. A chip-installation tool is not required, but it can make inserting the chips into sockets much easier. To remove chips, use a chip extractor or small screwdriver. Never try removing a RAM chip with your fingers, because you can bend the chip's pins or poke a hole in your finger with one of the pins. You remove SIMMs and DIMMs by releasing the locking tabs and either pulling or rolling them out of their sockets.

After adding the memory and putting the system back together, you may have to run the CMOS setup and resave with the new amount of memory. Most newer systems automatically detect the new amount of memory and reconfigure this for you. Most newer systems also don't require setting any jumpers or switches on the motherboard to configure them for your new memory. Older motherboards that used individual RAM chips rather than SIMMs or DIMMs for memory are more likely to need changes to jumper and switch settings. If you install individual RAM chips on a motherboard and the CMOS does not recognize the new RAM, check the system documentation to see if changes to motherboard jumpers or switches are required.

> **Note**
>
> Information on installing memory on older memory-expansion cards can be found in Chapter 7 of the sixth Edition of *Upgrading and Repairing PCs* on the CD-ROM accompanying this book.

After configuring your system to work properly with the additional memory, you should run a memory-diagnostics program to ensure the proper operation of the new memory. At least two and sometimes three memory-diagnostic programs are available for all systems. In order of accuracy, these programs are:

- POST (Power-On Self Test)

- Disk-based advanced diagnostics software

The POST is used every time you power up the system.

Many additional diagnostics programs are available from aftermarket utility software companies. More information on aftermarket testing facilities can be found in Chapter 17, "Diagnostics, Testing, and Maintenance."

The System Logical Memory Layout

The original PC had a total of 1M of addressable memory, and the top 384K of that was reserved for use by the system. Placing this reserved space at the top (between 640K and 1024K instead of at the bottom, between 0K and 640K) led to what today is often called the *conventional memory barrier*. The constant pressures on system and peripheral manufacturers to maintain compatibility by never breaking from the original memory scheme of the first PC has resulted in a system memory structure that is (to put it kindly) a mess. Almost two decades after the first PC was introduced, even the newest Pentium II-based systems are limited in many important ways by the memory map of the first PCs.

Someone who wants to become knowledgeable about personal computers must at one time or another come to terms with the types of memory installed on his system—the small and large pieces of different kinds of memory, some accessible by software application programs, and some not. The following sections detail the different kinds of memory installed on a modern PC. The kinds of memory covered in the following sections include the following:

- Conventional (Base) memory

- Upper Memory Area (UMA)

- High Memory Area (HMA)

- Extended memory (XMS)

- Expanded memory (obsolete)

- Video RAM memory (part of UMA)

- Adapter ROM and Special Purpose RAM (part of UMA)

- Motherboard ROM BIOS (part of UMA)

Subsequent sections also cover preventing memory conflicts and overlap, using memory managers to optimize your system's memory, and making better use of memory. In a 16-bit or higher system, the memory map extends beyond the 1M boundary and can continue to 16M on a system based on the 286 or higher processor, 4G (4,096M) on a 386DX or higher, or as much as 64G (65,536M) on a Pentium II. Any memory past 1M is called *extended memory*.

Figure 5.14 shows the logical address locations for a 16-bit or higher system. If the processor is running in real mode, only the first megabyte is accessible. If the processor is in protected mode, the full 16M, 4,096M, or 65,536M are accessible. Each symbol is equal to 1K of memory, and each line or segment is 64K. This map shows the first two megabytes of system memory.

◀◀ See "Processor Modes," p. 43

Note

To save space, this map is ended after the end of the second megabyte. In reality, this map continues to the maximum of addressable memory.

Conventional (Base) Memory

The original PC/XT-type system was designed to use 1M of memory workspace, sometimes called *RAM (random access memory)*. This 1M of RAM is divided into several sections, some of which have special uses. DOS can read and write to the entire megabyte, but can manage the loading of programs only in the portion of RAM space called *conventional memory*, which was 512K at the time the first PC was introduced. The other 512K was reserved for use by the system, including the motherboard and adapter boards plugged into the system slots.

After introducing the system, IBM decided that only 384K was needed for these reserved uses, and the company began marketing PCs with 640K of user memory. Thus, 640K became the standard for memory that can be used by DOS for running programs, and is often termed the *640K memory barrier*. The remaining memory after 640K was reserved for use by the graphics boards, other adapters, and the motherboard ROM BIOS.

This barrier largely affects 16-bit software such as DOS and Windows 3.1, and is much less of a factor with 32-bit software and operating systems such as Windows 95/98, NT, and so on.

Upper Memory Area (UMA)

The term *Upper Memory Area (UMA)* describes the reserved 384K at the top of the first megabyte of system memory on a PC/XT and the first megabyte on an AT-type system. This memory has the addresses from A0000 through FFFFF. The way the 384K of upper memory is used breaks down as follows:

■ The first 128K after conventional memory is called *video RAM*. It is reserved for use by video adapters. When text and graphics are displayed onscreen, the electronic impulses that contain their images reside in this space. Video RAM is allotted the address range from A0000-BFFFF.

```
   . = Program-accessible memory (standard RAM)
   G = Graphics Mode Video RAM
   M = Monochrome Text Mode Video RAM
   C = Color Text Mode Video RAM
   V = Video ROM BIOS (would be "a" in PS/2)
   a = Adapter board ROM and special-purpose RAM (free UMA space)
   r = Additional PS/2 Motherboard ROM BIOS (free UMA in non-PS/2 systems)
   R = Motherboard ROM BIOS
   b = IBM Cassette BASIC ROM (would be "R" in IBM compatibles)
   h = High Memory Area (HMA), if HIMEM.SYS is loaded.

Conventional (Base) Memory:

        : 0---1---2---3---4---5---6---7---8---9---A---B---C---D---E---F---
 000000: ................................................................
 010000: ................................................................
 020000: ................................................................
 030000: ................................................................
 040000: ................................................................
 050000: ................................................................
 060000: ................................................................
 070000: ................................................................
 080000: ................................................................
 090000: ................................................................

Upper Memory Area (UMA):

        : 0---1---2---3---4---5---6---7---8---9---A---B---C---D---E---F---
 0A0000: GGGGGGGGGGGGGGGGGGGGGGGGGGGGGGGGGGGGGGGGGGGGGGGGGGGGGGGGGGGGGGGGG
 0B0000: MMMMMMMMMMMMMMMMMMMMMMMMMMMMMMMMCCCCCCCCCCCCCCCCCCCCCCCCCCCCCCCCC
        : 0---1---2---3---4---5---6---7---8---9---A---B---C---D---E---F---
 0C0000: VVVVVVVVVVVVVVVVVVVVVVVVVVVVVVVVVaaaaaaaaaaaaaaaaaaaaaaaaaaaaaaaa
 0D0000: aaaaaaaaaaaaaaaaaaaaaaaaaaaaaaaaaaaaaaaaaaaaaaaaaaaaaaaaaaaaaaaa
        : 0---1---2---3---4---5---6---7---8---9---A---B---C---D---E---F---
 0E0000: rrrrrrrrrrrrrrrrrrrrrrrrrrrrrrrrrrrrrrrrrrrrrrrrrrrrrrrrrrrrrrrrr
 0F0000: RRRRRRRRRRRRRRRRRRRRRRRRRRRbbbbbbbbbbbbbbbbbbbbbbbbbbbbbbRRRRRRRR

Extended Memory:

        : 0---1---2---3---4---5---6---7---8---9---A---B---C---D---E---F---
 100000: hhhhhhhhhhhhhhhhhhhhhhhhhhhhhhhhhhhhhhhhhhhhhhhhhhhhhhhhhhhhhhhhh

Extended Memory Specification (XMS) Memory:

 110000: ................................................................
 120000: ................................................................
 130000: ................................................................
 140000: ................................................................
 150000: ................................................................
 160000: ................................................................
 170000: ................................................................
 180000: ................................................................
 190000: ................................................................
 1A0000: ................................................................
 1B0000: ................................................................
 1C0000: ................................................................
 1D0000: ................................................................
 1E0000: ................................................................
 1F0000: ................................................................
```

FIG. 5.14 The logical memory map of the first 2M.

- The next 128K is reserved for the adapter BIOS that resides in read-only memory chips on some adapter boards plugged into the bus slots. Most VGA-compatible video adapters use the first 32K of this area for their onboard BIOS. The rest can be used by any other adapters installed. Many network adapters also use this area for special-purpose RAM called Shared Memory. Adapter ROM and special-purpose RAM is allotted the address range from C0000-DFFFF.

- The last 128K of memory is reserved for motherboard BIOS (the basic input/output system, which is stored in read-only RAM chips or ROM). The POST (Power-On Self Test) and bootstrap loader, which handles your system at bootup until the operating system takes over, also reside in this space. Most systems only use the last 64K (or less) of this space, leaving the first 64K or more free for remapping with memory managers. Some systems also include the CMOS Setup program in this area. The motherboard BIOS is allotted the address range from E0000-FFFFF.

Not all the 384K of reserved memory is fully used on most 16-bit and higher systems. For example, according to the PC standard, reserved video RAM begins at address A0000, which is right at the 640K boundary. Normally, this is used for VGA graphics modes, while the monochrome and color text modes use B0000-B7FFF and B8000-BFFFF, respectively. Older non-VGA adapters only used memory in the B0000 segment. Different video adapters use varying amounts of RAM for their operations, depending mainly on the mode they are in. To the processor, however, it always appears as the same 128K area no matter how much RAM is really on the video card. This is managed by bank switching areas of memory on the card in and out of the A0000-BFFFF segments.

Although the top 384K of the first megabyte was originally termed *reserved memory*, it is possible to use previously unused regions of this memory to load 16-bit device drivers (such as ANSI.SYS) and memory-resident programs (such as MOUSE.COM), which frees up the conventional memory they would otherwise require. Note that 32-bit device drivers such as those used with Windows 95/98, NT, and so forth are not affected by this as they load into extended memory. The amount of free UMA space varies from system to system, depending on the adapter cards installed on the system. For example, most SCSI adapters and network adapters require some of this area for built-in ROMs or special-purpose RAM use.

Segment Addresses and Linear Addresses. One thing that can be confusing is the difference between a segment address and a full linear address. The use of segmented address numbers comes from the internal structure of the Intel processors, and is used primarily by older, 16-bit operating systems. They use a separate register for the segment information and another for the offset. The concept is very simple. For example, assume that I am staying in a hotel room, and somebody asks for my room number. The hotel has 10 floors, numbered from zero through nine; each floor has 100 rooms, numbered from 00 to 99. A segment is defined as any group of 100 rooms starting at a multiple of 10, and indicated by a two-digit number. So, a segment address of 54 would indicate the actual room 540, and you could have an offset of 00 to 99 rooms from there.

Thus in this hotel example, each segment is specified as a two-digit number from 00 to 99, and an offset can be specified from any segment starting with a number from 00 to 99 as well.

As an example, let's say I am staying in room 541. If the person needs this information in segment:offset form, and each number is two digits, I could say that I am staying at a room segment starting address of 54 (room 540), and an offset of 01 from the start of that segment. I could also say that I am in room segment 50 (room 500), and an offset of 41. You could even come up with other answers, such as I am at segment 45 (room 450) offset 91 (450+91=541). Here is an example of how this adds up:

Segment	Offset	Total
54	01	541
50	41	541
45	91	541

As you can see, although the particular segment and offset are different, they all add up to the same room address. In the Intel x86 processors, a similar scheme is used where a segment and offset are added internally to produce the actual address. It can be somewhat confusing, especially if you are writing assembly language or machine language software!

This is exactly how segmented memory in an Intel processor works. Notice that the segment and offset numbers essentially overlap on all digits except the first and last. By adding them together with the proper alignment, you can see the linear address total.

With 32-bit operating systems, segment addresses are not an issue. A linear address is one without segment:offset boundaries, such as saying room 541. It is a single number and not comprised of two numbers added together. For example, a SCSI host adapter might have 16K ROM on the card addressed from D4000 to D7FFF. These numbers expressed in segment:offset form are D400:0000 to D700:0FFF. The segment portion is composed of the most significant four digits, and the offset portion is composed of the least significant four digits. Because each portion overlaps by one digit, the ending address of its ROM can be expressed in four different ways, as follows:

```
D000:7FFF =     D000   segment          D7F0:00FF =    D7F0   segment
            +   7FFF   offset                       +  00FF   offset
                -----                                  -----
            = D7FFF    total                        = D7FFF   total

D700:0FFF =     D700   segment          D7FF:000F =    D7FF   segment
            +   0FFF   offset                       +  000F   offset
                -----                                  -----
            = D7FFF    total                        = D7FFF   total
```

As you can see in each case, although the segment and offset differ slightly, the total ends up being the same. Adding together the segment and offset numbers makes possible even more combinations, as in the following examples:

```
D500:2FFF  =    D500   segment
              +  2FFF   offset
                 -----
              = D7FFF   total

D6EE:111F  =    D6EE   segment
              +  111F   offset
                 -----
              = D7FFF   total
```

As you can see, several combinations are possible. The correct and generally accepted way to write this address as a linear address is D7FFF, whereas most would write the segment:offset address as D000:7FFF. Keeping the segment mostly zeros makes the segment:offset relationship easier to understand and the number easier to comprehend. If you understand the segment:offset relationship to the linear address, you now know why when a linear address number is discussed it is five digits, whereas a segment number is only four.

Video RAM Memory. A video adapter installed in your system uses a portion of your system's low memory to hold graphics or character information for display, but normally only when in basic VGA mode. A video card may have 4M or 8M on board, but most of that is used by the video chipset on the card and not directly accessed by your processor. When in basic VGA mode, such as when at a DOS prompt or when running in Windows safe mode, your processor can directly access up to 128K of the video RAM from address A0000-BFFFFh. All modern video cards also have onboard BIOS normally addressed at C0000-C7FFFh, which is part of the memory space reserved for adapter card BIOS. Generally, the higher the resolution and color capabilities of the video adapter, the more system memory the video adapter uses, but again that additional memory (past 128K) is not normally accessible by the processor. Instead, the system tells the video chip what should be displayed, and the video chip generates the picture by putting data directly into the video RAM on the card.

In the standard system-memory map, a total of 128K is reserved for use by the video card to store currently displayed information when in basic VGA mode. The reserved video memory is located in segments A000 and B000. The video adapter ROM uses additional upper memory space in segment C000. Even with the new multiple monitor feature in Windows 98, only one video card (the primary video card) is in the memory map; all others use no low system memory.

The location of video adapter RAM is responsible for the 640K DOS *conventional memory barrier*. DOS can use all available contiguous memory in the first megabyte of memory until the video adapter RAM is encountered. The use of ancient video adapters such as the MDA and CGA allows DOS access to more than 640K of system memory. The video memory *wall* begins at A0000 for the EGA, MCGA, and VGA systems, but the MDA and CGA do not use as much video RAM, which leaves some space that can be used by DOS and programs. The previous segment and offset examples show that the MDA adapter enables DOS to use an additional 64K of memory (all of segment A000), bringing the total for DOS program space to 704K. Similarly, the CGA enables a total of 736K of possible contiguous memory. The EGA, VGA, or MCGA is limited to the normal maximum of 640K of contiguous memory because of the larger amount used by video RAM. The maximum DOS-program memory workspace, therefore, depends on which video adapter is installed. Table 5.11 shows the maximum amount of memory available to DOS using the referenced video card.

Table 5.11 DOS Memory Limitations Based on Video Adapter Type	
Video Adapter Type	**Maximum DOS Memory**
Monochrome Display Adapter (MDA)	704K
Color Graphics Adapter (CGA)	736K
Enhanced Graphics Adapter (EGA)	640K
Video Graphics Array (VGA)	640K
Super VGA (SVGA)	640K
eXtended Graphics Array (XGA)	640K

Using this memory to 736K might be possible depending on the video adapter, the types of memory boards installed, ROM programs on the motherboard, and the type of system. You can use some of this memory if your system has a 386 or higher processor. With memory manager software (such as EMM386 that comes with DOS and Windows), which can operate the Memory Management Unit (MMU) found in those processors, you can remap extended memory into this space. Remember that Windows 9x will automatically use this memory if available.

The following sections examine how standard video adapters use the system's memory. This map is important because it may be possible to recognize some of this as unused in some systems, which may free up more space for software drivers to be loaded.

Obsolete Video Adapter Types. The MDA, CGA, and EGA video adapter types are not used in any current systems. The following sections give a brief description of the memory usage of these adapters so that you can see the progression of memory usage as adapters have evolved. If you still service or use systems with these video adapters, please see the Sixth edition of the book on the CD-ROM for the complete memory maps for this obsolete hardware.

Monochrome Display Adapter Memory (MDA). The original Monochrome Display Adapter (MDA) uses only a 4K portion of the reserved video RAM from B0000-B0FFF. Because the ROM code used to operate this adapter is actually a portion of the motherboard ROM, no additional ROM space is used in segment C000.

Note that although the original Monochrome Display Adapter only used 4K of memory starting at B0000, a VGA adapter running in Monochrome emulation mode (Mono Text Mode) activates 32K of RAM at this address. A true Monochrome Display Adapter has no onboard BIOS, and instead is operated by driver programs found in the primary motherboard BIOS.

Color Graphics Adapter (CGA) Memory. The Color Graphics Adapter (CGA) uses a 16K portion of the reserved video RAM from B8000-BBFFF. Because the ROM code used to operate this adapter is a portion of the motherboard ROM, no additional ROM space is used in segment C000.

The CGA card leaves memory from A0000-B7FFF free, which can be used by memory managers for additional DOS memory space. However, this precludes using any graphics mode software such as Windows. The original CGA card only used 16K of space starting at B8000, whereas a VGA adapter running in CGA emulation (Color Text) mode can activate 32K of RAM at this address. The original CGA card has no onboard BIOS and is instead operated by driver programs found in the primary motherboard BIOS.

Enhanced Graphics Adapter (EGA) Memory. The Enhanced Graphics Adapter (EGA) uses all 128K of the video RAM from A0000-BFFFF. The ROM code used to operate this adapter is on the adapter and consumes 16K of memory from C0000-C3FFF.

The original IBM EGA card only used 16K of ROM space at C0000. Aftermarket compatible EGA adapters can use additional ROM space up to 32K total. The most interesting thing to note about EGA (and this applies to VGA adapters, as well) is that segments A000 and B000 are not all used at all times. For example, if the card is in a graphics mode, only segment A000 would appear to have RAM installed, whereas segment B000 would appear completely empty. If you switched the mode of the adapter (through software) into Color Text mode, segment A000 would instantly appear empty, and the last half of segment B000 would suddenly "blink on." The monochrome text mode RAM area would practically never be used on a modern system, because little or no software would ever need to switch the adapter into that mode.

The EGA card became somewhat popular after it appeared, but this was quickly overshadowed by the VGA card that followed. Most of the VGA characteristics with regard to memory are the same as the EGA because the VGA is backward compatible with EGA.

Video Graphics Array (VGA) Memory. All VGA-compatible cards, including Super VGA cards, are almost identical to the EGA in terms of memory use. Just as with the EGA, they use all 128K of the video RAM from A0000-BFFFF, but not all at once. Again, the video RAM area is split into three distinct regions, and each of these regions is used only when the adapter is in the corresponding mode. One minor difference with the EGA cards is that virtually all VGA cards use the full 32K allotted to them for onboard ROM (C0000 to C7FFF). Figure 5.15 shows the VGA adapter memory map.

You can see that the typical VGA card uses a full 32K of space for the onboard ROM containing driver code. Some VGA cards may use slightly less, but this is rare. Just as with the EGA card, the video RAM areas are only active when the adapter is in the particular mode designated. In other words, when a VGA adapter is in graphics mode, only segment A000 is used; when it is in color text mode, only the last half of segment B000 is used. Because the VGA adapter is almost never run in monochrome text mode, the first half of segment B000 remains unused (B0000-B7FFF). Figure 5.15 also shows the standard motherboard ROM BIOS so that you can get a picture of how the entire UMA is laid out with this adapter.

```
.  = Empty Addresses
G  = Video Graphics Array (VGA) Adapter Graphics Mode Video RAM
M  = VGA Monochrome Text Mode Video RAM
C  = VGA Color Text Mode Video RAM
V  = Standard VGA Video ROM BIOS
R  = Standard Motherboard ROM BIOS


        : 0---1---2---3---4---5---6---7---8---9---A---B---C---D---E---F---
0A0000:  GGGGGGGGGGGGGGGGGGGGGGGGGGGGGGGGGGGGGGGGGGGGGGGGGGGGGGGGGGGGGGGG
0B0000:  MMMMMMMMMMMMMMMMMMMMMMMMMMMMMMMMMMMMCCCCCCCCCCCCCCCCCCCCCCCCCCCCCC
        : 0---1---2---3---4---5---6---7---8---9---A---B---C---D---E---F---
0C0000:  VVVVVVVVVVVVVVVVVVVVVVVVVVVVVVVVV...............................
0D0000:  ................................................................
        : 0---1---2---3---4---5---6---7---8---9---A---B---C---D---E---F---
0E0000:  ................................................................
0F0000:  RRRRRRRRRRRRRRRRRRRRRRRRRRRRRRRRRRRRRRRRRRRRRRRRRRRRRRRRRRRRRRRR
```

FIG. 5.15 The VGA (and Super VGA) adapter memory map.

Systems that use the LPX (Low Profile) motherboard design in an LPX- or Slimline-type case incorporate the video adapter into the motherboard. In these systems, even though the video BIOS and motherboard BIOS may be from the same manufacturer, they are always set up to emulate a standard VGA-type adapter card. In other words, the video BIOS appears in the first 32K of segment C000 just as if a standalone VGA-type card were plugged into a slot. The built-in video circuit in these systems can be easily disabled via a switch or jumper, which then allows a conventional VGA-type card to be plugged in. By having the built-in VGA act exactly as if it were a separate card, disabling it allows a new adapter to be installed with no compatibility problems that might arise if the video drivers had been incorporated into the motherboard BIOS.

If you were involved with the PC industry in 1987, you might remember how long it took for clone video card manufacturers to accurately copy the IBM VGA circuits. It took nearly two years (almost to 1989) before you could buy an aftermarket VGA card and expect it to run everything an IBM VGA system would with no problems. Some of my associates who bought some of the early cards inadvertently became members of the video card manufacturer's "ROM of the week" club! They were constantly finding problems with the operation of these cards, and many updated and patched ROMs were sent to try and fix the problems. Not wanting to pay for the privilege of beta testing the latest attempts at VGA compatibility, I bit the bullet and took the easy way out. I bought the IBM VGA card (PS/2 Display Adapter) for $595. Note that a top line AGP video card today normally runs for less than this!

Although the card worked very well in most situations, I did find compatibility problems with the memory use of this card and a few other cards, mainly SCSI adapters. This was my first introduction to what I call *scratch pad memory* use by an adapter. I found that many different types of adapters may use some areas in the UMA for mapping scratch pad memory. This refers to memory on the card that stores status information, configuration data, or any other temporary type information of a variable nature. Most cards keep this scratch pad memory to themselves and do not attempt to map it into the processor's address space. But some cards do place this type of memory in the address space so that the driver programs for the card can use it. Figure 5.16 shows the memory map of the IBM PS/2 Display Adapter (IBM's original VGA card).

```
        . = Empty Addresses
        G = Video Graphics Array (VGA) Adapter Graphics Mode Video RAM
        M = VGA Monochrome Text Mode Video RAM
        C = VGA Color Text Mode Video RAM
        V = IBM VGA Video ROM BIOS
        v = IBM VGA Scratch Pad memory (used by the card)
        R = Standard Motherboard ROM BIOS

       : 0---1---2---3---4---5---6---7---8---9---A---B---C---D---E---F---
0A0000: GGGGGGGGGGGGGGGGGGGGGGGGGGGGGGGGGGGGGGGGGGGGGGGGGGGGGGGGGGGGGGGGG
0B0000: MMMMMMMMMMMMMMMMMMMMMMMMMMMMMMMMCCCCCCCCCCCCCCCCCCCCCCCCCCCCCCCCC
       : 0---1---2---3---4---5---6---7---8---9---A---B---C---D---E---F---
0C0000: VVVVVVVVVVVVVVVVVVVVVVVVV..vvvvvv........vv.....................
0D0000: ...............................................................
       : 0---1---2---3---4---5---6---7---8---9---A---B---C---D---E---F---
0E0000: ...............................................................
0F0000: RRRRRRRRRRRRRRRRRRRRRRRRRRRRRRRRRRRRRRRRRRRRRRRRRRRRRRRRRRRRRRRRR
```

FIG. 5.16 IBM's ISA-bus VGA card (PS/2 Display Adapter) memory map.

There is nothing different about this VGA card and any other with respect to the video RAM area. What is different is that the ROM code that operates this adapter only consumes 24K of memory from C0000-C5FFF. Also strange is the 2K "hole" at C6000, and the 6K of scratch pad memory starting at C6800, and the additional 2K of scratch pad memory at CA000. In particular, the 2K "straggler" area really caught me off guard when I installed a SCSI host adapter in this system that had a 16K onboard BIOS with a default starting address of C8000. I immediately ran into a conflict that completely disabled the system. In fact, it would not boot, had no display at all, and could only beep out error codes that indicated that the video card had failed. I first thought that I had somehow "fried" the card, but removing the new SCSI adapter had everything functioning normally. I also could get the system to work with the SCSI adapter and an old CGA card substituting for the VGA, so I immediately knew a conflict was afoot. This scratch pad memory use was not documented clearly in the technical-reference information for the adapter, so it was something that I had to find out by trial and error. If you have ever had two cards that don't work together in the same system, this is one example of a potential conflict that can disable the system completely!

▶▶ See "Adapter Memory Configuration and Optimization," p. 385

Needless to say, nothing could be done about this 2K of scratch pad memory hanging out there, and I had to work around it as long as I had this card in the system. I solved my SCSI adapter problem by merely moving the SCSI adapter BIOS to a different address.

> **Note**
>
> I have seen other VGA-type video adapters use scratch pad memory, but they have all kept it within the C0000-C7FFF 32K region allotted normally for the video ROM BIOS. By using a 24K BIOS, I have seen other cards with up to 8K of scratch pad area, but none—except for IBM's—in which the scratch pad memory goes beyond C8000.

Adapter ROM and Special Purpose RAM Memory. The second 128K of upper memory beginning at segment C000 is reserved for the software programs, or BIOS (basic input/output system), on the adapter boards plugged into the system slots. These BIOS programs are stored on special chips known as read-only memory (ROM). Most adapters today use EEPROM (Electrically Erasable Programmable ROM) or flash ROM, which can both be erased and reprogrammed right in the system without removing the chip or card. Updating the flash ROM is as simple as running the update program you get from the manufacturer and following the directions onscreen. It pays to check periodically with your card manufacturers to see if they have flash ROM updates for their cards.

ROM is useful for semi-permanent programs that always must be present while the system is running, and especially for booting. Graphics boards, hard disk controllers, communications boards, and expanded memory boards, for example, are adapter boards that might have adapter ROM. These adapter ROMs are in a separate area of memory from the VGA video RAM area and the motherboard ROM as well.

On systems based on the 386 CPU chip or higher, memory managers that are included with DOS 6 or third-party programs can load device drivers and memory-resident programs into unused regions in the UMA.

To actually move the RAM usage on any given adapter requires that you consult the documentation for the card. Most older cards require that specific switches or jumpers be changed, and the settings will probably not be obvious without the manual. Most newer cards, especially those that are Plug and Play, allow these settings to be changed by software that either comes with the card, or the Device Manager program that goes with some of the newer operating systems such as Windows 95/98 or NT 5.0 and newer.

Video Adapter BIOS. The video adapter BIOS handles the translation between the video card and basic VGA mode graphics instructions. Remember that your system is in a basic VGA mode during boot, and whenever you are running Windows in safe mode. Although 128K of upper memory beginning at segment C000 is reserved for use by adapter BIOSs, not all this space is used by various video adapters commonly found on PCs. Table 5.12 details the amount of space used by the BIOS on each type of common video adapter card.

Table 5.12 Memory Used by Different Video Cards	
Type of Adapter	**Adapter BIOS Memory Used**
Monochrome Display Adapter (MDA)	None - Drivers in Motherboard BIOS
Color Graphics Adapter (CGA)	None - Drivers in Motherboard BIOS
Enhanced Graphics Adapter (EGA)	16K onboard (C0000-C3FFF)
Video Graphics Array (VGA)	32K onboard (C0000-C7FFF)
Super VGA (SVGA)	32K onboard (C0000-C7FFF)

Depending on the basic VGA mode selected (Color Text, Monochrome Text, or VGA Graphics), the video card will use all the 128K of upper memory beginning at segment C000. In addition, these graphics cards may contain up to 8M or more of onboard memory for use in their native high-resolution modes in which to store currently displayed data and more quickly fetch new screen data for display.

Hard Disk Controller and SCSI Host Adapter BIOS. The upper memory addresses C0000 to DFFFF also are used for the built-in BIOS contained on many hard drive and SCSI controllers. Table 5.13 details the amount of memory and the addresses commonly used by the BIOS contained on hard drive adapter cards.

Table 5.13 Memory Addresses Used by Different Hard Drive Adapter Cards		
Disk Adapter Type	**Onboard BIOS Size**	**BIOS Address Range**
Most XT Compatible Controllers	8K	C8000-C9FFF
Most AT Controllers	None	Drivers in Motherboard BIOS
Most Standard IDE Adapters	None	Drivers in Motherboard BIOS
Most Enhanced IDE Adapters	16K	C8000-CBFFF
Some SCSI Host Adapters	16K	C8000-CBFFF
Some SCSI Host Adapters	16K	DC000-DFFFF

The hard drive or SCSI adapter card used on a particular system may use a different amount of memory, but it is most likely to use the memory segment beginning at C800 because this address is considered part of the IBM standard for personal computers. Virtually all the disk controller or SCSI adapters today that have an onboard BIOS allow the BIOS starting address to be easily moved in the C000 and D000 segments. The locations listed in Table 5.13 are only the default addresses that most of these cards use. If the default address is already in use by another card, you have to consult the documentation for the new card to see how to change the BIOS starting address to avoid any conflicts.

Figure 5.17 shows an example memory map for an Adaptec AHA-2940 SCSI adapter.

```
 . = Empty Addresses
 G = Video Graphics Array (VGA) Adapter Graphics Mode Video RAM
 M = VGA Monochrome Text Mode Video RAM
 C = VGA Color Text Mode Video RAM
 V = Standard VGA Video ROM BIOS
 S = SCSI Host Adapter ROM BIOS
 R = Standard Motherboard ROM BIOS


        : 0---1---2---3---4---5---6---7---8---9---A---B---C---D---E---F---
 0A0000: GGGGGGGGGGGGGGGGGGGGGGGGGGGGGGGGGGGGGGGGGGGGGGGGGGGGGGGGGGGGGGGGGG
 0B0000: MMMMMMMMMMMMMMMMMMMMMMMMMMMMMMMMCCCCCCCCCCCCCCCCCCCCCCCCCCCCCCCCCC
        : 0---1---2---3---4---5---6---7---8---9---A---B---C---D---E---F---
 0C0000: VVVVVVVVVVVVVVVVVVVVVVVVVVVVVVVV................................
 0D0000: ........................................SSSSSSSSSSSSSSSSSS
        : 0---1---2---3---4---5---6---7---8---9---A---B---C---D---E---F---
 0E0000: ................................................................
 0F0000: RRRRRRRRRRRRRRRRRRRRRRRRRRRRRRRRRRRRRRRRRRRRRRRRRRRRRRRRRRRRRRRRRR
```

FIG. 5.17 Adaptec AHA-2940U SCSI adapter default memory use.

Note how this SCSI adapter fits in here. Although no conflicts are in the UMA memory, the free regions have been fragmented by the placement of the SCSI BIOS. Because most systems do not have any BIOS in segment E000, that remains as a free 64K region. With no other adapters using memory, this example shows another free UMB (Upper Memory Block) starting at C8000 and continuing through DBFFF, which represents an 80K free region. Using the EMM386 driver that comes with DOS or Windows, memory can be mapped into these two regions for loading 16-bit memory-resident drivers and programs. Note that this will have no effect on 32-bit Windows 95/98 or NT drivers, as those are loaded into extended memory automatically. Unfortunately, because programs cannot be split across regions, the largest 16-bit driver program you could load is 80K, which is the size of the largest free region. It would be much better if you could move the SCSI adapter BIOS so that it was next to the VGA BIOS, as this would bring the free UMB space to a single region of 144K. It is much easier and more efficient to use a single 144K region than two regions of 80K and 64K, respectively. Note again that manipulating memory in this manner is not necessary with 32-bit drivers, because they are automatically loaded into extended memory anyway.

Fortunately, it is possible to move this particular SCSI adapter because it is a Plug-and-Play card. This means you can control the resource settings via the Win95/98 Device Manager.

If you have an older non–Plug-and-Play card, then you will likely need the documentation to discover the switch and jumper settings for the card, as most manufacturers don't clearly label them. If you can't find your original documentation, you can consult the Micro House PC Hardware Library on the CD with this book, which contains an extensive database of adapter cards, motherboards, and hard drives showing jumper settings, configuration information, manufacturer information, and so on.

Most cards sold since '96 have been Plug and Play, meaning that they are fully software configurable.

After changing the appropriate switches to move the SCSI adapter BIOS to start at C8000, the optimized map would look like Figure 5.18.

```
     . = Empty Addresses
     G = Video Graphics Array (VGA) Adapter Graphics Mode Video RAM
     M = VGA Monochrome Text Mode Video RAM
     C = VGA Color Text Mode Video RAM
     V = Standard VGA Video ROM BIOS
     S = SCSI Host Adapter ROM BIOS
     R = Standard Motherboard ROM BIOS


        : 0---1---2---3---4---5---6---7---8---9---A---B---C---D---E---F---
0A0000: GGGGGGGGGGGGGGGGGGGGGGGGGGGGGGGGGGGGGGGGGGGGGGGGGGGGGGGGGGGGGGGGG
0B0000: MMMMMMMMMMMMMMMMMMMMMMMMMMMMMMMMMCCCCCCCCCCCCCCCCCCCCCCCCCCCCCCCCC
        : 0---1---2---3---4---5---6---7---8---9---A---B---C---D---E---F---
0C0000: VVVVVVVVVVVVVVVVVVVVVVVVVVVVVVVVVSSSSSSSSSSSSSSSS................
0D0000: ................................................................
        : 0---1---2---3---4---5---6---7---8---9---A---B---C---D---E---F---
0E0000: ................................................................
0F0000: RRRRRRRRRRRRRRRRRRRRRRRRRRRRRRRRRRRRRRRRRRRRRRRRRRRRRRRRRRRRRRRRRR
```

FIG. 5.18 Adaptec AHA-2940U SCSI adapter with optimized memory use.

Notice how the free space is now a single contiguous block of 144K. This represents a far more optimum setup than the default settings.

Network Adapters. Network adapter cards also can use upper memory in segments C000 and D000. The exact amount of memory used and the starting address for each network card vary with the type and manufacturer of the card. Some network cards do not use any memory at all. A network card might have two primary uses for memory. They are as follows:

- IPL (Initial Program Load or Boot) ROM

- Shared Memory (RAM)

An *IPL ROM* is usually an 8K ROM that contains a bootstrap loader program that allows the system to boot directly from a file server on the network. This allows the removal of all disk drives from the PC, creating a diskless workstation. Because no floppy or hard disk would be in the system to boot from, the IPL ROM gives the system the instructions necessary to locate an image of the operating system on the file server and load it as if it were on an internal drive. If you are not using your system as a diskless workstation, it would be beneficial to disable any IPL ROM or IPL ROM socket on the adapter card. Note that many network adapters do not allow this socket to be disabled, which means that you lose the 8K of address space for other hardware, even if the ROM chip is removed from the socket!

Shared memory refers to a small portion of RAM contained on the network card that is mapped into the PC's upper memory area. This region is used as a memory window onto the network and offers very fast data transfer from the network card to the system. IBM pioneered the use of shared memory for its first Token Ring network adapters, and now shared memory is in common use among other companies' network adapters. Shared memory was first devised by IBM because it found that transfers using the DMA channels were not fast enough in most systems. This had mainly to do with some quirks in the DMA controller and bus design, which especially affected 16-bit ISA bus systems. Network adapters that do not use shared memory will either use DMA or Programmed I/O (PIO) transfers to move data to and from the network adapter.

Although shared memory is faster than either DMA or PIO for ISA systems, it does require 16K of UMA space to work. Most standard performance network adapters use PIO because this makes them easier to configure, and they require no free UMA space, whereas most high performance adapters will use shared memory. The shared memory region on most network adapters that use one is usually 16K in size and may be located at any user-selected 4K increment of memory in segments C000 or D000.

Figure 5.19 shows the default memory addresses for the IPL ROM and shared memory of an IBM Token Ring network adapter, although many other network adapters such as Ethernet adapters would be similar. One thing to note is that most Ethernet adapters use either a DMA channel or standard PIO (Programmed I/O) commands to send data to and from the network, and don't use shared memory like many Token Ring cards.

```
        . = Empty Addresses
        G = Video Graphics Array (VGA) Adapter Graphics Mode Video RAM
        M = VGA Monochrome Text Mode Video RAM
        C = VGA Color Text Mode Video RAM
        V = Standard VGA Video ROM BIOS
        I = Token Ring Network Adapter IPL ROM
        N = Token Ring Network Adapter Shared RAM
        R = Standard Motherboard ROM BIOS


        : 0---1---2---3---4---5---6---7---8---9---A---B---C---D---E---F---
0A0000: GGGGGGGGGGGGGGGGGGGGGGGGGGGGGGGGGGGGGGGGGGGGGGGGGGGGGGGGGGGGGGGGGG
0B0000: MMMMMMMMMMMMMMMMMMMMMMMMMMMMMMMMMCCCCCCCCCCCCCCCCCCCCCCCCCCCCCCCCC
        : 0---1---2---3---4---5---6---7---8---9---A---B---C---D---E---F---
0C0000: VVVVVVVVVVVVVVVVVVVVVVVVVVVVVVVV................IIIIIIII........
0D0000: ..............................NNNNNNNNNNNNNNNN................
        : 0---1---2---3---4---5---6---7---8---9---A---B---C---D---E---F---
0E0000: ................................................................
0F0000: RRRRRRRRRRRRRRRRRRRRRRRRRRRRRRRRRRRRRRRRRRRRRRRRRRRRRRRRRRRRRRRRRR
```

FIG. 5.19 Network adapter default memory map.

I have also included the standard VGA video BIOS in Figure 5.19 because nearly every system would have a VGA-type video adapter as well. Note that these default addresses for the IPL ROM and the shared memory can easily be changed by reconfiguring the adapter. Most other network adapters are similar in that they also would have an IPL ROM and a shared memory address, although the sizes of these areas and the default addresses may be different. Most network adapters that incorporate an IPL ROM option can disable the ROM and socket such that those addresses are not needed at all. This helps to conserve UMA space and prevent possible future conflicts if you are never going to use the function.

Notice in this case that the SCSI adapter used in Figure 5.20 would fit both at its default BIOS address of DC000, and the optimum address of C8000. The Token-Ring shared memory location is not optimum and causes the UMB space to be fragmented. By adjusting the location of the shared memory, this setup can be greatly improved. Figure 5.20 shows an optimum setup with both the Token-Ring adapter and the SCSI adapter in the same machine.

```
     . = Empty Addresses
     G = Video Graphics Array (VGA) Adapter Graphics Mode Video RAM
     M = VGA Monochrome Text Mode Video RAM
     C = VGA Color Text Mode Video RAM
     V = Standard VGA Video ROM BIOS
     S = SCSI Host Adapter ROM BIOS
     I = Token Ring Network Adapter IPL ROM
     N = Token Ring Network Adapter Shared RAM
     R = Standard Motherboard ROM BIOS


        : 0---1---2---3---4---5---6---7---8---9---A---B---C---D---E---F---
0A0000: GGGGGGGGGGGGGGGGGGGGGGGGGGGGGGGGGGGGGGGGGGGGGGGGGGGGGGGGGGGGGGGGG
0B0000: MMMMMMMMMMMMMMMMMMMMMMMMMMMMMMMMCCCCCCCCCCCCCCCCCCCCCCCCCCCCCCCCC
        : 0---1---2---3---4---5---6---7---8---9---A---B---C---D---E---F---
0C0000: VVVVVVVVVVVVVVVVVVVVVVVVVVVVVVVVVSSSSSSSSSSSSSSSSSSSNNNNNNNNNNNNN
0D0000: IIIIIIII.........................................................
        : 0---1---2---3---4---5---6---7---8---9---A---B---C---D---E---F---
0E0000: .........................................................
0F0000: RRRRRRRRRRRRRRRRRRRRRRRRRRRRRRRRRRRRRRRRRRRRRRRRRRRRRRRRRRRRRRRRR
```

FIG. 5.20   Adaptec AHA-2940U SCSI adapter and network adapter with optimized memory use.

This configuration allows a single 120K UMB that can very efficiently be used to load software drivers. Notice that the IPL ROM was moved to D0000, which places it as the last item installed before the free memory space. This is because if the IPL function is not needed, it can be disabled and the UMB space would increase to 128K and still be contiguous. If the default settings are used for both the SCSI and network adapters, the UMB memory would be fragmented into three regions of 16K, 40K, and 64K. The memory would still function, but it is hardly an optimum situation.

Note that the Plug-and-Play feature in Win95/98 and NT 5.0 does not attempt to optimize memory use, only to resolve conflicts. Of course, with 32-bit drivers, the location and size of free Upper Memory Blocks don't really matter, as 32-bit drivers will be loaded into extended memory. If you are still occasionally running DOS-based programs such as games, you will want to manually optimize the upper memory area configuration for maximum memory and performance.

Other ROMs in the Upper Memory Area. In addition to the BIOS for hard drive controllers, SCSI adapters, and network cards, upper memory segments C000 and D000 are used by some terminal emulators, security adapters, memory boards, and various other devices and adapter boards. Some adapters may require memory only for BIOS information, and others may require RAM in these upper memory segments. For information on a specific adapter, consult the manufacturer's documentation.

Motherboard BIOS Memory. The last 128K of reserved memory is used by the motherboard BIOS. The BIOS programs in ROM control the system during the boot-up procedure and remain as drivers for various hardware in the system during normal operation. Because these programs must be available immediately, they cannot be loaded from a device such as a disk drive. Four main programs stored in most motherboard ROMs are as follows:

- *Power-On Self Test*, the POST, is a set of routines that tests the motherboard, memory, disk controllers, video adapters, keyboard, and other primary system components. This routine is useful when you troubleshoot system failures or problems.

▶▶ See "The Power-On Self Test (POST)," p. 984

- The *bootstrap loader* routine initiates a search for an operating system on a floppy disk or hard disk. If an operating system is found, it is loaded into memory and given control of the system.

▶▶ See "The Boot Process," p. 1042

- The *BIOS* is the software interface to all the hardware in the system. The BIOS is a collection of individual drivers for the hardware in the system. With the BIOS, a program easily can access features in the system by calling on a standard BIOS driver function instead of talking directly to the device.

◀◀ See "BIOS," p. 208

- The *CMOS Setup* program is a menu-driven application that is used for system configuration and setup. It is normally activated at boot time by pressing the proper key. This program is used to set basic system configuration parameters and BIOS features, motherboard and chipset features, user preferences and security features (passwords), and in some cases to run limited diagnostics. Not all systems have the CMOS Setup program in ROM; some must load it from a floppy disk or hard disk instead.

Both segments E000 and F000 in the memory map are considered reserved for the motherboard BIOS, but only some systems actually use this entire area. Older 8-bit systems require only segment F000 and enable adapter card ROM or RAM to use segment

E000. Most 16-bit or greater systems use all of F000 for the BIOS, and may decode but not use any of segment E000. By decoding an area, the motherboard essentially grabs control of the addresses, which precludes installing any other hardware in this region. In other words, it is not possible to configure adapter cards to use this area. That is why you will find that most adapters that use memory simply do not allow any choices for memory use in segment E000. Although this may seem like a waste of 64K of memory space, any 386 or higher system can use the powerful MMU in the processor to map RAM from extended memory into segment E000 as an Upper Memory Block, and subsequently use it for loading 16-bit driver software if necessary. This is a nice solution to what otherwise would be wasted memory, although it is not important if you use 32-bit drivers.

Many different ROM-interface programs are in the IBM motherboards, but the location of these programs is mostly consistent.

Figure 5.21 shows the motherboard ROM BIOS memory use of most 16-bit or greater systems.

```
   . = Empty Addresses
   R = Standard Motherboard ROM BIOS

       : 0---1---2---3---4---5---6---7---8---9---A---B---C---D---E---F---
0E0000: ................................................................
0F0000: RRRRRRRRRRRRRRRRRRRRRRRRRRRRRRRRRRRRRRRRRRRRRRRRRRRRRRRRRRRRRRRRRR
```

FIG. 5.21 Motherboard ROM BIOS memory use of most systems.

Note that the standard system BIOS uses only segment F000 (64K). In almost every case, the remainder of the BIOS area (segment E000) is completely free and can be used as UMA block space.

Extended Memory

As mentioned previously in this chapter, the memory map on a system based on the 286 or higher processor can extend beyond the 1M boundary that exists when the processor is in real mode. On a 286 or 386SX system, the extended memory limit is 16M; on a 386DX, 486, Pentium, Pentium MMX, or Pentium Pro system, the extended memory limit is 4G (4,096M). Systems based on the Pentium II processor have a limit of 64G (65,536M).

For a system to address memory beyond the first megabyte, the processor must be in *protected mode*—the native mode of 286 and higher processors. On a 286, only programs designed to run in protected mode can take advantage of extended memory. 386 and higher processors offer another mode, called *virtual real mode*, which enables extended memory to be, in effect, chopped into 1M pieces (each its own real-mode session). Virtual real mode also allows for several of these sessions to be running simultaneously in protected areas of memory. These can be seen as DOS prompt sessions or windows within Windows 95/98, NT, or OS/2. Although several DOS programs can be running at once, each still is limited to a maximum of 640K of memory because each session simulates a real-mode environment, right down to the BIOS and Upper Memory Area. Running several programs at once in virtual real mode, called *multitasking*, requires software that can manage each program and keep them from crashing into one another. OS/2, Windows 95/98, and Windows NT all do this.

The 286 and higher CPU chips also run in what is termed *real mode*, which enables full compatibility with the 8088 CPU chip installed on the PC/XT-type computer. Real mode enables you to run DOS programs one at a time on an AT-type system just like you would on a PC/XT. However, an AT-type system running in real mode, particularly a 386-, 486-, Pentium-, Pentium Pro-, or Pentium II-based system, is really functioning as little more than a turbo PC. In real mode, these processors can emulate the 8086 or 8088, but they cannot operate in protected mode at the same time. For that reason, the 386 and above also provide a virtual real mode that operates under protected mode. This allows for the execution of real-mode programs under the control of a protected-mode operating system, such as Win95/98, NT, or OS/2.

> **Note**
>
> Extended memory is basically all memory past the first megabyte, which can only be accessed while the processor is in protected mode.

XMS Memory. The extended memory specification (XMS) was developed in 1987 by Microsoft, Intel, AST Corp., and Lotus Development to specify how programs would use extended memory. The XMS specification functions on systems based on the 286 or higher and allows real-mode programs (those designed to run in DOS) to use extended memory and another block of memory usually out of the reach of DOS.

Before XMS, there was no way to ensure cooperation between programs that switched the processor into protected mode and used extended memory. There was also no way for one program to know what another had been doing with the extended memory because none of them could see that memory while in real mode. HIMEM.SYS becomes an arbitrator of sorts that first grabs all the extended memory for itself and then doles it out to programs that know the XMS protocols. In this manner, several programs that use XMS memory can operate together under DOS on the same system, switching the processor into and out of protected mode to access the memory. XMS rules prevent one program from accessing memory that another has in use. Because Windows 3.x is a program manager that switches the system to and from protected mode in running several programs at once, it has been set up to require XMS memory to function. Windows 95 operates mostly in protected mode, but still calls on real mode for access to many system components. Windows NT is a true protected-mode operating system, as is OS/2.

Extended memory can be made to conform to the XMS specification by installing a device driver in the CONFIG.SYS file. The most common XMS driver is HIMEM.SYS, which is included with Windows 3.x and later versions of DOS, starting with 4.0 and up. Windows 95/98 and NT automatically allow XMS functions in DOS prompt sessions, and you can configure full-blown DOS-mode sessions to allow XMS functions as well.

High Memory Area (HMA) and the A20 line. The High Memory Area (HMA) is an area of memory 16 bytes short of 64K in size, starting at the beginning of the first megabyte of extended memory. It can be used to load device drivers and memory-resident programs to free up conventional memory for use by real-mode programs. Only one device driver or memory-resident program can be loaded into HMA at one time, no matter what its size. Originally, this could be any program, but Microsoft decided that DOS could get there first, and built capability into DOS 5 and newer versions.

The HMA area is extremely important to those who use DOS 5 or higher because these DOS versions can move their own kernel (about 45K of program instructions) into this area. This is accomplished simply by first loading an XMS driver (such as HIMEM.SYS) and adding the line **DOS=HIGH** to your CONFIG.SYS file. Taking advantage of this DOS capability frees another 45K or so of conventional memory for use by real-mode programs by essentially moving 45K of program code into the first segment of extended memory. Although this memory was supposed to be accessible in protected mode only, it turns out that a defect in the design of the original 286 (which, fortunately, has been propagated forward to the more recent processors as a "feature") accidentally allows access to most of the first segment of extended memory while still in real mode.

The use of the HMA is controlled by the HIMEM.SYS or equivalent driver. The origins of this memory usage are interesting because they are based on a bug in the original 286 processor carried forward through even the Pentium II.

The problem started from the fact that memory addresses in Intel processors are dictated by an overlapping segment and offset address. By setting the segment address to FFFF—which itself specifies an actual address of FFFF0, which is 16 bytes from the end of the first megabyte—and then specifying an offset of FFFF, which is equal to 64K, you can create a memory address as follows:

```
    FFFF    segment
+   FFFF    offset
    ------
= 10FFEF    total
```

This type of address is impossible on an 8088 or 8086 system that has only 20 address lines and therefore cannot calculate an address that large. By leaving off the leading digit, these processors interpret the address as 0FFEF, in essence causing the address to "wrap around" and end up 16 bytes from the end of the first 64K segment of the first megabyte. The problem with the 286 and higher was that when they were in real mode, they were supposed to operate the same way, and the address should wrap around to the beginning of the first megabyte also. Unfortunately, a "bug" in the chip left the 21st address line active (called the A20 line), which allowed the address to end up 16 bytes from the end of the first 64K segment in the second megabyte. This memory was supposed to be addressable only in protected mode, but this bug allowed all but 16 bytes of the first 64K of extended memory to be addressable in real mode.

Because this bug caused problems with many real-mode programs that relied on the wrap to take place, when IBM engineers designed the AT, they had to find a way to disable the A20 line while in real mode, but then re-enable it when in protected mode. They did this by using some unused pins on the 8042 keyboard controller chip on the motherboard. The 8042 keyboard controller was designed to accept scan codes from the keyboard and transmit them to the processor, but there were unused pins not needed strictly for this function. So IBM came up with a way to command the keyboard controller to turn on and off the A20 line, thus enabling the "defective" 286 to truly emulate an 8088 and 8086 while in real mode.

Microsoft realized that you could command the 8042 keyboard controller to turn back on the A20 line strictly for the purpose of using this "bug" as a feature, which enabled you to access the first 64K of extended memory (less 16 bytes) without having to go through the lengthy and complicated process of switching into protected mode. Thus, HIMEM.SYS and the High Memory Area was born! HIMEM.SYS has to watch the system to see if the A20 line should be off for compatibility, or on to enable access to the HMA or while in protected mode. In essence, HIMEM becomes a control program that manipulates the A20 line through the 8042 keyboard controller chip.

Expanded Memory

Some older programs can use a type of memory called *Expanded Memory Specification* or EMS memory. Unlike conventional (the first megabyte) or extended (the second through 16th or 4,096th megabytes) memory, expanded memory is *not* directly addressable by the processor. Instead, it can only be accessed through a 64K window and small 16K pages established in the UMA. Expanded memory is a segment or bank-switching scheme in which a custom memory adapter has a large number of 64K segments onboard, combined with special switching and mapping hardware. The system uses a free segment in the UMA as the home address for the EMS board. After this 64K is filled with data, the board rotates the filled segment out and a new, empty segment appears to take its place. In this fashion, you have a board that can keep on rotating in new segments to be filled with data. Because only one segment can be seen or operated on at one time, EMS is very inefficient for program code and is normally only used for data.

Figure 5.22 shows how expanded memory fits with conventional and extended memory.

Intel originally created a custom-purpose memory board that had the necessary EMS bank-switching hardware. They called these boards *Above Boards*, and they were widely sold many years ago. EMS was designed with 8-bit systems in mind and was appropriate for them because they had no capability to access extended memory. 286 and newer systems, however, possess the capability to have 15 or more megabytes of extended memory, which is much more efficient than the goofy (and slow) bank-switching EMS scheme. The Above Boards are no longer being manufactured, and EMS memory—as a concept and functionally—is extremely obsolete.

If you have any antique software that still requires EMS memory, you are advised to upgrade to newer versions that can use extended memory directly. It is also possible to use the powerful MMU of the 386 and higher processors to convert extended memory to function like LIM EMS, but this should only be done if there is no way to use the extended memory directly. EMM386 can convert extended to expanded, and in fact was originally designed for this purpose, although today it is more likely to be used to map extended memory into the UMA for the purposes of loading drivers and not for EMS. The EMM386 driver is included with DOS versions 5 and newer as well as with Windows. If you have several versions on hand, as a rule, always use the newest one.

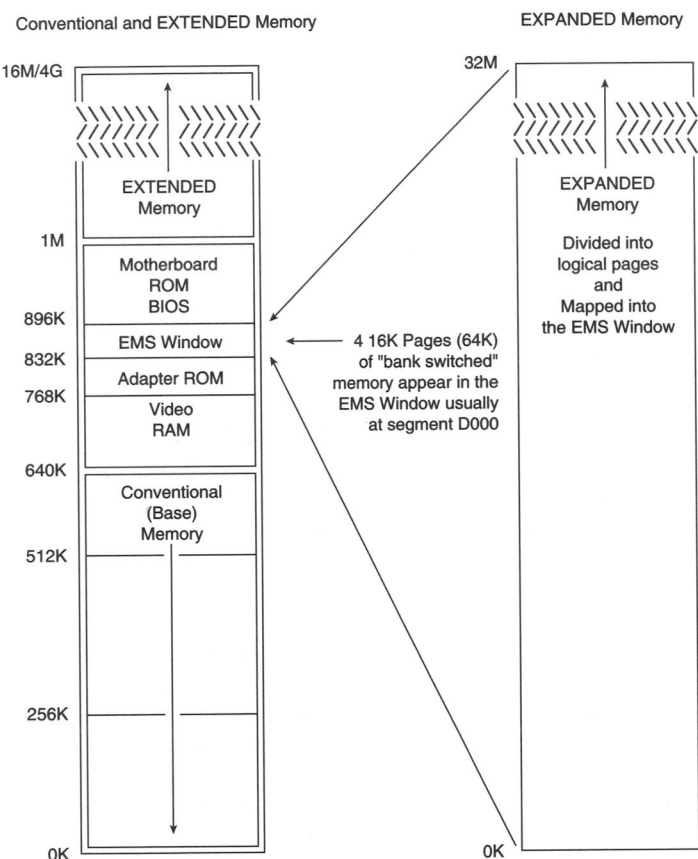

FIG. 5.22 Conventional, extended, and expanded memory.

Preventing ROM BIOS Memory Conflicts and Overlap

As detailed in previous sections, C000 and D000 are reserved for use by adapter-board ROM and RAM. If two adapters have overlapping ROM or RAM addresses, usually neither board operates properly. Each board functions if you remove or disable the other one, but they do not work together.

With many adapter boards, you can change the actual memory locations to be used with jumpers, switches, or driver software, which might be necessary to allow two boards to coexist in one system. This type of conflict can cause problems for troubleshooters. You must read the documentation for each adapter to find out what memory addresses the adapter uses and how to change the addresses to allow coexistence with another adapter.

Most of the time, you can work around these problems by reconfiguring the board or changing jumpers, switch settings, or software-driver parameters. This change enables the two boards to coexist and stay out of each other's way.

Additionally, you must ensure that adapter boards do not use the same IRQ (Interrupt Request Line), DMA (direct memory access) channel, or I/O Port address. You can easily avoid adapter board memory, IRQ, DMA channel, and I/O Port conflicts by creating a chart or template to mock up the system configuration by penciling on the template the resources already used by each installed adapter. You end up with a picture of the system resources and the relationship of each adapter to the others. This procedure helps you anticipate conflicts and ensures that you configure each adapter board correctly the first time. The template also becomes important documentation when you consider new adapter purchases. New adapters must be configurable to use the available resources in your system.

◀◀　See "System Resources," p. 269

If your system has Plug-and-Play capabilities, and you use PnP adapters, it will be able to resolve conflicts between the adapters by moving the memory usage on any conflict. Unfortunately, this routine is not intelligent and still requires human intervention—that is, manual specification of addresses in order to achieve the most optimum location for the adapter memory.

ROM Shadowing

Computers based on the 386 or higher CPU chip, which provides memory access on a 32- or 64-bit path, often use a 16-bit data path for system ROM BIOS information. In addition, adapter cards with onboard BIOS may use an 8-bit path to system memory. On these high-end computers, using a 16- or 8-bit path to memory is a significant bottleneck to system performance. In addition to these problems of width, most actual ROM chips are available in maximum speeds far less than what is available for the system's dynamic RAM. For example, the fastest ROMs available are generally 150ns to 200ns, whereas the RAM in a modern system is rated at 60ns or faster in most cases.

Because of the fact that ROM is so slow, any system accesses to programs or data in ROM cause many additional wait states to be inserted. These wait states can slow the entire system down tremendously, especially considering that many of the 16-bit driver programs used constantly by DOS reside in the BIOS chips found on the motherboard and many of the installed adapters. Fortunately, a way was found to transfer the contents of the slow 8- or 16-bit ROM chips into much faster 32-bit main memory. This is called *shadowing the ROMs*.

Virtually all 386 and higher systems enable you to use what is termed *shadow memory* for the motherboard and possibly some adapter ROMs as well. Shadowing essentially moves the programming code from slow ROM chips into fast 32-bit system memory. Shadowing slower ROMs by copying their contents into RAM can greatly speed up these BIOS routines—sometimes making them four to five times faster.

Shadowing is accomplished by using the powerful MMU in the 386 and higher processors. With the appropriate instructions, the MMU can take a copy of the ROM code, place it in RAM, and enable the RAM such that it appears to the system in exactly the same addresses at which it was originally located. This actually disables the ROM chips themselves, which are essentially shut down. The system RAM that is now masquerading as ROM is fully write-protected so that it acts in every way just like the real ROM, with the exception of being much faster, of course! Most systems have an option in the system setup to enable shadowing for the motherboard BIOS (usually segment F000) and the video BIOS (usually the first 32K of segment C000). Some systems will go further and offer you the capability to enable or disable shadowing in increments (usually 16K) throughout the remainder of the C000 and D000 segments.

> **Note**
>
> The important thing to note about shadowing is that if you enable shadowing for a given set of addresses, anything found there when the system is booting will be copied to RAM and locked in place. If you were to do this to a memory range that had a network adapter's shared memory mapped into it, the network card would cease to function. You must only shadow ranges that contain true ROM and no RAM.

Some systems do not offer shadowing for areas other than the motherboard and video BIOS. In these systems, you can use a memory manager such as EMM386 (which comes with DOS and Windows) to enable shadowing for any range you specify. It is preferable to use the system's own internal shadowing capabilities first because the system shadowing uses memory that would otherwise be discarded. Using an external memory manager such as EMM386 for shadowing costs you a small amount of extended memory, equal to the amount of space you are shadowing.

If you enable shadowing for a range of addresses, and one or more adapters or the system in general no longer works properly, you may have scratch pad memory or other RAM within the shadowed area, which is not accessible as long as the shadowing remains active. In this case, you should disable the shadowing for the system to operate properly. If you can figure out precisely which addresses are ROM and which are RAM within the Upper Memory Area, you can selectively shadow only the ROM for maximum system performance.

Note that shadowing ROMs is not very important when running a 32-bit operating system such as Win95/98 or NT. This is because those operating systems only use the 16-bit BIOS driver code during booting; then they load 32-bit replacement drivers into faster extended memory and use them. Thus, shadowing normally only affects DOS or other 16-bit software and operating systems.

Total Installed Memory Versus Total Usable Memory
One thing that most people don't realize is that not all the SIMM or other RAM memory you purchase and install in a system will be available. Because of some quirks in system design, the system usually has to "throw away" up to 384K of RAM to make way for the Upper Memory Area.

For example, most systems with 16M of RAM (which is 16,384K) installed show a total of only 16,000K installed during the POST or when running Setup. This indicates that 16,384K–16,000K = 384K of missing memory! Some systems may show 16,256K with the same 16M installed, which works out to 16,384K–16,256K = 128K missing.

If you run your Setup program and check out your base and extended memory values, you will find more information than just the single figure for the total shown during the POST. In most systems with 4,096K (4M), you have 640K base and 3,072K extended. In some systems, Setup reports 640K base and 3,328K extended memory, which is a bonus. In other words, most systems come up 384K short, but some come up only 128K short.

This shortfall is not easy to explain, but it is consistent from system to system. Say that you have a 486 system with two installed 72-pin (32-bit) 16M SIMMs. This results in a total installed memory of 32M in two separate banks because the processor has a 32-bit data bus. Each SIMM is a single bank in this system. Note that most cheaper 486 systems use the 30-pin (8-bit) SIMMs, of which four are required to make a single bank. The first bank (or SIMM, in this case) starts at address 0000000h (the start of the first megabyte), and the second starts at 1000000 (the start of the 17th megabyte).

One of the cardinal rules of memory is that you absolutely cannot have two hardware devices wired to the same address. This means that 384K of the first memory bank in this system would be in direct conflict with the video RAM (segments A000 and B000), any adapter card ROMs (segments C000 and D000), and of course the motherboard ROM (segments E000 and F000). This means that all SIMM RAM that occupies these addresses must be shut off or the system will not function! Actually, a motherboard designer can do three things with the SIMM memory that would overlap from A0000-FFFFF:

- Use the faster RAM to hold a copy of any slow ROMs (shadowing), disabling the ROM in the process.

- Turn off any RAM not used for shadowing, eliminating any UMA conflicts.

- Remap any RAM not used for shadowing, adding to the stack of currently installed extended memory.

Most systems shadow the motherboard ROM (usually 64K), the video ROM (32K), and simply turn off the rest. Some motherboard ROMs allow additional shadowing to be selected between C8000-DFFFF, usually in 16K increments.

> **Note**
>
> You can only shadow ROM, never RAM, so if any card (such as a network card) has a RAM buffer in the C8000-DFFFF area, you must not shadow the RAM buffer addresses or the card will not function. For the same reason, you cannot shadow the A0000-BFFFF area because this is the video adapter RAM buffer.

Most motherboards do not do any remapping, which means that any of the 384K not shadowed is simply turned off. That is why enabling shadowing does not seem to use any memory. The memory used for shadowing would otherwise be discarded in most systems. These systems would appear to be short by 384K compared to what is physically installed in the system. For example, in a system with 32M, no remapping would result in 640K of base memory and 31,744K of extended memory, for a total of 32,384K of usable RAM—384K short of the total (32,768K–384K).

Some systems shadow what they can and then remap any segments that do not have shadowing into extended memory so as not to waste the non-shadowed RAM. PS/2 systems, for example, shadow the motherboard BIOS area (E0000-FFFFF or 128K in these systems) and remap the rest of the first bank of SIMM memory (256K from A0000-DFFFF) to whatever address follows the last installed bank.

> **Note**
>
> Note that most new systems don't allow selecting ROM shadowing functions, nor do they do any remapping. These days, the small amount of memory gain just isn't worth the trouble in system engineering and design to accomplish it.

In my example system with two 16M 32-bit SIMMs, the 256K not used for shadowing would be remapped to 2000000-203FFFF, which is the start of the 33rd megabyte. This affects diagnostics because if you had any memory error reported in those addresses (2000000-203FFFF), it would indicate a failure in the first SIMM, even though the addresses point to the end of installed extended memory. The addresses from 1000000-1FFFFFF would be in the second SIMM, and the 640K base memory 0000000-009FFFF would be back in the first SIMM. As you can see, figuring out how the SIMMs are mapped into the system is not easy!

Most systems that do remapping can only remap an entire segment if no shadowing is going on within it. The video RAM area in segments A000 and B000 can never contain shadowing, so at least 128K can be remapped to the top of installed extended memory in any system that supports remapping. Because most systems shadow in segments F000 (motherboard ROM) and C000 (video ROM), these two segments cannot be remapped. This leaves 256K maximum for remapping. Any system remapping the full 384K must not be shadowing at all, which would slow down the system and is not recommended. Shadowing is always preferred over remapping, and remapping what is not shadowed is definitely preferred over simply turning off the RAM.

Systems that have 384K of "missing" memory do not do remapping. If you want to determine if your system has any missing memory, all you need to know are three things. One is the total physical memory actually installed. The other two items can be discovered by running your Setup program. You want to know the total base and extended memory numbers recognized by the system. Then simply subtract the base and extended memory from the total installed to determine the missing memory. You will usually find that your system is "missing" 384K, but you may be lucky and have a system that remaps 256K of what is missing and thus shows only 128K of memory missing.

Virtually all systems use some of the missing memory for shadowing ROMs, especially the motherboard and video BIOS, so what is missing is not completely wasted. Systems "missing" 128K will find that it is being used to shadow your motherboard BIOS (64K from F0000-FFFFF) and video BIOS (32K from C0000-C8000). The remainder of segment C0000 (32K from C8000-CFFFF) is simply being turned off. All other segments (128K from A0000-BFFFF and 128K from D0000-EFFFF) are being remapped to the start of the fifth megabyte (400000-43FFFF). Most systems simply disable these remaining segments rather then take the trouble to remap them. Remapping requires additional logic and BIOS routines to accomplish, and many motherboard designers do not feel that it is worth the effort to reclaim 256K.

> **Note**
>
> If your system is doing remapping, any errors reported near the end of installed extended memory are likely in the first bank of memory because that is where they are remapped from. The first bank in a 32-bit system would be constructed of either four 30-pin (8-bit) SIMMs or one 72-pin (32-bit) SIMM. The first bank in a 64-bit system would be constructed of either two 72-pin (32-bit) SIMMs or one 168-pin (64-bit) DIMM.

Adapter Memory Configuration and Optimization

Ideally, all adapter boards would be Plug-and-Play devices that require you to merely plug the adapter into a motherboard slot and then use it. With the new Plug-and-Play specification, we are moving toward that goal. However, sometimes it almost seems that adapter boards are designed as if they were the only adapter likely to be present on a system. They usually require you to know the upper memory addresses and IRQ and DMA channels already on your system, and how to configure the new adapter so that it does not conflict with your already-installed adapters.

Adapter boards use upper memory for their BIOS and as working RAM. If two boards attempt to use the same BIOS area or RAM area of upper memory, a conflict occurs that can keep your system from booting. The following sections cover ways to avoid these potential conflicts and how to troubleshoot if they do occur. In addition, these sections discuss moving adapter memory to resolve conflicts and provide some ideas on optimizing adapter memory use.

How to Determine What Adapters Occupy the UMA. You can determine what adapters are using space in upper memory in the following two ways:

- Study the documentation for each adapter on your system to determine the memory addresses they use.

- Use a software utility that can quickly determine for you what upper memory areas your adapters are using.

The simplest way (although by no means always the most foolproof) is to use a software utility to determine the upper memory areas used by the adapters installed on your system. One such utility, Microsoft Diagnostics (MSD), comes with Windows 3.x and DOS 6 or higher versions. The Device Manager under System in the Windows 95 Control Panel also provides this information, as does the new System Information utility that comes with Windows 98. These utilities examine your system configuration and determine not only the upper memory used by your adapters, but also the IRQs used by each of these adapters.

True Plug-and-Play systems will also shut down one of the cards involved in a conflict to prevent a total system lockup. This may cause Windows to boot in safe mode.

After you run MSD, Device Manager, or another utility to determine your system's upper memory configuration, make a printout of the memory addresses used. Thereafter, you can quickly refer to the printout when you are adding a new adapter to ensure that the new board does not conflict with any devices already installed on your system.

Moving Adapter Memory to Resolve Conflicts. After you identify a conflict or potential conflict by studying the documentation for the adapter boards installed on your system or using a software diagnostic utility to determine the upper memory addresses used by your adapter boards, you may have to reconfigure one or more of your adapters to move the upper memory space used by a problem adapter.

Most adapter boards make moving adapter memory a somewhat simple process, enabling you to change a few jumpers or switches to reconfigure the board; in Plug-and-Play cards, you can use the configuration program that comes with the board or the Windows Device Manager to make the changes. The following steps help you resolve most conflicts that arise because adapter boards conflict with one another:

1. Determine the upper memory addresses currently used by your adapter boards and write them down.

2. Determine if any of these addresses are overlapping, which results in a conflict.

3. Consult the documentation for your adapter boards to determine which boards can be reconfigured so that all adapters have access to unique memory addresses.

4. Configure the affected adapter boards so that no conflict in memory addresses occurs.

For example, if one adapter uses the upper memory range C8000-CBFFF and another adapter uses the range CA000-CCFFF, you have a potential address conflict. One of these must be changed. Note that Plug-and-Play cards allow these changes to be made directly from the Windows Device Manager.

Optimizing Adapter Memory Use. On an ideal PC, adapter boards would always come configured so that the upper memory addresses they use immediately follow the upper memory addresses used by the previous adapter, with no overlap that would cause conflicts. Such an upper memory arrangement would not only be "clean," but would make it much more simple to use available upper memory for loading device drivers and memory-resident programs. However, this is not the case. Adapter boards often leave gaps of unused memory between one another—this is, of course, preferable to an overlap, but still is not the best use of upper memory.

Someone who wanted to make the most of their upper memory might consider studying the documentation for each adapter board installed on his or her system to determine a way to compact the upper memory used by each of these devices. For example, if it were possible on a particular system using the adapters installed on it, the use of upper memory could be more simple if you configured your adapter boards so that the blocks of memory they use fit together like bricks in a wall, rather than like a slice of Swiss cheese, as is the case on most systems. The more you can reduce your free upper memory to as few contiguous chunks as possible, the more completely and efficiently you can take advantage of the UMA.

Memory optimization in this manner is not really necessary if you are running 32-bit drivers as you would in a normal Win95/98 or NT system. This is mostly useful for running older DOS applications, games, and so on.

Taking Advantage of Unused Upper Memory

On systems using an older 16-bit operating system such as Windows 3.1 or DOS, memory-resident programs and device drivers can be moved into the UMA by using a memory manager such as the MEMMAKER utility or some other aftermarket utility. These memory management utilities examine the memory-resident programs and device drivers installed on your system, determine their memory needs, and then calculate the best way to move these drivers and programs into upper memory, thus freeing the conventional memory they used.

Using MEMMAKER is quite simple. Make a backup of your CONFIG.SYS and AUTOEXEC.BAT files so that you have usable copies if you need them to restore your system configuration; then run MEMMAKER from the DOS prompt. MEMMAKER will install required device drivers in your CONFIG.SYS file, and then begin optimizing your memory configuration. It does a decent job of freeing up conventional memory; however, with careful fine-tuning, an individual can perform feats of memory management using only the raw DOS HIMEM.SYS and EMM386.EXE drivers that no automatic program can do.

Only driver programs that run in the processor's real mode must be loaded within the first megabyte of memory. Because real-mode drivers are made up of 16-bit real mode program code, they cannot reside in extended memory, because only the first megabyte (base memory) is accessible when in real mode. DOS and Windows 3.x are 16-bit programs and utilize drivers that run in real mode, hence the need for the base memory optimization. With the number of drivers that people are using today, it can be difficult to fit them all in the available UMA space while leaving enough base memory free to run applications.

Things are different with the newer operating systems. Windows 95/98, for example, uses primarily 32-bit protected mode drivers and program code, although there is still some 16-bit real-mode program code left. Windows NT and OS/2 are full 32-bit operating systems, and all their drivers and applications are made up of 32-bit protected mode instruction code. If you are using all 32-bit programs, then virtually no memory optimization is necessary in the first megabyte, as 32-bit programs are free to run in extended memory.

The following sections cover using memory-management software to optimize conventional memory, and additional ways to configure your system memory to make your system run as efficiently as possible. It is important to note that the DOS HIMEM.SYS and EMM386.EXE play an integral role in MEMMAKER's capability to move device drivers and memory-resident programs into upper memory. The next two sections describe using HIMEM.SYS and EMM386.EXE to configure extended and expanded memory.

> **Note**
>
> If you are running older 16-bit DOS applications under Windows 95, Windows NT, or OS/2, then you still need to know about base memory optimization. In these cases, you will be running the application in a DOS window, which, using the virtual real mode of the processor, can emulate the first megabyte of real-mode workspace. Using these 32-bit operating systems, you can customize how the application running in the DOS window sees the system, and how the system memory appears to be organized.

Using HIMEM.SYS (DOS). The DOS device driver HIMEM.SYS, which has been included with Windows and DOS 4.0 and higher, is used to configure extended memory to the XMS specification, as well as to enable the use of the first 64K of extended memory as the high memory area (HMA). HIMEM.SYS is installed by adding a line invoking the device driver to your CONFIG.SYS file.

Using EMM386.EXE (DOS). The program EMM386.EXE, which is included with DOS 5.0 and higher, is used primarily to map XMS memory (extended memory managed by HIMEM.SYS) into unused regions of the UMA. This allows programs to be loaded into these regions for use under DOS. EMM386 also has a secondary function of using XMS memory to emulate EMS version 4 memory, which can then be used by programs that need expanded memory. For more information on using EMM386.EXE, refer to Que's *Special Edition Using MS-DOS 6.2* or your DOS manual.

MS-DOS 6.x MEMMAKER. If you still run DOS applications and games that run in DOS, you can increase the amount of conventional memory available to software running in DOS on systems based on the 386 chip and above by running the MS DOS 6.x utility MEMMAKER. DOS 5 had the capability, using EMM386, to map extended memory into the UMA so that DOS could load memory-resident programs and drivers into the UMA. Unfortunately, this required an extensive knowledge of the upper memory configuration of a particular system, and trial and error to see what programs could fit into the available free regions. This process was difficult enough that many people were not effectively using their memory under DOS (and Windows).

To make things easier, when DOS 6 was released, Microsoft included a menu-driven program called MEMMAKER that determines the system configuration, automatically creates the proper EMM386 statements, and inserts them into the CONFIG.SYS file. By manipulating the UMA manually or through MEMMAKER and loading device drivers and memory-resident programs into upper memory, you can have more than 600K of free conventional memory.

Over the course of months or years of use, the installation programs for various software utilities often install so many memory-resident programs and device drivers in your AUTOEXEC.BAT and CONFIG.SYS files that you have too little conventional memory left to start all the programs you want to run. You may want to use MEMMAKER to free up more conventional memory for your programs. You can get help on MEMMAKER by typing **HELP MEMMAKER** at the DOS prompt. When you run the MEMMAKER utility, it automatically performs the following functions to free up more memory:

- Moves a portion of the DOS kernel into the HMA.

- Maps free XMS memory into unused regions in the UMA as UMBs, into which DOS can then load device drivers and memory-resident programs to free up the conventional memory these drivers and programs otherwise use.

- Modifies CONFIG.SYS and AUTOEXEC.BAT to cause DOS to load memory-resident programs and device drivers into UMBs.

Before running MEMMAKER, carefully examine your CONFIG.SYS and AUTOEXEC.BAT files to identify unnecessary device drivers and memory-resident programs. For example, the DOS device driver ANSI.SYS is often loaded in CONFIG.SYS to enable you to use color and other attributes at the DOS prompt and to remap the keys on your keyboard. If you are primarily a Windows user and do not spend much time at the DOS prompt, you can eliminate ANSI.SYS from your CONFIG.SYS file to free up the memory the driver is using.

Tip

SETVER is another often-loaded driver that most people don't need. If you don't run utilities or programs that require a specific version of DOS, you can remove SETVER from your CONFIG.SYS file.

After you strip down CONFIG.SYS and AUTOEXEC.BAT to their bare essentials (it is advisable to make backup copies first), you are ready to run MEMMAKER to optimize your system memory. To run MEMMAKER, follow these steps:

1. Exit from any other programs you are running.

2. Start your network or any memory-resident programs and device drivers you absolutely need.

3. At the DOS prompt, type **MEMMAKER.**

The MEMMAKER setup runs in two modes—Express and Custom. Express setup is preferable for users who want to enable MEMMAKER to load device drivers and memory-resident programs into high memory with the minimum amount of user input, unless they have an EGA or VGA (but not a Super VGA) monitor. If you have an EGA or VGA monitor, choose Custom Setup and answer Yes in the advanced options screen where it asks whether MEMMAKER should use monochrome region (B0000-B7FFF) for running programs. Use the defaults for the rest of the options in Custom setup unless you are sure that one of the defaults is not correct for your system. Custom setup is probably not a good idea unless you are knowledgeable about optimizing system memory, particular device drivers, and memory-resident programs on the system.

When MEMMAKER finishes optimizing the system memory, the following three lines are added to CONFIG.SYS:

```
DEVICE=C:\DOS\HIMEM.SYS
DEVICE=C:\DOS\EMM386.E XE NOEMS
DOS=HIGH,UMB
```

In addition, MEMMAKER modifies each line in CONFIG.SYS and AUTOEXEC.BAT that loads a device driver or memory-resident program now being loaded into UMBs. Various DEVICE= lines in your CONFIG.SYS are changed to DEVICEHIGH=, and various lines in your AUTOEXEC.BAT have the LH (LoadHigh) command inserted in front of them. For example, the line DEVICE=ANSI.SYS is changed to DEVICEHIGH=ANSI.SYS. In your AUTOEXEC.BAT, lines such as C:\DOS\DOSKEY are changed to LH C:\DOS\DOSKEY. The DEVICEHIGH and LH commands load the device drivers and memory-resident programs into UMBs. MEMMAKER also adds codes to specify where in upper memory each program will be loaded. For example, after you run MEMMAKER, a statement like this might be added to your AUTOEXEC.BAT:

```
LH /L:1 C:\DOS\DOSKEY
```

The /L:1 causes the resident program DOSKEY to load into the first UMB region. On many systems, MEMMAKER configures the system to free up 620K of conventional memory.

Chapter 6

Power Supply and Case

The power supply is a critical component in a PC because it supplies electrical power to every system component that needs it. In my experience, it is also one of the most failure-prone components in any computer system. A malfunctioning power supply can damage the other components in your computer by delivering an improper or erratic voltage. Because of its importance to proper and reliable system operation, you should understand both the function and limitations of a power supply, as well as its potential problems and their solutions.

Power Supply Function and Operation

The basic function of the power supply is to convert the type of electrical power available at the wall socket to the type the computer circuitry can use. The power supply in a conventional desktop system is designed to convert the American 120-volt, 60Hz, AC current into +3.3v, +5v, and +12v DC current. Usually, the digital electronic components and circuits in the system (motherboard, adapter cards, and disk drive logic boards) use the +3.3v or +5v power, and the motors (disk drive motors and any fans) use the +12v power. The power supply must deliver a good, steady supply of DC current so that the system can operate properly.

If you look at a specification sheet for a typical PC power supply, you can see that the supply generates not only +3.3v, +5v, and +12v, but also –5v and –12v. The positive voltages seemingly power everything in the system (logic and motors), so what are the negative voltages used for? The answer is, not much! These additional negative voltages are not used at all in many modern systems, although they are still required for backward compatibility. Because the +3.3v signal is a relatively recent addition, power supplies do not generate a –3.3v signal DC current.

> **Note**
>
> When Intel began releasing processors that required a +3.3v power source, power supplies that supplied the additional output voltage were not yet available. As a result, motherboard manufacturers began adding voltage regulators to their products, which convert +5v current to +3.3v. Voltage regulators, however, also generate a lot of heat, which should always be avoided in a PC. Now that you can obtain power supplies and motherboards designed to supply and use +3.3v, you should not have to purchase a system that converts voltages on the motherboard.

◀◀   See "CPU Operating Voltages," p. 72

Although –5v and –12v are supplied to the motherboard via the power supply connectors, the motherboard uses only the +5v. The –5v signal is simply routed to the ISA bus on pin B5. The motherboard does not use it. Originally, the analog data separator circuits found in older floppy controllers used –5v, so it was supplied to the bus. Because modern controllers do not need the –5v, systems no longer use it. It is still required, however, because it is part of the ISA bus standard.

> **Note**
>
> Power supplies in systems with a Micro Channel Architecture (MCA bus) do not have –5v. This power signal was never needed in these systems because they always used a more modern floppy controller design. IBM no longer uses the MCA bus in its PCs, but you may encounter it on legacy systems. Also, certain PCI-only systems are now being produced that do not need –5v current.

The motherboard logic doesn't use the +12v and –12v signals either. They are routed to pins B9 and B7 of the ISA bus (respectively). Any adapter card on the bus can make use of these voltages if needed, but typically they are used by serial port driver/receiver circuits. If the motherboard has integrated serial ports, then it may use the +12v and –12v signals for those ports.

> **Note**
>
> The load placed on the +12v and –12v signals by a serial port is very small. For example, the PS/2 Dual Async adapter uses only 35mA of +12v and 35mA of –12v (0.035 amps each) to operate two ports.

Most newer serial port circuits no longer use 12v driver/receiver circuits. Instead, they now use circuits that run on only +3.3 or +5v. If you have serial ports such as these in your system, the –12v signal from your power supply will probably not be used.

The main function of the +12v power is to run disk drive motors. Usually, a large amount of current is available, especially in systems with a large number of drive bays (such as in a tower configuration). Besides disk drive motors, the +12v supply is used by any cooling fans in the system—which, of course, should always be running. A single cooling fan can draw between 100mA and 250mA (0.1 to 0.25 amps); however, most newer fans use the lower 100mA figure. Note that although most fans in desktop systems run on +12v, port-able systems may use fans that run on +5v, or even +3.3v.

In addition to supplying power to run the system, the power supply also ensures that the system does not run unless the power supplied is sufficient to operate the system properly. In other words, the power supply actually prevents the computer from starting up or operating until all the correct power levels are present.

Each power supply completes internal checks and tests before allowing the system to start. If the tests are successful, the power supply sends a special signal to the motherboard called *Power_Good*. If this signal is not present continuously, the computer does not run. Therefore, when the AC voltage dips and the power supply becomes overstressed or overheated, the Power_Good signal goes down and forces a system reset or complete shutdown. If you have ever worked on a system that seems dead when the power switch is on and the fan and hard disks are running, you know the effects of losing the Power_Good signal.

IBM originally implemented this conservative design so that the computer would not operate if the power became low or the supply, overheated or overstressed, caused output power to falter.

> **Note**
>
> You even can use the Power_Good feature as a method of designing and implementing a reset switch for the PC. The Power_Good line is wired to the clock generator circuit, which controls the clock and reset lines to the microprocessor. When you ground the Power_Good line with a switch, the chip and related circuitry stop the processor. They do so by killing the clock signal and then resetting the processor when the Power_Good signal appears after you release the switch. The result is a full hardware reset of the system. Later in this chapter, you can find instructions for installing such a reset switch in a system not already equipped with one.

Systems with newer motherboard form factors, such as the ATX and the LPX, include another special signal. This feature, called *PS_ON*, can be used to turn the power supply (and thus the system) off via software. It is sometimes known as the *soft-off feature*. PS_ON is most evident when you use it with an operating system that supports the Advanced Power Management (APM) standard such as Windows 9x. When you select the Shut Down the Computer option from the Start menu, the power supply soft-offs—that is, Windows automatically turns the computer completely off after it completes the OS shutdown sequence. A system without this feature only displays a message that it's safe to shut down the computer.

Power Supply Form Factors

The shape and general physical layout of a component is called the *form factor*. Items that share a form factor are generally interchangeable, at least as far as their size is concerned. When designing a PC, the engineers can choose to use one of the popular standard PSU (power supply unit) form factors, or they can elect to build their own.

Choosing the former means that a virtually inexhaustible supply of inexpensive replacement parts will be available in a variety of quality and power output levels. Going the custom route means additional time and expense for development. In addition, the PSU will be unique to the system and available only from the original manufacturer.

If you can't tell already, I am a fan of the industry-standard form factors! In the early days of PCs, the computer industry was dominated by companies—such as IBM—that manufactured most of their own proprietary components. When other manufacturers began to "clone" PCs on a large scale, this philosophy became increasingly impractical. The drive toward the standardization of PC components, which began at that time, continues today.

Until the introduction of Intel's ATX architecture in 1995, the form factors of the power supplies used in PC systems differed primarily in their size and their orientation in the computer case. ATX and related standards introduced some new features (such as the PS_ON signal), but virtually all the power supplies used in PCs now conform to the same basic electronic design.

Technically, the PSU in your PC is described as a *constant voltage half-bridge forward converting switching power supply*. *Constant voltage* means that the PSU puts out the same voltage to the computer's internal components, no matter what the voltage of AC current running it or the capacity (wattage) of the power supply. *Half-bridge forward converting* refers to the PSU's switching design and its power regulation technique. This type of power supply is sometimes known as a *switching supply*. Compared to other types of power supplies, this design provides an efficient power source and generates a minimum amount of heat. It also maintains a small size and a low price.

> **Note**
>
> Although two power supplies may share the same basic design and form factor, they can differ greatly in quality and efficiency. Later in this chapter, you'll learn about some of the features and specifications to look for when evaluating PC power supplies.

Currently, eight power supply form factors can be called *industry standard*. These different form factors are as follows:

PC/XT style	LPX style
AT/Desk style	ATX style
AT/Tower style	NLX style
Baby AT style	SFX style

Each of these power supply types is available in numerous different configurations and power output levels. The new PCs on the market today generally use the ATX or Mini-style power supply. The earlier form factors are largely obsolete, and the NLX and SFX styles are only just beginning to gain popularity in new systems.

◀◀ See "Motherboard Form Factors," p. 167

PC/XT Style. IBM's XT used the same basic power supply shape as the original PC, except that the new XT supply had more than double the power output capability. Because they were identical in both external appearance and in the type of connectors they used, you could easily install the better XT supply as an upgrade for a PC system. The tremendous popularity of the original PC and XT design led a number of manufacturers to begin building systems that mimicked their shape and layout. These *clones*, as they have been called, could interchange virtually all components with the IBM systems, including the power supply. Numerous manufacturers then began producing these components. Most of these components follow the form factor of one or more IBM systems. The PC/XT power supply and connectors are shown in Figure 6.1.

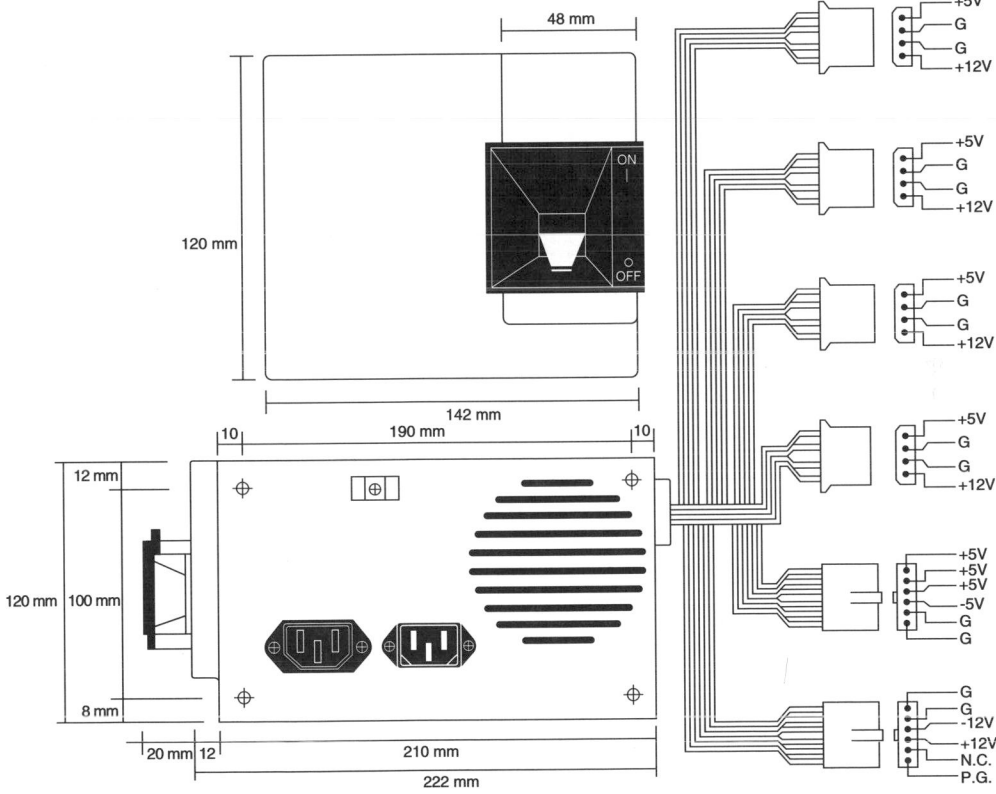

FIG. 6.1 PC/XT form factor power supply.

AT/Desk Style. The AT desktop system, introduced by IBM after the XT, had a larger power supply and a different form factor than the original PC/XT. This system, which was rapidly cloned, represented the basis for many IBM-compatible designs. The power supply used in these systems was called the *AT/Desktop-style power supply* (see Figure 6.2). Hundreds of manufacturers began making motherboards, power supplies, cases, and other components that were physically interchangeable with the original IBM AT.

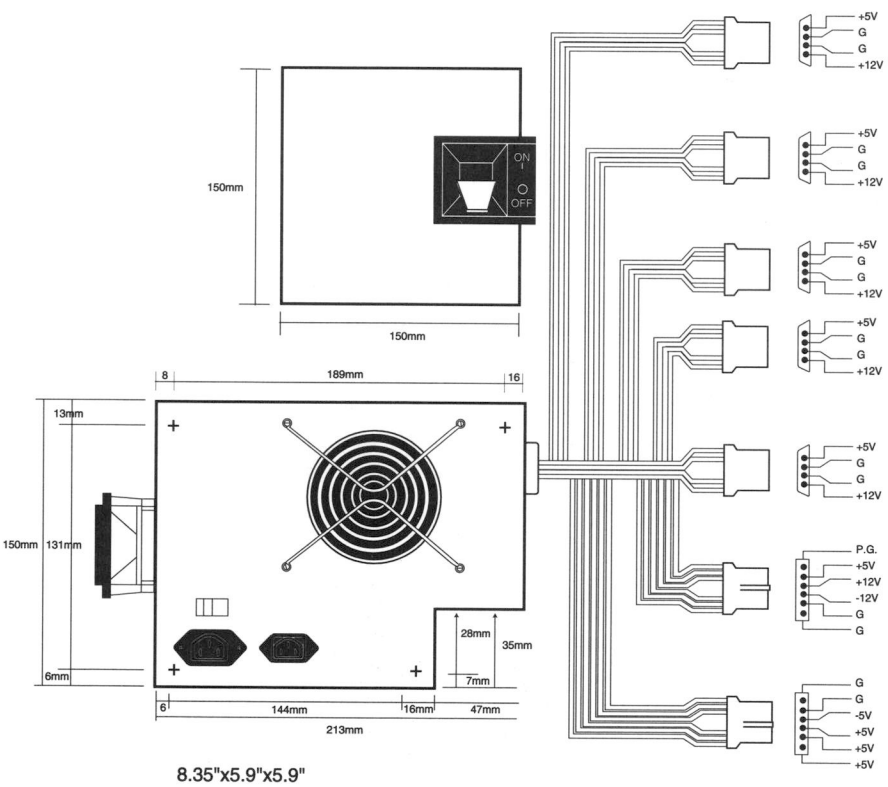

FIG. 6.2 AT/Desktop form factor power supply.

AT/Tower Style. The early PC-compatible market came up with some other variations on the AT theme that became quite popular. The *AT/Tower configuration* was basically a full-sized AT-style desktop system running on its side. The power supply and motherboard form factors were largely the same in the tower system as they were in the desktop. The tower configuration is not new; in fact, even IBM's original AT had a specially mounted logo that could be rotated when you ran the system on its side in the tower configuration.

The type of power supply used in a tower system is identical to that used in a desktop system, except for the location of the power switch. On most AT/Desktop systems, the power switch is located on the power supply (usually in the form of a large toggle switch). Most AT/Tower systems use an external switch attached to the power supply through a short four-wire cable. A full-sized AT power supply with a remote switch is called an *AT/Tower form factor power supply* (see Figure 6.3).

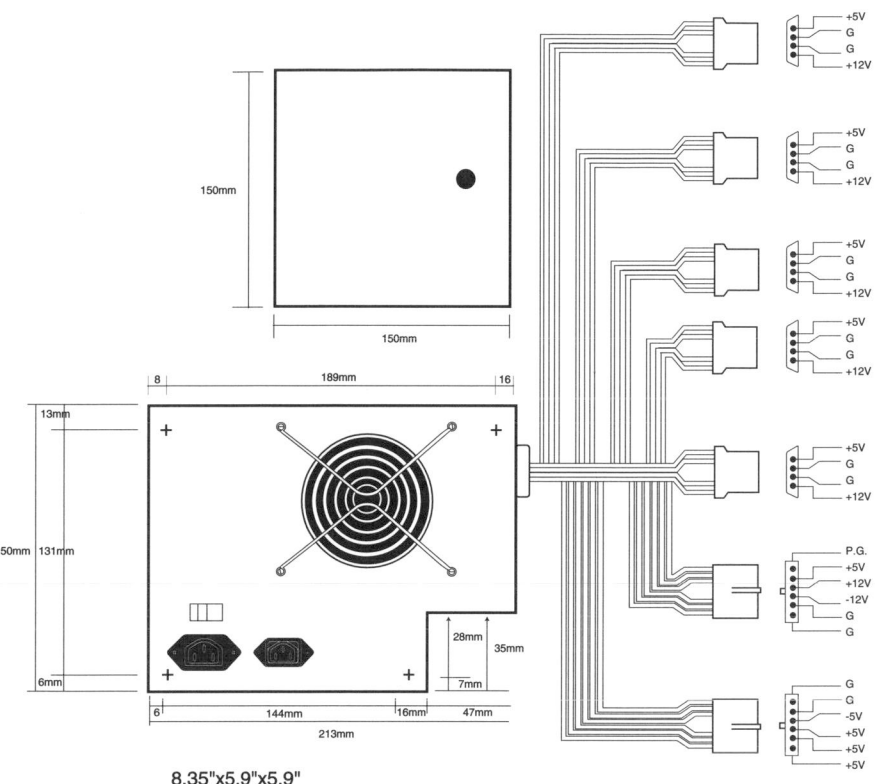

8.35"x5.9"x5.9"

FIG. 6.3 AT/Tower form factor power supply.

Baby AT Style. Another type of AT-based form factor is the so-called *Baby AT*, which is a shortened version of the full-sized AT system. The power supply in these systems is shortened in one dimension but matches the AT design in all other respects. Baby AT–style power supplies can fit into both a Baby AT chassis and the larger AT-style chassis; however, the full-sized AT/Tower power supply does not fit in the Baby AT chassis (see Figure 6.4). Because the Baby AT PSU performed all the same functions as the AT-style power supply, but was in a smaller package, it became the preferred form factor until overtaken by later designs.

LPX Style. The next PSU form factor to gain popularity was the *LPX* style, also called the *mini* and the *slimline* (see Figure 6.5). LPX systems are designed to have a smaller footprint and a lower height than AT-sized systems. These computers use a different motherboard configuration that mounts the expansion bus slots on a "riser" card that plugs into the motherboard. The expansion cards plug into this riser and are mounted sideways in the system, parallel to the motherboard. Because of its smaller case, an LPX system needs a smaller power supply. The PSU designed for LPX systems is smaller than the Baby AT style in every dimension and takes up less than half the space of its predecessor.

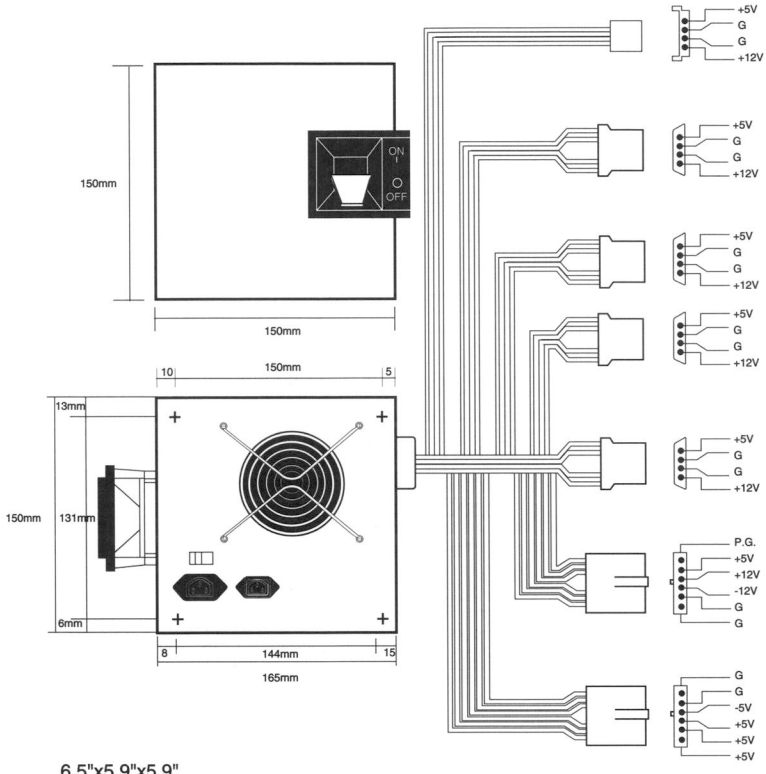

FIG. 6.4 Baby AT form factor power supply.

As with the Baby AT design in its time, the LPX power supply does the same job as its predecessor, but comes in a smaller package. The LPX power supply quickly found its way into many manufacturers' systems, soon becoming a *de facto* standard. It is still used in many of the PCs produced today, even in full-sized desktop and tower cases that can accept a larger form factor. Only in the last two years has the popularity of LPX been seriously challenged by the increasing acceptance of the ATX design.

ATX Style. One of the newer standards in the industry today is the *ATX form factor* (see Figure 6.6). The ATX specification, now in version 2.01, defines a new motherboard shape, as well as a new case and power supply form factor. The ATX power supply is based on the LPX design, but its differences are worth noting.

One difference is that the ATX specification originally called for the fan to be mounted along the inner side of the supply, where it could blow air across the motherboard and draw it in from outside the case at the rear. This kind of airflow runs in the opposite direction as most standard supplies, which blow air out the back of the supply through a hole in the case where the fan protrudes. The reverse-flow cooling provided by the ATX design forces air over the hottest components of the board, such as the processor, memory modules, and expansion slots, which are located in such a way as to take maximum advantage of the airflow. This eliminates the need for multiple fans in the system—including the CPU fans common in many systems today—the amount of noise produced by the system, and the amount of power needed to run the system.

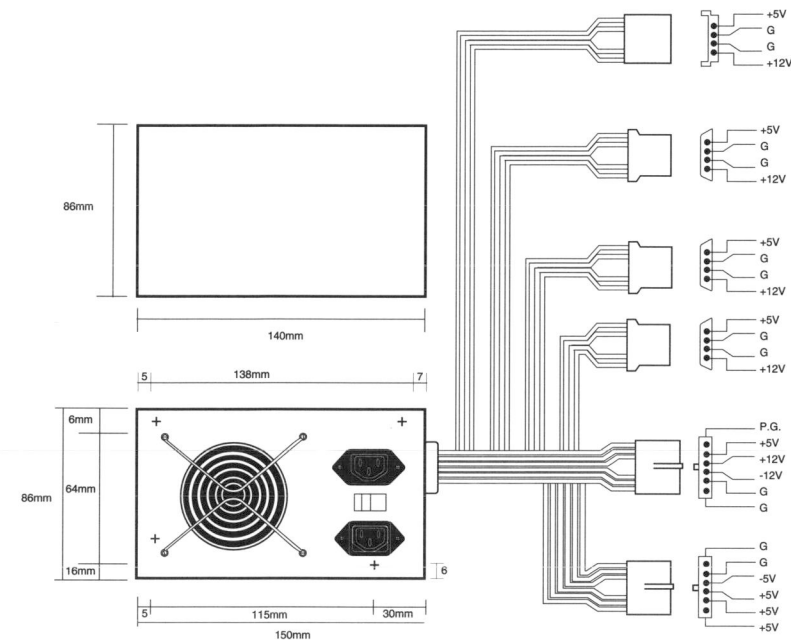

5.9"x5.5"x3.4"

FIG. 6.5 LPX form factor power supply.

Another benefit of the reverse-flow cooling is that the system remains cleaner, free from dust and dirt. The case is essentially pressurized, so air is continually forced out of the cracks in the case—the opposite of what happens with earlier designs. For this reason, the reverse-flow cooling design is often referred to as a *positive-pressure-ventilation* design. For example, if you held a lit cigarette in front of your floppy drive on a normal system, the smoke would be sucked in through the front of the drive and could contaminate the heads. On an ATX system with reverse-flow cooling, the smoke would be blown out away from the drive because the only air intake would be the single fan vent on the power supply at the rear. For systems that operate in extremely harsh environments, you can add a filter to the fan intake vent to further ensure that all the air entering the system is clean and free of dust.

Although this is theoretically the best way to ventilate a system, a properly designed positive-pressure system needs to use a more powerful fan to pull the required amount of air through a filter. Also, the filter has to be serviced on a periodic basis—depending upon operating conditions, it may need changing or cleaning as often as every week.

In addition, the heat load from the power supply on a fully loaded system exhausts heated air over the CPU, reducing its cooling capability. As newer CPUs create more and more heat, the cooling capability of the airflow becomes absolutely critical. In common practice, using a standard negative-pressure system with an exhaust fan on the power supply and a high-quality CPU cooling fan is the best solution. For this reason, the ATX power supply specification has been amended to allow for the older method of negative-pressure ventilation.

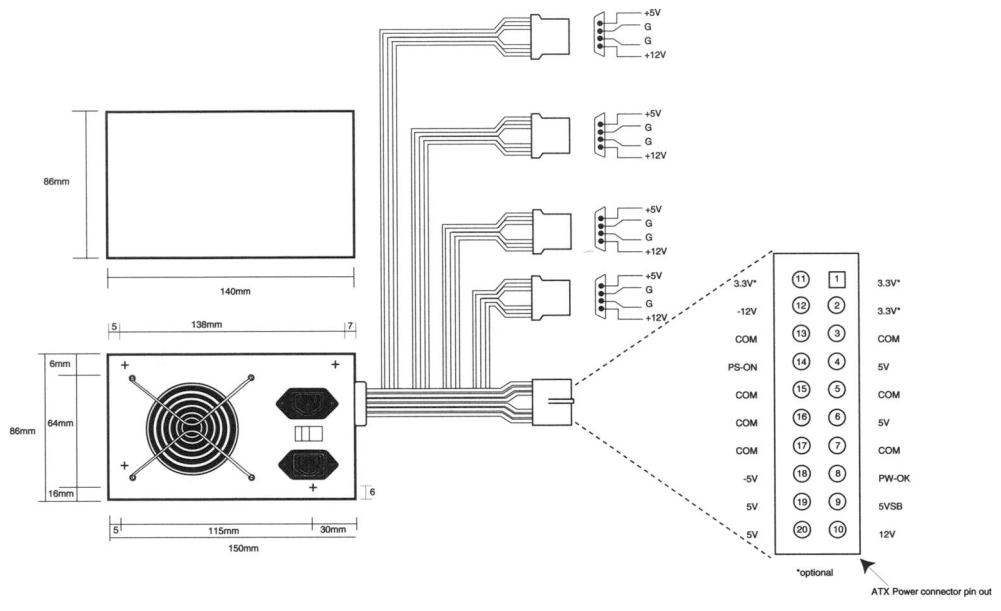

FIG. 6.6 ATX form factor power supply.

The ATX specification was first released by Intel in 1995. In 1996 it became increasingly popular in Pentium and Pentium Pro-based PCs, capturing 18% of the motherboard market. By the year 2000, this figure is expected to increase to 80%, with most Pentium and Pentium II systems using ATX motherboards, case designs, and power supplies.

The ATX form factor addresses several problems with the Baby AT and mini form factors. Two main problems with the power supply persist. One is that the traditional PC power supply has two connectors that plug into the motherboard. If you insert these connectors backward or out of their normal sequence, you will fry the motherboard. Most responsible system manufacturers "key" the motherboard and power supply connectors so that you cannot install them backward or out of sequence. However, some vendors of cheaper systems do not feature this keying on the boards or supplies they use.

The ATX form factor includes a new power plug for the motherboard to prevent users from plugging in their power supplies incorrectly. This new connector has 20 pins and is single-keyed. This makes it virtually impossible to plug it in backward. Because there is one connector instead of two almost identical ones, it is impossible to plug them in out of sequence. The new connector also supplies +3.3v, eliminating the need for voltage regulators on the motherboard to power the CPU and other +3.3v circuits.

Besides the new +3.3v signals, another set of signals is furnished by the ATX PSU that is not normally seen on standard power supplies. The set consists of the *Power_On* (PS_On) and *5v_Standby* (5VSB) signals, known collectively as *Soft Power*. Power_On is a motherboard signal that operating systems such as Windows 9x use to power the system down via software. These signals can also allow for the optional use of the keyboard to power the system back on—exactly like Apple Macintosh systems. The 5v_Standby signal is always active, giving the motherboard a limited source of power even when off.

The other problem solved by an ATX form factor power supply with reverse-cooling airflow is that of keeping today's system processors cool. But it only works in industrial applications, in which an industrial-duty power supply has been designed properly for the heat-load of the intended system and in which constant maintenance is provided. Most of the high-end Pentium and Pentium Pro systems on the market use active heat sinks on the processor, which means there is a small fan on the CPU designed to cool it. Intel and other manufacturers now package cooling fans with the CPU—some are actually permanently mounted on the CPU. For best results, use CPU fans only from reputable manufacturers because a CPU fan can be one of the most critical components for reliable operation.

> **Note**
>
> The cooling method described here is recommended by the ATX specification, but it is not required. Manufacturers can use alternative methodologies, such as the traditional outblowing fan arrangement, as well as active and/or passive heat sinks, on a system with an ATX motherboard. In fact, this may be a better solution for nonindustrial applications for which periodic maintenance of the power-supply filter is not assured. It is possible to modify a standard Baby AT or LPX power supply for use in an ATX system by adding the PS_ON and 5VSB signals and a +3.3v supply rail. If you plan to purchase a system with an ATX motherboard, don't automatically assume that you are getting an ATX power supply. If a vendor is unable to supply you with answers to technical questions such as this, it may be a good idea to try another vendor.

NLX Style. The NLX specification, also developed by Intel, defines a low-profile case and motherboard with many of the same attributes as the ATX. It uses a smaller form factor, however. As in previous slimline systems, the NLX motherboard uses a riser board for the expansion bus slots. The NLX motherboard is also designed for easy maintenance access; releasing a simple catch enables you to slide the entire motherboard out of the chassis. Just as the ATX architecture functionally replaced the Baby AT form factor in full-sized desktop and tower systems, NLX is intended to replace the LPX form factor.

The NLX specification does not define a new power supply form factor, but a separate NLX power supply recommendations document describes the features needed. To fit into an NLX case, a computer needs a power supply that is comparable to the LPX form factor in size, but which uses the same 20-pin connector, voltage signals, and fan arrangement as an ATX-style PSU. Although it's possible to modify an LPX power supply to support the new motherboard features, some manufacturers have begun producing power supplies specifically designed for use in NLX systems.

NLX is targeted more at the corporate computer market, which has feature and maintenance requirements quite different from those of home users. Adoption of the NLX standard is dragging slightly behind that of ATX, but quite a few computer manufacturers have announced systems that take advantage of the lower prices, smaller footprints, and easier maintenance that the new form factor can provide.

SFX Style (microATX Motherboards). Intel has released a third new motherboard specification, called microATX, that is intended for low-end systems that are designed with an even smaller footprint than NLX and with smaller power supply requirements. Because the microATX document defines only the motherboard form factor, Intel has also released the specification for a new power supply called SFX (see Figure 6.7).

The SFX power supply is specifically designed for use in small systems containing a limited amount of hardware. The PSU can provide 90 watts of continuous power (135 watts at its peak) in four voltages (+5, +12, –12, and +3.3v). This amount of power has proved to be sufficient for a small system with a Pentium II processor, an AGP interface, three expansion slots, and three peripheral devices—such as hard drives and CD-ROMs.

> **Note**
>
> The SFX power supply does not provide the –5v current required for full compliance with the ISA bus standard. MicroATX systems are supposed to use the PCI bus or the AGP interface for all the expansion cards installed in the computer, omitting the ISA bus entirely.

Although Intel designed the SFX power supply specification with the microATX motherboard form factor in mind, SFX is a wholly separate standard that is compliant with other motherboards as well. SFX power supplies use the same 20-pin connector defined in the ATX standard and include both the Power_On and 5v_Standby signals. The fan arrangement is different, however. Some modification to the power supply's metal housing is required in order to accommodate the ATX architecture.

On an SFX power supply, the fan is located on the surface of the housing, facing the inside of the computer's case. The fan draws the air into the power supply housing from the system cavity and expels it through a port at the rear of the system. Internalizing the fan in this way reduces system noise, but it also signifies a return to the pre-ATX airflow design model, in which the fan draws air into the case through the drive slots and other openings.

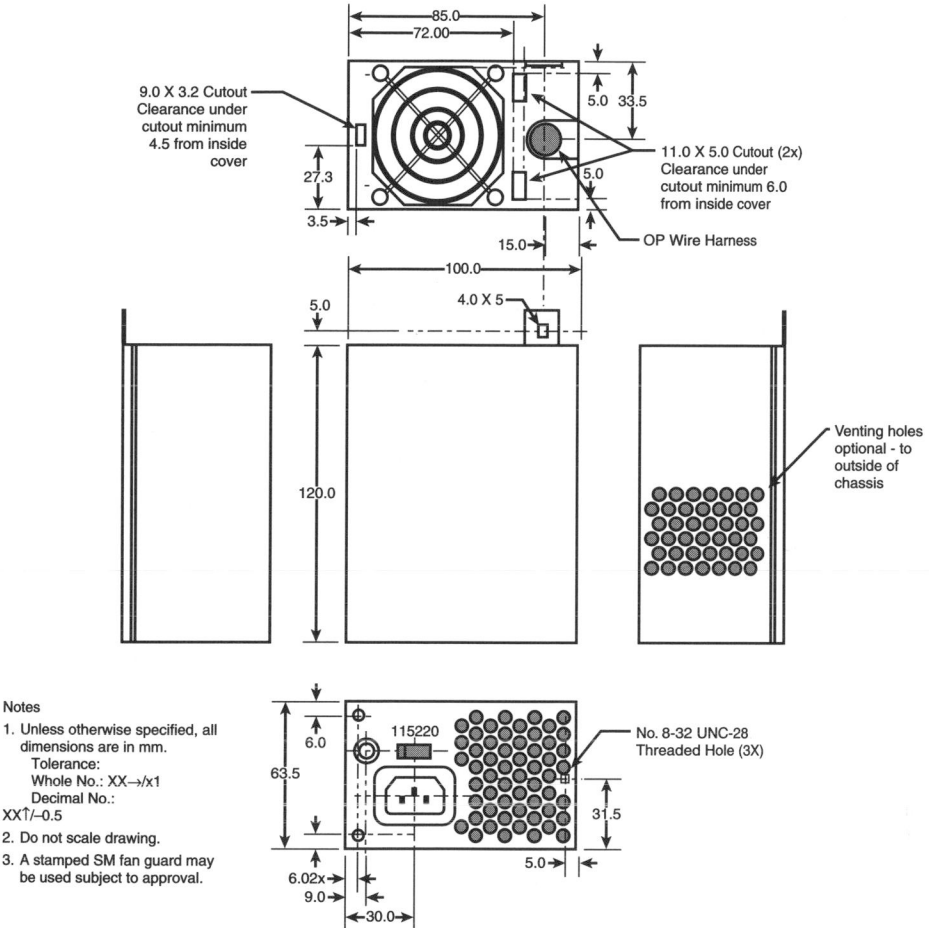

FIG. 6.7 SFX form factor power supply.

Power Supply Connectors

Table 6.1 shows the pinouts for most LPX, Baby AT, standard AT, and PC/XT-compatible systems. The two six-pin connectors (P8 and P9) attach the power supply to the motherboard, while P10 through P13 are identical four-pin connectors that you use to supply power to internal peripherals, such as floppy and hard disk drives.

All standard PC power supplies that use the P8 and P9 connectors have them installed end-to-end so that the two black-colored wires (ground connections) on both power cables are next to each other. Because the connectors usually have a clasp that prevents them from being inserted backward on the pins on the motherboards, the major concern is getting them in the correct order. Following the "black on black" rule keeps you safe. You must take care, however, to make sure no unconnected motherboard pins are between the two connectors when you install them. A properly installed connector connects to and covers every motherboard power pin—if any power pins are showing on either side of the connectors, the entire connector assembly is installed incorrectly, which can result in catastrophic failure for the motherboard and everything plugged into it at the time of power-up.

Some systems may have more or fewer drive connectors. For example, IBM's AT system power supplies have only three disk drive power connectors, although most AT/Tower-type power supplies have four drive connectors. Depending on their power ratings, some ATX supplies have as many as eight drive connectors.

If you are adding drives and need additional disk drive power connectors, "Y" splitter cables are available from many electronics supply houses (including Radio Shack). These cables can adapt a single power connector to service two drives. As a precaution, make sure that your total power supply output is capable of supplying the additional power.

Table 6.1   Typical PC/XT and AT Power Supply Connections

Connector	AT Type	PC/XT Type
P8-1	Power_Good (+5v)	Power_Good (+5v)
P8-2	+5v	Key (No connect)
P8-3	+12v	+12v
P8-4	–12v	–12v
P8-5	Ground (0)	Ground (0)
P8-6	Ground (0)	Ground (0)
P9-1	Ground (0)	Ground (0)
P9-2	Ground (0)	Ground (0)
P9-3	–5v	–5v
P9-4	+5v	+5v
P9-5	+5v	+5v
P9-6	+5v	+5v
P10-1	+12v	+12v
P10-2	Ground (0)	Ground (0)
P10-3	Ground (0)	Ground (0)
P10-4	+5v	+5v
P11-1	+12v	+12v
P11-2	Ground (0)	Ground (0)
P11-3	Ground (0)	Ground (0)
P11-4	+5v	+5v
P12-1	+12v	—
P12-2	Ground (0)	—
P12-3	Ground (0)	—
P12-4	+5v	—
P13-1	+12v	—
P13-2	Ground (0)	—
P13-3	Ground (0)	—
P13-4	+5v	—

Notice that the Baby AT and LPX power supplies also use the AT/Desktop or Tower pin configuration. The only other industry standard PSU-to-motherboard connector is the Molex 39-29-9202 (or equivalent). First used in the ATX form factor power supply, it is now used by the NLX and SFX form factors. This is a 20-pin keyed connector with pins configured, as shown in Table 6.2. The colors for the wires are those recommended by the ATX standard; however, they are not required for compliance to the specification (in other words, the colors could vary from manufacturer to manufacturer).

Tip

Although the PC/XT power supplies do not have any signal on pin P8-2, you can still use them on AT-type motherboards, or vice versa. The presence or absence of the +5v signal on that pin has little or no effect on system operation.

Table 6.2   ATX Power Supply Connections

Color	Signal	Pin	Pin	Signal	Color
Orange	+3.3v*	11	1	+3.3v*	Orange
Blue	−12v	12	2	+3.3v*	Orange
Black	GND	13	3	GND	Black
Green	PS_On	14	4	+5v	Red
Black	GND	15	5	GND	Black
Black	GND	16	6	+5v	Red
Black	GND	17	7	GND	Black
White	−5v	18	8	Power_Good	Gray
Red	+5v	19	9	+5VSB (Standby)	Purple
Red	+5v	20	10	+12v	Yellow

= Optional signal

Note

The ATX supply features several signals not seen before, such as the +3.3v, Power_On, and +5v_Standby signals. Therefore, it is difficult to adapt a standard LPX form factor supply to make it work properly in an ATX system, even though the shapes of the power supplies themselves are virtually identical.

ATX Optional Power Connector. In addition to the main 20-pin power connector, the ATX specification defines an optional six-pin connector (two rows of three pins each) as using 22 AWG wire to provide the signals shown in Table 6.3. The computer can use these signals to monitor and control the cooling fan, monitor the voltage of the +3.3v signal to the motherboard, and provide power and grounding to devices compliant with the IEEE 1394 (FireWire) standard.

Table 6.3 ATX Optional Power Supply Connections

Pin	Signal	Color
1	FanM	White
2	FanC	White w/blue stripe
3	+3.3v sense	White w/brown stripe
4	1394R	White w/black stripe
5	1394V	White w/red stripe
6	Reserved	

The FanM signal enables the operating system to monitor the status of the power supply's cooling fan so that it can take appropriate actions, such as shutting down the system if the fan fails.

An operating system can use the FanC signal with variable voltages to control the operation of the power supply's fan, shifting it into a low power state or shutting it off completely when the system is in sleep or standby mode. The ATX standard specifies that a voltage of +1v or less indicates that the fan is to shut down, while +10.5v or more instruct the fan to operate at full speed. The system designer can define intermediate voltages to operate variable-speed fans at various levels. If the power supply does not include a variable-speed fan circuit, any voltage level higher than +1v on the FanC signal is interpreted as a command to run the fan at its full (and only) speed.

> **Note**
>
> The SFX specification also defines the use of a six-pin control connector, but uses it only to provide a fan control signal on one pin. The other five pins are all reserved for future use.

Power Switch Connectors. Most of the power supplies used today employ a remote power switch that is accessible from the front of the computer case. In contrast, earlier form factors, such as the AT desktop and Baby AT, used a switch that was integrated into the power supply housing. Because the power supply was mounted in a rear corner of the case, the switch was inconveniently located on the back of the computer case.

Pre-ATX power supplies use a remote switch that is connected to the power supply through a standard four-wire cable. The ends of the cable are fitted with spade connector lugs, which plug onto the spade connectors on the power switch. The switch is usually a part of the case, so the power supply comes with the cable and no switch.

The cable from the power supply to the switch in the case contains four color-coded wires. There may also be a fifth wire supplying a ground connection to the case.

> **Caution**
>
> The remote power switch leads carry 110v AC current at all times. You could be electrocuted if you touch the ends of these wires with the power supply plugged in! Always make sure the power supply is unplugged before connecting or disconnecting the remote power switch.

The four or five wires are color coded as follows:

- The brown and blue wires are the live and neutral feed wires from the 110v power cord to the power supply. These wires are always hot when the power supply is plugged in.

- The black and white wires carry the AC feed from the switch back to the power supply. These leads should be hot only when the power supply is plugged in and the switch is turned on.

- A green wire or a green wire with a yellow stripe is the ground lead. It should be connected to the PC case, and should help ground the power supply to the case.

On the switch, the tabs for the leads are usually color coded; if not, you can still connect them easily. If no color coding is on the switch, then plug the blue and brown wires onto the tabs that are parallel to each other and the black and white wires to the tabs that are angled away from each other. See Figure 6.8 as a guide.

> ### Caution
>
> Although these wire color codings are used on most power supplies, they are not universal. I have encountered power supplies that did not use the same coloring scheme described here. Unless you can verify the color codes with the power supply manufacturer, always disconnect the power supply from the wall socket before handling any of these wires.

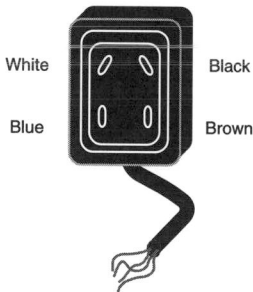

FIG. 6.8 Power supply remote switch connections.

As long as the blue and brown wires are on the one set of tabs and the black and white leads are on the other, the switch and supply will work properly. If you incorrectly mix the leads, you will likely blow the circuit breaker for the wall socket, because mixing them can create a direct short circuit.

All ATX and subsequent power supplies that employ the 20-pin motherboard connector use the PS_ON signal to power up the system. As a result, the remote switch does not physically control the power supply's access to the 110v AC power, as in the older style PSUs. Instead, the power supply's on or off status is toggled by a PS_ON signal received on pin 14 of the ATX connector.

The PS_ON signal can be generated physically by the computer's power switch or electronically by the operating system. PS_ON is an active low signal, meaning that all the DC power signals generated by the PSU are deactivated when PS_ON is held high, with the exception of the +5VSB (standby) signal on pin 9, which is active whenever the power supply is connected to an AC power source. The +5VSB signal provides the power for the remote switch on the case to operate while the computer is off. Thus, the remote switch in an ATX-style system (which should include most NLX and SFX systems) carries only +5v of DC power, rather than the full 110v AC current that is in the older form factors.

> **Caution**
>
> The continuous presence of the +5VSB signal on pin 9 of the ATX connector means that the motherboard is always receiving power from the PSU when connected to an AC source, even when the computer is turned off. As a result, it is even more crucial to unplug an ATX system from the power source before working inside the case than it is on an earlier model system.

Disk Drive Power Connectors. The disk drive connectors on power supplies are fairly universal with regard to pin configuration, and even wire color. Table 6.4 shows the standard disk drive power connector pinout and wire colors.

Pin	Wire Color	Signal
Table 6.4	**Disk Drive Power Connector Pinout**	
1	Yellow	+12v
2	Black	Gnd
3	Black	Gnd
4	Red	+5v

This information applies whether the drive connector is the larger Molex version or the smaller mini-version used on most 3 1/2-inch floppy drives. In each case, the pinouts and wire colors are the same. To determine the location of pin 1, look at the connector carefully. It is usually embossed in the plastic connector body; however, it is often tiny and difficult to read. Fortunately, these connectors are keyed and therefore difficult to insert incorrectly. Figure 6.9 shows the keying with respect to pin numbers on the larger drive power connector.

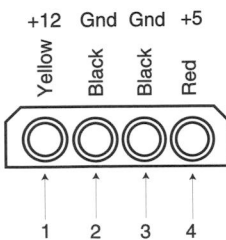

FIG. 6.9 A disk drive female power supply cable connector.

> **Note**
>
> Some drive connectors may supply only two wires—usually the +5v and a single ground (pins 3 and 4)—because the floppy drives in most newer systems run on only +5v and do not use the +12v at all.

Physical Connector Part Numbers. The physical connectors used in industry-standard PC power supplies were originally specified by IBM for the supplies used in the original PC/XT/AT systems. They used a specific type of connector between the power supply and the motherboard (the P8 and P9 connectors) and specific connectors for the disk drives. The motherboard connectors used in all the industry-standard power supplies were unchanged from 1981 (when the IBM PC appeared) until 1995 (when Intel released the ATX standard). The original PC's four-pin disk drive connector was augmented by a smaller (also four-pin) power connector when 3 1/2-inch floppy drives appeared in 1986. Table 6.5 lists the standard connectors used for motherboard and disk drive power.

Table 6.5   Physical Power Connectors

Connector Description	Female (on Power Cable)	Male (on Component)
ATX/NLX/SFX (20-pin)	Molex 39-29-9202	Molex 39-01-2200
ATX Optional (6-pin)	Molex 39-01-2960	Molex 39-30-1060
PC/AT/LPX Motherboard P8/P9	Burndy GTC6P-1	Burndy GTC 6RI
Disk Drive (large style)	AMP 1-480424-0	AMP 1-480426-0
Disk Drive (small style)	AMP 171822-4	AMP 171826-4

You can get these raw connectors through the electronics supply houses (Allied, Newark, and Digi-Key, for example) found in Appendix A, "Vendor List." You also can get complete cable assemblies, including drive adapters that convert the large connectors into small connectors; disk drive "Y" splitter cables; and motherboard power extension cables from a number of the cable and miscellaneous supply houses, such as Ci Design and Key Power.

> **Caution**
>
> Before you install additional connectors to your power supply using "Y" splitters or any other type of connector, be sure your power supply is capable of delivering sufficient power for all your internal peripherals. Overloading the power supply can cause damage to electrical components and stored data.

The Power_Good Signal

The Power_Good signal (sometimes called Power_OK or POK) is a +5v signal (with variation from +3.0 through +6.0v generally being considered acceptable) generated in the power supply when it has passed its internal self tests and the outputs have stabilized. This normally takes place anywhere from 0.1 to 0.5 seconds after you turn on the power supply switch. This power supply sends the signal to the motherboard, where it is received by the processor timer chip, which controls the reset line to the processor.

In the absence of Power_Good, the timer chip continuously resets the processor, which prevents the system from running under bad or unstable power conditions. When the timer chip receives the Power_Good signal, it stops resetting the processor, and the processor begins executing whatever code is at address FFFF:0000 (usually the ROM BIOS).

If the power supply cannot maintain proper outputs (such as when a brownout occurs), the Power_Good signal is withdrawn, and the processor is automatically reset. When the power output returns to its proper levels, the PSU regenerates the Power_Good signal and the system again begins operation (as if you had just powered on). By withdrawing Power_Good, the system never "sees" the bad power because it is "stopped" quickly (reset) rather than being allowed to operate using unstable or improper power levels, which can cause parity errors and other problems.

On pre-ATX systems, the Power_Good connection is made via connector P8-1 (P8 Pin 1) from the power supply to the motherboard. ATX and later systems use pin 8 of the 20-pin connector.

A well-designed power supply delays the arrival of the Power_Good signal until all the PSU's voltages stabilize after you turn the system on. Badly designed power supplies, which are found in *many* low-cost systems, often do not delay the Power_Good signal properly and enable the processor to start too soon. (The normal Power_Good delay is from 0.1 to 0.5 seconds.) Improper Power_Good timing also causes CMOS memory corruption in some systems. If you find that a system consistently fails to boot up properly the first time you turn on the switch but that it subsequently boots up if you press the reset or Ctrl+Alt+Delete warm boot command, you likely have a problem with the Power_Good timing. You must install a new, high-quality power supply and see whether it solves the problem.

Some cheaper power supplies do not have proper Power_Good circuitry and may just tie any +5v line to that signal. Some motherboards are more sensitive to an improperly designed or improperly functioning Power_Good signal than others. Intermittent startup problems are often the result of improper Power_Good signal timing. A common example is when you replace a motherboard in a system and then find that the system intermittently fails to start properly when you turn the power on. This can be very difficult to diagnose, especially for the inexperienced technician, because the problem appears to be caused by the new motherboard. Although it seems as if the new motherboard is defective, it usually turns out that the power supply is poorly designed. It either cannot produce stable enough power to properly operate the new board, or it has an improperly wired or timed Power_Good signal (which is more likely). In these situations, replacing the supply with a high-quality unit, in addition to the new motherboard, is the proper solution.

Power Supply Loading

PC power supplies are of a switching rather than a linear design. The switching type of design uses a high-speed oscillator circuit to generate different output voltages. It is very efficient in size, weight, and energy in comparison to the standard linear design, which uses a large internal transformer to generate different outputs. This type of transformer design is inefficient in at least three ways. First, the output voltage of the transformer linearly follows the input voltage (hence the name, linear), so any fluctuations in the AC power going into the system can cause problems with the output. Second, the high current requirements of a PC system require the use of heavy wiring in the transformer. Third, the 60Hz (hertz) frequency of the AC power supplied from your building is difficult to filter out inside the power supply, requiring large and expensive filter capacitors.

The switching supply, on the other hand, uses a switching circuit that "chops up" the incoming power at a relatively high frequency. This allows for the use of high-frequency transformers that are much lighter. Also, the higher frequency is much easier and cheaper to filter out at the output, and the input voltage can vary widely. Input ranging from 90 to 135 volts still produces the proper output levels, and many switching supplies can automatically adjust to 220-volt input.

One characteristic of all switching-type power supplies is that they do not run without a load. This means that you must have the supply plugged into something drawing power for the supply to work. If you simply have the power supply on a bench with nothing plugged into it, the supply either burns up or its protection circuitry shuts it down. Most power supplies are protected from no-load operation and shut down automatically. Some of the cheap clone supplies, however, lack the protection circuit and relay. They are destroyed after a few seconds of no-load operation. A few power supplies have their own built-in load resistors, so they can run even though no normal load is plugged in.

According to IBM specifications for the standard 192-watt power supply used in the original AT, a minimum load of 7.0 amps was required at +5v and a minimum of 2.5 amps was required at +12v for the supply to work properly.

Because floppy drives present no +12v load unless they are spinning, systems without a hard disk drive often do not operate properly. Some power supplies have a minimum load requirement for both the +5v and +12v sides. If you fail to meet this minimum load, the supply shuts down.

Because of this characteristic, when IBM used to ship AT systems without a hard disk, they plugged the hard disk drive power cable into a large 5-ohm 50-watt sandbar resistor, which was mounted in a little metal cage assembly where the drive would have been. The AT case had screw holes on top of where the hard disk would go, specifically designed to mount this resistor cage. Several computer stores I knew of in the mid-80s would order the diskless AT and install their own 20M or 30M drives, which they could get more cheaply from other sources than from IBM. They were throwing away the load resistors by the hundreds! I managed to grab a couple at the time, which is how I know the type of resistor they used.

This resistor would be connected between pin 1 (+12v) and pin 2 (Ground) on the hard disk power connector. This would place a 2.4-amp load on the supply's +12v output, drawing 28.8 watts of power—it would get hot!—and thus enabling the supply to operate normally. Note that the cooling fan in most power supplies draws approximately 0.1 to

0.25 amps, bringing the total load to 2.5 amps or more. If the load resistor were missing, the system would intermittently fail to start up or operate properly. The motherboard would draw +5v at all times, but +12v would normally be used only by motors, and the floppy drive motors would be off most of the time.

Most of the power supplies in use today do not require as much of a load as the original IBM AT power supply. In most cases, a minimum load of 0 to 0.3 amp at +3.3v, 2.0 to 4.0 amps at +5v, and 0.5 to 1.0 amps at +12v is considered acceptable. Most motherboards easily draw the minimum +5v current by themselves. The standard power supply cooling fan draws only 0.1 to 0.25 amps, so the +12v minimum load may still be a problem for a diskless workstation. Generally, the higher the rating on the supply, the more minimum load required; however, there are exceptions, so this is a specification you want to check when evaluating power supplies.

Some high-quality switching power supplies have built-in load resistors and can run under a no-load situation because the supply loads. Other high-quality power supplies, such as those from PC Power and Cooling, have no internal load resistors. They only require a small load on the +5 supply to operate properly. Many of the cheaper clone supplies, which often do not have built-in load resistors, may require +3.3v, +5v, and +12v loads to work.

If you want to bench test a power supply, make sure you place loads on all the PSU's positive voltage outputs. This is one reason why it is best to test the supply while it is installed in the system instead of testing it separately on the bench. For impromptu bench testing, you can use a spare motherboard and hard disk drive to load the outputs.

Power-Supply Ratings

A system manufacturer should be able to provide you with the technical specifications of the power supplies they use in their systems. This type of information may be found in the system's technical-reference manual, as well as on stickers attached directly to the power supply. Power-supply manufacturers can also supply this data, which is preferable if you can identify the manufacturer and contact them directly.

Tables 6.6 and 6.7 list power-supply specifications for several of IBM's units, from which the power supplies of many other systems are derived. The input specifications are listed as voltages, and the output specifications are listed as amps at several voltage levels. IBM reports output wattage level as "specified output wattage." If your manufacturer does not list the total wattage, you can convert amperage to wattage by using the following simple formula:

Watts = Volts × Amps

By multiplying the voltage by the amperage available at each output and then adding the results up, you can calculate the total capable output wattage of the supply.

Table 6.6 Power-Supply Output Ratings for IBM "Classic" Systems					
	PC	**Port-PC**	**XT**	**XT-286**	**AT**
Minimum Input Voltage	104	90	90	90	90
Maximum Input Voltage	127	137	137	137	137
110/220v Switching	No	Yes	No	Auto	Yes
Output Current (amps):					
+5v	7.0	11.2	15.0	20.0	19.8
−5v	0.3	0.3	0.3	0.3	0.3
+12v	2.0	4.4	4.2	4.2	7.3
−12v	0.25	0.25	0.25	0.25	0.3
Calculated output wattage	63.5	113.3	129.9	154.9	191.7
Specified output wattage	63.5	114.0	130.0	157.0	192.0

Table 6.6 shows the standard power supply output levels available in industry-standard form factors. Most manufacturers offer supplies with ratings from 100 watts to 450 watts or more. Table 6.7 shows the rated outputs at each of the voltage levels for supplies with different manufacturer-specified output ratings. To compile the table, I referred to the specification sheets for supplies from Astec Standard Power and PC Power and Cooling. Although most of the ratings are accurate, they are somewhat misleading for the higher wattage units.

Table 6.7 Typical Compatible Power-Supply Output Ratings							
Specified Output Wattage	**100W**	**150W**	**200W**	**250W**	**300W**	**375W**	**450W**
Output Current (amps):							
+5v	10.0	15.0	20.0	25.0	32.0	35.0	45.0
−5v	0.3	0.3	0.3	0.5	1.0	0.5	0.5
+12v	3.5	5.5	8.0	10.0	10.0	13.0	15.0
−12v	0.3	0.3	0.3	0.5	1.0	0.5	1.0
Calculated output wattage	97.1	146.1	201.1	253.5	297.0	339.5	419.5

Adding a +3.3v signal to the power supply modifies the equation significantly. Table 6.8 contains data for various ATX power supplies that include a +3.3v signal.

Table 6.8 ATX Power-Supply Output Ratings				
Specified Output Wattage	**235W**	**275W**	**300W**	**400W**
Output Current (amps):				
+3.3v	14.0	14.0	14.0	28.0
+5v	22.0	30.0	30.0	30.0

(continues)

Table 6.8 ATX Power-Supply Output Ratings Continued				
Specified Output Wattage	**235W**	**275W**	**300W**	**400W**
Max +3.3/+5v	125	150	150	215
–5v	0.5	0.5	0.5	1.0
+12v	8.0	10.0	12.0	14.0
–12v	1.0	1.0	1.0	1.0

If you compute the total output in the usual way, these PSUs seem to produce an output that is much higher than their ratings. The 300W model, for example, comes out at 354.7 watts. However, notice that the supply also has a maximum combined output for the +3.3v and +5v signals of 150 watts. This brings the total output to a more logical 308.5 watts.

Most PC power supplies have ratings between 150 and 300 watts. Although lesser ratings are not usually desirable, it is possible to purchase heavy-duty power supplies for most systems that have outputs as high as 500 watts.

The 300-watt and larger units are excellent for enthusiasts who are building fully optioned desktops or tower systems. These supplies run any combination of motherboard and expansion card, as well as a large number of disk drives and other peripherals. In most cases, you cannot exceed the ratings on these power supplies—the system will be out of room for additional items first!

Most power supplies are considered to be *universal*, or *worldwide*. That is, they can also run on the 220v, 50-cycle current used in Europe and many other parts of the world. Many power supplies that can switch from 110v to 220v input do so automatically, but a few require you to set a switch on the back of the power supply to indicate which type of power you will access.

If your supply does not switch automatically, make sure the voltage setting is correct. If you plug the power supply into a 110v outlet while set in the 220v setting, no damage will result, but the supply will certainly not operate properly until you correct the setting. On the other hand, if you are in a foreign country with a 220v outlet and have the switch set for 110v, you may cause some damage.

Power-Supply Specifications

In addition to power output, many other specifications and features go into making a high-quality power supply. I have had many systems over the years. My experience has been that if a brownout occurs in a room with several systems running, the systems with higher-quality power supplies and higher output ratings are far more likely to make it through the power disturbances unscathed, whereas others choke.

High-quality power supplies also help protect your systems. A power supply from a vendor such as Astec or PC Power and Cooling will not be damaged if any of the following conditions occur:

■ A 100 percent power outage of any duration

■ A brownout of any kind

■ A spike of up to 2,500v applied directly to the AC input (for example, a lightning strike or a lightning simulation test)

Decent power supplies have an extremely low current leakage to ground of less than 500 microamps. This safety feature is important if your outlet has a missing or improperly wired ground line.

As you can see, these specifications are fairly tough and are certainly representative of a high-quality power supply. Make sure that your supply can meet these specifications.

You can also use many other criteria to evaluate a PSU. The power supply is a component many users ignore when shopping for a PC, and it is therefore one that some system vendors may choose to skimp on. After all, a dealer is far more likely to be able to increase the price of a computer by spending money on additional memory or a larger hard drive than by installing a better power supply.

When buying a computer (or a replacement PSU), it is always a good idea to learn as much as possible about the power supply. However, many consumers are intimidated by the vocabulary and the statistics found in a typical PSU specification. Here are some of the most common parameters found on power supply specification sheets, along with their meanings:

■ *Mean Time Between Failures (MTBF) or Mean Time To Failure (MTTF)*. The (calculated) average interval, in hours, that the power supply is expected to operate before failing. Power supplies typically have MTBF ratings (such as 100,000 hours or more) that are clearly not the result of real-time empirical testing. In fact, manufacturers use published standards to calculate the results, based on the failure rates of the power supply's individual components. MTBF figures for power supplies often include the load to which the PSU was subjected (in the form of a percentage) and the temperature of the environment in which the tests were performed.

■ *Input Range (or Operating Range)*. The range of voltages that the power supply is prepared to accept from the AC power source. For 110v AC current, an input range of 90 to 135v is common; for 220v current, a 180 to 270v range is typical.

■ *Peak Inrush Current*. The greatest amount of current drawn by the power supply at a given moment immediately after it is turned on, expressed in terms of amps at a particular voltage. The lower the current, the less thermal shock the system experiences.

■ *Holdup Time*. The amount of time (in milliseconds) that a power supply's output remains within the specified voltage ranges after its input ceases. Values of 15–25 milliseconds are common for today's PSUs.

- *Transient Response.* The amount of time (in microseconds) a power supply takes to bring its output back the specified voltage ranges after a steep change of the output current. In other words, the amount of time it takes for the output power levels to stabilize after a device in the system starts or stops drawing power. Power supplies sample the current being used by the computer at regular intervals. When a device stops drawing power during one of these intervals (such as when a floppy drive stops spinning), the PSU may supply too high a voltage to the output for a brief time. This excess voltage is called *overshoot,* and the transient response is the time that it takes for the voltage to return to the specified level. Once a major problem that came with switching power supplies, overshoot has been greatly reduced in recent years. Transient response values are sometimes expressed in time intervals, and at other times are expressed in terms of a particular output change, such as "power output levels stay within regulation during output changes of up to 20%."

- *Overvoltage Protection.* The trip points for each output at which the power supply shuts down or squelches the signal for that output. Values can be expressed as a percentage (for example, 120% for +3.3 and +5v) or as raw voltages (for example, +4.6v for the +3.3v output and 7.0v for the +5v output).

- *Maximum Load Current.* The largest amount of current (in amps) that can be safely delivered through a particular output. Values are expressed as individual amperages for each output voltage. With these figures, you can calculate not only the total amount of power the PSU can supply, but also how many devices using those various voltages it can support.

- *Minimum Load Current.* The smallest amount of current (in amps) that must be drawn from a particular output for that output to function. If the current drawn from an output falls below the minimum, the power supply could be damaged or could automatically shut down.

- *Load Regulation (or Voltage Load Regulation).* When the current drawn from a particular output increases or decreases, the voltage changes slightly as well, usually increasing as the current rises. Load regulation is the change in the voltage for a particular output as it transitions from its minimum load to its maximum load (or vice versa). Values, expressed in terms of a +/– percentage, typically range from +/–1% to +/–5% for the +3.3, +5, and +12v outputs.

- *Line Regulation.* The change in output voltage as the AC input voltage transitions from the lowest to the highest value of the input range. A power supply should be capable of handling any AC voltage in its input range with a change in its output of 1 percent or less.

- *Efficiency.* The ratio of a PSU's power input to its power output, expressed in terms of a percentage. Values of 65–85% are common for power supplies today. The remaining 15–35% of the power input is converted to heat during the AC/DC conversion process. Although greater efficiency means less heat inside the computer (always a good thing) and lower electric bills, it should not be emphasized at the expense of precision, as evidenced in the PSU's load regulation and other parameters.

■ *Ripple (or Ripple and Noise, or AC Ripple, or PARD [Periodic and Random Deviation]).* The average voltage of all AC components' effects on the power supply's outputs, measured in millivolts peak-to-peak (RMS) for each output voltage. The effects can be caused by internal switching transients, feed through of the rectified line frequency, and other random noise.

Power-Supply Certifications

Many agencies around the world certify electric and electronic components for safety and quality. The most commonly known agency in the United States is Underwriters Laboratories, Inc. (UL). UL standard #1950; the *Standard for Safety of Information Technology Equipment, Including Electrical Business Equipment, Third Edition*; covers power supplies and other PC components. It is always a good idea to purchase power supplies and other devices that are UL-certified. It has often been said that although not every good product is UL-certified, no bad products are.

In Canada, electric and electronic products are certified by the Canadian Standards Agency (CSA). The German equivalents are TÜV Rheinland and VDE. NEMKO operates in Norway. These three agencies are responsible for certification of products throughout Europe. Power supply manufacturers that sell to an international market should have products that are certified at least by UL, the CSA, and TÜV—if not by all of the agencies listed, and more.

Apart from UL-type certifications, many power-supply manufacturers, even the most reputable ones, claim that their products have a Class B certification from the Federal Communications Commission, meaning that they meet FCC standards for electromagnetic and radio frequency interference (EMI/RFI). This is a contentious point, however, because the FCC does not certify power supplies as individual components. Title 47 of the Code of Federal Regulations, Part 15, Section 15.101(c) states as follows:

> "The FCC does NOT currently authorize motherboards, cases, and internal power supplies. Vendor claims that they are selling 'FCC-certified cases', 'FCC-certified motherboards' or 'FCC-certified internal power supplies' are false."

In fact, an FCC certification can be issued collectively only to a base unit consisting of a computer case, motherboard, and a power supply. Thus, a power supply purported to be FCC-certified was actually certified along with a particular case and motherboard—not necessarily the same case and motherboard you are using in your system. This does not mean, however, that the manufacturer is being deceitful, or that the power supply is inferior. If anything, this means that when evaluating power supplies, you should place less weight on the FCC certification than on other factors, such as UL certification.

Power-Use Calculations

When expanding or upgrading your PC, it is important to be sure your power supply is capable of providing sufficient current to power all the system's internal devices. One way to see whether your system is capable of expansion is to calculate the levels of power drain in the different system components and deduct the total from the maximum power supplied by the PSU. This calculation can help you decide whether you must upgrade the power supply to a more capable unit. Unfortunately, these calculations can be difficult to make because many manufacturers do not publish power consumption data for their products.

It can be difficult to get power-consumption data for many +5v devices, including motherboards and adapter cards. Motherboards can consume different power levels, depending on numerous factors. Most motherboards consume about 5 amps or so, but try to get information on the one you are using. For adapter cards, if you can find the actual specifications for the card, use those figures. To be on the conservative side, however, I usually go by the maximum available power levels set forth in the respective bus standards.

For example, consider the power-consumption figures for components in a modern PC, such as a desktop or slimline system with a 200-watt power supply rated for 20 amps at +5v and 8 amps at +12v. The ISA specification calls for a maximum of 2.0 amps of +5v and 0.175 amps of +12v power for each slot in the system. Most systems have eight slots, and you can assume that four are filled for the purposes of calculating power draw. The following calculation shows what happens when you subtract the amount of power necessary to run the different system components:

5v Power:	**20.0 Amps**
Less:	Motherboard –5.0
	4 slots filled at 2.0 each –8.0
	3 1/2- and 5 1/4-inch floppy drives –1.5
	3 1/2-inch hard disk drive –0.5
	CD-ROM drive –1.0
=Remaining power:	4.0 amps

12v Power:	**8.0 Amps**
Less:	4 slots filled at 0.175 each –0.7
	3 1/2-inch hard disk drive –1.0
	3 1/2- and 5 1/4-inch floppy drives –1.0
	Cooling fan –0.1
	CD-ROM drive –1.0
=Remaining power:	4.2 amps

In the preceding example, everything seems all right for the present. With half the slots filled, two floppy drives, and one hard disk, the system still has room for more. Problems with the power supply could come up, however, if this system were expanded to the extreme. With every slot filled and two or more hard disks, there definitely would be problems with the +5v current. However, the +12v does seem to have room to spare. You could add a CD-ROM drive or a second hard disk without worrying too much about the +12v power, but the +5v power would be strained.

If you anticipate loading up a system to the extreme—as in a high-end multimedia system, for example—you may want to invest in the insurance of a higher output power supply. For example, a 250-watt supply usually has 25 amps of +5v and 10 amps of +12v current, whereas a 300-watt unit has 32 amps of +5v power. These supplies enable you to fully load the system and are likely to be found in full-sized desktop or tower case configurations in which this type of expansion is expected.

Motherboards can draw anywhere from four to fifteen amps or more of +5v power to run. In fact, a single Pentium 66MHz CPU draws up to 3.2 amps of +5v power all by itself. A 200MHz Pentium Pro CPU or 400MHz Pentium II consumes up to 15 amps. Considering that systems with two or more processors are now becoming common, you could have 30 amps or more drawn by the processors alone. A motherboard such as this—with two CPUs and 128M or more of RAM for each CPU—might draw more than 40 amps all by itself. Very few "no-name" power supplies can supply this kind of current. For these applications, you should consider only high-quality, high-capacity power supplies from a reputable manufacturer, such as PC Power and Cooling.

In these calculations, bus slots are allotted maximum power in amps, as shown in Table 6.9.

Table 6.9   Maximum Power Consumption in Amps per Bus Slot

Bus Type	+5v Power	+12v Power	+3.3v Power
ISA	2.0	0.175	N/A
EISA	4.5	1.5	N/A
VL-Bus	2.0	N/A	N/A
16-Bit MCA	1.6	0.175	N/A
32-Bit MCA	2.0	0.175	N/A
PCI	5	0.5	7.6

As you can see from the table, ISA slots are allotted 2.0 amps of +5v and 0.175 amp of +12v power. Note that these are maximum figures. All cards do not draw this much power. If the slot has a VL-Bus extension connector, an additional 2.0 amps of +5v power are allowed for the VL-Bus.

Floppy drives can vary in power consumption, but most of the newer 3 1/2-inch drives have motors that run on +5v current in addition to the logic circuits. These drives usually draw 1.0 amps of +5v power and use no +12v at all. 5 1/4-inch drives use standard +12v motors that draw about 1.0 amps. These drives also require about 0.5 amps of +5v for the logic circuits. Most cooling fans draw about 0.1 amps of +12v power, which is negligible.

Typical 3 1/2-inch hard disks today draw about 1 amp of +12v power to run the motors—and only about 0.5 amp of +5v power for the logic. 5 1/4-inch hard disks, especially those that are full-height, draw much more power. A typical full-height hard drive draws 2.0 amps of +12v power and 1.0 amps of +5v power.

Another problem with hard disks is that they require much more power during the spinup phase of operation than during normal operation. In most cases, the drive draws double the +12v power during spinup, which can be 4.0 amps or more for the full-height drives. This tapers off to normal after the drive is spinning.

The figures that most manufacturers report for maximum power supply output are full duty-cycle figures. The PSU can supply these levels of power continuously. You usually can expect a unit that continuously supplies a given level of power to be capable of exceeding this level for some noncontinuous amount of time. A supply usually can offer 50% greater output than the continuous figure indicates for as long as one minute. Systems often use this cushion to supply the necessary power to spin up a hard disk drive. After the drive has spun to full speed, the power draw drops to a value within the system's continuous supply capabilities. Drawing anything over the rated continuous figure for any extended length of time causes the power supply to run hot and fail early, and can also create nasty symptoms in the system.

Tip

If you are using internal SCSI hard drives, you can ease the startup load on your power supply. The key is to enable the SCSI drives Remote Start option, which causes the drive to start spinning only when it receives a startup command over the SCSI bus. The effect is that the drive remains stationary (drawing very little power) until the very end of the POST and spins up right when the SCSI portion of the POST is begun.

If you have multiple SCSI drives, they all spin up sequentially based on their SCSI ID setting. This is designed so that only one drive is spinning up at any one time and so that no drives start spinning until the rest of the system has had time to start. This greatly eases the load on the power supply when you first power the system on.

In most cases, you enable Remote Start through your SCSI host adapter's setup program. This program may be supplied with the adapter on separate media, or it may be integrated into the adapter's BIOS and activated with a specific key combination at boot time.

The biggest cause of power-supply overload problems has historically been filling up the expansion slots and adding more drives. Multiple hard drives, CD-ROM drives, and floppy drives can create quite a drain on the system power supply. Make sure that you have enough +12v power to run all the drives you plan to install. Tower systems can be especially problematic because they have so many drive bays. Just because the case has room for the devices doesn't mean the power supply can support them. Make sure you have enough +5v power to run all your expansion cards, especially PCI cards. It pays to be conservative, but remember that most cards draw less than the maximum allowed. Today's newest processors can have very high current requirements for the +5 or +3.3-volt supplies. When selecting a power supply for your system, be sure to take into account any future processor upgrades.

Many people wait until an existing component fails before they replace it with an upgraded version. If you are on a tight budget, this "if it ain't broke, don't fix it" attitude may be necessary. Power supplies, however, often do not fail completely all at once; they can fail in an intermittent fashion or allow fluctuating power levels to reach the system, which results in unstable operation. You might be blaming system lockups on software bugs when the culprit is an overloaded power supply. If you have been running your original power supply for a long time and have upgraded your system in other ways, you should expect some problems.

Although there is certainly an appropriate place for the exacting power-consumption calculations you've read about in this section, a great many experienced PC users prefer the "don't worry about it" power calculation method. This technique consists of buying a system with a good quality 300- or 350-watt power supply (or installing such a supply yourself) and then upgrading the system freely, without concern for power consumption. Unless you plan to build a system with six SCSI drives and a dozen other peripherals, you will probably not exceed the capabilities of the PSU, and this method certainly requires far less effort.

Leave It On or Turn It Off?

Should you turn off a system when it is not in use? To answer this frequent question, you should understand some facts about electrical components and what makes them fail. Combine this knowledge with information on power consumption, cost, and safety, in order to come to your own conclusion. Because circumstances can vary, the best answer for your own situation might be different than for others, depending on your particular needs and applications.

Frequently, powering a system on and off does cause deterioration and damage to the components. This seems logical, but the simple reason is not obvious to most people. Many believe that flipping system power on and off frequently is harmful because it electrically "shocks" the system. The real problem, however, is temperature or thermal shock. As the system warms up, the components expand; and as it cools off, the components contract. In addition, various materials in the system have different thermal expansion coefficients, which means that they expand and contract at different rates. Over time, thermal shock causes deterioration in many areas of a system.

From a pure system-reliability viewpoint, it is desirable to insulate the system from thermal shock as much as possible. When a system is turned on, the components go from ambient (room) temperature to as high as 185 degrees F (85 degrees C) within 30 minutes or less. When you turn the system off, the same thing happens in reverse, and the components cool back to ambient temperature in a short period of time.

Thermal expansion and contraction remain the single largest cause of component failure. Chip cases can split, allowing moisture to enter and contaminate them. Delicate internal wires and contacts can break, and circuit boards can develop stress cracks. Surface-mounted components expand and contract at different rates than the circuit board they are mounted on, which causes enormous stress at the solder joints. Solder joints can fail due to the metal hardening from the repeated stress, resulting in cracks in the joint. Components that use heat sinks, such as processors, transistors, or voltage regulators, can overheat and fail because the thermal cycling causes heat sink adhesives to deteriorate, breaking the thermally conductive bond between the device and the heat sink. Thermal cycling also causes socketed devices and connections to loosen or "creep," which can cause a variety of intermittent contact failures.

Thermal expansion and contraction affect not only chips and circuit boards, but also things such as hard disk drives. Most hard drives today have sophisticated thermal compensation routines that make adjustments in head position relative to the expanding and contracting platters. Most drives perform this thermal compensation routine once every five minutes for the first 30 minutes the drive is running, and then every 30 minutes thereafter. In many drives, this procedure can be heard as a rapid "tick-tick-tick-tick" sound.

In essence, anything you can do to keep the system at a constant temperature prolongs the life of the system, and the best way to accomplish this is to leave the system either permanently on or off. Of course, if the system is never turned on in the first place, it should last a long time indeed!

Now, I am not saying that you should leave all systems on 24 hours a day. A system powered on and left unattended can be a fire hazard (I have had monitors spontaneously catch fire—luckily, I was there at the time), is a data security risk (from cleaning crews and other nocturnal visitors), can be easily damaged if moved while running, and wastes electrical energy.

I currently pay $0.11 for a kilowatt-hour of electricity. A typical desktop-style PC with display consumes at least 300 watts (0.3 kilowatt) of electricity (and that is a conservative estimate). This means that it would cost 3.3 cents to run my typical PC for an hour. Multiplying by 168 hours in a week means that it would cost $5.54 per week to run this PC continuously. If the PC were turned on at 9 a.m. and off at 5 p.m., it would be on only 40 hours per week and would cost only $1.32—a savings of $4.22 per week! Multiply this savings by 100 systems, and you are saving $422 per week. Multiply this by 1,000 systems, and you are saving $4,220 per week! Using systems certified under the new EPA Energy Star program (that is, "Green" PCs) would account for an additional savings of around $1 per system per week—or $1,000 per week for 1,000 systems. The great thing about Energy Star systems is that the savings are even greater if the systems are left on for long periods of time because the power management routines are automatic.

Based on these facts, my recommendations are that you power the systems on at the beginning of the workday and off at the end of the workday. Do not power the systems off for lunch, breaks, or any other short durations of time. Servers, of course, should be left on continuously. This seems to be the best compromise of system longevity with pure economics.

Power Management

As the standard PC configuration has grown to include capabilities formerly considered options, the power requirements of the system have increased steadily. Larger displays, CD-ROM drives, and audio adapters all need more power to run, and the cost of operating a PC rises steadily. To address these concerns, several programs and standards are now being developed that are intended to reduce the power needed to run a PC as much as possible.

For standard desktop systems, power management is a matter of economy and convenience. By turning off specific components of the PC when they are not in use, you can reduce the electric bill and avoid having to power the computer up and down manually.

For portable systems, power management is far more important. Adding CD-ROMs, speakers, and other components to a laptop or notebook computer reduces what is in many cases a short battery life even further. By adding new power management technology, a portable system can supply power only to the components it actually needs to run, thus extending the life of the battery charge.

Energy Star Systems

The EPA has started a certification program for energy-efficient PCs and peripherals. To be a member of this program, the PC or display must drop to a power draw at the outlet of 30 watts or less during periods of inactivity. Systems that conform to this specification get to wear the Energy Star logo. This is a voluntary program; however, many PC manufacturers are finding that it helps them sell their systems if they can advertise these systems as energy-efficient.

One problem with this type of system is that the motherboard and disk drives literally can *go to sleep*, which means they can enter a standby or sleep mode, in which they draw very little power. This causes havoc with some of the older power supplies because the low power draw does not provide enough of a load for them to function properly. Most of the newer supplies on the market, which are designed to work with these systems, have a very low minimum load specification. I suggest that you ensure that the minimum load will be provided by the equipment in your system if you buy a power supply upgrade. Otherwise, when the PC goes to sleep, it may take a power switch cycle to wake it up again. This problem would be most noticeable if you invested in a very high output supply and used it in a system that draws very little power to begin with.

Advanced Power Management

Advanced Power Management (APM) is a specification jointly developed by Intel and Microsoft that defines a series of interfaces between power management-capable hardware and a computer's operating system. When it is fully implemented, APM can automatically switch a computer between five states, depending on the system's current activity. Each state represents a further reduction in power use, accomplished by placing unused components into a low-power mode. The five system states are as follows:

- *Full On*. The system is completely operational, with no power management occurring.

- *APM Enabled*. The system is operational, with some devices being power managed. Unused devices may be powered down and the CPU clock slowed or stopped.

- *APM Standby*. The system is not operational, with most devices in a low power state. The CPU clock may be slowed or stopped, but operational parameters are retained in memory. When triggered by a specific user or system activities, the system can return to the APM Enabled state almost instantaneously.

- *APM Suspend*. The system is not operational, with most devices unpowered. The CPU clock is stopped and operational parameters are saved to disk for later restoration. When triggered by a wakeup event, the system returns to the APM Enabled state relatively slowly.

- *Off*. The system is not operational. The power supply is off.

APM requires support from both hardware and software to function. In this chapter, you've already seen how ATX-style power supplies can be controlled by software commands using the Power_On signal and the six-pin optional power connector. Manufacturers are also integrating the same sort of control features into other system components, such as motherboards, monitors, and disk drives.

Operating systems that support APM, such as Windows 9x, trigger power management events by monitoring the activities performed by the computer user and the applications running on the system. However, the OS does not address the power management capabilities of the hardware directly.

A system can have many different hardware devices and many different software functions participating in APM functions, which makes communication difficult. To address this problem, both the operating system and the hardware have an abstraction layer that facilitates communication between the various elements of the APM architecture.

The operating system runs an APM driver that communicates with the various applications and software functions that trigger power management activities, while the system's APM-capable hardware devices all communicate with the system BIOS. The APM driver and the BIOS communicate directly, completing the link between the OS and the hardware.

Thus, for APM to function, there must be support for the standard built into the system's individual hardware devices, the system BIOS, and the operating system (which includes the APM driver). Without all of these components, APM activities cannot occur.

> **Tip**
>
> If, for any reason, you find that power management activities cause problems on your system, such as operating system freeze-ups or hardware malfunctions, the easiest way to disable APM is through the system BIOS. Most BIOSs that support APM include an option to disable it. This breaks the chain of communication between the operating system and the hardware, causing all power management activities to cease. Although it is also possible to achieve the same end by removing the APM driver from the operating system, Windows 9x's Plug-and-Play (PnP) feature detects the system's APM capabilities whenever you restart the computer and attempts to reinstall the APM driver.

Power Supply Problems

A weak or inadequate power supply can put a damper on your ideas for system expansion. Some systems are designed with beefy power supplies, as if to anticipate a great deal of system add-ons and expansion components. Most desktop or tower systems are built in this manner. Some systems have inadequate power supplies from the start, however, and cannot adequately service the power-hungry options you might want to add.

The wattage rating can sometimes be very misleading. Not all 300-watt supplies are created the same. People familiar with high-end audio systems know that some watts are better than others. Cheap power supplies may in fact put out the rated power, but what about noise and distortion? Some of the supplies are under-engineered to just barely meet their specifications, whereas others may greatly exceed their specifications. Many of the cheaper supplies supply noisy or unstable power, which can cause numerous problems with the system. Another problem with under-engineered power supplies is that they can run hot and force the system to do so as well. The repeated heating and cooling of solid-state components eventually causes a computer system to fail, and engineering principles dictate that the hotter a PC's temperature, the shorter its life. Many people recommend replacing the original supply in a system with a heavier duty model, which solves the problem. Because power supplies come in common form factors, finding a heavy-duty replacement for most systems is easy, as is the installation process.

Some of the available replacement power supplies have higher-capacity cooling fans than the originals, which can greatly prolong system life and minimize overheating problems, especially for the newer, hotter-running processors. If system noise is a problem, models with special fans can run more quietly than the standard models. These PSUs often use larger-diameter fans that spin more slowly, so they run more quietly and move the same amount of air as the smaller fans. PC Power and Cooling specializes in heavy-duty and quiet supplies; Astec has several heavy-duty models as well.

Ventilation in a system is also important. You must ensure adequate airflow to cool the hotter items in the system. Many processors today use passive heat sinks that require a steady stream of air to cool the chip. If the processor heat sink has its own fan, this is not much of a concern. If you have free expansion slots, it's a good idea to space out the boards in your system to permit airflow between them. Place the hottest running boards nearest the fan or the ventilation holes in the system. Make sure that there is adequate airflow around the hard disk drive, especially for those that spin at high rates of speed. Some hard disks can generate quite a bit of heat during operation. If the hard disks overheat, data can be lost.

Always make sure you run your computer with the case cover on, especially if you have a loaded system. Removing the cover can actually cause a system to overheat. With the cover off, the power supply fan no longer draws air through the system. Instead, the fan ends up cooling the supply only, and the rest of the system must be cooled by simple convection. Although most systems do not immediately overheat for this reason, several of my own systems, especially those that are fully expanded, have overheated within 15 to 30 minutes when run with the case cover off.

In addition, be sure that any empty slot positions have the filler brackets installed. If you leave these brackets off after removing a card, the resultant hole in the case disrupts the internal airflow and may cause higher internal temperatures.

If you experience intermittent problems that you suspect are related to overheating, a higher-capacity replacement power supply is usually the best cure. Specially designed supplies with additional cooling fan capacity also can help. At least one company sells a device called a *fan card,* but I am not convinced these are a good idea. Unless the fan is positioned to draw air to or from outside the case, all it does is blow hot air around inside the system and provide a spot cooling effect for anything it is blowing on. In fact, adding fans in this manner contributes to the overall heat inside the system because the fan consumes power and generates heat.

CPU-mounted fans are an exception because they are designed only for spot cooling of the CPU. Many of the newer processors run so much hotter than the other components in the system that a conventional finned aluminum heat sink cannot do the job. In this case, a small fan placed directly over the processor provides a spot cooling effect that keeps the processor temperatures down. One drawback to these active processor cooling fans is that the processor overheats instantly and can even be damaged if they fail. Whenever possible, try to use the biggest passive (finned aluminum) heat sink you can find and purchase a CPU fan from a reputable vendor.

Power Supply Troubleshooting

Troubleshooting the power supply basically means isolating the supply as the cause of problems within a system and, if necessary, replacing it.

> **Caution**
>
> It is rarely recommended that an inexperienced user open a power supply to make repairs because of the dangerous high voltages present. Even when unplugged, power supplies can retain dangerous voltage and must be discharged (like a monitor) before service. Such internal repairs are beyond the scope of this book and are specifically not recommended unless the technician knows what he or she is doing.

Many symptoms lead me to suspect that the power supply in a system is failing. This can sometimes be difficult for an inexperienced technician to see because at times there appears to be little connection between the symptom and the cause—the power supply.

For example, in many cases a "parity check" error message can indicate a problem with the power supply. This may seem strange because the parity check message specifically refers to memory that has failed. The connection is that the power supply powers the memory, and memory with inadequate power fails.

It takes some experience to know when this type of failure is power related, not caused by the memory. One clue is the repeatability of the problem. If the parity check message (or other problem) appears frequently and identifies the same memory location each time, I would suspect defective memory is the problem. However, if the problem seems random, or if the memory location the error message cites as having failed seems random, I would suspect improper power as the culprit. The following is a list of PC problems that often are power supply–related:

- Any power-on or system startup failures or lockups.
- Spontaneous rebooting or intermittent lockups during normal operation.
- Intermittent parity check or other memory-type errors.
- Hard disk and fan simultaneously failing to spin (no +12v).
- Overheating due to fan failure.
- Small brownouts cause the system to reset.
- Electric shocks felt on the system case or connectors.
- Slight static discharges disrupt system operation.

In fact, just about any intermittent system problem can be caused by the power supply. I always suspect the supply when flaky system operation is a symptom. Of course, the following fairly obvious symptoms point right to the power supply as a possible cause:

- System is completely dead (no fan, no cursor)
- Smoke
- Blown circuit breakers

If you suspect a power supply problem, some of the simple measurements and the more sophisticated tests outlined in this section can help you determine whether the power supply is at fault. Because these measurements may not detect some intermittent failures, you might have to use a spare power supply for a long-term evaluation. If the symptoms and problems disappear when a "known good" spare unit is installed, you have found the source of your problem.

Digital Multi-Meters

One simple test you can perform on a power supply is to check the output voltages. This shows whether a power supply is operating correctly and whether the output voltages are within the correct tolerance range. Note that you must measure all voltages with the power supply connected to a proper load, which usually means testing while the power supply is still installed in the system.

Selecting a Meter. You need a simple *Digital Multi-Meter (DMM)* or *Digital Volt-Ohm Meter (DVOM)* to perform voltage and resistance checks on electronic circuits (see Figure 6.10). You should use only a DMM instead of the older needle-type multi-meters because the older meters work by injecting a 9v signal into the circuit when measuring resistance, which damages most computer circuits.

A DMM uses a much smaller voltage (usually 1.5v) when making resistance measurements, which is safe for electronic equipment. You can get a good DMM with many different features from several sources. I prefer the small pocket-sized meters for computer work because they are easy to carry around.

Some features to look for in a good DMM are as follows:

- *Pocket size.* This is self-explanatory, but small meters are available that have many, if not all, the features of larger ones. The elaborate features found on some of the larger meters are not really needed for computer work.

- *Overload protection.* This means that if you plug the meter into a voltage or current beyond the meter's capability to measure, the meter protects itself from damage. Cheaper meters lack this protection and can be easily damaged by reading current or voltage values that are too high.

- *Autoranging.* This means that the meter automatically selects the proper voltage or resistance range when making measurements. This is preferable to the manual range selection; however, really good meters offer both autoranging capability and a manual range override.

- *Detachable probe leads.* The leads can be easily damaged, and sometimes a variety of differently shaped probes are required for different tests. Cheaper meters have the leads permanently attached, which means that you cannot easily replace them. Look for a meter with detachable leads that plug into the meter.

- *Audible continuity test.* Although you can use the ohm scale for testing continuity (0 ohms indicates continuity), a continuity test function causes the meter to produce a beep noise when continuity exists between the meter test leads. By using the sound, you can quickly test cable assemblies and other items for continuity. After you use this feature, you will never want to use the ohms display for this purpose again.

- *Automatic power off.* These meters run on batteries, and the batteries can easily be worn down if the meter is accidentally left on. Good meters have an automatic shutoff that turns off the unit when it senses no readings for a predetermined period of time.

■ *Automatic display hold.* This feature enables you to hold the last stable reading on the display even after the reading is taken. This is especially useful if you are trying to work in a difficult-to-reach area single-handedly.

■ *Minimum and maximum trap.* This feature enables the meter to trap the lowest and highest readings in memory and hold them for later display, which is especially useful if you have readings that are fluctuating too quickly to see on the display.

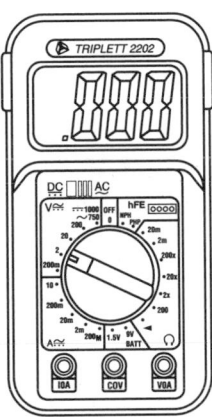

FIG. 6.10 A typical Digital Multi-Meter.

Although you can get a basic pocket DMM for as little as $20, one with all of these features is priced in the $100–$200 range. Radio Shack carries some nice inexpensive units, and you can purchase the high-end models from electronics supply houses, such as Newark or Digi-Key.

Measuring Voltage. To measure voltages on a system that is operating, you must use a technique called *back probing* on the connectors. You cannot disconnect any of the connectors while the system is running, so you must measure with everything connected. Nearly all the connectors you need to probe have openings in the back where the wires enter the connector. The meter probes are narrow enough to fit into the connector alongside the wire and make contact with the metal terminal inside. The technique is called *back probing* because you are probing the connector from the back. You must use this back probing technique to perform virtually all of the following measurements.

To test a power supply for proper output, check the voltage at the Power_Good pin (P8-1 on AT, Baby AT, and LPX supplies; pin 8 on the ATX-type connector) for +3v to +6v of power. If the measurement is not within this range, the system never sees the Power_Good signal and therefore does not start or run properly. In most cases, the power supply is bad and must be replaced.

Continue by measuring the voltage ranges of the pins on the motherboard and drive power connectors. If you are measuring voltages for testing purposes, any reading within 10% of the specified voltage is considered acceptable, although most manufacturers of high-quality power supplies specify a tighter 5% tolerance. For ATX power supplies, the specification requires that voltages must be within 5% of the rating, except for the 3.3v current, which must be within 4%.

Desired Voltage	Loose Tolerance		Tight Tolerance	
	Min. (–10%)	Max. (+8%)	Min. (–5%)	Max. (+5%)
+3.3v	2.97v	3.63v	3.135	3.465
+/–5.0v	4.5v	5.4v	4.75	5.25
+/–12.0v	10.8v	12.9v	11.4	12.6

The Power_Good signal has tolerances that are different from the other signals, although it is nominally a +5v signal in most systems. The trigger point for Power_Good is about +2.5v, but most systems require the signal voltage to be within the tolerances listed:

Signal	Minimum	Maximum
Power_Good (+5v)	3.0v	6.0v

Replace the power supply if the voltages you measure are out of these ranges. Again, it is worth noting that any and all power-supply tests and measurements must be made with the power supply properly loaded, which usually means that it must be installed in a system and the system must be running.

Specialized Test Equipment

You can use several types of specialized test gear to test power supplies more effectively. Because the power supply is one of the most failure-prone items in PCs today, it is wise to have these specialized items if you service many PC systems.

Load Resistors for Bench Testing a Power Supply. Bench testing a power supply requires some special setup because all PC power supplies require a load to operate.

Variable Voltage Transformer. When testing power supplies, it is sometimes desirable to simulate different AC voltage conditions at the wall socket to observe how the supply reacts. A *variable voltage transformer* is a useful test device for checking power supplies because it enables you to exercise control over the AC line voltage used as input for the power supply (see Figure 6.11). This device consists of a large transformer mounted in a housing with a dial indicator that controls the output voltage. You plug the line cord from the transformer into the wall socket and plug the PC power cord into the socket provided on the transformer. The knob on the transformer can be used to adjust the AC line voltage received by the PC.

Most variable transformers can adjust their AC output from 0v to 140v, no matter what the AC input (wall socket) voltage is. Some can cover a range from 0v to 280v as well. You can use the transformer to simulate brownout conditions, enabling you to observe the PC's response. Thus, you can check a power supply for proper Power_Good signal operation, among other things.

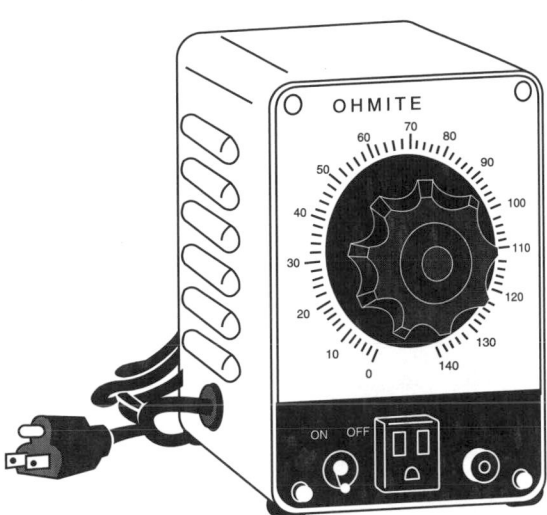

FIG. 6.11   A variable voltage transformer.

By running the PC and dropping the voltage until the PC shuts down, you can see how much "reserve" is in the power supply for handling a brownout or other voltage fluctuations. If your transformer can output voltages in the 200v range, you can test the capability of the power supply to run on foreign voltage levels. A properly functioning supply should operate between 90v to 135v but should shut down cleanly if the voltage is outside that range.

One indication of a problem is seeing "parity check" type error messages when you drop the voltage to 80v. This indicates that the Power_Good signal is not being withdrawn before the power supply output to the PC fails. The PC should simply stop operating as the Power_Good signal is withdrawn, causing the system to enter a continuous reset loop.

Variable voltage transformers are sold by a number of electronic parts supply houses, such as Newark and Digi-Key. You should expect to pay anywhere from $100 to $300 for this device.

Repairing the Power Supply

Hardly anyone actually repairs power supplies anymore, primarily because it is usually cheaper simply to replace the supply with a new one. Even high-quality power supplies are not that expensive when compared to the labor required to repair them.

A defective power supply is usually discarded unless it happens to be one of the higher-quality or more expensive units. In that case, it is usually wise to send the supply out to a company that specializes in repairing power supplies and other components. These companies usually provide what is called *depot repair,* which means you send the supply to them; they repair it and return it to you. If time is of the essence, most of the depot repair companies immediately send you a functional equivalent to your defective supply and take yours in as a core charge. Depot repair is the recommended way to service many PC components, such as power supplies, monitors, and printers. If you take your PC in to a conventional service outlet, they often determine which component has the problem and send it out to be depot repaired. You can do that yourself and save the markup that the repair shop normally charges in such cases.

For those with experience around high voltages, it might be possible to repair a failing supply with two relatively simple operations; however, these require opening the supply. I do not recommend doing so but I mention it only as an alternative to replacement in some cases.

Most manufacturers try to prevent you from entering the supply by sealing it with special tamper-proof Torx screws. These screws use the familiar Torx star driver, but also have a tamper-prevention pin in the center that prevents a standard driver from working. Most tool companies such as Jensen or Specialized sell sets of *TT (tamperproof Torx) bits*, which remove the tamper-resistant screws. Other manufacturers rivet the power supply case shut, which means you must drill out the rivets to gain access.

> **Caution**
>
> The manufacturers place these obstacles there for a reason—to prevent entry by those who are inexperienced with high voltage. Consider yourself warned!

Most power supplies have an internal fuse that is part of the overload protection. If this fuse is blown, the supply does not operate. It is possible to replace this fuse if you open the supply. Be aware, however, that in most cases an underlying power supply problem caused the fuse to blow, and replacing it only causes it to blow again until you address the root cause of the problem. In this case, you are better off sending the unit to a professional depot repair company. The vendor list in Appendix A lists several companies that do depot repair on power supplies and other components.

PC power supplies have an internal voltage adjustment control that the manufacturer calibrates and sets at the factory. Over time, the condition of some of the components in the supply can change, thus altering the output voltages. If this is the case, you may be able to access the adjustment control and tweak it to bring the voltages back to where they should be.

Several adjustable controls are in the supply—usually small variable resistors that you can turn with a screwdriver.

> **Caution**
>
> You should use a nonconductive tool, such as a fiberglass or plastic screwdriver designed for this purpose. If you dropped a metal tool into an operating supply, dangerous sparks and possibly fire could result—not to mention the danger of electrocution and damage to the supply.

You also have to figure out which of the adjustments are for voltage and which are for each voltage signal. This requires some trial-and-error testing. You can mark the current positions of all the resistors, begin measuring a single voltage signal, and try moving each adjuster slightly until you see the voltage change. If you move an adjuster and nothing changes, put it back to the original position you marked. Through this process, you can locate and adjust each of the voltages to the standard 3.3v, 5v, and 12v levels.

Obtaining Replacement Units

Most of the time, it is simply easier, safer, or less expensive (considering the time and materials involved) to replace the power supply rather than to repair it. As mentioned earlier, replacement power supplies are available from many manufacturers. Before you can shop for a supplier, however, you should consider other purchasing factors.

Deciding on a Power Supply

When you are shopping for a new power supply, you should take several factors into account. First, consider the power supply's shape, or form factor. For example, the power supply used in an AT-style system differs in size from the one used in a slimline computer. The larger AT form factor power supplies simply will not fit into a slimline case.

Apart from electrical considerations, power supply form factors can differ physically in their size, shape, screw-hole positions, connector type, number of connectors, fan location, and switch position. However, systems that use the same form factor can easily interchange power supplies. When ordering a replacement supply, you need to know which form factor your system requires.

Some systems use proprietary power supply designs, which makes replacement more difficult. If a system uses one of the common form factor power supplies, replacement units are available from hundreds of vendors. An unfortunate user of a system with a nonstandard form factor supply does not have this kind of choice and must get a replacement from the original manufacturer of the system—and usually pay through the nose for the unit. Although you can find standard form factor supplies for under $100, the proprietary units from some manufacturers run as high as $400 or more. PC buyers often overlook this and discover too late the consequences of having nonstandard components in a system.

◀◀ See "Power Supply Form Factors," p. 393

IBM, for example, used a number of PSU designs for the PS/2 systems, with little interchangeability possible between them. Some of the supplies do interchange, especially between any that have the same or similar cases, such as the Model 60, 65, and 80. Another example of a PC manufacturer that has sometimes used proprietary power supply designs is Compaq. Some of their systems do not use standard form factor PSUs, which means that Compaq usually is the only place from which you can get a replacement. If the power supply in some Compaq Deskpro systems "goes south," you can expect to pay over $400 for a replacement, and the replacement unit will be no better or quieter than the one you are replacing. You have little choice in the matter because almost no one offers Compaq form factor power supplies except for Compaq. One exception is that PC Power and Cooling offers excellent replacement power supplies for the earlier Compaq Portable systems and for the Deskpro series. These replacement power supplies have higher-output power levels than the original supplies from Compaq and cost much less.

Sources for Replacement Power Supplies

Because one of the most failure-prone items in PC systems is the power supply, I am often asked to recommend a replacement. Literally hundreds of companies manufacture PC power supplies, and I certainly have not tested them all. I can, however, recommend some companies whose products I have come to know and trust.

Although other high-quality manufacturers are out there, at this time I recommend power supplies from either Astec Standard Power or PC Power and Cooling.

Astec makes the power supplies used in most of the high-end systems by IBM, Hewlett-Packard, Apple, and many other name-brand systems. They have power supplies available in a number of standard form factors (AT/Tower, Baby AT, LPX, and ATX) and a variety of output levels. They have power supplies with ratings of up to 450 watts and power supplies especially designed for "green" PCs, which meet the EPA Energy Star requirements for low-power consumption. Their "green" power supplies are specifically designed to achieve high efficiency at low-load conditions. Be aware that high-output supplies from other manufacturers may have problems with very low loads. Astec also makes a number of power supplies for laptop and notebook PC systems and has numerous non-PC type supplies.

PC Power and Cooling has a complete line of power supplies for PC systems. They make supplies in all the standard PC form factors used today. Versions are available in a variety of different quality and output levels, from inexpensive replacements to very high-quality high-output models with ratings of up to 450 watts. They even have versions with built-in battery backup, redundant power systems, and a series of special models with high-volume, low-speed (quiet) fan assemblies. Their quiet models are especially welcome to people who work in quiet homes or offices and are annoyed by the fan noise that some power supplies emanate.

PC Power and Cooling also has units available that fit some of Compaq's proprietary designs. This can be a real boon if you have to service or repair Compaq systems because the PC Power and Cooling units are available in higher output ratings than Compaq's. These units cost much less than Compaq and bolt in as direct replacements.

The support offered by PC Power and Cooling is excellent also, and they have been in business a long time, which is rare in this industry. Besides power supplies, they also have an excellent line of cases.

A high-quality power supply from either of these vendors can be one of the best cures for intermittent system problems and can go a long way toward ensuring trouble-free operation in the future.

Using Power-Protection Systems

Power-protection systems do just what the name implies: They protect your equipment from the effects of power surges and power failures. In particular, power surges and spikes can damage computer equipment, and a loss of power can result in lost data. In this section, you learn about the four primary types of power-protection devices available and when you should use them.

Before considering any further levels of power protection, you should know that a good quality power supply already affords you a substantial amount of protection. High-end power supplies from the vendors I recommend are designed to provide protection from higher-than-normal voltages and currents, and they provide a limited amount of power-line noise filtering. Some of the inexpensive aftermarket power supplies probably do not have this sort of protection. If you have an inexpensive computer, further protecting your system might be wise.

Caution

All the power protection features in this chapter and the protection features in the power supply inside your computer require that the computer's AC power cable be connected to a ground.

Many older homes do not have three-prong (grounded) outlets to accommodate grounded devices.

Do not use a three-pronged adapter (that bypasses the three-prong requirement and enables you to connect to a two-prong socket) to plug in a surge suppressor, computer, or UPS into a two-pronged outlet. They often don't provide a good ground and can inhibit the capabilities of your power-protection devices.

It is also a good idea to test your power sockets to make sure they are grounded. Sometimes outlets, despite having three-prong sockets, are not connected to a ground wire; an inexpensive socket tester (available at most hardware stores) can detect this condition.

Of course, the easiest form of protection is to turn off and unplug your computer equipment (including your modem) when a thunderstorm is imminent. When this is not possible, however, there are other alternatives.

Power supplies should stay within operating specifications and continue to run a system if any of these power line disturbances occur:

- Voltage drop to 80v for up to 2 seconds

- Voltage drop to 70v for up to .5 seconds

- Voltage surge of up to 143v for up to 1 second

IBM also states that neither their power supplies, nor systems will be damaged by the following occurrences:

- Full power outage

- Any voltage drop (brownout)

- A spike of up to 2,500v

Because of their internal protection, many computer manufacturers that use high-quality PSUs state in their documentation that external surge suppressors are not needed with their systems.

To verify the levels of protection built into the existing power supply in a computer system, an independent laboratory subjected several unprotected PC systems to various spikes and surges of up to 6,000v—considered the maximum level of surge that can be transmitted to a system through an electrical outlet. Any higher voltage would cause the power to arc to the ground within the outlet. None of the systems sustained permanent damage in these tests. The worst thing that happened was that some of the systems rebooted or shut down if the surge was more than 2,000v. Each system restarted when the power switch was toggled after a shutdown.

I do not use any real form of power protection on my systems, and they have survived near-direct lightning strikes and powerful surges. The most recent incident, only 50 feet from my office, was a direct lightning strike to a brick chimney that blew the top of the chimney apart. None of my systems (which were running at the time) were damaged in any way from this incident; they just shut themselves down. I was able to restart each system by toggling the power switches. An alarm system located in the same office, however, was destroyed by this strike. I am not saying that lightning strikes or even much milder spikes and surges cannot damage computer systems—another nearby lightning strike did destroy a modem and serial adapter installed in one of my systems. I was just lucky that the destruction did not include the motherboard.

This discussion points out an important oversight in some power-protection strategies: Do not forget to provide protection from spikes and surges on the phone line.

The automatic shutdown of a computer during power disturbances is a built-in function of most high-quality power supplies. You can reset the power supply by flipping the power switch from on to off and back on again. Some power supplies even have an auto-restart function. This type of power supply acts the same as others in a massive surge or spike situation: It shuts down the system. The difference is that after normal power re-sumes, the power supply waits for a specified delay of three to six seconds and then resets itself and powers the system back up. Because no manual switch resetting is re-quired, this feature may be desirable in systems functioning as network servers or in those found in other unattended locations.

The first time I witnessed a large surge cause an immediate shutdown of all my systems, I was extremely surprised. All the systems were silent, but the monitor and modem lights were still on. My first thought was that everything was blown, but a simple toggle of each system-unit power switch caused the power supplies to reset, and the units powered up with no problem. Since that first time, this type of shutdown has happened to me several times, always without further problems.

The following types of power-protection devices are explained in the sections that follow:

- Surge suppressors
- Line conditioners
- Standby power supplies (SPS)
- Uninterruptible power supplies (UPS)

Surge Suppressors (Protectors)

The simplest form of power protection is any one of the commercially available surge protectors—that is, devices inserted between the system and the power line. These devices, which cost between $20 and $200, can absorb the high-voltage transients produced by nearby lightning strikes and power equipment. Some surge protectors can be effective for certain types of power problems, but they offer only very limited protection.

Surge protectors use several devices, usually *metal-oxide varistors (MOVs)*, that can clamp and shunt away all voltages above a certain level. MOVs are designed to accept voltages as high as 6,000v and divert any power above 200v to ground. MOVs can handle normal surges, but powerful surges such as a direct lightning strike can blow right through them. MOVs are not designed to handle a very high level of power and self-destruct while shunting a large surge. These devices therefore cease to function after either a single large surge or a series of smaller ones. The real problem is that you cannot easily tell when they no longer are functional. The only way to test them is to subject the MOVs to a surge, which destroys them. Therefore, you never really know if your so-called surge protector is protecting your system.

Some surge protectors have status lights that let you know when a surge large enough to blow the MOVs has occurred. A surge suppressor without this status indicator light is useless because you never know when it has stopped protecting.

Underwriters Laboratories has produced an excellent standard that governs surge suppressors, called *UL 1449*. Any surge suppressor that meets this standard is a very good one, and definitely offers a line of protection beyond what the power supply in your PC already offers. The only types of surge suppressors worth buying, therefore, should have two features:

- Conformance to the UL 1449 standard
- A status light indicating when the MOVs are blown

Units that meet the UL 1449 specification say so on the packaging or directly on the unit. If this standard is not mentioned, it does not conform. Therefore, you should avoid it.

Another good feature to have in a surge suppressor is a built-in circuit breaker that can be manually reset rather than a fuse. The breaker protects your system if it or a peripheral develops a short. These better surge suppressors usually cost about $40.

Phone Line Surge Protectors

In addition to protecting the power lines, it is critical to provide protection to your systems from any connected phone lines. If you are using a modem or fax board that is plugged into the phone system, any surges or spikes that travel through the phone line can damage your system. In many areas, the phone lines are especially susceptible to lightning strikes, which are the largest cause of fried modems and damage to the computer equipment attached to them.

Several companies manufacture or sell simple surge protectors that plug in between your modem and the phone line. These inexpensive devices can be purchased from most electronics supply houses. Most of the cable and communication products vendors listed in Appendix A sell these phone line surge protectors. Some of the standard power line surge protectors include connectors for phone line protection as well.

Line Conditioners

In addition to high-voltage and current conditions, other problems can occur with incoming power. The voltage might dip below the level needed to run the system, resulting in a brownout. Forms of electrical noise other than simple voltage surges or spikes might travel through the power line, such as radio-frequency interference or electrical noise caused by motors or other inductive loads.

Remember two things when you wire together digital devices (such as computers and their peripherals):

■ Any wire can act as an antenna and have voltage induced in it by nearby electromagnetic fields, which can come from other wires, telephones, CRTs, motors, fluorescent fixtures, static discharge, and, of course, radio transmitters.

■ Digital circuitry responds with surprising efficiency to noise of even a volt or two, making those induced voltages particularly troublesome. The electrical wiring in your building can act as an antenna, picking up all kinds of noise and disturbances.

A line conditioner can handle many of these types of problems. A *line conditioner* is designed to remedy a variety of problems. It filters the power, bridges brownouts, suppresses high-voltage and current conditions, and generally acts as a buffer between the power line and the system. A line conditioner does the job of a surge suppressor, and much more. It is more of an active device, functioning continuously, rather than a passive device that activates only when a surge is present. A line conditioner provides true power conditioning and can handle myriad problems. It contains transformers, capacitors, and other circuitry that can temporarily bridge a brownout or low-voltage situation. These units usually cost from $100 to $300, depending on the power-handling capacity of the unit.

Backup Power

The next level of power protection includes *backup power-protection devices*. These units can provide power in case of a complete blackout, which provides the time needed for an orderly system shutdown. Two types are available: the *standby power supply* (*SPS*) and the *uninterruptible power supply* (*UPS*). The UPS is a special device because it does much more than just provide backup power: It is also the best kind of line conditioner you can buy.

Standby Power Supplies (SPS). A standby power supply is known as an *offline device*: It functions only when normal power is disrupted. An SPS system uses a special circuit that can sense the AC line current. If the sensor detects a loss of power on the line, the system quickly switches over to a standby battery and power inverter. The power inverter converts the battery power to 110v AC power, which is then supplied to the system.

SPS systems do work, but sometimes a problem occurs during the switch to battery power. If the switch is not fast enough, the computer system shuts down or reboots anyway, which defeats the purpose of having the backup power supply. A truly outstanding SPS adds to the circuit a *ferroresonant transformer*, a large transformer with the capability to store a small amount of power and deliver it during the switch time. This device functions as a buffer on the power line, giving the SPS almost uninterruptible capability.

SPS units also may or may not have internal line conditioning of their own. Under normal circumstances, most cheaper units place your system directly on the regular power line and offer no conditioning. The addition of a ferroresonant transformer to an SPS gives it additional regulation and protection capabilities because of the buffer effect of the transformer. SPS devices without the ferroresonant transformer still require the use of a line conditioner for full protection. SPS systems usually cost from a couple hundred to several thousands of dollars, depending on the quality and power-output capacity.

Uninterruptible Power Supplies (UPS). Perhaps the best overall solution to any power problem is to provide a power source that is conditioned and that cannot be interrupted—which is the definition of an uninterruptible power supply. UPSs are known as *online systems* because they continuously function and supply power to your computer systems. Because some companies advertise ferroresonant SPS devices as though they were UPS devices, many now use the term *true UPS* to describe a truly online system. A true UPS system is constructed in much the same way as an SPS system; however, because the computer is always operating from the battery, there is no switching circuit.

In a true UPS, your system always operates from the battery. A voltage inverter converts from 12v DC to 110v AC. You essentially have your own private power system that generates power independently of the AC line. A battery charger connected to the line or wall current keeps the battery charged at a rate equal to or greater than the rate at which power is consumed.

When the AC current supplying the battery charger fails, a true UPS continues functioning undisturbed because the battery-charging function is all that is lost. Because the computer was already running off the battery, no switch takes place, and no power disruption is possible. The battery begins discharging at a rate dictated by the amount of load your system places on the unit, which (based on the size of the battery) gives you plenty of time to execute an orderly system shutdown. Based on an appropriately scaled storage battery, the UPS functions continuously, generating power and preventing unpleasant surprises. When the line power returns, the battery charger begins recharging the battery, again with no interruption.

> **Note**
>
> Occasionally, a UPS can accumulate too much storage and not enough discharge. When this occurs, the UPS emits a loud alarm, alerting you that it's full. Simply unplugging the unit from the AC power source for a while can discharge the excess storage (as it powers your computer) and drain the UPS of the excess.

Many SPS systems are advertised as though they were true UPS systems. The giveaway is the unit's *switch time*. If a specification for switch time exists, the unit cannot be a true UPS because UPS units never switch. However, a good SPS with a ferroresonant transformer can virtually equal the performance of a true UPS at a lower cost.

> **Note**
>
> Many UPSs today come equipped with a cable and software that enables the protected computer to shut down in an orderly manner on receipt of a signal from the UPS. This way, the system can shut down properly even if the computer is unattended. Some operating systems, such as Windows NT, contain their own UPS software components.

UPS cost is a direct function of both the length of time it can continue to provide power after a line current failure and how much power it can provide. You should therefore purchase a UPS that provides you with enough power to run your system and peripherals and enough time to close files and provide an orderly shutdown. Remember, however, to manually perform a system shutdown procedure during a power outage. You will probably need your monitor plugged into the UPS and the computer. Be sure the UPS you purchase can provide sufficient power for all the devices you must connect to it.

Because of a true UPS's almost total isolation from the line current, it is unmatched as a line conditioner and surge suppressor. The best UPS systems add a ferroresonant transformer for even greater power conditioning and protection capability. This type of UPS is the best form of power protection available. The price, however, can be high. To find out just how much power your computer system requires, look at the UL sticker on the back of the unit. This sticker lists the maximum power draw in watts, or sometimes in just volts and amperes. If only voltage and amperage are listed, multiply the two figures to calculate the wattage.

As an example, if the documentation for a system indicates that the computer can require as much as 110v at a maximum current draw of 5 amps, the maximum power the system can draw is about 550 watts. This wattage is for a system with every slot full, two hard disks, and one floppy—in other words, a system at the maximum possible level of expansion. The system should never draw any more power than that; if it does, a 5-ampere fuse in the power supply will blow. This type of system normally draws an average of 300 watts; to be safe when you make calculations for UPS capacity, however, be conservative. Use the 550-watt figure. Adding a monitor that draws 100 watts brings the total to 650 watts or more. Therefore, to run two fully loaded systems, you'll need an

1100-watt UPS. Don't forget two monitors, each drawing 100 watts. Therefore, the total is 1,300 watts. A UPS of that capacity or greater will cost approximately $500–$700. Unfortunately, that is what the best level of protection costs. Most companies can justify this type of expense only for critical-use PCs, such as network servers.

> **Note**
>
> The highest-capacity UPS sold for use with a conventional 15-amp outlet is about 1,400 watts. If it's any higher, you risk tripping a 15-amp circuit when the battery is charging heavily and the inverter is drawing maximum current.

In addition to the total available output power (wattage), several other factors can differentiate one UPS from another. The addition of a ferroresonant transformer improves a unit's power conditioning and buffering capabilities. Good units also have an inverter that produces a true sine wave output; the cheaper ones may generate a square wave. A *square wave* is an approximation of a sine wave with abrupt up-and-down voltage transitions. The abrupt transitions of a square wave signal are not compatible with some computer equipment power supplies. Be sure that the UPS you purchase produces a signal compatible with your computer equipment. Every unit has a specification for how long it can sustain output at the rated level. If your systems draw less than the rated level, you have some additional time.

> **Caution**
>
> Be careful. Most UPS systems are not designed for you to sit and compute for hours through an electrical blackout. They are designed to provide power only to essential components and to remain operating long enough to allow for an orderly shutdown. You pay a large amount for units that provide power for more than 15 minutes or so. At some point, it becomes more cost effective to buy a generator than to keep investing in extended life for a UPS.

Some of the many sources of power protection equipment include American Power Conversion (APC), Tripp Lite, and Best Power. These companies sell a variety of UPS, SPS, line, and surge protector products.

> **Caution**
>
> Don't connect a laser printer to a backed-up socket in any SPS or UPS unit. They are both "electrically noisy" and have widely varying current draws. This can be hard on the inverter in an SPS or UPS, frequently causing the inverter to fail or detect an overload and shut down. Either case means that your system will lose power, too.
>
> Printers are normally noncritical because whatever is being printed can be reprinted. Don't connect them to a UPS unless there's a good business need to do so.
>
> Some UPSs and SPSs have sockets that are conditioned, but not backed up—that is, they do not draw power from the battery. In cases such as this, you can safely plug printers and other peripherals into these sockets.

RTC/NVRAM Batteries

All 16-bit and higher systems have a special type of chip in them that combines a Real Time Clock (RTC) with at least 64 bytes (including the clock data) of Non-Volatile RAM (NVRAM) memory. This chip is officially called the *RTC/NVRAM chip*, but is often referred to as the *CMOS chip* or *CMOS RAM* because the type of chip used is produced using a CMOS (Complementary Metal Oxide Semiconductor) process. CMOS design chips are known for very low power consumption. This special RTC/NVRAM chip is designed to run off of a battery for several years.

The original chip of this type used in the IBM AT was the Motorola 146818 chip. Although the chips used today have different manufacturers and part numbers, they are all designed to be compatible with this original Motorola part.

These chips include a real-time clock. Its function should be obvious. The clock enables software to read the date and time and preserves the date and time data even when the system is powered off or unplugged.

The NVRAM portion of the chip has another function. It is designed to store basic system configuration, including the amount of memory installed, types of floppy and hard disk drives, and other information. Some of the more modern motherboards use extended NVRAM chips with as much as 2K or more of space to hold this configuration information. This is especially true for Plug-and-Play systems, which store not only the motherboard configuration, but also the configuration of adapter cards. This system can then read this information every time you power on the system.

These chips are normally powered by some type of battery while the system is off. This battery preserves the information in the NVRAM and powers the clock. Most systems use a lithium-type battery because they have a very long life, especially at the low power draw from the typical RTC/NVRAM chip.

Most of the higher-quality modern systems sold today have a new type of chip that has the battery embedded within it. These are made by several companies—including Dallas Semiconductor and Benchmarq. These chips are notable for their long life. Under normal conditions, the battery will last for 10 years—which is, of course, longer than the useful life of the system. If your system uses one of the Dallas or Benchmarq modules, the battery and chip must be replaced as a unit because they are integrated. Most of the time, these chip/battery combinations are installed in a socket on the motherboard just in case a problem requires an early replacement. You can get new modules direct from the manufacturers for $18 or less, which is often less than the cost of the older separate battery alone.

Some systems do not use a battery at all. Hewlett-Packard, for example, includes a special capacitor in many of their systems that is automatically recharged anytime the system is plugged in. Note that the system does not have to be running for the capacitor to charge; it only has to be plugged in. If the system is unplugged, the capacitor will power the RTC/NVRAM chip for up to a week or more. If the system remains unplugged for a duration longer than that, the NVRAM information is lost. In that case, these systems can reload the NVRAM from a backup kept in a special flash ROM chip contained on the motherboard. The only pieces of information that will actually be missing when you repower the system will be the date and time, which will have to be re-entered. By using the capacitor combined with a NVRAM backup in flash ROM, these systems have a very reliable solution that will last indefinitely.

Many systems use only a conventional battery, which may be either directly soldered into the motherboard or plugged in via a battery connector. For those systems with the battery soldered in, there is normally a spare battery connector on the motherboard where you can insert a conventional plug-in battery, should the original ever fail. In most cases, you would never have to replace the motherboard battery, even if it were completely dead.

Conventional batteries come in many forms. The best are of a lithium design because they will last from two to five years or more. I have seen systems with conventional alkaline batteries mounted in a holder; these are much less desirable because they fail more frequently and do not last as long. Also, they can be prone to leak, and if a battery leaks on the motherboard, the motherboard may be severely damaged.

Besides the different battery types, the chip can require any one of several different voltages. The batteries in PCs are normally 3.6v, 4.5v, or 6v. If you are replacing the battery, make sure that your replacement is the same voltage as the one you removed from the system. Some motherboards can use batteries of several different voltages. Use a jumper or switch to select the different settings. If you suspect your motherboard has this capability, consult the documentation for instructions on changing the settings. Of course, the easiest thing to do is to replace the existing battery with another of the same type.

Symptoms that indicate that the battery is about to fail include having to reset the clock on your PC every time you shut down the system (especially after moving it) and problems during the system's POST, such as drive-detection difficulties. If you experience problems such as these, it is a good idea to make note of your system's CMOS settings and replace the battery as soon as possible.

> ### Caution
>
> When you replace a PC battery, be sure that you get the polarity correct, or you will damage the RTC/NVRAM (CMOS) chip. Because the chip is soldered onto most motherboards, this can be an expensive mistake! The battery connector on the motherboard and the battery are normally keyed to prevent a backward connection. The pinout of this connector is in Appendix A, but should also be listed in your system documentation.

When you replace a battery, in most cases the existing data stored in the NVRAM is lost. Sometimes, however, the data will remain intact for several minutes (I have observed NVRAM retain information with no power for an hour or more), so if you make the battery swap quickly, the information in the NVRAM might be retained. Just to be sure, it is recommended that you record all the system configuration settings stored in the NVRAM by your system Setup program. In most cases, you would want to run the BIOS Setup program and copy or print out all the screens showing the different settings. Some Setup programs offer the capability to save the NVRAM data to a file for later restoration if necessary.

Tip

If your system BIOS is password protected and you forget the password, one possible way to bypass the block is to remove the battery for a few minutes and then replace it. This will reset the BIOS to its default settings, removing the password protection.

After replacing a battery, power up the system and use the Setup program to check the date and time setting and any other data that was stored in the NVRAM.

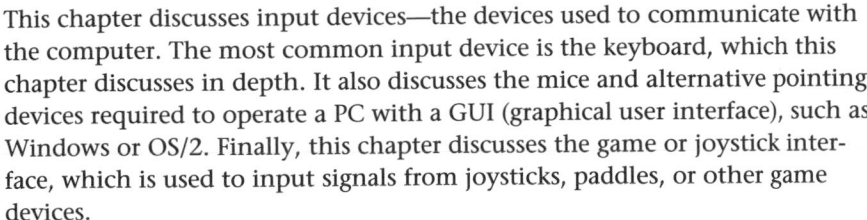

Chapter 7

Input Devices

This chapter discusses input devices—the devices used to communicate with the computer. The most common input device is the keyboard, which this chapter discusses in depth. It also discusses the mice and alternative pointing devices required to operate a PC with a GUI (graphical user interface), such as Windows or OS/2. Finally, this chapter discusses the game or joystick interface, which is used to input signals from joysticks, paddles, or other game devices.

Keyboards

One of the most basic system components is the *keyboard*, which is the primary input device. It is used for entering commands and data into the system. This section looks at the keyboards available for PC-compatible systems, examining the different types of keyboards, how the keyboard functions, the keyboard-to-system interface, and keyboard troubleshooting and repair.

Types of Keyboards

In the years since the introduction of the original IBM PC, IBM has created three different keyboard designs for PC systems, and Microsoft has augmented one of them. These designs have become *de facto* standards in the industry and are shared by virtually all PC manufacturers. More recently, with the introduction of Windows 95, a modified version of the standard 101-key design (created by Microsoft) has appeared, called the 104-key Windows keyboard.

The primary keyboard types are as follows:

- 83-key PC and XT keyboard

- 84-key AT keyboard

- 101-key Enhanced keyboard

- 104-key Enhanced Windows keyboard

This section discusses each keyboard type and shows its layout and physical appearance. Of the four designs listed, only the last two are still in general use, although you can still find old systems that utilize the 83-key and 84-key designs. Because all new systems to-day use the 101- and 104-key Enhanced keyboard designs, these versions are emphasized.

83-Key PC and XT Keyboard. When the original PC was introduced, it had something that few other personal computers had at the time: an external detachable keyboard. Most other small personal computers of the time, such as the Apple II, had built-in keyboards. Although the external design was a good move on IBM's part, the keyboard design was not without its drawbacks. One of the most criticized components of the original 83-key keyboard was the awkward layout (see Figure 7.1). The Shift keys in this model were small and were in the wrong place on the left side. The Enter key was also too small. These oversights were especially irritating at the time because IBM had recently produced the Selectric typewriter, perceived as a standard for good keyboard layout.

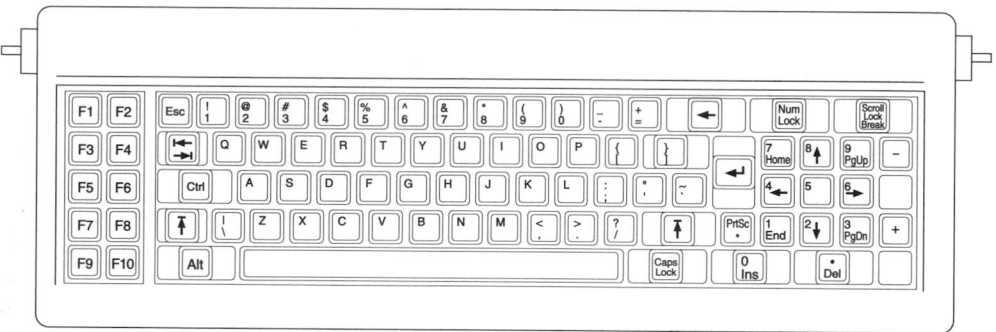

FIG. 7.1   PC and XT 83-key keyboard layout.

The PC keyboard has a built-in processor that communicates with the motherboard via a special serial data link. The communication is one-way, which means that the motherboard cannot send commands or data back to the keyboard. For this reason, IBM 83-key keyboards have no Light Emitting Diode (LED) indicator lights. Because the status of the Caps Lock, Num Lock, and Scroll Lock functions are maintained by the motherboard, there is no way to make sure that any LED indicator lights remain in sync with the actual status of the function.

Many aftermarket (non-IBM) PC keyboards added the lights, and the keyboard attempted to keep track of the three functions independently of the motherboard. This worked in most situations, but sometimes the LEDs would get out of sync with the actual function status. Rebooting corrected this temporary problem, but it was annoying process none-theless.

The original 83-key PC/XT keyboard is no longer used and is not electrically compatible with AT-compatible motherboards, although some aftermarket units may be compatible if an XT/AT switch usually found on the bottom of the keyboard is moved.

◀◀ See "System Types," p. 21

84-Key AT Keyboard. When the AT was introduced in 1984, it included a new keyboard—the 84-key unit (see Figure 7.2). This keyboard corrected many problems of the original PC and XT keyboards. The position and arrangement of the numeric keypad were modified. The Enter key was made much larger, like that of a Selectric typewriter. The Shift key positions and sizes were corrected. IBM also finally added LED indicators for the status of the Caps Lock, Scroll Lock, and Num Lock toggles.

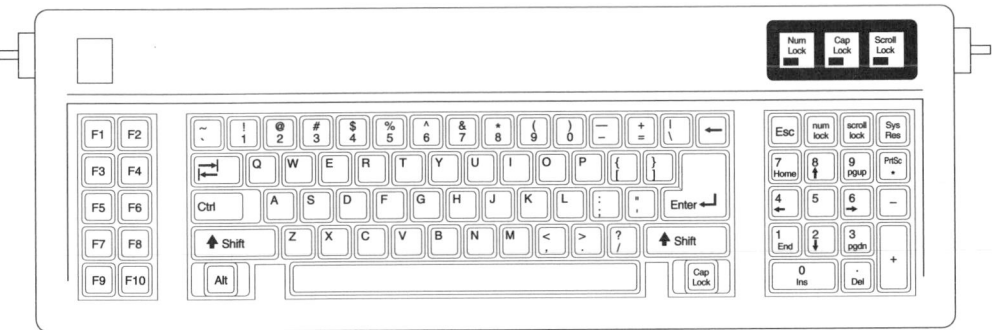

FIG. 7.2 AT 84-key keyboard layout.

These keyboards use a slightly modified, bidirectional interface protocol. This means that the processor built into the keyboard can talk to another processor (called the 8042 *keyboard controller chip*) that is built into the motherboard. The keyboard controller on the motherboard can send commands and data to the keyboard, which allows for functions such as changing the keyboard typematic (or repeat) rate and the delay before repeating begins. The keyboard controller on the motherboard also performs *scan code translations*, which allows for a much easier integration of foreign language keyboards into the system. *Scan codes* are the hexadecimal codes actually sent by the keyboard to the motherboard. The bidirectional interface can be used to control the LED indicators on the keyboard, thus ensuring that the status of a particular function and the corresponding indicator are always in sync.

The 84-key unit that came with the original AT system is no longer used, although its electrical design is compatible with newer systems. It lacks some of the keys found in the newer keyboards and does not have as nice a numeric keypad section, but many users prefer the more Selectric-style layout of the alphanumeric keys. Likewise, some users prefer to have the 10 function keys arranged on the left side instead of the enhanced arrangement, in which 12 function keys are lined up along the top.

For users accustomed to the newer keyboard layouts, the most obvious problem with the AT keyboard is the lack of dedicated cursor keys. Because the cursor keys are integrated into the numeric keypad, the status of the Num Lock function is crucial to the operation of the system and continues to be a source of constant exasperation to users. When you consider the importance of spreadsheet applications such as Lotus 1-2-3 in the early history of personal computing, it is easy to see why users who rely heavily on both the numeric keypad and the cursor keys welcomed the 101-key keyboard as a boon.

Enhanced 101-Key (or 102-Key). In 1986, IBM introduced the "corporate" enhanced 101-key keyboard for the newer XT and AT models (see Figure 7.3). I use the word "corporate" because this unit first appeared in IBM's RT PC, which is a *RISC (Reduced Instruction Set Computer)* system designed for scientific and engineering applications. Keyboards with this design were soon supplied with virtually every type of system and terminal that IBM sold. Other companies quickly copied this design, which has been the standard on Intel-based PC systems ever since.

The layout of this universal keyboard has improved over that of the 84-key unit—with perhaps the exception of the Enter key, which reverted to a smaller size. The 101-key Enhanced keyboard was designed to conform to international regulations and specifications for keyboards. In fact, other companies, such as Digital Equipment Corporation (DEC) and Texas Instruments (TI), had already been using designs similar to the IBM 101-key unit. The IBM 101-key units originally came in versions with and without the status indicator LEDs, depending on whether the unit was sold with an XT or AT system. Now there are many other variations to choose from, including some with integrated pointing devices.

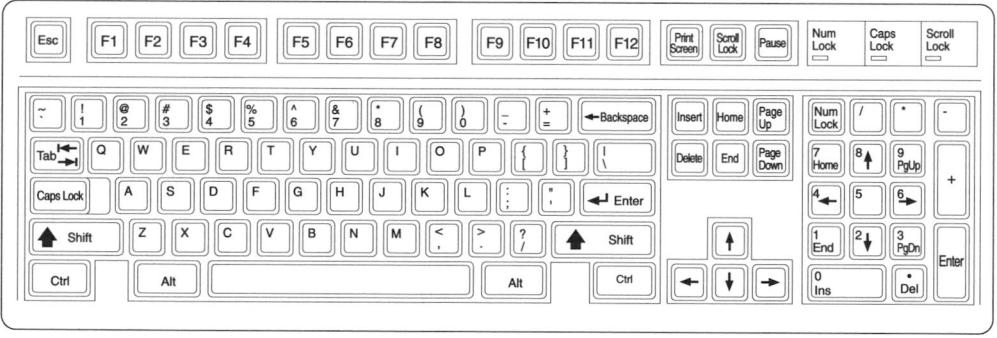

FIG. 7.3   101-key Enhanced keyboard layout.

The Enhanced keyboard is available in several different variations, but all are basically the same electrically and all can be interchanged. IBM and its Lexmark keyboard and printer subsidiary have produced a number of versions, including keyboards with built-in pointing devices and new ergonomic layouts. Some of the Enhanced keyboards still attach to the system via the five-pin DIN (an acronym from the German Deutsche Industrie Norm) connector, but most today come with cables for the six-pin mini-DIN connector introduced on the IBM PS/2s. Although the connectors may be physically different, the keyboards are not, and you can either interchange the cables or use a cable adapter to plug one type into the other.

The 101-key keyboard layout can be divided into the following four sections:

- Typing area
- Numeric keypad
- Cursor and screen controls
- Function keys

The 101-key arrangement is similar to the Selectric keyboard layout, with the exception of the Enter key. The Tab, Caps Lock, Shift, and Backspace keys have a larger striking area and are located in the familiar Selectric locations. Ctrl and Alt keys are on each side of the Spacebar. The typing area and numeric keypad have home-row identifiers for touch typing.

The cursor and screen-control keys have been separated from the numeric keypad, which is reserved for numeric input. (As with other PC keyboards, you can use the numeric keypad for cursor and screen control when the keyboard is not in Num Lock mode.) A division-sign key and an additional Enter key have been added to the numeric keypad.

The cursor-control keys are arranged in the inverted T format that is now expected on all computer keyboards. The Insert, Delete, Home, End, Page Up, and Page Down keys, located above the dedicated cursor-control keys, are separate from the numeric keypad. The function keys, spaced in groups of four, are located across the top of the keyboard. The keyboard also has two additional function keys: F11 and F12. The Esc key is isolated in the upper-left corner of the keyboard. Dedicated Print Screen/Sys Req, Scroll Lock, and Pause/Break keys are provided for commonly used functions.

Foreign language versions of the Enhanced keyboard include 102 keys and a slightly different layout from the 101-key U.S. versions.

One of the many useful features of the enhanced keyboard is removable keycaps. This permits the replacement of broken keys and provides access for easier cleaning. Also, with clear keycaps and paper inserts, you can customize the keyboard. Keyboard templates are also available to provide specific operator instructions.

The 101-key Enhanced keyboard or one of its variations will probably continue to be furnished with all desktop PC systems for some time to come. It is by far the most popular design and does not show any signs of being replaced in the future. Because most PCs use this same type of keyboard, it is easy to move from one system to another without relearning the layout. Also, as a relatively inexpensive component, you can easily replace a broken or uncomfortable keyboard.

104-Key (Windows Keyboard). If you are a touch typist like I am, then you really hate to take your hands off of the keyboard to use a mouse. Windows 95 makes this even more of a problem because it exploits both mouse buttons. Many new keyboards, especially those in portable computers, include a variation of the IBM TrackPoint or the Alps

Glidepoint pointing devices (discussed later in this chapter), which allow touch typists to keep their hands on the keyboard even while moving the pointer. However, there is still another alternative that can help. Microsoft has come up with a specification that calls for three new Windows-specific keys to be added to the keyboard. These new keys help with functions that would otherwise require multiple keystrokes or mouse clicks.

The Microsoft Windows keyboard specification outlines a set of new keys and key combinations. The familiar 101-key layout has now grown to 104 keys, with the addition of left and right Windows keys and an Application key. These keys are used for operating-system and application-level keyboard combinations, similar to today's Ctrl and Alt combinations. You don't need the new keys to use Windows 95 or NT, but software vendors are starting to add specific functions to their Windows products that make use of the new Application key (which provides the same functionality as clicking the right mouse button). Figure 7.4 shows the standard Windows keyboard layout, including the three new keys.

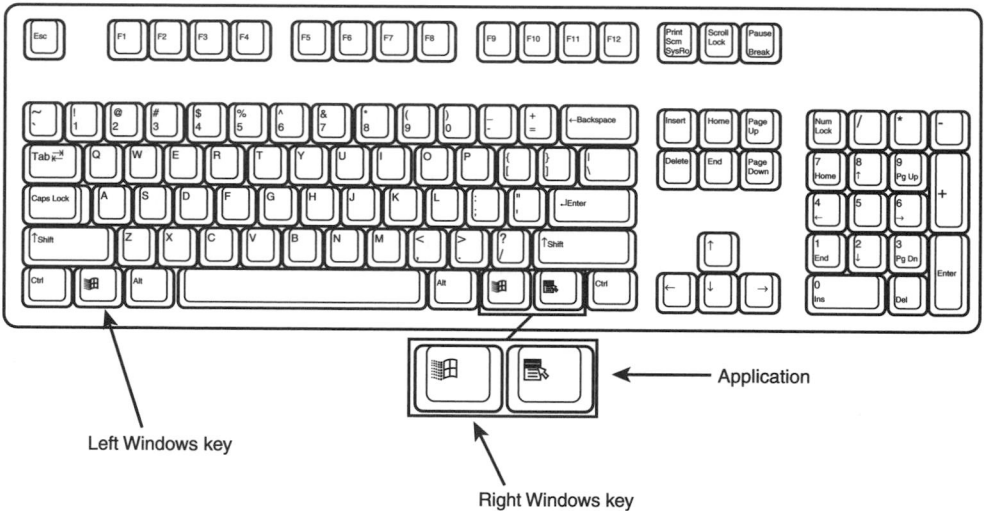

FIG. 7.4 104-key Windows keyboard layout.

The recommended Windows keyboard layout calls for the Left and Right Windows keys (called *WIN keys*) to flank the Alt keys on each side of the Spacebar, as well as an Application key on the right of the Right Windows key. Note that the exact placement of these keys is up to the keyboard designer, so you will see variations from keyboard to keyboard.

The WIN keys open the Windows 95 Start menu, which you can then navigate with the cursor keys. The Application key simulates the right mouse button; in most applications, it brings up a context-sensitive pop-up menu. Several WIN key combinations offer preset macro commands as well. For example, you press WIN+E to launch the Windows Explorer application. The following table shows a list of all the new Windows 95 key combinations:

Key Combination	Action
WIN+R	Displays the Run dialog box
WIN+M	Minimizes All
Shift+WIN+M	Undoes Minimize All
WIN+F1	Starts Help
WIN+E	Starts Windows Explorer
WIN+F	Finds files or folders
Ctrl+WIN+F	Finds the computer
WIN+Tab	Cycles through Taskbar buttons
WIN+Break	Displays the System Properties dialog box

The Windows keyboard specification requires that keyboard makers increase the number of trilograms in their keyboard designs. A *trilogram* is a combination of three rapidly pressed keys that perform a special function, such as Ctrl+Alt+Delete. Designing a keyboard so that the switch matrix will correctly registers trilograms is expensive, and this feature, plus the additional Windows keys, will cause the price of these keyboards to rise. Volume sales, however, as well as the natural market competition, should keep the price reasonable.

Virtually every keyboard manufacturer is now producing keyboards with these Windows-specific keys. Some are also combining these new keys with other features. For example, besides the new Windows keys, the *Microsoft Natural Keyboard* includes ergonomic features, such as split keypads that are rotated out from the middle to encourage a straight wrist position. For users accustomed to the standard key arrangement, these designs can take some getting used to. Unfortunately, this keyboard (made by Keytronics for Microsoft) does not have nearly as comfortable a feel as the mechanical switch designs such as Alps, Lite-On, or NMB. Nor does it have the extremely high-quality feel of the Lexmark and Unicomp keyboards. In addition to the Windows keys, other companies, such as Lexmark, NMB, and Alps, have licensed a new Spacebar design from Keyboard Enhancements, Inc. called *Erase-Ease*. This new design splits the Spacebar into two parts, using the shorter left (or optionally the right) half as an additional Backspace key. If you see a keyboard advertising 105 keys, then it probably has both the three additional Windows keys and the extra Backspace key next to the Spacebar.

Although the new Windows keys are not mandatory when running Windows, and are not yet universally accepted by PC manufacturers, more and more new PC systems include keyboards with these extra keys. They can make it easier for both experienced touch typists and novice users to access some of the functions of Windows and their applications.

Portable Keyboards. One of the biggest influences on keyboard design in recent years has been the proliferation of laptop and notebook systems. Because of size limitations, it is obviously not possible to utilize the standard keyboard layout for a portable computer. Manufacturers have come up with many different solutions. Unfortunately, none of these solutions has become an industry standard, as is the 101-key layout. Because of the variations in design, and because a portable system keyboard is not as easily replaceable as that of a desktop system, the keyboard arrangement should be an important part of your purchasing decision.

Early laptop systems often used smaller than normal keys to minimize the size of the keyboard, which resulted in many complaints from users. Today, the keytops on portable systems are usually comparable in size to that of a desktop keyboard, although some systems include half-sized keytops for the function keys and other lesser-used keyboard elements. In addition, consumer demand has caused most manufacturers to retain the inverted T design for the cursor keys after a few abortive attempts at changing their arrangement.

Of course, the most obvious difference in a portable system keyboard is the sacrifice of the numeric keypad. Most systems now embed the keypad into the standard alphabetical part of the keyboard, as shown in Figure 7.5. To switch the keys from their standard values to their keypad values, you typically must press a key combination involving a proprietary function key, often labeled Fn.

FIG. 7.5   Most portable systems today embed the numeric keypad into an oddly shaped block of keys on the alphabetical part of the keyboard.

This is an extremely inconvenient solution, and many users abandon their use of the keypad entirely on portable systems. Unfortunately, some activities, such as the entry of ASCII codes using the Alt key, require the use of the keypad numbers, which can be quite frustrating on systems using this arrangement.

In addition to keypad control, the Fn key is often used to trigger other proprietary features in portable systems, such as toggling between an internal and external display and controlling screen brightness and sound volume.

Some portable system manufacturers have gone to great lengths to provide users with adequate keyboards. For a short time, IBM marketed systems with a keyboard that used a "butterfly" design. The keyboard was split into two halves that rested on top of one another when the system was closed. When you opened the lid, the two halves separated to rest side-by-side, forming a keyboard that was actually larger than the computer case.

Ironically, the trend toward larger-sized displays in portable systems has made this sort of arrangement unnecessary. Many manufacturers have increased the footprint of their computers to accommodate 12- and even 14-inch display panels, leaving more room for the expansion of the keyboard.

▶▶ See "Keyboards," p. 937

Compatibility

The 83-key PC/XT type is different from all the others. It normally plugs into only 8-bit PC/XT systems that do not use the motherboard-based 8042-type keyboard controller chip. This is definitely true for IBM's keyboards, as well as for many compatible units. Some compatibles may be switchable to work with an AT-type motherboard via an XT/ AT switch.

The 84-key unit from IBM works on only AT-type 16-bit (or greater) motherboards. It does not work at all with PC/XT systems. Again, some aftermarket designs may have an XT/AT switch to allow for compatibility with PC/XT-type systems. If you have the keyboard set in the wrong mode, it will not work, but no damage will occur.

The Enhanced keyboards from IBM are universal. They are also *auto-switching*, which means that they work in virtually any system—from the XT to the PS/2 or any PC-compatible—after you plug them in. Some may also require that a switch be moved on the keyboard to make it compatible with PC/XT systems that do not have the 8042-type keyboard controller on the motherboard. In some cases, you may also need to switch to a different cable with the proper system end connector or use an adapter.

Although the Enhanced keyboard is electrically compatible with any AT-type motherboard and even most PC/XT-type motherboards, many older systems will have software problems using these keyboards. IBM changed the ROM on the systems to support the new keyboard properly, and the compatible vendors followed suit. Very old (1986 or earlier) machines may require a ROM upgrade to properly use some of the features on the 101-key Enhanced keyboards, such as the F11 and F12 keys. If the individual system ROM BIOS is not capable of operating the 101-key keyboard correctly, the 101-key keyboard may not work at all (as with all three ROM versions of the IBM PC). The additional keys (F11 and F12 function keys) may not work, or you may have problems with keyboard operation in general. In some cases, these compatibility problems cause improper characters to appear when keys are typed (causing the system to beep), and general keyboard operation is a problem. These problems can often be solved by a ROM upgrade to a newer version that has proper support for the Enhanced keyboard.

In an informal test, I plugged the new keyboard into an earlier XT. The keyboard seemed to work well. None of the keys that did not exist previously, such as F11 and F12, were operable, but the new arrow keys and numeric keypad worked. The Enhanced keyboard seems to work on XT or AT systems, but it does not function on the original PC systems because of BIOS and electrical interface problems. Many compatible versions of the 101-key Enhanced keyboards have a manual XT/AT switch on the bottom that may enable the keyboard to work in an original PC system.

> **Tip**
>
> If you have an older IBM system, you can tell whether your system has complete ROM BIOS support for the 101-key unit: When you plug in the keyboard and turn on the system unit, the Num Lock light automatically comes on and the numeric keypad portion of the keyboard is enabled. This method of detection is not 100% accurate, but if the light goes on, your BIOS generally supports the keyboard. A notable exception is the IBM AT BIOS, dated 06/10/85. It turns on the Num Lock light, but still does not properly support the Enhanced keyboard. All IBM BIOS versions dated since 11/15/85 have proper support for the Enhanced keyboards.

Num Lock

On IBM systems that support the Enhanced keyboard, when the system detects the keyboard on power-up, it enables the Num Lock feature and the light goes on. If the system detects an older 84-key AT-type keyboard, it does not enable the Num Lock function because these keyboards do not have cursor keys separate from the numeric keypad. When the Enhanced keyboards first appeared in 1986, many users (including me) were irritated to find that the numeric keypad was automatically enabled every time the system booted. Most system manufacturers subsequently began integrating a function into the BIOS setup that enabled you to specify the Num Lock status imposed during the boot process.

Some users thought that the automatic enabling of Num Lock was a function of the Enhanced keyboard because none of the earlier keyboards seemed to operate in this way. Remember that this function is not really a keyboard function but instead a function of the motherboard ROM BIOS, which identifies an Enhanced 101-key unit and turns on the Num Lock as a "favor." In systems with a BIOS that cannot control the status of the numeric keypad, you can use the DOS 6.0 or higher version NUMLOCK= parameter in CONFIG.SYS to turn Num Lock on or off, as desired. If you are running a version of DOS earlier than 6.0, you can use one of the many public domain programs available for controlling the Num Lock function. Running the program from the AUTOEXEC.BAT file can set the numeric keypad status whenever the system reboots.

Keyboard Technology

The technology that makes up a typical PC keyboard is very interesting. This section focuses on all of the aspects of keyboard technology and design, including the keyswitches, the interface between the keyboard and the system, scan codes, and the keyboard connectors.

Keyswitch Design. Today's keyboards use any one of several switch types to create the action for each key. Most keyboards use a variation of the mechanical keyswitch. A *mechanical keyswitch* relies on a mechanical momentary contact type switch to make the electrical contact that forms a circuit. Some high-end keyboards use a totally different nonmechanical design that relies on capacitive switches. This section discusses these switches and the highlights of each design.

The most common type of keyswitch is the mechanical type, available in the following variations:

- Pure mechanical
- Foam element
- Rubber dome
- Membrane

The *pure mechanical* type is just that—a simple mechanical switch that features metal contacts in a momentary contact arrangement. The switch often includes a *tactile feedback mechanism,* consisting of a clip and spring arrangement designed to give a "clicky" feel to the keyboard and offer some resistance to the keypress. Several companies, including Alps Electric, Lite-On, and NMB Technologies, manufacture this type of keyboard using switches obtained primarily from Alps Electric. Mechanical switches are very durable, usually have self-cleaning contacts, and are normally rated for 20 million keystrokes, which is second only to the capacitive switch in longevity. They also offer excellent tactile feedback.

Foam element mechanical switches were a very popular design in some older keyboards. Most of the older PC keyboards, including those made by Keytronics and many others, use this technology. These switches are characterized by a foam element with an electrical contact on the bottom. This foam element is mounted on the bottom of a plunger that is attached to the key (see Figure 7.6).

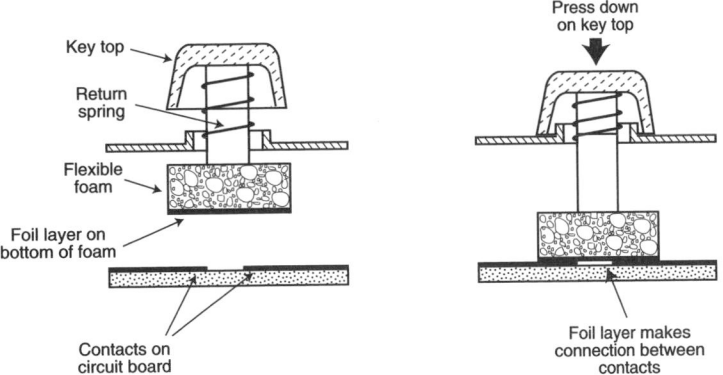

FIG. 7.6 Typical foam element mechanical keyswitch.

When the switch is pressed, a foil conductor on the bottom of the foam element closes a circuit on the printed circuit board below. A return spring pushes the key back up when the pressure is released. The foam dampens the contact, helping to prevent bounce, but unfortunately gives these keyboards a "mushy" feel. The big problem with this type of keyswitch design is that there is often little tactile feedback. Systems with these keyboards sometimes resort to tricks, such as clicking the PC's speaker to signify that contact has been made. Compaq has used keyboards of this type (made by Keytronics) in many of their systems. Preferences in keyboard feel are somewhat subjective; I personally do not favor the foam element switch design.

Another problem with this type of design is that it is more subject to corrosion on the foil conductor and the circuit board traces below. When this happens, the key strikes may become intermittent, which can be frustrating. Fortunately, these keyboards are among the easiest to clean. By disassembling the keyboard completely, you can usually remove the circuit board portion—without removing each foam pad separately—and expose the bottoms of all the pads. Then you can easily wipe the corrosion and dirt off the bottom of the foam pads and the circuit board, thus restoring the keyboard to a "like-new" condition. Unfortunately, over time, the corrosion problem will occur again. I recommend using some Stabilant 22a from D.W. Electrochemicals to improve the switch contact action and to prevent future corrosion. Because of such problems, the foam element design is not used much anymore and has been superseded in popularity by the rubber dome design.

Rubber dome switches are mechanical switches that are similar to the foam element type but are improved in many ways. Instead of a spring, these switches use a rubber dome that has a carbon button contact on the underside. As you press a key, the key plunger presses on the rubber dome, causing it to resist and then collapse all at once, much like the top of an oil can. As the rubber dome collapses, the user feels the tactile feedback, and the carbon button makes contact between the circuit board traces below. When the key is released, the rubber dome re-forms and pushes the key back up.

The rubber eliminates the need for a spring and provides a reasonable amount of tactile feedback without any special clips or other parts. Rubber dome switches use a carbon button because it is resistant to corrosion and because it has a self-cleaning action on the metal contacts below. The rubber domes themselves are formed into a sheet that completely protects the contacts below from dirt, dust, and even minor spills. This type of switch design is the simplest, and it uses the fewest parts. This makes the rubber dome keyswitch very reliable and helps make the keyboards that use it the most popular in service today.

If the rubber dome keyboard has any drawback, it is that the tactile feedback is not as good as many users would like. Although many people find its touch acceptable, some users prefer more tactile feedback than rubber dome keyboards normally provide.

The *membrane* keyboard is a variation on the rubber dome type. The keys themselves are no longer separate, but instead are formed together in a sheet that sits on the rubber dome sheet. This arrangement severely limits key travel. For this reason, membrane keyboards are not considered usable for normal touch typing. However, they are ideal for use in extremely harsh environments. Because the sheets can be bonded together and sealed from the elements, membrane keyboards can be used in situations in which no other type could survive. Many industrial applications use membrane keyboards for terminals that do not require extensive data entry but are used instead to operate equipment, such as cash registers.

Capacitive switches are the only nonmechanical types of keyswitch in use today (see Figure 7.7). The capacitive switch is the Cadillac of keyswitches. It is much more expensive than the more common mechanical rubber dome, but is more resistant to dirt and corrosion and offers the highest-quality tactile feedback of any type of switch.

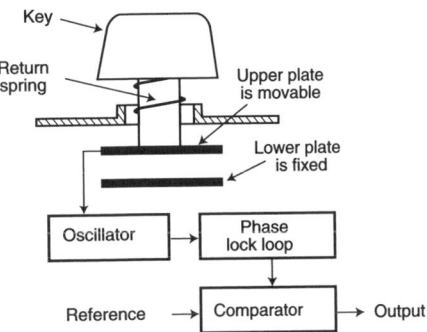

FIG. 7.7 A capacitive keyswitch.

A capacitive switch does not work by making contact between conductors. Instead, two plates usually made of plastic are connected in a switch matrix that is designed to detect changes in the capacitance of the circuit.

When the key is pressed, the plunger moves the top plate relative to the fixed bottom plate. Usually a mechanism provides for a distinct over-center tactile feedback with a resounding "click." As the top plate moves, the capacitance between the two plates changes. The comparator circuitry in the keyboard detects this change.

Because this type of switch does not rely on metal contacts, it is nearly immune to corrosion and dirt. These switches are very resistant to the key bounce problems that result in multiple characters appearing from a single strike. They are also the most durable in the industry—rated for 25 million or more keystrokes, as opposed to 10 to 20 million for other designs. The tactile feedback is unsurpassed because the switch provides a relatively loud click and a strong over-center feel. The only drawback to the design is the cost. Capacitive switch keyboards are among the most expensive designs. The quality of the feel and their durability make them worth the price, however.

Traditionally, the only vendors of capacitive keyswitch keyboards have been IBM and the inheritors of its keyboard technology, Lexmark and Unicomp.

The Keyboard Interface. A keyboard consists of a set of switches mounted in a grid or array called the *key matrix*. When a switch is pressed, a processor in the keyboard identifies which key is pressed by determining which grid location in the matrix shows continuity. The keyboard processor, which also interprets how long the key is pressed, can even handle multiple keypresses at the same time. A 16-byte hardware buffer in the keyboard can handle rapid or multiple keypresses, passing each one to the system in succession.

When you press a key, the contact bounces slightly in most cases, meaning that there are several rapid on-off cycles just as the switch makes contact. This is called *bounce*. The processor in the keyboard is designed to filter this, or *debounce* the keystroke. The keyboard processor must distinguish bounce from a double keystrike that the keyboard operator intends to make. This is fairly easy because the bouncing is much more rapid than a person could simulate by striking a key quickly several times.

The keyboard in a PC is actually a computer itself. It communicates with the main system through a special serial data link. This link transmits and receives data in 11-bit packets of information, consisting of eight data bits, plus framing and control bits. Although it is indeed a serial link (in that the data flows on one wire), the keyboard interface is not compatible with the standard RS-232 serial port commonly used to connect modems.

The processor in the original PC keyboard was an Intel 8048 microcontroller chip. Newer keyboards often use an 8049 version that has built-in ROM or other microcontroller chips compatible with the 8048 or 8049. For example, in its Enhanced keyboards, IBM has always used a custom version of the Motorola 6805 processor, which is compatible with the Intel chips. The keyboard's built-in processor reads the key matrix, debounces the keypress signals, converts the keypress to the appropriate scan code, and transmits the code to the motherboard. The processors built into the keyboard contain their own RAM, possibly some ROM, and a built-in serial interface.

In the original PC/XT design, the keyboard serial interface is connected to an 8255 Programmable Peripheral Interface (PPI) chip on the motherboard of the PC/XT. This chip is connected to the interrupt controller IRQ1 line, which is used to signal to the system that keyboard data is available. The data is sent from the 8255 to the processor via I/O port address 60h. The IRQ1 signal causes the main system processor to run a subroutine (INT 9h) that interprets the keyboard scan code data and decides what to do.

In an AT-type keyboard design, the keyboard serial interface is connected to a special keyboard controller on the motherboard. This controller is an Intel 8042 Universal Peripheral Interface (UPI) slave microcontroller chip in the original AT design. This microcontroller is essentially another processor that has its own 2K of ROM and 128 bytes of RAM. An 8742 version that uses *EPROM (Erasable Programmable Read Only Memory)* can be erased and reprogrammed. In the past, when you purchased a motherboard ROM upgrade from a motherboard manufacturer for an older system, the upgrade included a new keyboard controller chip as well because it had somewhat dependent and updated ROM code in it. Some systems may use the 8041 or 8741 chips, which differ only in the amount of built-in ROM or RAM, whereas other systems now have the keyboard controller built into the main system chipset.

In an AT system, the (8048-type) microcontroller in the keyboard sends data to the (8042-type) keyboard controller on the motherboard. The motherboard-based controller can also send data back to the keyboard. When the keyboard controller on the motherboard receives data from the keyboard, it signals the motherboard with an IRQ1 and sends the data to the main motherboard processor via I/O port address 60h, just as in the PC/XT. Acting as an agent between the keyboard and the main system processor, the 8042-type keyboard controller can translate scan codes and perform several other functions as well. The system can also send data to the 8042 keyboard controller via port 60h, which then passes it on to the keyboard. Additionally, when the system needs to send commands to or read the status of the keyboard controller on the motherboard, it reads or writes through I/O port 64h. These commands are usually followed by data sent back and forth via port 60h.

In older systems, the 8042 keyboard controller is also used by the system to control the A20 memory address line, which provides access to system memory greater than 1M. More modern motherboards usually incorporate this functionality directly into the motherboard chipset.

◀◀ See "High Memory Area (HMA) and the A20 Line," p. 378

Typematic Functions. If a key on the keyboard is held down, it becomes *typematic*, which means that the keyboard repeatedly sends the keypress code to the motherboard. In the AT-style keyboards, the typematic rate is adjusted by sending the appropriate commands to the keyboard processor. This is not possible for the earlier PC/XT keyboard types because the keyboard interface for these types is not bidirectional.

AT-style keyboards have programmable typematic repeat rate and delay parameters. Most operating systems include functions that enable you to adjust these parameters to your own specifications. In Windows 9x and Windows NT, you use the Keyboard Control Panel. In DOS, you use the MODE command.

Adjusting Keyboard Parameters in Windows 9x/NT/3.x. To modify the default values for the typematic repeat rate and delay parameters in any version of Windows, you open the Keyboard Control Panel. In Windows 95, 98, and NT, the controls are located on the Speed page, as shown in Figure 7.8. The Repeat Delay slider controls the amount of time a key must be pressed before the character begins to repeat, and the Repeat Rate slider controls how fast the character repeats after the delay has elapsed.

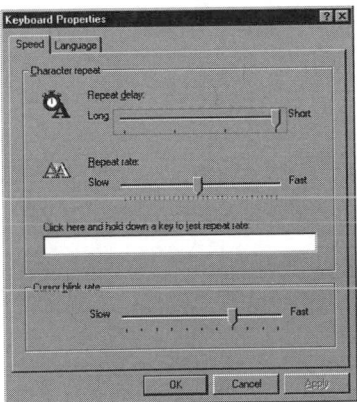

FIG. 7.8 Windows 9x and NT provide graphical controls for the keyboard typematic parameters.

> **Note**
>
> The increments on the Repeat Delay and Repeat Rate sliders in the Keyboard Control Panel corre-spond to the timings given for the MODE command's RATE and DELAY values, as listed in Tables 7.1 and 7.2 later in this chapter.

The dialog box also contains a text box you can use to test the settings you have chosen before committing them to your system. When you click in the box and press a key, the keyboard reacts using the settings currently specified by the sliders, even if you have not yet applied the changes to the Windows environment.

> **Note**
>
> In Windows 3.1, the settings in the Keyboard Control Panel override any typematic settings that you may have applied in DOS using the MODE command.

Adjusting Keyboard Parameters in DOS. In DOS versions 4.0 and later, the MODE command enables you to set the keyboard typematic (repeat) rate, as well as the delay, before typematic action begins. The default value for the RATE parameter (r) is 20 for most PC systems and 21 for IBM PS/2 systems. The default value for the DELAY parameter (d) is 2. Thus, for most systems, the standard keyboard typematic speed is 10cps (charac-ters per second), and the delay before typematic action occurs is 0.5 seconds.

To use the DOS MODE command to reset the keyboard typematic rate and delay, use the following command:

```
MODE CON[:] [RATE=r DELAY=d]
```

The acceptable values for the rate r and the resultant typematic rate in cps are shown in Table 7.1.

Table 7.1 DOS 4.0+ *MODE* Command Keyboard Typematic Rate Parameters

Rate No.	Rate ± 20%	Rate No.	Rate ± 20%
32	30.0cps	16	7.5cps
31	26.7cps	15	6.7cps
30	24.0cps	14	6.0cps
29	21.8cps	13	5.5cps
28	20.0cps	12	5.0cps
27	18.5cps	11	4.6cps
26	17.1cps	10	4.3cps
25	16.0cps	9	4.0cps
24	15.0cps	8	3.7cps
23	13.3cps	7	3.3cps

Rate No.	Rate ± 20%	Rate No.	Rate ± 20%
22	12.0cps	6	3.0cps
21	10.9cps	5	2.7cps
20	10.0cps	4	2.5cps
19	9.2cps	3	2.3cps
18	8.6cps	2	2.1cps
17	8.0cps	1	2.0cps

Table 7.2 shows the values for DELAY and the resultant delay time in seconds.

Table 7.2 DOS *MODE* Command Keyboard Typematic Delay Parameters	
DELAY No.	**Delay Time**
1	0.25sec
2	0.50sec
3	0.75sec
4	1.00sec

For example, when running DOS, I always place the following command in my AUTOEXEC.BAT file:

```
MODE CON: RATE=32 DELAY=1
```

This command sets the typematic rate to the maximum speed possible, or 30cps. It also trims the delay to the minimum of 0.25 seconds before repeating begins. This command "turbocharges" the keyboard and makes operations requiring repeated keystrokes work much faster, such as moving within a file by using arrow keys. The quick typematic action and short delay can be disconcerting to some keyboard operators. Slower typists might want to leave their keyboard speed at the default until they become more proficient.

Note

Note that if you are working on a very old system or keyboard, you may receive the following message:

```
Function not supported on this computer
```

This indicates that your system, keyboard, or both do not support the bidirectional interface or the commands required to change the typematic rate and delay. Upgrading the BIOS or the keyboard may enable this function, but it is probably not cost effective to do this on an older system.

> **Note**
>
> Some BIOS versions feature keyboard speed selection capability; however, not all of them allow for full control over the speed and delay.

Keyboard Key Numbers and Scan Codes. When you press a key on the keyboard, the processor built into the keyboard (8048- or 6805-type) reads the keyswitch location in the keyboard matrix. The processor then sends to the motherboard a serial packet of data that contains the scan code for the key that was pressed. In AT-type motherboards that use an 8042-type keyboard controller, the 8042 chip translates the actual keyboard scan code into one of up to three different sets of system scan codes, which are sent to the main processor. It can be useful in some cases to know what these scan codes are, especially when troubleshooting keyboard problems or when reading the keyboard or system scan codes directly in software.

When a keyswitch on the keyboard sticks or otherwise fails, the scan code of the failed keyswitch is usually reported by diagnostics software, including the *POST (Power-On Self Test)*, as well as conventional disk-based diagnostics. This means that you have to identify the malfunctioning key by its scan code. Tables 7.3 through 7.7 list all the scan codes for every key on the 83-, 84-, and 101-key keyboards. By looking up the reported scan code on these charts, you can determine which keyswitch is defective or needs to be cleaned.

> **Note**
>
> 101-key Enhanced keyboards are capable of three different scan code sets. Set 1 is the default. Some systems, including some of the IBM PS/2 machines, use one of the other scan code sets during the POST. For example, my IBM P75 uses Scan Code Set 2 during the POST but switches to Set 1 during normal operation. This is rare, and it really threw me off in diagnosing a stuck key problem at one time. It is useful to know if you are having difficulty interpreting the Scan Code number, however.

IBM also assigns each key a unique key number to distinguish it from the others. This is important when you are trying to identify keys on foreign keyboards, which may use different symbols or characters from the U.S. models. In the case of the Enhanced keyboard, most foreign models are missing one of the keys (key 29) found on the U.S. version and have two other additional keys (keys 42 and 45). This accounts for the 102-key total rather than the 101 keys found on the U.S. version.

Figure 7.9 shows the keyboard numbering and character locations for the original 83-key PC keyboard. Table 7.3 shows the scan codes for each key relative to the key number and character.

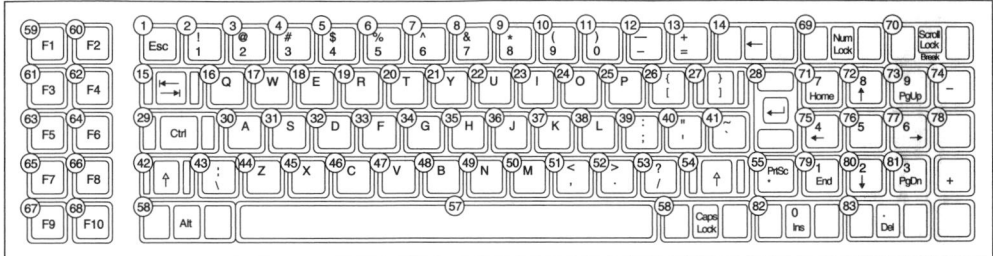

FIG. 7.9 83-key PC keyboard key number and character locations.

Table 7.3 83-Key (PC/XT) Keyboard Key Numbers and Scan Codes					
Key Number	**Scan Code**	**Key**	**Key Number**	**Scan Code**	**Key**
1	01	Esc	29	1D	Ctrl
2	02	1	30	1E	a
3	03	2	31	1F	s
4	04	3	32	20	d
5	05	4	33	21	f
6	06	5	34	22	g
7	07	6	35	23	h
8	08	7	36	24	j
9	09	8	37	25	k
10	0A	9	38	26	l
11	0B	0	39	27	;
12	0C	-	40	28	'
13	0D	=	41	29	`
14	0E	Backspace	42	2A	Left Shift
15	0F	Tab	43	2B	\
16	10	q	44	2C	z
17	11	w	45	2D	x
18	12	e	46	2E	c
19	13	r	47	2F	v
20	14	t	48	30	b
21	15	y	49	31	n
22	16	u	50	32	m
23	17	i	51	33	,
24	18	o	52	34	.
25	19	p	53	35	/
26	1A	[	54	36	Right Shift
27	1B	]	55	37	*
28	1C	Enter	56	38	Alt
					(continues)

Table 7.3   83-Key (PC/XT) Keyboard Key Numbers and Scan Codes Continued

Key Number	Scan Code	Key	Key Number	Scan Code	Key
57	39	Spacebar	71	47	Keypad 7 (Home)
58	3A	Caps Lock	72	48	Keypad 8 (Up arrow)
59	3B	F1	73	49	Keypad 9 (PgUp)
60	3C	F2	74	4A	Keypad -
61	3D	F3	75	4B	Keypad 4 (Left arrow)
62	3E	F4	76	4C	Keypad 5
63	3F	F5	77	4D	Keypad 6 (Right arrow)
64	40	F6	78	4E	Keypad +
65	41	F7	79	4F	Keypad 1 (End)
66	42	F8	80	50	Keypad 2 (Down arrow)
67	43	F9	81	51	Keypad 3 (PgDn)
68	44	F10	82	52	Keypad 0 (Ins)
69	45	Num Lock	83	53	Keypad . (Del)
70	46	Scroll Lock			

Figure 7.10 shows the keyboard numbering and character locations for the original 84-key AT keyboard. Table 7.4 shows the scan codes for each key relative to the key number and character.

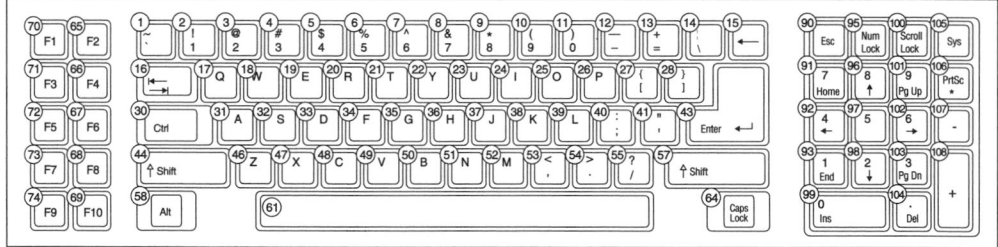

FIG. 7.10 84-key AT keyboard key number and character locations.

Table 7.4   84-Key AT Keyboard Key Numbers and Scan Codes

Key Number	Scan Code	Key	Key Number	Scan Code	Key
1	29	`	8	08	7
2	02	1	9	09	8
3	03	2	10	0A	9
4	04	3	11	0B	0
5	05	4	12	0C	-
6	06	5	13	0D	=
7	07	6	14	2B	\

Key Number	Scan Code	Key	Key Number	Scan Code	Key
15	0E	Backspace	53	33	,
16	0F	Tab	54	34	.
17	10	q	55	35	/
18	11	w	57	36	Right Shift
19	12	e	58	38	Alt
20	13	r	61	39	Spacebar
21	14	t	64	3A	Caps Lock
22	15	y	65	3C	F2
23	16	u	66	3E	F4
24	17	i	67	40	F6
25	18	o	68	42	F8
26	19	p	69	44	F10
27	1A	[	70	3B	F1
28	1B	]	71	3D	F3
30	1D	Ctrl	72	3F	F5
31	1E	a	73	41	F7
32	1F	s	74	43	F9
33	20	d	90	01	Escape
34	21	f	91	47	Keypad 7 (Home)
35	22	g	92	4B	Keypad 4 (Left arrow)
36	23	h	93	4F	Keypad 1 (End)
37	24	j	95	45	Num Lock
38	25	k	96	48	Keypad 8 (Up arrow)
39	26	l	97	4C	Keypad 5
40	27	;	98	50	Keypad 2 (Down arrow)
41	28	'	99	52	Keypad 0 (Ins)
43	1C	Enter	100	46	Scroll Lock
44	2A	Left Shift	101	49	Keypad 9 (PgUp)
46	2C	z	102	4D	Keypad 6 (Right arrow)
47	2D	x	103	51	Keypad 3 (PgDn)
48	2E	c	104	53	Keypad . (Del)
49	2F	v	105	54	SysRq
50	30	b	106	37	Keypad *
51	31	n	107	4A	Keypad -
52	32	m	108	4E	Keypad +

Figure 7.11 shows the keyboard numbering and character locations for the 101-key Enhanced keyboard. Table 7.5 shows each of the three scan code sets for each key relative to the key number and character. Scan Code Set 1 is the default; the other two are rarely used. Figure 7.12 shows the layout of a typical foreign language 102-key version of the Enhanced keyboard—in this case, a U.K. version.

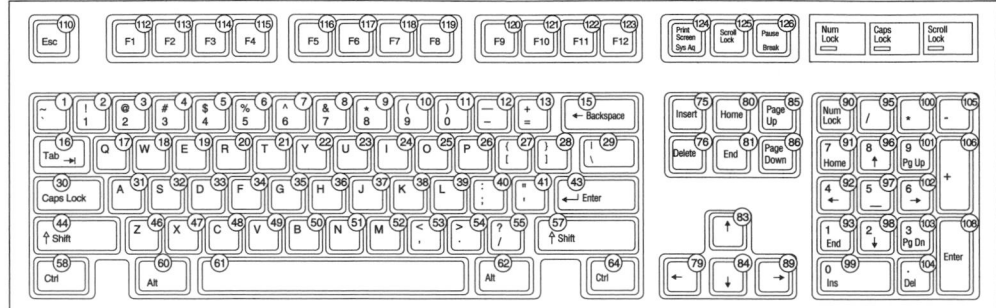

FIG. 7.11   101-key Enhanced keyboard key number and character locations (U.S. version).

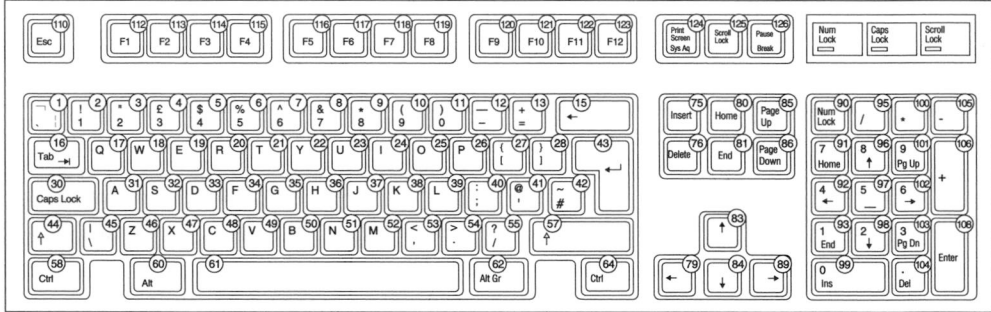

FIG. 7.12   102-key Enhanced keyboard key number and character locations (U.K. English version).

Table 7.5 101/102-Key (Enhanced) Keyboard Key Numbers and Scan Codes				
Key Number	**Key/Character**	**Scan Code Set 1**	**Scan Code Set 2**	**Scan Code Set 3**
1	'	29	0E	0E
2	1	2	16	16
3	2	3	1E	1E
4	3	4	26	26
5	4	5	25	25
6	5	6	2E	2E
7	6	7	36	36
8	7	8	3D	3D
9	8	9	3E	3E
10	9	0A	46	46
11	0	0B	45	45
12	-	0C	4E	4E
13	=	0D	55	55
15	Backspace	0E	66	66
16	Tab	0F	0D	0D

Key Number	Key/Character	Scan Code Set 1	Scan Code Set 2	Scan Code Set 3
17	q	10	15	15
18	w	11	1D	1D
19	e	12	24	24
20	r	13	2D	2D
21	t	14	2C	2C
22	y	15	35	35
23	u	16	3C	3C
24	i	17	43	43
25	o	18	44	44
26	p	19	4D	4D
27	[	1A	54	54
28	]	1B	5B	5B
29	\ (101-key only)	2B	5D	5C
30	Caps Lock	3A	58	14
31	a	1E	1C	1C
32	s	1F	1B	1B
33	d	20	23	23
34	f	21	2B	2B
35	g	22	34	34
36	h	23	33	33
37	j	24	3B	3B
38	k	25	42	42
39	l	26	4B	4B
40	;	27	4C	4C
41	'	28	52	52
42	# (102-key only)	2B	5D	53
43	Enter	1C	5A	5A
44	Left Shift	2A	12	12
45	\ (102-key only)	56	61	13
46	z	2C	1A	1A
47	x	2D	22	22
48	c	2E	21	21
49	v	2F	2A	2A
50	b	30	32	32
51	n	31	31	31
52	m	32	3A	3A
53	,	33	41	41
54	.	34	49	49
55	/	35	4A	4A

(continues)

Table 7.5   101/102-Key (Enhanced) Keyboard Key Numbers and Scan Codes Continued

Key Number	Key/Character	Scan Code Set 1	Scan Code Set 2	Scan Code Set 3
57	Right Shift	36	59	59
58	Left Ctrl	1D	14	11
60	Left Alt	38	11	19
61	Spacebar	39	29	29
62	Right Alt	E0,38	E0,11	39
64	Right Ctrl	E0,1D	E0,14	58
75	Insert	E0,52	E0,70	67
76	Delete	E0,53	E0,71	64
79	Left arrow	E0,4B	E0,6B	61
80	Home	E0,47	E0,6C	6E
81	End	E0,4F	E0,69	65
83	Up arrow	E0,48	E0,75	63
84	Down arrow	E0,50	E0,72	60
85	Page Up	E0,49	E0,7D	6F
86	Page Down	E0,51	E0,7A	6D
89	Right arrow	E0,4D	E0,74	6A
90	Num Lock	45	77	76
91	Keypad 7 (Home)	47	6C	6C
92	Keypad 4 (Left arrow)	4B	6B	6B
93	Keypad 1 (End)	4F	69	69
95	Keypad /	E0,35	E0,4A	77
96	Keypad 8 (Up arrow)	48	75	75
97	Keypad 5	4C	73	73
98	Keypad 2 (Down arrow)	50	72	72
99	Keypad 0 (Ins)	52	70	70
100	Keypad *	37	7C	7E
101	Keypad 9 (PgUp)	49	7D	7D
102	Keypad 6 (Left arrow)	4D	74	74
103	Keypad 3 (PgDn)	51	7A	7A
104	Keypad . (Del)	53	71	71
105	Keypad -	4A	7B	84
106	Keypad +	4E	E0,5A	7C
108	Keypad Enter	E0,1C	E0,5A	79
110	Escape	1	76	8
112	F1	3B	5	7
113	F2	3C	6	0F
114	F3	3D	4	17
115	F4	3E	0C	1F

Key Number	Key/Character	Scan Code Set 1	Scan Code Set 2	Scan Code Set 3
116	F5	3F	3	27
117	F6	40	0B	2F
118	F7	41	83	37
119	F8	42	0A	3F
120	F9	43	1	47
121	F10	44	9	4F
122	F11	57	78	56
123	F12	58	7	5E
124	Print Screen	E0,2A,E0,37	E0,12,E0,7C	57
125	Scroll Lock	46	7E	5F
126	Pause	E1,1D,45,E1,9D,C5	E1,14,77,E1,F0,14,F0,77	62

The new keys found on a 104-key Windows keyboard have their own unique scan codes. Table 7.6 shows the scan codes for the new keys.

Table 7.6   104-Key Windows Keyboard New Key Scan Codes

New Key	Scan Code Set 1	Scan Code Set 2	Scan Code Set 3
Left Windows	E0,5B	E0,1F	8B
Right Windows	E0,5C	E0,27	8C
Application	E0,5D	E0,2F	8D

Knowing these key number figures and scan codes are useful when you are troubleshooting stuck or failed keys on a keyboard. Diagnostics can report the defective keyswitch by the scan code, which varies from keyboard to keyboard on the character it represents and its location.

International Keyboard Layouts. After the keyboard controller in the system receives the scan codes generated by the keyboard and passes them to the main processor, the operating system converts the codes into the appropriate alphanumerical characters. In the United States, these characters are the letters, numbers, and symbols found on the standard American keyboard.

However, no matter what characters you see on the keytops, it is a relatively simple matter to adjust the scan code conversion process to map different characters to the keys. Windows 9x and Windows NT take advantage of this capability by enabling you to install multiple keyboard layouts to support different languages.

When you open the Keyboard Control Panel and select the Language page, you see a screen like Figure 7.13. The Language box should display the keyboard layout you selected when you installed the operating system. By clicking the Add button, you can select any one of several additional keyboard layouts supporting other languages.

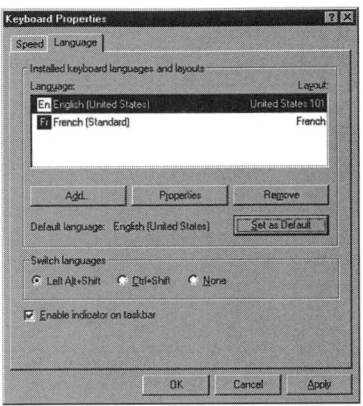

FIG. 7.13 The Language page of the Keyboard Control Panel provides support for multiple character sets.

These keyboard layouts map different characters to certain keys on the standard keyboard. The standard French layout provides easy access to the accented characters commonly used in that language. For example, pressing the 2 key produces the é character. To type the numeral 2, you press the Shift+2 key combination. Other French-speaking countries have different keyboard conventions for the same characters, so Windows includes support for several keyboard layout variations for some languages, based on nationality.

> **Note**
>
> It is important to understand that this feature is not the same as installing the operating system in a different language. These keyboard layouts do not modify the text already displayed on the screen; they only alter the characters generated when you press certain keys.

The alternative keyboard layouts also do not provide support for non-Roman alphabets, such as Russian and Chinese. The accented characters and other symbols used in languages such as French and German are part of the standard ASCII character set. They are always accessible to English-language users through the Windows Character Map utility or through the use of Alt+keypad combinations. An alternative keyboard layout simply provides an easier way to access the characters used in certain languages.

If you work on documents using more than one language, you can install as many keyboard layouts as necessary and switch between them at will. When you click the Enable Indicator on Taskbar checkbox on the Language page of the Keyboard Control Panel, a selector appears in the Taskbar's tray area that enables you to switch languages easily. On the same page, you can enable a key combination that switches between the installed keyboard layouts.

Keyboard/Mouse Interface Connectors. Keyboards have a cable with one of two primary types of connectors at the system end. On most aftermarket keyboards, the cable is connected inside the keyboard case on the keyboard end, requiring you to open up the keyboard case to disconnect or test it. Enhanced keyboards manufactured by IBM use a unique cable assembly that plugs into both the keyboard and the system unit. This makes cable interchange or replacement an easy plug-in affair. A special connector called an *SDL (Shielded Data Link)* is used at the keyboard end, and the appropriate DIN connector is used at the PC end. Any IBM keyboard or cable can be ordered separately as a spare part. The newer Enhanced keyboards come with an externally detachable keyboard cable that plugs into the keyboard port with a special connector, much like a telephone connector. The other end of the cable is of one of the following two types:

- *5-pin DIN connector.* Used on most PC systems with Baby-AT form factor motherboards.

- *6-pin mini-DIN connector.* Used on PS/2 systems and most PCs with LPX, ATX, and NLX motherboards.

Figure 7.14 and Table 7.7 show the physical layout and pinouts of all the respective keyboard connector plugs and sockets.

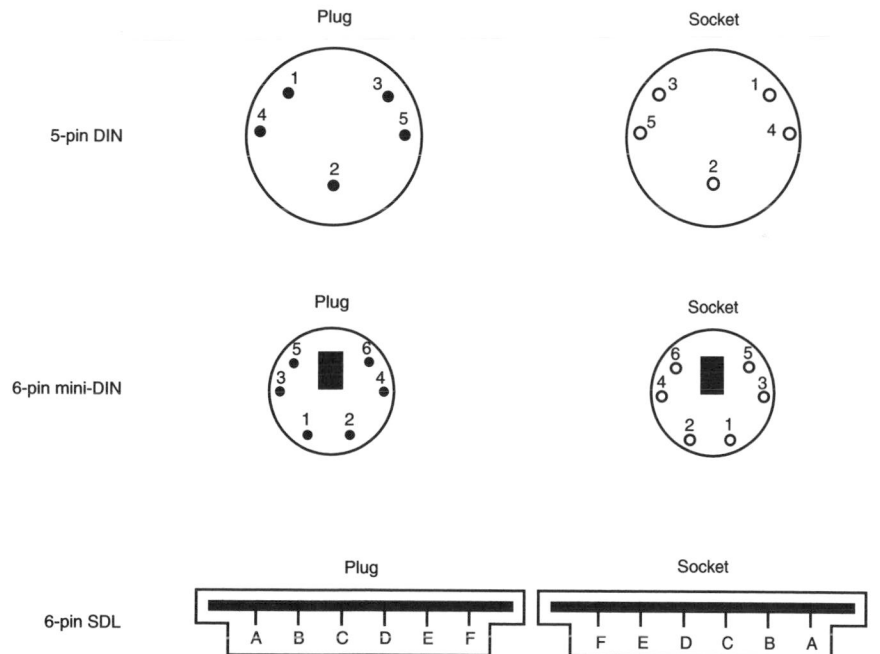

FIG. 7.14 Keyboard and mouse connectors.

Table 7.7	Keyboard Connector Signals		
Signal Name	**5-Pin DIN**	**6-Pin Mini-DIN**	**6-Pin SDL**
Keyboard Data	2	1	B
Ground	4	3	C
+5v	5	4	E

(continues)

Table 7.7 Keyboard Connector Signals Continued			
Signal Name	**5-Pin DIN**	**6-Pin Mini-DIN**	**6-Pin SDL**
Keyboard Clock	1	5	D
Not Connected	—	2	A
Not Connected	—	6	F
Not Connected	3	—	—

DIN = German Industrial Norm (Deutsche Industrie Norm), a committee that sets German dimensional standards
SDL = Shielded Data Link, a type of shielded connector created by AMP and used by IBM and others for keyboard cables

Motherboard mouse connectors also use the 6-pin mini-DIN connector and have the same pinout and signal descriptions as the keyboard connector; however, the data packets are incompatible. This means that you can easily plug a motherboard mouse (PS/2 style) into a mini-DIN keyboard connector or plug the mini-DIN type keyboard connector into a motherboard mouse port; however, neither one will work properly in this situation.

> **Caution**
>
> I have also seen PCs with external power supplies that used the same standard DIN connectors to attach the keyboard and the power supply. Although cross-connecting the mini-DIN connectors of a mouse and a keyboard is a harmless annoyance, connecting a power supply to a keyboard socket can be disastrous.

Keyboards with Special Features. A number of keyboards on the market have special features not found in the standard designs. These additional features range from simple things, such as built-in calculators and clocks, to more complicated features, such as integrated pointing devices, special character layouts, shapes, and even programmable keys.

The Dvorak Keyboard. Over the years, many people have attempted to change the design of the standard keyboard in order to improve typing speed and ergonomics. The standard QWERTY layout (so named for the first six letters below the number keys) that we are all familiar with today was designed primarily to facilitate the mechanical needs of early manual typewriters. The arrangement of the letters helped prevent the keys from jamming together as they flew up to strike the paper. Around 1936, August Dvorak and William L. Dealy developed a modified character layout for the keyboard that was intended to replace the QWERTY layout. It was designed with the typist's needs in mind.

The Dvorak-Dealy keyboard design is normally called the Dvorak design. It featured different character positions on the keys that were designed to promote the alternation of hands during typing. The characters are arranged so that the vowels are in the home row under the left hand, while the consonants used most frequently are placed in the home row under the right hand. The theory was that this format would dramatically improve typing speed; however, most tests show only modest improvements. The Dvorak keyboard design still has its devotees, but it has not achieved widespread popularity, largely due to the difficulty of switching from the familiar QWERTY layout, which is still by far the most commonly used design.

Ergonomic Keyboards. A more recent trend is to change the shape of the keyboard instead of altering the character layout. This has resulted in a number of different so-called ergonomic designs. The goal is to shape the keyboard to better fit the human hand. The most common of these designs splits the keyboard in the center, bending the sides outward. Some of these designs allow the angle between the sides to be adjusted, such as the Lexmark Select-Ease design. Others, such as the Microsoft Natural Keyboard, are fixed. These split or bent designs more easily conform to the natural angle of the hands while typing than the standard keyboard. They can improve productivity and typing speed and help prevent repetitive strain injuries, such as carpal tunnel syndrome (tendon inflammation).

Virtually every keyboard company now has some form of similar ergonomic keyboard, and the same criteria apply with respect to quality and feel as with the standard keyboard designs. One of the most popular ergonomic keyboards, the Microsoft Natural Keyboard, is manufactured for Microsoft by Keytronics. It uses the inexpensive keyswitches they are known for. For those who prefer a more rugged keyboard with higher-quality switches, I recommend the Lexmark Select-Ease, Alps, NMB Technologies, or Lite-On keyboards. These keyboards are available with very high-quality mechanical switches that have a positive tactile feel to them. The Lexmark design, in particular, allows you to adjust the angle between the two sides of the keyboard from fully closed like a standard keyboard, to split at virtually any angle. You can even separate the two halves completely. It also features built-in palm rests, an oversized Spacebar, and cursor keys on both sides of the keyboard.

Because of their novelty and their trendy appeal, some ergonomic keyboards can be considerably more expensive than traditional designs, but for users with medical problems caused or exacerbated by improper positioning of the wrists at the keyboard, they can be an important remedy to a serious problem. General users, however, are highly resistant to change, and these designs have yet to significantly displace the standard keyboard layout.

Programmable Keyboards. Several companies, including Maxi-Switch, have introduced keyboards that feature programmable keys. You can assign different keystrokes or macros to keys, or even reprogram the entire keyboard layout. This type of keyboard has been supplied in the past by some of the major PC vendors, such as Gateway 2000.

At one time I used a number of these keyboards in the seminars I teach. Unfortunately, I found the programming functions difficult to remember. Accidentally pressing the programming control keys would often put the keyboard into an altered state, requiring it to be reset. In a business environment, this phenomenon resulted in an annoying number of technical support calls from mystified users who were wondering why their keyboards were locked up.

One other problem was that the extra keys added width to the keyboard, making it wider than most other standard designs. I quickly decided that the programming functions were so rarely used that they were simply not worth the hassle and specified standard keyboards for future purchases.

Keyboard Troubleshooting and Repair

Keyboard errors are usually caused by two simple problems. Other more difficult, intermittent problems can arise, but they are much less common. The most frequent problems are as follows:

- Defective cables
- Stuck keys

Defective cables are easy to spot if the failure is not intermittent. If the keyboard stops working altogether or every keystroke results in an error or incorrect character, the cable is likely the culprit. Troubleshooting is simple, especially if you have a spare cable on hand. Simply replace the suspected cable with one from a known, working keyboard to verify whether the problem still exists. If it does, the problem must be elsewhere. You also can test the cable for continuity when it is removed from the keyboard by using a *Digital Multi-Meter (DMM)*. DMMs that have an audible continuity tester built in make this procedure much easier to perform. Wiggle the ends of the cable as you check each wire to make sure there are no intermittent connections. If you discover a problem with the continuity in one of the wires, replace the cable or the entire keyboard, whichever is cheaper. Because replacement keyboards are so inexpensive, sometimes it can be cheaper to replace the entire unit than to get a new cable.

Many times you first discover a problem with a keyboard because the system has an error during the POST. Most systems use error codes in a 3xx numeric format to distinguish the keyboard. If you have any such errors during the POST, write them down. Some BIOS versions do not use cryptic numeric error codes; they simply state something like the following:

```
Keyboard stuck key failure
```

This message normally would be displayed by a system with a Phoenix BIOS if a key were stuck. Unfortunately, the message does not identify which key it is!

If your system displays a 3xx (keyboard) error that is preceded by a two-digit hexadecimal number, the number is the scan code of a failing or stuck keyswitch. Look up the scan code in the tables provided in this section to determine which keyswitch is the culprit. By removing the keycap of the offending key and cleaning the switch, you can often solve the problem.

For a simple test of the motherboard keyboard connector, you can check voltages on some of the pins. Using Figure 7.14 as a guide, measure the voltages on various pins of the keyboard connector. To prevent possible damage to the system or keyboard, turn off the power before disconnecting the keyboard. Then unplug the keyboard and turn the power back on. Make measurements between the ground pin and the other pins according to Table 7.8. If the voltages are within these specifications, the motherboard keyboard circuitry is probably okay.

Table 7.8 Keyboard Connector Specifications			
DIN Connector Pin	**Mini-DIN Connector Pin**	**Signal**	**Voltage**
1	5	Keyboard Clock	+2.0v to +5.5v
2	1	Keyboard Data	+4.8v to +5.5v

DIN Connector Pin	Mini-DIN Connector Pin	Signal	Voltage
3	-	Reserved	—
4	3	Ground	—
5	4	+5v Power	+2.0v to +5.5v

If your measurements do not match these voltages, the motherboard might be defective. Otherwise, the keyboard cable or keyboard might be defective. If you suspect that the cable is the problem, the easiest thing to do is to replace the keyboard cable with a known good one. If the system still does not work normally, you may have to replace either the entire keyboard or the motherboard.

In many newer systems, the motherboard's keyboard and mouse connectors are protected by a fuse that can be replaced. Look for any type of fuse on the motherboard in the vicinity of the keyboard or mouse connectors. Other systems may have a socketed keyboard controller chip (8042-type). In that case, it may be possible to repair the motherboard keyboard circuit by replacing this chip. Because these chips have ROM code in them, it is best to get the replacement from the motherboard or BIOS manufacturer.

Following is a list of standard POST and diagnostics keyboard error codes:

Error Code	Description
3xx	Keyboard errors
301	Keyboard reset or stuck-key failure (XX 301, XX = scan code in hex)
302	System unit keylock switch is locked
302	User-indicated keyboard test error
303	Keyboard or system-board error; keyboard controller failure
304	Keyboard or system-board error; keyboard clock high
305	Keyboard +5v error; PS/2 keyboard fuse (on motherboard) blown
341	Keyboard error
342	Keyboard cable error
343	Keyboard LED card or cable failure
365	Keyboard LED card or cable failure
366	Keyboard interface cable failure
367	Keyboard LED card or cable failure

Disassembly Procedures and Cautions. Repairing and cleaning a keyboard often requires you to take it apart. When performing this task, you must know when to stop! Some keyboards come apart into literally hundreds of little pieces that are almost impossible to reassemble. An IBM keyboard generally has these four major parts:

■ Cable

■ Case

■ Keypad assembly

■ Keycaps

You easily can break down a keyboard into these major components and replace any of them, but don't disassemble the keypad assembly, or you will be showered with hundreds of tiny springs, clips, and keycaps. Finding all these parts—several hundred of them—and piecing the unit back together is not a fun way to spend your time. You also may not be able to reassemble the keyboard properly. Figure 7.15 shows a typical keyboard with the case opened.

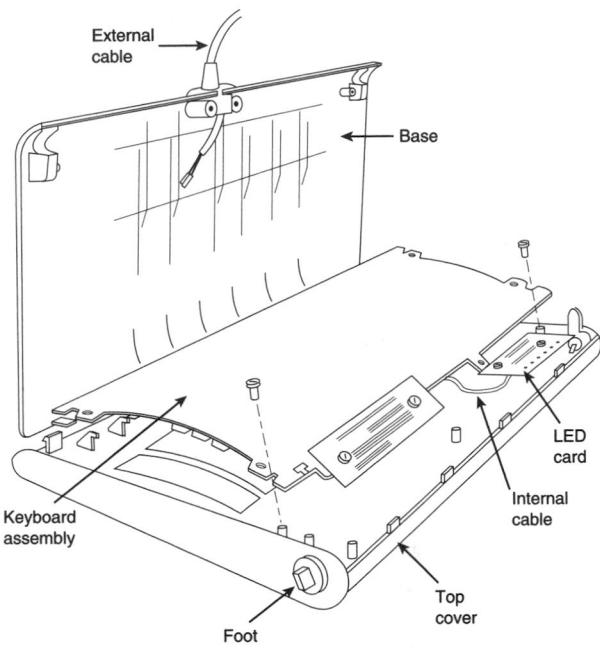

FIG. 7.15 Typical keyboard components.

Another problem is that you cannot purchase the smaller parts separately, such as contact clips and springs. The only way to obtain these parts is from another keyboard. If you ever have a keyboard that is beyond repair, keep it around for these parts. They might come in handy someday.

Most repair operations are limited to changing the cable or cleaning some component of the keyboard, from the cable contact ends to the key contact points. The keyboard cable takes quite a lot of abuse and, therefore, can fail easily. The ends are stretched, tugged, pulled, and generally handled roughly. The cable uses strain reliefs, but you still might have problems with the connectors making proper contact at each end or even with wires that have broken inside the cable. You might want to carry a spare cable for every type of keyboard you have.

All keyboard cables plug into the keyboard and PC with connectors, and you can change the cables easily without having to splice wires or solder connections. With the earlier 83-key PC and 84-key AT keyboards, you must open the case to access the connector to which the cable attaches. On the newer 101-key Enhanced keyboards from IBM, Lexmark, and Unicomp, the cable plugs into the keyboard from the outside of the case, using a modular jack and plug similar to a telephone jack. This design also makes the IBM/Lexmark/Unicomp keyboards universally usable on nearly any system (except the original PC) by simply switching the cable.

The only difference, for example, between the Enhanced keyboards for an IBM AT and an IBM PS/2 system is the attached cable. PS/2 systems use a tan cable with a smaller plug on the computer side. The AT cable is black and has the larger DIN-type plug on the computer side. You can interchange the Enhanced keyboards as long as you use the correct cable for the system.

The only feasible way to repair a keyboard is to replace the cable and to clean the individual keyswitch assemblies, the entire keypad, or the cable contact ends. Other than cleaning a keyboard, the only thing that you can do is replace the entire keypad assembly (virtually the entire keyboard) or the cable.

Cleaning a Keyboard. One of the best ways to keep a keyboard in top condition is periodic cleaning. As preventive maintenance, you should vacuum the keyboard weekly, or at least monthly. You can also use canned compressed air to blow the dust and dirt out instead of using a vacuum. Before you dust a keyboard with the compressed air, turn the keyboard upside down so that the particles of dirt and dust collected inside can fall out.

On all keyboards, each keycap is removable, which can be handy if a key sticks or acts erratically. For example, a common problem is a key that does not work every time you press it. This problem usually results from dirt collecting under the key. An excellent tool for removing keycaps on almost any keyboard is the U-shaped chip-puller included in many computer tool kits. Simply slip the hooked ends of the tool under the keycap, squeeze the ends together to grip the underside of the keycap, and lift up. IBM sells a tool designed specifically for removing keycaps from its keyboards, but the chip puller works even better. After removing the cap, spray some compressed air into the space under the cap to dislodge the dirt. Then replace the cap and check the action of the key.

> ### Caution
>
> When you remove the keycaps, be careful not to remove the Spacebar on the original 83-key PC and the 84-key AT-type keyboards. This bar is very difficult to reinstall. The newer 101-key units use a different wire support that can be removed and replaced much more easily.

Spills also can be a problem. If you tip a soft drink or cup of coffee into a keyboard, you do not necessarily have a disaster. You should immediately (or as soon as possible) flush out the keyboard with distilled water. Partially disassemble the keyboard and use the water to wash the components. (See the following section for disassembly instructions.) If the spilled liquid has dried, soak the keyboard in some of the water for a while. When you are sure that the keyboard is clean, pour another gallon or so of distilled water over it and through the keyswitches to wash away any residual dirt. After the unit dries completely, it should be perfectly functional. You may be surprised to know that drenching your keyboard with water will not harm the components. Just make sure that you use distilled water, which is free from residue or mineral content. Also make sure that the keyboard is fully dry before you attempt to use it, or some of the components might short out.

Replacement Keyboards. In most cases, it is cheaper or more cost effective to replace a keyboard rather than repair it. This is especially true if the keyboard has an internal malfunction or if one of the keyswitches is defective. Replacement parts for keyboards are almost impossible to procure, and in most cases the installation of any repair part is difficult. In addition, many of the keyboards supplied with lower-cost PCs leave much to be desired. They often have a mushy feel, with little or no tactile feedback. A poor keyboard can make using a system a frustrating experience, especially if you are a touch typist. For all these reasons, it is often a good idea to replace an existing keyboard with something better.

Perhaps the highest-quality keyboards in the entire computer industry are those made by IBM, or, more accurately, Unicomp. Several years ago, IBM spun off its keyboard and printer divisions as a separate company called Lexmark. Lexmark used to manufacturer most IBM-brand keyboards and printers and sold them not only to IBM, but also to other PC vendors and end users. In 1996, Lexmark sold its keyboard technology to a company called Unicomp, which now maintains an extensive selection of over 1,400 keyboards.

Table 7.9 shows the part numbers of all IBM-labeled keyboards and cables. These numbers can serve as a reference when you are seeking a replacement IBM keyboard from IBM directly or from third-party companies. Many third-party companies sell IBM label keyboards for much less than IBM, in both new and refurbished form. Remember that you can also purchase these same keyboards through Unicomp, although they do not come with an IBM label.

Table 7.9   IBM Keyboard and Cable Part Numbers

Description	Part Number
83-key U.S. PC keyboard assembly with cable	8529297
Cable assembly for 83-key PC keyboard	8529168
84-key U.S. AT keyboard assembly with cable	8286165
Cable assembly for 84-key keyboard	8286146
101-key U.S. keyboard without LED panel	1390290
101-key U.S. keyboard with LED panel	6447033
101-key U.S. keyboard with LED panel (PS/2 logo)	1392090
6-foot cable for Enhanced keyboard (DIN plug)	6447051
6-foot cable for Enhanced keyboard (mini-DIN plug)	61X8898
6-foot cable for Enhanced keyboard (shielded mini-DIN plug)	27F4984
10-foot cable for Enhanced keyboard (mini-DIN plug)	72X8537

Notice that the original 83/84-key IBM keyboards are sold with a cable that has the larger, five-pin DIN connector already attached. IBM Enhanced keyboards are always sold (at least by IBM) without a cable. You must order the proper cable as a separate item. Cables are available to connect the keyboards to either the older system units that use the larger DIN connector or to PS/2 systems (and many compatibles) that use the smaller mini-DIN connector.

Recently, IBM has started selling complete keyboard assemblies under a program called *IBM Options*. This program is designed to sell these components in the retail channel to end users of both IBM and compatible systems from other vendors. Items under the IBM Options program are sold through normal retail channels, such as CompUSA and Computer Discount Warehouse (CDW). These items are also priced much cheaper than items purchased as spare parts. They include a full warranty and are sold as complete packages, including cables. Table 7.10 lists some of the IBM Options keyboards and part numbers.

Table 7.10 IBM Options Keyboards (Sold Retail)	
Description	**Part Number**
IBM Enhanced keyboard (cable w/DIN plug)	92G7454
IBM Enhanced keyboard (cable w/mini-DIN plug)	92G7453
IBM Enhanced keyboard, built-in Trackball (cable w/DIN plug)	92G7456
IBM Enhanced keyboard, built-in Trackball (cable w/mini-DIN plug)	92G7455
IBM Enhanced keyboard, integrated TrackPoint II (cables w/mini-DIN plugs)	92G7461

The extremely positive tactile feedback of the IBM/Lexmark/Unicomp design is also a benchmark of comparison for the rest of the industry. Although keyboard feel is an issue of personal preference, I have never used a keyboard that feels better than the IBM/Lexmark/Unicomp designs. I now equip every system I use with a Unicomp keyboard, including the many non-IBM systems I use. You can purchase these keyboards directly from Unicomp at very reasonable prices. Also, you can sometimes find IBM-labeled models selling for under $100 available from advertisers in computer magazines.

▶▶ An online catalog of Unicomp keyboard products is available on the World Wide Web at **http://www.pckeyboard.com.**

Unicomp sells other keyboards for very reasonable prices as well. Many different models are available, including some with a built-in trackball or even the revolutionary TrackPoint pointing device. (TrackPoint refers to a small stick mounted between the G, H, and B keys.) This device was first featured on the IBM ThinkPad laptop systems, although the keyboards are now sold for use on other manufacturers' PCs. The technology is being licensed to many other manufacturers, including Toshiba. Other manufacturers of high-quality keyboards that are similar in feel to the IBM/Lexmark/Unicomp units are Alps, Lite-On, and NMB Technologies. These keyboards have excellent tactile feedback, with a positive click sound. They are my second choice, after a Unicomp unit. Maxi-Switch also makes a high-quality aftermarket keyboard, which is used by a number of PC manufacturers, including Gateway 2000. These also have a good feel and are recommended. Many of these companies can make their keyboards with your own company logo on them (such as the Maxi-Switch models used by Gateway 2000), which is ideal for clone manufacturers looking for name-brand recognition.

Reference Material

If you are interested in more details about keyboard design or interfacing, a company called Annasoft Systems publishes a book/disk package called *PC Keyboard Design*. This document defines the protocol between the keyboard and computer for both XT and AT types and includes schematics and keyboard controller source code. The kit, which includes a license to use the source code, costs $249.

Other excellent sources of information are the various technical reference manuals put out by IBM. Appendix A, "Vendor List," contains a list of important IBM reference manuals, in which you can find much valuable information. This information can be especially valuable to owners of non-IBM systems because other manufacturers often do not put out the same level of technical information as IBM, and many PC designs are similar or even identical to one or more IBM systems. After all, that is why these designs were referred to as IBM-compatibles for so long. Much of my personal knowledge and expertise comes from poring over the various IBM technical reference manuals.

Mice

The mouse was invented in 1964 by Douglas Englebart, who at the time was working at the *Stanford Research Institute (SRI)*, a think tank sponsored by Stanford University. The mouse was officially called an *X-Y Position Indicator for a Display System*. Xerox later applied the mouse to its revolutionary Alto computer system in 1973. At the time, unfortunately, these systems were experimental and used purely for research.

In 1979, several people from Apple, including Steve Jobs, were invited to see the Alto and the software that ran the system. Steve Jobs was blown away by what he saw as the future of computing, which included the use of the mouse as a pointing device and the GUI it operated. Apple promptly incorporated these features into what was to become the Lisa computer and lured away 15 to 20 Xerox scientists to work on the Apple system.

Although Xerox released the Star 8010 computer that used this technology in 1981, it was expensive, poorly marketed, and perhaps way ahead of its time. Apple released the Lisa computer, its first system that used the mouse, in 1983. It also was not a runaway success, largely because of its $10,000 list price, but by then Jobs already had Apple working on the low-cost successor to the Lisa, the Macintosh. The Apple Macintosh was introduced in 1984. Although it was not an immediate hit, the Macintosh has grown in popularity since that time.

Many credit the Macintosh with inventing the mouse and GUI, but as you can see, this technology was actually borrowed from others, including SRI and Xerox. Certainly the Macintosh, and now Microsoft Windows and OS/2, have gone on to popularize this interface and bring it to the legion of Intel-based PC systems.

Although the mouse did not catch on quickly in the PC marketplace, today the GUIs for PC systems such as Windows and OS/2 virtually demand the use of a mouse. Therefore, it is common for a mouse to be sold with nearly every new system on the market.

Mice come in many shapes and sizes from many different manufacturers. Some have taken the standard mouse design and turned it upside down, creating the *trackball*. In the trackball devices, you move the ball with your hand directly rather than the unit itself. IBM even produced a very cool mouse/trackball convertible device called the TrackPoint (p/n 1397040). The TrackPoint could be used as either a mouse (ball side down), or as a trackball (ball side up). In most cases, the dedicated trackballs have a much larger ball than would be found on a standard mouse. Other than the orientation and perhaps the size of the ball, a trackball is identical to a mouse in design, basic function, and electrical interface.

The largest manufacturers of mice are Microsoft and Logitech. Even though mice may come in different varieties, their actual use and care differ very little. The standard mouse consists of several components:

- A housing that you hold in your hand and move around on your desktop

- A roller ball that signals movement to the system

- Buttons (usually two) for making selections

- A cable for connecting the mouse to the system

- An interface connector to attach the mouse to the system

The housing, which is made of plastic, consists of very few moving parts. On top of the housing, where your fingers normally reside, are buttons. There may be any number of buttons, but in the PC world, there are typically only two. If additional buttons are on your mouse, specialized software is required for them to operate. On the bottom of the housing is a small rubber ball that rolls as you move the mouse across the tabletop. The movements of this rubber ball are translated into electrical signals transmitted to the computer across the cable. Some mice use a special optical sensor that detects movement over a grid. These optical mice have fallen into disfavor because they work only if you use a special grid pad underneath them.

The cable can be any length, but it is typically between four and six feet long.

Tip

If you have a choice on the length of cable to purchase, go for a longer one. This allows easier placement of the mouse in relation to your computer.

After the mouse is connected to your computer, it communicates with your system through the use of a *device driver*, which can be either loaded explicitly or built into the operating system software. For example, no separate drivers are needed to use a mouse with Windows or OS/2, but using the mouse with most DOS-based programs requires a separate driver to be loaded from the CONFIG.SYS or AUTOEXEC.BAT file. Regardless of whether it is built in or not, the driver translates the electrical signals sent from the mouse into positional information and indicates the status of the buttons.

Internally, a mouse is very simple as well. The ball usually rests against two rollers, one for translating the X-axis movement and the other for translating the Y-axis movement. These rollers are usually connected to small disks with shutters that alternately block and allow the passage of light. Small optical sensors detect movement of the wheels by watching an internal infrared light blink on and off as the shutter wheel rotates and "chops" the light. These blinks are translated into movement along the axes. This type of setup, called an *opto-mechanical mechanism,* is by far the most popular in use today (see Figure 7.16).

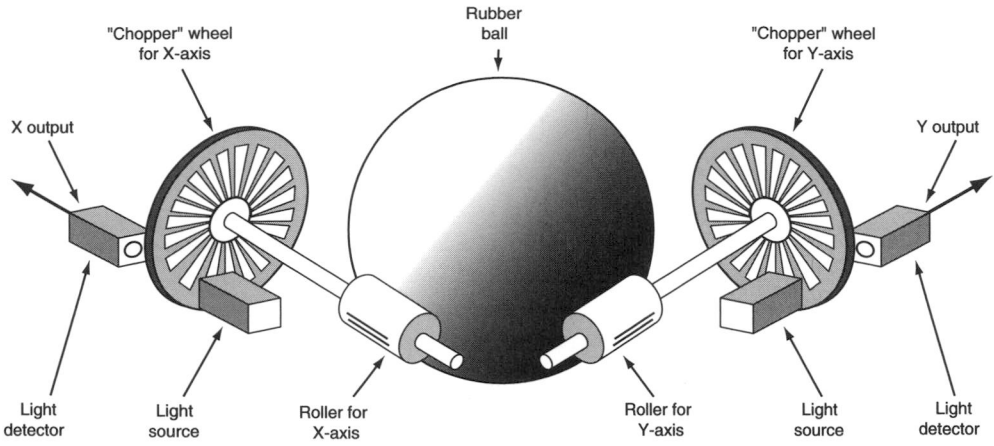

FIG. 7.16 Typical opto-mechanical mouse mechanism.

Mouse Interface Types

The connector used to attach your mouse to the system depends on the type of interface you are using. Three basic interfaces are used for mouse connections, with a fourth combination device possible as well. Mice are most commonly connected to your computer through the following three interfaces:

- Serial interface

- Dedicated motherboard mouse port

- Bus-card interface

Serial. A popular method of connecting a mouse to older PCs is through the standard *serial* interface. As with other serial devices, the connector on the end of the mouse cable is either a 9-pin or 25-pin male connector. Only a couple of pins in the DB-9 or DB-25 connectors are used for communications between the mouse and the device driver, but the mouse connector typically has all nine or 25 pins present.

Because most PCs come with two serial ports, a serial mouse can be plugged into either COM1: or COM2:. The device driver, when initializing, searches the ports to determine which one the mouse is connected to.

Because a serial mouse does not connect to the system directly, it does not use system resources by itself. Instead, the resources used are those used by the serial port to which it is connected. For example, if you have a mouse connected to COM2, it most likely uses IRQ3 and I/O port addresses 2F8h-2FFh.

▶▶ See "Serial Ports," p. 583

Motherboard Mouse Port (PS/2). Most newer computers now come with a dedicated mouse port built into the motherboard. This practice was introduced by IBM with the PS/2 systems in 1987, so this interface is often referred to as a *PS/2 mouse interface*. This term does not imply that such a mouse can work only with a PS/2; instead, it means that the mouse can connect to any system that has a dedicated mouse port on the motherboard.

From a hardware perspective, a motherboard mouse connector usually is exactly the same as the mini-DIN connector used for newer keyboards. In fact, the motherboard mouse port is connected to the 8042-type keyboard controller found on the motherboard. All the PS/2 computers include mini-DIN keyboard and mouse port connectors on the back. Most compatible slimline computers also have these same connectors for space reasons. Other motherboards have a pin-header type connector for the mouse port because most standard cases do not have a provision for the mini-DIN mouse connector. If that is the case, an adapter cable is usually supplied with the system. This cable adapts the pin-header connector on the motherboard to the standard mini-DIN type connector used for the motherboard mouse.

> **Caution**
>
> As mentioned in the "Keyboard/Mouse Interface Connectors" section earlier in this chapter, the mini-DIN sockets used for both keyboard and mouse connections on many systems are physically and electrically interchangeable, but the data packets they carry are not. Be sure to plug each device into the correct socket or neither will function correctly.

Connecting a mouse to the built-in mouse port is the best method of connection because you do not sacrifice any of the system's interface slots or any serial ports, and the performance is not limited by the serial port circuitry. The standard resource usage for a motherboard (or PS/2) mouse port is IRQ 12, as well as I/O port addresses 60h and 64h. Because the motherboard mouse port uses the 8042-type keyboard controller chip, the port addresses are those of this chip. IRQ 12 is an interrupt that is usually free on most systems and it, of course, must remain free on any ISA bus systems that have a motherboard mouse port because interrupt sharing is not allowed with the ISA bus.

Serial and Motherboard Mouse Port (PS/2). A hybrid type of mouse can plug into a serial port or a motherboard mouse port connection. This combination serial-PS/2 mouse is more flexible than the single design types. Circuitry in this mouse automatically detects the type of port to which it is connected and configures the mouse automatically. These mice usually come with a mini-DIN connector on the end of their cable and an adapter that converts the mini-DIN to a 9- or 25-pin serial port connector.

Sometimes people use adapters to try to connect a serial mouse to a motherboard mouse port or a motherboard mouse to a serial port. That this does not work is not the fault of the adapter. If the mouse does not explicitly state that it is both a serial and a PS/2-type mouse, it does not work on either interface, but instead works only on the single interface for which it was designed. Most of the time, you find the designation for what type of mouse you have printed on its underside.

Bus. A *bus* mouse is typically used in systems that do not have a motherboard mouse port or any available serial ports. The name *bus mouse* is derived from the fact that the mouse requires a special bus interface board, which occupies a slot in your computer and communicates with the device driver across the main motherboard bus. Although the use of a bus mouse is transparent to the user (there is no operational difference between a bus mouse and other types of mice), many people view a bus mouse as less desirable than other types because it occupies a slot that could be used for other peripherals.

Another drawback to the bus mouse is that it is electrically incompatible with the other types of mice. Because they are not very popular, bus mice can be hard to find in a pinch. Likewise, the bus adapters are typically available only for ISA slots; because they are always 8-bit cards, you are limited in the choice of nonconflicting hardware interrupts. A bus mouse can also be dangerous because it uses a mini-DIN connector—just like the motherboard (PS/2)-type mouse—although they are totally incompatible. I have even heard of people damaging motherboards by plugging a bus mouse into a motherboard mouse connector.

Bus mouse adapter cards usually have a selectable interrupt and I/O port address setting, but the IRQ selection is limited to 8-bit interrupts. This usually means that you must choose IRQ 5 in most systems that already have two serial ports because all the other 8-bit interrupts are in use. If you are already using another 8-bit-only card that needs an interrupt, like some sound cards, you will not be able to run both devices in the same system without conflicts. All in all, I think bus mice should be avoided.

> **Note**
>
> Microsoft sometimes calls a bus mouse an *inport mouse*, which is its proprietary name for a bus mouse connection.

USB. The newest interface for PC keyboards, and virtually every other type of peripheral you can name, is the Universal Serial Bus (USB). USB keyboards connect to a PC through the universal four-wire connector used by all USB devices. Because you can plug up to 127 devices into a single USB port on your PC, these keyboards frequently include additional USB sockets built into the housing, enabling them to function as hubs for other USB devices.

Alternatively, the USB plug that connects to your PC may have a "pass-through" connector. This is a standard USB plug with an integrated USB socket, so you can connect another device using the same port on the computer. Some USB keyboards also include a standard PS/2 mouse port, so you can connect your existing mouse directly to the keyboard instead of to the computer.

Mouse Calibration

Most mouse drivers include parameters that you can adjust to modify the performance of the device to your specifications. These adjustments do not alter the physical performance of the mouse; instead, they control the way that the operating system interprets the signals that it receives from the hardware. The Windows operating systems include a Mouse Control Panel that provides the interface for these control parameters.

On a PC running Windows 9x with the operating system's standard PS/2 port mouse driver installed, the Mouse Control Panel appears as shown in Figure 7.17.

The Buttons Page. On the Mouse Control Panel's Buttons page, you can select whether your mouse should operate in Right-handed or Left-handed mode. On the standard, two-button mouse used with Windows, the left mouse button is traditionally the primary button. It is used for selecting and dragging, while the right button is the secondary button, which provides access to context menus and other special features. In many contexts, the terms primary and secondary are preferable to left and right because the driver can switch the functions of the two buttons to accommodate left-handed users.

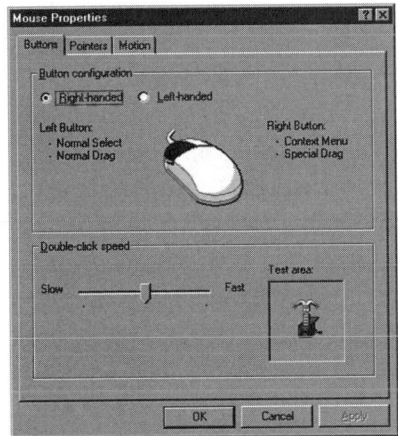

FIG. 7.17 The Windows 9x Mouse Control Panel enables you to adjust mouse performance attributes to your specifications.

Mouse design is a sore point among many left-handed users because a great deal of documentation and even some mouse hardware favor the right-handed. Manuals often refer to the left or right mouse button instead of the primary or secondary, which can be confusing to the uninformed. Worse, the so-called Microsoft Ergonomic Mouse included with a great many of the new systems sold today has a curved design that favors right-handed users. I have seen many users become accustomed to using this mouse with the left hand, but in my experience, an equal number of left-handed people get into the habit of operating the mouse right-handed.

Also on the Buttons page is a slider that enables you to adjust the mouse's double-click speed. This adjustment controls the time interval between two clicks of the primary mouse button enabling you to distinguish two single clicks from one double click. When using applications such as Windows Explorer, this distinction can be important, for it signals the difference between launching a file and renaming it.

Many users are frustrated by the minuscule click timing differences that distinguish one mouse function from another and are unaware that they can easily modify the behavior of the mouse to provide them with a greater margin of error. The test area of the dialog box contains an animation of a jack-in-the-box that lets you test your adjustments before committing them to the system configuration.

The Pointers Page. On the Pointers page, you can select the cursors that Windows 9x displays during specific system events. The operating system includes a large selection of amusing cursors, some of which are animated. However, this capability to select cursors also has a functional use. Windows 9x also includes cursors that are designed using sizes and colors intended to accommodate certain screen types (such as older, less visible portable system displays), long-distance viewing (such as at presentations), and users with visual disabilities.

The Motion Page. On the Motion page (see Figure 7.18), you can control how the distance that you move the mouse relates to the distance the pointer moves on the computer screen. If, for example, your work surface provides only a small area in which to move the mouse, you can move the Pointer Speed slider to the right to increase the speed. This can prevent you from having to lift the mouse off of the work surface to move the pointer across the whole screen. Some mouse types, such as the TrackPoint included on many portable systems, are designed to react to very subtle touches, and you can easily fine-tune their movements by using this control.

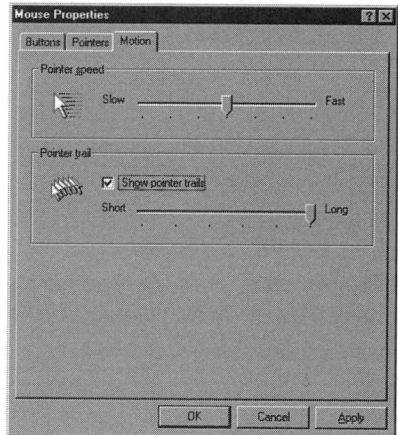

FIG. 7.18 On the Motion page, you can control the relationship between the movement of the mouse and that of the pointer.

The Pointer Trail control enables you to configure your mouse to leave a series of pointer images behind it as it moves across the screen, forming a trail of adjustable length. Again, this feature has a practical use in situations in which pointer visibility is a problem. However, some users simply enjoy the effect, while others are profoundly irritated by it.

The General Page. On the General page, you select the mouse driver used by your system. In most cases, Windows 9x automatically detects and identifies the mouse during the operating system installation and supplies the correct driver. However, in cases in which you are installing a new or unusual pointing device, you can use this page to install a new or updated mouse driver.

Mouse Troubleshooting

If you are experiencing problems with your mouse, you need to look in only two general places—hardware or software. Because mice are basically simple devices, looking at the hardware takes very little time. Detecting and correcting software problems can take a bit longer, however.

Hardware Problems. Two types of hardware problems can crop up when you are using a mouse. The most common is a dirty mouse, which is fixed by doing some "mouse cleaning." The other problem, which relates to interrupt conflicts, is more difficult to solve.

Cleaning Your Mouse. If you notice that the mouse pointer moves across the screen in a jerky fashion, it may be time to clean your mouse. This jerkiness is caused when dirt and dust get trapped around the mouse's ball-and-roller assembly, thereby restricting its free movement.

From a hardware perspective, the mouse is a simple device, and cleaning it is also very simple. The first step is to turn the mouse housing over so that you can see the ball on the bottom. Notice that surrounding the ball is an access panel that you can open. Some instructions may even indicate how the panel is to be opened. (Some off-brand mice may require you to remove some screws to get at the roller ball.) Remove the panel to see more of the roller ball and the socket in which it rests.

If you turn the mouse back over, the rubber roller ball should fall into your hand. Take a look at the ball. It may be gray or black, but it should have no visible dirt or other con-tamination. If it does, wash it in soapy water or a mild solvent, such as contact lens cleaner solution or alcohol, and dry it off.

Now take a look at the socket in which the roller ball normally rests. You will see two or three small wheels or bars against which the ball normally rolls. If you see dust or dirt on or around these wheels or bars, you need to clean them. The best way is to use a com-pressed air duster, which can blow out any dust or dirt. You also can use some electrical contact cleaner to clean the rollers. Remember, any remaining dirt or dust impedes the movement of the roller ball and results in the mouse not working as it should.

Put the mouse back together by inserting the roller ball into the socket and then securely attaching the cover panel. The mouse should look just like it did before you removed the panel, except that it will be noticeably cleaner.

Interrupt Conflicts. *Interrupts* are internal signals used by your computer to indicate when something needs to happen. With a mouse, an interrupt is used whenever the mouse has information to send to the mouse driver. If a conflict occurs and the same interrupt used by the mouse is used by a different device, the mouse will not work prop-erly—if at all.

Interrupt conflicts do not normally occur if your system uses a mouse port, but they can occur with the other types of mouse interfaces. Mouse ports built into modern motherboards are almost always set to IRQ 12. Be sure if your system has a motherboard mouse port that you don't set any other adapter cards to IRQ 12, or a conflict will result.

When you are using a serial mouse, interrupt conflicts typically occur if you add a third and fourth serial port, using either an expansion card or an internal serial device, such as a modem. This is because in ISA bus systems, the odd-numbered serial ports (1 and 3) are usually configured to use the same interrupts, as are the even-numbered ports (2 and 4). Thus, if your mouse is connected to COM2: and an internal modem uses COM4:, they both may use the same interrupt, and you cannot use them at the same time.

Because the mouse generates interrupts only when it is moved, you may find that the modem functions properly until you touch the mouse, at which point the modem is disconnected. You may be able to use the mouse and modem at the same time by moving one of them to a different serial port. For instance, if your mouse uses COM1: and the modem still uses COM4:, you can use them both at once because odd and even ports use different interrupts.

The best way around these interrupt conflicts is to make sure no two devices use the same interrupt. Serial port adapters are available for adding COM3: and COM4: serial ports that do not share the interrupts used by COM1: and COM2:. These boards enable the new COM ports to use other normally available interrupts, such as IRQs 10, 11, 12, 15, or 5. I never recommend configuring a system with shared interrupts; it is a sure way to run into problems later.

If you suspect an interrupt problem with a bus-type mouse, you can use the Device Manager built into Windows 9x (which is accessible from the System Control Panel) or even a program such as MicroSoft Diagnostics (MSD) to help you identify what interrupt is being used by the mouse. You get MSD free with Windows 3.0 or later, as well as with MS-DOS 6.0 or later.

▶▶ See "Operating System Diagnostics," p. 995

Be aware that programs that attempt to identify IRQ usage such as MSD are not always 100 percent accurate—in fact, they are inaccurate in many cases—and they usually require that the device driver for the particular device be loaded to work.

The Device Manager in Windows 9x is part of the Plug-and-Play (PnP) software for the system, and it is usually 100 percent accurate on PnP hardware. Although some of these interrupt-reporting programs can have problems, most will easily identify the mouse IRQ if the mouse driver has been loaded. After the IRQ is identified, you may need to change the IRQ setting of the bus mouse adapter or one or more other devices in your system so that everything works together properly.

If your driver refuses to recognize the mouse at all, regardless of its type, try using a different mouse that you know works. Replacing a defective mouse with a known good one may be the only way to know whether the problem is indeed caused by a bad mouse.

I have had problems in which a bad mouse caused the system to lock right as the driver loaded or even when diagnostics such as MSD attempted to access the mouse. You can easily ferret out this type of problem by loading MSD with the /I option, which causes

MSD to bypass its initial hardware detection. Then run each of the tests separately, including the mouse test, to see whether the system locks. If the system locks during the mouse test, you have found a problem with either the mouse or the mouse port. Try replacing the mouse to see whether that helps. If it does not, you may need to replace the serial port or bus mouse adapter. If a motherboard-based mouse port goes bad, you can replace the entire motherboard—which is usually expensive—or you can just disable the motherboard mouse port via jumpers or the system BIOS setup program and install a serial or bus mouse instead. This enables you to continue using the system without having to replace the motherboard.

Software Problems. Software problems can be a little trickier than hardware problems. Software problems generally manifest themselves as the mouse "just not working." In such instances, you need to check the driver and your software applications before assuming that the mouse has gone bad.

Driver Software. To function properly, the mouse requires the installation of a device driver. In DOS, you have to load the driver manually through your CONFIG.SYS or AUTOEXEC.BAT file, but the driver is automatically loaded in all versions of Windows. I normally recommend using the default drivers built into the Windows or OS/2 operating systems. In those environments, no additional external driver is necessary. The only reason for loading an external driver (via CONFIG.SYS) is if you want the mouse to work with DOS applications in Windows 3.1. Windows 9x drivers support the use of the mouse in DOS applications by default.

If you need the mouse to work in standard DOS—in other words, outside Windows or OS/2—you must load a device driver through either your CONFIG.SYS file or your AUTOEXEC.BAT file. This driver, if loaded in the CONFIG.SYS file, is typically called MOUSE.SYS. The version that loads in the AUTOEXEC.BAT file is called MOUSE.COM. (It is possible that your mouse drivers have different names, depending on who manufactured your mouse.) Again, remember that if you use a mouse only in Windows or OS/2, no external drivers are required because the mouse driver is built in.

The first step to installing a DOS mouse driver is to make sure the proper command to load the driver is in your CONFIG.SYS or AUTOEXEC.BAT file. If it isn't, add the proper line, according to the information supplied with your mouse. For instance, the proper command to load the mouse driver through the CONFIG.SYS file for a Microsoft mouse is as follows:

```
DEVICEHIGH=\DOS\MOUSE.SYS
```

The actual syntax of the command may vary, depending on whether you are loading the device into upper memory and where the device driver is located on your disk.

One of the biggest problems with the separate mouse driver is getting it loaded into an Upper Memory Block (UMB). The older Microsoft mouse drivers—versions 9.0 and earlier—require a very large block of 40–56K UMB to load, and upon loading they shrink down to less than 20K. Even though they take only 20K or less after loading, you still need a very large area to get them "in the door."

The best tip I can give you with respect to these separate drivers is to use the newest drivers available from Microsoft. These drivers are included with the newer Microsoft mice and are sold separately as an upgrade. The Microsoft driver works with any type of Microsoft-compatible mouse, which basically means just about any mouse at all. Microsoft requires that you pay about $50 for an upgrade to the newer versions of the mouse driver. You can also get the new driver with a new mouse for $35 or less, which makes the driver-only purchase not very cost effective. Microsoft still includes only the older driver with MS-DOS 6.22 or earlier. IBM included the new driver with PC DOS 6.3 but switched back to the 8.2 driver in PC DOS 7.0.

If you use version 9.01 or later, the driver requires less memory than previous versions and automatically loads into high memory. One of the best features is that the driver first loads into low memory, shrinks down to about 24K, and then moves into upper memory automatically. In addition, the driver seeks out the smallest UMB that can hold it instead of trying only the largest, as would happen if you used the DEVICEHIGH, LOADHIGH, or LH commands to load the driver. Previous versions of the driver could not fit into an upper memory block unless that block was at least 40–56K or larger in size, and they would certainly not move into upper memory automatically. The enhanced self-loading capability of the Microsoft DOS mouse driver 9.01 and higher can save much memory space. It is well worth having.

◄◄ See "Taking Advantage of Unused Upper Memory," p. 387

After placing the proper driver load command in your CONFIG.SYS or AUTOEXEC.BAT file, reboot the system with the mouse connected and make sure the driver loads properly. If the proper command is in place and the driver is not loading, watch your video screen as your system boots. At some point, you should see a message from the mouse driver indicating that it is loaded. If you see a message indicating that the driver failed to load instead, you must determine why. For example, the driver may not be able to load because not enough memory is available. After you determine why the driver is not loading, you need to rectify the situation and make sure the driver loads.

DOS Application Software. If your mouse does not work with a specific piece of DOS application software, check the setup information or configuration section of the program. Make sure you indicated to the program (if necessary) that you are using a mouse. If it still does not work and the mouse works with other software you are using, contact the technical support department of the application software company.

Microsoft IntelliMouse

Late in 1996, Microsoft introduced a new variation of its popular mouse, called the *IntelliMouse*. This device looks exactly like the standard Microsoft mouse except for a miniature gray wheel rising up between the two buttons. This wheel represents the only major change in external mouse design in many years.

The wheel has two main functions. The primary function is to act as a scrolling device, enabling you to scroll through documents or Web pages by manipulating the wheel with your index finger. The wheel also functions as a third mouse button when you press it.

Although three-button mice have been available for years, the scrolling function is a real breakthrough. No longer do you have to move the mouse pointer to click the scrollbar on the right side of your screen or take your hand off of the mouse to use the arrow keys on the keyboard. You just push or pull on the wheel. This is a major convenience, especially when browsing Web pages or working with word processing documents or spreadsheets. Also, unlike three-button mice from other vendors, the IntelliMouse's wheel-button doesn't seem to get in the way and you are less likely to click it by mistake.

The major drawback to the IntelliMouse is that the wheel functions only in software that is written to support it. At the time the IntelliMouse debuted, Microsoft Internet Explorer had already been modified to use the new wheel, and all the applications in Office 97 support it as well. For example, most Office 97 applications allow you to hold down the Ctrl key while turning the wheel to zoom in and out. Manipulating the wheel while holding down the Shift key expands and collapses outlines. As new and updated versions of other software come out, you can expect that they will also support the new wheel functions.

The IntelliMouse 2.0 driver combines features from earlier versions of Microsoft's mouse driver with some interesting new functions. A feature called *ClickLock* allows you to drag items without holding down the primary mouse button. You can customize this feature by specifying how long you have to hold the button down to activate ClickLock. You can also configure the wheel to scroll a specified number of lines or scroll a screen with each click of the wheel.

You can also set the driver software so that the wheel-button ignores all application-specific functions and instead performs one of four preset functions in all Windows applications. The four choices are as follows:

- Double-left-click
- Open an application's Help file
- Switch to Windows Explorer
- Bring up the Windows Start menu

Other driver features retained from earlier versions include a Snap To feature, which moves the pointer to the default button of a dialog box, and functions that add trails when the pointer moves and make the pointer disappear when you start typing.

TrackPoint II/III
On October 20, 1992, IBM introduced a revolutionary new pointing device called *TrackPoint II* as an integrated feature of its new ThinkPad 700 and 700C computers. Often referred to as a *pointing stick* device, it consists primarily of a small rubber cap that appears on the keyboard right above the B key, between the G and H keys. This was the first significant new pointing device since the mouse had been invented nearly 30 years earlier!

This device occupies no space on a desk, does not have to be adjusted for left-handed or right-handed use, has no moving parts to fail or become dirty, and—most importantly—does not require you to move your hands from the home row to use. This is an absolute boon for touch typists.

I was fortunate enough to meet the actual creator and designer of this device in early 1992 at the spring Comdex/Windows World in Chicago. He was in a small corner of the IBM booth showing off his custom-made keyboards with a small silicone rubber nub in the middle. In fact, the devices he had were hand-built prototypes installed in standard desktop keyboards, and he was there trying to get public reaction and feedback on his invention.

I was invited to play with one of the keyboards, which was connected to a demonstration system. By pressing on the stick with my index finger, I could move the mouse pointer on the screen. The stick itself did not move, so it was not a joystick. Instead, it had a silicone rubber cap that was connected to pressure transducers that measured the amount of force my finger was applying and the direction of the force and moved the mouse pointer accordingly. The harder I pressed, the faster the pointer moved. I could move the pointer in any direction smoothly by slightly changing the direction of push or pull. The silicone rubber gripped my finger even though I had been sweating from dashing about the show. After playing around with it for just a few minutes, the movements became automatic—almost as if I could just "think" about where I wanted the pointer to go.

After reflecting on this for a minute, it really hit me: This had to be the most revolutionary pointing device since the mouse itself! Not only would this be a natural replacement for a mouse, but it would also be a boon for touch typists like me who don't like to take their hands off of the keyboard.

The gentleman at the booth turned out to be Ted Selker, the primary inventor of the device. He and Joseph Rutledge created this integrated pointing device at the IBM T.J. Watson Research Center. When I asked him when such keyboards would become available, he could not answer. At the time, there were apparently no plans for production, and he was only trying to test user reaction to the device.

Just over six months later, IBM announced the *ThinkPad 700*, which included this revolutionary device, then called the TrackPoint II Integrated Pointing Device. Since the original version came out, an enhanced version with greater control and sensitivity called the TrackPoint *III* has been available.

> **Note**
>
> The reason the device was called TrackPoint II is that IBM had previously been selling a convertible mouse/trackball device called the TrackPoint. No relationship exists between the original TrackPoint mouse/trackball, which has since been discontinued, and the TrackPoint II integrated device. Since the original TrackPoint II came out, an improved version called TrackPoint III is now available. It is basically an improved version of the same design. In the interest of simplicity, I will refer to all of the TrackPoint II, III, and successive devices as just TrackPoint.

In its final production form, the TrackPoint consists of a small red silicone rubber knob nestled between the G, H, and B keys on the keyboard. The primary and secondary mouse buttons are placed below the Spacebar where you can easily reach them with your thumbs without taking your hands off the keyboard.

IBM studies conducted by Selker found that the act of removing your hand from the keyboard to reach for a mouse and replacing the hand on the keyboard takes approximately 1.75 seconds. If you type 60wpm, that can equal nearly two lost words per minute, not including the time lost while you regain your train of thought. Almost all this time can be saved each time you use the track point to either move the pointer or make a selection (click or double-click). The combination of the buttons and the positioning knob also enable you to perform drag-and-drop functions easily.

IBM's research also found that people can get up to 20 percent more work accomplished using the TrackPoint instead of a mouse, especially when the application involves a mix of typing and pointing activities, such as with word processing, spreadsheets, and other typical office applications. In usability tests with the TrackPoint III, IBM provided a group of desktop computer users with both a TrackPoint and a traditional mouse. After two weeks, 80 percent of the users had unplugged their mice and switched solely to the TrackPoint device. Selker is convinced (as am I) that the TrackPoint is the best pointing solution for both laptop and desktop systems.

Another feature of the TrackPoint is that a standard mouse can be connected to the system at the same time to allow for dual-pointer use. In this case, a single mouse pointer would still be on the screen but both the TrackPoint and the simultaneously connected mouse could move the pointer. This not only enables a single person to use both devices, but also enables two people to use the TrackPoint and the mouse simultaneously to move the pointer on the screen. The first pointing device that moves (thus issuing a system interrupt) takes precedence and retains control over the mouse pointer on the screen until it completes its movement action. The second pointing device is automatically locked out until the primary device is stationary. This enables the use of both devices, while preventing each one from interfering with the other.

Recognizing the significance of the TrackPoint, especially for portable systems, several other manufacturers of laptop and notebook portable computers, such as Toshiba and Texas Instruments, have licensed the TrackPoint pointing device from IBM. They often give the device a different name, but the technology and operation are the same. For example, Toshiba calls its pointing stick the Accupoint.

I have compared the TrackPoint device to other pointing devices for notebooks, such as the trackballs and even the capacitive touch pads. But nothing compares in terms of accuracy and control, and, of course, you don't have to take your hands off of the keyboard!

Unfortunately, many of the lower-end portable system manufacturers have chosen not to license the IBM TrackPoint technology, but instead have attempted to copy it using inferior transducers and control software. The major drawback to these nonlicensed TrackPoint type devices is that they simply do not perform as well as the official versions licensed from IBM. They are usually slow to respond, sluggish in operation, and lack the sensitivity and accuracy found in the IBM-designed versions.

One way of telling that the TrackPoint device is licensed from IBM and uses the IBM technology is that it will accept IBM TrackPoint II or III rubber caps. These have a square hole in them and will properly lock on to any of the licensed versions, such as those found in Toshiba systems.

IBM recently upgraded its pointing stick and now calls it TrackPoint III. There are two main differences in the III system, but the one that is most obvious is in the rubber cap. IBM always uses red caps in their TrackPoint device, while other companies use different colors (Toshiba uses green or gray, for example). However, the main difference in the new TrackPoint III caps is in the rubber composition, not the color.

The IBM TrackPoint II and Toshiba Accupoint caps are made out of silicone rubber, which is grippy and works well in most situations. However, if the user has greasy fingers, the textured surface of the rubber can absorb some of the grease and become slippery. Cleaning the cap (and the user's hands) solves the problem, but it can be annoying at times. The new TrackPoint III caps are made out of a different type of rubber, which Selker calls "plastic sandpaper." This type of cap is much more grippy, and does not require cleaning except for cosmetic purposes. I have used both types of caps and can say for certain that the TrackPoint III cap is superior!

> **Note**
>
> Because the Accupoint device used in the Toshiba notebooks is licensed from IBM, it uses the same hardware (a pressure transducer called a *strain gauge*) and takes the same physical caps. I ordered a set of the new TrackPoint III caps and installed them on my Toshiba portable systems, which dramatically improved the grip. You can get these caps by ordering them from IBM Parts directly or from others who sell IBM parts, such as DakTech, under IBM part number 84G6536. The cost is approximately $9 for a set of two "plastic sandpaper" red caps.

Replacing the cap is easy—simply grab the existing cap with your fingers and pull straight up; it will pop right off. Then push on the new red IBM TrackPoint III cap in its place. You will thank me when you feel how you can grip the new IBM cap much more easily than you can grip the designs used by others.

The other difference between the TrackPoint II and III from IBM is in the control software. IBM added routines that implement a subtle technique Selker calls "negative inertia," but which is marketed under the term *QuickStop response*. This software not only takes into account how far you push the pointer in any direction, but also how quickly you push or release it. Selker found that this improved software (and the sandpaper cap) allows people to make selections up to 8% faster.

The TrackPoint is obviously an ideal pointing device for a portable system in which lugging around an external mouse or trackball can be inconvenient. The trackballs and mini-trackballs built into some laptop keyboards are very difficult to use and usually require removing your hands from the home row. Mouse and trackball devices are notorious for becoming "sticky" as the ball picks up dirt that affects the internal roller motion. This is especially noticeable with the smaller mini-trackball devices.

Many newer notebook systems include a touch pad, and although this seemed like a good idea at first, it pales in comparison with the TrackPoint. The touch pads are based on a capacitive effect, and pointer operation can become erratic if your skin is either too dry or too moist. Their biggest drawback is that they are positioned on the keyboard below the Spacebar, which means you either have to remove your hand from the home row to place your index finger on the pad, or try to use the pad with your thumb, which has too wide a contact area for precise movement and control.

The bottom line is that anyone who touch types should strongly consider only portable systems that include an IBM-licensed TrackPoint device (such as Toshiba). TrackPoints are far superior to other pointing devices, such as the touch pads, because the TrackPoint is faster to use (you don't have to take your hands off of the home row on the keyboard), easier to adapt to (especially for speedy touch typists), and far more precise.

But the benefits of the TrackPoint are not limited to portable systems. Because I use a notebook so often and have found the TrackPoint so fast and easy to use, I wanted to use it on my desktop systems as well. For desktop systems, I use a Lexmark keyboard with the IBM-licensed TrackPoint device built in. This makes for a more consistent interface between desktop and notebook use because I can use the same pointing device in both environments. One drawback for some older systems is that the TrackPoint device in these keyboards works only with systems that used a PS/2- or motherboard-type mouse connector—no serial version is available. I list the part number for the IBM Enhanced keyboard with the TrackPoint in the section "Replacement Keyboards" earlier in this chapter. You can also purchase these keyboards directly from Unicomp, which has purchased Lexmark's keyboard technology.

Glidepoint

In response to the TrackPoint, other companies have adopted new pointing device technologies as well. For example, Alps Electric has introduced a touch pad pointing device called the *Glidepoint*. The Glidepoint uses a flat, square pad that senses finger position through body capacitance. This is similar to the capacitance-sensitive elevator button controls you sometimes encounter in office buildings or hotels. Instead of sitting in between the keys, the Glidepoint is mounted below the Spacebar, and it detects pressure applied by your thumbs or fingers. Transducers under the pad convert finger movement into pointer movement. Several laptop and notebook manufacturers have licensed this technology from Alps and are incorporating it into their portable systems. Apple was one of the first to adopt it in its portable systems.

Although it seems to have gained wide acceptance, this technology has a number of drawbacks. Operation of the device can be erratic, depending on skin resistance and moisture content. The biggest drawback is that to operate the touch pad, users have to remove their hands from the home row on the keyboard, which dramatically slows their progress. In addition, the operation of the touch pad can be imprecise, depending on how pointy your finger or thumb is!

On the other hand, if you're not a touch typist, then removing your hands from the keyboard to operate the touch pad may be easier than using a TrackPoint. Even with their drawbacks, touch pad type pointing devices are still vastly preferable for portable systems to using a trackball or a cumbersome external mouse.

The Future. Pointer technology is progressing in ways that were undreamed of when the first mice were developed. Hardware developers are beginning to take advantage of the bidirectional interfaces on PCs to develop input devices that react to a user's actions. A company called Immersion Corp. is planning to release a mouse called FEELit in late 1998. FEELit is permanently mounted to a specially designed pad that houses a processor for generating real-time simulations.

An electromagnetic drive inside the pad generates sensations, enabling you to feel three-dimensional icons, window edges, scroll buttons, and other Windows artifacts. You can click and drag objects with variable pressure and feel the elasticity of shapes as you stretch them. Developers can write applications using special function calls that allow them to incorporate the feelings generated by textures, surfaces, liquids, and vibrations into their programs.

This type of technology has great promise for making computers truly interactive and for enhancing the reality of games and other simulated environments.

Game Adapter (Joystick) Interface

The *game control* or *joystick* adapter is a special input device that enables you to attach up to four paddles or two joysticks to a PC system. The term *paddle* is used to refer to a knob that can be rotated to move an object on the screen. It was named after the first popular video game, called Pong, in which the knob moved the game paddles.

You can find the game adapter function on a dedicated ISA bus adapter card, or it can be combined with other functions on a multifunction card. The game connector on the card is a female 15-pin D-Shell type socket (see Figure 7.19).

The game adapter can recognize up to four simple contact switches (called *buttons*) and four resistive inputs. Each paddle normally has one button and one knob that controls a variable resistor, whereas a joystick normally has two buttons and a central stick that controls two variable resistors. In a joystick, the variable resistors are tied to the central stick. One indicates the relative horizontal position (or x-coordinate) of the stick, and the other indicates its relative vertical position (or y-coordinate).

More advanced controllers track the rotational movement (R-axis) of the joystick, and some also track the position of the "top hat," an additional control that sits atop the stick and is maneuvered with the thumb. Also, some digital joysticks sense position using crystals in the top hat to generate an electrical current when it is pressed or distorted. Digital joysticks also allow for the use of more than two pairs of X-Y axes; in fact, joysticks are now being designed that include a Z-axis, to track movement in the third dimension.

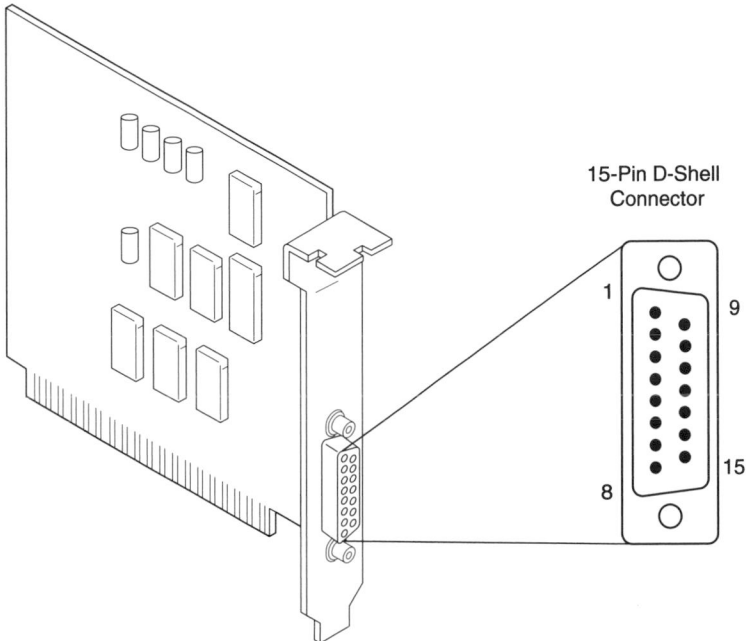

15-Pin D-Shell
Connector

FIG. 7.19   Typical game adapter and 15-pin connector.

The Universal Serial Bus also promises to improve the gaming experience by providing a bidirectional interface through which you will be able to feel a response in a joystick to an artificial stimulus. By integrating servo mechanisms into the joystick, you can be made to feel bumps in the road while playing a driving game and wind resistance in a flight simulator. This technique is called *force feedback*; it is already being assimilated into products such as the Microsoft Sidewinder Force Feedback Pro game controller.

Resistor inputs are variable, from 0 to 100K ohms. The adapter converts the resistive value to a digital pulse with a duration proportional to the resistive load. Software can time these pulses to determine the relative resistance value. The game adapter does not use much in the way of system resources. The card does not use an IRQ, DMA channel, or memory, and it requires only a single I/O address (port) 201h. The adapter is controlled by reading and writing data to and from port 201h.

Note that joystick resistance is read by polling the adapter; the game port interface is not interrupt driven. This means that a program has to scan the device by sending an I/O command for input rather than by receiving an interrupt, as with other (such as serial) devices.

Table 7.11 shows the interface connector pinout specification for a PC-compatible game adapter.

Table 7.11	PC-Compatible Game Adapter Connector		
Pin	**Signal**	**Function**	**I/O**
1	+5v	Paddle 1, Joystick A	Out
2	Button 4	Paddle 1 button, Joystick A button #1	In
3	Position 0	Paddle 1 position, Joystick A x-coordinate	In
4	Ground	—	—
5	Ground	—	—
6	Position 1	Paddle 2 position, Joystick A y-coordinate	In
7	Button 5	Paddle 2 button, Joystick A button #2	In
8	+5v	Paddle 2	Out
9	+5v	Paddle 3 and Joystick B	Out
10	Button 6	Paddle 3 button, Joystick B button #1	In
11	Position 2	Paddle 3 position, Joystick B x-coordinate	In
12	Ground	—	—
13	Position 3	Paddle 4 position, Joystick B y-coordinate	In
14	Button 7	Paddle 4 button, Joystick B button #2	In
15	+5v	Paddle 4	Out

Because this adapter actually reads resistance and can be easily manipulated with standard programming languages, the game adapter serves as a poor man's data acquisition board or real-time interface card. With it, you can hook up to four sensors and four switches and easily read the data on the PC.

Game adapters are available for ISA bus systems from a number of vendors, and joysticks using the Universal Serial Bus should be available by the time you read this. Consult Appendix A for some companies that may offer these types of adapters. Generally, the best place to look is one of the larger mail order system and peripheral vendors.

Some manufacturers have produced specialized joysticks that really don't look like joysticks at all. Perhaps the best known of these is the steering wheel and pedal control set sold for use with driving and flight simulator games. However, these devices are exactly the same as the standard joystick and paddles as far as your system is concerned. Instead of paddle knobs, they have steering wheels and pedals controlling the variable resistors in the circuit. A number of these devices are on the market for the popular driving and flight simulator games, and they can make these games much more realistic. Because the different controls can be connected to different paddle inputs on the game adapters, make sure that your software will support the particular control device you select.

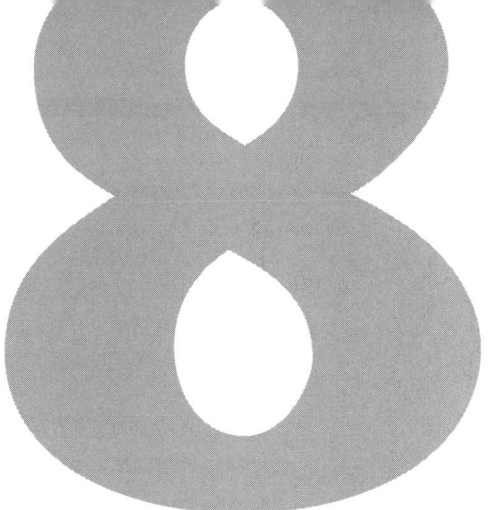

Chapter 8

Video Hardware

As the visual link between you and your computer, the video display is one of the most important components of your PC. Before CRT monitors came into general use, the teletypewriter was the standard computer interface—a large, loud device that printed the input and output characters on a roll of paper. The first CRT displays were primitive by today's standards; they displayed only text in a single color, but to users at the time they were a great improvement.

Today, PC video displays are much more sophisticated, but you must be careful when selecting video hardware for your computer. Working with even the fastest and most powerful PC can be a chore when the display slows the system down, causes eyestrain, or is not suitable for the tasks you want to accomplish.

The video subsystem of a PC consists of two main components:

- Monitor (or video display)
- Video adapter (also called the video card or graphics adapter)

This chapter explores the range of PC video adapters on the market today, and the displays that work with them.

> **Note**
>
> The term *video*, as it is used in this context, does not necessarily imply the existence of a moving image, such as on a television screen. All adapters that feed signals to a monitor or other display are video adapters, whether or not they are used with applications that display moving images, such as multimedia or videoconferencing software.

Monitors

A monitor requires a source of input. The signals that run to your monitor come from a video adapter inside or plugged into your computer. Some computers—such as those that use the low profile (LPX) or new low profile (NLX) motherboard form factor—contain this adapter circuitry on the motherboard. Most systems, however, use Baby-AT or ATX-style motherboards and normally incorporate the video adapter on a separate circuit board that is plugged into an expansion or bus slot. The expansion cards that produce video signals are called *video cards*, or *graphics cards*. The term video adapter is applicable to either integrated or separate video circuitry. Whether the video adapter is built into the motherboard or found on a separate card, the circuitry operates the same way and generally uses the same components.

> **Note**
>
> One product, the Cyrix MediaGX, actually incorporates video adapter (and audio adapter and RAM controller) functionality into the system processor. The processor's XpressGRAPHICS feature eliminates the delays incurred by the constant transfer of data to and from the video adapter. Also, because it does not use dedicated memory, the video adapter functions can self-adjust to use as much main system memory as needed for the selected video resolution. Obviously, this is a radical approach to video display technology that requires a motherboard that is built around this special processor.

Display Technologies

A monitor may use one of several display technologies. By far the most popular is cathode ray tube (CRT) technology, the same technology used in television sets. CRTs consist of a vacuum tube enclosed in glass. One end of the tube contains an electron gun; the other end contains a screen with a phosphorous coating.

When heated, the electron gun emits a stream of high-speed electrons that are attracted to the other end of the tube. Along the way, a focus control and deflection coil steer the beam to a specific point on the phosphorous screen. When struck by the beam, the phosphor glows. This light is what you see when you watch TV or your computer screen.

The phosphor chemical has a quality called *persistence*, which indicates how long this glow will remain onscreen. Persistence is what causes a faint image to remain on your TV screen for a few seconds after you turn the set off. The *scanning frequency* of the display specifies how often the image is refreshed. You should have a good match between persistence and scanning frequency so the image has less flicker (which occurs when the persistence is too low) and no ghost images (as when the persistence is too high).

The electron beam moves very quickly, sweeping the screen from left to right in lines from top to bottom, in a pattern called a *raster*. The *horizontal scan rate* refers to the speed at which the electron beam moves laterally across the screen.

During its sweep, the beam strikes the phosphor wherever an image should appear onscreen. The beam also varies in intensity to produce different levels of brightness. Because the glow begins to fade almost immediately, the electron beam must continue to sweep the screen to maintain an image—a practice called *redrawing* or *refreshing* the screen.

Most displays have an ideal *refresh rate* (also called the *vertical scan frequency*) of about 70 hertz (Hz), meaning that the screen is refreshed 70 times per second. Refresh rates that are too low cause the screen to flicker, contributing to eyestrain. The higher the refresh rate, the better for your eyes.

It is important that the refresh rates expected by your monitor match those produced by your video card. If you have mismatched rates, you will not see an image and may actually damage your monitor.

Some monitors have a fixed refresh rate. Other monitors may support a range of frequencies; this support provides built-in compatibility with future video standards (described in the "Video Display Adapters" section later in this chapter). A monitor that supports many video standards is called a *multiple-frequency monitor*. Most monitors today are multiple-frequency monitors, which means they support operation with a variety of popular video signal standards. Different vendors call their multiple-frequency monitors by different trade names, including multisync, multifrequency, multiscan, autosynchronous, and autotracking.

Phosphor-based screens come in two styles—*curved* and *flat*. The typical display screen is curved, meaning that it bulges outward from the middle of the screen. This design is consistent with the vast majority of CRT designs (the same as the tube in most television sets).

The traditional screen is curved both vertically and horizontally. Some models use the *Trinitron design*, which is curved only horizontally and is flat vertically. Many people prefer this flatter screen because it shows less glare and a higher-quality, more accurate image. The disadvantage is that the technology required to produce flat-screen displays is more expensive, resulting in higher prices for the monitors.

LCD Displays. Alternative display designs are available, as well. Borrowing technology from laptop manufacturers, some companies market monitors with LCD (liquid-crystal display) displays. LCDs have low-glare screens that are completely flat, and low power requirements (five watts versus nearly 100 watts for an ordinary monitor). The color quality of an active-matrix LCD panel actually exceeds that of most CRT displays.

At this point, however, LCD screens usually are more limited in resolution than typical CRTs and are more expensive; for example, a 14-inch LCD screen can cost more than $1,000, more than the cost of a high-quality 17-inch CRT monitor. However, it is important to consider that an LCD screen provides a larger viewable image than a CRT monitor of the same size. There are three basic LCD choices: passive-matrix monochrome, passive-matrix color, and active-matrix color. The passive-matrix designs are also available in single- and dual-scan versions.

In an LCD, a polarizing filter creates two separate light waves. The polarizing filter allows light waves that are aligned only with the filter to pass through. After passing through the polarizing filter, the remaining light waves are all aligned in the same direction. By aligning a second polarizing filter at a right angle to the first, all those waves are blocked. By changing the angle of the second polarizing filter, the amount of light allowed to pass can be changed. It is the role of the liquid crystal cell to change the angle of polarization and control the amount of light that passes. In a color LCD, there is an additional filter that has three cells for each pixel—one each for displaying red, green, and blue.

The light wave passes through a liquid-crystal cell, with each color segment having its own cell. The liquid crystals are rod-shaped molecules that flow like a liquid. They enable light to pass straight through, but an electrical charge alters their orientation and the orientation of light passing through them. Although monochrome LCDs do not have color filters, they can have multiple cells per pixel for controlling shades of gray.

In a passive-matrix LCD, each cell is controlled by the electrical charges of two transistors, determined by the cell's row and column positions on the display. The number of transistors along the screen's horizontal and vertical edges determines the resolution of the screen. For example, a screen with an 800×600 resolution has 800 transistors on its horizontal edge and 600 on the vertical, for a total of 1,400. As the cell reacts to the pulsing charge from its two transistors, it twists the light wave, with stronger charges twisting the light wave more. *Supertwist* refers to the orientation of the liquid crystals, comparing on mode to off mode—the greater the twist, the higher the contrast.

Charges in passive-matrix LCDs are pulsed, so the displays lack the brilliance of active-matrix, which provides a constant charge to each cell. To increase the brilliance, some vendors have turned to a new technique called *double-scan LCD*, which splits passive-matrix screens into a top half and bottom half, reducing the time between each pulse. Besides increasing the brightness, dual-scan designs also increase the response time and therefore the perceptible speed of the display, making this type more usable for full-motion video or other applications where the displayed information changes rapidly.

In an active-matrix LCD, each cell has its own dedicated transistor behind the panel to charge it and twist the light wave. Thus, an 800×600 active-matrix display has 480,000 transistors. This provides a brighter image than passive-matrix displays because the cell can maintain a constant, rather than a momentary, charge. However, active-matrix technology uses more energy than passive-matrix. With a dedicated transistor for every cell, active-matrix displays are more difficult and expensive to produce.

> **Note**
>
> Because an LCD display requires a specified number of transistors to support each cell, there are no multiple frequency displays of this type. All the pixels on an LCD screen are of a fixed size, although CRT pixels are variable. Thus, LCD displays are designed to be operated at a specific resolution. Before purchasing this type of display, be sure your video adapter supports the same resolution as the screen, and that the resolution will be sufficient for your needs throughout the life of the monitor.

In both active- and passive-matrix LCDs, the second polarizing filter controls how much light passes through each cell. Cells twist the wavelength of light to closely match the filter's allowable wavelength. The more light that passes through the filter at each cell, the brighter the pixel.

Monochrome LCDs achieve grayscales (up to 64) by varying the brightness of a cell or dithering cells in an on-and-off pattern. Color LCDs, on the other hand, dither the three-color cells and control their brilliance to achieve different colors on the screen. Double-scan passive-matrix LCDs have recently gained in popularity because they approach the quality of active-matrix displays, but do not cost much more to produce than other passive-matrix displays.

The big problem with active-matrix LCDs is that the manufacturing yields are low, forcing higher prices. This means many of the panels produced have more than a certain maximum number of failed transistors. The resulting low yields limit the production capacity and incurs higher prices.

In the past, several hot CRTs were needed to light an LCD screen, but portable computer manufacturers now use a single tube the size of a cigarette. Fiber-optic technology evenly spreads light emitted from the tube across an entire display.

Thanks to supertwist and triple-supertwist LCDs, today's screens enable you to see the screen clearly from more angles with better contrast and lighting. To improve readability, especially in dim light, some laptops include *backlighting* or *edgelighting* (also called *sidelighting*). Backlit screens provide light from a panel behind the LCD. Edgelit screens get their light from the small fluorescent tubes mounted along the sides of the screen. Some older laptops excluded such lighting systems to lengthen battery life. Most modern laptops enable you to run the backlight at a reduced power setting that dims the display, but allows for longer battery life.

The best color displays are *active-matrix* or *thin-film transistor (TFT)* panels, in which each pixel is controlled by three transistors (for red, green, and blue). Active-matrix-screen refreshes and redraws are immediate and accurate, with much less ghosting and blurring than in passive-matrix LCDs (which control pixels via rows and columns of transistors along the edges of the screen). Active-matrix displays are also much brighter and can easily be read at an angle.

Gas Plasma Displays. An alternative to LCD screens is gas-plasma technology, typically known for its black and orange screens in some of the older Toshiba notebook computers. Some companies are incorporating gas-plasma technology for desktop screens and possibly color high-definition television (HDTV) flat-panel screens.

Monochrome Versus Color

During the early years of the IBM PC and the compatibles that followed, owners had only two video choices—color using a CGA display adapter and monochrome using an MDA display adapter. Since then, many adapter and display options have hit the market.

Monochrome monitors produce images of one color. The most popular is amber, followed by white and green. The color of the monitor is determined by the color of the phosphors on the CRT screen. Some monochrome monitors with white phosphors can support many shades of gray.

Color monitors use more sophisticated technology than monochrome monitors, which accounts for their higher prices. Whereas a monochrome picture tube contains one electron gun, a color tube contains three guns arranged in a triangular shape referred to as a *delta configuration*. Instead of amber, white, or green phosphors, the monitor screen contains phosphor triads, which consist of one red phosphor, one green phosphor, and one blue phosphor arranged in the same pattern as the electron guns. These three primary colors can be mixed to produce all other colors.

Monochrome monitors are difficult to find these days, which is a shame because they do still have applications. It has always seemed wasteful to me to devote a color monitor to a system running an OS with a mono-color display, such as on a NetWare server.

The Right Size

Monitors come in different sizes, ranging from 9-inch to 42-inch diagonal measure. The larger the monitor, the higher the price tag—once you get beyond 17 inch displays, the prices skyrocket. The most common monitor sizes are 14, 15, 17, and 21 inches. These diagonal measurements, unfortunately, often represent not the size of the actual image that the screen displays, but the size of the tube.

As a result, comparing one company's 15-inch monitor to that of another may be unfair unless you actually measure the active screen area. The active screen area refers to the diagonal measure of the lighted area on the screen. In other words, if you are running Windows, the viewing area is the actual diagonal measure of the desktop.

This area can vary widely from monitor to monitor, so one company's 17-inch monitor may display a 15.0-inch image, and another company's 17-inch monitor may present a 15.5-inch image.

The following table shows the monitor's advertised diagonal screen size, along with the approximate diagonal measure of the actual active viewing area for the most common display sizes.

Monitor Size (in Inches)	Viewing Area (in Inches)
12	10.5
14	12.5
15	13.5
16	14.5
17	15.5
18	16.5
19	17.5
20	18.5
21	19.5

The size of the actual viewable area varies from manufacturer to manufacturer, but tends to be approximately 1.5 inches less than the actual screen size. However, you can adjust some monitors—such as some models made by NEC, for example—to display a high-quality image that completely fills the tube from edge to edge. Other makes can fill the screen also, but some of them do so only by pushing the monitor beyond its comfortable limits. The result is a distorted image that is worse than the monitor's smaller, properly adjusted picture.

This phenomenon is a well-known monitor purchasing caveat and, as a result, some manufacturers and vendors have begun advertising the size of the active viewing area of their monitors along with the screen size. This makes it easier for consumers to get what they are paying for.

In most cases, the 17-inch monitor is currently the best bargain in the industry. A 17-inch monitor is recommended for new systems, especially when running Windows, and is not much more expensive than a 15-inch display. I recommend a 17-inch monitor as the minimum you should consider for most normal applications. Low-end applications can still get away with a 15-inch display, but you will be limited in the screen resolutions that you can view comfortably. Eighteen–21-inch or larger displays are recommended for high-end systems, especially where graphics applications are the major focus.

Larger monitors are particularly handy for applications such as CAD and desktop publishing, in which the smallest details must be clearly visible. With a 17-inch or larger display, you can see nearly an entire 8 1/2×11-inch print page in 100% view—in other words, what you see onscreen virtually matches the page that will be printed. This feature is called *WYSIWYG*—short for "what you see is what you get." If you can see the entire page at its actual size, you can save yourself the trouble of printing several drafts before you get it right.

With the popularity of the Internet, monitor size and resolution become even more of an issue. Many Web pages are being designed for 1,024×768 resolution, which requires a 17-inch CRT display as a minimum to handle without eyestrain and inadequate focus. Because of their much tighter dot pitch, LCD displays in laptop computers can handle that resolution easily on 13.3– or even some 12.1-inch displays. Using 1,024×768 resolution means you will be able to view most Web pages without scrolling sideways, which is a major convenience.

> **Note**
>
> Although many monitors smaller than 17 inches are physically capable of running at 1,024×768 and even higher resolutions, most people have trouble reading print at that size.

Monitor Resolution

Resolution is the amount of detail a monitor can render. This quantity is expressed in the number of horizontal and vertical picture elements, or *pixels*, contained in the screen. The greater the number of pixels, the more detailed the images. The resolution required depends on the application. Character-based applications (such as DOS command-line programs) require little resolution, whereas graphics-intensive applications (such as desktop publishing and Windows software) require a great deal.

As PC video technology developed, the screen resolutions supported by video adapters grew at a steady pace. The following table lists some standard resolutions used in PC video adapters and the terms that were used to commonly describe them:

Resolution	Acronym	Standard Designation
640×480	VGA	Video Graphics Array
800×600	SVGA	Super VGA
1,024×768	XGA	eXtended Graphics Array
1,280×1,024	UVGA	Ultra VGA

Today, the term VGA is still in common usage as a reference to the standard 640×480 16-color display that the Windows operating systems use as their default. The 15-pin connector to which you connect the monitor on most video adapters is also often called a VGA plug.

However, the terms SVGA, XGA, and UVGA have fallen into disuse. The industry now describes screen resolutions simply by citing the number of pixels. Nearly all the video adapters sold today support the 640×480, 800×600, and 1,024×768 pixel resolutions at several color depths, and many support 1,280×1,024 and higher as well.

Dot Pitch

Another important specification that denotes the quality of a given monitor is its dot pitch. In a monochrome monitor, the picture element is a screen phosphor, but in a color monitor, the picture element is a phosphor triad. Dot pitch, which applies only to color monitors, is the distance (in millimeters) between phosphor triads. Screens with a small dot pitch have a smaller space between the phosphor triads. As a result, the picture elements are closer together, producing a sharper picture on the screen. Conversely, screens with a large dot pitch tend to produce images that are less clear.

The original IBM PC color monitor had a dot pitch of 0.43mm, which is considered to be poor by almost any standard. The state-of-the-art monitors marketed today have a dot pitch of 0.25mm or less; I would not recommend buying a monitor with a dot pitch of more than 0.28mm in most cases. Although you can save money by picking a smaller monitor or one with a higher dot pitch, the trade off is not usually worth it.

Interlaced Versus Noninterlaced

Monitors and video adapters may support interlaced or noninterlaced resolution. In *noninterlaced* (conventional) mode, the electron beam sweeps the screen in lines from top to bottom, one line after the other, completing the screen in one pass. In *interlaced* mode, the electron beam also sweeps the screen from top to bottom, but it does so in two passes—sweeping the odd lines first and the even lines second. Each pass takes half the time of a full pass in noninterlaced mode. Therefore, both modes refresh the entire screen in the same amount of time.

This technique redraws the screen faster and provides more stable images, but also produces what is often a very noticeable flicker. If you switch your video adapter to a higher screen resolution, and you find that your solid, satisfactory picture suddenly seems flickery, you have probably switched to a resolution that your hardware only supports in interlaced mode. Different users react to interlaced displays differently. To some people, it is hardly noticeable, while to others, looking at the screen is unbearable.

Caution

It's not unheard of for people with neurological disorders such as epilepsy to be profoundly affected by the flicker produced by monitors running in interlaced mode or at low refresh rates. These people should take adequate precautions before adjusting their video display setting and, if possible, be aware of their physical limitations.

Monitors that use interlacing can use lower refresh rates, thus lessening their cost. The drawback is that interlacing depends on the ability of the eye to combine two nearly identical lines, separated by a gap, into one solid line. If you are looking for high-quality video, however, you should avoid interlacing at all costs and get a video adapter and monitor that support high-resolution, noninterlaced displays.

Energy and Safety

A properly selected monitor can save energy. Many PC manufacturers are trying to meet the Environmental Protection Agency's Energy Star requirements. Any PC-and-monitor combination that consumes less than 60 watts (30 watts apiece) during idle periods can use the Energy Star logo. Some research shows that such "green" PCs can save each user about $70 per year in electricity costs.

Power Management. Monitors, being one of the most power-hungry computer components, can contribute to those savings. One of the first energy-saving standards for monitors was VESA's Display Power-Management Signaling (DPMS) spec, which defines the signals that a computer sends to a monitor to indicate idle times. The computer or video card decides when to send these signals.

Since then, Intel and Microsoft have jointly developed the Advanced Power Management (APM) specification, which defines a BIOS-based interface between hardware that is capable of power management functions and an operating system that implements power management policies. In short, this means that you can configure an OS such as Windows 9x to switch your monitor into a low-power mode after an interval of nonuse, and even to shut it off entirely. For these actions to occur, however, the monitor, the system BIOS, and the operating system must all support the APM standard.

For displays, power management is implemented when DPMS signals the monitor to enter into the various APM modes. The basis of the DPMS standard is the condition of the synchronization signals being sent to the display. By altering these signals, a DPMS-compatible monitor can be forced into the various APM modes by an operating system that supports the power management standard. You can configure the monitor to enter the stand-by and suspend modes at predefined intervals when the computer is not in use, and even shift back to the on mode when certain events occur, such as when a modem phone line rings.

The defined monitor states in DPMS are as follows:

- *On.* Refers to the state of the display when it is in full operation.

- *Stand-By.* Defines an optional operating state of minimal power reduction with the shortest recovery time.

- *Suspend.* Refers to a level of power management in which substantial power reduction is achieved by the display. The display can have a longer recovery time from this state than from the Stand-By state.

- *Off.* Indicates that the display is consuming the lowest level of power and is non-operational. Recovery from this state may optionally require the user to manually power on the monitor.

Table 8.1 summarizes the DPMS modes.

Table 8.1	Display Power Management Signaling				
State	**Horizontal**	**Vertical**	**Video**	**Power Savings**	**Recovery Time**
On	Pulses	Pulses	Active	None	Not Applicable
Stand-By	No Pulses	Pulses	Blanked	Minimal	Short
Suspend	Pulses	No Pulses	Blanked	Substantial	Longer
Off	No Pulses	No Pulses	Blanked	Maximum	System Dependent

Emissions. Another trend in green monitor design is to minimize the user's exposure to potentially harmful electromagnetic fields. Several medical studies indicate that these electromagnetic emissions may cause health problems, such as miscarriages, birth defects, and cancer. The risk may be low, but if you spend a third of your day (or more) in front of a computer monitor, that risk is increased.

The concern is that VLF (very low frequency) and ELF (extremely low frequency) emissions might affect the body. These two emissions come in two forms—*electric* and *magnetic*. Some research indicates that ELF magnetic emissions are more threatening than VLF emissions, because they interact with the natural electric activity of body cells. Monitors are not the only culprits; significant ELF emissions also come from electric blankets and power lines.

> **Note**
>
> ELF and VLF are a form of electromagnetic radiation; they consist of radio frequencies below those used for normal radio broadcasting.

These two frequencies are covered by the new Swedish monitor-emission standard called *SWEDAC,* named after the Swedish regulatory agency. In many European countries, government agencies and businesses buy only low-emission monitors. The degree to which emissions are reduced varies from monitor to monitor. The Swedish government's MPR I standard, which dates back to 1987, is the least restrictive. MPR II, established in

1990, is significantly stronger (adding maximums for ELF and VLF emissions) and is the level that you will most likely find in low-emission monitors today.

A more stringent 1992 standard called *TCO* further tightens the MPR II requirements. In addition, it is a more broad-based environmental standard that includes power-saving requirements and emission limits. Most of the major manufacturers currently offer monitors that meet the TCO standard.

A low-emission monitor costs about $20 to $100 more than similar regular-emission monitors. When you shop for a low-emission monitor, don't just ask for a low-emission monitor; also find out whether the monitor limits specific types of emissions. Use as your guideline the three electromagnetic-emission standards described in this section.

If you decide not to buy a low-emission monitor, you can take other steps to protect yourself. The most important is to stay at arm's length (about 28 inches) from the front of your monitor. When you move a couple of feet away, ELF magnetic emission levels usually drop to those of a typical office with fluorescent lights. Likewise, monitor emissions are weakest at the front of a monitor, so stay at least three feet from the sides and backs of nearby monitors and five feet from any photocopiers, which are also strong sources of ELF.

Electromagnetic emissions should not be your only concern; you also should be concerned about screen glare. In fact, some of the antiglare panels that fit in front of a monitor screen not only reduce eyestrain, but also cut ELF and VLF emissions.

Monitor Buying Criteria

A monitor may account for a large part of the price of your computer system. What should you look for when you shop for a monitor?

Frequencies. One essential trick is to choose a monitor that works with your selected video adapter. You can save money by purchasing a single-standard (fixed-frequency) monitor and a matching video card; for example, you can order a VGA monitor and a VGA video card. For greatest flexibility, however, you should buy a multiple-frequency (also called multiscanning and multifrequency) monitor that accommodates a range of standards, including those that are not yet standardized.

> **Tip**
>
> High-quality monitors retain their value longer than most other computer components. Although it's common for a newer, faster processor to come out right after you have purchased your computer, or to find the same model with a bigger hard disk for the same money, a good quality monitor should outlast your computer. If you purchase a unit with the expectation that your own personal requirements will grow over the years, you may be able to save money on your next system by reusing your old monitor.

With multiple-frequency monitors, you must match the range of horizontal and vertical frequencies the monitor accepts with those generated by your video adapter. The wider the range of signals, the more expensive—and more versatile—the monitor. Your video adapter's vertical and horizontal frequencies must fall within the ranges supported by your monitor. The *vertical frequency* (or refresh/frame rate) determines how stable your image will be. The higher the vertical frequency, the better. Typical vertical frequencies range from 50Hz to 160Hz, but multiple-frequency monitors support different vertical frequencies at different resolutions. You may find that a bargain monitor has a respectable 100Hz vertical frequency at 640×480, but drops to a less desirable 50Hz at 1,024×768. The *horizontal frequency* (or line rate) typically ranges from 31.5KHz to 90KHz or more.

To keep the frequency low, some video adapters use interlaced signals, alternately displaying half the lines of the total image. As discussed earlier in this chapter, interlacing produces a pronounced flicker in the display on most monitors, unless the phosphor is designed with a very long persistence. For this reason, you should avoid using interlaced video modes if possible. Some older adapters and displays used interlacing as an inexpensive way to attain a higher resolution than otherwise would be possible. For example, the original IBM XGA adapters and monitors used an interlaced vertical frame rate of 43.5Hz in 1,024×768 mode, instead of the higher frame rate that most other adapters and displays use at that resolution.

In my experience, a 60Hz vertical scan frequency (frame rate) is the minimum anybody should use, and even at this frequency a flicker will be noticed by most people. Especially on a larger display, this can cause eyestrain and fatigue. If you can select a frame rate (vertical scan frequency) of 72Hz or higher, most people will not be able to discern any flicker. Most modern displays easily handle vertical frequencies of up to 85Hz or more, which greatly reduces the flicker seen by the user. However, note that increasing the frame rate, while improving the quality of the image, can also slow down the video hardware, because it now needs to display each image more times per second. In general, I recommend you set the lowest frame rate that you find comfortable.

When you shop for a VGA monitor, make sure the monitor supports a horizontal frequency of at least 31.5KHz—the minimum that a VGA card needs to paint a 640×480 screen. The 800×600 resolution requires at least a 72Hz vertical frequency and a horizontal frequency of at least 48KHz. The sharper 1,024×768 image requires a vertical frequency of 60Hz and a horizontal frequency of 58KHz. If the vertical frequency increases to 72Hz, the horizontal frequency must be 58KHz. For a super-crisp display, look for available vertical frequencies of 75Hz or higher and horizontal frequencies of up to 90KHz or more. My favorite 17-inch NEC monitor supports vertical resolutions of up to 75Hz at 1,600×1,200 pixels, 117Hz at 1,024×768, and 160Hz at 640×480!

Most of the analog monitors on the market today are, to one extent or another, multiple-frequency. Because literally hundreds of manufacturers produce thousands of monitor models, it is impractical to discuss the technical aspects of each monitor model in detail. Suffice it to say that before investing in a monitor, you should check the technical specifications to make sure that the monitor meets your needs. If you are looking for a place to start, check out some of the different magazines, which periodically features reviews of monitors. If you can't wait for a magazine review, investigate monitors at the Web sites run by any of the following vendors:

IBM   Sony

Mitsubishi   Viewsonic

NEC

Each of these manufacturers creates monitors that set the standards by which other monitors can be judged. Although you typically pay a bit more for these manufacturers' monitors, they offer a known high level of quality and compatibility, as well as service and support.

Dot Pitch. You also should check the dot pitch of the monitor. The *dot pitch* (also called phosphor pitch) is the diagonal distance between phosphor dots of the same color, measured in millimeters. Smaller pitch values indicate sharper images. Most monitors have a dot pitch between 0.25 and 0.30mm. To avoid grainy images, look for a dot pitch of 0.26mm or smaller. Be wary of monitors with anything larger than a 0.28mm dot pitch; they lack clarity for fine text and graphics.

The dot pitch is one of the most important specifications of any monitor, but it is not the only specification. It is entirely possible that you may find the image on a monitor with a slightly higher dot pitch superior to that of a monitor with a lower pitch.

Screen Size. What resolution do you want for your display? Generally, the higher the resolution, the larger the display you will want. If you are operating at 640×480 resolution, for example, you should find a 14- or 15-inch monitor to be comfortable. At 1,024×768, you probably will find that the display of a 15-inch monitor is too small and will therefore prefer to use a larger one, such as a 17-inch monitor.

Here are the minimum sized monitors I recommend to properly display the resolutions that users typically select:

Resolution	Minimum Recommended Monitor
640×480	13-inch
800×600	15-inch
1,024×768	17-inch
1,280×1,024	21-inch

These minimum recommended display sizes are the advertised diagonal display dimension of the monitor. Note that these are not necessarily the limits of the given monitors' capabilities, but are what I recommend. In other words, most 15-inch monitors are able to display resolutions at least up to 1,024×768, but the characters, icons, and other information are too small for most users and can cause eyestrain if you try to run beyond the recommended 800×600 resolution. One exception to this rule is with the LCD displays used in portable systems and a few desktop monitors. LCD-type displays are always crisp and perfectly focused by nature. Also, the dimensions advertised for the LCD screens represent the exact size of the viewable image, unlike most conventional CRT-based monitors. So, the 12.1-inch LCD panels found on many notebook systems today actually have a viewable area with a 12.1-inch diagonal measurement. This measurement is comparable to a 14-inch or even 15-inch CRT display in most cases. Not only that, but the LCD is so crisp that screens of a given size can easily handle resolutions that are higher than otherwise would be acceptable on a CRT. For example, many of the high-end notebook systems now use 13.3-inch LCD panels that feature 1,024×768 resolution. Although this resolution would be unacceptable on a 14-inch or 15-inch CRT display, it works well on the 13.3-inch LCD panel due to the crystal clear image.

Controls. Most of the newer monitors now use digital controls instead of analog controls. This has nothing to do with the signals that the monitor receives from the computer, but only the controls (or lack of them) on the front panel that enable you to adjust the display. Monitors with digital controls have a built-in menu system that allows you to set parameters such as brightness, contrast, screen size, vertical and horizontal shifts, and even focus. The menu is brought up on the screen by a button, and you use controls to make menu selections and vary the settings. When you complete your adjustments, the monitor saves the settings in NVRAM (Nonvolatile RAM) located inside the monitor. This type of memory provides permanent storage for the settings with no battery or other power source. You can unplug the monitor without losing your settings, and alter them at any time in the future. Digital controls provide a much higher level of control over the monitor, and are highly recommended.

> **Tip**
>
> Get a monitor with positioning and image controls that are easy to reach, preferably on the front of the case. Look for more than just basic contrast and brightness controls; a good monitor should enable you to adjust the width and height of your screen images, and the placement of the image on the screen. The monitor should also be equipped with a tilt-swivel stand, so you can adjust the monitor to the best angle for your use.

Environment. One factor that you may not consider when shopping for a monitor is the size of the desk that you intend to put it on. Before you think about purchasing a monitor larger than 15 inches, be aware that a 17-inch monitor can be 18 inches to two feet deep and weigh upwards of 40 pounds; 21-inch and larger monitors can be truly huge! Some of the rickety computer stands and mechanical arms used to keep monitors off the desktop may not be able to safely hold or support a large unit.

Another important consideration is the lighting in the room where you will use the monitor. The appearance of a CRT display in the fluorescent lighting of an office will be markedly different from that in your home. The presence or absence of sunlight in the room also makes a big difference. Office lighting and sunlight can produce glare that becomes incredibly annoying when you are forced to stare at it for hours on end. Some monitors are equipped with an anti-glare coating that can help in these instances. Many manufacturers and third-party vendors also produce aftermarket filters designed to reduce glare.

Many inexpensive monitors are curved because it is easier to send an electron beam across them. Flat-screen monitors, which are a bit more expensive, look better to most people. As a general rule, the less curvature a monitor has, the less glare it will reflect.

Testing. Unlike most of the other components of your computer, you can't really tell whether a monitor will suit you by examining its technical specifications. Price may not be a reliable indicator either. Testing monitors is a highly subjective process, and it is best to "kick the tires" of a few at a dealer showroom or (with a liberal return policy) in the privacy of your home or office.

Testing should also not be simply a matter of looking at whatever happens to be displayed on the monitor at the time. Many computer stores display movies, scenic photos, or other flashy graphics that are all but useless for a serious evaluation and comparison. If possible, you should look at the same images on each monitor you try, and compare the manner in which they perform a specific series of tasks.

One good series of tasks is as follows:

- Draw a perfect circle with a graphics program. If the displayed result is an oval, not a circle, this monitor will not serve you well with graphics or design software.

- Using a word processor, type some words in 8- or 10-point type (1 point equals 1/72 inch). If the words are fuzzy, or if the black characters are fringed with color, select another monitor.

- Turn the brightness up and down while examining the corner of the screen's image. If the image blooms or swells, it is likely to lose focus at high brightness levels.

- Display a screen with as much white space as possible and look for areas of color variance. This may indicate a problem only with that individual unit or its location, but if you see it on more than one monitor of the same make, it may be indicative of a manufacturing problem.

- Load Microsoft Windows to check for uniform focus. Are the corner icons as sharp as the rest of the screen? Are the lines in the title bar curved or wavy? Monitors usually are sharply focused at the center, but seriously blurred corners indicate a poor design. Bowed lines may be the result of a poor video adapter, so don't dismiss a monitor that shows those lines without using another adapter to double-check the effect.

- A good monitor will be calibrated so that rays of red, green, and blue light hit their targets (individual phosphor dots) precisely. If they don't, you have bad convergence. This is apparent when edges of lines appear to illuminate with a specific color. If you have good convergence, the colors will be crisp, clear, and true, provided there isn't a predominant tint in the phosphor.

Video Display Adapters

A *video adapter* provides the interface between your computer and your monitor and transmits the signals that appear as images on the display. Throughout the history of the PC, there have been a succession of standards for video display characteristics that represent a steady increase in screen resolution and color depth. The following list of standards can serve as an abbreviated history of PC video display technology:

MDA (Monochrome Display Adapter)

CGA (Color Graphics Adapter)

EGA (Enhanced Graphics Adapter)

VGA (Video Graphics Array)

SVGA (Super VGA)

XGA (eXtended Graphics Array)

Most of these standards were pioneered by IBM, but were also adopted by the manufacturers of compatible PCs as well. Today, IBM is no longer the industry leader that it once was, and many of these standards are obsolete. Those that aren't obsolete are seldom referred to by these names anymore. The sole exception to this is VGA, which is a term that is still used to refer to a baseline graphic display capability supported by virtually every video adapter on the market today.

When you shop for a video adapter today, you are more likely to see specific references to the screen resolutions and color depths that the device supports than a list of standards such as VGA, SVGA, and XGA. However, reading about these standards gives you a good idea of how video display technology developed over the years, and prepares you for any close encounters you may have with legacy equipment from the dark ages.

Obsolete Display Adapters

Although many types of display systems were at one time considered to be industry standards, few of these are viable standards for today's hardware and software. For example, the CGA standard works, but it is unacceptable for running the graphics-intensive programs on which many users now rely. In fact, Microsoft Windows 3.1 does not work with any PC that has less-than-EGA resolution, and Windows 9x and Windows NT require VGA as an absolute minimum. The next several sections discuss the display adapters that are viewed as being obsolete in today's market, although you may still find them in use in some places.

Monochrome Display Adapter (MDA) and Display. The simplest (and first available) display type was the IBM *Monochrome Display Adapter (MDA)*. It was introduced along with the IBM PC in 1981. The MDA video card displayed text only at a 720×350 resolution. One interesting point is that the MDA card also incorporated a printer port and was the first multi-function adapter card available.

As a character-only system, the MDA display had no inherent graphics capabilities. The display originally was a top-selling option because it was fairly cost-effective. As a bonus, the MDA provided a printer interface, thus conserving an expansion slot.

For its time, the MDA display was known for clarity and high resolution, making it ideal for business use—especially for businesses using DOS-based word processing or spreadsheet programs.

Because the monochrome display is a character-only display, you cannot use it with software that requires graphics. Originally, that drawback kept users only from playing games on a monochrome display, but today even the most serious business software uses graphics and color to great advantage. With the 9×14 dot character box (*matrix*), the IBM monochrome monitor displays attractive characters.

Later, a company named Hercules released a video card called the *Hercules Graphics Card (HGC)*. This card could display sharper text and handle graphics, such as the charts produced by spreadsheet applications.

Color Graphics Adapter (CGA) and Display. The *Color Graphics Adapter (CGA)* was introduced along with the IBM PC in 1981 and for many years was the most commonly used video adapter. Of course, by today's standards, its capabilities leave much to be desired. The CGA adapter has two basic modes of operation: alphanumeric (A/N) or all points addressable (APA). In *A/N mode*, the card operates in 40-column by 25-line mode or 80-column by 25-line mode with 16 colors. In APA and A/N modes, the character set is formed with a resolution of 8×8 pixels. In *APA* mode, two resolutions are available: medium-resolution color mode (320×200), with four colors available from a palette of 16; and two-color high-resolution mode (640×200).

Most of the monitors sold for use with the CGA adapter were RGBs, not composite monitors. The color signal of a composite monitor contains a mixture of colors that must be decoded or separated. RGB monitors receive red, green, and blue separately, and combine the colors in different proportions to generate other colors. RGB monitors offer better resolution than composite monitors, and they do a much better job of displaying 80-column text.

One severe drawback of the CGA video adapter was the fact that it was prone to producing flicker and snow. *Flicker* is the annoying tendency of the text to flash as you move the image up or down. *Snow* is the flurry of bright dots that can appear anywhere on the screen.

Most companies that sold CGA-type adapters have long since discontinued those products. With VGA adapters available for less than $100, recommending a CGA makes little sense, even if you could find one.

Enhanced Graphics Adapter (EGA) and Display. The IBM Enhanced Graphics Adapter was introduced in 1984, just after the IBM AT system. It was discontinued when the PS/2 systems were introduced in April 1987. The EGA package consisted of a graphics board, a graphics memory-expansion board, a graphics memory-module kit, and a high-resolution color monitor. The whole package originally cost about $1,800! The aftermarket gave IBM a great deal of competition in this area; it was possible to put together a similar system from non-IBM vendors for much less money. One advantage of EGA, however, was that you could build your system in modular steps. Because the card worked with any of the monitors IBM produced at the time, you could use it with the IBM Monochrome Display, the earlier IBM Color Display, or the IBM Enhanced Color Display.

With the EGA adapter, the IBM color monitor displays 16 colors in 320×200 or 640×200 mode, and the IBM monochrome monitor shows a resolution of 640×350 with a 9×14 character box (text mode).

With the EGA adapter, the IBM Enhanced Color Display is capable of displaying 640×350 pixels in 16 colors from a palette of 64. The character box for text is 8×14, compared with 8×8 for the earlier CGA board and monitor. The 8×8 character box can be used, however, to display 43 lines of text. Through software, the character box can be manipulated up to the size of 8×32.

You can enlarge the RAM-resident, 256-member character set to 512 characters by using the IBM memory expansion card, and add a 1,024-character set by installing the IBM graphics memory-module kit. These character sets are loaded from programs.

All of this memory fits in the unused space between the end of the RAM user memory and the current display-adapter memory. The EGA has a maximum 128K of memory that maps into the RAM space just above the 640K boundary. If you install more than 640K, you will probably lose the extra memory after installing the EGA. The graphics memory-expansion card adds 64K to the standard 64K, for a total of 128K. The IBM graphics memory-module kit adds another 128K, for a total of 256K. This second 128K of memory is only on the card and does not consume any of the PC's memory space. (Because almost every aftermarket EGA card comes configured with the full 256K of memory, expansion options are not necessary.)

The VGA system supersedes the EGA in many respects. The EGA has problems emulating the earlier CGA or MDA adapters, and some software that works with the earlier cards will not run on the EGA until the programs are modified.

Professional Color Display and Adapter. The Professional Graphics Display System is a video display product that IBM introduced in 1984. At $4,290, the system was too expensive to become a mainstream product and never achieved any significant popularity. It was the first processor-based video adapter for PCs; it actually incorporated an Intel 8088 processor on the card.

The system consisted of a Professional Graphics Monitor and a Professional Graphics Card Set. When fully expanded, the card set used three slots in an XT or AT system—a high price to pay, but the features were impressive. The Professional Graphics Adapter (PGA) offered three-dimensional rotation and clipping as a built-in hardware function. The adapter could run 60 frames of animation per second because the PGA used a built-in dedicated microcomputer.

The Professional Graphics card and monitor was intended for engineering and scientific use rather than for financial or business applications. The VGA and other higher-resolution graphics standards designed for these newer systems replaced this system, which was discontinued when the PS/2 was introduced.

8514 Display Adapter. The PS/2 Display Adapter 8514/A, introduced in 1987 along with the PS/2 systems, offered higher resolution and more colors than the standard VGA. This adapter, designed for use with the PS/2 Color Display 8514, plugs into a Micro Channel slot in any PS/2 model so equipped.

With the 8514/A installed, all operational modes of the PS/2's built-in VGA continue to be available. An IBM 8514 memory-expansion kit was also available for the 8514/A, providing increased color and grayscale support.

To take full advantage of the 8514/A adapter, you had to use the 8514 display because it was matched to the capabilities of the adapter. Note that IBM has long since discontinued the 8514/A adapter, and specified the XGA in its place.

MultiColor Graphics Array (MCGA). The *MultiColor Graphics Array (MCGA)* graphics adapter was integrated into the motherboard of the PS/2 Models 25 and 30. The MCGA supported all CGA modes when an IBM analog display was attached, but any previous IBM display was not compatible. In addition to providing existing CGA mode support, the MCGA included four additional modes.

The MCGA used as many as 64 shades of gray in converting color modes for display on monochrome monitors, so users who preferred a monochrome display could execute color-based applications.

VGA Adapters and Displays

When IBM introduced the PS/2 systems on April 2, 1987, it also introduced the Video Graphics Array (VGA) display. On that day, in fact, IBM also introduced the lower-resolution MultiColor Graphics Array (MCGA) and higher-resolution 8514 adapters. The MCGA and 8514 adapters did not become popular standards like the VGA, and both were discontinued.

Digital Versus Analog Signals. Unlike earlier video standards, which are digital, the VGA is an analog system. Why are displays going from digital to analog when most other electronic systems are going digital? Compact-disc players (digital) have replaced most turntables (analog), and newer VCRs and camcorders have digital picture storage for smooth slow-motion and freeze-frame capability. With a digital television set, you can watch several channels on a single screen by splitting the screen or placing a picture within another picture.

Most personal computer displays introduced before the PS/2 are digital. This type of display generates different colors by firing the RGB electron beams in on-or-off mode, which allows for the display of up to eight colors (2 to the third power). In the IBM displays and adapters, another signal doubles the number of color combinations from 8 to 16 by displaying each color at one of two intensity levels. This digital display is easy to manufacture and offers simplicity with consistent color combinations from system to system. The real drawback of the digital display system is the limited number of possible colors.

In the PS/2 systems, IBM went to an analog display circuit. Analog displays work like the digital displays that use RGB electron beams to construct various colors, but each color in the analog display system can be displayed at varying levels of intensity—64 levels, in the case of the VGA. This versatility provides 262,144 possible colors (64^3). For realistic computer graphics, color depth is often more important than high resolution, because the human eye perceives a picture that has more colors as being more realistic. IBM moved to analog graphics to enhance the color capabilities of their systems.

Video Graphics Array (VGA). PS/2 systems incorporate the primary display adapter circuitry onto the motherboard. A single custom VLSI chip designed and manufactured by IBM implements the circuits, or VGA. To adapt this new graphics standard to the earlier systems, IBM introduced the PS/2 Display Adapter. Also called a VGA card, this adapter contains the complete VGA circuit on a full-length adapter board with an 8-bit interface. IBM has since discontinued its VGA card, but many third-party units are available.

The VGA *BIOS (Basic Input/Output System)* is the control software residing in the system ROM for controlling VGA circuits. With the BIOS, software can initiate commands and functions without having to manipulate the VGA directly. Programs become somewhat hardware-independent and can call a consistent set of commands and functions built into the system's ROM-control software.

◀◀ See "Video Adapter BIOS," p. 369

Other implementations of the VGA differ in their hardware but respond to the same BIOS calls and functions. New features are added as a superset of the existing functions, and VGA remains compatible with the graphics and text BIOS functions built into the PC systems from the beginning. The VGA can run almost any software that originally was written for the MDA, CGA, or EGA.

In a perfect world, software programmers would write to the BIOS interface rather than directly to the hardware and would promote software interchanges between different types of hardware. More frequently, however, programmers want the software to perform better, so they write the programs to control the hardware directly. As a result, these programmers achieve higher-performance applications that are dependent on the hardware for which they were first written.

When bypassing the BIOS, a programmer must ensure that the hardware is 100% compatible with the standard so that software written to a standard piece of hardware runs on the system. Just because a manufacturer claims this register level of compatibility does not mean that the product is 100% compatible or that all software runs as it would on a true IBM VGA. Most manufacturers have "cloned" the VGA system at the register level, which means that even applications that write directly to the video registers will function correctly. Also, the VGA circuits themselves emulate the older adapters even to the register level and have an amazing level of compatibility with these earlier standards. This compatibility makes the VGA a truly universal standard.

The VGA displays up to 256 colors onscreen, from a palette of 262,144 (256K) colors. Because the VGA outputs an analog signal, you must have a monitor that accepts an analog input.

VGA displays come not only in color but also in monochrome VGA models, using color summing. With *color summing*, 64 gray shades are displayed instead of colors; the translation is performed in the ROM BIOS. The summing routine is initiated if the BIOS detects a monochrome display when the system boots. This routine uses an algorithm that takes the desired color and rewrites the formula to involve all three color guns, producing varying intensities of gray. Users who prefer a monochrome display, therefore, can execute color-based applications.

Table 8.2 lists the VGA display modes.

| Table 8.2 | VGA Display Modes | | | | | | | |
Resolution	Colors	Mode Type	BIOS Mode	Character Format	Character Box	Vertical (Hz)	Horizontal (KHz)
360×400	16	Text	00/01h	40×25	9×16	70	31.5
720×400	16	Text	02/03h	80×25	9×16	70	31.5
320×200	4	APA	04/05h	40×25	8×8	70	31.5
640×200	2	APA	06h	80×25	8×8	70	31.5
720×400	16	Text	07h	80×25	9×16	70	31.5
320×200	16	APA	0Dh	40×25	8×8	70	31.5
640×200	16	APA	0Eh	80×25	8×8	70	31.5
640×350	4	APA	0Fh	80×25	8×14	70	31.5
640×350	16	APA	10h	80×25	8×14	70	31.5
640×480	2	APA	11h	80×30	8×16	60	31.5
640×480	16	APA	12h	80×30	8×16	60	31.5
320×200	256	APA	13h	40×25	8×8	70	31.5

APA = All points addressable (graphics)
— = Not supported

Few video adapters on the market today are limited only to support for the VGA standard. Instead, VGA, at its 16-color 640×480 resolution, has come to be the baseline for PC graphical display configurations. VGA is accepted as the least common denominator for all Windows systems, and is expected to be supported by the video adapters in all systems running Windows. The installation programs of all Windows versions use these VGA settings as their default video configuration. In addition to VGA, most adapters support a range of higher screen resolutions and color depths, depending on the capabilities of the hardware.

XGA and XGA-2

IBM announced the PS/2 XGA Display Adapter/A on October 30, 1990, and the XGA-2 in September 1992. Both adapters are high-performance, 32-bit bus-mastering adapters for Micro Channel-based systems. These video subsystems, evolved from the VGA, provide greater resolution, more colors, and much better performance.

Combine fast VGA, more colors, higher resolution, a graphics coprocessor, and bus-mastering, and you have XGA. Being a bus-mastering adapter means that the XGA can take control of the system as though it were the motherboard. In essence, a bus master is an adapter with its own processor that can execute operations independent of the motherboard.

The XGA was introduced as the default graphics-display platform with the Model 90 XP 486 and the Model 95 XP 486. In the desktop Model 90, the XGA is on the motherboard; in the Model 95 (a tower unit), it is located on a separate add-in board. This board—the XGA Display Adapter/A—also is available for other 386- and 486-based Micro Channel systems. The XGA adapter can be installed in any MCA systems that have 80386, 80386SX, 80386SLC, 486SLC2, 486SLC3, or 80486 processors, including PS/2 Models 53, 55, 57, 65, 70, and 80.

The XGA comes standard with 512K of graphics memory, which can be upgraded to 1M with an optional video-memory expansion.

In addition to all VGA modes, the XGA adapter offers several new modes of operation, which are listed in Table 8.3.

Table 8.3 XGA Unique Modes of Operation		
Maximum Resolution	**Maximum Colors**	**Required VRAM**
1,024×768	256 colors	1M
1,024×768	64 gray shades	1M
1,024×768	16 colors	512K
1,024×768	16 gray shades	512K
640×480	65,536 colors	1M
640×480	64 gray shades	512K

The reason for the different memory requirements is explained in the "The Video RAM" section, later in this chapter. The 65,536-color mode provides near photographic quality output. The 16-bit pixel is laid out as 5 bits of red, 6 bits of green, and 5 bits of blue (5-6-5)—in other words, 32 (2^5) shades of red, 64 (2^6) shades of green, and 32 shades of blue. (The eye notices more variations in green than in red or blue.)

The XGA-2 improves on the performance of the original XGA in several ways. To begin with, the XGA-2 increases the number of colors supported at 1,024×768 resolution to 65,536 (64K). In addition, because of the circuitry of the XGA-2, it can process data at twice the speed of the XGA. The XGA-2 also works in noninterlaced mode, so it produces less flicker than the XGA does.

Both the XGA and XGA-2 support all existing VGA and 8514/A video modes. Quite a few popular applications were developed to support the 8514/A high-resolution 1,024×768 mode. These applications were written to the *8514/A Adapter interface*, which is a software interface between the application and the 8514/A hardware. The XGA's extended graphics function maintains compatibility at the same level. Because of the power of the XGA and XGA-2, VGA and 8514/A applications run much faster.

Much of the speed of the XGA and XGA-2 also can be attributed to its *video RAM (VRAM)*, a type of dual-ported RAM designed for graphics-display systems. This memory can be accessed both by the processor on the graphics adapter and the system CPU simultaneously, providing nearly instantaneous data transfers. The XGA VRAM is mapped into the system's address space. The VRAM normally is located in the top addresses of the 386's 4G address space. Because no other adapters normally use this area, conflicts are rare. The adapters also have an 8K ROM BIOS extension that must be mapped somewhere in segment C000 or D000. (The integrated motherboard implementation of the XGA does not require its own ROM, because the motherboard BIOS contains all the necessary code.)

◀◀ See "Video RAM Memory," p. 364

Table 8.4 summarizes the XGA modes.

Table 8.4   IBM eXtended Graphics Array (XGA) Specifications

Resolution	Colors	Mode Type	BIOS Mode	Character Format	Character Box	Vertical (Hz)	Horizontal (KHz)
360×400	16	Text	00/01h	40×25	9×16	70	31.5
720×400	16	Text	02/03h	80×25	9×16	70	31.5
320×200	4	APA	04/05h	40×25	8×8	70	31.5
640×200	2	APA	06h	80×25	8×8	70	31.5
720×400	16	Text	07h	80×25	9×16	70	31.5
320×200	16	APA	0Dh	40×25	8×8	70	31.5
640×200	16	APA	0Eh	80×25	8×8	70	31.5
640×350	4	APA	0Fh	80×25	8×14	70	31.5
640×350	16	APA	10h	80×25	8×14	70	31.5
640×480	2	APA	11h	80×30	8×16	60	31.5
640×480	16	APA	12h	80×30	8×16	60	31.5
320×200	256	APA	13h	40×25	8×8	70	31.5
1,056×400	16	Text	14h	132×25	8×16	70	31.5
1,056×400	16	Text	14h	132×43	8×9	70	31.5
1,056×400	16	Text	14h	132×56	8×8	70	31.5
1,056×400	16	Text	14h	132×60	8×6	70	31.5
1,024×768	256	APA*	14h	85×38	12×20	43.48	35.52
640×480	65,536	APA	14h	80×34	8×14	60	31.5
1,024×768	256	APA*	14h	128×54	8×14	43.48	35.52
1,024×768	256	APA*	14h	146×51	7×15	43.48	35.52

APA = All points addressable (graphics)
* = Interlaced

Super VGA (SVGA)

When IBM's XGA and 8514/A video cards were introduced, competing manufacturers chose not to attempt to clone these incremental improvements on their VGA products. Instead, they began producing lower-cost adapters that offered even higher resolutions. These video cards fall into a category loosely known as *Super VGA (SVGA)*.

SVGA provides capabilities that surpass those offered by the VGA adapter. Unlike the display adapters discussed so far, SVGA refers not to an adapter that meets a particular specification but to a group of adapters that have different capabilities.

For example, one card may offer several resolutions (such as 800×600 and 1,024×768) that are greater than those achieved with a regular VGA, whereas another card may offer the same or even greater resolutions but also provide more color choices at each resolution. These cards have different capabilities; nonetheless, both are classified as SVGA.

The SVGA cards look much like their VGA counterparts. They have the same connectors, including the feature adapter shown. Because the technical specifications from different SVGA vendors vary tremendously, it is impossible to provide a definitive technical overview in this book. The pinouts for the standard VGA and SVGA video connector (see Figure 8.1) are shown in the following table.

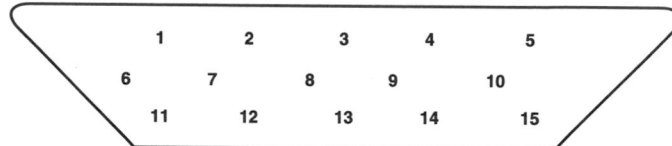

FIG. 8.1 The standard 15-pin VGA connector.

Pin	Function	Direction
1	Red Video	Out
2	Green Video	Out
3	Blue Video	Out
4	Monitor ID 2	In
5	TTL Ground (monitor self-test)	-_
6	Red Analog Ground	-_
7	Green Analog Ground	-_
8	Blue Analog Ground	-_
9	Key (Plugged Hole)	-_
10	Sync Ground	-_
11	Monitor ID 0	In
12	Monitor ID 1	In
13	Horizontal Sync	Out
14	Vertical Sync	Out
15	Monitor ID 3	In

On the VGA cable connector that plugs into your video adapter, pin 9 is always pinless. Pin 5 is used only for testing purposes and pin 15 is rarely used; these are often pinless as well. To identify the type of monitor connected to the system, some manufacturers use the presence or absence of the monitor ID pins in various combinations.

VESA SVGA Standards

The Video Electronics Standards Association (VESA) includes members from various companies associated with PC and computer video products. In October 1989, VESA, recognizing that programming applications to support the many SVGA cards on the market was virtually impossible, proposed a standard for a uniform programmer's interface for SVGA cards.

The SVGA standard is called the *VESA BIOS Extension*. If a video card incorporates this standard, a program easily can determine the capabilities of the card and access them. The benefit of the VESA BIOS Extension is that a programmer needs to worry about only one routine or driver to support SVGA. Different cards from different manufacturers are accessible through the common VESA interface.

When first proposed, this concept met with limited acceptance. Several major SVGA manufacturers started supplying the VESA BIOS Extension as a separate memory-resident program that you could load when you booted your computer. Over the years, however, other vendors started supplying the VESA BIOS Extension as an integral part of their SVGA BIOS. Obviously, from a user's perspective, support for VESA in BIOS is a better solution. You do not have to worry about loading a driver or other memory-resident program whenever you want to use a program that expects the VESA extensions to be present.

The current VESA SVGA standard covers just about every video resolution and color-depth combination currently available, up to 1,280×1,024 with 16,777,216 (24-bit) colors. Even if an SVGA video adapter claims to be VESA-compatible, however, it still may not work with a particular driver, such as the 800×600, 256-color, SVGA driver that comes with Microsoft Windows. In practice, however, manufacturers continue to provide their own driver software.

Table 8.5 lists the video modes of the Chips and Technologies 65554 SVGA graphics accelerator, a typical chipset used today.

Table 8.5 Chips and Technologies 65554 Graphics Accelerator Chipset Video Modes

BIOS Mode	Mode Type	Resolution	Character	Colors	Scan Freq (hor/vert)
0, 1	VGA Text	40×25 char	9×16	16/256K	31.5KHz/70Hz
2, 3	VGA Text	80×25 char	9×16	16/256K	31.5KHz/70Hz
4, 5	VGA Graph	320×200 pels	8×8	4/256K	31.5KHz/70Hz
6	VGA Graph	640×200 pels	8×8	2/256K	31.5KHz/70Hz
7	VGA Text	80×25 char	9×16	Mono	31.5KHz/70Hz
D	VGA Graph	320×200 pels	8×8	16/256K	31.5KHz/70Hz
E	VGA Graph	640×200 pels	8×8	16/256K	31.5KHz/70Hz
F	VGA Graph	640×350 pels	8×14	Mono	31.5KHz/70Hz

(continues)

Table 8.5   Chips and Technologies 65554 Graphics Accelerator Chipset Video Modes Continued

BIOS Mode	Mode Type	Resolution	Character	Colors	Scan Freq (hor/vert)
10	VGA Graph	640×350 pels	8×14	16/256K	31.5KHz/70Hz
11	VGA Graph	640×480 pels	8×16	2/256K	31.5KHz/60Hz
12	VGA Graph	640×480 pels	8×16	16/256K	31.5KHz/60Hz
13	VGA Graph	320×200 pels	8×8	256/256K	31.5KHz/70Hz
20	SVGA Graph	640×480 pels	8×16	16/256K	31.5KHz/60Hz
					37.6KHz/75Hz
					43.2KHz/85Hz
22	SVGA Graph	800×600 pels	8×8	16/256K	37.9KHz/60Hz
					46.9KHz/75Hz
					53.7KHz/85Hz
24	SVGA Graph	1024×768 pels	8×16	16/256K	35.5KHz/87Hz*
					48.5KHz/60Hz
					60.0KHz/75Hz
					68.8KHz/85Hz
28	SVGA Graph	1280×1024 pels	8×16	16/256K	35.5KHz/87Hz*
					35.5KHz/60Hz
30	SVGA Graph	640×480 pels	8×16	256/256K	31.5KHz/60Hz
					37.6KHz/75Hz
					43.2KHz/85Hz
32	SVGA Graph	800×600 pels	8×16	256/256K	37.9KHz/60Hz
					46.9KHz/75Hz
					53.7KHz/85Hz
34	SVGA Graph	1024×768 pels	8×16	256/256K	35.5KHz/87Hz*
					48.5KHz/60Hz
					60.0KHz/75Hz
					68.8KHz/85Hz
38	SVGA Graph	1280×1024 pels	8×16	256/256K	35.5KHz/87Hz*
					35.5KHz/60Hz
40	SVGA Graph	640×480 pels	8×16	32K/32K	31.5KHz/60Hz
					37.6KHz/75Hz
					43.2KHz/85Hz
41	SVGA Graph	640×480 pels	8×16	64K/64K	31.5KHz/60Hz
					37.6KHz/75Hz
					43.2KHz/85Hz
42	SVGA Graph	800×600 pels	8×16	32K/32K	37.9KHz/60Hz
					46.9KHz/75Hz
					53.7KHz/85Hz

BIOS Mode	Mode Type	Resolution	Character	Colors	Scan Freq (hor/vert)
43	SVGA Graph	800×600 pels	8×16	64K/64K	37.9KHz/60Hz
					46.9KHz/75Hz
					53.7KHz/85Hz
44	SVGA Graph	1024×768 pels	8×16	32K/32K	48.5KHz/60Hz
45	SVGA Graph	1024×768 pels	8×16	64K/64K	48.5KHz/60Hz
50	SVGA Graph	640×480 pels	8×16	16M/16M	31.5KHz/60Hz
52	SVGA Graph	800×600 pels	8×16	16M/16M	37.9KHz/60Hz

= interlaced

Video Adapter Components

All video display adapters contain certain basic components, such as the following:

- The video BIOS
- The video processor
- The video memory
- The digital-to-analog converter (DAC)
- The bus connector
- The video driver

Many of the popular adapters on the market today include additional modules intended for special purposes, such as 3D acceleration. The following sections examine these components in greater detail.

The Video BIOS. Video adapters include a BIOS (basic input/output system) that is similar in construction, but completely separate from the main system BIOS. (Other devices in your system, such as SCSI adapters, may also include their own BIOS.) If you turn your monitor on first and look quickly, you may see an identification banner for your adapter's video BIOS at the very beginning of the system startup process.

Like the system BIOS, the video adapter's BIOS takes the form of a ROM (read-only memory) chip containing basic instructions that provide an interface between the video adapter hardware and the software running on your system. The software that makes calls to the video BIOS can be a standalone application, an operating system, or the main system BIOS. It is the programming in the BIOS chip that enables your system to display information on the monitor during the system POST and boot sequences, before any other software drivers have been loaded from disk.

The video BIOS is also upgradable, just like a system BIOS, in one of two ways. Either the BIOS uses a rewritable chip called an EEPROM *(electrically erasable programmable read-only memory)*, that you can upgrade with a utility that the adapter manufacturer provides, or you can completely replace the chip with a new one, again supplied by the manufacturer. A BIOS that you can upgrade using software is referred to as a *flash BIOS*.

Video BIOS upgrades are sometimes necessary to use an existing adapter with a new operating system, or when the manufacturer encounters a significant bug in the original programming. As a general rule, the video BIOS is a component that falls into the "if it ain't broke, don't fix it" category. Try not to let yourself be tempted to upgrade just because you've discovered that a new BIOS revision is available. Check the documentation for the upgrade, and unless you are experiencing a problem that the upgrade addresses, leave it alone.

◀◀ See "Video Adapter BIOS," p. 369

The Video Processor. The video processor, or *chipset*, is the heart of any video adapter and essentially defines the card's functions and performance levels. Two video adapters built using the same chipset often have many of the same capabilities and deliver comparable performance. Also, the software drivers that operating systems and applications use to address the video adapter hardware are written primarily with the chipset in mind. You can often use a driver intended for an adapter with a particular chipset on any other adapter using the same chipset. Of course, cards built using the same chipset can differ in the amount and type of memory installed, so performance may vary.

There are three main types of processors used in video adapters:

- Frame buffers
- Coprocessors
- Accelerators

The oldest technology used in creating a video adapter is known as *frame-buffer technology*. In this scheme, the video adapter is responsible for displaying the individual frames of an image. The video adapter maintains each frame, but it is the main system CPU that performs the calculations necessary to create the frame. This arrangement places a heavy burden on the CPU, which could be busy doing other program-related computing.

At the other end of the spectrum is a chipset technology known as *coprocessing*. In this scheme, the video adapter includes its own processor, which performs all video-related computations. This arrangement reduces the burden on the system's main CPU, enabling it to perform other tasks. Theoretically, this type of chipset provides the fastest overall system throughput, but performance is, of course, dependent on the hardware being used.

Between these two arrangements is a middle ground—a fixed-function *accelerator chip*. In this scheme, which is used in many of the graphics accelerator boards on the market today, the circuitry on the video adapter does many of the more time-consuming video tasks (such as drawing lines, circles, and other objects); however, the main CPU still directs the adapter by passing graphics-primitive commands from applications, such as an instruction to draw a rectangle of a given size and color.

When you evaluate video adapters for purchase, you should always know which chipset the devices use. This information gives you a much better basis for comparing that card against others. Product literature and Web sites that provide technical specifications for video adapters should always specify the chipsets used on the devices.

Also, you can often find reviews or opinions concerning specific chipsets that can influence your purchasing decision. You may, for example, read about a great new chipset that has recently been released by a particular manufacturer and, as a result, seek out video adapters using that chipset.

Identifying the chipset on your video adapter also provides you with an additional avenue for drivers and technical support. Most chipset manufacturers maintain Web sites and tech support departments, just as adapter manufacturers do. If you do not receive adequate service from one of the companies, you can always try the other.

The vendor list in Appendix A has information on most of the popular video chipset manufacturers, including how to contact them.

The Video RAM. Video adapters rely on their own on-board memory that they use to store video images while processing them. The amount of memory on the adapter determines the maximum screen resolution and color depth that the device can support. You can often select how much memory you want on a particular video adapter—for example, 256K, 512K, 1M, 2M, 4M, or 8M are common choices today. Most cards today come with at least 2M, and many have 4M. Adding more memory does not speed up your video adapter; instead, it enables the card to generate more colors and/or higher resolutions.

Many different types of memory are used on video adapters today. These memory types are summarized in Table 8.6 and examined more fully in upcoming sections.

Table 8.6 Memory Types Used in Video Display Adapters				
Memory Type	**I/O Bus**	**Total Frequency (MHz)**	**Net Latency (ns)**	**Bandwidth (M/sec)**
FPM DRAM	Fast Page-Mode RAM	25-33	80	80
VRAM	Video RAM	25-33	*	100
WRAM	Window RAM	>50	*	120
EDO DRAM	Extended Data Out DRAM	40-50	100	105
SDRAM	Synchronous DRAM	66-100	102-75	166-253
MDRAM	Multibank DRAM	125-166	22-19	405-490
SGRAM	Synchronous Graphics DRAM	>125	100-75	200-300

VRAM and WRAM are dual-ported memory types that can read and write data simultaneously.

RAM Calculations. The amount of memory that a video adapter needs to display a particular resolution and color depth is based on a mathematical equation. There has to be a location in the adapter's memory array to display every pixel on the screen, and the number of total pixels is determined by the resolution. For example, a screen resolution of 1,024×768 requires a total of 786,432 pixels.

If you were to display that resolution with only two colors, you would need only one bit of memory space to represent each pixel. If the bit has a value of 0, the dot is black, and if its value is 1, the dot is white. If you use four bits of memory space to control each pixel, you can display 16 colors, because there are 16 possible combinations with a 4-digit binary number (2 to the 4th power equals 16). If you multiply the number of pixels needed for the screen resolution by the number of bits required to represent each pixel, you have the amount of memory that the adapter needs to display that resolution. Here is how the calculation works:

$$1,024 \times 768 = 786,432 \text{ pixels} \times 4\text{-bits per pixel}$$

$$= 3,145,728 \text{ bits}$$

$$= 393,216 \text{ bytes}$$

$$= 384K$$

As you can see, displaying 16 colors at 1,024×768 resolution requires exactly 384K of RAM on the video adapter. Because most adapters support memory amounts of only 256K, 512K, 1M, 2M, or 4M, you would have to install 512K to run your system using that resolution and color depth. Increasing the color depth to 8 bits per pixel results in 256 possible colors, and a memory requirement of 786,432 bytes or 768K. Again, because no video adapters are equipped with that exact amount, you would have to purchase an adapter with 1M of memory.

To use the higher resolution modes and greater numbers of colors that are common today, you will need much more memory on your video adapter than the 256K found on the original IBM VGA. Table 8.7 shows the memory requirements for some of the most commonly used screen resolutions and color depths.

Table 8.7 Video Display Adapter Minimum Memory Requirements				
Resolution	**Color Depth**	**No. Colors**	**Video**	**Memory Required**
640×480	4-bit	16	256K	153,600 bytes
640×480	8-bit	256	512K	307,200 bytes
640×480	16-bit	65,536	1M	614,400 bytes
640×480	24-bit	16,777,216	1M	921,600 bytes
800×600	4-bit	16	256K	240,000 bytes
800×600	8-bit	256	512K	480,000 bytes
800×600	16-bit	65,536	1M	960,000 bytes
800×600	24-bit	16,777,216	2M	1,440,000 bytes
1,024×768	4-bit	16	512K	393,216 bytes
1,024×768	8-bit	256	1M	786,432 bytes
1,024×768	16-bit	65,536	2M	1,572,864 bytes
1,024×768	24-bit	16,777,216	4M	2,359,296 bytes
1,280×1,024	4-bit	16	1M	655,360 bytes
1,280×1,024	8-bit	256	2M	1,310,720 bytes
1,280×1,024	16-bit	65,536	4M	2,621,440 bytes
1,280×1,024	24-bit	16,777,216	4M	3,932,160 bytes

From this table, you can see that a video adapter with 2M can display 65,536 colors in 1,024×768 resolution mode, but for a true color (16.8M colors) display, you would need to upgrade to 4M.

> **Note**
>
> Although some adapters can operate in a 32-bit mode, this does not necessarily mean that they can produce more than the 16,277,216 colors of a 24-bit true color display. Many video processors and video memory buses are optimized to move data in 32-bit words, and actually display 24-bit color while operating in a 32-bit mode, instead of the 4,294,967,296 colors that you would expect from a true 32-bit color depth.

If you spend a lot of time working with graphics, you may want to invest in a 24-bit video card with 4M of RAM. Many of the cards today can easily handle 24-bit color, but you will need 4M of RAM to get that capability in the higher resolution modes.

> **Note**
>
> You can upgrade the RAM on some video adapters by installing a separate module containing the additional memory chips. The module usually takes the form of a *daughter card*; that is, a small circuit board that plugs into a socket on the video adapter. The design of the daughter board is proprietary, even if the type of memory chips on the board are not. You will have to purchase the module from the manufacturer of the video adapter.

Video Bus Width. Another issue with respect to the memory on the video adapter is the width of the bus connecting the graphics chipset and the memory on the adapter. The chipset is usually a single large chip on the card that contains virtually all of the adapter's functions. It is wired directly to the memory on the adapter through a local bus on the card. Most of the high-end adapters use an internal memory bus that is 64 bits or even 128 bits wide. This jargon can be confusing, because video adapters that take the form of separate expansion cards also plug into the main system bus, which has its own speed rating. When you read about a 64-bit or 128-bit video adapter, you must understand that this refers to the local video bus, and that the bus connecting the adapter to the system is actually the 32- or 64-bit PCI or AGP bus on the system's motherboard.

◄◄ See "System Bus Functions and Features," p. 233

DRAM. Historically, most video adapters have used regular *dynamic RAM (DRAM)* for this purpose. This type of RAM, although inexpensive, is rather slow. The slowness can be attributed to the need to constantly refresh the information contained within the RAM, and to the fact that DRAM cannot be read at the same time it is being written.

Modern PC graphics adapters need extremely high data transfer rates to and from the video memory. At a resolution of 1,024×768 and a standard refresh rate of 72Hz, the digital-to-analog converter (DAC) on the card needs to read the contents of the video memory frame buffer 72 times per second. In true color (24-bits per pixel) mode, this means that the DAC must be able to read from the video memory at a rate of about 170M/sec, which is just about the maximum available from a conventional DRAM design. Because of the high bandwidth required, a number of competing memory technologies have emerged over the past several years to meet the performance needs of high-end video memory.

◀◀ See "DRAM," p. 311

EDO DRAM. One of the more recent memory designs to be incorporated into video adapters is *EDO (Extended Data Out)* DRAM. EDO provides a wider effective bandwidth by offloading memory precharging to separate circuits, meaning that the next access can begin before the last access has finished. As a result, EDO offers a 10% speed boost over DRAM, at a similar cost. EDO DRAM was introduced by Micron Technologies, and was originally designed for use in a PC's main RAM array, but it is now also being used for video adapter memory. EDO chips are constructed using the same dies as conventional DRAM chips, and they differ from DRAMs only in how they are wired in final production. This method enables manufacturers to make EDO chips on the same production lines and at the same relative costs as DRAM.

◀◀ See "EDO RAM," p. 315

VRAM. *VRAM (Video RAM)* is another popular type of memory that manufacturers have been using in video adapters for some time now. VRAM is designed to be *dual-ported*, which enables the processor or accelerator chip on the adapter and the DAC or even the PC's own processor to access the RAM simultaneously. This provides much greater performance than standard DRAM or even EDO, but it comes at a higher price.

WRAM. *WRAM*, or *Windows RAM*, is a modified VRAM-type dual-ported memory technology developed by Samsung that is aimed specifically at graphics adapters. WRAM offers marginally better performance than standard VRAM at a lower cost. Many makers of high-end video adapters are now using WRAM as a replacement for VRAM.

MDRAM. *MDRAM (Multibank DRAM)* is a new type of memory that is also explicitly aimed at graphics and video applications. Developed by MoSys Inc., MDRAMs consist of a large number of small (32K) banks. Traditionally, DRAM or VRAM is logically organized as a single, monolithic bank. Organizing the memory into small banks makes it possible for manufacturers to easily supply adapters with any amount of MDRAM that is an integral multiple of 32K, instead of being restricted to the traditional binary multiple sizes found in many video cards. This is a significant advantage for the cost-sensitive PC marketplace.

For example, a 1,024×768 true color (24-bit) graphics system requires 2.3M for the frame buffer plus some extra memory for off-screen storage. For an adapter using 256K×16 DRAMs and a 64-bit bus, the only workable memory size that accommodates this frame buffer is 4M, constructed of two banks of four chips each. However, with MDRAM, it is no problem to construct an adapter with a memory system of 2.5M, that is composed of only two or three individual chips. This eliminates the wasted extra 1.5M, and the total memory cost can be significantly reduced.

In addition to the better memory sizing, MDRAM organizes its internal banks off of a narrow central bus, which permits access to each bank individually. As a result, this design can complete a burst to or from one bank and then begin a burst to or from another, all in a single clock cycle, offering much higher performance than VRAM or WRAM.

SGRAM. *SGRAM*, or *Synchronous Graphics RAM*, is a high-end solution for very fast video adapter designs. Like the SDRAM used in motherboard memory arrays, SGRAM can synchronize itself with the speed of the bus, up to 100MHz. This type of memory can be up to four times as fast as conventional DRAM and operate at speeds up to 125MHz or faster and is now being used in many of the highest quality PCI and AGP adapters. SGRAM is one of the most expensive memory technologies now used in video adapters, but it offers superior performance for graphics-intensive applications.

◀◀ See "SDRAM," p. 316

The Digital-to-Analog Converter. The digital-to-analog converter on a video adapter (commonly called a RAMDAC) does exactly as its name describes. The RAMDAC is responsible for converting the digital images that your computer generates into analog signals that the monitor can display. The speed of the RAMDAC is measured in MHz; the faster the conversion process, the higher the adapter's vertical refresh rate. The speeds of the RAMDAC's used in today's high performance video adapters can exceed 200MHz.

The Bus. You've learned in this chapter that certain video adapters were designed for use with certain system buses. For example, the VGA and XGA were both originally designed for use with IBM's MCA bus. The bus that you use in your computer affects the speed at which your system processes video information. For example, the ISA bus offers a 16-bit data path at speeds of 8.33MHz. The EISA or MCA buses can process 32 bits of data at a time, but they also run at speeds up to 10MHz. These three buses are no longer used for video adapters, because IBM has discontinued the MCA bus and the others are too slow.

> **Note**
>
> Don't confuse the system bus speed with the system processor speed, even though they are both measured in megahertz (MHz). System processors run at speeds upward of 300MHz, but the system bus is much slower.

The next major improvement in bus speed came with the *VESA local bus* (VL-Bus) standard. The VL-Bus standard typically is an addition to an existing bus technology. For example, you might have an ISA system that also contains a VL-Bus slot. Even if it is used in an ISA system, the VL-Bus processes 32 bits of data at a time and at the full-rated external speed of the CPU—up to 40MHz. Thus, you can achieve much greater speeds by using a well implemented VL-Bus in your system.

In July 1992, Intel Corporation introduced Peripheral Component Interconnect (PCI) as a blueprint for directly connecting microprocessors and support circuitry; it then extended the design to a full expansion bus with Release 2 in 1993. Popularly termed a *mezzanine bus,* PCI combines the speed of a local bus with microprocessor independence. PCI video adapters, like VL-Bus adapters, can increase video performance dramatically. PCI video adapters, by their design, are meant to be *Plug and Play (PnP)*, meaning that they require little configuration. The PCI standard virtually replaced the older VL-Bus standard overnight and is now found in nearly all new PCs. The vast majority of the video adapters on the market today use the PCI bus.

◀◀ See "Accelerated Graphics Port (AGP)," p. 268

◀◀ See "The PCI Bus," p. 256

The most recent system bus innovation is the Accelerated Graphics Port (AGP), a dedicated video bus designed by Intel that delivers a maximum bandwidth four times larger than that of a comparable PCI bus. AGP is essentially an enhancement to the existing PCI bus, intended for use only with video adapters, and providing them with high-speed access to the main system memory array. This enables the adapter to process certain 3D video elements, such as texture maps, directly from system memory, rather than having to copy the data to the adapter memory before the processing can begin. This saves time and eliminates the need to upgrade the video adapter memory to better support 3D functions.

Although it was designed with the Pentium II in mind, AGP is not processor-dependent. However, it does require support from the motherboard chipset, which means that you cannot upgrade an existing system to use AGP without replacing the motherboard. Currently, Pentium II motherboards with the Intel 440LX, 440EX, and 440BX chipsets support AGP. Intel is also currently developing an AGP chipset for use on socket 7 motherboards, so systems with processors other than the Pentium II can use AGP. Acer Laboratories Inc. (ALi) also has the Aladdin Pro II chipset that supports AGP X2 for Pentium II Slot 1 motherboards and the Aladdin V Pentium chipset that supports AGP X2 for Pentium Socket 7 motherboards. VIA Technologies' Apollo VP3 and Apollo MVP3 both support AGP for Socket 7 motherboards. And, SiS has their SiS 5591 which also supports AGP on a socket 7 motherboard.

Even with the proper chipset, however, you cannot take full advantage of AGP's capabilities without the proper operating system support. AGP's DIrect Memory Execute (DIME) feature uses main memory instead of the video adapter's memory for certain tasks, to lessen the traffic to and from the adapter. Windows 98 supports this feature, as will Windows NT 5, but Windows 95 does not.

◀◀ See "Chipsets," p. 183

It is always wise to be cautious before adopting any new technology, and AGP is no exception. There have been problems reported with some of the early AGP implementations to reach the market. Also, version 2.0 of the AGP specification is currently in the preliminary draft stage. The new spec includes support for 2x and 4x data transfer modes that promise to improve the performance of the bus still further. After AGP technology has matured a bit, however, it is very likely to become the industry standard bus for video adapters.

Many of the high-end video adapters on the market today are already available in both PCI and AGP versions. If your computer has a chipset that supports AGP, you are likely to be well served by taking advantage of its capabilities.

VL-Bus, PCI, and AGP have some important differences, as Table 8.8 shows.

Table 8.8 Local Bus Specifications			
Feature	**VL-Bus**	**PCI**	**AGP**
Theoretical maximum throughput	132M/sec	132M/sec*	533M/sec
Slots**	3 (typical)	4/5 (typical)	1
Plug and Play support	No	Yes	Yes
Cost	Inexpensive	Slightly higher	Slightly higher than PCI
Ideal use	Low cost 486	High-end 486, Pentium, P6	Pentium II

*At the 66MHz bus speed and 32 bits. Throughput will be higher on the 100MHz system bus.
**More slots are possible through the use of PCI bridge chips.

The Video Driver. The software driver is an essential, and often a problematic, element of a video display subsystem. The driver enables your software to communicate with the video adapter. You can have a video adapter with the fastest processor and the most efficient memory on the market, but still have poor video performance because of a badly written driver.

DOS applications address the video display hardware directly, and typically include their own drivers for various types of video adapters. All versions of Windows, however, use a driver that is installed in the operating system. Applications then can use operating system function calls to access the video hardware.

Video drivers are generally designed to support the processor on the video adapter. All video adapters come equipped with drivers supplied by the manufacturer, but you often can use a driver created by the chipset manufacturer as well. Sometimes you may find that one of the two provides better performance than the other, or resolves a particular problem you are experiencing.

Most manufacturers of video adapters and chipsets maintain Web sites from which you can obtain the latest drivers. A driver from the chipset manufacturer can be a useful alternative, but you should always try the adapter manufacturer's driver first. Before purchasing a video adapter, it is a good idea to check out the manufacturer's site and see whether you can determine how many driver releases there have been for the adapter you're considering. Frequent driver revisions can be a sign that many users are experiencing problems. Although it may be a good thing to see that the company is responding to complaints, it may also indicate that the hardware is not dependable.

The video driver also provides the interface that you can use to configure the display produced by your adapter. On a Windows 98 system, the Settings page of the Display Control Panel (shown in Figure 8.2) identifies the monitor and video adapter installed on your system, and enables you to select the color depth and screen resolution that you prefer. The driver controls the options that are available for these settings, so you can't choose parameters that aren't supported by the hardware. For example, the controls would not allow you to select a 1024×768 resolution with 24-bit color if the adapter had only 1M of memory.

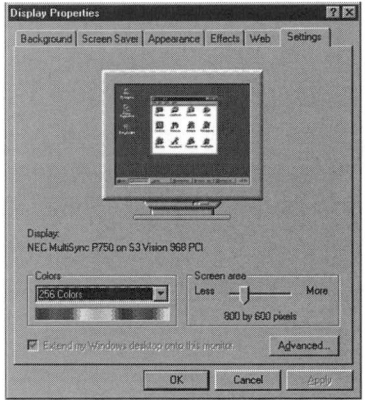

FIG. 8.2 From the Windows 98 Control Panel, you can set the screen resolution and color depth for your display.

When you click the Advanced button on the Settings page, you see the Properties dialog box for your particular video display adapter. The contents of this dialog box can vary, depending on the driver and the capabilities of the hardware. Typically, on the General page of this dialog box, you can select the size of the fonts (large or small) to use with the resolution you've chosen. Windows 98 also adds a control to activate a very convenient feature. The Show Settings Icon on Task Bar checkbox activates a tray icon that enables you to quickly and easily change resolutions and color depths without having to open the Control Panel.

The Adapter page displays detailed information about your adapter and the drivers installed on the system, and enables you to set the Refresh Rate for your display. If your adapter includes a graphics accelerator, the Performance page (see Figure 8.3) contains a Hardware Acceleration slider that you can use to control the degree of graphic display assistance provided by your adapter hardware.

Setting the Hardware Acceleration slider to the Full position activates all the adapter's hardware acceleration features.

Moving the slider one notch to the left addresses mouse display problems by disabling the hardware's cursor support in the display driver. This is the equivalent of adding the SWCursor=1 directive to the [Display] section of the System.ini file.

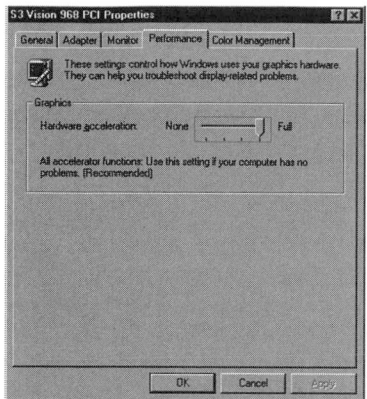

FIG. 8.3 Windows 98 displays detailed information about your video display adapter and its driver support.

Moving the slider another notch (to the second notch from the right) prevents the adapter from performing certain bit block transfers. With some drivers, this setting also disables memory-mapped I/O. This is the equivalent of adding the `Mmio=0` directive to the `[Display]` section of System.ini and the `SafeMode=1` directive to the `[Windows]` section of Win.ini (and the `SWCursor` directive mentioned previously).

Moving the slider to the None setting (the far left) adds the `SafeMode=2` directive to the `[Windows]` section of the Win.ini file. This disables all hardware acceleration support and forces the operating system to use only the device-independent bitmap (DIB) engine to display images, rather than bit-block transfers. Use this setting when you experience frequent screen lockups or when you receive `invalid page fault` error messages.

Video Cards for Multimedia

Multimedia has become an important element of the personal computing industry. Technology that was at first relegated to entertainment uses, and therefore dismissed by many computing professionals, has now been assimilated into the corporate world. Live data feeds, videoconferencing, and animated presentations are just a few of the technologies that are now commonplace elements of business computing.

As the demand for multimedia content increases, so do the capabilities of the hardware and software used to produce the content. Video is just one, albeit important, element of the multimedia experience, and the graphics adapters on the market today reflect the demand for these increased capabilities. Producing state-of-the-art multimedia content today often requires that the PC be capable of interfacing with other devices, such as cameras, VCRs, and television sets, and many video adapters are now equipped with this capability.

Other multimedia technologies, such as 3D animation, place an enormous burden on a system's processing and data-handling capabilities, and many manufacturers of video adapters are redesigning their products to shoulder this burden more efficiently. The following sections examine some of the video adapter components that make these technologies possible and practical.

Video Feature Connectors. One often overlooked part of the VGA standard that IBM released in 1987 was the *Video Feature Connector*, or *VFC*. This was a 26-pin connector that enabled other video cards to connect to a VGA adapter directly. Unfortunately, this standard was poorly documented by IBM and poorly implemented by most VGA adapter manufacturers. In fact, many VGA cards did not implement the VFC at all, basically ignoring the need. That may have been fine in the early days of VGA, because there were few multimedia products that needed to tap into the VGA signal. Today, however, there are many types of multimedia add-on boards that have features such as full-motion video, video capture, video compression, and television tuners that need the services of this connector to do their job.

Unfortunately, there was another problem with the VFC besides it not being there or being implemented incorrectly. The problem was one of performance. The original VGA adapter was designed as an 8-bit bus adapter, and functioned at a maximum resolution of only 640×480 pixels. Thus, the VFC had these same limitations, which put a damper on the type of video signal that could be transferred directly from one card to another. Because most of the technologies today that require communication between adapters involve full-motion video and other bandwidth-intensive applications, this was a major problem.

In November 1983, the problems with the VFC were addressed by the Video Electronics Standards Association's (VESA) announcement of the VESA Advanced Feature Connector (VAFC) and the VESA Media Channel (VMC) video bus standards. These new standards were designed to provide compatibility and performance for interconnected multimedia adapters and video adapters. The result is the rapid growth in the adoption of new applications such as interactive video, video presentation, video conferencing, and desktop video editing.

The *VESA Advanced Feature Connector (VAFC)* provides an extension of the industry standard VFC found on many graphics boards. The VAFC solves high bandwidth requirements by widening the current feature connector's data path from 16/32 to 8 bits and adding additional signals, which provide more reliable operation. The VAFC delivers 75M/sec throughput in its 16-bit baseline configuration, and up to 150M/sec in the 32-bit configuration. Other features include multiple pixels per clock, color space data, genlocking, and asynchronous video input. The VAFC also overcomes the current 640×480 pixel 256-color resolution limitations of most video overlay products.

Unfortunately, while the VAFC successfully addresses the performance and compatibility issues of the VFC, it has not turned out to be a cost-effective solution, and has not been adopted by many video adapter manufacturers.

The *VESA Media Channel (VMC)* is a dedicated multimedia bus that provides an independent path for the simultaneous processing of several high bandwidth video streams. The VMC directly addresses the current limitations of running video across a computer's system bus. This design solves the universal bandwidth bottleneck and latency issues that exist in all system or processor bus architectures including ISA, EISA, MicroChannel, VL-Bus, and PCI.

To correct these problems, the *VESA Media Channel* is designed to enable the transparent integration of video and graphics without the interference of processor interrupts or bus contention. VESA Media Channel provides the option for a 68-pin multi-drop cable, enabling the combination of up to 15 devices in a modular fashion with data transfer rates of up to 132M/sec. For example, a graphics system supporting the VESA Media Channel can easily and cost-effectively be configured as a capture, decode only, encode only, or a full encode/decode video system. This is important in applications such as video teleconferencing, and provides flexible, cost-effective engineering of a particular system.

> ### Tip
>
> If you intend to use your PC for video applications that require the use of additional adapters for services like video capture or MPEG compression, it is a good idea to select a video adapter that supports the 68-pin VMC connector. If you see only a 26-pin connector on the adapter, then the card supports only the standard VFC. Most of the higher-quality multimedia adapters will require a VMC connection for high performance video signal transfer.

Because none of these specifications for internal video feature connectors have become industry standards, some manufacturers of auxiliary video products such as dedicated 3D accelerator boards and MPEG decoders have taken an alternate route through the standard VGA connector.

The Diamond Monster 3D (and 3D II), for example, works in addition to a system's standard 2D video adapter, not in place of it. However, instead of requiring that the 2D adapter have a particular internal connector, the Monster 3D includes an external pass-through cable. This cable connects the Monster 3D card to your 2D adapter, after which you plug your monitor into the VGA port on the Monster 3D card. Games and any other applications that support the Monster 3D can address that device directly through the PCI bus, and all of the signals generated by the 2D adapter pass through the Monster 3D card and are relayed to the monitor.

Video Output Devices. When video technology was first introduced, it was based on television. There is a difference between the signals used by a television and the signals used by a computer. In the United States, the National Television System Committee (NTSC) established color TV standards in 1953. Some other countries, such as Japan, followed this standard. Many countries in Europe developed more sophisticated standards, including Phase Alternate Line (PAL) and SEquential Couleur Avec Mémoire (SECAM). Table 8.9 shows the differences among these standards.

Table 8.9	Television Versus Computer Monitors			
Standard	**Yr. Est.**	**Country**	**Lines**	**Rate**
Television				
NTSC	1953 (color)	U.S., Japan	525	60Hz
	1941 (b&w)			
PAL	1941	Europe*	625	50Hz
SECAM	1962	France	625	25Hz
Computer				
VGA	1987	U.S.	640×480**	72Hz

England, Holland, West Germany.
**VGA is based upon more lines and uses pixels (480) versus lines; genlocking is used to lock pixels into lines and synchronize computers with TV standards.

A video-output (or VGA-to-NTSC) adapter enables you to display computer screens on a TV set or record them onto videotape for easy distribution. These products fall into two categories: those with *genlocking* (which enables the board to synchronize signals from multiple video sources or video with PC graphics) and those without. Genlocking provides the signal stability you need to obtain adequate results when recording to tape, but is not necessary for using a television as a video display.

VGA-to-NTSC converters are available both as internal expansion boards or external boxes that are portable enough to use with a laptop for presentations on the road. Indeed, many laptop and notebook systems these days come equipped with a built in VGA-to-NTSC converter.

The converter does not replace your existing video adapter but instead connects to the adapter using an external cable. In addition to VGA input and output ports, a video output board has a video output interface for S-Video and composite video.

Most VGA-to-TV converters support the standard NTSC television format and may also support the European PAL format. The resolution that these devices display on a TV set or record on videotape is often limited to straight VGA at 640×480 pixels. The converter may also contain an anti-flicker circuit to help stabilize the picture, because VGA-to-TV products often suffer from a case of the jitters.

Still-Image Video Capture Cards. You can install a board into your PC that enables you to capture individual screen images for later editing and playback. There are also external devices that plug into a PC's parallel port. These units capture still images from NTSC video sources such as camcorders or VCRs. Although image quality is limited by the input signal, the results are still good enough for presentations and desktop publishing applications. These devices work with 8-, 16-, and 24-bit VGA cards and usually accept video input from VHS, Super VHS, and Hi-8 devices. As you might expect, however, Super VHS and Hi-8 video sources give better results, as do configurations using more than 256 colors.

Multiple Monitors. Windows 98 includes a video display feature that Macintosh systems have had for years: the capability to use multiple monitors on one system. Windows 98 supports up to nine monitors (and video adapters), each of which can provide a different view of the desktop. When you configure a Windows 98 system to do this, the operating system creates a *virtual desktop*; that is, a display that exists in video memory that can be larger than the image actually displayed on a single monitor. You use the multiple monitors to display various portions of the virtual desktop, enabling you to place the windows for different applications on separate monitors, and move them around at will.

Of course, each monitor that you connect to the system requires its own video adapter, so unless you have nine bus slots free, the prospects of seeing a nine-screen windows display are slim, for now. However, even two monitors can be a boon to computing productivity.

On a multi-monitor Windows 98 system, there is always one display that is considered to be the primary display. The primary display can use any PCI VGA video adapter that uses a Windows 98 minidriver with a linear frame buffer and a packed (non-planar) format, meaning that most of the brand name adapters sold today are eligible. Additional monitors are called secondaries, and are much more limited in their hardware support. A secondary must use one of the following video adapters:

- The S3-ViRGE series
- S3Trio-64V+
- S3 Aurora
- Cirrus 5436, 5446, 7548
- ET6000
- ATI Mach 64, Rage I, II
- Imagine i128(2)

It's important that the computer correctly identify which one of the video adapters is the primary. This is a function of the system BIOS and, if the BIOS on your computer does not let you select which device should be the primary VGA display, then it decides based on the order of the PCI slots in the machine. You should therefore install the primary adapter in the highest priority PCI slot.

◀◀ See "The PCI Bus," p. 256

After the hardware is in place, you can configure the display for each monitor from the Display Control Panel's Settings page. The primary display is always fixed in the upper-left corner of the virtual desktop, but you can move the secondary displays to view any area of the desktop you like. You can also set the screen resolution and color depth for each display individually.

Desktop Video (DTV) Boards. You can also capture NTSC (television) signals to your computer system for display or editing. In other words, you can literally watch TV in a window on your computer. When capturing video, you should think in terms of digital versus analog. The biggest convenience of an analog TV signal is efficiency; it is a compact way to transmit video information through a low-bandwidth pipeline. The disadvantage is that while you can control how the video is displayed, you can't edit it.

Actually capturing and recording video from external sources and saving the files onto your PC requires special technology. To do this, you need a device called a *video capture board,* also called a *TV tuner, video digitizer,* or *video grabber.*

> **Note**
>
> In this context, the technical nomenclature again becomes confusing, because the term video here has its usual connotation; that is, it refers to the display of full-motion photography on the PC monitor. When evaluating video hardware, be sure to distinguish between devices that capture still images from a video source, and those that capture full-motion video streams.

One of the uses for analog video is with interactive Computer-Based Training (CBT) programs in which your application sends start, stop, and search commands to a laserdisc player that plays discs you have mastered. The software controls the player via an interface that also converts the laserdisc's NTSC signal into a VGA-compatible signal for display on your computer's monitor. These types of applications require NTSC-to-VGA conversion hardware.

Whereas a computer can display up to 16 million colors, the NTSC standard allows for approximately only 32,000 colors. Affordable, high-quality video is the Achilles' heel of multimedia. The images are often jerky or less than full-screen. The reason is because full-motion video, such as that which you see on TV, requires 30 images or frames per second (fps), which can be an enormous amount of data.

The typical computer screen was designed to display mainly static images. The storing and retrieving of these images requires managing huge files. Consider this: A single, full-screen color image in an uncompressed format can require as much as 2M of disk space; a one-second video would therefore require 45M. Likewise, any video transmission that you want to capture for use on your PC must be converted from an analog NTSC signal to a digital signal that your computer can use. On top of that, the video signal must be moved inside your computer at 10 times the speed of the conventional ISA bus structure. You need not only a superior video card and monitor but also an excellent expansion bus, such as PCI or AGP.

Considering the fact that full-motion video can consume massive quantities of disk space, it becomes apparent that data compression is all but essential. Compression and decompression (or *codec*) applies to both video and audio. Not only does a compressed file take up less space, it also performs better; there is simply less data to process. When you are ready to replay the video/audio, the application decompresses the file during playback. In any case, if you are going to work with video, be sure that your hard drive is large enough and fast enough to handle the huge files that can result. There are two types of codecs: *hardware-dependent codecs* and *software* (or *hardware-independent*) *codecs*. Hardware codecs typically perform better; however, they require additional hardware. Software codes do not require hardware for compression or playback, but they typically do not deliver the same quality or compression ratio. Two of the major codec algorithms are:

- *JPEG (Joint Photographic Experts Group)*. Originally developed for still images, JPEG can compress and decompress at rates acceptable for nearly full-motion video (30fps). JPEG still uses a series of still images, which makes editing easier. JPEG is typically lossy (meaning that a small amount of the data is lost during the compression process, slightly diminishing the quality of the image), but it can also be lossless. JPEG compression functions by eliminating redundant data for each individual image (intraframe). Compression efficiency is approximately 30:1 (20:1–40:1).

- *MPEG (Motion Pictures Experts Group)*. MPEG by itself compresses video at approximately a 30:1 ratio, but with pre-compression through oversampling, the ratio can climb to 100:1 and higher, while retaining high quality. Thus, MPEG compression results in better, faster videos that require less storage space. MPEG is an interframe compressor. Because MPEG stores only incremental changes, it is not used during editing phases. MPEG decoding can be performed in software on high-performance Pentium systems.

If you will be capturing, compressing, and playing video, you will need Microsoft Video for Windows (VFW), which is included with the Windows 9x and NT operating systems, or QuickTime, which is available as a free download from Apple's Web site. The following codecs are provided along with VFW:

- *Cinepak*. Although Cinepak can take longer to compress, it can produce better quality and higher compression than Indeo. It is also referred to as *Compact Video Coded (CVC)*.

- *Indeo*. Indeo can outperform Cinepak and is capable of real-time compression. An Intel Smart Video board is required for real-time compression.

- *Microsoft Video 1*. Developed by MediaVision (MotiVE) and renamed MS Video 1, this codec is a DCT-based post-processor. A file is compressed after capture.

Many other codecs are freely available from various vendors, providing support for other video formats. Many of the video plug-ins that work with Web browsers supply their codecs and automatically install them on your system. If you look on the Devices page of the Windows 98 Multimedia Control Panel (or the Advanced page in Windows 95) under Video Compression Codecs (see Figure 8.4), you can view and manage the codecs installed on your computer.

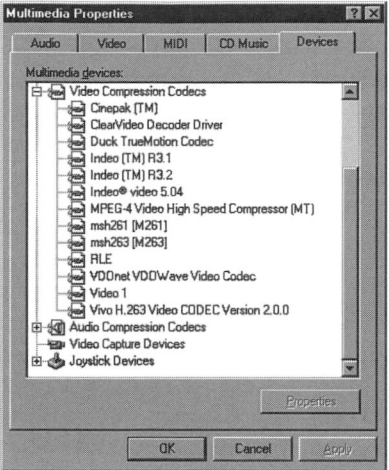

FIG. 8.4 In the Windows 9x Multimedia Control Panel, you can see the video compression codecs installed on your system.

To play or record video on your multimedia PC (MPC), you will need some extra hardware and software:

- Video system software, such as Apple's QuickTime for Windows or Microsoft's Video for Windows.

- A compression/digitization video adapter that enables you to digitize and play large video files.

- An NTSC-to-VGA adapter that combines TV signals with computer video signals for output to a VCR. Video can come from a variety of sources: TV, VCR, video camera, or laserdisc player. When you record an animation file, you can save it in a variety of different file formats: AVI (Audio Video Interleave), MOV (Apple QuickTime format), or MPG (MPEG format).

When you connect video devices, use the S-Video (S-VHS) connector whenever available. This cable provides the best signal because separate signals are used for color (*chroma*) and brightness (*luma*). Otherwise, you will have to use *composite video*, which mixes luma and chroma. This results in a lower-quality signal. The better your signal, the better your video quality will be.

You can also purchase devices that display just NTSC signals on your computer. The way that multimedia technology is advancing, you will soon not be able to tell whether you are using a computer screen or a television. Digital video, in-screen filling, and full-motion color has arrived on desktop platforms with titles, playback boards, and encoding equipment. Soon, MPEG movie clip libraries will be the next form of clip art on CD-ROM. Hardware advances such as the MMX instructions incorporated into the Pentium architecture are helping to make motion video more of a useful reality rather than just a novelty.

3D Graphics Accelerators

The latest trend in PC graphic display technology is the expanded use of three dimensional images. Three-dimensional—or 3D—imagery has been used for years in the computer gaming world, and has even made its way into business computing. Spreadsheet programs such as Microsoft Excel have for years used 3D charts to display spreadsheet data. Of course, the images are not truly three-dimensional, because the monitor screen is a 2-D medium, but software can produce 3D effects using perspective, textures, and shading.

Abstract shapes such as Excel's 3D bar graphs are not difficult to produce, because they consist solely of polygons and other shapes with solid color fills of various shades. You find the truly innovative side of 3D graphics in the so-called virtual reality environments created in games and other applications. As with other types of multimedia, however, the techniques that originate in games and other entertainment software will eventually be assimilated into mainstream use.

A 3D image can contain an immense amount of detail, and an animated 3D sequence like those of many games requires a great many images. Obviously, the more images that are needed, the more disk space is required to store them, and the more processing and image-handling speed is needed to display them. To manage all that detail, 3D applications usually store and work with abstractions of the images, rather than the actual images themselves. In essence, the 3D images are actually generated—or *rendered*—as needed, rather than simply read from a storage medium.

To construct an animated 3D sequence, a computer can mathematically animate the sequences between keyframes. A *keyframe* identifies specific points. A bouncing ball, for example, can have three keyframes: up, down, and up. Using these frames as a reference point, the computer can create all the interim images between the top and the bottom. This creates the effect of a smooth bouncing ball.

After it has created the basic sequence, the system can then refine the appearance of the images by filling them in with color. The most primitive and least effective fill method is called *flat shading*, in which a shape is simply filled with a solid color. *Gouraud shading*, a slightly more effective technique, involves the assignment of colors to specific points on a shape. The points are then joined using a smooth gradient between the colors.

The most processor intensive, and by far the most effective type of fill, is called *texture mapping*. The 3D application includes patterns—or textures—in the form of small bitmaps that it tiles onto the shapes in the image, just as you can tile a small bitmap to form the wallpaper for your Windows desktop. The primary difference is that the 3D application can modify the appearance of each tile by applying perspective and shading to achieve 3D effects.

Until recently, 3D applications had to rely on support from software routines to convert these abstractions into live images. This places a heavy burden on the system processor in the PC, which has a significant impact on the performance not only of the visual display, but also of any other applications that the computer may be running. Now, there is a new breed of video accelerator chipsets found on many video adapters that can take on a lot of the tasks involved in rendering 3D images, greatly lessening the load on the system processor and overall system performance.

Prices are dropping rapidly on these 3D accelerators and more and more software titles are making use of them. Technology that was once available only on high-end graphics workstations is now available on PCs. By rendering images right on the adapter, 3D graphics accelerator adapters can create smooth, photo-realistic 3D images on a PC at speeds that rival those of low-end graphics workstations.

3D technology has added an entirely new vocabulary to the world of video display adapters. Before purchasing a 3D accelerator adapter, it is a good idea to familiarize yourself with the some of the terms and concepts involved in the 3D image generation process.

The basic function of 3D software is to convert image abstractions into the fully realized images that are then displayed on the monitor. The image abstractions typically consist of the following elements:

- *Vertices*. Locations of objects in three dimensional space, described in terms of their X, Y, and Z coordinates on three axes representing height, width, and depth.

- *Primitives*. The simple geometric objects that the application uses to create more complex constructions, described in terms of the relative locations of their vertices. This serves not only to specify the location of the object in the 2D image, but also provides perspective, as the three axes can define any location in three-dimensional space.

- *Textures*. Two-dimensional bitmap images or surfaces that are designed to be mapped onto primitives. The software enhances the 3D effect by modifying the appearance of the textures depending on the location and attitude of the primitive; this process is called *perspective correction*. Some applications use another process called *MIP mapping*, which utilizes different versions of the same texture that contain varying amounts of detail, depending on how close the object is to the viewer in the three-dimensional space. Another technique, called *depth cueing*, reduces the color and intensity of an object's fill as the object moves farther away from the viewer.

Using these elements, the abstract image descriptions must then be *rendered*, meaning that they are converted to visible form. Rendering depends on two standardized functions that convert the abstractions into the completed image that is displayed onscreen. The standard functions performed in rendering are:

- *Geometry*. The sizing, orienting, and moving of primitives in space and the calculation of the effects produced by the virtual light sources that illuminate the image.

- *Rasterization*. The converting of primitives into pixels on the video display by filling the shapes with properly illuminated shading, textures, or a combination of the two.

A modern video adapter that includes a chipset capable of 3D video acceleration will have special built-in hardware that can perform the rasterization process much faster than if it is done by software (using the system processor) alone. Most chipsets with 3D acceleration perform the following rasterization functions right on the adapter:

- *Scan conversion.* The determination of which onscreen pixels fall into the space delineated by each primitive.

- *Shading.* The process of filling pixels with smoothly flowing color using the flat or Gouraud shading technique.

- *Texturing.* The process of filling pixels with images derived from a 2D sample picture or surface image.

- *Visible surface determination.* The identification of which pixels in a scene are obscured by other objects closer to the viewer in three-dimensional space.

- *Animation.* The process of switching rapidly and cleanly to successive frames of motion sequences.

Compared to software-only rendering, hardware-accelerated rendering provides better image quality and faster animation than with software alone. Using special drivers, these 3D adapters can take over the intensive calculations needed to render a 3D image that were formerly performed by software running on the system processor. This is particularly useful if you are creating your own 3D images and animations, but it is also a great enhancement to the many modern games that rely extensively on 3D effects.

3D Chipsets. As with standard 2D video adapters, there are several manufacturers of popular 3D video chipsets, and many more manufacturers of video adapters that use them. Table 8.10 lists the major 3D chipset manufacturers, the various chipsets they make, and the video adapters that use them.

Table 8.10 3D Video Chipset Manufacturers		
Manufacturer	**Chipset**	**Available Boards**
3Dfx Interactive	Voodoo Graphics*(3D only)*	A-Trend Helios 3D
		Canopus Pure 3D
		Deltron Flash 3D
		Diamond Monster 3D
		Guillemot MAXI Gamer 3Dfx
		Orchid Righteous 3D
		Quantum 3D Obsidian series
		Skywell Magic 3D
3Dfx Interactive	Voodoo Rush*(2D/3D)*	California Graphics Emotion 3D
		Deltron Flash AT3D Rush
		Hercules Stingray 128/3D
		Intergraph Intense 3D
		Jazz Adrenaline Rush
		Viewtop Rush 3D
3D labs	Permedia 2*(2D/3D)*	Creative G.B. Extreme
		Diamond FireGL 1000Pro

(continues)

Table 8.10 Continued		
Manufacturer	**Chipset**	**Available Boards**
ATi	RAGE PRO TURBO *(2D/3D)*	ALL-IN-WONDER PRO
		XPERT@PLAY 98
ATi	RAGE II+ *(2D/3D)*	3D XPRESSION+
ATi	3D RAGE II+DVD *(2D/3D)*	3D PRO TURBO PC2TV
nVidia	RIVA 128*(2D/3D)*	ASUS 3D Explorer
		Canopus Total 3D 128V
		Diamond Viper330
		Elsa Erazor Victory
		STB Velocity 128
Rendition	Vérité 2100*(2D/3D)*	Diamond Stealth S220
Rendition	Vérité 2200*(2D/3D)*	DSystems Gladiator
		Hercules Thriller 3D
		Jazz Outlaw 3D
S3	ViRGE *(2D/3D)*	*Cardex Genesis SV*
		Dataexpert Expertcolor DSV3325P
		Diamond Stealth 3D 2000 Pro
		Elsa Victory 3D
		Expert EVP ViRGE
		Genoa Phantom 3D
		Hercules Terminator 64/3D
		Number Nine 9FX Reality 332
		Orchid Fahrenheit Video3D
		STB Powergraph 64 3D
VideoLogic/NEC	PowerVR PCX2*(3D only)*	Matrox m3D
		VideoLogic 3Dx
		VideoLogic 5D
		VideoLogic 5D Sonic

Adapter and Display Troubleshooting

Solving most graphics adapter and monitor problems is fairly simple, although costly, because replacing the adapter or display is the usual procedure. However, before you take this step, make sure that you have exhausted all of your other options. One embarrassingly obvious fix to monitor display problems that is often overlooked by many users is to adjust the controls on the monitor, such as the contrast and the brightness. While most monitors today have a control panel on the front of the unit, other adjustments may be possible as well.

Some NEC monitors, for example, have a focus adjustment screw on the left side of the unit. Because the screw is deep inside the case, the only evidence of its existence is a hole in the plastic grillwork on top of it. To adjust the monitor's focus, you have to stick a long-shanked screwdriver about two inches into the hole and feel around for the screw head. This type of adjustment can save you both an expensive repair bill and the humiliation of being ridiculed by the repair technician. Always examine the monitor case, the documentation, and the manufacturer's Web site or other online services for the locations of adjustment controls.

A defective or dysfunctional adapter or display usually is replaced as a single unit, rather than repaired. Most of today's adapters cost more to service than to replace, and the documentation required to service the hardware properly is not always available. You usually cannot get schematic diagrams, parts lists, wiring diagrams, and other documents for most adapters or monitors. Also, many adapters now are constructed with surface-mount technology that requires a substantial investment in a rework station before you can remove and replace these components by hand. You cannot use a $25 pencil-type soldering iron on these boards!

Servicing monitors is a slightly different proposition. Although a display often is replaced as a whole unit, many displays are too expensive to replace. Your best bet is to either contact the company from which you purchased the display, or to contact one of the companies that specializes in monitor depot repair.

Depot repair means that you send in your display to repair specialists who either fix your particular unit or return an identical unit they have already repaired. This is normally accomplished for a flat-rate fee; in other words, the price is the same no matter what they have done to repair your actual unit.

Because you will usually get a different (but identical) unit in return, they can ship out your repaired display immediately on receiving the one you sent in, or even in advance in some cases. This way, you have the least amount of downtime, and can receive the repaired display as quickly as possible. In some cases, if your particular monitor is unique or one they don't have in stock, then you will have to wait while they repair your specific unit.

Troubleshooting a failed monitor is relatively simple. If your display goes out, for example, a swap with another monitor can confirm that the display is the problem. If the problem disappears when you change the display, the problem is almost certainly in the original display or the cable; if the problem remains, it is likely in the video adapter or PC itself.

The monitor cable can sometimes be the source of display problems. A bent pin in the DB-15 connector that plugs into the video adapter can prevent the monitor from displaying images. Most of the time, you can repair the connector by carefully straightening the bent pin with sharp-nosed pliers.

If the pin breaks off, or the connector is otherwise damaged, you can sometimes replace the monitor cable. Some monitor manufacturers use cables that disconnect from the monitor and the video adapter, whereas others are permanently connected. Depending on the type of connector the device uses at the monitor end, you may have to contact the manufacturer for a replacement.

If you narrow down the problem to the display, consult the documentation that came with the monitor or call the manufacturer for the location of the nearest factory repair depot. There are also alternative third-party depot repair service companies that can repair most displays (if they are no longer covered by a warranty); their prices often are much lower than factory service. Check the vendor list in Appendix A for several companies who do depot repair of computer monitors and displays.

Caution

You should never attempt to repair a CRT monitor yourself. Touching the wrong component can be fatal. The display circuits can hold extremely high voltages for hours, days, or even weeks after the power is shut off. A qualified service person should discharge the cathode ray tube and power capacitors before proceeding.

For most displays, you are limited to making simple adjustments. For color displays, the adjustments can be quite formidable if you lack experience. Even factory service technicians often lack proper documentation and service information for newer models; they usually exchange your unit for another and repair the defective one later. Never buy a display for which no local factory repair depot is available.

If you have a problem with a display or adapter, it pays to call the manufacturer who might know about the problem and make repairs available. Sometimes, when manufacturers encounter numerous problems with a product, they may offer free repair, replacements, or another generous offer that you would never know about if you did not call.

Remember also that many of the problems you may encounter with modern video adapters and displays are related to the drivers that control these devices, rather than to the hardware. Be sure you have the latest and proper drivers before you attempt to have the hardware repaired; there may already be a solution available.

DisplayMate

DisplayMate is a unique diagnostic and testing program designed to thoroughly test your video adapter and display. It is somewhat unique in that most conventional PC hardware diagnostics programs do not emphasize video testing as this program does.

I find it useful not only in testing if a video adapter is functioning properly, but also in examining video displays. You can easily test the image quality of a display, which allows you to make focus, centering, brightness and contrast, color level, and other adjustments much more accurately than before. If you are purchasing a new monitor, you can use the program to evaluate the sharpness and linearity of the display, and to provide a consistent way of checking each monitor that you are considering. If you use projection systems for presentations as I do in my PC hardware seminars, you will find it invaluable for setting up and adjusting the projector.

DisplayMate can also test a video adapter thoroughly. It will set the video circuits into each possible video mode, so you can test all of its capabilities. It will also help you to determine the performance level of your card, both with respect to resolution and colors as well as to speed. You can then use the program to benchmark the performance of the display, which enables you to compare one type of video adapter system to another.

See the vendor list in Appendix A for more information on Sonera Technologies, the manufacturer and distributor of DisplayMate.

Chapter 9

Audio Hardware

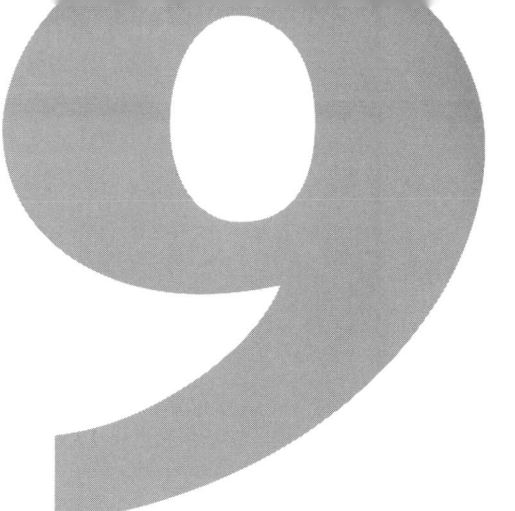

When the PC was first created, it did not include audio capabilities other than rudimentary beeping or tone generation. Part of the reason for this was that the PC standard originated in '81, and most of the other computers of that time had similar rudimentary capabilities. Another reason was that there really were no important applications for anything other than the most basic sounds. Computers used beeps to signal problems such as a full keyboard buffer or errors during the POST (power on self test) sequence and little else.

Systems that were designed later, such as the Macintosh that debuted in '84, did include high-quality audio capabilities as an integral part of the system hardware and software. Although there still is no universal audio hardware and software standard for PC-compatible systems, the inherent expandability of the PC platform enables users to easily add audio capability to existing systems, and at least one de facto audio standard has emerged.

Today's PC audio hardware usually takes the form of an audio adapter on an expansion card that you install into a bus slot in the computer. As with video adapters, some systems today include the audio hardware directly on the motherboard. The adapter provides jacks for speakers, a microphone, and sometimes other devices such as joysticks and MIDI hardware. On the software side, the audio adapter requires the support of a driver that you install either directly from an application or in your computer's operating system. This chapter focuses on the audio products found in today's PCs, their uses, and how you install and operate them.

Audio Adapter Applications

At first, consumer audio adapters were used only for games. Several companies, including AdLiB, Roland, and Creative Labs, released products by the late '80s. In '89, Creative Labs introduced the Game Blaster, which provided stereo sound to a handful of computer games. The question for many buyers was: "Why spend $100 for a card that adds sound to a $50 game?" More importantly, because no sound standards existed at the time, the sound card you selected might turn out to be useless with other games.

> **Note**
>
> About the same time as the release of the Game Blaster, hardware supporting the Musical Instrument Digital Interface (MIDI) became available for the PC. At this time, however, such hardware was used only in very specialized recording applications. As MIDI support became a more common feature in musical instruments, it also became a more affordable PC add-on.

A few months after releasing the Game Blaster, Creative Labs announced the Sound Blaster audio adapter. The Sound Blaster was compatible with the AdLiB sound card and Creative Labs' own Game Blaster card. It included a built-in microphone jack and a MIDI port for connecting the PC to a synthesizer or other electronic musical instrument. Finally, the audio adapter had the potential for uses other than games.

Unfortunately, as in '89, there is still no official standard for PC audio adapters. In many areas of the computer industry, standards often evolve informally due to the widespread acceptance of the market leader's products in a particular segment of the marketplace. These are called *de facto standards*, as contrasted with *de jure standards*, which are officially ratified by the manufacturers involved in the development process. For example, Hewlett-Packard printers use a page description language called PCL that has become a de facto standard because a great many of their printers have been sold and most software supports them. Other printer manufacturers then strive to create products that emulate the Hewlett-Packard printers so that they don't require unique commands and can use the same drivers as a Hewlett-Packard printer. This is how a de facto standard is born. The process is essentially based on popularity and economic factors. Although other standards for page description languages exist, Hewlett-Packard's standard is supported by most PC-compatible printers because failure to support it would all but guarantee a marketing disaster.

Over the past few years, some manufacturers of audio adapters have fought for dominance over the market, and there are several popular brands. However, there is no question that the leader in the field is Creative Labs, whose Sound Blaster audio adapters dominate the marketplace and have become the de facto standard for the industry. As a result, virtually all the audio adapters on the market today emulate the Creative Labs Sound Blaster. As with the Hewlett-Packard printer standard, the Creative Labs Sound Blaster interface is the one that most hardware products emulate, and the one for which most drivers are written. Failure to support this de facto standard would be all but suicidal for a commercial audio adapter product.

Today, audio adapters have many uses, including the following:

- Adding stereo sound to multimedia entertainment (game) software
- Increasing the effectiveness of educational software, particularly for young children

■ Adding sound effects to business presentations and training software

■ Creating music by using MIDI hardware and software

■ Adding voice notes to files

■ Audioconferencing and network telephony

■ Adding sound effects to operating system events

■ Enabling a PC to read

■ Enabling PC use by handicapped individuals

■ Playing audio CDs

Games

As with other multimedia technologies, audio adapters were originally designed to play games. In fact, many adapters include a *game adapter interface*, which is a connector for adding a game control device (usually a joystick or control paddles). Some adapters also use this interface to connect a plug providing a MIDI connector. The game port is a potential area of conflict because other cards, such as the multi-I/O type cards that many PCs use to provide serial and parallel ports, also have a game interface. This can result in an I/O port address conflict because most game interfaces use the same I/O port addresses. In these cases, it is usually best to use the game adapter interface on the audio adapter and disable any other in your system, especially if you plan to use MIDI devices.

By adding an audio adapter, game playing takes on a new dimension. Sound adds a level of realism that would otherwise be impossible, even with the best graphics. For example, some games use digitized human voices or real recorded dialog. In addition to realistic sounds and effects, games can also have musical scores, which add to the excitement and entertainment.

Multimedia

A sound card is a prerequisite if you want to turn your PC into a *Multimedia PC (MPC)*. What is multimedia? The term embraces a number of PC technologies, but primarily deals with video, sound, and storage. Basically, PC multimedia means the capability to merge images, data, and sound on a computer into a unified perceptual experience. In a practical sense, multimedia usually means adding an audio adapter and a CD-ROM drive to your system.

An organization called the Multimedia PC (MPC) Marketing Council was originally formed by Microsoft to generate standards for MPCs. They have created several MPC standards and license their logo and trademark to manufacturers whose hardware and software conform to these standards.

More recently, the MPC Marketing Council formally transferred responsibility for their standards to the Software Publishers Association's Multimedia PC Working Group. This group includes many of the same members as the original MPC, and is now the body governing the MPC specifications. The first thing this group did was create a new MPC standard.

The MPC Marketing Council originally developed two primary standards for multimedia. They are called the *MPC Level 1* and *MPC Level 2* standards. Now under the direction of the Software Publishers Association (SPA), these first two standards have been augmented by a third standard called *MPC Level 3*, which was introduced in June 1995. These standards define the minimum capabilities for an MPC. Table 9.1 shows these standards.

Table 9.1 Multimedia Standards	MPC Level 1	MPC Level 2	MPC Level 3
Processor	16MHz 386SX	25MHz 486SX	75MHz Pentium
RAM	2M	4M	8M
Hard disk	30M	160M	540M
Floppy disk	1.44M 3 1/2-inch	1.44M 3 1/2-inch	1.44M 3 1/2-inch
CD-ROM drive	Single-speed	Double-speed	Quad-speed
Audio	8-bit	16-bit	16-bit
VGA video	640×480	640×480	640×480
Resolution	16K colors	64K colors	64K colors
Other I/O	Serial, Parallel, MIDI, Game	Serial, Parallel, MIDI, Game	Serial, Parallel, MIDI, Game
Software	Microsoft Windows 3.1	Microsoft Windows 3.1	Microsoft Windows 3.1
Date introduced	1990	May 1993	June 1995

The MPC-3 specifications should be considered the absolute bare minimums for any multimedia system. In fact, most of the new computers sold today exceed the Level 3 specification by a substantial margin in almost every area. With Windows 95 or 98 as the standard operating system, I would normally recommend a system that includes at least 32M of RAM, a 200MHz Pentium processor, and 2G of hard drive space. A faster CD-ROM drive and a higher video resolution also enhance the multimedia experience. Note that although speakers or headphones are technically not a part of the MPC specification, they are certainly required for sound reproduction.

In addition to hardware specifications, the MPC specifications also define the audio capabilities of a multimedia system. These capabilities must include digital audio recording and playback (linear PCM sampling), music synthesis, and audio mixing.

Sound Files

You can use two basic types of files to store audio on your PC. One type is generically called a *sound file* and uses formats like WAV, VOC, AU, and AIFF. Sound files contain *waveform data*, which means they are analog audio recordings that have been digitized for storage on a computer. Just as you can store graphic images at different resolutions, you can have sound files that use various resolutions, trading off sound quality for file size. The three default sound resolution levels used in Windows 9x are shown in Table 9.2.

Table 9.2   Windows 9x Sound File Resolutions

Resolution	Frequency	Bandwidth	File Size
Telephone quality	11,025Hz	8-bit mono	11K/sec
Radio quality	22,050Hz	8-bit mono	22K/sec
CD quality	44,100Hz	16-bit stereo	172K/sec

As you can see, the difference in file sizes between the highest and lowest audio resolution levels is substantial. CD quality sound files can occupy enormous amounts of disk space. At this rate, just 60 seconds of audio would require over 10M of storage. For applications that don't require or benefit from such high resolution, such as voice annotation, telephone quality audio is sufficient, and generates much smaller files.

MIDI Files

The second type of audio file is a MIDI file, which is as different from a WAV as a vector graphic is from a bitmap. MIDI files, which use MID or RMI extensions, are wholly digital files that do not contain recordings of sound; instead, they contain the instructions that the audio hardware uses to create the sound. Just as 3D video adapters use instructions and textures to create images for the computer to display, MIDI-capable audio adapters use MIDI files to synthesize music.

MIDI is a powerful programming language developed in the '80s to permit electronic musical instruments to communicate. MIDI was the breakthrough standard in the electronic music industry, an industry that to this day shuns nearly all attempts at hardware standardization in favor of proprietary systems. With MIDI you can create, store, edit, and play back music files on your computer either in tandem with a MIDI-compatible electronic musical instrument, typically a keyboard synthesizer, or with just the computer.

Unlike the other types of sound files, MIDI messages require relatively little storage space. An hour of stereo music stored in MIDI format requires less than 500K. Many games use MIDI sounds instead of recorded ones to supply large amounts of music while conserving disk space. Because they are not recordings, the use of various resolutions does not apply to MIDI files.

A MIDI file is actually a digital representation of a musical score. It is composed of a collection of separate *channels*, each of which represents a different musical instrument or type of sound. Each channel specifies the frequencies and duration of the notes to be "played" by that instrument, just like a piece of sheet music does. Thus, a MIDI file of a string quartet contains four channels, representing two violins, a viola, and a cello.

> **Note**
>
> MIDI files are not intended to be a replacement for sound files such as WAVs; they should be considered a complementary technology. The biggest drawback of MIDI is that the playback technology is limited to sounds that are readily synthesizable. The most obvious shortcoming is
>
> (continues)

(continued)

that MIDI files are incapable of producing voices (except for synthesized choir effects). Therefore, when you download a MIDI file of your favorite song from the Internet, you'll have to do the singing.

All three of the MPC specifications call for all audio adapters to support MIDI. The general MIDI standard used by most of the audio adapters on the market allows for up to 16 channels in a single MIDI file, but this does not necessarily limit you to 16 instruments. A single channel can represent the sound of a group of instruments, such as a violin section, enabling you to synthesize an entire orchestra.

Because MIDI files consist of digital instructions, you can edit them much more easily than you can a sound file such as a WAV file. With the appropriate software, you can select any channel of a MIDI file and change the notes, the instrument used to play them, and many other attributes that affect the sound the PC produces.

Some software packages can even produce a manuscript of the music in a MIDI file by using standard musical notation. A composer can write a piece of music directly on the computer, edit it as needed, and then print out sheet music for live musicians to read. This is an enormous benefit for professional musicians who, throughout history, have had to either employ music copyists or publishers or spend long hours copying music by hand.

Playing MIDI Files. When you play a MIDI file on your PC, you are not playing back a recording. Your system is actually creating music from scratch. To do this, the computer requires a synthesizer, and every MIDI-capable audio adapter has one. As the system reads the MIDI file, the synthesizer generates the appropriate sound for each channel, using the instructions in the file to create the proper pitches and note lengths, and using a predefined patch to simulate the sound of a specific musical instrument. A *patch* is a set of instructions that the synthesizer uses to create sound similar to a particular instrument. You can control the speed at which the music plays and its volume in real time with the MIDI player software.

The synthesizer on an audio adapter is similar electronically to those found in actual electronic keyboard instruments, but it is usually not as capable. The MPC specifications call for audio adapters to contain FM synthesizer chips that are capable of playing at least six melodic notes and two percussive notes simultaneously.

FM Synthesis. Most sound boards generate sounds by using *FM synthesis*, a technology first pioneered in 1976. By using one sine wave operator to modify another, FM synthesis creates an artificial sound that mimics an instrument. The MIDI standard supported by the adapter specifies an array of preprogrammed sounds containing most of the instruments used by pop bands and orchestras.

Over the years, the technology has progressed (some FM synthesizers now use four operators) to a point where FM synthesis can sound moderately good, but is still noticeably artificial. The trumpet sound, for example, is vaguely similar to that of a trumpet, but would never be confused with the real thing.

Wavetable Synthesis. As you move up to the higher end of the audio adapter market, fewer devices use FM synthesis because, even at its best, the sound it produces is not a realistic simulation of a musical instrument. More realistic, inexpensive sound was pioneered by Ensoniq Corp., the makers of professional keyboards, in 1984.

Using a technology that was theorized at about the same time as FM synthesis, Ensoniq developed a method of sampling any instrument—including pianos, violins, guitars, flutes, trumpets, and drums—and storing the digitized sound in a wavetable. Stored either in ROM chips or on disk, the wavetable supplies an actual digitized sound of an instrument that the audio adapter can manipulate as needed. Soon after Ensoniq's discovery, other keyboard makers replaced their FM synthesizers with wavetable synthesis.

A wavetable synthesizer can take a sample of an instrument playing a single note and modify its frequency to play any note on the scale. Some adapters produce better sound by using several samples of the same instrument. The highest note on a piano differs from the lowest note in more than just pitch, and the closer the pitch of the sample is to the note being synthesized, the more realistic the sound is.

Thus, the size of the wavetable has a powerful effect on the quality and variety of sounds that the synthesizer can produce. The best quality wavetable adapters on the market usually have several megabytes of memory on the card for storing samples. Some support optional daughtercards for the installation of additional memory and enable you to customize the samples in the wavetable to your own specifications.

MIDI Connectivity. The advantages of MIDI go beyond the internal functions of your computer. You can also use your audio adapter's MIDI interface to connect an electronic keyboard, sound generator, drum machine, or other MIDI device to your computer. You can then play MIDI files by using the synthesizer in the keyboard instead of the one on your adapter—or create your own MIDI files by playing notes on the keyboard. With the right software, you can compose an entire symphony by playing the notes of each instrument separately into its own channel, and then playing back all the channels together. Many professional musicians and composers use MIDI to create music directly on computers, bypassing traditional instruments altogether.

Some manufacturers even offer high-end MIDI cards that can operate in full-duplex mode, meaning that you can play back prerecorded audio tracks as you record a new track into the same MIDI file. This is technology that only a few years ago required the services of a professional recording studio with equipment costing hundreds of thousands of dollars.

To connect a MIDI device to your PC, you need an audio adapter that has the MIDI ports defined by the MIDI specification. MIDI uses two round 5-pin DIN ports (see Figure 9.1) for separate input (MIDI-IN) and output (MIDI-OUT). Many devices also have a MIDI-THRU port that passes the input from a device directly to output, but audio adapters generally do not have this. Interestingly, MIDI sends data through only pins 1 and 3 of the connector. Pin 2 is shielded and pins 4 and 5 are unused.

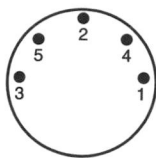

FIG. 9.1   The MIDI specification calls for the use of two or three 5-pin DIN connectors.

The primary function of the audio adapter's MIDI interface is to convert the parallel data bytes used on a computer's system bus into the serial MIDI data format. MIDI uses asynchronous serial ports that run at 31.25kbaud. MIDI communications use 8 data bits, with one start and one stop bit, for a speed of 320 microseconds per serial byte.

> **Note**
>
> You can obtain the most recent specifications for the MIDI standard, for a modest fee, from the International MIDI Association, 23634 Emelita Street, Woodland Hills, California 91367 USA.

MIDI runs over special unshielded twisted-pair cables that can have a maximum length of up to 50 feet (although most of the cables sold are 10 or 20 feet long). You can also daisy chain multiple MIDI devices together to combine their capabilities. The total length of the MIDI chain is not limited, as long as each individual cable is less than 50 feet.

Many audio adapters do not have MIDI ports directly on the adapter card. Instead, they use a separate connector that plugs into the adapter's game port and provides the MIDI ports. Unfortunately, this connector is rarely included in the box with the adapter. You have to purchase it separately from the manufacturer.

MIDI Software. Windows 9x includes basic software that enables you to play MIDI files, in the form of its Media Player application, and also includes a selection of MIDI music files. For full MIDI capabilities, however, you'll need sequencing software to manipulate the tempo of MIDI files and the sounds used to play them, or to cut and paste together various prerecorded music sequences.

Many audio adapters come with a selection of software products that provide some MIDI capabilities, and there are shareware and freeware tools available on the Internet, but the truly powerful software that enables you to create, edit, and manipulate MIDI files must be purchased separately.

Presentations

Businesses are rapidly discovering that integrating graphics, animation, and sound into their presentations is more impressive than a simple slide show, and more likely to keep their audiences awake. An audio adapter adds impact to any presentation or classroom.

A variety of business-presentation software and high-end training and authoring packages that can take advantage of a PC's audio capabilities already exist, and you don't have to be a programmer to get your own show on the road. Popular software packages such as Microsoft PowerPoint now include sound and animation features for their presentation files.

Presentation software packages support WAV, AVI, and MIDI files. With these products, you can synchronize sounds with objects. When a presentation displays a picture of your new product, for example, you can add a roaring round of applause. You can even pull in sound from an audio CD in your CD-ROM drive. Many presentation software packages also include clip-media libraries with audio files that you can use license-free.

You can even take your show on the road. Many laptop and notebook computers include sound capability and even have built-in CD-ROM drives and speakers. There are also external audio adapters and even CD-ROM drives available to provide multimedia on the go.

An audio adapter can make many computing tasks (such as learning how to use software) easier. PC software manufacturers have taken an early lead in this area. Many publishers are taking advantage of the space on the CD-ROMs they now use to distribute their products by including animated tutorials and online help, replete with music.

Sound has also found its place on the World Wide Web. Because of their relatively small size, MIDI files are an excellent choice for providing background music when users arrive at your Web site. A catchy tune can help people remember your site out of the many others they see each day.

Recording

Virtually all audio adapters have an audio input jack. With a microphone, you can record your voice. Using the Sound Recorder application included with all versions of Microsoft Windows, you can play, edit, or record a sound file in the WAV format. From the Windows Sounds Control Panel, you can assign specific WAV files to certain Windows events (see Figure 9.2). I always get a laugh when I exit Windows and hear the sound of a flushing toilet!

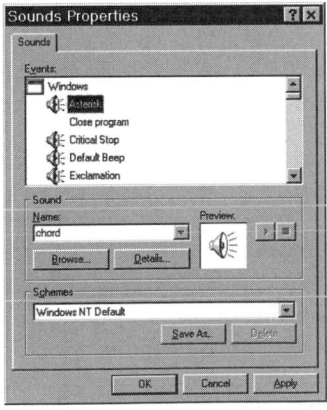

FIG. 9.2 The Windows 9x Sounds Control Panel adds sound to different Windows events.

This capability is not just an entertaining novelty, however. You can also use specific sounds to notify you of important events, such as when your system experiences an error or when you receive new e-mail. The Windows operating system ships with a collection of basic WAV files that you can assign as needed. Windows 9x also includes collections of WAV files called sound schemes that provide a unified environment for your system, based on a given subject. The Musica sound scheme, for example, automatically assigns sound files of various musical instruments to many of the standard system events. Many applications add their own events to the operating system, enabling you to configure sounds for activities specific to that product.

By recording the sound of your own voice, or anything else, you can create your own WAV files and assign them to certain events, instead of using the default Windows WAVs. On most multimedia systems, you can record directly from an audio CD in your CD-ROM drive to the WAV format. You can also attach your stereo system or VCR to the audio input jack and record any sound to a WAV file.

With this simple connection, users have amassed libraries consisting of thousands of WAV files celebrating popular songs, movies, and TV shows.

Voice Annotation

By using WAV files, you can record voice messages and embed them into your Windows documents. For example, a business executive could pick up a microphone and, by embedding a message in a contract or spreadsheet, give his or her secretary explicit instructions. This message is called a *voice annotation*. I like to think of it as a verbal Post-It Note.

With voice annotation, you can embed voice messages, suggestions, or questions in a document and send it to a colleague. To leave such messages, your Windows application must support Windows' Object Linking and Embedding (OLE). OLE is a technology that enables you to take objects created by one application and embed them into a document created in another application. Activating the embedded object in the target application by double-clicking it automatically launches the object's source application.

For example, if you embed a portion of a Microsoft Excel spreadsheet into a Word document, you will see the grid of the spreadsheet on the page in Word. However, when you double-click the spreadsheet, Excel launches and temporarily replaces the Word menu and button bars with those of Excel. Clicking another part of the Word document returns you to the normal Word environment.

Embedding a sound in a document works the same way. Imagine that you're editing an Excel spreadsheet and you want to insert a voice note next to a total that looks questionable. Place the cursor in the cell next to the total, then select Edit, Insert, Object, Sound to call up Windows' Sound Recorder. Click the Record button and begin speaking. After you've finished recording, the sound appears as an icon in the selected cell. Because the sound file is actually an embedded part of the spreadsheet file, you can copy it to a disk or e-mail it to another user. That user can then double-click the icon and hear your voice.

Tip

Voice annotation is typically an area where sound quality is not a major issue. Be sure to configure your system to use telephone-quality (that is, the lowest quality) audio for this purpose, or you could end up with files that are enormously inflated in size by the addition of embedded audio.

Voice Recognition

Some audio adapters are equipped with software that is capable of voice recognition. You can also get voice recognition for your current adapter in the form of add-on software. Voice-recognition, as the name implies, is when your computer is "taught" to recognize spoken word forms and react to them. Voice recognition products generally take two forms: those that are designed to provide a simple voice interface to basic computer functions, and those that can accept vocal dictation and insert the spoken text into an application such as a word processor.

Voice Command Software. The voice interface application is clearly the simpler of the two, as the software only has to recognize a limited vocabulary of words. With this type of software, you can sit in front of your computer and say the words "file open" to access the menu in your active Windows application.

For the average user, this type of application is of dubious value. For a time, Compaq was shipping computers to corporate clients with a microphone and an application of this type, at little or no additional cost. The phenomenon of dozens of users in an office, talking to their computers, was interesting, to say the least. The experiment resulted in virtually no increased productivity, a lot of wasted time as users experimented with the software, and a noisier office.

However, for users with physical handicaps that limit their ability to use a keyboard, this type of software can represent a whole new avenue of communication. For this reason alone, continued development of voice recognition technology is essential.

Note

Voice recognition applications, by necessity, have to be somewhat limited in their scope. For example, it quickly becomes a standard office joke for someone to stick their head into another person's cubicle and call out "Format C!," as though this command would erase the user's hard drive. Obviously, the software must not be able to damage a user's system because of a misinterpreted voice command.

Voice Dictation Software. The other type of voice recognition software is far more complex. Converting standard speech into text is an extraordinarily difficult task, given the wide variation in human speech patterns. For this reason, nearly all software of this type (and some of the basic voice command applications, as well) must be "trained" to understand a particular user's voice. You do this training by reading prepared text samples supplied with the software to the computer. Because the software knows what you're supposed to be saying beforehand, it can associate certain words with the manner in which you speak them.

Users' results with this sort of application vary widely, probably due in no small part to their individual speech patterns. I've heard people rave about being able to dictate pages of text without touching the keyboard, while others claim that correcting the many typographical errors is more trouble than typing the text manually.

Voice recognition technology is still in its infancy, and is sensitive to changes in a person's voice. Illness and stress can often change a person's voice enough to throw off most of the "consumer" voice recognition products. You will also need a fast computer, at least a Pentium, to achieve response times that are quick enough to keep up with your speech. However, advances in this technology may develop to a point that we'll be able to use continuous speech to control computers, rather than typing.

Conferencing

One of the newest applications in the world of multimedia is video and audio conferencing over the Internet. These applications range from point-to-point products, such as VocalTec's Internet Phone, to multiuser-conferencing packages, such as Microsoft's NetMeeting. Other applications, such as RealNetworks' Real Player, can play back audio (with or without video) as it is received over the Internet, a process called *streaming*.

For all these applications, the audio adapter is an integral part of the technology. Depending on the speed of your Internet connection, the data compression technology that the software uses, and whether or not you elect to stream video along with audio, the quality of the sound delivered by conferencing software can range from poor to rather good.

As with voice recognition, this is a technology that is still very young. Over a 33.6Kbps modem connection (which frequently does not reach a full 33.6), one-way audio and video streaming generally works tolerably well, but full-duplex communications, even when audio-only, tend to drop words. However, as faster Internet connections and better data compression techniques become available, audioconferencing and videoconferencing are likely to become as reliable as the telephone network.

Proofreading

You can also use an audio adapter as an inexpensive proofreading tool. Many adapters include a text-to-speech utility that you can use to read a list of numbers or text back to you. This type of software can read back highlighted words or even an entire file.

Having text read back to you enables you to more easily spot forgotten words or awkward phrases. Accountants can double-check numbers, and busy executives can listen to their e-mail while they are doing paperwork.

Audio CDs

One convenient and entertaining use of a CD-ROM drive is to play audio CDs while you are working on something else. Virtually all CD-ROM drives support audio CDs, and the music can be piped not only through a pair of speakers (and even a subwoofer) connected to the audio adapter, but also through headphones plugged into the jack provided on most CD-ROM drives. Most sound cards include a CD-player utility, as does Windows 9x, and free versions are available for download on the Internet. These programs usually present a visual display similar to the Control Panel of an audio CD player. You operate the controls with a mouse or the keyboard, and can listen to audio CDs as you work on other things.

Sound Mixer

On a multimedia PC, it is often possible for two or more sound sources to require the services of the audio adapter at the same time. Any time you have multiple sound sources that you want to play through a single set of speakers, a mixer is necessary.

Most audio adapters include a mixer that enables all the different audio sources, MIDI, WAV, line in, and the CD to use the single line out jack. Normally, the adapter ships with software that displays visual sliders like you would see on an actual audio mixer in a recording studio. With these controls, you can set the relative volume of each of the sound sources.

Is an Audio Adapter Necessary?

In the preceding sections, you read about the various ways that high-quality audio can improve the computing experience. Certainly, for recreational computer users, audio greatly enhances the entertainment value of games and other multimedia software. The question still remains, however, of whether audio is suited to the business world.

There are definitely applications, such as voice annotation and audioconferencing, that can be useful to business computer users. In training and other educational environments, audio can be a necessity in some cases. However, three other factors that can make the assimilation of PC audio into the business office problematic are the following:

- Expense
- Productivity
- Noise

The price of adding basic audio capabilities to a PC, like that of virtually all computer hardware, has plummeted during the past few years. Business applications do not require high-end audio features such as wavetable synthesis, so a simple adapter that conforms to the MPC specification is sufficient. You can usually buy a serviceable audio adapter and speakers for about $100, or less when you are buying in volume.

However, this is not an insignificant expenditure when you are talking about hundreds or thousands of PCs. Added to that is the cost of the manpower needed to install and configure all this new hardware.

The easiest solution to this problem is to purchase PCs with integrated audio adapters on the motherboard. Because these systems usually arrive preconfigured, or are automatically configured by the operating system, integrated audio eliminates the time and expense of installation, and provides basic audio capabilities at the lowest possible cost.

Employee productivity is another important concern. Many network administrators and company executives are only now coming to grips with the effect that Internet access has had on the workforce. Audio definitely has its uses in the business world, as does the World Wide Web, but the question remains as to whether it will be seen by many supervisors as just another time-wasting toy.

The answer to this problem is not so simple. Administrators can take steps to limit users' access to the operating system's sound configuration controls, using Windows 9x system policies, but they cannot easily prevent users from downloading or recording sound files and playing them back, without limiting the audio hardware's usefulness. As with the Web, however, it is likely that once the novelty of the new capabilities wears off, users will waste less time playing with audio and more time using it productively.

The final problem is the obvious one of the noise produced by the individual speakers attached to a large fleet of PCs. The degree of difficulty is, of course, dependent on the architectural layout of the workplace. For users working in small or private offices, the noise level should be minimal. For workers in cubicles, the situation should be tolerable, as long as the users exercise some restraint in the volume. In an open office with many computers, however, the noise could be a severe problem.

Network administrators should consider these factors when deciding which users should be furnished with audio hardware.

Audio Adapter Concepts and Terms

To fully understand audio adapters and their functions, you need to understand various concepts and terms. Terms like *16-bit*, *CD quality*, and *MIDI port* are just a few. Concepts such as *sampling* and *digital-to-audio conversion (DAC)* are often sprinkled throughout stories about new sound products. You've already learned about some of these terms and concepts; the following sections describe many others.

The Nature of Sound

To understand an audio adapter, you have to understand the nature of sound. Every sound is produced by vibrations that compress air or other substances. These sound waves travel in all directions, expanding in balloon-like fashion from the source of the sound. When these waves reach your ear, they cause vibrations that you perceive as sound.

Two of the basic properties of any sound are its pitch and its intensity.

Pitch is the rate at which vibrations are produced. It is measured in the number of *hertz (Hz)*, or cycles per second. One cycle is a complete vibration back and forth. The number of Hz is the frequency of the tone; the higher the frequency, the higher the pitch.

Humans cannot hear all possible frequencies. Very few people can hear sounds with frequencies less than 16Hz or more than about 20KHz (kilohertz; 1KHz equals 1,000Hz). In fact, the lowest note on a piano has a frequency of 27Hz, and the highest note a little more than 4KHz. Frequency-modulation (FM) radio stations can broadcast notes with frequencies as high as 15KHz.

The intensity of a sound is called its *amplitude*. This intensity determines the sound's volume, and depends upon the strength of the vibrations producing the sound. A piano string, for example, vibrates gently when the key is struck softly. The string swings back and forth in a narrow arc, and the tone it sends out is soft. If the key is struck more forcefully, however, the string swings back and forth in a wider arc, producing a greater amplitude and a greater volume. The loudness of sounds is measured in *decibels (db)*. The rustle of leaves is rated at 20db, average street noise at 70db, and nearby thunder at 120db.

Game Standards

Most audio adapters support the Sound Blaster, by Creative Labs, which is the current entertainment audio standard. *AdLiB* was a company whose audio adapters at one time rivaled those of Creative Labs in the PC game industry. They were involved in the development of the MSC Level 1 and 2 standards and, for some time, AdLiB and Creative Labs were running neck and neck as the *de facto* standard, until AdLiB declined and went out of business for a time. Now, the company is back in business as AdLiB Multimedia, but they no longer hold a position comparable to that of Creative Labs.

To hear sounds in most DOS games, you must configure the game by selecting one of the audio adapter drivers included with the program. Sticking with a popular sound card product like one of the Sound Blaster models will ensure that you always have software support, because most software supports them. Even if you don't have an actual Sound Blaster, however, nearly all other audio adapters on the market today emulate them. If you have some old or off-brand adapter that does not emulate the Sound Blaster, then you may find many software products that do not specifically support your card.

Many games are now being written for the Windows 9x operating system, which eliminates the problem of audio adapter compatibility. In Windows 9x, you install the driver in the operating system, and any application can take advantage of it. As long as you have a Windows 9x driver for your adapter, you can run any game designed for the OS.

Frequency Response

The quality of an audio adapter is often measured by two criteria: frequency response (or range) and total harmonic distortion.

The *frequency response* of an audio adapter is the range in which an audio system can record and/or play at a constant and audible amplitude level. Many cards support 30Hz to 20KHz. The wider the spread, the better the adapter.

The *total harmonic distortion* measures an audio adapter's *linearity*, the straightness of a frequency response curve. In layman's terms, the harmonic distortion is a measure of accurate sound reproduction. Any nonlinear elements cause distortion in the form of harmonics. The smaller the percentage of distortion, the better.

Sampling

With an audio adapter, a PC can record waveform audio. *Waveform audio* (also known as *sampled* or *digitized sound*) uses the PC as a recording device (such as a tape recorder). Small computer chips built into the adapter, called *analog-to-digital converters (ADCs)*, convert analog sound waves into digital bits that the computer can understand. Likewise, *digital-to-analog converters (DACs)* convert the recorded sounds to an audible analog format.

Sampling is the process of turning the original analog sound waves (see Figure 9.3) into digital (binary) signals that the computer can save and later replay. The system samples the sound by taking snapshots of its frequency and amplitude at regular intervals. For example, at time X the sound may be measured with an amplitude of Y. The higher (or more frequent) the sample rate, the more accurate the digital sound is to its real-life source, and the larger the amount of disk space needed to store it.

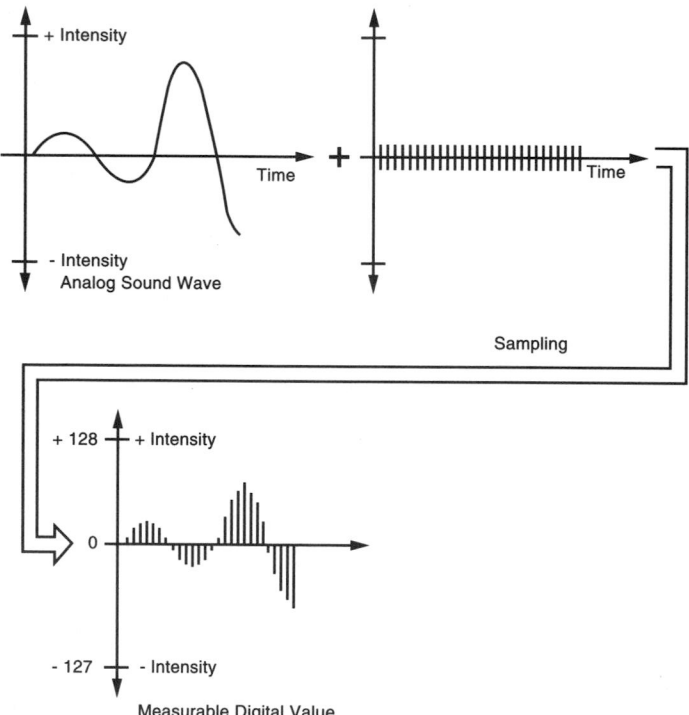

FIG. 9.3 Sampling turns a changing sound wave into measurable digital values.

8-Bit Versus 16-Bit

The original MPC specifications required audio adapters to provide 8-bit sound. This doesn't mean the audio adapter must fit into an 8-bit instead of a 16-bit expansion slot. Rather, *8-bit audio* means that the adapter uses eight bits to digitize each sound sample.

This translates into 256 (2^8) possible digital values to which the sample can be pegged (less quality than the 65,536 values possible with a 16-bit sound card). Generally, 8-bit audio is adequate for recorded speech, while 16-bit sound is best for the demands of music. Figure 9.4 shows the difference between 8- and 16-bit sound.

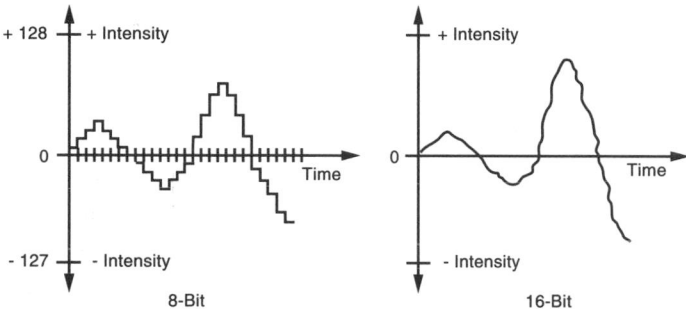

FIG. 9.4   16-bit resolution allows more accurate sound reproduction than 8-bit resolution.

Many of the older audio adapters did only 8-bit sound reproduction. Today, I would not recommend anything less than a 16-bit card, which offers very high resolution.

Besides resolution, the sampling rate or frequency determines how often the audio adapter measures the level of the sound being recorded or played back. Basically, you have to sample at about two times the highest frequency you want to produce, plus an extra 10 percent to keep out unwanted signals. Humans can hear up to 20,000 cycles per second, or 20KHz. If you double this number and add 10%, you get a 44.1KHz sampling rate, the same sampling rate used by high-fidelity audio CDs.

Sound recorded at the telephone quality rate of 11KHz (capturing 11,000 samples per second) is fuzzier than sound sampled at the radio quality rate of 22KHz. A sound sampled in 16-bit stereo (two channel) at 44KHz (CD-audio quality) requires as much as 10.5M per minute of disk space. The same sound sample in 8-bit mono (single channel) at 11KHz takes 1/16th the space.

Audio Adapter Features

To make an intelligent purchasing decision, you should be aware of some audio adapter basic components and the features they provide. The following sections discuss the features you should consider while evaluating audio adapters for your PC.

Connectors

Most audio adapters have the same connectors. These 1/8-inch minijack connectors provide the means of passing sound signals from the adapter to speakers, headphones, and stereo systems, and of receiving sound from a microphone, CD player, tape player, or stereo. The four types of connectors your audio adapter should have are shown in Figure 9.5.

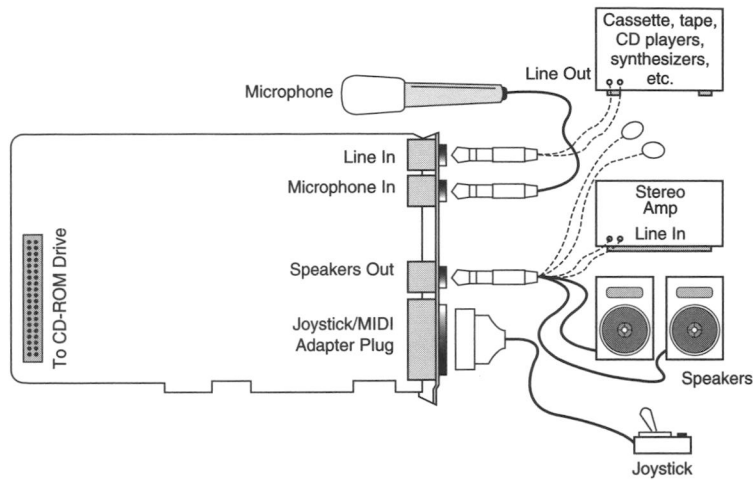

FIG. 9.5 The basic input and output connectors that most audio adapters have in common.

■ *Stereo line, or audio, out connector.* The line out connector is used to send sound signals from the audio adapter to a device outside the computer. You can hook up the cables from the line out connector to stereo speakers, a headphone set, or your stereo system. If you hook up the PC to your stereo system, you can have amplified sound. Some adapters , such as the Microsoft Windows Sound System, provide two jacks for line out. One is for the left channel of the stereo signal; the other is for the right channel.

■ *Stereo line, or audio, in connector.* With the line in connector, you can record or mix sound signals from an external source, such as a stereo system or VCR, to the computer's hard disk.

■ *Speaker/headphone connector.* The speaker/headphone connector is provided on most audio adapters, but not necessarily all of them. Instead, the line out (described earlier) doubles as a way to send stereo signals from the adapter to your stereo system or speakers. When the adapter provides both a speaker/headphone and a line out connector, the speaker/headphone connector provides an amplified signal that can power your headphones or small bookshelf speakers. Most adapters can provide up to four watts of power to drive your speakers. The signals that the adapter sends through the line out connector are not amplified. The line out connector generally provides better sound reproduction because it relies on the external amplifier built-in to your stereo system or speakers, which is typically more powerful than the small amplifier on the audio adapter.

■ *Microphone, or mono, in connector.* The mono in connector is used to connect a microphone for recording your voice or other sounds to disk. This microphone jack records in mono, not in stereo, and is therefore not suitable for high-quality music recordings. Many audio adapters cards use *Automatic Gain Control (AGC)* to improve recordings. This feature adjusts the recording levels on-the-fly. A 600ohm to 10K ohm dynamic or condenser microphone works best with this jack. Some inexpensive audio adapters use the line in connector instead of a separate microphone jack.

■ *Joystick connector.* The joystick connector is a 15-pin, D-shaped connector that can connect to any standard joystick or game controller. Sometimes the joystick port can accommodate two joysticks if you purchase an optional Y-adapter. Many computers already contain a joystick port as part of a multi-function I/O circuit on the motherboard or an expansion card. If this is the case, you must take note of which port your operating system or application is configured to use when connecting the game controller.

■ *MIDI connector.* Audio adapters typically use the same joystick port as their MIDI connector. Two of the pins in the connector are designed to carry signals to and from a MIDI device, such as an electronic keyboard. In most cases, you must purchase a separate MIDI connector from the audio adapter manufacturer that plugs into the joystick port and contains the two round, 5-pin DIN connectors used by MIDI devices, plus a connector for a joystick. Because their signals use separate pins, you can connect the joystick and a MIDI device at the same time. You need only this connector if you plan to connect your PC to external MIDI devices. You can still play the MIDI files found on many Web sites by using the audio adapter's internal synthesizer.

■ *Internal pin-type connector.* Most audio adapters have an internal pin-type connector that you can use to plug an internal CD-ROM drive directly into the adapter, using a ribbon cable. This connection enables you to channel audio signals from the CD-ROM directly to the audio adapter, so you can play the sound through the computer's speakers. Note that this connector is different from the CD-ROM controller connector found on some audio adapters. This connector does not carry data from the CD-ROM to the system bus; it only provides the CD-ROM drive with direct audio access to the speakers. If your adapter lacks this connector, you can still play CD audio through the computer speakers by connecting the CD-ROM drive's headphone jack to the audio adapter's line in jack with an external cable.

Tip

The line in, line out, and speaker connectors on an audio adapter all use the same 1/8-inch minijack socket. The three jacks are usually labeled, but when setting up a computer on or under a desk, these labels on the back of the PC can be difficult to read. One of the most common reasons why a PC fails to produce any sound is that the speakers are plugged into the wrong socket.

Volume Control

Some audio adapters include a thumbwheel volume control next to the input/output jacks, although sophisticated sound cards have no room for it. This control is usually redundant, as the operating system or the software included with the adapter typically provides a combination of keys or a visual slider control that you can use to adjust the volume. In fact, the volume wheel can be troublesome; if you aren't aware of its existence and it is turned all the way down, you may be puzzled by the adapter's failure to produce sufficient sound.

Synthesis

At one time, when evaluating audio adapters, you had to decide whether to buy a mono-phonic or stereophonic card. Today, virtually all audio adapters are stereophonic.

Stereophonic cards produce many voices concurrently and from two different sources. A *voice* is a single sound produced by the adapter. A string quartet uses four voices, one for each instrument, while a polyphonic instrument such as a piano requires one voice for each note of a chord. Thus, to fully reproduce the capabilities of a pianist requires ten voices, one for each finger. The more voices an audio adapter is capable of producing, the better the sound fidelity. The best audio adapters on the market today can produce up to 128 simultaneous voices.

Most of the audio adapters that use FM synthesis to imitate musical instruments use synthesizer chips developed by Yamaha. Older and less-expensive adapters use the monophonic 11-voice YM3812 or OPL2 chip. Better models use the stereophonic 20-voice YMF262 or OPL3 chip.

Imitated musical instruments are not as impressive as the real thing. Wavetable audio adapters use digital recordings of real instruments and sound effects. Often, several megabytes of these sound clips are embedded in ROM chips on the card. For example, some sound cards use the Ensoniq chip set (a type of circuit design) that does wavetable synthesis of musical instruments. Instead of synthesizing the sound of a trombone play-ing a D flat, the Ensoniq chip set accesses a digitized sample of an actual trombone play-ing that note.

If your primary interest in an audio adapter is for entertainment or for use in educational or business settings, FM synthesis quality may be good enough. If you are a music enthu-siast or plan to work extensively with MIDI, then a wavetable adapter is preferable.

> **Note**
>
> To enhance the MIDI capabilities of Sound Blaster adapters that use FM synthesis, Creative Labs offers the *Wave Blaster*. The Wave Blaster is a daughtercard that plugs into the Sound Blaster card. When the system plays MIDI music, the adapter looks to the Wave Blaster for any of 213 CD-quality digitally recorded musical instrument sounds. Without the Wave Blaster, the Sound Blaster would imitate these sounds through FM synthesis. With the Wave Blaster, the music sounds as though it's being played by real instruments—because it is.

Data Compression

Most sound cards today can easily produce CD-quality audio, which is sampled at 44.1KHz. At this rate, recorded files (even of your own voice) can consume over 10M for every minute of recording. To counter this demand for disk space, many audio adapters include their own data-compression capability. For example, the Sound Blaster ASP 16 includes on-the-fly compression of sound files in ratios of 2:1, 3:1, or 4:1.

Some manufacturers of audio adapters use an algorithm called *Adaptive Differential Pulse Code Modulation (ADPCM) compression* to reduce file size by more than 50%. However, a simple fact of audio technology is that when you use such compression, you lose sound quality.

Because it degrades sound quality, there is no standard for the use of ADPCM. Creative Labs uses a proprietary hardware approach, while Microsoft is promoting the Business Audio ADPCM design, developed with Compaq.

The most popular compression standard is the *Motion Pictures Experts Group (MPEG) standard*, which works with both audio and video compression and is gaining support in the non-PC world from products such as the new crop of DVD players now hitting the market. MPEG by itself provides a potential compression ratio of 30:1, and largely because of this, full-motion-video MPEG DVD and CD-ROM titles are now available.

Multi-Purpose Digital Signal Processors

Many audio adapters use *digital signal processors (DSPs)* to add intelligence to the adapter, freeing the system processor from work-intensive tasks, such as filtering noise from recordings or compressing audio on-the-fly.

The Sound Blaster AWE32's programmable DSP, for example, features compression algorithms for processing text-to-speech data and enables the card's QSound surround-sound 3D audio, along with reverb and chorus effects. DSPs enable an audio adapter to be a multi-purpose device. IBM uses its DSP to add a fax modem and digital answering machine to its WindSurfer Communications Adapter.

CD-ROM Connectors

Some audio adapters double as a CD-ROM controller, or interface, cards. Before the EIDE interface made the CD-ROM a ubiquitous PC component, connecting the drive to the audio adapter was an inexpensive means of adding multimedia capabilities to a system. Although some adapters provide a SCSI port that you can theoretically use to connect any SCSI device, others use a proprietary connection that accommodates only a select few CD-ROM drives that support the same interface.

If you're seeking to add both an audio adapter and a CD-ROM drive to an existing system, then you might want to consider using an adapter with a CD-ROM connector. Some manufacturers market multimedia upgrade kits that bundle an audio adapter, CD-ROM drive, CD-ROM titles, software, and cables in an attractively priced package. By purchasing a multimedia upgrade kit rather than separate components, you may save some money, and you can be certain that all the components will work together.

If you already own a CD-ROM drive, make sure it's compatible with the audio adapter you plan to buy. If you plan to add a CD-ROM drive or expect to upgrade your drive, keep in mind that a proprietary interface will limit your choices, perhaps to a single CD-ROM brand.

Although an integrated audio/CD-ROM controller can be a quick and easy multimedia solution for older systems, I generally recommend that users connect the CD-ROM through a standard EIDE or SCSI interface, and avoid the CD-ROM connector on the audio adapter. Virtually all new systems sold today include an EIDE interface, and a SCSI adapter enables you to attach other devices to the same interface, such as hard disks, tape drives, and scanners. The software driver support and performance of a dedicated driver interface will be much better than those provided by audio/CD-ROM combination cards.

▶▶ For more information on adding a CD-ROM drive to your system, see Chapter 13, "Optical Storage."

Sound Drivers

As with many PC components, a software driver provides a vital link between an audio adapter and the application or operating system that uses it. Operating systems such as Windows 9x and Windows NT include a large library of drivers for most of the audio adapters on the market. In most cases, these drivers are written by the manufacturer of the audio adapter and only distributed by Microsoft. You may find that the drivers that ship with the adapter are more recent than those included with the operating system. As always, the best place to find the most recent drivers for a piece of hardware is the manufacturers own Web site or other online service.

DOS applications do not usually include as wide a range of driver support as an operating system, but you should find that most games and other programs support the Sound Blaster adapters. If you are careful to buy an adapter that is Sound Blaster-compatible, you should have no trouble finding driver support for all your applications.

Choosing an Audio Adapter

What are some key features to consider in a sound card? Although some aspects are subjective, the following sections describe some key buying points.

Consumer or Producer?

Different users require varying degrees of performance and different features from an audio adapter. One simple way of classifying audio users is to divide them into consumers and producers of sound.

Many users need only basic audio capabilities. They want to hear sound effects and music when they play games or view Web sites, and maybe listen to audio CDs as they work. These are consumers of sound. They obtain audio from outside sources such as CD-ROMs and the Internet and play them over their speakers. For this type of user, a modest audio adapter is all that is needed. The adapter should provide 16-bit audio, but an FM synthesizer should be sufficient for sound production. Users of this type that are hard-core gamers may want to move up to an adapter with a wavetable synthesizer, but they do not require a top-of-the-line model.

Producers are people who intend to create their own sound files. These can range from casual business users recording low-fidelity voice annotations to professional musicians and MIDI-maniacs. These users need an adapter that can perform as much of the audio processing as possible itself, so as not to place an additional burden on the system processor. Adapters that use DSPs to perform compression and other tasks are highly recommended in this case. Musicians will certainly want an adapter with as many voices as possible and a wavetable synthesizer. Adapters with expandable memory arrays and the capability to create and modify custom wavetables are also preferable.

Compatibility

Although there are no official audio adapter standards, Creative Labs' popular Sound Blaster line has become a *de facto* standard. The Sound Blaster—the first widely distributed audio adapter—is supported by the greatest number of software programs. An audio adapter advertised as Sound Blaster-compatible should be able to run with virtually any application that supports sound. Most adapters also support the MPC Level 2 or Level 3 specifications, enabling you to play sound files in Windows and more.

Caution

Beware of audio adapters that require special drivers to be Sound Blaster-compatible. These drivers can cause problems and will take up additional memory that otherwise would be available to your applications.

Bundled Software

A software bundle can sometimes make the difference between a good buy on an audio adapter and a great one. Audio adapters usually include several sound utilities so you can begin using your adapter right away. Some of the types of software you may receive are as follows:

- Text-to-speech conversion programs
- Applications for playing, editing, and recording audio files
- Audio CD-player programs
- Stereo sound-mixer programs
- Sequencer software, which helps you create, edit, and play back MIDI music files
- Various sound clips

Audio Adapter Installation

Installing an audio adapter is no more intimidating than installing an internal modem or a video adapter, especially if you are using Windows 9x and the adapter conforms to the Plug-and-Play specification, as most do. Typically, you follow these steps:

1. Open your computer.
2. Configure your sound card (if it isn't Plug and Play).
3. Insert the audio adapter into a bus slot and attach the CD-ROM drive to the CD Audio In connector, if present.

4. Close your computer.

5. Boot the system, causing Windows 9x to locate and install the driver for the adapter (or install the sound card software for non–Plug-and-Play devices).

6. Attach your speakers and other sound accessories.

Installing the Sound Card

After your computer is open, you can install the audio adapter. Most adapters today use a 16-bit ISA slot, although some high-end adapters use the PCI bus. The migration from ISA to PCI in the audio-adapter industry has been slower than that for other components, such as video-display adapters. The first PCI audio cards were much more expensive than standard commercial models and intended for professional applications, but several manufacturers, including Cirrus Logic and VideoLogic, are now marketing PCI adapters for the home PC market.

If you have several empty bus slots from which to choose, install the audio adapter in the slot that is as far away as possible from the other cards in the computer. This reduces any possible electromagnetic interference; that is, it reduces stray radio signals from one card that might affect the sound card. The analog components on audio adapters are highly susceptible to interference and, even though they are shielded, they should be protected as well as possible.

Next, you must remove the screw that holds the metal cover over the empty expansion slot you've chosen. Remove your audio adapter from its protective packaging. When you open the bag, carefully grab the card by its metal bracket and edges. Do not touch any of the components on the card. Any static electricity you may transmit can damage the card. Also, do not touch the gold-edge connectors. You may want to invest in a grounding wrist strap, which continually drains you of static build-up as you work on your computer.

If your adapter is not Plug and Play, you may have to set jumpers or DIP switches to configure the adapter to use the appropriate hardware resources in your computer. For example, you may have to adjust an IRQ or DMA setting, or turn off the adapter's joystick port because your joystick is already connected to your PC elsewhere. See the instructions that came with your audio adapter.

If your system has an internal CD-ROM drive with an audio cable, connect it to the adapter's CD Audio In connector. This connector is keyed so that you can't insert it improperly. Note that there is no true standard for this audio cable, so be sure that you get the right one that matches your drive and adapter.

Next, insert the adapter's edge connector into the bus slot, but first touch a metal object, such as the inside of the computer's cover, to drain yourself of static electricity. When the card is firmly in place, attach the screw to hold the expansion card and then reassemble your computer.

After the adapter card is installed, you can connect small speakers to the speaker jack. Typically, sound cards provide four watts of power per channel to drive bookshelf speakers. If you are using speakers rated for less than four watts, do not turn up the volume on your sound card to the maximum; your speakers may burn out from the overload. You'll get better results if you plug your sound card into powered speakers—that is, speakers with built-in amplifiers.

Using Your Stereo Instead of Speakers

Another alternative is to patch your sound card into your stereo system for greatly amplified sound. Check the plugs and jacks at both ends of the connection. Most stereos use *pin plugs*—also called *RCA* or *phono plugs*—for input. Although pin plugs are standard on some sound cards, most use miniature 1/8-inch phono plugs, which require an adapter when connecting to your stereo system. From Radio Shack, for example, you can purchase an audio cable that provides a stereo 1/8-inch miniplug on one end and phono plugs on the other (Cat. No. 42-2481A).

Make sure that you get stereo, not mono, plugs, unless your sound card supports only mono. To ensure that you have enough cable to reach from the back of your PC to your stereo system, get a six-foot long cable.

Hooking up your stereo to an audio adapter is a matter of sliding the plugs into proper jacks. If your audio adapter gives you a choice of outputs—speaker/headphone and stereo line out—choose the stereo line out jack for the connection. This will give you the best sound quality because the signals from the stereo line out jack are not amplified. The amplification is best left to your stereo system.

Connect this cable output from your audio adapter to the auxiliary input of your stereo receiver, preamp, or integrated amplifier. If your stereo doesn't have an auxiliary input, other input options include—in order of preference—tuner, CD, or Tape 2. (Do not use phono inputs, however, because the level of the signals will be uneven.) You can connect the cable's single stereo miniplug to the sound card's Stereo Line Out jack, for example, and then connect the two RCA phono plugs to the stereo's Tape/VCR 2 Playback jacks.

The first time you use your audio adapter with a stereo system, turn down the volume on your receiver to prevent blown speakers. Barely turn up the volume control and then select the proper input (such as Tape/VCR 2) on your stereo receiver. Finally, start your PC. Never increase the volume to more than three-fourths of the way up. Any higher and the sound may become distorted.

Tricks for Using the Tape Monitor Circuit of Your Stereo

Your receiver might be equipped with something called a *tape monitor*. This outputs the sound coming from the tuner, tape, or CD to the tape out port on the back, and then expects the sound to come back in on the tape in port. These ports, in conjunction with the line in and line out ports on your audio adapter, enable you to play computer sound and the radio through the same set of speakers.

(continues)

(continued)

Here's how you do it:

1. Turn off the tape monitor circuit on your receiver.

2. Turn down all the controls on the sound card's mixer application.

3. Connect the receiver's tape out ports to the audio adapter's line in port.

4. Connect the audio adapter's line out port to the receiver's tape in ports.

5. Turn on the receiver, select some music, and set the volume to a medium level.

6. Turn on the tape monitor circuit.

7. Slowly adjust the line in and main out sliders in the audio adapter's mixer application until the sound level is about the same as before.

8. Disengage and re-engage the tape monitor circuit while adjusting the output of the audio adapter so that the sound level is the same, whether the tape monitor circuit is engaged or not.

9. Start playing a WAV file.

10. Slowly adjust up the volume slider for the WAV file in the audio adapter's mixer application until it plays at a level (slightly above, or below the receiver) that is comfortable.

Now you can get sounds from your computer, and the radio through the receiver's speakers.

Troubleshooting Sound Card Problems

To operate, an audio adapter needs hardware resources, such as IRQ numbers, a base I/O address, and DMA channels that don't conflict with other devices. Most adapters come preconfigured to use the standard Sound Blaster resources that have come to be associated with audio adapters. However, problems occasionally arise, even with Plug-and-Play adapters. Troubleshooting may mean that you have to change board jumpers or switches, or even reconfigure the other devices in your computer. No one said life was fair.

Hardware (Resource) Conflicts

The most common problem for audio adapters is that they conflict with other devices installed in your PC. You may notice that your audio adapter simply doesn't work (no sound effects or music), repeats the same sounds over and over, or causes your PC to freeze. This situation is called a *device*, or *hardware conflict*. What are they fighting over? Mainly the same bus signal lines or channels (called *resources*) used for talking to your PC. The sources of conflict in audio adapter installations are generally threefold:

- *Interrupt ReQuests (IRQs)*. Hardware devices use IRQs to "interrupt" your PC and get its attention.

- *Direct Memory Access (DMA) channels*. DMA channels move information directly to your PC's memory, bypassing the system processor. DMA channels enable sound to play while your PC is doing other work.

■ *Input/Output (I/O) port addresses.* Your PC uses I/O port addresses to channel information between the hardware devices on your audio adapter and your PC. The addresses usually mentioned in a sound card manual are the starting or base addresses. An audio adapter has several devices on it, and each one uses a range of addresses starting with a particular base address.

Most audio adapters include installation software that analyzes your PC and attempts to notify you should any of the standard settings be in use by other devices. The Windows 9x Device Manager (accessed from the System Control Panel) can also help you to resolve conflicts. Although these detection routines can be fairly reliable, unless a device is operating during the analysis, it may not always be detectable.

Table 9.3 shows the default resources used by the components on a typical Sound Blaster 16 card.

Table 9.3 Default Sound Blaster Resource Assignments				
Device	**Interrupt**	**I/O Ports**	**16-Bit DMA**	**8-Bit DMA**
Audio	IRQ 5	220h-233h	DMA 5	DMA 1
MIDI Port	—	330h-331h	—	—
FM Synthesizer	—	388h-38Bh	—	—
Game Port	—	200h-207h	—	—

All these resources are used by a *single* sound card in your system. No wonder many people have conflicts and problems with audio adapter installations! In reality, working out these conflicts is not all that hard, as we shall see. You can change most of the resources that audio adapters use to alternate settings, should there be conflicts with other devices; even better, you can change the settings of the other device to eliminate the conflict. Note that some devices on the audio adapter such as the MIDI Port, FM Synthesizer, and Game Port do not use resources like IRQs or DMA channels.

It is always best to install an audio adapter by using the default settings whenever possible. This is mainly because of poorly written software that cannot work properly with alternate settings, even if they do not cause conflicts. In other words, if you are having a conflict with another type of adapter, modify the settings of the other device rather than those of the audio adapter. Take this from experience; otherwise, you will have to explain to your five-year old why the new Dinosaur program you just installed does not make any sounds!

Resolving Resource Conflicts. The audio portion of a sound card has a default IRQ setting, but also supports any of several alternate interrupts. As stated earlier, you should endeavor to leave the audio IRQ at the default setting (usually IRQ 5) and change those of other adapters where possible.

If your audio adapter is set to the same IRQ as another device in your system, you may see symptoms such as skipping, jerky sound, or system lockups.

A typical audio adapter requires the use of *two* simultaneous DMA channels. These are usually split into a requirement for an 8-bit DMA and a 16-bit DMA channel. Most adapters use DMA 1 for 8-bit sound (Creative Labs calls this *Low DMA*), and DMA 5 for 16-bit sound (*High DMA*). The primary symptom of a DMA conflict in your system is that you hear no sound at all.

Solving Hardware Conflicts. If you use Windows 9x, the Device Manager application can tell you which devices are using a particular resource. If not, you may have to manually resolve any resource conflicts you find.

The best way to manually locate a hardware conflict is to gather all the documentation for your PC and its various devices, such as the SCSI interface adapters, CD-ROM drives, and so on. This topic is discussed more completely in Chapter 10, "I/O Interfaces."

The most common causes of system resource conflicts are the following:

- SCSI host adapters
- Network interface cards
- Bus mouse adapter cards
- Serial port adapter cards for COM3: or COM4:
- Parallel port adapter cards for LPT2:
- Internal modems
- Scanner interface cards

One way to find which device is conflicting with your audio adapter is to temporarily remove all the expansion cards from your system except for the audio adapter and essential devices (such as the video adapter). Then, replace each of the cards you removed, one at a time, until your audio adapter no longer works. The last card you added is the troublemaker.

Having found the card that's causing the conflict, you can either switch the settings for the device that is conflicting with your audio adapter or change the settings of the audio adapter. In either case, you will have to change the IRQ, DMA, or I/O address. To do this, you may have to set jumpers or DIP switches on the adapter, or use a configuration program supplied with the adapter to change its settings.

Other Sound Card Problems

Like the common cold, audio adapter problems have common symptoms. Use the following sections to diagnose your problem.

No Sound. If you don't hear anything from your audio adapter, consider these solutions:

- Make sure that the audio adapter is set to use all default resources, and that all other devices using these resources have been either reconfigured or removed.
- Are the speakers connected? Check that the speakers are plugged into the sound card's Stereo Line Out or speaker jack (not the Line In or microphone jack).

- If you're using amplified speakers, are they powered on? Check the strength of the batteries or the AC adapter's connection to the electrical outlet.

- Are the speakers stereo? Check that the plug inserted into the jack is a stereo plug, not mono.

- Are the mixer settings high enough? Many audio adapters include a sound mixer application. The mixer controls the volume settings for various sound devices, such as the microphone or CD player. There may be separate controls for both recording and playback. Increase the master volume or speaker volume when you are in the play mode.

- Use your audio adapter's setup or diagnostic software to test and adjust the volume of the adapter. Such software usually includes sample sounds used to test the adapter.

- Turn off your computer for one minute and then turn it back on. A hard reset (as opposed to pressing the Reset button or pressing Ctrl+Alt+Delete) may clear the problem.

- If your computer game lacks sound, check that it is designed to work with your audio adapter. For example, some games may require the exact settings of IRQ 7, DMA 1, and address 220 to be Sound Blaster-compatible.

One-Sided Sound. If you hear sound coming from only one speaker, check out these possible causes:

- Are you using a mono plug in the stereo jack? A common mistake is to use a mono plug into the sound card's speaker or stereo out jacks. Seen from the side, a stereo connector has two darker stripes. A mono connector has only one stripe.

- Is the audio adapter driver loaded? Some sound cards provide only left-channel sound if the driver is not loaded correctly. Re-run your adapter's setup software or re-install it in the operating system.

Volume Is Low. If you can barely hear your sound card, try these solutions:

- Are the speakers plugged into the proper jack? Speakers require a higher level of drive signal than headphones. Again, adjust the volume level in your mixer application.

- Are the mixer settings too low? Again, adjust the volume level in your mixer application.

- Is the initial volume too low? If your audio adapter has a thumbwheel volume control, check to make sure that it is not turned down too low.

- Are the speakers too weak? Some speakers may need more power than your audio adapter can produce. Try other speakers or put a stereo amplifier between your sound card and speakers.

Scratchy Sound. Scratchy or staticy sound can be caused by several different problems. Improving the sound may be as simple as rearranging your hardware components. The following list suggests possible solutions to the problem of scratchy sound:

- Is your audio adapter near other expansion cards? The adapter may be picking up electrical interference from other expansion cards inside the PC. Move the audio card to an expansion slot as far away as possible from other cards.

- Are your speakers too close to your monitor? The speakers may pick up electrical noise from your monitor. Move them farther away.

- Are you using a cheaper audio adapter with an FM synthesizer? Some of the adapters that use FM synthesis instead of wavetable sound generation have very poor quality output. Many people have been fooled into thinking they had a defective sound card, when in reality it was just a poor-quality FM synthesis card that simply does not sound good. You can test this by comparing the sound of a MIDI file (which uses the FM synthesizer) with that of a sound file like a WAV (which doesn't). If the problem is the synthesizer, then I recommend upgrading to an adapter that does wavetable synthesis so you can get the full benefit of high quality sound.

Your Computer Won't Start. If your computer won't start at all, you may not have inserted the audio adapter completely into its slot. Turn off the PC and then press firmly on the card until it is seated correctly.

Parity Errors or Other Lockups. Your computer may display a memory parity error message or simply "crash." This is normally caused by resource conflicts in one of the following areas:

- IRQ (Interrupt ReQuest)
- DMA (Direct Memory Access)
- I/O (Input/Output) ports

If other devices in your system are using the same resources as your audio adapter, crashes, lockups, or parity errors can result. You must ensure that multiple devices in your system do not share these resources. Follow the procedures outlined earlier in this chapter to resolve the resource conflicts.

Joystick Troubleshooting. If your joystick won't work, consider the following list of cures:

- Are you using two game ports? If you already have a game port installed in your PC, the game or joystick port provided on your audio adapter may conflict with it. Usually it is best to disable any other game ports and use the one on the audio adapter. Many of the Multi-I/O or Super-I/O adapters that come in PC-compatible systems feature game ports that you should disable when you install an audio adapter.

■ Is your computer too fast? Some fast computers get confused by the inexpensive game ports. During the heat of virtual combat, for example, you may find yourself flying upside down or spiraling out of control. This is one sign that your game port is inadequate. Most of the game adapters built into audio adapters work better than the ones on the Multi-I/O adapters. There are also dedicated game cards available, which can work with faster computers. These game cards include software to calibrate your joystick and dual ports so that you can enjoy a game with a friend. Another solution is to run your computer at a slower speed, which on some systems is as easy as pressing some type of "de-turbo" button on the case.

Other Problems. Sometimes sound problems can be difficult to solve. Due to quirks and problems with the way DMA is implemented in some motherboard chipsets, there can be problems interacting with certain cards or drivers. Sometimes altering the Chipset Setup options in your CMOS settings can resolve problems. These kinds of problems can take a lot of trial and error to solve.

The PC "standard" is based loosely on the cooperation among a handful of companies. Something as simple as one vendor's BIOS or motherboard design can make the standard nonstandard.

Speakers

Successful business presentations, multimedia applications, and MIDI work demand external high-fidelity stereo speakers. Although you can use standard stereo speakers, they are often too big to fit on or near your desk. Smaller bookshelf speakers are better.

Sound cards offer little or none of the amplification needed to drive external speakers. Although some sound cards have small 4-watt amplifiers, they are not powerful enough to drive quality speakers. Also, conventional speakers sitting near your display may create magnetic interference, which can distort colors and objects on-screen or jumble the data recorded on nearby floppy disks or other magnetic media.

To solve these problems, computer speakers need to be small, efficient, and self-powered. Also, they should be provided with magnetic shielding, either in the form of added layers of insulation in the speaker cabinet or electronic cancellation of the magnetic distortion.

> **Caution**
>
> Although most computer speakers are magnetically shielded, do not leave recorded tapes, watches, credit cards, or floppy disks in front of the speakers for long periods of time.

Quality sound depends on quality speakers. A 16-bit audio adapter may provide better sound to computer speakers, but even an 8-bit adapter sounds good from a good speaker. Conversely, an inexpensive speaker makes both 8-bit and 16-bit adapters cards sound tinny.

There are now dozens of models of PC speakers on the market ranging from inexpensive minispeakers from Sony, Koss, and LabTech to larger self-powered models from prestigious audio companies such as Bose and Altec Lansing. Many of the higher-end speaker systems even include subwoofers to provide additional bass response. To evaluate speakers, it helps to know the jargon. Speakers are measured by three criteria:

- *Frequency response.* A measurement of the range of high and low sounds a speaker can reproduce. The ideal range is from 20Hz to 20KHz, the range of human hearing. No speaker system reproduces this range perfectly. In fact, few people hear sounds above 18KHz. An exceptional speaker may cover a range of 30Hz to 23,000KHz. Lesser models may cover only 100Hz to 20,000Hz. Frequency response is the most deceptive specification, because identically rated speakers can sound completely different.

- *Total Harmonic Distortion (THD).* An expression of the amount of distortion or noise created by amplifying the signal. Simply put, distortion is the difference between the sound sent to the speaker and the sound you hear. The amount of distortion is measured in percentages. An acceptable level of distortion is below .1 percent (one-tenth of 1 percent). For some CD-quality recording equipment, a common standard is .05 percent. Some speakers have a distortion of 10 percent or more. Headphones often have a distortion of about 2 percent or less.

- *Watts.* Usually stated as *watts per channel*, the amount of amplification available to drive the speakers. Check that the company means "per channel" (or RMS) and not total power. Many audio adapters have built-in amplifiers, providing up to eight watts per channel (most provide four watts). This wattage is not enough to provide rich sound, however, which is why many speakers have built-in amplifiers. With the flick of a switch or the press of a button, these speakers amplify the signals they receive from the audio adapter. If you do not want to amplify the sound, you typically leave the speaker switch set to "direct." In most cases, you'll want to amplify the signal.

PC speakers often use batteries to power the amplifiers. Because these speakers require so much power, you may want to invest in an AC adapter, or purchase speakers that use AC power. With an AC adapter, you won't have to buy new batteries every few weeks. If your speakers didn't come with an AC adapter, you can pick one up from your local Radio Shack or hardware store. Be sure that the adapter you purchase matches your speakers in voltage and polarity.

You can control the volume and other sound attributes of your speakers in various ways, depending on their complexity and cost. Typically, each speaker has a volume knob, although some share a single volume control. If one speaker is farther away than the other, you may want to adjust the volume accordingly. Many computer speakers include a *dynamic bass boost (DBB) switch.* This button provides a more powerful bass and clearer treble, regardless of the volume setting. Other speakers have separate bass and treble boost switches or a three-band equalizer to control low, middle, and high frequencies.

When you rely on your audio adapter's power rather than your speakers' built-in amplifier, the volume and dynamic bass boost controls have no effect. Your speakers are at the mercy of the adapter's power.

An 1/8-inch stereo minijack connects from the audio adapter's output jack to one of the speakers. The speaker then splits the signal and feeds through a separate cable from the first speaker to the second one (often referred to as the "satellite speaker").

Before purchasing a set of speakers, check that the cables between the speakers are long enough for your computer setup. For example, a tower case sitting alongside one's desk may require longer speaker wires than a desktop computer.

Beware of speakers that have a tardy built-in "sleep" feature. Such speakers, which save electricity by turning themselves off when they are not in use, may have the annoying habit of clipping the first part of a sound after a period of inactivity.

Headphones are an option when you can't afford a premium set of speakers. Headphones also provide privacy and allow you to play your PC audio as loud as you like.

Microphones

Some audio adapters come complete with a microphone, but most do not. You'll need one to record your voice to a WAV file. Selecting a microphone is quite simple. You need one that has an 1/8-inch minijack to plug into your audio adapter's microphone, or audio in, jack. Most microphones have an on/off switch.

Like speakers, microphones are measured by their frequency range. This is not an important buying factor, however, because the human voice has a limited range. If you are recording only voices, consider an inexpensive microphone that covers a limited range of frequencies. An expensive microphone's recording capabilities extend to frequencies outside the voice's range. Why pay for something you won't be needing?

If you are recording music, invest in an expensive microphone, but make sure that your audio adapter can do justice to the signal produced by the microphone. A high-quality microphone can produce mediocre results when paired with a cheap 8-bit audio adapter.

Your biggest decision is to select a microphone that suits your recording style. If you work in a noisy office, you may want an unidirectional microphone that will prevent extraneous noises from being recorded. An omnidirectional microphone is best for recording a group conversation.

Most higher-priced audio adapters include a microphone of some type. This can be a small lapel microphone, a hand-held microphone, or one with a desktop stand. If you want to leave your hands free, you may want to shun the traditional hand-held microphone for a lapel or desktop model. If your audio adapter does not come with a microphone, see your local stereo or electronics parts store. Be sure that any microphone you purchase has the correct impedance to match the audio adapter's input.

Chapter 10

I/O Interfaces

When thinking about Input/Output devices, it's easy to categorize only serial ports, parallel ports, Universal Serial Bus, and FireWire (IEEE-1394) as being I/O interfaces. I cover these topics in-depth in this chapter. It's important to remember that SCSI and IDE are I/O interfaces too.

This chapter covers the major I/O interfaces used in PCs today. When discussing I/O interfaces for drives, I talk mostly about SCSI and IDE because these are the most popular high-speed storage interfaces used today.

Serial and Parallel Ports

The most basic communications ports in any PC system are the serial and parallel ports. The serial ports were originally used for devices that must communicate bidirectionally with the system. Such devices include modems, mice, scanners, digitizers, and any other devices that "talk to" and receive information from the PC. Newer parallel port standards now allow the parallel port to perform high-speed bidirectional communications.

Several companies manufacture communications programs that perform high-speed transfers between PC systems using serial or parallel ports. Versions of these file transfer programs have been included with DOS 6.0 and higher (Interlink), and Windows 95 and newer versions (DCC—Direct Cable Connection). Several products are currently on the market that make non-traditional use of the parallel port. You can purchase network adapters, high-capacity floppy disk drives, CD-ROM drives, or tape backup units that attach to the parallel port, for example.

Serial Ports

The *asynchronous serial interface* was designed as a system-to-system communications port. *Asynchronous* means that no synchronization or clocking signal is present, so characters may be sent with any arbitrary time spacing.

Each character sent over a serial connection is framed by a standard start-and-stop signal. A single 0 bit, called the *start bit*, precedes each character to tell the receiving system that the next 8 bits constitute a byte of data. One or two stop bits follow the character to signal that the character has been sent. At the receiving end of the communication, characters are recognized by the start-and-stop signals instead of by the timing of their arrival. The asynchronous interface is character-oriented and has about a 20% overhead for the extra information needed to identify each character.

Serial refers to data sent over a single wire, with each bit lining up in a series as the bits are sent. This type of communication is used over the phone system, because this system provides one wire for data in each direction. Add-on serial ports for the PC are available from many manufacturers. You usually can find these ports on one of the multifunction boards available or on a board with at least a parallel port. Virtually all modern motherboards include a built-in Super I/O chip that adds one or two serial ports to the motherboard, meaning no additional interface card is required. Older systems normally have the serial ports on a card. Note that card-based modems also incorporate a built-in serial port on the card as part of the modem circuitry. Figure 10.1 shows the standard 9-pin connector used with most modern external serial ports. Figure 10.2 shows the original standard 25-pin version.

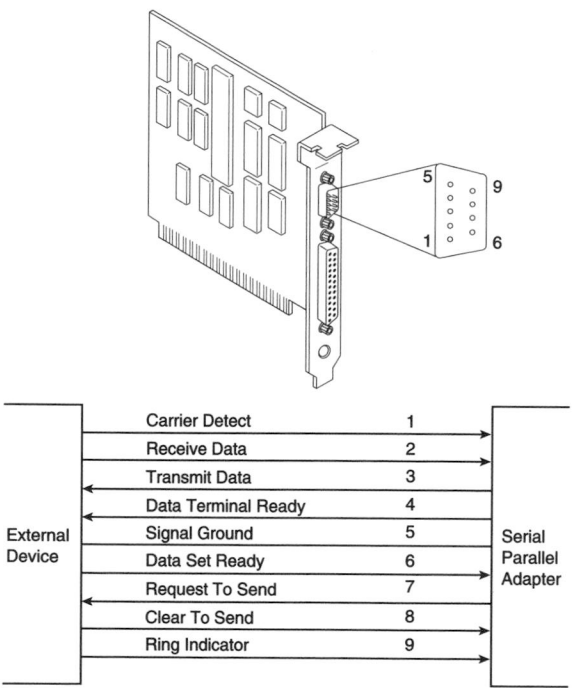

External Device	Carrier Detect	1	Serial Parallel Adapter
	Receive Data	2	
	Transmit Data	3	
	Data Terminal Ready	4	
	Signal Ground	5	
	Data Set Ready	6	
	Request To Send	7	
	Clear To Send	8	
	Ring Indicator	9	

FIG. 10.1   AT-style 9-pin serial-port connector specifications.

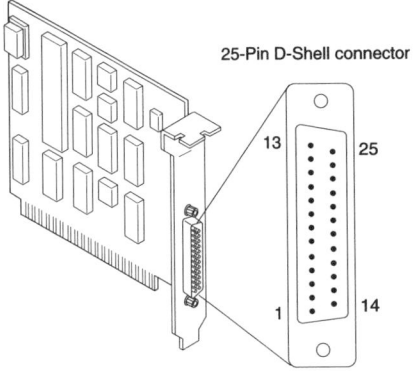

Description	Pin	
NC	1	
Transmitted Data	2	
Received Data	3	
Request to Send	4	
Clear to Send	5	
Data Set Ready	6	
Signal Ground	7	
Received Line Signal Detector	8	
+ Transmit Current Loop Data	9	
NC	10	
- Transmit Current Loop Data	11	
NC	12	Asynchronous
NC	13	Communications
NC	14	Adapter
NC	15	(RS-232C)
NC	16	
NC	17	
+ Receive Current Loop Data	18	
NC	19	
Data Terminal Ready	20	
NC	21	
Ring Indicator	22	
NC	23	
NC	24	
- Receive Current Loop Return	25	

External Device

FIG. 10.2 Standard 25-pin serial-port connector specifications.

Serial ports may connect to a variety of devices such as modems, plotters, printers, other computers, bar code readers, scales, and device control circuits. Basically, anything that needs a two-way connection to the PC uses the industry-standard Reference Standard number 232 revision C (RS-232C) serial port. This device enables data transfer between otherwise incompatible devices.

The official specification recommends a maximum cable length of 50 feet. The limiting factor is the total load capacitance of cable and input circuits of the interface. The maximum capacitance is specified as 2500 pF. Special low-capacitance cables are available that can effectively increase the maximum cable length greatly, to as much as 500 feet or more. Also line drivers (amplifier/repeaters) are available that can extend cable length even further.

Tables 10.1, 10.2, and 10.3 show the pinouts of the 9-pin (AT-style), 25-pin, and 9-pin-to-25-pin serial connectors.

Table 10.1   9-Pin (AT) Serial Port Connector

Pin	Signal	Description	I/O
1	CD	Carrier detect	In
2	RD	Receive data	In
3	TD	Transmit data	Out
4	DTR	Data terminal ready	Out
5	SG	Signal ground	—
6	DSR	Data set ready	In
7	RTS	Request to send	Out
8	CTS	Clear to send	In
9	RI	Ring indicator	In

Table 10.2   25-Pin (PC, XT, and PS/2) Serial Port Connector

Pin	Signal	Description	I/O
1	—	Chassis ground	—
2	TD	Transmit data	Out
3	RD	Receive data	In
4	RTS	Request to send	Out
5	CTS	Clear to send	In
6	DSR	Data set ready	In
7	SG	Signal ground	—
8	CD	Carrier detect	In
9	—	+Transmit current loop return	Out
11	—	–Transmit current loop data	Out
18	—	+Receive current loop data	In
20	DTR	Data terminal ready	Out
22	RI	Ring indicator	In
25	—	-Receive current loop return	In

Table 10.3 9-Pin to 25-Pin Serial Cable Adapter Connections

9-Pin	25-Pin	Signal	Description
1	8	CD	Carrier detect
2	3	RD	Receive data
3	2	TD	Transmit data
4	20	DTR	Data terminal ready
5	7	SG	Signal ground
6	6	DSR	Data set ready
7	4	RTS	Request to send
8	5	CTS	Clear to send
9	22	RI	Ring indicator

Note

Macintosh systems use a similar serial interface defined as RS-422. Most external modems in use today can interface with either RS-232 or RS-422, but it is safest to make sure that the external modem you get for your PC is designed for a PC, not a Macintosh.

UARTs. The heart of any serial port is the *Universal Asynchronous Receiver/Transmitter (UART) chip*. This chip completely controls the process of breaking the native parallel data within the PC into serial format, and later converting serial data back into the parallel format.

There are several types of UART chips on the market. The original PC and XT used the 8250 UART, which was used for many years in low-priced serial cards. Starting with the first 16-bit systems, the 16450 UART was normally used. The only difference between these chips is their suitability for high-speed communications. The 16450 is better suited for high-speed communications than the 8250; otherwise, both chips appear identical to most software.

The 16550 UART was the first serial chip used in the IBM PS/2 line, and other 386 and higher systems rapidly adopted it. This chip could function as the earlier 16450 and 8250 chips, but it also included a 16-byte buffer that aided in faster communications. This is sometimes referred to as a *FIFO (first in/first out) buffer*. Unfortunately, the early 16550 chips had a few bugs, particularly in the buffer area. These bugs were corrected with the release of the 16550A. The most current version of the chip is the 16550D, which is produced by National Semiconductor.

Tip

The high-speed buffered 16550A (or newer) UART chip is pin-for-pin compatible with the 16450 UART. If your 16450 UART is socketed, it is a cheap and easy way to improve serial performance to install a 16550 UART chip in the socket.

Because the 16550 is a faster, more reliable chip than its predecessors, it is best to ensure your serial ports either have that chip or an equivalent. Most motherboards today that have built-in serial ports use a Super I/O chip that contains the serial port UARTs within it. If you are in doubt about which type of UART you have in your system, you can use the Microsoft MSD program (provided with Windows, MS DOS 6.x, and Windows 95) to determine the type of UART you have.

> **Note**
>
> Another way to tell if you have a 16650 UART in Windows 95 or 98 is to click the Start menu, choose Settings, Control Panel, double-click Modems, then click the Diagnostics tab. The Diagnostics tab shows a list of all COM ports in the system, even if they don't have a modem attached to them. Select the port you want to check in the list and click More Info. Windows 95 or 98 will communicate with the port to determine the UART type and that information will be listed in the Port Information portion of the More Info box. If a modem was attached, then you will see additional information about the modem displayed.

The original designer of these UARTs is National Semiconductor (NS). Many other manufacturers are producing clones of these UARTs, such that you probably don't have an actual NS brand part in your system. Even so, the part you have will be compatible with one of the NS parts, hopefully the 16550. In other words, you should check to see that whatever UART chip you do have does indeed feature the 16-byte FIFO buffer as found in the NS 16550 part.

Most motherboards now include Super I/O integrated chips that take on the functions of multiple separate chips. Most of these integrated chips function as a 16550 would; however, some used on older motherboards may not.

◀◀ See "Super I/O Chips" p. 207

Table 10.4 lists the standard UART chip types used in PC systems.

Table 10.4 UART Chips in PC Systems

Chip	Description
8250	IBM used this original chip in the PC serial port card. This chip has no transmit/receive buffer, which means it is very slow. The chip has several bugs, none of which is serious. The PC and XT ROM BIOS are written to anticipate at least one of the bugs. This chip was replaced by the 8250B.
8250A	Do not use the second version of the 8250 in any system. This upgraded chip fixes several bugs in the 8250, including one in the interrupt enable register, but because the PC and XT ROM BIOS expect the bug, this chip does not work properly with those systems. The 8250A should work in an AT system that does not expect the bug, but does not work adequately at 9600bps.
8250B	The last version of the 8250 fixes bugs from the previous two versions. The interrupt enable bug in the original 8250, expected by the PC and XT ROM BIOS software, has been put back into this chip, making the 8250B the most desirable chip for any non-AT serial port application. The 8250B chip may work in an AT under DOS, but does not run properly at 9600bps because like all 8250s it has no transmit/receive buffer.

Chip	Description
16450	IBM selected the higher-speed version of the 8250 for the AT. The higher performance mainly comes from a 1-byte transmit/receive buffer contained within the chip. Because this chip has fixed the interrupt enable bug mentioned earlier, the 16450 does not operate properly in many PC or XT systems, because they expect this bug to be present. OS/2 requires this chip as a minimum, or the serial ports do not function properly. It also adds a scratch-pad register as the highest register. The 16450 is used primarily in AT systems because of its increase in throughput over the 8250B.
16550A	This chip is pin-compatible with the 16450, but is much faster due to a built-in 16-character Transmit and Receive FIFO (First In First Out) buffer. It also allows multiple DMA channel access. The original version of this chip would not allow the buffer to work but all 16550A or later revisions had the bug fixed. The last version produced by National Semiconductor was called the 16550D. You should use a version of this UART in your serial port if you do any communications at 9600bps or higher. If your communications program makes use of the FIFO, which all do today, it can greatly increase communications speed and eliminate lost characters and data at the higher speeds. Virtually all Super I/O chips contain the equivalent of dual 16550A or later chips. Most 16550 UARTs have a maximum communications speed of 115Kbps (bits per second).
16650	Several companies have produced versions with larger buffers that they have called 16650 and 16750. These chips are not from National Semiconductor and the designations are only to imply that they are compatible with the 16550 but have a larger buffer. The 16650 chips normally have a 32-byte buffer while the 16750 chips have a 64-byte buffer. These larger buffered versions allow speeds of 230K or 460Kbps and are recommended when running a high-speed external communications link such as an ISDN terminal adapter. These are discussed more in the following section.

High-Speed Serial Ports. Some modem manufacturers have gone a step further on improving serial data transfer by introducing *Enhanced Serial Ports (ESP)* or *Super High Speed Serial Ports*. These ports enable a 28.8Kbps or faster modem to communicate with the computer at data rates up to 921.6Kbps. The extra speed on these ports is generated by increasing the buffer size. These ports are usually based on a 16550, 16650, or 16750 UART and some even include more buffer memory on the card. Most will allow raw port speed settings of 230Kbps or 460Kbps, which is very valuable when connecting a PC to a high-speed external component connected to a serial port, such as an ISDN terminal adapter. You can't really get the full-speed benefit of an external ISDN modem (terminal adapter) unless your serial port can go at least 230Kbps. Lava Computer Mfg. is one company that offers a complete line of high-speed serial and parallel port cards (see Appendix A, "Vendor List").

As the need for additional serial devices continues to increase, users are beginning to need more than the standard two COM ports that are built into most modern motherboards. As a result, *multi-port serial cards* were created. These cards generally have 2–32 ports on them. Often, they also provide higher baud rates than can be achieved on a standard serial port.

Most of the multi-port serial cards on the market use standard 16550 UARTs with a processor (typically an 80×86 based processor) and some memory. These cards can improve performance slightly because the processor is dedicated to handling serial information. However, it's not always the best method for high-performance applications.

Some of the better multi-port serial cards have broken the model of the 16550 UART in favor of a single integrated circuit. These cards have the advantage of higher sustainable throughput without loss.

Various manufacturers make versions of the 16550; National Semiconductor was the first. The current version is a 40-pin DIP (Dual In-line Pin package) chip called the NS16550D. You can contact Fry's Electronics or Jameco Electronics to obtain the NS16550D, for example.

Serial-Port Configuration. Each time a character is received by a serial port, it has to get the attention of the computer by raising an *Interrupt Request Line (IRQ)*. Eight-bit ISA bus systems have eight of these lines, and systems with a 16-bit ISA bus have 16 lines. The 8259 interrupt controller chip usually handles these requests for attention. In a standard configuration, COM1 uses IRQ4, and COM2 uses IRQ3.

When a serial port is installed in a system, it must be configured to use specific I/O addresses (called *ports*), and interrupts (called *IRQs* for Interrupt Request). The best plan is to follow the existing standards for how these devices should be set up. For configuring serial ports, you should use the addresses and interrupts indicated in Table 10.5.

Table 10.5 Standard Serial I/O Port Addresses and Interrupts			
System	**COMx**	**Port**	**IRQ**
All	COM1	3F8-3FFh	IRQ4
All	COM2	2F8-2FFh	IRQ3
ISA bus	COM3	3E8-3EFh	IRQ4*
ISA bus	COM4	2E8-2EFh	IRQ3*

Note that although many serial ports can be set up to share IRQ 3 and 4 with COM1 and COM2, it is not recommended. The best recommendation is setting COM3 to IRQ 10 and COM4 to IRQ 11 (if available). If ports above COM3 are required, it is recommended that you purchase a special multi-port serial board.

You should ensure that if you are adding more than the standard COM1 and COM2 serial ports, they use unique and non-conflicting interrupts. If you purchase a serial port adapter card and intend to use it to supply ports beyond the standard COM1 and COM2, be sure that it can use interrupts other than IRQ3 and IRQ4.

Another problem if you are still using DOS or DOS-based 16-bit programs is that the BIOS manufacturers never built support for COM3 and COM4 into the BIOS. Therefore, the DOS MODE command cannot work with serial ports above COM2 because DOS gets its I/O information from the BIOS. The BIOS finds out what is installed in your system and where it is installed during the POST (Power On Self Test). The POST checks only for the first two installed ports. This is not a problem at all under Windows because both Windows 95 and 98 have built-in support for up to 128 ports.

To get around this problem in a DOS environment, most communications software and some serial peripherals (such as mice) support higher COM ports by addressing them directly, rather than making DOS function calls. The popular DOS communications program Procomm, for example, supports the additional ports even if your BIOS or DOS does not. Of course, if your system or software does not support these extra ports or you need to redirect data using the MODE command, trouble arises. Because Windows 95/98 support 128 ports, special drivers or communications software is not normally necessary.

With support for up to 128 serial ports in Windows 95 and Windows 98, it is much easier to use multi-port boards in the system. *Multi-port boards* give your system the capability to collect or share data with multiple devices, while using only one slot and one interrupt.

> **Caution**
>
> Sharing interrupts between COM ports or any devices can function properly sometimes and not others. It is recommended that you *never* share interrupts between multiple serial ports. It will cause you hours of frustration trying to track down drivers, patches, and updates to allow this to work successfully—if it's even possible at all in your system.

◀◀ See "Resolving Resource Conflicts," p. 281

Testing Serial Ports

You can perform several tests on serial and parallel ports. The two most common types of tests involve software only, or both hardware and software. The software-only tests are done with diagnostic programs such as Microsoft's MSD, while the hardware and software tests involve using a wrap plug to perform loopback testing.

Microsoft Diagnostics (MSD). MSD is a diagnostic program supplied with MS-DOS 6.x, Microsoft Windows, and Windows 95. Early versions of the program also were shipped with some Microsoft applications such as Microsoft Word for DOS. Note that with Windows 95, this program can be found on the CD in the \other\msd directory. In Windows 98, you can find it on the CD in the \tools\oldmsdos directory. MSD is not automatically installed when you install the operating system. To use it, you must run it from the CD directly or copy the program from the CD to your hard disk.

Many diagnostics programs such as MSD are best run in a DOS-only environment for the most accurate results. Because of this, you should restart the machine in DOS mode before using them. Then to use MSD, switch to the directory in which it is located. This is not necessary, of course, if the directory containing the program is in your search path—which is often the case with the DOS 6.x or Windows-provided versions of MSD. Then simply type **MSD** at the DOS prompt and press Enter. Soon you see the MSD screen.

Choose the Serial Ports option. Notice that you are provided information about which type of serial chip you have in your system, and information about which ports are available. If any of the ports are in use (with a mouse, for example), that information is provided as well.

MSD is helpful in at least determining whether your serial ports are responding. If MSD cannot determine the existence of a port, it does not provide the report indicating that the port exists. This sort of "look-and-see" test is the first action I usually take to determine why a port is not responding.

Windows 95/98 Diagnostics. Windows 95/98 also show whether or not your ports are functioning. To check your ports, right-click My Computer and choose Properties. Choose the Device Manager tab. On the Device Manager screen, if a device is not working properly there will be an exclamation point in a yellow circle next to the device on the list. You can also double-click Ports (COM & LPT), and then double-click the desired port to see whether Windows 95/98 says that the port is functioning or not. In many cases, it tells you what is conflicting with that specific port.

Advanced Diagnostics Using Loopback Testing. One of the most useful tests is the *loopback test*, which can be used to ensure the correct function of the serial port, and any attached cables. Loopback tests basically are internal (digital), or external (analog). Internal tests can be run simply by unplugging any cables from the port and executing the test via a diagnostics program.

The external loopback test is more effective. This test requires that a special loopback connector or wrap plug be attached to the port in question. When the test is run, the port is used to send data out to the loopback plug, which simply routes the data back into the port's receive pins so that the port is transmitting and receiving at the same time. A loopback or wrap plug is nothing more than a cable doubled back on itself. Most diagnostics programs that run this type of test include the loopback plug, and if not, these types of plugs can be purchased easily or even built.

The wiring needed to construct your own loopback or wrap plugs is as follows:

- Standard IBM type 25-Pin Serial (Female DB25S) Loopback Connector (Wrap Plug). Connect these pins:

  1 to 7
  2 to 3
  4 to 5 to 8
  6 to 11 to 20 to 22
  15 to 17 to 23
  18 to 25

- Norton Utilities (Symantec) 25-Pin Serial (Female DB25S) Loopback Connector (Wrap Plug). Connect these pins:

  2 to 3
  4 to 5
  6 to 8 to 20 to 22

- Standard IBM type 9-Pin Serial (Female DB9S) Loopback Connector (Wrap Plug). Connect these pins:

  1 to 7 to 8
  2 to 3
  4 to 6 to 9

- Norton Utilities (Symantec) 9-Pin Serial (Female DB9S) Loopback Connector (Wrap Plug). Connect these pins:

  2 to 3
  7 to 8
  1 to 4 to 6 to 9

One advantage of using loopback connectors is that you can plug them into the ends of a cable that includes the cable in the test. This can verify that both the cable and the port are working properly.

If you need to test serial ports further, refer to Chapter 17 "Diagnostics, Testing, and Maintenance," which describes third-party testing software.

Parallel Ports

A *parallel port* has eight lines for sending all the bits that comprise 1 byte of data simultaneously across eight wires. This interface is fast and has traditionally been used for printers. However, programs that transfer data between systems have always used the parallel port as an option for transmitting data because it can do so 4 bits at a time rather than 1 bit at a time with a serial interface.

In the following section, we'll look at how these programs transfer data between parallel ports. The only problem with parallel ports is that their cables cannot be extended for any great length without amplifying the signal or errors occur in the data. Table 10.6 shows the pinout for a standard PC parallel port.

Table 10.6	25-Pin PC-Compatible Parallel Port Connector	
Pin	**Description**	**I/O**
1	–Strobe	Out
2	+Data Bit 0	Out
3	+Data Bit 1	Out
4	+Data Bit 2	Out
5	+Data Bit 3	Out
6	+Data Bit 4	Out
7	+Data Bit 5	Out
8	+Data Bit 6	Out
9	+Data Bit 7	Out

(continues)

Table 10.6 25-Pin PC-Compatible Parallel Port Connector Continued		
Pin	Description	I/O
10	–Acknowledge	In
11	+Busy	In
12	+Paper End	In
13	+Select	In
14	–Auto Feed	Out
15	–Error	In
16	–Initialize Printer	Out
17	–Select Input	Out
18	–Data Bit 0 Return (GND)	In
19	–Data Bit 1 Return (GND)	In
20	–Data Bit 2 Return (GND)	In
21	–Data Bit 3 Return (GND)	In
22	–Data Bit 4 Return (GND)	In
23	–Data Bit 5 Return (GND)	In
24	–Data Bit 6 Return (GND)	In
25	–Data Bit 7 Return (GND)	In

Over the years, several types of parallel ports have evolved. Here are the primary types of parallel ports found in systems today:

- Unidirectional (4-bit)

- Bidirectional (8-bit)

- Enhanced Parallel Port (EPP)

- Enhanced Capabilities Port (ECP)

The following sections discuss each of these types of parallel ports.

Unidirectional (4-bit). Older PCs did not have different types of parallel ports available. The only port available was the parallel port used to send information from the computer to a device, such as a printer. This is not to say that bidirectional parallel ports were not available; indeed, they were common in other computers on the market and in hobbyist computers at the time.

The unidirectional nature of the original PC parallel port is consistent with its primary use—that is, of sending data to a printer. There were times, however, when it was desirable to have a bidirectional port—for example, when you need feedback from a printer, which is common with PostScript printers. This could not be done easily with the original unidirectional ports.

Although it was never intended to be used for input, a clever scheme was devised where four of the signal lines could be used as a 4-bit input connection. Thus, these ports can do 8-bit byte output and 4-bit (nibble) input. This is still very common on low-end desktop systems. Systems built after 1993 are likely to have more capable parallel ports, such as 8-bit, EPP, or ECP.

4-bit ports are capable of effective transfer rates of about 40–60K/sec with typical devices and can be pushed to upwards of 140K/sec with certain design tricks.

Bidirectional (8-bit). With the introduction of the PS/2 in 1987, IBM introduced the bidirectional parallel port. These are commonly found in PC-compatible systems today, and may be designated "PS/2 type," "bidirectional," or "extended" parallel port. On newer systems with multi-mode ports, this mode is often called "standard" or "Centronics" mode, and represents the lowest performance setting. This port design opened the way for true communications between the computer and the peripheral across the parallel port. This was done by defining a few of the previously unused pins in the parallel connector, and defining a status bit to indicate in which direction information was traveling across the channel.

These ports can do both 8-bit input and output using the standard eight data lines, and are considerably faster than the 4-bit ports when used with external devices. 8-bit ports are capable of speeds ranging from 80–300K/sec, depending on the speed of the attached device, the quality of the driver software, and the port's electrical characteristics.

Enhanced Parallel Port (EPP). EPP is a newer specification sometimes referred to as the *Fast Mode parallel port.* The EPP was developed by Intel, Xircom, and Zenith Data Systems and announced in October 1991. The first products to offer EPP were ZDS laptops, Xircom Pocket LAN Adapters, and the Intel 82360 SL I/O chip.

EPP operates almost at ISA bus speed, and offers a 10-fold increase in the raw throughput capability over a conventional parallel port. EPP is especially designed for parallel port peripherals such as LAN adapters, disk drives, and tape backups. EPP has been included in the new IEEE 1284 Parallel Port standard. Transfer rates of 1 to 2M/sec are possible with EPP.

Since the original Intel 82360 SL I/O chip in 1992, other major chip vendors (such as National Semiconductor, SMC, Western Digital, and VLSI) have also produced I/O chipsets offering some form of EPP capability. One problem is that the procedure for enabling EPP across the various chips differs widely from vendor to vendor, and many vendors offer more than one I/O chip.

EPP version 1.7 (March 1992) identifies the first popular version of the hardware specification. With minor changes, this has since been abandoned and folded into the IEEE 1284 standard. Some technical reference materials have erroneously made reference to "EPP specification version 1.9" causing confusion about the EPP standard. Note that "EPP version 1.9" does not exist, and any EPP specification after the original version 1.7 is technically a part of the IEEE 1284 specification.

Unfortunately, this has resulted in two somewhat incompatible standards for EPP parallel ports: the original EPP Standards Committee version 1.7 standard, and the IEEE 1284 Committee standard. The two standards are sufficiently similar that new peripherals may be designed in such a way as to support both standards, but existing EPP 1.7 peripherals may not operate with EPP 1284 ports.

EPP ports were more common with IBM machines than other hardware manufacturers who seemed to stay away from the printer port issue until the Enhanced Capabilities Port (ECP) was introduced by Microsoft and Hewlett-Packard (HP). However, because the EPP port is defined in the IEEE 1284 standard, it has gained software and driver support, including support in Windows NT.

Enhanced Capabilities Port (ECP). Another type of high-speed parallel port called the *ECP (Enhanced Capabilities Port)* was jointly developed by Microsoft and Hewlett-Packard, and formally announced in 1992. Like EPP, ECP offers improved performance for the parallel port and requires special hardware logic.

Since the original announcement, ECP is included in IEEE 1284 just like EPP. Unlike EPP, ECP is not tailored to support portable PCs' parallel port peripherals; its purpose is to support an inexpensive attachment to a very high-performance printer. Further, ECP mode requires the use of a DMA channel, which EPP did not define, and which can cause troublesome conflicts with other devices that use DMA. Most PCs with newer "super I/O" chips will be able to support either EPP or ECP mode.

Most new systems are being delivered with ECP ports that support high throughput communications. In most cases, the ECP ports can be turned into EPP, or standard unidirectional parallel ports via BIOS. However, it's recommended that the port be placed in ECP mode for the best throughput.

IEEE 1284. The IEEE 1284 standard called "Standard Signaling Method for a Bidirectional Parallel Peripheral Interface for Personal Computers" was approved for final release in March 1994. This standard defines the physical characteristics of the parallel port, including data transfer modes and physical and electrical specifications.

IEEE 1284 defines the electrical signaling behavior external to the PC for a multimodal parallel port that may support 4-bit and modes of operation. Not all modes are required by the 1284 specification, and the standard makes some provision for additional modes.

The IEEE 1284 specification is targeted at standardizing the behavior between a PC and an attached device, most specifically attached printers. Although, the specification is of interest to vendors of parallel port peripherals (disks, LAN adapters, and so on).

IEEE 1284 is a hardware and line control-only standard and does not define how software should talk to the port. An offshoot of the original 1284 standard has been created to define the software interface. The IEEE 1284.3 committee was formed to develop a standard for software used with IEEE 1284-compliant hardware. This standard, designed to address the disparity among providers of parallel port chips, contains a specification for supporting EPP mode via the PC's system BIOS.

IEEE 1284 allows for much higher throughput in a connection between a computer and a printer, or two computers. The result is that the printer cable is no longer the standard printer cable. The IEEE 1284 printer cable uses twisted-pair technology, the same technology that allows Category 5 cabling to carry speeds up to 100Mbps.

IEEE 1284 also defined a new port—a fact that most people aren't familiar with. A type A connector in the IEEE 1284 standard is defined as a DB25 pin connector. A type B connector is defined as a Centronics 36 connector. The new connector, referred to as type C is a high-density connector that is already beginning to be installed in HP's printer line. The three connectors are shown in Figure 10.3.

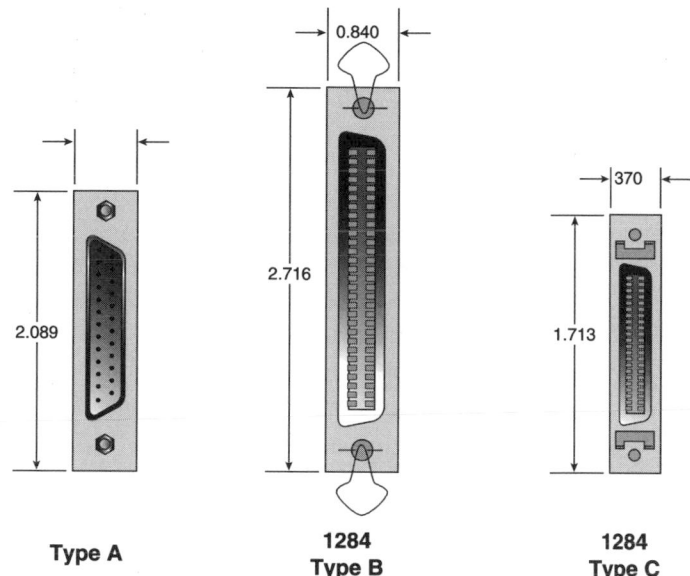

FIG. 10.3   The three different IEEE 1284 connectors.

Upgrading to EPP/ECP Ports. If you are purchasing a system today, I would recommend one that has a so-called "Super I/O" chip that supports both EPP and ECP operation. If you want to test the parallel ports in a system, especially to determine what type they are, I highly recommend a utility called *Parallel*. This is a handy parallel port information utility that examines your system's parallel ports and reports the Port Type, IO address, IRQ level, BIOS name, and an assortment of informative notes and warnings in a compact and easy-to-read display. The output may be redirected to a file for tech support purposes. Parallel uses very sophisticated techniques for port and IRQ detection, and is aware of a broad range of quirky port features. You can get it from Parallel Technologies (see Appendix A).

If you have an older system that does not include an EPP/ECP port and you would like to upgrade, there are several companies now offering boards with the correct Super I/O chips that implement these features. I recommend you check with Farpoint Communications, Byterunner Technologies, or Lava Computer Mfg.; they are listed in the vendor list in Appendix A.

Parallel-Port Configuration

Parallel-port configuration is not as complicated as it is for serial ports. Even the original IBM PC has BIOS support for three LPT ports, and DOS has always had this support as well. Table 10.7 shows the standard I/O address and interrupt settings for parallel port use.

Table 10.7 Parallel Interface I/O Port Addresses and Interrupts				
System	**LPTx Std.**	**Alt**	**I/O Port**	**IRQ**
8/16-bit ISA	LPT1	—	3BCh	IRQ7
8/16-bit ISA	LPT1	LPT2	378h	IRQ5
8/16-bit ISA	LPT2	LPT3	278h	None

Because the BIOS and DOS always have provided three definitions for parallel ports, problems with older systems are infrequent. Problems can arise, however, from the lack of available interrupt-driven ports for ISA bus systems. Normally, an interrupt-driven port is not absolutely required for printing operations; in fact, many programs do not use the interrupt-driven capability. Many programs do use the interrupt, however, such as network print programs and other types of background or spooler-type printer programs.

Also, high-speed, laser-printer utility programs often use the interrupt capabilities to allow for printing. If you use these types of applications on a port that is not interrupt driven, you see the printing slow to a crawl, if it works at all. The only solution is to use an interrupt-driven port. MS-DOS and Windows 95/98 now support up to 128 parallel ports.

To configure parallel ports in ISA bus systems, you probably will have to set jumpers and switches. Because each board on the market is different, you always should consult the OEM manual for that particular card if you need to know how the card should be configured.

Linking Systems with Parallel Ports. The original IBM PC designers envisioned that the parallel port would be used only for communicating with a printer. Over the years, the number of devices that can be used with a parallel port has increased tremendously. You now can find everything from tape backup units to LAN adapters to CD-ROMs that connect through your parallel port. Some modem manufacturers now have modems that connect to the parallel port instead of the serial port for faster data transfer.

Perhaps one of the most common uses for bidirectional parallel ports is to transfer data between your system and another, such as a laptop computer. If both systems use an EPP/ECP port, you can actually communicate at rates of up to 2M/sec, which rivals the speed of some hard disk drives. This capability has led to an increase in software to serve this niche of the market. If you are interested in such software (and the parallel ports necessary to facilitate the software), you should refer to the reviews that periodically appear in sources such as *PC Magazine*.

Connecting two computers with standard unidirectional parallel ports requires a special cable, known as a null modem cable. Most programs sell or provide these cables with their software. However, if you need to make one for yourself, Table 10.8 provides the wiring diagram you need.

Table 10.8 Null Modem/Lap Link Cable Wiring				
25-pin	**Signal Descriptions**		**Signal Descriptions**	**25-pin**
pin 2	Data Bit 0	↔	–Error	pin 15
pin 3	Data Bit 1	↔	Select	pin 13
pin 4	Data Bit 2	↔	Paper End	pin 12
pin 5	Data Bit 3	↔	–Acknowledge	pin 10
pin 6	Data Bit 4	↔	Busy	pin 11
pin 15	–Error	↔	Data Bit 0	pin 2
pin 13	Select	↔	Data Bit 1	pin 3
pin 12	Paper End	↔	Data Bit 2	pin 4
pin 10	–Acknowledge	↔	Data Bit 3	pin 5
pin 11	Busy	↔	Data Bit 4	pin 6
pin 25	Ground	↔	Ground	pin 25

Tip

Even though cables are most often provided for data transfer programs, notebook users may want to look for an adapter that makes the appropriate changes to a standard parallel cable. This can make traveling lighter by preventing the need for additional cables. Most of the time, these adapters attach to the Centronics end of the cable, and provide a standard DB25 connection on the other end. They're sold under a variety of names; however, null modem cable, Laplink adapter, or Laplink converter are the most common.

Although the wiring configuration and premade interlink cables given in Table 10.8 will work for connecting two machines with ECP/EPP ports, they won't be able to take advantage of the advanced transfer rates of these ports. Special cables are needed to communicate between ECP/EPP ports. Parallel Technologies is a company that sells ECP/EPP cables for connecting to other ECP/EPP computers, and also sells a universal cable for connecting any two parallel ports together to use the highest speed. Connect Air is listed in Appendix A.

Windows 95 and newer versions include a special program called DCC (Direct Cable Connection), which allows two systems to be networked together via a null modem/ LapLink cable. Consult the Windows documentation for information on how to establish a DCC connection. A company called Parallel Technologies (see Appendix A) has been contracted by Microsoft to supply the special DCC cables used to connect the systems. They have one special type of cable that uses active electronics to ensure a reliable high-speed interconnection.

Testing Parallel Ports

Testing parallel ports is, in most cases, simpler than testing serial ports. The procedures you use are effectively the same as those used for serial ports, except that when you use the diagnostics software, you choose the obvious choices for parallel ports rather than serial ports.

Not only are the software tests similar, but the hardware tests require the proper plugs for the loopback tests on the parallel port. Several different loopback plugs are required depending on what software you are using to test. Most use the IBM style loopback, but some use the style originated in the Norton Utilities diagnostics.

The wiring needed to construct your own loopback or wrap plugs is as follows:

- IBM 25-Pin Parallel (Male DB25P) Loopback Connector (Wrap Plug). Connect these pins:

  1 to 13
  2 to 15
  10 to 16
  11 to 17

- Norton Utilities 25-Pin Parallel (Male DB25P) Loopback Connector (Wrap Plug). Connect these pins:

  2 to 15
  3 to 13
  4 to 12
  5 to 10
  6 to 11

Serial and Parallel Port Replacements

Two new high-speed serial-bus architectures for desktop and portable are becoming available, called the *Universal Serial Bus (USB)* and *FireWire* or *IEEE 1394*. These are high-speed communications ports that far outstrip the capabilities of the standard serial and parallel ports most systems contain today, and may be used as an alternative to SCSI for high-speed peripheral connections. In addition to performance, these new ports will offer I/O device consolidation, meaning all types of external peripherals will connect to these ports.

The recent trend in high-performance peripheral bus design is to use a serial architecture, where one bit is sent at a time down a wire. Parallel architecture uses 8, 16, or more wires to send bits simultaneously. At the same clock speed, the parallel bus is faster; however, it is much easier to increase the clock speed of a serial connection than a parallel one.

Parallel connections suffer from several problems, the biggest being signal skew and jitter. Skew and jitter are the reasons that high-speed parallel buses like SCSI are limited to short distances of 3 meters or less. The problem is that although the 8 or 16 bits of data are fired from the transmitter at the same time, by the time they reach the receiver, propagation delays have conspired to allow some bits to arrive before the others. The longer the cable, the longer the time between the arrival of the first and last bits at the other end! This *signal skew*, as it is called, either prevents you from running a high-speed transfer rate, a longer cable, or both. *Jitter* is the tendency for the signal to reach its target voltage and float above and below for a short period of time.

With a serial bus, the data is sent one bit at a time. Because there is no worry about when each bit will arrive, the clocking rate can be increased dramatically.

With a high clock rate, parallel signals tend to interfere with each other. Serial again has an advantage in that with only one or two signal wires, crosstalk and interference between the wires in the cable are negligible.

Parallel cables are very expensive. In addition to the many additional wires needed to carry the multiple bits in parallel, the cable also needs to be specially constructed to prevent crosstalk and interference between adjacent data lines. This is one reason external SCSI cables are so expensive. Serial cables, on the other hand, are very inexpensive. For one thing, they have very few wires, plus the shielding requirements are far simpler, even at very high speeds. Because of this, it is also easier to transmit serial data reliably over longer distances, which is why parallel interfaces have shorter recommended cable lengths than serial interfaces. If you go by specifications, serial cables should be no longer than 10 feet while parallel cables should be no longer than 50 feet.

It is for these reasons, plus the need for new Plug-and-Play external peripheral interfaces, and the elimination of the physical port crowding on portable computers, that these new high-performance serial buses have been developed. Both USB and 1394 are available on desktop and portable PCs today.

USB (Universal Serial Bus)

USB is peripheral bus standard developed by PC and telecom industry leaders including Compaq, DEC, IBM, Intel, Microsoft, NEC, and Northern Telecom, that will bring Plug and Play of computer peripherals outside of the PC. USB will eliminate the need to install cards into dedicated computer slots and reconfigure the system, saving on important system resources such as Interrupts (IRQs). Personal computers equipped with USB will allow computer peripherals to be automatically configured as soon as they are physically attached, without the need to reboot or run setup. USB will also allow up to 127 devices to run simultaneously on a computer, with peripherals such as monitors and keyboards acting as additional plug-in sites, or hubs.

Intel has been the primary proponent of USB, and all their new PC chipsets, starting with the PIIX3 South Bridge component used with the 430HX Triton II, will include USB support as standard. Six other companies have worked with Intel in co-developing the USB, including Compaq, Digital, IBM, Microsoft, NEC, and Northern Telecom. Together, these companies have established the USB Implementers Forum to develop, support, and promote the USB architecture.

◀◀ See "Chipsets," p. 183

The USB is a 12Mbit/sec (1.5M/sec) interface over a simple 4-wire connection. The bus supports up to 127 devices and uses a tiered star topology built on expansion hubs that can reside in the PC, any USB peripheral, or even standalone hub boxes. A sample USB configuration is shown in Figure 10.4. For low-performance peripherals such as pointing devices and keyboards, the USB also has a slower 1.5Mbit/sec subchannel. The subchannel connection is used for slower interface devices such as keyboards and mice.

Maximum cable length between two full-speed (12Mbit/sec) devices or a device and a hub is five meters using twisted pair shielded cable with 20 gauge wire. Maximum cable length for low speed (1.5Mbit/sec) devices using nontwisted pair wire is three meters. These distance limits are shorter if smaller-gauge wire is used, according to Table 10.9:

Table 10.9   Maximum Cable Lengths Versus Wire Gauge

Gauge	Resistance (in Ohms/meter Ω/m)	Length (Max.)
28	0.232 Ω/m	0.81m
26	0.145 Ω/m	1.31m
24	0.091 Ω/m	2.08m
22	0.057 Ω/m	3.33m
20	0.036 Ω/m	5.00m

Although USB is not as fast at data transfer as FireWire or SCSI, it is still more than adequate for the types of peripherals for which it is designed.

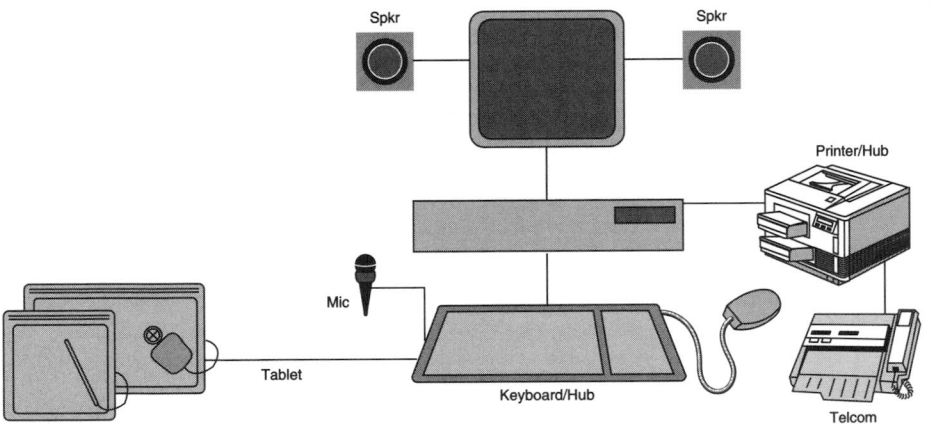

FIG. 10.4   A PC can use multiple USB hubs to support a variety of different peripherals connected to whichever hub is most convenient.

The physical USB plug is small and, unlike a typical serial or parallel cable, the plug is not attached by screws or thumbscrews. The USB plug (shown in Figure 10.5) snaps into place on the USB connector on the PC. Table 10.10 shows the pinout for the USB 4-wire connector and cable.

FIG. 10.5   The slots on the USB plug snap it into place on the spring-loaded tabs in a USB connector.

Table 10.10	USB Connector Pinout	
Pin	**Signal Name**	**Comment**
1	VCC	Cable power
2	– Data	
3	+ Data	
4	Ground	Cable ground

USB conforms to Intel's Plug and Play (PnP) specification, including *hot plugging*, which means that devices can be plugged in dynamically without powering down or rebooting the system. Simply plug in the device, and the USB controller in the PC will detect the device and automatically determine and allocate the resources and drivers required. Microsoft has USB drivers developed and has included them in existing versions of Windows 95 and NT. Note that the Windows 95b release or later is required for USB support; the necessary drivers are not present in the original Windows 95 or 95a. USB support will also be required in the BIOS, which will be included in newer systems with USB ports built in. Aftermarket boards are also available for adding USB to systems that don't include it as standard on the motherboard. USB peripherals will include modems, telephones, joysticks, keyboards, and pointing devices such as mice and trackballs.

One interesting feature of USB is that all attached devices will be powered by the USB bus. The PnP aspects of USB allow the system to query the attached peripherals as to their power requirements and issue a warning if available power levels are being exceeded. This will be important for USB when used in portable systems, because battery power to run the external peripherals may be limited.

Another benefit of the USB specification is self-identifying peripherals, a feature that should greatly ease installations. This means that you don't have to set unique IDs or identifiers for each peripheral, the USB handles that automatically. Also, USB devices can be "hot" plugged or unplugged, meaning that you will not have to turn off your computer or reboot every time you want to connect or disconnect a peripheral. As of this writing, USB-compatible devices are still hard to find, although most newer motherboards are being made to support them. One thing to keep in mind before purchasing USB peripherals is that your operating system must offer USB support. Whereas the original Windows 95 upgrade and Windows NT 4.0 do not support USB, the later OSR-2 (OEM Service Release 2) release of Windows 95 (also called 95B) does. Windows 98 and Windows NT 5.0 have full support for USB. Because the USB standard shows promise, it should become an important bus technology in the years to come.

One of the biggest advantages to an interface such as USB is that USB only requires a single interrupt from the PC. This means that you can connect up to 127 devices and they will not use separate interrupts as they might if each were connected over a separate interface. With modern PCs suffering from an interrupt shortage, this is a major benefit, and should spur the adoption of this interface for lower-speed peripherals.

FireWire (IEEE 1394)

FireWire is a relatively new bus technology; it is the result of the large data-moving demands of today's audio and video multimedia devices. It is extremely fast, with data transfer rates up to an incredible 400M/sec, and even faster speeds are being developed. The IEEE-1394 (as it is officially known) specification was published by the IEEE Standards Board in late 1995.

The IEEE-1394 standard currently exists with three different signaling rates: 100-, 200-, and 400Mbits/sec (12.5-, 25-, 50MBytes/sec), with gigabit-per-second versions in the works! Most PC adapter cards support the 200M/sec rate, even though current devices generally only operate at 100M/sec. A maximum of 63 devices can be connected to a single IEEE-1394 adapter card by daisy chaining. Cables for IEEE-1394 devices use Nintendo GameBoy-derived connectors and consist of six conductors; four wires are used for data transmission, and two conduct power. Connection with the motherboard is made either by a dedicated IEEE-1394 interface or by a PCI adapter card.

This bus was derived from the FireWire bus originally developed by Apple and Texas Instruments, and is also a part of the new Serial SCSI standard that is discussed later in this chapter in the section titled "SCSI-3."

1394 uses a simple six-wire cable with two differential pairs of clock and data lines plus two power lines. Just as with USB, 1394 is fully PnP, including the capability for hot plugging (insertion and removal of components without powering down). Unlike the much more complicated parallel SCSI bus, 1394 does not require complicated termination, and devices connected to the bus can draw up to 1.5 amps of electrical power. 1394 offers equal or greater performance compared to Ultra-Wide SCSI, with a much less expensive and less complicated connection.

1394 is built on a daisy-chained and branched topology and allows up to 63 nodes with a chain of up to 16 devices on each node. If this is not enough, the standard also calls for up to 1,023 bridged buses, which can interconnect more than 64,000 nodes! Additionally, 1394 can support devices with different data rates on the same bus, just as with SCSI.

The types of devices that will be connected to the PC via 1394 include practically anything that might use SCSI today. This includes all forms of disk drives, including hard disk, optical, floppy, CD-ROM, and the new DVD (Digital Video Disc) drives. Also, digital cameras, tape drives, and many other high-speed peripherals featuring 1394 have interfaces built in. Expect the 1394 bus to be implemented in both desktop and portable computers as a replacement for other external high-speed buses like SCSI.

Chipsets and PCI adapters for the 1394 bus are already available. Microsoft has developed drivers to support 1394 in Windows 95/98 and Windows NT. As of this writing, devices that conform to the IEEE-1394 standard are limited primarily to camcorders and VCRs with digital video (DV) capability. Sony was among the first to release such devices, although its products have a unique four-wire connector that requires an adapter cord to be used with IEEE-1394 PC cards. DV products are also available from Panasonic and Matsushita, and future IEEE-1394 applications should include DV conferencing devices, satellite audio and video data streams, audio synthesizers, DVD, and other high-speed disc drives.

Because of the current DV emphasis for IEEE-1394 peripherals, most PC cards currently offered by Adaptec, FAST Multimedia, Matrox, and others involve DV capturing and editing. If you're willing to spend $1,000 or more on DV equipment, these items should provide substantial video editing and dubbing capabilities on your PC. Of course, you will need IEEE-1394 I/O connectivity, which is still a rarity on current motherboards. Fortunately, Adaptec and Texas Instruments both offer PCI adapter cards that support IEEE-1394.

IEEE-1394 stands to offer unprecedented multimedia capabilities to current and future PC users. Current peripherals—particularly DV devices—are expensive, but as with any emerging technology, prices should come down in the future, opening the door wide for new PC uses both in the home and office. A great number of people would gain the ability to do advanced audio and video editing. If you anticipate having multimedia needs on your PC in the future, IEEE-1394 connectivity is a must.

Storage Device Interfaces

The remainder of this chapter describes interfaces used commonly by storage devices—mainly disk drives. It covers the disk interface from the drives to the cables and controllers that run them. You learn about the various disk interfaces you can select, and the shortcomings and strengths of each type. As these interfaces have evolved, they are now much more versatile. The IDE interface, which is the most widely used storage device interface in modern systems, has evolved from a hard disk only interface to one that supports hard disks and many different types of removable media such as tape, CD-ROM, CD-RW, Zip, and others. The SCSI interface has always been much more than a drive interface and is even more versatile than IDE, allowing nonstorage devices such as scanners to be attached.

A variety of hard disk interfaces are available today. As time has passed, the number of choices has increased, and many of the older designs are no longer viable in newer systems. You need to know about all these interfaces, from the oldest to the newest designs, because you will encounter all of them whenever upgrading or repairing systems is necessary.

The interfaces have different cabling and configuration options, and the setup and format of drives will vary as well. Special problems may arise when you are trying to install more than one drive of a particular interface type or (especially) when you are mixing drives of different interface types in one system.

This section covers the different hard disk drive interfaces, giving you all the technical information you need to deal with them in any way—troubleshooting, servicing, upgrading, and even mixing the different types.

This section also examines the standard controllers and describes how you can work with these controllers, and replace them with much faster units. Also discussed are the different types of drive interfaces: ST-506/412, ESDI, IDE, and SCSI. Choosing the proper interface is important, because your choice also affects your disk drive purchase and the ultimate speed of the disk subsystem.

The primary job of the hard disk controller or interface is to transmit and receive data to and from the drive. The different interface types limit how fast data can be moved from the drive to the system and offer different levels of performance. If you are putting together a system in which performance is a primary concern, you need to know how these different interfaces affect performance and what you can expect from them. Many of the statistics that appear in technical literature are not indicative of the real performance figures you will see in practice. I will separate the myths presented by some of these overly optimistic figures from the reality of what you will actually see.

With regard to disk drives, and especially hard disk drives, the specification on which people seem to focus the most is the drive's reported *average seek time*, the (average) time it takes for the heads to be positioned from one track to another. Unfortunately, the importance of this specification often is overstated, especially in relation to other specifications, such as the data transfer rate.

The transfer rate of data between the drive and the system is more important than access time, because most drives spend more time reading and writing information than they do simply moving the heads around. The speed at which a program or data file is loaded or read is affected most by the data transfer rate. Specialized operations such as sorting large files, which involves a lot of random access to individual records of the file (and, therefore, many seek operations), are helped greatly by a faster-seeking disk drive. Seeking performance is important in these cases. Most normal file load and save operations, however, are affected most by the rate at which data can be read and written to and from the drive. The data transfer rate depends on both the drive and the interface.

Several types of hard disk interfaces have been used in PC systems over the years, as shown in the following table.

Interface	When Used:
ST-506/412	1978–1985
ESDI	1986–1989
SCSI	1986–Present
IDE	1988–Present

As you can see, only IDE and SCSI remain popular today. Of these interfaces, only ST-506/412 and ESDI are what you could call true disk-controller-to-drive interfaces. SCSI and IDE are system-level interfaces that usually incorporate a chipset-based variation of one of the other two types of disk controller interfaces internally. For example, most SCSI and IDE drives incorporate the same basic controller circuitry used in separate ESDI controllers. The SCSI interface adds another layer of interface that attaches the controller to the system bus, whereas IDE is a direct bus-attachment interface. Even so, virtually all modern disk drives use either IDE or SCSI interfaces to connect to a system.

In data recovery, it helps to know the disk interface you are working with, because many data-recovery problems involve drive setup and installation problems. Each interface requires a slightly different method of installation and drive configuration. If the installation or configuration is incorrect or accidentally altered by the system user, it may prevent access to data on a drive. Accordingly, anyone who wants to become proficient in data recovery must be an expert on installing and configuring various types of hard disks and controllers.

IBM's reliance on industry-standard interfaces such as those listed here was a boon for everybody in the IBM-compatible industry. These standards allow a great deal of cross-system and cross-manufacturer compatibility. The use of these industry-standard interfaces allows you to pick up a mail-order catalog, purchase a hard disk for the lowest possible price, and be assured that it will work with your system. This Plug-and-Play capability results in affordable hard disk storage and a variety of options in capacities and speed.

The ST-506/412 Interface

The ST-506/412 interface was developed by Seagate Technologies around 1980. The interface originally appeared in the Seagate ST-506 drive, which was a 5M formatted (or 6M unformatted) drive in a full-height, 5 1/4-inch form factor. By today's standards, this drive is a tank! In 1981, Seagate introduced the ST-412 drive, which added a feature called *buffered seek* to the interface. This drive was a 10M formatted (12M unformatted) drive that also qualifies as a tank by today's standards. Besides the Seagate ST-412, IBM also used the Miniscribe 1012 as well as the International Memories, Inc. (IMI) model 5012 drive in the XT. IMI and Miniscribe are long gone, but Seagate remains as one of the largest drive manufacturers. Since the original XT, Seagate has supplied drives for numerous systems made by many different manufacturers.

Most drive manufacturers that made hard disks for PC systems adopted the Seagate ST-506/412 standard, a situation that helped make this interface popular. One important feature is the interface's Plug-and-Play design. No custom cables or special modifications are needed for the drives, which means that virtually any ST-506/412 drive will work with any ST-506/412 controller. The only real compatibility issue with this interface is the level of BIOS support provided by the system.

When introduced to the PC industry by IBM in 1983, ROM BIOS support for this hard disk interface was provided by a BIOS chip on the controller. Contrary to what most believed, the PC and XT motherboard BIOS had no inherent hard disk support. When the AT system was introduced, IBM placed the ST-506/412 interface support in the motherboard BIOS and eliminated it from the controller. All 16-bit and higher systems since then have an enhanced version of the same support in the motherboard BIOS as well. Because this support was somewhat limited, especially in the older BIOS versions, many disk controller manufacturers also placed additional BIOS support for their controllers directly on the controllers themselves. In some cases, you would use the controller BIOS and motherboard BIOS together; in other cases, you would disable the controller or motherboard BIOS and then use one or the other. These issues will be discussed more completely later in this chapter in the section "System Configuration."

The ST-506/412 interface does not quite make the grade in today's high-performance PC systems. This interface was designed for a 5M drive, and I have not seen any drives larger than 152M (Modified Frequency Modulation encoding) or 233M (Run-Length Limited encoding) available for this type of interface. Because the capacity, performance, and expandability of ST-506/412s are so limited, this interface is obsolete and generally unavailable in new systems. However, many older systems still use drives that have this interface.

Disk Drive Encoding Schemes and Problems. As indicated in Chapter 12, "Magnetic Storage" in the section "Data Encoding Schemes," *encoding schemes* are used in communications for converting digital data bits to various tones for transmission over a telephone line. For disk drives, the digital bits are converted, or *encoded*, in a pattern of magnetic impulses, or *flux transitions* (also called *flux reversals*), which are written on the disk. These flux transitions are decoded later, when the data is read from the disk.

A device called an *endec (encoder/decoder)* accomplishes the conversion to flux transitions for writing on the media and the subsequent reconversion back to digital data during read operations. The function of the endec is very similar to that of a modem (modulator/demodulator) in that digital data is converted to an analog waveform, which then is converted back to digital data. Sometimes, the endec is called a *data separator*, because it is designed to separate data and clocking information from the flux-transition pulse stream read from the disk.

One of the biggest problems with the original ST-506/412 interface used in the first PC hard disks was the fact that this endec resided on the disk controller (rather than the drive), which resulted in the possibility of corruption of the analog data signal before it reached the media. This problem became especially pronounced when the ST-506/412 controllers later switched to using RLL endecs to store 50 percent more data on the drive. With the RLL encoding scheme, the actual density of magnetic flux transitions on the disk media remains the same as with MFM encoding, but the timing between the transitions must be measured much more precisely.

In *RLL encoding*, the intervals between flux changes are approximately the same as with MFM, but the actual timing between them is much more critical. As a result, the transition cells in which signals must be recognized are much smaller and more precisely placed than with MFM. RLL encoding places more stringent demands on the timing of the controller and drive electronics. With RLL encoding, accurately reading the timing of the flux changes is paramount. Additionally, because RLL encodes variable-length groups of bits rather than single bits, a single error in one flux transition can corrupt 2 to 4 bits of data. For these reasons, an RLL controller usually has a more sophisticated error-detection and error-correction routine than an MFM controller.

The bottom line is that other than improved precision, there is no real difference between an ST-506/412 drive that is sold as an MFM model and one that is sold as an RLL model.

One method for avoiding reliability problems in the conversion process is to place an endec directly on the drive rather than on the controller. This method reduces the susceptibility to noise and interference that can plague some drive systems running RLL encoding. IDE and SCSI drives both have the endec (and, often, the entire controller) built into the drive by default. Because the endec is attached to the drive without cables and with an extremely short electrical distance, the propensity for timing- and noise-induced errors is greatly reduced or eliminated. This situation is analogous to a local telephone call between the endec and the disk platters. This local communication makes the ESDI, IDE, and SCSI interfaces much more reliable than the older ST-506/412 interface; they share none of the reliability problems that were once associated with RLL encoding over the ST-506/412 interface. Virtually all ESDI, IDE, and SCSI drives use RLL encoding today with tremendously increased reliability over even MFM ST-506/412 drives.

For a complete historical reference covering the original ST-506/412 controllers used in the PC environment, see *Upgrading and Repairing PCs Sixth Edition*, found in its entirety on the CDs included with this book.

The ESDI Interface

ESDI, or *Enhanced Small Device Interface*, is a specialized hard disk interface established as a standard in 1983, primarily by Maxtor Corporation. Maxtor led a consortium of drive manufacturers to adopt its proposed interface as a high-performance standard to succeed ST-506/412. ESDI later was adopted by the ANSI (American National Standards Institute) organization and published under the ANSI X3T9.2 Committee. The latest version of the ANSI ESDI document is known as X3.170a-1991. You can obtain this document, and other ANSI-standard documents, from ANSI or from Global Engineering Documents. These companies are listed in Appendix A.

Compared with ST-506/412, ESDI has provisions for increased reliability, such as building the endec into the drive. ESDI was much faster than the older ST-506/412 that preceded it, and was capable of a maximum 24Mbit/sec transfer rate. Most drives running ESDI, however, are limited to a maximum 10- or 15Mbit/sec. Unfortunately, compatibility problems between different ESDI implementations combined with pressure from low-cost, high-performance IDE interface drives served to make the ESDI interface obsolete by the early '90s. ESDI became somewhat popular in high-end (especially file server) systems during the late '80s.

Enhanced commands enabled some ESDI controllers to read a drive's capacity parameters directly from the drive, and to control defect mapping, but several manufacturers had different methods for writing this information on the drive. When you install an ESDI drive, in some cases the controller automatically reads the parameter and defect information directly from the drive. In other cases, however, you still have to enter this information manually, as with ST-506/412.

The ESDI's enhanced defect-mapping commands provide a standard way for the PC system to read a defect map from a drive, which means that the manufacturer's defect list can be written to the drive as a file. The defect-list file then can be read by the controller and low-level format software, eliminating the need for the installer to type these entries from the keyboard and enabling the format program to update the defect list with new entries if it finds new defects during the low-level format or the surface analysis.

Most ESDI implementations have drives formatted to 32 sectors per track or more (80 or more sectors per track are possible)—many more sectors per track than the standard ST-506/412 implementation of 17 to 26. The greater density results in two or more times the data-transfer rate, with a 1:1 interleave. Almost without exception, ESDI controllers support a 1:1 interleave, which allows for a transfer rate of 1M/sec or greater.

Because ESDI is much like the ST-506/412 interface, it can replace that interface without affecting software in the system. Most ESDI controllers are register-compatible with the older ST-506/412 controllers, which enables OS/2 and other non-DOS operating systems to run with few or no problems. The ROM BIOS interface to ESDI is similar to the ST-506/412 standard, and many low-level disk utilities that run on one interface will run on the other. To take advantage of ESDI defect mapping and other special features, however, use a low-level-format and surface-analysis utility designed for ESDI (such as the ones usually built into the controller ROM BIOS and called by DEBUG).

During the late 1980s, most high-end systems from major manufacturers were equipped with ESDI controllers and drives. Starting with the early 1990s, manufacturers began equipping high-end systems such as network file servers and workstations with SCSI. The SCSI interface allows for much greater expandability, supports more types of devices than ESDI does, and offers equal or greater performance.

The IDE Interface

Integrated Drive Electronics (IDE) is a generic term applied to any drive with an integrated (built-in) disk controller. The IDE interface as we know it is officially called *ATA (AT Attachment)*, and is an ANSI standard; however, IDE can roughly apply to any disk drive with a built-in controller.

The first drives with integrated controllers were *hardcards*; today, a variety of drives with integrated controllers is available. In a drive with IDE, the disk controller is integrated into the drive, and this combination drive/controller assembly usually plugs into a bus connector on the motherboard or bus adapter card. Combining the drive and controller greatly simplifies installation, because there are no separate power or signal cables from the controller to the drive. Also, when the controller and the drive are assembled as a unit, the number of total components is reduced, signal paths are shorter, and the electrical connections are more noise-resistant, resulting in a more reliable design than is possible when a separate controller, connected to the drive by cables, is used.

Placing the controller (including endec) on the drive gives IDE drives an inherent reliability advantage over interfaces with separate controllers. Reliability is increased because the data encoding, from digital to analog, is performed directly on the drive in a tight noise-free environment; the timing-sensitive analog information does not have to travel along crude ribbon cables that are likely to pick up noise and insert propagation delays into the signals. The integrated configuration allows for increases in the clock rate of the encoder and the storage density of the drive.

Integrating the controller and drive also frees the controller and drive engineers from having to adhere to the strict standards imposed by the earlier interface standards. Engineers can design what essentially are custom drive and controller implementations because no other controller would ever have to be connected to the drive. The resulting drive and controller combinations can offer higher performance than earlier standalone controller and drive setups. IDE drives sometimes are called drives with embedded controllers.

The IDE connector on motherboards in many systems is nothing more than a stripped-down bus slot. In ATA IDE installations, these connectors normally contain a 40-pin subset of the 98 pins that would be available in a standard 16-bit ISA bus slot. The pins used are only the signal pins required by a standard-type XT or AT hard disk controller. For example, because an AT-style disk controller uses only interrupt line 14, the motherboard ATA IDE connector supplies only that interrupt line; no other interrupt lines are needed. The XT IDE motherboard connector supplies interrupt line 5 because that is what an XT controller would use. Note that even if your ATA interface is connected to the South Bridge chip and runs at PCI bus speeds, the pinout and functions of the pins are still the same.

◀◀ See "Motherboard Interface Connectors," p. 228

◀◀ See "The ISA Bus," p. 239

> **Note**
>
> Many people who use systems with IDE connectors on the motherboard believe that a hard disk controller is built into their motherboard, but the controller really is in the drive. I do not know of any PC systems that have hard disk controllers built into the motherboard.

When IDE drives are discussed, the ATA IDE variety usually is the only kind mentioned because it is so popular. But other forms of IDE drives exist, based on other buses. For example, several PS/2 systems came with Micro-Channel (MCA) IDE drives that plug directly into a Micro-Channel Bus slot (through an angle adapter or interposer card). An 8-bit ISA form of IDE also existed but was never very popular. Most IBM-compatible systems with the ISA or EISA bus use AT-Bus (16-bit) IDE drives. The ATA IDE interface is by far the most popular type of drive interface available.

> **Note**
>
> ATA is a specific interface, which is commonly called IDE. As such, they are often (technically incorrectly, I might add) used interchangeably. IDE is a generic name that could be given to any interface where the controller portion of the circuit is on the drive.

The primary advantage of IDE drives is cost. Because the separate controller or host adapter is eliminated and the cable connections are simplified, IDE drives cost much less than a standard controller-and-drive combination. These drives also are more reliable, because the controller is built into the drive. Therefore, the endec or data separator (the converter between the digital and analog signals on the drive) stays close to the media. Because the drive has a short analog-signal path, it is less susceptible to external noise and interference.

Another advantage is performance. IDE drives are some of the highest-performance drives available—but they also are among the lowest-performance drives. This apparent contradiction is a result of the fact that all IDE drives are different. You cannot make a blanket statement about the performance of IDE drives because each drive is unique. The high-end models, however, offer performance that is equal or superior to that of any other type of drive on the market for a single-user, single-tasking operating system.

IDE Origins

Technically, the first IDE drives were hardcards. Companies such as the Plus Development division of Quantum took small 3 1/2-inch drives (either ST-506/412 or ESDI) and attached them directly to a standard controller. The assembly then was plugged into a bus slot as though it were a normal disk controller. Unfortunately, the mounting of a heavy, vibrating hard disk in an expansion slot with nothing but a single screw to hold it in place left a lot to be desired—not to mention the possible interference with adjacent cards due to the fact that many of these units were much thicker than a controller card alone.

Several companies got the idea that you could redesign the controller to replace the logic-board assembly on a standard hard disk and then mount it in a standard drive bay just like any other drive. Because the built-in controller in these drives still needed to plug directly into the expansion bus just like any other controller, a cable was run between the drive and one of the slots.

These connection problems were solved in different ways. Compaq was the first to incorporate a special bus adapter in its system to adapt the 98-pin AT bus edge connector on the motherboard to a smaller 40-pin header style connector that the drive would plug into. The 40-pin connectors were all that was needed, because it was known that a disk controller never would need more than 40 of the bus lines.

In 1987, IBM developed its own MCA IDE drives and connected them to the bus through a bus adapter device called an *interposer card*. These bus adapters (sometimes called *paddle boards* or *angle boards*) needed only a few buffer chips and did not require any real circuitry because the drive-based controller was designed to plug directly into the bus. The paddle board nickname came from the fact that they resembled game paddle or joystick adapters, which do not have much circuitry on them. Another 8-bit variation of IDE appeared in 8-bit ISA systems such as the PS/2 Model 30. The XT IDE interface uses a 40-pin connector and cable that is similar to, but not compatible with, the 16-bit version.

IDE Bus Versions

Three main types of IDE interfaces are available, with the differences based on three different bus standards:

- AT Attachment (ATA) IDE (16-bit ISA)

- XT IDE (8-bit ISA)

- MCA IDE (16-bit Micro Channel)

> **Note**
>
> Many people are confused about 16- versus 32-bit bus connections and 16- versus 32-bit hard drive connections. A PCI connection allows for a 32-bit (and possibly 64-bit in the future) bandwidth from the bus to the IDE host interface, which is normally in the motherboard chipset South Bridge. However, the actual ATA-IDE interface between the host connector on the motherboard and the drive (or drives) themselves is only a 16-bit interface. Thus, in an IDE (or EIDE) drive configuration, you are still getting only 16-bit bandwidth between the drive and the motherboard-based host interface. This usually does not create a bottleneck, because one or two hard drives cannot supply the controller enough data to saturate even a 16-bit channel.

The XT and ATA versions have standardized on 40-pin connectors and cables, but the connectors have slightly different pinouts, rendering them incompatible with one another. MCA IDE uses a completely different 72-pin connector and is designed for MCA bus systems only.

In most cases, you must use the type of IDE drive that matches your system bus. This situation means that XT IDE drives work only in XT-class 8-bit ISA slot systems, AT IDE (ATA) drives work only in AT-class 16-bit or greater ISA/PCI or EISA slot systems, and MCA IDE drives work only in Micro-Channel systems (such as the IBM PS/2 Model 50 or higher). A company called Silicon Valley offers adapter cards for XT systems that will run ATA IDE drives. Other companies, such as Arco Electronics and Sigma Data, have IDE adapters for Micro-Channel systems that allow ATA IDE drives to be used on these systems. (You can find these vendors in Appendix A.) These adapters are very useful for XT or PS/2 systems, because there is a very limited selection of XT or MCA IDE drives, whereas the selection of ATA IDE drives is virtually unlimited.

In most modern ISA/PCI systems, you will find an ATA connector on the motherboard. If your motherboard does not have one of these connectors and you want to attach an AT IDE drive to your system, you can purchase an adapter card that adds an ATA interface (or two) to a system via the ISA or PCI bus slots. Some of the cards offer additional features, such as an on-board ROM BIOS or cache memory.

ATA IDE

CDC, Western Digital, and Compaq actually created what could be called the first ATA-type IDE interface drive and were the first to establish the 40-pin IDE connector pinout. The first ATA IDE drives were 5 1/4-inch half-height CDC 40M units with integrated WD controllers sold in the first Compaq 386 systems in 1986.

Eventually, the 40-pin IDE connector and drive interface method was placed before one of the ANSI standards committees which, in conjunction with drive manufacturers, ironed out some deficiencies, tied up some loose ends, and published what is known as the *CAM ATA (Common Access Method AT Attachment) interface.* The CAM Committee was formed in October 1988, and the first working document of the AT Attachment interface was introduced in March 1989. Before the CAM ATA standard, many companies that followed CDC, such as Conner Peripherals, made proprietary changes to what had been done by CDC. As a result, many older ATA drives from the late '80s are very difficult to integrate into a dual-drive setup that has newer drives. By the early '90s, most drive manufacturers brought their drives into full compliance with the official standard, which eliminated many of these compatibility problems.

Some areas of the ATA standard have been left open for vendor-specific commands and functions. These vendor-specific commands and functions are the main reason why it is so difficult to low-level format IDE drives. To work properly, the formatter that you are using usually must know the specific vendor-unique commands for rewriting sector headers and remapping defects. Unfortunately, these and other specific drive commands differ from OEM to OEM, clouding the "standard" somewhat.

Note

It is important to note that only the ATA IDE interface has been standardized by the industry. The XT IDE and MCA IDE never were adopted as industry-wide standards and never became very popular. These interfaces no longer are in production, and no new systems of which I am aware come with these nonstandard IDE interfaces.

The ATA Specification

The ATA specification was introduced in March 1989 as an ANSI standard. ATA-1 was finally approved in 1994, and ATA-2 (also called *Enhanced IDE*) was approved in 1995. ATA-3 was approved in 1997, and ATA-4 is in development. You can obtain the current version of these standards from Global Engineering Documents, which is listed in Appendix A. The ATA standards have gone a long way toward eliminating incompatibilities and problems with interfacing IDE drives to ISA/PCI bus systems. The ATA specifications define the signals on the 40-pin connector, the functions and timings of these signals, cable specifications, and so on. The following section lists some of the elements and functions defined by the ATA specification.

Dual-Drive Configurations. Dual-drive ATA installations can be problematic because each drive has its own controller, and both controllers must function while being connected to the same bus. There has to be a way to ensure that only one of the two controllers will respond to a command at a time.

The ATA standard provides the option of operating on the AT Bus with two drives in a daisy-chained configuration. The primary drive (drive 0) is called the *master*, and the secondary drive (drive 1) is the *slave*. You designate a drive as being master or slave by setting a jumper or switch on the drive or by using a special line in the interface called the *Cable Select (CSEL) pin,* and by setting the CS jumper on the drive.

When only one drive is installed, the controller responds to all commands from the system. When two drives (and, therefore, two controllers) are installed, all commands from the system are received by both controllers. Each controller then must be set up to respond only to commands for itself. In this situation, one controller then must be designated as the master and the other as the slave. When the system sends a command for a specific drive, the controller on the other drive must remain silent while the selected controller and drive are functioning. Setting the jumper to master or slave allows discrimination between the two controllers by setting a special bit (the *DRV bit*) in the Drive/Head Register of a command block.

ATA I/O Connector. The ATA interface connector is a 40-pin header-type connector that should be keyed to prevent the possibility of installing it upside down. A key is provided by the removal of pin 20, and the corresponding pin on the cable connector should be plugged in to prevent a backward installation. The use of keyed connectors and cables is highly recommended, because plugging an IDE cable in backward can damage both the drive and the bus adapter circuits (although I have done it myself many times with no smoked parts yet!).

Table 10.11 shows the ATA-IDE interface connector pinout.

Table 10.11	ATA Connector		
Signal Name	**Pin**	**Pin**	**Signal Name**
–RESET	1	2	GROUND
Data Bit 7	3	4	Data Bit 8
Data Bit 6	5	6	Data Bit 9
Data Bit 5	7	8	Data Bit 10
Data Bit 4	9	10	Data Bit 11
Data Bit 3	11	12	Data Bit 12
Data Bit 2	13	14	Data Bit 13
Data Bit 1	15	16	Data Bit 14
Data Bit 0	17	18	Data Bit 15

(continues)

Table 10.11	ATA Connector Continued		
Signal Name	**Pin**	**Pin**	**Signal Name**
GROUND	19	20	KEY (pin missing)
DRQ 3	21	22	GROUND
–IOW	23	24	GROUND
–IOR	25	26	GROUND
I/O CH RDY	27	28	SPSYNC:CSEL
–DACK 3	29	30	GROUND
IRQ 14	31	32	–IOCS16
Address Bit 1	33	34	–PDIAG
Address Bit 0	35	36	Address Bit 2
–CS1FX	37	38	–CS3FX
–DA/SP	39	40	GROUND
+5 Vdc (Logic)	41	42	+5 Vdc (Motor)
GROUND	43	44	–TYPE (0=ATA)

Note that the connector pinout shows 44 total pins, although only the first 40 are used on most 3 1/2 inch or larger ATA drives. The additional 4 pins shown (pins 41-44) are found primarily on the smaller 2 1/2 inch drives used in notebook and laptop systems. Those drives don't have room for a separate power connector, so the additional pins are primarily designed to supply power to the drive.

ATA I/O Cable. A 40-conductor ribbon cable is specified to carry signals between the bus adapter circuits and the drive (controller). To maximize signal integrity and to eliminate potential timing and noise problems, the cable should not be longer than 0.46 meters (18 inches).

Note that the newer high-speed IDE interfaces are especially susceptible to cable problems, and cables that are too long. If the cable is too long, you will experience data corruption and other errors that can be maddening. I always keep a special high-quality short IDE cable in my toolbox for testing drives where I suspect this problem.

ATA Signals. This section describes some of the most important signals in more detail.

Pin 20 is used as a key pin for cable orientation and is not connected through in the interface. This pin should be missing from any ATA connectors, and the cable should have the pin-20 hole in the connector plugged off to prevent the cable from being plugged in backward.

Pin 39 carries the *Drive Active/Slave Present (DASP) signal*, which is a dual-purpose, time-multiplexed signal. During power-on initialization, this signal indicates whether a slave drive is present on the interface. After that, each drive asserts the signal to indicate that it is active. Early drives could not multiplex these functions and required special jumper settings to work with other drives. Standardizing this function to allow for compatible dual-drive installations is one of the features of the ATA standard.

Pin 28 carries the *Cable Select* or *Spindle Synchronization signal (CSEL or SPSYNC)*, which is a dual-purpose conductor; a given installation, however, may use only one of the two functions. The CSEL function is the most widely used and is designed to control the designation of a drive as master (drive 0) or slave (drive 1) without requiring jumper settings on the drives. If a drive sees the CSEL as being grounded, the drive is a master; if CSEL is open, the drive is a slave.

You can install special cabling to ground CSEL selectively. This installation normally is accomplished through a Y-cable arrangement, with the IDE bus connector in the middle and each drive at opposite ends of the cable. One leg of the Y has the CSEL line connected through, indicating a master drive; the other leg has the CSEL line open (conductor interrupted or removed), making the drive at that end the slave.

ATA Commands. One of the best features of the ATA IDE interface is the enhanced command set. The ATA IDE interface was modeled after the WD1003 controller that IBM used in the original AT system. All ATA IDE drives must support the original WD command set (eight commands), with no exceptions, which is why IDE drives are so easy to install in systems today. All IBM-compatible systems have built-in ROM BIOS support for the WD1003, which means that, essentially, they support ATA IDE as well.

In addition to supporting all the WD1003 commands, the ATA specification added numerous other commands to enhance performance and capabilities. These commands are an optional part of the ATA interface, but several of them are used in most drives available today and are very important to the performance and use of ATA drives in general.

Perhaps the most important is the Identify Drive command. This command causes the drive to transmit a 512-byte block of data that provides all details about the drive. Through this command, any program (including the system BIOS) can find out exactly what type of drive is connected, including the drive manufacturer, model number, operating parameters, and even the serial number of the drive. Many modern BIOSs use this information to automatically receive and enter the drive's parameters into CMOS memory, eliminating the need for the user to enter these parameters manually during system configuration. This arrangement helps prevent mistakes that can later lead to data loss when the user no longer remembers what parameters he or she used during setup.

The Identify Drive data can tell you many things about your drive, including the following:

- Number of cylinders in the recommended (default) translation mode
- Number of heads in the recommended (default) translation mode
- Number of sectors per track in the recommended (default) translation mode
- Number of cylinders in the current translation mode
- Number of heads in the current translation mode
- Number of sectors per track in the current translation mode

- Manufacturer and model number

- Firmware revision

- Serial number

- Buffer type, indicating sector buffering or caching capabilities

Several public-domain programs can execute this command to the drive and report the information onscreen. I use the IDEINFO (available at **http://www.dc.ee/Files/ Utils/IDEINFO.ARJ**) or IDEDIAG (available from many of the popular shareware sites) program. I find these programs especially useful when I am trying to install IDE drives and need to know the correct parameters for a user-definable BIOS type. These programs get the information directly from the drive.

Two other very important commands are the Read Multiple and Write Multiple commands. These commands permit multiple-sector data transfers and, when combined with block-mode Programmed I/O (PIO) capabilities in the system, can result in incredible data-transfer rates many times faster than single-sector PIO transfers.

Tip

If you want the ultimate in IDE performance and installation ease, make sure that your motherboard BIOS and IDE adapter support ATA-2 or EIDE. This support allows your BIOS to execute data transfers to and from the IDE drive several times faster than normal, and also makes installation and configuration easier because the BIOS will be able to detect the drive-parameter information automatically. The most recent South Bridge chipsets found on motherboards today implement the Ultra-DMA (UDMA or Ultra-33) 33M/sec interface, which is part of the most recent ATA-3 standard.

There are many other enhanced commands, including room for a given drive manufacturer to implement what are called *vendor-unique commands*. These commands often are used by a particular vendor for features unique to that vendor. Often, features such as low-level formatting and defect management are controlled by vendor-unique commands. This is why low-level format programs can be so specific to a particular manufacturer's IDE drives and why many manufacturers make their own LLF programs available.

ATA IDE Drive Categories

ATA-IDE drives can be divided into three main categories. These categories separate the drives by function (such as translation capabilities) and design (which can affect features such as low-level formatting):

- Non-Intelligent ATA-IDE drives

- Intelligent ATA-IDE drives

- Intelligent Zoned Recording ATA-IDE drives

Non-Intelligent IDE. As I stated earlier, the ATA standard requires that the built-in controller respond exactly as though it were a Western Digital WD1003 controller. This controller responds to a command set of eight commands. Early IDE drives supported these commands and had few, if any, other options. These early drives actually were more like regular ST-506/412 or ESDI controllers bolted directly into the drive than the more intelligent drives that we consider today to be IDE.

These drives were not considered to be intelligent IDE drives; an intelligent drive is supposed to have several capabilities that these early IDE drives lacked. The drives could not respond to any of the enhanced commands that were specified as (an optional) part of the ATA IDE specification, including the Identify Drive command. These drives also did not support *sector translation*, in which the physical parameters could be altered to appear as any set of logical cylinders, heads, and sectors. Enhanced commands and sector-translation support are what make an IDE drive an intelligent IDE drive, and these features were not available in the early IDE drives.

These drives could be low-level formatted in the same manner as any normal ST-506/412 or ESDI drive. They were universally low-level formatted at the factory, with factory-calculated optimum interleave (usually 1:1) and head- and cylinder-skew factors. Also, factory defects were recorded in a special area on the drive; they no longer were written on a sticker pasted to the exterior. Unfortunately, this arrangement means that if you low-level format these drives in the field, you most likely will alter these settings (especially the skew factors) from what the factory set as optimum, and wipe out the factory-written defect table.

Some manufacturers released special low-level format routines that would reformat the drives while preserving these settings, but others did not make such programs available. Because they did not want you to overwrite the defect list or potentially slow the drive, most manufacturers stated that you should never low-level format their IDE drives.

This statement started a myth that the drives could somehow be damaged or rendered inoperable by such a format, which truly is not the case. One rumor was that the servo information could be overwritten, which would mean that you would have to send the drive back to the manufacturer for re-servoing. This also is not true; the servo information is protected and cannot be overwritten. The only consequence of an improper low-level format of these drives is the possible alteration of the skew factors and the potential loss of the factory defect maps.

The Disk Manager program by Ontrack is the best special-purpose format utility to use on these drives for formatting because it is aware of these types of drives and often can restore the skew factors and preserve the defect information. If you are working with a drive that already has had the defect map overwritten, Disk Manager can perform a very good surface analysis that will mark off any of these areas that it finds. Disk Manager allows you to specify the skew factors and to mark defects at the sector level so that they will not cause problems later. Other general-purpose diagnostics that work especially well with IDE drives such as this include the PC-Technician program by Windsor Technologies and Microscope by Micro 2000. Another alternative is the Drive Pro software from MicroHouse.

Intelligent IDE. Later IDE drives became known as *intelligent IDE drives*. These drives support enhanced ATA commands, such as the `Identify Drive` command, and sector-translation capabilities.

These drives can be configured in two ways: in raw physical mode or in translation mode. To configure the drive in raw physical mode, you simply enter the CMOS drive parameters during setup so that they match the true physical parameters of the drive. For example, if the drive physically has 800 cylinders, 6 heads, and 50 sectors per track, you enter these figures during setup. To configure the drive in translation mode, you simply enter any combination of cylinders, heads, and sectors that adds up to equal or less than the true number of sectors on the drive.

In the example I just used, the drive has a total of 240,000 sectors (800×6×50). All I have to do is figure out another set of parameters that adds up to equal or less than 240,000 sectors. The simplest way to do this is to cut the number of cylinders in half and double the number of heads. Thus, the new drive parameters become 400 cylinders, 12 heads, and 50 sectors per track. This method adds up to 240,000 sectors and enables the drive to work in translation mode.

When these drives are in translation mode, a low-level format cannot alter the interleave and skew factors, nor can it overwrite the factory defect-mapping information. A low-level format program can, however, perform additional defect mapping or sector sparing while in this mode.

If the drive is in true physical mode, a low-level format rewrites the sector headers and modifies the head and cylinder skewing. If performed incorrectly, the format can be repaired by a proper low-level format program that allows you to set the correct head and cylinder skew. This task can be accomplished automatically by the drive manufacturer's recommended low-level format program (if available) or by other programs, such as Disk Manager by Ontrack. When you use Disk Manager, you have to enter the skew values manually; otherwise, the program uses predetermined defaults. To obtain the correct skew values, it is best to contact the drive manufacturer's technical support department. You can calculate the skew values if the manufacturer cannot provide them. Skew values normally only apply to non-IDE or non-SCSI drives, as IDE and SCSI drives normally don't allow a true physical format; that can only be done at the factory.

▶▶ See "Hard Drive Parameters," p. 1353

To protect the skew factors and defect information on intelligent IDE drives, all you have to do is run them in translation mode. In translation mode, this information cannot be overwritten.

Intelligent Zoned Recording IDE. Most modern IDE drives combine intelligence with Zoned Recording. With *Zoned Recording*, the drive has a variable number of sectors per track in several zones across the surface of the drive. Because the PC BIOS can handle only a fixed number of sectors on all tracks, these drives always must run in translation mode. Because these drives are always in translation mode, you cannot alter the factory-set interleave and skew factors or wipe out the factory defect information.

You still can low-level format these drives, however, and use such a format to map or spare additional defective sectors that crop up during the life of the drive. To low-level format intelligent Zoned Recording drives, you need either a specific utility from the drive manufacturer or an IDE-aware program, such as Disk Manager by Ontrack, PC-Technician by Windsor Technologies, Microscope by Micro 2000, or Drive Pro by MicroHouse.

ATA-2 and ATA-3 (Enhanced IDE)

ATA-2 and *ATA-3* are extensions of the original ATA (IDE) specification. The most important additions are performance-enhancing features such as fast PIO and DMA modes. ATA-2 also features improvements in the Identify Drive command allowing a drive to tell the software exactly what its characteristics are; this is essential for both Plug and Play (PnP) and compatibility with future revisions of the standard. ATA-3 adds improved reliability, especially of the faster mode 4 transfers; note that ATA-3 does not define any faster modes. ATA-3 also adds a simple password-based security scheme, more sophisticated power management, and Self Monitoring Analysis and Report Technology (SMART). This allows a drive to keep track of problems that might result in a failure.

ATA-2 and 3 are often called Enhanced IDE (or EIDE). EIDE is technically a marketing program from Western Digital. Fast-ATA and Fast-ATA-2 are similar Seagate-inspired marketing programs, which are also endorsed by Quantum. As far as the hard disk and BIOS are concerned, these are all different terms for basically the same thing.

There are four main areas where ATA-2 (EIDE), ATA-3, and ATA-4 have improved the original ATA/IDE interface in several ways:

- Increased maximum drive capacity
- Faster data transfer
- Secondary two-device channel
- ATAPI (ATA Program Interface)

The following sections describe these improvements.

Increased Drive Capacity. ATA-2/EIDE allows for increased drive capacity over the original ATA/IDE specification. This is done through an Enhanced BIOS, which makes it possible to use hard disks exceeding the 504M barrier. The origin of this limit is the disk geometry (cylinders, heads, sectors) supported by the combination of an IDE drive and the BIOS' software interface. Both IDE and the BIOS are capable of supporting huge disks, but their combined limitations conspire to restrict the useful capacity to 504M.

An Enhanced BIOS circumvents this by using a different geometry when talking to the drive than when talking to the software. What happens in between is called *translation*. For example, if your drive has 2,000 cylinders and 16 heads, a translating BIOS will make programs think that the drive has 1,000 cylinders and 32 heads.

▶▶ See "Hard Drive Parameters," p. 1353

You can usually tell if your BIOS is enhanced by the capability to specify more than 1,024 cylinders in the BIOS setup, although this is inconclusive. If you see drive-related settings like LBA, ECHS, or even Large, these are telltale signs of a BIOS with translation support. Most BIOSs with a date of 1994 or later are enhanced. If your system currently does not have an Enhanced BIOS, you may be able to get an upgrade.

There are three ways today's BIOSs can handle translation: Standard CHS addressing, Extended CHS addressing, and LBA addressing. They are summarized in the following table.

BIOS Mode	Operating System to BIOS	BIOS to Drive Ports
Standard CHS	Logical CHS Parameters	Logical CHS Parameters
Extended CHS	Translated CHS Parameters	Logical CHS Parameters
LBA	Translated CHS Parameters	LBA Parameters

In Standard CHS, there is only one possible translation step internal to the drive. The drive's actual, physical geometry is completely invisible from the outside with all zoned recorded ATA drives today. The Cylinders, Heads, and Sectors printed on the label for use in the BIOS setup are purely logical geometry, and do not represent the actual physical parameters. Standard CHS addressing is limited to 16 heads and 1,024 cylinders, which gives us a limit of 504M.

This is often called "Normal" in the BIOS setup, and causes the BIOS to behave like an old-fashioned one without translation. Use this setting if your drive has fewer than 1,024 cylinders or if you want to use the drive with a non-DOS operating system that doesn't understand translation.

In Extended CHS, a translated logical geometry is used to communicate between the drive and the BIOS, while a different translated geometry is used to communicate between the BIOS and everything else. In other words, there are normally two translation steps. The drive still translates internally, but has logical parameters that exceed the 1,024 cylinder limitation of the standard BIOS. In this case, the drive's cylinder count is usually divided by 2, and the head count is multiplied by 2 to get the translated values from those actually stored in the CMOS Setup. This type of setting breaks the 504/528M barrier.

This is often called "Large" or "ECHS" in the BIOS setup, and tells the BIOS to use Extended CHS translation. It uses a different geometry (cylinders/heads/sectors) when talking to the drive than when talking to the BIOS. This type of translation should be used with drives that have more than 1,024 cylinders but that do not support LBA (Logical Block Addressing). Note that the geometry entered in your BIOS setup is the logical geometry, not the translated one.

LBA is a means of linearly addressing sector addresses, beginning at Cylinder 0, Head 0, Sector 1 as LBA 0, and proceeding on to the last physical sector on the drive. This is new in ATA-2, but has always been the one and only addressing mode in SCSI.

With LBA, each sector on the drive is numbered starting from 0. The number is a 28-bit binary number internally, which translates to a sector number from 0 to 268,435,456. Because each sector represents 512 bytes, this results in a maximum drive capacity of exactly 128G, or 137 billion bytes. Unfortunately, the operating system still needs to see a translated CHS, so the BIOS determines how many sectors there are, and comes up with Translated CHS to match. The BIOS CHS limits are 1,024 cylinders, 256 heads, and 63 sectors per track, which limits total drive capacity to just under 8G.

In other words, this breaks the 528M barrier in essentially the same way as Extended CHS does. Because it is somewhat simpler to use a single linear number to address a sector on the hard disk compared to a CHS type address, this is the preferred method if the drive supports LBA.

> **Caution**
>
> A word of warning with these BIOS translation settings: If you switch between Standard CHS, Extended CHS, or LBA, the BIOS may change the (translated) geometry. The same thing may happen if you transfer a disk that has been formatted on an old, non-LBA computer to a new one that uses LBA. This will cause the logical CHS geometry seen by the operating system to change, and will cause the data to appear in the wrong locations from where it actually is! This can cause you to lose access to your data if you are not careful. I always recommend recording the CMOS Setup screens associated with the hard disk configuration so that you can properly match the setup of a drive to the settings it was originally at.

Faster Data Transfer. ATA-2/EIDE and ATA-3 define several high-performance modes for transferring data to and from the drive. These faster modes are the main part of the new specifications and were the main reason they were initially developed. Most of the faster drives on the market today will support either PI/O transfer Mode 3 or Mode 4, which results in a very fast transfer. The following section discusses these modes.

The PIO mode determines how fast data is transferred to and from the drive. In the slowest possible mode, PIO mode 0, the data cycle time cannot exceed 600 nanoseconds (ns). In a single cycle, 16 bits are transferred into or out of the drive making the theoretical transfer rate of PIO Mode 0 (600ns cycle time) 3.3M/sec. Most of the high-performance ATA-2 (EIDE) drives today support PIO Mode 4, which offers a 16.6M/sec transfer rate.

The following table shows the PIO modes, with their respective transfer rates.

PIO Mode	Cycle Time (ns)	Transfer Rate (M/sec)	Specification
0	600	3.33	ATA
1	383	5.22	ATA
2	240	8.33	ATA
3	180	11.11	ATA-2
4	120	16.67	ATA-2

To run in Mode 3 or 4 requires that the IDE port on the system be a local bus port. This means that it must operate through either a VL-Bus or PCI bus connection. Most motherboards with ATA-2/EIDE support have dual IDE connectors on the motherboard, and most of them now allow full throughput. Older 486 and some early Pentium boards have only the primary connector running through the system's PCI local bus. The secondary connector on those boards usually runs through the ISA bus, and therefore supports up to Mode 2 operation only.

When interrogated with an Identify Drive command, a hard disk returns, among other things, information about the PIO and DMA modes it is capable of using. Most enhanced BIOSs will automatically set the correct mode to match the capabilities of the drive. If you set a mode faster than the drive can handle, data corruption will result.

ATA-2 and newer drives also perform *Block Mode PIO*, which means that they use the Read/Write Multiple commands that greatly reduce the number of interrupts sent to the host processor. This lowers the overhead, and the resulting transfers are even faster.

DMA Transfer Modes. Although it is not used by most operating systems or BIOSs, ATA-2 drives also support Direct Memory Access transfers. DMA means that the data is transferred directly between drive and memory without using the CPU as an intermediary, as opposed to PIO.

There are two distinct types of direct memory access: *DMA* and *busmastering DMA*. Ordinary DMA relies on the DMA controller on the system's mainboard to perform the complex task of arbitration, grabbing the system bus and transferring the data. In the case of busmastering DMA, all this is done by logic on the interface card. Of course, this adds considerably to the complexity and the price of a busmastering interface.

Systems using the Intel PIIX (PCI IDE ISA eXcelerator) and later South Bridge chips have the capability of supporting Bus Master IDE. This uses the busmaster mode on the PCI bus to execute data transfers. The busmaster IDE modes and transfer rates are shown in the following table.

BMIDE Mode	Cycle Time (ns)	Transfer Rate (M/sec)	Specifications
0	480	4.16	ATA-2
1	150	3.33	ATA-2
2	120	16.67	ATA-2

Unfortunately, even the fastest busmaster IDE mode 2 results in the same 16.67M/sec transfer speed as PIO Mode 4, so busmaster IDE never really caught on as being desirable, and most of the time it is recommended to stick with the standard PIO Mode 4 on drives that support it. Busmaster IDE modes were never very effective and have now been superseded by the newer Ultra-DMA modes supported in ATA-4 compatible devices.

ATAPI (ATA Packet Interface). *ATAPI* is a standard designed for devices such as CD-ROMs and tape drives that plug into an ordinary ATA (IDE) connector. The principal advantage of ATAPI hardware is that it's cheap and works on your current adapter. For CD-ROMs, it has a somewhat lower CPU usage compared to proprietary adapters, but there's no performance gain otherwise. For tape drives, ATAPI has potential for superior performance and reliability compared to the popular floppy controller attached tape devices. ATAPI is also used to run other removable storage devices such as the LS-120 superdisk drives and internal Iomega Zip and Jaz drives.

Although ATAPI CD-ROMs use the hard disk interface, this does not mean they look like ordinary hard disks; to the contrary, from a software point of view, they are a completely different kind of animal. They actually most closely resemble a SCSI device.

> **Caution**
>
> ATAPI support is not found directly in the BIOS of many systems. Systems without ATAPI support in the BIOS cannot boot from an ATAPI CD-ROM and you still must load a driver to use it under DOS or Windows. Windows 95 and Windows NT have native ATAPI support, and newer systems with ATAPI-aware BIOS which will even allow booting from an ATAPI CD-ROM are now available. The Windows 98 and NT 5.0 CD-ROMs will be directly bootable on those systems, greatly easing installation.

Another note is that I normally recommend keeping different types of IDE devices on separate channels. Some older chipsets cannot support setting different transfer rates for different devices, which means the channel must be set to the speed of the slowest device. Because most CD-ROM and tape drives run at lower IDE mode speeds, this would force your hard disk to run slower if they shared a single cable. Even if the chipset you have supports separate speed settings for devices on the same channel (cable), I still recommend keeping them separate as IDE does not normally support overlapping access such as SCSI. In other words, when one drive is running, the other cannot be accessed. By keeping the CD-ROM and hard disk on separate channels, you can more effectively overlap accessing between them.

ATA-4

ATA-4 is the latest revision of ATA and should receive final approval in 1998. Even so, numerous drives and interfaces already fully support the latest version. The newer PIIX4 and later South Bridge chips from the Intel motherboard chipsets support ATA-4, and many of the new drives support the high-speed UDMA (Ultra-DMA) transfer mode.

◄◄ See "Chipsets," p. 183

ATA-4 makes ATAPI (ATA Packet Interface) support a full part of the ATA standard, and thus ATAPI is no longer an auxiliary interface to ATA but is merged completely within. This should promote ATA for use as an interface for many other types of devices. ATA-4 also adds support for new Ultra-DMA modes (also called Ultra-ATA) for even faster data transfer. The highest-performance mode, called DMA/33, has 33M/second bandwidth, twice that of the fastest programmed I/O mode or DMA mode previously supported.

Also included is support for queuing commands, which is similar to that provided in SCSI-2. This allows for better multitasking as multiple programs make requests for IDE transfers.

▶▶ See "IDE Versus SCSI," p. 646

Obsolete IDE Versions

As mentioned earlier, other versions of the IDE interface were used in some early systems. While you may find some systems based on these interfaces if you are supporting legacy hardware, none of these has been used in any new system since the approval of the ATA-1 standard in 1994.

XT-Bus (8-Bit) IDE. Many systems with XT ISA bus architecture used XT IDE hard drives. The IDE interface in these systems usually is built into the motherboard. The IBM PS/2 Models 25, 25-286, 30, and 30-286 systems used an 8-bit XT IDE interface. These 8-bit XT IDE drives are difficult to find; few manufacturers other than IBM, Western Digital, and Seagate made them; none of these drives were available in capacities beyond 40M.

Because the ATA IDE interface is a 16-bit design, it could not be used in 8-bit (XT type) systems, so some of the drive manufacturers standardized an XT-Bus (8-bit) IDE interface for XT class systems. These drives were never very popular, and were usually only available in capacities from 20M to 40M.

MCA IDE. The IBM PS/2 Models 50 and higher come with Micro-Channel Architecture (MCA) bus slots. IBM used a type of MCA IDE drive in many of these systems. MCA IDE is a form of IDE interface, but it is designed for the MCA bus and is not compatible with the more industry-standard ATA IDE interface. Few companies other than IBM and Western Digital make replacement MCA IDE drives for these systems. I recommend replacing these drives with ATA IDE drives, using adapters from Arco Electronics or Sigma Data, or switching to SCSI drives instead. The IBM MCA IDE drives are expensive for the limited capacity that they offer.

Small Computer System Interface (SCSI)

SCSI (pronounced "scuzzy") stands for *Small Computer System Interface*. This interface has its roots in *SASI*, the *Shugart Associates System Interface*. SCSI is not a disk interface, but a systems-level interface. SCSI is not a type of controller, but a bus that supports as many as 8 or 16 total devices. One of these devices, the host adapter, functions as the gateway between the SCSI bus and the PC system bus. The SCSI bus does not talk directly with devices such as hard disks; instead, it talks to the controller that is built into the drive.

A single SCSI bus can support as many as 8 or 16 physical units, usually called *SCSI IDs*. One of these units is the adapter card in your PC; the other seven can be other peripherals. You could have hard disks, tape drives, CD-ROM drives, a graphics scanner, or other devices (up to seven or fifteen total) attached to a single SCSI host adapter. Most systems support up to four host adapters, each with up to 15 devices, for a total of 60 devices!

When you purchase a SCSI device, you usually are purchasing the device, controller, and SCSI adapter in one circuit. This type of drive usually is called an *embedded SCSI device*; the SCSI interface is built in. For example, most SCSI hard drives are technically the same as their IDE counterparts except for the addition of the SCSI bus adapter circuits added. You do not need to know what type of controller is inside the SCSI drive, because your system cannot talk directly to the controller as though it were plugged into the system bus, like on a standard IDE drive. Instead, communications go through the SCSI host adapter installed in the system bus. You can access the drive only with the SCSI protocols.

Apple originally rallied around SCSI as being an inexpensive way out of the bind in which it put itself with the Macintosh. When the engineers at Apple realized the problem in making the Macintosh a closed system (with no slots), they decided that the easiest way to gain expandability was to build a SCSI port into the system, which is how external peripherals can be added to the slotless Macs. Because PC systems always have been expandable, the push toward SCSI has not been as urgent. With up to eight bus slots supporting different devices and controllers in PC compatible systems, it seemed as though SCSI was not needed as much.

SCSI has since become popular in the PC-based computer world because of the great expandability that it offers and the number of devices that are available with built-in SCSI. One block that stalled acceptance of SCSI in the PC marketplace was the lack of a real standard; the SCSI standard was designed primarily by a committee. No single manufacturer has led the way, at least in the PC arena; each company has its own interpretation of how SCSI should be implemented, particularly at the host-adapter level.

SCSI is a standard, in much the same way that RS-232 is a standard. The SCSI standard (like the RS-232 standard), however, defines only the hardware connections, not the driver specifications required to communicate with the devices. Software ties the SCSI subsystem into your PC, but unfortunately, most of the driver programs work only for a specific device and a specific host adapter. With a SCSI driver for most common adapters and devices built into Windows 95 and 98, it is now much easier to get multiple SCSI devices to work using a single adapter.

> **Note**
>
> Some SCSI host adapters bundled with hardware such as graphics scanners or a "bargain" SCSI CD-ROM drive, will not include all the features needed to support multiple SCSI devices or bootable SCSI hard drives. This has nothing to do with any limitations in the SCSI specification. The situation is simply that the manufacturer has included the most stripped-down version of a SCSI adapter available to save money. It has all the functionality needed to support the device it came with, but nothing else. Fortunately, with the right adapter and drivers, one card could do it all, most likely the one used for the hard disk as it would be the most full-featured of the bunch.

SCSI can be troublesome at times because of the lack of a single host-adapter standard, a software interface standard, and standard ROM BIOS support for hard disk drives attached to the SCSI bus. Fortunately, some simple recommendations can keep you from living this compatibility nightmare!

In the beginning, SCSI lacked the capability to run hard disks off the SCSI bus. To boot from these drives and use a variety of operating systems was a problem that resulted from the lack of an interface standard. The standard IBM XT and AT ROM BIOS software was designed to talk to ST-506/412 hard disk controllers. The software easily was modified to work with ESDI because ESDI controllers are similar to ST-506/412 controllers at the register level. (This similarity at the register level enabled manufacturers to easily design self-booting, ROM-BIOS-supported ESDI drives.) The same can be said of IDE, which completely emulates the WD1003 ST-506/412 controller interface and works perfectly with the existing BIOS as well. SCSI is so different from these other standard disk interfaces that a new set of ROM BIOS routines are necessary to support the system so it can self-boot. SCSI host adapters are available with BIOS support on the SCSI host adapter.

Because of the lead taken by Apple in developing systems software (operating systems and ROM) support for SCSI, peripherals connect to Apple systems in fairly standard ways. Until recently, this kind of standard-setting leadership was lacking for SCSI in the PC world. This situation changed dramatically with Windows 95, which included drivers for most standard SCSI adapters and peripherals on the market.

Many PC manufacturers have standardized SCSI for high-end systems. In these systems, a SCSI host adapter card is in one of the slots, or the system has a SCSI host adapter built into the motherboard. This arrangement is similar in appearance to the IDE interface, because a single cable runs from the motherboard to the SCSI drive. Although, SCSI supports as many as seven or fifteen additional devices (some of which may not be hard disks), whereas IDE supports only four devices (two per controller). Additionally, SCSI supports more types of devices other than hard disks than IDE supports which IDE devices must be either a hard disk, IDE-type CD-ROM drive, or a tape drive, LS-120 superdisk drive, Zip drive, and so on. Systems with SCSI drives are easy to upgrade, because virtually any third-party SCSI drive will plug in and function.

ANSI SCSI standards

The SCSI standard defines the physical and electrical parameters of a parallel I/O bus used to connect computers and peripheral devices in daisy-chain fashion. The standard supports devices such as disk drives, tape drives, and CD-ROM drives. The original SCSI standard (ANSI X3.131-1986) was approved in 1986, SCSI-2 was approved in January 1994, and a new revision called SCSI-3 is still under development.

The SCSI interface is defined as a standard by ANSI. The X3 Task Group operates as an ASC (Accredited Standards Committee) under ANSI to develop Information Processing System standards. X3T9 is the I/O Interfaces group, and X3T9.2 specifically is in charge of low-level interfaces such as SCSI and ATA-IDE (among others). The original SCSI-1 standard was published by the X3T9 ANSI group in 1986, and is officially published by ANSI as X3.131-1986.

One problem with the original SCSI-1 document was that many of the commands and features were optional, and there was little or no guarantee that a particular peripheral would support the expected commands. This problem caused the industry as a whole to define a set of 18 basic SCSI commands called the *Common Command Set (CCS)*, which would become the minimum set of commands supported by all peripherals. CCS became the basis for what is now the SCSI-2 specification.

In addition to formal support for CCS, SCSI-2 provided additional definitions for commands to access CD-ROM drives (and their sound capabilities), tape drives, removable drives, optical drives, and several other peripherals. In addition, an optional higher speed called Fast SCSI-2 and a 16-bit version called Wide SCSI-2 were defined. Another feature of SCSI-2 is *command queuing*, which enables a device to accept multiple commands and execute them in the order that the device deems to be most efficient. This feature is most beneficial when you are using a multitasking operating system that could be sending several requests on the SCSI bus at the same time.

The X3T9 group approved the SCSI-2 standard as X3.131-1990 in August 1990, but the document was recalled in December 1990 for changes before final ANSI publication. Final approval for the SCSI-2 document was finally made in January 1994, although it has changed little from the original 1990 release. The SCSI-2 document is now called ANSI X3.131-1994. The official document is available from Global Engineering Documents or the ANSI committee, which are listed in Appendix A. You can also download working drafts of these documents from the NCR SCSI BBS, listed in Appendix A under "NCR Microelectronics."

Most companies indicate that their host adapters follow both the ANSI X3.131-1986 (SCSI-1) as well as the x3.131-1994 (SCSI-2) standards. Note that because virtually all parts of SCSI-1 are supported in SCSI-2, virtually any SCSI-1 device is also considered SCSI-2 by default. Many manufacturers advertise that their devices are SCSI-2, but this does not mean that they support any of the additional optional features that were incorporated in the SCSI-2 revision.

For example, an optional part of the SCSI-2 specification includes a fast synchronous mode that doubles the standard synchronous transfer rate from 5M/sec to 10M/sec. This Fast SCSI transfer mode can be combined with 16-bit Wide SCSI for transfer rates of up to 20M/sec. There was an optional 32-bit version defined in SCSI-2, but component manufacturers have shunned this as too expensive. In essence, 32-bit SCSI was a stillborn specification. Most SCSI implementations are 8-bit standard SCSI or Fast/Wide SCSI. Even devices which support none of the Fast or Wide modes can still be considered SCSI-2.

The SCSI-3 standard should be approved in '98. Even before it was fully completed, portions of this specification, although not final, have been sold in products. One of these developments is the Fast-20 mode, which is also called *Ultra-SCSI*. This essentially is quad-speed SCSI, and will run 20M/sec on an 8-bit standard SCSI bus, and 40M/sec on Wide (16-bit) SCSI.

Table 10.12 shows the maximum transfer rates for the SCSI bus at various speeds and widths, and the cable type required for the specific transfer widths.

Table 10.12	SCSI Data-Transfer Rates				
Bus Width	**Standard SCSI**	**Fast SCSI**	**Fast-20 (Ultra)**	**Fast-40 (Ultra 2)**	**Cable Type**
8-bit	5M/sec	10M/sec	20M/sec	40M/sec	A (50-pin)
16-bit (Wide)	10M/sec	20M/sec	40M/sec	80M/sec	P (68-pin)

> **Note**
>
> The A cable is the standard 50-pin SCSI cable, whereas the P cable is a 68-pin cable designed for 16-bit. Maximum cable length is 6m (about 20 feet) for standard speed SCSI, and only 3m (about 10 feet) for Fast/Fast-20/Fast-40 (Ultra) SCSI. Pinouts for these cable connections are listed in this chapter in Tables 10.13 through 10.17.

So-called SCSI-1 adapters have no problems with SCSI-2 peripherals. In fact, as was stated earlier, virtually any SCSI-1 device can also legitimately be called SCSI-2 (or even SCSI-3). You can't take advantage of Fast, Fast-20, or Wide transfer capabilities, but the extra commands defined in SCSI-2 can be sent by means of a SCSI-1 controller. In other words, nothing is different between SCSI-1- and SCSI-2-compliant hardware. For example, I am running a Seagate Barracuda 4G Fast SCSI-2 drive with my standard IBM SCSI-1 host adapter, and it runs fine. Most adapters are similar, in that they actually are SCSI-2 compatible, even if they advertise only SCSI-1 support.

Because the SCSI-2 standard was not actually approved before January 1994, any devices that claimed to be SCSI-2 before that time were not officially in compliance with the standard. This is really not a problem, however, because the SCSI-2 document had not changed appreciably since it was nearly approved in 1990. The same thing is currently happening with advertisers listing devices as "SCSI-3." The SCSI-3 specification is not yet approved, although certain areas are being worked out.

Single-ended or Differential SCSI

"Normal" SCSI also is called *single-ended SCSI*. For each signal that needs to be sent across the bus, a wire exists to carry it. With differential SCSI, for each signal that needs to be sent across the bus, a pair of wires exists to carry it. The first in this pair carries the same type of signal that the single-ended SCSI carries. The second in this pair, however, carries the logical inversion of the signal. The receiving device takes the difference of the pair (hence the name *differential*), which makes it less susceptible to noise and allows for greater cable length. Because of this, differential SCSI can be used with cable lengths of up to 25m, whereas single-ended SCSI is good only for 6m with standard asynchronous or synchronous transfers or for only 3m for Fast SCSI.

You cannot mix single-ended and differential devices on a single SCSI bus; the result would be catastrophic. (That is to say, you probably will see smoke!) Notice that the cables and connectors are the same, so it's entirely possible to make this mistake. This usually is not a problem, however, because very few differential SCSI implementations exist. Especially with SCSI in the PC environment, single-ended is about all you will ever see. If, however, you come upon a peripheral that you believe might be differential, there are a few ways to tell. One way is to look for a special symbol on the unit; the industry has adopted different universal symbols for single-ended and differential SCSI. Figure 10.6 shows these symbols.

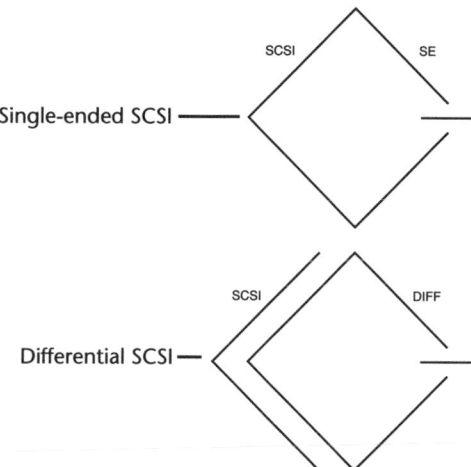

FIG. 10.6   Single-ended and differential SCSI universal symbols.

If you do not see such symbols, you can tell whether you have a differential device by using an ohmmeter to check the resistance between pins 21 and 22 on the device connector. On a single-ended system, the pins should be tied together and also tied to the ground. On a differential device, the pins should be open or have significant resistance between them. Again, this generally should not be a problem, because virtually all devices used in the PC environment are single-ended.

SCSI-1 and SCSI-2

The SCSI-2 specification essentially is an improved version of SCSI-1 with some parts of the specification tightened and with several new features and options added. Normally, SCSI-1 and SCSI-2 devices are compatible, but SCSI-1 devices ignore the additional features in SCSI-2.

Some of the changes in SCSI-2 are very minor. For example, SCSI-1 allowed SCSI Bus parity to be optional, whereas parity must be implemented in SCSI-2. Another requirement is that initiator devices, such as host adapters, provide terminator power to the interface; most devices already did so.

SCSI-2 also has several optional features:

■ Fast SCSI

■ Wide SCSI

■ Command queuing

■ High-density cable connectors

■ Improved Active (Alternative 2) termination

These features are not required; they are optional under the SCSI-2 specification. If you connect a standard SCSI host adapter to a Fast SCSI drive, for example, the interface will work, but only at standard SCSI speeds.

SCSI-3. *SCSI-3* is a term used to describe a set of standards currently being developed. Simply put, it is the next generation of documents a product conforms to. See the section "New Commands" later in this chapter.

Fast and Fast-Wide SCSI. *Fast SCSI* refers to high-speed synchronous transfer capability. Fast SCSI achieves a 10M/sec transfer rate on the standard 8-bit SCSI cabling. When combined with a 16-bit Wide SCSI interface, this configuration results in data-transfer rates of 20M/sec (called *Fast/Wide*).

Fast-20 (Ultra) SCSI. *Fast-20* or *Ultra SCSI* refers to high-speed synchronous transfer capability that is twice as fast as Fast-SCSI. This has been introduced in the Draft (unfinished) SCSI-3 specification and has already been adopted by the marketplace, especially for high-speed hard disks. Ultra SCSI achieves a 20M/sec transfer rate on the standard 8-bit SCSI cabling. When combined with a 16-bit Wide SCSI interface, this configuration results in data-transfer rates of 40M/sec (called *Ultra/Wide*).

Fast-40 SCSI. Fast-40 SCSI is a future revision of SCSI-3 (mentioned earlier in the chapter) capable of achieving a 40M/sec transfer rate.

Wide SCSI. *Wide SCSI* allows for parallel data transfer at a bus width of 16 bits. The wider connection requires a new cable design. The standard 50-conductor 8-bit cable is called the *A cable*. SCSI-2 originally defined a special 68-conductor B cable that was supposed to be used in conjunction with the A cable for wide transfers, but the industry ignored this specification in favor of a newer 68-conductor P cable that was introduced as part of the SCSI-3 specification. The P cable superseded the A and B cable combination because the P cable can be used alone (without the A cable) for 16-bit Wide SCSI.

A 32-bit Wide SCSI version was originally defined on paper as a part of the SCSI-2 specification, but has not found popularity and probably never will in the PC environment. Theoretically, 32-bit SCSI implementations would require two cables: a 68-conductor P cable and a 68-conductor Q cable.

Fiber Channel SCSI. Fiber Channel SCSI is a specification for a serial interface using a fiber channel physical and protocol characteristic, with SCSI command set. It can achieve 100M/sec over either fiber or coaxial cable.

Termination. The single-ended SCSI bus depends on very tight termination tolerances to function reliably. Unfortunately, the original 132-ohm passive termination defined in the SCSI-1 document was not designed for use at the higher synchronous speeds now possible. These passive terminators can cause signal reflections to generate errors when transfer rates increase or when more devices are added to the bus. SCSI-2 defines an active (voltage-regulated) terminator that lowers termination impedance to 110 ohms and improves system integrity.

Command Queuing. In SCSI-1, an initiator device, such as a host adapter, was limited to sending one command per device. In SCSI-2, the host adapter can send as many as 256 commands to a single device, which will store and process those commands internally before responding on the SCSI bus. The target device even can resequence the commands to allow for the most efficient execution or performance possible. This feature is especially useful in multitasking environments, such as OS/2 and Windows NT, which can take advantage of this feature.

New Commands. SCSI-2 took the Common Command Set that was being used throughout the industry and made it an official part of the standard. The CCS was designed mainly for disk drives and did not include specific commands designed for other types of devices. In SCSI-2, many of the old commands are reworked, and several new commands have been added. New command sets have been added for CD-ROMs, optical drives, scanners, communications devices, and media changers (jukeboxes).

SCSI-3

Even though the SCSI-2 specification has only recently been approved (although it has remained stable for some time), the SCSI-3 specification is already being developed. SCSI-3 will have everything that SCSI-2 has and definitely will add new commands, features, and implementations. For example, SCSI-3 will provide support for up to 32 devices on the bus instead of only eight.

One of the most exciting things about SCSI-3 is the proposed *Serial SCSI*, a scheme that may use only a six-conductor cable and that will be able to transfer data at up to 100M/sec! The switch to serial instead of parallel is designed to control the delay, noise, and termination problems that have plagued SCSI-2, as well as to simplify the cable connection. Serial SCSI will be capable of transferring more data over six wires than 32-bit Fast Wide SCSI-2 can over 128 wires! The intention is that Serial SCSI be implemented on the motherboard of future systems, giving them incredible expansion and performance capabilities.

Although Serial SCSI may not make the older host adapters and cables obsolete overnight, it does make future cabling possibilities even more of a puzzle. Serial SCSI offers the possibility of longer cable lengths, less electromagnetic interference, and easier connections on laptops, notebooks, and docking stations. Expect SCSI-3 to offer almost pain-free installations with automatic PnP SCSI ID setup and termination schemes.

In any practical sense, SCSI-3 is still a bit away from being approved. Because the standard exists in draft documents before being officially approved, if the portions of the standard become stable, we may very well see products claiming SCSI-3 compatibility well before the standard truly exists. Because SCSI-3 actually incorporates all of what is in SCSI-2, technically anybody can call any SCSI-1 or SCSI-2 device a SCSI-3 device as well. Beware of product hype along these lines. Some of the new SCSI-3 features will likely be incompatible with previous SCSI implementations, and may take a while to appear on the market.

SCSI Cables and Connectors

The SCSI standards are very specific when it comes to cables and connectors. The most common connectors specified in this standard are the 50-position unshielded pin header connector for internal SCSI connections and the 50-position shielded Centronics latch-style connectors for external connections. The shielded Centronics style connector also is called *Alternative 2* in the official specification. Passive or Active termination (Active is preferred) is specified for both single-ended and differential buses. The 50-conductor bus configuration is defined in the SCSI-2 standard as the A-cabled.

The SCSI-2 revision added a high-density, 50-position, D-shell connector option for the A-cable connectors. This connector now is called *Alternative 1*. The Alternative 2 Centronics latch-style connector remains unchanged from SCSI-1. A 68-conductor B-cable specification was added to the SCSI-2 standard to provide for 16- and 32-bit data transfers; the connector, however, had to be used in parallel with an A cable. The industry did not widely accept the B-cable option, which has been dropped from the SCSI-3 standard.

To replace the ill-fated B cable, a new 68-conductor P cable was developed as part of the SCSI-3 specification. Shielded and unshielded high-density D-shell connectors are specified for both the A cable and P cable. The shielded high-density connectors use a squeeze-to-release latch rather than the wire latch used on the Centronics-style connectors. Active termination for single-ended buses is specified, providing a high level of signal integrity.

SCSI Cable and Connector Pinouts

The following section details the pinouts of the various SCSI cables and connectors. There are two electrically different versions of SCSI, *Single-ended* and *Differential*. These two versions are electrically incompatible, and must not be interconnected or damage will result. Fortunately, there are very few Differential SCSI applications available in the PC industry, so you will rarely (if ever) encounter it. Within each electrical type (Single-ended or Differential), there are basically three SCSI cable types:

- A Cable (Standard SCSI)
- P Cable (16- and 32-bit Wide SCSI)
- Q Cable (32-bit Wide SCSI)

The A cable is used in most SCSI-1 and SCSI-2 installations, and is the most common cable you will encounter. SCSI-2 Wide (16-bit) applications use a P cable instead, which completely replaces the A cable. You can intermix standard and Wide SCSI devices on a single SCSI bus by interconnecting A and P cables with special adapters. 32-bit wide SCSI-3 applications use both the P and Q cables in parallel to each 32-bit device. Today there are virtually no PC applications for 32-bit Wide SCSI-3, and because of the two-cable requirement, it is not likely to catch on.

The A cables can have Pin Header (Internal) type connectors or External Shielded connectors, each with a different pinout. The P and Q cables feature the same connector pinout on either Internal or External cable connections.

Single-Ended SCSI Cables and Connectors. The single-ended electrical interface is the most popular type for PC systems. Tables 10.13 and 10.14 show all the possible single-ended cable and connector pinouts. The A cable is available in both internal unshielded and external shielded configurations. A hyphen preceding a signal name indicates the signal is Active Low. The RESERVED lines have continuity from one end of the SCSI bus to the other. In an A cable bus, the RESERVED lines should be left open in SCSI devices (but may be connected to ground), and are connected to ground in the bus terminator assemblies. In the P and Q cables, the RESERVED lines are left open in SCSI devices and in the bus terminator assemblies.

Table 10.13	A-Cable (Single-Ended) Internal Unshielded Header Connector		
Signal Name	**Pin**	**Pin**	**Signal Name**
GROUND	1	2	–DB(0)
GROUND	3	4	–DB(1)
GROUND	5	6	–DB(2)
GROUND	7	8	–DB(3)
GROUND	9	10	–DB(4)
GROUND	11	12	–DB(5)
GROUND	13	14	–DB(6)
GROUND	15	16	–DB(7)
GROUND	17	18	–DB(Parity)
GROUND	19	20	GROUND
GROUND	21	22	GROUND
RESERVED	23	24	RESERVED
Open	25	26	TERMPWR
RESERVED	27	28	RESERVED
GROUND	29	30	GROUND
GROUND	31	32	–ATN
GROUND	33	34	GROUND
GROUND	35	36	–BSY
GROUND	37	38	–ACK
GROUND	39	40	–RST
GROUND	41	42	–MSG
GROUND	43	44	–SEL
GROUND	45	46	–C/D
GROUND	47	48	–REQ
GROUND	49	50	–I/O

Table 10.14   A-Cable (Single-Ended) External Shielded Connector

Signal Name	Pin	Pin	Signal Name
GROUND	1	26	–DB(0)
GROUND	2	27	–DB(1)
GROUND	3	28	–DB(2)
GROUND	4	29	–DB(3)
GROUND	5	30	–DB(4)
GROUND	6	31	–DB(5)
GROUND	7	32	–DB(6)
GROUND	8	33	–DB(7)
GROUND	9	34	–DB(Parity)
GROUND	10	35	GROUND
GROUND	11	36	GROUND
RESERVED	12	37	RESERVED
Open	13	38	TERMPWR
RESERVED	14	39	RESERVED
GROUND	15	40	GROUND
GROUND	16	41	–ATN
GROUND	17	42	GROUND
GROUND	18	43	–BSY
GROUND	19	44	–ACK
GROUND	20	45	–RST
GROUND	21	46	–MSG
GROUND	22	47	–SEL
GROUND	23	48	–C/D
GROUND	24	49	–REQ
GROUND	25	50	–I/O

IBM used the SCSI interface in virtually all PS/2 systems introduced after 1990. These systems use a Micro-Channel SCSI adapter or have the SCSI Host Adapter built into the motherboard. In either case, IBM's SCSI interface uses a special 60-pin mini-Centronics type external shielded connector that is unique in the industry. A special IBM cable is required to adapt this connector to the standard 50-pin Centronics style connector used on most external SCSI devices. The pinout of the IBM 60-pin mini-Centronics style External Shielded connector is shown in Table 10.15. Notice that although the pin arrangement is unique, the pin-number-to-signal designations correspond with the standard unshielded internal pin header type of SCSI connector.

Table 10.15   IBM PS/2 SCSI External Shielded 60-Pin Connector

Signal Name	Pin	Pin	Signal Name
GROUND	1	60	Not Connected
–DB(0)	2	59	Not Connected

Signal Name	Pin	Pin	Signal Name
GROUND	3	58	Not Connected
–DB(1)	4	57	Not Connected
GROUND	5	56	Not Connected
–DB(2)	6	55	Not Connected
GROUND	7	54	Not Connected
–DB(3)	8	53	Not Connected
GROUND	9	52	Not Connected
–DB(4)	10	51	GROUND
GROUND	11	50	–I/O
–DB(5)	12	49	GROUND
GROUND	13	48	–REQ
–DB(6)	14	47	GROUND
GROUND	15	46	–C/D
–DB(7)	16	45	GROUND
GROUND	17	44	–SEL
–DB(Parity)	18	43	GROUND
GROUND	19	42	–MSG
GROUND	20	41	GROUND
GROUND	21	40	–RST
GROUND	22	39	GROUND
RESERVED	23	38	–ACK
RESERVED	24	37	GROUND
Open	25	36	–BSY
TERMPWR	26	35	GROUND
RESERVED	27	34	GROUND
RESERVED	28	33	GROUND
GROUND	29	32	–ATN
GROUND	30	31	GROUND

The P cable (Single-ended) and connectors are used in 16-bit wide SCSI-2 applications (see Table 10.16 for the pinout).

Table 10.16 P Cable (Single-ended) Internal or External Shielded Connector

Signal Name	Pin	Pin	Signal Name
GROUND	1	35	–DB(12)
GROUND	2	36	–DB(13)
GROUND	3	37	–DB(14)
GROUND	4	38	–DB(15)

(continues)

Table 10.16   P Cable (Single-ended) Internal or External Shielded Connector Continued

Signal Name	Pin	Pin	Signal Name
GROUND	5	39	–DB(Parity 1)
GROUND	6	40	–DB(0)
GROUND	7	41	–DB(1)
GROUND	8	42	–DB(2)
GROUND	9	43	–DB(3)
GROUND	10	44	–DB(4)
GROUND	11	45	–DB(5)
GROUND	12	46	–DB(6)
GROUND	13	47	–DB(7)
GROUND	14	48	–DB(Parity 0)
GROUND	15	49	GROUND
GROUND	16	50	GROUND
TERMPWR	17	51	TERMPWR
TERMPWR	18	52	TERMPWR
RESERVED	19	53	RESERVED
GROUND	20	54	GROUND
GROUND	21	55	–ATN
GROUND	22	56	GROUND
GROUND	23	57	–BSY
GROUND	24	58	–ACK
GROUND	25	59	–RST
GROUND	26	60	–MSG
GROUND	27	61	–SEL
GROUND	28	62	–C/D
GROUND	29	63	–REQ
GROUND	30	64	–I/O
GROUND	31	65	–DB(8)
GROUND	32	66	–DB(9)
GROUND	33	67	–DB(10)
GROUND	34	68	–DB(11)

The Q Cable (Single-ended) and connector is defined only for 32-bit SCSI implementations, which also require a P cable as well (see Table 10.17 for the pinout). 32-bit SCSI applications are virtually nonexistent.

Table 10.17   Q Cable (Single-Ended) Internal or External Shielded Connector

Signal Name	Pin	Pin	Signal Name
GROUND	1	35	–DB(28)
GROUND	2	36	–DB(29)

Signal Name	Pin	Pin	Signal Name
GROUND	3	37	−DB(30)
GROUND	4	38	−DB(31)
GROUND	5	39	−DB(Parity 3)
GROUND	6	40	−DB(16)
GROUND	7	41	−DB(17)
GROUND	8	42	−DB(18)
GROUND	9	43	−DB(19)
GROUND	10	44	−DB(20)
GROUND	11	45	−DB(21)
GROUND	12	46	−DB(22)
GROUND	13	47	−DB(23)
GROUND	14	48	−DB(Parity 2)
GROUND	15	49	GROUND
GROUND	16	50	GROUND
TERMPWRQ	17	51	TERMPWRQ
TERMPWRQ	18	52	TERMPWRQ
RESERVED	19	53	RESERVED
GROUND	20	54	GROUND
GROUND	21	55	TERMINATED
GROUND	22	56	GROUND
GROUND	23	57	TERMINATED
GROUND	24	58	−ACKQ
GROUND	25	59	TERMINATED
GROUND	26	60	TERMINATED
GROUND	27	61	TERMINATED
GROUND	28	62	TERMINATED
GROUND	29	63	−REQQ
GROUND	30	64	TERMINATED
GROUND	31	65	−DB(24)
GROUND	32	66	−DB(25)
GROUND	33	67	−DB(26)
GROUND	34	68	−DB(27)

Differential SCSI Signals. Differential SCSI is not normally used in a PC environment, but is very popular with minicomputer installations due to the very long bus lengths that are allowed.

Termination. All buses need to be electrically terminated at each end; the SCSI bus is no exception. Improper termination still is one of the most common problems in SCSI installations. Three types of terminators typically are available for the SCSI bus:

- Passive

- Active (also called Alternative 2)

- Forced Perfect Termination (FPT): FPT-3, FPT-18, and FPT-27

Typical passive terminators (a network of resistors) allow signal fluctuations in relation to the terminator power signal on the bus. Usually, passive terminating resistors suffice over short distances, such as two or three feet, but for longer distances, active termination is a real advantage. Active termination is required with Fast SCSI.

An active terminator actually has one or more voltage regulators to produce the termination voltage, rather than resistor voltage dividers. This arrangement helps ensure that the SCSI signals always are terminated to the correct voltage level. Active terminators will usually have some sort of LED indicating the termination activity. The SCSI-2 specification recommends active termination on both ends of the bus and requires active termination whenever Fast or Wide SCSI devices are used. Most high-performance host adapters have an "auto-termination" feature so if it is the end of a chain, it will terminate itself.

A variation on active termination is available: Forced Perfect Termination. *Forced Perfect Termination* is an even better form of active termination, in which diode clamps are added to eliminate signal overshoot and undershoot. The trick is that instead of clamping to +5 and Ground, these terminators clamp to the output of two regulated voltages. This arrangement enables the clamping diodes to eliminate signal overshoot and undershoot, especially at higher signaling speeds and over longer distances.

FPT terminators are available in several versions. FPT-3 and FPT-18 versions are available for 8-bit standard SCSI, while the FPT-27 is available for 16-bit (Wide) SCSI. The FPT-3 version forces perfect the three most highly active SCSI signals on the 8-bit SCSI bus, while the FPT-18 forces perfect all the SCSI signals on the 8-bit bus except grounds. FPT-27 also forces perfect all the 16-bit Wide SCSI signals except grounds.

> **Note**
>
> Several companies make high-quality terminators for the SCSI bus, including Aeronics and the Data Mate division of Methode. Both of these companies make a variety of terminators, but Aeronics is well-noted for some unique FPT versions that are especially suited to problem configurations that require longer cable runs or higher signal integrity. One of the best investments that you can make in any SCSI installation is in high-quality cables and terminators. Contact information for both of these companies is listed in Appendix A.

SCSI Drive Configuration

SCSI drives are not too difficult to configure, but they are more complicated than IDE drives. The SCSI standard controls the way that the drives must be set up. You need to set two or three items when you configure an SCSI drive:

- SCSI ID setting (0–7 or 0–15)

- Terminating resistors

The SCSI ID setting is very simple. Up to eight SCSI devices can be used on a single narrow SCSI bus or up to fifteen devices on a wide SCSI bus, and each device must have a unique SCSI ID address. The host adapter takes one address, so the rest are free for up to seven SCSI peripherals. Most SCSI host adapters are factory-set to ID 7 or 15, which is the highest-priority ID. All other devices must have unique IDs that do not conflict with one another. Some host adapters boot only from a hard disk set to a specific ID. Older Adaptec host adapters required the boot hard disk to be ID 0; newer ones can boot from any ID.

Setting the ID usually involves changing jumpers on the drive. If the drive is installed in an external chassis, the chassis may have an ID selector switch that is accessible at the rear. This selector makes ID selection a simple matter of pressing a button or rotating a wheel until the desired ID number appears. If no external selector is present, you must open the external device chassis and set the ID via the jumpers on the drive.

Three jumpers are required to set the SCSI ID; the particular ID selected actually is derived from the binary representation of the jumpers themselves. For example, setting all three ID jumpers off results in a binary number of 000b, which translates to an ID of 0. A binary setting of 001b equals ID 1, 010b equals 2, 011b equals 3, and so on. (Notice that as I list these values, I append a lowercase b to indicate binary numbers.)

Unfortunately, the jumpers can appear either forward or backward on the drive, depending on how the manufacturer set them up. To keep things simple, I have recorded all the different ID jumper settings in the following tables. Table 10.18 shows the settings for drives that order the jumpers with the Most Significant Bit (MSB) to the left; Table 10.19 shows the settings for drives that have the jumpers ordered so that the MSB is to the right.

Table 10.18 SCSI ID Jumper Settings with the Most Significant Bit to the Left			
SCSI	**ID**	**Jumper**	**Settings**
0	0	0	0
1	0	0	1
2	0	1	0
3	0	1	1
4	1	0	0
5	1	0	1
6	1	1	0
7	1	1	1

1 = Jumper On, 0 = Jumper Off

Table 10.19	SCSI ID Jumper Settings with the Most Significant Bit to the Right		
SCSI	**ID**	**Jumper**	**Settings**
0	0	0	0
1	1	0	0
2	0	1	0
3	1	1	0
4	0	0	1
5	1	0	1
6	0	1	1
7	1	1	1

1 = Jumper On, 0 = Jumper Off

SCSI termination is very simple. Termination is required at both ends of the bus; there are no exceptions. If the host adapter is at one end of the bus, it must have termination enabled. If the host adapter is in the middle of the bus, and if both internal and external bus links are present, the host adapter must have its termination disabled, and the devices at each end of the bus must have terminators installed. Unfortunately, the majority of problems that I see with SCSI installations are the result of improper termination.

When installing an external SCSI device, you will usually find the device in a storage enclosure with both input and output SCSI connectors, so that you can use the device in a daisy chain. If the enclosure is at the end of the SCSI bus, an external terminator module most likely will have to be plugged into the second (outgoing) SCSI port to provide proper termination at that end of the bus (see Figure 10.7).

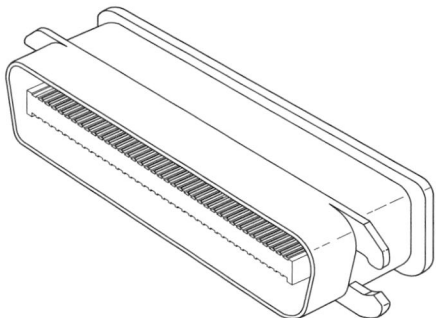

FIG. 10.7 External SCSI device terminator.

External terminator modules are available in a variety of connector configurations, including pass-through designs, which are needed if only one port is available. Pass-through terminators also are commonly used in internal installations in which the device does not have built-in terminating resistors. Many hard drives use pass-through terminators for internal installations to save space on the logic-board assembly (see Figure 10.8).

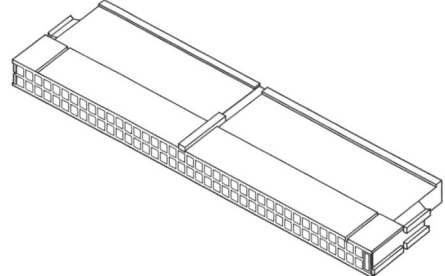

FIG. 10.8 Internal pin-header connector pass-through SCSI terminator.

The pass-through models are required when a device is at the end of the bus and only one SCSI connector is available.

Other configuration items on a SCSI drive can be set via jumpers. Following are several of the most common additional settings that you will find:

■ Start on Command (delayed start)

■ SCSI Parity

■ Terminator Power

■ Synchronous Negotiation

These configuration items are described in the following sections.

Start On Command (Delayed Start). If you have multiple drives installed in a system, it is wise to set them up so that all the drives do not start to spin immediately when the system is powered on. A hard disk drive can consume three or four times more power during the first few seconds after power-on than during normal operation. The motor requires this additional power to get the platters spinning quickly. If several drives are drawing all this power at the same time, the power supply may be overloaded, which can cause the system to hang or to have intermittent startup problems.

Nearly all SCSI drives provide a way to delay drive spinning so that this problem does not occur. When most SCSI host adapters initialize the SCSI bus, they send out a command called Start Unit to each of the ID addresses in succession. By setting a jumper on the hard disk, you can prevent the disk from spinning until it receives the Start Unit command from the host adapter. Because the host adapter sends this command to all the ID addresses in succession, from the highest-priority address (ID 7) to the lowest (ID 0), the higher-priority drives can be made to start first, with each lower-priority drive spinning up sequentially. Because some host adapters do not send the Start Unit command, some drives may simply delay spinup for a fixed number of seconds rather than wait for a command that never will arrive.

If drives are installed in external chassis with separate power supplies, you need not implement the delayed-start function. This function is best applied to internal drives that must be run from the same power supply that runs the system. For internal installations, I recommend setting Start on Command (delayed start) even if you have only one SCSI drive; this setting will ease the load on the power supply by spinning the drive up after the rest of the system has full power. This method is especially good for portable systems and other systems in which the power supply is limited.

SCSI Parity. SCSI Parity is a limited form of error checking that helps ensure that all data transfers are reliable. Virtually all host adapters support SCSI parity checking, so this option should be enabled on every device. The only reason why it exists as an option is that some older host adapters do not work with SCSI parity, so the parity must be turned off.

Terminator Power. The terminators at each end of the SCSI bus require power from at least one device on the bus. In most cases, the host adapter supplies this terminator power; in some cases, however, it does not. For example, parallel port SCSI host adapters typically do not supply terminator power. It is not a problem if more than one device supplies terminator power because each source is diode-protected. For simplicity's sake, many will configure all devices to supply terminator power. If no device supplies terminator power, the bus will not be terminated correctly and will not function properly.

SCSI Synchronous Negotiation. The SCSI bus can run in two modes: *asynchronous* (the default) and *synchronous*. The bus actually switches modes during transfers through a protocol called *synchronous negotiation*. Before data is transferred across the SCSI bus, the sending device (called the *initiator*) and the receiving device (called the *target*) negotiate how the transfer will take place. If both devices support synchronous transfers, they will discover this fact through the negotiation, and the transfer will take place at the faster synchronous rate.

Unfortunately, some older devices do not respond to a request for synchronous transfer and can actually be disabled when such a request is made. For this reason, both host adapters and devices that support synchronous negotiation often have a jumper that can be used to disable this negotiation so it can work with older devices. By default, all devices today should support synchronous negotiation, and this function should be enabled.

Plug-and-Play (PnP) SCSI

Plug-and-Play SCSI was originally released in April 1994. This specification allows SCSI device manufacturers to build PnP peripherals that will automatically configure when used with a PnP operating system. This will allow you to easily connect or reconfigure external peripherals, such as hard disk drives, backup tapes, and CD-ROMs.

To connect SCSI peripherals to the host PC, the specification requires a PnP SCSI host adapter such as PnP ISA or PCI. PnP add-in cards enable a PnP operating system to automatically configure software device drivers and system resources for the host bus interface.

The PnP SCSI specification version 1.0 includes these technical highlights:

■ A single cable-connector configuration

■ Automatic termination of the SCSI bus

■ SCAM (SCSI Configured Automagically) automatic ID assignment

■ Full backward compatibility of PnP SCSI devices with the installed base of SCSI systems.

This should go a long way in making SCSI easier to use for the normal user.

Each SCSI peripheral that you add to your SCSI bus (other than hard disk drives) requires an external driver to make the device work. Hard disks are the exception; driver support for them normally is provided as part of the SCSI host adapter BIOS. These external drivers are specific not only to a particular device, but also to the host adapter.

Recently, two types of standard host adapter interface drivers have become popular, greatly reducing this problem. By having a standard host adapter driver to write to, peripheral makers can more quickly create new drivers that support their devices and then talk to the universal host adapter driver. This arrangement eliminates dependence on one particular type of host adapter. These primary or universal drivers link the host adapter and the operating system.

The *Advanced SCSI Programming Interface (ASPI)* currently is the most popular universal driver, with most peripheral makers writing their drivers to talk to ASPI. The A in ASPI used to stand for Adaptec, the company that introduced it, but other SCSI device vendors have licensed the right to use ASPI with their products. DOS does not support ASPI directly, but it does when the ASPI driver is loaded. Windows 95, Windows NT, and OS/2 2.1 and later versions provide automatic ASPI support for several SCSI host adapters.

Future Domain and NCR have created another interface driver called the *Common Access Method (CAM)*. CAM is an ANSI-approved protocol that enables a single driver to control several host adapters. In addition to ASPI, OS/2 2.1 and later versions currently offer support for CAM. Future Domain also provides a CAM-to-ASPI converter in the utilities that go with its host adapters.

SCSI Configuration Tips

When you are installing a chain of devices on a single SCSI bus, the installation can get complicated very quickly. Here are some tips for getting your setup to function quickly and efficiently:

■ *Start by adding one device at a time.* Rather than plug numerous peripherals into a single SCSI card and then try to configure them at the same time, start by installing the host adapter and a single hard disk. Then you can continue installing devices one at a time, checking to make sure that everything works before moving on.

- *Keep good documentation.* When you add a SCSI peripheral, write down the SCSI ID address and any other switch and jumper settings, such as SCSI Parity, Terminator Power, and Delayed or Remote Start. For the host adapter, record the BIOS addresses, Interrupt, DMA channel, and I/O Port addresses used by the adapter, and any other jumper or configuration settings (such as termination) that might be important to know later.

- *Use proper termination.* Each end of the bus must be terminated, preferably with active or Forced Perfect (FPT) terminators. If you are using any Fast SCSI-2 device, you must use active terminators rather than the cheaper passive types. Even with standard (slow) SCSI devices, active termination is highly recommended. If you have only internal or external devices on the bus, the host adapter and last device on the chain should be terminated. If you have external and internal devices on the chain, you generally will terminate the first and last of these devices but not the SCSI host adapter (which is in the middle of the bus).

- *Use high-quality shielded SCSI cables.* Make sure that your cable connectors match your devices. Use high-quality shielded cables, and observe the SCSI bus-length limitations. Use cables designed for SCSI use, and if possible, stick to the same brand of cable throughout a single SCSI bus. Different brands of cables have different impedance values; this situation sometimes causes problems, especially in long or high-speed SCSI implementations.

Following these simple tips will help minimize problems and leave you with a trouble-free SCSI installation.

IDE Versus SCSI

When you compare the performance and capabilities of IDE and SCSI interfaced drives, you need to consider several factors. These two types of drives are the most popular drives used in PC systems today, and a single manufacturer may make identical drives in both interfaces. Deciding which drive type is best for your system is a difficult decision that depends on many factors.

In most cases, you will find that an IDE drive outperforms an equivalent SCSI drive at a given task or benchmark, and that IDE drives usually cost less than SCSI drives, thus offering better value. In some cases, however, SCSI drives have significant performance and value advantages over IDE drives.

It is interesting to see that SCSI really evolved from IDE, or you could say that both evolved from the ST-506/412 and ESDI interfaces that were once used.

SCSI Hard Disk Evolution and Construction

SCSI is not a disk interface, but a bus that supports SCSI bus interface adapters connected to disk and other device controllers. The first SCSI drives for PCs were standard ST-506/412 or ESDI drives with a separate SCSI bus interface adapter (sometimes called a *bridge controller*) that converted the ST-506/412 or ESDI interfaces to SCSI. This interface originally was in the form of a secondary logic board, and the entire assembly often was mounted in an external case.

The next step was to build the SCSI bus interface "converter" board directly into the drive's own logic board. Today, we call these drives *embedded SCSI drives*, because the SCSI interface is built in.

At that point, there was no need to conform to the absolute specifications of ST-506/412 or ESDI on the internal disk interface, because the only other device that the interface ever would have to talk to was built in as well. Thus, the disk-interface and controller-chipset manufacturers began to develop more customized chipsets that were based on the ST-506/412 or ESDI chipsets already available but offered more features and higher performance. Today, if you look at a typical SCSI drive, you often can identify the chip or chipset that serves as the disk controller on the drive as being exactly the same kind that would be used on an ST-506/412 or ESDI controller or as some evolutionary customized variation thereof.

Consider some examples. An ATA IDE drive must fully emulate the system-level disk-controller interface introduced with the Western Digital WD1003 controller series that IBM used in the AT. These drives must act as though they have a built-in ST-506/412 or ESDI controller; in fact, they actually do. Most of these built-in controllers have more capabilities than the original WD1003 series (usually in the form of additional commands), but they must at least respond to all the original commands that were used with the WD1003.

If you follow the hard drive market, you usually will see that drive manufacturers offer most of their newer drives in both ATA-IDE and SCSI versions. In other words, if a manufacturer makes a particular 500M IDE drive, you invariably will see that the company also make a SCSI model with the same capacity and specifications, which uses the same HDA (Head Disk Assembly) and even looks the same as the IDE version. If you study these virtually identical drives, the only major difference you will find is the additional chip on the logic board of the SCSI version, called a *SCSI Bus Adapter Chip (SBIC)*.

Figures 10.9 and 10.10 show the logic-block diagrams of the WD-AP4200 (a 200M ATA-IDE drive) and WD-SP4200 (a 200M SCSI drive), respectively. These drives use the same HDA; they differ only in their logic boards, and even the logic boards are the same except for the addition of an SBIC on the SCSI drive's logic board.

Notice that even the circuit designs of these two drives are almost identical. Both drives use an LSI (Large Scale Integrated circuit) chip called the WD42C22 Disk Controller and Buffer manager chip. In the ATA drive, this chip is connected through a DMA control chip directly to the AT bus. In the SCSI version, a WD33C93 SCSI bus interface controller chip is added to interface the disk-controller logic to the SCSI bus. In fact, the logic diagrams of these two drives differ only in the fact that the SCSI version has a complete subset of the ATA drive, with the SCSI bus interface controller logic added. This essentially is a very condensed version of the separate drive and bridge controller setups that were used in the early days of PC SCSI.

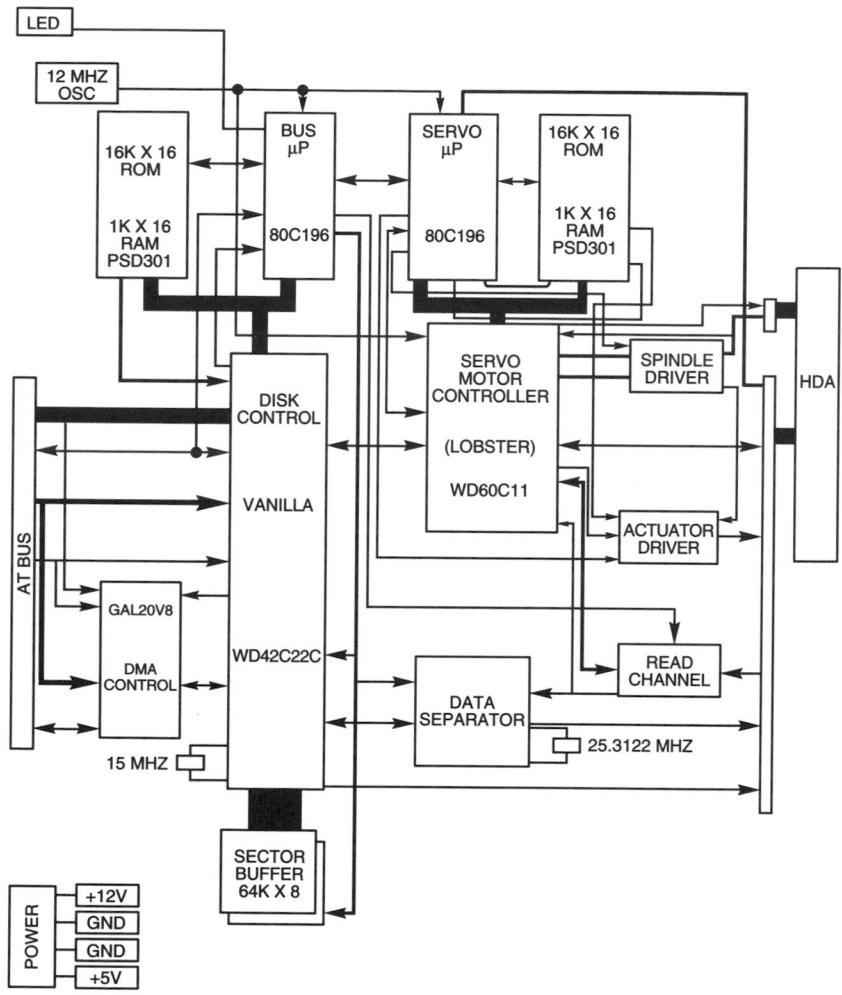

FIG. 10.9 Western Digital WD-AP4200 200M ATA-IDE drive logic-board block diagram.

To top off this example, study the following logic diagram for the WD 1006V-MM1, which is an ST-506/412 controller (see Figure 10.11).

You can clearly see that the main LSI chip onboard is the same WD42C22 disk controller chip used in the IDE and SCSI drives. Here is what the technical reference literature says about that chip:

> *The WD42C22 integrates a high performance, low cost Winchester controller's architecture. The WD42C22 integrates the central elements of a Winchester controller subsystem such as the host interface, buffer manager, disk formatter/controller, encoder/decoder, CRC/ECC (Cyclic Redundancy Check/Error Correction Code) generator/checker, and drive interface into a single 84-pin PQFP (Plastic Quad Flat Pack) device.*

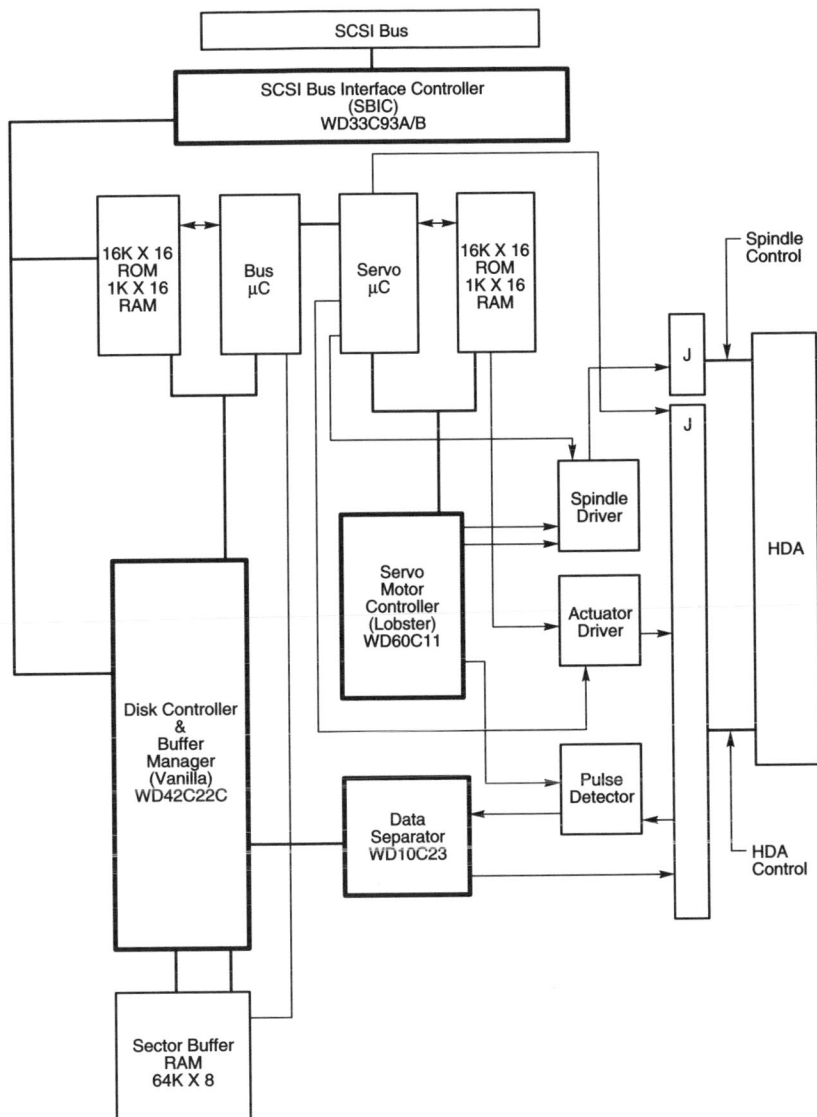

FIG. 10.10   Western Digital WD-SP4200 200M SCSI drive logic-board block diagram.

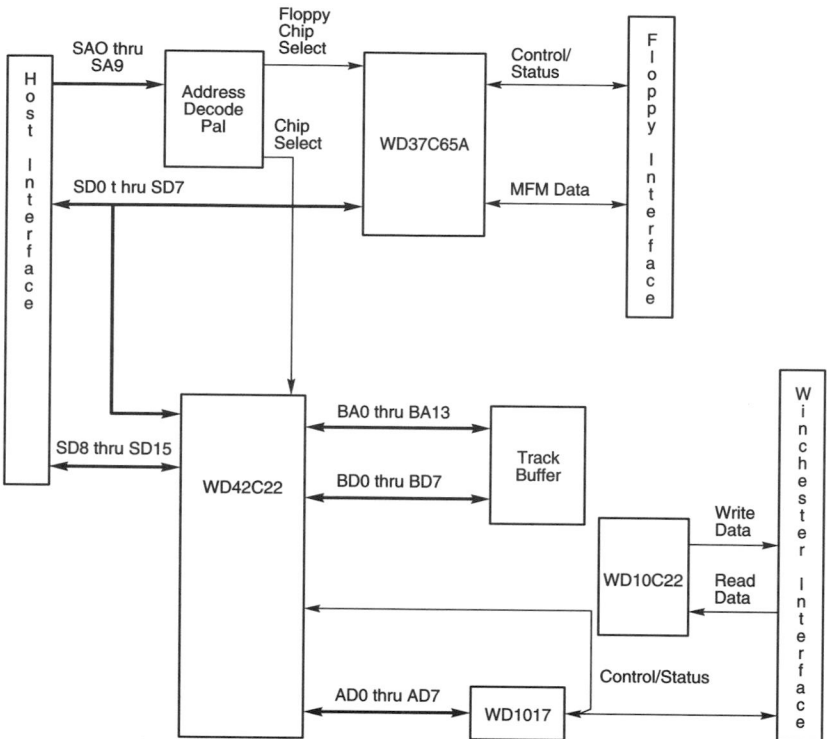

FIG. 10.11   Western Digital WD1006V-MM1 ST-506/412 Disk Controller block diagram.

The virtually identical design of ATA-IDE and SCSI drives is not unique to Western Digital. Most drive manufacturers design their ATA-IDE and SCSI drives the same way, often using these very same WD chips, and disk controller and SCSI bus interface chips from other manufacturers. You now should be able to understand that most SCSI drives are "regular" ATA-IDE drives with SCSI bus logic added. This fact will come up again later in this chapter in the section "SCSI Versus IDE: Advantages and Limitations," which discusses performance and other issues differentiating these interfaces.

For another example, I have several IBM 320M and 400M embedded SCSI-2 hard disks; each of these drives has onboard a WD-10C00 Programmable Disk Controller in the form of a 68-pin PLCC (Plastic Leaded Chip Carrier) chip. The technical literature states:

> *This chip supports ST412, ESDI, SMD and Optical interfaces. It has 27Mbit/sec maximum transfer rate and an internal, fully programmable 48- or 32-bit ECC, 16-bit CRC-CCITT or external user defined ECC polynomial, fully programmable sector sizes, and 1.25 micron low power CMOS design.*

In addition, these particular embedded SCSI drives include the 33C93 SCSI Bus Interface Controller chip, which also is used in the other SCSI drive that I mentioned. Again, there is a distinctly separate disk controller, and the SCSI interface is added on.

So again, most embedded SCSI drives have a built-in disk controller (usually based on previous ST-506/412 or ESDI designs) and additional logic to interface that controller to the SCSI bus (a built-in bridge controller, if you like). Now think about this from a performance standpoint. If virtually all SCSI drives really are ATA-IDE drives with a SCSI Bus Interface Controller chip added, what conclusions can you draw?

First, no drive can perform sustained data transfers faster than the data can actually be read from the disk platters. In other words, the HDA limits performance to whatever it is capable of achieving. Drives can transmit data in short bursts at very high speeds, because they often have built-in cache or read-ahead buffers that store data. Many of the newer high-performance SCSI and ATA-IDE drives have 1M or more of cache memory onboard. No matter how big or intelligent the cache is, however, sustained data transfer still will be limited by the HDA.

Data from the HDA must pass through the disk controller circuits, which, as you have seen, are virtually identical between similar SCSI and ATA-IDE drives. In the ATA-IDE drive, this data then is presented directly to the system bus. In the SCSI drive, however, the data must pass through a SCSI Bus Interface adapter on the drive, travel through the SCSI bus, and then pass through another SCSI Bus Interface controller in the SCSI host adapter card in your system. The longer route that a SCSI transfer must take makes this type of transfer slower than the much more direct ATA-IDE transfer.

The conventional wisdom has been that SCSI always is much faster than IDE; unfortunately, this wisdom is usually wrong. This incorrect conclusion was derived by looking at the raw SCSI and ISA bus performance capabilities. An 8-bit Fast SCSI-2 bus can transfer data at 10M/sec, whereas the 16-bit ISA bus used directly by IDE drives can transfer data at rates ranging from 2M to 8M/sec. Based on these raw transfer rates, SCSI seems to be faster, but the raw transfer rate of the bus is not the limiting factor. Instead, the actual HDA and disk-controller circuitry place the limits on performance. Another point to remember is that unless you are using a PCI, VL-Bus, EISA, or 32-bit MCA SCSI adapter, the SCSI data-transfer speeds will be limited by the host bus performance and by the drive performance.

However, modern operating systems are multitasking, and SCSI devices (with all their additional controller circuitry) function independently of one another, unlike IDE. Therefore, data can be read and written to any of the SCSI devices *simultaneously*. This allows for smoother multitasking and increased overall data throughput. The most advanced operating systems such as Windows NT even allow drive striping. A *striped drive set* is two or more drives that appear to the user as one drive. Data is split between the drives equally, again increasing overall throughput.

Performance

ATA IDE drives currently are used in most PC configurations on the market, because the cost of an IDE-drive implementation is low and the performance capabilities are high. In comparing any given IDE and SCSI drive for performance, you have to look at the capabilities of the HDAs that are involved.

To minimize the variables in this type of comparison, it is easiest to compare IDE and SCSI drives from the same manufacturer that also use the identical HDA. You will find that in most cases, a drive manufacturer makes a given drive available in both IDE and SCSI forms. For example, most hard drive companies make similar SCSI and IDE drives that use identical HDAs and that differ only in the logic board. The IDE version has a logic board with a built-in disk controller and a direct AT Bus interface. The SCSI version has the same built-in disk controller and bus interface circuits, and also a SBIC chip. The SBIC chip is a SCSI adapter that places the drive on the SCSI bus. What you will find, in essence, is that virtually all SCSI drives actually are IDE drives with the SBIC chip added.

The HDAs in these example drives are capable of transferring data at a sustained rate of up to 8M/sec or more. Because the SCSI version always has the additional overhead of the SCSI bus to go through, in almost all cases the directly attached IDE version performs slightly faster.

SCSI Versus IDE: Advantages and Limitations

IDE drives have much less command overhead for a given sector transfer than do SCSI drives. In addition to the drive-to-controller command overhead that both IDE and SCSI must perform, a SCSI transfer involves negotiating for the SCSI bus; selecting the target drive; requesting data; terminating the transfer over the bus; and finally converting the logical data addresses to the required cylinder, head, and sector addresses. This arrangement gives IDE an advantage in sequential transfers handled by a single-tasking operating system. In a multitasking system that can take advantage of the extra intelligence of the SCSI bus, SCSI can have the performance advantage.

SCSI drives offer significant architectural advantages over IDE and other drives. Because each SCSI drive has its own embedded disk controller that can function independently from the system CPU, the computer can issue simultaneous commands to every drive in the system. Each drive can store these commands in a queue and then perform the commands simultaneously with other drives in the system. The data could be fully buffered on the drive and transferred at high speed over the shared SCSI bus when a time slot was available.

Although IDE drives also have their own controllers, they do not operate simultaneously, and command queuing is not supported. In effect, the dual controllers in a dual-drive IDE installation work one at a time so as not to step on each other.

What are the limitations of IDE?

■ IDE does not support overlapped, multitasked I/O.

■ IDE does not support command queuing.

As you can see, SCSI has some advantages over IDE, especially where expansion is concerned, and also with regard to support for multitasking operating systems. Unfortunately, it also costs more to implement.

One final advantage of SCSI is in the portability of external devices. It is easy to take an external SCSI CD-ROM, tape drive, scanner, or even a hard disk and quickly move it to another system. This allows moving peripherals more freely between systems and can be a bonus if you have several systems with which you might want to share a number of peripherals. It is easier to install a new external SCSI device on a system because you will not normally need to open it up at all.

Recommended SCSI Host Adapters

For SCSI host adapters, I normally recommend Adaptec. Their adapters work well and come with the necessary formatting and operating software. Windows 95, Windows 98, Windows NT, and OS/2 have built-in support for Adaptec SCSI adapters. This support is a consideration in many cases, because it frees you from having to deal with additional drivers.

Standard or Fast SCSI is adequately supported by the ISA bus, but if you are going to install a Fast-Wide SCSI bus, or especially an Ultra-Wide bus, then you should consider some form of local bus SCSI adapter, normally PCI. This is because the ISA bus supports a maximum transfer speed of about 8M/sec, while a Fast-Wide SCSI bus runs up to 20M/sec, and an Ultra-Wide SCSI bus runs up to a blazing 40M/sec! In most cases, a local bus SCSI adapter would be a PCI bus version, which is supported in most current PC systems.

One example of a popular SCSI adapter for the PCI bus is the Adaptec AHA-2940AU (see Figure 10.12) and 2940UW. The 2940AU is an Ultra-SCSI adapter and the 2940UW is Ultra-Wide. These adapters are most notable for their ease of installation and use. Virtually all functions on the card can be configured and set through software. No more digging through manuals or looking for Interrupt, DMA, I/O Port, and other jumper settings—everything is controlled by software and saved in a flash memory module on the card. Following are some of the features of this card:

- Complete configuration utility built into the adapter's ROM
- Software-configurable IRQ, ROM addresses, DMA, I/O Port addresses, SCSI Parity, SCSI ID, and other settings
- Software-selectable termination (no resistors to pull out!)
- Enhanced BIOS support for up to 15 drives
- No drivers required for more than two hard disks
- Drive spinup on a per-drive basis available
- Boots from any SCSI ID

Adaptec has full PnP support on all their SCSI adapters. These adapters will be automatically configured in any PC that supports the PnP specification, or they can be configured manually through supplied software in non-PnP systems. The PnP SCSI adapters are highly recommended because they can be configured without opening up the PC! All functions are set by software, and there are no jumpers or switches to attend to. Most peripheral manufacturers write drivers for Adaptec's cards first, so you will not have many compatibility or driver-support problems with any Adaptec card.

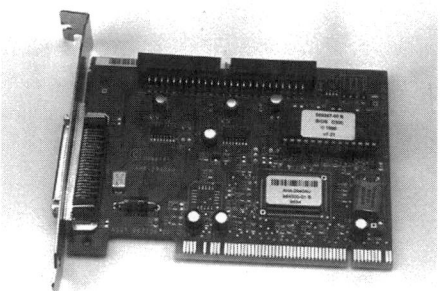

FIG. 10.12 An Adaptec AHA-2940AU SCSI host adapter.

Chapter 11

Communications and Networking

Communications between computers is a major part of the PC computing industry. Whether by using a modem or a network, the majority of PCs are somehow connected to other computers, enabling them to share files, send and receive electronic mail, and access the Internet. This chapter explores the various technologies you can use to expand the reach of your PC across the room or around the world.

It may surprise you to see modems and networking covered in the same chapter of this book, but a modem connection is really just another form of networking. In fact, the Windows 9x and Windows NT operating systems have all but blended the two services into a single entity.

The reason for this combination is that the typical target for a modem connection has changed over the years. For a long time, PC users dialed in to *bulletin board systems* (or BBSs)—proprietary services that provided terminal access to other computers. Online services such as America Online and CompuServe have also been around for many years, but they use proprietary clients and protocols, quite different from those found on local area networks.

With the explosive growth of the Internet, modem and network technologies were joined, because both could use the same client software and protocols. Today, the most popular suite of networking protocols—TCP/IP—is used on both local area networks and the Internet. When you dial into an Internet service provider (or ISP), you are actually connecting to a network, using a modem instead of a network interface card.

> **Note**
>
> Computer networking is an enormous subject, worthy of far more coverage than can be provided here. For a much more detailed examination of networking concepts, refer to Que's *Upgrading and Repairing Networks*, ISBN 0-7897-0181-2. An electronic copy of *Upgrading and Repairing Networks* is included on the CD-ROM with this book.

Asynchronous Modems

For PCs that are not connected to a network by some other means, a modem has become virtually a standard piece of equipment. For many home users, connecting to the Internet is their primary reason for owning a computer. Whether for business, entertainment, or just keeping in touch with friends and family, a modem connection takes an isolated system and makes it a part of a worldwide network.

The word *modem* (from MOdulator/DEModulator) basically describes a device that converts the digital data used by computers into analog signals suitable for transmission over a telephone line, and converts the analog signals back to digital data at the destination. The typical PC modem is an *asynchronous* device, meaning that it transmits data in an intermittent stream of small packets. The receiving system takes the data in the packets and reassembles it into a form the computer can use.

Asynchronous modems transmit each byte of data individually as a separate packet. One byte equals 8 bits, which using the standard ASCII codes is enough data to transmit a single alphanumeric character. For a modem to transmit asynchronously, it must identify the beginning and the end of each byte to the receiving modem. It does this by adding a *start bit* before and a *stop bit* after every byte of data, thus using 10 bits to transmit each byte (see Figure 11.1). For this reason, asynchronous communications have sometimes been referred to as *start-stop communications*. This is in contrast to synchronous communications, in which a continuous stream of data is transmitted at a steady rate.

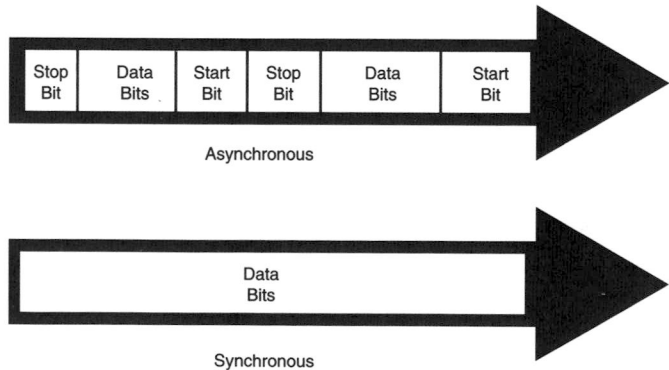

FIG. 11.1 Asynchronous modems frame each byte of data with a start bit and a stop bit, while synchronous communications use an uninterrupted stream of data.

Note

During high-speed modem communications, the start and stop bits are usually not transmitted over the telephone line. Instead, they are eliminated by the data compression algorithm implemented by the modem. However, these bits are part of the data packets generated by the communications software in the computer, and they exist until they reach the modem hardware.

The use of a single start bit is required in all forms of asynchronous communication, but some protocols use more than one stop bit. To accommodate systems with different protocols, communications software products usually enable you to modify the format of the frame used to transmit each byte. The standard format used to describe an asynchronous communications format is *parity–data bits–stop bits*. Almost all asynchronous connections today are therefore abbreviated as N-8-1 (No parity/8 data bits/1 stop bit). The meanings for each of these parameters and their possible variations are as follows:

- *Parity*. Before error-correction protocols became standard modem features, a simple parity mechanism was used to provide basic error checking at the software level. Today, this is almost never used, and the value for this parameter is nearly always set to *none*. Other possible parity values that you might see in a communications software package are *odd*, *even*, *mark*, and *space*.

- *Data Bits*. This parameter indicates how many bits are actually carried in the data portion of the packet (exclusive of the start and stop bits). PCs typically use 8 data bits, but some types of computers use a 7-bit byte, and others may call for other data lengths. Communications programs provide this option to prevent a system from confusing a stop bit with a data bit.

- *Stop Bits*. This parameter specifies how many stop bits are appended to each byte. PCs typically use one stop bit, but other types of protocols may call for the use of 1.5 or 2 stop bits.

In most situations, you will never have to modify these parameters manually, but the controls are almost always provided. In Windows 9x, for example, if you open the Modems Control Panel and look at the Connection page of your modem's Properties dialog box, you will see Data Bits, Parity, and Stop Bits selectors, as shown in Figure 11.2.

Note

Because it has become such a familiar term, even to inexperienced computers users, the word *modem* is frequently used to describe devices that are, strictly speaking, not modems at all. Later in this chapter, you will learn about ISDN and cable modems, neither of which convert digital information to analog signals. However, because these devices look something like a standard modem and are used to connect PCs to the Internet or to other networks, they are called modems.

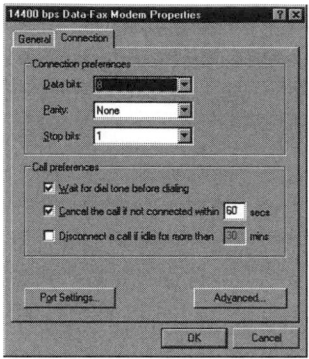

FIG. 11.2 The Windows 9x Control Panel enables you to adjust the connection preferences for your modem.

Modem Standards

For two modems to communicate, they must share the same protocol. A *protocol* is simply a specification that determines how two entities will communicate. Just as humans must share a common language and vocabulary to speak with each other, two computers or two modems must share a common protocol. In the case of modems, the protocol determines the nature of the analog signal that the device creates from the computer's digital data.

Through the years, there have been many standards for modem communications, most of them developed by bipartisan committees and accepted by nearly all modem manufacturers. As the hardware technology has improved, modem communications have become faster and more efficient, and new standards are constantly being developed to take advantage of the hardware's capabilities.

Bell Labs and the CCITT are two of the bodies that have set standards for modem protocols. *CCITT* is an acronym for *Comité Consultatif International Téléphonique et Télégraphique,* a French term that translates into English as the *Consultative Committee on International Telephone and Telegraph.* The organization was renamed the International Telecommunications Union (ITU) in the early 1990s, but the protocols developed under the old name are often referred to as such. Newly developed protocols are referred to as ITU-T standards, which refers to the *Telecommunication Standardization Sector* of the ITU. Bell Labs no longer sets new standards for modems, although several of its older standards are still used. Most modems built in recent years conform to the standards developed by the CCITT.

The ITU is an international body of technical experts responsible for developing data communications standards for the world. The group falls under the organizational umbrella of the United Nations, and its members include representatives from major modem manufacturers, common carriers (such as AT&T), and governmental bodies. The ITU establishes communications standards and protocols in many areas, so one modem often adheres to many different standards, depending on its various features and capabilities. Modem standards can be grouped into the following three areas:

- Modulation standards

  Bell 103
  Bell 212A
  CCITT V.21
  CCITT V.22bis
  CCITT V.29
  CCITT V.32
  CCITT V.32bis
  CCITT V.34
  ITU V.90

- Error-correction

  CCITT V.42

- Data-compression

  V.42bis

Other standards have been developed by different companies (not Bell Labs or the ITU). These are sometimes called *proprietary standards*, even though most of these companies publish the full specifications of their protocols so that other manufacturers can develop modems to work with them. The following list shows some of the proprietary standards that have been popular over the years:

- Modulation

  HST
  PEP
  DIS
  X2
  K56flex

- Error correction

  MNP 1-4
  Hayes V-series

- Data compression

  MNP 5
  CSP

In the interests of backward-compatibility, modem manufacturers typically add support for new standards as they are developed, leaving the support for the old standards in place. As a result, when you evaluate modems, you are likely to see long lists of the standards they support, like those just shown. In most cases, you will want to know whether a modem supports the most recent standards, so support for an archaic and seldom-used protocol should not govern your purchasing decision.

Almost all modems today claim to be *Hayes-compatible*, a phrase that has come to be as meaningless as *IBM-compatible* when referring to PCs. It does not refer to any communication protocol, but instead to the AT command set that operates the modem. AT commands are text strings sent to the modem by software to activate the modem's features. For example, the ATDT command, followed by a telephone number, causes the modem to dial that number using tone dialing mode. Applications that use modems typically generate AT commands for you, but you can control a modem directly using a communications program with a terminal mode, or even the DOS ECHO command.

Assuming that you have a modem connected to your PC's COM2 port, you can demonstrate this capability by issuing the following command from the DOS command line:

    ECHO ATH1 > COM2

This command sends the ATH1 command string out through your computer's COM2 port to the modem, causing it to go "off hook." If your modem has a speaker, you should hear a dial tone. To hang up, issue the following command:

    ECHO ATH0 > COM2

Because almost every modem uses the Hayes command set, this compatibility is a given and should not really affect your purchasing decisions about modems. The basic modem commands may vary slightly from manufacturer to manufacturer, depending on a modem's special features, but the basic AT command set is all but universal. Some modems, most notably U.S. Robotics, allow you to query the command set by simply sending the string **AT$** to the modem.

Note

A list of the basic AT commands can be found in Appendix D, "Technical Reference." However, the best source for the commands used by your modem is the manual that came with the device.

Baud Versus Bits per Second (bps)

When discussing modem transmission speeds, the terms *baud rate* and *bit rate* are often confused. *Baud rate* is the rate at which a signal between two devices changes in one second. If a signal between two modems can change frequency or phase at a rate of 300 times per second, for example, that device is said to communicate at 300 baud.

Sometimes a single modulation change is used to carry a single bit. In that case, 300 baud also equals 300 bits per second (bps). If the modem could signal two bit values for each signal change, the bits per second rate would be twice the baud rate, or 600bps at 300 baud. Most modems transmit several bits per baud, so that the actual baud rate is much slower than the bits per second rate. In fact, people often use the term *baud* incorrectly. We normally are not interested in the raw baud rate, but in the bits per second rate, which is the true gauge of communications speed.

Modulation Standards. Modems start with *modulation*, which is the electronic signaling method used by the modem (from modulator to demodulator). Modulation is a variance in some aspect of the transmitted signal. By modulating the signal using a predetermined pattern, the modem encodes the computer data and sends it to another modem that demodulates (or decodes) the signal. Modems must use the same modulation method to understand each other. Each data rate uses a different modulation method, and sometimes more than one method exists for a particular rate.

The three most popular modulation methods are

- *Frequency-shift keying (FSK).* A form of frequency modulation, otherwise known as *FM*. By causing and monitoring frequency changes in a signal sent over the phone line, two modems can send information.

- *Phase-shift keying (PSK).* A form of phase modulation, in which the timing of the carrier signal wave is altered and the frequency stays the same.

- *Quadrature amplitude modulation (QAM).* A modulation technique that combines phase changes with signal-amplitude variations, resulting in a signal that can carry more information than the other methods.

Table 11.1 lists the protocols that define the modulation standards used by asynchronous modems, along with their maximum transmission rates and duplex modes. A *full duplex* protocol is one in which communications can travel in both directions at the same time and at the same speed. A telephone call, for example, is full duplex, because both parties can speak at the same time. In *half duplex* mode, communications can travel in both directions, but only one side can transmit at a time. A radio call in which only one party can speak at a time is an example of half duplex communications.

Table 11.1   Modem Modulation Standards and Transmission Rates

Protocol	Maximum Transmission Rate (Bits per Second)	Duplex Mode
Bell 103	300bps	Full
CCITT V.21	300bps	Full
Bell 212A	1200bps	Full
ITU V.22	1200bps	Half
ITU V.22bis	2400bps	Full
ITU V.23	1200/75bps	Pseudo-Full
ITU V.29	9600bps	Half
ITU V.32	9600bps	Full
ITU V.32bis	14400bps (14.4Kbps)	Full
ITU V.32fast	28800bps (28.8Kbps)	Full
ITU V.34	28800bps (28.8Kbps)	Full
ITU V.90	56000bps (56Kbps)	Full

Bell 103. Bell 103 is a U.S. and Canadian 300bps modulation standard. It uses FSK modulation at 300 baud to transmit 1 bit per baud. Most higher-speed modems are still capable of communicating using this protocol, even though it is obsolete.

V.21. V.21 is an international data-transmission standard for 300bps communications, similar to Bell 103. Because of some differences in the frequencies they use, Bell 103 modems are not compatible with V.21 modems. This standard was used primarily outside the United States.

Bell 212A. Bell 212A is the U.S. and Canadian 1200bps modulation standard. It uses differential phase-shift keying (DPSK) at 600 baud to transmit 2 bits per baud.

V.22. V.22 is an international 1200bps data-transmission standard. This standard is similar to the Bell 212A standard but is incompatible in some areas, especially in answering a call. This standard was used primarily outside the United States.

V.22bis. V.22bis is a data-transmission standard for 2400bps communications. *Bis* is derived from the Latin meaning *second*, indicating that this data transmission is an improvement to, or follows, V.22. This international standard is used inside and outside the United States. V.22bis uses QAM at 600 baud and transmits 4 bits per baud to achieve 2400bps.

V.23. V.23 is a split data-transmission standard, operating at 1,200bps in one direction and 75bps in the reverse direction. Therefore, the modem is only *pseudo-full-duplex*, meaning that it can transmit data in both directions simultaneously, but not at the maximum data rate. This standard was developed to lower the cost of 1200bps modem technology, which was expensive in the early 1980s. This standard was used primarily in Europe.

V.29. V.29 is a data-transmission standard for 9600bps communications, which defines a half-duplex (one-way) modulation technique. This standard generally is used in Group III facsimile (fax) transmissions, and only rarely in modems. Because V.29 is a half-duplex method, it is substantially easier to implement this high-speed standard than a high-speed full-duplex standard. As a modem standard, V.29 has not been fully defined, so V.29 modems of different brands seldom can communicate with each other. This does not affect fax machines, however, which have a fully defined standard.

V.32. V.32 is a full-duplex (two-way) data transmission standard that runs at 9600bps. It is a full modem standard and also includes forward error-correcting and negotiation standards. V.32 uses *TCQAM (trellis coded quadrature amplitude modulation)* at 2400 baud to transmit 4 bits per baud, resulting in the 9600bps transmission speed.

The trellis coding is a special forward error-correction technique that creates an additional bit for each packet of 4. This extra check bit is used to allow on-the-fly error correction to take place at the receiving end of the transmission. It also greatly increases the resistance of V.32 to noise on the telephone line.

In the past, V.32 has been expensive to implement because the technology it requires is complex. Because a one-way, 9600bps stream uses almost the entire bandwidth of the phone line, V.32 modems implement echo cancellation, meaning that they cancel out the overlapping signal that their own modems transmit and just listen to the other modem's signal. This procedure is complicated and was at one time costly. Advances in lower-cost chipsets then made these modems inexpensive, and they were the *de facto* 9,600bps standard for some time.

V.32bis. V.32bis is a 14,400bps extension to V.32. This protocol uses TCQAM modulation at 2,400 baud to transmit 6 bits per baud, for an effective rate of 14,400bps. The trellis coding makes the connection more reliable. This protocol is also a full-duplex modulation protocol, with a fallback to V.32 if the phone line is impaired.

V.32fast. V.32fast, or V.FC (Fast Class) as it is also called, is a standard that was developed by Rockwell and introduced before V.34. V.32fast is an extension to V.32 and V.32bis, but offers a transmission speed of 28,800bps. It has since been superseded by V.34. If you buy a used 28,800bps modem, make sure that it is not one of the devices that supports V.32fast and not V.34. Modems like this are incompatible with many of the V.34 devices now in general use.

V.34. V.34 has superseded all the other 28.8Kbps standards and is the current state-of-the-art in purely analog modem communications. It has been proven as the most reliable standard of communication at 28.8Kbps. A recent annex to the V.34 standard also defines optional higher speeds of 31.2 and 33.6Kbps. Most of the V.34 modems now being produced are capable of transmitting at these higher speeds, and existing V.34 modems that are designed using sophisticated Digital Signal Processors (DSPs) can easily be upgraded to 33.6Kbps. In most cases, you do this by downloading a Modem ROM upgrade from the manufacturer and then running a program to "flash" the modem's ROM with the new code.

V.34 is the fastest communication now possible over an analog serial connection. Because of limitations inherent in the telephone system, it is also very likely to be the fastest that purely analog communications are going to get. The 56k standards that represent the next increment in modem communication speed require a digital connection at one end, and are therefore not purely analog. Other high-speed communication technologies such as ISDN and cable network connections eschew analog communications entirely, so they cannot be called modems.

V.90. V.90 is the ITU-T designation for a 56Kbps communication standard that reconciles the conflict between the U.S. Robotics (3Com) X2 and Rockwell K56Flex modem specifications. See "56K Modems," later in this chapter, for more information.

Error-Correction Protocols. *Error correction* refers to the capability of some modems to identify errors during a transmission, and to automatically resend data that appears to have been damaged in transit. Although it is also possible to implement error correction using software, this places an additional burden on the computer's expansion bus and processor. By performing error correction using dedicated hardware in the modem, errors are detected and corrected before any data is passed to the computer's CPU.

As with modulation, both modems must adhere to the same standard for error correction to work. Fortunately, most modem manufacturers use the same error correction protocols.

MNP 1-4. This is a proprietary standard that was developed by Microcom to provide basic error correction. The Microcom Networking Protocol (MNP) is examined in greater detail in the "Proprietary Standards" section, later in this chapter.

V.42. V.42 is an error-correction protocol, with fallback to MNP 4, and version 4 is an error-correction protocol as well. Because the V.42 standard includes MNP compatibility through Class 4, all MNP 4-compatible modems can establish error-controlled connections with V.42 modems.

This standard uses a protocol called *LAPM (Link Access Procedure for Modems)*. LAPM, like MNP, copes with phone-line impairments by automatically retransmitting data corrupted during transmission, assuring that only error-free data passes between the modems. V.42 is considered to be better than MNP 4 because it offers approximately a 20% higher transfer rate due to its more intelligent algorithms.

Data-Compression Standards. *Data compression* refers to a built-in capability in some modems to compress the data they're sending, thus saving time and money for modem users. Depending on the type of files the modem is sending, data can be compressed to nearly one-fourth its original size, effectively quadrupling the speed of the modem. For example, a 14400bps modem with compression can yield transmission rates of up to 57600bps, and a 28800bps can yield up to 115200bps.

As with error correction, data compression can also be performed with software. Data can only be compressed once, so if you are transmitting files that are already in a compressed form, such as ZIP archives or GIF images, there will be no palpable increase in speed from the modem's hardware compression. The transmission of plain text files and uncompressed bitmaps, however, is accelerated greatly by modem compression.

MNP 5. Microcom continued the development of its MNP protocols to include a compression protocol called MNP 5. This protocol is examined more fully in the section "Proprietary Protocols," later in this chapter.

V.42bis. V.42bis is a CCITT data-compression standard similar to MNP Class 5, but providing about 35% better compression. V.42bis is not actually compatible with MNP Class 5, but nearly all V.42bis modems include the MNP 5 data-compression capability as well.

This protocol can sometimes quadruple throughput, depending on the compression technique. This fact has led to some deceptive advertising; for example, a 2400bps V.42bis modem might advertise "9600bps throughput" by including V.42bis as well, but this would be possible in only extremely optimistic cases, such as when sending text files that are very loosely packed. In the same manner, many 9600bps V.42bis makers now advertise "up to 38.4Kbps throughput" by virtue of the compression. Just make sure that you see the truth behind such claims.

V.42bis is superior to MNP 5 because it analyzes the data first and then determines whether compression would be useful. V.42bis only compresses data that needs compression. MNP 5 always attempts to compress the data, which slows down throughput on previously compressed files.

To negotiate a standard connection using V.42bis, V.42 also must be present. Therefore, a modem with V.42bis data compression is assumed to include V.42 error correction. When combined, these two protocols result in an error-free connection that has the maximum data compression possible.

Proprietary Standards. In addition to the industry-standard protocols for modulation, error correction, and data compression that are generally defined and approved by the ITU-T, several protocols in these areas were invented by various companies and included in their products without any official endorsement by any standards body. Some of these protocols have been quite popular at times and became pseudo-standards of their own.

The most successful proprietary protocols are the MNP (Microcom Networking Protocol) standards developed by Microcom. These error-correction and data-compression protocols are supported widely by other modem manufacturers as well.

Another company that has been successful in establishing proprietary protocols as limited standards is U.S. Robotics (now part of 3COM), with its HST (high-speed technology) modulation protocols. Because of an aggressive marketing campaign with BBS operators, HST modems captured a large portion of the market in the 1980s.

The following sections examine these and other proprietary modem protocols.

HST. HST is a 14,400bps and 9,600bps modified half-duplex proprietary modulation protocol developed by U.S. Robotics. Although commonly used by BBSs in the 1980s, the HST was made all but extinct by the introduction of V.32 modems at very competitive prices. HST modems run at 9,600bps or 14,400bps in one direction and 300bps or 450bps in the other direction. This is an ideal protocol for interactive sessions. Because echo-cancellation circuitry is not required, costs are lower.

U.S. Robotics also marketed modems that used the ITU-T standard protocols and the U.S. Robotics proprietary standard. These dual-standard modems incorporated both V.32bis and HST protocols, giving you the best of the standard and proprietary worlds and enabling you to connect to virtually any other system at the maximum communications rate. They were at one time among the best modems available; I used and recommended them for many years.

DIS. DIS is a 9,600bps proprietary modulation protocol by CompuCom, which uses *dynamic impedance stabilization (DIS)*, with claimed superiority in noise rejection over V.32. Implementation was very inexpensive, but like HST, only one company made modems that supported the DIS standard. Because of the lower costs of V.32 and V.32bis, this proprietary standard quickly disappeared.

MNP. MNP offers end-to-end error correction, meaning that the modems are capable of detecting transmission errors and requesting retransmission of corrupted data. Some levels of MNP also provide data compression.

As MNP evolved, different classes of the standard were defined, describing the extent to which a given MNP implementation supports the protocol. Most current implementations support Classes 1 through 5. Higher classes usually are unique to modems manufactured by Microcom, Inc. because they are proprietary.

MNP generally is used for its error-correction capabilities, but MNP Classes 4 and 5 also provide performance increases, with Class 5 offering real-time data compression. The lower classes of MNP are not important to today's modem user, but they are included in the following list for the sake of completeness:

- *MNP Class 1 (block mode)* uses asynchronous, byte-oriented, half-duplex (one-way) transmission. This method provides about 70% efficiency and error correction only, so it's rarely used today.

- *MNP Class 2 (stream mode)* uses asynchronous, byte-oriented, full-duplex (two-way) transmission. This class also provides error correction only. Because of protocol overhead (the time it takes to establish the protocol and operate it), throughput at Class 2 is only about 84% of that for a connection without MNP, delivering about 202 cps (characters per second) at 2,400bps (240 cps is the theoretical maximum). Class 2 is used rarely today.

- *MNP Class 3* incorporates Class 2 and is more efficient. It uses asynchronous, bit-oriented, full-duplex method. The improved procedure yields throughput about 108% of that of a modem without MNP, delivering about 254 cps at 2,400bps.

- *MNP Class 4* is a performance-enhancement class that uses Adaptive Packet Assembly and Optimized Data Phase techniques. Class 4 improves throughput and performance by about 5%, although actual increases depend on the type of call and connection, and can be as high as 25% to 50%.

- *MNP Class 5* is a data-compression protocol that uses a real-time adaptive algorithm. It can increase throughput up to 50%, but the actual performance of Class 5 depends on the type of data being sent. Raw text files allow the highest increase, although program files cannot be compressed as much and the increase in throughput is smaller. On precompressed data (files already compressed with PKZIP, for example), MNP 5 decreases performance, and therefore was often disabled on BBS systems and online services that dealt primarily with precompressed files.

V-Series. The Hayes V-series is a proprietary error-correction protocol by Hayes that was used in some of its modems. However, the advent of lower-cost V.32 and V.32bis modems (even from Hayes) made the V-series all but extinct. These modems used a modified V.29 protocol, which is sometimes called a *ping-pong protocol* because it has one high-speed channel and one low-speed channel that alternate back and forth.

CSP. The *CSP (CompuCom Speed Protocol)* is an error-correction and data-compression protocol available on CompuCom DIS modems.

Fax Modem Standards. Facsimile technology is a science unto itself, although it has many similarities to data communications. These similarities have led to the combination of data and fax capabilities into the same modem. Virtually all the modems on the market today support fax and data communications.

Over the years, the CCITT has set international standards for fax transmission. This has led to the grouping of faxes into one of four groups. Each group (I through IV) uses different technology and standards for transmitting and receiving faxes. Groups I and II are relatively slow and provide results that are unacceptable by today's standards, and are therefore not discussed in detail here. Group III is the universal standard in use today by virtually all fax machines, including those combined with modems.

The Group III Fax Protocol. The Group III protocol specifies a maximum fax transmission rate of 9,600 baud and two levels of image resolution: standard (203×98 pixels) and fine (303×196 pixels). The protocol also calls for the use of a data-compression protocol defined by the CCITT (called T.4.) and V.29 modulation.

There are two general subdivisions within the Group III fax standard—Class 1 and Class 2. The difference between the two is that in Class 1 faxing, the fax software generates the images and handles the session protocol and timing with the receiving system. In Class 2, the software generates an image for each page and passes it to the fax modem, which handles the session protocol and timing. Thus, with Class 1, compatibility with other fax devices is more the responsibility of the software, while with Class 2, compatibility is more the responsibility of the modem. While both classes call for additional fax-related AT commands to be recognized and acted upon by the modem, the Class 2 command set is much larger, consisting of over 40 new instructions.

The Class 1 specification was readily accepted and ratified by the CCITT in 1988, but the Class 2 document was rejected repeatedly. However, some manufacturers have designed Class 2 modems using the draft (that is, unratified) version of the standard. Today, nearly all fax modems support the Group III, Class 1 standard, and this should be the minimum acceptable requirement for any fax modem you intend to purchase. Class 2 support is an additional benefit, but by itself does not provide the almost universal compatibility of Class 1.

The Group IV Fax Protocol. Whereas Groups I through III are analog in nature (such as modems) and are designed to use standard analog telephone lines, the Group IV specification calls for the digital transmission of fax images and requires an ISDN or other digital connection to the destination system. Group IV supports fax resolutions of up to 400 dpi and uses a newer CCITT data compression protocol called T.6.

For a digital solution such as Group IV faxing to function, the connection between the source and the destination system must be fully digital. This means that even though your office may use a PBX-based telephone system that is digital, and your telephone carrier may use digital connections, it is very likely that there is at least some analog communication involved in the circuit, such as between the PBX and the local telephone service. Until the telephone system has been converted to a fully digital network (a monumental task), Group IV fax systems will not be able to replace Group III systems.

56K Modems

In the ever-continuing quest for speed, modem manufacturers have overcome what was considered to be an unbreakable ceiling for asynchronous data transfer rates over standard telephone lines, and have released modems that support speeds of up to 56,000bps (or 56Kbps). To understand how this additional speed was achieved, you must consider the basic principle of modem technology, that is, the digital-to-analog conversion.

As you've learned, a traditional modem converts data from digital to analog form so it can travel over the Public Switched Telephone Network (PSTN). At the destination system, another modem converts the analog data back to its digital form. This conversion from digital to analog and back causes some speed loss. Even though the phone line is physically capable of carrying data at 56Kbps or more, the effective maximum speed because of the conversions is about 33.6Kbps. A man by the name of Shannon came up with a law (Shannon's Law) stating that the maximum possible error-free data communications rate over the PSTN is approximately 35Kbps, depending on the noise present.

However, Shannon's Law assumes a fully analog connection between the two modems. That is not the case in most of the United States today. In urban areas, most circuits are digital until they reach the telephone company's central office (CO), to which your phone line is connected. The CO converts the digital signal into an analog signal before sending it to your home.

Considering the fact that the phone system is largely digital, you can—in some cases—omit the initial digital-to-analog conversion and send a purely digital signal over the PSTN to the recipient's CO. Thus, there is only one digital-to-analog conversion needed, instead of two or more. The result is that you can theoretically increase the speed of the data transmission, in one direction only, beyond the 35Kbps specified by Shannon's Law, to nearly the 56Kbps speed supported by the telephone network. The transmission in the other direction is still limited to the V.34 maximum of 33.6Kbps.

56K Limitations. Thus, 56K modems can increase data transfer speeds beyond the limits of V.34 modems, but they are subject to certain limitations. Unlike standard modem technologies, you cannot buy two 56K modems, install them on two computers, and achieve 56Kbps speeds. One side of the connection must use a special digital modem that connects directly to the PSTN without a digital-to-analog conversion.

56K modems, therefore, can be used only to connect to Internet service providers or other hosting services that have invested in the necessary infrastructure to support the connection. Because the ISP has the digital connection to the PSTN, its downstream transmissions to your computer are accelerated, while your communications back to the ISP are not. On a practical level, this means you can surf the Web and download files more quickly, but if you host a Web server on your PC, your users will realize no speed gain, because the upstream traffic is not accelerated.

Also, there can only be one digital-to-analog conversion in the downstream connection from the ISP to your computer. This is dictated by the nature of the physical connection to your local telephone carrier. If additional conversions are involved in your connection, then 56K technology will not work for you; 33.6Kbps will be your maximum possible speed. Several modem manufacturers have made software available on the Internet that tests your phone line and determines whether it can accommodate 56Kbps connections.

> **Caution**
>
> 56K modem communications are also highly susceptible to slowdowns caused by line noise. Your telephone line may be perfectly adequate for voice communications, and even lower-speed modem communications, but inaudible noise can easily degrade a 56K connection to the point at which there is only a marginal increase over a 33.6Kbps modem, or even no increase at all.

56K Standards. To achieve a high-speed connection, both modems and your ISP's (or other hosting service to which you connect), must support the same 56K technology, and here rises the biggest issue surrounding 56K compatibility. As is often the case, modem manufacturers were anxious to bring the latest technology to market, so two companies released products using competing 56K standards. U.S. Robotics (now part of 3COM) introduced a line of 56K modems using Texas Instruments chipsets that they called *X2*, while Rockwell, a manufacturer of modem chipsets, released another 56K standard that it called *K56flex*. Naturally, these two standards were not compatible, and the rest of the modem industry rapidly polarized, supporting one standard or the other. The result was a latter-day version of the Beta-VHS conflict of the 1970s.

> **Note**
>
> To complicate matters further, it was discovered only days before U.S. Robotics shipped its first X2 modems that an old FCC regulation known as Part 68 specifies the maximum amount of power that you can run through a PSTN phone line. Because faster communications require more power, this regulation effectively limits modem communications to a maximum speed of approximately 53Kbps. The regulation was created because increasing the power transmitted over a line beyond a certain point causes increased interference, called *crosstalk*, on neighboring lines. The FCC implemented this regulation long ago, not intending it to apply specifically to modems, and is currently re-evaluating its position.

As a result of having two standards, users were forced either to wait and see which technology their ISPs would adopt, or commit to one of the two standards and then find an ISP that supported it. Because the investment in 56K technology was so much more substantial for an ISP, many of them waited to see which of the two standards would win out by becoming either a *de facto* or a *de jure* standard.

V.90. Fortunately, this problem is in the process of being resolved. On February 5, 1998, the ITU-T approved a "determination" for a 56K modem standard called V.90. A determination indicates that the technical aspects of the standard are in place, and final ratification of the standard is expected in the fall of 1998. Now that an official standard exists, all modem manufacturers will upgrade their products to support V.90, and interoperability between devices supporting the two earlier standards should be possible.

Because the X2 and K56flex implementations are fundamentally similar in the hardware requirements described earlier, it should be possible to modify existing modems of either type to support V.90 by upgrading their firmware using a flash update or a simple chip replacement. However, this is for the individual modem manufacturers to decide.

Modem Recommendations

A modem for a PC can take the form either of an external device with its own power supply that plugs into a PC's serial port, or an internal expansion card that you insert into a bus slot inside the computer. Most manufacturers of modems have both internal and external versions of the same models.

External versions are slightly more expensive because they include a separate case and power supply. Both are equally functional, however, and the decision as to which type you use should typically depend on whether you have a free bus slot or serial port, how much room you have on your desk, the capabilities of your system's internal power supply, and how comfortable you are with opening up your computer.

I have often preferred external modems because of the visual feedback they provide through indicator lights. These lights make it easy to see if the modem is still connected and transmitting or receiving data. However, some communication programs today include onscreen simulations of the lights, providing the same information.

There are other situations, too, where an internal modem is preferable. In case your computer's serial ports do not have buffered UART chips such as the 16550, many internal modems include an onboard 16550 UART. This onboard UART with the modem saves you the trouble of upgrading the UART serial port. Also, external 56K modems can be hampered from achieving their full speed by the limitations of the computer's serial port. An internal model may be preferable instead.

◄◄ See "UARTs," p. 587

Not all modems that function at the same speed have the same functionality. Many modem manufacturers produce modems running at the same speed, but with different feature sets at different price points. The more expensive modems usually support advanced features such as distinctive ring support and caller ID. When purchasing a modem, be sure that it supports all the features you need. It's also a good idea to make sure the software you plan to use, including the operating system, has been certified for use with the modem you select.

Most of the brand-name modems on the market today support a wide range of modulation, error-correction, and data-connection standards. This is because most modems are *auto-negotiating*; that is, when they connect to another modem they implement the most efficient set of protocols they have in common. Even if the two modems do not agree on the most advanced protocol of a particular type, they are likely to have at least one protocol in common.

As to speed, the only reason to avoid a 56K modem was the conflict between the X2 and K56flex standards. Once the manufacturers on both sides have implemented V.90, there will be no reason not to buy these modems. The price difference between a V.90 and a V.34 will be minimal, and even if you cannot immediately make use of 56K capabilities, you still get the 33.6Kbps speed provided by V.34 and the capability to run at 56K when your situation allows it.

Integrated Services Digital Network (ISDN)

To get past the speed limitations of asynchronous modems, you have to go completely digital, and *ISDN* is the next step in telecommunications. ISDN makes the break from the old technology of analog data transfer to the newer digital data transfer. With ISDN, you can connect to the Internet at speeds of up to 128Kbps.

ISDN has been available for over 10 years but has only recently become a practical solution for private users. This was mostly due to the difficulties involved in arranging for the installation of the service with the telephone company. Two years ago, it was difficult to find someone at most regional phone companies who had even heard of ISDN, but there are now quite a few businesses that provide turnkey solutions, including ISP services, ISDN hardware, and negotiations with the phone company.

While it can be used for voice communications, ISDN is not like a normal telephone connection, even though it uses your existing telephone wiring. To achieve high speeds, both ends of the connection must be digital, so you would typically set up an ISDN line specifically for connecting to an Internet service provider that also uses ISDN. Businesses also use higher bandwidth ISDN connections for Internet access or to connect local area networks in remote offices.

ISDN is also not like a leased telephone line, however, which permanently connects two specific locations. Your software still dials the number of your intended destination (although it is a special ISDN number), and breaks the connection (that is, hangs up) when the session is finished. Thus, you can change to a different ISP that supports ISDN, if necessary, without dealing with the phone company again.

ISDN Services

On an ISDN connection, bandwidth is divided into *bearer channels* (B channels) that run at 64Kbps and a *delta channel* (D channel) that runs at 16Kbps or 64Kbps, depending on the type of service. The B channels carry voice transmissions or user data, and the D channel carries control traffic.

There are two types of ISDN service: Basic Rate Interface (BRI) and Primary Rate Interface (PRI). The BRI service is intended for private and home users and consists of two B channels and one 16Kbps D channel, for a total of 144Kbps. The PRI service is oriented more toward business use, such as for PBX connections to the telephone company's CO. In North America and Japan, the PRI service consists of 23 B channels and one 64Kbps D channel for a total of 1536Kbps, running over a standard T1 interface. In Europe, the PRI service is 30 B channels and one 64Kbps D channel, totaling 1,984Kbps, corresponding to the E1 telecommunications standard. For businesses that require more bandwidth than one PRI connection provides, it's possible to use one D channel to support multiple PRI channels using *Non-Facility Associated Signaling* (NFAS).

> **Note**
>
> When speaking of ISDN connections, one kilobyte equals 1,000 bytes, not 1,024 bytes as in standard computer applications.

It is possible to aggregate the bandwidth of multiple B channels using a protocol such as *Multilink PPP* or *BONDING* (developed by the Bandwidth ON Demand INteroperability Group), so you can use the BRI service to establish a single 128Kbps connection to the Internet. You can also connect multiple devices to a single ISDN connection and transmit multiple signals to different destinations at the same time, thus replacing several standard telephone lines.

To have an ISDN connection installed, you must be within 18,000 feet (about 3.4 miles or 5.5 km) of the CO for the BRI service. For greater distances, expensive repeater devices are needed, and some telephone companies may not offer the service at all. Most of the existing telephone wiring in the United States is capable of supporting ISDN communications, so you usually need not pay for the installation of new telephone cable.

Prices for ISDN service vary widely, depending on your location. In the United States, the initial installation fee can be in the area of $100–$150, depending on whether you are converting an existing line or installing a new one. The monthly charges are typically $30–$50, and often there is a connect-time charge as well, ranging from 1 to 6 cents per minute. Keep in mind that you also must purchase an ISDN terminal adapter for your PC and possibly other hardware as well, and that these charges are only for the telephone company's ISDN service. You must also pay your ISP for access to the Internet at ISDN speeds.

ISDN Hardware

To connect a PC to an ISDN connection, you must have a hardware component called a *terminal adapter (TA)*. The terminal adapter takes the form of an expansion board or an external device connected to a serial port, much like a modem. In fact, terminal adapters are often mistakenly referred to as ISDN modems. Actually, they are not modems at all, because they do not perform analog/digital conversions.

There are two different interfaces to the ISDN service. The *U-Interface* consists of a single pair of wires leading to the telephone company's CO. The *Subscriber/Termination (S/T) Interface* consists of two pairs of wires that typically run from a wall jack to your terminal adapter. The device that converts the U-Interface signal to the S/T Interface is called a *network termination device*, or *NT-1*.

Some terminal adapters include an NT-1 integrated into the hardware, enabling you to connect the U-Interface directly to the computer. This is an excellent solution as long as the computer is the only device that you plan to connect to the ISDN line. If you want to connect multiple devices, or if your terminal adapter does not include an NT-1, then you must purchase an NT-1 separately. Another alternative is to get a network-ready terminal adapter that you can connect to your current NIC. This is an especially good alternative if you have several PCs, as you can share one TA among them.

> **Caution**
>
> When purchasing an ISDN terminal adapter, you will almost always want to purchase an internal version. A terminal adapter with compression can easily exceed a serial port's capability to reliably send and receive data. Consider that even a moderate 2:1 compression ratio exceeds the maximum rated speed of 232Kbps that most high-speed COM ports support.

Leased Lines

For users with high bandwidth requirements (and deep pockets), dedicated leased lines provide digital service between two locations at speeds that can far exceed ISDN. A leased line is a permanent 24-hour connection to a particular location that can only be changed by the telephone company. Businesses use leased lines to connect LANs in remote locations or to connect to the Internet through a service provider. Leased lines are available at various speeds, as described in the following sections.

T-1 Connections

To connect networks in distant locations, networks that must support a large number of Internet users, or especially organizations that will be hosting their own Internet services, a T-1 connection may be the wise investment. A *T-1* is a digital connection running at 1.55Mbps. This is more than 10 times faster than an ISDN link. A T-1 may be split (or *fractioned*), depending on how it is to be used. It can be split into 24 individual 64Kbps lines, or left as a single high-capacity pipeline. Some Internet service providers allow you to lease any portion of a T-1 connection that you want (in 64Kbps increments).

T-1 links in the United States usually cost several thousand dollars per month, plus a substantial installation fee. But, for a large organization that requires a lot of bandwidth, it can be more economical to install a higher-capacity service and grow into it, rather than constantly upgrade the link.

T-3 Connections

Equivalent in throughput to approximately 30 T-1 lines, a T-3 connection runs at 45Mbps, and is suitable for use by very large networks and university campuses. Pricing information falls into the "if you have to ask, you can't afford it" category.

CATV Networks

Although ISDN represents a significant increase in speed over standard modem technologies, the installation difficulties and the expense (especially when there are connect-time charges) may not be justified. The next step up in speed is a cable TV (CATV) network connection, and this service, when available, is usually less expensive than ISDN.

Cable Modems

As with ISDN, the device used to connect a PC to a CATV network is somewhat inaccurately called a modem. In fact, the so-called cable modem (a name I will continue to use, for the sake of convenience) is actually a great deal more. The device does indeed modulate and demodulate, but it also functions as a tuner, a network bridge, an encryptor, an SNMP agent, and a hub.

To connect your PC to a CATV network, you do not use a serial port as with standard modem technologies. Instead, you must install a standard Ethernet network interface adapter into a bus slot. The Ethernet adapter connects to the cable modem with the same type of twisted-pair cable used on local area networks. In fact, your PC and the cable modem actually form a two-node LAN, with the modem functioning as a *hub*.

The cable modem also connects to the CATV network using the same coaxial cable connection as your cable TV service. Thus, the cable modem functions as a *bridge* between the tiny twisted-pair network in your home and the *hybrid fiber/coax* (HFC) network that connects all the cable customers in your neighborhood.

CATV Bandwidth

Cable TV uses what is known as a *broadband* network, meaning that the bandwidth of the connection is split to carry many signals at the same time. These various signals correspond to the various channels you see on your TV. A typical HFC network provides approximately 750MHz of bandwidth, and each channel requires 6MHz. Therefore, since the television channels start at about 50MHz, you would find channel 2 in the 50MHz–56MHz range, channel 3 at 57MHz–63MHz, and continuing on up the frequency spectrum. At this rate, an HFC network can support about 110 channels.

For data networking purposes, cable systems typically allocate one channel's worth of bandwidth in the 50MHz–750MHz range for downstream traffic (that is, traffic coming into the cable modem from the CATV network). In this way, the cable modem functions as a *tuner*, just like your cable TV box, ensuring that your PC receives signals from the correct frequency.

Upstream traffic (data sent from your PC to the network) uses a different channel. Cable TV systems commonly reserve the bandwidth from 5MHz to 42MHz for upstream signals of various types (such as those generated by cable TV boxes that enable you to order pay-per-view programming). Depending on the bandwidth available, you may find that your CATV provider does not furnish the same high speed upstream as it does downstream. This is called an *asymmetrical* network.

Note

Because the upstream speed often does not match the downstream speed, and for other network-related reasons, cable TV connections are usually not practical for hosting World Wide Web servers and other Internet services. This is largely deliberate, as most CATV providers are currently targeting their traditional home user market. As the technology matures, however, this type of Internet connection is likely to spread to the business world as well.

The amount of data throughput that the single 6MHz downstream channel can support is dependent on the type of modulation used at the *head end* (that is, the system to which your PC connects over the network). Using a technology called *64 QAM* (quadrature amplitude modulation), the channel may be able to carry up to 27Mbps of downstream data. A variant called *256 QAM* can boost this to 36Mbps.

You must realize, however, that you will not achieve anything even approaching this throughput on your PC. First of all, the Ethernet adapter used to connect to the cable modem is limited to 10Mbps, but even this is well beyond the real-life results you will achieve. As with any local area network, you are sharing the available bandwidth with other users. All of your neighbors who also subscribe to the service make use of the same 6MHz channel. As more users are added, more systems are contending for the same bandwidth, and throughput goes down.

CATV Security

Because your PC is sharing a network with other users in your neighborhood, and because the traffic is bidirectional, the security of your PC and the network becomes an issue. In most cases, some form of encryption is involved to prevent unauthorized access to the network. As with your cable TV box, the cable modem may contain encryption circuitry that is needed to access the network. Your CATV provider may also supply encryption software that uses a special protocol to log you on to the network. This protects the CATV provider from non-paying users, but it doesn't protect you.

If you use an operating system such as Windows 9x that has built-in peer networking capabilities, you may be able to see your neighbors' computers on the network. The operating system has settings that enable you to specify whether other network users can access your drives. If these settings are configured improperly, your neighbors may be able to view, access, and even delete the files on your hard drives. Be sure that the technician from the cable company installing the service addresses this problem.

CATV Performance

The fact that you are sharing the CATV network with other users doesn't mean that the performance of a cable modem isn't usually spectacular. Typically, the realized throughput hovers around 512Kbps, almost 10 times that of the fastest modem connection and four times that of ISDN. You will find the World Wide Web to be an entirely new experience at this speed. Those huge audio and video clips you avoided in the past now download in seconds, and you will soon fill your hard drives with all the free software available.

Add to this the fact that the service is typically quite reasonably priced. Remember that the CATV provider is replacing both the telephone company and your ISP in your Internet access solution. The price may be about $40 per month, twice that of a normal dial-up ISP account, but it is far less than ISDN, does not require a telephone line, and provides you with 24-hour access to the Internet. The only drawback is that the service may not yet be available in your area. In my opinion, this technology exceeds all the other Internet access solutions available today in speed, economy, and convenience.

Direct Cable Connections

When you have a large amount of data that you want to transfer from one computer to another in the same room, you have several possible solutions. You can copy the data to floppy disks, but for any more than a few megabytes, this is not convenient. Zip drives and other removable disk technologies hold more data, but you must have the same type of drive on both systems, or move the drive from one system to another. A network connection would be the fastest solution but is not worth setting up for occasional or one-time use. Finally, you could use modems to dial up one computer from the other and transfer files. This method also works, but requires two modems and two telephone lines. As an alternative, you can establish a "modem" connection between the two computers without using modems! Using a special type of cable called a *null modem* (or *laplink*) *cable*, you can connect the serial or parallel ports on two computers, forming a simple two-node network, and transfer files between them. This is particularly useful when you have both a desktop and a laptop system on which you want to use the same data.

Null Modem Cables

A null modem cable is a special cable that has its circuits crossed so the transmit data (TD) pin on each serial port connector leads to the receive data (RD) pin on the other. A cable that connects the systems' parallel ports in this way is called a bidirectional parallel cable. Cables like these are usually available at any computer store that sells cables. They are sometimes called laplink cables, after one of the first software products to introduce the concept of the direct cable connection.

You can also build your own null modem or bidirectional parallel cable using the wiring diagrams that follow. Table 11.2 shows the pins that you must connect for a serial cable, using either DB-9 (9-pin) or DB-25 (25-pin) connectors. Table 11.3 shows the connections for a parallel port cable. The parallel cable is slightly harder to build, but is recommended because of its higher transfer speed and because it will not interfere with existing modems and mouse drivers on the computers.

Table 11.2 3-Wire Serial Null Modem Cable Pinouts					
PC#1	**DB-9**	**DB-25**	**DB-25**	**DB-9**	**PC#2**
TD	3	2 <———> 3		2	RD
RD	2	3 <———> 2		3	TD
SG	5	7 <———> 7		5	SG

Table 11.3 11-Wire Parallel Null Modem Cable Pinouts	
PC #1	**PC #2**
2 <———————> 15	
15 <———————> 2	
3 <———————> 13	

PC #1	PC #2
13 <————————> 3	
4 <————————> 12	
12 <————————> 4	
5 <————————> 10	
10 <————————> 5	
6 <————————> 11	
11 <————————> 6	
25 <————————> 25	

Direct Connect Software

After you have the hardware in place, you need the proper software for the two systems to communicate. At one time, you had to purchase a third-party product (such as LapLink) to do this, but the capability is now part of most operating systems, including DOS 6, Windows 9x, and Windows NT.

In DOS, the software consists of two executable files, called INTERSVR.EXE and INTERLNK.EXE. On Windows 9x and Windows NT, the feature is called Direct Cable Connection. The software functions in basically the same way in either case. One computer is designated the *host*, and the other the *guest*. The software enables a user, working at the guest machine, to transfer files to and from the host.

In the DOS version, you run the INTERSVR program on the host computer. This system can be running a different version of DOS; you simply have to copy the INTERSVR.EXE program to it from a DOS 6 machine (using a floppy disk). On Windows 98, you click the Start menu and then select Programs, Accessories, Communications, Direct Cable Connection. Then choose the Host option button (see Figure 11.3). In both cases, you are prompted to select the COM or LPT port to which you have connected the cable.

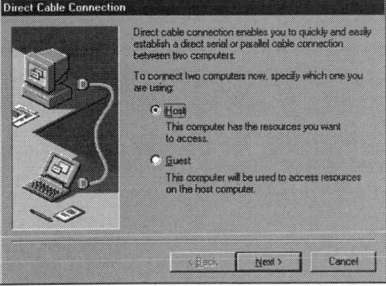

FIG. 11.3 Windows 9x enables you to access another computer using a serial or parallel connection.

On the other computer, you run the INTERLNK.EXE program in DOS or select the same Direct Cable Connection menu item in Windows 9x and choose the *Guest* option button. Again, you are prompted to choose the correct port, after which the software establishes a connection between the two machines. After this is done, the guest computer mounts the drives from the host in its own file system, assigning them the next available drive letters.

At this point, you can use the drive letters representing the host system just as though they were local resources. You can copy files back and forth using any standard file-management tool, such as the DOS COPY command or Windows Explorer. The only difference is that file transfers will, of course, be slower than local hard drive operations.

Local Area Networks

A local area network (LAN) enables you to share files, applications, printers, disk space, modems, faxes, and CD-ROM drives among different systems; use client/server software products; send electronic mail; and otherwise make a collection of computers work as a team.

In today's world, there are many ways to construct a LAN. As you have seen, a LAN can be as simple as two computers connected via either their serial or parallel ports. Although the term *network* is not often used for this sort of arrangement, it does satisfy the definition.

Networking Basics

In most cases, however, computers are connected to a network using a *network interface adapter* that either takes the form of an expansion card (called a network interface card, or NIC) or is integrated into the computer's motherboard. The adapter in each computer then connects to a cable installation in such a way as to permit any computer on the network to communicate with any other.

> **Note**
>
> Although the vast majority of networked computers are connected by cables, it is also possible to use various wireless technologies such as infrared, lasers, or microwaves as the network medium.

Nearly all LANs are *baseband* networks, meaning that when a computer transmits its data, the signal occupies the entire bandwidth of the network medium. This is in contrast to a *broadband* network, on which multiple signals can travel as one. A cable TV network is an example of a broadband network, because the signals carrying many different TV channels are all transmitted simultaneously.

Client/Server Versus Peer-to-Peer. Although every computer on a LAN is connected to every other, they do not necessarily all communicate with each other. There are two basic types of LANs, based on the communication patterns between the machines, called client/server networks and peer-to-peer networks.

On a *client/server network*, every computer has a distinct role, either that of a client or a server. A server is designed to share its resources among the client computers on the network. Typically, servers are located in secured areas, such as locked closets and data centers, because they hold the organization's most valuable data and do not have to be accessed by operators on a continuous basis. The rest of the computers on the network function as clients (see Figure 11.4).

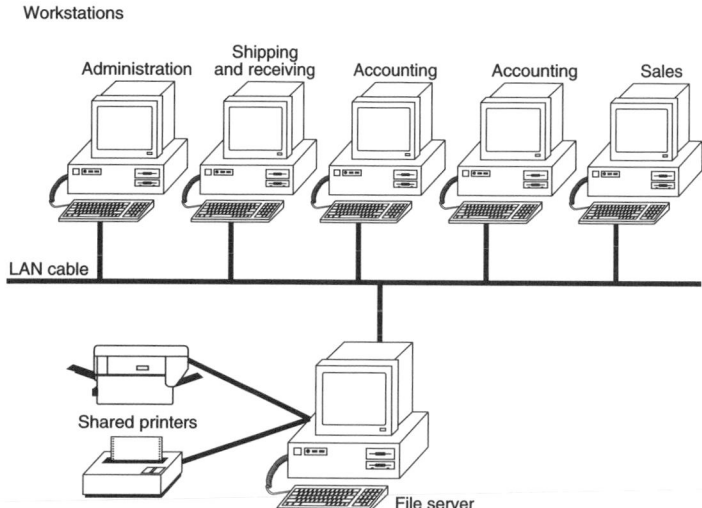

FIG. 11.4   The components of a client/server LAN.

A dedicated server computer typically has a faster processor, more memory, and more storage space than a client, as it may have to service dozens or even hundreds of users at the same time. The server runs a special network operating system, such as NetWare, that is designed solely to facilitate the sharing of its resources.

A client computer communicates only with servers, not with other clients. A client system is a standard PC, running an operating system such as DOS or Windows. The only difference is the addition of a client software package that enables the computer to access the resources shared by servers.

By contrast, on a peer-to-peer network, every computer is equal and can communicate with any other computer on the network to which it has been granted access rights (see Figure 11.5). Essentially, every computer on a peer-to-peer network functions as both a server and a client. This is why you may hear about client and server activities, even when the discussion is about a peer-to-peer network. Peer-to-peer networks can be as small as two computers or as large as hundreds of units.

Peer-to-peer networks are more common in small offices or within a single department of a larger organization. The advantage of a peer-to-peer network is that you don't have to dedicate a computer to function as a file server. Instead, every computer can share its resources with any other. The potential disadvantages to a peer-to-peer network are that there is typically less security and less control because users normally administer their own systems, while client/server networks have the advantage of centralized administration.

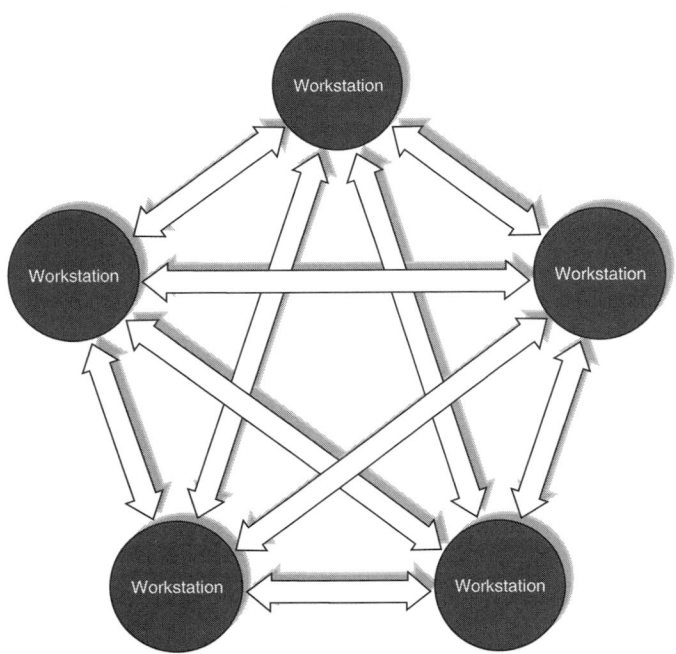

FIG. 11.5 The logical architecture of a typical peer-to-peer network.

Windows 9x and Windows NT have peer-to-peer networking capabilities built into them. Because of Plug-and-Play technology, it is a relatively easy matter to install network interface cards in a collection of Windows 9x systems, connect them with the right kind of cable, and build your own peer-to-peer network.

You can also network two Windows 9x or Windows NT PCs using modems and the operating system's Dial-Up Networking feature. Dial-Up Networking uses the same network client software as standard Windows 9x networking, but substitutes a modem connection for the network interface adapter. You can use this technology to connect to your office PC from your home computer, and even access other resources on your office network.

It is important to know that client/server and peer-to-peer networks are not mutually exclusive. You can have dedicated servers on your network and still share your local resources with other users, for example. In fact, this type of mixed network is very popular today, as many organizations are running both NetWare (a client/server operating system) and Windows NT (a peer-to-peer operating system).

Network Client Software. To access network resources with a PC, whether it is connected to a client/server or a peer-to-peer network, you must install network client software on the computer. The network client can be part of the operating system or a separate product, but it is this software that enables the system to use the network interface adapter to communicate with other machines.

On a properly configured network workstation, accessing network resources is no different from accessing local ones (except that they may be slightly slower). You can open a file on a network drive just as you would open the same file on your local hard disk. This is because the network client software is completely integrated into every level of the computer's operating system.

In most cases, the network client software is part of the operating system. Windows 9x, for example, includes all the software you need to participate in a peer-to-peer Windows network or to connect to Windows NT and NetWare servers. To connect to a network using DOS or Windows 3.1, however, you must install a separate client software package.

Packet Switching Versus Circuit Switching. The computers on a LAN must share the same baseband medium, so their communications have to be designed to provide each system with the opportunity to transmit its data. To make this possible, computers break down the data to be transmitted into individual units called *packets*. The system transmits the packets one at a time, and they travel over the network to the destination, intermingled with packets generated by other machines. At the destination system, the packets are reassembled into their original form. This type of network is called a *packet switching network*.

By contrast, a *circuit switching network* establishes a connection between the two communicating systems that fully occupies a designated bandwidth all during the session. The two systems transmit their signals over this connection in an unbroken stream, because they do not have to share the medium with other systems. The telephone system is an example of a circuit switching network.

The Networking Stack. Because network client software operates at many levels within each computer, it is often referred to as a *stack*, that is, a series of modules and services layered atop one another. Earlier in this chapter, you learned about the different types of protocols that modems use to communicate with one another. Networked computers use protocols, too, and for the same reason. For two systems to communicate, they must be speaking the same language.

A LAN connection is more complicated than a modem connection, however, and there are many more protocols involved at every layer of the networking stack. For this reason, the networking software is sometimes called the *protocol stack*. When designing a LAN, there are different protocols available at the various layers of the stack that a network administrator can select to suit a particular environment.

The OSI Reference Model. One of the most commonly used teaching and reference tools in local area networking is called the *OSI (Open Systems Interconnection) Reference Model*. Developed by the International Organization for Standardization (abbreviated as the ISO) in the 1980s, the OSI model splits a computer's networking stack into seven discrete layers (see Figure 11.6). Each layer provides specific services to the layers above and below it.

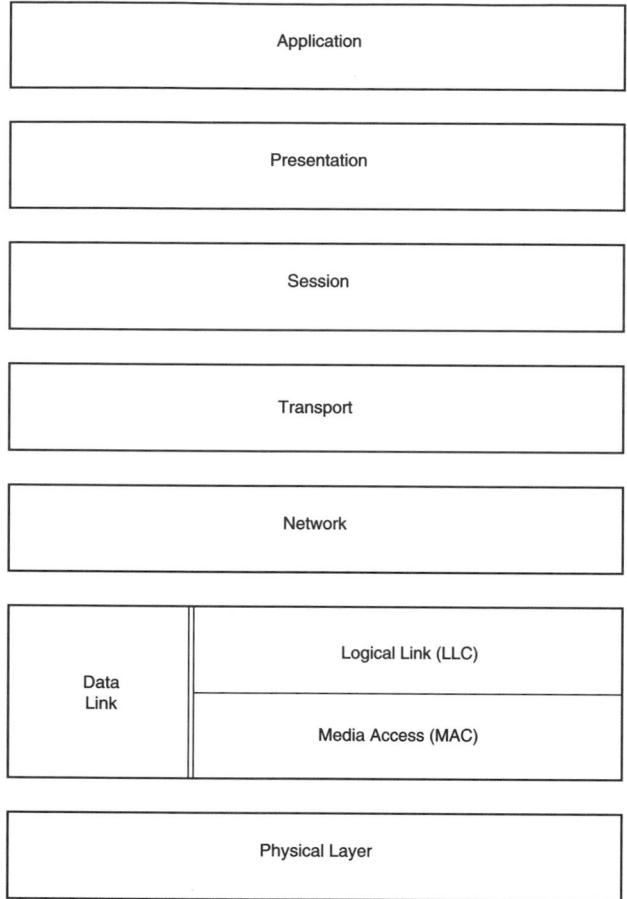

FIG. 11.6 The OSI reference model.

At the bottom of the model is the physical side of the network, including cables, NICs, and other hardware. At the top of the model is the application interface that enables you to use your word processor to open a file on a network drive as easily as you can open one on your local drive. In between are layers describing additional services, all of which combine to make network communications possible. Descriptions of the seven layers follow:

- *Physical.* This part of the OSI model specifies the physical and electrical characteristics of the connections that make up the network (twisted-pair cables, fiber-optic cables, coaxial cables, connectors, repeaters, and other hardware). You can think of this layer as the hardware layer. Although the rest of the layers may be implemented as firmware (that is, chip-level functions on the network adapter) rather than actual software, the other layers are software in relation to this first layer.

■ *Data Link*. This layer controls how the electrical impulses enter or leave the network cable. The network's electrical representation of your data (bit patterns, encoding methods, and tokens) is known to this layer and only to this layer. It is here that most errors are detected and corrected (by requesting retransmissions of corrupted packets). In some networking systems, the data link layer is subdivided into a Media Access Control (MAC) layer and a Logical Link Control (LLC) layer. The MAC layer deals with network access (token-passing or collision-sensing) and network control. The LLC layer, operating just above the MAC layer, is concerned with sending and receiving the user data messages. Ethernet and Token Ring are data link-layer protocols.

■ *Network*. This layer switches and routes the packets as necessary to get them to their destinations and is responsible for addressing and delivering message packets. While the data link layer is conscious only of the immediately adjacent computers on the network, the network layer is responsible for the entire route of a packet, from source to destination. IP and IPX are examples of network-layer protocols.

■ *Transport*. When more than one packet is in process at any time, such as when a large file must be split into multiple packets for transmission, the transport layer controls the sequencing of the message components and regulates inbound traffic flow. If a duplicate packet arrives, this layer recognizes it as a duplicate and discards it. TCP and SPX are transport-layer protocols.

■ *Session*. The functions in this layer enable applications running at two workstations to coordinate their communications into a single session (which you can think of in terms of a highly structured dialogue). The session layer supports the creation of the session, the management of the packets sent back and forth during the session, and the termination of the session.

■ *Presentation*. When IBM, Apple, DEC, NeXT, and Burroughs computers want to talk to one another, obviously a certain amount of translation and byte reordering needs to be done. The presentation layer converts data into an interim format for transmission over the network, and back into the machine's native format afterward.

■ *Application*. This layer defines the interface to the applications running on a networked computer. Application-layer protocols can be programs in themselves (such as FTP), or they can be used by other programs (as SMTP, the Simple Mail Transfer Protocol, is used by most e-mail applications) to redirect data to the network.

It is important to understand that while the OSI model was designed to be a model for the development of actual networking software, the products used on today's LANs do not exactly correspond to these layers. While you may find that certain protocols fall neatly within the boundaries between the layers, others may overlap or provide services that span several layers. As mentioned earlier, the model is primarily used as a tool for teaching networking and as a reference tool for networking professionals.

Data Encapsulation. The data packets transmitted over a LAN originate at the top of a computer's protocol stack, at the application layer of the OSI model. This is the application data in its simplest form, such as a request for a file stored on another machine or a print job destined for a network printer. As the data travels down through the layers of the protocol stack, it is packaged for its trip across the network. This packaging consists of information provided by each protocol in the stack, and intended for the equivalent protocol in the destination computer. Each protocol adds its own information to the data it receives from the layer above in the form of a *frame*. A frame consists of a header and sometimes a footer added to the beginning (and possibly the end) of a packet. The header and footer are simply additional bytes of data containing specialized control information used to get the packet to its destination.

Thus, when a file request is passed down from the application layer, the next protocol it encounters is usually at the transport layer (because there are no specific presentation-layer and session-layer protocols). The transport layer takes the data from the application layer, adds its own header, and passes it down to the network layer. The network takes the transport-layer data (including the transport header) and adds its own header before passing it down to the data link layer. The data link-layer protocol is unique in that it adds a footer in addition to a header.

This process is called *data encapsulation.* By the time the packet is introduced to the network cable, it has been encapsulated three times or more, and consists of a frame within a frame within a frame (see Figure 11.7).

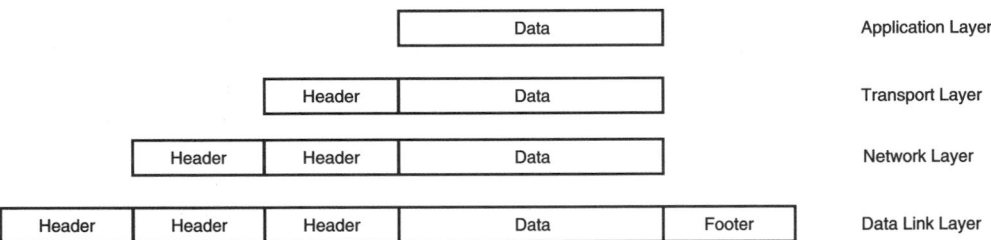

FIG. 11.7 Each protocol in a computer's networking stack encapsulates the data it receives from the layer above by adding its own header.

When the packet arrives at its destination, it travels up through the protocol stack and each frame is removed in the reverse order from which it was applied. In this way, the protocols at each layer in the stack communicate indirectly with their equivalent protocols in the other computer (see Figure 11.8).

LAN Hardware Components
Although you can connect virtually any PC to a network, you should use a different set of hardware evaluation criteria when building or purchasing a computer specifically for network use. The following sections examine the types of computers typically found on networks, and the other hardware involved, such as network interface adapters and cable types.

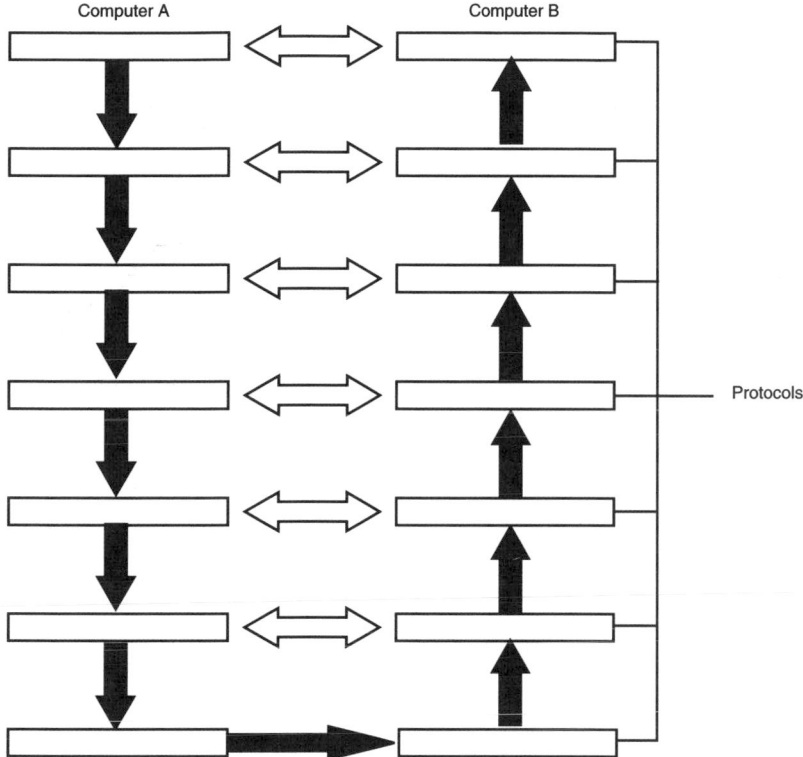

FIG. 11.8 Protocols in the networking stack communicate indirectly with their equivalent protocols in other computers.

Although all the PCs on a network use the same basic components as a standalone system, tradition and experience have resulted in two major hardware profiles: workstations and servers. Workstations are usually operated by users on their individual desktops, while servers are usually located in a secured area. On a client/server network, the workstation is used only by the person sitting in front of it, while a server allows many people to share its resources. As a general rule, servers are more powerful machines than workstations, because they must service many different users at once.

On a peer-to-peer network, however, the distinction begins to blur. Since workstations may also function as servers, it can be necessary to equip them with more powerful components. Technically, there is no reason why you cannot buy a PC marketed as a workstation or a standalone system and use it as a server, as long as it has sufficient resources to run the server software. However, most PC manufacturers sell computers that are specifically designed to function as servers. These machines may have specialized components designed for heavy use and fault tolerance, and you pay more as a result.

Workstations. The configuration of a workstation PC is largely dependent on the operating system that you intend to use. DOS and Windows 3.1, for example, can get by on 8M of RAM, while Windows 9x needs at least 16–32M, and Windows NT should have a minimum of 32M. In the same way, a Windows NT machine should have a faster processor and more hard drive space. Today, it is difficult to buy a new system that has anything less than a Pentium processor, but workstations tend to use the lower-speed versions that have been on the market for a while and are therefore lower in price. The big difference between a workstation and a standalone system, however, is that you should consider what resources will be available on the network. If you plan to have users storing their data on network drives, for example, you can equip workstations with smaller hard drives. In the same way, you might want to question whether your workstations need CD-ROMs if you can provide access to networked units.

You also should consider the environment in which the workstations will be used. It may not be a good idea to equip PCs with audio adapters and speakers if you are going to have a lot of computers in a single room. Also, computers that use a slimline case might be appreciated by users with limited workspace.

Servers. A network server is far more likely to be a top-of-the-line PC, with the fastest processor available, a lot of RAM, and a large amount of hard disk space. Servers must be high-quality, heavy-duty machines because, in serving the whole network, they do many times the work of an ordinary workstation computer. You may type on the server's keyboard only a couple of times a day, and you may glance at its monitor only infrequently. The server's CPU and hard disk drives, however, take the brunt of responding to the file-service requests of all the workstations on the LAN.

Server Processors. The processor in a server should be the most advanced and the fastest that you can afford. Right now, a Pentium II is preferable, but new models are being released at shorter and shorter intervals. Servers do more multitasking than any workstation, and the faster the processor, the more efficient the server will be. However, reliability should also be a major concern. A server is not the place to test out new technology.

◄◄ See "P6 (686) Sixth-Generation Processors," p. 127

Server Memory. Servers often require large amounts of memory, much more than workstations. The minimum is usually 64M these days, but you may need more, depending on the software you intend to run and how much disk space you have installed in the server. Both Windows NT and NetWare run better when they have more than the recommended amount of memory.

It's also a good idea, when shopping for a server, to be aware of the number of memory slots on the motherboard and the maximum amount of RAM that it supports. Check also how the memory that comes with the computer is configured. A machine with a single 64M DIMM is easier to upgrade than one with 16M modules filling all four slots.

◀◀ See "Physical Memory," p. 323

Server Storage. Hard disk drives are often the most important components in a server. File sharing is one of the primary reasons for networking computers, and the server's hard drives need to be durable and reliable, and geared to the task of serving multiple users simultaneously. For this reason, SCSI hard drives are preferred over IDE drives in today's servers.

◀◀ See "Small Computer System Interface (SCSI)," p. 626

The hard disk drives should be large and fast, although in some cases the highest capacity drive available is not necessarily the best choice. When you consider that the server will be processing the file requests of many users simultaneously, it can be more efficient to have, for example, nine 1G SCSI hard drives rather than one 9G drive. That way, the requests can be spread across several different units, rather than queued up waiting for one device.

Aside from standard hard disk drives, there are also more elaborate mass storage products on the market that are specifically designed for use with servers. Hard drive arrays can house large numbers of drives and use disk mirroring or RAID (Redundant Array of Inexpensive Disks) to provide fault tolerance. These are technologies that automatically store multiple copies of the server data on various hard drives, so in the event of a drive failure, all the data remains available to users. On some of these arrays, the drives may even be *hot-swappable*, meaning that you can replace a malfunctioning drive while the machine is still running.

While a server will usually have a CD-ROM drive in it to install software, if nothing else, you may want to have additional CD-ROM drives to share with network users. There are many CD-ROM changer and drive array products on the market that enable you to provide users with continuous access to large amounts of CD-ROM-based information.

A CD-ROM changer is a device that holds multiple disks and swaps them in and out of one or more drives. A CD-ROM drive array is a collection of drives in a single housing that share one power supply. A drive array is more expensive than a changer, but all the disks are immediately available.

Server Backups. If you value the data stored on your server at all, then making regular backups of your server drives is a necessity. For this purpose, you will probably want to install a SCSI tape drive on your server. Not every server needs its own tape drive, however, because network backup software products can use a single drive to protect data from multiple servers and workstations.

Server Power Supplies. In a server, the power supply is an important but often overlooked item. As with any PC, be sure that the power supply delivers enough current to run all the devices in the computer. On a server, this may require a 400-watt supply or more, as servers typically contain more drives than workstation PCs do.

Power supply failures and malfunctions can also cause problems elsewhere in the computer that are difficult to diagnose. Your file server may display a message indicating that a RAM chip has failed, and then stop; the cause of the problem may indeed be a failed RAM chip, or the problem may be in the power supply.

◄◄ See "Power Supply Troubleshooting," p. 426

Power supply fans sometimes stop working or become obstructed with dust and dirt. As a result, the computer overheats and fails completely or acts strangely. Cleaning the fan(s)—after unplugging the computer from the wall outlet, of course—should be a part of the regular maintenance of your file server.

Some servers include redundant fans and power supplies that enable the computer to keep running even when a power supply fails. In other models, the redundant power supplies are hot-swappable, providing even more fault tolerance.

You should also take steps to protect your server from variances in the voltage of its AC power supply (sags and spikes). To make your server as reliable as possible, you should install an uninterruptible power supply (UPS) between the electric power source and the server. The UPS not only provides electricity in case of a power failure, but also conditions the line to protect the server from voltage fluctuations.

Many UPSs also include a cable that connects to the server's serial port and software that automatically shuts down the operating system when the AC power fails for a given period of time. This ensures that server data is not corrupted by an improper system shutdown.

Server Keyboards, Monitors, and Mice. One area where you can safely skimp when purchasing a server is the user interface components, such as the keyboard, monitor, and mouse (if any). Because these items receive far less use than their workstation counterparts, you can use lower quality, less-expensive components here. A typical file server runs unattended and may go for hours or days without interaction from you. You can turn off the monitor for these long periods.

Network Interface Adapters. The network interface adapter is the PC's link to all the other computers on the network. All file requests and other network communications enter and leave the computer through the network adapter. Figure 11.9 shows a typical network interface adapter card that you might install in a server or workstation. Unlike many other components, the adapters in servers and workstations are usually the same. It serves no purpose to install a high-speed adapter in a server if the network workstations do not also support that same speed. The only difference that you may find is that a server might have more than one adapter, to connect to multiple networks.

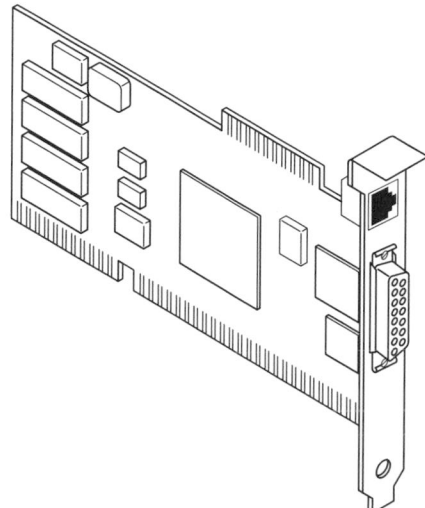

FIG. 11.9 The network interface adapter sends and receives messages to and from all the computers on the LAN.

All the network interface adapters on a LAN are designed to use Ethernet, Token Ring, or some other data link-layer protocol. Before you purchase adapter cards (or network cables, for that matter), you must decide which data link protocol you want to use. You can find network interface adapters for each of these protocols, however, that perform better than others. A particular network adapter may be faster at processing messages because it has a large amount of onboard memory (RAM); because it contains its own microprocessor; or perhaps because the adapter uses a PCI bus rather than ISA, and thus can transfer more data to and from the CPU at one time.

On most computers, the network interface adapter takes the form of a *network interface card*, or *NIC*, that fits into a slot in each computer. Some systems incorporate the network interface adapter onto the motherboard, but this practice is more commonly found in workstations and rarely in servers, because most network administrators prefer to select their own.

Ethernet and Token Ring adapters have unique hardware addresses coded into their firmware. The data link-layer protocol uses these addresses to identify the other systems on the network. A packet gets to the right destination because its data link-layer protocol header contains the hardware addresses of both the sending and receiving systems.

Network adapters range in price from well under $100 to as much as $1,000. What do you get for your money? Primarily speed. The faster adapters can push data faster onto the cable, which means that a server can receive a request more quickly and send back a response more quickly.

> **Data-Transfer Speeds on a LAN**
>
> Electrical engineers and networking professionals measure the speed of a network in megabits per second (Mbps). Because a byte of information consists of 8 bits, you can divide the megabits per second rating by 8 to find out how many millions of characters (bytes) per second the network can theoretically handle. In practice, however, a LAN is slower than its rated speed. In fact, a LAN is no faster than its slowest component. A slow hard disk drive can make it seem as though the LAN is performing poorly, when the problem is actually inside one of the computers. This multitude of possible causes can make diagnosing networking problems difficult.

Network Adapter Connectors. Ethernet adapters typically have a connector that looks like a large telephone jack called an RJ45 (for 10BaseT cables), a single BNC connector (for Thinnet), or a D-shaped 15-pin connector called a DB15 (for Thicknet). Some adapters have a combination of two or all three of these connector types. Token Ring adapters can have a 9-pin connector called a DB9, or sometimes an RJ45 jack. Figure 11.10 shows a high-performance Token Ring adapter with both kinds of connectors.

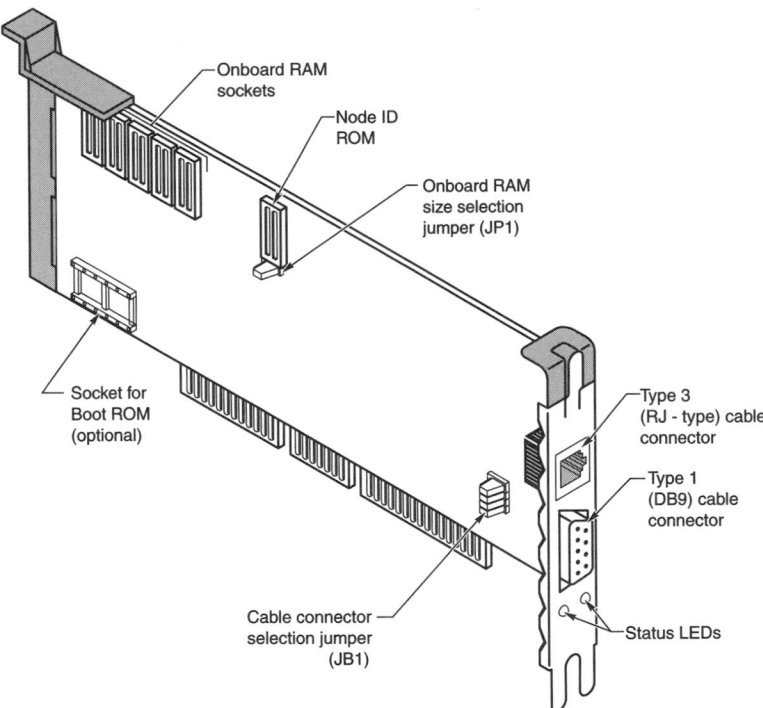

FIG. 11.10   The Thomas-Conrad 16/4 Token Ring adapter (with DB9 and RJ45 connectors).

Cards with two or more connectors enable you to choose from a wider variety of LAN cables. An Ethernet card with two connectors, for example, may enable you to use either unshielded twisted-pair (UTP) or thin Ethernet (Thinnet) cable. You cannot use both connectors at the same time, however, except on special adapters designed specifically for this purpose.

Network Adapter Functions. The LAN adapter card in your PC receives all the traffic going by on the network cable, accepts only the packets destined for your computer, and discards the rest. The adapter then hands these packets over to the system CPU for further processing. The packets then begin their journey up the rest of the networking stack to the application that is their final destination.

When your computer wants to transmit data, the network adapter waits for the appropriate time (determined by which data link-layer protocol it uses), and inserts the packets into the data stream. The receiving system notifies your computer as to whether the message arrived intact; if it was garbled, your machine resends.

The network adapter, along with the adapter driver installed on the computer, also participates in the preparation of the data for transmission. A network adapter performs seven major functions during the process of sending or receiving every packet. When sending data out to the network, the adapter performs the steps in the order presented in the following list. When it receives data, the steps are reversed. The seven steps are as follows:

1. *Data transfer.* Data is transferred from PC memory (RAM) to the network interface adapter or from the adapter to PC memory via DMA, shared memory, or programmed I/O.

2. *Buffering.* While being processed by the network adapter, data is stored in a buffer. The buffer enables the adapter to access an entire frame at once so that it can manage the difference between the data rate of the network and the rate at which the PC can process data.

3. *Frame formation.* The network adapter breaks up the data into manageable chunks (or, on reception, reassembles it). On an Ethernet network, these chunks are about 1,500 bytes. Token Ring networks generally use a frame size of about 4K. The adapter encapsulates the data packet with a header and footer, forming the data link-layer frame. At this point, the packet is complete and ready for transmission. (For inbound packets, the adapter reads and removes the header and footer at this stage.)

4. *Media access.* The network adapter uses the appropriate media access control mechanism for the data link-layer protocol to regulate its transmissions. On an Ethernet network, the network adapter ensures that the line is quiet before sending its data (or retransmits its data if a collision occurs). On a Token Ring network, the adapter waits until it receives a token that it can claim. Once it has a token, the adapter can transmit its data. (These steps are not applicable to incoming traffic, of course.)

5. *Parallel/serial conversion.* The network adapter receives (or sends) data over the system bus in parallel fashion, either 16 or 32 bits at a time, and stores it in the buffer. The data in the buffer must be sent or received through the network cables in serial fashion, with one bit following the next. The adapter card converts between these two formats in the split second before transmission (or after reception).

6. *Encoding/decoding.* The network adapter encodes the data it receives over the system bus into the electrical signals that are carried by the network cable, and decodes the signals arriving from the network. Ethernet adapters use a technique called *Manchester encoding*, while Token Ring adapters use a slightly different scheme called *Differential Manchester*. These techniques have the advantage of incorporating timing information into the data through the use of bit periods. Instead of representing a 0 as the absence of electricity and a 1 as its presence, the 0s and 1s are represented by changes in polarity as they occur in relation to very small time periods.

7. *Sending/receiving impulses.* The adapter takes the electrically encoded impulses that comprise the data (frame), amplifies them, and sends them through the wire. (On reception, the adapter passes the incoming impulses to the decoding step.)

Of course, the execution of all of these steps takes only a fraction of a second. While you were reading about these steps, thousands of frames could have been sent across the LAN.

Network adapter cards and the support software recognize and handle errors that occur when electrical interference, packet collisions (in Ethernet networks), or malfunctioning equipment cause some portion of a frame to be corrupted. Adapters generally detect errors through the use of a *cyclic redundancy check (CRC)* value computed by the sending system and included in the outgoing frame's footer. The same CRC calculation is performed by the receiving system. If its own calculated CRC doesn't match the value of the CRC in the frame, the receiver tells the sender about the error and requests retransmission of the bad frame.

Cables and Connectors. Generally speaking, the cabling systems described in the next few sections use one of three distinct cable types. These are twisted-pair (in shielded and unshielded varieties known as STP and UTP, 10BaseT, or 100BaseT), coaxial in thin and thick varieties (known as 10Base2 and 10Base5, respectively), and fiber-optic. The kind of cable you use depends mostly on the data link-layer protocol that you elect to use, the conditions at the network site, and, of course, your budget. All the major data link-layer protocols used on LANs (such as Ethernet and Token Ring) include highly specific guidelines for the installation of the network cable as part of their specifications. Technically, these guidelines are part of the physical layer, but this is one example of how protocols in the real world do not conform exactly to the OSI model.

Twisted-Pair Cable. *Twisted-pair* cable is just what its name implies: insulated wires within a protective casing, with a specified number of twists per foot. Twisting the wires reduces the effect of electromagnetic interference (that can be generated by nearby cables, electric motors, and fluorescent lighting) on the signals being transmitted.

Shielded twisted pair (STP) refers to the amount of insulation around the cluster of wires and therefore its immunity to noise. You are probably familiar with *unshielded twisted-pair (UTP)* cable; it is often used for telephone wiring. Figure 11.11 shows unshielded twisted-pair cable; Figure 11.12 illustrates shielded twisted-pair cable.

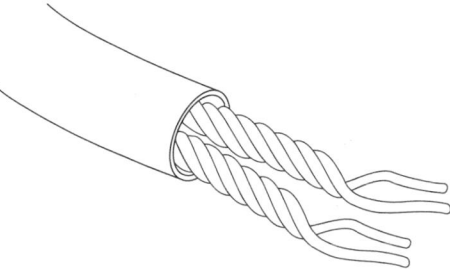

FIG. 11.11   An unshielded twisted-pair cable.

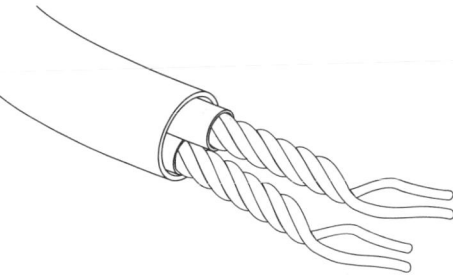

FIG. 11.12   A shielded twisted-pair cable.

Shielded Versus Unshielded Twisted Pair

When cabling was being developed for use with computers, it was first thought that shielding the cable from external interference was the best way to reduce interference and allow for greater transmission speeds. However, it was discovered that twisting the pairs of wires is a more effective way to prevent interference from disrupting transmissions. As a result, earlier cabling scenarios relied on shielded cables rather than the unshielded cables more commonly in use today.

Shielded cables also have some special grounding concerns because one—and only one—end of a shielded cable should be connected to an earth ground; issues arose where people inadvertently caused grounding loops to occur by connecting both ends, or caused the shield to act as an antenna because it wasn't grounded.

Grounding loops are situations where two different grounds are tied together. This is a bad situation because each ground can have a slightly different potential, resulting in a circuit that has very low voltage but infinite amperage. This causes undue stress on electrical components and can be a fire hazard.

Coaxial Cable. *Coaxial cable* is fairly prevalent in your everyday life, as it is the standard medium used by cable TV networks and for antenna connections. Thin and thick, of course, refer to the diameter of the coaxial cable itself. Standard Ethernet cable (Thick Ethernet), rarely used for networking today, is as thick as your thumb. Thin Ethernet cable (sometimes called Thinnet or CheaperNet) is slightly narrower than your little finger. The thick cable has a greater degree of noise immunity, is more difficult to damage, and requires a *vampire tap* (a connector with teeth that pierce the tough outer insulation) and a drop cable to connect to a workstation. Although thin coaxial cable carries the signal over shorter distances than the thick cable, it is lower in cost (hence the name CheaperNet) and uses a simple, bayonet-locking connector called a BNC (Bayonet-Neill-Concelman) connector to attach to workstations. Thin Ethernet was at one time the standard for Ethernet networking, but it has since been replaced by 10BaseT (unshielded twisted pair). Thinnet is wired directly to the back of each computer on the network and generally installs much more easily than Thicknet, but it is more prone to signal interference and physical connection problems.

Figure 11.13 shows an Ethernet BNC coaxial T-connector, and Figure 11.14 illustrates the design of coaxial cable.

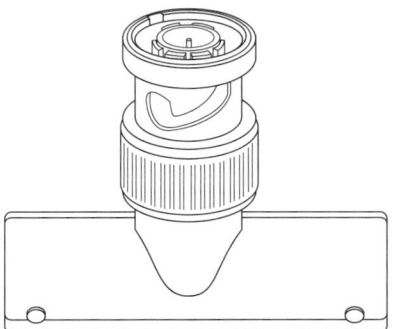

FIG. 11.13 An Ethernet coaxial cable T-connector.

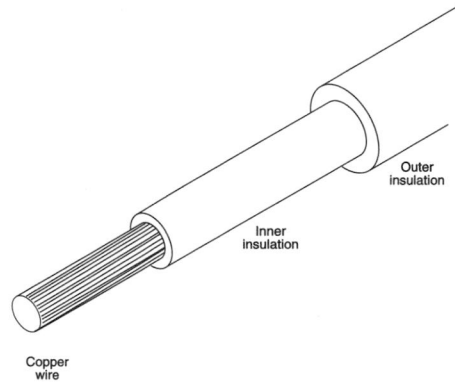

FIG. 11.14 Coaxial cable.

Fiber-Optic Cable. Fiber-optic cable uses pulses of light rather than electrical signals to carry information. It is therefore completely resistant to the electromagnetic interference that limits the length of copper cables. *Attenuation* (the weakening of a signal as it traverses the cable) is also less of a problem, enabling fiber to send data over huge distances at high speeds. It is, however, very expensive and difficult to install and maintain. Splicing the cable, installing connectors, and using the few available diagnostic tools for finding cable faults are skills that very few people have.

> **Tip**
>
> Fiber-optic cable is often used to connect buildings together in a campus network environment for two very important reasons. One is that fiber can travel approximately 2.2 km, while copper-based technologies are significantly more restricted. The other reason is that, because fiber does not use electrical signals, it eliminates the problems with differing ground sources.

Fiber-optic cable is simply designed, but unforgiving of bad connections. It usually consists of a core of glass thread with a diameter measured in microns (millionths of a meter), surrounded by a solid glass cladding. This, in turn, is covered by a protective sheath. The first fiber-optic cables were made of glass, but plastic fibers also have been developed. The light source for fiber-optic cable is a light-emitting diode (LED); information usually is encoded by varying the intensity of the light. A detector at the other end of the cable converts the incoming signal back into electrical impulses. Two types of fiber-optic cable exist: single mode and multimode. *Single mode* has a smaller diameter, is more expensive, and can carry signals over a greater distance.

Figure 11.15 illustrates fiber-optic cables and their connectors. Multimode has a diameter five to ten times greater than single mode, making it easier to connect. This ease of use makes it the most commonly used fiber. However, multimode suffers from higher distortion and lower bandwidth.

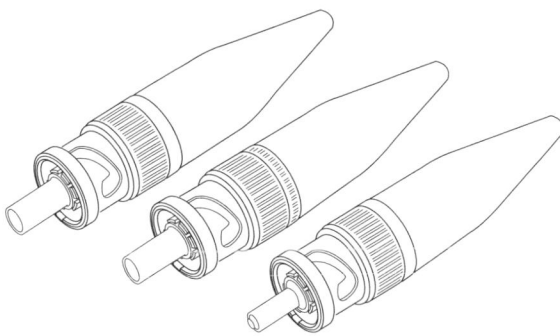

FIG. 11.15   Fiber-optic cables use light to carry LAN messages. The ST connector is commonly used with fiber-optic cables.

Network Topologies. Each computer on the network is connected to the other computers with cable (or some other medium). Sometimes a single piece of cable winds from station to station, visiting all of the network's computers along the way. This cabling arrangement is called a *bus topology*, as shown in Figure 11.16. (A *topology* is simply a description of the way the workstations and servers are physically connected.) The potential disadvantage to this type of wiring is that if one computer or cable connection malfunctions, it can cause all the stations beyond it on the bus to lose their network connections. Thin and thick Ethernet coaxial cables are typically installed using a bus topology.

FIG. 11.16 The linear bus topology, attaching all network devices to a common cable.

Another type of topology uses separate cables to connect each computer to a central wiring nexus, often called a *hub* or a *concentrator*. Figure 11.17 shows this arrangement, which is called a *star topology*. Because each computer uses a separate cable, the failure of a network connection affects only the single machine involved. The other computers can continue to function normally. Bus cabling schemes use less cable than the star, but are harder to diagnose or bypass when problems occur. At this time, Ethernet using 10BaseT cable in a star topology is the most commonly implemented type of LAN.

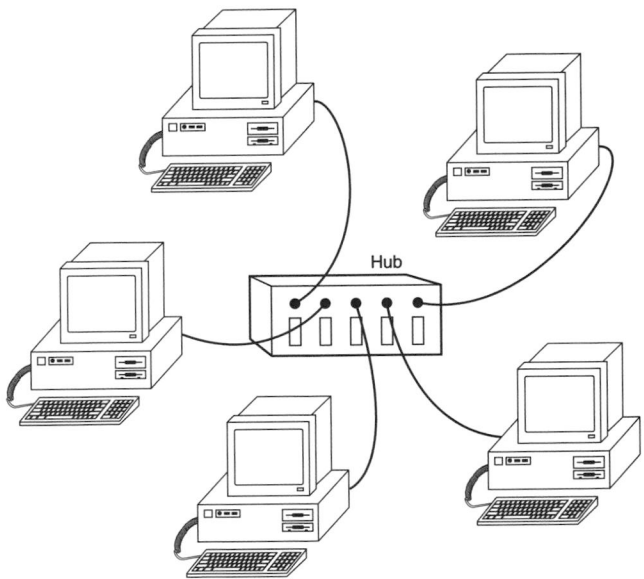

FIG. 11.17 The star topology, linking the LAN's computers and devices to one or more central hubs, or access units.

The other topology often listed in discussions of this type is a *ring*, in which each workstation is connected to the next, and the last workstation is connected to the first again (essentially a bus topology with the two ends connected). Data travels around a Token Ring network in this fashion, for example. However, the ring is not physically evident in the cabling layout for the network. In fact, the ring exists only within the hub (called a *multistation access unit* or *MSAU* on a Token Ring network).

Signals generated from one computer travel to the hub, are sent out to the next computer, and then back to the hub again. The data is then passed to each system in turn until it arrives back at the computer that originated it, where it is removed from the network. Therefore, although the physical wiring topology is a star, the data path is theoretically a ring. This is called a *logical ring*.

The logical ring is preferable to a physical ring topology because it affords a greater degree of fault tolerance. As on a bus network, a cable break anywhere in a physical ring would affect the entire network. On a Token Ring network, the MSAU can effectively remove a malfunctioning computer from the logical ring, allowing the rest of the network to function normally.

These different topologies are often mixed, forming what is called a *hybrid network*. For example, you can link the hubs of several star networks together with a bus, forming a star-bus network. Rings can be connected in the same way.

Network Cable Installations. If you have to run cables (of any type) through existing walls and ceilings, the cable installation can be the most expensive part of setting up a LAN. At every branching point, special fittings connect the intersecting wires. Sometimes you also need various additional components along the way, such as hubs, repeaters, or MSAUs.

> **Note**
>
> A few companies, such as Motorola, market LAN technologies that do not require cables at all. Wireless LAN uses infrared, lasers, or radio waves to carry network signals from computer to computer. These technologies are uniquely suited to certain specialized environments, but have not yet achieved the speed and reliability needed for general use.

Planning the cable layout, cutting the cable, attaching connectors, and installing the cables and fittings are jobs usually best left to experienced workers. If the fittings are not perfect, you may get electronic echoes on the network, which cause transmission errors. There are also a great many physical specifications for each network type that must be observed if the network is to function properly. One of the advantages of using UTP cable is that a great many telephone system contractors are familiar with the medium. In new construction, you can have your network cabling installed along with the telephone cable. However, make sure that the contractor you hire is aware of the requirements for data networking, which are typically far more stringent than those for telephone wiring.

Building codes almost always require you to use fireproof plenum cables. (A *plenum* is the air space between a drop ceiling and the floor above it.) Plenum cables are more fire-resistant than some other cables. A professional cable installer should be familiar with the building codes in your area, but make sure of this before signing a contract. You would be very upset if you were to have ordinary cable installed and were later told by a building inspector to rip out the cable and start over again with the proper kind.

Because of the expense and the mess of a cable installation, it is a good idea to have the installer run more cable than you initially need so that you won't have to install more later. Consideration for your network's growth potential should be a part of every step in the planning of your network.

The only time that you might consider installing LAN cable yourself is when you have a small group of computers located on adjacent desks and you do not have to pull cable through the walls or ceiling. Even in this case, however, make sure that you are aware of the guidelines for the cable type you select, such as the minimum and maximum allowed cable lengths.

Selecting the Proper Cable. As the demands of network users continue for ever-increasing amounts of bandwidth, and as manufacturers develop new networking systems to accommodate them, it soon becomes necessary to examine the capabilities of the most fundamental part of the network infrastructure: the cable itself. Ethernet over UTP cable, or 10BaseT, is the medium of choice in the majority of LAN installations today, although 100BaseT (Fast Ethernet) networks are becoming increasingly popular.

The UTP cable used for Ethernet networks was originally the same as that used for business telephone wiring. This is known as *Category 3*, or *voice grade UTP cable*, measured according to a scale that quantifies the cable's data-transmission capabilities. The cable itself is 24 AWG (American Wire Gauge, a standard for measuring the diameter of a wire), copper tinned, with solid conductors, 100–105 ohm characteristic impedance, and a minimum of two twists per foot. Category 3 cable is adequate for networks running at up to 16Mbps.

Newer, faster network types require greater performance levels, however. Fast Ethernet technologies that run at 100Mbps using the same number of wires as standard Ethernet need a greater resistance to signal crosstalk and attenuation. Therefore, the use of Category 5 UTP cabling is essential. If, when you are building a LAN, you can use Category 3 wiring that is already in place, by all means do so. If, however, you are pulling new cable for your network, the use of Category 5 cable is recommended. Even if you are not running a high-speed network today, you will probably want to consider it in the future.

> **Caution**
>
> A chain is only as strong as its weakest link, and the same rule holds true for a network cable installation. If you choose to install Category 5 UTP cable, make sure that all the connectors, wall plates, and other hardware components involved are also Category 5.

The people who design computer systems love to find ways to circumvent limitations. Manufacturers of Ethernet products have made it possible to build networks in star, branch, and tree designs that overcome the basic limitations already mentioned. You can have thousands of computers on a complex Ethernet network.

LANs are local because the network adapters and other hardware components typically cannot send LAN messages more than a few hundred feet. Table 11.4 lists the distance limitations of different kinds of LAN cable. In addition to the limitations shown in the table, keep in mind that you cannot connect more than 30 computers on a single Thinnet Ethernet segment, more than 100 computers on a Thicknet Ethernet segment, more than 72 computers on a UTP Token Ring cable, or more than 260 computers on an STP Token Ring cable.

Table 11.4 Network Distance Limitations

Network Adapter	Cable Type	Maximum	Minimum
Ethernet	Thin	607 ft.	20 in.
	Thick (drop cable)	164 ft.	8 ft.
	Thick (backbone)	1,640 ft.	8 ft.
	UTP	328 ft.	8 ft.
Token Ring	STP	328 ft.	8 ft.
	UTP	148 ft.	8 ft.
ARCnet (passive hub)		393 ft.	Depends on cable
ARCnet (active hub)		1,988 ft.	Depends on cable

Data Link-Layer Protocols

The protocol that you choose to run at the data link layer is the single most important decision you make when designing a local area network. This protocol defines the speed of the network, the medium access control mechanism it uses, the types of cables you can use, the network interface adapters that you must buy, and the adapter drivers that you install in the network client software.

The Institute of Electrical and Electronic Engineers (IEEE) has defined and documented a set of standards for the physical characteristics of both collision-sensing and token-passing networks. These standards are known as IEEE 802.3 (Ethernet) and IEEE 802.5 (Token Ring). Be aware, however, that the colloquial names Ethernet and Token Ring actually refer to earlier versions of these protocols, upon which the IEEE standards were based. There are minor differences between the frame definitions for true Ethernet and true IEEE 802.3. In terms of the standards, IBM's 16Mbps Token Ring products are an extension of the IEEE 802.5 standard. There is also an older data link protocol called ARCnet that is now rarely used.

The following sections examine these data link-layer protocols.

ARCnet. *ARCnet* is one of the oldest types of LAN. It originally was a proprietary scheme of the Datapoint Corporation, but other companies also began to manufacture ARCnet-compatible hardware. By modern standards, ARCnet is very slow, but it is forgiving of minor errors in installation. It is known for solid reliability, and ARCnet cable/adapter problems are easy to diagnose. ARCnet generally costs less than Ethernet, but hardware prices for Ethernet adapters have plummeted so much in recent years that the difference in price between the two is no longer that great an issue. ARCnet operates something like Token Ring, but at the slower rate of 2.5Mbps.

Ethernet. With over 20 million installed computers, Ethernet is the most widely used data link-layer protocol in the world. Ethernet-based LANs enable you to interconnect a wide variety of equipment, including UNIX workstations, Apple computers, printers, and PCs. You can buy Ethernet adapters from dozens of competing manufacturers, support-ing all three of the cable types defined in the standard: Thinnet, Thicknet, and UTP. Traditional Ethernet operates at a speed of 10Mbps, but the more recent "Fast Ethernet" standards push this speed to 100Mbps.

Fast Ethernet requires adapters, hubs, and cables designed to support the higher speed, but you can buy combination devices that run at both 10Mbps and 100Mbps, enabling you to gradually upgrade your network by installing new NICs and hubs over an ex-tended period of time.

The Ethernet specification consists of three elements:

- *Physical-layer specifications.* A set of cabling guidelines for the installation of UTP, Thinnet, or Thicknet cable.

- *The Ethernet Frame.* A frame format that defines what information goes into the header and footer applied to every packet of network-layer data by the Ethernet protocol. The frame includes the hardware addresses of the systems sending and receiving the packet and the CRC value used for error correction.

- *Media Access Control.* A mechanism used to regulate access to the shared network medium by multiple computers.

Because computers on a LAN share a common network medium (usually a cable), there must be a scheme to arbitrate each system's access to the network. If two computers transmit a packet at the same time, a *collision* can result, garbling both packets and caus-ing data loss. This arbitration scheme is called a *media access control* (or MAC) mecha-nism, and Ethernet networks use a MAC mechanism called *Carrier Sense, Multiple Access with Collision Detection (CSMA/CD).*

When a computer on an Ethernet network wants to transmit, it first listens to the net-work to see if the network is currently in use. If another computer is transmitting, the system waits for a while and then listens again. If the network is clear, the system trans-mits its data. This is not a foolproof method, however, as it is possible for two computers to detect a clear network and transmit at the same time, causing a collision.

Collisions are a regular and accepted occurrence on an Ethernet LAN, and a good deal of the technology is devoted to detecting them. When a computer realizes that its transmission has collided with another packet, it waits for a random period of time (called a *backoff interval*) and transmits the same packet again. Since the two computers involved in the collision use different backoff intervals, the chances of a second collision are reduced.

While a certain number of collisions are normal and expected on an Ethernet network, with higher amounts of traffic the frequency of collisions rises, and response times increase. A saturated Ethernet network actually can spend more time recovering from collisions than it does sending data. For this reason, it is important not to overburden a single Ethernet segment with too many computers.

On an Ethernet network, the number of computer connections and their intervening distances are the network's limiting factors. Each cable type is subject to its own distance limitations, beyond which an electrical device called a *repeater* is needed to amplify the signal. Without repeaters, standing waves (additive signal reflections) would distort the signal and cause errors.

Because the Ethernet collision-detection mechanism is highly dependent on timing, you can have only five 200-meter segments and four repeaters wired in series, with a maximum of three segments connected to computers, before the signal propagation delay becomes longer than the maximum allowed period for the detection of a collision. Otherwise, the computers farthest from the sender would be unable to determine whether a collision had occurred. This is known as the *Ethernet 5-4-3 rule*.

Token Ring. Token Ring networks differ substantially from Ethernet. Originally designed by IBM to run at 4Mbps over STP or UTP cable in a logical ring topology, the standard was revised to include a 16Mbps version, which is what most installations use today. Token Ring adapters and hubs (MSAUs) are considerably more expensive than their Ethernet counterparts, but this cost can often be justified by the protocol's greater speed and its excellent performance even at high traffic levels.

It takes several seconds to open the adapter connection on a Token Ring LAN. During this time, the MSAU and the Token Ring adapter perform a small diagnostic check, after which the MSAU establishes the computer as a new neighbor on the ring. After being established as an active workstation, your computer is linked on both sides to your upstream and downstream neighbors (as defined by your position on the MSAU). In its turn, your Token Ring adapter card accepts the token or frame, regenerates its electrical signals, and sends the token or frame through the MSAU in the direction of your downstream neighbor.

Token Ring networks use a different type of MAC mechanism than Ethernet LANs, called *token passing*. On a Token Ring network, computers continuously pass a special packet called a *token* among themselves. The token is just a short message indicating that the computer possessing it is allowed to transmit. If a computer has no data to send, it passes the token on to the next downstream computer as soon as it receives it. Only the computer holding the token can transmit data onto the LAN.

Every packet transmitted on the network circulates through all the computers on the ring, including its intended destination, and eventually ends up back at the computer that sent it. The sender is then responsible for removing the packet from the network and generating a new token, thus releasing control of the network to the next system.

Because it is not possible for two computers to transmit at the same time on a properly functioning Token Ring network, there are no collisions, and because every computer has an equal opportunity to transmit, network performance does not degrade at high traffic levels. In special situations, it is also possible to assign priorities to certain computers so they get more frequent access to the LAN. Sometimes a station fumbles and "drops" the token, however. When this happens, the computers on the LAN monitor each other and use a procedure called *beaconing* to detect the location of the problem and regenerate a lost token.

Early Token Release

On a momentarily idle Token Ring LAN, workstations circulate a token. The LAN becomes busy (carries information) when a computer takes possession of the token and transmits a data frame targeted at another computer on the network. After receipt by the target node, the data frame continues circulating around the LAN until it returns to its source node. The source node removes the data frame and generates a new token that circulates until a downstream node needs it. So far, so good—these are just standard Token Ring concepts.

When a client sends a file request to a server, it consists of only a few bytes, far fewer than the transmission that returns the actual file to the client. If the request packet has to pass through many other systems to circulate the ring, and if the data frame is small, latency occurs. *Latency* is the unproductive delay that occurs while the source node waits for its upstream neighbor to return the data frame.

During the latency period, the source node appends idle characters onto the LAN following the data frame until the frame circulates the entire LAN and arrives back at the source node. The typical latency period of a 16Mbps ring will result in the transmission of 400 or more bytes' worth of idle characters.

Early Token Release, available only on 16Mbps networks, is a feature that enables the originating workstation to transmit a new token immediately after sending its data frame, thus avoiding the latency period. Downstream nodes pass along the data frame and then receive the token, giving them the opportunity to transmit data themselves. If you were to perform a protocol analysis of a network using Early Token Release, you would see tokens and other data frames immediately following the file request, instead of a long trail of idle characters.

High-Speed Networking Technologies

If you have fast computers on your network, you may want a fast network as well. Even the 16Mbps of a Token Ring network may be too slow if your applications are data-intensive. The explosive growth of multimedia, groupware, and other technologies that require enormous amounts of data has forced network administrators to consider the need for high-speed network connections to individual desktop systems.

Networking technologies that run at speeds above 16Mbps have been around for several years, but they have primarily been limited to high-speed backbone connections between servers, due to the additional expense. Several new technologies are available today, however, that are designed to deliver data at high speeds—up to 100Mbps and more—to standard user workstations. Real-time data feeds from financial services, videoconferencing, video editing, and high-color graphics processing are just some of the tasks now being performed on PCs that would benefit greatly from an increase in network transmission speed.

Fiber Distributed Data Interface. FDDI has been available for several years, but it is still a much newer protocol than Ethernet or Token Ring. Designed by the X3T9.5 Task Group of ANSI (the American National Standards Institute), FDDI passes tokens and data frames around a double ring of optical fiber cable at a rate of 100Mbps. Two separate rings (called the *primary* and the *secondary*) with traffic traveling in opposite directions provide fault tolerance in case of a cable break or other malfunction. FDDI classifies the computers on the network as either Class A (connected to both rings) or Class B (connected to the primary ring only).

FDDI was designed to be as much like the IEEE 802.5 Token Ring standard as possible, above the physical layer. Differences occur only where necessary to support the faster speeds and longer transmission distances of FDDI.

If FDDI were to use the same bit-encoding scheme used by Token Ring, every bit would require two optical signals: a pulse of light and then a pause of darkness. This means that FDDI would need to send 200 million signals per second to have a 100Mbps transmission rate. Instead, the scheme used by FDDI—called NRZI 4B/5B—encodes 4 bits of data into 5 bits for transmission so that fewer signals are needed to send a byte of information. The 5-bit codes (symbols) were chosen carefully to ensure that they meet network timing requirements. The NRZI 4B/5B scheme, at a 100Mbps transmission rate, sends 125 million signals per second (this is 125 megabaud). Also, because each carefully selected light pattern symbol represents 4 bits (a half byte, or *nibble*), FDDI hardware can operate at the nibble and byte level rather than at the bit level, making it easier to achieve the high data rate.

There are two major differences in the way that FDDI and IEEE 802.5 Token Ring manage their respective tokens. In traditional Token Ring, a new token is circulated only after a sending system gets back the frame that it sent. In FDDI, a new token is circulated immediately by the sending system after it finishes transmitting a frame, a technique that has since been adapted for use in Token Ring networks and called *Early Token Release*. FDDI classifies the computers on the network as either *asynchronous* (systems that are not rigid about the time periods that occur between network accesses) or *synchronous* (systems having very stringent requirements regarding the timing between transmissions). FDDI uses a complex algorithm to allocate network access to the two classes of devices.

Although it provides superior performance, FDDI's acceptance as a desktop networking solution has been hampered by its higher installation and maintenance costs. An alternative using a more conventional copper cable, called CDDI (Copper Distributed Data Interface), is easier to install and maintain, but does not provide the resistance to interference that enables fiber-optic cable to span such long distances.

100Mbps Ethernet

One of the largest barriers to the implementation of high-speed networking has been the need for a complete replacement of the networking infrastructure. Most companies cannot afford the downtime needed to rewire the entire network, replace all the hubs and NICs, and then configure everything to operate properly. As a result of this, some of the new 100Mbps technologies are designed to make the upgrade process easier in several ways. First, they can often use the network cable that is already in place, and second, they are compatible enough with the existing installation to allow a gradual changeover to the new technology, system by system. Obviously, these factors also minimize the expense associated with such an upgrade.

The two systems that take this approach are *100BaseT*, also known as Fast Ethernet, first developed by the Grand Junction Corp., and *100VG AnyLAN*, advocated by Hewlett-Packard and AT&T. Both of these systems run at 100Mbps over standard UTP cable, but that is where the similarities end. In fact, of the two, only 100BaseT can truly be called an Ethernet network. 100BaseT uses the same CSMA/CD media access control mechanism and the same frame layout defined in the IEEE 802.3 standard. In fact, 100BaseT has been ratified as an extension to that standard, called *802.3u*.

To accommodate existing cable installations, the 802.3u document defines three different cabling standards, as shown in Table 11.5.

Table 11.5 100BaseT Cabling Standards		
Standard	**Cable Type**	**Segment Length**
100BaseTX	Category 5 (2 pairs)	100 meters
100BaseT4	Category 3, 4, or 5 (4 pairs)	100 meters
100BaseFX	62.6 micrometer Multimode fiber (2 strands)	400 meters

Sites with Category 3 cable already installed can use the system without the need for rewiring, as long as the full four pairs in a typical run are available.

Note

Despite the apparent wastefulness, it is not recommended that data and voice traffic be mixed within the same cable, even if sufficient wire pairs are available. Digital phone traffic could possibly coexist, but normal analog voice lines will definitely inhibit the performance of the data network.

100BaseT also requires the installation of new hubs and new NICs, but because the frame type used by the new system is identical to that of the old, this replacement can be performed gradually, to spread the labor and expense over a protracted period of time. You could replace one hub with a 100BaseT model and then switch computers over to it, one at a time, as time permits. You can even purchase NICs that can operate at both 10Mbps and 100Mbps speeds to make the changeover even easier.

100VG (voice grade) AnyLAN also runs at 100Mbps, and is specifically designed to use existing Category 3 UTP cabling. Like 100BaseT4, it requires four pairs of cable strands for its communications. There is also a separate Category 5 cable option in the standard. Beyond the cabling, 100VG AnyLAN is quite different from 100BaseT and indeed from Ethernet.

While 10BaseT and 100BaseT networks both reserve one pair of wires for collision detection, 100VG-AnyLAN is able to transmit over all four pairs simultaneously. This technique is called *quartet signaling*. 100VG-AnyLAN also uses a different signal-encoding scheme called 5B/6B NRZ, which sends 2.5 times more bits per cycle than an Ethernet network's Manchester encoding scheme. Multiplied by the four pairs of wires (as compared to 10BaseT's one), you have a tenfold increase in transmission speed.

The fourth pair of wires is available for transmitting data because there is no need for collision detection on a 100VG-AnyLAN network. Instead of the CSMA/CD media access system that defines an Ethernet network, 100VG-AnyLAN uses a brand-new technique called *demand priority*. Individual network computers have to request and be granted permission to transmit by the hub before they can send their data.

100VG-AnyLAN can use the same frame formats as IEEE 802.3 Ethernet and IEEE 802.5 Token Ring so that its traffic can coexist on a LAN with that of existing Ethernet or Token Ring systems. Like 100BaseT, combination 10/100Mbps NICs are available, and the network can be gradually migrated to the new technology.

Support for 100VG-AnyLAN has almost completely disappeared from the market due to the cost of the adapters and the popularity of 10/100Mbps Fast Ethernet adapters.

Asynchronous Transfer Mode

Asynchronous Transfer Mode, or ATM, is one of the newest of the high-speed technologies. It has been in an "emerging" state for some time now, without having developed into its full potential. ATM defines a physical-layer protocol in which a standard-size 53-byte packet (called a *cell*) is used to transmit voice, data, and real-time video over the same cable, simultaneously. The cells contain identification information that allows high-speed ATM switches (*wiring hubs*) to separate the data types and ensure that the cells are reassembled in the right order.

The basic ATM standard runs at 155Mbps, but some implementations can go as high as 660Mbps. There is also an ATM desktop standard that runs at 25Mbps, but this doesn't seem to be enough of a gain over Token Ring's 16Mbps to be worth the adoption of an entirely new networking technology.

ATM is a radically different concept, and there are no convenient upgrade paths as there are with the 100Mbps standards described earlier. All the networking hardware must be replaced, and the prices of ATM products are significantly higher than those of Fast Ethernet and other high-speed technologies. For this reason, ATM is being used primarily for WAN links at this time. When the delivery of real-time video over the network becomes more of a practical reality than it is now, ATM might find its rightful place. For now, it remains a niche technology.

Upper-Layer Protocols

When you add network client software to a PC, the first step is to install a driver for the network interface adapter in the machine. This driver not only identifies the adapter hardware, but it implements the data link-layer protocol. The next step is to install support for the protocols running above the data link layer. There are usually several different protocols operating at the upper layers, but for the purposes of a client installation they are treated as a single entity.

For example, after installing a driver for the Ethernet adapter in your PC, you can select a protocol suite such as TCP/IP or IPX to work at the upper layers. Both TCP/IP and IPX actually consist of several different protocols, but you install them as one module that operating systems such as Windows 9x and Windows NT somewhat confusingly refer to by the term *protocol*.

In nearly all cases, you can also install multiple protocol suites to support different networking clients on the same computer. For example, a single Ethernet adapter can use IPX to access NetWare servers and TCP/IP to share Windows NT resources, both at the same time.

The following sections examine the upper-layer protocols most commonly used on today's LANs.

TCP/IP

TCP/IP stands for *Transmission Control Protocol/Internet Protocol*. TCP and IP are separate transport- and network-layer protocols, respectively, but TCP/IP is the colloquial name given to the entire suite of networking protocols developed for use by the Internet, of which TCP and IP are only two. Later, the TCP/IP protocols were adopted by the UNIX operating systems, and they have now become the most commonly used protocol suite on PC LANs. Virtually every operating system with networking capabilities supports TCP/IP, and it is well on its way to displacing all the other competing protocols.

TCP/IP is an extensive collection of protocols operating at the application, transport, network, and data link layers. The protocols were originally developed by the U.S. Department of Defense in the 1970s as a platform- and hardware-independent medium for communication over what was to become known as the Internet. A good example of this independence is the capability of DOS, Windows 3.1, Windows 9x, and Windows NT systems to access information and transfer files on the Internet, which is a mixed-platform environment. The primary advantages of TCP/IP are

- *Platform Independence*. TCP/IP is not designed for use in any single hardware or software environment. It can be used and is being used on computers and networks of all types.

- *Absolute Addressing*. TCP/IP provides a means of uniquely identifying every machine on the Internet.

- *Open Standards*. The TCP/IP specifications are publicly available to users and developers alike. Suggestions for changes to the standard can be submitted by anyone.

- *Application Protocols*. TCP/IP allows dissimilar environments to communicate. High-level protocols such as FTP and Telnet have become ubiquitous in TCP/IP environments on all platforms.

Although they have been the protocols of choice on UNIX networks for many years, the explosive growth of the Internet has brought the TCP/IP protocols onto all kinds of LANs as well. Many network administrators are finding that they can configure all their network operating systems to use TCP/IP and thus lessen the network traffic problems that can be caused by running several different sets of protocols on the same network.

Some of the most important protocols of the TCP/IP suite are as follows:

- *Internet Protocol (IP)*. Operating at the network layer, IP is the main protocol of the TCP/IP suite. It supplies network data with addressing and routing information, and splits packets into smaller fragments as needed during the trip to their destination. The data generated by nearly all the other TCP/IP protocols is carried within IP packets, called *datagrams*.

- *Transmission Control Protocol (TCP)*. TCP is a reliable, connection-oriented protocol operating at the transport layer. A *reliable* protocol is one in which the destination system returns acknowledgment messages to the sender, verifying that the packets were received without errors. A *connection-oriented* protocol is one in which the two computers exchange messages before transmitting any user data. These messages establish a connection that remains open until the data transmission is completed. TCP is used to transmit relatively large amounts of data, such as FTP file transfers and HTTP Web page transactions.

- *User Datagram Protocol*. Also operating at the transport layer, UDP is a connectionless, unreliable protocol, and the counterpart to TCP. A *connectionless* protocol transmits its data without knowing if the destination system is ready to receive it, or even if the destination system exists. An *unreliable* protocol is one in which the destination system does not transmit explicit acknowledgment messages. Actually, UDP is far from unreliable in the literal sense, because it is mostly used for short query/response transactions in which the response functions as an acknowledgment. The Internet's Domain Name System (DNS) uses UDP for much of its communications.

- *Internet Control Message Protocol (ICMP)*. ICMP does not carry user data, but is instead a control and diagnostic protocol that is used to inform other systems of conditions and errors on the network. The TCP/IP PING utility uses ICMP to determine if another system on a TCP/IP network is functioning.

- *Address Resolution Protocol (ARP)*. ARP is a protocol that IP uses to convert its own network-layer addresses into data link-layer hardware addresses.

- ■ *Point-to-Point Protocol (PPP)*. PPP is a data link-layer protocol, but not for use on LANs. PPP is used to establish a direct connection between two computers, usually using a modem connection. If you use Windows 9x or Windows NT's Dial-Up Networking feature to connect to the Internet, then you are probably using PPP.

- ■ *File Transfer Protocol (FTP)*. FTP is an application-layer protocol used to transfer files between TCP/IP systems. Unlike most protocols, FTP actually defines the user interface for an application. Virtually every TCP/IP implementation includes a text-based FTP program, and many of the commands are the same no matter what operating system you are using.

- ■ *Hypertext Transfer Protocol (HTTP)*. Operating at the application layer, HTTP is the fundamental protocol of the World Wide Web. When you type a URL in your Web browser, the program transmits an HTTP request to the server you've specified. The server then responds with an HTTP reply containing the file you requested.

- ■ *Simple Mail Transfer Protocol (SMTP)*. SMTP is the application-layer protocol used by most e-mail applications to send mail over the Internet.

IPX. The IPX protocol suite is the collective term for the proprietary protocols created by Novell for their NetWare operating system. Although based loosely on some of the TCP/IP protocols, the IPX protocol standards are privately held by Novell. However, this has not prevented Microsoft from creating its own IPX-compatible protocol for the Windows operating systems.

IPX (Internetwork Packet Exchange) itself is a connectionless, unreliable, network-layer protocol, equivalent in function to IP. The suite's equivalent to TCP is the Sequenced Packet Exchange (SPX) protocol, which provides connection-oriented, reliable service at the transport layer.

The IPX protocols are typically used today only on networks with NetWare servers, and are often installed along with another protocol suite such as TCP/IP. Even NetWare, however, is phasing out its use of IPX and making the move over to TCP/IP, along with the rest of the networking industry.

NetBEUI. NetBEUI (NetBIOS Extended User Interface) is a protocol used primarily on small Windows NT networks. It was the default protocol in Windows NT 3.1, the first version of that operating system. Later versions, however, use the TCP/IP protocols as their default.

NetBEUI is a simple protocol that lacks many of the features that enable protocol suites like TCP/IP to support networks of almost any size. NetBEUI is not routable, so it cannot be used on large internetworks. It is suitable for small peer-to-peer networks, but any serious Windows NT network installation should use TCP/IP.

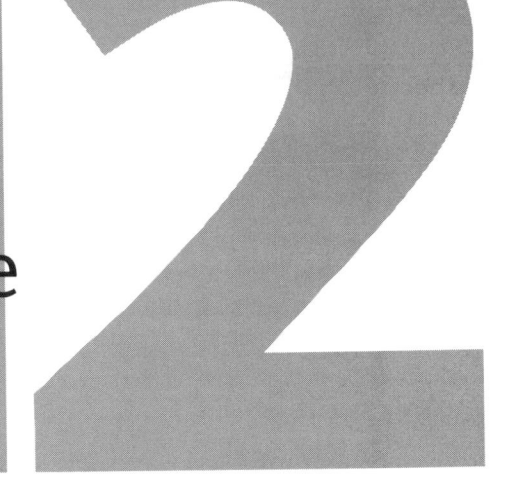

Chapter 12

Magnetic Storage

Most of the storage media in personal computer systems operate on magnetic principles. Purely optical devices like CD-ROMs are often used as a secondary form of storage, but the average PC typically relies on a magnetic medium for its primary disk storage. Due to the high performance and density capabilities of magnetic storage, optical disk drives and media probably will never totally replace magnetic storage in PC systems.

This chapter examines the various forms of magnetic storage media used in computer systems, from the floppy disk drives and hard disk drives found in virtually every PC to the removable mass storage media, like cartridge and tape drives, that are becoming increasingly popular options. In this chapter you learn about how magnetic data storage works and how it can help you develop a feel for the way your computer's drives operate.

▶▶ See "CD-ROM Disc and Drive Formats," p. 838

Principles of Magnetic Storage

All magnetic storage devices, such as floppy disk drives and hard disk drives, read and write data by using *electromagnetism*. This basic principle of physics states that as an electric current flows through a conductor, a magnetic field is generated around the conductor. This magnetic field can then exert an influence on magnetic material in the field. When the direction of the flow of electric current is reversed, the magnetic field's polarity also is reversed. For example, an electric motor uses electromagnetism to exert pushing and pulling forces on magnets attached to a rotating shaft.

Another effect of electromagnetism is that if a conductor is passed through a changing magnetic field, an electrical current is generated. As the polarity of the magnetic field changes, so does the direction of the electric current's flow. For example, a type of electrical generator used in automobiles, called an *alternator*, operates by rotating electromagnets past coils of wire conductors that contain large amounts of electrical current. When applied to magnetic storage devices, this two-way operation of electromagnetism makes it possible to record data on a disk and read that data back later.

The read/write heads in a magnetic storage device are U-shaped pieces of conductive material, with the ends of the U situated directly above (or next to) the surface of the actual data storage medium. The U-shaped head is wrapped with coils of conductive wire, through which an electric current can flow. When the drive logic passes a current through these coils, it generates a magnetic field in the drive head. Reversing the polarity of the electric current causes the polarity of the generated field to change also. In essence, the heads are electromagnets whose voltage can be switched in polarity very quickly.

The disk or tape that constitutes the actual storage medium consists of some form of substrate material (such as Mylar for floppy disks or aluminum or glass for hard disks) on which a layer of magnetizable material has been deposited. This material usually is a form of iron oxide with various other elements added. Each of the individual magnetic particles on the storage medium has its own magnetic field. When the medium is blank, the polarities of those magnetic fields are normally in a state of random disarray. Because the fields of the individual particles point in random directions, each tiny magnetic field is canceled out by one that points in the opposite direction; the cumulative effect of this is a surface with no observable field polarity.

When a magnetic field is generated by the drive's read/write head, the field jumps the gap between the ends of the U-shape. Because a magnetic field passes through a conductor much more easily than through the air, the field bends outward from the head and actually uses the adjacent storage medium as the path of least resistance to the other side of the gap. As the field passes through the medium directly under the gap, it polarizes the magnetic particles that it touches so they are aligned with the field. The field's polarity—and, therefore, the polarity of the magnetic medium—are based on the direction of the flow of electric current through the coils.

When the magnetic field passes through the medium, the particles in the area below the head gap are aligned in the same direction as the field emanating from the gap. When the individual magnetic domains of the particles are in alignment, they no longer cancel one another out, and an observable magnetic field exists in that region of the medium. This local field is generated by the many magnetic particles that now are operating as a team to produce a detectable cumulative field with a unified direction.

The term *flux* describes a magnetic field that has a specific direction. As the surface of the medium moves across the drive head, the head can create a magnetic flux over a specific region of the medium. When the flow of electric current through the coils in the head is reversed, so is the magnetic field polarity in the head gap. This reversal also causes the polarity of the flux being created on the medium to reverse.

The *flux reversal* or *flux transition* is a change in the polarity of the aligned magnetic particles on the surface of the storage medium. A drive head creates flux reversals on the medium to record data. For each data bit (or bits) that a drive writes, it creates a pattern of positive-to-negative and negative-to-positive flux reversals on the medium in specific areas known as bit or transition cells. A *bit cell* or *transition cell* is a specific area of the medium—controlled by the time and speed at which the medium travels—in which the drive head creates flux reversals. The particular pattern of flux reversals within the transition cells that are used to store a given data bit (or bits) is called the *encoding method*. The drive logic or *controller* takes the data to be stored and encodes it as a series of flux reversals over a period of time, according to the pattern dictated by the encoding method it uses.

> **Note**
>
> The two most popular encoding methods for magnetic media are *Modified Frequency Modulation (MFM)* and *Run Length Limited (RLL)*. All floppy disk drives and some older hard disk drives use the MFM scheme. Today's hard disk drives use one of several variations on the RLL encoding method. These encoding methods are described in more detail in the next section, "Data Encoding Schemes."

During the write process, voltage is applied to the head, and as the polarity of this voltage changes, the polarity of the magnetic field being recorded also changes. The flux transitions are written precisely at the points where the recording polarity changes. Strange as it may seem, during the read process, a head does not generate exactly the same signal that was written. Instead, the head generates a voltage pulse or spike only when it crosses a flux transition. When the transition changes from positive to negative, the pulse that the head detects is a negative voltage. When the transition changes from negative to positive, the pulse is a positive voltage spike.

In essence, while reading from the medium, the head becomes a flux transition detector, emitting voltage pulses whenever it crosses a transition. Areas of no transition generate no pulse. Figure 12.1 shows the relationship between the read and write waveforms and the flux transitions recorded on a storage medium.

You can think of the write pattern as being a square waveform that is at a positive or negative voltage level and that continuously polarizes the storage medium in one direction or another. Where the waveform transitions go from positive to negative voltage, or vice versa, the magnetic flux on the disk also changes polarity. During a read, the head senses the flux transitions and generates a pulsed waveform. In other words, the signal is zero volts unless the head detects a positive or negative transition, in which case it generates a positive or negative pulse. Pulses appear only when the head is passing over flux transitions on the medium. By knowing the clock timing the drive uses, the controller circuitry can determine whether a pulse (and therefore a flux transition) falls within a given transition cell.

The electrical pulse currents that are generated in the head while it is passing over the storage medium in read mode are very weak and can contain significant noise. Sensitive electronics in the drive and controller assembly amplify the signal above the noise level and decode the train of weak pulse currents back into binary data that is (theoretically) identical to the data originally recorded.

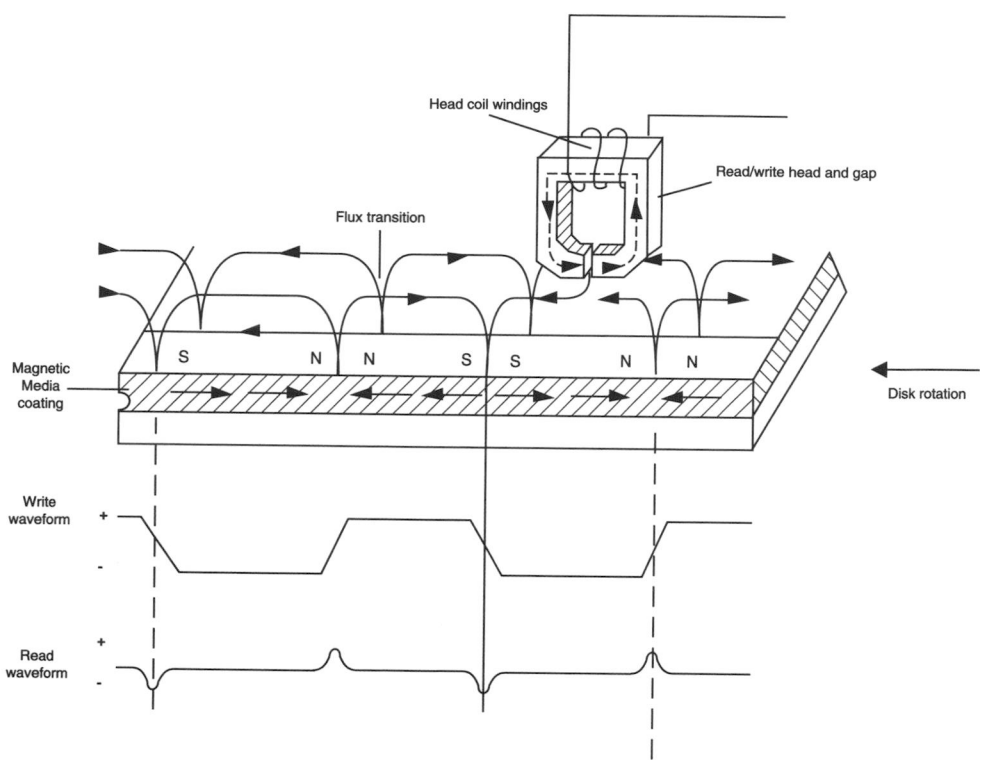

FIG. 12.1   Magnetic write and read processes.

So as you can see, hard disk drives and other storage devices read and write data by means of basic electromagnetic principles. A drive writes data by passing electrical currents through an electromagnet (the drive head), generating a magnetic field that is stored on the medium. The drive reads data by passing the head back over the surface of the medium. As the head encounters changes in the stored magnetic field, it generates a weak electrical current that indicates the presence or absence of flux transitions in the signal as it was originally written.

Data Encoding Schemes

Magnetic storage is essentially an analog medium. The data that a PC stores on it, however, is digital information—that is, ones and zeros. When the drive sends digital information to a magnetic recording head, the head creates magnetic domains on the storage medium with specific polarities corresponding to the positive and negative voltages that the drive applies to the head. It is the flux reversals that form the boundaries between the areas of positive and negative polarity that the drive controller uses to encode the digital data onto the analog medium. During a read operation, each flux reversal that the drive detects generates a positive or negative pulse that the device uses to reconstruct the original binary data.

To optimize the placement of flux transitions during magnetic storage, the drive passes the raw digital input data through a device called an *encoder/decoder (endec)*, which converts the raw binary information to a waveform that is more conducive to the optimum placement of the flux transitions (pulses). During a read operation, the endec reverses the process and decodes the pulse train back into the original binary data. Over the years, several different schemes for encoding data in this manner have been developed; some are better or more efficient than others, which you see later in this section.

Other descriptions of the data encoding process may be much simpler, but they omit the facts that make some of the issues related to hard drive reliability so critical—namely, timing. Engineers and designers are constantly "pushing the envelope" to stuff more and more bits of information into the limited quantity of magnetic flux reversals per inch. What they came up with, essentially, is a design in which the bits of information are not only decoded from the presence or absence of flux reversals, but from the timing between them. The more accurately they can time the reversals, the more information that can be encoded (and subsequently decoded) from that timing information.

In any form of binary signaling, the use of timing is significant. When interpreting a read or write waveform, the timing of each voltage transition event is critical. If the timing is off, a given voltage transition may be recognized at the wrong time, and bits may be missed, added, or misinterpreted. To ensure that the timing is precise, the transmitting and receiving devices must be in synch. For example, a consecutive series of ten 0 bits can be interpreted as nine or eleven bits if the timing is not exactly synchronized. This synchronization is often accomplished by adding a separate timing signal, called a *clock signal*, to the transmission between the two devices. It is also possible for the clock and data signals to be combined and transmitted as a single signal. Most magnetic data encoding schemes use this type of combination of clock and data signals.

Adding a clock signal to the data ensures that the communicating devices can accurately interpret the individual bit cells. Each bit cell is bounded by two other cells containing the clock transitions. By sending clock information along with the data, the clocks remain in synch, even if the medium contains a long string of identical 0 bits. Unfortunately, the transition cells that are used solely for timing take up space on the medium that could otherwise be used for data.

Because the number of flux transitions that a drive can record on a particular medium is limited by the physical nature of the medium and the head technology, drive engineers have developed various ways of encoding the data by using a minimum number of flux reversals (taking into consideration the fact that some flux reversals used solely for clocking are required). Signal encoding enables the system to make the maximum use of a given drive hardware technology.

Although various encoding schemes have been tried, only a few are popular today. Over the years, these three basic types have been the most popular:

- Frequency Modulation (FM)
- Modified Frequency Modulation (MFM)

■ Run Length Limited (RLL)

The following sections examine these codes, discusses how they work, where they are used, and any advantages or disadvantages that apply to them.

FM Encoding. One of the earliest techniques for encoding data for magnetic storage is called *Frequency Modulation (FM)* encoding. This encoding scheme, sometimes called *Single Density* encoding, was used in the earliest floppy disk drives installed in PC systems. The original Osborne portable computer, for example, used these Single Density floppy disk drives, which stored about 80K of data on a single disk. Although it was popular until the late 1970s, FM encoding is no longer used.

MFM Encoding. *Modified Frequency Modulation (MFM)* encoding was devised to reduce the number of flux reversals used in the original FM encoding scheme and, therefore, to pack more data onto the disk. MFM encoding minimizes the use of clock transition cells, leaving more room for the data. MFM records clock transitions only when a stored 0 bit is preceded by another 0 bit; in all other cases, a clock transition is not required. Because MFM minimizes the use of clock transitions, it can double the clock frequency used by FM encoding, enabling it to store twice as many data bits in the same number of flux transitions.

Because it is twice as efficient as FM encoding, MFM encoding also has been called *Double Density recording*. MFM is used in virtually all PC floppy disk drives today and was used in nearly all PC hard disks for a number of years. Today, virtually all hard disks use RLL (Run Length Limited) encoding, which provides even greater efficiency than MFM.

Because MFM encoding writes twice as many data bits by using the same number of flux reversals as FM, the clock speed of the data is doubled, so the drive actually sees the same number of total flux reversals as with FM. This means that a drive using MFM encoding reads and writes data at twice the speed of FM, even though the drive sees the flux reversals arriving at the same frequency as in FM.

The only caveat is that MFM encoding requires improved disk controller and drive circuitry, because the timing of the flux reversals must be more precise than in FM. These improvements were not difficult to achieve, and MFM encoding became the most popular encoding scheme for many years.

Table 12.1 shows the data bit to flux reversal translation in MFM encoding.

Table 12.1 MFM Data to Flux Transition Encoding	
Data Bit Value	**Flux Encoding**
1	NT
0 preceded by 0	TN
0 preceded by 1	NN

T = Flux transition
N = No flux transition

RLL Encoding. Today's most popular encoding scheme for hard disks, called *RLL (Run Length Limited)*, packs up to 50% more information on a given disk than MFM does and three times as much information as FM. In RLL encoding, the drive combines groups of bits into a unit to generate specific patterns of flux reversals. By combining the clock and data signals in these patterns, the clock rate can be further increased while maintaining the same basic distance between the flux transitions on the storage medium.

IBM invented RLL encoding and first used the method in many of its mainframe disk drives. During the late 1980s, the PC hard disk industry began using RLL encoding schemes to increase the storage capabilities of PC hard disks. Today, virtually every drive on the market uses some form of RLL encoding.

Instead of encoding a single bit, RLL normally encodes a group of data bits at a time. The term *Run Length Limited* is derived from the two primary specifications of these codes, which is the minimum number (the run length) and maximum number (the run limit) of transition cells allowed between two actual flux transitions. Several variations of the scheme are achieved by changing the length and limit parameters, but only two have achieved any real popularity: RLL 2,7 and RLL 1,7.

You can even express FM and MFM encoding as a form of RLL. FM can be called RLL 0,1, because there are as few as zero and as many as one transition cells separating two flux transitions. MFM can be called RLL 1,3, because there are as few as one and as many as three transition cells separating two flux transitions. (Although these codes can be expressed as variations of RLL form, it is not common to do so.)

RLL 2,7 was initially the most popular RLL variation because it offers a high density ratio with a transition detection window that is the same relative size as that in MFM. This method provides high storage density and fairly good reliability. In very high-capacity drives, however, RLL 2,7 did not prove to be reliable enough. Most of today's highest-capacity drives use RLL 1,7 encoding, which offers a density ratio 1.27 times that of MFM and a larger transition detection window relative to MFM. Because of the larger relative window size within which a transition can be detected, RLL 1,7 is a more forgiving and more reliable code, which is important when media and head technology are being pushed to their limits.

Another little-used RLL variation called RLL 3,9—sometimes called *ARLL (Advanced RLL)*—allows an even higher density ratio than RLL 2,7. Unfortunately, reliability suffered too greatly under the RLL 3,9 scheme; the method was used by only a few controllers and has all but disappeared.

It is difficult to understand how RLL codes work without looking at an example. Within a given RLL variation such as RLL 2,7 or 1,7, you can construct many different flux transition encoding tables to demonstrate how particular groups of bits are encoded into flux transitions.

In the conversion table shown in Table 12.2, specific groups of data bits 2, 3, and 4 bits long are translated into strings of flux transitions 4, 6, and 8 transition cells long,

PRML (Partial-Response, Maximum-Likelihood)

Another new feature in high-end hard disk drives involves the disk read circuitry. Read channel circuits using Partial-Response, Maximum-Likelihood (PRML) technology enable disk drive manufacturers to increase the amount of data stored on a disk platter by up to 40%. PRML replaces the standard "detect one peak at a time" approach of traditional analog peak-detect, read/write channels with digital signal processing.

As the data density of hard disks increases, the drive must necessarily record the flux reversals closer together on the medium. This makes it more difficult to read the data on the disk, because the magnetic peaks can begin to interfere with each other. PRML modifies the way that the drive reads the data from the disk. The controller analyzes the analog data stream it receives from the heads by using digital signal sampling, processing, and detection algorithms (this is the *partial response* element) and predicts the sequence of bits that the data stream is most likely to represent (the *maximum likelihood* element).

This may not sound like a very precise method of reading data that must be bit-perfect to be usable, but the aggregate effect of the digital signal processing filters out the noise efficiently enough to enable the drive to place the flux change pulses much closer together on the platter, thus achieving greater densities.

Capacity Measurements

The industry standard abbreviations for the units used to measure the capacity of magnetic (and other) drives are shown in Table 12.3.

Table 12.3   Standard Abbreviations and Meanings

Abbreviation	Description	Decimal Power	Decimal Value	Binary Power	Binary Value
Kbit or Kb	Kilobit	10^3	1,000	2^{10}	1,024
K or KB	Kilobyte	10^3	1,000	2^{10}	1,024
Mbit or Mb	Megabit	10^6	1,000,000	2^{20}	1,048,576
M or MB	Megabyte	10^6	1,000,000	2^{20}	1,048,576
Gbit or Gb	Gigabit	10^9	1,000,000,000	2^{30}	1,073,741,824
G or GB	Gigabyte	10^9	1,000,000,000	2^{30}	1,073,741,824
Tbit or Tb	Terabit	10^{12}	1,000,000,000,000	2^{40}	1,099,511,627,776
T or TB	Terabyte	10^{12}	1,000,000,000,000	2^{40}	1,099,511,627,776

As you can see, each of these units of measurement has two possible values: a decimal (or metric) one and a binary one. Unfortunately, there are no differences in the abbreviations used to indicate these two types of values. In other words, M can indicate both "millions of bytes" and megabytes. In general, memory values are expressed by using the binary values, although disk capacities can go either way. This often leads to confusion in reporting disk capacities, because many manufacturers tend to use whichever value makes their products look better. Note also that when bits and bytes are used as part of some other measurement, the difference between bits and bytes is often distinguished by the use of a lower- or uppercase *B*. For example, megabits are typically abbreviated with a lowercase *b*, resulting in the abbreviation Mbps for megabits per second, while MBps indicates megabytes per second.

I hope that this examination of the basic principles of magnetic storage and the different encoding schemes that magnetic devices use has taken some of the mystery out of the way data is recorded on a drive. The following sections examine the specific devices that use these principles, such as hard disk, floppy disk, removable cartridge, and tape drives.

Hard Disk Drives

To many users, the hard disk drive is the most important, and yet the most mysterious, part of a computer system. A *hard disk drive* is a sealed unit that a PC uses for nonvolatile data storage. Nonvolatile, or permanent storage, in this case, means that the storage device retains the data even when there is no power supplied to the computer. Because the hard disk drive is expected to retain its data until a user deliberately erases it, the PC uses it to store its most crucial programming and data. As a result, when the hard disk fails, the consequences are usually very serious. To maintain, service, and expand a PC system properly, you must understand how the hard disk unit functions.

Most computer users want to know how hard disk drives work and what to do when a problem occurs. However, few books about hard disks cover this subject in the detail necessary for the PC technician or sophisticated user. This section corrects that situation, by thoroughly describing the hard disk drive from a physical, mechanical, and electrical point of view.

Definition of a Hard Disk

A hard disk drive contains rigid, disk-shaped platters, usually constructed of aluminum or glass. Unlike floppy disks, the platters cannot bend or flex—hence the term *hard disk*. In most hard disk drives, you cannot remove the platters, which is why they are sometimes called *fixed disk drives*. Removable hard disk drives are also available. Sometimes this term refers to a device in which the entire drive unit (that is, the disk and the drive) is removable, but it is more commonly used to refer to cartridge drives, such as the Iomega Zip and Jaz drives, that have removable storage media.

Note

Hard disk drives were at one time called *Winchester drives*. This term dates back to the 1960s, when IBM developed a high-speed hard disk drive that had 30M of fixed-platter storage and 30M of removable-platter storage. That drive, the *30-30 drive*, soon received the nickname *Winchester* after the famous Winchester 30-30 rifle. For a time after that, all drives that used a high-speed spinning platter with a floating head were known colloquially as *Winchester drives*.

Hard Drive Advancements. In the 15 or more years that hard disks have commonly been used in PC systems, they have undergone tremendous changes. To give you an idea of how far hard drives have come in that time, the following are some of the most profound changes in PC hard disk storage:

- Maximum storage capacities have increased from the 10M 5 1/4-inch full-height drives available in 1982 to 20G or more for small 3 1/2-inch half-height drives, and 10G or more for notebook system 2 1/2-inch drives. Hard drives smaller than 2G are rare in today's personal computers.

- Data transfer rates from the media (sustained) have increased from 85 to 102K/sec for the original IBM XT in 1983 to 30M/sec or more for some of the fastest drives today.

- Average seek times have decreased from more than 85ms (milliseconds) for the 10M XT hard disk in 1983 to fewer than 8ms for some of the fastest drives today.

- In 1982, a 10M drive cost more than $1,500 ($150 per megabyte). Today, the cost of hard drives has dropped to 3 cents per megabyte or less!

Areal Density. Areal density is often used as a technology-growth-rate indicator for the hard disk drive industry. *Areal density* is defined as the product of the linear bits per inch (BPI), measured along the length of the tracks around the disk, multiplied by the number of tracks per inch (TPI) measured radially on the disk. The results are expressed in units of megabits or gigabits per square inch (Mbit/sq-inch or Gbit/sq-inch) and are used as a measure of efficiency in drive recording technology. Current high-end 3 1/2-inch drives record at areal densities of nearly 3Gb/sq-inch. Prototype drives with densities as high as 10Gbit/sq-inch now exist, providing capacities of more than 20G on a single 2 1/2-inch platter.

Areal density (and, therefore, drive capacity) has been doubling approximately every two to three years, which will soon enable manufacturers to build 20 or 30G drives that fit in the palm of your hand. Companies are also developing new media and head technologies to support these higher areal densities, such as ceramic or glass platters, MR (Magneto-Resistive) heads, pseudo-contact recording, and PRML (Partial-Response, Maximum-Likelihood) electronics. The primary challenge in achieving higher densities is manufacturing drive heads and disks to operate at closer tolerances. To fit more data on a platter of a given size, the tracks must be placed closer together, and the heads must be able to achieve greater precision in their placement over the tracks. This means that as hard disk capacities increase, heads must ride ever closer to the disk surface.

Hard Disk Drive Operation

The basic physical construction of a hard disk drive consists of spinning disks with heads that move over the disks and store data in tracks and sectors. The heads read and write data in concentric rings called *tracks*, which are divided up into segments called *sectors*, which normally store 512 bytes each (see Figure 12.3).

Hard disk drives usually have multiple disks, called *platters*, that are stacked on top of each other and spin in unison, each with two sides on which the drive stores data. Most drives have at least two or three platters, resulting in four or six sides, and some drives have up to 11 or more platters. The identically positioned tracks on each side of every platter together make up a *cylinder* (see Figure 12.4). A hard disk drive normally has one head per platter side, with all the heads mounted on a common carrier device, or *rack*.

The heads move radially in and out across the disk in unison; they cannot move independently, because they are mounted on the same rack.

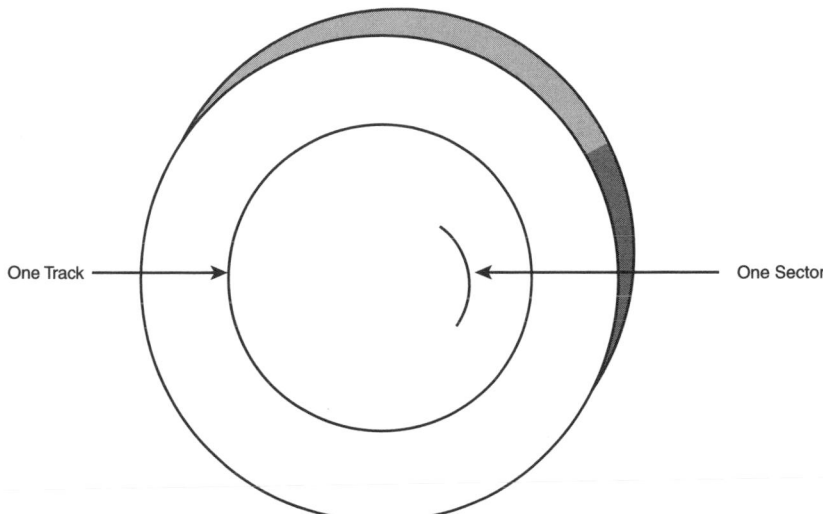

One Track

One Sector

FIG. 12.3 The tracks and sectors of a hard disk drive.

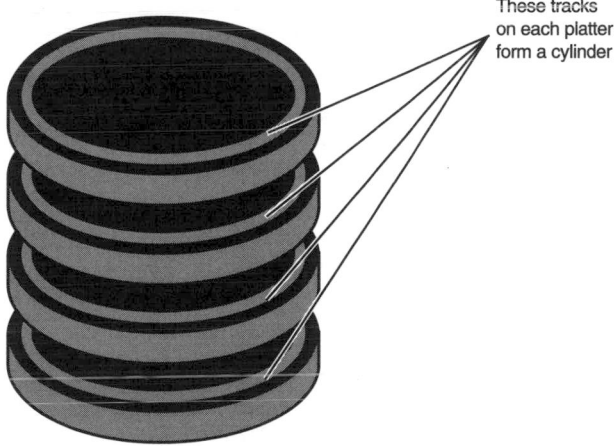

These tracks on each platter form a cylinder

FIG. 12.4 A hard disk cylinder.

Originally, most hard disks spun at 3,600 RPM—approximately 10 times faster than a floppy disk drive. Until recently, 3,600 RPM was pretty much a constant among hard drives. Now, however, quite a few hard drives spin the disks even faster. The Toshiba 3.3G drive in my notebook computer spins at 4,852 RPM; other drives spin as fast as 5,400, 5,600, 6,400, 7,200, and even 10,000 RPM. High rotational speeds combined with a fast head-positioning mechanism and more sectors per track are what make one hard disk faster than another.

The heads in most hard disk drives do not (and should not!) touch the platters during normal operation. When the heads are powered off, however, they land on the platters as they stop spinning. While the drive is running, a very thin cushion of air keeps each head suspended a short distance above or below the platter. If the air cushion is disturbed by a particle of dust or a shock, the head may come into contact with the platter while it is spinning at full speed. When contact with the spinning platters is forceful enough to do damage, the event is called a *head crash*. The result of a head crash may be anything from a few lost bytes of data to a completely ruined drive. Most drives have special lubricants on the platters and hardened surfaces that can withstand the daily "takeoffs and landings" as well as more severe abuse.

Because the platter assemblies are sealed and non-removable, the track densities on the disk can be very high. Many drives have 3,000 or more TPI (tracks per inch) of media. *Head Disk Assemblies (HDAs)*, which contain the platters, are assembled and sealed in clean rooms under absolutely sanitary conditions. Because few companies repair HDAs, repair or replacement of the parts inside a sealed HDA can be expensive. Every hard disk ever made eventually fails. The only questions are when the failure will occur and whether your data is backed up.

> **Caution**
>
> It is strongly recommended that you do not even attempt to open a hard disk drive's HDA unless you have the equipment and the expertise to make repairs inside. Most manufacturers deliberately make the HDA difficult to open, to discourage the intrepid do-it-yourselfer, and opening the HDA almost certainly voids the drive's warranty.

Many PC users think that hard disks are fragile, and comparatively speaking, they are one of the more fragile components in your PC. In my weekly PC Hardware and Troubleshooting or Data Recovery seminars, however, I have run various hard disks for days with the lids off, and have even removed and installed the covers while the drives were operating. Those drives continue to store data perfectly to this day with the lids either on or off. Of course, I do not recommend that you try this test with your own drives, nor would I do this with my larger, more expensive drives.

The Ultimate Hard Disk Drive Analogy. I'm sure that you have heard the traditional analogy that compares the interaction of the heads and the medium in a typical hard disk drive as being similar in scale to a 747 flying a few feet off the ground at cruising speed (500+ mph). I have heard this analogy used over and over again for years, and I've even used it in my seminars many times without checking to see whether the analogy is technically accurate with respect to modern hard drives. It isn't.

One highly inaccurate aspect of the 747 analogy has always bothered me—the use of an airplane of any type to describe the head-and-platter interaction. This analogy implies that the heads fly very low over the surface of the disk—but technically, this is not true. The heads do not fly at all, in the traditional aerodynamic sense; instead, they float on a cushion of air that's being dragged around by the platters.

A much better analogy would use a hovercraft instead of an airplane; the action of a hovercraft much more closely emulates the action of the heads in a hard disk drive. Like a hovercraft, the drive heads rely somewhat on the shape of the bottom of the head to capture and control the cushion of air that keeps them floating over the disk. By nature, the cushion of air on which the heads float forms only in very close proximity to the platter and is often called an *air bearing* by the disk drive industry.

I thought it was time to come up with a new analogy that more correctly describes the dimensions and speeds at which a hard disk drive operates today. I looked up the specifications on a specific hard disk drive, and then magnified and rescaled all the dimensions involved to make the head floating height equal to 1 inch. For my example, I used a Seagate model ST-12550N Barracuda 2 drive, which is a 2G (formatted capacity), 3 1/2-inch SCSI-2 drive, hardly state of the art by today's rapidly changing standards. Table 12.4 shows the specifications of the Barracuda drive, as listed in the technical documentation.

Table 12.4 Seagate ST-12550N Barracuda 2, 3 1/2-inch, SCSI-2 Drive Specifications		
Specification	**Value**	**Unit of Measure**
Linear density	52,187	Bits Per Inch (BPI)
Bit spacing	19.16	Micro-inches (μ-in)
Track density	3,047	Tracks Per Inch (TPI)
Track spacing	328.19	Micro-inches (μ-in)
Total tracks	2,707	Tracks
Rotational speed	7,200	Revolutions per minute (RPM)
Average head linear speed	53.55	Miles per hour (MPH)
Head slider length	0.08	Inches
Head slider height	0.02	Inches
Head floating height	5	Micro-inches (μ-in)
Average seek time	8	Milliseconds (ms)

By interpreting these specifications, you can see that in this drive, the head sliders are about 0.08-inch long and 0.02-inch high. The heads float on a cushion of air about 5 μ-in (millionths of an inch) from the surface of the disk while traveling at an average speed of 53.55 MPH (figuring an average track diameter of 2 1/2 inches). These heads

Table 12.5 shows the format for each track and sector on a typical hard disk drive with 17 sectors per track.

Table 12.5 Typical 17-Sector/17-Track Disk Sector Format		
Bytes	**Name**	**Description**
16	POST INDEX GAP	All 4Eh, at the track beginning after the Index mark.
The following sector data (shown between the lines in this table) is repeated 17 times for an MFM encoded track.		
13	ID VFO LOCK	All 00h; synchronizes the VFO for the sector ID.
1	SYNC BYTE	A1h; notifies the controller that data follows.
1	ADDRESS MARK	FEh; defines that ID field data follows.
2	CYLINDER NUMBER	A value that defines the actuator position.
1	HEAD NUMBER	A value that defines the head selected.
1	SECTOR NUMBER	A value that defines the sector.
2	CRC	Cyclic Redundancy Check to verify ID data.
3	WRITE TURN-ON GAP	00h written by format to isolate the ID from DATA.
13	DATA SYNC VFO LOCK	All 00h; synchronizes the VFO for the DATA.
1	SYNC BYTE	A1h; notifies the controller that data follows.
1	ADDRESS MARK	F8h; defines that user DATA field follows.
512	DATA	The area for user DATA.
2	CRC	Cyclic Redundancy Check to verify DATA.
3	WRITE TURN-OFF GAP	00h; written by DATA update to isolate DATA.
15	INTER-RECORD GAP	All 00h; a buffer for spindle speed variation.
693	PRE-INDEX GAP	All 4Eh, at track end before Index mark.
571	*Total bytes per sector*	
512	*Data bytes per sector*	
10,416	*Total bytes per track*	
8,704	*Data bytes per track*	

This table refers to a hard disk track with 17 sectors. Although this capacity was typical during the mid 1980s, modern hard disks place as many as 150 or more sectors per track, and the specific formats of those sectors may differ slightly from this example. As you can see, the usable space on each track is about 16% less than its unformatted capacity. This is true for most disks, although the percentage may vary slightly. The following paragraphs detail each piece of the sector data listed in Table 12.5.

The POST INDEX GAP provides a head-switching recovery period, so when switching from one track to another, the heads can read sequential sectors without waiting for an additional revolution of the disk. Because the disk is continuously spinning and the heads take some small amount of time to move radially from track to track, it is not possible to read consecutive sectors on two different tracks one right after the other. By the time the head moves to the new track, the beginning of the second sector has already spun past it. Leaving a gap between sectors provides the heads with time to move to another track.

In some drives, this gap does not provide sufficient time for the heads to move. When this is the case, it is possible for a drive to gain additional time by skewing the sectors on different tracks so the arrival of the first sector is delayed. In other words, the low-level formatting process offsets the sector numbering, so instead of the same numbered sectors on each track being adjacent to each other, sector 9 on one track may be next to sector 8 of the next track, which is next to sector 7 on the next, and so forth. The optimum skew value is based on the rotational speed of the disk as compared to the lateral speed of the heads.

Note

At one time, the head skew was a parameter that you could set yourself while low-level formatting a drive. Today's IDE and SCSI drives are low-level formatted at the factory with the optimum skew values.

The Sector ID data consists of the Cylinder, Head, and Sector Number fields, as well as a CRC field used to verify the ID data. Most controllers use bit 7 of the Head Number field to mark a sector as bad during a low-level format or surface analysis. This convention is not absolute, however. Some controllers use other methods to mark a bad sector, but usually the mark involves one of the ID fields.

The WRITE TURN-ON GAP follows the ID field's CRC bytes and provides a pad to ensure a proper recording of the user data area that follows, as well as to allow full recovery of the ID CRC.

The user DATA field consists of all 512 bytes of data stored in the sector. This field is followed by a CRC field to verify the data. Although many controllers use two bytes of CRC here, the controller may implement a longer Error Correction Code (ECC) that requires more than two CRC bytes to store. The ECC data stored here provides the possibility of correcting errors in the DATA field as well as detecting them. The correction/detection capabilities depend on the ECC code the drive uses and on its implementation by the controller. The WRITE TURN-OFF GAP is a pad that enables the ECC (CRC) bytes to be fully recovered.

The INTER-RECORD GAP provides a means to accommodate variances in drive spindle speeds. A track may have been formatted while the disk was running slightly slower than normal and then written to while the disk was running slightly faster than normal. In such cases, this gap prevents the accidental overwriting of any information in the next sector. The actual size of this padding varies, depending on the speed of the DATA disk's rotation when the track was formatted and each time the DATA field is updated.

The PRE-INDEX GAP allows for speed tolerance over the entire track. This gap varies in size, depending on the variances in disk-rotation speed and write-frequency tolerance at the time of formatting.

This sector prefix information is extremely important, because it contains the numbering information that defines the cylinder, head, and sector. So this information—except the

DATA field, DATA CRC bytes, and WRITE TURN-OFF GAP—is written only during a low-level format.

Disk Formatting. There are two formatting procedures required before you can write user data to a disk:

- Physical, or *low-level* formatting
- Logical, or *high-level* formatting

When you format a floppy disk, the Windows 9x Explorer or the DOS FORMAT command performs both kinds of formats simultaneously. A hard disk, however, requires two separate formatting operations. Moreover, a hard disk requires a third step, between the two formatting procedures, to write the partitioning information to the disk. *Partitioning* is required because a hard disk is designed to be used with more than one operating system. It is possible to use multiple operating systems on one hard drive by separating the physical formatting into a procedure that is always the same, regardless of the operating system used and the high-level format (which is different for each operating system). Partitioning enables a single hard disk drive to run more than one type of operating system or it can enable a single operating system to use the disk as several volumes or logical drives. A *volume* or *logical drive* is any section of the disk to which the operating system assigns a drive letter or name.

Consequently, preparing a hard disk drive for data storage involves three steps:

1. Low-Level Formatting (LLF)
2. Partitioning
3. High-Level Formatting (HLF)

Low-Level Formatting. During a low-level format, the formatting program divides the disk's tracks into a specific number of sectors, creating the intersector and intertrack gaps and recording the sector header and trailer information. The program also fills each sector's data area with a dummy byte value or a pattern of test values. For floppy disks, the number of sectors recorded on each track depends on the type of disk and drive. For hard disks, the number of sectors per track depends on the drive and the controller interface.

Originally, PC hard disk drives used a separate controller that took the form of an expansion card or was integrated into the motherboard. Because the controller could be used with various disk drives and may even have been made by a different manufacturer, there had to be some uniformity in the communications between the controller and the drive. For this reason, the number of sectors written to a track tended to be relatively consistent.

The original ST-506/412 MFM controllers always placed 17 sectors per track on a disk, although ST-506/412 controllers with RLL encoding increased the number of sectors to 25 or 26 per track and ESDI drives had 32 or more sectors per track. The IDE and SCSI drives found in PCs today can have anywhere from 17 to 100 or more sectors per track because these drives have the controller integrated into the drive unit. This is what Integrated Drive Electronics (IDE) means. A SCSI drive is basically the same as an IDE, except for the addition of a SCSI Bus Adapter circuit. Because the drive and the controller are a matched set, there is no need for manufacturers to maintain any uniformity in the communications between them, and they can use any number of sectors per track they want.

Virtually all IDE and SCSI drives use a technique called *Zoned Recording*, which writes a variable number of sectors per track. The outermost tracks hold more sectors than the inner tracks do because they are longer. Because of limitations in the PC BIOS, these drives still have to behave as though they have a fixed number of sectors per track. This situation is handled by translation algorithms that are implemented in the controller.

One way to increase the capacity of a hard drive during the low-level format is to create more sectors on the disks' outer cylinders than on the inner ones. Because they have a larger circumference, the outer cylinders can hold more data. Drives without Zoned Bit Recording store the same amount of data on every cylinder, even though the tracks of the outer cylinders may be twice as long as those of the inner cylinders. The result is wasted storage capacity, because the disk media must be capable of storing data reliably at the same density as on the inner cylinders. When the number of sectors per track is fixed, as in older controllers, the drive capacity is limited by the density of the innermost (shortest) track.

Drives that use Zoned Bit Recording split the cylinders into groups called *zones*, with each successive zone having more sectors per track as you move outwards from the center of the disk. All the cylinders in a particular zone have the same number of sectors per track. The number of zones varies with specific drives, but most drives have 10 or more zones.

Another effect of Zoned Bit Recording is that transfer speeds vary depending on what zone the heads are in. The rotational speed of the disk is always the same, but because there are more sectors in the outer zones, the transfer rate is higher there.

As an example, see Table 12.6, which shows the zones defined for one particular 3.8G Quantum drive, the sectors per track for each zone, and its data transfer rate.

Table 12.6 Zoned Bit Recording Information for the Quantum Fireball 3.8G Hard Disk Drive

Zone	Tracks in Zone	Sectors Per Track	Data Transfer Rate (Mbit/s)
0	454	232	92.9
1	454	229	91.7
2	454	225	90.4
3	454	225	89.2
4	454	214	85.8

(continues)

Table 12.6 Zoned Bit Recording Information for the Quantum Fireball 3.8G Hard Disk Drive Continued			
Zone	**Tracks in Zone**	**Sectors Per Track**	**Data Transfer Rate (Mbit/s)**
5	454	205	82.1
6	454	195	77.9
7	454	185	74.4
8	454	180	71.4
9	454	170	68.2
10	454	162	65.2
11	454	153	61.7
12	454	142	57.4
13	454	135	53.7
14	454	122	49.5

This drive has a total of 6,810 tracks on each platter surface and, as you can see, the tracks are divided into 15 zones of 454 tracks each. It is not essential for all the zones to be the same size; this is simply how this drive is arranged. Zone 0 consists of the outermost 454 tracks, which are the longest and contain the most sectors: 232. Each track in this zone can therefore provide 118,784 bytes or 116K of user data storage, although the 122 sector tracks in zone 14 can hold only 62,464 bytes, or 61K.

Thus, with Zoned Bit Recording, each platter surface in this disk drive contains 1,259,396 sectors, for a storage capacity of 644,810,752 bytes or 614.94M. Without Zoned Bit Recording, the number of sectors per track would be limited to 122 over the entire surface of each platter, for a total of 830,820 sectors, storing 425,379,840 bytes or 405.67M. Zoned Bit Recording, therefore, provides a 51.59% increase in the storage capacity of this particular drive.

Notice also the difference in the data transfer rates for each of the zones. The tracks in the outermost zone (0) yield a transfer rate of 92.9 Mbit/sec, which is 87.67% higher than the 49.5 Mbit/sec of the innermost zone (14). This is one reason why you may notice huge discrepancies in the results produced by disk drive benchmark programs. A test that reads or writes files on the outer tracks of the disk naturally yields far better results than one conducted on the inner tracks. It may appear as though your drive is running slower, when the problem is actually that the test results you are comparing result from disk activity on different zones. The drives with separate controllers used in the past could not handle Zoned Bit Recording because there was no standard way to communicate information about the zones from the drive to the controller. With SCSI and IDE disks, however, it is possible to format individual tracks with different numbers of sectors, due to the fact that these drives have the disk controller built in. The built-in controllers on these drives are fully aware of the zoning algorithm, and can translate the physical Cylinder, Head, and Sector numbers to logical Cylinder, Head, and Sector numbers so the drive appears to have the same number of sectors on each track. Because the

PC BIOS is designed to handle only a single number of sectors per track throughout the entire drive, a zoned drive must run by using a sector translation scheme.

The use of Zoned Bit Recording enables drive manufacturers to increase the capacity of their hard drives by between 20% and 50% compared with a fixed-sector-per-track arrangement. Virtually all IDE and SCSI drives today use Zoned Bit Recording.

Partitioning. Creating a partition on a hard disk drive enables it to support separate file systems, each in its own partition. Each file system can then use its own method to allocate file space in logical units called *clusters* or *allocation units*. Every hard disk drive must have at least one partition on it and can have up to four partitions, each of which can support the same or different type file systems. There are three common file systems used by PC operating systems today:

- *FAT (File Allocation Table)*. The standard file system supported by DOS, Windows 9x, and Windows NT. FAT partitions support file names of 11 characters maximum (8+3 character extension) under DOS, and 255 characters under Windows 9x or Windows NT 4.0 (or later). The standard FAT file system uses 12- or 16-bit numbers to identify clusters, resulting in a maximum volume size of 2G. You can create only two physical FAT partitions on a hard disk drive, called primary and extended, but you can subdivide the extended partition into as many as 25 logical volumes.

- *FAT32 (File Allocation Table, 32-bit)*. An optional file system supported by Windows 95 OSR2 (OEM Service Release 2), Windows 98, and Windows NT 5.0. FAT32 uses 32-bit numbers to identify clusters, resulting in a maximum single volume size of 2T or 2,048G in size.

- *NTFS (Windows NT File System)*. The native file system for Windows NT that supports file names up to 256 characters long and partitions up to (a theoretical) 16 exabytes (1 exabyte = 2^{64} bytes = 17,179,869,184 terabytes). NTFS also provides extended attributes and file system security features that do not exist in the FAT file system. Of these three file systems, the FAT file system still is by far the most popular and is accessible by nearly every operating system, which makes it the most compatible as well. FAT32 and NTFS provide additional features but are not universally accessible by other operating systems.

▶▶ See "FAT Disk Structures," p. 1065 and "FAT32," p. 1082

High-Level Formatting. During the high-level format, the operating system (such as Windows 9x, Windows NT, or DOS) writes the structures necessary for managing files and data on the disk. FAT partitions have a Volume Boot Sector (VBS), two copies of a file allocation table (FAT), and a root directory on each formatted logical drive. These data structures enable the operating system to manage the space on the disk, keep track of files, and even manage defective areas so they do not cause problems.

High-level formatting is not really a physical formatting of the drive, but rather the creation of a table of contents for the disk. In low-level formatting, which is the real physical formatting process, tracks and sectors are written on the disk. As mentioned, the DOS FORMAT command can perform both low-level and high-level format operations on a floppy disk, but it performs only the high-level format for a hard disk. Low-level formats of IDE and SCSI hard disk drives are performed by the manufacturer, and should almost never be performed by the end user.

Basic Hard Disk Drive Components

Many types of hard disk drives are on the market, but nearly all of them share the same basic physical components. There may be some differences in the implementation of these components (and in the quality of the materials used to make them), but the operational characteristics of most drives are similar. The basic components of a typical hard disk drive (see Figure 12.5) are as follows:

- Disk platters
- Read/write heads
- Head actuator mechanism
- Spindle motor
- Logic board
- Cables and connectors
- Configuration items (such as jumpers or switches)

The platters, spindle motor, heads, and head actuator mechanisms are usually contained in a sealed chamber called the *Head Disk Assembly (HDA)*. The HDA is usually treated as a single component; it is rarely opened. Other parts external to the drive's HDA—such as the logic boards, bezel, and other configuration or mounting hardware—can be disassembled from the drive.

Hard Disk Platters (Disks). A typical hard disk drive has one or more platters, or *disks*. Hard disks for PC systems have been available in a number of form factors over the years. Normally, the physical size of a drive is expressed as the size of the platters. Following are the platter sizes that have been associated with PC hard disk drives:

- 5 1/4-inch (actually 130mm, or 5.12 inches)
- 3 1/2-inch (actually 95mm, or 3.74 inches)
- 2 1/2-inch
- 1.8-inch

Larger hard disk drives that have 8-inch, 14-inch, or even larger platters are available, but these drives are not used with PC systems. Currently, the 3 1/2-inch drives are the most popular for desktop and some portable systems, while the 2 1/2-inch and smaller drives are very popular in portable or notebook systems. These little drives are quite amazing, with current capacities typically in the 1G–4G range, and capacities of 20G expected by the year 2000.

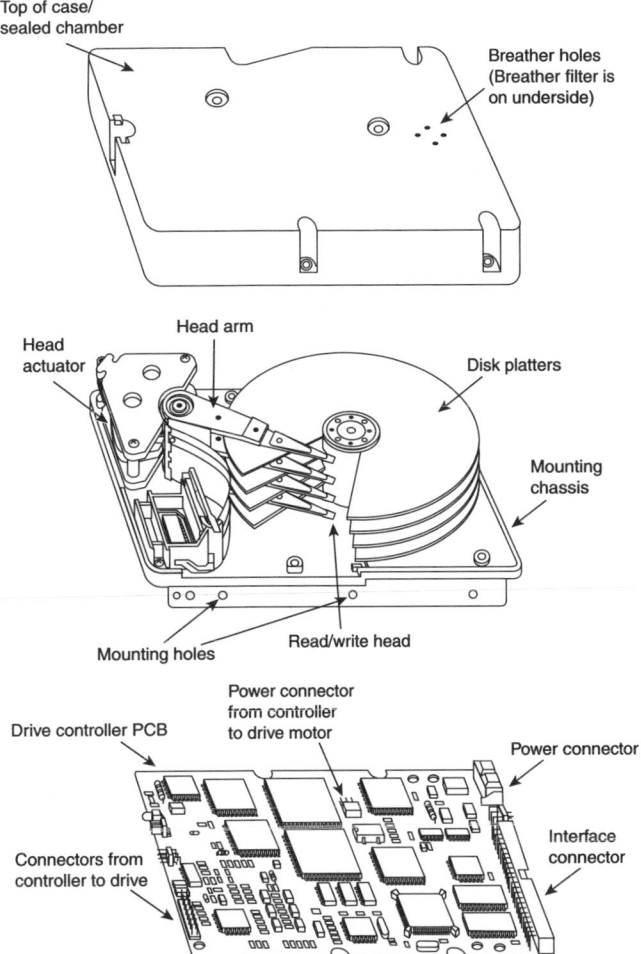

FIG. 12.5 Hard disk drive components.

Most hard disk drives have two or more platters, although some of the smaller drives have only one. The number of platters that a drive can have is limited by the drive's vertical physical size. The maximum number of platters that I have seen in any 3 1/2-inch drive is 11.

Platters have traditionally been made from an aluminum alloy that provides both strength and light weight. However, manufacturers' desire for higher and higher densities and smaller drives has led to the use of platters made of glass (or, more technically, a glass-ceramic composite). One such material, produced by the Dow Corning Corporation, is called MemCor. MemCor is composed of glass with ceramic implants, enabling it to resist cracking better than pure glass. Glass platters offer greater rigidity than metal (because metal can be bent and glass cannot) and can therefore be machined to one-half the thickness of conventional aluminum disks—sometimes less. Glass platters are also much more thermally stable than aluminum platters, which means that they do not expand or contract very much with changes in temperature. Several hard disk drives made by companies such as Seagate, Toshiba, Areal Technology, Maxtor, and Hewlett-Packard currently use glass or glass-ceramic platters. For most manufacturers, glass disks will probably replace the standard aluminum substrate over the next few years, especially in high-performance 2 1/2- and 3 1/2-inch drives.

Recording Media. No matter what substrate is used, the platters are covered with a thin layer of a magnetically retentive substance, called the medium, on which magnetic information is stored. Two popular types of magnetic media are used on hard disk platters:

- Oxide media
- Thin-film media

The *oxide media* is made of various compounds, containing iron oxide as the active ingredient. The magnetic layer is created on the disk by coating the aluminum platter with a syrup containing iron-oxide particles. This syrup is spread across the disk by spinning the platters at high speed; centrifugal force causes the material to flow from the center of the platter to the outside, creating an even coating of the material on the platter. The surface is then cured and polished. Finally, a layer of material that protects and lubricates the surface is added and burnished smooth. The oxide coating is normally about 30 millionths of an inch thick. If you could peer into a drive with oxide-coated platters, you would see that the platters are brownish or amber.

As drive density increases, the magnetic media needs to be thinner and more perfectly formed. The capabilities of oxide coatings have been exceeded by most higher-capacity drives. Because the oxide media is very soft, disks that use it are subject to head-crash damage if the drive is jolted during operation. Most older drives, especially those sold as low-end models, use oxide media on the drive platters. Oxide media, which have been used since 1955, remained popular because of their relatively low cost and ease of application. Today, however, very few drives use oxide media.

The *thin-film media* is thinner, harder, and more perfectly formed than oxide media. Thin film was developed as a high-performance medium that enabled a new generation of drives to have lower head floating heights, which in turn made increases in drive density possible. Originally, thin-film media were used only in higher-capacity or higher-quality drive systems, but today, virtually all drives use thin-film media.

The thin-film media is aptly named. The coating is much thinner than can be achieved by the oxide-coating method. Thin-film media are also known as *plated*, or *sputtered*, media because of the various processes used to deposit the thin film on the platters.

Thin-film plated media are manufactured by depositing the magnetic media on the disk with an electroplating mechanism, in much the same way that chrome plating is deposited on the bumper of a car. The aluminum platter is immersed in a series of chemical baths that coat the platter with several layers of metallic film. The magnetic medium layer itself is a cobalt alloy about 3 μ-in thick.

Thin-film sputtered media are created by first coating the aluminum platters with a layer of nickel phosphorus and then applying the cobalt-alloy magnetic material in a continuous vacuum-deposition process called *sputtering*. This process deposits magnetic layers as thin as 1 or 2 μ-in on the disk, in a fashion similar to the way that silicon wafers are coated with metallic films in the semiconductor industry. The same sputtering technique is then used again to lay down an extremely hard, 1 μ-in protective carbon coating. The need for a near-perfect vacuum makes sputtering the most expensive of the processes described here.

The surface of a sputtered platter contains magnetic layers as thin as 1 μ-in. Because this surface also is very smooth, the head can float closer to the disk surface than was possible previously. Floating heights as small as 3 μ-in above the surface are possible. When the head is closer to the platter, the density of the magnetic flux transitions can be increased to provide greater storage capacity. Additionally, the increased intensity of the magnetic field during a closer-proximity read provides the higher signal amplitudes needed for good signal-to-noise performance.

Both the sputtering and plating processes result in a very thin, very hard film of magnetic media on the platters. Because the thin-film media is so hard, it has a better chance of surviving contact with the heads at high speed. In fact, modern thin-film media are virtually uncrashable. If you could open a drive to peek at the platters, you would see that platters coated with the thin-film media look like the silver surfaces of mirrors.

The sputtering process results in the most perfect, thinnest, and hardest disk surface that can be produced commercially, which is why it has largely replaced plating as the preferred method of creating thin-film media. Having a thin-film media surface on a drive results in increased storage capacity in a smaller area with fewer head crashes—and in a drive that typically will provide many years of trouble-free use.

Read/Write Heads. A hard disk drive usually has one read/write head for each platter surface (meaning that each platter has two sets of read/write heads—one for the top side and one for the bottom side of the platter). These heads are connected, or *ganged*, on a single movement mechanism. The heads, therefore, move across the platters in unison.

Mechanically, read/write heads are simple. Each head is on an actuator arm that is spring-loaded to force the head into contact with a platter. Few people realize that each platter actually is "squeezed" by the heads above and below it. If you could open a drive safely and lift the top head with your finger, the head would snap back down into the platter when you released it. If you could pull down on one of the heads below a platter, the spring tension would cause it to snap back up into the platter when you released it.

Figure 12.6 shows a typical hard disk head-actuator assembly from a voice coil drive.

MIG heads are designed with a layer of magnetic alloy placed along the trailing edge of the gap. Double-sided MIG designs apply the layer to both sides of the gap. The metal alloy is applied through a vacuum-deposition process called sputtering, which was discussed in the previous section on recording media.

This magnetic alloy has twice the magnetization capability of raw ferrite and enables the head to write to the higher-coercivity thin-film media needed at the higher densities. MIG heads also produce a sharper gradient in the magnetic field for a better-defined magnetic pulse. Double-sided MIG heads offer even higher coercivity capability than the single-sided designs do.

Because of these increases in capabilities through improved designs, MIG heads were for a time the most popular head design, and were used in all but very high-capacity drives. Due to market pressures demanding higher and higher densities, however, MIG heads have been largely displaced in favor of thin-film heads.

Thin Film. *Thin-film (TF) heads* are manufactured in much the same manner as a semiconductor chip—that is, through a photolithographic process. This process creates many thousands of heads on a single circular wafer, and produces a very small, high-quality product.

TF heads have an extremely narrow and controlled head gap that is created by sputtering a hard aluminum material. Because this material completely encloses the gap, the area is very well protected, minimizing the chance of damage from contact with the spinning disk. The core is a combination of iron and nickel alloy that has two to four times more magnetic power than a ferrite head core.

TF heads produce a sharply defined magnetic pulse that enables them to write at extremely high densities. Because they do not have a conventional coil, TF heads are more immune to variations in coil impedance. These small, lightweight heads can float at a much lower height than the ferrite and MIG heads; in some designs, the floating height is 2 μ-in or less. Because the reduced height enables the heads to pick up and transmit a much stronger signal from the platters, the signal-to-noise ratio increases, improving accuracy. At the high track and linear densities of some drives, a standard ferrite head would not be able to pick out the data signal from the background noise. Another advantage of TF heads is that their small size enables the platters to be stacked closer together, making it possible to fit more platters into the same space.

Until the past few years, TF heads were relatively expensive compared with older technologies, such as ferrite and MIG. Better manufacturing techniques and the need for higher densities, however, have driven the market to TF heads. The widespread use of these heads has also made them cost-competitive with, if not cheaper than, MIG heads.

Many of the drives in the 100M to 1,000M range manufactured today use TF heads, especially in the smaller form factors. TF heads displaced MIG heads as the most popular head design, but they are now themselves being displaced by newer technologies, such as magneto-resistive heads.

Magneto-Resistive. *Magneto-Resistive (MR) heads* are the latest technology. Invented and pioneered by IBM, MR heads currently offer the highest performance available. Most 3 1/2-inch drives with capacities in excess of 1G currently use MR heads. As areal densities continue to increase, the MR head eventually will become the head of choice for nearly all hard drives, displacing the popular MIG and TF head designs.

MR heads rely on the fact that the resistance of a conductor changes slightly when an external magnetic field is present. Rather than put out a voltage by passing through a magnetic-field flux reversal, as a normal head would, the MR head senses the flux reversal and changes resistance. A small current flows through the heads, and this sense current measures the change in resistance. This design provides an output that is three or more times more powerful than a TF head during a read. In effect, MR heads are power-read heads, acting more like sensors than generators.

MR heads are more costly and complex to manufacture than other types of heads, because several special features or steps must be added. Among them are

- Additional wires must be run to and from the head to carry the sense current.

- Four to six more masking steps are required.

- Because MR heads are so sensitive, they are very susceptible to stray magnetic fields and must be shielded.

Because the MR principle can only read data and is not used for writing, MR heads really are two heads in one. The assembly includes a standard inductive TF head for writing data, and an MR head for reading. Because two separate heads are built into one assembly, each head can be optimized for its task. Ferrite, MIG, and TF heads are known as *single-gap heads* because the same gap is used for both reading and writing, while the MR head uses a separate gap for each operation.

The problem with single-gap heads is that the gap length is always a compromise between what is best for reading and what is best for writing. The read function needs a thin gap for higher resolution; the write function needs a thicker gap for deeper flux penetration to switch the medium. In a dual-gap MR head, the read and write gaps can be optimized for both functions independently. The write (TF) gap writes a wider track than the read (MR) gap reads. Thus, the read head is less likely to pick up stray magnetic information from adjacent tracks.

Drives with MR heads require better shielding from stray magnetic fields, which can affect these heads more easily than they do the other head designs. All in all, however, the drawback is minor compared with the advantages that the MR heads offer.

Head Sliders. The term *slider* is used to describe the body of material that supports the actual drive head itself. The slider is what actually floats or slides over the surface of the disk, carrying the head at the correct distance from the medium for reading and writing. Most sliders resemble a catamaran, with two outboard pods that float along the surface of the disk media and a central "rudder" portion that actually carries the head and the read/write gap.

The trend toward smaller and smaller form factor drives has forced sliders to become smaller and smaller as well. The typical mini-Winchester slider design is about .160×.126×.034 inches in size. Most head manufacturers have now shifted to 50% smaller nanosliders, which have dimensions of about .08×.063×.017 inches. The nanoslider is being used in both high-capacity and small-form-factor drives. The next evolution in slider design, called the *picoslider*, is smaller still: 70% smaller than the original design. Picosliders are assembled by using flex interconnect cable (FIC) and chip on ceramic (COC) technology that enables the process to be completely automated.

Smaller sliders reduce the mass carried at the end of the head actuator arms, providing increased acceleration and deceleration, leading to faster seek times. The smaller sliders also require less area for a landing zone, thus increasing the usable area of the disk platters. Further, the smaller slider contact area reduces the slight wear on the platter surface that occurs during normal startup and spindown of the drive platters.

The newer nanoslider designs also have specially modified surface patterns that are designed to maintain the same floating height above the disk surface, whether the slider is positioned above the inner or outer cylinders. Conventional sliders increase or decrease their floating height considerably, according to the velocity of the disk surface traveling beneath them. Above the outer cylinders, the velocity and floating height are higher. This arrangement is undesirable in newer drives that use Zoned Bit Recording, in which the bit density is the same on all the cylinders. When the bit density is uniform throughout the drive, the head floating height should be relatively constant as well for maximum performance. Special textured surface patterns and manufacturing techniques enable the nanosliders to float at a much more consistent height, making them ideal for Zoned Bit Recording drives.

Head Actuator Mechanisms. Possibly more important than the heads themselves is the mechanical system that moves them: the *head actuator*. This mechanism moves the heads across the disk and positions them accurately above the desired cylinder. There are many variations on head actuator mechanisms in use, but all of them fall into one of two basic categories:

- Stepper motor actuators
- Voice coil actuators

The use of one or the other type of actuator has profound effects on a drive's performance and reliability. The effects are not limited to speed; they also include accuracy, sensitivity to temperature, position, vibration, and overall reliability. The head actuator is the single most important specification in the drive, and the type of head actuator mechanism in a drive tells you a great deal about the drive's performance and reliability characteristics. Table 12.7 shows the two types of hard disk drive head actuators and the affected performance characteristics.

Table 12.7 Characteristics of Stepper Motor Versus Voice Coil Drives

Characteristic	Stepper Motor	Voice Coil
Relative access speed	Slow	Fast
Temperature sensitive	Yes (very)	No
Positionally sensitive	Yes	No
Automatic head parking	Not usually	Yes
Preventive maintenance	Periodic format	None required
Relative reliability	Poor	Excellent

Generally, a stepper motor drive has a slower average access rating, is temperature-sensitive during read and write operations, is sensitive to physical orientation during read and write operations, does not automatically park its heads above a save zone during power-down, and usually requires annual or biannual reformats to realign the sector data with the sector header information due to mistracking. To put it bluntly, a drive equipped with a stepper motor actuator is much less reliable (by a large margin) than a drive equipped with a voice coil actuator.

Floppy disk drives position their heads by using a stepper motor actuator. The accuracy of the stepper mechanism is suited to a floppy disk drive, because the track densities are usually nowhere near those of a hard disk. The track density of a 1.44M floppy disk is 135 tracks per inch, while hard disk drives have densities of over 5000 tracks per inch. Virtually all the hard disk drives being manufactured today use voice coil actuators, because stepper motors cannot achieve the degree of accuracy needed.

Stepper Motor Actuators. A *stepper motor* is an electrical motor that can "step," or move from position to position, with mechanical detents or click-stop positions. If you were to grip the spindle of one of these motors and spin it by hand, you would hear a clicking or buzzing sound as the motor passed each detent position with a soft click.

Stepper motors cannot position themselves between step positions; they can stop only at the predetermined detent positions. The motors are small (between 1 and 3 inches) and can be square, cylindrical, or flat. Stepper motors are outside the sealed HDA, although the spindle of the motor penetrates the HDA through a sealed hole.

Stepper motor mechanisms are affected by a variety of problems. The greatest problem is temperature. As the drive platters heat and cool, they expand and contract, and the tracks on the platters move in relation to a predetermined track position. The stepper mechanism cannot move in increments of less than a single track to correct for these temperature-induced errors. The drive positions the heads to a particular cylinder according to a predetermined number of steps from the stepper motor, with no room for nuance.

Voice Coil Actuators. The *voice coil actuators* used in virtually all hard disk drives made today, unlike stepper motor actuators, use a feedback signal from the drive to accurately determine the head positions and to adjust them, if necessary. This arrangement provides significantly greater performance, accuracy, and reliability than traditional stepper motor actuator designs.

A voice coil actuator works by pure electromagnetic force. The construction of the mechanism is similar to that of a typical audio speaker, from which the term *voice coil* is derived. An audio speaker uses a stationary magnet surrounded by a voice coil, which is connected to the speaker's paper cone. Energizing the coil causes it to move relative to the stationary magnet, which produces sound from the cone. In a typical hard disk drive's voice coil system, the electromagnetic coil is attached to the end of the head rack and placed near a stationary magnet. There is no physical contact between the coil and the magnet; instead, the coil moves by pure magnetic force. As the electromagnetic coils are energized, they attract or repulse the stationary magnet and move the head rack. Systems like these are extremely quick and efficient, and usually much quieter than systems driven by stepper motors.

Unlike a stepper motor, a voice coil actuator has no click-stops, or detent positions; rather, a special guidance system stops the head rack above a particular cylinder. Because it has no detents, the voice coil actuator can slide the heads in and out smoothly to any position desired. Voice coil actuators use a guidance mechanism called a *servo* to tell the actuator where the heads are in relation to the cylinders and to place the heads accurately at the desired positions. This positioning system often is called a *closed loop feedback mechanism*. This system works by sending the index (or servo) signal to the positioning electronics, which return a feedback signal that is used to position the heads accurately. The system is also called *servo-controlled,* which refers to the index or the servo information that is used to dictate or control head-positioning accuracy.

A voice coil actuator with servo control is not affected by temperature changes, as a stepper motor is. When temperature changes cause the disk platters to expand or contract, the voice coil system compensates automatically because it never positions the heads in predetermined track positions. Rather, the voice coil system searches for the specific track, guided by the prewritten servo information, and then positions the head rack precisely above the desired track, wherever it happens to be. Because of the continuous feedback of servo information, the heads adjust to the current position of the track at all times. For example, as a drive warms up and the platters expand, the servo information enables the heads to "follow" the track. As a result, a voice coil actuator is sometimes called a *track following system.*

The two main types of voice-coil positioner mechanisms are

- ■ Linear voice-coil actuators
- ■ Rotary voice-coil actuators

The two types differ only in the physical arrangement of the magnets and coils.

A *linear actuator* (see Figure 12.7) moves the heads in and out over the platters in a straight line. The coil moves in and out on a track surrounded by the stationary magnets. The primary advantage of the linear design is that it eliminates the head azimuth variations that occur with rotary positioning systems. (*Azimuth* refers to the angular measurement of the head position relative to the tangent of a given cylinder.) A linear actuator does not rotate the head as it moves from one cylinder to another, thus eliminating this problem.

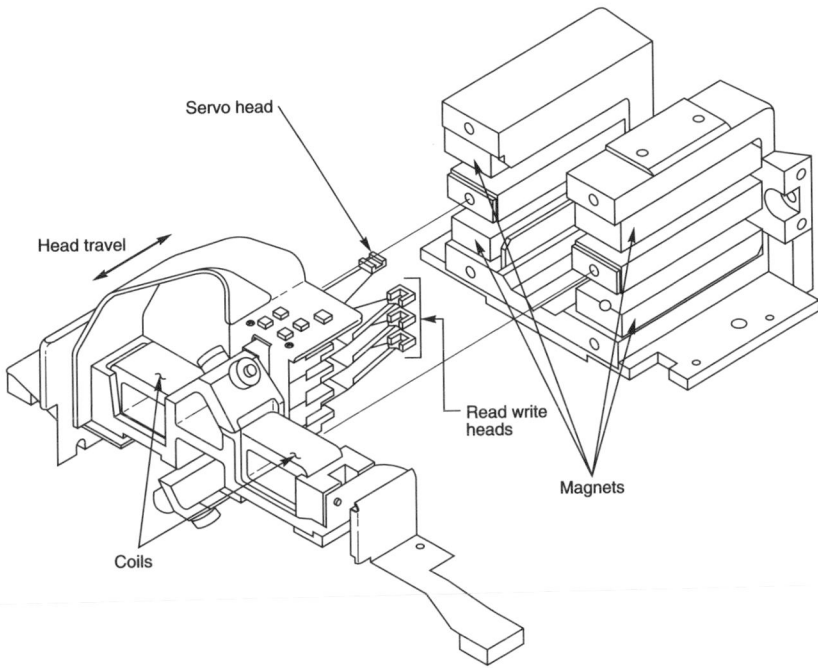

Servo head

Head travel

Read write
heads

Magnets

Coils

FIG. 12.7 A linear voice coil actuator.

Although the linear actuator seems to be a good design, it has one fatal flaw: The devices are much too heavy. As drive performance has increased, the desire for lightweight actuator mechanisms has become very important. The lighter the mechanism, the faster it can accelerate and decelerate from one cylinder to another. Because they are much heavier than rotary actuators, linear actuators were popular only for a short time; they are virtually nonexistent in drives manufactured today.

Rotary actuators (refer to Figure 12.6) also use stationary magnets and a movable coil, but the coil is attached to the end of an actuator arm. As the coil moves relative to the stationary magnet, it swings the head arms in and out over the surface of the disk. The primary advantage of this mechanism is its light weight, which means that the heads can accelerate and decelerate very quickly, resulting in very fast average seek times. Because of the lever effect on the head arm, the heads move faster than the actuator, which also helps to improve access times.

The disadvantage of a rotary system is that as the heads move from the outer to the inner cylinders, they rotate slightly with respect to the tangent of the cylinders. This rotation results in an azimuth error and is one reason why the area of the platter in which the cylinders are located is somewhat limited. By limiting the total motion of the actuator, the azimuth error is contained to within reasonable specifications. Virtually all voice coil drives today use rotary actuator systems.

Servo Mechanisms. Three servo mechanism designs have been used to control voice coil positioners over the years:

- Wedge servo
- Embedded servo
- Dedicated servo

The three designs are slightly different, but they accomplish the same basic task: They enable the head positioner to adjust continuously so it is precisely positioned above a given cylinder on the disk. The main difference between these servo designs is where the gray code information is actually written on the drive.

All servo mechanisms rely on special information that is written to the disk when it is manufactured. This information is usually in the form of a special code called a gray code. A *gray code* is a special binary notational system in which any two adjacent numbers are represented by a code that differs in only one bit place or column position. This system makes it easy for the head to read the information and quickly determine its precise position.

At the time of manufacture, a special machine called a *servowriter* writes the servo gray code on the disk. The servowriter is basically a jig that mechanically moves the heads to a given reference position and then writes the servo information at that position. Many servowriters are themselves guided by a laser-beam reference that calculates its own position by calculating distances in wavelengths of light. Because the servowriter must be capable of moving the heads mechanically, the process requires either that the lid of the drive be removed or that access be available through special access ports in the HDA. After the servowriting is complete, these ports are usually covered with sealing tape. You often see these tape-covered holes on the HDA, usually accompanied by warnings that you will void the warranty if you remove the tape. Because servowriting exposes the interior of the HDA, it requires a clean-room environment.

A servowriter is an expensive piece of machinery, costing up to $50,000 or more, and often must be custom-made for a particular make or model of drive. Some drive-repair companies have *servowriting capability*, which means that they can rewrite the servo information on a drive if it becomes damaged. If a servowriter is not available, a drive with servo-code damage must be sent back to the drive manufacturer for the servo information to be rewritten.

Fortunately, it is impossible to damage the servo information through disk read and write processes. Drives are designed so the heads cannot overwrite the servo information, even during a low-level format. One myth that has been circulating (especially with respect to IDE drives) is that you can damage the servo information by improper low-level formatting. This is not true. An improper low-level format may compromise the performance of the drive, but the servo information is totally protected and cannot be overwritten.

The track-following capabilities of a servo-controlled voice coil actuator eliminates the positioning errors that occur over time with stepper motor drives. Voice coil drives are not affected by conditions such as thermal expansion and contraction of the platters. In fact, many voice coil drives today perform a special thermal-recalibration procedure at predetermined intervals while they run. This procedure usually involves seeking the heads from cylinder 0 to some other cylinder one time for every head on the drive. As this sequence occurs, the control circuitry in the drive monitors how much the track positions have moved since the last time the sequence was performed, and a thermal-recalibration adjustment is calculated and stored in the drive's memory. This information is then used every time the drive positions the heads to ensure the most accurate positioning possible.

Most drives perform the thermal-recalibration sequence every five minutes for the first half-hour that the drive is powered on and then once every 25 minutes after that. With some drives, this thermal-recalibration sequence is very noticeable; the drive essentially stops what it is doing, and you hear rapid ticking for a second or so. Some people think that this is an indication that their drive is having a problem reading something and perhaps is conducting a read retry, but this is not true. Most of the newer intelligent drives (IDE and SCSI) employ this thermal-recalibration procedure to maintain positioning accuracy.

As multimedia applications grew in popularity, thermal recalibration became a problem with some manufacturers' drives. The thermal-recalibration sequence sometimes interrupted the transfer of a large data file, such as an audio or video file, which resulted in audio or video playback jitter. Some companies released special A/V (Audio Visual) drives that hide the thermal-recalibration sequences so they never interrupt a file transfer. Most of the newer IDE and SCSI drives are A/V capable, which means that the thermal-recalibration sequences will not interrupt a transfer such as a video playback.

While we are on the subject of automatic drive functions, most of the drives that perform thermal-recalibration sequences also automatically perform a function called a *disk sweep*. Also called *wear leveling* by some manufacturers, this procedure is an automatic head seek that occurs after the drive has been idle for a period of time. The disk-sweep function moves the heads to a cylinder in the outer portion of the platters, which is where the head float-height is highest (because the head-to-platter velocity is highest). Then, if the drive continues to remain idle for another period, the heads move to another cylinder in this area, and the process continues indefinitely as long as the drive is powered on.

The disk-sweep function is designed to prevent the head from remaining stationary above one cylinder in the drive for too long, where friction between the head and platter eventually would dig a trench in the medium. Although the heads are not in direct contact with the medium, they are so close that the constant air pressure from the head floating above a single cylinder could cause friction and excessive wear.

Wedge Servo. Some early servo-controlled drives used a technique called a *wedge servo*. In these drives, the gray-code guidance information is contained in a "wedge" slice of the drive in each cylinder immediately preceding the index mark. The index mark indicates the beginning of each track, so the wedge-servo information was written in the PRE-INDEX GAP, which is at the end of each track. This area is provided for speed tolerance and normally is not used by the controller. Figure 12.8 shows the servo-wedge information on a drive.

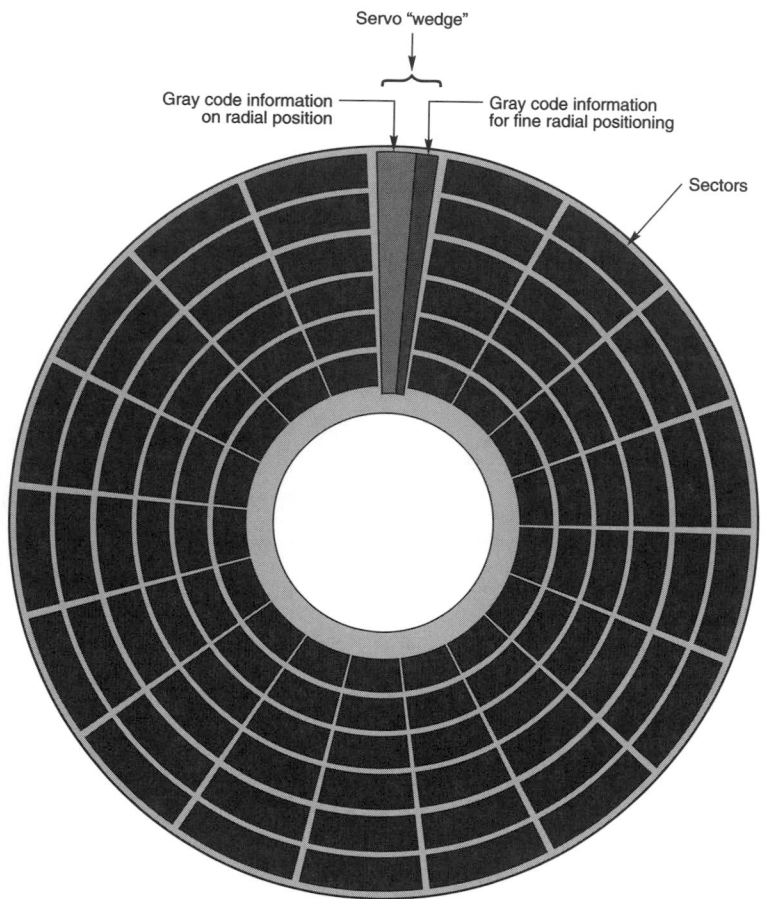

FIG. 12.8 A wedge servo.

Some controllers had to be notified that the drive was using a wedge servo so they could shorten the sector timing to allow for the wedge-servo area. If they were not correctly configured, these controllers would not work properly with the drive.

Another problem was that the servo information appears only one time every revolution, which means that the drive often needed several revolutions before it could accurately determine and adjust the head position. Because of these problems, the wedge servo never was a popular design; it no longer is used in drives.

Embedded Servo. An *embedded servo* (see Figure 12.9) is an enhancement of the wedge servo. Instead of placing the servo code before the beginning of each cylinder, an embedded servo design writes the servo information before the start of each sector. This arrangement enables the positioner circuits to receive feedback many times in a single revolution, making the head positioning much faster and more precise. Another advantage is that every track on the drive has its own positioning information, so each head can quickly and efficiently adjust position to compensate for any changes in the platter or head dimensions, especially for changes due to thermal expansion or physical stress.

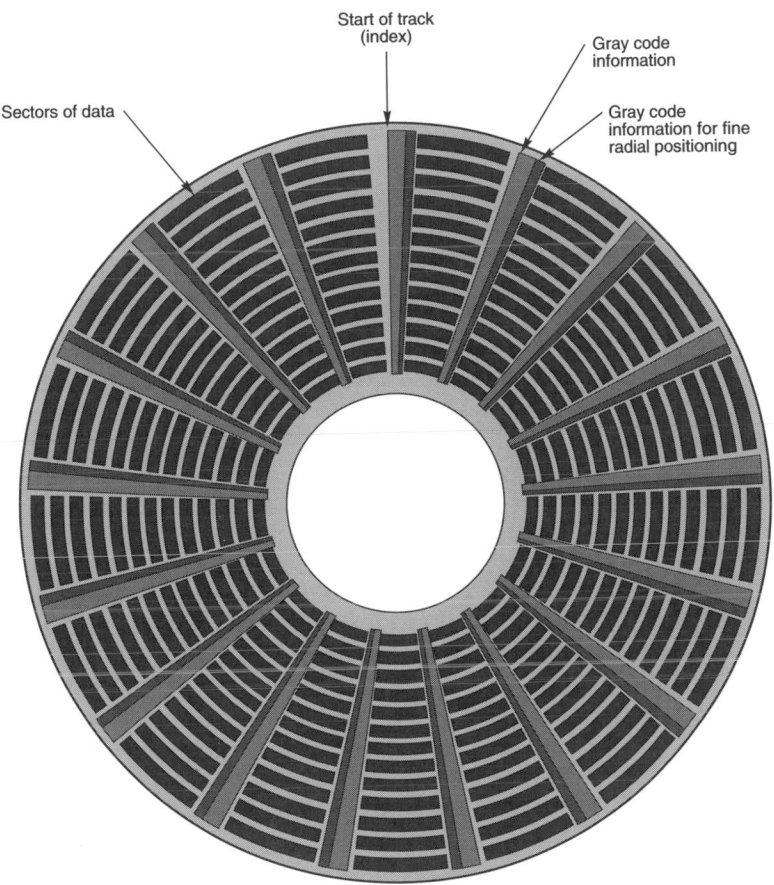

FIG. 12.9   An embedded servo.

Most drives today use an embedded servo to control the positioning system. As in the wedge servo design, the embedded servo information is protected by the drive circuits, and any write operations are blocked whenever the heads are above the servo information. Thus, it is impossible to overwrite the servo information with a low-level format, as some people incorrectly believe.

Although the embedded servo works much better than the wedge servo because the servo feedback information is made available several times in a single disk revolution, a system that offered continuous servo feedback information would be better.

Dedicated Servo. A *dedicated servo* is a design in which the servo information is written continuously throughout the entire track, rather than just once per track or at the beginning of each sector. Unfortunately, if this procedure were used on the entire drive, no room would be left for data. For this reason, a dedicated servo uses one side of one of the platters exclusively for the servo-positioning information. The term *dedicated* comes from the fact that this platter side is completely dedicated to the servo information and cannot contain any data.

When building a dedicated servo drive, the manufacturer deducts one side of one platter from normal read/write usage, and records a special set of gray-code data there that indicates the proper track positions. Because the head that rests above this surface cannot be used for normal reading and writing, the gray code can never be erased, and the servo information is protected, as in the other servo designs. No low-level format or other procedure can possibly overwrite the servo information.

When the drive moves the heads to a specific cylinder, the internal drive electronics use the signals received by the servo head to determine the position of the read/write heads. As the heads move, the track counters are read from the dedicated servo surface. When the servo head detects the requested track, the actuator stops. The servo electronics then fine-tune the position so the heads are positioned precisely above the desired cylinder before any writing is permitted. Although only one head is used for servo tracking, the other heads are attached to the same rack so if one head is above the desired cylinder, all the others will be as well.

One way of telling if a drive uses a dedicated servo platter is if it has an odd number of heads. For example, the Toshiba MK-538FB 1.2G drive that I have on my computer has 8 platters, but only 15 read/write heads. The drive uses a dedicated-servo positioning system, and the 16th head is the servo head. The advantage of the dedicated servo concept is that the servo information is continuously available to the drive, making the head positioning process faster and more precise. The drawback is that dedicating an entire platter surface to servo information can be wasteful. More drives today use embedded servo information than dedicated servo. Some drives combine a dedicated servo with an embedded servo, but this type of hybrid design is rare.

Of course, as mentioned earlier, today's IDE and SCSI drives have head, track, and sector-per-track parameters that are translated from the actual physical numbers. Therefore, it is not usually possible to tell from the published numbers exactly how many heads or platters are contained within a drive.

Automatic Head Parking. When you power off a hard disk drive, the spring tension in each head arm pulls the heads into contact with the platters. The drive is designed to sustain thousands of takeoffs and landings, but it is wise to ensure that the landing occurs at a spot on the platter that contains no data. Some amount of abrasion occurs during the landing and takeoff process, removing just a "micro puff" from the magnetic medium; but if the drive is jarred during the landing or takeoff process, real damage can occur.

One benefit of using a voice coil actuator is *automatic head parking*. In a drive that has a voice coil actuator, the heads are positioned and held by magnetic force. When the power to the drive is removed, the magnetic field that holds the heads stationary over a particular cylinder dissipates, enabling the head rack to skitter across the drive surface and potentially cause damage. In the voice coil design, the head rack is attached to a weak spring at one end and a head stop at the other end. When the system is powered on, the spring is overcome by the magnetic force of the positioner. When the drive is powered off, however, the spring gently drags the head rack to a park-and-lock position before the drive slows down and the heads land. On some drives, you can actually hear the "ting…ting…ting…ting" sound as the heads literally bounce-park themselves, driven by this spring.

On a drive with a voice coil actuator, you activate the parking mechanism by turning off the computer; you do not need to run a program to park or retract the heads. In the event of a power outage, the heads park themselves automatically. (The drives unpark automatically when the system is powered on.)

Air Filters. Nearly all hard disk drives have two air filters. One filter is called the *recirculating filter*, and the other is called either a *barometric* or *breather filter*. These filters are permanently sealed inside the drive and are designed never to be changed for the life of the drive, unlike many older mainframe hard disks that had changeable filters.

A hard disk on a PC system does not circulate air from inside to outside the HDA, or vice versa. The recirculating filter that is permanently installed inside the HDA is designed to filter only the small particles scraped off the platters during head takeoffs and landings (and possibly any other small particles dislodged inside the drive). Because PC hard disk drives are permanently sealed and do not circulate outside air, they can run in extremely dirty environments (see Figure 12.10).

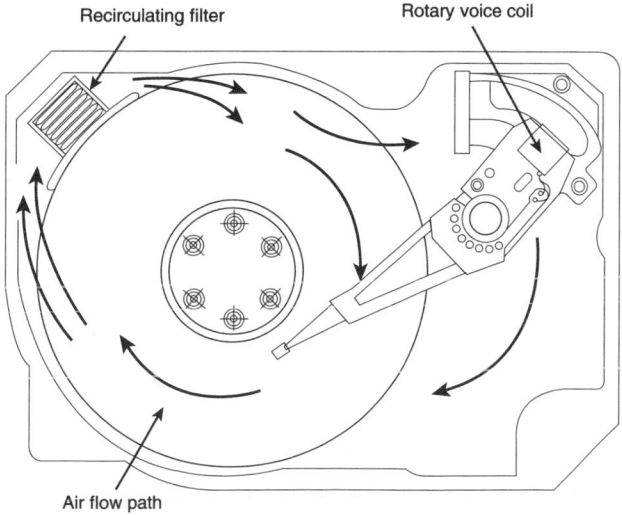

Recirculating filter

Rotary voice coil

Air flow path

FIG. 12.10 Air circulation in a hard disk.

The HDA in a hard disk drive is sealed but not airtight. The HDA is vented through a barometric or breather filter element that allows for pressure equalization (breathing) between the inside and outside of the drive. For this reason, most hard drives are rated by the drive's manufacturer to run in a specific range of altitudes, usually from 1,000 feet below to 10,000 feet above sea level. In fact, some hard drives are not rated to exceed 7,000 feet while operating, because the air pressure would be too low inside the drive to float the heads properly. As the environmental air pressure changes, air bleeds into or out of the drive so internal and external pressures are identical. Although air does bleed through a vent, contamination usually is not a concern, because the barometric filter on this vent is designed to filter out all particles larger than 0.3 microns (about 12 μ-in) to meet the specifications for cleanliness inside the drive. You can see the vent holes on most drives, which are covered internally by this breather filter. Some drives use even finer-grade filter elements to keep out even smaller particles.

I conducted a seminar in Hawaii several years ago, and several of the students were from the Mauna Kea astronomical observatory. They indicated that virtually all the hard disk drives they had tried to use at the observatory site had failed very quickly, if they worked at all. This was no surprise, because the observatory is at the 13,800-foot peak of the mountain, and at that altitude, even people don't function very well! At the time, it was suggested that the students look into solid-state (RAM) disks, tape drives, or even floppy disk drives as their primary storage medium. Since this time, IBM's Adstar division (which produces all IBM hard drives) introduced a line of rugged 3 1/2-inch drives that are hermetically sealed (airtight), although they do have air inside the HDA. Because they carry their own internal air under pressure, these drives can operate at any altitude, and can also withstand extremes of shock and temperature. The drives are designed for military and industrial applications, such as systems used aboard aircraft and in extremely harsh environments.

Hard Disk Temperature Acclimation. Because hard drives have a filtered port to bleed air into or out of the HDA, moisture can enter the drive, and after some period of time, it must be assumed that the humidity inside any hard disk is similar to that outside the drive. Humidity can become a serious problem if it is allowed to condense—and especially if you power up the drive while this condensation is present. Most hard disk manufacturers have specified procedures for acclimating a hard drive to a new environment with different temperature and humidity ranges, and especially for bringing a drive into a warmer environment in which condensation can form. This situation should be of special concern to users of laptop or portable systems. If you leave a portable system in an automobile trunk during the winter, for example, it could be catastrophic to bring the machine inside and power it up without allowing it to acclimate to the temperature indoors.

The following text and Table 12.8 are taken from the factory packaging that Control Data Corporation (later Imprimis and eventually Seagate) used to ship its hard drives:

If you have just received or removed this unit from a climate with temperatures at or below 50°F (10°C) do not open this container until the following conditions are met, otherwise condensation could occur and damage to the device and/or media may result. Place this package in the operating environment for the time duration according to the temperature chart.

Table 12.8 Hard Disk Drive Environmental Acclimation Table	
Previous Climate Temperature	**Acclimation Time**
+40°F (+4°C)	13 hours
+30°F (–1°C)	15 hours
+20°F (–7°C)	16 hours
+10°F (–12°C)	17 hours
0°F (–18°C)	18 hours
–10°F (–23°C)	20 hours
–20°F (–29°C)	22 hours
–30°F (–34°C) or less	27 hours

As you can see from this table, you must place a hard disk drive that has been stored in a colder-than-normal environment into its normal operating environment for a specified amount of time to allow it to acclimate before you power it on.

Spindle Motors. The motor that spins the platters is called the *spindle motor* because it is connected to the spindle around which the platters revolve. Spindle motors in hard disk drives are always connected directly; there are no belts or gears involved. The motor must be free of noise and vibration; otherwise, it can transmit a rumble to the platters that can disrupt reading and writing operations.

The spindle motor must also be precisely controlled for speed. The platters in hard disk drives revolve at speeds ranging from 3,600 to 7,200 RPM or more, and the motor has a control circuit with a feedback loop to monitor and control this speed precisely. Because the speed control must be automatic, hard drives do not have a motor-speed adjustment. Some diagnostics programs claim to measure hard drive rotation speed, but all that these programs do is estimate the rotational speed by the timing at which sectors pass under the heads.

There is actually no way for a program to measure the hard disk drive's rotational speed; this measurement can be made only with sophisticated test equipment. Don't be alarmed if some diagnostics program tells you that your drive is spinning at an incorrect speed; most likely the program is wrong, not the drive. Platter rotation and timing information is not provided through the hard disk controller interface. In the past, software could give approximate rotational speed estimates by performing multiple sector read requests and timing them, but this was valid only when all drives had the same number of sectors per track and spun at the same speed. Zoned Bit Recording—combined with the many different rotational speeds used by modern drives, not to mention built-in buffers and caches—means that these calculation estimates cannot be performed accurately by software.

On most drives, the spindle motor is on the bottom of the drive, just below the sealed HDA. Many drives today, however, have the spindle motor built directly into the platter hub inside the HDA. By using an internal hub spindle motor, the manufacturer can stack more platters in the drive, because the spindle motor takes up no vertical space.

> **Note**
>
> Spindle motors, particularly on the larger form-factor drives, can consume a great deal of 12-volt power. Most drives require two to three times the normal operating power when the motor first spins the platters. This heavy draw lasts only a few seconds, or until the drive platters reach operating speed. If you have more than one drive, you should try to sequence the start of the spindle motors so the power supply does not have to provide such a large load to all the drives at the same time. Most SCSI and IDE drives have a delayed spindle-motor start feature.

Logic Boards. All hard disk drives have one or more logic boards mounted on them. The *logic boards* contain the electronics that control the drive's spindle and head actuator systems and that present data to the controller in some agreed-upon form. On IDE drives, the boards include the controller itself, while SCSI drives include the controller and the SCSI bus adapter circuit.

Many disk drive failures occur in the logic board, not in the mechanical assembly. (This statement does not seem logical, but it is true.) Therefore, you can sometimes repair a failed drive by replacing just the logic board, rather than the entire drive. Replacing the logic board, moreover, enables you to regain access to the data on the drive—something that replacing the entire drive does not.

In many cases, logic boards plug into the drive and are easily replaceable. These boards are usually mounted with standard screw hardware. If a drive is failing and you have a spare, you may be able to verify a logic-board failure by taking the board off the known good drive and mounting it on the bad one. If your suspicions are confirmed, you can order a new logic board from the drive manufacturer, but unless you have data on the drive you need to recover, it may make more sense to just buy a new drive, considering today's low disk drive costs.

To reduce costs further, many third-party vendors can also supply replacement logic-board assemblies. These companies often charge much less than the drive manufacturers for the same components. (See Appendix A, "Vendor List," for vendors of drive components, including logic boards.)

Cables and Connectors. Hard disk drives typically have several connectors for interfacing to the computer, receiving power, and sometimes grounding to the system chassis. Most drives have at least these three types of connectors:

- Interface connector(s)

- Power connector

- Optional ground connector (tab)

Of these, the *interface connectors* are the most important, because they carry the data and command signals between the system and the drive. In most cases, the drive interface cables can be connected in a *daisy chain* or bus-type configuration. Most interfaces support at least two devices, and SCSI (Small Computer System Interface) can support up to seven (Wide SCSI-2 can support up to 15) devices in the chain, in addition to the host adapter. Older interfaces, such as ST-506/412 or ESDI (Enhanced Small Device Interface), used separate cables for data and control signals, but today's SCSI and IDE (Integrated Drive Electronics) drives have a single connector.

◀◀ See "ATA I/O Connector," p. 615, and "SCSI Cables and Connectors," p. 634

The *power connector* is usually the same 4-pin type that is used in floppy disk drives, and the same power-supply connector plugs into it. Most hard disk drives use both 5- and 12-volt power, although some of the smaller drives designed for portable applications use only 5-volt power. In most cases, the 12-volt power runs the spindle motor and head actuator, and the 5-volt power runs the circuitry. Make sure that your power supply can supply adequate power for the hard disk drives installed in your system.

The 12-volt power consumption of a drive usually varies with the physical size of the unit. The larger the drive is, the faster it spins, and the more platters there are to spin, the more power that it requires. For example, most of the 3 1/2-inch drives on the market today use roughly one-half to one-fourth the power (in watts) of the older 5 1/4-inch drives. Some of the very small (2 1/2- or 1.8-inch) hard disks barely sip electrical power and actually use 1 watt or less!

A *grounding tab* provides a positive ground connection between the drive and the system's chassis. In most computers, the hard disk drive is mounted directly to the chassis using screws so the ground wire is unnecessary. On some systems, the drives are installed on plastic or fiberglass rails, which do not provide proper grounding. These systems must provide a grounding wire plugged into the drive at this grounding tab. Failure to ground the drive may result in improper operation, intermittent failure, or general read and write errors.

Configuration Items. To configure a hard disk drive for installation in a system, you usually must set several jumpers (and, possibly, terminating resistors) properly. These items vary from interface to interface and often from drive to drive as well. A complete discussion of the configuration settings for each interface appears in the section "Hard Disk Installation Procedures" later in this chapter.

The Faceplate or Bezel. Many hard disk drives offer as an option a front faceplate, or *bezel* (see Figure 12.11). A bezel usually is supplied as an option for the drive rather than as a standard item. In most cases today, the bezel is a part of the case and not the drive itself.

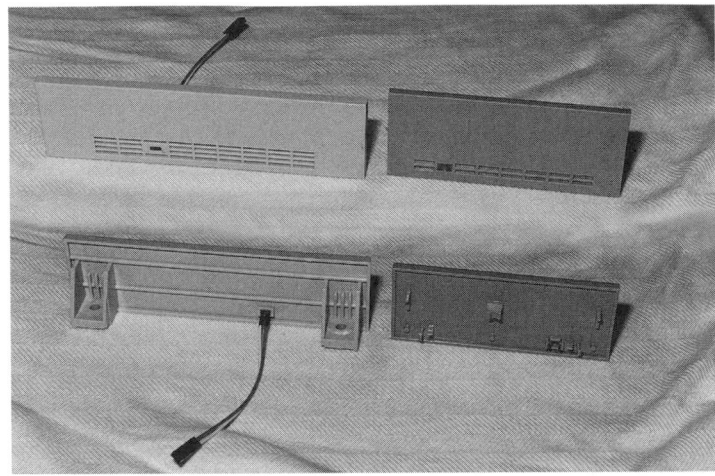

FIG. 12.11 Typical 5 1/4- and 3 1/2-inch hard drives bezel shown from the front (as seen on the outside of the PC case) (top) and from the back (bottom) (the inside mounting and LED wiring).

Older systems had the drive installed so it was visible outside the system case. To cover the hole in the case, you would use an optional bezel or faceplate. Bezels often come in several sizes and colors to match various PC systems. Many faceplate configurations for 3 1/2-inch drives are available, including bezels that fit 3 1/2-inch drive bays as well as 5 1/4-inch drive bays. You even have a choice of colors (usually black, cream, or white).

Some bezels feature a Light-Emitting Diode (LED) that flickers when your hard disk is in use. The LED is mounted in the bezel; the wire hanging off the back of the LED plugs into the drive. In some drives, the LED is permanently mounted on the drive, and the bezel has a clear or colored window so you can see the LED flicker while the drive is being accessed.

In systems in which the hard disk is hidden by the unit's cover, a bezel is not needed. In fact, using a bezel may prevent the cover from resting on the chassis properly, in which case the bezel will have to be removed. If you are installing a drive that does not have a proper bezel, frame, or rails to attach to the system, check Appendix A of this book; several listed vendors offer these accessories for a variety of drives.

Hard Disk Features

To make the best decision in purchasing a hard disk for your system, or to understand what differentiates one brand of hard disk from another, you must consider many features. This section examines some of the issues that you should consider when you evaluate drives:

- Reliability
- Speed
- Shock mounting
- Cost

Reliability. When you shop for a drive, you may notice a statistic called the *Mean Time Between Failures (MTBF)* described in the drive specifications. MTBF figures usually range from 20,000 hours to 500,000 hours or more. I usually ignore these figures because they are derived theoretically.

In understanding the MTBF claims, it is important to understand how the manufacturers arrive at them and what they mean. Most manufacturers have a long history of building drives and their drives have seen millions of hours of cumulative use. They can look at the failure rate for previous drive models with the same components and calculate a failure rate for a new drive based on the components used to build the drive assembly. For the electronic circuit board, they can also use industry standard techniques for predicting the failure of the integrated electronics. This enables them to calculate the predicted failure rate for the entire drive unit.

To understand what these numbers mean, it is important to know that the MTBF claims apply to a *population* of drives, not an individual drive. This means that if a drive claims to have a MTBF of 500,000 hours, you can expect a failure in that population of drives in 500,000 hours of total running time. If there are 1,000,000 drives of this model in service and all 1,000,000 are running at once, you can expect one failure out of this entire population every 1/2 hour. MTBF statistics are not useful for predicting the failure of any individual drive or a small sample of drives.

It is also important to understand the meaning of the word *failure* in this use. In this sense, a failure is a fault that requires the drive to be returned to the manufacturer for repair, not an occasional failure to read or write a file correctly.

Finally, as some drive manufacturers point out, this measure of MTBF should really be called *mean time to first failure*. "Between failures" implies that the drive fails, is returned for repair, and then at some point fails again. The interval between repair and the second failure here would be the MTBF. Because in most cases, a failed hard drive that would need manufacturer repair is replaced rather than repaired, the whole MTBF concept is misnamed.

The bottom line is that I do not really place much emphasis on MTBF figures. For an individual drive, they are not accurate predictors of reliability. However, if you are an information systems manager considering the purchase of thousands of PCs or drives per year, or a system vendor building and supporting thousands of systems, it is worth your while to examine these numbers and study the methods used to calculate them by each vendor. If you can understand the vendor's calculations and compare the actual reliability of a large sample of drives, then you can purchase more reliable drives and save time and money in service and support.

Performance. When you select a hard disk drive, one of the important features you should consider is the performance (speed) of the drive. Hard drives can have a wide range of performance capabilities. As is true of many things, one of the best indicators of a drive's relative performance is its price. An old saying from the automobile-racing industry is appropriate here: "Speed costs money. How fast do you want to go?"

When an application program wants to read data from a hard drive, the cache program intercepts the read request, passes the read request to the hard drive controller in the usual way, saves the data read from the disk in its cache memory buffer, and then passes the data back to the application program. Depending on the size of the cache buffer, data from numerous sectors can be read into and saved in the buffer.

When the application wants to read more data, the cache program again intercepts the request and examines its buffers to see whether the requested data is still in the cache. If so, the program passes the data back from the cache to the application immediately, without another hard drive operation. Because the cached data is stored in memory, this method speeds access tremendously and can greatly affect disk drive performance measurements.

Most controllers now have some form of built-in hardware buffer or cache that doesn't intercept or use any BIOS interrupts. Instead, the drive caches data at the hardware level, which is invisible to normal performance-measurement software. Manufacturers originally included track read-ahead buffers in controllers to permit 1:1 interleave performance. Some manufacturers now increase the size of these read-ahead buffers in the controller, while others add intelligence by using a cache instead of a simple buffer.

Many IDE and SCSI drives have cache memory built directly into the drive's on-board controller. For example, the Seagate Hawk 4G drive on which I am saving this chapter has 512K of built-in cache memory. Other drives have even larger built-in caches, such as the Seagate Barracuda 4G with 1M of integrated cache memory. I remember when 640K was a lot of memory for an entire system. Now, tiny 3 1/2-inch hard disk drives have more than that built right in! These integrated caches are part of the reason many IDE and SCSI drives perform so well.

Although software and hardware caches can make a drive faster for routine transfer operations, a cache will not affect the true maximum transfer rate that the drive can sustain.

Interleave Selection. In a discussion of disk performance, the issue of interleave often comes up. Although traditionally this was more a controller performance issue than a drive issue, modern IDE and SCSI hard disk drives with built-in controllers are fully capable of processing the data as fast as the drive can send it. In other words, virtually all modern IDE and SCSI drives are formatted with no interleave (sometimes expressed as a 1:1 interleave ratio). On older hard drive types, such as MFM and ESDI, you could modify the interleave during a low-level format to optimize the drive's performance. Today, drives are low-level formatted at the factory and interleave adjustments are a moot topic.

Head and Cylinder Skewing. Another performance adjustment that you could make at one time during a low-level format of a drive was to adjust the skew of the drive's heads and cylinders. *Head skew* is the offset in logical sector numbering between the same physical sectors on two tracks below adjacent heads of the same cylinder. The number of sectors skewed when switching from head to head within a single cylinder compensates for head switching and controller overhead time. *Cylinder skew* is the offset in logical sector numbering between the same physical sectors on two adjacent tracks on two adjacent cylinders.

Today's IDE and SCSI drives have their interleave and skew factors set to their optimum values by the manufacturer. In most cases, you cannot even change these values. In the cases where you can, the most likely result is decreased performance. For this reason, most IDE drive manufacturers recommend against low-level formatting their drives. With some IDE drives, unless you use the right software, you might alter the optimum skew settings and slow down the drive's transfer rate. Drives that use Zoned Bit Recording cannot ever have the interleave or skew factors changed, and as such, they are fully protected. No matter how you try to format these drives, the interleave and skew factors cannot be altered.

Shock Mounting. Most hard disks manufactured today have a *shock-mounted* HDA, which means that there is a rubber cushion placed between the disk drive body and the mounting chassis. Some drives use more rubber than others, but for the most part, a shock mount is a shock mount. Some drives do not have a shock-isolated HDA due to physical or cost constraints. Be sure that the drive you are using has adequate shock-isolation mounts for the HDA, especially if you are using the drive in a portable PC system or in a system used in a non-office environment where conditions may be less favorable. I usually never recommend a drive that lacks at least some form of shock mounting.

Cost. The cost of hard disk storage is continually falling and can now be as little as 4 cents per megabyte or less. You can now purchase a 4G IDE drive for under $170. That places the value of the 10M drive I bought in 1983 at about 42 cents. (Too bad that I paid $1,800 for it at the time!)

Of course, the cost of drives continues to fall, and eventually, even 4 cents per megabyte will seem expensive. Because of the low costs of disk storage today, not many drives with capacities of less than 1G are even being manufactured.

Capacity. There are four figures commonly used in advertising drive capacity:

- Unformatted capacity, in millions of bytes
- Formatted capacity, in millions of bytes
- Unformatted capacity, in megabytes
- Formatted capacity, in megabytes

The term formatted, in these figures, refers to the low-level (or physical) formatting of the drive. Most manufacturers of IDE and SCSI drives now report only the formatted capacities because these drives are delivered preformatted. Most of the time, advertisements and specifications refer to the unformatted or formatted capacity in millions of bytes, because these figures are larger than the same capacity expressed in megabytes. This situation generates a great deal of confusion when the user runs FDISK (which reports total drive capacity in megabytes) and wonders where the missing space is. This question can seem troubling. Fortunately, the answer is easy; it only involves a little math to figure it out.

Perhaps the most common questions I get are concerning "missing" drive capacity. Consider the following example: "I just installed a new Western Digital AC2200 drive, billed as 212M. When I entered the drive parameters (989 cylinders, 12 heads, 35 sectors per track), both the BIOS Setup routine and FDISK report the drive as only 203M! What happened to the other 9M?"

The answer is only a few calculations away. By multiplying the drive specification parameters, you get this result:

Cylinders:	989
Heads:	12
Sectors per track:	35
Bytes per sector:	512
Total bytes (in millions):	212.67
Total megabytes:	202.82

The result figures to a capacity of 212.67 million bytes or 202.82 megabytes. Drive manufacturers usually report drive capacity in millions of bytes, because they result in larger, more impressive sounding numbers, although your BIOS and the FDISK program usually report the capacity in megabytes. One megabyte equals 1,048,576 bytes (or 1,024K in which each kilobyte is 1,024 bytes). So the bottom line is that, because the same abbreviations are often used for both millions of bytes and megabytes, this 212.67M drive also is a 202.82M drive!

One additional item to note about this particular drive is that it is a Zoned Bit Recording drive and the actual physical parameters are different. Physically, this drive has 1,971 cylinders and 4 heads; however, the total number of sectors on the drive (and, therefore, the capacity) is the same no matter how you translate the parameters.

Although Western Digital does not report the unformatted capacity of this particular drive, unformatted capacity usually works out to be about 19% larger than a drive's formatted capacity. The Seagate ST-12550N Barracuda 2G drive, for example, is advertised as having the following capacities:

Unformatted capacity:	2,572.00 million bytes
Unformatted capacity:	2,452.85 megabytes
Formatted capacity:	2,139.00 million bytes
Formatted capacity:	2,039.91 megabytes

Each of these four figures is a correct answer to the question "What is the storage capacity of the drive?" As you can see, however, the numbers are very different. In fact, there is yet another number you can use. Divide the 2,039.91 megabytes by 1,024, and the drive's capacity is 1.99G! So when you are comparing or discussing drive capacities, make sure that you are working with a consistent unit of measure, or your comparisons will be meaningless.

Specific Recommendations. If you are going to add a hard disk to a system today, I can give you a few recommendations. For the drive interface, there really are only two types to consider:

- IDE (Integrated Drive Electronics)
- SCSI (Small Computer System Interface)

SCSI offers great expandability, cross-platform compatibility, high capacity, performance, and flexibility. IDE is less expensive than SCSI and also offers a very high-performance solution, but expansion, compatibility, capacity, and flexibility are more limited when compared with SCSI. I usually recommend IDE for most people for two reasons. First, the interface is already integrated into virtually every motherboard and BIOS sold today. Second, most users will not need more capacity than the four devices supported by the standard primary and secondary IDE interfaces found in most systems. SCSI offers additional performance potential with a multithreaded operating system like Windows NT, as well as support for more devices, but it also requires the purchase of a separate host adapter card, which is in addition to the higher cost for the drive itself.

> **Note**
>
> Note that the current IDE standard is ATA-4 (AT Attachment), otherwise loosely called Fast ATA or Enhanced IDE. SCSI-3 is the most current SCSI standard, which although not fully approved, is nearing completion.

Hard Disk Installation Procedures

This section describes the hard disk drive installation process, particularly the configuration, physical installation, and formatting of a hard disk drive.

To install a hard drive in a PC, you must perform some or all of the following procedures:

- Configure the drive
- Configure the host adapter
- Physically install the drive
- Configure the system
- Partition the drive
- High-level format the drive

As you perform the setup procedure, you may need to know various details about the hard disk drive, the host adapter, and the system ROM BIOS, as well as many of the other devices in the system. This information usually appears in the various OEM manuals that come with these devices. Make sure when you purchase these items that the vendor includes these manuals. (Many vendors do not include the manuals unless you ask for them.) For most equipment sold today, you will get enough documentation from the vendor or reseller of the equipment to enable you to proceed.

If you are like me, however, and want all the technical documentation on the device, you will want to contact the original manufacturer of the device and order the technical specification manual. For example, if you purchase a system that comes with a Western Digital IDE hard disk, the seller probably will give you some limited information on the drive, but not nearly the amount that the actual Western Digital technical specification manual provides. To get this documentation, you have to call Western Digital and order it. The same rule applies for any of the other components in most of the systems sold today. I find the OEM technical manuals to be essential in providing the highest level of technical support possible.

For reference, you can look up the hard disk manufacturer names in Appendix A, "Vendor List," and you will find numbers to call for technical support, as well as URLs for their Web sites.

Drive Configuration

Before you physically install a hard disk drive into the computer, you must be sure that it is properly configured. For an IDE drive, this generally means designating the drive as a master or a slave, depending on whether there are other devices installed in the system. For SCSI drives, you must set the device's SCSI ID and possibly its SCSI bus termination state.

◀◀ These procedures are covered in "The IDE Interface," p. 610, and "SCSI Drive Configuration," p. 640

Host Adapter Configuration

Older hard disk drive types used separate disk controller cards that you had to install in a bus slot. The IDE and SCSI hard disk drives used in today's PCs have the disk controller integrated into the drive assembly. For IDE drives, the I/O interface is nearly always integrated into the system's motherboard, and you configure the interface through the system BIOS. There is no separate host adapter, therefore, if you have an IDE drive you can proceed to "Physical Installation," later in this chapter.

SCSI drives, however, usually require a host adapter card that you must install in a bus slot like any other card. A few motherboards have integrated SCSI adapters, but these are rare. Configuring a SCSI host adapter card involves setting the different system resources that the adapter requires. As with most expansion cards, a SCSI host adapter will require some combination of the following system resources:

■ ROM addresses

- Interrupt requests (IRQ)

- DMA (Direct Memory Access) channel (DRQ)

- I/O port addresses

Not all adapters use every one of these resources, but some may use them all. In most cases, you must configure these resources so they are unique and cannot be shared with other devices. For example, if a disk controller is using I/O port addresses from 1F0 to 1F7h, no other device in the system can use those addresses.

When you install a host adapter that supports Plug and Play in a system with a Plug-and-Play BIOS and operating system, like Windows 9x, the configuration process is completely automatic. The computer sets the required hardware resource settings to values that do not conflict with other devices in the computer.

If your hardware or operating system does not support Plug and Play, you have to manually configure the adapter to use the appropriate resources. Some adapters provide software that enables you to reconfigure or change the hardware resources, while others use jumpers or DIP switches.

◀◀ See "System Resources," p. 269

The IDE interface is part of the standard PC BIOS, which makes it possible to boot from an IDE drive. The BIOS provides the device driver functionality that the system needs to access the drive before any files can be loaded from disk. The SCSI interface is not part of the standard PC BIOS, so most SCSI host adapters have their own ROM BIOS that enables SCSI drives to function as boot devices.

Use of the SCSI BIOS is usually optional. If you are not booting from a SCSI drive, you can load a standard device driver for your operating system to access the SCSI devices. Most host adapters have DIP switches that you use to enable or disable SCSI BIOS support.

In addition to providing boot functionality, the SCSI BIOS can provide many other functions, including any or all of the following:

- Low-level formatting

- Drive-type (parameter) control

- Host adapter configuration

- SCSI diagnostics

- Support for nonstandard I/O port addresses and interrupts

If the adapter's on-board BIOS is enabled, it will use specific memory address space in the Upper Memory Area (UMA). The UMA is the top 384K in the first megabyte of system memory. The UMA is divided into three areas of two 64K segments each, with the first and last areas being used by the video-adapter circuits and the motherboard BIOS, respectively. Segments C000h and D000h are reserved for use by adapter ROMs such as those found on disk controllers or SCSI host adapters.

> **Note**
>
> You must ensure that any adapters using space in these segments of the HMA (High Memory Area) do not overlap with another adapter that uses this space. No two adapters can share this memory space. Most adapters have software, jumpers, or switches that can adjust the configuration of the board and change the addresses it uses to prevent conflict.

Physical Installation

The procedure for the physical installation of a hard disk drive is much the same as that for installing a floppy disk drive. You must have the correct screws, brackets, and faceplates for the specific drive and system before you can install the drive.

Some computer cases require plastic rails that are secured to the sides of a hard disk drive so it can slide into the proper place in the system (see Figure 12.12). When you purchase a drive, vendors often give you the option to purchase a kit as opposed to the bare drive. For slightly more money, the kit includes mounting rails, screws, and often a ribbon cable that you should be able to use in most systems. Be careful when purchasing a SCSI drive, however, as the kit may include a host adapter that can add substantially to the price.

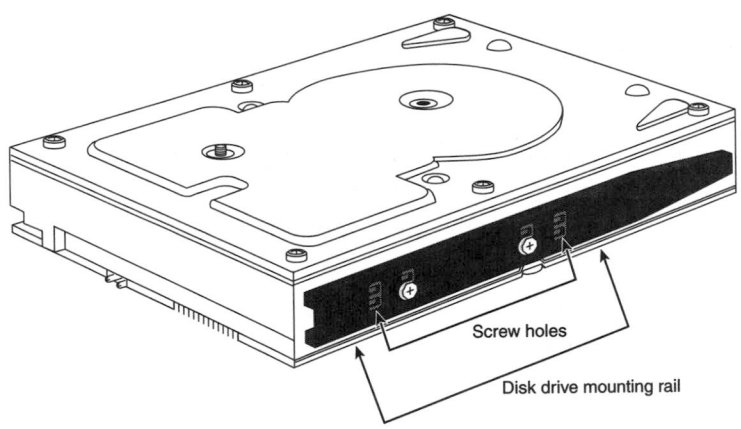

Screw holes

Disk drive mounting rail

FIG. 12.12   A typical hard disk with mounting rails.

If you cannot purchase a drive kit, there are several companies listed in Appendix A that specialize in drive-mounting brackets, cables, and other hardware accessories. Also, many newer after-market computer cases have eliminated the need for drive rails altogether by building the expansion slot itself to the 3 1/2- or 5 1/4-inch drive specification, enabling you to bolt the new drive directly to the case itself. Most 3 1/2-inch hard drives sold in boxed packaging in retail outlets do include the mounting bracket required to mount a 3 1/2-inch drive in a 5 1/4-inch bay (as shown in Figure 12.13).

> **Note**
>
> You should also note the length of the drive cable itself when you plan on adding a hard disk drive. It can be very annoying to assemble everything that you think you'll need to install a drive, and then find that the drive cable is not long enough to reach the new drive location. You can try to reposition the drive to a location closer to the interface connector on the host adapter or motherboard, or just get a longer cable.

FIG. 12.13   A typical bracket used to mount a 3 1/2-inch drive in a 5 1/4-inch drive bay. The bracket is screwed to the drive and then mounted in the bay by using screws or rails as determined by the case.

Different faceplate, or bezel, options are also available. Make sure that you have the correct bezel for your application. Some systems, for example, do not need a bezel; if there is a bezel on the drive, you must remove it.

> **Caution**
>
> Make sure you use only the screws that come with your new drive. Many drives come with a special short-length screw that can have the same size thread as other screws you might use in your system. If you use screws that are too long, they might protrude too far into the drive casing and cause problems.

System Configuration

Once your drive is physically installed, you can begin configuring the system to use it. You have to provide the computer with basic information about the drive so the system can access it and boot from it. How you set and store this information depends on the type of drive and system you have. Standard (IDE) setup procedures apply for most hard disks except SCSI drives. SCSI drives normally follow a custom setup procedure that varies depending on the host adapter that you are using. If you have a SCSI drive, follow the instructions included with the host adapter to configure the drives.

Automatic Drive Typing. For IDE drives, virtually all new BIOS versions in today's PCs have automatic typing. The BIOS sends a special Identify Drive command to all the devices connected to the IDE interface during the system startup sequence, and the drives are intelligent enough to respond with the correct parameters. The BIOS then automatically enters the parameter information returned by the drive. This procedure eliminates errors or confusion in parameter selection. However, even with automatic drive typing, some BIOSs will alert you that you need to enter the system setup program and configure the drive. In these situations, just enter the system BIOS configuration utility and save the settings that the BIOS has detected for the drive. You don't need to enter any settings yourself.

Manual Drive Typing. If you are dealing with a motherboard that does not support automatic typing, you must enter the appropriate drive information in the system BIOS manually. The BIOS has a selection of pre-configured drive types, but these are woefully outdated in most cases, providing support only for drives holding a few hundred megabytes or less. In nearly every case, you will have to select the user-defined drive type and provide values for the following settings:

- Cylinders
- Heads
- Sectors per track
- Write precompensation

The values that you use for these settings should be provided in the documentation for the hard disk drive, or may even be printed on the drive itself. It's a good idea to check for these settings and write them down, because they may not be visible once you've installed the drive in the computer. You should also maintain a copy of these settings in case your system BIOS should lose its data due to a battery failure. One of the best places to store this information is inside the computer itself. Taping a note with vital settings like these to the inside of the case can be a lifesaver.

> **Note**
>
> The setup parameters for over 1,000 popular drive models are included in Appendix D, "Technical Reference." Additionally, there is a generic table of parameters included in the appendix that will work (although they may not work optimally) with any IDE drive up to 528M.

Depending on the maker and the version of your system BIOS, there may be other settings to configure as well, such as what transfer mode to use, and whether or not the BIOS should use Logical Block Addressing.

◀◀ See "Increased Drive Capacity," p. 621

Formatting

Proper setup and formatting are critical to a drive's performance and reliability. This section describes the procedures used to format a hard disk drive correctly. Use these procedures when you install a new drive in a system or immediately after you recover data from a hard disk that has been exhibiting problems.

There are three major steps in the formatting process for a hard disk drive subsystem:

1. Low-level formatting

2. Partitioning

3. High-level formatting

Low-Level Formatting. All new hard disk drives are low-level formatted by the manufacturer, and you do not have to perform another LLF before you install the drive. In fact, under normal circumstances, you should not ever have to perform a low-level format on an IDE or SCSI drive. Most manufacturers no longer recommend that you low-level format any IDE type drive.

This recommendation has been the source of some myths about IDE. Many people say, for example, that you cannot perform a low-level format on an IDE drive, and that if you do, you will destroy the drive. This statement is untrue! What can happen is that you may lose the optimal head and cylinder skew factors for the drive that were set by the manufacturer, as well as the map of drive defects. This situation is not good and will definitely have a negative effect on the drive's performance, but you still can use the drive with no problems.

Despite this recommendation, however, there may be times when you must perform a low-level format on an IDE or SCSI drive. The following sections discuss the software that you can use to do this.

SCSI Low-Level Format Software. If you are using a SCSI drive, you must use the LLF program provided by the manufacturer of the SCSI host adapter. The design of these devices varies enough that a register-level program can work only if it is tailored to the individual controller. Fortunately, all SCSI host adapters include low-level format software, either in the host adapter's BIOS or in a separate disk-based program.

The interface to the SCSI drive is through the host adapter. SCSI is a standard, but there are no true standards for what a host adapter is supposed to look like. This means that any formatting or configuration software will be specific to a particular host adapter.

Note

Notice that SCSI format and configuration software is keyed to the host adapter and is not specific in any way to the particular SCSI hard disk drive that you are using.

IDE Low-Level Format Software. IDE drive manufacturers have defined extensions to the standard WD1002/1003 AT interface, which was further standardized for IDE drives as the ATA (AT Attachment) interface. The ATA specification provides for vendor-unique commands, which are manufacturer proprietary extensions to the standard. To prevent improper low-level formatting, many of these IDE drives have special codes that must be sent to the drive to unlock the format routines. These codes vary among manufacturers. If possible, you should obtain LLF and defect-management software from the drive manufacturer; this software usually is specific to that manufacturer's products.

Most ATA IDE drives are protected from any alteration to the skew factors or defect map erasure because they are in a translated mode. Zoned Bit Recording drives are always in translation mode and are fully protected. Most ATA drives have a custom command set that must be used in the format process; the standard format commands defined by the ATA specification usually do not work, especially with intelligent or Zoned Bit Recording IDE drives. Without the proper manufacturer-specific format commands, you can't perform the defect management by the manufacturer-specified method, in which bad sectors often can be spared.

If formatting software is not available from your drive's manufacturer, I recommend Disk Manager by Ontrack, as well as the MicroScope program by Micro 2000. These programs can format many IDE drives because they know the manufacturer-specific IDE format commands and routines. They also can perform defect-mapping and surface-analysis procedures.

Nondestructive Formatters. General-purpose, BIOS-level, nondestructive formatters, such as Calibrate and SpinRite, are not recommended in most situations where a real LLF is required. These programs have several limitations and problems that limit their effectiveness; in some cases, they can even cause problems with the way that defects are handled on a drive. These programs attempt to perform a track-by-track LLF by using BIOS functions, while backing up and restoring the track data as they go. These programs do not actually perform a complete LLF, because they do not even try to low-level format the first track (Cylinder 0, Head 0) due to problems with some controller types that store hidden information on the first track.

These programs also do not perform defect mapping in the way that standard LLF programs do, and they can even remove the carefully applied sector header defect marks during a proper LLF. This situation potentially allows data to be stored in sectors that originally were marked defective and may actually void the manufacturer's warranty on some drives. Another problem is that these programs only work on drives that have already been formatted and can format only drives that are formattable through BIOS functions.

A true LLF program bypasses the system BIOS and sends commands directly to the disk controller hardware. For this reason, many LLF programs are specific to the disk controller hardware for which they are designed. It is virtually impossible to have a single format program that will run on all different types of controllers. Many hard drives have been incorrectly diagnosed as being defective because the wrong format program was used and the program did not operate properly.

Drive Partitioning with FDISK. *Partitioning* a hard disk is the act of defining areas of the disk for an operating system to use as a volume.

When you partition a disk, the partitioning software writes a master partition boot sector at cylinder 0, head 0, sector 1—the first sector on the hard disk. This sector contains data that describes the partitions by their starting and ending cylinder, head, and sector locations. The partition table also indicates to the ROM BIOS which of the partitions is bootable and, therefore, where to look for an operating system to load.

▶▶ See "File Systems and Data Recovery," p. 1065

The FDISK program is the accepted standard for partitioning hard disk drives for use with all versions of Windows 9x and DOS. Partitioning prepares the boot sector of the disk in such a way that the FORMAT.COM program or the Windows GUI Format utility can operate correctly. FDISK also makes it possible for different operating systems to coexist on a single hard disk.

High-Level (Operating-System) Formatting. The final step in the installation of a hard disk drive is the high-level format. Like the partitioning process, the high-level format is specific to the file system you've chosen to use on the drive. On Windows 9x and DOS systems, the primary function of the high-level format is to create a FAT and a directory system on the disk so the operating system can manage files.

Usually, you perform the high-level format with the FORMAT.COM program or the formatting utility in Windows 9x Explorer. FORMAT.COM uses the following syntax:

```
FORMAT C: /S /V
```

This command high-level formats drive C, writes the hidden operating-system files in the first part of the partition, and prompts for the entry of a volume label to be stored on the disk at the completion of the process.

The FAT high-level format program performs the following functions and procedures:

1. Scans the disk (read only) for tracks and sectors marked as bad during the LLF, and notes these tracks as being unreadable.

2. Returns the drive heads to the first cylinder of the partition, and at that cylinder (head 1, sector 1) writes a DOS volume boot sector.

3. Writes a FAT at head 1, sector 2. Immediately after this FAT, it writes a second copy of the FAT. These FATs essentially are blank except for bad-cluster marks noting areas of the disk that were found to be unreadable during the marked-defect scan.

4. Writes a blank root directory.

5. If the /S parameter is specified, copies the system files, IO.SYS and MSDOS.SYS (or IBMBIO.COM and IBMDOS.COM, depending on which DOS you run) and COMMAND.COM to the disk (in that order).

6. If the /V parameter is specified, prompts the user for a volume label, which is written as the fourth file entry in the root directory.

Now, the operating system can use the disk for storing and retrieving files, and the disk is a bootable disk.

During the first phase of the high-level format, the program performs a marked defect scan. Defects marked by the LLF operation show up during this scan as being unreadable tracks or sectors. When the high-level format encounters one of these areas, it automatically performs up to five retries to read these tracks or sectors. If the unreadable area was marked by the LLF, the read fails on all attempts.

After five retries, the DOS FORMAT program gives up on this track or sector and moves to the next one. Areas that remain unreadable after the initial read and the five retries are noted in the FAT as being bad clusters.

Hard Disk Drive Troubleshooting and Repair

If a hard disk drive has a problem inside its sealed HDA, repairing the drive usually is not feasible. If the failure is in the logic board, you can replace that assembly with a new or rebuilt assembly easily and at a much lower cost than replacing the entire drive.

Most hard disk problems really are not hardware problems; instead, they are soft problems that can be solved by a new LLF and defect-mapping session. *Soft problems* are characterized by a drive that sounds normal but produces various read and write errors.

Hard problems are mechanical, such as when the drive sounds as though it contains loose marbles. Constant scraping and grinding noises from the drive, with no reading or writing capability, also qualify as hard errors. In these cases, it is unlikely that an LLF will put the drive back into service. If a hardware problem is indicated, first replace the logic-board assembly. You can make this repair yourself and, if successful, you can recover the data from the drive.

If replacing the logic assembly does not solve the problem, contact the manufacturer or a specialized repair shop that has clean-room facilities for hard disk repair. (See Appendix A for a list of drive manufacturers and companies that specialize in hard disk drive repair.)

Floppy Disk Drives

This section examines floppy disk drives and disks. It explores how floppy disk drives and disks function, what types of disk drives and disks are available, and how to properly install and service drives and disks.

Development of the Floppy Disk Drive

Alan Shugart is generally credited with inventing the floppy disk drive in 1967 while working for IBM. One of Shugart's senior engineers, David Noble, actually proposed the flexible media (then 8 inches in diameter) and the protective jacket with the fabric lining. Shugart left IBM in 1969, and in 1974, his company, Shugart Associates, introduced the mini-floppy (5 1/4-inch) disk drive, which, of course, became the standard eventually used by personal computers, rapidly replacing the 8-inch drives. He also helped create the Shugart Associates System Interface (SASI), which was later renamed SCSI (Small Computer System Interface) when approved as an ANSI standard.

Shugart left Shugart Associates in 1974 and together with Finis Conner formed Seagate Technology in 1978. At Seagate, he created the ST-506/412 interface, which became the de facto standard PC hard disk interface, and which also served as the basis for the later ESDI and even the IDE interface. Seagate went on to become the world's largest manufacturer of hard disk drives. Note that all PC floppy disk drives are still based on (and mostly compatible with) the original Shugart designs. Compared to other parts of the PC, the floppy disk drive has undergone relatively few changes.

Drive Components

This section describes the components that make up a typical floppy disk drive and examines how these components operate together to read and write data—the physical operation of the drive. All floppy disk drives, regardless of type, consist of several basic common components. To properly install and service a disk drive, you must be able to identify these components and understand their function (see Figure 12.14).

Read/Write Heads. A floppy disk drive normally has two read/write heads, one for each side of the disk, with both heads being used for reading and writing on their respective disk sides (see Figure 12.15). At one time, single-sided drives were available for PC systems (the original PC had such drives), but today single-sided drives are a fading memory.

> **Note**
>
> Many people do not realize that the first head on a floppy disk drive is the bottom one. Single-sided drives, in fact, used only the bottom head; the top head was replaced by a felt pressure pad. Another bit of disk trivia is that the top head (Head 1) is not directly over the bottom head (Head 0)—the top head is located either four or eight tracks inward from the bottom head, depending on the drive type.

The head mechanism is moved by a motor called a *head actuator*. The heads can move in and out over the surface of the disk in a straight line to position themselves over various tracks. The heads move in and out tangentially to the tracks that they record on the disk. Because the top and bottom heads are mounted on the same rack, or mechanism, they move in unison and cannot move independently of each other. The heads are made of soft ferrous (iron) compounds with electromagnetic coils. Each head is a composite design, with a read/write head centered within two tunnel-erase heads in the same physical assembly (see Figure 12.16).

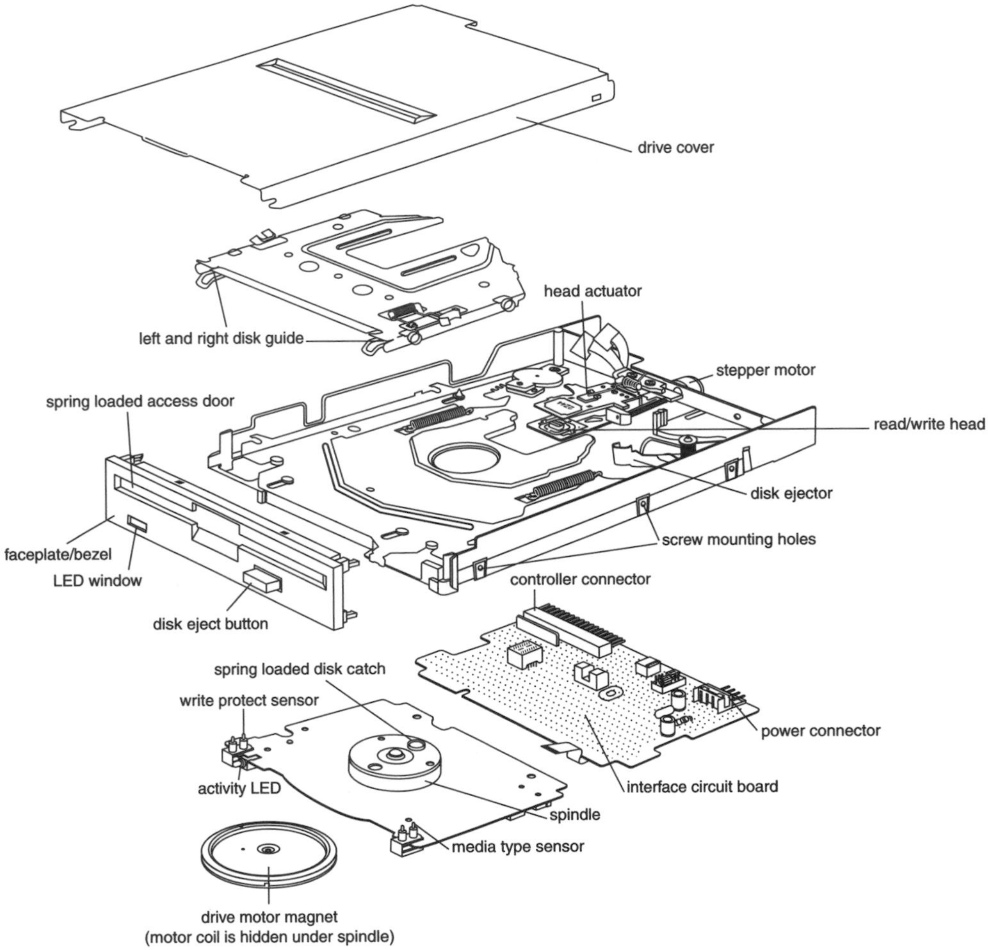

drive cover

head actuator

stepper motor

left and right disk guide

read/write head

spring loaded access door

disk ejector

screw mounting holes

faceplate/bezel

LED window

controller connector

disk eject button

spring loaded disk catch

write protect sensor

power connector

activity LED

interface circuit board

spindle

media type sensor

drive motor magnet
(motor coil is hidden under spindle)

FIG. 12.14 A typical floppy disk drive.

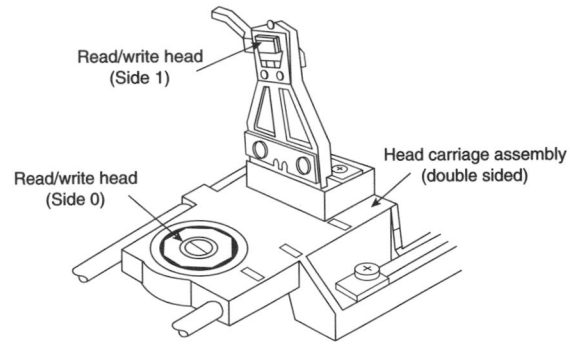

Read/write head
(Side 1)

Head carriage assembly
(double sided)

Read/write head
(Side 0)

FIG. 12.15 A double-sided drive head assembly.

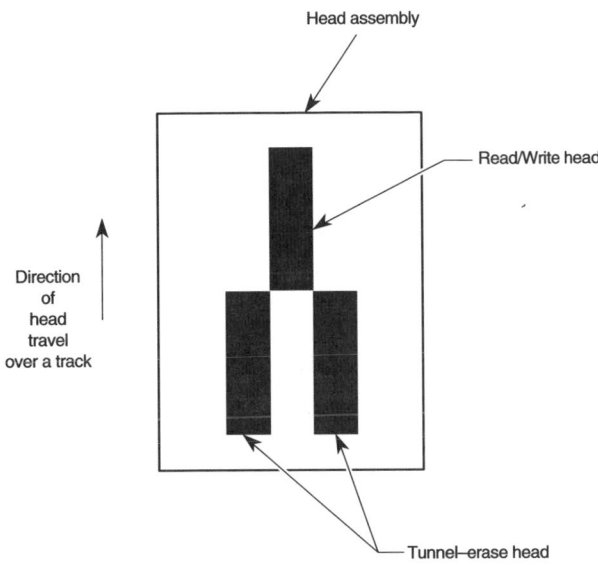

FIG. 12.16 Composite construction of a typical floppy disk drive head.

Floppy disk drives use a recording method called *tunnel erasure*. As the drive writes to a track, the trailing tunnel-erase heads erase the outer bands of the track, trimming it cleanly on the disk. The heads force the data into a specified narrow "tunnel" on each track. This process prevents the signal from one track from being confused with the signals from adjacent tracks, which would happen if the signal were allowed to naturally "taper off" to each side. *Alignment* is the placement of the heads with respect to the tracks they must read and write. Head alignment can be checked only against some sort of reference-standard disk recorded by a perfectly aligned machine. These types of disks are available, and you can use one to check your drive's alignment. However, this is usually not practical for the end user, because one calibrated analog alignment disk can cost more than a new drive.

The floppy disk drive's two heads are spring-loaded and physically grip the disk with a small amount of pressure, which means that they are in direct contact with the disk surface while reading and writing to the disk. Because floppy disk drives spin at only 300 or 360 RPM, this pressure does not present an excessive friction problem. Some newer disks are specially coated with Teflon or other compounds to further reduce friction and enable the disk to slide more easily under the heads. Because of the contact between the heads and the disk, a buildup of the magnetic material from the disk eventually forms on the heads. The buildup should periodically be cleaned off the heads as part of a preventive-maintenance or normal service program.

To read and write to the disk properly, the heads must be in direct contact with the magnetic medium. Very small particles of loose oxide, dust, dirt, smoke, fingerprints, or hair can cause problems with reading and writing the disk. Disk and drive manufacturers' tests have found that a spacing as little as .000032 inch (32 millionths of an inch) between the heads and the medium can cause read/write errors. You now can understand why it is important to handle disks carefully and avoid touching or contaminating the surface of the disk medium in any way. The rigid jacket and protective shutter for the head access aperture on 3 1/2-inch disks is excellent for preventing problems caused by contamination. 5 1/4-inch disks do not have the same protective elements, which is one reason why they have fallen into disuse. If you still use 5 1/4-inch floppy disks, you should exercise more care in their handling.

The Head Actuator. The *head actuator* for a floppy disk drive uses a special kind of motor, a *stepper motor*, that moves in both directions in an increment called a *step*. This type of motor does not spin around continuously; rather, the motor turns a precise specified distance and stops. Stepper motors are not infinitely variable in their positioning; they move in fixed increments, or *detents*, and must stop at a particular detent position. The location of each track on the disk is defined by one or more increments of the motor's motion. The disk controller can instruct the motor to position itself according to any relative increment within the range of its travel. To position the heads at track 25, for example, the controller instructs the motor to go to the 25th detent position.

The stepper motor can be linked to the head rack in one of two ways. In the first, the link is a coiled, split-steel band. The band winds and unwinds around the spindle of the stepper motor, translating the rotary motion into linear motion. Some drives, however, use a worm-gear arrangement rather than a band. In this type of drive, the head assembly rests on a worm gear driven directly off the stepper motor shaft. Because this arrangement is more compact, you normally find worm-gear actuators on the smaller 3 1/2-inch drives.

Most stepper motors used in floppy disk drives can step in specific increments that relate to the track spacing on the disk. Older 48 Track Per Inch (TPI) drives have a motor that steps in increments of 3.6°. This means that each 3.6° of stepper motor rotation moves the heads from one track to the next. Most 96 or 135 TPI drives have a stepper motor that moves in 1.8° increments, which is exactly half of what the 48 TPI drives use. Sometimes you see this information actually printed or stamped right on the stepper motor itself, which is useful if you are trying to figure out what type of drive you have. 5 1/4-inch 360K drives were the only 48 TPI drives that used the 3.6° increment stepper motor. All other drive types normally use the 1.8° stepper motor. On most drives, the stepper motor is a small cylindrical object near one corner of the drive.

A stepper motor usually has a full travel time of about 1/5 of a second—about 200ms. On average, a half-stroke is 100ms, and a one-third stroke is 66ms. The timing of a one-half or one-third stroke of the head-actuator mechanism is often used to determine the reported average-access time for a disk drive. *Average-access time* is the normal amount of time the heads spend moving at random from one track to another.

The Spindle Motor. The *spindle motor* spins the disk. The normal speed of rotation is either 300 or 360 RPM, depending on the type of drive. The 5 1/4-inch high-density (HD) drive is the only drive that spins at 360 RPM; all others, including the 5 1/4-inch double-density (DD), 3 1/2-inch DD, 3 1/2-inch HD, and 3 1/2-inch extra-high density (ED) drives, spin at 300 RPM. This is quite a slow speed when compared to a hard disk drive, which helps to explain why floppy disk drives have much lower data transfer rates. However, this slow speed also makes it possible for the drive heads to be in physical contact with the disk while it is spinning, without causing friction damage.

Most earlier drives used a mechanism by which the spindle motor physically turned the disk spindle with a belt, but all modern drives use a direct-drive system with no belts. The direct-drive systems are more reliable and less expensive to manufacture, as well as smaller in size. The earlier belt-driven systems did have more rotational torque available to turn a sticky disk because of the torque multiplication factor of the belt system. Most newer direct-drive systems use an automatic torque-compensation capability that automatically sets the disk-rotation speed to a fixed 300 or 360 RPM, and compensates with additional torque for sticky disks or less torque for slippery ones. This arrangement eliminates the need to adjust the rotational speed of the drive.

Circuit Boards. A disk drive always incorporates one or more *logic boards*, which are circuit boards that contain the circuitry used to control the head actuator, read/write heads, spindle motor, disk sensors, and other components on the drive. The logic board implements the drive's interface to the controller board in the system unit.

The standard interface used by all PC floppy disk drives is the Shugart Associates SA-400 interface, which was invented in the 1970s and is based on the NEC 765 controller chip. This industry-standard interface is why you can purchase "off-the-shelf" drives (raw, or bare, drives) that can plug directly into your controller.

> **Tip**
>
> Logic boards for a drive can fail and usually are difficult to obtain as a spare part. One board often costs more than replacing the entire drive. I recommend keeping failed or misaligned drives that might otherwise be discarded so they can be used for their remaining good parts—such as logic boards. You can use the parts to restore a failing drive very cost-effectively.

The Controller. At one time, the controller for a computer's floppy disk drives took the form of a dedicated expansion card installed in an ISA bus slot. Later implementations used a multifunction card that provided the IDE/ATA, parallel, and serial port interfaces in addition to the floppy disk drive controller. Today's PCs have the floppy controller integrated into the motherboard, usually in the form of a Super I/O chip that also includes the parallel and serial interfaces.

Unlike the motherboard's IDE interface, the floppy disk controller has not changed very much in recent years. Virtually the only thing that has changed is the controller's maximum speed. As the data density of floppy disks (and their capacity) has increased over the years, the controller speed has had to increase, as well. Nearly all floppy disk controllers in computers today support speeds of up to 1Mbit/sec, which supports all the standard floppy disk drives. 500Kbit/sec controllers can support all floppy disk drives except for the 2.88M extra-high density models. Older computers used 250Kbit/sec controllers that could support only 360K 5 1/4-inch and 720K 3 1/2-inch drives. To install a standard 1.44M 3 1/2-inch drive in an older machine, you may have to replace the floppy controller with a faster model.

Tip

The best way to determine the speed of the floppy disk drive controller in your computer is to examine the floppy disk drive options provided by the system BIOS.

Even if you do not intend to use a 2.88M floppy disk drive, you still may want to make sure that your computer has the fastest possible controller. Some of the tape drives on the market use the floppy disk interface to connect to the system, and in this case the controller has a profound effect on the overall throughput of the drive.

The Faceplate. The *faceplate*, or *bezel*, is the plastic piece that comprises the front of the drive. These pieces, usually removable, come in different colors and configurations.

Most drives use a bezel that is slightly wider than the drive. You have to install these types of drives from the front of a system because the faceplate is slightly wider than the hole in the computer case. Other drive faceplates are the same width as the drive's chassis; you can install these drives from the rear—an advantage in some cases.

Connectors. Nearly all floppy disk drives have two connectors—one for power to run the drive, and the other to carry the control and data signals to and from the drive. These connectors are fairly standardized in the computer industry; a four-pin in-line connector (called Mate-N-Lock, by AMP), in both a large and small style, is used for power (see Figure 12.17); and a 34-pin connector in both edge and pin header designs is used for the data and control signals. 5 1/4-inch drives normally use the large style power connector and the 34-pin edge type connector, while most 3 1/2-inch drives use the smaller version of the power connector and the 34-pin header type logic connector. The drive controller and logic connectors and pinouts are detailed later in this chapter as well as in Appendix A.

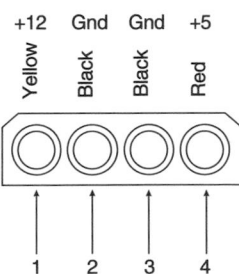

FIG. 12.17 A disk drive female power supply cable connector.

Both the large and small power connectors from the power supply are female plugs. They plug into the male portion, which is attached to the drive itself. One common problem with upgrading an older system with 3 1/2-inch drives is that your power supply only has the large style connectors, while the drive has the small style. An adapter cable is available from Radio Shack (Cat. No. 278-765) and other sources that converts the large-style power connector to the proper small style used on most 3 1/2-inch drives.

Most standard PCs use 3 1/2-inch drives with a 34-pin signal connector and a separate small-style power connector. For older systems, many drive manufacturers also sell 3 1/2-inch drives installed in a 5 1/4-inch frame assembly with a special adapter built in that enables you to use the larger power connector and standard edge-type signal connectors. Because no cable adapters are required and they install in a 5 1/4-inch half-height bay, these types of drives are ideal for upgrading earlier systems. Most 3 1/2-inch drive-upgrade kits sold today are similar and include the drive, appropriate adapters for the power and control and data cables, a 5 1/4-inch frame adapter and faceplate, and mounting rails. The frame adapter and faceplate enable you to install the drive where a 5 1/4-inch half-height drive would normally go.

The Floppy Disk Drive Cable. The 34-pin connector on a floppy disk drive takes the form of either an edge connector (on 5 1/4-inch drives) or a pin connector (on 3 1/2-inch drives). The pinouts for the connector are shown in Table 12.9.

Table 12.9 Pinouts for the Standard Floppy Disk Drive Connector			
Pin	**Signal**	**Pin**	**Signal**
1	Ground	18	Direction (Stepper Motor)
2	Unused	19	Ground
3	Ground	20	Step Pulse
4	Unused	21	Ground
5	Ground	22	Write Data
6	Unused	23	Ground
7	Ground	24	Write Enable
8	Index	25	Ground
9	Ground	26	Track 0
10	Motor Enable A	27	Ground
11	Ground	28	Write Protect
12	Drive Select B	29	Ground
13	Ground	30	Read Data
14	Drive Select A	31	Ground
15	Ground	32	Select Head 1
16	Motor Enable B	33	Ground
17	Ground	34	Ground

The cable used to connect the floppy disk drive(s) to the controller on the motherboard is quite strange. To support various drive configurations, the cable typically has five connectors on it, two edge connectors and two pin connectors to attach to the drives, and one pin connector to connect to the controller. The cable has redundant connectors for each of the two drives (A and B) supported by the standard floppy disk drive controller, so you can install any combination of 5 1/4-inch and 3 1/2-inch drives (see Figure 12.18).

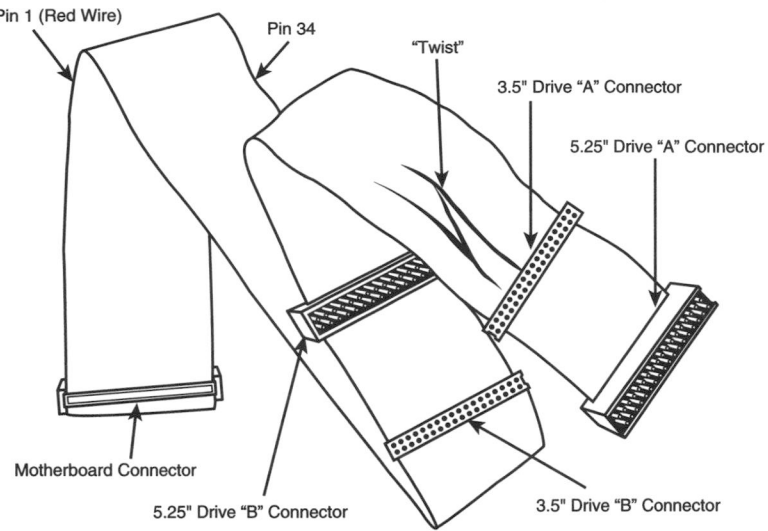

Pin 1 (Red Wire)

Pin 34

"Twist"

3.5" Drive "A" Connector

5.25" Drive "A" Connector

Motherboard Connector

5.25" Drive "B" Connector

3.5" Drive "B" Connector

FIG. 12.18   Standard five-connector floppy interface cable.

In addition to the connectors, the cable on most systems has a special twist that inverts the signals of wires 10 through 16. These are the wires carrying the Drive Select and Motor Enable signals for each of the two drives. Floppy disk drives have DS (Drive Select) jumpers that were designed to enable you to select whether a given drive should be recognized as A or B.

You may not even know that these jumpers exist, because the twist in the cable prevents you from having to adjust them. When installing two floppy disk drives in one system (admittedly a rarity nowadays), the cable electrically changes the DS configuration of the drive that is plugged in after the twist. Thus, the twist causes a drive physically set to the second DS position (B) to appear to the controller to be set to the first DS position (A) and vice versa. The adoption of this cable has made it possible to use a standard jumper configuration for all floppy disk drives, regardless of whether you install one or two drives in a computer.

If you install only a single floppy disk drive, you use the connector after the twist, which will cause the drive to be recognized as drive A.

Disk Physical Specifications and Operation
Most of the PCs sold today are equipped with a 3 1/2-inch 1.44M floppy disk drive. You may run into an older system that has a 5 1/4-inch 1.2M drive instead of, or in addition to, the 3 1/2-inch drive. There are also PC systems that have a 2.88M 3 1/2-inch drive that can also read and write 1.44M disks. The older drive types: 5 1/4-inch 360K and 3 1/2-inch 720K drives are obsolete, and rarely found anymore.

> **Note**
>
> For information on older floppy disk drives and media, see Chapter 13, "Floppy Disk Drives," in *Upgrading and Repairing PCs, Eighth Edition*, found on the CD included with this book.

The physical operation of a disk drive is fairly simple to describe. The disk rotates in the drive at either 300 or 360 RPM. Most drives spin at 300 RPM; only the 5 1/4-inch 1.2M drives spin at 360 RPM. With the disk spinning, the heads can move in and out approximately 1 inch and write 80 tracks. The tracks are written on both sides of the disk and are therefore sometimes called *cylinders*. A single cylinder comprises the tracks on the top and bottom of the disk. The heads record by using a tunnel-erase procedure that writes a track to a specified width, and then erases the edges of the track to prevent interference with any adjacent tracks.

Different drives record tracks at different widths. Table 12.10 shows the track widths in both millimeters and inches for the different types of floppy disk drives found in modern PC systems.

Table 12.10 Floppy Disk Drive Track-Width Specifications			
Drive Type	**No. of Tracks**	**Track Width**	
5 1/4-inch 360K	40 per side	0.300 mm	0.0118 in.
5 1/4-inch 1.2M	80 per side	0.155 mm	0.0061 in.
3 1/2-inch 720K	80 per side	0.115 mm	0.0045 in.
3 1/2-inch 1.44M	80 per side	0.115 mm	0.0045 in.
3 1/2-inch 2.88M	80 per side	0.115 mm	0.0045 in.

How the Operating System Uses a Disk. To the operating system, data on your PC disks is organized in tracks and sectors, just as on a hard disk drive. *Tracks* are narrow, concentric circles on a disk. *Sectors* are pie-shaped slices of the individual tracks.

Table 12.11 summarizes the standard disk formats for PC floppy disk drives.

Table 12.11 3 1/2-Inch and 5 1/4-Inch Floppy Disk Drive Formats		
5.25-Inch Floppy Disks	**Double Density 360K (DD)**	**High Density 1.2M (HD)**
Bytes per Sector	512	512
Sectors per Track	9	15
Tracks per Side	40	80
Sides	2	2
Capacity (Kilobytes)	360	1,200
Capacity (Megabytes)	0.352	1.172
Capacity (Million Bytes)	0.369	1.229

(continues)

Table 12.11   3 1/2-Inch and 5 1/4-Inch Floppy Disk Drive Formats Continued

3 1/2-Inch Floppy Disks	Double Density 720K (DD)	High Density 1.44M (HD)	Extra-High Density 2.88M (ED)
Bytes per Sector	512	512	512
Sectors per Track	9	18	36
Tracks per Side	80	80	80
Sides	2	2	2
Capacity (Kilobytes)	720	1,440	2,880
Capacity (Megabytes)	0.703	1.406	2.813
Capacity (Million Bytes)	0.737	1.475	2.949

You can calculate the capacity differences between different formats by multiplying the sectors per track by the number of tracks per side together with the constants of two sides and 512 bytes per sector.

Note that the floppy disk's capacity can actually be expressed in different ways. The traditional method is to refer to the capacity of a floppy by the number of kilobytes (1,024 bytes equals 1K). This works fine for the old-style 360K and 720K disks but is strange when applied to the 1.44M and 2.88M disks. As you can see, a 1.44M disk is really 1,440K, and not actually 1.44 megabytes. Because a megabyte is 1,024K, what we call a 1.44M disk actually has a capacity of 1.406M.

Another way of expressing disk capacity is in millions of bytes. In that case, the 1.44M disk has 1.475 million bytes of capacity. Again, as with hard disk drives, both megabyte and millions of bytes are abbreviated as MB or M, often resulting in a great deal of confusion.

Like blank sheets of paper, new disks contain no information. Formatting a disk is similar to adding lines to the paper so you can write straight across. Formatting the disk writes the information that the operating system needs to maintain a directory and file table of contents. On a floppy disk, there is no distinction between a high-level and a low-level format, nor do you have to create any partitions. When you format a floppy disk with Windows 9x Explorer or the DOS FORMAT.COM program, both the high- and low-level formats are performed at the same time.

When you format a floppy disk, the operating system reserves the track nearest to the outside edge of a disk (track 0) almost entirely for its purposes. Track 0, Side 0, Sector 1 contains the *DOS Boot Record (DBR)*, or Boot Sector, that the system needs to begin operation. The next few sectors contain the FATs, which keeps records of which clusters or allocation units on the disk contain file information and which are empty. Finally, the next few sectors contain the root directory, in which the operating system stores information about the names and starting locations of the files on the disk.

Cylinders. The *cylinder* number is sometimes used in place of *track number*. A *cylinder* is all the tracks under a drive's read/write heads at one time. Because a disk cannot have more than two sides and the drive has two heads, there are always two tracks per cylinder for floppy disks. Hard disk drives, you will recall, can have many disk platters, each with two (or more) heads, for many tracks per single cylinder. In either case, because a cylinder is comprised of all tracks with the same number, the cylinder number and track number (of all the tracks in that cylinder) will always be the same.

Clusters or Allocation Units. A *cluster* also is called an *allocation unit* in DOS version 4.0 and higher. The term is appropriate because a single cluster is the smallest unit of the disk that DOS can allocate when it writes a file. A cluster or allocation unit consists of one or more sectors—usually a power of two (1, 2, 4, 8, and so on). Having more than one sector per cluster reduces the FAT size and enables DOS to run faster because it has fewer individual clusters to manage. The tradeoff is in some wasted disk space. Because DOS can manage space only in the cluster size unit, every file consumes space on the disk in increments of one cluster.

Table 12.12 lists the default cluster sizes used by DOS and Windows for different floppy disk formats.

Table 12.12 Default Cluster and Allocation Unit Sizes		
Floppy Disk Capacity	**Cluster/Allocation Unit Size**	**FAT Type**
5 1/4-inch, 360K	2 sectors	1,024 bytes 12-bit
5 1/4-inch, 1.2M	1 sector	512 bytes 12-bit
3 1/2-inch, 720K	2 sectors	1,024 bytes 12-bit
3 1/2-inch, 1.44M	1 sector	512 bytes 12-bit
3 1/2-inch, 2.88M	2 sectors	1,024 bytes 12-bit

K = 1,024 bytes
M = 1,048,576 bytes

Diskette Changeline. The standard PC floppy controller and drive use a special signal on pin 34 called *Diskette Changeline* to determine whether the disk has been changed, or more accurately, whether the same disk loaded during the previous disk access is still in the drive. *Disk Change* is a pulsed signal that changes a status register in the controller to let the system know that a disk has been either inserted or ejected. This register is set to indicate that a disk has been inserted or removed (changed) by default.

The register is cleared when the controller sends a step pulse to the drive and the drive responds, acknowledging that the heads have moved. At this point, the system knows that a specific disk is in the drive. If the disk change signal is not received before the next access, the system can assume that the same disk is still in the drive. Any information read into memory during the previous access can therefore be reused without rereading the disk.

Because of this process, systems can buffer or cache the contents of the file allocation table (FAT) or directory structure of a disk in the system's memory. By eliminating unnecessary rereads of these areas of the disk, the apparent speed of the drive is increased. If you move the door lever or eject button on a drive that supports the disk change signal, the DC pulse is sent to the controller, thus resetting the register and indicating that the disk has been changed. This procedure causes the system to purge buffered or cached data that had been read from the disk because the system then cannot be sure that the same disk is still in the drive.

One interesting problem can occur when certain drives are installed in a 16-bit or greater system. As mentioned, some drives use pin 34 for a "Ready" (RDY) signal. The RDY signal is sent whenever a disk is installed and rotating in the drive. If you install a drive that has pin 34 set to send RDY, the system "thinks" that it is continuously receiving a disk change signal, which causes problems. Usually the drive fails with a Drive not ready error and is inoperable. The only reason that the RDY signal exists on some drives is that it happens to be a part of the standard Shugart SA-400 disk interface; however, it has never been used in PC systems.

The biggest problem occurs if the drive is not sending the DC signal on pin 34, and it should. If a system is told (through CMOS setup) that the drive is any other type than a 360K (which cannot ever send the DC signal), the system expects the drive to send DC whenever a disk has been ejected. If the drive is not configured properly to send the signal, the system never recognizes that a disk has been changed. Therefore, even if you do change the disk, the system still acts as though the first disk is in the drive and holds the first disk's directory and FAT information in RAM. This can be dangerous because the FAT and directory information from the first disk can be partially written to any subsequent disks written to in the drive.

> ### Caution
>
> If you ever have seen a system with a floppy disk drive that shows "phantom directories" of the previously installed disk, even after you have changed or removed it, you have experienced this problem firsthand. The negative side effect is that all disks after the first one you place in this system are in extreme danger. You likely will overwrite the directories and FATs of many disks with information from the first disk.
>
> If even possible at all, data recovery from such a catastrophe can require quite a bit of work with utility programs such as Norton Utilities. These problems with Disk Change most often are traced to an incorrectly configured drive.

If the drive you are installing is a 5 1/4-inch 1.2M or 3 1/2-inch 720K, 1.44M, or 2.88M drive, be sure to set pin 34 to send the Disk Change (DC) signal.

Types of Floppy Disk Drives

The characteristics of the floppy disk drives you might encounter in PC-compatible systems are summarized in Table 12.13. As you can see, the different disk capacities are determined by several parameters, some of which seem to remain constant on all drives, although others change from drive to drive. For example, all drives use 512-byte physical sectors, which is true for hard disks, as well.

Table 12.13 Floppy Disk Logical Formatted Parameters	Current Formats					Obsolete Formats		
Disk Size (inches)	3 1/2	3 1/2	3 1/2	5 1/4	5 1/4	5 1/4	5 1/4	5 1/4
Disk Capacity (K)	2,880	1,440	720	1,200	360	320	180	160
Media Descriptor Byte	F0h	F0h	F9h	F9h	FDh	FFh	FCh	FEh
Sides (Heads)	2	2	2	2	2	2	1	1
Tracks per Side	80	80	80	80	40	40	40	40
Sectors per Track	36	18	9	15	9	8	9	8
Bytes per Sector	512	512	512	512	512	512	512	512
Sectors per Cluster	2	1	2	1	2	2	1	1
FAT Length (Sectors)	9	9	3	7	2	1	2	1
Number of FATs	2	2	2	2	2	2	2	2
Root Dir. Length (Sectors)	15	14	7	14	7	7	4	4
Maximum Root Entries	240	224	112	224	112	112	64	64
Total Sectors per Disk	5,760	2,880	1,440	2,400	720	640	360	320
Total Available Sectors	5,726	2,847	1,426	2,371	708	630	351	313
Total Available Clusters	2,863	2,847	713	2,371	354	315	351	313

The 1.44M 3 1/2-Inch Drive. The 3 1/2-inch, 1.44M, High Density (HD) drives first appeared from IBM in the PS/2 product line introduced in 1987. Most other computer vendors started offering the drives as an option in their systems immediately afterwards. This type of drive is still the most popular in systems today.

The drive records 80 cylinders consisting of two tracks each with 18 sectors per track, resulting in a formatted capacity of 1.44M. Some disk manufacturers label these disks as 2.0M disks, and the difference between this unformatted capacity and the formatted usable result is lost during the format. Note that the 1,440K of total formatted capacity does not account for the areas that the FAT file system reserves for file management, leaving only 1423.5K of actual file-storage area.

The drive spins at 300 RPM, and in fact must spin at that speed to operate properly with existing high- and low-density controllers. To use the 500KHz data rate (the maximum from most standard high- and low-density floppy controllers), these drives must spin at a maximum of 300 RPM. If the drives were to spin at the faster 360 RPM rate of the 5 1/4-inch drives, they would have to reduce the total number of sectors per track to 15, or else the controller could not keep up. In short, the 1.44M 3 1/2-inch drives store 1.2 times the data of the 5 1/4-inch 1.2M drives, and the 1.2M drives spin exactly 1.2 times faster than the 1.44M drives. The data rates used by both of these HD drives are identical and compatible with the same controllers. In fact, because these 3 1/2-inch HD drives can run at the 500KHz data rate, a controller that can support a 1.2M 5 1/4-inch drive can support the 1.44M drives also.

The 2.88M 3 1/2-Inch Drive. The 3 1/2-inch, 2.88M drive was developed by Toshiba Corporation in the 1980s and was officially announced in 1987. Toshiba began production manufacturing of the drives and disks in 1989, and several vendors began selling the drives as upgrades for their systems. IBM officially adopted these drives in their PS/2 systems in 1991, and a number of manufacturers began making them, including Toshiba, Mitsubishi, Sony, and Panasonic. Because a 2.88M drive can fully read and write 1.44M disks, the change is an easy one but, unfortunately, due to high media costs, these drives have not caught on widely, although virtually all systems today have built-in support for them. DOS version 5.0 or later is required to support the 2.88M drives.

The 2.88M Extra-high Density (ED) drive uses a technique called *vertical recording* to achieve its great linear density of 36 sectors per track. This technique increases density by magnetizing the domains perpendicular to the recording surface. By essentially placing the magnetic domains on their ends and stacking them side by side, the disk density increases enormously.

The technology for producing heads that can perform a vertical or perpendicular recording has been around for some time, but it is not the heads or even the drive that represent the major breakthrough in technology; rather, it is the media that is special. Standard disks have magnetic particles shaped like tiny needles that lie on the surface of the disk. Orienting these acicular particles in a perpendicular manner to enable vertical recording is very difficult. The particles on a barium-ferrite floppy disk are shaped like tiny, flat, hexagonal platelets that can more easily be arranged to have their axes of magnetization perpendicular to the plane of recording.

Toshiba perfected a glass-crystallization process for manufacturing the ultra-fine platelets used in coating the barium-ferrite disks. This technology, patented by Toshiba, is being licensed to a number of disk manufacturers, all of whom are producing barium-ferrite disks by using Toshiba's process. Toshiba also made certain modifications to the design of standard disk drive heads to enable them to read and write the new barium-ferrite disks, as well as standard cobalt or ferrite disks. This technology is being used not only in floppy disk drives but also is appearing in a variety of tape drive formats.

The disks are called *4M disks* in reference to their unformatted capacity. The actual formatted capacity is 2,880K, or 2.88M. Because of space lost in the formatting process, as well as space occupied by the volume boot sector, FATs, and root directory, the total usable storage space is 2,863K.

To support the 2.88M drive, modifications to the disk controller circuitry were required, because these drives spin at the same 300 RPM but have an astonishing 36 sectors per track. Because all floppy disks are formatted with consecutively numbered sectors (1:1 interleave), the drive has to read and write 36 sectors in the same time it takes a 1.44M drive to read and write 18 sectors. This requires that the controller support a much higher data transmission rate of 1MHz (1 million bps). Most older floppy controllers support only the maximum of 500KHz data rate used by the 1.44M drives. To upgrade to a 2.88M drive requires that the controller be changed to one that supports the higher 1MHz data rate.

An additional support issue is the ROM BIOS. The BIOS must have support for the controller and the capability to specify and accept the 2.88M drive as a CMOS setting. Some newer motherboard BIOS sets from companies like Phoenix, AMI, and Award have support for ED controllers.

Virtually all modern PCs have built-in floppy controllers and ROM BIOS software that fully support the 2.88M drives. Adding or upgrading to a 2.88M drive in these systems is as easy as plugging in the drive and running the CMOS Setup program. For systems that do not have this built-in support, the upgrade process is much more difficult. Several companies offer new controllers and BIOS upgrades as well as the 2.88M drives specifically for upgrading older systems.

Although the 2.88M drives themselves are not much more expensive than the 1.44M drives they replace, the disk media can be expensive and hard to find, as this format never really caught on in the mainstream, although all modern PCs support it.

The 720K 3 1/2-Inch Drive. The 720K, 3 1/2-inch, DD drives first appeared in an IBM system with the IBM Convertible laptop system introduced in 1986. In fact, all IBM systems introduced since that time have 3 1/2-inch drives as the standard supplied drives. This type of drive also is offered by IBM as an internal or external drive for the AT or XT systems.

> **Note**
>
> Outside the PC-compatible world, other computer-system vendors (Apple, Hewlett-Packard, and so on) offered 3 1/2-inch drives for their systems well before the PC-compatible world "caught on."

The 720K, 3 1/2-inch, DD drive normally records 80 cylinders of two tracks each, with nine sectors per track, resulting in the formatted capacity of 720K.

It is interesting to note that many disk manufacturers label these disks as 1.0M disks, which is true. The difference between the actual 1.0M of capacity and the usable 720K after formatting is that some space on each track is occupied by the header and trailer of each sector, the inter-sector gaps, and the index gap at the start of each track before the first sector. These spaces are not usable for data storage, and account for the differences between the unformatted and formatted capacities. Most manufacturers report the unformatted capacities because they do not know on which type of system you will format the disk. Apple Macintosh systems, for example, can store 800K of data on the same disk because of a different formatting technique.

Note also that the 720K of usable space does not account for the disk areas DOS reserves for managing the disk (boot sectors, FATs, directories, and so on) and that because of these areas, only 713K remains for file data storage.

PC-compatible systems have used 720K, 3 1/2-inch, DD drives primarily in XT-class systems because the drives operate from any low-density controller. The drives spin at 300

RPM, and therefore require only a 250KHz data rate from the controller to operate properly. This data rate is the same as the 360K disk drives, which means that any controller that supports a 360K drive also supports the 720K drives.

An IBM system with a ROM BIOS date of 06/10/85 or later has built-in support for 720K drives and requires no driver to use them. If your system has an earlier ROM BIOS date, the DRIVER.SYS program from DOS V3.2 or later—as well as the DRIVPARM CONFIG.SYS command in some OEM DOS versions—is all you need to provide the necessary software support to operate these drives.

The 1.2M 5 1/4-Inch Drive. The 1.2M high-density floppy disk drive first appeared in the IBM AT system introduced in August 1984. The drive required the use of a new type of disk to achieve the 1.2M format capacity, but it still could read and write (although not always reliably) the lower-density 360K disks.

The 1.2M 5 1/4-inch drive normally recorded 80 cylinders of two tracks each, starting with cylinder 0, at the outside of the disk. This situation differs from the low-density 5 1/4-inch drive in its capability to record twice as many cylinders in approximately the same space on the disk. This capability alone suggests that the recording capacity for a disk would double, but that is not all. Each track normally is recorded with 15 sectors of 512 bytes each, increasing the storage capacity even more. In fact, these drives store nearly four times the data of the 360K disks. The density increase for each track required the use of special disks with a modified media designed to handle this type of recording. Because these disks initially were expensive and difficult to obtain, many users attempted incorrectly to use the low-density disks in the 1.2M 5 1/4-inch drives and format them to the higher 1.2M-density format, which results in data loss and unnecessary data-recovery operations.

A compatibility problem with the 360K drives stems from the 1.2M drive's capability to write twice as many cylinders in the same space as the 360K drives. The 1.2M drives position their heads over the same 40 cylinder positions used by the 360K drives through *double stepping*, a procedure in which the heads are moved every two cylinders to arrive at the correct positions for reading and writing the 40 cylinders on the 360K disks. The problem is that because the 1.2M drive normally has to write 80 cylinders in the same space in which the 360K drive writes 40, the heads of the 1.2M units had to be made dimensionally smaller. These narrow heads can have problems overwriting tracks produced by a 360K drive that has a wider head because the narrower heads on the 1.2M drive cannot "cover" the entire track area written by the 360K drive.

The 1.2M 5 1/4-inch drives spin at 360 RPM, or six revolutions per second, or 166.67ms per revolution. The drives spin at this rate no matter what type of disk is inserted—either low- or high-density. To send or receive 15 sectors (plus required overhead) six times per second, a controller must use a data-transmission rate of 500,000bps (500KHz). All standard high- and low-density controllers support this data rate and, therefore, these drives.

This support depends also on proper ROM BIOS support of the controller in this mode of operation. When a standard 360K disk is running in an HD drive, it also is spinning at 360 RPM; a data rate of 300,000bps (300KHz), therefore, is required to work properly. All standard AT-style low- and high-density controllers support the 250KHz, 300KHz, and 500KHz data rates. The 300KHz rate is used only for HD 5 1/4-inch drives reading or writing to low-density 5 1/4-inch disks.

Virtually all standard AT-style systems have a ROM BIOS that supports the controller's operation of the 1.2M drive, including the 300KHz data rate.

The 360K 5 1/4-Inch Drive. The 5 1/4-inch double-density drive is designed to create a standard-format disk with 360K capacity. The term *double-density* arose from the use of the term *single density* to indicate a type of drive that used frequency modulation (FM) encoding to store approximately 90K on a disk. This type of obsolete drive never was used in any PC-compatible systems, but was used in some older systems such as the original Osborne-1 portable computer. When drive manufacturers changed the drives to use Modified Frequency Modulation (MFM) encoding, they began using the term *double-density* to indicate it, as well as the (approximately doubled) increase in recording capacity realized from this encoding method.

The 360K 5 1/4-inch drives spin at 300 RPM, which equals exactly five revolutions per second, or 200ms per revolution. All standard floppy controllers support a 1:1 interleave, in which each sector on a specific track is numbered (and read) consecutively. To read and write to a disk at full speed, a controller sends data at a rate of 250,000bps.

All standard PC-compatible systems include ROM BIOS support for these drives; therefore, you usually do not need special software or driver programs to use them.

Analyzing Floppy Disk Construction

The 5 1/4-inch and 3 1/2-inch disks each have unique construction and physical properties.

The flexible (or floppy) disk is contained within a plastic jacket. The 3 1/2-inch disks are covered by a more rigid jacket than the 5 1/4-inch disks; the disks within the jackets, however, are virtually identical except, of course, for the size.

When you look at a typical 5 1/4-inch floppy disk, you see several things (see Figure 12.19). Most prominent is the large round hole in the center. When you close the disk drive's "door," a cone-shaped clamp grabs and centers the disk through the center hole. Many disks come with *hub-ring reinforcements*—thin, plastic rings that help the disk withstand the mechanical forces of the clamping mechanism. The HD disks usually lack these reinforcements because the difficulty in accurately placing them on the disk means they can cause alignment problems.

On the right side, just below the center of the hub hole, is a smaller round hole called the *index hole*. If you carefully turn the disk within its protective jacket, you can see a small hole in the disk itself. The drive uses the index hole as the starting point for all the sectors on the disk—sort of the "prime meridian" for the disk sectors. A disk with a single index hole is a soft-sectored disk; the software (operating system) decides the actual number of sectors on the disk. Some older equipment, such as Wang word processors, use hard-sectored disks, which have an index hole to demarcate individual sectors. Do not use hard-sectored disks in a PC.

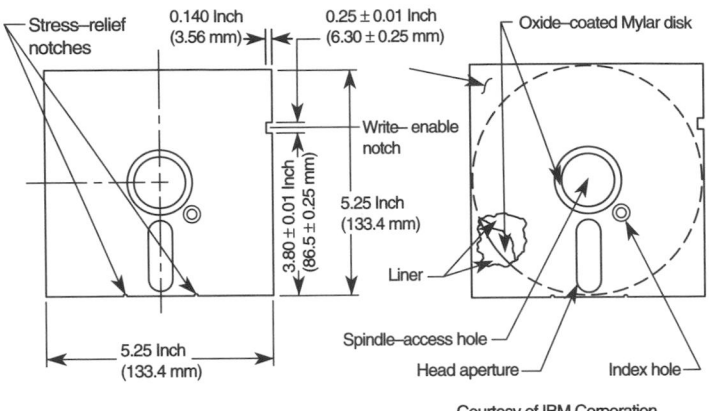

FIG. 12.19   Construction of a 5 1/4-inch floppy disk.

Below the hub hole is a slot shaped somewhat like a long racetrack through which you can see the disk surface. Through this media-access hole, the disk drive heads read and write data to the disk surface.

On the right side, about one inch from the top, is a rectangular punch from the side of the disk cover. If this write-enable notch is present, writing to the disk has been enabled. Disks without this notch (or with the notch taped over) are write-protected disks. The notch might not be present on all disks, particularly those purchased with programs on them.

On the rear of the disk jacket at the bottom, two very small oval notches flank the head slot. These notches relieve stress on the disk and help prevent it from warping. The drive might also use these notches to assist in keeping the disk in the proper position in the drive.

Because the 3 1/2-inch disks use a much more rigid plastic case, which helps stabilize the magnetic medium inside, these disks can record at track and data densities greater than the 5 1/4-inch disks (see Figure 12.20). A metal shutter protects the media-access hole. The drive manipulates the shutter, leaving it closed whenever the disk is not in a drive. The media is then completely insulated from the environment and from your fingers. The shutter also obviates the need for a disk jacket.

Because the shutter is not necessary for the disk to work, you can remove it from the plastic case if it becomes bent or damaged. Pry it off of the disk case; it will pop off with a snap. You should remove the spring that pushes it closed, as well. After removing the damaged shutter, it would be a good idea to copy the data from the damaged disk to a new one.

Rather than an index hole in the disk, the 3 1/2-inch disks use a metal center hub with an alignment hole. The drive "grasps" the metal hub, and the hole in the hub enables the drive to position the disk properly.

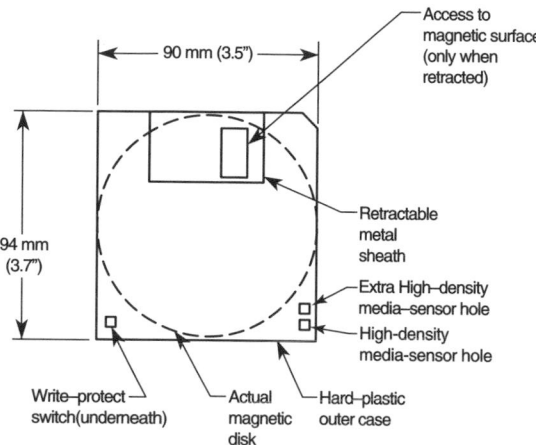

FIG. 12.20 Construction of a 3 1/2-inch floppy disk.

On the lower-left part of the disk is a hole with a plastic slider—the *write-protect/-enable hole*. When the slider is positioned so the hole is visible, the disk is write-protected; the drive is prevented from recording on the disk. When the slider is positioned to cover the hole, writing is enabled, and you can save data to the disk. For more permanent write-protection, some commercial software programs are supplied on disks with the slider removed so you cannot easily enable recording on the disk, which is exactly opposite of a 5 1/4-inch floppy in which Covered equals Write Protect, not Write Enable.

On the other (right) side of the disk from the write-protect hole, there is usually another hole called the *media-density-selector hole*. If this hole is present, the disk is constructed of a special medium and is therefore an HD or ED disk. If the media-sensor hole is exactly opposite the write-protect hole, it indicates a 1.44M HD disk. If the media-sensor hole is located more toward the top of the disk (the metal shutter is at the top of the disk), it indicates an ED disk. No hole on the right side means that the disk is a low-density disk. Most 3 1/2-inch drives have a media sensor that controls recording capability based on the absence or presence of these holes.

The actual magnetic medium in both the 3 1/2-inch and 5 1/4-inch disks is constructed of the same basic materials. They use a plastic base (usually Mylar) coated with a magnetic compound. High density disks use a cobalt-ferric compound, and extended density disks use a barium-ferric media compound. The rigid jacket material on the 3 1/2-inch disks often causes people to believe incorrectly that these disks are some sort of "hard disk" and not really a floppy disk. The disk "cookie" inside the 3 1/2-inch case is just as floppy as the 5 1/4-inch variety.

Floppy Disk Media Types and Specifications. This section examines the types of disks you can purchase for your system. Especially interesting are the technical specifications that can separate one type of disk from another, as Table 12.14 shows. The following sections define all the specifications used to describe a typical disk.

Table 12.14 Floppy Disk Media Specifications

| | 5 1/4-Inch | | | 3 1/2-Inch | | |
Media Parameters	Double Density (DD)	Quad Density (QD)	High Density (HD)	Double Density (DD)	High Density (HD)	Extra-High Density (ED)
Tracks Per Inch (TPI)	48	96	96	135	135	135
Bits Per Inch (BPI)	5,876	5,876	9,646	8,717	17,434	34,868
Media Formulation	Ferrite	Ferrite	Cobalt	Cobalt	Cobalt	Barium
Coercivity (Oersteds)	300	300	600	600	720	750
Thickness (Micro-In.)	100	100	50	70	40	100
Recording Polarity	Horiz.	Horiz.	Horiz.	Horiz.	Horiz.	Vert.

Density. *Density*, in simplest terms, is a measure of the amount of information that can be packed reliably into a specific area of a recording surface. The keyword here is *reliably*.

Disks have two types of densities: longitudinal density and linear density. *Longitudinal density* is indicated by how many tracks can be recorded on the disk, often expressed as a number of tracks per inch (TPI). *Linear density* is the capability of an individual track to store data, often indicated as a number of bits per inch (BPI). Unfortunately, these types of densities are often confused when discussing different disks and drives.

Media Coercivity and Thickness. The coercivity specification of a disk refers to the magnetic-field strength required to make a proper recording. *Coercivity*, measured in oersteds, is a value indicating magnetic strength. A disk with a higher coercivity rating requires a stronger magnetic field to make a recording on that disk. With lower ratings, the disk can be recorded with a weaker magnetic field. In other words, the lower the coercivity rating, the more sensitive the disk.

HD media demands higher coercivity ratings so the adjacent magnetic domains don't interfere with each other. For this reason, HD media is actually less sensitive and requires a stronger recording signal strength.

Another factor is the thickness of the disk. The thinner the disk, the less influence a region of the disk has on another adjacent region. The thinner disks, therefore, can accept many more bits per inch without eventually degrading the recording.

Caring for and Handling Floppy Disks and Drives. Most computer users know the basics of disk care. Disks can be damaged or destroyed easily by the following:

- Touching the recording surface with your fingers or anything else
- Writing on a disk label with a ball-point pen or pencil
- Bending the disk
- Spilling coffee or other substances on the disk

- Overheating a disk (leaving it in the hot sun or near a radiator, for example)

- Exposing a disk to stray magnetic fields

Despite all these cautions, disks are rather hardy storage devices; I can't say that I have ever destroyed one by just writing on it with a pen, because I do so all the time. I am careful, however, not to press too hard, which can put a crease in the disk. Also, touching a disk does not necessarily ruin it but rather gets the disk and your drive head dirty with oil and dust. The real danger to your disks comes from magnetic fields that, because they are unseen, can sometimes be found in places you never imagined.

For example, all color monitors (and color TV sets) have a degaussing coil around the face of the tube that demagnetizes the shadow mask when you turn the monitor on. If you keep your disks anywhere near (within one foot) of the front of the color monitor, you expose them to a strong magnetic field every time you turn on the monitor. Keeping disks in this area is not a good idea because the field is designed to demagnetize objects, and indeed works well for demagnetizing disks. The effect is cumulative and irreversible.

Another source of powerful magnetic fields is an electric motor, found in vacuum cleaners, heaters or air conditioners, fans, electric pencil sharpeners, and so on. Do not place these devices near areas where you store disks. Audio speakers also contain magnets, but most of the speakers sold for use with PCs are shielded to minimize disk corruption.

Airport X-Ray Machines and Metal Detectors. People associate myths with things they cannot see, and we certainly cannot see data as it is stored on a disk, nor the magnetic fields that can alter the data.

One of my favorite myths to dispel is that the airport X-ray machine somehow damages disks. I have a great deal of experience in this area from having traveled around the country for the past 10 years or so with disks and portable computers in hand. I fly about 150,000 miles per year, and my portable computer equipment and disks have been through X-ray machines more than 100 times each year.

The biggest problem people have when they approach the airport X-ray machines with disks or computers is that they don't pass the stuff through! Seriously, X-rays are essentially just a form of light, and disks and computers are not affected by X-rays at anywhere near the levels found in these machines.

What can damage your magnetic media is the metal detector. Time and time again, someone with magnetic media or a portable computer approaches the security check. They freeze and say, "Oh no, I have disks and a computer—they have to be hand-inspected." The person then refuses to place the disk and computer on the X-ray belt, and either walks through the metal detector with disks and computer in hand or passes the items over to the security guard, in very close proximity to the metal detector.

Metal detectors work by monitoring disruptions in a weak magnetic field. A metal object inserted in the field area causes the field's shape to change, which the detector observes. This principle, which is the reason that the detectors are sensitive to metal objects, can be dangerous to your disks; the X-ray machine, however, is the safest area through which to pass either your disk or your computer.

The X-ray machine is not dangerous to magnetic media because it merely exposes the media to electromagnetic radiation at a particular (very high) frequency. *Blue light* is an example of electromagnetic radiation of a different frequency. The only difference between X-rays and blue light is in the frequency, or wavelength, of the emission.

Some people worry about the effect of X-ray radiation on their system's *EPROM (Erasable Programmable Read-Only Memory) chips*. This concern might actually be more valid than worrying about disk damage because EPROMs are erased by certain forms of electromagnetic radiation. In reality, however, you do not need to worry about this effect, either. EPROMs are erased by direct exposure to very intense ultraviolet light. Specifically, to be erased, an EPROM must be exposed to a 12,000 uw/cm2 UV light source with a wavelength of 2,537 angstroms for 15 to 20 minutes, and at a distance of 1 inch. Increasing the power of the light source or decreasing the distance from the source can shorten the erasure time to a few minutes.

The airport X-ray machine is different by a factor of 10,000 in wavelength, and the field strength, duration, and distance from the emitter source are nowhere near what is necessary for EPROM erasure. Many circuit-board manufacturers even use X-ray inspection on circuit boards (with components including EPROMs installed) to test and check quality control during manufacture.

In my own experiences, I have passed one disk through different airport X-ray machines for two years, averaging two or three passes a week. The same disk still remains intact with all the original files and data and has never been reformatted. I also have a portable computer that has gone through X-ray machines safely every week for more than four years. I prefer to pass computers and disks through the X-ray machine because it offers the best shielding from the magnetic fields produced by the metal detector standing next to it. Doing so may also lessen the "hassle factor" with the security personnel because if I have the computer X-rayed, they often do not require that I unpack it and turn it on. Unfortunately, with the greater emphasis on airport security these days, even when the computer is X-rayed, some airlines require that the system be demonstrated (turned on) anyway.

Now you may not want to take my word for it, but there has been scientific research published that corroborates what I have stated. A few years ago, a study was published by two scientists, one of whom actually designs X-ray tubes for a major manufacturer. Their study was titled "Airport X-rays and floppy disks: no cause for concern," and was published in 1993 in the journal *Computer Methods and Programs in Biomedicine*. According to the abstract,

> A controlled study was done to test the possible effects of X-rays on the integrity of data stored on common sizes of floppy disks. Disks were exposed to doses of X-rays up to seven times that to be expected during airport examination of baggage. The readability of nearly 14 megabytes of data was unaltered by X-irradiation, indicating that floppy disks need not be given special handling during X-ray inspection of baggage.

In fact, the disks were retested after two years of storage, and there has still been no measurable degradation since the exposure.

Drive-Installation Procedures

In most cases, installing a floppy disk drive is a matter of attaching the drive to the computer chassis or case and then plugging the power and signal cables into the drive. Some type of bracket and screws are normally required to attach the drive to the chassis. These are normally included with the chassis or case itself. Several companies listed in Appendix A, "Vendor List," specialize in cases, cables, brackets, screw hardware, and other items useful in assembling systems or installing drives.

> **Note**
>
> Because floppy disk drives are generally installed into the same half-height bays as hard disk drives, the physical mounting of the drive in the computer case is the same for both units. See "Hard Disk Installation Procedures," earlier in this chapter, for more information on the process.

When you connect a drive, make sure the power cable is installed properly. The cable is normally keyed so you cannot plug it in backward. Also, install the data and control cable. If there is no key is in this cable, use the colored wire in the cable as a guide to the position of pin 1. This cable is oriented correctly when you plug it in so the colored wire is plugged into the disk drive connector toward the cut-out notch in the drive edge connector.

Repairing Floppy Disk Drives

Attitudes about repairing floppy disk drives have changed over the years, primarily because of the decreasing cost of drives. When drives were more expensive, people often considered repairing the drive rather than replacing it. With the cost of drives decreasing every year, however, certain labor- or parts-intensive repair procedures have become almost as expensive as replacing the drive with a new one. Because of cost considerations, repairing floppy disk drives usually is limited to cleaning the drive and heads and lubricating the mechanical mechanisms.

Cleaning Floppy Disk Drives. Sometimes read and write problems are caused by dirty drive heads. Cleaning a drive is easy; you can proceed in two ways:

- Use one of the simple head-cleaning kits available from computer- or office-supply stores. These devices are easy to operate and don't require you to open the computer case to access the drive.

- The manual method: Use a cleaning swab with a liquid such as pure alcohol or trichloroethane. With this method, you must open the system unit to expose the drive and, in many cases (especially in earlier full-height drives), also remove and partially disassemble the drive.

The manual method can result in a better overall job, but usually the work required is not worth the difference.

The cleaning kits come in two styles: The wet type uses a liquid squirted on a cleaning disk to wash off the heads; the dry kit relies on abrasive material on the cleaning disk to remove head deposits. I recommend that you never use the dry drive-cleaning kits. Always use a wet system in which a liquid solution is applied to the cleaning disk. The dry disks can prematurely wear the heads if used improperly or too often; wet systems are very safe to use.

The manual drive-cleaning method requires that you have physical access to the heads to swab them manually with a lint-free foam swab soaked in a cleaning solution. This method requires some level of expertise: Simply jabbing at the heads incorrectly with a cleaning swab might knock the drive heads out of alignment. You must use a careful in-and-out motion, and lightly swab the heads. No side-to-side motion (relative to the way the heads travel) should be used; this motion can snag a head and knock it out of alignment. Because of the difficulty and danger of this manual cleaning, for most applications I recommend a simple wet-disk cleaning kit because it is the easiest and safest method.

One question that comes up repeatedly in my seminars is "How often should you clean a disk drive?" Only you can answer that question. What type of environment is the system in? Do you smoke cigarettes near the system? If so, more frequent cleaning is required. Usually, a safe rule of thumb is to clean drives about once a year if the system is in a clean office environment in which no smoke or other particulate matter is in the air. In a heavy-smoking environment, you might have to clean every six months or perhaps even more often. In dirty industrial environments, you might have to clean every month or so. Your own experience is your guide in this matter. If the operating system reports drive errors such as the familiar DOS Abort, Retry, Ignore prompt, you should clean your drive to try to solve the problem. If cleaning does solve the problem, you probably should step up the interval between preventive-maintenance cleanings.

In some cases, you might want to place a very small amount of lubricant on the door mechanism or other mechanical contact point inside the drive. Do not use oil; use a pure silicone lubricant. Oil collects dust rapidly after you apply it and usually causes the oiled mechanism to gum up later. Silicone does not attract dust in the same manner and can be used safely. Use very small amounts of silicone; do not drip or spray silicone inside the drive. You must make sure that the lubricant is applied only to the part that needs it. If the lubricant gets all over the inside of the drive, it may cause unnecessary problems.

Aligning Floppy Disk Drives. If your disk drives are misaligned, you will notice that other drives cannot read disks created in your drive, and you might not be able to read disks created in other drives. This situation can be dangerous if you allow it to progress unchecked. If the misalignment is bad enough, you will probably notice it first in the drive's inability to read original application-program disks, while still being able to read the disks you have created yourself.

To solve this problem, you can have the drive realigned. I usually don't recommend realigning drives because of the low cost of replacing the drive compared to aligning one. Also, an unforeseen circumstance catches many people off-guard: You might find that your newly aligned drive might not be able to read all the disks you created while the drive was out of alignment. If you replace the misaligned drive with a new one and keep the misaligned drive, you can use it for DISKCOPY purposes to transfer the data to newly formatted disks in the new drive.

Aligning disk drives is usually no longer performed because of the high relative cost. In the past, aligning a drive properly required access to an oscilloscope (for about $500), a special analog-alignment disk ($75), and the OEM service manual for the drive; also, you must spend half an hour to an hour aligning the drive.

Some programs on the market evaluate the condition of floppy disk drives by using a disk created or formatted on the same drive. A program that uses this technique cannot make a proper evaluation of a disk drive's alignment. To do this, you must use a specially created disk produced by a tested and calibrated machine. You can use this type of disk as a reference standard by which to judge a drive's performance. Accurite, the primary manufacturer of reference standard floppy disks, helps specify floppy disk industry standards. Accurite produces the following three main types of reference standard disks used for testing drive function and alignment:

- Digital Diagnostic Diskette (DDD)

- Analog Alignment Diskette (AAD)

- High-Resolution Diagnostic Diskette (HRD)

The HRD disk, introduced in 1989, represented a breakthrough in floppy disk drive testing and alignment. The disk is accurate to within 50 µ-inches (millionths of an inch)—accurate enough to use not only for precise testing of floppy disk drives, but also for aligning drives. With software that uses this HRD disk, you can align a floppy disk drive without having to use special tools or an oscilloscope. Other than the program and the HRD disk, you need only a PC to which to connect the drive. This product has significantly lowered the cost of aligning a floppy disk drive and has eliminated the need for special test equipment.

The Accurite program Drive Probe is designed to work with the HRD disks. Drive Probe is the most accurate and capable floppy disk testing program on the market, thanks to the use of HRD disks. Until other programs utilize the HRD disks for testing, Drive Probe is my software of choice for floppy disk drive testing and alignment. Because the Drive Probe software also acts as a disk exerciser, for use with AAD disks and an oscilloscope, you can move the heads to specific tracks for controlled testing.

With the price of most types of floppy disk drives hovering at or below the $35 mark, aligning drives usually is not a cost-justified alternative to replacement. The Drive Probe and HRD system can make alignment more cost-effective than before, but it is still a labor- and cost-intensive operation. Weigh this cost against the replacement cost and age of the drive. I have purchased brand-new 1.44M floppy disk drives for as low as $25. At these prices, alignment is no longer a viable option.

Removable Storage Drives

The reason for the shortage of storage space on today's PCs is easy enough to understand. Just take a look at the sheer number and size of the files stored in the two main directories used by Windows 9x (usually C:\WINDOWS and C:\WINDOWS\SYSTEM). The amount of disk space used by the files in those two directories alone can quickly balloon to 100M or more after you also install a few Windows applications. The reason is simple: Nearly all Windows applications place files in one of the Windows directories that the application will use later. These files include those with extensions like DLL, 386, VBX, DRV, TTF, and many others. Similarly, Windows NT, OS/2, and UNIX, as well as the software applications that run in these operating systems, can require enormous amounts of storage space.

This section focuses on some of the more advanced data storage options on the market: removable media large-capacity cartridge drives. Some removable media drives use media as small as a 3 1/2-inch floppy disk, while others use media about the size of a 5 1/4-inch floppy.

These drives, whose capacities range from 35M to 2G or more, offer fairly speedy performance, the capability to store data or less frequently used programs on a removable disk, and the capability to easily transport huge data files—Computer Aided Drawing (CAD) files and graphics files, for example—from one computer to another. Or, you can use a removable cartridge to take sensitive data away from your office so you can lock it safely away from prying eyes.

> **Note**
>
> Removable media drives can also be used as system backup devices. However, the higher price of the medium itself (disks or cartridges) can make this use somewhat prohibitive.

> **Tip**
>
> There are literally dozens of removable storage devices currently on the market. Be sure to compare your chosen solution against the competition before making a final purchase. Be especially wary of missing statistics in press releases and product packaging—manufacturers are apt to omit a specification if their drive doesn't measure up to the competition.

Types of Removable Media Drives

There are two commonly used types of removable media drives: magnetic media and optical media, also called *magneto-optical media*. Magnetic media drives use technology very much like that of a floppy or hard disk drive to encode data for storage. Magneto-optical media drives encode information on disk by using newer technology, a combination of traditional magnetic and laser technologies.

Magnetic media drives are considerably faster than magneto-optical drives and offer similar capacities. The Syquest magnetic media drives, for example, offer 14ms average access times, compared to the 30ms (or slower) access times of magneto-optical drives.

Magneto-optical drives can also be more than twice as expensive as magnetic media drives. If you have a great deal of data to store, however, the comparative cost of using a magneto-optical drive drops because magneto-optical media cartridges are considerably less expensive than magnetic media. For example, 270M Syquest cartridges can cost roughly $40 each, while 230M magneto-optical cartridges can cost as little as $13 apiece.

There are also several connection options for the leading removable drives. Although SCSI has been, and continues to be, a popular solution, many drives today connect to the computer's parallel port. This option allows you to share one drive between several different computers, but the parallel port drives generally provide relatively poor performance levels. Of course, internal SCSI and IDE solutions remain just as popular for the single machine installation.

> **Note**
>
> Connection and/or installation of removable media drives is very similar to connecting and installing other internal and external peripherals.
>
> The installation of an external parallel port drive is the simplest of the available interfaces, requiring a special cable that comes with the drive and installation of special software drivers. See the instructions that come with each drive for the specifics of its installation.

The following sections provide information on magnetic media and magneto-optical drive types.

Magnetic Media Drives

A small group of companies dominate the market for magnetic removable media drives. 3M's spinoff company Imation, Iomega, and Syquest are the leading names in removable magnetic media drives.

Removable magnetic media drives are usually floppy or hard disk based. For example, the popular Zip drive is a 3 1/2-inch version of the original Bernoulli floppy disk drive made by Iomega. The new 3M LS-120 drive is a floppy-based drive that stores 120M on a disk that looks exactly like a 1.44M floppy! The Syquest drive and Iomega Jaz drive are both hard disk-based designs.

Both the Iomega and Syquest designs are their own proprietary standard, while the LS-120 is a true industry standard supported by many companies. However, the Iomega Zip drive is well on its way to becoming a de facto standard in the industry. Many of the new PCs sold today include a Zip drive as standard equipment.

Floptical Drives. There is a special type of high-capacity floppy disk drive being marketed by several companies that is called a *floptical drive*. These drives are unique in that they can both read and write standard floppy disks as well as higher-capacity floptical disks. A 21M version was originally available but more recently a 120M version has become popular, and the 21M version has become obsolete. The older 21M version was created by Insite Peripherals, and packed 21M of data on the same size disk as a 3 1/2-inch floppy. More recently, 3M and Matsushita have introduced a drive called the LS-120 that can store 120M on a single 3 1/2-inch floppy disk! In addition, all floptical drives can read and write 1.44M and 720K floppy disks (although they cannot handle 2.88M disks). Because of their greatly increased storage capacity and capability to use common floppy disks, the newer 120M flopticals are considered by many as the perfect replacement floppy disk drive.

The name "floptical" might suggest the use of laser beams to burn or etch data onto the disk or to excite the media in preparation for magnetic recording—as is the case with the CD-R and Write Once, Read Many (WORM) drives, but this suggestion is erroneous. The read/write heads of a floptical drive use magnetic recording technology, much like that of floppy disk drives. The floptical disk itself is composed of the same ferrite materials common to floppy and hard disks. Floptical drives are capable of such increased capacity because many more tracks are packed on each disk, compared with a standard 1.44M floppy. Obviously, to fit so many tracks on the floptical disk, the tracks must be much more narrow than those on a floppy disk.

That's where optical technology comes into play. Flopticals use a special optical mechanism to properly position the drive read/write heads over the data tracks on the disk. *Servo information*, which specifically defines the location of each track, is embedded in the disk during the manufacturing process. Each track of servo information is actually etched or stamped on the disk and is never disturbed during the recording process. Each time the floptical drive writes to the disk, the recording mechanism (including the read/write heads) is guided by a laser beam precisely into place by this servo information. When the floptical drive reads the encoded data, the laser uses this servo information again to guide the read/write heads precisely into place.

21M Floptical Drives. The original Insite 21M floptical disks used tracks formatted to 27 sectors of 512 bytes. The disks revolved at 720 RPM. Flopticals are capable of nearly 10M per minute data throughput, using a SCSI interface.

Unfortunately, the 21M drives by Insite never really caught on due to several reasons. One is that no leading manufacturer has included these drives in a standard configuration with built-in BIOS drivers and support. Also, Microsoft, IBM, and Apple have not built support for these drives directly into their operating systems.

LS-120 (120M) Floptical Drives. The LS-120 drive (also called a SuperDisk drive) was designed to become the new standard floppy disk drive in the PC industry. LS-120 technology was developed by Imation (3M) Corporation, Matsushita-Kotobuki Industries, Ltd. (MKE), and O.R. Technology, and stores 120M of data, or about 83 times more data than current 1.44M floppy disks. In addition to storing more, these drives read and write at up to five times the speed of standard floppy disk drives.

The LS-120 floppy disk drive can act as the PC's bootable A: drive and is fully compatible with Windows NT, Windows 95 OSR2, and Windows 98. In addition to the new 120M floppy disks, the LS-120 drive accepts standard 720K and 1.44M floppy disks, and actually reads and writes those disks up to three times faster than standard floppy disk drives. Iomega Zip drives are not backward-compatible and cannot use existing floppy disks; the proprietary Zip media stores less and is more expensive than the 3M LS-120 media. Many people in the computer industry believe that LS-120 technology will replace the 1.44M floppy disk in new computers.

The LS-120 uses the standard IDE interface, which is already built into most existing systems, and it is perfect for portable systems. The LS-120 provides a solution that not only replaces the existing floppy, but it can even replace the floppy disk drive internally. Having one of these high-capacity drives in a portable allows the use of the relatively inexpensive 120M removable disks while on the road. They are perfect for storing entire applications or datasets and can be removed and secured when the portable system is not in use.

LS-120 specifications are compared to standard 1.44M floppy disks in Table 12.15.

Table 12.15 LS-120 Specifications		
Drive Type	**LS-120 Floppy**	**Standard 1.44M Floppy Disk**
Formatted Capacity	120M	1.44M
Transfer Rate: parallel port	290K/sec	45K/sec
Transfer Rate: internal IDE	484K/sec	Not Applicable
Average seek time	70ms	84ms
Disk rotational speed	720 RPM	300 RPM
Track density	2,490 TPI	135 TPI
Number of tracks	1,736 X 2 sides	80 X 2 sides

The 3M LS-120 disk has the same shape and size as a standard 1.44M 3 1/2-inch floppy disk; however, it uses a combination of magnetic and optical technology to enable greater capacity and performance. Named after the Laser Servo (LS) mechanism it employs, LS-120 technology places optical reference tracks on the disk that are both written and read by a laser system. The optical sensor in the drive enables the read-write head to be precisely positioned over the magnetic data tracks, enabling track densities of 2,490 TPI versus the 135 TPI for a 1.44M floppy disk.

Virtually all new PCs now come with LS-120 support directly in the BIOS, which means that these drives are not only easy to install, but they can directly replace the A: floppy disk drive and are bootable, as well. Many newer laptop systems come with LS-120 drives that replace and yet are fully compatible with the standard floppy disk drive. Unlike Zip, you can install the LS-120 in your laptop and leave the standard floppy disk drive at home. Many PC manufacturers are incorporating LS-120 drives in their products as standard equipment. Besides coming in new systems, these drives are also available separately at a cost of about $75 or less in internal or external versions for upgrading older systems. The 120M floppy disks are available for about $10 per disk or less, almost half the cost of the proprietary Zip media.

Removable Cartridge Drives. Back in the early 1980s, Iomega introduced the Bernoulli drive. The disk used in the original Bernoulli drive was a thick cartridge roughly the same size as a 5 1/4-inch floppy disk, although a large shutter, similar to the shutter on a

3 1/2-inch floppy disk, easily differentiated Bernoulli disks from standard floppy disks. Bernoulli cartridges were originally available in 10M capacities, but those were replaced by 35M, 65M, 105M, and 150M capacities.

Bernoulli disks are widely known as the most durable of the removable media drive types. It is probably safer to mail a Bernoulli cartridge than another type of removable disk because the media is well-protected inside the cartridge. Bernoulli encases a magnetic-media-covered flexible disk (in effect, a floppy disk) in a rigid cartridge in the same way the thin disk of a 1.44M floppy is encased in a rigid plastic shell.

When it rotates in the drive, the disk is pulled by air pressure toward the drive heads. Many people do not think that there is head-to-disk contact in a Bernoulli drive, but indeed there is. As the disk spins, the airflow generated by the disk movement encounters what is called a *Bernoulli plate*, a stationary plate designed to control the air flow so the disk is pulled toward the read/write head. At full speed, the head does touch the disk, which causes wear. Bernoulli drives have built-in random seek functions that prevent any single track on the disk from wearing excessively during periods of inactivity. Bernoulli disk cartridges should be replaced periodically because they can wear out. The disk itself spins at speeds approaching the 3,600 RPM of relatively slow hard drives. The drive has an average seek time of 18ms, not a great deal slower than today's medium-priced hard drives.

Zip Drives. Another form of Bernoulli drive from Iomega is the popular Zip drive. This device is available as a internal SCSI or IDE unit, or as an external SCSI or parallel port device. There is also a low-power version designed for use in notebook computers. The drive is capable of storing up to 100M of data on a small removable magnetic cartridge that resembles a 3 1/2-inch floppy disk, and has approximately a 29ms access time and a 1M/sec transfer rate when used with a SCSI connection. When using the parallel connection, the drive's speed is often limited by the speed of the parallel port.

The Zip drives use a proprietary 3 1/2-inch disk made by Iomega. It is about twice as thick as a standard 3 1/2-inch floppy disk. The Zip drives do not accept standard 1.44M or 720K floppy disks, making this an unlikely candidate for a floppy disk drive replacement. Internal Zip drives have become popular options in new PCs, and the external models are an effective solution for exchanging data between systems, but the major PC manufacturers have not recognized the proprietary format directly in the system BIOS, meaning you cannot boot from a Zip drive, nor can it replace the A: floppy disk drive. Zip drives have also suffered from reliability problems, such as the so called "click death," which occurs when the drive begins a rhythmic ticking sound. At this point, the data on the disk can be corrupted and both the drive and the media must be replaced. Finally, the media costs of Zip are almost double that of the higher-capacity LS-120 drives, which are an industry standard fully supported by the system BIOS in modern PCs. Table 12.16 lists the Zip specifications.

Table 12.16 Zip Specifications		
Model (Interface)	**SCSI and/or Parallel**	**EIDE**
Formatted Capacity	100 M	100 M
Sustained transfer rate maximum	1.40 M/sec	1.40 M/sec
Sustained transfer rate minimum	0.79 M/sec	0.79 M/sec
Maximum Throughput	60 M/min (SCSI); 20 M/min (parallel)	84M/min
Average seek time	29 msec	29 msec
Disk Rotational speed	2941 RPM	2941 RPM
Buffer size	32 K	16 K

Syquest Drives. Syquest manufactures some drives that use 5 1/4-inch cartridges and others that use 3 1/2-inch cartridges. But the Syquest disks, like the Bernoulli cartridges, are easily differentiated from floppy disks. The 5 1/4-inch 44M and 88M cartridges used in some SyDOS drives are encased in clear plastic, as are the SyDOS 3 1/2-inch 105M and Syquest 270M cartridges. The disk spins inside the cartridge at several thousand RPM. Syquest claims a 14ms average access time for the drives it manufactures.

The disks for the Syquest and SyDOS drives are composed of a rigid platter inside a plastic cartridge but are not as well-protected as the disk in a Bernoulli cartridge. Some people consider these disks fragile. If the Syquest and SyDOS cartridges are not severely jostled or dropped, however, they can be transported safely. These cartridges must be carefully protected when you mail or ship them.

The Syquest/SyDOS drives are available in internal and external models. The internal models require a connection to the existing IDE hard drive interface card. The external models require a SCSI interface card with an external connector and are powered by a transformer that connects to a grounded AC wall plug.

Jaz Drives. Another type of removable hard disk drive is the *Jaz drive* from Iomega. This is physically and functionally identical to the Syquest drives in that it is a true removable cartridge hard disk, except that the capacity of the cartridge has been increased; 1G and 2G models are available. Unfortunately, the cartridges themselves cost $100 to $125, which is about seven times the cost of a DAT (Digital Audio Tape) cartridge that stores up to four times more data! The high cost of the media makes the Jaz drive unsuitable for backup when compared to traditional tape media, but possibly useful as an add-on external SCSI hard disk drive. Table 12.17 lists the specifications for Jaz drives.

Table 12.17 Jaz Specifications		
Model	**1 Gig**	**2 Gig**
Formatted Capacity	1070 million bytes	2000 million bytes
Transfer rate:		
Maximum	6.62 M/sec	8.7 M/sec
Average	5.4 M/sec	7.35 M/sec

(continues)

Table 12.17 Jaz Specifications Continued		
Model	**1 Gig**	**2 Gig**
Minimum	3.41 M/sec	3.41 M/sec
Burst	10 M/sec	20 M/sec
Average seek time read	10 msec	10 msec
Average seek time write	12 msec	12 msec
Access Time	15.5–17.5 msec	15.5–17.5 msec
Disk Rotational speed	5400 RPM	5394 RPM
Buffer size	256 K	512 K
Interface	Fast SCSI II	Ultra SCSI

SparQ Drives. The SparQ drive is a removable hard disk drive by Syquest that is de-signed to be a low-cost alternative to other technologies with similar capacities, such as the Jaz and the SyJet. The medium is a proprietary cartridge containing a single disk platter with a 1G capacity. At $99 for a three-pack of cartridges, the cost per megabyte of the SparQ is substantially less than that of comparable removable hard disk media, al-though it still does not approach that of tape or CD-R.

The drive is available in internal IDE and external parallel port versions. The parallel port version, like all drives using this interface, is limited by the throughput of the port itself, but the IDE version of the SparQ provides data transfer rates that are faster than most competing drives. EIDE burst transfer rates can be as high as 16.6M/sec by using PIO mode 4, with sustained rates ranging from 3.7 to 6.8M/sec. Table 12.18 lists the specifica-tions for the SparQ drive.

Table 12.18 SparQ Specifications	
Formatted Capacity	**1008 million bytes**
Transfer rate: EIDE version	
Maximum	6.9 M/sec
Minimum	3.7 M/sec
Burst (PIO mode 4)	16.6 M/sec
Sustained Transfer rate: parallel version	1.25 M/sec
Average seek time	12 msec
Disk Rotational speed	5400 RPM

Comparing Removable Drives. Deciding on a removable drive is getting tougher, as there are many removable drives currently on the market. Iomega and Syquest lead the pack, but new entries from Exabyte and Avatar Peripherals provide their own proprietary drives, as well. Unfortunately, all these drives use their own proprietary media that are universally incompatible. If you want to exchange files with another user, they must have a drive made by the same manufacturer. The ease of portability is one reason why the parallel port models of many of these drives are popular.

Table 12.19 shows a direct comparison between the most popular removable drives on the market.

Table 12.19 Removable Drive Specifications			
Drive Type	**Disk/Cartridge Capacity**	**Average Seek Time**	**Data Transfer Rate**
Iomega Zip Parallel	100M	29ms	1.4M/sec
Iomega Zip IDE	100M	29ms	1.4M/sec
Iomega Zip SCSI	100M	29ms	1.4M/sec
Imation LS-120 Internal	120M	70ms	4.0M/sec
Syquest 235 Parallel	235M	13.5ms	1.25M/sec
Avatar Shark 250 Parallel	250M	12ms	1.2 M/sec
Avatar Shark PCMCIA	250M	12ms	2.0M/sec
Syquest 235 SCSI/IDE	235M	13.5ms	2.4M/sec
Iomega Jaz (SCSI)	2G	12ms	5.4M/sec
Avatar Shark IDE	250M	12ms	2.5M/sec
Syquest Syjet SCSI	1.5G	12ms	5.3M/sec
Syquest Syjet IDE	1.5G	12ms	5.3M/sec
Syquest SparQ IDE	1G	12ms	6.9M/sec
Syquest SparQ Parallel	1G	12ms	1.25M/sec
CD-R Drives	650M	<150ms	150K/sec–2.4M/sec

When shopping for a removable drive, keep the following in mind:

■ *Price per megabyte of storage.* Take the cost of the drive's cartridge or disk and divide it by the storage capacity to see how much you are paying per megabyte of storage. This difference in price will become quite apparent as you buy more cartridges or disks for the drive. (Don't forget to factor in the cost of the drive itself!)

■ *Access time versus need of access.* The access and data transfer speeds are only important if you need to access the data frequently or quickly. If your primary use is archiving data, a slower drive may be fine. However, if you plan on running programs off of the drive, choose a faster drive instead.

■ *Compatibility and portability.* Opt for an external SCSI or parallel port solution if you will need to move the drive between various computers. Also verify that there are drivers available for each type of machine and operating system you want to use with the drive. Also consider whether you will have to exchange disks with other users. The Iomega Zip disk is rapidly becoming the standard for removable cartridge media, but the graphic design industry has long used Syquest drives. For some users, this may be the most important factor in choosing a drive.

Tape Drives

The data backup and archive needs of a personal computer can be overwhelming. People with large hard drives and numerous application programs installed, and those who generate a large amount of data, may find it necessary to back up their computers on a weekly or even a daily basis.

In addition, a critical need on today's PCs is data storage space. Sometimes it seems as though the storage requirements of a PC can never be satisfied. On nearly any PC used for business, study, or even for fun, the amount of software installed can quickly overwhelm even a large hard drive. To save space on the primary storage devices, you can archive infrequently used data to another storage medium.

This section focuses on tape backup drives, which you can use to solve the problems of the growing need for data storage space and the need for a fast and efficient way to back up many megabytes of data.

Any computer book worth reading warns repeatedly that you should back up your system regularly. Backups are necessary because at any time a major problem, or even some minor ones, can corrupt the important information and the programs stored on your computer's hard disk drive, rendering this information useless. A wide range of problems can damage the data on your hard drive. Here is a list of some of these data-damaging problems:

■ Sudden fluctuations in the electricity that powers your computer (*power spikes*) resulting in data damage or corruption.

■ Overwriting a file by mistake.

■ Mistakenly formatting your hard disk when you meant to format a floppy.

■ Hard drive failure resulting in loss of data that has not been backed up. Not only do you have to install a new drive but, because you have no backup, you also must reinstall all your software.

■ Catastrophic damage to your computer (storm, flood, lightning strike, fire, theft). A single lightning strike near your office or home can destroy the circuitry of your computer, including your hard drive. Theft of your computer, of course, is equally devastating. A recent, complete backup greatly simplifies the process of setting up a replacement computer.

■ Loss of valuable data due to a computer-related virus. One single download or floppy disk can contain a virus that can damage valuable files and even your entire hard disk. With several hundred new viruses appearing each month, no anti-virus software program can keep you entirely safe. A recent backup of noninfected, critical files can help repair even the worst damage.

Backups are also the cure for such common headaches as a full hard drive and the need to transfer data between computers. By backing up data you rarely use, then deleting the original data from your hard drive, you free up the space once occupied by that data. If you later need a particular data file, you can retrieve that file from your backup. You can also more easily share large amounts of data between computers—as when you send data from one city to another, for example—by backing up the data to a tape and sending the tape.

Regardless of how important regular backups are, many people avoid making them. A major reason for this lapse is that for many people, backing up their system is tedious work when they have to use floppy disks or other low-capacity media. When you use these media, you may have to insert and remove many disks to back up all the important programs and data.

Tape backup drives are the most simple and efficient device for backing up your system. With a tape backup drive installed in your computer, you insert a tape into the drive, start your backup software, and select the drive and files you want to back up. The backup software copies your selected files onto the tape while you attend to other business. Later, when you need to retrieve some or all the files on the backup tape, you insert the tape in the drive, start your backup program, and select the files you want to restore. The tape backup drive takes care of the rest of the job.

This section examines the various types of tape backup drives on the market, describing the capacities of different drives as well as the system requirements for installation and use of a tape drive. The following topics are covered in this section:

■ Common standards for tape backup drives

■ Common backup tape capacities

■ Newer higher-capacity tape drives

■ Common tape drive interfaces

- The QIC standards for tape backup drives
- Portable tape drives
- Tape backup software

The Origins of Tape Backup Standards

The evolution of tape backup standards is similar to that of standards for many computer components. Using tape to back up computer data became a common practice long before accepted tape backup standards existed. At first, computers used reel-to-reel tape systems (somewhat similar to old reel-to-reel audio tape recorders) to store data. The most commonly used tape—*quarter-inch*—eventually developed into a de facto standard. But each tape system manufacturer used its own data-encoding specifications for backup tapes. Variations included not only the number of tracks and data density on the tape, but also the interface used to connect the drive to the computer.

In 1972, more than a decade before the introduction of the first IBM-PC, the 3M company introduced the first quarter-inch tape cartridge designed for data storage. The cartridge measured 6×4×5/8 inches. Inside this cartridge, the tape was threaded onto two reels. The tape was moved from one reel to another during the recording or read-back process by a drive belt. Because of the reliability of this tape cartridge, the demand for tape backup systems began to grow, despite the lack of established standards for storing data on these cartridges.

The result of this lack of standardization was that quarter-inch tapes written on one manufacturer's tape backup drive generally could not be read on by manufacturer's quarter-inch tape drive. One problem created by this situation was that the way particular manufacturers encoded data on a tape continued to change. If a particular model of tape drive became disabled and the manufacturer had discontinued that particular drive and no longer used its encoding format, the data stored on tapes written on the disabled drive would be unavailable until the drive was repaired. In the event the manufacturer could not repair the drive, the data was lost forever.

Table 12.20   Specifications of QIC-Standard Quarter-Inch Tape Cassettes and Minicartri

QIC Minicartridge Tape Standards

DC-2000 QIC Tape Standards (Approximate Dimensions 3 1/4 by 2 1/2 by 3/5)

QIC Standard Number	Capacity (w/o Compression) (1)	Tracks	Data Transfer Rate (Approximate)
QIC-40	40M/60M	20	2M-to-8M/minute
QIC-80	80M/120M	28	3M-to-9M/minute
QIC-100 (obsolete)	20M/40M	12 or 24	—
QIC-128	86M/128M	32	—
QIC-3010	255M	40	9M/minute
QIC-3020	500M	40	9M/minute
QIC-3030	555M	40	—

As with other computer components, such as hard drive interface cards, consumers were the force behind standardization. Consumers clamored for standardized tape drives that could read tapes created on different tape drives manufactured by different companies.

The QIC Standards

In response to this demand for standardization, the tape drive industry formed the Quarter-Inch Cartridge Drive Standards Inc., sometimes referred to as the *Quarter-Inch Committee (QIC)*. In 1983–84, the first tape drive based on a QIC standard was shipped: the *QIC-02*, which stored 60M of data encoded in nine data tracks on roughly 300 feet of tape.

As the technology improved, and because the 4×6×5/8-inch size of the first tape cartridges was difficult to adapt to the 5 1/2-inch drive bays in most PCs, QIC adopted a second standard for tape cartridges roughly the size of an audio cassette. These mini-cartridges measure 3 1/4×2 1/2×3/5 inches.

These two cartridge sizes are currently used in various QIC-standard tape drives. A two-letter code at the end of the QIC standard number designates whether the tape standard is based on the full-sized cartridge or the minicartridge. These two-letter codes are as follows:

- *DC* in a QIC standard number stands for *data cartridge*, the 4×6×5/8-inch cassette.
- *MC* in a QIC standard number stands for *minicartridge*, the 3 1/4×2 1/2×3/5-inch cassette.

The new QIC-5B-DC, for example, is a 5G-capacity tape based on the QIC standard for the full-sized cartridge. The new QIC-5010-MC, which has 13G capacity, is based on the minicartridge standard.

Table 12.20 shows the common QIC-standard tape formats and their technical specifications.

Data Density	Tape Length (2)	Encoding Method	Interface Type
—	205 ft. or 307.5 ft.	MFM	Floppy or optional adapter card
—	205 ft. or 307.5 ft.	MFM	Floppy or optional adapter card
10,000bpi	—	MFM	SCSI (4) or QIC
16,000bpi	—	MFM	SCSI or QIC
22,000bpi	300 ft.	MFM	Floppy or IDE
42,000bpi	400 ft.	MFM	Floppy or IDE
51,000bpi	275 ft.	MFM	SCSI-2 or QIC

(continues)

Table 12.20   Specifications of QIC-Standard Quarter-Inch Tape Cassettes and Minicartri

QIC Minicartridge Tape Standards

DC-2000 QIC Tape Standards (Approximate Dimensions 3 1/4 by 2 1/2 by 3/5)

QIC Standard Number	Capacity (w/o Compression) (1)	Tracks	Data Transfer Rate (Approximate)
QIC-3040	840M (3)	42 or 52	—
QIC-3050	750M	40	—
QIC-3060 (inactive)	875M	38	—
QIC-3070	4G	144	—
QIC-3080	1.6G	50	—
QIC-3095	2–5G	72	30–60M*
QIC-3110	2G	48	—
QIC-3210	2.3/5.7G	72	30M*
QIC-5010	13G	144	—

(1) Tape capacity may vary according to tape length.
(2) Tape lengths may vary by manufacturer.
(3) 1G with drives based on 0.315-inch tape cartridge
(4) SCSI: Small Computer Systems Interface
*Compressed

QIC Full-Sized Data Cartridge Standards

DC-300a/DC-600/DC-6000 QIC Tape Standards (Approximate Dimensions 4 by 6 by 5/8

QIC Standard Number	Capacity (w/o Compression)	Tracks	Max. Data Transfer Rate (Approximate)
QIC-11 (DC-300)	45M	9	—
QIC-24	45M/60M	9	—
QIC-120	125M	15	—
QIC-150	150M/250M	18	—
QIC-525	320M/525M	26	12M/minute
QIC-1000	1G	30	18M/minute
QIC-1350	1.35G	30	18M/minute
QIC-2100	2.1G	30	18M/minute
QIC-2GB	2.0G	42	18M/minute
QIC-5GB	5G	44	18M/minute
QIC-5010	13G	144	18M/minute
QIC-5210	25G	144	120M/minute

(1) Tape capacity may vary according to tape length.
(2) Tape lengths may vary by manufacturer.

Data Density	Tape Length (2)	Encoding Method	Interface Type
41,000bpi	400 ft.	RLL	SCSI-2 or QIC
—	295 ft.	RLL	SCSI-2 or QIC
—	295 ft.	RLL	—
68,000bpi	295 ft.	RLL	SCSI-2 or QIC
60,000bpi	—	RLL	SCSI-2 or QIC
67,733bpi	Various	RLL	IDE or SCSI
—	—	RLL	SCSI-2 or QIC
60,960bpi	740 ft.	GCR	SCSI or SCSI-2
—	—	RLL	SCSI-2 or QIC

Data Density	Tape Length (1)	Encoding Method	Interface Type
—	450 ft.	MFM	QIC-02
8,000	450 ft. or 600 ft.	MFM	SCSI or QIC-02
10,000	600 ft.	MFM	SCSI or QIC-02
10,000bpi	600 ft. or 1,000 ft.	MFM	SCSI or QIC-02
16,000bpi	1,000 ft.	MFM	SCSI or SCSI-2
36,000bpi	760 ft.	MFM	SCSI or SCSI-2
51,000bpi	760 ft.	RLL	SCSI-2
68,000bpi	875 ft.	RLL	SCSI-2
40,640bpi	900 ft.	MFM	SCSI-2
96,000bpi	1,200 ft.	RLL	SCSI-2
68,000bpi	—	RLL	SCSI-2
101,600bpi	1,200-1,500 ft.	RLL	SCSI or SCSI-2

Unlike software with version numbers (1.0, 1.1, 2.0, 2.1) that tell you which version of the software is the most recent, the QIC number designation does not serve as an accurate guide to understanding which QIC-standard tape drives are the latest technology. The designations QIC-100 and QIC-128, for example, were used for tape drives marketed long before today's QIC-40 and QIC-80 drives. Furthermore, the QIC-standard version numbers frequently have no correlation with the capacity of the tape cassettes or minicartridges used by the drive. For example, the QIC-40 tapes have a capacity of 60M; the QIC-80 tapes, a capacity of 120M.

QIC-standard backup tapes are magnetic media, primarily ferric oxide, and are recorded in a manner similar to the way data is encoded on your hard drive, using either Modified Frequency Modulation (MFM) or Run-Length Limited (RLL) technology.

Early QIC Tape Backup Types. The original QIC-standard drives, QIC-40 and QIC-80, are based on minicartridges. There are several reasons for the success of QIC-40 and QIC-80, not the least of which is that these two standards resulted in the first generation of economically attractive tape drives that store data in a manner that is compatible with products made by different manufacturers. In other words, QIC-40 and QIC-80 tape drives and tapes are quite affordable, and backups made on one QIC-40 or QIC-80 tape drive can be read in a tape drive built by another manufacturer.

In addition, the compact size of the minicartridge used for QIC-40 and QIC-80 tapes has resulted in drives made by numerous manufacturers that fit easily into both 5 1/2-inch half-height drive bays and 3 1/2×1-inch drive bays.

Backup tapes, like floppy disks and hard drives, must be formatted before use, and one aspect of using a QIC-80 tape drive that was never improved was the time it takes to format a tape. Formatting a 125M length QIC-80 tape can take more than three hours. It's almost impossible to find a preformatted tape because of these long format times. The industry has been preformatting tapes since 1994. Other tape formats have the capability to format on-the-fly, which means they don't require preformatted tapes.

Data is stored on QIC-40 and QIC-80 tapes in MFM format, the format used on floppy disks (and older hard drives). Another similarity between formatting a backup tape, floppy disks, and a hard drive is that the formatting process creates a record-keeping system. The record-keeping system used on QIC-40 and QIC-80 tapes is similar to that on a hard drive or floppy disk.

The QIC standard calls for a file allocation table (FAT) that keeps track of where data is stored on the tape and keeps bad sectors from being used for data storage. A QIC-40 tape is divided into 20 tracks, with each track divided into 68 segments of 29 sectors each. Each sector stores 1K (1,024 bytes). This record-keeping system and the error-correcting system that ensures reliably stored backup data use a total of 30% or more of each QIC-40 tape.

Despite the slow backup speeds of tape backup drives on some computers and the time it takes to format tapes, the ease of using a backup tape drive makes it easy to understand why the QIC-40 and QIC-80 tape drives were very popular.

High-Capacity QIC-Standard Drives. Using a QIC-80 tape drive to back up a network server's 4G drive or other large hard drive packed with data can be nearly as frustrating as swapping floppy disks during a backup, because you have to switch media many times to protect the whole drive.

The solution to this tape-swapping problem is to use a larger-capacity tape drive system. QIC has established a number of standards for higher-capacity tape drive systems ranging from 86M to 13G. Generally, these larger-capacity systems pack data more densely on the tape, using as many as 144 tracks to pack 60,000 bits per inch (bpi) or more onto the tape (compared to the QIC-40's 20 tracks and 10,000 bpi). To achieve these higher capacities, QIC-standards call for tape media with a higher coercivity level of 1,300 oersteds or more (compared to QIC-40 and QIC-80 tape media, which has a coercivity level of 550 oersteds). High-capacity tapes are also longer. QIC-5010 tapes, for example, are 1,200 feet long (compared to QIC-40 and QIC-80 tapes, both of which are roughly 300 feet long).

> **Note**
>
> Just as the higher coercivity level of 1.44M floppy disks enables an HD drive to write more densely packed tracks than is possible with 720K floppy disks, higher-coercivity tape media enables higher densities, as well.

Although tape systems based on the minicartridge dominate the market for lower-capacity tape drives, high-capacity tape backup systems are based on both minicartridge-sized tapes and full-sized data cartridge tapes. For example, the QIC-525 standard, which has a capacity of 525M (without data compression), is based on the full-sized (4×6×5/8) cartridge. The QIC-5010 standard is based on a minicartridge (3 1/4×2 1/2×3/5).

QIC-Tape Compatibility. Although QIC-standard drives are based on the standard mini-cartridge and the full-sized data cartridge, it would be a mistake to assume that tapes based on the same cartridge standard are always compatible. For example, QIC-5010-standard tapes are incompatible with QIC-40 and QIC-80 tape backup systems, although both standards are based on the minicartridge. Similarly, QIC-525-standard tapes are incompatible with earlier standards based on the full-sized data cartridge. The lack of compatibility between tapes based on the same sized cartridge is due to differences in tape drive mechanisms, as well as the coercivity differences between tape standards. Table 12.21 shows the compatibility of common QIC-standard backup tapes.

Table 12.21 QIC-Tape-Standard Compatibility	
QIC Minicartridge Standard	**Compatibility**
QIC-40	N/A
QIC-80	QIC-40 (read-only)
QIC-3010	QIC-40 and QIC-80 (read only)
QIC-3020	QIC-40, QIC-80, and QIC-3010 (read only)
QIC-3030	QIC-3010 (read-only)
QIC-3040	
QIC-3050	
QIC-3070	QIC-3030 (read-only)
QIC-3080	
QIC-3095	QIC-3010 and QIC-3020 (read-only)
QIC-3210	QIC-3040 (read-only)
QIC-3230	QIC-3040, QIC-3095, and QIC-3210 (read-only)
QIC Full-Sized Cartridge Standard	**Compatibility**
QIC-24	N/A
QIC-120	QIC-24 (read-only)
QIC-150	QIC-24 and QIC-120 (read-only)
QIC-525	QIC-24, QIC-120, and QIC-150 (read-only)
QIC-1000	QIC-120, QIC-150, and QIC-525 (read-only)
QIC-1350	QIC-525 and QIC-1000 (read-only)
QIC-2G	QIC-120, QIC-150, QIC-525, and QIC-1000 (read-only)
QIC-2100	QIC-525 and QIC-1000 (read-only)
QIC-5G	QIC-24, QIC-120, QIC-150, QIC-525, and QIC-1000 (read-only)
QIC-5010	QIC-150, QIC-525, and QIC-1000 (read-only)

Tape compatibility is an important issue to consider when you choose a tape backup system. For example, as you can see from Table 12.21, the 4G QIC-3070-standard drive can read only its own tapes and those that conform to the QIC-3030 standard. If you have many QIC-80 tapes containing data that you must continue to access, a better choice might be a drive based on the 2G QIC-3010 standard. The QIC-3010 can read QIC-40 and QIC-80 tapes.

Other High-Capacity Tape Drive Standards
Ferric oxide QIC-standard tapes have declined in popularity in recent years, while two other types of tape backup systems are becoming increasingly popular for backing up networks and other systems with large amounts of data: 4mm digital audio tape (DAT) and 8mm videotape.

Sony introduced DAT tape, and licenses DAT tape technologies to other manufacturers, in effect setting the standard for drives and tapes manufactured by those companies. There is only one company, Exabyte, that manufactures 8mm tape drive assemblies. As a result, you're assured compatibility. Table 12.22 shows the basic specifications of the DAT and 8mm technology tapes.

Table 12.22 DAT and 8mm Tape Specifications							
Tape Standard	**Capacity (w/o Com- pression)**	**Data Density**	**Tracks (Approx- imate)**	**Tape Length**	**Recording Technology**	**Encoding Format**	**Interface**
DAT tape (4mm metal particle)	2G/4G	114Mb	1,869	195 ft./ 300 ft.	Helical Scan DataDAT	DDS*	SCSI
8mm video tape	14G	NA	NA	120m	Helical Scan		

DDS: Digital data storage

Helical scan recording is similar in many ways to the way video images are recorded to videotape. As with QIC-standard tape drives, DAT and 8mm tapes move past the record-ing heads, which are mounted on a drum. These read/write heads rotate at a slight angle to the tape, writing a section of a *helix*, or spiral. The tape drive mechanism wraps the tape about halfway around the read/write heads, causing the heads to touch the tape at an angle. With helical scan technology, the entire surface of the tape is used to record data, unlike other technologies in which data tracks are separated by areas of unrecorded tape. This use of the entire tape surface enables helical scan backup drives to pack a much greater amount of data on a particular length of tape.

The DAT Tape Drive Standard. *DAT (Digital Audio Tape)* is a tape standard that has primarily been developed and marketed by Hewlett-Packard. HP chairs the DDS (Digital Data Storage) Manufacturers Group, and has led the development of the DDS standards.

The technology behind digital audio tape is similar in many ways to the techniques used to record music and encode it on audio compact discs (CDs). DAT drives do not record data on the tape in the MFM or RLL formats used by QIC-standard drives; rather, bits of data received by the tape drive are assigned numerical values, or digits. Then the drive translates these digits into a stream of electronic pulses that are written to the tape. Later, when you restore information to a computer from the tape, the DAT tape drive translates these digits back into the original binary bits.

DAT tapes can store up to 12G of uncompressed data, or about 24G compressed. Two types of data formats—digital data storage (DDS) and DataDAT—are used for DAT tapes; however, DDS type drives are by far the most common. DDS drives are available in three types:

- *DDS-1 drives* store 2G of uncompressed data (4G compressed).

- *DDS-2 drives* can store 4G of uncompressed data (up to 8G with compression).

■ *DDS-3 drives* have a native 12M capacity, or 24M compressed.

DDS-3 drives offer full read and write compatibility with all DDS-2 and DDS-1 drives, as well as three times the capacity and double the data-transfer rate of current DDS-2 drives. DDS-3 drives are designed to provide reliable high-performance backup for medium to large networks at a substantially lower price than 8mm or DLT (digital linear tape) products with similar capacities.

The new HP DDS-3 drive (Model C1537A) has a native capacity of 12G with a transfer rate of 1M/sec. The DDS-3 drive typically can store 24G on a single 125m tape at a rate of 2M/sec by using built-in hardware data compression. The new HP DDS-3 drive incorporates several innovations, including the use of a partial response maximum likelihood (PRML) data-channel detection scheme that enables the tape's read head to differentiate between bits of data picked up simultaneously.

A typical DDS-2 drive costs about $800, while DDS-3 drives are approximately $1,300. DDS technology has an excellent track record and a reputation for reliability that has made it the technology of choice for workstation, end user, and network backups.

The 8mm Tape Drive. A single manufacturer, Exabyte, offers tape backup drives that use 8mm tape cartridges like those used for videotape. However, while the cartridge design is the same as a videotape, the actual magnetic medium is not. It is strongly recommended that you do not use videotapes for backing up your data. You should use only tapes that are intended for use as a data storage medium. Exabyte offers drives in several capacities—1.5G (3G with hardware data compression), 5G (10G with hardware compression), 7G (14G with hardware compression), and 20G (40G with hardware compression).

Although these drives use 8mm videotapes, they do not use video technology for the process of writing computer data to the tape. Rather, Exabyte developed its own technology for encoding information on the tapes, using the helical scan method to record the data.

The 6M/sec data throughput rate of the Exabyte 8mm tape backup drive, compared with the 10M per minute throughput of the DAT drive, makes the 8mm tape drive a more attractive choice. The extraordinary speed and huge capacity of these 8mm tape drives makes them extremely attractive for backing up network servers and for backing up workstations from the server.

DLT (Digital Linear Tape). *Digital linear tape (DLT)* is now considered one of the hottest products in the high-end tape-backup market, because of its capability to provide high-capacity, high-speed, and highly reliable backups. DLT started as a proprietary technology belonging to Digital Equipment Corporation. The technology has been on the market since 1991, but in December 1994, Quantum purchased Digital's DLT and magneto-resistive drive technology.

DLT has a capacity of up to 35–70G compressed, and a data-transfer rate of 5–10M/sec or more. This is approximately the same speed as a high-speed 8mm drive; however, 8mm has a slight performance advantage in real-world tests.

DLT segments the tape into parallel horizontal tracks and records data by streaming the tape across a single stationary head at 100–150 inches/sec during read/write operations. This is a dramatic contrast to traditional helical-scan technology, in which the data is recorded in diagonal stripes with a rotating drum head while a much slower tape motor draws the media past the recording head.

The result is a very durable drive and a robust medium. DLT drive heads have a minimum life expectancy of 15,000 hours under worst-case temperature and humidity conditions, and the tapes have a life expectancy of 500,000 passes. DLT drives are designed primarily for network server backup, and cost $6,000 to $8,000 or more depending on capacity. With automatic tape changers, DLT drives can be left unattended for many network backup tasks.

Travan Cartridge Tape. 3M has created an entirely new tape cartridge standard based on the QIC format called *Travan*. Tape drives based on Travan technology have had a significant impact on the tape market for PCs and workstations, and drives based on this technology should have a prominent place in this market over the next several years.

The Travan platform features a unique drive/minicartridge interface that is patented by 3M. The Travan platform fits in a 3 1/2-inch form factor, making it easy to install in a variety of systems and enclosures. Travan drives can accept current QIC and Travan minicartridges—a critical need for users, given the installed base of more than 200 million QIC-compatible minicartridges worldwide.

Travan cartridges contain 750 feet of .315-inch wide tape. There are currently several different levels of Travan cartridges and drives available called TR-1 through TR-4, each based on a particular QIC standard:

- The TR-1 minicartridge provides users with 400M of uncompressed storage, more than doubling the capacity of the QIC-80 minicartridge (125M).

- The TR-2 minicartridge, a new modified QIC-3010 drive/cartridge, stores 800M of uncompressed data, which is significantly more than the 340M capacity of QIC-3010 tapes.

- The capacity of the TR-3 minicartridge, a new modified 3020 drive/cartridge, is 1.6G of uncompressed data (up from 670M in the QIC-3020).

- The newest Travan cartridge, TR-4, stores 4G of uncompressed data and is compatible with the QIC-3095 standard.

Notice that virtually all Travan drives offer 2:1 data compression, which doubles the uncompressed native capacity. This means that a Travan TR-4 drive can store up to 8G on a single cartridge! A typical TR-4 based drive, like those from Hewlett-Packard's Colorado Memory Systems Division, sell for about $300. Because Travan tapes sell in the $35 price range and are available through many distributors and resellers, the low cost and high availability of these drives and cartridges make Travan one of the best backup solutions possible for most individuals.

The TR-1 through TR-3 drives usually interface to the system via the floppy controller or parallel port. I recommend using an EPP or ECP parallel port for ease of use and performance. The higher end TR-4 drives often use a SCSI-2 interface, which offers greater performance than either the floppy or parallel port interface. A typical TR-4 system such as the HP T4000 drive operates at 514K/sec, which is approximately four times faster than floppy-interface systems, providing backup speeds up to 31M per minute native and up to 62M per minute with 2:1 data compression. Using a typical Pentium system, users can back up a 1G hard drive in about 30 minutes. If you are using the floppy controller or parallel port, you can expect backup times about four times longer or about two hours for a 1G drive.

Storage industry leaders such as 3M, HP/Colorado, Iomega, Exabyte, Tandberg Data, and Sony offer Travan drives and support future development of Travan drive and recording formats.

Choosing a Tape Backup Drive

Choosing a tape backup drive can be a simple job if you need to back up a single standalone system with a relatively small hard drive. The decision becomes more complex if the system has a larger hard drive, or if you must back up not only a desktop system but also a laptop. Choosing a tape backup drive type can be an even more complex program if you must back up a network server's hard drives and perhaps even back up the workstations from the server. As you ponder which backup tape drive type you should choose, consider the following factors:

- The amount of data you must back up
- The data throughput you need
- The tape standard that is best for your needs
- The cost of the drive and tapes
- The capabilities and compatibility of the included driver and backup software

By balancing the considerations of price, capacity, throughput, compatibility, and tape standard, you can find a tape drive that best meets your needs.

Note

When purchasing a tape backup drive, take the time to look through magazines where dealers or distributors advertise. Several publications specialize in PCs and carry advertising from many hardware and software distributors. I recommend publications such as the *Computer Reseller News* and *Computer Shopper*. These publications cater to people or companies willing to go around the middlemen and buy direct. By reading such publications, you can get an excellent idea of the drives available and the price you can expect to pay.

While reading about drive capabilities and prices, don't neglect to read reviews of the software included with each drive. Verify that the software capabilities match your expectations and needs. This is especially important if you intend to use the drive on a non-Windows 9x system, because most backup software today is tailored for Windows 9x.

Capacity. The first rule for choosing a tape backup drive is to buy a drive whose capacity is large enough for your needs, now and for the foreseeable future. The ideal is to buy a drive with enough capacity so you can start your backup software, insert a blank tape in the drive, walk away from the system, and find the backup completed when you return.

No matter what the capacity needs for a workstation, I generally recommend either DAT drives or the newer Travan drives. These are the most cost-effective, highest-performing drives on the market today. The tapes are preformatted, which saves a lot of time, and can store up to 8G on a single Travan TR-4 tape or 24G on a single DDS-3 DAT tape.

You should always make sure that your tape backup medium supports a capacity larger than your largest single drive or partition. This will make automated backups possible because you won't have to change a tape in the middle of a backup. Because the DAT drives normally interface via SCSI, you can use a parallel port SCSI adapter to connect the drive to a system's parallel port or a standard internal SCSI adapter. Of course, the internal adapter will perform better, but a portable DAT drive connected via the parallel port can be used to back up many different systems. The DAT medium is also cheaper than any other tape medium on the market when you consider its cost per megabyte.

Tape Standards. The next most important consideration, after adequate capacity, is choosing a drive whose tapes meet a standard that is useful to you. For example, if you must be able to restore backup data by using any of a number of different tape backup drives, you should make sure that all of these drives can at least read the tapes. For this reason, if you have several systems to work with, you should choose a tape standard that will work in them all.

There is no quick, simple answer as to which standard is the best. Many people stick with QIC-standard drives because QIC created the first standards and continues to develop new standards for large-capacity tape backups. But if you need a large-capacity backup tape system, DAT or 8mm may be the correct choice.

If you need backward compatibility with tapes or tape drives you already have, you will need to buy drives that are the same standard or a higher compatible standard. For example, if you need a large-capacity tape drive that is backward compatible with your QIC-80 tapes, you should consider the 2G-capacity QIC-3010, which reads QIC-40 and QIC-80 tapes. If, on the other hand, you don't have to worry about data already stored on old tapes, the important considerations may be capacity and performance. Therefore, DAT or 8mm drives may be the best choice.

> **Tip**
>
> It is important that you make a choice you can live with. If you manage a large installation of computers, mixing QIC, Travan, DAT, and 8mm drives among systems is seldom a good idea.

Software Compatibility. Equally important to your consideration is the software required to operate each drive. Currently, most drives come with software that runs under the Windows 9x operating system. However, finding software that runs equally well under Windows NT or UNIX might be difficult.

Most operating systems have their own software for backing up data to a tape drive. If you intend to use this software, you should verify that the drive you purchase is supported by each piece of software on each system that you intend to use with the drive.

Data Throughput. You should consider the 8mm or DLT drives if performance is more important to you than price or compatibility. These drives offer huge capacity and tremendous data throughput—as high as 6M/sec. Large-capacity drives based on newer QIC-standards are capable of 18M per minute throughput. DAT tape drives offer throughput of 10M per minute.

The low end of the tape backup drive performance spectrum is the older QIC-80 standard drives. When linked to a floppy controller, these drives achieve 3M to 4M per minute throughput. Even with a dedicated interface card purchased at added cost, QIC-80 drives are lucky to achieve their advertised throughput of 9M per minute. Portable QIC-80 drives are advertised at 3M to 8M per minute, but 2M or 3M a minute is a more realistic figure.

The Cost of the Drive and Tapes. The price of tape drives varies considerably based upon where you buy, so it pays to shop enthusiastically for a good price after you have settled on the type of drive you want to buy.

The cost of backup tapes also varies widely, depending on where you buy. Because many computer retailers and direct channel vendors offer lower prices when you buy three or more tapes at a time, it pays to shop for price and buy the largest quantity of tapes you expect to need.

> **Tip**
>
> One point worth remembering when you evaluate whether to buy a tape drive is that the cost of the tapes and drive, taken as a whole, is nowhere near as high as the costs (in terms of frustration and lost productivity) of a single data-damaging hard drive problem. Considering that most people are more likely to back up their system if they have a tape drive installed than if they must use another medium for the backup, the cost of a drive and tapes is quite small, even on a standalone PC used mostly for fun.

Portable Tape Drives. The *portable tape drive* is one of the most popular tape drive configurations because portables can be moved easily from system to system—desktops, laptops, a single system, or multisystem installations. Portable tape drives are particularly useful to people who use laptops (in which an internal tape backup drive will not fit) and those who want to back up a number of systems on a single tape backup drive. Portable tape drives are good also for people who want to use a tape backup drive for their desktop system but whose system has no available drive bay, as is often the case with small profile, or slimline, desktop systems.

Portable tape drives can meet so many needs because these drives are self-contained. The unit connects to the computer's parallel port and is powered by a transformer that plugs into a standard AC socket.

To set up a portable tape drive, you plug the transformer cord into the system unit and an AC socket, connect the data cable to the computer's parallel port, and run the backup software. One limitation of portable units is availability of compatible backup software. Although portable tape drive manufacturers include software that operates the drive, some popular third-party backup software cannot be used with portable drives.

Tape Drive Installation Issues

Each of the tape drive standards covered in this chapter provides a range of options for installation, usually including both internal and external models. Whether to choose an internal or external drive, and which external drive to choose if that appears to be the best choice for you, is not always a cut-and-dried issue. If you must back up a single computer with a relatively small hard drive, an internal drive might be your best choice. If you have to back up several computers, or if you must be able to share data between several computers, a portable would be preferable. If your backup needs are not that simple, however, here are some additional considerations:

- If your computer has a large hard drive and you back up often, or if you administer a large number of systems, you should consider installing large-capacity QIC, DAT or 8mm tape drives. Using these tape formats minimizes the amount of work you must do and the number of tapes you have to store for each computer.

- If your best choice is a large capacity QIC, DAT, or 8mm tape drive and almost all the computers you administer have an available drive bay, you might choose a portable DAT or 8mm tape system, which you can move from system to system.

The following sections cover some important installation issues for internal and external mounted drives.

Internal Installation. Virtually all internal tape backup drives available today are designed to be installed in a half-height drive bay. Many are designed to be installed in either half-height drive bays or the smaller drive bays generally used for 3 1/2-inch floppy disk drives. Drives that can be installed in 3 1/2-inch floppy disk drive bays generally are shipped in a *cage*, or frame, that also enables them to be installed in a 5 1/4-inch bay. To install the drive in a 3 1/2-inch bay, you remove the cage and the 5 1/4-inch bay faceplate. Most tape drives are between 5 and 9 inches deep and require that much clearance inside the system case. To mount tape drives inside the system, use the same rails or cage apparatus used for floppy disk drives, hard drives, and other devices such as CD-ROM drives.

Internal tape drives require a spare power connector, usually the larger connector used for hard drives, although some may require the smaller power connector used by 3 1/2-inch floppy disk drives. If a power connector is not available inside your system, you can buy a power splitter from a computer store or cable supply vendor.

Internal tape drives also require an interface to the system. QIC-40 and QIC-80 drives most often connect to the system through the floppy controller. On a system with only one floppy disk drive, you connect the tape drive to an unused connector on the floppy disk data cable. On systems with two floppy disk drives, you use a special cable linked to the floppy disk data cable, in effect a splitter cable.

Internal drives other than QIC-40s and QIC-80s usually connect to either a SCSI adapter or the IDE interface integrated into the system's motherboard.

External Installation. If you want to move an external tape drive from computer to computer, you must have the appropriate interface installed in each system on which you want to use the drive. Portable tape backup drives like the DAT portables use either a standard SCSI connection or have a SCSI-to-parallel port converter that uses the computer's parallel port connector. There are no external IDE devices.

Power is supplied to external units by a transformer that plugs into an ordinary 120v AC wall socket. Generally, the transformer connects to the external tape drive with a small connector. When you choose an external tape drive, be sure you have enough AC power sockets available for your computer, its peripherals, and the tape drive.

Tape Drive Backup Software

The most important decision you can make after you choose the tape standard and capacity of your backup tape drive is the backup software you will use with it. Most tape drives are shipped with backup software that generally is adequate for your basic backup needs.

Often, however, third-party software compatible with the drive you have chosen gives you greater flexibility and functionality. For example, some tape drives may not ship with software for the operating system that you want to use. If you want to use one of these drives with another operating system, you may need to purchase third-party backup software. And if you will be backing up network workstations from a server, you must make sure that the drive is shipped with software capable of performing this function; otherwise, you will need to acquire third-party software. The most important issue when selecting a third-party backup software package is compatibility with your drive. Be sure to check the software company's list of certified tape drives for the exact manufacturer and model number for your unit before you make a purchase. Some software manufacturers even certify specific firmware revisions in a tape drive.

One important issue with backup software is *data compression*, special programming that stores data on the backup tape in less space than is needed on the original source disk. Some companies produce backup software that is well-known for especially efficient data compression. In other words, backup software produced by these companies does a better job of compressing large data files into a small amount of space. However, if your tape drive provides compression at the hardware level, then this point is moot, as far as the software is concerned. You can only compress data once, and hardware compression is always preferable to software compression.

You may want to take the time to read reviews on backup software in one of the many monthly computer magazines, such as *PC Magazine, Windows Magazine,* or *BYTE Magazine.* The reviews can help you determine which backup software does the best job of compressing data; they also provide information on how quickly backup software programs perform a typical backup. The speed of the backup software and its data-compression capabilities are important considerations. Also of great importance is whether the software is easy to use. If your backup software makes backing up more difficult than it has to be, chances are you won't back up as often as you should.

> **Tip**
>
> Some of the more recent software for tape drives include a "Disaster Recovery" feature. This feature creates a boot disk (floppy) that can be used to quickly reformat a drive and perform a basic operating system installation. Look for this feature when considering your purchase decision.

Bundled Software. Before you buy a backup tape drive, you should always check whether the drive includes software that will meet your needs and, if it doesn't, be sure to buy third-party software that does the job. Generally, the software bundled with most tape backup drives will do the job for you—provided that you don't plan to place great demands on the tape drive.

Third-Party Software. A large number of companies manufacture backup software designed for different types of tape drives and different uses. For example, many manufacturers design their backup software to be compatible with most networks. Others specialize in DOS and Windows backup software. Some specialize in OS/2 software. Others are well-known among those whose computers run in UNIX. You may need to call the software company to determine whether a particular type of software is compatible not only with the tape drive you have chosen, but also with your network and operating environment.

Often, third-party software is easier to use than the software designed by a tape manufacturer. The tape manufacturer's software may have an unfamiliar interface or its commands may seem cryptic to you, even if you have used backup software for years. It is not uncommon for tape manufacturers to include inadequate or even incomplete documentation for the backup software included with the drive, although this is generally the case only with lower-cost models. In such a case, you may be able to solve the problem by purchasing third-party software.

Third-party software often does a better job of data compression than the software designed by a tape manufacturer. In addition, third-party software often includes capabilities not included with the software bundled with many drives. Some of the capabilities you might want to look for include the following:

- *Unattended backup scheduling.* Enables you to schedule a backup for a time when you won't need to use your computer.

- *Macro capability.* Use when selecting options and the files to back up.

- *A quick tape-erase capability.* Use when erasing the entire contents of a tape.

- *Partial tape-erase capability.* Use when erasing only part of a tape.

- *Tape unerase capability.* Use when recovering erased data.

- *Password-protect capability.* Enables you to protect backup data from access by unauthorized persons.

You can find backup software manufacturers by reading some of the many monthly computer magazines, paying particular attention to their usability reviews. Generally, if a backup software product gets good reviews, works on a system configuration like yours, and has the features you need, it is worth the price you pay.

Chapter 13

Optical Storage

Within minutes of inserting an aluminum-coated, 5-inch plastic data disc into your computer, you have access to information that might have taken you days or even weeks to find a few short years ago. Science, medicine, law, business profiles, and educational materials—every conceivable form of human endeavor or pursuit of knowledge—are making their way to *CD-ROM*, or *compact disc read-only memory*. Other formats such as CD-R and CD-RW are expanding the compact disc's capabilities by making them writable, and new technologies such as DVD are making it possible to store more data than ever on the same size disc.

CD-ROM drives are now considered standard equipment on most PCs. The primary exception to this rule is PCs that are intended for use on business networks. Server hard drives and shared network CD-ROMs can be much more economical than individual CD-ROM drives on every computer. However, nearly all standalone systems can benefit from some sort of optical storage device.

What Is CD-ROM?

The CD-ROM is a read-only optical storage medium capable of holding up to 682M of data (approximately 333,000 pages of text), 74 minutes of high-fidelity audio, or some combination of the two, on a single side of a 5-inch disc. The CD-ROM is very similar to the familiar audio compact disc and can, in fact, play in a normal audio player. The result, however, would be noise—unless audio accompanies the data on the CD-ROM (see the CD PLUS coverage, later in this chapter). Accessing data from a CD-ROM is quite a bit faster than floppy disk but considerably slower than a modern hard drive. The term *CD-ROM* refers to both the discs themselves and the drive that reads them.

Although only a few dozen CD-ROM discs, or titles, were published for personal computer users in all of 1988, there are currently thousands of individual titles containing data and programs, ranging from worldwide the inside of the disc and ends as close as 5mm from the edge of the disc. This single spiral track is nearly three miles long!

When a CD—audio or data—seeks out a specific datum on the disc, it looks up the address of the datum from a table of contents and positions itself near the beginning of this datum across the spiral, waiting for the right string of bits to flow past the laser beam.

CD-ROM data is recorded using a technique called *Constant Linear Velocity (CLV)*. This means that the track data is always moving past the read laser at the same linear speed. In other words, the disk must spin faster when reading the inner track area and slower when reading the outer track area. Because CDs were originally designed to record audio, the speed at which the drive reads the data had to be constant. Thus, each disc is broken up into blocks, or sectors, that are stored at the rate of 75 blocks per second on a disc that can hold a total of 74 minutes of information, resulting in a maximum of 333,000 blocks (sectors).

New multi-speed CD-ROM readers still read the same CLV recorded CDs, but play them back at a *Constant Angular Velocity (CAV)*. This means that the track data is moving past the read laser at a different speed, depending on where the track is physically located on the CD (inner or outer track). This type of drive reads the tracks at the edge of the disk faster than ones near the center, because the CD is rotating at a constant speed, similar to old record players. CAV drives are also quieter than CLV drives, as a rule. A drive that combines CLV and CAV technologies is referred to as *P-CAV* or *Partial-CAV*.

In an audio disc, each block stores 2,352 bytes. In a CD-ROM, 304 of these bytes are used for Sync (Synchronizing bits), ID (Identification bits), ECC (Error Correcting Code), and EDC (Error Detection Code) information, leaving 2,048 bytes for user data. Because these blocks are read at a constant speed of 75 per second, this results in a standard CD-ROM transfer rate of 153,600 bytes per second, which is exactly 150K/sec.

Because a typical disc can hold a maximum of 74 minutes of data, and each second contains 75 blocks of 2,048 bytes each, you can calculate the absolute maximum storage capacity of a CD-ROM at 681,984,000 bytes (rounded as 682M or 650M).

Inside Data CDs

The microprocessor that decodes the electrical impulses is the key difference between audio CD players and CD-ROM drives. Audio CDs convert the digital information stored on the disc into analog signals for a stereo amplifier to process. In this scheme, some imprecision is acceptable, because it would be virtually impossible to hear in the music. CD-ROMs, however, cannot tolerate any imprecision. Each bit of data must be read accurately. For this reason, CD-ROM discs have a great deal of additional *Error Correcting Code (ECC)* information written to the disc along with the actual stored information. The ECC can be used to detect and correct most minor errors, improving the reliability and precision to levels that are acceptable for data storage.

CD-ROM drives operate in the following manner:

1. The *laser diode* emits a low-energy infrared beam toward a reflecting mirror.

2. The *servo motor*, on command from the microprocessor, positions the beam onto the correct track on the CD-ROM by moving the reflecting mirror.

3. When the beam hits the disc, its refracted light is gathered and focused through the first lens beneath the platter, bounced off the mirror, and sent toward the beam splitter.

4. The *beam splitter* directs the returning laser light toward another focusing lens.

5. The last lens directs the light beam to a photo detector that converts the light into electric impulses.

6. These incoming impulses are decoded by the microprocessor and sent along to the host computer as data.

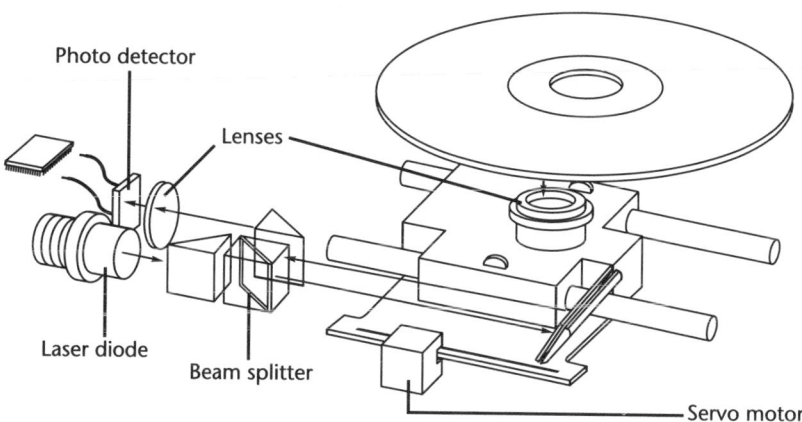

FIG. 13.1   Typical components inside a CD-ROM drive.

The pits that are etched into the CD-ROM vary in length. The reflected light beam changes in intensity as it crosses over from a land to a pit area. The corresponding electrical signal from the photodetector varies with the reflected light intensity. The transitions between high and low signals, physically recorded as the start and end of each pit area, form a signaling code that the drive interprets as data bits.

Because a single bit error can be disastrous in a program or data file, the error detection and correction algorithms used by a CD-ROM drive are extensive. These routines allow for the probability of a non-detected error to be less than 1 in 10^{25}. In more physical terms, this means that there would be only one undetected error in 2 quadrillion discs (this would form a stack 1 billion miles high!).

The error-correction data alone requires 288 bytes for every 2,048 bytes of informational content on the disc. This allows for the correction of numerous bad bits, including bursts of bad data over 1,000 bits long. This powerful error-correction capability is required because physical defects can cause errors, and because the CD medium was originally designed for audio reproduction, in which minor errors or even missing data are tolerable.

In the case of an audio CD, missing data can be *interpolated*—that is, the information follows a predictable pattern that enables the drive to guess the missing values. For example, if three values are stored on an audio disc, say 10, 13, and 20 appearing in a series, and the middle value is missing—due to damage or dirt on the CD's surface—you can interpolate a middle value of 15, which is midway between 10 and 20. Although this may not be exactly correct, in the case of audio recording it will not be noticeable to the listener. If those same three values appear on a CD-ROM in an executable program, there is no way to guess at the correct value for the middle sample. Interpolation cannot work because executable program data follows no natural law; the data is a series of values. To guess 15 is not just slightly off; it is completely wrong.

Because of the need for such precision, CD-ROM drives for use on PCs were later to market than their audio counterparts. When first introduced, CD-ROM drives were too expensive for widespread adoption. In addition, drive manufacturers were slow in adopting standards, causing a lag time for the production of CD-ROM titles. Without a wide base of software to drive the industry, acceptance was slow.

After the production costs of both drives and discs began to drop, however, CD-ROMs were rapidly assimilated into the PC world. This was particularly due to the ever-expanding size of PC applications. Virtually all software is now supplied on CD-ROM, even if the disc doesn't contain data representing a tenth of its potential capacity. As the industry stands now, if a software product requires more than two or three floppy disks, it is more economical to put it on a CD-ROM.

For large programs, the advantage is obvious. The Windows 98 operating system would require more than 70 floppy disks, and even that is only when Microsoft uses its proprietary 1.71M disk format. The cost of producing, packaging, and shipping that many floppy disks instead of a single CD-ROM would drive up the price of the product substantially.

What Types of Drives Are Available?

When purchasing a CD-ROM drive for your PC, you should consider three distinct sets of criteria, as follows:

- The drive's performance specifications

- The interface the drive requires for connection to your PC

■ The physical disc-handling system the drive uses

The variance in all these categories is enormous; in fact, single vendors offer entire lines of drives that vary in performance specifications, disc-handling mechanisms, and type of interface to the PC. For these reasons, drive prices can also vary widely. Before you buy, know the drive's characteristics.

CD-ROM Drive Specifications

Drive specifications tell you the drive's performance capabilities. If you're shopping for a sports car, for example, and the dealer tells you the car can accelerate from a standing stop to 60 miles per hour in five seconds, you know you've got a hot car. You can use the car's horsepower, weight, suspension design, and other specifications to understand more about the vehicle's performance.

CD-ROM drive specifications tell the shopper much the same thing. Typical performance figures published by manufacturers are the data transfer rate, access time, internal cache or buffers (if any), and the interface the drive uses.

Data Transfer Rate. The data transfer rate tells you how much data the drive can read from a CD-ROM and transfer to the host computer when it is reading one large, sequential stream of data. The standard measurement in the industry is kilobytes per second, usually abbreviated as K/sec or, for today's faster drives, megabytes per second (M/sec). If a manufacturer claims a drive can transfer data at 150K/sec, it means that a drive reading a sequential stream of data from the CD will achieve 150K/sec after it has come up to speed. Note that this is a sustained and sequential read, as of a single large file, not access across the data disc from different portions of the platter. Obviously, the data transfer specification is meant to convey the drive's peak data-reading capabilities. A higher rate of transfer might be better, but a number of other factors come into play as well.

The standard compact disc format dictates that there should be 75 blocks (or sectors) of data per second, with each block containing 2,048 bytes of data. This gives a transfer rate of exactly 150K/sec. This is the standard for CD-DA (Digital Audio) drives, and is also called *single-speed* in CD-ROM drives. The term single-speed is used to refer to the original 150K/sec drives, because CDs are recorded in a Constant Linear Velocity (CLV) format, which means that the rotational speed of the disc varies to keep the track speed constant. A double-speed (or 2x) drive simply attains a transfer rate of 300K/sec, two times that of the single-speed drive.

Because CD-ROM drives do not read and play data in real time like audio drives, it is possible to speed up the data transfer rate by spinning the disc at a higher linear velocity. CD-ROM drive speeds have accelerated rapidly over the years, and there are currently many different drive speeds available, all of which are multiples of the original single-speed drives. Table 13.1 shows the speeds at which CD-ROM drives can operate.

Table 13.1   CD-ROM Drive Speeds and Data Transfer Rates

Drive Speed	Transfer Rate (bps)	Transfer Rate (K/sec)
Single-speed (1x)	153,600	150
Double-speed (2x)	307,200	300
Triple-speed (3x)	460,800	450
Quad-speed (4x)	614,400	600
Six-speed (6x)	921,600	900
Eight-speed (8x)	1,228,800	1,200
Ten-speed (10x)	1,536,000	1,500
Twelve-speed (12x)	1,843,200	1,800
Sixteen-speed (16x)	2,457,600	2,400
Eighteen-speed (18x)	2,764,800	2,700
Twenty-four-speed (24x)	3,686,400	3,600
Thirty-two-speed (32x)	4,915,200	4,800
One-hundred-speed (100x)	15,360,000	15,000
CAV drives (12x–24x)	1,843,200–3,686,400	1,800–3,600

bps = bytes per second
K/sec = kilobytes per second

The 24x and 32x drives are currently the most popular, and are standard equipment in most new PCs on the market today. A 4x drive is the minimum required to meet the MPC-3 (Multimedia Personal Computer) standard, and the fact that 100x drives are now available goes to show that the hardware industry moves much more quickly than the standards-making process. In fact, it would probably be relatively difficult to find a new 4x drive today. New systems typically include a 24x or 32x CD-ROM drive.

The way that CD-ROM drive speeds have constantly increased makes the thought of performing upgrades problematic. The drive speed of a CD-ROM has a different effect on different types of users. If you use CDs primarily to install applications or look up textual information in reference products like dictionaries and telephone directories, the speed of the drive is not critical. A few more seconds spent performing a one-time program installation is not worth making sure you always have the fastest drive on the market.

Multimedia and game titles that contain a lot of music, animation, and video are another story, however. The multimedia experience can be greatly enhanced by a faster CD-ROM drive, and some software products specify a recommended minimum drive speed. It certainly is not necessary, however, to buy a new drive each time a faster speed is introduced. For gamers and other heavy CD-ROM users, a good rule of thumb is that an upgrade is not worthwhile unless you would be at least doubling your present speed. For light CD-ROM users, upgrading may never be necessary. I still have a single-speed CD-ROM drive that is perfectly adequate for performing software installations.

Despite these speed increases, however, even the fastest CD-ROM drives pale in comparison to hard disk drive transfer rates, which can be as high as 21M/sec. The SCSI or

ATA/IDE interfaces that CD-ROM drives use today support data transfer rates reaching 80M/sec, meaning that they are more than up to the task of maintaining CD-ROM transfer rates. If you expect to run a variety of CD-based software on your system, you need a drive with a high data-transfer rate. Applications that employ full-motion video, animation, and sound require high transfer rates, and you'll be disappointed in the results with a slower drive.

Access Time. The access time for a CD-ROM drive is measured the same way as for PC hard disk drives. In other words, the *access time* is the delay between the drive receiving the command to read, and its actual first reading of a bit of data. The time is recorded in milliseconds; a typical manufacturer's rating for a 24x drive would be listed as 95ms. This is an average access rate; the true access rate depends entirely on where the data is located on the disc. When the read mechanism is positioned to a portion of the disc nearer to the narrower center, the access rate is faster than when it is positioned at the wider outer perimeter. Access rates quoted by many manufacturers are an average taken by calculating a series of random reads from a disc.

Obviously, a faster (that is, a lower) average access rate is desirable, especially when you are relying on the drive to locate and pull up data quickly. Access times for CD-ROM drives are steadily improving, and the advancements are discussed later in this chapter. Note that these average times are significantly slower than PC hard drives, ranging from 200ms to below 100ms, compared to the 8ms access time of a typical hard disk drive. Most of the speed difference lies in the construction of the drive itself. Hard drives have multiple read heads that range over a smaller surface area of the medium; CD-ROM drives have only one laser read beam, and it must be able to access the entire range of the disc. In addition, the data on a CD is organized in a single long spiral. When the drive positions its head to read a track, it must estimate the distance into the disc and skip forward or backward to the appropriate point in the spiral. Reading off the outer edge requires a longer access time than the inner segments, unless you have a CAV (Constant Angular Velocity) drive, which spins at a constant rate so the access time to the outer tracks is equal to that of the inner tracks.

Access times have been falling since the original single-speed drives came out. With each increase in data transfer speed, we have usually seen an increase in access time as well. But as you can see in Table 13.2, these improvements are much less significant because of the physical limitation of the drive's single read mechanism design.

Table 13.2 Typical CD-ROM Drive Access Times

Drive Speed	Access Time (ms)
Single-speed (1x)	400
Double-speed (2x)	300
Triple-speed (3x)	200
Quad-speed (4x)	150
Six-speed (6x)	150
Eight-speed (8x)	100

(continues)

Table 13.2 Typical CD-ROM Drive Access Times Continued	
Drive Speed	**Access Time (ms)**
Ten-speed (10x)	100
Twelve-speed (12x)	100
Sixteen-speed (16x)	90
Eighteen-speed (18x)	90
Twenty-four-speed (24x)	90
Thirty-two-speed (32x)	85
One-hundred-speed (100x)	80
CAV (12/24x)	150-90

The times listed here are typical examples for good drives; within each speed category there will be drives that are both faster and slower.

Buffer/Cache. Most CD-ROM drives include internal buffers or caches of memory installed on-board. These *buffers* are actual memory chips installed on the drive's circuit board that enable it to stage or store data in larger segments before sending it to the PC. A typical buffer for a CD-ROM drive is 256K, although drives are available that have either more or less (more is usually better!). Generally, the faster drives will come with more buffer memory to handle the higher transfer rates.

Having buffer or cache memory for the CD-ROM drive offers a number of advantages. Buffers can ensure that the PC receives data at a constant rate; when an application requests data from the CD-ROM, the data may be found in files scattered across different segments of the disc. Because the drive has a relatively slow access time, the pauses between data reads can cause a drive to send data to the PC sporadically. You might not notice this in typical text applications, but on a drive with a slower access rate coupled with no data buffering, it is very noticeable—and even irritating—during the display of video or some audio segments. In addition, a drive's buffer, when under the control of sophisticated software, can read and have ready the disc's table of contents, speeding up the first request for data. A minimum size of 512K for a built-in buffer or cache is recommended, and is standard on most 24x drives.

Interface

A CD-ROM's *interface* is the physical connection of the drive to the PC's expansion bus. The interface is the data pipeline from the drive to the computer, and its importance shouldn't be minimized. There are three different types of interfaces available for attaching a CD-ROM drive to your system:

- SCSI/ASPI (Small Computer System Interface/Advanced SCSI Programming Interface)

- IDE/ATAPI (Integrated Drive Electronics/AT Attachment Packet Interface)

- Parallel port

The following sections examine these different interface choices.

SCSI/ASPI. *SCSI* (pronounced SKUH-zee), or the *Small Computer System Interface,* is a name given to a special interface bus that allows many different types of peripherals to communicate. The current implemented version of the standard is called *SCSI-2.* A standard software interface called *ASPI (Advanced SCSI Programming Interface)* enables CD-ROM drives (and other SCSI peripherals) to communicate with the SCSI host adapter installed in the computer. SCSI offers the greatest flexibility and performance of the interfaces available for CD-ROM drives, and can be used to connect many other types of peripherals to your system as well.

The SCSI bus enables computer users to string a group of devices along a chain from one SCSI host adapter, avoiding the complication of installing a separate adapter card into the PC bus slots for each new hardware device, such as a tape unit or additional CD-ROM drive added to the system. These traits make the SCSI interface preferable for connecting a peripheral such as a CD-ROM to your PC.

All SCSI adapters are not created equal, however. Although they may share a common command set, they can implement these commands differently, depending on how the adapter's manufacturer designed the hardware. ASPI was created to eliminate these incompatibilities. ASPI stands for Advanced SCSI Programming Interface and was originally developed by Adaptec, Inc., a leader in the development of SCSI controller cards and adapters who originally named it the Adaptec SCSI Programming Interface before it became a *de facto* standard. ASPI consists of two main parts. The primary part is an ASPI-Manager program, which is a driver that functions between the operating system and the specific SCSI host adapter. The ASPI-Manager sets up the ASPI interface to the SCSI bus.

The second part of an ASPI system is the individual ASPI device drivers. For example, you would get an ASPI driver for your SCSI CD-ROM drive. You can also get ASPI drivers for your other SCSI peripherals, such as tape drives and scanners. The ASPI driver for the peripheral talks to the ASPI-Manager for the host adapter. This is what enables the devices to communicate together on the SCSI bus.

The bottom line is that if you are getting a SCSI interface CD-ROM, make sure that it includes an ASPI driver that runs under your particular operating system. Also, be sure that your SCSI host adapter has the corresponding ASPI-Manager driver as well.

The SCSI interface offers the most powerful and flexible connection for CD-ROMs and other devices. It provides better performance, and seven or more drives can be connected to a single host adapter. The drawback is cost. If you do not need SCSI for other peripherals and intend on connecting only one CD-ROM drive to the system, then you will be spending a lot of money on unused potential. In that case, an IDE/ATAPI interface CD-ROM drive would be a more cost-effective choice.

IDE/ATAPI. The *IDE/ATAPI (Integrated Drive Electronics/AT Attachment Packet Interface)* is an extension of the same ATA (AT Attachment) interface most computers use to connect to their hard disk drives. Specifically, ATAPI is an industry-standard Enhanced IDE interface for CD-ROM drives. ATAPI is a software interface that adapts the SCSI/ASPI commands to the IDE/ATA interface. This has enabled drive manufacturers to take their high-end CD-ROM drive products and quickly adapt them to the IDE interface. This also enables the IDE CD-ROM drives to remain compatible with the MSCDEX (Microsoft CD-ROM Extensions) that provide a software interface with DOS. With Windows 9x, the CD-ROM extensions are contained in the CDFS (CD File System) VxD (virtual device) driver.

ATAPI drives are sometimes also called *Enhanced IDE* (*EIDE*) drives, because this is an extension of the original IDE (technically the ATA) interface. In most cases, an IDE/ATA CD-ROM drive will connect to the system via a second IDE interface connector and channel, leaving the primary one for hard disk drives only. This is preferable because IDE does not share the single channel well, and would cause a hard disk drive to wait for CD-ROM commands to complete and vice versa. SCSI does not have this problem, because a SCSI host adapter can send commands to different devices without having to wait for each previous command to complete.

> ### Caution
>
> If you decide to purchase a writable CD-ROM drive, such as a CD-R or CD-RW, the SCSI interface is most definitely recommended over IDE/ATA because of IDE's problems in sharing a channel between two devices. Writing to a compact disc requires a steady stream of data that the IDE interface often is not capable of delivering.

The IDE/ATAPI interface represents the most cost-effective yet high-performance interface for CD-ROM drives. Most new systems that include a CD-ROM drive will have it connected through IDE/ATAPI. To prevent performance problems, be sure that your CD-ROM drive is connected on the secondary IDE channel, which is separate from the primary channel used by your hard disk drive(s). Some sound cards include an ATAPI interface driver and the requisite secondary IDE interface connector specifically for a CD-ROM drive. You can connect up to two drives to the secondary IDE connector; for more than that, SCSI is your only choice, and provides better performance as well.

Parallel Port. By far the easiest type of CD-ROM drive to install is one that uses a parallel port interface. Rather than opening the case to insert a SCSI adapter or connect an internal drive, you can install some CD-ROM drives simply by connecting a cable to the PC's parallel port and loading the appropriate software.

Obviously, the advantages of CD-ROMs that use the parallel port interface are their ease of installation and their portability. In an office environment where the primary function of CD-ROMs is to install software, you can easily move one parallel port drive from machine to machine, rather than purchase a drive for each system. If you use an operating system that supports Plug and Play (PnP), such as Windows 9x, simply plugging a Plug- and-Play drive into the parallel port causes the OS to detect the new hardware and load the appropriate driver for you automatically.

> **Note**
>
> Parallel port CD-ROM drives nearly always include a cable with a *pass-through* connector. This connector plugs into the parallel port and, if necessary, a printer cable can plug into the connector. This enables you to continue using the port to connect to your printer while sharing the interface with the CD-ROM drive.

Not surprisingly, you pay a price for all this convenience. Parallel port drives typically have somewhat lower data-transfer rates and higher access times than their SCSI or IDE/ATA counterparts, they are slightly more expensive, and, of course, they require their own external power supply. Parallel port devices can also be subject to compatibility problems, particularly on older systems. These performance levels may make the drives unsuitable for high-end gaming and multimedia applications, but for general use they are more than adequate.

I generally do not recommend that you purchase a parallel port device simply to save the trouble of opening up the computer. Installing an internal drive is not terribly difficult, and the performance increase is more than worth the extra effort. However, if you can take advantage of the portability that these devices provide, they are an excellent CD-ROM solution.

Loading Mechanism

There are two distinctly different mechanisms for loading a CD into a CD-ROM drive: the caddy and the tray. Each one offers some benefits and features. Which type you select will have a major impact on your use of the drive, because you will interact with this mechanism every time you load a disc.

There are multiple disc drives on the market that allow you to insert more than one disc at a time. Most of these use a special cartridge that you fill with discs, much like a multi-disc CD-DA player for automotive use.

Caddy. At one time, the *caddy system* was used on most high-end CD-ROM drives. It has since declined in popularity due to the convenience of the tray. The caddy system requires that you place the CD itself into a special caddy, which is a sealed container with a metal shutter. The caddy has a hinged lid that you open to insert the CD, but after that the lid remains shut. When you insert the caddy containing the CD into the drive, the drive opens a metal shutter on the bottom of the caddy, allowing access to the CD by the laser.

The caddy is not the most convenient loading mechanism, although if all your CDs are in their own caddies, then all you have to do is grab the caddy containing the disc you want and shove it into the drive. This makes the CD operate much like a 3.5-inch diskette. You can handle the caddy without worrying about touching or contaminating the disc or the drive, making this the most accurate and durable mechanism as well. Young children can easily handle the caddies and don't have to touch the compact discs themselves.

Because the caddy is sealed, the discs are protected from damage caused by handling. The only time you actually handle the disc is when you first put it into the caddy. The caddy loading system also ensures that the disc is properly located when inside the drive. This allows for more accurate laser-head positioning mechanisms, and caddy drives generally have faster access times, as well.

The drawbacks to the caddy system are the expense and the inconvenience. You only get one caddy with the drive, so if you want to store your CD-ROMs in their own caddies, you must buy many more. Additional caddies can cost from $4 to $10 each, which can lead to a significant expense if you have a large number of CD-ROMs. Most people do not buy caddies for all their discs. The alternative is that each time you insert a new disc into the drive, you first have to eject the caddy/disc, remove the disc from the caddy, put the disc back into the original jewel case, open the jewel case for the new disc, put the new disc into the caddy, and finally insert the caddy/disc back into the drive.

A final advantage of caddy-loaded drives is that they can function when mounted either horizontally or vertically, meaning that the drive can be installed sideways. You cannot do this with the cheaper tray-loaded drives, although some newer tray-loaded drives have small retaining tabs that allow both horizontal or vertical mounting.

Tray. Many CD-ROM drives use a *tray loading* mechanism. This is similar to the mechanism used with a stereo system. Because you don't need to put each disc into a separate caddy, this mechanism is much less expensive overall. However, it also means that you have to handle each disc every time you insert or remove it.

Tray loading is more convenient than a caddy system, because you don't need a caddy. However, this can make it much more difficult for young children to use the discs without smudging or damaging them due to the excess handling.

The tray loader itself is also subject to damage. The trays can easily break if bumped or if something is dropped on them while they are extended. Also, any contamination you place on the tray or disc is brought right into the drive when the tray is retracted. Tray-loaded drives should not be used in a harsh environment such as a commercial or industrial application.

> **Note**
>
> One of the classic legends among PC technical support engineers is that of the user who called to complain that the cup-holder on his computer retracted every time he restarted the machine. After careful questioning, the puzzled engineer determined that the caller had been using the CD-ROM tray to hold his coffee cup. Needless to say, this practice is not recommended.

The tray mechanism also does not hold the disc as securely as the caddy. If you don't have the disc placed in the tray properly when it retracts, then the disc or tray can be damaged. Even a slight misalignment can prevent the drive from reading the disc properly, forcing you to open the tray and reset the disc.

Some tray drives cannot operate in a vertical (sideways) position, as gravity would prevent proper loading and operation. Check to see if the drive tray has retaining clips on the outer edge of the CD seat, like the Hitachi drive I have in my HP Vectra. If so, you can run the drive in either horizontal or vertical position.

Apart from the convenience, the other advantage to the tray mechanism over the caddy system is in cost, and that is a big factor. If you do not have young children and you plan to use the drive in a clean environment where careful handling and cleanliness can be assured, then the tray mechanism would be recommended due to its significantly lower cost.

Other Drive Features

Although drive specifications are of the utmost importance, you should also consider other factors and features when evaluating CD-ROM drives. Besides quality of construction, the following criteria bear scrutiny when making a purchasing decision:

- Drive sealing
- Self-cleaning lenses
- Internal versus external drive

Drive Sealing. Dirt is your CD-ROM's biggest enemy. Dust or dirt, when it collects on the lens portion of the mechanism, can cause read errors or severe performance loss. Many manufacturers seal off the lens and internal components from the drive bay in airtight enclosures. Other drives, although not sealed, have double dust doors—one external and one internal—to keep dust from the inside of the drive. All these features help prolong the life of your drive.

Caddy-loaded drives are inherently sealed better and are much more resistant to the external environment than tray-loaded drives. Always use a caddy-loaded drive in harsh industrial or commercial environments.

Self-Cleaning Lenses. If the laser lens gets dirty, so does your data. The drive will spend a great deal of time seeking and reseeking, or finally giving up. Lens-cleaning discs are available, but built-in cleaning mechanisms are now included on virtually all good-quality drives. This may be a feature you'll want to consider, particularly if you work in a less-than-pristine work environment, or you have trouble keeping your desk clean, let alone your CD-ROM drive lens.

Internal Versus External Drives. When deciding whether you want an internal or external drive, think about where and how you're going to use your CD-ROM drive. What about the future expansion of your system? Both types of drives have advantages and disadvantages, such as the following:

- *External Enclosure*. These tend to be rugged, portable, and large—in comparison to their internal versions. Buy an external drive only if you lack the space inside the system or if your computer's power supply cannot support the additional load. You might also consider an external if you want to be able to move the drive from one

PC to another easily. Parallel port drives are the most portable, but if each PC has its own SCSI adapter, all you need to do is unplug the drive from one adapter and plug it in to the other. Only parallel port and SCSI CD-ROM drives can be external, so if you are looking for an IDE type interface, you must go internal.

■ *Internal Enclosure.* Internal drives will clear off a portion of your desk. Buy an internal drive if you have a free drive bay and a sufficient power supply, and you plan on keeping the CD-ROM drive exclusively on one machine. The internal drives are also nice because you can connect the audio connector to your sound card and leave the external audio connectors free for other inputs. Internal drives can be IDE or SCSI.

CD-ROM Disc and Drive Formats

Compact discs are pitted to encode the binary bit values 0 and 1. Without a logical organization to this disc full of digits, the CD-ROM drive and PC would be at a loss to find any discernible data amid all those numbers. To this end, the data is encoded to conform to particular standards. When a drive encounters particular patterns, it—and the PC—can recognize the organization of the disc and find its way around the platter. Without standard data formats, the CD-ROM industry would be dead in the water; vendors of discs and disc drives would be producing hardware and software that was incompatible with that of other vendors, thereby limiting the number of units that could be sold.

Formats are also needed to advance the technology. For example, hard rubber wheels and no suspension were just fine for the first automobiles as they cruised along at the breakneck speed of 30 miles an hour. But hitting a pothole at 60 could cause serious damage to the vehicle—and the riders. Inflatable tires and shock absorbers became necessary components of the modern car.

Similarly, the standards for disc formats have evolved as well. The first compact data discs stored only text information, which is relatively easy to encode. Graphics produced a greater challenge, and the standards evolved to accommodate them. The use of animation with synchronized sound, and then live-motion video, called for other expansions to the standards by which data is stored on CDs.

It is extremely important to note that advanced CD-ROM standards are in the process of evolution right now. Multiple vendors are deploying a number of different techniques for expanding the capabilities of CD-ROM technology. They may be incompatible with each other or immature in their development, but acceptance of these newer standards by software vendors is essential to the widespread use of these standards. It is important that you be familiar with these issues before you purchase a drive. Consider the formats it is capable of reading now—and in the future.

The majority of drives available today, however, do comply with earlier CD-ROM formats, ensuring that the vast library of CD-ROM titles available today can be used on these drives.

Data Standard: ISO 9660

Manufacturers of the first CD-ROM data discs produced their discs for one particular drive. In other words, a data disc produced for company A's drive could not be read by anyone who had purchased company B's CD-ROM drive—the disc needed to be formatted for each manufacturer's drive. Obviously, this stalled the development of the industry. Philips and Sony developed the "Yellow Book" specifications for data CD-ROMs.

When Philips and Sony first published the audio CD specifications, the material was released in a red binder and became known as the "Red Book." Subsequent CD-ROM specifications have been dubbed by color as well, such as the "Orange Book" and the "Green Book."

The Yellow Book specifications are an extension of the way in which audio data can be stored on disc, and detail how data—rather than audio—can be organized on a disc for its later retrieval. The International Organization for Standardization (ISO) refined this specification (called ISO 9660) so that every vendor's products could expect to find a table of contents in the same place on a data disc. This is known as a *Volume Table of Contents*, and is quite similar in theory to a printed book's table of contents. ISO 9660 did not completely solve compatibility problems, however. The method for incorporating additional data to aid and refine the disc search process, and even the format of the data blocks, were still left to each separate vendor's design.

High Sierra Format

It was in all manufacturers' interests to resolve this standardization issue. In a meeting in 1985 at the High Sierra Hotel and Casino in Lake Tahoe, California, leading manufacturers of CD-ROM drives and CD-ROM discs came together to resolve the differences in their implementation of the ISO 9660 format. The agreement has become known as the *High Sierra format* and is now a part of the ISO 9660 specification document. This agreement enabled all drives to read all ISO 9660-compliant discs, opening the way for the mass production of CD-ROM software publishing. Adoption of this standard also enabled disc publishers to provide cross-platform support for their software, easily manufacturing discs for DOS, UNIX, and other operating system formats. Without this agreement, the maturation of the CD-ROM marketplace would have taken years longer and stifled the production of CD-ROM–based information.

The exact and entire specifications for how to format the compact disc medium are complex, strewn with jargon you may never need, and superfluous to your understanding of a drive's capabilities. You should know the basics, however, because you get a glimpse into the inner workings of how data can be retrieved so quickly from such an enormous well.

To put the basic High Sierra format in perspective, the disc layout is roughly analogous to that of a floppy disk. A floppy disk has a system track that not only identifies itself as a floppy disk and reveals its density and operating system, but also tells the computer how it's organized—into directories, which are made up of files.

Basic CD-ROM formats are much the same. The initial track of a data CD identifies it as a CD and begins the synchronization between the drive and the disc. Beyond the synchronization lies a system area that details how the entire disc is structured. This system area identifies the location of the volume area—where the actual data is stored. The system area also lists the directories in this volume, with pointers or addresses to various named areas, as illustrated in Figure 13.2. A significant difference between the CD directory structure and that of DOS is that the CD's system area also contains direct addresses of the files within the subdirectories, allowing the CD to seek specific locations on the spiral data track.

Because the CD data is all on one long spiral track, when speaking of tracks in the context of a CD, we're actually talking about sectors or segments of data along that spiral.

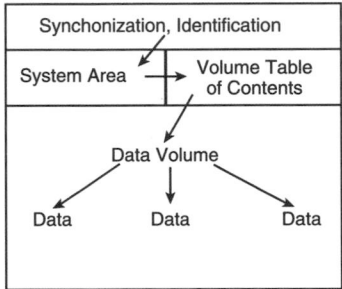

FIG. 13.2   A diagram of CD-ROM basic file organizational format.

CD-DA (Digital Audio)
Data drives that can read both data and audio are called *CD-DA*. Virtually all the data drives now being sold read both types of discs. When you insert a disc, the drive reads the first track to determine what type of disc you've loaded. Most drives ship with audio CD software that enables you to play music CDs from your PC; Windows 9x and Windows NT have this capability built in. You can use headphones or, with an installed sound card, connect speakers to the system. Some external drives ship with standard Left/Right audio plugs; just plug them into any external amplifier.

CD-ROM XA or Extended Architecture
CD-ROM XA, or *Extended Architecture*, is backward-compatible with the earlier High Sierra or ISO 9660 CD-ROMs. It adds another dimension to the world of CD-ROM technology: multiple-session recording.

Multiple Sessions. You will remember from the High Sierra format discussion that each CD-ROM disc has a VTOC (or Volume Table of Contents) in its system area, which tells the CD reader where and how the data is laid out on disc. Until this point, CD data was single-session in its encoding. In other words, when a CD was mastered, all the data that will ever reside on the disc had to be recorded in one session. The format, or the medium, had no provision for returning later to append more information.

Single-session CDs are no longer the only option, however. The CD-ROM XA format includes the capability to create multiple sessions on a single disc, each with its own VTOC. A drive that is CD-ROM XA–compliant is capable of finding the multiple VTOCs located on different areas of the disc and reading the data from those multiple sessions. This means that you can record a small amount of data on a CD, remove it from the drive, and then return to it later to record more data, until the disc is filled. This is a vast improvement over the single-session concept, which forced you to wait until you had a sufficient amount of data to make burning a disc worthwhile.

Interleaving. CD-ROM XA drives employ a technique known as *interleaving*. The specification calls for the capability to encode on disc whether the data directly following an identification mark is graphics, sound, or text. Graphics can include standard graphics pictures, animation, or full-motion video. In addition, these blocks can be *interleaved*, or interspersed, with each other. For example, a frame of video may start a track followed by a segment of audio, which would accompany the video, followed by yet another frame of video. The drive picks up the audio and video sequentially, buffering the information in memory, and then sending it along to the PC for synchronization.

In short, the data is read off the disc in alternating pieces and then synchronized at playback so that the result is a simultaneous presentation of the data. Without interleaving, it would be necessary for the drive to read and buffer the entire video track before it could read the audio track and synchronize the two for playback.

Mode 1 and Mode 2, Form 1 and Form 2. To achieve this level of sophistication, the CD format is broken up so that the data types are layered. *Mode 1* is the standard Yellow Book CD sector format with error correction. Each 2,352-byte sector consists of four fields (see Figure 13.3), as follows:

- Synchronization (12 bytes)

- Header (8 bytes)

- User Data (2,048 bytes)

- Error Correction Code (ECC) and Error Detection Code (EDC) (284 bytes)

Synchronization (12 bytes)	Header (8 bytes)	User Data (2048 bytes)	ECC & EDC (284 bytes)

FIG. 13.3 CD-ROM Yellow Book (Mode 1) sector format.

Mode 2, which was newly defined for the XA format, is CD data without error correction. The Mode 2 track, however, allows what are called *Form 1* and *Form 2* tracks to exist one after the other on the Mode 2 track, thereby permitting the interleaving. These interleaved tracks may include their own error correction and can contain any type of data. Figure 13.4 shows a visual representation of the breakdowns of Mode and Form structure.

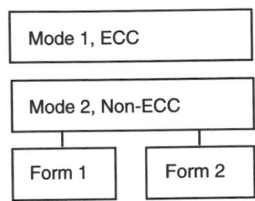

FIG. 13.4   A diagrammatic view of Mode and Form format for CD-ROM XA.

A Mode 2, Form 1 sector contains six fields (see Figure 13.5), as follows:

- Synchronization (12 bytes)

- Header (8 bytes)

- Subheader (8 bytes)

- User Data (2048 bytes)

- Error Correction Code (280 bytes)

- Error Detection Code (4 bytes)

Synchronization (12 bytes)	Header (8 bytes)	Subheader (8 bytes)	User Data (2048 bytes)	ECC (280 bytes)	EDC (4 bytes)

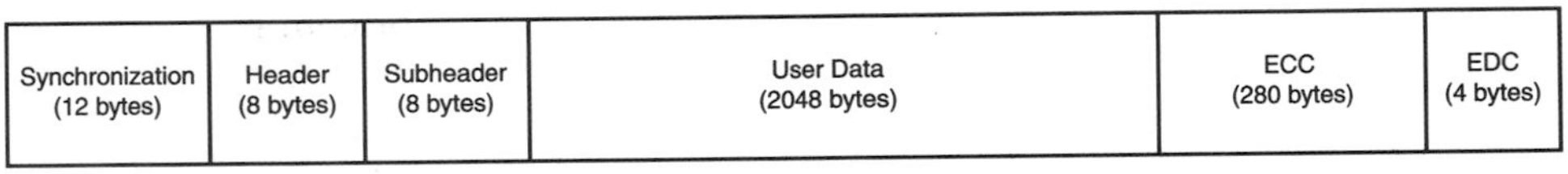

FIG. 13.5   CD-ROM Yellow Book (Mode 2, Form 1) sector format.

A Mode 2, Form 2 sector contains only five fields (see Figure 13.6), as follows:

- Synchronization (12 bytes)

- Header (8 bytes)

- Subheader (8 bytes)

- User Data (2324 bytes)

- Error Detection Code (4 bytes)

Synchronization (12 bytes)	Header (8 bytes)	Subheader (8 bytes)	User Data (2324 bytes)	EDC (4 bytes)

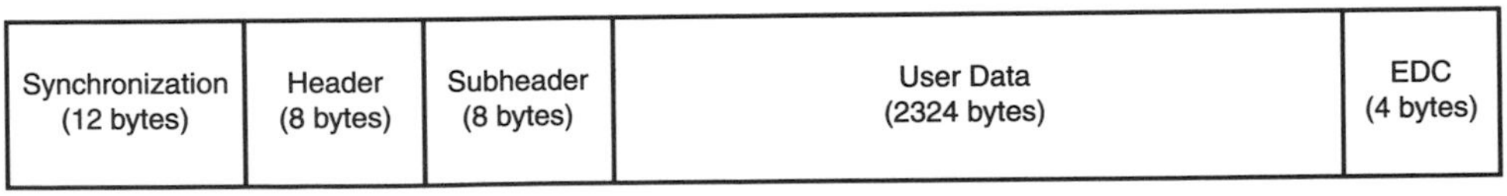

FIG. 13.6   CD-ROM Yellow Book (Mode 2, Form 2) sector format.

Both sector formats add a subheader field that identifies the type of information (such as audio or video) carried in the user data field. The Form 2 sector lacks the Error Correction Code of the Form 1 sector, and increases the size of the user data field instead.

Because they use less control data, CD-ROMs that use the Mode 2, Form 2 sector format (such as MPEG video CDs) can hold more user information than other CD-ROM types in the same number of sectors, resulting in a data transfer rate of 172K/sec instead of the standard 150K/sec.

For a drive to be truly XA-compatible, the Form 2 data encoded on the disc as audio must be *ADPCM (Adaptive Differential Pulse Code Modulation) audio*—specially compressed and encoded audio. This requires that the drive or the SCSI controller have a signal processor chip that can decompress the audio during the synchronization process.

What all this translates into is that many of the CD-ROM drives currently available are only partially XA-compliant. They might be capable of reading the interleaved data and multisession discs but may not have the ADPCM audio component on the disc or its controller.

Presently, the only drives with full XA compliance are produced by Sony and IBM. The Sony drive incorporates the ADPCM chip on its drive. The IBM XA drive is for IBM's proprietary Micro Channel bus and is designed for its high-end PS/2 Model computers.

Manufacturers may claim that their drives are "XA-ready," which means that they are capable of multisession and Mode 1 and Mode 2, Form 1 and Form 2 reading, but they do not incorporate the ADPCM chip. This is not a devastating shortcoming, however, because the CD-ROM XA format has not been very successful in itself. Software developers have not produced many XA software titles. IBM has a few under its Multimedia program, but when compared to the thousands of CD-ROM titles produced each year, very few of them take full advantage of XA capabilities.

However, while you may not find many XA discs on the market, the multisession capabilities and the Mode 2 sector formats defined by the standard are the basis for other CD-ROM formats that have been somewhat more successful, such as *CD Extra* (or *CD PLUS*) and *PhotoCD*.

If you purchase a drive that is fully mode-and form-compatible and is capable of reading multiple sessions, then you have the technology needed to take advantage of the most popular formats available at this time. Audio and video interleaving is possible without full XA compliance, as MPC (Multimedia PC) applications under Microsoft Windows demonstrate.

Mixed-Mode CDs

There are several CD-ROM formats that combine different mode sectors on a single disc. Usually, these discs include both standard CD audio and CD-ROM data sectors, and originate from the music side (rather than the data side) of the compact disc industry. The intention is for a user to be able to play only the audio tracks in a standard audio CD player while remaining unaware of the data track. However, a user with a PC or a dedicated combination audio/data player can access both the audio and data tracks on the same disc. The audio portion of the disc can consist of up to 98 standard Red Book audio tracks, while the data track is typically composed of XA Mode 2 sectors, and may contain video, song lyrics, still images, or other multimedia content.

The fundamental problem with these mixed-mode CDs is that when an audio player tries to play the data track, the result is static that could conceivably damage speakers. Different manufacturers have addressed this problem in different ways, resulting in a number of format names, including *CD-ROM Ready, Enhanced Music CDs, CD Extra*, and *CD Plus*.

CD-ROM Ready. One solution, the *CD-ROM Ready* disk, hides the data track in a pause before the first audio track on the disc. Inserting the CD into an audio player and pressing the "play" button simply skips past the pause and plays the first audio track. However, if you start the audio playing and then rewind past the beginning of the first audio track, the player will access the data track, possibly with disastrous results (depending on the volume level). CD-ROM Ready is therefore not a completely effective solution.

Enhanced Music CDs. Philips and Sony, in conjunction with other companies such as Microsoft and Apple, have developed another solution, the *Enhanced Music CD* specification, as defined in the Blue Book standard. Enhanced music CDs are often marketed under the names *CD Plus* (CD PLUS) or *CD Extra* and use the multisession technology defined in the CD-ROM XA standard to separate the audio and data tracks. Sometimes the markings are quite obscure, and you may not know that an audio CD contains data tracks until you play it in a CD-ROM drive.

The first session on an Enhanced Music CD contains up to 98 standard Red Book audio tracks, while the second session contains a single track of CD-ROM XA Mode 2 sectors. Since audio CD players are only single-session capable, they play only the audio tracks and ignore the additional session containing the XA data. An XA-ready CD-ROM drive in a PC, however, can see both of the sessions on the disc and access both the audio and data tracks.

PhotoCD

First announced back in 1990 but not available until 1992, CD drives or players that display your own CD-ROM-recorded photographs over your television are now being sold by Kodak. You simply drop off a roll of film at a participating Kodak developer; later you take home a PhotoCD and drop it into your PC or a Kodak PhotoCD-compatible disc player.

A PhotoCD-compatible player is a home A/V (audio/visual) entertainment system component that is designed to play both PhotoCDs and audio CDs.

Because virtually all data-ready CD drives can also interpret audio, it was not difficult for Kodak to design the CD players to play audio discs as well. The player merely reads the first track and determines what type of disc you've fed it.

Using the PhotoCD player, you can view your photographs at any one of several resolutions; with a PC, you can both view your images and manipulate them using standard graphics software packages.

When you drop off your roll of film, the Kodak developers produce prints, just as they normally do. After prints are made, however, the process goes high-tech. Using high-speed SUN SparcStations, they scan the prints with ultra–high-resolution scanners. To give you an idea of the amount of information each scan carries, one color photograph can take 15–20M of storage. The compressed, stored images are then encoded onto special writable CDs. The finished product is packaged in a familiar CD case and shipped back to your local developer for pickup.

PhotoCD Disc Types. The images on the disc are compressed and stored using Kodak's own PhotoYCC encoding format, which includes up to six different resolutions for each image, as shown in Table 13.3. Kodak has defined several different types of PhotoCD discs to accommodate the needs of different types of users. The *PhotoCD Master* disc is the standard consumer format, and contains up to 100 of your photos in all the resolutions shown in the table except for base x64.

Table 13.3 PhotoCD Resolutions		
Base	**Resolution (pixels)**	**Description**
/16	128×192	Thumbnail
/4	256×384	Thumbnail
x1	512×768	TV Resolution
x4	1024×1536	HDTV Resolution
x16	2048×3072	Print Size
x64	4096×6144	Pro PhotoCD Master only

The different resolutions are intended to supply you with images appropriate for different applications. If, for example, you wanted to include a PhotoCD image on a Web page, you would choose a low-resolution image. A professional photographer shooting photos for a print ad would want to use the highest resolution possible.

The *Pro PhotoCD Master* disc is intended for professional photographers using larger film formats, such as 70mm, 120mm, or 4×5 inch. This type of disc adds an even higher-resolution image (4096×6144 pixels) to those already furnished on the PhotoCD Master disc. Because of this added high-res image, this type of disk may hold anywhere from 25 to 100 images, depending on the film format.

The *PhotoCD Portfolio* disc is designed for interactive presentations that include sound and other multimedia content. The high-resolution images that take up the most space are not needed here, so this type of disc can contain up to 700 images, depending on how much other content is included.

The *PhotoCD Catalogue* disc uses even lower-resolution images, designed for use in thumbnail displays. Up to 600 images of this type can be stored on a single disc.

The *Print PhotoCD* disc is intended for users in the printing industry and includes the same five resolutions as the PhotoCD Master disc, plus a platform-independent CMYK image that can be used by virtually any imaging software or publishing system.

Multiple Sessions. One of the breakthroughs of the PhotoCD concept is that each of the disc types is capable of containing multiple sessions. Because the average consumer would not usually have enough film processed to fill an entire disc, you can bring back your partially filled CDs each time you have more film to develop. A new session is then added to your existing CD until the entire disc is filled. You pay less for the processing because a new CD is not needed, and all your images are stored on a smaller number of disks.

Any XA-compliant or XA-ready CD-ROM drive can read the multiple sessions on a PhotoCD disc, and even if your drive is not multisession capable, it can still read the first session on the disc. If this is the case, you'll have to purchase a new disc for each batch of film you process, but you can still take advantage of PhotoCD technology.

Kodak provides software that enables you to view the PhotoCD images on your PC, and licenses a PhotoCD import filter to the manufacturers of many different desktop publishing, image editing, and paint programs. This means that you can modify your PhotoCD images using a program like Adobe Photoshop, and integrate them into documents for printing or electronic publication with a page layout program like Adobe PageMaker.

Writable CD-ROM Drives

It is now possible to create your own CD-ROMs—and audio CDs as well—using one of the new breeds of recordable CD-ROM devices. By purchasing writable CD-ROM disks and recording (or *burning*) your own CDs, you can store large amounts of data at a cost that is lower than any other removable, random-access medium.

You may find that cartridge drives like Iomega's Zip and Jaz are priced comparably to writable CD-ROM drives, but recordable CD-ROM disks typically cost from $3 to $10 each, while a 1G Jaz cartridge costs over $100. Also, if you want to transport the data, the other system must have the same type of drive, as there is no industry standard for cartridge data formats.

Magnetic tape media may provide a lower cost per megabyte, but tapes are linear-access devices. Accessing files from tape is a time-consuming process and does not provide anywhere near the convenience of a CD-ROM.

Compared with either tape or other removable media, using a CD-ROM burner is a very cost-effective and easy method for transporting large files or making archival copies. Another benefit of the CD for archiving data is that CDs have a much longer shelf life than tapes or other removable media.

Most writable CD-ROM drives are WORM (write-once, read many) devices, meaning that once you fill a CD with data, it is permanently stored. The *de facto* standard for this technology is the CD-R (CD-Recordable) drive. The write-once limitation makes this type of device less than ideal for system backups or other purposes in which it would be preferable to reuse the same media over and over. However, because of its low media costs, you may find that making permanent backups to CD-ROMs is as economically feasible as tape or other media.

In any case, there are now also CD-ROM burners on the market that are rewritable. CD-RW (CD ReWritable) drives can reuse the same discs, making them suitable for almost any type of data storage task. The following sections examine these two standards and how you can use them for your own data storage needs.

CD-R

CD-R drives are indeed WORM devices; however, they use a special recordable CD-ROM disc that, once recorded, can be played back or read in any standard CD-ROM drive. CD-R drives are very useful for archival storage or for creating master CDs, which can be duplicated for distribution within a company.

> **Note**
>
> Because of the technical changes in the way the CD is made, there can sometimes be problems reading CDs made by CD-R devices in a standard CD-ROM player. Most of these problems just result in poor play performance as the CD-ROM drive tries to align itself to the CD. However, some very old CD-ROM drives can't handle CD-R media.

CD-Rs function using the same principle as standard CD-ROMs, by reading the light reflected by a laser striking the surface of the disc. Light is either returned from the disc or not, forming a binary code. However, the CD-R disc itself is different from a standard CD-ROM.

Instead of the recording beam burning pits into a metallic or glass strata, the CD-R media is coated with a photosensitive organic dye that has the same reflective properties as a "virgin" CD. In other words, a CD reader would see an unrecorded CD-R disc as one long land. When the recording laser begins to burn data into the CD-R media, it heats the gold layer and the dye layer beneath. The result of heating these areas causes the dye and gold areas to diffuse light in exactly the same way that a pit would on a glass master disc or a mass-produced CD. The reader is fooled into thinking a pit exists, but there is no actual pit, just a spot of less-reflective disc caused by the chemical reaction of heating the dye and gold. This use of heat to create the pits in the disc is why the recording process is often referred to as "burning" a CD.

Most recordable CD-ROM drives can write discs using any of the formats discussed thus far—from ISO 9660 all the way through CD-ROM XA. In addition, these drives can read the formats as well, and therefore serve as general purpose CD-ROM readers. Prices have been falling steadily and now can be $500 or less for a drive, and under $5 for the blank media.

Writing a CD with a CD-R Drive. CD-R drives come in slower speeds than their CD-ROM reader counterparts. The fastest CD-R drives write at 4x normal speed—given the system performance to do so. However, some can read at up to 6x normal speed. This is obviously no competition for the 24x and 32x CD-ROM reader drives on the market today, but many CD-R users already have a read-only CD-ROM drive.

Whenever a CD-R is writing data, it is creating one long spiral track on the CD, alternating on and off to etch the pattern into the raw media. Because the CD-R can't realign itself like a hard drive, once it starts writing it must continue until it's finished with the track, or the CD is ruined. This means that the CD-R recording software, in combination with your system hardware, must be able to deliver a consistent stream of data to the CD-R drive while it's writing. To aid in this effort, the software uses a buffer that it creates on your hard disk to temporarily store the data as it is being sent to the CD-R drive.

You'll recall that the normal data transfer rate for a single-speed CD-ROM is 150K/sec. When writing at a 4x speed, the computer must feed data to the CD-R drive at 600K/sec. If any part of the computer isn't able to maintain that data rate, you'll receive a `buffer under-run` message, and the recording attempt will fail.

The `buffer under-run` message indicates that the CD-R had to abort recording because it ran out of data in its buffer to write to the CD. This is the biggest problem that people have with CD-R devices. Providing a fast source to write from—usually a fast SCSI drive—on a system with plenty of RAM will generally help avoid buffer under-runs.

CD-R Software. Another difficulty with CD-R devices is that they require special software to write them. Although most cartridge drives and other removable media mount as standard devices in the system and can be accessed just like a hard drive, the CD-R drive uses special CD-ROM burning software to write to the disk.

This software handles the differences between how data is stored on a CD and how it is stored on a hard drive. As you learned earlier, there are several CD-ROM standards for storing information. The CD-ROM burning software arranges the data into one of these formats so the CD can be read later by a CD-ROM reader.

At one time, CD recording technology required that you have what amounted to a replica of the CD on a local hard drive. In fact, some software packages even required a separate, dedicated disk partition for this purpose. You would copy all the files to the appropriate place on the hard drive, creating the directory structure for the CD, and then the software would create an exact replica of every sector for the proposed CD-ROM—including every file, all the directory information, and the volume information—and copy it to the CD-R drive. The result was that you had to have about 1.5G of storage to burn a single CD (650M/CD $\times$ 2 = 1.3G + overhead $\approx$ 1.5G). This is no longer a requirement, as most software supports virtual images. You select the files and directories that you want to write to the CD from your hard drive and create a virtual directory structure for the CD-ROM in the software. This means that you can select files from different directories on different hard drives, or even files from network or other CD-ROM drives, and combine them any way you wish on the CD-R.

The software assembles the directory information and burns it onto the CD, then opens each file on the CD and copies the data directly from the original source. This generally works well, but you must be aware of the access times for the media you select as data sources. If, for example, you select directories from a slow hard drive or from a busy network, the software might not be able to read the data fast enough to maintain a consistent stream to the recorder. This causes the write to fail, resulting in a wasted disc.

CD-R drives that support several writing speeds typically come equipped with software that can simulate the recording process for testing purposes. The software reads the source data from the various media you've selected and determines the maximum possible speed for the recording process. Even this is not foolproof, however. Conditions may change between the time of the test and the actual disc write process, resulting in a failed recording attempt. For this reason, it is best to burn CDs from source data on a local hard drive rather than network drives. SCSI is preferable to IDE for both the CD-R burner and the source drive, because SCSI is better suited to devices sharing the same interface.

Multiple Sessions. Although it is true that a CD-R disc can only be filled with data once, most of the CD-R drives and software packages support multiple sessions on a single disk. This means you can partially fill a disk and then add other sessions later. As with any multisession disk, you must have an XA-compliant or XA-ready CD-ROM drive to read all the sessions on a CD-R disc. Otherwise, your access is limited to the data in the first session.

CD-RW

CD-RW (CD-ReWritable) drives, as defined in Part III of the Orange Book standard, are rapidly becoming a popular alternative to CD-Rs. CD-RWs use a different type of disc that the drive can rewrite at least one thousand times. While slightly more expensive than CD-R media, CD-RWs are still far cheaper than optical cartridges and other removable formats. This makes CD-RW a viable technology for system backups, file archiving, and virtually any other data storage task.

> **Note**
>
> CD-RW drives are sometimes referred to as *erasable CD* or *CD-E*.

The drawback of the CD-RW is that the lower reflectivity of the disc itself limits its readability. Many standard CD-ROM and CD-R drives cannot read CD-RWs. However, a new multiread capability is rapidly being integrated into many standard CD-ROM drives, enabling them to read CD-RWs. What's more, CD-RW drives are also capable of writing to CD-R discs and of reading standard CD-ROM discs. This means that by spending a little bit more for a CD-RW drive, you can get the best of both worlds: fully compatible WORM capability as well as rewritable storage.

The CD-RW Medium. The photosensitive dye within a CD-R disk changes from a reflective state to a non-reflective state when it is exposed to the laser recording beam of a CD-R drive. The change of state is permanent, which is why CD-R is a WORM medium. CD-RW disks also contain a substance that changes its reflective state when exposed to a laser, but unlike a CD-R, the change is not permanent.

The active layer of a CD-RW disk is an Ag-In-Sb-Te (silver-indium-antimony-tellurium) alloy that, in its original state, has a polycrystalline structure that makes it reflective. The active material is deposited on top of a polycarbonate substrate that is grooved in a spiral pattern to ensure precise servo guidance, resulting in accurate alignment of the lands and pits and absolute time information.

When the CD-RW drive writes to the disk, the laser uses its highest power setting, known as *Pwrite*, to heat the active material to a temperature between 500 and 700 degrees Celsius, causing it to liquefy. In its liquid state, the molecules of the active material flow freely, losing their polycrystalline structure and taking on an amorphous state. When the material solidifies in this amorphous state, it loses its reflectivity. By selectively firing the laser, the drive leaves parts of the disc in the polycrystalline state, forming the lands, and parts in the amorphous state, forming the pits.

To reverse the phase of a specific area on a disc, the laser operates at a lower power setting (*Perase*) and heats the active material to approximately 200 degrees Celsius, well below its liquification temperature, but above the temperature at which it reverts back from its amorphous to its polycrystalline state and becomes reflective again.

Note that despite the name of the Perase power setting, there is no explicit erasure performed to a CD-RW disk when it is rewritten. The drive pulses the laser at the appropriate power levels to produce polycrystalline and amorphous areas (lands and pits) at the appropriate locations, regardless of the previous state of those locations. Thus, the drive is writing both lands and pits. It is not possible to "erase" a CD-RW disk without writing new data over the old.

Reading CD-RW Discs. The original CD standards specify that on a compact disc the lands should have a minimum reflectance value of 70%, meaning that the area of a disc that represents a land should reflect back no less than 70% of the light directed at it. The pits should have a maximum reflectance value of 28%. In the early 1980s when these standards were developed, the photodiodes used in CD players were relatively insensitive, and these reflectance requirements were deliberately made stringent to accommodate them.

On a CD-RW disk, the reflectance of a land is approximately 15% to 25%, obviously well below the original minimum requirement. All the reflectance levels of CD-RW disks are approximately one-third of those defined in the original standard. However, the difference in the reflectance of a CD-RW disc's lands and the pits meets the 60% required by the original CD-ROM standard, and the photodiodes available today are more than capable of discerning between the CD-RW reflectance values. Thus, while some CD-ROM drives are not capable of reading CD-RW discs, it is not a difficult matter to modify the existing designs to make it possible for them to do so.

Philips, the company that is largely responsible for the development of CD-RW technology, in conjunction with Hewlett-Packard, has developed a *multiread* specification that has been approved by the Optical Storage Technology Association. This specification defines the levels of amplification needed for standard CD-ROM drives to read CD-RW discs. If the popularity of CD-RW continues to increase at its present rate, it is very likely that before long, most of the standard CD-ROM drives on the market will be multiread-capable, enabling them to read CD-RW drives. Until then, it is entirely possible that you may find your CD-RW disks readable only by other CD-RW drives.

DVD (Digital Versatile Disc)

The future of CD-ROM is called DVD (Digital Versatile Disc). This is a new standard that dramatically increases the storage capacity of, and therefore the useful applications for, CD-ROM–size disks. A CD-ROM can hold a maximum of about 680M of data, which may sound like a lot but is simply not enough for many up-and-coming applications, especially where the use of video is concerned.

One of the primary applications envisioned for the new DVD standard is a replacement for videotapes. In the future, instead of renting a tape at your local video store, you will be able to rent or purchase a movie on a CD-ROM disc! As such, DVD will have applications not only in computers, but in the consumer entertainment market as well.

DVD History

DVD had a somewhat confusing beginning. During 1995, two competing standards for high-capacity CD-ROM drives emerged to compete with each other for future market share. A standard called Multimedia CD was introduced and backed by Sony and Philips Electronics, while a competing standard called the Super Density (SD) disk was introduced and backed by Toshiba, Time Warner, and several other companies. If both of these standards had hit the market as is, consumers as well as entertainment and software producers would have been in a quandary over which one to choose.

Fearing a repeat of the Beta/VHS situation, several organizations, including the Hollywood Video Disc Advisory Group and the Computer Industry Technical Working Group, banded together. They insisted on a single format and refused to endorse either competing proposal. With this incentive, both groups worked out an agreement on a single, new, high-capacity CD-ROM in September of 1995. The new standard combined elements of both previously proposed standards and was called DVD, which originally stood for Digital Video Disk, but which has since been changed to Digital Versatile Disc. The single DVD standard has avoided a confusing replay of the VHS/Beta fiasco and has given the software, hardware, and movie industries a single, unified standard to support.

DVD Specifications

DVD offers an initial storage capacity of 4.7G of digital information on a single-sided, single-layer disc the same diameter and thickness of a current CD-ROM. With MPEG-2 (Motion Picture Experts Group) compression, that's enough to contain 135 minutes of video, enough for a full-length, full-screen, full-motion feature film—including three channels of CD-quality audio and four channels of subtitles. With only one audio track, a single disk could easily hold 160 minutes of video or more. This initial capacity is no coincidence; the creation of DVD was driven by the film industry, which has long sought a storage medium cheaper and more durable than videotape.

> **Note**
>
> It is important to know the difference between the DVD-Video and DVD-ROM standards. DVD-Video discs contain only video programs and are intended to be played in a DVD player, connected to a television and possibly an audio system. DVD-ROM is a data storage medium intended for use by PCs and other types of computers. The distinction is much like that between an audio CD and a CD-ROM. Computers may be able to play audio CDs as well as CD-ROMs, but dedicated audio CD players cannot make use of a CD-ROM's data tracks.

Future plans for DVD include 8.5G dual-layer discs as well as double-sided discs that will store 9.4G in a single layer and 17G in a dual-layer format.

DVD's initial storage capacity is made possible by several factors, including

- A smaller pit length (~2.08x, from 0.972 to 0.4 microns)

- A reduced track pitch (~2.16x, from 1.6 to 0.74 microns)

- A larger data area on the disc (~1.02x, from 86 to 87.6 square centimeters)

- More efficient channel bit modulation (~1.06x)

- More efficient error correction code (~1.32x)

- Less sector overhead (~1.06x, from 2048/2352 to 2048/2060 bytes)

The drive uses a shorter wavelength laser to read these smaller pits and lands. DVD can double its initial capacity by using both sides of the disc, and double it again by writing two separate layers of data on each side. The second data layer is written to a separate substrate below the first layer, which is semi-reflective to allow the laser to penetrate to the substrate beneath it. By focusing the laser on one of the two substrates, the drive can read roughly twice the amount of data from the same surface area.

With advancements coming in blue light lasers, this capacity may be increased several-fold in the future. DVD drives are also very fast compared to current CD-ROM technology. The standard transfer rate is 1.3M/sec, which is approximately equivalent to that of a 9x CD-ROM drive. Access times are typically in the 150–200ms range, with burst transfer rates of 12M/sec or higher. DVD drives spin at a base speed that is about three times as fast as a single speed CD-ROM. 2x DVD drives are available now, and 5x drives have been announced. DVD drives use either the IDE/ATA or SCSI interface, just like CD-ROMs, and include audio connectors for playing audio CDs through headphones or speakers.

DVD drives will be fully backward-compatible, and as such will be able to play today's CD-ROMs as well as audio CDs. When playing existing CDs, the performance will be equivalent to a 4x CD-ROM drive. As such, users who currently own 4x CD-ROM drives may want to consider a DVD drive instead of upgrading to a 6x or faster drive. Several manufacturers have announced plans to phase out their CD-ROM products in favor of DVD. In a few years, DVDs may make CD-ROMs obsolete, just as audio CDs displaced vinyl records in the 1980s.

Many PC vendors have integrated DVD-ROM drives into their new high-end computers, usually as an option. The typical package also includes an MPEG-2 decoder board for processing the compressed video on DVD disks. This offloads the intensive MPEG calculations from the system processor and makes it possible to display full-screen, full-motion video on a PC.

Some manufacturers of video display adapters have begun to include MPEG decoder hardware on their products. These adapters are called "DVD MPEG-2 accelerated," and call for some of the MPEG decoding tasks to be performed by software. Any software decoding involved in an MPEG solution places a greater burden on the main system processor, and may therefore yield less satisfactory results.

DVD Standards

DVD is young technology, and the standards situation is more confused than usual. Just about the only certain element in the DVD picture is the DVD-ROM format itself. Just about all the other aspects of the technology are caught up in conflicts between rival standards.

DVD video currently exists as a standard supported by approximately half of the movie industry. Movie titles have begun appearing in North America and Japan, and the first DVD players are now available. However, several major movie industry players, including Paramount, Disney, and Fox, have announced their support for an alternative system called Divx developed by Digital Video Express (DVE).

Divx requires a different player—the DVD players available now cannot play Divx discs—and, even more shocking, requires that the player be connected to DVE's computerized billing system via a built-in modem to play a Divx disc. Although the player can also play standard DVD and audio CDs, the intention is to add further copy protection security to Divx disc releases by requiring the modem connection. It seems highly unlikely that Divx will become an industry standard, but even an impractical alternative like this can delay the acceptance of a competing technology, sometimes for years.

There are also conflicts between standards for writable versions of DVD drives. Right now, the most likely candidates for acceptance are DVD-R and DVD-RAM, both based on specifications published in August 1997. DVD-R is comparable to CD-R in that it is a WORM technology that uses an organic dye as its active medium. The first DVD-R drives were released by Pioneer in October 1997 with a price of $17,000; blank discs are about $50.

DVD-RAM is a rewritable drive type that uses a phase-change technology like that of CD-RW. However, DVD-RAM discs cannot be read by standard DVD-ROM drives because of differences in both reflectivity of the medium and the data format. (DVD-R, by comparison, is backward-compatible with DVD-ROM.) DVD-ROM drives that can read DVD-RAM discs are expected in the future. Neither DVD-R nor DVD-RAM can write disks using dual layers, but there will be double-sided DVD-RAM discs available. Some manufacturers have matched the standard 4.7G capacity for a single-sided, single-layer disc with their DVD-R and DVD-RAM products, but most implementations hold slightly less.

Apart from DVD-R and DVD-RAM, several other writable DVD standards are in various stages of development. DVD+RW, also called *DVD Phase Change Rewritable*, is a competing rewritable format championed by Philips, Sony, and Hewlett-Packard. It is more closely based on CD-RW and is incompatible with DVD-RAM, although DVD+RW drives can read DVD-ROMs and CDs.

Pioneer has its own rewritable format, called DVD-R/W, that also uses a phase-change technology and is somewhat more compatible than DVD-RAM. The main problem with having so many specifications for the same basic technology is that it splinters the industry. Even the introduction of a superior specification complicates the process of accepting one specification as an industry standard.

Installing an Optical Drive

Installation of a CD-ROM or DVD-ROM drive can be as difficult or as easy as you make it. If you plan ahead, the installation should go smoothly.

This section walks you through the installation of a typical internal (SCSI or IDE) and external (SCSI only) optical drive, with tips that often aren't included in the manufacturer's installation manuals. After you install the hardware, your job may be finished if you are running Windows 9x and using a Plug-and-Play drive, or you may have to manually load the software needed to access the drive.

> **Note**
>
> CD-ROM and DVD-ROM drives use the same IDE and SCSI system interfaces and can be installed using the same basic procedures. Some DVD-ROM drives come with an MPEG-2 decoder board that enables you to view DVD movies and video on your PC. This board installs in a PCI bus slot like any other expansion card and performs the video decoding process that would otherwise fall to the system processor.

Avoiding Conflict: Get Your Cards in Order

Regardless of the type of installation—internal or external drive—you must have a functioning IDE or SCSI host adapter before the drive can function. In most cases, you will be connecting the optical drive to an existing IDE or SCSI adapter. If so, the adapter should already be configured not to conflict with other devices in your system. All you have to do is connect the drive with the appropriate cable and proceed from there.

Most computers today have an IDE adapter integrated into the motherboard. However, if you are adding SCSI to your system for the first time, you must install a SCSI host adapter into an expansion slot and make sure it is configured to use the appropriate hardware resources, such as the following:

- IRQ
- DMA channel
- I/O port address

As always, Windows 9x and PnP hardware can completely automate this process, but if you're using another operating system, you may have to configure the adapter manually.

Drive Configuration

Configuration of your new optical drive is paramount to its proper functioning. Examine your new drive (see Figure 13.7) and locate any jumpers. For an IDE drive, here are the typical ways to jumper the drive:

- As the primary (master) drive on the secondary IDE connection

- As the secondary (slave) drive to a current hard disk drive

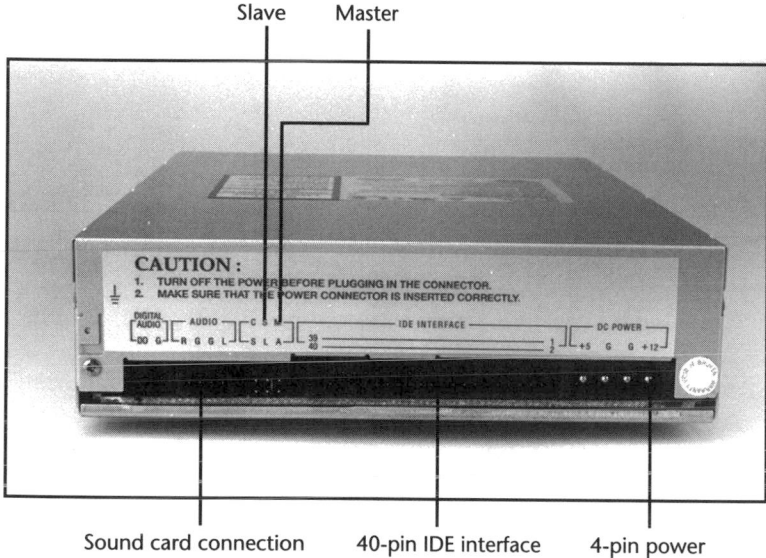

FIG. 13.7   The rear connection interfaces of a typical IDE internal CD-ROM drive.

If the drive is to be the *only* device on your secondary EIDE interface, the factory settings are usually correct. Consult the manual to make sure this is so.

When you use the CD-ROM or DVD-ROM as a secondary drive—that is, the second drive on the same ribbon cable with another device—make sure it is jumpered as the slave drive, and configure the other device so it is the master drive (see Figure 13.8). In most cases, the drive will show up as the next logical drive, or the D: drive.

> **Caution**
>
> Whenever possible, you should not connect a CD-ROM or DVD-ROM drive to the same channel as a hard disk drive, as sharing the channel can slow down both devices. If your computer has the two IDE channels standard in systems today, you should connect the optical drive to the secondary channel, even if you only have one hard disk drive on the primary.

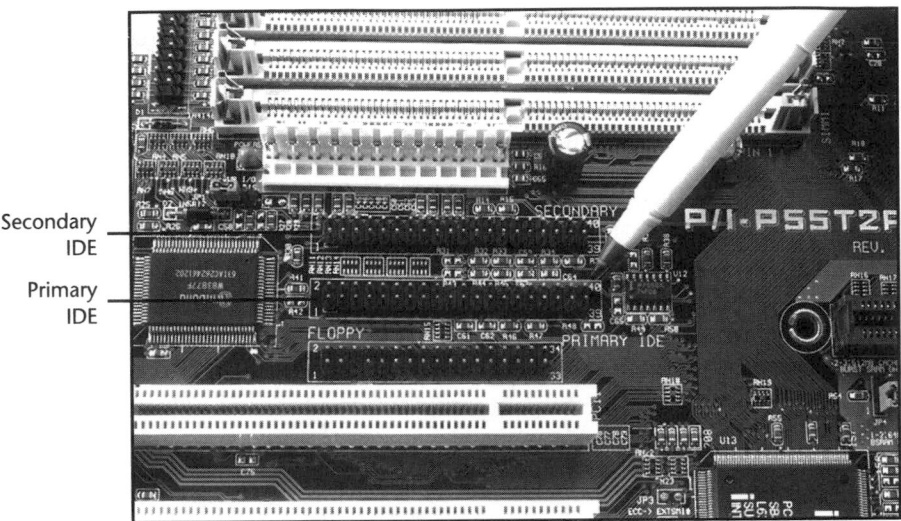

Secondary IDE

Primary IDE

FIG. 13.8 An embedded EIDE interface with a primary and secondary IDE connection.

SCSI drives are a bit easier to configure, because you need only to select the proper SCSI ID for the drive. By convention, the boot disk (the C: drive) in a SCSI system is set as ID0, and the host adapter has the ID of 7. You are free to choose any ID in between that is not being used by another device. Most SCSI devices use some sort of rotating or pushbutton selector to cycle between the SCSI IDs, but some may use jumpers.

SCSI devices are cabled together in a bus configuration. If your new SCSI drive falls at the end of the SCSI bus, you will also need to terminate the drive. Note that the SCSI bus refers to the physical arrangement of the devices, and not the SCSI IDs selected for each one.

> **Note**
>
> IDE/EIDE discs and SCSI optical drives can easily coexist in the same system. The optical drive will need to be connected to a SCSI host adapter separate from the IDE subsystem. Some audio adapters have a SCSI interface built in.

External (SCSI) Drive Hook-Up

Unpack the drive carefully. With the purchase of an external drive, you should receive the following items:

- CD-ROM or DVD-ROM drive

- SCSI adapter cable

With the exception of the SCSI host adapter, this is the bare minimum you need to get the drive up and running. You'll probably also find a CD caddy, documentation for the drive, driver software, a SCSI terminator plug, and possibly a sampling of CDs to get you started. SCSI drives almost never come with the SCSI host adapter that you need to connect them to the system. Because SCSI is designed to support up to 7 devices on the same system (or up to 15 devices for Ultra2 SCSI), it would be impractical to include a host adapter with every peripheral. Although a few computers have SCSI interfaces integrated into the motherboard, in most cases you have to purchase a SCSI adapter as a separate expansion card.

To begin the installation, take a look at your work area and the SCSI cable that came with the drive. Where will the drive find a new home? You're limited by the length of the cable. Find a spot for the drive, and insert the power cable into the back of the unit. Make sure that you have an outlet, or preferably a free socket in a surge-suppressing power strip to plug in the new drive.

SCSI devices generally use one of two cable types. Some older drives use a 50-pin Centronics cable, referred to as an *A-cable*, while most drives today use a 68-connector D-shell cable called a *P-cable*. Plug one end of the supplied cable into the connector socket of the drive, and one into the SCSI connector on the adapter card. Most external drives have two connectors on the back—either connector can be hooked to the PC (see Figure 13.9). You use the other connector to attach another SCSI device or, if the drive is at the end of the bus, to connect a terminator plug. Secure the cable with the guide hooks on both the drive and adapter connector, if provided.

> **Note**
>
> A SCSI device should include some means of terminating the bus, when necessary. The terminator may take the form of a cableless plug that you connect to the second SCSI connector on the drive, or the drive may be self-terminating, in which case there should be a jumper or a switch that you can set to activate termination.

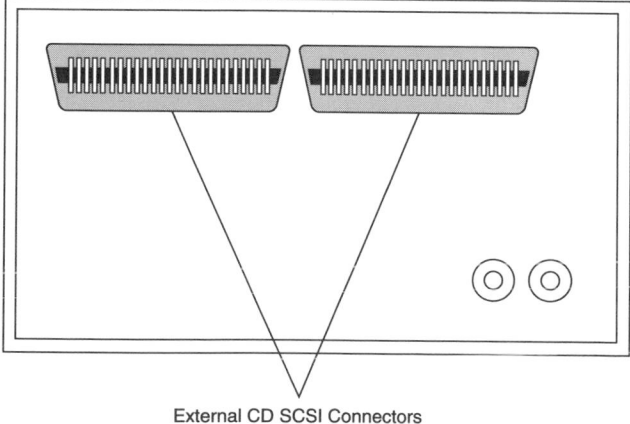

External CD SCSI Connectors

FIG. 13.9   Older Centronics-style external CD-ROM drive SCSI connectors.

Finally, your external drive should have a SCSI ID select switch on the back. This switch sets the identification number that the host adapter uses to distinguish the drive from the other devices on the bus. The host adapter, by most manufacturers' defaults, should be set for SCSI ID 7, and some (but not all) manufacturers reserve the IDs 0 and 1 for use by hard disk drives. Make sure you set the SCSI ID for the CD-ROM or DVD-ROM drive to any other number—6, 5, or 4, for example. The only rule to follow is to make sure that you do not set the drive for an ID that is already occupied—by either the adapter or any other SCSI peripheral on the bus.

Internal Drive Installation

Unpack your internal drive kit. You should have the following pieces:

- The drive

- Internal CD-audio cable

- Floppy disks/CD-ROM with device driver software and manual

- Drive rails and/or mounting screws

Your manufacturer also may have provided a *power cable splitter*—a bundle of wires with plastic connectors on each of three ends. A disc caddy and owner's manual may also be included. If you do not already have one in the computer, you will also need a SCSI host adapter to connect SCSI peripherals.

Make sure the PC is turned off, and remove the cover from the case. Before installing a SCSI adapter into the PC's expansion bus, connect the SCSI ribbon cable onto the adapter card (see Figure 13.10).

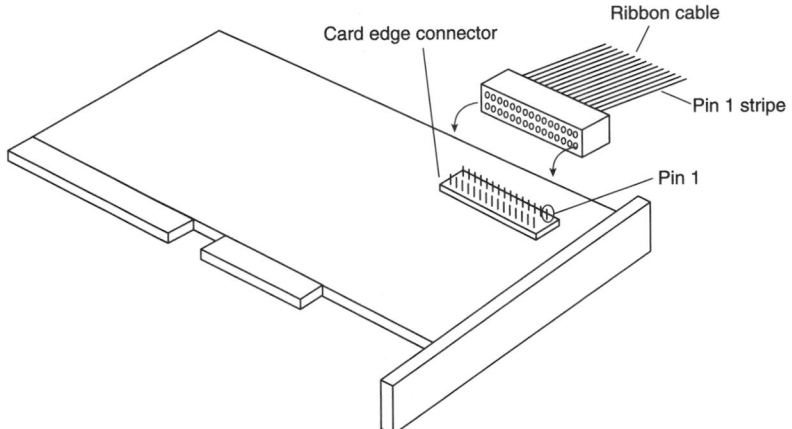

FIG. 13.10 Connecting a ribbon cable to a SCSI adapter.

Ribbon Cable and Card Edge Connector

The ribbon cable should be identical on both ends. You'll find a red stripe or dotted line down one side of the outermost edge of the cable. This stripe indicates a pin-1 designation and ensures that the SCSI cable is connected properly into the card and into the drive. If you're lucky, the manufacturer supplied a cable with notches or keys along one edge of the connector. With such a key, you can insert the cable into the card and drive in only one way. Unkeyed cables must be hooked up according to the pin-1 designation.

Along one edge of your SCSI adapter, you'll find a double row of 50 brass-colored pins. This is the card edge connector. In small print along the base of this row of pins you should find at least two numbers next to the pins—1 and 50. Aligning the ribbon cable's marked edge over pin 1, carefully and evenly insert the ribbon cable connector.

Now insert the adapter card into a free bus slot in the computer, leaving the drive end of the cable loose for the time being.

Choose a bay in the front of your computer's case for your internal drive. Make sure it's easily accessible from outside and not blocked by other items on your desk. You'll be inserting the CDs or DVDs here, and you'll need the elbow room.

Remove the drive bay cover from the computer case. You may have to loosen some screws to do this, or the cover may just pop out. Inside the drive bay, you should find a metal enclosure with screw holes for mounting the drive. If the drive has mounting holes along its side and fits snugly into the enclosure, you won't need mounting rails. If it's a loose fit, however, mount the rails along the sides of the drive with the rail screws, and then slide the drive into the bay. Secure the drive into the bay with four screws— two on each side. If the rails or drive don't line up evenly with four mounting holes, make sure that you use at least two—one mounting screw on each side. Because you'll be inserting and ejecting many discs over the years, mounting the drive securely is a must.

Once again, find the striped side of the ribbon cable and align it with pin 1 on the drive's edge connector. Either a diagram in your owner's manual or a designation on the connector itself tells you which is pin 1.

The back of the drive has a 4-pin power connector outlet. Inside the case of your PC, at the back of your floppy or hard disk, are power cords—bundled red and yellow wires with plastic connectors on them. You may already have an open power connector lying open in the case. Take the open connector and plug it into the back of the power socket on the CD-ROM or DVD-ROM drive. These connectors can only go in one way. If you do not have an open connector, use the splitter (see Figure 13.11). Disconnect a floppy drive power cord. Attach the splitter to the detached power cord. Plug one of the free ends into the floppy drive, the other into the CD-ROM or DVD-ROM drive.

Note

It's preferable to "borrow" power from the floppy drive connector in this way, rather than from another device. Your hard drive may require more power or be more sensitive to sharing this line than the floppy. If you have no choice—if the splitter and ribbon cable won't reach, for example— you can split off any power cord that hasn't already been split. Check the power cable to ensure that you have a line not already overloaded with another splitter.

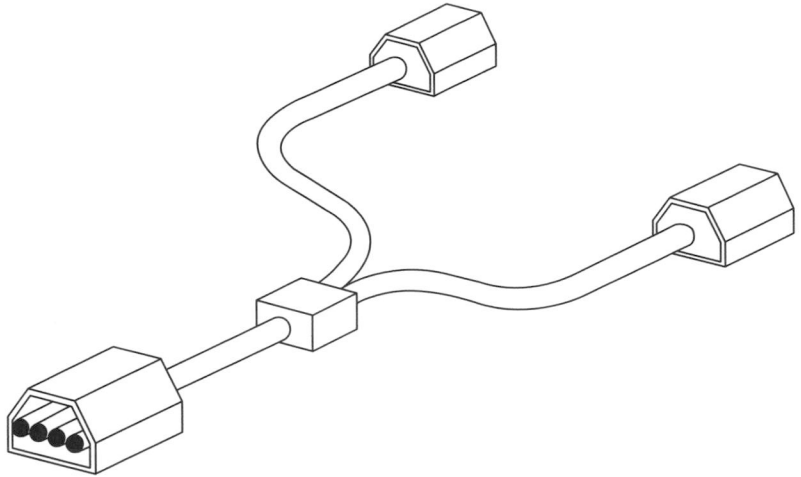

FIG. 13.11 Power cord splitter and connector.

Do *not* replace the PC cover yet—you need to make sure that everything is running perfectly before you seal the case. You're now ready to turn on the computer.

SCSI Chains: Internal, External, a Little of Both

Remember, one of the primary reasons for using the SCSI interface for your CD-ROM or DVD-ROM drive is the ability to connect a string of peripherals from one adapter, thus saving card slots inside the PC and limiting the nightmare of tracking IRQs, DMAs, and I/O memory addresses.

You can add hard drives, scanners, tape backup units, and other SCSI peripherals to this chain (see Figure 13.12). You must keep a few things in mind, however, and chief among them is SCSI termination.

◀◀ See "Termination," p. 639

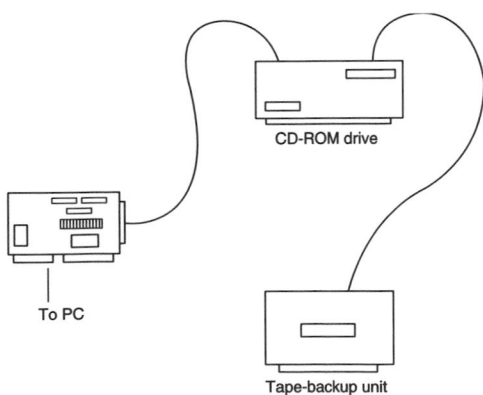

CD-ROM drive

To PC

Tape-backup unit

FIG. 13.12 A SCSI chain of devices on one adapter card.

Example One: All External SCSI Devices. Say that you installed your CD-ROM or DVD-ROM drive and added a tape device to the SCSI bus with the extra connector on the back of the optical drive. The first device in this SCSI bus is the adapter card itself. Most modern host adapters are *auto terminating*, meaning they will terminate themselves without your intervention if they are at the end of the bus.

From the card, you ran an external cable to the optical drive, and from the optical drive, you added another cable to the back of the tape unit. You must now terminate the tape unit as well. Most external units are terminated with a SCSI cap—a small connector that plugs into the unused external SCSI connector. These external drive connectors come in two varieties: a SCSI cap and a pass-through terminator. The cap is just that; it plugs over the open connector and covers it. The pass-through terminator, however, plugs into the connector and has an open end into which you can plug the SCSI cable. This type of connector is essential if your external drive has only one SCSI connector; you can plug the drive in and make sure that it's terminated—all with one connector.

Example Two: Internal Chain and Termination. On an internal SCSI bus, the same rules apply: All the internal devices must have unique SCSI ID numbers, and the first and last devices must be terminated. In the case of internal devices, however, you must check for termination. Internal devices typically have DIP switches or terminator packs similar to those on your adapter card. If you install a tape unit as the last device on the chain, it must have some means of terminating the bus. If you place your optical drive in the middle of the bus, you must deactivate its termination. The host adapter at the end of the chain must still be terminated.

> **Note**
>
> Most internal SCSI devices ship with terminating resistors and/or DIP switches on board, usually the latter. Check your user's manuals for their locations. Any given device may have one, two, or even three such resistors.

Example Three: Internal and External SCSI Devices. If you mix and match external as well as internal devices, follow the same rules. The bottom example shown in Figure 13.13 has an internal CD-ROM drive, terminated and set for SCSI ID 6; the external tape unit also is terminated, and it is using SCSI ID 5. The SCSI adapter itself is set for ID 7 and, most importantly, its termination has been disabled, because it is no longer at the end of the bus.

> **Note**
>
> As with any adapter card, be careful when handling the card itself. Make sure that you ground yourself first.

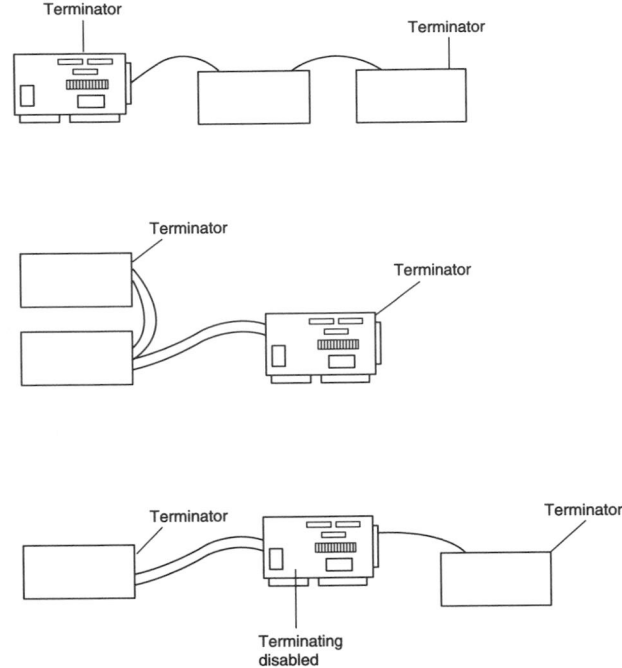

FIG. 13.13 Examples of various SCSI termination scenarios.

CD-ROM Software on Your PC

After you've configured the controller card, you're ready for the last step—installation of the drivers and other CD-ROM/DVD-ROM software. As usual, this process can be very simple with a PnP operating system like Windows 9x, or rather painful with DOS and Windows 3.1. The optical drive needs the following three software components for it to operate on a PC:

- A SCSI adapter driver (not needed for ATAPI IDE CD-ROM drives). Most popular SCSI adapter drivers are built into Windows 9x.

- A SCSI driver for the specific CD-ROM drive you've installed. An ASPI driver is built into Windows 9x, as is an ATAPI IDE CD-ROM driver.

- MSCDEX—Microsoft CD Extensions for DOS, which is built into Windows 9x as the CDFS VxD.

If you are still using DOS, you can have the first two drivers—the SCSI adapter driver and CD-ROM driver—load into your system at startup by placing command lines in your CONFIG.SYS file. The MSCDEX, or DOS extension, is an executable file added into your system through your AUTOEXEC.BAT file. This is not required in Windows 9x; the operating system will auto-detect the drive upon startup and prompt you to install the correct drivers if it can't find them in its standard arsenal of device drivers.

Using Windows 9x along with a CD-ROM or DVD-ROM drive that conforms to the ATAPI (AT Attachment Packet Interface) IDE specification does not require you to do anything. All the driver support for these drives is built into Windows 9x, including the ATAPI driver and the CDFS VxD driver.

If you are running a SCSI CD-ROM drive under Windows 9x, you will still need the ASPI (Advanced SCSI Programming Interface) driver that goes with your drive. The ASPI driver for your drive will normally come from the drive manufacturer and is included with the drive in most cases. However, by arrangement with hardware manufacturers, Windows 9x usually includes the ASPI driver for most SCSI host adapters, and also automatically runs the CDFS VxD virtual device driver. In some rare cases, you may have to install an updated driver that you have obtained from the manufacturer.

When you install a PnP SCSI host adapter in a Windows 9x system, simply booting the computer should cause the operating system to detect, identify, and install drivers for the new device. Once the driver for the host adapter is active, the system should detect the SCSI devices connected to the adapter and again load the appropriate drivers automatically.

The only problem you may encounter is if you are installing a new device, like a DVD-ROM drive, on an older version of Windows. Windows 98 includes drivers for most of the DVD-ROM drives on the market, but Windows 95 was released before these devices existed. In this case, you will probably have to supply a device driver on floppy disk, in response to a request from the OS, during the installation process.

DOS SCSI Adapter Driver. For DOS users, of course, the installation process is not so easy. Each SCSI adapter model has a specific driver that enables communication between the PC and the SCSI interface. Normally, these drivers conform to the ASPI. The ASPI driver for the drive connects with the ASPI driver for the SCSI host adapter; this is how the adapter and the drive communicate. An ASPI driver should be provided both with your SCSI drive and with the host adapter. Documentation should also have been included that walks you through the installation of the software.

Most SCSI adapters come with an installation program that automates the process of installing the appropriate ASPI drivers, both for the adapter and for the devices connected to the SCSI bus. However, you can manually add the SCSI device driver to your CONFIG.SYS file. In the CONFIG.SYS file, add the name and path of the appropriate driver with the DEVICE= command:

```
DEVICE=C:\DRIVERS\MYSCSI.SYS
```

C:\DRIVERS is the subdirectory into which you copied the SCSI ASPI device drivers. Some drivers have option switches or added commands that, for example, enable you to view the progress of the driver being loaded.

DOS CD-ROM Device Driver. This driver should be a part of your basic installation kit as well. If not, contact the drive's manufacturer for the proper device driver for your SCSI card.

The device driver should come with an installation program that prompts you for the memory I/O address for the SCSI adapter to which you've connected the CD-ROM drive. This device driver enables the adapter to communicate with the drive through the SCSI bus. Installation programs add a line similar to the following to your CONFIG.SYS file:

```
DEVICE=C:\DRIVERS\MYCDROM.SYS /D:mscd001
```

`C:\DRIVERS` is the subdirectory that contains the driver MYCDROM.SYS, the driver for your specific CD-ROM drive.

Note the `/D:mscd001` option after the preceding statement. This designation, called the *device signature*, identifies this CD-ROM driver as controlling the first (001), and only, CD-ROM drive on the system. This portion of the device driver statement is for the Microsoft DOS Extensions driver, which designates CD-ROM drives in this fashion. In fact, you could use any designation here, as long as the MSCDEX command line uses the same one.

MSCDEX: Adding CDs to DOS. The Microsoft CD Extensions for DOS allow the DOS operating system (and by extension, Windows 3.1) to identify and use data from CD-ROMs attached to the system. The original DOS operating system had no provisions for this technology, so "hooks" or handling of this unique media are not part of the basic operating environment. Using these extensions is convenient for all involved, however. As CD-ROM technology changes, the MSCDEX can be changed, independently of DOS. For example, most PhotoCD, multiple-session CD-ROM drives require MSCDEX.EXE version 2.21, which has been modified from earlier versions to accommodate the newer CD-ROM format.

MSCDEX.EXE should be in your software kit with your drive. If not, you can obtain the latest copy directly from Microsoft. If you are a registered user of DOS or Windows 3.1, MSCDEX.EXE is free. Read the licensing agreement that appears on the disc or in your manual concerning the proper licensing of the MSCDEX files.

Your installation software should add a line similar to the following to your AUTOEXEC.BAT file:

```
C:\WINDOWS\COMMAND\MSCDEX.EXE /d:mscd001
```

`C:\WINDOWS\COMMAND` is the directory in which the MSCDEX.EXE file is located by default. The `/d:mscd001` portion of the command line supplies the MSCDEX extension with the device signature defined in the CD-ROM device driver of your CONFIG.SYS file.

Note

The MSCDEX and CD-ROM device signatures must match. The defaults that most installations provide are used in this example. As long as the two names are the same, the drivers can find one another.

As long as you have these three drivers—the SCSI adapter driver, the CD-ROM driver, and the DOS CD extensions—loaded properly in your system, the CD-ROM drive will operate as transparently as any other drive in your system.

Table 13.4 lists the options that you can add to the MSCDEX.EXE command line.

Table 13.4 MSCDEX Command-Line Options	
Switch	**Function**
/V	Called *Verbose*; when this option is added to the command line displays information about memory allocation, buffers, drive letter assignments, and device driver names on your screen at boot time.
/L:<letter>	Designates which DOS drive letter you want to assign to the drive. For example, /L:G assigns the drive letter G: to your CD-ROM drive. Two conditions apply: First, you must not have another drive assigned to that letter; and second, your lastdrive= statement in your CONFIG.SYS file must be equal to or greater than the drive letter you're assigning. LASTDRIVE=G would be fine. LASTDRIVE=F would cause an error if you attempt to assign the CD-ROM drive to the G: drive with the /L: switch.
/M:<buffers>	Enables you to buffer the data from the CD-ROM drive. This is useful if you want faster initial access to the drive's directory. Buffers of 10 to 15 are more than enough for most uses. Any more is overkill. Each buffer, however, is equal to 2K of memory. So a /M:10 buffer argument, for example, would take 20K of memory. Note that this does not significantly increase the overall performance of the drive, just DOS's initial access to the drive and the access of large data blocks when the drive is reading live-motion video files, for example. You can't turn a 400ms drive into a speed demon by adding a 200K buffer. With no /M: argument added, MSCDEX will add six buffers as a default. That may be fine for most PCs and CD-ROM drives.
/E	Loads the aforementioned buffers into DOS high memory, freeing up space in the conventional 640K. Early versions of MSCDEX—anything below version 2.1—do not load into extended memory. You must have DOS 5.0 for this option to load.
/K	Provides Kanji (Japanese) language support.
/S	Enables you to share your CD-ROM drive on a peer-to-peer network, such as Windows for Workgroups.

Note that Windows 9x uses a built-in CDFS (CD File System) driver that takes the place of MSCDEX. It is configured through the Windows 9x Registry and requires no AUTOEXEC.BAT command.

Software Loading

As mentioned earlier, your drive should come with installation software that copies the device driver files to your hard drive. It should also add the necessary command lines to your CONFIG.SYS and AUTOEXEC.BAT files.

When the process is complete, you can reboot your machine and look for signs that all went smoothly in the software installation.

Following is a series of sample portions of your bootup screens to give you an idea of what messages you'll receive when a given driver is properly loaded into the system.

When you're sure that the software is loaded correctly, try out the drive by inserting a disc into the drive. Then get a directory of the disc from the DOS prompt by issuing the following command:

```
DIR/w G:
```

This command gives you a directory of the CD you've inserted, if your CD has been assigned the drive letter G.

You can log in to the CD-ROM drive, just as you would any DOS drive. The only DOS commands not possible on a CD-ROM drive are those that write to the drive. Remember that CDs are media that cannot be overwritten, erased, or formatted.

If you logged in to the CD-ROM and received a directory of a sample CD, you're all set.

Now you can power down the PC and replace the cover.

CD-ROM in Microsoft Windows 3.x

When your drive is added to your system, Windows already knows about it through the device drivers and DOS. The CD-ROM drive is accessible through File Manager by double-clicking its file cabinet icon. You see your CD-ROM drive among the drive icons across the top. Windows knows that the drive is a CD-ROM drive through the DOS extensions discussed earlier.

You can set your CD-ROM player to play audio CDs while you are working in Windows. You need to hook up your drive to a sound card and speakers, or connect the CD's audio ports to a stereo first. Go to Windows' Control Panel and select Drivers. If you do not see [MCI] CD Audio among the files in the driver's list, choose Add. Insert the Windows installation disk that contains the CDAUDIO driver and add the driver. When the driver appears on the list, close the Drivers and Control Panel windows.

Double-click the Media Player icon. Under Devices, select CD. A listing of the track numbers on your audio CD appears along the bottom edge of the Media Player. The controls on Media Player are similar to those of an audio CD player, including track select, continuous play, and pause.

Many drive manufacturers supply DOS-based CD audio players with their systems. Check your installation manual and software discs for these utilities.

Optical Drives in Windows 9x and Windows NT 4.0

As stated earlier, Windows 9x and Windows NT include virtually all the drivers you will need to run your optical drive, making the software installation automatic. Windows automatically recognizes most IDE drives, and with the addition of the appropriate drive-specific ASPI driver, most SCSI drives as well.

There are several new capabilities with CDs and DVDs in Windows 9x/NT. The most dramatic is the Autoplay feature. Autoplay is a feature integrated into Windows 9x that enables you to simply insert a disc into the drive, and Windows will automatically run it without any user intervention. It will also detect whether that particular disc has already been installed on your system, and if not, it will automatically start the install program. If the disc has already been installed, it will start the application program on the disc.

The Autoplay feature is simple. When you insert a disc, Windows 9x automatically spins it and looks for a file called AUTORUN.INF. If this file exists, Windows 9x opens it and follows the instructions contained within. As you can see, this Autoplay feature will only work on discs that have this file. Most software companies are now shipping CD-ROM and DVD-ROM titles that incorporate the Autoplay feature.

> **Tip**
>
> You can disable the Autoplay feature by opening the Windows 9x System Control Panel to the Device Manager page, highlighting your CD-ROM drive, and clicking the Properties button. The Properties dialog box for the drive has a Settings page that contains an Auto Insert Notification checkbox. Clearing this box prevents the operating system from processing the AUTORUN.INF file.

Windows 9x/NT includes a new version of the Media Player found in Windows 3.x called the CD Player. This application allows you to play audio CDs in your drive while you work at the computer. The CD Player features graphical controls that look like a standard audio CD-ROM drive, and even has advanced features found in audio drives, like random play, programmable playback order, and the ability to save *playlist* programs.

Troubleshooting CD-ROMs

Some people believe that optical discs and drives are indestructible when compared to their magnetic counterparts. Actually, modern optical drives are far less reliable than modern hard disk drives! Reliability is the bane of any removable media, and CD-ROMs and DVD-ROMs are no exception.

By far the most common causes of problems with optical discs and drives are scratches, dirt, and other contamination. Small scratches or fingerprints on the bottom of the disc should not affect performance because the laser focuses on a point inside the actual disk, but dirt or deep scratches can interfere with reading a disc.

To remedy this type of problem, you can clean the bottom surface of the CD with a soft cloth, but be careful not to scratch the surface in the process. The best technique is to wipe the disc in a radial fashion, using strokes that start from the center of the disc and emanate toward the outer edge. This way, any scratches will be perpendicular to the tracks rather than parallel to them, minimizing the interference they might cause. You can use any type of solution on the cloth to clean the disc, so long as it will not damage plastic. Most window cleaners are excellent at removing fingerprints and other dirt from the disc, and will not damage the plastic surface.

If there are deep scratches, they can often be buffed or polished out. A commercial plastic cleaner like that sold in auto parts stores for cleaning plastic instrument cluster and tail lamp lenses is very good for removing these types of scratches. This type of plastic polish or cleaner has a very mild abrasive that serves to polish scratches out of a plastic surface. Products labeled as *cleaners* are usually designed for more serious scratches, while those labeled as *polishes* are usually milder and work well as a final buff after using the cleaner. Polishes can be used alone if the surface is not scratched very deeply.

Read errors can also occur when dust accumulates on the read lens of your CD-ROM drive. You can try to clean out the drive and lens with a blast of "canned air," or by using a drive cleaner (which can be purchased at most music stores that sell audio CDs).

If your discs and your drive are clean, but you still can't read a particular disc, then your trouble might be due to disc capacity. Early CD-ROM discs had a capacity of about 550M (equivalent to about 60 minutes of CD audio). More recently, the capacity of a standard CD has been pushed to 680M (74 minutes of CD audio). Many older CD-ROM drives are unreliable when they try to read the outermost tracks of newer discs where the last bits of data are stored. You're more likely to run into this problem with a CD that has lots of data—including some Microsoft multimedia titles such as Ancient Lands, Art Gallery, and Complete Baseball. If you have this problem, you may be able to solve it with a firmware or driver upgrade for your CD-ROM drive, but it's possible that the only solution will be to replace the drive.

Sometimes too little data on the disc can be problematic as well. Some older CD-ROM drives use an arbitrary point on the disc's surface to calibrate their read mechanism, and if there happens to be no data at that point on the disc, the drive will have problems calibrating successfully. For example, some CD-ROM drives are not able to calibrate successfully with the Microsoft Flight Simulator 5.1 CD-ROM, because that disc does not have very much data on it. Fortunately, this problem can usually be corrected by a firmware or driver upgrade for your drive.

Many older drives have had problems working under Windows 9x. If you are having problems, contact your drive manufacturer to see if there is a firmware or software driver upgrade that may take care of your problem. With new high-speed drives available for well under $100, it may not make sense to spend any time messing with an older drive that is having problems. It would be more cost-effective to simply upgrade to a new drive instead!

If you are having problems with only one particular disc and not the drive in general, then you may find that your difficulties are in fact caused by a defective disc. See if you can exchange the disc for another to determine if that is indeed the cause.

Chapter 14

Printers

The capability to produce a printed version (often called a *hard copy*) of a document is a primary function of a PC, and along with modems, printers are becoming a required accessory. This is not to say, however, that every PC requires its own printer. One of the main reasons for the rise in local area networking in the business world has been the ability to share printers among multiple users.

Due in part to this network market, there is a wide variety of printers on the market supporting a multitude of both features and speeds. This chapter examines the underlying concepts of all printer technology, the basic types of printers available today and how they function, and how to install and troubleshoot a printer on your PC.

Printer Technology

There are three basic types of printer technologies used with PCs, defined by the method in which the image is produced on the paper. These three technologies are as follows:

- *Laser*. Laser printers function by creating an electrostatic image of an entire page on a photosensitive drum with a laser beam. When an ultrafine colored powder called a *toner* is applied to the drum, it adheres only to the sensitized areas corresponding to the letters or images on the page. The drum spins and is pressed against a sheet of paper, transferring the toner to the page and creating the image. This is the same basic technology used by copiers.

- *Inkjet*. Inkjet printers, as their name implies, have tiny nozzles that spray ionized ink onto a page. Magnetized plates direct the ink onto the page in the proper pattern to form letters and images.

- *Dot Matrix*. Dot matrix printers use an array of round-headed pins to press an inked ribbon against a page. The pins are arranged in a rectangular grid (called a *matrix*); different combinations of pins form the various characters and images.

In general, laser printers provide the best quality output, followed closely by inkjet, with dot matrix printers coming in a distant third. As with most computer equipment, the prices of printers have dropped tremendously in recent years, making the laser printers that were once a high-ticket item accessible to users at almost every level. Inkjet and dot matrix printers have become largely relegated to specialized uses: inkjet to budget color printing and dot matrix to commercial applications requiring continuous feed and multipart forms.

Except for these specialized uses, laser printers are superior to inkjet and dot matrix printers in almost every way. Most printers use the same basic terminology to describe their features and capabilities. The following sections examine some of this technology, how (or if) it applies to the various printer types, and what you should look for when shopping for a printer.

Print Resolution

The term *resolution* is used to describe the sharpness and clarity of the printed output. All these printer technologies create images by laying down a series of dots on the page. The size and number of these dots determine the printer's resolution and the quality of the output. If you look at a page of text produced by a low-resolution dot matrix printer, for example, the pattern of dots that forms the individual characters is immediately obvious to the naked eye. This is because the dots are relatively large and of a uniform size. On high-resolution laser printer output, however, the characters look solid, because the dots are much smaller, and often can be of different sizes.

Printer resolution is usually measured in *dots per inch (dpi)*. This refers to the number of separate dots that the printer can produce in a straight line one inch long. Most printers function at the same resolution both horizontally and vertically, so a specification such as 300 dpi implies a 300×300 dot one-inch square. A 300 dpi printer can therefore print 90,000 dots in a square inch of space. There are some printers, however, that specify different resolutions in each direction, such as 600×1200 dpi, which means that the printer can produce 720,000 dots in one square inch.

It's important to realize that the resolution of a printed page is far higher than that of a typical PC monitor. The word *resolution* is used to quantify PC video displays also, usually in terms of the number of pixels, such as 640×480 or 800×600. By print standards, however, the typical PC video display has a resolution of only 50–80 dpi. By measuring the actual height and width of an image on your screen and comparing it to the image's dimensions in pixels, you can determine the dpi for your display.

As a result, the claims of WYSIWYG (what you see is what you get) output by software and hardware manufacturers are valid only in the roughest sense. All but the lowest resolution printers should produce output that is far superior to that of your screen display.

90,000 dots per square inch may sound like an extraordinary amount of detail, but at 300 dpi, printed characters can have noticeably jagged diagonal lines (see Figure 14.1). There are two ways to improve the quality of the printed output and eliminate the "jaggies." One way is to increase the resolution. Today's laser printers usually operate at a minimum of 300 dpi, most use 600 dpi, and high-end models can reach as high as 1,200 dpi. Commercial offset printing (as used in the printing of this book, for example), by contrast, usually runs from 1,200 to 2,400 dpi. 600 dpi resolution, by itself, is sufficient to eliminate the obvious jaggedness in the print output.

FIG. 14.1 Because printed characters are composed of individual dots, lower resolution images can contain diagonal lines in which a jagged effect is quite obvious.

Resolution Enhancement. It is also possible to increase the quality of the print output without increasing the resolution, by varying the size of the dots. This is a technique that was originated by Hewlett Packard that they call *Resolution Enhancement Technology (RET)*. RET uses smaller dots to fill in the jagged edges created by larger dots, as shown in Figure 14.2.

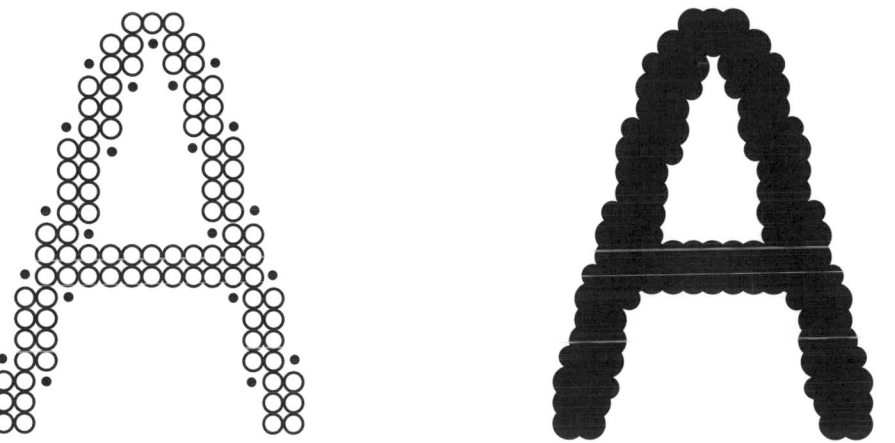

FIG. 14.2 Resolution Enhancement Technology mixes dots of different sizes to lessen the jagged effect seen in low resolution images.

Because the dots are so small, the cumulative effect to the naked eye is a straight diagonal line. Other manufacturers have developed their own versions of this concept by using other names, such as "edge enhancement." This type of enhancement is only possible for laser and inkjet printers. Because dot matrix printers produce images by having pins physically strike the page (through an inked ribbon), it is not possible to use variable-sized dots.

Interpolation. There are also many printers that produce higher resolution output by means of a process called *interpolation*. Printer resolution is not just a physical matter of how small the dots created by a laser or inkjet can be; a higher resolution image also means that the printer must process more data. A 600 dpi printer has to work with up to 360,000 dots per square inch, whereas a 300 dpi printer uses only 90,000 dots.

The higher resolution image, therefore, requires four times more memory than its low-resolution counterpart (at minimum), and a great deal more processing time. Some printers are built with the capability to physically print at a higher resolution, but without the required memory and processing power. Thus, the printer may process an image at 600 dpi, and then interpolate (or scale) the results up to 1200 dpi. Although an interpolated 1200 dpi image is better than a 600 dpi image without interpolation, a printer that operates at a true 1200 dpi resolution should produce noticeably better output than an interpolated 1200 dpi, and will probably cost significantly more as well. It is important when you evaluate printers that you check to see whether the resolution specified by the manufacturer is interpolated.

Dot Matrix Print Quality. Dot matrix printers are different from inkjet and laser printers in several fundamental ways. Most important, dot matrix printers do not process an entire page's worth of data at a time like lasers and inkjets, but rather work with streams of characters. The print resolution of a dot matrix printer is based not on its memory or its processing power, but rather on its mechanical capabilities. The grid of dots that a dot matrix printer uses to create characters is not a data set in a memory array or a pattern on a photosensitive drum; rather, the grid is formed by a set of metal pins that physically strike the page in various combinations. The resolution of the printer is therefore determined by the quantity of its pins, which is usually either 9 or 24.

Because it uses more pins to create characters of the same size, a 24-pin printer has pins that are necessarily smaller than those of a 9-pin printer, and the dots they create are smaller as well. As with the other printer types, smaller dots result in fewer jagged edges to the printed characters, and a better appearance to the document overall. However, techniques such as resolution enhancement and interpolation do not apply to dot matrix technology, making the resolution of the printer a far less important statistic. Beyond checking to see whether the printer has 9 or 24 pins, you will not see differences in print quality that are the result of print resolution technology.

> **Note**
>
> 24-pin dot matrix printers are often described by manufacturers as producing "near letter quality" output. In a literal sense I suppose this is true, because the output that these printers produce is near (but not quite) what you would want to send to a correspondent. Dot matrix printers still have their place in the professional world, such as for printing multipart forms and carbon copies, but when it comes to printing letters and other general office documents, they lack the resolution needed to produce a professional-looking product.

Page Description Languages (PDL)

Both laser and inkjet printers are known as page printers, because they assemble an entire page in memory before committing it to paper. This is in contrast to dot matrix printers, which are character-based. When your PC communicates with a page printer, it does so using a specialized language called a *page description language*, or *PDL*. A PDL is simply a means of coding every aspect of a printed document into a data stream that can be transmitted to the printer. After the PDL code arrives at the printer, internal firmware converts the code to the pattern of dots that are printed on the page. There are currently two PDLs in use today that have become de facto standards in the computer industry: PCL and PostScript. These languages are discussed in the following sections.

Printers that do not support a PDL use *escape code sequences* to control the printer's features, in combination with standard ASCII text for the body of the document (see "Escape Codes" later in this chapter). It is the printer driver loaded on your PC that is responsible for producing print output that is understood by your printer, whether it uses escape codes or a PDL. No matter what the source of the document you are printing, and no matter what format is used to store the original document, the data must be converted into a PDL data stream or an ASCII text stream with escape codes to be printed.

PCL (Printer Control Language). PCL is a page description language that was developed by Hewlett Packard for use in its printers in the early 1980s. As a result of HP's dominance in the printer market, PCL has become a standard that is emulated by many other printer manufacturers. Apart from the actual text being printed, PCL consists largely of commands that are designed to trigger various features and capabilities of the printer. These commands fall into four categories:

- *Control codes*. Standard ASCII codes that represent a function rather than a character, such as Carriage Return (CR), Form Feed (FF), and Line Feed (LF).

- *PCL commands*. Basically the same type of *escape code sequences* used by dot matrix printers. These commands comprise the majority of a PCL file's control code and include printer-specific equivalents to document parameters such as page formatting and font selection.

- *HP-GL/2 (Hewlett Packard Graphics Language) commands.* Commands that are specific to the printing of vector graphics as part of a compound document. An HP-GL/2 command consists of a two-letter mnemonic that may be followed by one or more parameters that specify how the printer should process the command.

- *PJL (Printer Job Language) commands.* Enable the printer to communicate with the PC bidirectionally, exchange job status and printer identification information, and control the PDL that the printer should use for a specific job and other printer control panel functions. PJL commands are limited to job-level printer control and are not involved in the printing of individual documents.

PCL has evolved over the years as printer capabilities have improved. PCL versions 1 and 2 were used by Hewlett Packard inkjet and daisywheel impact printers in the early 1980s, and could not be considered to be full-fledged page description languages. The first LaserJet printer released in 1984 used PCL 3, and the latest models contain PCL 6. Table 14.1 lists the various versions of PCL, the major capabilities added to each new version, and the HP laser printer models that use them.

Table 14.1	Hewlett Packard Printer Control Language (PCL) Versions		
Version	**Date**	**Models**	**Benefits**
PCL 3	May 1984	LaserJet LaserJet Plus	Full page formatting; vector graphics
PCL 4	Nov 1985	LaserJet Series II	Added typefaces; downloadable macros; support for larger bitmapped fonts and graphics
PCL 4e	Sep 1989	LaserJet IIP, raster IIP Plus	Compressed bitmap fonts; images
PCL 5	Mar 1990	LaserJet III, IIID, IIIP, IIIsi, HP-GL/2	Scalable typefaces; outline fonts; (vector) graphics
PCL 5e	Oct 1992	LaserJet 4, 4M, 4L, 4ML, 4P, 4MP, 4 Plus, 4M Plus, 5P, 5MP, 5L, 5L-FS, 5Lxtra, 6L, 6Lxi, 6Lse, 6P, 6MP, 6Psi, 6Pse	600 dpi support; bidirectional communication between printer and PC; additional fonts for Microsoft Windows
PCL 5c	Oct 1994	Color LaserJet Color LaserJet 5, 5M	Color extensions
PCL 6	Apr 1996	LaserJet 5, 5se, LaserJet 6, 6Pse, 6Psi, 6MP	Faster graphics printing & return to application

Although PCL is wholly owned and developed by Hewlett Packard, this company's long-term dominance in the printer market has made it a *de facto* standard. Many other companies manufacture printers that use PCL, and often advertise these printers as being compatible with a specific Hewlett Packard model.

PostScript. PostScript is a page description language that was developed by Adobe and first introduced in the Apple LaserWriter printer in 1985. PostScript possessed capabilities at its inception, such as scalable type and vector graphics support, that were only added to PCL years later. For this reason, PostScript quickly became, and still remains, the industry standard for desktop publishing and graphics work. Adobe licenses the PostScript language to many different printer manufacturers, including those that make the high-resolution imagesetters used by service bureaus to produce camera-ready output for the offset printing processes used by newspaper, magazine, and book printers.

PostScript does not use escape code sequences such as PCL; it is more like a standard programming language. PostScript is called an *object-oriented* language because the printer sends images to the printer as geometrical objects rather than bitmaps. This means that to produce type using a particular font, the printer driver specifies a font outline and a specific size. The font outline is a template for the creation of the font's characters at any size. The printer actually generates the images of the characters from the outline, rather than calling on a stored bitmap of each character at each size. This type of image that is generated specifically for use on a particular page is called a *vector graphic*, as opposed to a *bitmap graphic*, which arrives at the printer as a fully formed dot pattern. PCL did not have the capability to print scalable type until version 5 was introduced in 1990.

When it comes to printing fonts, outlines simplify the process by enabling printers to be equipped with more internal fonts that can be printed at any size. Bitmapped fonts, on the other hand, usually must be downloaded to the printer from the PC. When graphic images are involved, the difference between a vector-based object and a bitmap can often be seen in the printed output. Because a vector image is actually generated inside the printer, its quality is based on the printer's capabilities. Printing a vector image on a 600 dpi printer produces a much better quality product than printing the same image on a 300 dpi printer. A bitmap image, on the other hand, will generate the same output on either printer.

At first, modifications to the PostScript language were based on the evolving capabilities of the Apple laser printers that were its primary outlet. These minor modifications eventually became numerous enough for Adobe to release a new baseline version of the language, called PostScript Level 2, in 1992. The evolution continued, and PostScript 3 was introduced in 1997. These updates improved the speed and performance of PostScript printers and accommodated their physical changes, such as increased amounts of memory and added paper trays, but they did not introduce revolutionary new features the way that the PCL updates did. PostScript had its most powerful features from the very beginning, and the succeeding revisions of the language remain backward compatible.

PDL Support. When you are evaluating printers, the decision as to what PDL you want to use should be based primarily on your interaction with other parties, their documents, and their printers. Today, PCL and PostScript are comparable in their capabilities (although this was not always the case), and for your own personal use either one can produce excellent printed output. However, if you plan to produce documents that are to be passed on to other parties, such as service bureaus for pre-press work, PostScript support is strongly recommended, because it is still the dominant standard in the world of professional graphics, printing, and publishing.

You may also come across documents on the Internet and in other places that are provided in the PostScript format. For a long time, a PostScript output file (usually with a .PS extension) was the most convenient, platform-independent format for distributing a document containing graphical content.

For example, the specifications for the TCP/IP networking protocols are freely distributed on the Internet in ASCII text form. A few of the documents, however, have diagrams and other graphics that can't be represented in ASCII, so they are published in PostScript format. Any user with a PostScript printer, regardless of the computing platform, can simply copy the file to the printer and produce a hard copy of the document, including all the graphics and fonts found in the original. Although the practice of releasing raw PostScript files is less frequent now that platform-independent formats such as Adobe Acrobat are available, this can still be a valid reason for having a PostScript printer available.

Both PCL and PostScript are available in a wide variety of printers. The Macintosh printing platform is designed around PostScript, which is standard equipment in all Apple's laser printers. Obviously, since Hewlett Packard developed the PCL standard, all their printers use that PDL by default. However, most of the HP models are available in a version with PostScript, as well. In addition, most HP printers can accept a special add-on module that provides the printer with PostScript support.

Many other manufacturers also use PCL or PostScript (or both) for their printers, which they have either licensed from HP or Adobe, or emulated themselves. The question of whether a printer has genuine, licensed versions of its PDLs can be very important. There have been numerous instances throughout the history of these PDLs in which unauthorized or poorly emulated versions of PCL and PostScript have been foisted on the public as the real thing. In the mid-1980s, the term "LaserJet Plus Emulation" came to have as little meaning as "Hayes compatible" did for modems. Nowadays, most of the PCL (usually version 5) emulations used in other manufacturers' printers are quite good, but PostScript is a far more complex language, and is more difficult to emulate. It is still possible to find discrepancies between an emulated version of a PDL and the real thing that result in visible differences in the printed output.

Here again, the PDL emulation issue is largely dependent on your interactions with other users. If you have a printer with an emulated version of PostScript and a printer driver that accurately addresses that emulated printer firmware, it matters little if the language does not conform precisely to the Adobe specifications. If you are sending your PostScript output to a service bureau for printing on an imagesetter, however, the discrepancies between an emulated PostScript and the real thing can make a vast difference.

Whenever possible, it is recommended that you purchase a printer that uses the genuine PDL licensed from its creator. A minimum of PCL 5 and/or PostScript Level 2 is preferable.

Many printers support both PCL and PostScript, and you should check to see how a printer handles mixed jobs using different PDLs. The best printers detect the PDL of each job as it arrives in the printer and automatically switch to the appropriate language. If a printer does not have this feature, you may have to send a command with each print job triggering the mode change. For a single user on a standalone system, this is not much of a problem, but for a printer connected to a network, it is often hard to be certain of the order in which jobs are printed unless someone constantly monitors the print queue, and manual mode changes can be difficult to organize.

Escape Codes

Virtually all laser printers and most inkjet printers support at least one page description language, but some printers (especially dot matrix) do not, and in this case the printer driver usually communicates with the printer using escape code sequences. Similar to the PCL commands described earlier, *escape codes* are control sequences used to activate the features of a particular printer. Escape codes are so named because the ASCII value for the Escape key is used as the first character of the code, to signal to the printer that what follows is an instruction code, and not a textual element of the document being printed.

On a dot matrix printer, it may be possible to select different resolutions, fonts, and speeds, depending on the printer's capabilities. The printer driver that you install on your PC is designed to generate the appropriate escape codes based on the options you specify in your application and your printer driver configuration.

Escape codes are not as standardized as PDLs; you may see different printers use different codes for the same function. Epson, for example, has long been a market leader in the dot matrix printer industry, and their escape codes have come to be accepted by some other manufacturers, but the acceptance of the codes has not been general enough for them to be called an industry standard.

Printer Memory

Printers have memory chips in them just as PCs do, and laser and inkjet printers usually have a processor as well, making the printer a computer unto itself, albeit a highly specialized one. Printers can use their internal memory for several purposes: as a buffer to hold print job data while it is being fed to the actual print engine; as a workspace to hold data during the processing of images, fonts, and commands; and as permanent and semi-permanent storage for outline fonts and other data.

For laser and inkjet printers, the amount of memory in a page printer is an extremely important gauge of its capabilities. The printer must be able to assemble a bitmap image of an entire page to print it, and the graphic images and fonts that are used on that page all take up memory. Even vector graphics and outline fonts must be processed into bitmaps before they can be printed. The larger the graphics on the page and the more fonts used, the more memory is required. This is in addition to the memory needed to store the PDL interpreter and the printer's permanent fonts.

You may find that your printer has sufficient memory to print an average page of mixed text and graphics, but not enough to print a full-page graphic or a page with many different fonts. The result of this may be a graphic split in half over two pages, missing fonts, or even no output at all. Fortunately, most printers can accept additional memory to extend their capabilities.

Expansion memory for printers can come in many different forms. Some printers use standard memory modules such as SIMMs or DIMMs, whereas others use proprietary designs that you must purchase from the manufacturer (at an inflated price, of course). As with a PC, extra memory installed in a printer is almost never wasted. In addition to the capability of processing larger graphics and more fonts, printers may be able to use extra memory to process the data for one page while printing another, and to buffer larger amounts of data received from the PC.

A printer with additional memory can accept more data from the PC at one time. Depending on your PC's operating system and its printer driver configuration, this can result in a noticeable difference to your system's performance. When you print a document in a DOS application, you cannot proceed with your work (in most cases) until the entire print job has been transmitted to the printer. Multitasking operating systems such as Windows 9x can usually print in the background, enabling work to proceed as the PC processes the print job, but performance may still suffer until the print job is completed. The larger the printer's memory buffer, the faster the print job data leaves the PC, returning the PC to its normal operation.

Simply learning how much memory is installed in the printer you plan to buy is not sufficient to make an intelligent purchasing decision. You must also be aware of how much memory is utilized by the PDL's and resident fonts, and how much is left free for print job data. Different PDLs, page sizes, and resolutions require different amounts of memory. As an example, for a 300 dpi letter size (8 1/2"×11") printer using PCL, 12M is a great deal of memory. For a 600 dpi tabloid size (11"×17") PostScript printer, it is barely enough.

> **Note**
>
> The issue of memory expansion is applicable only to page printers such as lasers and inkjets. Most dot matrix printers receive data from the PC as a stream of ASCII characters, and because they do not have to assemble an entire page at a time, they can maintain a much smaller buffer, usually only a few kilobytes. Even graphic images are processed by the PC and transmitted to the printer as a bit stream, so it is rarely possible to augment a dot matrix printer's memory.

Fonts

Fonts are one of the most commonly used, and most entertaining, printer features. Having quality fonts and using them correctly can make the difference between a professional-looking document and an amateurish one. The term *font* refers to a particular typeface in a particular typestyle at a particular size. A *typeface* is a design for a set of alphanumeric characters, in which the letters, numbers, and symbols all work well together to form an attractive and readable presentation. There are thousands of typefaces available, with many new designs being produced all the time. Some of the basic typefaces included with the Windows operating systems are called Times New Roman, Arial, and Courier (see Figure 14.3). A *typestyle* is a variation on a typeface, such as bold or italic. A typeface can have only one style, or it can have a dozen or more.

Times New Roman

Arial

Courier

FIG. 14.3 Examples of the Times New Roman, Arial, and Courier typefaces.

Typefaces are often classified by characteristics they have in common. For example, Times New Roman is known as a *serif* typeface, because all its characters have little decorative strokes known as serifs. A typeface like Arial, which lacks these strokes, is called a *sans serif* typeface. Courier is called a *monospaced* typeface, because all its letters occupy the same width on the page, as on a typewriter. In contrast, Arial and Times New Roman are both *proportional* typefaces, because the characters are designed to fit together, based on their widths. The letter "i" in a proportional typeface occupies less horizontal space on the page than the letter "w."

Technically, the term *font* refers to a typeface at a particular size, usually measured in *points* (72 points equals one inch). 10-point Courier and 12-point Courier would be considered two separate fonts. This is because in traditional printing, and in the first PC printers, each size of a particular typeface was a separate entity. On an old-time printing press, each character on a page was printed by a separate wood or metal slug that would be pressed against the paper to make an impression. Slugs of different sizes were needed to produce different sized characters. In the same way, printers originally used bitmaps to create type. In this printing technique, every character of a typeface exists as a separate pattern of dots, ready to be sent to the printer. In essence, each character existed as an individual, tiny graphic. To print the same typeface at various sizes requires individual graphics for each different size. These are called *bitmap fonts*.

Today, printers nearly always use *scalable fonts*. This is a technology in which a typeface requires only a single outline for each character to produce type of any size. The printer retains the outline in memory, and generates bitmaps of the text characters at the size required for each job. The bitmaps are stored in a temporary font cache, but only for the duration of the job. The printer can also rotate a scalable font to any angle, whereas bitmaps can be rotated only in 90 degree increments. Outline fonts take up less memory space in the printer and provide a wider range of variations for each typeface. Also, because they utilize what amounts to a vector graphic technology, scalable fonts can take advantage of the printer's full resolution, whereas bitmap fonts look the same at any resolution. The drawback to scalable fonts is that they require more processing power from the print engine, but when compared to the advantages they offer, this is a small sacrifice.

> **Note**
>
> Although bitmap fonts are seldom used any longer for normal business documents, some professionals prefer them for certain high resolution printing tasks, because they can be customized to suit a particular need. Bitmap fonts are also sometimes used by graphical operating systems such as Windows 3.1 for screen displays, because scalable fonts do not look good at the low resolution of the typical monitor. However, a technology called *anti-aliasing* that uses pixels of varying shades of gray (instead of just black and white) to smooth out jagged lines, has begun to replace the use of bitmap fonts on screen displays.

As a result of this evolution in technology, the terms font and typeface have come to be confused. In the old days, when you purchased a typeface, you would receive the same character set in a variety of sizes, with each size being called a font. Today, when you purchase a typeface, you receive only a single outline font that your printer can scale to any size.

In the days when bitmap fonts were common, there were several different ways to get the bitmaps to the printer. Because bitmap fonts take up more memory space than outlines, it is not practical to store a large number of fonts in the printer permanently. You could buy bitmap fonts as software (called *soft fonts*) and use a special utility to download them to the printer when needed, or you could purchase fonts on cartridges that you could insert into the printer and remove at will.

Few (if any) of the printers manufactured today have cartridge slots anymore, and the process of manually downloading soft fonts, although still technologically possible, is too much trouble to be worthwhile. Today, scalable type is all but universal, and although printers are usually equipped with a selection of font outlines permanently stored in memory, this is more for reasons of speed and convenience than necessity. The printer driver on your PC can automatically download font outlines to the printer as needed or generate scalable type just as your printer can. Technologies such as the TrueType fonts found on both Windows and Macintosh systems can provide you with access to hundreds of typefaces in many styles and at almost any size.

▶▶ See "Driver Problems," p. 907

Although all outline fonts function in basically the same way, there are different types of scalable fonts available. PostScript was the original scalable font technology, and Adobe has built up a library of typefaces over the years that is without peer in the digital type industry. Most PostScript printers are equipped with a collection of 39 basic fonts stored internally, but you can choose from thousands of others by browsing Adobe's online services or their Type On Call CD-ROM. In either case, after you purchase these PostScript Type 1 font outlines, you install them on your computer along with a utility called Adobe Type Manager, which is responsible for downloading the appropriate font outlines to your printer as needed.

The other major scalable font technology in use today is TrueType. Developed about six years after PostScript, TrueType is the result of a joint project between Apple and Microsoft. Both companies wanted to integrate a PostScript-style scalable font engine into their respective operating systems, but neither of whom wanted to delegate the control over an important element of their OS to a third-party company such as Adobe.

Although there are substantial technical differences in the way that their font outlines are created, PostScript and TrueType function in much the same way. The primary advantage of TrueType is that it is already integrated into the Windows and Macintosh operating systems, and does not require external software such as Adobe Type Manager. Most type foundries now produce their fonts in both PostScript Type 1 and TrueType versions, and any difference between the two in the final product is usually quite difficult to spot.

As with PostScript, many printers include an internal collection of TrueType fonts that the operating system makes available to your applications. You should consider the number of fonts supplied with your printer primarily as a bonus when you evaluate various products. Any typeface provided as an internal TrueType font in your printer can just as easily be produced using a software version, although you may have to purchase it separately.

> **Note**
>
> There are thousands of TrueType and PostScript Type 1 fonts available today, at a wide range of prices. Many fonts are available free for the downloading from the Internet, or on bargain CD-ROMs, whereas others (such as those offered by Adobe) are quite expensive by comparison. Be aware that there can be profound differences in the quality of these fonts, and although it is not always true that more expensive is better, there are a great many more cheap bad fonts than there are expensive bad fonts.

Printer Drivers

As with many peripherals, printers are highly reliant on a driver installed on the PC. The printer driver provides the software interface between the printer and your application or operating system. The primary function of the driver is to inform the PC about the capabilities of the printer, such as the PDLs it uses, the types of paper it handles, and the fonts installed. When you print a document in an application, the print options you select are supplied by the printer driver, although they appear to be part of the application.

In DOS, printer drivers are integrated into individual applications. A few major software packages provide drivers for a full range of printers, but most include only a few generic drivers. At times like these, the best thing to do is to select a driver that supports the same PDL revision as your printer. For example, a LaserJet III driver uses PCL 5, which will support all the LaserJet III and 4 models, even if it does not utilize all the printer's features. It is quite possible that a DOS application that doesn't have a driver for your exact printer model might not be able to take advantage of all your printer's capabilities.

In all versions of Windows, you install the printer driver as part of the operating system, not in the individual applications. The Windows product includes drivers for a wide range of printers, and individual drivers are almost always available from the printer manufacturer's online services. Note that the drivers included with Windows are usually developed by the manufacturer of the printer, not by Microsoft, and are included in the Windows package for the sake of convenience. This means there are usually no problems resulting from drivers produced by two different manufacturers.

PostScript Printer Descriptions. Whereas printers that use PCL or escape sequences all have completely separate Windows drivers, PostScript printers use a single generic driver to support the PDL. For all versions of Windows, this driver is called PSCRIPT.DRV. To support the various capabilities of individual printers, the driver uses plug-in modules called PPDs (PostScript Printer Descriptions). The PPD provides information on the specific mechanical capabilities of the printer, such as paper trays and sizes, whereas the language support is provided by the PostScript driver. To support multiple PostScript printers in Windows, you install additional PPDs to the existing driver architecture.

In addition to the module included with Windows, there is also a PostScript driver called AdobePS that is freely available from Adobe, the owners of the PostScript language. If you have a printer that uses true Adobe PostScript, this driver is recommended because it provides more complete support for the language and all its capabilities. Although the PostScript driver is provided by Microsoft or Adobe, you typically obtain new PPDs from the manufacturer of your printer.

How Printers Work

Each of the three main printer types uses a different method to create images on a page, as well as a different substance: powdered toner, liquid ink, or a fabric ribbon. The following sections examine how each type of printer creates images on the page.

Laser Printers

The process of printing a document on a laser printer consists of the following stages:

- Communications
- Processing
- Formatting
- Rasterizing
- Laser scanning
- Toner application
- Toner fusing

Different printers perform these procedures in various ways, but the steps are fundamentally the same. Less expensive printers, for example, may rely on the PC to perform more of the processing tasks, whereas others have the internal hardware to do the processing themselves.

Communications. The first step in the printing process is to get the print job data from the PC to the printer. PCs traditionally use the parallel port to communicate with a printer, although many printers can use a serial port. Some devices can even use both types of ports at the same time to connect to two different computers. Network printers often bypass these ports entirely and use an internal adapter to connect directly to the network cable.

◄◄ See "Parallel Ports," p. 593

Communications between the printer and the PC obviously consist largely of print job data sent from the computer to the printer. However, communications flow in the other direction, as well. The printer also sends signals back to the PC for the purpose of flow control, that is, to inform the computer when to stop sending data and when to resume. The printer typically has an internal memory buffer that is smaller than the average print job, and can only handle a certain amount of data at a time. As pages are actually printed, the printer purges data from its buffer and signals the PC to continue transmitting. This is commonly called *handshaking*. The handshaking protocols used for this communication are dependent on the port used to connect the printer to the PC.

The amount of data that a printer can hold varies widely, and you read earlier in this chapter how you can often enlarge the buffer by installing additional memory. Some printers even contain internal hard disk drives, and can store large amounts of print data and collections of fonts. The process of temporarily storing multiple print jobs as they await processing is known as *print spooling*.

Many printers today support even more advanced communications with a PC, enabling a user to interrogate the printer for its current status using a software application, and even to configure parameters that previously were accessible only from the control panel on the printer. This type of communication requires that the PC have a bidirectional, ECP, or EPP port.

Processing. After the printer receives the data from the PC, it begins the process of interpreting the code. Most laser printers are really computers in themselves, containing a microprocessor and a memory array that functions much like the equivalent components in your PC. This part of the printer is often called the *controller* or the *interpreter*, and includes the firmware supporting the page description language(s) that the printer uses.

The first step of the interpretation process is the examination of the incoming data to distinguish the control commands from the actual content of the document. The printer's processor reads the code and evaluates the commands that it finds, organizing those that are to be part of the formatting process and executing others that require physical adjustments to the printer configuration, such as paper tray selection and simplex (single sided) or duplex (double sided) printing. Some printers also convert the document formatting commands into a specialized code that streamlines the formatting process to come, whereas others leave these commands in their raw form.

Formatting. The formatting phase of the data interpretation process involves the interpretation of the commands that dictate how the content is to be placed on the page. Again, this is a process that can differ depending on the processing capabilities of the printer. With low-end printers, the PC does much of the formatting, sending highly specific instructions to the printer that describe the exact placement of every character on the page. More capable printers perform these formatting tasks themselves, and you may be surprised to find just how much work your printer does, in this respect.

Your application may display your document in a WYSIWYG format that looks very much like the printed output, but this is not necessarily how the printer driver sends the document data to the printer. In most cases, the printer actually lays out the document all over again by interpreting a series of commands that dictate parameters such as the paper size, the location of the margins, and the line spacing. The controller then places the text and graphics on the page within these guidelines, often performing complex procedures such as text justification within the printer.

The formatting process also includes the processing of outline fonts and vector graphics to convert them into bitmaps. In response to a command specifying the use of a particular font at a particular size, for example, the controller accesses the font outline and generates a set of character bitmaps at the correct size. These bitmaps are stored in a temporary font cache where the controller can access them as needed while laying out the text on the page.

Rasterizing. The result of the formatting process is a detailed set of commands defining the exact placement of every character and graphic on each page of the document. In the final stage of the data interpretation process, the controller processes the formatting commands to produce the pattern of tiny dots that will be applied to the page. This process is called *rasterization*. The array of dots is typically stored in a page buffer while it awaits the actual printing process.

The efficiency of this buffering process depends on the amount of memory in the printer and the resolution of the print job. On a monochrome printer, each dot requires one bit of memory, so a letter-sized page at 300 dpi requires 1,051,875 bytes of memory ($[\{8\ 1/2 \times 11\} \times 300^2]/8$), or just over 1M. At 600 dpi, the memory requirement jumps to 4,207,500 bytes—over 4M. Some printers have sufficient memory to buffer an entire page while the formatting of the next page proceeds. Others may lack even enough memory to store even one full page, and use what are called *band buffers* instead.

Printers that use band buffers divide a page into several horizontal strips, or bands. The controller rasterizes one band's worth of data at a time and sends it to the print engine, clearing the buffer for the next band. This way, the printer can process a page gradually, with the entire array only coming together on the photosensitive drum in the print engine. The band buffer method is cheaper than a full page buffer because it uses less memory, but it is also slower and more prone to errors. In recent years, the price of memory has dropped so much that band buffers are rarely used in laser printers.

Tip

Some printer drivers enable you to control whether graphics are sent to the printer in vector or raster form. In general, vector graphics provide better speed, but if you experience problems with the placement of the graphics on the page, you can switch to the raster option. Most printer drivers that offer this feature place the control on the Graphics page of the printer's Properties dialog box. However, some drivers may place the control elsewhere, or not provide it at all.

Laser Scanning. After the rasterized image of a page is created by the controller and stored in memory, the processing of that page passes to the print engine, the physical part of the printing process. *Print engine* is a collective term that is used to refer to the actual imaging technology in the printer, including the laser scanning assembly, the photoreceptor, the toner container, the developer unit, the corotrons, the discharge lamp, the fuser, and the paper transport mechanisms. These components are often treated as a collective unit because the print engine is essentially the same hardware used in copy machines. Most printer manufacturers build their products around a print engine that they obtain from another manufacturer, such as Canon. A PC printer differs from a copy machine primarily in its data acquisition and processing procedures. A copier has a built-in scanner, while a printer receives and processes digital data from the PC. After the raster image reaches the print engine, however, the procedure that produces the actual document is fundamentally identical.

The laser assembly in a laser printer, sometimes called a *raster output scanner (ROS)*, is used to create an electrostatic pattern of dots on a photosensitive drum (called the *photoreceptor*) that corresponds to the image stored in the page buffer. The laser assembly consists of the laser, a rotating mirror, and a lens. The laser always remains stationary, so to create the pattern of dots across the horizontal width of the drum, the mirror rotates laterally and the lens adjusts to focus the beam so that the dots on the outer edges of the drum are not distorted by having been farther from the light source. The vertical motion is provided by the slow and steady turning of the drum.

Caution

Because the drum is sensitive to any form of light, it should not be exposed to room light or daylight for extended periods of time. Some printers have a protective mechanism that shields the drum from exposure to light whenever you open up the printer's service compartment. Even when this is the case, however, you should leave the compartment open long enough only to service the printer or change the toner cartridge.

The photoreceptor drum, which in some printers may actually be a belt, is coated with a smooth material that holds an electrostatic charge that can be discharged on specific areas of its surface by exposure to light. The initial charge over the entire surface of the drum is applied by a device called the charger corotron. A *corotron* is a wire carrying a very high voltage that causes the air immediately around it to ionize. This ionization charges the drum's surface and also produces ozone, the source of the smell that is characteristic of laser printers. Some smaller printers use charged rollers instead of corotrons, specifically to avoid the production of ozone.

> **Caution**
>
> *Ozone* is a noxious and corrosive gas that should be avoided in closed, unventilated spaces. Although ozone is used to deodorize air and purify water, working in close proximity to laser printers for extended periods of time without a sufficient fresh air supply can cause health problems.

The drum is sensitive to any type of light, but a laser can produce fine enough dots to support the high resolutions required for professional looking documents. Every spot that the laser light touches on the drum is electrically discharged, leaving the pattern of the page's characters and images on its surface. The laser in a printer discharges the areas of the drum corresponding to the black parts of the page, that is, the characters and images that comprise the document's content. This is known as *write-black* printing. By contrast, copiers discharge the background areas of the page, a process called *write-white* printing.

Toner Application. As the photoreceptor drum rotates, the portion of its surface that the laser has discharged next passes by the developer unit (see Figure 14.4). The *developer* is a roller coated with fine magnetic particles that function as a "brush" for the toner. *Toner* is an extremely fine black plastic powder that will actually form the image on the printed page. As the developer roller rotates, it passes by the toner container and picks up an even coating of the particles on its magnetic surface. This same developer roller is also located right next to the photoreceptor drum, so that when its surface passes by the roller, the toner particles are attracted to the areas that have been discharged by the laser, thus forming the image of the page on the drum using the toner particles as a color medium.

As the drum continues its slow rotation, it next passes close to the surface of the paper. The printer has an entirely separate mechanism for extracting one sheet of paper at a time from the supply tray and passing it through the print engine so that its flat surface passes underneath the drum (without actually touching it) at the same speed that the drum is rotating. Beneath the sheet of paper, there is another corotron (called the *transfer corotron*) that charges the paper, causing it to attract the toner particles from the drum in the exact pattern of the document image. After the toner is transferred to the page, the continued rotation of the drum causes it to pass by a discharge lamp (usually a row of LEDs) that "erases" the image of the page by completely discharging the surface of the drum. By this time, the drum has completed a full revolution and the entire charging and discharging process can begin again for the next page of the document.

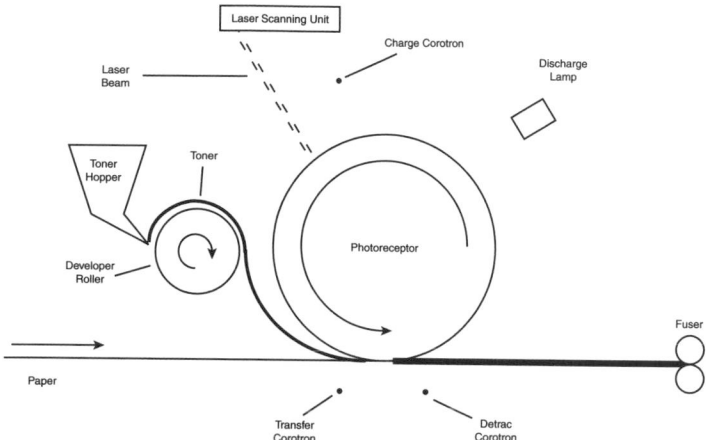

FIG. 14.4 A laser printer's print engine largely revolves around a photoreceptor drum that receives the document image from the laser and applies it to the page as it slowly rotates.

As you might imagine, these processes leave little margin for error when it comes to the proximity of the components involved. The drum must pass very close to the corotrons, the developer roller, and the paper surface for the toner to be applied properly. For this reason, many print engines combine these components into a single integrated cartridge that you replace every time you replenish the printer's toner supply. This increases the price of the toner cartridge, but it also enables you to easily replace the most sensitive parts of the printer on a regular basis, thus keeping the printer in good repair.

Toner Fusing. After the toner is transferred from the photoreceptor drum to the page, the page continues its journey through the printer by passing over yet another corotron, called the *detrac corotron*. This corotron essentially cancels the charge that was originally applied by the transfer corotron just before the application of the toner. This is necessary because an electrostatically charged piece of paper tends to stick to anything it contacts, such as the printer's paper handling rollers or other pieces of paper.

At this point in the printing process, you have a sheet of paper with toner sitting on it in the pattern of the printed page. The toner is still in its powdered form and, because the page is no longer statically charged, there is nothing holding it in place except gravity. A slight breeze or tremor can ruin the image at this point. To permanently fuse the toner to the page, it passes through a pair of rollers heated to 400 degrees Fahrenheit or more. This heat causes the plastic toner particles to melt and adhere to the fibers of the paper. At this point, the printing process is complete, and the page exits the printer. It is the nature of the toner and the fusing process that causes the characters of a laser printed document to have a raised feel and appearance to them that is very attractive, whereas an inked page feels perfectly flat.

Inkjet Printers

The data interpretation stages of the inkjet printing process are fundamentally similar to those of a laser printer. The main difference is that because many inkjets tend to occupy the low end of the printer market, they are less likely to have the powerful processors and large amounts of memory found in lasers. You are therefore likely to find more inkjet printers on the market with relatively small memory buffers that rely on the PC for the majority of their processing activities. These printers may print graphics using band buffers instead of full page buffers. Higher-end inkjets, however, can have virtually the same processing capabilities and memory capacities as laser printers.

The primary difference between an inkjet printer and a laser printer, however, is the way that the image is applied to the page. Inkjet printing technology is far simpler than laser printing, requires fewer and less expensive parts, and takes up much less space. Instead of an elaborate process by which toner is applied to a drum and then transferred from the drum to the page, inkjet printers use tiny nozzles to spray liquid ink directly onto the paper in the same dot patterns used by laser printers. For these reasons, inkjet technology is more easily adapted for use in portable printers.

There are two basic types of inkjet printing in use today: thermal and piezo (discussed in the following sections). These terms describe the technology used to force the ink out of the cartridge through the nozzles. The inkjet cartridge typically consists of a reservoir for the liquid ink and the tiny (as small as one micron) nozzles through which the ink is expelled onto the page. The number of nozzles is dependent on the printer's resolution; configurations using anywhere from 21 to 128 nozzles per color are common. Color inkjet printers use four reservoirs with different color inks (cyan, magenta, yellow, and black). By mixing the four inks, the printer can produce virtually any color. (Some inkjets use one replaceable cartridge to hold the reservoirs for the three colors cyan, magenta, and yellow.)

Thermal Inkjet Printing. *Thermal* inkjet printers function by superheating the ink in the cartridge to approximately 400 degrees. This causes vapor bubbles to form inside the cartridge that rise to the top of the reservoir. The pressure from the vapor forces ink out of the cartridge through the nozzles in tiny droplets that form the dots on the page. The vacuum caused by the expelled ink draws more ink down into the nozzles, making a constant stream of droplets as needed.

The thermal type of inkjet printing was the first to be developed and is still the most popular. Because of the vapor bubbles that form in the cartridge, Canon began calling its inkjet printers "BubbleJets," a name that has become almost synonymous with this technology.

Piezo Inkjet Printing. *Piezo* inkjet printing is a newer technology than thermal, and it presents distinct advantages. Instead of heat, these printers apply an electric charge to piezoelectric crystals inside the cartridge nozzles. These crystals change their shape as a result of the electric current, forcing the ink out through the nozzles.

Removing the high temperatures from the inkjet printing process presents two important advantages. First, the selection of inks that can withstand 400 degree heat is very limited; piezo technology enables printers to use ink formulations that are better suited to the printing process and less prone to smearing, which is a traditional problem with inkjet printing. Second, spray nozzles that are not exposed to extreme heat can last far longer than those traditional thermal cartridges.

Inkjet Limitations. Because it is more difficult to create fine dots with liquid ink than with toner, inkjet printers tend to have lower resolutions than lasers. Inkjet printing is also quite a bit slower than laser. Although it is possible to build high-end laser printers that can produce 16 pages per minute (ppm) or more, inkjets are limited in how fast they can actually dispense liquid ink, and rarely go above a maximum of 8 pages per minute, if that.

The biggest problem with most inkjet printers, however, is that the ink they use has a tendency to smear on standard paper stock. There are special inkjet papers that prevent this problem, but they are more expensive and offer far less variety than the laser printer papers on the market.

Dot Matrix Printers

Dot matrix printers were, at one time, the most popular type of printer on the market, because they were small, inexpensive to buy and to run, and fairly reliable. As the price of laser printers steadily dropped, however, and inkjet printers came to market that offered far superior output quality at virtually the same price, the market for dot matrix printers reduced dramatically. Although they continue to perform certain tasks quite well, dot matrix printers generally are too noisy, offer mediocre print quality, and poor paper handling.

Unlike lasers and most inkjets, dot matrix printers do not process documents a page at a time. Instead, they work primarily with a stream of ASCII characters up to a line at a time, and therefore require very small memory buffers. As a result, their speed is measured in characters per second (cps), instead of pages per minute (ppm). There is also very little processing performed in the printer, when compared to a laser. Dot matrix printers do not use complex page description languages such as PCL and PostScript. The data stream from the computer contains escape sequences used to set basic printer parameters such as page size and print quality, but any complex processing required is performed by the PC.

Dot matrix printers work by advancing paper vertically around a rubberized roller called a *platen*, one line at a time. At the same time, a print head travels back and forth horizontally on a metal bar. The print head contains a matrix of metal pins (usually either 9 or 24) that it extends in various combinations to make a physical impression on the paper. Between the pins and the paper is an inked ribbon, much like that used in a typewriter. The pins pressing through the ribbon onto the page make a series of small dots, forming typographic characters on the page. Dot matrix printers also usually have rudimentary graphical capabilities, enabling them to produce low-resolution bitmaps using their limited memory as a band buffer.

Dot matrix printers are usually associated with continuous sheet paper, driven by pinholes on the edges. Most models can also handle single sheets, although rarely with the accuracy found in most laser or inkjet printers. Because they are *impact printers*, meaning that there is actual physical contact between the print head and the paper, dot matrix printers can do one thing that lasers and inkjets can't: print multipart forms and carbon copies. Many printers enable you to adjust the pressure of the impact to support various numbers of copies. Dot matrix printers are rarely used for correspondence and general office printing anymore. Instead, they have found their place in commercial applications such as banks and hotels.

Color Printing

At one time limited to graphics professionals and other high-end users, color printers have now become a commonplace PC accessory. The simplicity of inkjet printer technology has made it possible for manufacturers to build very low-cost printers that produce color output that, while not up to professional standards, is sufficient for basic personal and business needs.

There are several different types of color printers, most of them adaptations of existing monochrome technologies. In most cases, color printers function by using the same printing medium in several colors (usually four). Thus, a color inkjet printer uses four colored inks and a color laser uses toner in four colors. As in process color offset printing, it is possible to create virtually any color by combining cyan, magenta, yellow, and black in various proportions. This is called the *CMYK color model* and is referred to as four-color printing. Some inexpensive printers (mostly inkjets) use only three colors, eliminating the black. These printers create a simulated black by combining the maximum proportions of the other three colors, but the result is far less effective than a true black medium.

Depending on the color medium, there are different processes for combining the four colors. For most color printers, it is not possible to actually mix the four colors to achieve the desired result, as you would mix paint. Instead, the printer applies the four colors very close to one another in the correct proportion to achieve the desired result. For example, an inkjet print works by creating an interlaced pattern of dots, with each dot using one of the four inks. This is known as *bi-level printing*. The proportion of dots of each color and the pattern in which they're interlaced dictates the final color. This process of mixing different colored dots to form another color is called *dithering*. The process is similar to the display on your color monitor that creates the color for each pixel by placing red, green, and blue dots of varying intensities very close to one another.

In most cases, dithering is only a moderately successful color process. The resolution of many color printers is not high enough to prevent you from seeing the individually colored dots if you look carefully. The cumulative effect, when seen from a distance, is of a solid color, but close up, the dithering pattern is discernible to the naked eye.

Printing in color necessarily complicates the language that the printer uses to communicate with the PC. Only the PostScript page description language has supported color from its inception. A version of PCL 5 with extensions to accommodate color, called PCL 5c, was introduced by Hewlett Packard in 1994. Many printer manufacturers, however, have their own proprietary color printing technologies, usually employing the printer driver to perform the additional processing required within the PC.

There are obviously many different applications for color printing, but the true test of any color printer is photographic reproduction. Dithered color that is acceptable for use in a bar chart, for example, may be totally inappropriate for printing photographs. Some relatively low-cost printers use special techniques, such as six inks instead of four, to produce better photographic reproductions, but the general rule is that to achieve photographic color prints that are comparable with those you see every day in magazines, you need equipment that is far beyond that which is typically used with PCs.

Graphics professionals, in most cases, use PC-based color printers as a proofing medium. In the past, it would often be necessary for an artist or designer to send a file to a service bureau for color printing, just to see a proof of the results of their work in hard copy. Now, rather than endure the delay and expense of that process, a relatively low-cost color printer can streamline the entire creative process.

> **Note**
>
> In the world of color printing, "low-cost" is a highly relative term. To a professional graphic artist or designer, a $5,000 color laser printer is a low-cost alternative to the enormously expensive print systems used by service bureaus. To the average PC user with far more modest color requirements, low-cost color inkjet printers are available in the $200-$300 range.

Color printing suffers in comparison to monochrome printing in two significant areas: speed and cost. In most cases, color printers are designed to sacrifice speed to achieve the best possible print quality. For this reason, it is a good idea to separate your color from your monochrome printing tasks in any sort of production environment. If you use inkjet printers in a business office, for example, it is usually better to have a separate printer dedicated to color output than force users to wait for a color job to complete to print a simple letter.

The cost of a color printer can range from a few hundred to many thousands of dollars, but one aspect of printing in color that many users do not anticipate is the cost of consumables. People accustomed with monochrome printing rarely contemplate the cost of the ink or toner the printer uses and the paper they print on. A single toner cartridge for a laser printer typically produces thousands of pages, and there is a wide range of paper types and qualities available at varying prices.

Color printers, however, are usually far more expensive to run than monochrome. Depending on the color technology it uses, the printer may require special paper that is more expensive than standard printer paper. In addition, the color medium, whether ink, toner, or ribbon, is usually far more expensive than the monochrome alternative, and yields fewer prints. The price of consumables per printed page is dependent on the coverage—a full page photograph obviously uses far more color than a page of text with a small color chart embedded in it, but color printing costs of fifty cents or more per page are common, as compared to a few pennies for monochrome printing.

The following sections examine the various color printer technologies intended for the PC market.

Color Inkjet Printers

Inkjet printers are the easiest to adapt to color use and the most inexpensive. In fact, most of the inkjet printers on the market are capable of printing in color; there are few that are monochrome only. The most typical arrangement is for the printer to use two cartridges, one containing black ink only and one containing the other three colors. The advantage of this arrangement is that you have fewer individual ink containers to re- place, but the disadvantage is that when any one of the color reservoirs is empty, you have to replace the entire three-color cartridge, thus driving up the cost. Some printers (such as a few of the HP DeskJet models) also accept a second three-color cartridge in place of the black one, providing a six-color printing solution that achieves better results in photographic printing.

Inkjet printers vary widely in their capabilities and their prices. Low-end models typically operate at 150 to 300 dpi, support only letter-sized paper, and print at 2 or 3 ppm. As you move up the price scale, resolutions and speeds increase, and printers may be able to use larger page sizes. One specialized breed of printer that often uses inkjet technology is designed to print poster-sized images on paper up to 36" wide.

One variation on the inkjet concept, called *solid inkjet*, *wax jet*, or *phase change* printing, uses solid, dyed wax as the color medium rather than liquid ink. As the printer works, it melts the wax and sprays it onto the page. Solid inkjet printers are generally slower and more expensive than traditional inkjets, but they tend to produce more vivid colors and are more resistant to smearing, enabling you to use virtually any type of paper.

Color Laser Printers

Color laser printers are a relatively new development, when compared to the other tech- nologies discussed here. The technology is the same as that of a monochrome laser printer, except that there are four toners in different colors. Unlike the other types of color printers, which apply all the colors at the same time, many color lasers actually print each color on the page individually. Because the printer has only a single photore- ceptor drum, the entire print engine cycle repeats four times for each page, applying the colored toners on top of each other.

This method greatly complicates the printer's paper handling. In a monochrome printer, the page passes beneath the photoreceptor drum at a speed equal to the drum's rotation, so that the toner can be applied evenly onto the page. In a color printer, the page must reverse so that it can pass under the drum four times. In addition, the page must be in precisely the same position for each pass, so that the individual dots of different colors fall directly on top of one another.

There are some lasers that mix the toner on the drum by applying each toner in turn, after which all four colors are laid onto the paper at once. This eases the paper handling difficulties, but presents other problems when applying the toner to the drum. In either case, the result is four toner colors mixed on the page and passing through the fuser assembly at once. This technique provides results that are vastly superior to dithered inks and other media. However, color laser printers are still very expensive, with prices start- ing at $3,000 to $4,000. Also, because the drum must rotate four times for each page, these printers are significantly slower than monochrome lasers.

Dye Sublimation Printers

Dye sublimation, also called *thermal dye transfer*, is a printing technique that uses ribbons containing four colored dyes that the printer heats directly into a gas. This way, the four colors are mixed before the printer applies them to the paper. These printers can produce 256 hues for each of the four colors, which combine into a palette totaling 16.7 million different colors. This results in *continuous tone* (that is, undithered) images that come very close to photographic quality.

Dye sublimation printers produce excellent output, but they suffer in almost every other way. They are slow and costly, both to buy and to run. They require a special paper type that is quite expensive, as are the ribbon cartridges they use. However, dye sublimation technology is quite compatible with thermal wax transfer printing—the two differ primarily in the color medium they use. Several manufacturers make dual mode printers that can use both thermal wax transfer, which is less expensive, and dye sublimation. This enables you to use the cheaper thermal wax mode for proofing and everyday printing, saving the dye sublimation mode for the final product and other special uses.

Thermal Wax Transfer Printers

Thermal wax transfer printers use wax-based inks, somewhat like those used in solid inkjets, that the printer melts before applying them to the page. The process is faster than dye sublimation and does not require a special type of paper, but the printer applies the inks as dots, meaning that the colors must be dithered. The print quality suffers as a result when compared to continuous tone output, but it is generally better than the output from inkjets and other dithered color technologies.

Choosing a Printer Type

There are hundreds of printers on the market, and you may have a tough time deciding which technology is best suited to your needs. Obviously, price is a major factor, but there are many other criteria that you should consider before making your decision, such as those presented in the following sections.

How Many Printers?

If you are buying a single printer for your own personal use, you should consider all your needs and try to find a product that satisfies them. For casual use, and particularly for families with kids, an inkjet printer with color capabilities can satisfy most serious needs and provide a lot of fun at the same time. If, however, you need top quality output for business correspondence or other professional documents, it may be a good idea to sacrifice the color capabilities and buy a laser printer. There are now small, personal models that are quite affordable for home use.

For businesses, you should consider whether it is a better idea to satisfy all your needs with one printer, or consider buying two units with complementary features, such as an inkjet for colored charts and reports and a laser for correspondence. Another consideration should be the proximity of the printer to its users. For example, consider whether it would be more convenient to have two 8 ppm printers at opposite ends of the office, rather than one 16 ppm printer in the middle.

Combination Devices

Sometimes, it's a good idea to consider your printing requirements in combination with other business needs. There are many devices on the market that combine the functions of several machines into one, for reasons of economy.

Fax Modem/Scanner/Printers. Combination fax/printer units have become very popular alternatives for home offices and telecommuters. The device generally consists of a laser or inkjet printer, a fax modem, and a scanner, all integrated into one unit. You can use the device to print hard copy from your PC, send faxes directly from the PC, print incoming faxes, and scan documents either for immediate faxing or storage as PC files.

You can achieve the same capabilities by purchasing a separate scanner, modem, and printer, but the combination unit ensures that all the modules will work properly together, and is usually significantly cheaper as well. The drawback of this concept is that you often cannot find a product that has all the features you want in your printer, your modem, and your scanner. If you want capabilities that go beyond the expected uses of the product, such as color printing or scanning, separate components may be preferable.

Printer/Copiers. As explained earlier in this chapter, laser printers and copiers use much of the same technology, and some manufacturers are taking advantage of this by manufacturing combination devices that function both as standalone copiers and high volume network printers. The device is essentially a copier to which the manufacturer has added the processor and memory needed for PC-based laser printing and a network interface adapter.

This strategy is particularly evident in the color printer market. Because color laser printers and color copiers are both high-ticket items, combining their functions into one unit is an ingenious solution.

Print Speed

Page printers such as lasers and inkjets measure their speed in *pages per minute* (ppm), whereas dot matrix printers use a *characters per second (cps)* measurement. Speed, along with resolution, usually increases steadily as you go up the price scale. For the home user, printer speed is usually not a major consideration, but for businesses it can be quite important, especially when multiple users are sharing one printer.

Typically, a laser or inkjet printer designed for personal use runs at about 4 ppm. The next higher size, suitable for small office or workgroup, runs at about 8 ppm. Large network printers can reach 16 ppm and more. These speeds are for monochrome printing; color printers are always far slower. As is usually the case, these figures are the manufacturers' estimations, which often run high. Your actual results depend on the nature of the documents you are printing. The more graphics and fonts you have on a page, the longer a page takes to print.

Another specification that is associated with the printer's speed is its duty cycle. The *duty cycle* is the number of pages that the printer is designed to print in a given period of time, usually a month. For example, the 12 ppm HP LaserJet 5 has a duty cycle of 35,000 pages per month, whereas the LaserJet 6L, a 6 ppm printer designed for personal use, has a duty cycle of 6,000 pages per month. There is no implicit rule saying that slower print-ers must have smaller duty cycles, but it is only logical that they should. Even if you are not overly concerned with speed, buying the LaserJet 6L and trying to get 20,000 pages per month out of it is not a good idea. Overtaxing the printer can shorten its life and diminish its output quality.

Paper Types

Another important factor in evaluating printers should be the types of paper that a printer can use. This refers not only to inkjets and other printer types that may require special papers, but to the paper sizes and weights that you will need for your work. Letter size paper (8 1/2×11 inches) is the standard in the United States, and A4 (210mm×297mm) in Europe, and virtually every printer supports one of these, but you should consider whether you will need larger sized pages, such as *legal* (8 1/2×14 inches) or *tabloid* (11 ×17 inches). Because it is the same width as letter size, support for legal sized printing does not usually add much to the price of the printer, but tabloid size printing does, because it requires major changes to the entire paper handling system.

Another question is just how the printer supports the various page sizes. Some printers use interchangeable paper trays, whereas others can use multiple trays at the same time. The capacity of the paper trays is also an issue. If you are buying a printer for office use, the less attention it needs, the better everyone will like it.

You might also want to consider the weight of the paper you will be printing on; some printers handle heavier card stock better than others. Envelope printing is another com-mon concern. Some printers use a multipurpose tray (that is, an open-ended, adjustable width tray) for this kind of work, whereas others may support envelope feeders (usually as an option).

Cost of Consumables

As mentioned earlier in this chapter, the cost of consumables can vary greatly, depend-ing on the kind of printer you choose. The printer's consumables include the paper, the color medium (either toner cartridges, ink cartridges, or inked ribbons), and even the electricity the printer uses.

Printers that require special papers add to the cost of consumables, because these papers are inevitably more expensive than standard stock. These printers also limit your selec-tion of papers. There are many grades of laser printer paper; you can switch from inex-pensive copier paper to more luxurious stock as the need arises. There is also a wide range of colored and textured papers that can add distinction to your documents. Spe-cialized papers for use in inkjet and other printers that require them are not available in anywhere near the same variety.

When you consider the cost of the color medium, you should calculate the price per page by dividing the cost of the cartridge by the number of pages it is expected to pro-duce. Like printer speeds, these figures are gross estimates, based on a specific percentage of ink or toner page coverage. Printing double-spaced text pages obviously requires less coverage than tightly spaced pages with a lot of graphics.

With laser printers, the price of toner can vary widely from printer to printer, depending on what other components are included in the cartridge. Clearly, a toner cartridge that includes a new photoreceptor drum and developer assembly will cost significantly more than a cartridge containing toner alone. However, in terms of printer maintenance and output quality, the extra expense may be justified.

Depending on the printer you select, there may be a competitive market for ink, toner, or ribbon cartridges. If you choose to try various brands, it's a good idea to record how many pages you get from each cartridge. It is often the case that cheaper cartridges are actually less economical because they produce fewer pages.

There is also is a large, even more volatile market for refilled toner and inkjet cartridges. Some vendors of toner cartridges for laser printers, for example, completely rebuild old cartridges by cleaning and repairing (or replacing) the photoreceptor and developer assemblies in addition to adding new toner. This can save you an enormous amount of money over the years and help the environment as well. Less reputable vendors, however, simply drill a hole into the cartridge, pour in some toner, and ship it out the door, which can result in a leaky cartridge and more problems than the savings are worth.

Use of electricity can also be a major concern. Laser printers in particular use a large amount of power, and many businesses leave them running continuously. Printers that have power saver features that automatically place the unit into a low-power standby mode after a period of inactivity can provide significant savings and, again, help the environment.

Installing Printer Support

As soon as you connect a printer to your PC's parallel or serial port, it is capable of receiving and processing ASCII text input. Even before you install a driver, you can issue a simple DOS command like the following:

```
dir > LPT1
```

The "greater than" sign in this command redirects the directory listing to the PC's parallel port. A printer connected to that port will receive and print the listing using the printer's default page format. If the printer connected to your PC processes data a page at a time, you will have to manually eject the current page to see the printed results. This is because the echo command does not include the form feed escape sequence that causes the printer to eject the page.

You can also redirect a text file to the printer port using a command like the following:

```
copy readme.txt > LPT1
```

These commands prove that the PC's parallel or serial port provides a fully functional interface to the printer, but to exercise any further control over the print job, you must install a printer driver. However, if you are troubleshooting a system problem that prevents you from loading the Windows printer drivers, this capability can be useful for printing documentation files or other documents.

DOS Drivers

Many DOS programs use no printer drivers, relying instead on the capabilities of the printer and the ASCII characters that represent control codes (such as carriage return and line feed). Larger applications, however, such as word processors and spreadsheets, typically do include drivers for specific printers. Normally, the driver selection is part of the program's installation process.

There are only a few DOS applications that provide driver support for a large selection of printers. WordPerfect, for example, traditionally took pride in its comprehensive printer support, but most applications tend to include a few generic drivers that enable you to specify your printer only in the most general sense. These days, the decline of DOS has resulted in the virtual cessation of DOS application development, meaning that you will probably have a difficult time finding support for a new model printer, even in a product such as WordPerfect.

If you have a laser printer that is not specified in the applications list of drivers, you should be able to use a driver supporting the same version of the page description language that your printer uses. A LaserJet III driver, for example, will function with any of the LaserJet III variants, such as the IIId and the IIIsi, because they all use PCL 5. The same driver should also work with the LaserJet 4 and 5 lines, if needed, because the versions of PCL these printers use are backward compatible with PCL 5.

These more generic drivers may not support all your printer's paper trays and the other features that distinguish the various models. For example, you will not be able to print at 600 dpi on your LaserJet 5 printer with a PCL 5 (not PCL 5e) driver. However, you should be able to expect reasonably good results with this type of driver support.

Windows Drivers

Printer drivers in Windows differ from those in DOS in that they are part of the operating system instead of the application, and in that you should always be able to find a driver for your exact model printer. Windows 3.1, Windows 9x, and Windows NT may use different drivers to support the same printer, and the interface you use to add printer support may be different in each operating system, but the process of installing a driver is fundamentally the same. The process consists mainly of a printer manufacturer and model selection, and the selection of an interface port.

All the Windows operating systems have a Printers Control Panel that is the central location for all printer driver configuration activities. You can install drivers for as many printers as you need, including multiple drivers for the same printer, drivers for network printers, and even drivers for printers that do not exist.

If you have a printer that offers a choice of PDLs, you can install a driver for each of the supported languages (typically PostScript and PCL), and select either one when you print a document. Experience will teach you that each language has its strengths and when to use a particular language.

If you have a network client installed on your system, you can install drivers for the printers that you regularly access on the network. The Printers Control Panel enables you to browse the network by using your client and select the objects representing your network printers.

You may also encounter situations in which it is convenient to "print" a document to an imaginary printer. If, for example, you have to submit a desktop publishing document for pre-press work, you can install the appropriate driver for their imagesetter on your PC and save the print job data to a file instead of sending it out through a parallel or serial port.

The PDL code created by a printer driver is simply ASCII text and, as such, you can store it as a normal file on your PC. All Windows and most DOS printer drivers enable you to select an output destination of FILE as an alternative to a parallel or serial port. When you actually print a document, the system prompts you for the name and location of the output file to be created.

You can then transport the print file to a system with the appropriate printer by using a disk, a modem, or any other standard medium. After the file is there, you can simply direct it out the appropriate printer port by using the COPY command shown earlier. Because the printer driver has already processed the job, you do not need to have the application that created the document or the printer driver installed on the system. All the commands are in the output file, and you simply have to get it to the printer.

Windows 9x Driver Installation. Windows 9x and Windows NT include a wizard for installing printer drivers that walks you through the entire process. The procedure in Windows 3.1 is fundamentally the same, although the screens are somewhat different in appearance. When you click the Add Printer icon in the Printers Control Panel, the wizard first asks whether you are installing a driver for a printer connected to the local machine or to the network. Then, you are presented with a dialog box like that in Figure 14.5, in which you can select the manufacturer of your printer and the specific model.

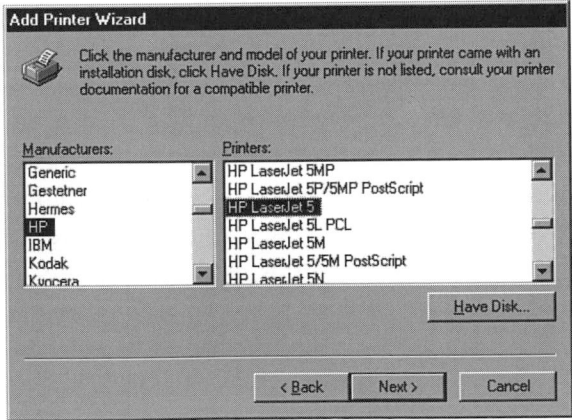

FIG. 14.5 The Printer Selector screen from the Windows 98 Add Printer Wizard.

The operating systems include a comprehensive selection of printer drivers and a Have Disk button that enables you to install drivers that you have obtained from the manufacturer of your printer or from other sources.

After selecting the printer type, you specify the port to which the printer is attached. The Available Ports option (see Figure 14.6) lists all the COM and LPT ports installed on your system and the FILE entry for saving print jobs to disk files.

The wizard also asks whether you intend to use the printer with DOS applications. If you answer yes, the wizard configures your system to redirect all output sent to the LPT1 printer port to the printer driver. This is needed when you are configuring a network printer because DOS applications usually do not have support for network printing.

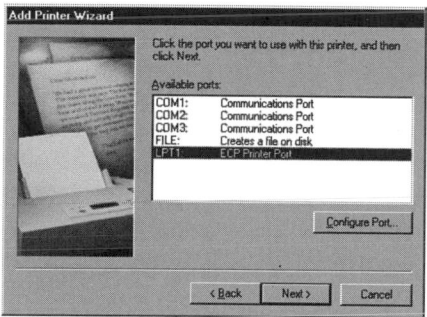

FIG. 14.6 The Add Printer Wizard's Available Ports dialog box.

After you specify whether you want to make the new printer your default Windows printer, the wizard creates a new icon in the Printers Control Panel. This makes the printer available to all your Windows applications, and provides access to the printer's Properties dialog box, which you can use to configure the driver and manipulate your print jobs.

Windows 9x Driver Configuration. The Properties dialog box for a particular printer typically contains numerous settings apart from those for selecting the port that the printer is to use. The features and the appearance of this dialog box are dependent on the printer driver you have installed; however, in most cases it enables you to select items such as the size and orientation of the paper that the printer will use, the tray that the paper is loaded in, and the number of copies of each page to print.

Many printer drivers provide settings that enable you to adjust the way that the driver handles print elements such as fonts and graphics. A typical Graphics page such as that for the HP LaserJet 5P driver may contain the following parameters:

- *Resolution.* Enables you to select from the print resolutions supported by the printer. A lower resolution provides faster printing and uses less printer memory.

- *Dithering.* Enables you to select various types of dithering for the shades of gray or colors produced by your printer. The various dithering types provide different results depending on the nature of the image and the resolution at which you are running the printer.

■ *Intensity*. Enables you to control how dark the graphic images in your documents should be printed.

■ *Graphics mode*. Enables you to select whether the driver should send graphic images to the printer as vectors to be rasterized by the printer, or whether the driver should rasterize the images in the computer and send the resulting bitmaps to the printer.

Many printer drivers include a Fonts page that lets you control how the driver treats the TrueType fonts in the documents you print. The usual options are as follows:

■ *Download TrueType fonts as outline soft fonts*. Causes the driver to send the fonts to the printer as vector outlines, so that the printer can rasterize them into bitmaps of the proper size. This option generally provides the fastest performance.

■ *Download TrueType fonts as bitmap soft fonts*. Causes the driver to rasterize the fonts in the computer and send the resulting bitmaps to the printer. This option is slightly slower than sending the font outlines, but uses less printer memory.

■ *Print TrueType as graphics*. Causes the driver to rasterize the fonts into bitmaps and send them to the printer as graphic images. This is the slowest of the three options, but it enables you to overlap text and graphics without blending them.

The Device Options page provided by many printer drivers lets you specify values for the following options:

■ *Print Quality*. Enables you to select the level of text quality for your documents. Lower qualities print faster, but have a coarser appearance.

■ *Printer Memory*. Enables you to specify how much memory is installed in the printer. The setting displays the amount of memory that ships with the printer, but if you install additional memory, be sure to modify this setting.

■ *Printer Memory Tracking*. Enables you to control how aggressively the printer driver will use the amount of memory configured in the printer memory parameter. When it processes a print job, the driver computes the amount of printer memory needed and compares it to the amount installed in the printer. If the job requires a great deal more memory than the printer has, it will abort the job and generate an error message. When the amount of memory required is close to the amount installed, this setting determines whether the driver will attempt to send the job to the printer, at the risk of incurring an out of memory error, or behave conservatively by aborting the job.

Printer Sharing. Windows 9x and Windows NT enable you to share local printers with other users on a Windows network. To do this, you must explicitly create a share representing the printer from the Sharing page of its Properties dialog box (see Figure 14.7). On this page, you specify a NetBIOS name that will become the share name for the printer and a password, if you want to limit access to certain users.

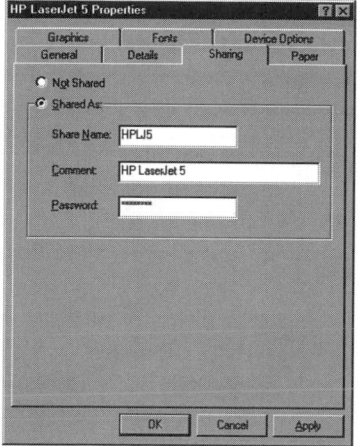

FIG. 14.7 Windows 9x and Windows NT can share printers with other network users.

After you have created the share, the printer appears to other users on the network just like a shared drive. To access the printer, a network user must install the appropriate driver for the printer and specify the name of the share instead of a local printer port. To avoid having to type out the path, you can drag an icon representing a network printer from the Network Neighborhood and drop it onto the Add New Printer icon in the Printers Control Panel. After this, you need only select the appropriate driver and answer the default printer and printer test page questions to complete the printer installation.

Remote Drivers. Windows NT 4.0 differs from Windows 9x in that it can store and distribute the printer drivers for multiple operating systems. When you share a printer in Windows NT, the dialog box contains an Alternate Drivers selector (see Figure 14.8) that enables you to choose the operating systems used by the other computers on your network.

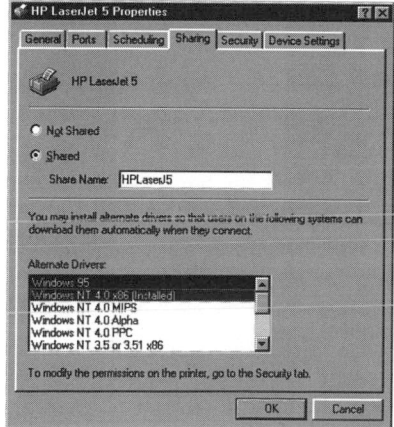

FIG. 14.8 Windows NT can automatically supply printer drivers to network client systems.

After the wizard installs the driver for the Windows NT system, it prompts you for the appropriate media containing the drivers for the other operating systems you've selected. This way, when a client selects that Windows NT printer share, it automatically downloads the proper driver from the Windows NT system and installs it, preventing the user from having to identify the printer manufacturer and model.

Preventive Maintenance

Printers are traditionally one of the most annoying components to troubleshoot for computer professionals because they are prone to many mechanical problems that PCs and other networking components are not. Variability in the quality of consumables and improper handling by users can exacerbate these problems, resulting in printers that require more attention and maintenance than other components.

As with PCs, preventive maintenance for printers is largely based on common sense. If you keep the unit clean and treat it properly, it will last longer and produce better quality output than if you don't.

Laser and Inkjet Printers

For laser printers, the best preventive maintenance regimen results from purchasing a printer that uses toner cartridges with photoreceptor and developer assemblies. These are the components that regularly come in contact with the toner, so replacing them on a regular basis ensures that these vital parts are clean and undamaged. If your printer does not use this type of cartridge, you should take extra care to clean the inside of the printer whenever you replenish the toner, following the manufacturer's recommendations. Some printers include a special brush or other tool for this purpose.

> **Caution**
>
> It is particularly important to follow the manufacturer's recommendations regarding safety whenever you are working inside a laser printer. Apart from the obvious danger caused by live electrical connections, be aware that some components are very delicate and can be damaged either by rough handling (such as the developer unit and the corotrons) or by excessive exposure to light (such as the photoreceptor). In addition, the printer's fusing mechanism is designed to heat up to 400 degrees F or more, and may remain very hot for some time after you unplug the unit. Always allow the printer to cool down for at least 15 minutes before performing any internal maintenance that brings you near the fusing rollers.

Most inkjet cartridges contain new nozzles and a new ink supply, which prevents problems caused by nozzles that have become clogged with dried ink. Like lasers, thermal inkjet printers also rely on a powerful heat source, so you should take precautions before touching the internal components.

Dot Matrix Printers

Dot matrix printers are more prone to collecting dirt and dust than any other type of printer. This is due both to the physical contact between the inked ribbon and the print head, and to the use of continuous feed paper. As the printer runs, a fabric ribbon turns within its cartridge to keep a freshly inked surface in front of the print head. This lateral movement of the ribbon, combined with the continuous high-speed back-and-forth motion of the pins within the print head, tends to produce an ink-saturated lint that can clog the print heads and smudge the printed characters. Film ribbons can help reduce these problems and provide better print quality, but at the cost of a shorter ribbon life.

Continuous feed paper presents another problem. This paper has perforated borders on both edges, with holes that the printer uses to pull the paper through the printer. Depending on the quality of the paper you purchase, some of the dots punched out to produce the holes may be left in the pad of paper. As the paper passes through the printer, these dots can be left behind, and can eventually interfere with the paper handling mechanism. Keep dot matrix printers clean by removing the dots and dust with canned air or a vacuum cleaner and swabbing the print heads regularly with alcohol.

Choosing the Best Paper

Both laser and inkjet printers use cut-sheet paper exclusively, and are therefore prone to paper handling problems such as paper jams and clumping (multiple sheets feeding at once). You can minimize these problems by making sure that you use paper that is intended for your printer type. This is especially true when you are printing on unusual media such as heavy card stock, adhesive labels, or transparencies.

Printer manufacturers usually specify a range of paper weights that the printer is designed to support, and exceeding these can affect the quality of your results. Even more dangerous, using labels or transparencies in a laser printer that are not designed for laser use can be catastrophic. These media are usually not capable of withstanding the heat generated by the fusing process, and may actually melt inside the printer, causing severe or irreparable damage.

It is also important to take precautions when storing your printer paper supply. Damp paper is one of the chief causes of paper jams, clumping, and bad toner coverage. Always store your paper in a cool, dry place, with the reams lying flat, and do not open a package until you are ready to use the paper. When you load paper into your printer, it's always a good idea to riffle through the pad first. This helps the individual pages to separate when the printer extracts them from the paper tray.

Common Printing Problems

You can avoid many printing problems with regular preventive maintenance procedures, but there are still likely to be occasions when you find that the output from your printer is not up to its usual standards or that the printer is not functioning at all. When you are faced with a printing problem, it can sometimes be difficult to determine whether the problem originates in your application, in the computer's printer driver, or in the printer hardware.

In many cases, you can apply standard troubleshooting methodology to printing problems. For example, if you experience the same printing problem when you generate a test page from the printer's control panel as when you print a document from your PC, then you can rule out the computer, the driver, and the printer connection as the source of the problem, and begin examining the printer. If you experience the same printing problem with different drivers, then you can probably rule out the driver as the cause (unless the manufacturer produced several versions of the driver with the same bug).

Consistency is also an important factor when troubleshooting printer problems. If one page in ten exhibits the problem, then you can generally rule out software as the cause, and begin looking at the hardware, such as the connecting cable and the printer.

The following sections examine some of the most commonly seen printer problems, categorizing them according to the source of the problem. However, these categories must be taken loosely, because some of the problems can have several different causes.

It's important to understand that none of the procedures described in the following sections should take the place of the maintenance and troubleshooting instructions provided with your printer. Your printer may use components and designs that differ substantially from those described in this chapter, and the manufacturer should always be the ultimate authority for hardware maintenance and problem solving procedures.

Printer Hardware Problems

Problems with the printer usually result from the consumables, such as toner and paper. If the toner cartridge is nearly empty, or if the printer's internal components become encrusted with loose toner, the quality of the print output can degrade in various ways. In the same way, paper that is damp, bent, wrinkled, or inserted into the tray improperly can cause myriad problems. You should always check these elements first before assuming that printer's internal hardware is at fault.

- *Fuzzy print.* On a laser printer, characters that are suddenly fuzzy or unclear are probably the result of using paper that is slightly damp. On an inkjet printer, fuzzy or smeary characters can result when you use various types of paper not specifically intended for inkjet printing.

- *Variable print density.* If, on a laser printer, you find that some areas of the page are darker than others, the problem is probably due to the distribution of the toner on the photoreceptor. The most common cause for this is uneven dispensation of the toner as its container empties. Removing the toner cartridge and shaking it from side to side redistributes the toner and should cause it to flow evenly. You can also use this technique to get a few more pages out of a toner cartridge after the printer has registered a "toner low" error. If your printer consistently produces pages with the same varied print density, the problem could be the printer's location. If the unit is not resting on a level surface, the toner can shift to one side of the cartridge, affecting the distribution of the toner on the page. It is also possible that your printer might have a light leak that is causing one area of the photoreceptor to be exposed to more ambient light than others. Moving the printer away from a bright light source can sometimes remedy this problem.

- *Dirty or damaged corotrons*. A laser printer's corotrons apply electrostatic charges to the photoreceptor and the paper. If the transfer corotron (which charges the paper) has clumps of toner or paper fragments on it, it can apply an uneven charge to the paper, and you may see faint or fuzzy white lines running vertically down your printed pages. All black or all white pages can be caused by a broken charger or transfer corotron (respectively). A toner cartridge that contains the photoreceptor drum typically includes the charger corotron as well, so replacing the cartridge can remedy some of these problems. You can also (gently!) clean a dirty corotron with a cotton swab or other material recommended by the manufacturer. The transfer corotron is usually built into the printer (and not the cartridge) and will require professional servicing if it is broken.

- *Sharp vertical white lines*. A sharp white line extending vertically down the entire length of your laser printed pages that does not go away when you shake the toner cartridge is probably caused by dirt or debris in the developer unit that is preventing the unit from evenly distributing the toner onto the photoreceptor. Again, if the toner cartridge includes the developer unit, replacing it is the simplest fix. If not, your printer may have a mechanism that enables you to remove the developer roller for cleaning, or even a tool designed to remove dirt from the roller while it is in place. It may also be possible to clean the roller by slipping the corner of a sheet of paper down the slots between the roller and the metal blades on either side of it.

- *Regularly spaced spots*. If your laser printed pages have a spot or spots that are consistently left unprinted, the cause may be a scratch or other flaw in the photoreceptor drum or a buildup of toner on the fusing roller. You can often tell the difference between these two problems by the distance between the spots on the page. If the spots occur less than three inches apart (vertically), then the problem is probably caused by the fusing roller. Because the photoreceptor drum has a larger diameter than the fusing roller, the spots it produces would be farther apart, or perhaps only one on a page. Replacing a toner cartridge that contains the photoreceptor drum and the fuser cleaning pad (an oil-impregnated pad that presses against the fuser roller to remove excess toner) should solve either of these problems. Otherwise, you will probably have to replace the drum assembly or the fuser cleaning pad separately. Some printers require professional servicing to replace the photoreceptor drum.

- *Gray print or gray background*. As the photoreceptor drum in a laser printer wears, it begins to hold less of a charge, and less toner adheres to the drum, resulting in printing that is gray rather than black. On printers that include the drum as part of the toner cartridge, this is not usually a problem because the drum is changed frequently. Printers that use the drum for longer periods of time often have a print density control that enables you to gradually increase the amount of toner dispensed by the developer unit as the drum wears. Eventually, however, you will have to replace the drum; at that point, you must lower the print density back to its original setting, or you may find that your prints have a gray background because the developer is applying too much toner to the photoreceptor drum.

- *Loose toner.* If the pages emerging from your laser printer have toner on them that you can rub or brush off, then they have not been properly fused. Usually, this means that the fuser is not reaching the temperature needed to completely melt the toner and fuse it to the page. A problem of this type nearly always requires professional service.

- *Solid vertical black line.* A vertical black line running down the entire length of several consecutive pages is a sign that your laser printer's toner cartridge may be nearly empty. Shaking the cartridge can usually eliminate the problem, but eventually you will have to replace it.

- *Frequent paper jams.* Paper handling can be a delicate part of the printer mechanism that is affected by several elements. Printer jams can result when paper is loaded incorrectly into the feed tray, when the paper is damp or wrinkled, or when you use the wrong kind of paper. Occasional jams are normal, but frequent jamming can indicate that you are using paper stock that is too heavy or textured in such a way as to be improper for laser printing. Jams can also result when the printer is not resting on a level surface.

- *Blank pages appear between printed pages.* Paper that is damp, wrinkled, or too tightly compressed can cause two or more sheets to run through the printer at one time. To prevent this, store your paper in a cool, dry place, don't stack the reams too high, and riffle through the stack of paper before you insert it in the feed tray.

- *Memory overflow/printer overrun errors.* These errors indicate that the job you sent to the printer was too complex or consisted of more data than its buffers could handle. This can be caused by the use of too many fonts, too dense text, or graphics that are too complex. You can resolve this problem by simplifying your document or installing more memory in the printer.

Connection Problems

- *Gibberish.* If your page printer produces page after page of seemingly random "garbage" characters, the problem is probably that the printer has failed to recognize the PDL used by the print job. For example, a PostScript print job must begin with the two characters %!. If the printer fails to receive these characters, all the remaining data in the job prints as ASCII. This kind of problem is usually the result of some sort of communications failure between the PC and the printer. Check that the cable connections are secure and the cable is not damaged. If the problem occurs consistently, it may be the result of an improperly configured port in the PC, particularly of you are using a serial port. Check the port's parameters in the operating system. A serial port should be configured to use 8 data bits, 1 stop bit, and no parity (N-8-1).

- *Printer not available error.* When Windows 9x does not receive a response from a printer over the designated port, it switches the driver to offline mode, which enables you to print jobs and store them in the print spooler until the printer is available. The printer may be unavailable because the parallel or serial port is incorrectly configured, the printer cable is faulty, or the printer is turned off, offline, or malfunctioning. A malfunctioning port can be caused by an IRQ conflict (LPT1 uses IRQ 7, and COM 1 and COM 2 use IRQs 4 and 3, by default) or in the case of a serial port, incorrect start/stop/parity bit settings could be the culprit.

- *Printer does not notify Windows when it is out of paper, jammed, or other problem.* This is usually indicative of a communications problem between the printer and the PC. Check the printer cable and its connections at both ends. Some manufacturers recommend that you use a cable that is compliant with the IEEE 1284 standard.

- *Intermittent or failed communications or a partial print job followed by gibberish.* Interruptions in the communication between the computer and the printer can cause data to be lost in transit, resulting in partial print jobs or no print output at all. Aside from a faulty cable, these problems can result from the use of additional hardware between the printer port and the printer. Switchboxes used to share a printer among several computers and peripherals that share the parallel port with the printer (such as CD-ROM drives) are particularly prone to causing problems such as this.

- *Port is busy error or printer goes offline.* These errors can occur when an ECP sends data to a printer at a rate faster than it can handle. You can remedy the problem by using the Windows 9x System Control Panel to load the standard printer port driver instead of the ECP driver.

Driver Problems

The best way to determine whether a printer driver is causing a particular problem is to stop using it. If a problem printing from a Windows application disappears when you print a directory listing by issuing the DIR > LPT1 command from the DOS prompt, then you can safely say that you need to install a new printer driver. Other driver problems include the following:

- *Form feed light comes on but nothing prints.* This indicates that the printer has less than a full page of data in its buffer and the computer has failed to send a form feed command to eject the page. This is a common occurrence when you print from a DOS prompt or application without the benefit of a printer driver, but it can also be the result of a malfunctioning driver. Some drivers (particularly PostScript drivers) provide an option to send an extra form feed at the end of every print job. Otherwise, you must eject the page manually from the printer's control panel.

- *Incorrect fonts printing.* Virtually all laser printers have a selection of fonts built into the printer, and by default most drivers use these fonts in place of similar TrueType or PostScript Type 1 fonts installed on the computer. Sometimes there can be noticeable differences between the two fonts, however, and the printed text may not look exactly like that on the screen. Slight size discrepancies between the fonts can also cause the page breaks in the printed output to differ from those on the screen.

Application Problems

■ *Margins out of range error.* Most laser printers have a border around all four sides of the page of approximately one third of an inch where the toner cannot reach. If you configure an application to use margins smaller than this border, some drivers can generate this error message, whereas others simply truncate the output to fit the maximum printable page size. If your application or driver does not generate an error message and give you an opportunity to enter a correct margin setting, be sure to check your printer manual to find the allowable margin settings before printing.

Chapter 15

Portable PCs

Portable computers, like their desktop counterparts, have evolved enormously since the days when the word *portable* could refer to a desktop-sized case with a handle on it. Today, portable systems can rival the performance of their desktop counterparts in nearly every way. It is to the point that many systems are now being marketed as "desktop replacements," which companies are providing to traveling employees as their primary systems. This chapter examines the types of portable computers available and the technologies designed specifically for use in mobile systems.

Portables started out as suitcase-sized systems that differed from desktops mainly in that all the components, including the monitor, were installed into a single case. Compaq was among the first to market portable computers like these in the 1980s, and although their size, weight, and appearance were almost laughable when compared to today's portables, they were cutting-edge technology for the time. The components themselves were not very different from those in standard computers. Most portable systems are now approximately the size of the notebook they are often named for, and are built using the clamshell design that has become an industry standard, with nearly every component developed specifically for use in mobile systems.

Portable computers have settled into a number of distinct roles that now determine the size and capabilities of the systems available. Traveling users have specific requirements of portable computers, and the added weight and expense incurred by additional features makes it less likely for a user to carry a system more powerful than is needed.

Form Factors

There are three basic form factors that describe most of the portable computers on the market today: laptops, notebooks, and subnotebooks. The definitions of the three types are fluid, however, with the options available on some systems causing particular models to ride the cusp of two categories.

The categories are based primarily on size and weight, but these factors have a natural relationship to the capabilities of the system, because a larger case obviously can fit more into it. The three form factors are described in the following sections.

Laptops

As the original name coined for the clamshell-type portable computer, the laptop is the largest of the three basic form factors. Typically, a laptop system weighs seven pounds or more, and is approximately 9×12×2 inches in size, although the larger screens now arriving on the market are causing all portable system sizes to increase. Originally the smallest possible size for a computer, laptops have today become the high-end machines, offering features and performance that are comparable to a desktop system.

Indeed, many laptops are being positioned in the market either as desktop replacements or as multimedia systems suitable for delivering presentations on the road. Because of their greater weight, laptops are typically used by salespeople and other travelers who require the features they provide. However, many high-performance laptops are now being issued to users as their sole computer, even if they only travel from the office to the home. Large displays, 16M or more of RAM, and hard drives up to 2G in size are all but ubiquitous, with many systems now carrying CD-ROM drives, onboard speakers, and connectivity options that enable the use of external display, storage, and sound systems.

To use them as a desktop replacement, you can equip many laptops with a docking station that functions as the user's "home base," enabling connection to a network and the use of a full-size monitor and keyboard. For a person who travels frequently, this arrangement often works better than separate desktop and portable systems, on which data must continually be kept in sync. Naturally, you pay a premium for all this functionality. Cutting-edge laptop systems can now cost as much as $4,000 to $6,000 or more, at least twice the price of a comparable desktop.

Notebooks

A notebook system is designed to be somewhat smaller than a laptop in nearly every way: size, weight, features, and price. Weighing five to seven pounds, notebooks typically have smaller and less capable displays and lack the high-end multimedia functions of laptops, but they need not be stripped-down machines. Many notebooks have hard drive and memory configurations comparable to laptops, and some are equipped with CD-ROM drives and sound capabilities.

Designed to function as an adjunct to a desktop system rather than a replacement, a notebook probably won't impress your clients but can be a completely serviceable road machine. Notebooks typically have a wide array of options, as they are targeted at a wider audience, from the power user that can't quite afford the top-of-the-line laptop, to the bargain hunter that requires only basic services. Prices can range from under $2,000 to over $4,000.

Subnotebooks

Subnotebooks are substantially smaller than both notebooks and laptops, and are intended for users who must enter and work with data on the road, as well as connect to the office network. Weighing four to five pounds, and often less than an inch thick, the subnotebook is intended for the traveler that feels overburdened by the larger machines, and doesn't need their high-end capabilities.

Usually, the first component omitted in a subnotebook design is the internal floppy drive, although some include external units. You also will not find CD-ROM drives and other bulky hardware components. However, many subnotebooks do include large, high-quality displays, plenty of hard drive space, and a full-size keyboard (by portable standards).

As is common in the electronics world, devices become more inexpensive as they get smaller, but only up to a certain point at which small size becomes a commodity and prices begin to go up. Some subnotebooks are intended (and priced) for the high-end market, such as for the executive who uses the system for little else but e-mail and scheduling, but wants a lightweight, elegant, and impressive-looking system. Subnotebooks can cost as much as $4,000. Others are much cheaper.

Portable System Designs

Obviously, portable systems are designed to be smaller and lighter than desktops, and much of the development work that has been done on desktop components has certainly contributed to this end. The 2 1/2-inch hard drives typically used in portables today are a direct extension of the size reductions that have occurred in all hard drives over the past few years. However, two other issues have created a need for the development of new technologies specifically for portable systems; those issues are power and heat.

Environmental concerns are leading to the development of more efficient power management technologies, but, obviously, operating a computer from a battery imposes system limitations that designers of desktop systems never had to consider before the advent of portable systems. What's more, the demand for additional features like CD-ROM drives, larger displays, and ever faster processors has increased the power drain on the typical system enormously. The problem of conserving power and increasing the system's battery life is typically addressed in three ways:

- *Low power components.* Nearly all the components in today's portable systems are specifically designed to use less power than their desktop counterparts.

- *Increased battery efficiency.* Newer battery technologies like lithium ion, while not keeping up with the power requirements of increasingly loaded systems, are making power supplies more consistent and reliable.

- *Power management.* Operating systems and utilities that turn off specific system components, such as disk drives when they are not in use, can greatly increase battery life.

Perhaps a more serious problem than battery life in portable systems is heat. The moving parts in a computer, such as disk drives, generate heat through friction, which must somehow be dissipated. In desktop systems, this is accomplished by using fans to continuously ventilate the empty spaces inside the system.

The worst culprit by far, however, as far as heat is concerned, is the system processor. When they were first released, the amount of heat generated by Intel's 80486 and Pentium processors was a problem even in desktop systems. Heat sinks and tiny fans mounted on top of the CPU became standard components in most systems.

Because many portable systems are now being designed as replacements for desktops, users are not willing to compromise on processing power. Even the newest and fastest processors designed for desktop systems, like the Pentium II, are quickly adapted for use in mobile systems. However, for reasons of power consumption, noise, and space, fans in portable computers must be much smaller or omitted entirely, and there is very little empty space within the case for ventilation.

To address this problem, Intel has created special methods for packaging its mobile processors that are designed to keep heat output to a minimum. Other components are also designed to withstand the heat within a portable computer, which is usually greater than that of a desktop, in any case.

Upgrading and Repairing Portables

The portable systems manufactured today are generally as upgradable and repairable as traditional desktop systems. In fact, the process of replacing a device is often simpler than on a desktop, because portable systems typically use modular components with snap-in connectors that eliminate the need for ribbon cables, mounting rails, and separate electrical connections. Thus, common upgrades like adding memory and swapping out a hard drive can usually be accomplished in seconds.

The problem with replacing components in portables is that the hardware tends to be much less generic in portable systems than it is in desktops. Except for PC Cards, which are interchangeable by definition, and in some cases hard drives, purchasing a component that is not specifically intended for use in your exact system model can be risky.

In some cases, these compatibility problems are a matter of simple logistics. Portable system manufacturers jam a great deal of machinery into a very small case, and sometimes a new device just will not fit in the space left by the old one. This is particularly true of devices that must be accessible from the outside of the case, like CD-ROM and floppy drives. Keyboards and monitors, the most easily replaceable of desktop components, are so completely integrated into the case of a portable system they may not be practically removed at all.

In other cases, your upgrade path may be deliberately limited by the options available in the system BIOS. For example, manufacturers may limit the hard drive types supported by the system to force you to buy a replacement drive from them (at an inflated price), and not a third party. This is something you should check when shopping for a portable system by asking whether the BIOS is upgradable and finding out how much the vendor charges for replacement components.

Most of the time, components for portable systems are sold by referencing the system model number, even when third parties are involved. If you look through a catalog for desktop memory, for example, you see parts listed generically by attributes like chip speed, form factor, and parity or non-parity. The memory listings for portable systems, on the other hand, will very likely consist of a series of systems manufacturers' names and model numbers, plus the amount of memory in the module.

There are always exceptions to the rule, of course. It is even possible to purchase a basic laptop case and populate it with individual components from various manufacturers. However, purchasing compatible components that fit together properly is certainly more of a challenge than it is for a desktop system.

> **Note**
>
> Generally speaking, purchasing a preassembled portable system from a reputable manufacturer is strongly recommended, as is purchasing only replacement components that are advertised as being specifically designed for your system.

Portable System Hardware

From a technical standpoint, some of the components used in portable systems are very similar to those in desktop computers, while others are completely different. The following sections examine the various subsystems found in portable computers and how they differ from their desktop counterparts.

Displays

Perhaps the most obvious difference between a portable system and a desktop is the display screen. Gone is the box with an emitter bombarding a concave glass tube with electrons. In its place is a flat screen, which is less than half an inch thick. This is called an *LCD*, or *liquid crystal display*. Virtually all the screens in portable systems today are color, although monochromes were at one point the industry standard, just as in standard monitors.

An LCD consists of two sheets of a flexible, polarizing material with a layer of liquid crystal solution between them. If you press gently on an LCD screen while it is lit, you can see how it gives slightly, displacing the liquid inside. When an electric current is passed through the liquid, the crystals align and become semi-permeable to light.

The display is usually the single most expensive component in a portable system, often costing the manufacturer $1,000 or more. In fact, it is sometimes more economical to replace the entire computer rather than have a broken display replaced. In the first laptops with color screens, the display was a poor replacement for a standard VGA monitor. Today's portable screens are much improved, with some high-end displays even rivaling the performance of a good monitor and providing excellent performance, suitable even for graphic-intensive applications like bitmap editing and videoconferencing. In fact, there are even LCD displays now being manufactured for use with non-portable systems.

The LCD display in a portable system is designed to operate at a specific resolution. This is because the size of the pixels on an LCD panel cannot be changed. On a desktop system, the signal output from the video adapter can change the resolution on the monitor, thus changing the number of pixels created on the screen. Obviously, as you switch from a resolution of 640×480 to 800×600, the pixels must be smaller to fit into the same space.

An LCD panel, on the other hand, should be thought of as a grid ruled off to a specified resolution, with transistors controlling the color displayed by each individual pixel. The arrangement of the transistors defines the two major types of LCD displays used in portable systems today: dual scan and active matrix.

Dual Scan (Passive Matrix) Displays. The *dual scan* display, sometimes called a *passive matrix* display, has an array of transistors running down the x and y axes of two sides of the screen. The number of transistors determines the screen's resolution. For example, a dual scan display with 640 transistors along the x axis and 480 along the y creates a grid like that shown in Figure 15.1. Each pixel on the screen is controlled by the two transistors representing its coordinates on the x and y axes.

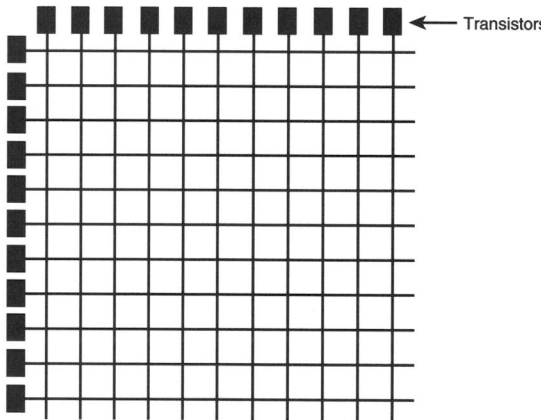

FIG. 15.1 Dual scan LCD displays use a combination of two transistors on intersecting axes to control the color of each pixel.

If a transistor in a dual scan display should fail, a whole line of pixels is disabled, causing a black line across the screen (either horizontally or vertically). There is no solution for this problem other than to replace the display or just live with it. The term *dual scan* comes from the fact that the processor redraws half of the screen at a time, which speeds up the refresh process somewhat.

Dual scan displays are generally inferior to active matrix screens. Dual scan displays tend to be dimmer, because the pixels work by modifying the properties of reflected light (either room light or, more likely, a white light source behind the screen), rather than generating their own. Dual scan panels are also prone to ghost images and are difficult to view from an angle, making it hard for two or more people to view the same screen.

However, newer passive matrix technologies like *color super-twist nematic* (CSTN), *double-layer super-twist nematic* (DSTN), and especially *high-performance addressing* (HPA) screens have come a long way in making passive matrix displays a viable, lower-cost alternative to active matrix technology. These newer displays offer better response rates and contrast—problems that plagued many of the earlier display types—but they are still not as sharp or as fast as an active matrix screen.

Of course, passive matrix displays are also far less expensive than active matrix screens. The drawbacks of a passive matrix display are most noticeable during video-intensive applications, such as presentations, full-color graphics, video, or fast-moving games. For computing tasks that consist largely of reading words on the screen, like word processing and e-mail, the passive matrix display is quite serviceable, even for long periods of time.

The standard size for a dual scan display is 10 1/2 inches (measured diagonally), running at 640×480, but there are now some systems with 12.1-inch displays that run at 800×600 resolution. If you are familiar with the dual scan display of an older portable, you will find that today's models are greatly improved.

Active Matrix Displays. An active matrix display differs from a dual scan in that it contains at least one transistor for every pixel on the screen, rather than just at the edges. The transistors are arranged on a grid of conductive material, with each connected to a horizontal and a vertical member (see Figure 15.2). Selected voltages are applied by electrodes at the perimeter of the grid to address each pixel individually.

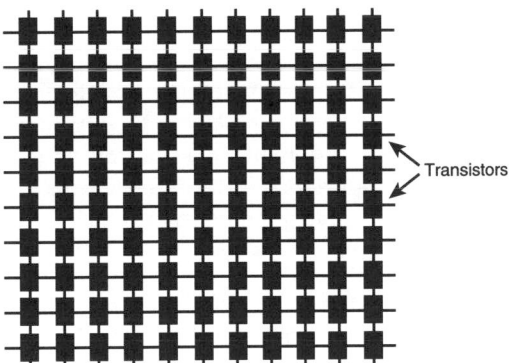

FIG. 15.2 Active matrix LCD displays contain a transistor for each pixel on the screen. The pixels generate their own light for a brighter display.

Most active matrix displays use a *thin film transistor* (TFT) array. TFT is a method for packaging one to four transistors per pixel within a flexible material that is the same size and shape as the display, so the transistors for each pixel lie directly behind the liquid crystal cells they control.

Two different TFT manufacturing processes account for most of the active matrix displays on the market today: hydrogenated amorphous silicon (a-Si) and low temperature polysilicon (p-Si). These processes differ primarily in their cost. At first, most TFT displays were manufactured using the a-Si process because it required lower temperatures (less than 400 degrees Celsius) than the p-Si process of the time. Now, lower temperature p-Si manufacturing processes are making this method an economically viable alternative to p-Si.

Although a TFT display has a great many transistors—from 480,000 to 1,920,000 for an 800×600 display—each pixel does not have its own signal connection. Instead, voltages are applied through connections for each row and column, much like the transistors in a passive matrix display.

Because every pixel is individually powered, each one generates its own light of the appropriate color, creating a display that is much brighter and more vivid than a dual scan panel. The viewing angle is also greater, allowing multiple viewers to gather around the screen, and refreshes are faster and crisper, without the fuzziness of the dual scans, even in the case of games or full-motion video.

On the downside, it should be no surprise that, with 480,000 or more transistors rather than 1,400 (on an 800×600 screen), an active matrix display requires a lot more power than a dual scan. It drains batteries faster and costs a great deal more, as well.

With all these transistors, it is not uncommon for failures to occur, resulting in displays with one or more "dead pixels," due to malfunctioning transistors. Unlike a dual scan display, in which the failure of a single transistor causes an immediate and obvious flaw, a single black pixel is far less noticeable. However, many buyers feel (and rightly so) that a computer costing thousands of dollars should be perfect, and have attempted to return systems to the manufacturer solely for this reason.

Because all the transistors of a TFT display are integrated into a single component, there is no way to remedy a dead pixel except by replacing the entire transistor array. Because this is one of the most expensive components in a portable system, many portable computer manufacturers refuse to accept returns of systems for less than a set number of bad pixels. This is another part of the vendor's purchasing policy that you should check before ordering a system with an active matrix display.

The 12.1-inch (diagonal) active matrix screen has become a standard on many portable systems, running at a resolution of 800×600 or even 1,024×768. High-end systems now include TFT screens as large as 14.1 inches. Many portable systems now also include PCI bus video adapters with 2M of RAM, providing extra speed, even at 16- or 24-bit color depths. A good TFT display and portable PCI adapter rival the quality and performance of a quality monitor and video adapter in a desktop system. In fact, a 12.1-inch TFT display (which, unlike most conventional monitors, describes the actual size of the image) generally has a better picture quality and usability than a similarly sized CRT-type display.

> **Note**
>
> Another flat-screen technology, called the *gas plasma display*, has been used in large display screens and a few portables. Plasma displays provide a CRT-quality picture on a thin flat screen using two glass panes filled with a neon/xenon gas mixture. Unfortunately, the displays require far more power than LCDs and have never become a practical alternative for the portable computer market.

Screen Resolution. The screen resolution of a portable system's display can be an important factor in your purchasing decision. If you are accustomed to working on desktop systems running at 800×600 or 1,024×768 pixels or more, you will find a 640×480 laptop screen to be very restrictive. Remember that an LCD screen's resolution is determined as much by the screen hardware as by the drivers and the amount of video memory installed in the system.

Some portables can use a *virtual screen* arrangement to provide an 800×600 (or larger) display on a 640×480 pixel screen. The larger display is maintained in video memory while the actual screen displays only the portion that fits into a 640×480 window (see Figure 15.3). When you move the cursor to the edge of the screen, the image pans, moving the 640×480 window around within the 800×600 display. The effect is difficult to get used to, rather like a "scan and pan" videotape of a wide-screen movie. The most serious problem with this arrangement is that some manufacturers have advertised it as an 800×600 display, without being more clear about its actual nature.

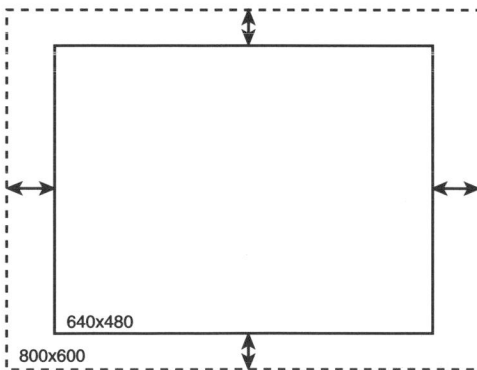

FIG. 15.3 A virtual screen lets you use a small display to view a portion of a larger screen.

Color depth, on the other hand, is affected by the amount of video memory in the system, just as in a desktop system. To operate any LCD screen in 16- or 24-bit color mode, you must have sufficient video memory available. Portables typically have the video adapter hardware permanently installed on the motherboard, leaving little hope for a video memory upgrade. There are, however, a few PC Card video adapters that you can use to connect to an external monitor and increase the system's video capabilities.

◀◀ See "RAM Calculations," p. 527

Processors

As with desktop systems, the majority of portables use Intel multiprocessors, and the creation of chips designed specifically for portable systems is a major part of the company's development effort. Intel has a complete line of Pentium processors optimized for mobile or portable use. Intel has focused on mobile processors since the 386SL, and has dramatically expanded mobile processor technology and features with the Pentium and the Pentium II. As with most portable system components, the main concerns with the mobile processors are reducing their size, power requirements, and heat generation.

Virtually all new portable systems sold today contain one of the Pentium family of processors, either a Pentium, a Pentium with MMX technology, or a Pentium II. (There are no mobile versions of the Pentium Pro.) The mobile versions of these processors have the same features and architecture as the full-sized models; they differ mainly in their packaging and their power consumption. The processor's packaging defines the type of casing used to enclose and protect the internal circuitry of the chip, as well as the type of connector that provides the processor's interface with the motherboard.

Mobile Pentium. The main idea for mobile processors is to shrink them as small as possible, which then lets them run at lower voltages. This saves power. The 200MHz- and 233MHz mobile Pentium processors with MMX technology (codenamed Tillamook) were the first products manufactured using Intel's advanced 0.25 micron process technology now used for the Pentium II, as well. Since then, Intel has added 266MHz and 166MHz mobile Pentium/MMX processors also made on the 0.25 micron process. Mobile processors in general provide notebook manufacturers with a unique opportunity to offer users better battery life along with features and functionality that are on par with desktop systems.

The 0.25 micron manufacturing process and Intel's Voltage Reduction Technology decrease the core voltage from 2.45 volts to 1.8 volts (2.0 volts for the 266MHz version) and the I/O interface from 3.3 volts to 2.5 volts, relative to previous generation processors. Intel's new 0.25 micron manufacturing process increases chip speed up to 60%, while reducing power consumption (up to 53%) when compared to 166MHz mobile Pentium processors with MMX technology on the 0.35 micron process. This reduction in voltages allows for higher speeds with less battery power use and less heat production. Typical power consumption can be reduced from 7.7 watts for 166MHz mobile Pentium processors with MMX technology on the 0.35 process to 3.9 watts for the 233MHz processor. These improvements represent nearly a 50% decrease in power consumption.

◀◀ See "Pentium," p. 105

◄◄ See "Pentium-MMX Processors," p. 113

> **Tip**
>
> The 166MHz chip is the slowest Pentium/MMX processor that Intel has manufactured using the 0.25 micron process, and the fastest one manufactured using the 0.35 micron process. If you consider buying a system based on this processor, try to get the 0.25 micron version. The other 0.35 Pentium/MMX processors all run at slower speeds (120MHz, 133MHz, and 150MHz), while the other 0.25 micron Pentium MMX chips run faster, at 200MHz, 233MHz, and 266MHz.

Intel also continues to manufacture regular (non-MMX) Pentium chips at speeds of 75-, 100-, 120-, 133-, and 150MHz for use in low-end portable systems. These chips also use Voltage Reduction Technology (VRT), which means that they draw the standard 3.3v from the motherboard, but internally they operate on only 2.9v (3.1v for the 150MHz model). Although not as dramatic a reduction as that evidenced in the 0.25 micron process chips, VRT still reduces the overall power consumption and heat production of these processors.

Mobile Pentium II. On April 2, 1998, Intel announced the first mobile Pentium II processors. Running at 233MHz and 266MHz, these processors are also manufactured using the 0.25 micron process. With a core voltage of 1.7v and an I/O buffer voltage of 1.8v, they run at even lower voltage levels than their Pentium/MMX counterparts. Although at 8.6 watts, a 266MHz Pentium II consumes more power overall than a Pentium/MMX running at the same speed, you must take into account that the Pentium II includes an integrated Level 2 cache, while the Pentium/MMX, at 4.5 watts, does not.

As with the other Pentium processors, the mobile versions of the Pentium II sacrifice none of the features of the full desktop versions and are expected to be 30%–35% faster than a comparable 0.25 micron Pentium/MMX.

◄◄ See "Pentium II," p. 140

Table 15.1 lists the speed, manufacturing process, and voltage specifications for the mobile Pentium, Pentium/MMX, and Pentium II processors currently manufactured by Intel.

Table 15.1   Intel Mobile Processor Specifications

Processor Voltage	Speed	Mfg. Process	Core Voltage	I/O Buffer
Pentium	75MHz	0.35 micron	2.9v	3.3v
Pentium	100MHz	0.35 micron	2.9v	3.3v
Pentium	120MHz	0.35 micron	2.9v	3.3v
Pentium	133MHz	0.35 micron	2.9v	3.3v

(continues)

Table 15.1	Intel Mobile Processor Specifications Continued			
Processor Voltage	**Speed**	**Mfg. Process**	**Core Voltage**	**I/O Buffer**
Pentium	150MHz	0.35 micron	3.1v	3.3v
Pentium/MMX	120MHz	0.35 micron	2.45v	3.3v
Pentium/MMX	133MHx	0.35 micron	2.45v	3.3v
Pentium/MMX	150MHx	0.35 micron	2.45v	3.3v
Pentium/MMX	166MHx	0.35 micron	2.45v	3.3v
Pentium/MMX	166MHx	0.25 micron	1.8v	2.5v
Pentium/MMX	200MHx	0.25 micron	1.8v	2.5v
Pentium/MMX	233MHx	0.25 micron	1.8v	2.5v
Pentium/MMX	266MHx	0.25 micron	2.0v	2.5v
Pentium II	233MHz	0.25 micron	1.7v	1.8v
Pentium II	266MHz	0.25 micron	1.7v	1.8v

Mobile Processor Steppings. As with Intel's desktop processor, the chips of the mobile processor line undergo continual development, and are modified in the form of steppings that incorporate corrections and refinements into the hardware manufacturing process. Tables 15.2 and 15.3 list the steppings for the mobile Pentium and Pentium/MMX processor lines, respectively.

Table 15.2	Mobile Pentium Processor Versions and Steppings						
Type	**Family**	**Model**	**Stepping**	**Mfg. Stepping**	**Speed**	**Spec. Number**	**Comments**
0	5	2	1	B1	75-50	Q0601	TCP
0	5	2	2	B3	75-50	Q0606	TCP
0	5	2	2	B3	75-50	SX951	TCP
0/2	5	2	4	B5	75-50	Q0704	TCP
0	5	2	4	B5	75-50	SX975	TCP
0	5	2	5	C2	75-50	Q0725	TCP
0	5	2	5	C2	75-50	SK079	TCP
0	5	2	5	mA1	75-50	Q0686	VRT,TCP
0	5	2	5	mA1	75-50	Q0689	VRT
0	5	2	5	mA1	90-60	Q0694	VRT,TCP
0	5	2	5	mA1	90-60	Q0695	VRT
0	5	2	5	mA1	75-50	SK089	VRT,TCP
0	5	2	5	mA1	75-50	SK091	VRT
0	5	2	5	mA1	90-60	SK090	VRT,TCP
0	5	2	5	mA1	90-60	SK092	VRT
0	5	2	B	mcB1	100-66	Q0884	VRT,TCP
0	5	2	B	mcB1	120-60	Q0779	VRT,TCP

Type	Family	Model	Stepping	Mfg. Stepping	Speed	Spec. Number	Comments
0	5	2	B	mcB1	120-60	Q0808	
0	5	2	B	mcB1	100-66	SY029	VRT,TCP
0	5	2	B	mcB1	120-60	SK113	VRT,TCP
0	5	2	B	mcB1	120-60	SK118	VRT,TCP
0	5	2	B	mcB1	120-60	SX999	
0	5	7	0	mA4	75-50	Q0848	VRT,TCP
0	5	7	0	mA4	75-50	Q0851	VRT
0	5	7	0	mA4	90-60	Q0849	VRT,TCP
0	5	7	0	mA4	90-60	Q0852	VRT
0	5	7	0	mA4	100-66	Q0850	VRT,TCP
0	5	7	0	mA4	100-66	Q0853	VRT
0	5	7	0	mA4	75-50	SK119	VRT,TCP
0	5	7	0	mA4	75-50	SK122	VRT
0	5	7	0	mA4	90-60	SK120	VRT,TCP
0	5	7	0	mA4	90-60	SK123	VRT
0	5	7	0	mA4	100-66	SK121	VRT,TCP
0	5	7	0	mA4	100-66	SK124	VRT
0	5	2	C	mcC0	100-66	Q0887	VRT,TCP
0	5	2	C	mcC0	120-60	Q0879	VRT,TCP
0	5	2	C	mcC0	120-60	Q0880	3.1v
0	5	2	C	mcC0	133-66	Q0881	VRT,TCP
0	5	2	C	mcC0	133-66	Q0882	3.1v
0	5	2	C	mcC0	150-60	Q024	VRT,TCP
0	5	2	C	mcC0	150-60	Q0906	TCP,3.1v
0	5	2	C	mcC0	150-60	Q040	VRT
0	5	2	C	mcC0	75-50	SY056	VRT/TCP
0	5	2	C	mcC0	100-66	SY020	VRT/TCP
0	5	2	C	mcC0	100-66	SY046	3.1v
0	5	2	C	mcC0	120-60	SY021	VRT,TCP
0	5	2	C	mcC0	120-60	SY027	3.1v
0	5	2	C	mcC0	120-60	SY030	
0	5	2	C	mcC0	133-66	SY019	VRT,TCP
0	5	2	C	mcC0	133-66	SY028	3.1v
0	5	2	C	mcC0	150-60	SY061	VRT,TCP
0	5	2	C	mcC0	150-60	SY043	TCP,3.1v
0	5	2	C	mcC0	150-60	SY058	VRT
0	5	2	6	E0	75-50	Q0846	TCP
0	5	2	6	E0	75-50	SY009	TCP

Table 15.3   Mobile Pentium MMX Processor Versions and Steppings

Type	Family	Model	Stepping	Mfg. Stepping	Speed	Spec. Number	Comments
0	5	4	4	mxA3	150-60	Q016	ES,TCP,2.285V
0	5	4	4	mxA3	150-60	Q061	ES,PPGA,2.285V
0	5	4	4	mxA3	166-66	Q017	ES,TCP,2.285V
0	5	4	4	mxA3	166-66	Q062	ES,PPGA,2.285V
0	5	4	4	mxA3	150-60	SL22G	TCP,2.285V
0	5	4	4	mxA3	150-60	SL246	PPGA,2.285V
0	5	4	4	mxA3	166-66	SL22F	TCP,2.285V
0	5	4	4	mxA3	166-66	SL23Z	PPGA,2.285V
0	5	4	3	mxB1	120-60	Q230	ES,TCP,2.2v
0	5	4	3	mxB1	133-66	Q130	ES,TCP,2.285V
0	5	4	3	mxB1	133-66	Q129	ES,PPGA,2.285V
0	5	4	3	mxB1	150-60	Q116	ES,TCP,2.285V
0	5	4	3	mxB1	150-60	Q128	ES,PPGA,2.285V
0	5	4	3	mxB1	166-66	Q115	ES,TCP,2.285V
0	5	4	3	mxB1	166-66	Q127	ES,PPGA,2.285V
0	5	4	3	mxB1	133-66	SL27D	TCP, 2.285V
0	5	4	3	mxB1	133-66	SL27C	PPGA,2.285V
0	5	4	3	mxB1	150-60	SL26U	TCP,2.285V
0	5	4	3	mxB1	150-60	SL27B	PPGA,2.285V
0	5	4	3	mxB1	166-66	SL26T	TCP,2.285V
0	5	4	3	mxB1	166-66	SL27A	PPGA,2.285V
0	5	8	1	myA0	166-66	Q255	TCP,1.8v
0	5	8	1	myA0	200-66	Q146	TCP,1.8v
0	5	8	1	myA0	233-66	Q147	TCP,1.8v
0	5	8	1	myA0	200-66	SL28P	TCP,1.8v
0	5	8	1	myA0	233-66	SL28Q	TCP,1.8v
0	5	8	1	myA0	266-66	Q250	TCP,2.0v

ES = Engineering Sample. These chips were not sold through normal channels, but were designed for development and testing purposes.

STP = The cB1 stepping is logically equivalent to the C2 step, but on a different manufacturing process. The mcB1 step is logically equivalent to the cB1 step (except it does not support DP, APIC, or FRC). The mcB1, mA1, mA4, and mcC0 steps also use Intel's VRT (Voltage Reduction Technology), and are available in the TCP or SPGA package, primarily to support mobile applications. The mxA3 is logically equivalent to the xA3 stepping (except it does not support DP or APIC).

TCP = Tape Carrier Package

PPGA = Plastic Pin Grid Array

VRT = Voltage Reduction Technology

2.285v = This is a mobile Pentium processor with MMX technology with a core operating voltage of 2.285v–2.665v.

1.8v = This is a mobile Pentium processor with MMX technology with a core operating voltage of 1.665v–1.935v and an I/O operating voltage of 2.375v–2.625v.

2.2v = This is a mobile Pentium processor with MMX technology with a core operating voltage of 2.10v–2.34v.

2.0v = This is a mobile Pentium Processor with MMX technology with a core operating voltage of 1.850v–2.150v and an I/O operating voltage of 2.375v–2.625v.

Table 15.4 lists the steppings for mobile Pentium II processors in both the mobile module and mobile mini-cartridge forms.

Table 15.4 Mobile Pentium II Processor Steppings										
Type	Family	Model	Stepping	Core Stepping	L1 Size (K)	TagRAM/ Stepping	S-Spec	ECC/ Non-ECC	Speed (MHz) Core/Bus	Notes
0	6	5	0	mdA0	512	T6P/A3	SL2KH	ECC	233/66	MC,1.7v
0	6	5	0	mdA0	512	T6P/A3	SL2KJ	ECC	266/66	MC,1.7v
0	6	5	0	mmdA0	512	T6P/A3	PMD233 05001AA	ECC	233/66	MMO,1.7v
0	6	5	0	mmdA0	512	T6P/A3	PMD266 05001AA	ECC	266/66	MMO,1.7v

1.7v = Core processor voltage is 1.7v for these mobile Pentium processors.
MC = Mobile cartridge Pentium II processor.
MMO = Mobile Pentium II processor mounted in a mobile module including the 440BX North Bridge.

◀◀ See "Pentium Processor Models and Steppings," p. 117

Mobile Processor Packaging

The heat generated by Pentium processors has been a concern since the first chips were released. In desktop systems, the heat problem is addressed, to a great extent, by computer case manufacturers. The use of multiple cooling fans and better internal layout designs can keep air flowing through the system to cool the processor, which is usually equipped with its own fan and heat sink.

For developers of portable systems, however, not as much can be accomplished with the case arrangement. So it was up to Intel to address the problem in the packaging of the chip. At the same time, users became increasingly unwilling to compromise on the clock speed of the processors in portable systems. Running a Pentium at 133Mhz or 166MHz requires more power and generates even more heat than the 75MHz Pentiums that were originally designed for mobile use.

Tape Carrier Packaging. Intel's solution to the size and heat problems for Pentium processors is the *tape carrier package (TCP)*, a method of packaging processors for use in portable systems that reduces the size, the power consumed, and the heat generated by the chip. A Pentium mounted onto a motherboard using TCP is much smaller and lighter than the standard SPGA (staggered pin grid array) Pentiums used in desktop systems. The 49mm square of the SPGA is reduced to 29mm in the TCP processor, the thickness to approximately 1mm, and the weight from 55 grams to under 1 gram.

◀◀ See "Physical Packaging," p. 53

Instead of metal pins inserted into a socket on the motherboard, a TCP processor is essentially a raw die encased in an oversized piece of polyamide film. The film is similar to photographic film. The die is attached to the film using a process called *tape automated bonding (TAB)*, the same process used to connect electrical connections to LCD panels. The film, called the *tape*, is laminated with copper foil that is etched to form the leads that will connect the processor to the motherboard (see Figure 15.4). This is similar to the way electrical connections are photographically etched onto a printed circuit board.

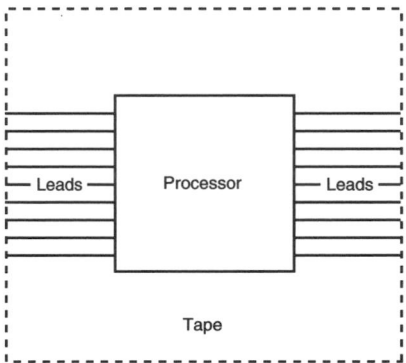

FIG. 15.4   A processor that is mounted using the tape carrier package is attached to a piece of copper-laminated film that replaces the pins used in standard desktop processors.

After the leads are formed, they are plated with gold to allow bonding to a gold bump on the silicon die and to guard against corrosion. Next, they are bonded to the processor chip itself, and then the whole package is coated with a protective polyamide siloxane resin and mounted on a filmstrip reel for machine assembly. To get a feel for the small size of this processor, look at Figure 15.5 where it is shown next to a standard-size push-pin for comparison.

After testing, the processor ships to the motherboard manufacturer in this form. The reels of TCP chips are loaded into special machines that stamp-solder them directly to the portable system's motherboard. As such, the installation is permanent; a TCP processor can never be removed from the board for repair or upgrade. Because there is no heat sink or physical container directly attached to the processor, the motherboard itself becomes the conduit to a heat sink mounted underneath it, thus using the portable system's chassis to pull heat away. Some faster portable systems include thermostatically controlled fans to further aid in heat removal.

Mounting the TCP to the system circuit board requires specific tooling available from all major board assembly equipment vendors. A special tool cuts the tape containing the processor to the proper size and folds the ends containing the leads into a modified gull wing shape that contacts the circuit board, leaving the processor itself suspended just above the board (see Figure 15.6). Another tool dispenses a thermally conductive paste to the circuit board prior to placement of the tape containing the processor. This is done so the heat can be dissipated through a sink on the underside of the motherboard itself while it is kept away from the soldered connections.

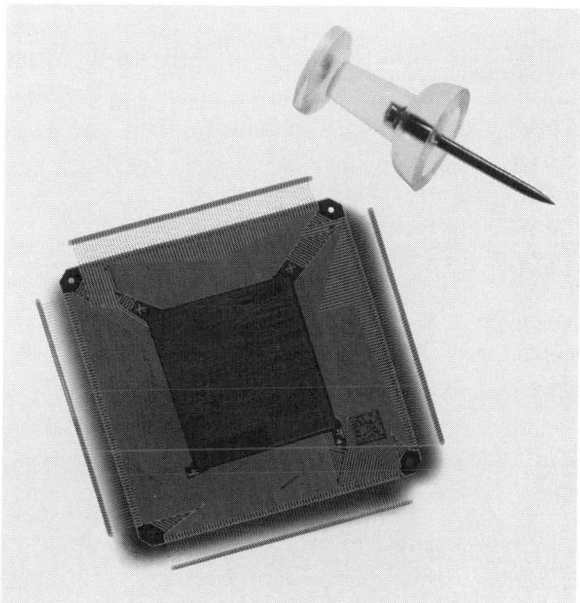

FIG. 15.5 Pentium MMX Processor in TCP Mobile Package. *Photograph used by permission of Intel Corporation.*

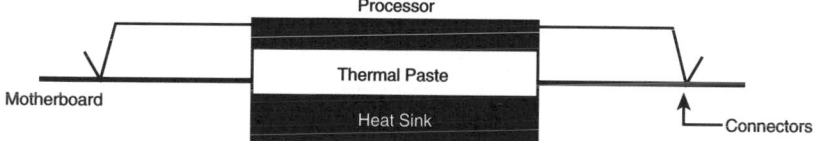

FIG. 15.6 The tape keeps the processor's connections to the motherboard away from the chip itself and allows the underside of the processor to be thermally bonded to the motherboard.

Finally, a hot bar soldering tool connects the leads on the tape to the circuit board. The pinouts for the mobile Pentium TCP are shown in Figure 15.7. The completed TCP assembly forms an efficient thermal contact directly from the die to the motherboard, allowing the processor to run within its temperature limits even in such a raw state. By eliminating the package and essentially bonding the die directly to the motherboard, a significant amount of size and weight are saved.

> **Note**
>
> It should be noted that there are manufacturers of portable systems who use standard desktop PGA processors, sometimes accompanied by fans. Apart from a greatly diminished battery life, systems like these can sometimes be too hot to touch comfortably. For this reason, it is a good idea to determine the exact model processor used in a system that you intend to purchase, and not just the speed.

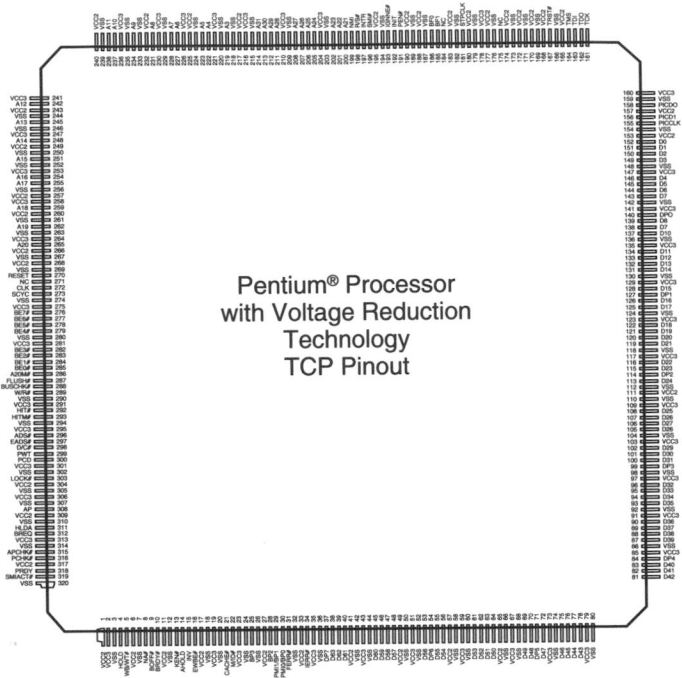

FIG. 15.7 Intel Mobile Pentium Tape Carrier Package Pinout.

Mobile Module. Portable system manufacturers can purchase Pentium processors in raw TCP form and mount the processors to their motherboards themselves. Intel has also introduced another form of processor packaging called the *mobile module*, or MMO (see Figure 15.8).

FIG. 15.8 Mobile Pentium Processors in mobile module or raw Tape Carrier Package form. *Photograph used by permission of Intel Corporation.*

The mobile module consists of a Pentium or Pentium II processor in its TCP form, mounted on a small daughterboard along with the power supply for the processor's unique voltage requirements, the system's Level 2 cache memory, and the "North Bridge" part of the motherboard chipset. This is the core logic that connects the processor to standard system buses containing the "South Bridge" part of the chipset, as shown in the block diagram in Figure 15.9. The terms *North Bridge* and *South Bridge* describe what has come to be an accepted method for dividing the functionality of the chipset into halves that are mounted on separate modules. In a typical portable system design, the manufacturer purchases the mobile module (complete with the North Bridge) from Intel, and uses a motherboard designed by another company that contains the South Bridge.

In many ways, the MMO is similar to the Pentium II Single Edge Cartridge (SEC) design, and in the future will allow the cache memory to run at higher speeds on a separate bus from the rest of the system.

◀◀ See "Intel Chipsets," p. 185

◀◀ See "Single Edge Cartridge (SEC)," p. 54

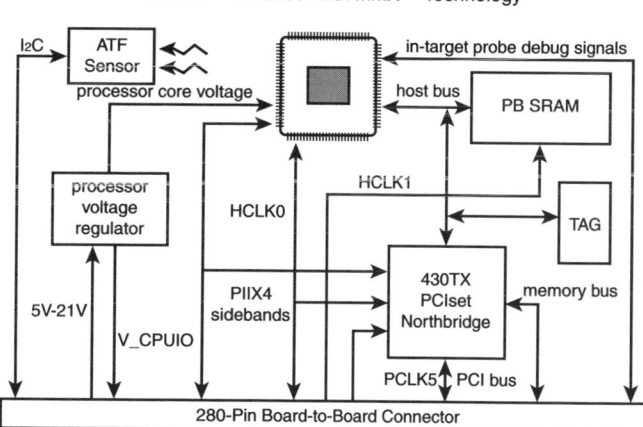

FIG. 15.9   Intel Pentium mobile module block diagram.

The module interfaces electrically to its host system via a 3.3-volt PCI bus, a 3.3-volt memory bus, and Intel chipset control signals bridging the half of the chipset on the module to the other half of the chipset on the system motherboard. The Intel mobile module also incorporates a single thermal connection that carries all of the module's thermal output to the mobile PC's main cooling mechanisms.

The MMO is mounted with screws and alignment guides to secure the module against the typical shock and vibration associated with mobile PC usage. The MMO (shown in Figure 15.10) is 4 inches (101.6mm) long by 2.5 inches (63.5mm) wide by 0.315 inch (8mm) high (0.39 inch or 10mm high at connector).

FIG. 15.10 Intel Pentium MMX mobile module, including the processor, chipset, and L2 cache. *Photograph used by permission of Intel Corporation.*

The mobile module greatly simplifies the process of installing a Pentium or Pentium II processor into a portable system, permits manufacturers to build more standardization into their portable computer designs, and eliminates the need for manufacturers to invest in the special tools needed to mount TCP processors on circuit boards themselves. The module also provides a viable processor upgrade path that was unavailable with a TCP processor permanently soldered to the motherboard.

IBM has adopted the MMO in the latest ThinkPad systems, which should allow them to come out with new designs more quickly because the MMO part of the system will remain an industry standard. The size of the MMO precludes its use in some very thin notebooks, so IBM and others still use the raw TCP processor version for many portable designs as well.

Mini-Cartridge. The mobile versions of the Pentium II processor are available in the mobile module package, with the North Bridge portion of the Intel 440BX AGP chipset. However, Intel has also introduced another new package for the Pentium II called the *mini-cartridge*. The mini-cartridge is designed especially for use in ultralight portable computers in which the height or bulk of the mobile module would interfere with the system design. It contains only the processor core itself and 512K of Level 2 cache memory in a stainless steel case that exposes the connector and the processor die.

◀◀ See "Intel 440BX," p. 205

The mini-cartridge is approximately 51mm×47mm in size and 4.5mm in height. Overall, the package is about one-fourth the weight, one-sixth the size, and consumes two-thirds of the power of a desktop Pentium II processor using the Single Edge Connector (SEC). To connect to the socket on the motherboard, the mini-cartridge has a 240-pin connector at one end of the bottom side, with the pins arranged in an 8×30 ball grid array (BGA), as shown in Figure 15.11.

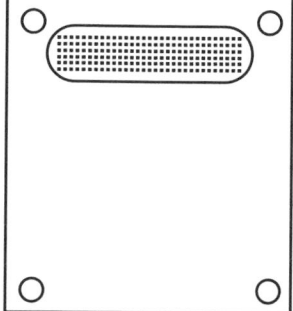

FIG. 15.11   Bottom side of the Pentium II mini-cartridge package.

Chipsets

As in the desktop market, Intel has come to dominate the mobile chipset industry by creating products that support the advanced features of each new processor they release. The recent mobile Pentium II processor releases were accompanied by the introduction of the Mobile 440BX AGPset, which provides support for the Accelerated Graphics Port, 100MHz memory and system buses, and processor power management capabilities designed to extend battery life.

Intel's other current chipsets intended for mobile systems are the 430TX PCIset for the Pentium/MMX and the 430MX PCIset for the Pentium.

◀◀ See "Fifth-Generation (P5 Pentium Class) Chipsets," p. 187

◀◀ See "Sixth-Generation (P6 Pentium Pro/Pentium II Class) Chipsets," p. 199

Intel's most recent chipset innovation, however, is intended to accommodate the mobile module package for the Pentium/MMX and Pentium II processors. In this design, the chipset's two halves, called the *North Bridge* and *South Bridge*, are located on the mobile module and the system motherboard, respectively.

In the 440BX AGPset, for example, the host bridge system controller consists of two VLSI devices. The first of these, the 443BX Host Bridge (the North Bridge) is part of the mobile module. The other device is the PIIX4 PCI/ISA bridge, which the system manufacturer must incorporate into the motherboard design for the portable computer. This forms the South Bridge. The mobile module connects to the motherboard through a 3.3v PCI bus, a 3.3v memory bus, and through some 443BX Host Bridge control signals. It is these signals that combine the North Bridge and the South Bridge into a single functional chipset.

Clearly, innovations like the mobile module accentuate the association between a computer's processor and its motherboard chipset. Now that the development cycles for new processors tend to be measured in months, not years, it is rapidly becoming a foregone conclusion that to get the most out of the latest Intel processor, you have to use an Intel chipset as well. As when shopping for a desktop system, you should be aware of what chipset is used in the portable computer you plan to buy, and whether it fully supports the capabilities of the processor and the system's other components.

Memory

Adding memory is one of the most common upgrades performed on computers, and portables are no exception. However, most portable systems are exceptional in the design of their memory chips. Unlike desktop systems, in which there are only a few basic types of slots for additional RAM, there are literally dozens of different memory chip configurations that have been designed to shoehorn RAM upgrades into the tightly packed cases of portable systems.

Some portables use extender boards like the SIMMs and DIMMs in desktop systems, while others use memory cartridges that look very much like PC Cards, but which plug into a dedicated IC (integrated circuit) memory socket. In any case, appearance is not a reliable measure of compatibility. It is strongly recommended that you install only memory modules that have been designed for your system, in the configurations specified by the manufacturer.

◀◀ See "SIMMs and DIMMs," p. 324

This recommendation does not necessarily limit you to purchasing memory upgrades only from the manufacturer. There are now many companies that manufacture memory upgrade modules for dozens of different portable systems, by reverse-engineering the original vendor's products. This adds a measure of competition to the market, usually making third-party modules much cheaper than those of a manufacturer that is far more interested in selling new computers for several thousand dollars rather than memory chips for a few hundred.

> **Note**
>
> Some companies have developed memory modules that exceed the original specifications of the system manufacturer, allowing you to install more memory than you could with the maker's own modules. Some manufacturers, such as IBM, have certification programs to signify their approval of these products. Otherwise, there is an element of risk involved in extending the system's capabilities in this way.

Inside the memory modules, the components are not very different from those of desktop systems. Portables use the same types of DRAM and SRAM as desktops, including the new memory technologies like EDO (Enhanced Data Out) and SDRAM (Synchronous DRAM). At one time, portable systems tended not to have memory caches because the SRAM chips typically used for this purpose generate a lot of heat. Advances in thermal management have now made this less of an issue, however, and you should expect a high-end system to include SRAM cache memory.

Hard Disk Drives

Hard disk drive technology is also largely unchanged in portable systems, except for the size of the disks and their packaging. Enhanced IDE drives are all but universal in portable computers. Internal hard drives typically use 2 1/2-inch platters and are 12.5mm or 19mm tall, depending on the size of the system.

As with memory modules, systems manufacturers have different ways of mounting hard drives in the system, which can cause upgrade compatibility problems. Some systems use a caddy to hold the drive and make the electrical and data connections to the system. This makes the physical part of an upgrade as easy as inserting a new drive into the caddy and then mounting it in the system. In other cases, you might have to purchase a drive that has been specifically designed for your system, with the proper connectors built into it.

In many portables, replacing a hard drive is much simpler than in a desktop system. Quite a few manufacturers now design their portable systems with external bays that let you easily swap out hard drives without opening the case. Multiple users can share a single machine by snapping in their own hard drives, or you can use the same technique to load different operating systems on the same computer.

The most important aspect of hard drive upgrades that you must be aware of is the drive support provided by the system's BIOS. The BIOS in some systems, and particularly older ones, may offer limited hard drive size options. This is particularly true if your system was manufactured before 1995, when EIDE hard drives came into standard use. BIOSs made before this time support a maximum drive size of 508M. In some cases, flash BIOS upgrades, which provide support for additional drives, may be available for your system.

Another option for extending hard drive space is PC Card hard drives. These are devices that fit into a type III PC Card slot that can provide as much as 450M of disk space in a remarkably tiny package (usually with a remarkably high price). You can also connect external drives to a portable PC, using a PC Card SCSI host adapter or specialized parallel port drive interface. This frees you from the size limitations imposed by the system's case, and you can use any size SCSI drive you want, without concern for BIOS limitations.

Removable Media

Apart from hard disk drives, portable systems are now being equipped with other types of storage media that can provide access to larger amounts of data. CD-ROM drives are now available in many laptop and notebook systems, while a few include removable cartridge drives, such as Iomega's Zip drive. This has been made possible by the Enhanced IDE specifications that let other types of devices share the same interface as the hard drive.

Another important issue is that of the floppy drive. Small subnotebook systems usually omit the floppy drive to save space, sometimes including an external unit. Some other systems enable you to substitute a second hard drive or battery for the floppy drive. For certain types of users, the lack of a floppy drive may or may not be an acceptable inconvenience. Many users of portables, especially those that frequently connect to networks, have little use for a floppy drive. This is now true even for the installation of applications, as virtually all software now ships on CD-ROMs.

One of the features that is becoming increasingly common in laptop and notebook systems is swappable drive bays that you can use to hold any one of several types of components. This arrangement lets you customize the configuration of your system to suit your immediate needs. For example, when traveling you might remove the floppy drive and replace it with an extra battery, or install a second hard drive when your storage needs increase. Notebook vendors and magazine reviews may refer to the number of *spindles* when discussing the number of drives a notebook can have installed simultaneously. For example, a computer that can use a floppy drive, CD-ROM, and hard drive simultaneously is a three-spindle system. If a system has two spindles, the most common configuration is a hard drive along with a bay that you can swap a floppy drive, CD-ROM drive, battery, or second hard drive in and out of. When evaluating your notebook needs and hardware, be sure to determine which devices included with a model can be used simultaneously and which require removing another device. If lightweight travel is a concern, determine which parts you don't need for travel that can be swapped out. Swappable bays should come with a cover or faceplate for the open bay to prevent dirt and foreign objects from entering when the bay is empty.

PC Cards

In an effort to give laptop and notebook computers the kind of expandability that users have grown used to in desktop systems, the Personal Computer Memory Card International Association (PCMCIA) has established several standards for credit card-size expansion boards that fit into a small slot on laptops and notebooks. The development of the PC Card interface is one of the few successful feats of hardware standardization in a market full of proprietary designs.

The PC Card standards, which were developed by a consortium of more than 300 manufacturers (including IBM, Toshiba, and Apple), have been touted as being a revolutionary advancement in mobile computing. PC Card laptop and notebook slots enable you to add memory expansion cards, fax/modems, SCSI adapters, network interface adapters, and many other types of devices to your system. If your computer has PC Card slots that conform to the standard developed by the PCMCIA, you can insert any type of PC Card (built to the same standard) into your machine and expect it to be recognized and usable.

The promise of PC Card technology is enormous. There are not only PC Card memory expansion cards, tiny hard drives, and wireless modems available, but also ISDN adapters, MPEG decoders, network interface adapters, sound cards, CD-ROM controllers, and even GPS systems that use global positioning satellites to help you find your way by locating your exact position on the earth.

Originally designed as a standard interface for memory cards, the PCMCIA document defines both the PC Card hardware and the software support architecture used to run it. The PC Cards defined in version 1 of the standard, called Type I, are credit card size

(3.4×2.1 inches) and 3.3mm thick. The standard has since been revised to support cards with many other functions. The third version, called PC Card Specification—February 1995, defines three types of cards, with the only physical difference being their thickness. This was done to support the hardware for different card functions.

Most of the PC Cards on the market today, such as modems and network interface adapters, are 5mm-thick Type II devices. Type III cards are 10.5mm thick, and are typically used for PC Card hard drives. All the card types are backward-compatible; you can insert a Type I card into a Type II or III slot. The standard PC Card slot configuration for portable computers is two Type II slots, with one on top of the other. This way, you can also insert a single Type III card, taking up both slots but using only one of the connectors.

Note

There is also a Type IV PC Card, thicker still than the Type III, that was designed for higher-capacity hard drives. This card type is not recognized by the PCMCIA, however, and is not included in the standard document. There is, therefore, no guarantee of compatibility between Type IV slots and devices, and they should generally be avoided.

The latest version of the standard, published in March 1997, includes many features designed to increase the speed and efficiency of the interface, such as

- DMA (direct memory access) support.

- 3.3v operation.

- Support for APM (Advanced Power Management).

- Plug-and-Play support.

- The PC Card ATA standard, which lets manufacturers use the AT Attachment protocols to implement PC CARD hard disk drives.

- Support for multiple functions on a single card (such as a modem and a network adapter).

- The Zoomed Video (ZV) interface, a direct video bus connection between the PC Card adapter and the system's VGA controller, allowing high-speed video displays for videoconferencing applications and MPEG decoders.

- A thermal ratings system that can be used to warn users of excessive heat conditions.

- CardBus, a 32-bit interface that runs at 33MHz and provides 32-bit data paths to the computer's I/O and memory systems, as well as a new shielded connector that prevents CardBus devices from being inserted into slots that do not support the latest version of the standard. This is a vast improvement over the 8- or 16-bit bus width and 8MHz speed of the original PC Card-16 interface. If you connect your portable computer to a 100Mbps network, CardBus can provide the high-speed interface that, in a desktop system, would be provided by PCI.

The PC Card itself usually has a sturdy metal case, and is sealed except for the interface to the PCMCIA adapter in the computer at one end, which consists of 68 tiny pinholes. The other end of the card may contain a connector for a cable leading to a telephone line, a network, or some other external device.

The pinouts for the PC Card interface are shown in Table 15.5.

Table 15.5 Pinouts for a PCMCIA Card

Pin	Signal Name	Pin	Signal Name
1	Ground	35	Ground
2	Data 3	36	–Card Detect 1
3	Data 4	37	Data 11
4	Data 5	38	Data 12
5	Data 6	39	Data 13
6	Data 7	40	Data 14
7	–Card Enable 1	41	Data 15
8	Address 10	42	–Card Enable 2
9	–Output Enable	43	Refresh
10	Address 11	44	RFU (–IOR)
11	Address 9	45	RFU (–IOW)
12	Address 8	46	Address 17
13	Address 13	47	Address 18
14	Address 14	48	Address 19
15	–Write Enable/–Program	49	Address 20
16	Ready/–Busy (IREQ)	50	Address 21
17	+5V	51	+5V
18	Vpp1	52	Vpp2
19	Address 16	53	Address 22
20	Address 15	54	Address 23
21	Address 12	55	Address 24
22	Address 7	56	Address 25
23	Address 6	57	RFU
24	Address 5	58	RESET
25	Address 4	59	–WAIT
26	Address 3	60	RFU (–INPACK)
27	Address 2	61	–Register Select
28	Address 1	62	Battery Voltage Detect 2 (–SPKR)
29	Address 0	63	Battery Voltage Detect 1 (–STSCHG)
30	Data 0	64	Data 8
31	Data 1	65	Data 9
32	Data 2	66	Data 10
33	Write Protect (–IOIS16)	67	–Card Detect 2
34	Ground	68	Ground

PC Card Software Support. PC Cards are by definition *hot-swappable*, meaning that with the proper software support you can remove a card from a slot and replace it with a different one without having to reboot the system. If your PC Card devices and your operating system conform to the Plug-and-Play standard, inserting a new card into the slot causes the appropriate drivers for the device to be loaded and configured automatically.

To make this possible, two separate software layers are needed on the computer that provide the interface between the PCMCIA adapter (that controls the card slots) and the applications that use the services of the PC Card devices (see Figure 15.12). These two layers are called *Socket Services* and *Card Services*. A third module, called an *enabler*, actually configures the settings of the PC Cards.

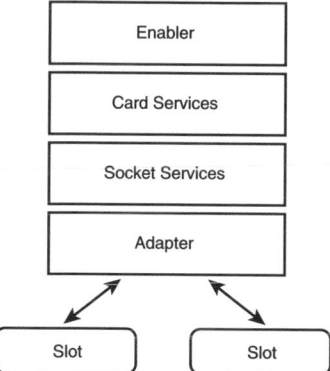

FIG. 15.12 The Card and Socket Services enable an operating system to recognize the PC Card inserted into a slot and configure the appropriate system hardware resources for the device.

Socket Services. The PCMCIA adapter that provides the interface between the card slots and the rest of the computer is one of the only parts of the PCMCIA architecture that is not standardized. There are many different adapters available to portable systems manufacturers and, as a result, an application or operating system cannot address the slot hardware directly, as it can a parallel or serial port.

Instead, there is a software layer called Socket Services that is designed to address a specific make of PCMCIA adapter hardware. The Socket Services software layer isolates the proprietary aspects of the adapter from all the software operating above it. The communications between the driver and the adapter may be unique, but the other interface, between the Socket Services driver and the Card Services software, is defined by the PCMCIA standard.

Socket Services can take the form of a device driver, a TSR program run from the DOS prompt (or the AUTOEXEC.BAT file), or a service running on an operating system like Windows 9x or Windows NT. It is possible for a computer to have PC Card slots with different adapters, as in the case of a docking station that provides extra slots in addition to those in the portable computer itself. In this case, the computer can run multiple Socket Services drivers, all of which communicate with the same Card Services program.

Card Services. The Card Services software communicates with Socket Services, and is responsible for assigning the appropriate hardware resources to PC Cards. PC Cards are no different from other types of bus expansion cards, in that they require access to specific hardware resources to communicate with the computer's processor and memory subsystems. If you have ever inserted an ISA network interface card into a desktop system, you know that you must specify a hardware interrupt, and maybe an I/O port or memory address for the card to operate.

A PC Card network adapter requires the same hardware resources, but you don't manually configure the device using jumpers or a software utility as you would an ISA card. The problem is also complicated by the fact that the PCMCIA standard requires that the computer be able to assign hardware resources to different devices as they are inserted into a slot. Card Services addresses this problem by maintaining a collection of various hardware resources that it allots to devices as needed, and reclaims as the devices are removed.

If, for example, you have a system with two PC Card slots, the Card Services software might be configured to use two hardware interrupts, two I/O ports, and two memory addresses, whether any cards are in the slots at boot time or not. No other devices in the computer can use those interrupts. When cards are inserted, Card Services assigns configuration values for the settings requested by the devices, ensuring that the settings allotted to each card are unique.

Card Services is not the equivalent of Plug and Play, although the two may seem similar. In fact, in Windows 9x, Card Services obtains the hardware resources it assigns to PC Cards using Plug and Play. For other operating systems, the resources may be allotted to the Card Services program using a text file or command-line switches. In a non–Plug-and-Play system, you must configure the hardware resources assigned to Card Services with the same care that you would configure an ISA board. Although Card Services won't allow two PC Cards to be assigned the same interrupt, there is nothing in the PCMCIA architecture to prevent conflicts between the resources assigned to Card Services and those of other devices in the system.

You can have multiple Socket Services drivers loaded on one system, but there can be only one Card Services program. Socket Services must always be loaded before Card Services.

Enablers. One of the oldest rules of PC configuration is that the software configuration must match that of the hardware. For example, if you configure a network interface card to use interrupt 10, then you must also configure the network driver to use the same interrupt, so it can address the device. Today, this can be confusing because most hardware is configured not by physically manipulating jumpers or DIP switches, but by running a hardware configuration utility.

In spite of their other capabilities, neither Socket Services nor Card Services is capable of actually configuring the hardware settings of PC Cards. This job is left to a software module called an *enabler*. The enabler receives the configuration settings assigned by Card

Services and actually communicates with the PC Card hardware itself to set the appropriate values.

Like Socket Services, the enabler must be designed to address the specific PC Card that is present in the slot. In most cases, a PCMCIA software implementation includes a *generic enabler*, that is, one that can address many different types of PC Cards. This, in most cases, lets you insert a completely new card into a slot and have it be recognized and configured by the software.

The problem with a generic enabler, and with the PCMCIA software architecture in general, is it requires a significant amount of memory to run. Because it must support many different cards, a generic enabler can require 50K of RAM or more, plus another 50K for the Card and Socket Services. For systems running DOS (with or without Windows 3.1), this is a great deal of conventional memory just to activate one or two devices. Once installed and configured, the PC Card devices may also require additional memory, for network, SCSI, or other device drivers.

Note

Windows 9x is definitely the preferred operating system for running PC Card devices. The combination of its advanced memory management, its Plug-and-Play capabilities, and the integration of the Card and Socket Services into the operating system makes the process of installing a PC Card usually as easy as inserting it into the slot.

With Windows NT 4.0, for example, you have to shut down the system and reboot to change the PC Card in a slot. What's more, it can be difficult to find Windows NT drivers for many of the PC Cards on the market.

When memory is scarce, there can be an alternative to the generic enabler. A *specific enabler* is designed to address only a single specific PC Card, and uses much less memory for that reason. Some PC Cards ship with specific enablers that you can use in place of a generic enabler. However, it is also possible to use a specific enabler when you have a PC Card that is not recognized by your generic enabler. You can load the specific enabler to address the unrecognized card, along with the generic enabler to address any other cards that you may use. This practice, of course, increases the memory requirements of the software.

Finally, you can avoid the overhead of generic enablers and the Card and Socket Services entirely, by using what is known as a *point enabler*. A point enabler is a software module that is included with some PC Cards that addresses the hardware directly, eliminating the need for Card and Socket Services. As a result, the point enabler removes the capability to hot swap PC Cards and have the system automatically recognize and configure them. If, however, you intend to use the same PC Cards all the time and have no need for hot swapping, point enablers can save you a tremendous amount of memory.

Keyboards

Unlike desktop systems, portables have keyboards that are integrated into the one-piece unit. This makes them difficult to repair or replace. The keyboard should also be an important element of your system purchasing decision, because manufacturers are forced to modify the standard 101-key desktop keyboard layout to fit in a smaller case.

The numeric keypad is always the first to go in a portable system's keyboard. Usually, its functionality is embedded into the alphanumeric keyboard and activated by a Function key combination. The Function (or Fn) key is an additional control key used on many systems to activate special features like the use of an alternate display or keyboard.

Most portable systems today have keyboards that approach the size and usability of desktop models. This is a vast improvement over some older designs in which the keys were reduced to a point at which you could not comfortably touch-type with both hands. Standard conventions like the "inverted T" cursor keys also were modified, causing extreme user displeasure.

Some systems still have half-sized function keys, but one of the by-products of the larger screens found in many of today's portable systems is more room for the keyboard. Thus, many manufacturers are taking advantage of the extra space.

Pointing Devices

As with the layout and feel of the keyboard, pointing devices are a matter of personal taste. Most portable systems have pointing devices that conform to one of the three following types:

- *Trackball.* A small ball (usually about 1/2-inch) embedded partially in the keyboard below the space bar, that is rolled by the user. While serviceable and accurate, trackballs have become unpopular, primarily due to their tendency to gather dust and dirt in the well that holds the ball, causing degraded performance.

- *Trackpoint.* Developed by IBM and adopted by many other manufacturers, the trackpoint is a small (about 1/4-inch) rubberized button located between the G, H, and B keys of the keyboard. It looks like a pencil eraser and can be nudged in any direction to move the cursor around the screen. The trackpoint is very convenient because you can manipulate it without taking your hands off of the keyboard. On some earlier models, the rubber cover tended to wear off after heavy use. Newer versions are made of sturdier materials.

- *Trackpad.* The most recent development of the three, the trackpad is an electromagnetically sensitive pad, usually about 1×2 inches, that responds to the movement of a finger across its surface. Mouse clicks can be simulated by tapping the pad. Trackpads have great potential, but tend to be overly sensitive to accidental touches, causing undesired cursor movements and especially unwanted mouse clicks. Trackpads are also sensitive to humidity and moist fingers, resulting in unpredictable performance.

The trackpad is still a relatively new innovation to the portable system market (although the technology has been around for years), and some systems allow users a choice by providing both a trackpoint and a trackpad. Unfortunately, on most of the systems that do this, the two devices use the same interrupt, forcing you to select one device or the other in the system BIOS, rather than letting you use both at the same time.

Another important part of the pointer arrangement is the location of the primary and secondary buttons. Some systems locate the buttons in peculiar configurations that require unnatural contortions to perform a click-and-drag operation. Pointing devices are definitely a feature of a portable system that you should test drive before you make a purchase. As an alternative, remember that nearly all portables have a serial port that you can use to attach an external mouse to the system, when your workspace permits.

Batteries

Battery life is one of the biggest complaints users have about portable systems. Although a great deal has been done to improve the power management capabilities of today's portable computers, the hardware configuration of a fully equipped portable system dissipates 90% more power than it did three years ago, and that trend is still continuing. The efficiency of a computer's power use may also have doubled in the last two years, but battery technology has not improved at anything approaching the same rate, leaving the battery life of a typical portable system approximately the same as it was before.

The goal sought by many mobile users has been the same for many years: a full-featured portable system that can run on a single battery for the entire duration of a transcontinental U.S. airplane flight. Unfortunately, the industry seems to be no closer to approaching this goal than it was several years ago. Users typically have to carry two or more battery packs for a six-hour flight, and while mobile power technologies are improving, so are the demands of today's systems. However, while typical battery life has remained in the two- to three-hour range for most reputable manufacturers, the new notebooks have the advantage of having larger hard drives, bigger and brighter screens, more RAM, faster processors, integrated speakers, and CD-ROM drives. Based on the increasing popularity of these notebook systems, the buying consumer has clearly voiced that a more powerful notebook with continuing average battery life is more important and useful than a system that would run for 6–10 hours but sacrifice features they have grown used to using.

Battery Types. The battery technology also plays a major role in the portable power issue, of course. Most portable systems today use one of four battery types:

- *Nickel Cadmium (NiCad).* As the oldest of the four technologies, nickel cadmium batteries are rarely used in portable systems today, because of their shorter life and their sensitivity to improper charging and discharging. The life of the battery's charge can be shortened by as much as 40% if the battery is not fully discharged before recharging, or if it is overcharged. Permanent damage to the cell can be prevented by periodically discharging it to 1 volt or less. Despite this "memory" effect, however, NiCad batteries hold a charge well when not in use, losing 10% of their capacity in the first 24 hours and approximately 10% per month after that, and can be recharged 1,500 times or more.

- *Nickel Metal-Hydride (NiMH).* More expensive than NiCads, NiMH batteries have approximately a 30% longer life than NiCads, are less sensitive to the memory effect caused by improper charging and discharging, and do not use the environmentally dangerous substances found in NiCads. They have a recommended discharge current that is lower than that of a NiCad battery (one-fifth to one-half of the rated capacity), a self-discharge rate that is 1 1/2 to 2 times greater than that of a NiCad, and can be recharged as many as 500 times. NiMH batteries also require nearly twice as long to recharge as NiCads. While they are still used in many portable systems, NiMH batteries are now found mostly in computers at the lower end of the price range.

■ *Lithium-Ion (Li-ion).* As the current industry standard, Li-ion batteries are longer-lived than either NiCad or NiMH technologies, cannot be overcharged, and hold a charge well when not in use. Batteries that use lithium—one of the lightest of all metals, with the greatest electrochemical potential, and providing the largest energy content—have been manufactured since the 1970s. However, lithium is also an unstable substance, and some battery explosions resulted in a large number of battery recalls in the early 1990s. Subsequent models were manufactured using lithium ions from chemicals like lithium-cobalt dioxide ($LiCoO_2$). Despite a slightly lower energy density, Li-ion batteries are much safer than the lithium designs. Various types of Li-ion batteries use different active materials for their negative electrodes; there are *coke* and two *graphite* versions that have slightly different voltage characteristics. Li-ion batteries can also support the heavy-duty power requirements of today's high-end systems. Unlike NiCad and NiMH batteries, which can be used in the same system without modification to the circuitry, Li-ion batteries can only be used in systems specifically designed for them. Inserting a Li-ion battery into a system designed for a NiCad or NiMH can result in a fire. Although the most expensive of the four technologies, Li-ion batteries have come to be used in all but the very low end of the portable system market.

■ *Lithium-Ion Polymer.* This is a fourth battery type that has been in development for several years, but which is only now appearing on the market. Lithium-ion polymer batteries are manufactured using a lithium ion and cobalt oxide cell with a proprietary polymer electrolyte, and can be formed into flat sheets as small as 1mm thick and of almost any size. Thus, a thin battery panel can be fitted into a portable computer behind the LCD panel. Lithium-ion polymer batteries provide an energy density that is four times better than a NiCad and a charge life that is 40% longer than a Li-ion battery, at one-fifth the weight. This battery technology provides up to 500 charges and is immune to the memory effect that can prevent NiCad and NiMH batteries from recharging fully. Once they are manufactured in sufficient quantities, lithium-ion polymer batteries could well replace the bulky battery packs used today in portable systems.

> **Note**
>
> All the battery types in use today function best when they are completely discharged before being recharged. Lithium-ion batteries are affected the least by incomplete discharging and have a higher discharge cut-off point (2.5–3v versus 1v for NiCads), but the effect on the life of future charges is still noticeable. When storing charged batteries, refrigerating them helps them to retain their charges for longer periods, although you should always allow the battery to return fully to room temperature and be sure that it is dry before putting it in the computer to prevent condensation from forming in the computer.

Unfortunately, buying a portable computer with a more efficient battery does not necessarily mean that you will realize a longer charge life. Power consumption depends on the components installed in the system, the power management capabilities provided by the system software, and the size of the battery itself. Some manufacturers, for example, when moving from NiMH to Li-ion batteries, see this as an opportunity to save some space inside the computer. They decide that because they are using a more efficient power storage technology, they can make the battery smaller and still deliver the same performance.

Battery technology trails behind nearly all the other subsystems found in a portable computer, as far as the development of new innovations is concerned. Due to the continuing trend of adding more features and components to mobile computers, their power consumption has risen enormously in recent years, and power systems have barely been able to keep up. On a high-end laptop system, a battery life of three hours is very good, even with all the system's power management features activated.

One other way that manufacturers are addressing the battery life problem is by designing systems that are capable of carrying two batteries. The inclusion of multipurpose bays within the system's case enables users to replace the floppy or CD-ROM drive with a second battery pack, effectively doubling the computer's charge life.

Power Management. There are various components in a computer that do not need to run continuously while the system is turned on. Mobile systems often conserve battery power by shutting down these components based on the activities of the user. If, for example, you open a text file in an editor and the entire file is read into memory, there is no need for the hard drive to spin while you are working on the file.

After a certain period of inactivity, a power management system can park the hard drive heads and stop the platters from spinning until you save the file to disk or issue any other command that requires drive access. Other components, such as floppy and CD-ROM drives and PC Cards, can also be powered down when not in use, resulting in a significant reduction of the power needed to run the system.

Most portables also have systemic power saver modes that suspend the operation of the entire system when it is not in use. The names assigned to these modes can differ, but there are usually two system states that differ in that one continues to power the system's RAM while the other does not. Typically, a "suspend" mode shuts down virtually the entire system after a preset period of inactivity except for the memory. This requires only a small amount of power and allows the system to be reawakened almost instantaneously.

Portable systems usually have a "hibernate" mode, as well, which writes the current contents of the system's memory to a special file on the hard disk and then shuts down the system, erasing memory as well. When the computer is reactivated, it reads the contents of the file back into memory and work can continue. The reactivation process takes a bit longer in this case, but the system conserves more power by shutting down the memory array.

Note

The memory swap file used for hibernate mode may, in some machines, be located in a special partition on the hard drive dedicated to this purpose. If you inadvertently destroy this partition, you may need a special utility from the system manufacturer to re-create the file.

In most cases, these functions are defined by the APM (Advanced Power Management) standard, a document developed jointly by Intel and Microsoft that defines an interface between an operating system power management policy driver and the hardware-specific software that addresses devices with power management capabilities. This interface is usually implemented in the system BIOS.

◀◀ See "Advanced Power Management," p. 423

However, as power management techniques continue to develop, it becomes increasingly difficult for the BIOS to maintain the complex information states needed to implement more advanced functions. There is, therefore, another standard under development by Intel, Microsoft, and Toshiba called *ACPI (the Advanced Configuration and Power Interface)*, which is designed to implement power management functions in the operating system.

Placing power management under the control of the OS allows for a greater interaction with applications. For example, a program can indicate to the operating system which of its activities are crucial, forcing an immediate activation of the hard drive, and which can be delayed until the next time that the drive is activated for some other reason.

Peripherals

There are a great many add-on devices available for use with portable systems that provide functions that cannot practically or economically be included inside the system itself. Many of the most common uses for portable systems may require additional hardware, either because of the computer's location or the requirements of the function itself. The following sections discuss some of the most common peripherals used with portable systems.

External Displays

High-end laptop systems are often used to host presentations to audiences that can range in size from the boardroom to the auditorium. For all but the smallest groups of viewers, some means of enlarging the computer display is needed. Most portable systems are equipped with a standard VGA jack that allows the connection of an external monitor.

Systems typically allow the user to choose whether the display should be sent to the internal, the external, or both displays, as controlled by a keystroke combination or the system BIOS. Depending on the capabilities of the video display adapter in the computer, you may be able to use a greater display resolution on an external monitor than you would on the LCD panel.

For environments where the display of a standard monitor is not large enough, there are several alternatives, as discussed in the following sections.

Overhead LCD Display Panels. An LCD display panel is something like the LCD screen in your computer except that there is no back on it, making the display transparent. The display technologies and screen resolution options are the same as those for the LCD displays in portable systems, although most of the products on the market use active matrix displays.

You use an LCD panel by placing it on an ordinary overhead projector, causing the image on the panel to be projected onto a screen (or wall). Because they are not intended solely for use with portable systems, these devices typically include a pass-through cable arrangement, allowing a connection to a standard external monitor, as well as the panel.

While they are serviceable for training and internal use, overhead display panels do not usually deliver the depth and vibrancy of color that can add to the excitement of a sales presentation. The quality of the image is also dependent on the brightness of the lamp used to display it. While the panel itself is fairly small and lightweight, overhead projectors frequently are not. If a projector is already available at the presentation site, the LCD panel is a convenient way of enlarging your display. If, however, you are in a position where you must travel to a remote location and supply the overhead projector yourself, you are probably better off with a self-contained LCD projector.

Overhead display panels are not cheap. You will probably have to pay more for one than you paid for your computer. However, on a few models of the IBM ThinkPad, you can remove the top cover that serves as the back of the display and use the computer's own LCD screen as an overhead panel.

LCD Projectors. An *LCD projector* is essentially a self-contained unit that is a combination of a transparent display panel and a projector. The unit connects to a VGA jack like a regular monitor and frequently includes speakers that connect with a separate cable. Not all LCD projectors are portable; some are intended for permanent installations. The portable models vary in weight, display technologies, and the brightness of the lamp, which is measured in lumens.

A 16-pound unit delivering 300–400 lumens is usually satisfactory for a conference room environment; a larger room may require a projector delivering 500 lumens or more and weighing up to 25 pounds. LCD projectors tend to deliver images that are far superior to those of overhead panels, and they offer a one-piece solution to the image-enlargement problem. However, you have to pay dearly for the convenience. Prices of LCD projectors can range from $4,000 to well over $10,000, but if your business relies on your presentations, the cost may be justified.

TV-Out. One of the simplest display solutions is a feature that is being incorporated into many of the high-end laptop systems on the market today. It allows you to connect the computer to a standard television set. Called *TV-out*, various systems provide support for either the North American NTSC television standard, the European PAL standard, or both. Once connected, a software program lets you calibrate the picture on the TV screen.

TV-out is becoming a popular feature on high-end video adapters for desktop systems as well as portables. There are also some manufacturers that are producing external boxes that plug into any computer's VGA port and a television set, to provide an external TV display solution. The products convert the digital VGA signal to an analog output that typically can be set to use the NTSC or PAL standard.

Obviously, TV-out is an extremely convenient solution, as it provides an image size that is limited only by the type of television available, costs virtually nothing, and adds no extra weight to the presenter's load (unless you have to bring the TV yourself). You can also connect your computer to a VCR and record your presentation on standard video-tape. However, the display resolution of a television set does not approach that of a computer monitor, and the picture quality suffers as a result. This is particularly noticeable when displaying images that contain a lot of text, such as presentation slides and Web pages. It is recommended that you test the output carefully with various size television screens before using TV-out in a presentation environment.

Docking Stations

Now that many portable systems are being sold as replacements for standard desktop computers, docking stations are becoming increasingly popular. A docking station is a desktop unit to which you attach (or dock) your portable system when you are at your home or office. At the very least, a docking station provides an AC power connection, a full-size keyboard, a standard desktop mouse, a complete set of input and output ports, and a VGA jack for a standard external monitor.

Once docked, the keyboard and display in the portable system are deactivated, but the other components—particularly the processor, memory, and hard drive—remain active. You are essentially running the same computer but using a standard full-size desktop interface. Docking stations can also contain a wide array of other features, such as a network interface adapter, external speakers, additional hard disk or CD-ROM drives, additional PC Card slots, and a spare battery charger.

An operating system like Windows 9x can maintain multiple hardware profiles for a single machine. A hardware profile is a collection of configuration settings for the devices accessible to the system. To use a docking station, you create one profile for the portable system in its undocked state, and another that adds support for the additional hardware available while docked.

The use of a docking station eliminates much of the tedium involved in maintaining separate desktop and portable systems. With two machines, you must install your applications twice and continually keep the data between the two systems synchronized. This is traditionally done using a network connection or the venerable null modem cable (a crossover cable used to transfer files between systems by connecting their parallel or serial ports). With a docking station and a suitably equipped portable, you can achieve the best of both worlds.

Docking stations are highly proprietary items that are designed for use with specific computer models. Prices vary widely depending on the additional hardware provided, but since a docking station lacks a CPU, memory, and a display, the cost is usually not excessive.

Connectivity

One of the primary uses for portable computers is to keep in touch with the home office while traveling by using a modem. Because of this, many hotels and airports are starting to provide telephone jacks for use with modems, but there are still many places where finding a place to plug into a phone line can be difficult. There are products on the market, however, that can help you overcome these problems, even if you are traveling overseas.

Line Testers. Many hotels use digital PBXs for their telephone systems, which typically carry more current than standard analog lines. This power is needed to operate additional features on the telephone itself, such as message lights and LCD displays. This additional current can permanently damage your modem without warning, and unfortunately, the jacks used by these systems are the same standard RJ-11 connectors used by traditional telephones.

To avoid this problem, you can purchase a line-testing device for about $50 that plugs into a wall jack and measures the amount of current on the circuit. It then informs you whether or not it is safe to plug in your modem.

Acoustic Couplers. On those occasions when you cannot plug your modem into the phone jack, or when there is no jack available (such as at a pay phone), the last resort is an acoustic coupler. The acoustic coupler is an ancient telecommunications device that predates the system of modular jacks used to connect telephones today. To connect to a telephone line, the coupler plugs into your modem's RJ-11 jack at one end and clamps to a telephone handset at the other end. A speaker at the mouthpiece and a microphone at the earpiece allow the audible signals generated by the modem and the phone system to interact.

The acoustic coupler may be an annoying bit of extra baggage to have to carry with you, but it is the one foolproof method for connecting to any telephone line without having to worry about international standards, line current, or wiring.

Chapter 16

Building or Upgrading Systems

In these days of commodity parts and component pricing, building your own system from scratch is no longer the daunting process it once was. Every component necessary to build an Intel-based PC system is available off the shelf at competitive pricing. In many cases, the system you build can use the same components as the top name-brand systems.

There are, however, some cautions to heed. The main thing to note is that you rarely save money when building your own system; Purchasing a complete system from a mail-order vendor or mass merchandiser is usually less expensive. The reason for this is simple: Most system vendors who build systems to order use many, if not all the same components you can use when building your own system. The difference is that they buy these components in quantity and receive a much larger discount than you can by purchasing only one of a particular item.

In addition, there is only one shipping and handling charge when you purchase a complete system instead of the multiple shipping charges when you purchase separate components. In fact, the shipping, handling, and phone charges from ordering all the separate parts needed to build a PC often add up to $100 or more. This cost rises if you encounter problems with any of the components and have to make additional calls or send improper or malfunctioning parts back for replacement.

It is clear that the reasons for building a system from scratch often have less to do with saving money and more to do with the experience you gain and the results you achieve. In the end, you have a custom system that contains the exact components and features you have selected. Most of the time when you buy a preconfigured system, you have to compromise in some way. For example, you may get the video adapter you want, but you would prefer a different make of motherboard. By building your own system, you can select the exact components you want and build the ultimate system for your needs. The experience is also very rewarding. You know exactly how your system is constructed and configured because you have done it yourself. This makes future support and installation of additional accessories much easier.

It may be possible to save some money using components of your current system when building your new system. You may have recently upgraded your hard drive and/or memory in an attempt to extend the life of your current computer. In most cases, you can take those components with you to the new system if you plan appropriately. For example, if you used 30-pin SIMMs in your old system, you can buy a new motherboard that supports both 72- and 30-pin SIMMs or buy a SIMM adapter to convert your 30-pin SIMMs to 72-pin.

So if you are interested in a rewarding experience, you want a customized system that is not exactly the same as that offered by any vendor, you want to save some money by reusing some of the components from your current system, and you are not in a hurry, then building your own PC may be the way to go. On the other hand, if you are interested in getting a PC for the best price, you want one-stop support for warranty claims and technical problems, and you need an operational system quickly, then building your own system should definitely be avoided.

This chapter details the components needed to assemble your own system, explains the assembly procedures, and lists some recommendations for components and their sources.

System Components

The components used in building a typical PC are

- Case and power supply
- Motherboard

    Processor

    Memory

    Serial ports

    Parallel port

    EIDE drive interface

    Floppy disk interface

- Floppy disk/Zip drive
- Hard disk drive(s)
- CD-ROM drive
- Keyboard and pointing device (mouse)
- Video card and display
- Sound card and speakers

■ Accessories

Heat sinks/cooling fans

Cables

Hardware

Operating system software

Each of these components is discussed in the following sections.

Case and Power Supply

The case and power supply are usually sold as a unit. There are several designs to choose from. For a custom-built system, an ATX case and power supply is the recommended choice. Cases designed for the Baby-AT motherboard are still available, but the ATX architecture offers considerable improvements. The size and shape of the case, power supply, and even the motherboard are called the *form factor*. The most popular case form factors are

■ Full Tower

■ Mini-Tower

■ Desktop

■ Low Profile (also called Slimline)

When deciding what type of case to purchase, you should consider where you will place your computer. Will it be on a desk? Or is it more feasible to put the system on the floor and just have the monitor, keyboard, and mouse on the desk? The amount of space you have available for the computer can affect other purchasing decisions, such as the length of the monitor, keyboard, and mouse cables.

Of the choices listed, it is recommended that you avoid the Low Profile systems. Designed primarily for use in business environments, these Slimline systems have a smaller footprint (meaning that they take up less space on your desk) than the typical desktop computer and are usually not designed with expansion in mind. These cases require a special type of motherboard called a *Low Profile* or *LPX board*. The low profile version of the ATX form factor is called the NLX. LPX and NLX motherboards often have virtually everything built in, including video, sound, and even network adapters.

LPX and NLX motherboards do not have any normal adapter slots. Instead, all the expansion slots are mounted on a "tree" board called a *riser card*, which plugs into a special slot on the motherboard. Adapter cards then plug sideways into the riser card (parallel to the motherboard), making expansion difficult and somewhat limited. In addition, the small size of the case makes it difficult to work inside the machine. Some designs force you to remove some components to gain access to others, making system maintenance inconvenient.

Many of the case designs other than the Low Profile (or Slimline) take a standard sized motherboard called a *Baby-AT* type. This designation refers to the form factor or shape of the motherboard, which is to say that it mimics the original IBM AT but is slightly smaller. Actually, the Baby-AT form factor is kind of a cross between the IBM XT and AT motherboard sizes.

◄◄ See "Motherboard Form Factors," p. 167

Many of the newer cases accept Baby-AT form factor motherboards as well as the new ATX-style boards that are rapidly becoming the standard for Pentium, Pentium Pro, and Pentium II systems. However, an older case designed for Baby-AT motherboards does *not* accept an ATX motherboard. The ATX form factor has replaced the Baby-AT style for most newer motherboards. If you are interested in the most flexible type of case and power supply that will support future upgrades, look for a unit that conforms to the ATX and Baby-AT motherboard form factors.

Whether you choose a desktop or one of the tower cases is really a matter of personal preference and system location. Most people feel that the tower systems are roomier and easier to work on, and the full-sized tower cases have lots of bays for different storage devices. Tower cases typically have enough bays to hold floppy drives, multiple hard disk drives, CD-ROM drives, tape drives, and anything else you might want to install. However, some of the desktop cases can have as much room as the towers, particularly the mini- or mid-Tower models. In fact, a tower case is sometimes considered to be a desktop case turned sideways or vice versa. Some cases are convertible—that is, they can be used in either a desktop or tower orientation.

As to the power supply, the most important consideration is how many devices you plan to install in the system and how much power they require. Chapter 6, "Power Supply and Case," describes the process for calculating the power required by your system hardware and selecting an appropriate power supply for your needs.

◄◄ See "Power-Use Calculations," p. 417

When you build your own system, you should always keep upgradability in mind. A properly designed custom PC should last you far longer than an off-the-shelf model because you can more easily add and substitute new components. When choosing a case and power supply, leave yourself some room for expansion, on the assumption that you will eventually need another hard drive or that some new device will appear on the market that you won't be able to live without.

Motherboard

Several compatible form factors are used for motherboards. The form factor refers to the physical dimensions and size of the board and dictates what type of case the board will fit into. The types of motherboard form factors generally available are the following:

- Full-size AT
- Baby-AT
- ATX
- Micro-ATX
- LPX
- NLX

The full-size AT motherboard is so named because it matches the original IBM AT motherboard design. This allows for a large board of up to 12 inches wide by 13.8 inches deep. The keyboard connector and slot connectors must conform to specific placement requirements to fit the holes in the case. This type of board will fit into the tower or full-sized desktop cases only. Because the cases that will fit these boards are more limited in availability, and due to component miniaturization, the full-size AT boards are no longer being produced by most motherboard manufacturers.

The Baby-AT form factor is essentially the same as the original IBM XT motherboard, with modifications in screw-hole positions to fit into an AT-style case (see Figure 16.1). These motherboards also have specific placement of the keyboard connector and slot connectors to match the holes in the case. Virtually all full-size AT and Baby-AT motherboards use the standard 5-pin DIN type connector for the keyboard.

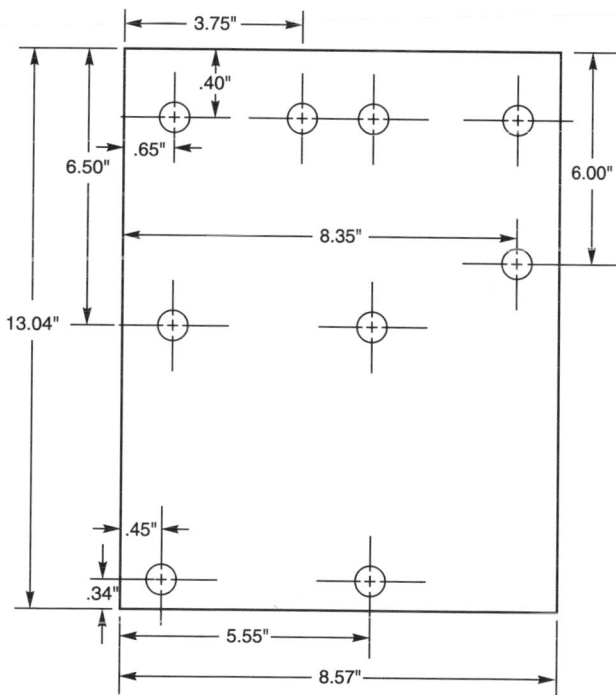

FIG. 16.1 Baby-AT motherboard form factor.

The Baby-AT form factor is currently being overtaken in popularity by the ATX form factor, which was released by Intel in July 1995 (see Figure 16.2). The ATX design is now used on all of Intel's Pentium, Pentium Pro, and Pentium II-based motherboards and has also been adopted by many other manufacturers.

ATX is an open architecture that improves on the Baby-AT design in many ways that affect other components of the computer, such as the case and the power supply. An ATX motherboard has the same basic dimensions as a Baby-AT; however, it is rotated 90 degrees in the case from the standard Baby-AT orientation. This places the expansion slots parallel to the short side of the board, allowing more space for other components without interfering with expansion boards.

Components that produce large amounts of heat, such as the CPU and memory, are located next to the power supply, which is redesigned to feature an internal fan blowing directly across the board. This cooling design requires only a single fan (instead of the two or three commonly found in Baby-AT systems) and provides easier access to the processor and memory sockets.

The ATX-style power supply features a redesigned, single-keyed (foolproof!) connector that cannot be plugged in backward. This power supply provides the motherboard with the 3.3v current used by many of the newer CPUs and other components. ATX power supplies are also designed to support the advanced power management features now found in system BIOS and operating systems.

The micro-ATX form factor is a further development of the ATX design, intended for use in lower-cost systems. The micro-ATX architecture is backward compatible with ATX and does not specify a motherboard that is physically smaller, as the name implies. Instead, the micro-ATX design allows for the use of more inexpensive components such as the smaller SFX power supply. Although it is physically possible to purchase a micro-ATX motherboard and later replace it with an ATX in the same case, this is hardly a cost-effective strategy when building your own system.

If you plan to build a full-sized desktop or tower system, the ATX motherboard is definitely the way to go. Virtually all motherboard manufacturers have committed to the new ATX design in the long run, as the ATX motherboard designs will be cheaper, easier to access, and more reliable.

Other form factors used in motherboards today are the LPX and NLX form factors. These form factors require the use of a Low-Profile case and are normally not recommended when building your own system. This is due to the number of different variations on case and riser card designs, the limited expandability imposed by the motherboard and case architecture, and the difficulty of working in such a small space.

There can be some differences among systems with LPX motherboards, so it is possible to find interchangebility problems among different motherboards and cases. The NLX form factor is another open standard developed by Intel, with features comparable to the ATX, but defining a Slimline-style case and motherboard arrangement. Systems based on the NLX standard should not experience the compatibility problems of LPX-based systems, but the inherent problems of the Low-Profile design remain. These types of form factors are popular with corporate clients and novice consumers because of the systems' small footprint and their "everything-on-the-motherboard" design.

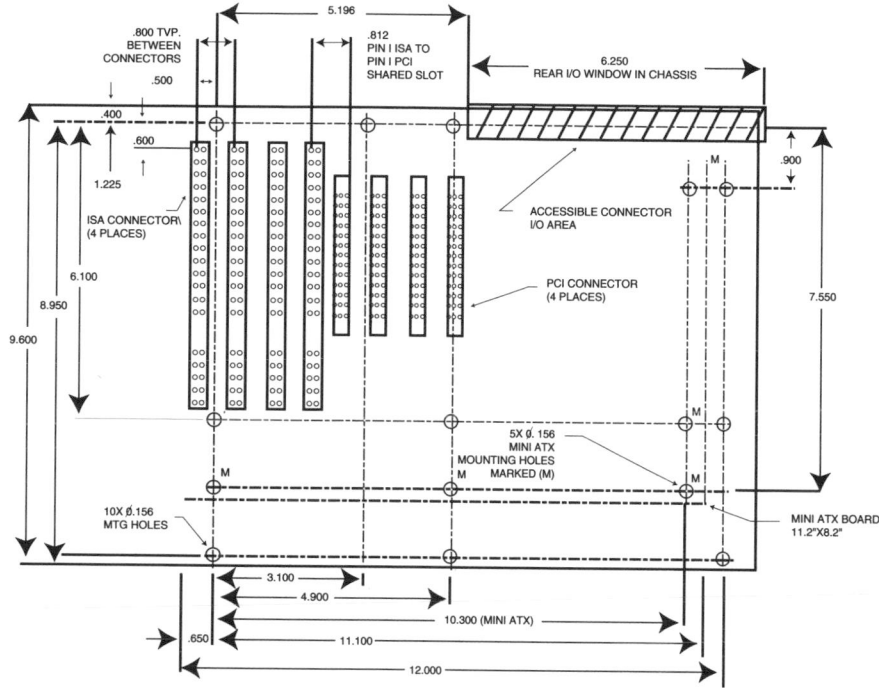

FIG. 16.2 ATX motherboard form factor.

In addition to the form factor, you should consider several other features when selecting a motherboard. The following sections examine each feature.

Processor. In most cases, your motherboard comes with the processor already installed. Most of the name-brand motherboard manufacturers like to install the processor and warranty the board and processor as a unit. This is not always the case, and it is definitely possible to purchase the motherboard and processor separately.

The motherboards you consider should have a socket for one of four different processor families:

- Pentium
- Pentium with MMX (MultiMedia eXtension)
- Pentium Pro
- Pentium II

Pentium motherboards normally have a Zero Insertion Force (ZIF) Socket 7 (321-pin), which supports processors with speeds from 120MHz to 233MHz. *MMX* is an extension of the Pentium line that includes additional instructions to handle and accelerate multimedia function calls, such as video and sound. Pentium Pro motherboards use the 387-pin Socket 8. The Pentium II is to the Pentium Pro as the Pentium with MMX is to the Pentium. The Pentium II processor, running at speeds up to 400MHz, is Intel's newest processor family and is rapidly becoming a popular alternative on high-end systems. Pentium II motherboards use a single-edge connector (SEC) processor slot rather than the standard pin-and-socket approach of the previous Intel processor designs.

◄◄ See "Processor Sockets," p. 54

◄◄ See "Sixth-Generation Processors," p. 127

◄◄ See "Processor Sockets/Slots," p. 182

Depending on the exact processor you install and the speed at which it is to run, there may be jumpers on the motherboard to set. There may also be jumpers to control the voltage supplied to the processor. You should carefully check that these settings are correct or the board and processor will not operate properly.

Chipsets. Aside from the processor, the main component on a motherboard is called the *chipset*. This is normally a set of one to five chips that contains the main motherboard circuits. These chipsets replace the 100 or more distinct components that were used in the original IBM AT systems and allow a motherboard designer to easily create a functional system. The chipset contains the local bus controller (usually PCI), the cache controller, main memory controller, DMA and interrupt controllers, and several other circuits.

The chipset used in a given motherboard has a profound effect on the performance of the board and dictates performance parameters and limitations, such as cache size and speed, main memory size and speed, processor types and speeds, and more. If you plan to incorporate new technologies such as the Accelerated Graphics Port (AGP) or the Universal Serial Bus (USB) into your system, you must be sure that your motherboard has a chipset that supports these features.

Because chipsets are constantly being introduced and improved over time, I cannot list all of them and their functions. There are several popular high-performance chipsets designed for Pentium motherboards on the market today. The best of these offer support for SDRAM (Synchronous DRAM) or EDO (Extended Data Out) RAM, pipeline burst cache SRAM (Static RAM), PCI local bus, Advanced Power Management (APM), and other functions, such as Ultra-DMA or other bus-mastering IDE interfaces.

Intel is currently the most popular manufacturer of chipsets, which is not surprising as the development of new chipsets parallels the introduction of new processors. There are other chipset manufacturers, but as Intel releases new processor models at an ever increasing rate, it becomes more difficult for other developers to keep up. In fact, in many cases you can use the Intel-compatible processors manufactured by other companies, such as AMD and Cyrix, with motherboards containing Intel chipsets.

◄◄ See "Chipsets," p. 183

Several of the Intel chipsets are available for Pentium, Pentium Pro, and Pentium II-based motherboards:

- *Intel 440BX AGPset.* Released in coordination with the 350- and 400MHz Pentium II processors, the 440BX chipset is the first to support both 66- and 100MHz system bus speeds and processor speeds of 233–400MHz. The chipset includes the 82443BX Host Bridge/Controller, which provides a Host-to-PCI bridge, an optimized DRAM controller and data path, and a 2× Accelerated Graphic Port (AGP) interface. Intended for 3-D graphics and multimedia applications, the chipset employs a technique called Quad Port Acceleration, which uses separate buffers and arbiters for the main processor bus, the PCI bus, the graphics port, and SDRAM. This chipset also supports the power management functions defined in Intel's Advanced Configuration and Power Interface (ACPI) specification.

- *Intel 440LX AGPset.* Designed for Pentium II systems, the 440LX chipset is Intel's first chipset to support the Accelerated Graphics Port (AGP) using the 8243LX PCI AGP Controller (PAC). The 440LX also uses Intel's Quad Port Acceleration, supports ACPI power management, and includes the Quantum Ultra DMA protocol which increases the transfer rate of the ATA/IDE interface to 33 megabytes per second.

- *Intel 440FX PCIset.* Code-named Natoma and designed for systems containing one or two Pentium II or Pentium Pro processors, the 440FX PCIset includes the 82441FX PCI and Memory Controller (PMC), the 82442FX Data Bus Accelerator (DBX), and the 82371SB PCI ISA IDE Xcelerator (PIIX3). The PMC and DBX function as a two-chip host-to-PCI bridge, and incorporate the PCI interface, the PCI arbiter, and DRAM control. The chipset also supports the Universal Serial Bus (USB).

- *Intel 430TX PCIset.* Designed for Pentium systems with MMX, the 430TX PCIset includes the 82439TX System Controller (MTXC) and the 82371AB PCI ISA IDE Xcelerator (PIIX4), supporting both desktop and mobile architectures.

- *Intel 430HX PCIset.* Code-named the Triton II, this chipset is designed for (non-MMX) Pentium-based systems, and includes the 82439HX System Controller (TXC) and the 82371SB PCI I/O IDE Xcelerator (PIIX3). The TXC provides second-level cache control and DRAM control functions, while functioning as a single-chip host-to-PCI bridge. The 430HX PCIset was released as a second-generation variant on the 430FX PCIset, which does not contain support for parity-checked RAM. The 430HX provides support for up to 512M of parity and/or ECC (Error Correcting Code) memory.

- *Intel 430VX PCIset.* Also intended for use with Pentium processors, the 430VX PCIset includes the 82437VX System Controller (TVX), two 82438VX Data Paths (TDX), and the 82371SB PCI ISA IDE Xcelerator (PIIX3). The chipset functions as a Host-to-PCI bridge, provides a full function 64-bit data path to main memory and second-level cache control, and supports the Universal Serial Bus.

- *Intel 430FX PCIset.* Code-named Triton and designed for Pentium systems, the 430FX PCIset includes the 82437FX Triton System Controller (TSC), two 82438FX Triton Data Paths (TDP), and the 82371FB PCI ISA IDE Xcelerator (PIIX). The TSC integrates the cache and main memory control functions and provides bus control for transfers between the CPU, cache, main memory, and the PCI Bus. The L2 cache controller in the TSC supports write-back cache for cache sizes of 256K and 512K and lower-cost cacheless designs. Cache memory can be implemented with either standard, burst, or pipeline burst SRAMs. The TSC and TDPs together support up to 128M of EDO or standard main memory. The PIIX acts as a PCI-to-ISA bridge and includes the DMA controllers, interrupt controllers, timer/counter, power management support, and an Enhanced IDE interface with up to two IDE connectors for four IDE devices.

Other manufacturers produce chipsets such as the following:

- *Opti Viper.* The 82C550 Viper-DP from Opti supports not only the Pentium, but also the AMD K5 and Cyrix M1 processors, in both single- and dual-processor configurations. The Viper-DP chipset consists of three chips: the 82C556 Data Buffer Controller (DBC), the 82C557 System Controller (SC), and the 82C558 Integrated Peripherals Controller (IPC). The SC is the main chip and contains the main memory controller, L2 cache controller, and the PCI and VL-Bus interfaces. The IPC contains the ISA bus controller, DMA and Interrupt controllers, and PCI-to-ISA bridge. The DBC buffers the CPU and main memory and contains the parity generation and checking circuits. Viper supports up to 512M of EDO or standard main memory with or without parity checking, and up to 2M of L2 write-back cache using either asynchronous, burst, or pipeline burst SRAMs.

- *ALi Aladdin.* The Aladdin M1510 chipset from Acer Laboratories, Inc. also supports the Pentium, AMD K5, and Cyrix M1 series processors in both single- and dual-processor configurations. Aladdin M1510 is a four-chip set. It includes the M1511 Memory/Cache Controller that supports EDO RAM and standard RAM up to 768M with or without parity checking.

  This chip also supports up to 1M of L2 write-back cache, including support for standard, burst, and pipeline burst SRAMs. The M1513 System I/O Controller contains the PCI bus interface, DMA and Interrupt controllers, timer circuits, PCI Enhanced IDE interface, and an integrated keyboard controller. Two M1512 data buffers are used to serve as an intermediate between the CPU and main memory.

- *AVI Apollo MVP3.* Designed for use with Socket 7 Pentiums, the MVP3 chipset supports system bus speeds up to 100MHz, AGP version 1.0, and the UltraDMA-33 EIDE interface. Based on the VT82C598AT system controller (476-pin BGA) and the VT82C586B PCI-to-ISA bridge (208 pin PQFP), the chipset supports ACPI power management, concurrent CPU and AGP access, and Fast Page Mode (FPM), EDO, SDRAM, and DDR SDRAM.

◄◄ See "Knowing What to Look For," p. 292

Clearly, the selection of a chipset must be based largely upon the processor you choose and the additional components you intend to install in the computer. At the time of this writing, a system with an ATX motherboard, a Pentium II processor, and the Intel 440LX AGPset chipset would be the top of the line, and could easily support the intensive graphics and multimedia functions of today's applications.

However, no matter what Pentium, Pentium Pro, or Pentium II class chipset you look for, I recommend checking for the following supported features:

- SDRAM or EDO RAM (main memory)

- Pipeline Burst (also called Synchronous) SRAM cache

- RAM parity generation and checking

- ECC memory support

- APM (Advanced Power Management) energy-saving functions

- MMX support (if you plan to do any multimedia)

- PCI Local Bus

Most of the better chipsets on the market today should have these features. If you are intent on building yourself the ultimate PC (at least by this week's standards), you will also want to consider the fastest Pentium II processors available. Chipsets designed for these processors should include support for the latest technologies, such as the 100MHz system bus and the accelerated graphics port (AGP). Be sure not to waste your investment on the most capable processor by using a chipset that doesn't fully exploit its capabilities.

Most motherboards manufactured today use both the ISA and PCI expansion buses, and the chipset dictates how these buses are implemented. When you are designing your system, carefully consider the number and type of expansion cards that you intend to install. Then, make sure that the motherboard you select has the correct number of slots and that they are of the correct bus type for your peripherals (ISA or PCI).

When you buy a motherboard, I highly recommend you contact the chipset manufacturer and obtain the documentation (usually called the data book) for your particular chipset. This will explain how the memory and cache controllers, as well as many other devices in the system, operate. This documentation should also describe the Advanced Chipset Setup functions in your system's Setup program. With this information, you may be able to fine-tune the motherboard configuration by altering the chipset features. Because chipsets are frequently discontinued and replaced with newer models, don't wait too long to get the chipset documentation, as most manufacturers make it available only for chips currently in production.

> **Note**
>
> One interesting fact about chipsets is that in the volume that the motherboard manufacturers purchase them, the chipsets usually cost about $40 each. If you have an older motherboard that needs repair, you normally cannot purchase the chipset because they are usually not stocked by the manufacturer after they are discontinued. The low-cost chipset is one of the reasons why motherboards have become disposable items which are rarely, if ever, repaired.

BIOS. Another important feature on the motherboard is the *BIOS (Basic Input Output System)*. This is also called the *ROM BIOS* because the code is stored in a Read Only Memory (ROM) chip. There are several things to look for here. One is that the BIOS be supplied by one of the major BIOS manufacturers such as AMI (American Megatrends International), Phoenix, Award, or Microid Research. Also, make sure that the BIOS is contained in a special type of reprogrammable chip called a *Flash ROM* or *EEPROM (Electrically Erasable Programmable Read Only Memory)*. This will allow you to download BIOS updates from the manufacturer and, using a program they supply, easily update the code in your BIOS. If you do not have the Flash ROM or EEPROM type, you will have to physically replace the chip if an update is required.

◄◄ See "Upgrading the ROM Bios," p. 215

Make sure that the motherboard and BIOS support the Plug-and-Play (PnP) specification. This will make installing new cards, especially PnP cards, much easier. PnP automates the installation and uses special software built into the BIOS and the operating system (such as Windows 95 and 98) to automatically configure adapter cards and resolve adapter resource conflicts.

Memory. Pentium systems require memory for the Level 2 (secondary) cache and the main memory. The cache memory will be in the form of individual SRAM chips or possibly in what is called *COAST (Cache On A STick)* or *CELP (Card Edge Low Profile)*. COAST and CELP are different names for the same thing. This is a new standard for cache SIMMs. COAST/CELP SIMMs have a different number of pins and pinout from standard main memory SIMMs, and are not interchangeable with them.

◄◄ See "Cache Memory—SRAM," p. 319

Most Pentium motherboards support at least 256–512K of cache memory. The chips themselves are available in three basic cache types—standard asynchronous, burst, and pipeline burst. The last offers the highest performance; choose it if your motherboard supports it. Most of the newer Pentium boards support the pipeline burst cache chips; most of the 486 boards didn't. This is because these faster cache chips are not really needed at the slower 33–40MHz memory bus speeds on the 486 compared to the 60- and 66MHz memory bus speeds in a Pentium system.

For Pentium Pro and Pentium II systems, no additional level 2 memory is needed because the processors have the cache memory integrated into the processor package.

Main memory is normally installed in the form of *SIMMs (Single Inline Memory Modules)* or in some cases the newer *DIMMs (Dual Inline Memory Modules)*. There are three different physical types of main memory modules used in PC systems today, with several variations of each. The three main types are as follows:

- 30-pin IMMs
- 72-pin SIMMs
- 168-pin DIMMs

The 72-pin SIMMs are by far the most common type of memory module used today; however, just a few years ago, most systems came with 30-pin modules. Many high-end systems use the DIMMs because they are 64 bits wide and can be used as a single bank on a Pentium, Pentium Pro, or Pentium II system. Depending on the type of processor, a different number of SIMMs must be installed to make a complete memory bank, and the 72-pin SIMMs are four times as dense as the 30-pin types.

◀◀ See "Physical Memory," p. 323

For example, in a 486-based system, you would need four 30-pin SIMMs to make a single bank of memory, while only one 72-pin SIMM would be required for a single bank. This is because the 72-pin SIMMs hold data 32 bits wide, while the 30-pin SIMMs hold data only 8 bits wide. A 64-bit Pentium system, then, would require two 72-pin SIMMs or a single 168-pin DIMM to make a single bank.

Memory modules can include an extra bit for each eight to be used for parity checking. These are called *parity SIMMs* or *parity DIMMs* and are required by most older boards. Many newer motherboards do not employ parity checking, which means that you will not be able to use the slightly more expensive parity SIMMs. You can install them, but the extra parity bits won't function. I don't necessarily agree with this philosophy, but nevertheless, many motherboards (such as those based on the Intel Triton chipset) simply cannot use parity checking at all! Most other chipsets, including the newer Triton II, do support memory parity checking.

Another thing to watch out for is the type of metal on the memory module contacts. They are available with either tin- or gold-plated contacts. Although it may seem that gold-plated contacts are better (they are), you should not use them in all systems. You should instead always match the type of plating on the module contacts to what is also used on the socket contacts. In other words, if the motherboard SIMM or DIMM sockets have tin-plated contacts, then you *must* use SIMMs or DIMMs with tin-plated contacts.

If you mix dissimilar metals (tin with gold), corrosion on the tin side is rapidly acceler-ated, and tiny electrical currents are generated. The combination of the corrosion and tiny currents causes havoc, and all types of memory problems and errors may occur. In some systems, I have observed that everything seems fine for about a year, during which the corrosion develops. After that, random memory errors result. Removing and cleaning the memory module and socket contacts postpones the problem for another year, upon which the problems return again. How would you like this problem if you had 100 or more systems to support? Of course, you can avoid these problems if you insist on using SIMMs with contacts whose metal matches the metal found in the sockets in which they will be installed.

Finally, some systems now use a special type of memory called *EDO (Extended Data Out)*. These memory chips are slightly redesigned and do not cost much more than standard non-EDO memory, but they can operate at increased efficiency in a motherboard with a chipset designed for them. The actual speed increase varies but is usually not more than a couple of percentage points. Motherboards that use EDO memory can also use standard non-EDO memory, but they will not enjoy the increased performance. You can install EDO memory in older systems that do not support it because EDO is backward-compat-ible with standard (called *fast page mode*) memory. Of course, installing the more expen-sive EDO modules in an older system will not improve performance.

I/O Ports. Most motherboards today have built-in I/O ports. If these ports are not built in, then they will have to be supplied via a plug-in expansion board that, unfortunately, wastes an expansion slot. The following ports should be included in any new system you assemble:

- Mouse port (so-called PS/2 type)
- Two local bus enhanced IDE ports (primary and secondary)
- Floppy controller
- Two serial ports (16550A buffered UART type)
- Parallel port (EPP/ECP type)

Many motherboards now include one or more USB (Universal Serial Bus) ports in addi-tion to the standard I/O ports listed.

The standard procedure is to include all of these ports directly on the motherboard. This is possible because there are several chip companies that have implemented all of these features except the mouse port (which uses the keyboard controller) on a single Super I/O chip. These chips often cost less than $5 in quantities of 1,000 or more; therefore, adding these items directly to the motherboard saves both money and the use of an expansion slot.

If these devices are not present on the motherboard, then various Super or Multi-I/O boards that implement all of these ports are available. Again, most of the newer versions of these boards use a single-chip implementation because it is cheaper and more reliable.

◄◄ See "Super I/O Chips," p. 207

It has become an increasingly popular practice in recent years (especially in Slimline-style systems) to integrate other standard computer functions into the motherboard design, such as video, sound, and even network adapters. The advantages of this practice are that it frees up expansion slots that would normally be occupied by separate adapter cards and that it saves money. The price difference between a motherboard with integrated video and sound and one without would be far less than the cost of good-quality sound and video cards.

The drawback, of course, is that you have little or no choice about the features or quality of the integrated adapters. Integrated components like these are nearly always of service-able quality, but they certainly do not push the performance envelope of higher-end expansion cards. Most people who decide to build a system themselves do so because they want optimum performance from every component, which you do not get from integrated video and sound.

Buying a motherboard with integrated adapters, however, does not preclude you from adding expansion devices of the same type. You can usually install a video or sound card into a system with an integrated adapter without major problems, except that the additional cost of the integrated component is wasted. You may also encounter difficulties with the automated hardware detection routines in operating systems like Windows 9x detecting the wrong adapter in your system, but you can remedy this by manually identifying the expansion card to the OS.

Floppy Disk and Removable Drives

Since the advent of the CD-ROM, the floppy disk drive has largely been relegated to a minor role as an alternative system boot device. Usually, today's systems are equipped with a 1.44M 3 1/2-inch drive, but the 2.88M drives pioneered by IBM are also available. The 2.88M drives are fully backward-compatible with 1.44M disks and do not cost that much more. However, before making your purchase, make sure that the drive controller and the ROM BIOS in your system fully support 2.88M drive.

Although the 1.2M 5 1/4-inch floppy disk drive is now all but obsolete, you should still be able to find them, if you have data stored in that format. Some floppy drive manufacturers also make combo drives that include both a 3 1/2-inch 1.44M and 5 1/4-inch 1.2M drive in a single unit, which installs in a half-height 5 1/4-inch bay. At least one company (Teac) offers a combo drive that combines a 1.44M floppy and a CD-ROM drive in a single unit. One drawback of these combo units is that if one of the components fails, the entire combo drive has to be replaced. Also, no one seems to make these with the more desirable 2.88M floppy drives.

For removable data storage and system backups, the 100M Iomega Zip drive is rapidly becoming a *de facto* standard on new PCs. Internal models use either the EIDE or SCSI interface. The drives and the media are inexpensive, and their 100M capacity is far more practical than a stack of floppy disks. You can also purchase combination floppy/Zip drives that fit into a standard half-height bay. Depending on your storage needs, there are other types of removable cartridge drives of varying capacities. At the high end, Iomega makes Jaz drives that are available in 1G and 2G models, while other manufacturers such as Syquest offer drives with a variety of disk sizes.

The Imation LS-120 is a good alternative to the Zip because it can store 120M on its own proprietary media and still accept standard 1.44M floppies in the same drives. With a recent BIOS by one of the major manufacturers (Award, Phoenix, or AMI), you can boot the system from these disks just as you would a normal floppy drive.

Hard Disk Drive

Your system also needs at least one hard disk drive. In most cases, a drive with a minimum capacity of 2G is recommended, although in some cases you can get away with less for a low-end configuration. High-end systems should have drives of 2–8G or higher. One of the cardinal rules of computer shopping is that you can never have too much hard disk space. Buy as much as you can afford, and you'll almost certainly end up filling it anyway.

> **Tip**
>
> If you are an Internet user, one informal method of estimating how much disk space you will need is to go by the speed of your Internet connection. If you have a high-speed link such as that provided by an ISDN connection, a cable modem, or a LAN, you will find that the ease of downloading large amounts of data fills disk drives amazingly quickly. I would recommend at least a 6G hard drive in these cases, and a removable storage system with a large capacity, such as a Jaz or CD-R drive, is also a good idea.

The most popular hard drive interface for desktop systems is EIDE, though SCSI is preferable for use with multitasking OSs. EIDE generally offers greater performance for single-drive installations, but SCSI is better for use with two or more drives or with multitasking operating systems such as Windows 95 and NT. This is due to the greater intelligence in the SCSI interface, which removes some of the I/O processing burden from the system's CPU.

> **Note**
>
> In most cases, a system's EIDE adapter is integrated into the motherboard. With SCSI, this is much less common. Although it is sometimes possible to purchase a motherboard with an integrated SCSI adapter, you are more likely to have to purchase a separate SCSI host adapter and install it into one of your system's expansion slots. It is recommended that you select a SCSI adapter that uses the fastest expansion bus that your system supports, which in most cases today is PCI. Good quality SCSI host adapters are considerably more complex than an EIDE adapter, and are therefore more expensive. Be sure to consider this additional expense and the need for an additional slot when deciding on a hard drive interface for your system.

SCSI adapters and hard disk drives cost considerably more than their EIDE counterparts, but they offer greater expandability (up to 7 or even 15 devices, depending on the SCSI type) and better performance when several different processes are accessing the same devices. If you are building a relatively simple standalone system containing one or two hard disk drives and a CD-ROM, EIDE is probably more than sufficient for your needs. However, if you plan on adding other peripherals such as tape drives, cartridge drives, and scanners, or if you plan to share your drives with other users over a network, then SCSI may be a worthwhile investment.

Tip

For removable storage devices that require a consistent stream of data to function properly, such as CD-R and tape drives, SCSI is strongly recommended. EIDE devices do not handle multiple tasks nearly as well as SCSI, and can result in slower data transfer rates and less efficient storage capacity when used with these types of devices.

There are several brands of high-quality hard disk drives to choose from, and most of them offer similar performance within their price and capacity categories. In fact, you may notice that the capacities and specifications of the various EIDE and SCSI drives offered by certain manufacturers are remarkably similar. This is because a single drive assembly is manufactured for use with both interfaces. The same 2G EIDE drive, for example, with the addition of a SCSI controller, becomes a SCSI drive, at a substantially higher price.

◄◄ See "Performance," p. 651

CD-ROM Drive

A CD-ROM drive should be considered a mandatory item in any PC you construct these days. This is because virtually all software is now being distributed on CD-ROM. Systems can now even boot from CD-ROM drives (using Windows NT 4.0, for example), as long as the system BIOS provides the proper support. There are several types of CD-ROM drives to consider these days, but I generally recommend a minimum of a 12- or 16X drive connected using an EIDE interface. This results in the best possible performance with the minimum amount of hassle. If you plan on using SCSI for your hard drives, however, you also should select a SCSI CD-ROM; you'll improve your multitasking performance and save money on an unneeded IDE controller.

There are several variations on the standard CD-ROM drive that you also may want to consider. For example, there is a combination drive developed by Panasonic that is called a PD-ROM. This drive reads standard CDs and also supports removable cartridges with the same capacity as a CD-ROM, approximately 660M. Unfortunately, you cannot use both media at the same time, preventing you from using the drive for its most obvious purpose, copying CDs.

You might also consider purchasing a writable CD-ROM drive, generally known as a CD-R. Burning your own CDs can be a convenient and relatively inexpensive data storage method. Most of the writable CD-ROM drives are WORM (write once/read many) devices that also provide read-only support for standard CD-ROM discs. There are now rewritable CD-ROM drives on the market, called CD-RWs, but unlike a CD-R, a CD-RW disc can be read only by "multi-read" drives because the reflection rate of the disc is only 25–35% that of a standard CD. DVD-ROM drives are the latest storage solution to hit the market and are dropping rapidly in price. DVD-ROM is a high-density data storage format that uses a CD-sized disc to store a great deal more data than a CD-ROM: from 4.7– 17G, depending on the format. This technology is still in its infancy, but the drives available now can read standard CD-ROMs and audio CDs.

◀◀ See "DVD (Digital Versatile Disk)," p. 851

Keyboard and Pointing Device (Mouse)

Obviously, your system needs a keyboard and some type of pointing device, such as a mouse. Different people prefer different types of keyboards, and the "feel" of one type can vary considerably from other types. If possible, I suggest that you try a variety of keyboards until you find the type that suits you best. I prefer a stiff action with tactile feedback myself, but others prefer a lighter, quieter touch.

Because two types of keyboard connectors are found in systems today, make sure that the keyboard you purchase matches the connector on your motherboard. Most Baby-AT boards use the larger 5-pin DIN connector, and most ATX boards use the 6-pin, mini-DIN connector; however, the trend now seems to be changing to the mini-DIN connector for all boards. On some motherboards, you have an option of choosing either connector when you purchase the board. If you end up with a keyboard and motherboard that do not match, there are several companies that sell adapters to mate either type of keyboard to either type of motherboard connector. You can also purchase extension cables for both keyboards and mice that enable you to comfortably place a tower system under a desk or table while the keyboard and mouse remain on the work surface.

◀◀ See "Types of Keyboards," p. 445
◀◀ See "Keyboard Technology," p. 454

The same selection concept also applies to mice or other pointing devices; there are a number of different choices that suit different individuals. Try several before deciding on the type you want. If your motherboard includes a built-in mouse port, make sure you get a mouse designed for that interface. This mouse is often called a *PS/2 type mouse* because the IBM PS/2 systems introduced this type of mouse port. Many systems use a serial mouse connected to a serial port, but a motherboard-integrated mouse port is preferable because it leaves both serial ports free for other devices.

> **Tip**
>
> You might be tempted to skimp on your keyboard and mouse in order to save a few dollars. *Don't.* You do all of your interacting with your new PC through these devices, and cheap ones make their presence known every time you use your system.

◀◀ See "Mice," p. 480

Video Card and Display

You need a video adapter and a monitor or display to complete your system. There are numerous choices in this area, but the most important piece of advice I have to give is to choose a good monitor. The display is your main interface to the system and can be the cause of many hours of either pain or pleasure, depending on what monitor you choose.

I usually recommend a minimum of a 17-inch display these days. Anything smaller cannot acceptably display a 1,024×768 pixel resolution. If you opt for a 15-inch or smaller display, you might find that the maximum tolerable resolution is 800×600. This may be confusing because many 15-inch monitors are capable of displaying 1,024×768 resolution or even higher, but the characters and features are so small onscreen at that resolution that excessive eyestrain and headaches are often the result. If you spend a lot of time in front of your system and want to work in the higher screen resolutions, a 17-inch display should be considered mandatory.

Your video card and monitor should be compatible in terms of refresh rate, and the minimum refresh rate for a solid, nonflickering display is 70–72Hz; the higher the better. If your new video card can display 16 million colors at a resolution of 1,024×768 and a refresh rate of 76Hz, but your monitor's maximum refresh rate at 1,024×768 is 56Hz, then you can't use the video card to its maximum potential. Configuring a video adapter to deliver signals that the monitor cannot support is one of the few software configuration processes that can physically damage the system hardware. Pushing a monitor beyond its capabilities can cause it irreparable harm.

Video adapters in recent years have become standardized on the PCI interface, but the introduction of the accelerated graphics port (AGP) is a serious challenge to PCI graphics. The AGP chipsets and adapters on the market are all relatively new products, meaning their prices are artificially high and that, as with any new technology, a period of maturation will probably improve their capabilities. Given today's graphic intensive applications and operating systems, the eventual adoption of AGP as an industry standard seems to be a virtual certainty.

◀◀ See "Accelerated Graphics Port (AGP)," p. 268

Sound Card and Speakers

You need a sound card and a set of external speakers for any system that you want to be multimedia capable. The sound card should be compatible with the Creative Labs Sound Blaster cards, which have set the standards in this area. Getting a sound card with an upgradable memory (the same SIMMs you use for your main memory) enables you to download additional sound samples.

Selection of a sound card can be said to depend largely on whether you are a "consumer" or a "producer" of computer sound. If you are interested only in playing WAV files on your machine and running multimedia or music CDs, then you don't require much from the card, although you may benefit from a better pair of speakers. If, on the other hand, you intend to make your own WAV (or other audio) files or work with MIDI, then a more capable sound card is probably in order.

Speakers designed for use with PCs range from tiny, underpowered devices to large audiophile systems. Many of the top manufacturers of stereo speakers are now producing speaker systems for PCs.

USB Peripherals

The Universal Serial Bus promises to render the standard I/O ports on the PC obsolete. Essentially, USB brings Plug-and-Play support to external peripherals by enabling you to plug up to 127 devices into a single port supporting data transfer rates up to 12Mbps. Typically, you plug a USB monitor or keyboard into a port integrated into the motherboard and plug other devices into that. Many of the current motherboards and chipsets support USB, but the actual USB devices are appearing on the market more slowly.

As to the types of devices planned for USB, there are virtually no limits. Modems, monitors, keyboards, mice, CD-ROM drives, speakers, joysticks, tape and floppy drives, scanners, cameras, and printers are all in various stages of development. However, before you start buying all USB peripherals for your new system, be aware that this technology is very young, and that compatibility problems between devices are common.

Accessories

Apart from the major components, you need a number of other accessories to complete your system. These are the small parts that can make the assembly process a pleasure or a chore. If you are purchasing your system components from mail-order sources, you should make a complete list of all the parts you need, right down to the last cable and screw, and be sure you have everything before you begin the assembly process. It is excruciating to have to wait several days with a half-assembled system for the delivery of a forgotten part.

Heat Sinks/Cooling Fans. Most of today's faster processors produce a lot of heat, and this heat has to be dissipated or your system will operate intermittently or even fail completely. Heat sinks are available in two main types: passive and active.

Passive heat sinks are simply finned chunks of metal (usually aluminum) that are clipped or glued to the top of the processor. They act as a radiator, and in effect give the processor more surface area to dissipate the heat. I normally recommend this passive-design type of heat sink because there are no mechanical parts to fail. In some cases, you should use a thermal transfer grease or sticky tape to fill any air gaps between the heat sink and the processor. This allows for maximum heat transfer and the best efficiency.

An *active heat sink* includes a fan. These can offer greater cooling capacity than the passive types, and some processors are sold with the fan already attached. If you rely on a CPU fan to cool your processor, be sure to buy a high quality one that runs from the computer's internal power. I've seen some battery-operated fans, and even some lower quality system-powered ones, fail without warning, and this can result in damage to the processor from excessive heat.

> **Note**
>
> The newer ATX form factor motherboards are designed to eliminate the troublesome and unreliable active heat sink (CPU fan). These systems feature a power supply with reverse-flow cooling that blows air directly over the CPU, which is relocated in these systems to take advantage of this design. Due to this architectural improvement, the ATX motherboard form factor eliminates the need for any sort of cooling fan mounted directly to the CPU. There are, however, some manufacturers who continue to use CPU fans in ATX systems, because they are unaware of this fact, they are not fully supporting the ATX standard, or they are simply being cautious.

Cables. PC systems need a number of different cables to hook up everything. These can include power cables or adapters, disk drive cables, internal or external CD-ROM cables, and many others. Most of the time, the devices you purchase come with included cables, but in some cases, they aren't supplied. The vendor list in Appendix B, "Useful Hardware Web Sites," lists several cable and small parts suppliers that can get you the cables or other parts you need to complete your system.

Another advantage of the ATX motherboard form factor is that these boards feature externally accessible I/O connectors directly mounted to the rear of the board. This eliminates the "rat's nest" of cables found in the common Baby-AT form factor systems. This feature also makes the ATX system a little cheaper and more reliable.

Hardware. You need screws, standoffs, mounting rails, and other miscellaneous hardware to assemble your system. Most of these parts come with the case or with your other system components. When you purchase a component such as a hard disk drive, some vendors offer you the option of purchasing the bare drive or a kit containing the required cables and mounting hardware for the device. Spending the few additional dollars for the complete kit is rarely a waste of money. Even if you're left with some extra bits and pieces after assembling your system, they will probably come in handy someday.

In situations where you need other hardware not included with your system components, you can consult the vendor list in Appendix B for suppliers of small parts and hardware needed to get your system operational.

Hardware and Software Resources

When you are planning to build a system, it is important to consider how all of your selected components will work together, and how the software you run must support them. It is not enough to be sure that you have sufficient slots on the motherboard for all of your expansion cards and enough bays in the case for all of your drives. You must also consider the resources required for all the components.

For example, not only should you be certain that you have enough hardware interrupts (IRQs) to support all of your components, you should also know which IRQs are supported by each device. Otherwise, you may find yourself stuck with hardware that you can't install, even though you have interrupts free. Essentially, you should completely configure the system before you begin ordering any parts. Planning a system to this level of detail can be a lot of work, which is one reason why the vast majority of PCs are prebuilt.

Another consideration is the operating system and other software you will need. Prebuilt systems nearly always arrive with the operating system installed, but when you build your own, you must be prepared with a copy of your selected operating system, including a system disk so you can boot the system the first time.

The operating system that you select for your new computer is another important decision. You must be certain that the OS supports all the hardware you've selected, which can occasionally be a difficult task. If, for example, you intend to use USB devices, you must run, at the very least, Windows 95 OSR 2.1, which consists of the operating system plus an additional USB support module. To obtain the Windows 95 OSR 2 release, you must purchase it with a new system or, alternatively, a new motherboard or hard drive. Fortunately, USB support is fully integrated into the Windows 98 retail product.

Drivers for specific hardware components may also be a problem. It is a good idea to gather all the latest driver revisions for your hardware, as well as BIOS flashes, firmware updates, and other software components and have them available when you begin the assembly process. Floppy disks are preferable for this, because your CD-ROM drive and connectivity hardware may not yet be operative.

System Assembly and Disassembly

Actually assembling the system is easy after you have lined up all the components! In fact, you may find the procurement phase the most lengthy and trying of the entire experience. Completing the system is basically a matter of screwing everything together, plugging in all the cables and connectors, and configuring everything to operate properly together.

In short order, you will find out whether your system operates as you had planned or whether there are some incompatibilities between some of the components. Be careful and pay attention to how you install all of your components. It is rare that a newly assembled system operates perfectly the first time, even for people who are somewhat experienced. It is very easy to forget a jumper, switch, or cable connection that later causes problems in system operation. Most people's first reaction when there are problems is to blame defective hardware, but that is usually not the source. Usually, the problem can be traced to some missed step or error made in the assembly process.

Above all, the most crucial rule of assembling your own system is to save every piece of documentation and software that comes with every component in your system. This material can be indispensable in troubleshooting problems you encounter during the assembly process or later on. You should also retain all the packing materials used to ship mail order components to you until you are certain that they will not have to be returned.

The process of physically assembling a PC requires only a few basic tools: a 1/4-inch nut driver or Phillips-head screwdriver for the external screws that hold the cover in place and a 3/16-inch nut driver or Phillips-head screwdriver for all the other screws. Needle-nose pliers can also help in removing motherboard standoffs, jumpers, and stubborn cable connectors. It is because of marketplace standardization that only a couple of different types and sizes of screws (with a few exceptions) are used to hold a system together. Also, the physical arrangement of the major components is similar even among different manufacturers.

This section covers the assembly and disassembly procedure in the following sections:

- Case or cover assembly   - Power supply
- Adapter boards   - Motherboard
- Disk drives

This section discusses how to install and remove these components for several different types of systems. With regard to assembly and disassembly, it is best to consider each system by the type of case that the system uses. All systems that have AT-type cases, for example, are assembled and disassembled in much the same manner. Tower cases are basically AT-type cases turned sideways, so the same basic instructions apply to those cases. Most Slimline and XT-style cases are similar; these systems are assembled and disassembled in much the same way.

The following section lists assembly and disassembly instructions for several case types.

Assembly Preparation

Before you begin assembling any system, one of the issues you must be aware of is *ESD (electrostatic discharge)* protection. The other is recording the configuration of the system, with regard to the physical aspects of the system (such as jumper or switch settings and cable orientations) and to the logical configuration of the system (especially in terms of elements such as CMOS settings).

ESD Protection. When you are working on the internal components of a computer, you need to take the necessary precautions to prevent accidental static discharges to the components. At any time, your body can hold a large static voltage charge that can easily damage components of your system. Before I ever put my hands into an open system, I first touch a grounded portion of the chassis, such as the power supply case, while the computer is plugged in. This action serves to equalize the charges that the device and I are carrying. By leaving the computer plugged in, you're allowing the static electricity to drain off safely to ground, rather than forcing the components of the system to accept the jolt.

For this reason, it is sometimes recommended that you leave an assembled computer plugged in while you are working inside the case. Although this practice can be safe in older systems, the ATX and NLX power supplies used in many systems today deliver a +5v current to the motherboard whenever they are plugged in. This current can be dangerous, so unplug the system before working inside and find another place to ground yourself.

High-end workbenches at repair facilities have the entire bench grounded, so it's not as big a problem; however, you need something to be a good ground source to prevent a current from building up in you.

A more sophisticated way to equalize the charges between you and any of the system components is to use an ESD protection kit. These kits consist of a wrist strap and mat, with ground wires for attachment to the system chassis. When you are going to work on a system, you place the mat next to or partially below the system unit. Next, you clip the ground wire to both the mat and the system's chassis, tying the grounds together. You then put on the wrist strap and attach that wire to a ground. Because the mat and system chassis are already wired together, you can attach the wrist-strap wire to the system chassis or to the mat. If you are using a wrist strap without a mat, clip the wrist-strap wire to the system chassis. When clipping these wires to the chassis, be sure to use an area that is free of paint so a good ground contact can be achieved. This setup ensures that any electrical charges are carried equally by you and any of the components in the system, preventing the sudden flow of static electricity that can damage the circuits.

As you install or remove disk drives, adapter cards, and especially delicate items such as the entire motherboard, SIMMs, or processors, you should place these components on the static mat. I see some people putting the system unit on top of the mat, but the unit should be alongside the mat so you have room to lay out all the components as you work with them. If you are going to remove the motherboard from a system, be sure that you leave enough room for it on the mat.

If you do not have such a mat, simply place the removed circuits and devices on a clean desk or table. Always pick up a loose adapter card by the metal bracket used to secure the card to the system. This bracket is tied into the ground circuitry of the card, so by touching the bracket first, you prevent a discharge from damaging the components of the card. If the circuit board has no metal bracket (a motherboard, for example), handle the board carefully by the edges, and try not to touch any of the connectors or components.

Caution

Some people have recommended placing loose circuit boards and chips on sheets of aluminum foil. *This procedure is absolutely not recommended and can actually result in an explosion!* Many motherboards, adapter cards, and other circuit boards today have built-in lithium or ni-cad batteries. These batteries react violently when they are shorted out, which is exactly what you would be doing by placing such a board on a piece of aluminum foil. The batteries will quickly overheat and possibly explode like a large firecracker (with dangerous shrapnel). Because you will not always be able to tell whether a board has a battery built into it somewhere, the safest practice is to never place any board on any conductive metal surface, such as foil.

Recording Physical Configuration. While you are assembling a system, it is a good idea to record all the physical settings and configurations of each component, including jumper and switch settings, cable orientations and placement, ground-wire locations, and even adapter-board placement. Keep a notebook handy for recording these items, and write down all the settings in the book.

It is especially important to record all the jumper and switch settings on every card that you install in the system, as well as those on the motherboard. If you accidentally disturb these jumpers or switches, you will know how they were originally set. This knowledge is very important if you do not have all the documentation for the system handy. Even if you do, undocumented jumpers and switches often do not appear in the manuals but must be set a certain way for the item to function. Also, record all cable orientations. Most name-brand systems use cables and connectors that are keyed so that they cannot be plugged in backward, but some generic PCs do not have this added feature. In addition, it is possible to mix up hard disk and floppy cables. You should mark or record what each cable was plugged into and its proper orientation. Ribbon cables usually have an odd-colored (red, green, blue, or black) wire at one end that indicates pin 1. There may also be a mark on the connector such as a triangle or even the number 1. The devices into which the cables are plugged are also marked in some way to indicate the orientation of pin 1. Often, there will be a dot next to the pin 1 side of the connector, or there may be a 1 or other mark.

Although cable orientation and placement seem to be very simple, we rarely get through the entire course of my PC troubleshooting seminars without at least one group of people having cable-connection problems. Fortunately, in most cases (excepting power cables), plugging any of the ribbon cables inside the system backward rarely causes any permanent damage.

Power and battery connections are exceptions; plugging them in backward in most cases will cause damage. In fact, plugging the motherboard power connectors in backward or in the wrong plug location will put 12v where only 5v should be—a situation that can cause components of the board to violently explode. I know of several people who have facial scars caused by shrapnel from exploding components caused by improper power supply connections! As a precaution, I always turn my face away from the system when I power it on for the first time.

Plugging the CMOS battery in backward can damage the CMOS chip, which usually is soldered into the motherboard; in such a case, the motherboard must be replaced.

Finally, it is a good idea to record miscellaneous items such as the placement of any ground wires, adapter cards, and anything else that you may have difficulty remembering later. Some configurations and setups may be particular about the slots in which the adapter cards are located; it usually is a good idea to put everything back exactly the way it was originally.

Motherboard Installation

When you are installing your system's motherboard, unpack the motherboard and check to make sure you have everything that should be included. If you purchase a new board, normally you get at least the motherboard, some I/O cables, and a manual. If you ordered the motherboard with a processor and/or memory, it will normally be installed on the board for you but may also be included separately. Some board kits will include an antistatic wrist strap to help prevent damage due to static electricity when installing the board.

Prepare the New Motherboard. Before a new motherboard can be installed, it must be set up properly to accept the processor. Most newer motherboards have jumpers that control both the CPU speed and the voltage supplied to it. If these are set incorrectly, the system may not operate at all, operate erratically, or possibly even damage the CPU. If you have any questions about the proper settings, contact the vendor who sold you the board before making any jumper changes.

◄◄ See "CPU Operating Voltages," p. 72

Most processors today run hot enough to require some form of heat sink to dissipate heat from the processor. To install the processor and heat sink, use the following procedures:

1. Take the new motherboard out of the antistatic bag it was supplied in, and set it on the bag or the antistatic mat, if you have one.

2. Refer to the motherboard manufacturer's manual to set the jumpers to match the CPU you are going to install. Look for the diagram of the motherboard to find the jumper location, and look for the tables for the right settings for your CPU. If the CPU was supplied already installed on the motherboard, then the jumpers should already be correctly set for you, but it is still a good idea to check them.

3. For socketed processors, find pin 1 on the processor; it is usually denoted by a corner of the chip that is marked by a dot or a bevel in that corner. Next, find the corresponding pin 1 of the ZIF socket for the CPU on the motherboard. Pin 1 is usually marked on the board, or there may be a bevel in one corner of the socket. Insert the CPU into the ZIF socket by lifting the release lever, aligning the pins on the processor with the holes in the socket, and pushing it down into place. If the

processor does not go all the way into the socket, then check for possible interference or pin alignment problems. When the processor is fully seated in the socket, push the locking lever on the socket down to secure the processor.

4. If the CPU does not already have a heat sink attached to it, then attach it now. Most heat sinks will either clip directly to the CPU or to the socket with one or more retainer clips. Be careful when attaching the clip to the socket; you don't want it to scrape against the motherboard, which might damage circuit traces or components. In most cases, it is a good idea to put a dab of heat sink thermal transfer compound (normally a white-colored grease) on the CPU before installing the heat sink. This prevents any air gaps and allows the heat sink to work more efficiently.

Install Memory Modules. In order to function, the motherboard must have memory installed on it. Modern motherboards use either SIMMs or DIMMs. Depending on the module type, it will have a specific method of sliding into and clipping to the sockets. Normally, you install modules in the lowest numbered sockets or banks first. Note that some boards will require modules to be installed in pairs or even four at a time. Consult the motherboard documentation for more information on which sockets to use first and in what order, and how to install the specific modules the board uses.

◀◀ See "Memory Banks," p. 338

Memory modules are normally keyed to the sockets by a notch on the side or on the bottom, so they can go in only one way.

> **Caution**
>
> Be careful not to damage the connector. If you damage the motherboard memory connector, you could be facing an expensive repair. Never force the module; it should come out easily. If it doesn't, you are doing something wrong.

Mount the New Motherboard in the Case. The motherboard attaches to the case with one or more screws and often several plastic standoffs. If you are using a new case, you may have to attach one or more metal spacers or plastic standoffs in the proper holes before you can install the motherboard. Use the following procedure to install the new motherboard in the case:

1. Find the holes in the new motherboard for the metal spacers and plastic standoffs. You should use metal spacers wherever there is a ring of solder around the hole. Use plastic standoffs where there is no ring of solder (see Figure 16.3). Screw any metal spacers into the new case in the proper positions to align with the screw holes in the motherboard.

2. Insert any plastic standoffs directly into the new motherboard from underneath until they snap into place.

3. Install the new motherboard into the case by setting it down so any standoffs engage the case. Often you will have to set the board into the case and slide it sideways to engage the standoffs into the slots in the case. When the board is in the proper position, the screw holes in the board should be aligned with all of the metal spacers or screw holes in the case.

4. Take the screws and any plastic washers that were supplied with the new motherboard, and screw the board into the case.

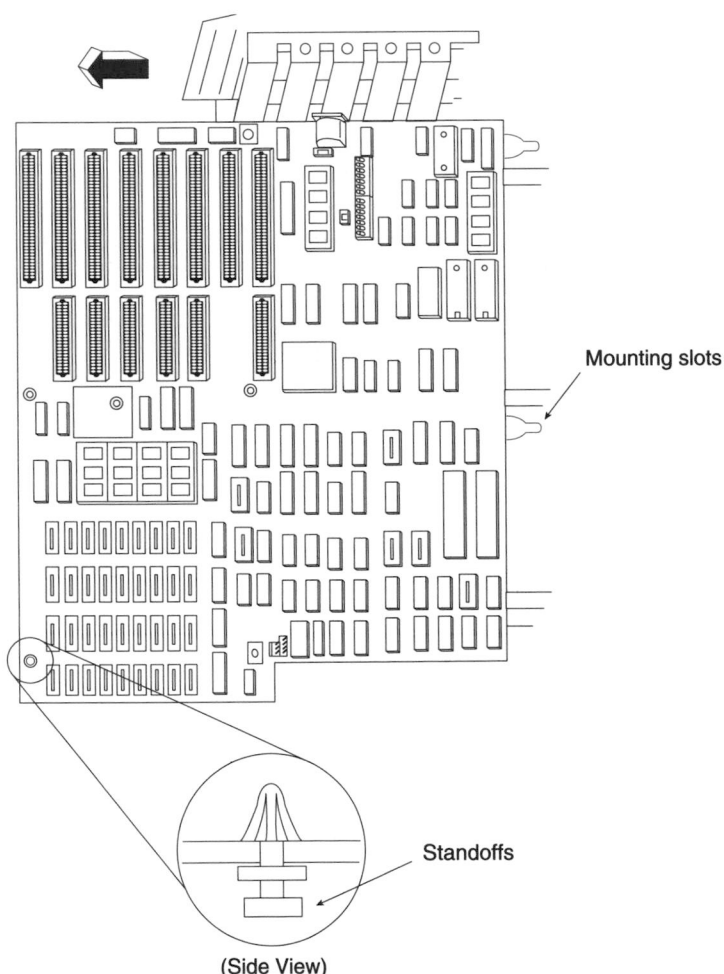

Mounting slots

Standoffs

(Side View)

FIG. 16.3   Insert standoffs into their mounting slots.

Connect the Power Supply. Newer ATX-style motherboards have a single-power connector that can go on only one way. Baby-AT and other-style board designs usually have two separate six-wire power connectors from the power supply to the board, which may not be keyed and therefore may be interchangeable (see Figure 16.4). Even though it may be possible to insert them several ways, only one way is correct! These power leads are usually labeled P8 and P9 in most systems. The order in which you connect them to the board is crucial; if you install them backward, you might cause damage to the motherboard when you power it up. Many systems use a CPU cooling fan, which should also be connected. To attach the power connectors from the power supply to the motherboard, do the following:

◀◀ See "Power Supply Connectors," p. 403

1. If the system uses a single ATX-style power connector, then plug it in; it can go on only one way.

   If two separate six-wire connectors are used, the two black ground wires on the ends of the connectors must meet in the middle. Align the power connectors such that the black ground wires are adjacent to each other and plug the connectors in. Consult the documentation with your board to make sure the power supply connection is correct.

2. Plug in the power lead for the CPU fan if one is used. The fan will either connect to the power supply via a disk drive power connector, or it may connect directly to a fan power connector on the motherboard.

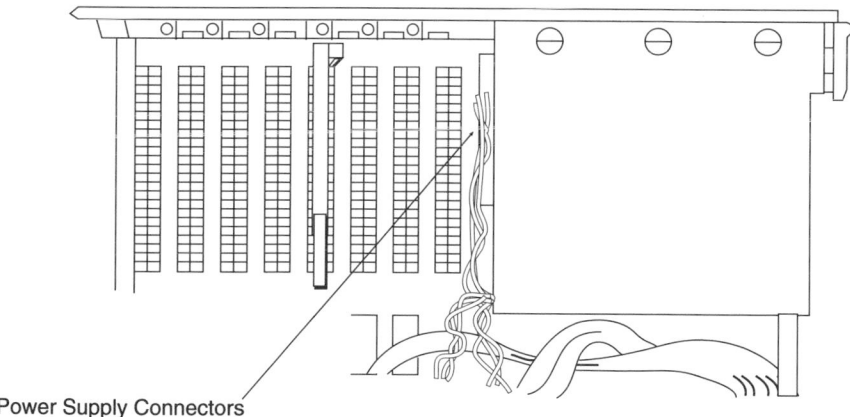

Power Supply Connectors

Used with permission
from IBM Corporation.

FIG. 16.4 Connect the cables from the power supply to the motherboard.

Connect I/O and Other Cables to the Motherboard. There are several connections that must be made between a motherboard and the case. These include LEDs for the hard disk and power, an internal speaker connection, a reset button, and a de-turbo button on some systems. Most modern motherboards also have several built-in I/O ports that have to be connected. This would include dual IDE host adapters, a floppy controller, dual serial ports, and a parallel port. Some boards will also include additional items such as built-in video, sound, or SCSI adapters.

If the board is an ATX type, the connectors for all of the external I/O ports are already built into the rear of the board. If you are using a Baby-AT type board, then you may have to install cables and brackets to run the serial, parallel, and other external I/O ports to the rear of the case. If your motherboard has onboard I/O, use the following procedures to connect the cables:

1. Connect the floppy cable between the floppy drives and the 34-pin floppy controller connector on the motherboard.

2. Connect the IDE cables between the hard disk, IDE CD-ROM, and the 40-pin primary and secondary IDE connectors on the motherboard. Normally, you will use the primary IDE channel connector for hard disks only and the secondary IDE channel connector to attach an IDE CD-ROM or other device, such as a tape drive.

3. On non-ATX boards, a 25-pin female cable port bracket is normally used for the parallel port. There are usually two serial ports: a 9-pin, and either another 9-pin or a 25-pin male connector port. Align pin 1 on the serial and parallel port cables with pin 1 on the motherboard connector and plug them in.

4. If the ports don't have card slot-type brackets or if you need all of your expansion slots, there may be port knockouts on the back of the case that you can use instead. Find ones that fit the ports, and push them out, removing the metal piece covering the hole. Unscrew the hex nuts on each side of the port connector and position the connector in the hole. Install the hex nuts back in through the case to hold the port connector in place.

5. Most newer motherboards also include a built-in mouse port. If the connector for this port is not built into the back of the motherboard (usually next to the keyboard connector), then you will probably have a card bracket type connector to install. In that case, plug the cable into the motherboard mouse connector and then attach the external mouse connector bracket to the case.

6. Attach the front panel switch, LED, and internal speaker wires from the case front panel to the motherboard. If they are not marked on the board, check where each one is on the diagram in the motherboard manual.

Install Bus Expansion Cards. Most systems use expansion cards for video, network interface, sound, and SCSI adapters. These cards are plugged into the bus slots present on the motherboard (see Figure 16.5). To install these cards, follow these steps:

1. Insert each card by holding it carefully by the edges, making sure not to touch the chips and circuitry. Put the bottom edge finger connector into a slot that fits. Firmly press down on the top of the card, exerting even pressure, until it snaps into place.

2. Secure each card bracket with a screw.

3. Attach any internal cables you may have removed earlier from the cards.

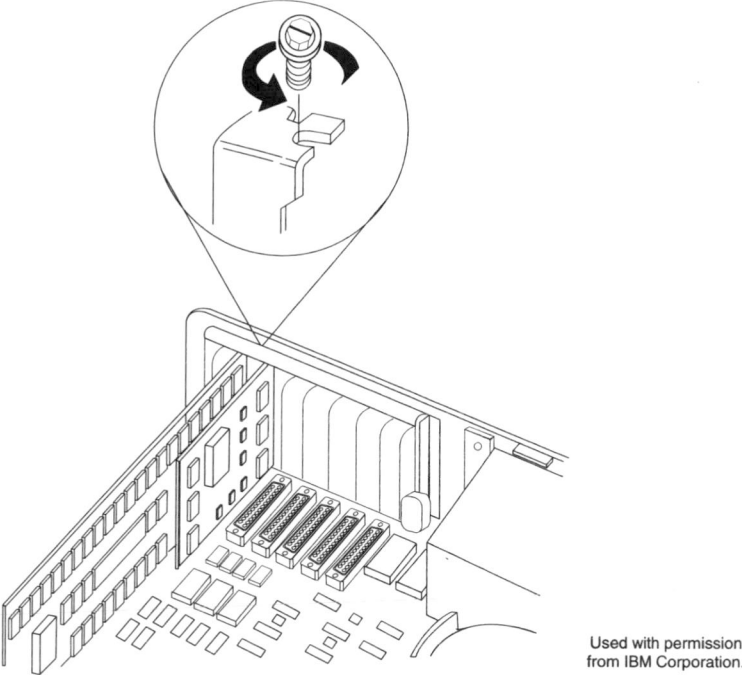

Used with permission
from IBM Corporation.

FIG. 16.5 Insert the adapter into a slot and screw it in place.

Replace the Cover and Connect External Cables. Now the system should be nearly
assembled. All that remains is installing the cover assembly and connecting any external
devices that are cabled to the system. I usually don't like to install the case cover screws
until I have tested the system and I am sure everything is working properly (see Figure
16.6). Often, I will find that a cable has been connected improperly, or some jumper
setting is not correct, requiring that I remove the cover to repair the problem. Use the
following procedure to complete the assembly:

1. Slide the cover onto the case.

2. Before powering up the system, connect any external cables. Most of the connectors are D-shaped and go in only one way.

3. Plug the 15-pin monitor cable into the video card female connector.

4. Attach the phone cord to the modem, if any.

5. Plug the round keyboard cable into the keyboard connector, and the mouse into
   the mouse port or serial port (if you are using a serial mouse).

6. If you have any other external cabling, such as joystick or audio jacks to a sound
   card, attach them now.

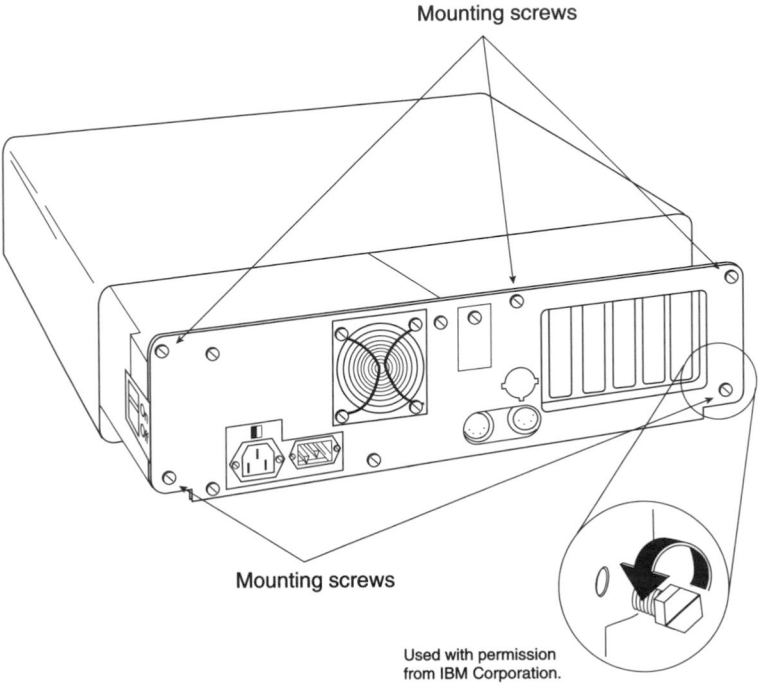

Mounting screws

Mounting screws

Used with permission
from IBM Corporation.

FIG. 16.6 Insert the screws that hold the cover in place.

Run the Motherboard BIOS Setup Program (CMOS Setup). Now that everything is connected, you can power up the system and run the system configuration or setup program. This will enable you to configure the motherboard to access the installed devices, and to set the system date and time. The system will also test itself to determine whether there are any problems:

1. Power on the monitor first, and then the system unit. Observe the operation via the screen and listen for any beeps from the system speaker.

2. The system should automatically go through a Power-On Self Test (POST) consisting of video BIOS checking, RAM test, and usually an installed component report. If there is a fatal error during the POST, you may not see anything on the screen and the system may beep several times, indicating a specific problem. Check the motherboard or BIOS documentation to determine what the beep codes mean.

3. If there are no fatal errors, you should see the POST display on the screen. Depending on the type of motherboard BIOS such as Phoenix, AMI, Award, or others, you need to press a key or series of keys to interrupt the normal boot sequence and get to the setup program screens that allow you to enter important system information. Normally, the system will indicate via the onscreen display which key to press to activate the BIOS setup program during the POST, but if not, then check the motherboard manual for the key(s) to press to enter the BIOS Setup.

4. After the setup program is running, use the setup program menus to enter the current date and time, your hard drive settings, floppy drive types, video cards, keyboard settings, and so on. Most newer motherboard BIOSs can autodetect the hard drive, so you should not have to manually enter any parameters for it.

5. Follow the instructions on the screen or in the motherboard manual to save the settings and exit the setup menu.

At this point, the system should boot normally from either a floppy disk or hard disk. If there are any problems, turn to the troubleshooting section of the motherboard manual. When you are sure the system is up and running successfully, power it off and screw the chassis cover securely to the case.

Now your new motherboard should be installed and your new system should be ready to go.

Disassembly Preparation

After you've built your system, you probably will have to open it up again sometime to perform a repair or upgrade. Before you power off the system for the last time and begin to open the case, you should learn and record several things about your computer. Often, when working on a system, you intentionally or accidentally wipe out the CMOS setup information. Most systems use a special battery-powered CMOS clock and data chip that is used to store the system's configuration information. If the battery is disconnected, or if certain pins are accidentally shorted, you can discharge the CMOS memory and lose the setup. The CMOS memory in most systems is used to store simple things such as how many and what type of floppy drives are connected, how much memory is in the system, and the date and time.

A critical piece of information is the hard disk type settings. Although you or the system can easily determine the other settings the next time you power on the system, the hard disk type information may be another story. Most modern BIOS software can read the type information directly from most IDE and all SCSI drives. With older BIOS software, however, you have to explicitly tell the system the parameters of the attached hard disk. This means that you need to know the current settings for cylinders, heads, and sectors per track.

Some BIOS software indicates the hard disk only by a type number, usually ranging from 1 to 50. Be aware that most BIOS programs use type 47 or higher for what is called a *user-definable type*, which means that the cylinder, head, and sector counts for this type were entered manually and are not constant. These user-definable types are especially important to write down because this information may be very difficult to figure out later when you need to start the system.

Modern Enhanced IDE drives will also have additional configuration items that you should record. These include the translation mode and transfer mode. With drives larger than 504M, it is important to record the translation mode, which will be expressed differently in different BIOS versions. Look for settings such as CHS (Cylinder Head Sector), ECHS (Extended CHS), Large (which equals ECHS), or LBA (Logical Block Addressing).

If you reconfigure a system and do not set the same drive translation as was used originally with that drive, then all the data may be inaccessible. Most modern BIOS have an autodetect feature that automatically reads the drive's capabilities and sets the CMOS settings appropriately. Even so, there have been some problems with the BIOS not reading the drive settings properly or where someone had overridden the settings in the previous installation. With translation, you have to match the setting to what the drive was formatted under previously if you want to read the data properly.

The speed setting is a little more straightforward. Older IDE drives can run up a speed of 8.3M/sec, which is called *PIO (Programmed I/O) mode 2*. Newer EIDE drives can run PIO Mode 3 (11.1M/sec) or PIO Mode 4 (16.6M/sec). Most BIOSs today allow you to set the mode specifically, or you can use the autodetect feature to automatically set the speed. For more information on the settings for hard disk drives, refer to Chapter 12, "Magnetic Storage."

If you do not enter the correct hard disk type information in the CMOS setup program, you will not be able to access the data on the hard disk. I know of several people who lost some or all of their data because they did not enter the correct type information when they reconfigured their systems. If this information is incorrect, the usual results are a `Missing operating system` error message when the systems starts and the inability to access the C drive.

Some people think that it's possible to figure out the parameters by looking up the particular hard disk in a table. (I have included a table of popular hard disk drive parameters in Appendix D, "Technical Reference," and this table has proved to be useful to me time and time again.) Unfortunately, this method works only if the person who set up the system originally entered the correct parameters. I have encountered a large number of systems in which the hard disk parameters were not entered correctly; the only way to regain access to the data is to determine, and then use, the same incorrect parameters that were used originally. As you can see, no matter what, you should record the hard disk information from your setup program.

Most systems have the setup program built right into the ROM BIOS software. These built-in setup programs are activated by a hotkey sequence such as Ctrl+Alt+Esc or Ctrl+Alt+S. Other ROMs prompt you for the setup program every time the system boots, such as with the popular AMI BIOS. With the AMI, you simply press the Delete key when the prompt appears onscreen during a reboot.

When you get the setup program running, record all the settings. The easiest way to do this is to print it out. If a printer is connected, press Shift+Print Screen; a copy of the screen display will be sent to the printer. Some setup programs have several pages of information, so you should record the information on each page.

Many setup programs, such as those in the AMI BIOS, allow for specialized control of the particular chipset used in the motherboard. These complicated settings can take up several screens of information, all of which should be recorded. Most systems will return all these settings to a default state when the battery is removed, and you lose any custom settings you specified earlier.

There are programs that advertise the capability to save all of your CMOS settings to disk, allowing you to reload them later. This works as long as the program is designed to work with your specific BIOS, but unfortunately there is no such program that works properly with all of the different BIOS versions on the market today. If you use such a program, be sure it is compatible with your system before proceeding.

Sources and Suppliers

One of the most valuable (to me, anyway) parts of this book is the vendor list in Appendix A. Here you will find a number of vendors of different PC components, including addresses, phone numbers, and other information as it is available. These vendors are in this list usually because I recommend their products, or because they are important companies whose products are very popular. There are companies listed in the vendor list covering all of the components needed to build your system. In some cases, the manufacturers of the components listed will not sell directly to end users, and you may find yourself purchasing through a distributor instead. That is okay; I normally include the actual manufacturers in my list because they can best recommend a distributor for their own products, and, of course, they should also support their own products.

Chapter 17

Diagnostics, Testing, and Maintenance

No matter how well-built your PC is, and how well-written its software, something is eventually going to go wrong, and there may not always be a support system available to resolve the problem for you. Diagnostic software, the kind that comes with your computer, as well as that available from third parties, can be vitally important to you any time your computer malfunctions or you begin the process of upgrading a system component or adding a new device. This chapter examines the types of software that are available, and particularly those that you might already own, because they are included with common operating system and hardware products.

You may also find that your system problems are caused by a hardware malfunction, and that you have to open up the computer case to perform repairs. This chapter also examines the tools and testers used to upgrade and repair PCs, both the basic items that every user should own, and some of the more advanced devices.

Of course, the best way to deal with a problem is to prevent it from happening in the first place. The preventive maintenance sections of this chapter describe the procedures that you should perform on a regular basis to keep your system in good working order.

This chapter describes three levels of diagnostic software (POST, system, and advanced) included with your computer or available from your computer manufacturer. The chapter describes how you can get the most from this software. It also details IBM's audio codes and error codes, which are similar to the error codes used by most computer manufacturers, and examines aftermarket diagnostics and public-domain diagnostic software.

Diagnostics Software

There are several types of diagnostic software available for PCs. Some diagnostic functions are integrated into the PC hardware or into peripheral devices such as expansion cards, whereas others take the form of operating system utilities or separate software products. This software, some of which is included with the system when purchased, assists users in identifying many problems that can occur with a computer's components. In many cases, these programs can do most of the work in determining which PC component is defective or malfunctioning. The types of diagnostic software are as follows:

- *POST.* The Power-On Self Test operates whenever any PC is powered up (switched on).

- *Manufacturer supplied diagnostics software.* Many of the larger manufacturers—especially high-end, name-brand manufacturers such as IBM, Compaq, Hewlett-Packard, Dell, and others—make special diagnostics software that is expressly designed for their systems. This manufacturer-specific software normally consists of a suite of tests that thoroughly examines the system. In some cases, you can download these diagnostics from the manufacturer's online services, or you may have to purchase them. Some vendors like Gateway include a limited version of one of the aftermarket packages that has been customized for use with their systems. In some cases, the diagnostic software is installed on a special partition on the hard drive and can be accessed during startup. This is a convenient way for system manufacturers to make sure that you always have diagnostics available.

- *Peripheral diagnostics software.* Many hardware devices ship with specialized diagnostics software designed to test their particular functions. Adaptec SCSI host adapters, for example, include diagnostic functions in the card's BIOS that you can access with a keystroke at boot time. Other devices may provide the software as a separate program on disk.

- *Operating system diagnostics software.* Operating systems such as Windows 9x and Windows NT include a wide variety of diagnostic software designed to identify and monitor the performance of various components in the computer.

- *Aftermarket diagnostics software.* There are a number of manufacturers making general purpose diagnostics software for PCs. This type of software is often bundled with other system maintenance and repair utilities to form a general PC software toolkit.

The Power-On Self Test (POST)

When IBM first began shipping the original PC in 1981, it included safety features that had never been seen in a personal computer. These features were the POST and parity-checked memory. Although parity-checked memory is being phased out on many systems, every PC still executes a POST when you turn it on. The following sections provide more detail on the POST, a series of program routines buried in the motherboard ROM-BIOS chip that tests all the main system components at power-on time. This series of routines is partially responsible for the delay when you turn on your PC; the computer executes the POST before loading the operating system.

◀◀ See "Memory Reliability," p. 344

What Is Tested? Whenever you start up your computer, it automatically performs a series of tests that check the primary components in your system, such as the CPU, ROM, motherboard support circuitry, memory, and major peripherals such as the expansion chassis. These tests are brief and are designed to catch hard (not intermittent) errors. The POST procedures are not very thorough compared with available disk-based diagnostics. The POST process provides error or warning messages whenever it encounters a faulty component.

Although the diagnostics performed by the system POST are not very thorough, they are the first line of defense, especially when it comes to detecting severe motherboard problems. If the POST encounters a problem severe enough to keep the system from operating properly, it halts the system boot process and generates an error message that often identifies the cause of the problem. These POST-detected problems are sometimes called fatal errors, because they prevent the system from booting. The POST tests normally provide three types of output messages: audio codes, onscreen text messages, and hexadecimal numeric codes that are sent to an I/O port address.

POST Audio Error Codes. POST audio error codes take the form of a series of beeps that identify the faulty component. When your computer is functioning normally, you should usually hear one short beep when the system starts up at the completion of the POST, although some systems (like Compaq's) do not do this. If a problem is detected, a different number of beeps sound—sometimes in a combination of short and long tones. These BIOS-dependent codes can vary among different BIOS manufacturers. Table 17.1 lists the beep codes for IBM systems and the problem indicated by each series of beeps. Award BIOS (from Award Software, Inc.) uses many of the same codes as the IBM BIOS.

Table 17.1 IBM POST Audio Error Codes and Indicated Problem

Audio Code	Sound	Problem (Fault Domain)
1 short beep	.	Normal POST-system OK
2 short beeps	..	POST error-error code
No beep		Power supply, system board
Continuous beep	————————	Power supply, system board
Repeating short beeps	......	Power supply, system board
One long, one short beep	-.	System board
One long, two short beeps	-..	Display adapter (MDA, CGA)
One long, three short beeps	-...	Enhanced Graphics Adapter (EGA)
Three long beeps	- - -	3270 keyboard card

. = *short beep*

- = *long beep*

In Table 17.2 the Audio POST Codes are listed for AMI BIOS. Tables 17.3 and 17.4 list audio codes for Phoenix BIOS. You'll notice that both lists are far superior to the IBM fatal error codes.

Table 17.2   AMI BIOS Audio POST Codes

Beep Code	Fatal Error
1 short	DRAM refresh failure
2 short	Parity circuit failure
3 short	Base 64K RAM failure
4 short	System timer failure
5 short	Processor failure
6 short	Keyboard controller Gate A20 error
7 short	Virtual mode exception error
8 short	Display memory Read/Write test failure
9 short	ROM BIOS checksum failure
10 short	CMOS Shutdown Read/Write error
11 short	Cache Memory error
Beep Code	**Nonfatal Errors**
1 long, 3 short	Conventional/extended memory failure
1 long, 8 short	Display/retrace test failed

For the 1-, 2-, and 3-beep errors, you may be able to resolve the problem by reseating the system's memory modules in their slots. If this fails, one or more of the memory modules themselves may be malfunctioning. For the six-beep error, you can try reseating the motherboard's keyboard controller chip in its socket, substituting a different keyboard, and checking the status of the keyboard fuse (if there is one). An eight-beep error indicates that the memory on the system's video display adapter is not functioning properly. If the video adapter is on a separate card, you can try reseating it in its slot or substituting another card to resolve the problem. All the other beep codes (4, 5, 7, 9, and 10 beeps) indicate the existence of a more serious motherboard problem that probably requires that the board be professionally repaired or replaced.

Table 17.3   Phoenix BIOS Fatal System Board Errors

Beep Code	Code at Port 80h	Description
None	01h	CPU register test in progress
1-1-3	02h	CMOS write/read failure
1-1-4	03h	ROM BIOS checksum failure
1-2-1	04h	Programmable interval timer failure
1-2-2	05h	DMA initialization failure
1-2-3	06h	DMA page register write/read failure
1-3-1	08h	RAM refresh verification failure

Beep Code	Code at Port 80h	Description
None	09h	First 64K RAM test in progress
1-3-3	0Ah	First 64K RAM chip or data line failure, multibit
1-3-4	0Bh	First 64K RAM odd/even logic failure
1-4-1	0Ch	Address line failure first 64K RAM
1-4-2	0Dh	Parity failure first 64K RAM
2-1-1	10h	Bit 0 first 64K RAM failure
2-1-2	11h	Bit 1 first 64K RAM failure
2-1-3	12h	Bit 2 first 64K RAM failure
2-1-4	13h	Bit 3 first 64K RAM failure
2-2-1	14h	Bit 4 first 64K RAM failure
2-2-2	15h	Bit 5 first 64K RAM failure
2-2-3	16h	Bit 6 first 64K RAM failure
2-2-4	17h	Bit 7 first 64K RAM failure
2-3-1	18h	Bit 8 first 64K RAM failure
2-3-2	19h	Bit 9 first 64K RAM failure
2-3-3	1Ah	Bit 10 first 64K RAM failure
2-3-4	1Bh	Bit 11 first 64K RAM failure
2-4-1	1Ch	Bit 12 first 64K RAM failure
2-4-2	1Dh	Bit 13 first 64K RAM failure
2-4-3	1Eh	Bit 14 first 64K RAM failure
2-4-4	1Fh	Bit 15 first 64K RAM failure
3-1-1	20h	Slave DMA register failure
3-1-2	21h	Master DMA register failure
3-1-3	22h	Master interrupt mask register failure
3-1-4	23h	Slave interrupt mask register failure
None	25h	Interrupt vector loading in progress
3-2-4	27h	Keyboard controller test failure
None	28h	CMOS power failure/checksum calculation in progress
None	29h	Screen configuration validation in progress
3-3-4	2Bh	Screen initialization failure
3-4-1	2Ch	Screen retrace failure
3-4-2	2Dh	Search for video ROM in progress
None	2Eh	Screen running with video ROM
None	30h	Screen operable
None	31h	Monochrome monitor operable
None	32h	Color monitor (40 column) operable
None	33h	Color monitor (80 column) operable

Table 17.4   Phoenix BIOS Nonfatal System Board Errors

Beep Code	Code at Port 80h	Description
4-2-1	34h	Timer tick interrupt test in progress or failure
4-2-2	35h	Shutdown test in progress or failure
4-2-3	36h	Gate A20 failure
4-2-4	37h	Unexpected interrupt in protected mode
4-3-1	38h	RAM test in progress or address failure > FFFFh
4-3-3	3Ah	Interval timer Channel 2 test or failure
4-3-4	3Bh	Time-of-day clock test or failure
4-4-1	3Ch	Serial port test or failure
4-4-2	3Dh	Parallel port test or failure
4-4-3	3Eh	Math coprocessor test or failure
Low 1-1-2	41h	System board select failure
Low 1-1-3	42h	Extended CMOS RAM failure

POST Visual Error Codes. On most PCs, the POST also displays the results of its system memory test on the monitor. The last number displayed is the amount of memory that tested successfully. For example, a system might display the following message:

```
32768 KB OK
```

The number displayed by the memory test should agree with the total amount of memory installed on the system motherboard. Some older systems display a slightly lower total because they deduct part or all of the 384K of UMA (Upper Memory Area) from the count. On old systems that use expanded memory cards, the memory on the card is not tested by the POST and does not count in the numbers reported. Also, this memory test is performed before any system software loads, so many memory managers or device drivers you may have installed do not affect the results of the test. If the POST memory test stops short of the expected total, the number displayed can indicate how far into the system memory array a memory error lies. This number can help you to identify the exact module that is at fault and can be a valuable troubleshooting aid in itself.

If an error is detected during the POST procedures, an error message may be displayed onscreen. These messages usually are in the form of a numeric code several digits long; for example, 1790-Disk 0 Error. You should check the documentation for your motherboard or system BIOS for information about these errors. The major BIOS manufacturers also maintain Web sites where this information should be available.

I/O Port POST Codes. A lesser-known feature of the POST is that at the beginning of each POST, the BIOS sends test codes to a special I/O port address. These POST codes can be read only by a special adapter card plugged into one of the system slots. These cards originally were designed to be used by system manufacturers for burn-in testing of the motherboard, to prevent the need for a video display adapter and display. Several companies now make these cards available to technicians. Micro 2000, JDR Microdevices, Data Depot, Ultra-X, and Trinitech are just a few manufacturers that market these POST cards.

When you plug one of these POST cards into a slot, during the POST you see two-digit hexadecimal numbers flash on the card's display. If the system stops unexpectedly or hangs, you can identify the test in progress during the hang from the two-digit code. This step usually identifies the malfunctioning component.

Most of the system BIOSs on the market in computers with an ISA or EISA bus output the POST codes to I/O port address 80h.

The two most common types of POST cards are those that plug into the 8-bit connector that is a part of the ISA or EISA bus, and those that plug into the MCA bus. Some companies offer both types of POST cards—one for MCA bus systems and one for ISA/EISA bus systems. Micro 2000 and Data Depot do not offer a separate MCA bus card; rather, they have slot adapters that enable their existing ISA bus cards to work in MCA bus systems and in ISA and EISA systems. Most other companies offer only ISA/EISA POST cards and ignore the MCA bus, which has now been discontinued. There are also POST cards that are designed to work in PCI slots. These will certainly become more prevalent as more PCI-only systems (no ISA slots) come on the market. The POSTPlus from ForeFront Direct has two edge connectors so it can be used in either an ISA or PCI slot.

The POST I/O port error codes for various BIOSs are listed in the 6th edition of this book, located on the CD.

Hardware Diagnostics

There are many types of diagnostic software that are intended for use with specific hardware products. This software may be integrated into the hardware, included with the hardware purchase, or sold as a separate product. The following sections examine several different types of hardware-specific diagnostics.

> **Note**
>
> IBM includes specialized diagnostic software with their PCs that is designed for use by both end users and repair technicians. For more information on this software, see the 6th edition of "Upgrading and Repairing PCs" on the CD-ROM included with this book.

SCSI Diagnostics. Unlike the IDE drive support that is built into the system BIOS of virtually every PC, SCSI is an add-on technology, and most SCSI host adapters contain their own BIOS that enables you to boot the system from a SCSI hard drive. In some cases, the SCSI BIOS also contains configuration software for the adapter's various features, and diagnostics software as well.

The most popular manufacturer of SCSI host adapters is Adaptec, and most of their host adapters contain these features. An Adaptec SCSI adapter typically contains a bank of eight DIP switches next to the external SCSI connector. Setting switches 6, 7, and 8 to the ON position enables the adapter's onboard BIOS. When the BIOS is activated, you see a message on the monitor as the system boots, identifying the model of the adapter and the revision number of the BIOS. The message also instructs you to press CTRL-A to access what Adaptec calls its SCSISelect™ utility.

The SCSISelect utility identifies the Adapter host adapters installed in the system, and if there is more than one, enables you to choose the adapter you want to work with by selecting its port address. After you do this, you are presented with a menu of the functions built into the adapter's BIOS. Every adapter BIOS contains a configuration program and a SCSI Disk Utilities feature that scans the SCSI bus, identifying the devices connected to it. For each hard disk drive connected to the bus, you can perform a low-level disk format or scan the disk for defects, remapping any bad blocks that are found.

For SCSI adapters that use DMA (Direct Memory Access), there is also a Host Adapter Diagnostics feature that tests the communication between the adapter and the main system memory array by performing a series of DMA transfers. If this test should fail, you are instructed how to configure the adapter to use a lower DMA transfer rate.

Network Interface Diagnostics. As with SCSI adapters, many network interface adapters are equipped with their own diagnostics, designed to test their own specialized functions. The EZSTART program included with all SMC network interface cards, for example, contains two adapter test modes. The Basic mode performs the following internal tests on the SMC8000 adapter:

- Bus Interface Controller Test
- LAN Address ROM Test
- Network Interface Controller Test
- RAM Test
- ROM Test
- Interrupt Generation
- Loopback Test

The Two Node test sequence requires that you have another node installed on the same network with an SMC adapter. By running the EZSTART software on both computers, you can configure one adapter as the Responder and the other as the Initiator. The Initiator transmits test messages to the Responder that echoes the same messages back again. If the adapters and the network are functioning properly, the messages should return to the Initiator system in exactly the same form as they were transmitted.

Other network adapters have similar testing capabilities, although the names of the tests may not be exactly the same. The software for the 3COM 3C509B adapter, for example, performs the following tests:

- Register Access Test

- EEPROM Vital Data Test

- EEPROM Configurable Data Test

- FIFO Loopback Test

- Interrupt Test

- Ethernet Core Loopback Test

- Encoder/Decoder Loopback Test

- Echo Exchange Test (requires two adapters on the same network)

Both the SMC and 3COM diagnostics programs are integrated into the software you use to configure the hardware resources used by the adapters and their other features. The software is not integrated into the hardware; it takes the form of a separate program that ships with the devices and that you can also download free of charge from the manufacturers' respective Web sites.

General-Purpose Diagnostics Programs

A large number of third-party diagnostics programs are available for PC systems. Specific programs are available also to test memory, floppy drives, hard disks, video adapters, and most other areas of the system. Although some of these utility packages should be considered essential in any toolkit, many fall short of the level needed by professional-level troubleshooters. Many products, geared more toward end users, lack the accuracy, features, and capabilities needed by technically proficient people who are serious about troubleshooting. Most of the better diagnostics on the market offer several advantages over end-user products. They are usually better at determining where a problem lies within a system, and often include the serial- and parallel-port loopback connectors that are required to properly diagnose and test serial and parallel ports.

Many of these programs can run in a batch mode, which enables you to run a series of tests without operator intervention. You then can set up automated test suites, which can be especially useful when burning in a system or executing the same tests on many systems.

These programs test all types of memory, including conventional (base) memory, extended memory, and expanded memory. Failures can usually be identified down to the individual memory chip or module (SIMM or DIMM).

Tip

Before trying a commercial diagnostic program to solve your problem, look in your operating system. Most operating systems today provide at least some of the diagnostic functions that diagnostic programs do. You may be able to save some time and money. Operating system-based diagnostics are covered in Chapter 18, "Operating Systems Software and Troubleshooting."

Unfortunately, there is no clear leader in the area of diagnostic software. Each program presented here has unique advantages. As a result, no program is universally better than another. When deciding which diagnostic programs, if any, to include in your arsenal, look for the features that you need.

AMIDiag. AMI (American Megatrends, Inc.) is one of the largest manufacturers of PC ROM BIOS software today. The AMI BIOS can be found on many PCs, and if you've seen the AMI BIOS, you know that most versions have a built-in diagnostic program. Few people know, however, that AMI also markets an enhanced disk-based version of the same diagnostic software that is built into the AMI ROM.

AMIDiag, as the program is called, has numerous features and enhancements not found in the simpler ROM version. AMIDiag is a comprehensive, general-purpose diagnostic that is designed for use on any PC, not just those with an AMI ROM BIOS. Regularly updated over the years, AMIDiag's extensive reporting and diagnostics functions support virtually all the latest hardware found in PCs today, including the latest MMX processors, systems with multiple (up to 16) processors, memory arrays up to 4G in size, the Intel Universal Serial Bus controller, SCSI devices, PCI, Advanced Power Management, and Plug and Play.

AMIDiag also provides an extensive suite of multimedia diagnostics that can isolate problems with CD-ROM drives, audio adapters, and video displays, as well as modem and network tests.

Checkit Pro. Touchstone Software Corporation's Checkit products offer an excellent suite of testing capabilities, including tests of the system CPU; conventional, extended, and expanded memory; hard and floppy drives; and video adapter and monitor (including VESA-Standard cards and monitors, mouse, and keyboard). Several versions of the Checkit product are available—Checkit Professional Edition is the company's most complete hardware diagnostic program. The package includes Checkit versions for both Windows 9x and DOS, Touchstone's PC-cillin anti-virus program, and loopback plugs for testing parallel and serial ports.

Checkit Professional Edition provides benchmarking capabilities and diagnostic tests for most system components, and gives detailed information about your system hardware such as total installed memory, hard drive type and size, current memory allocation (including upper memory usage), IRQ availability and usage, modem/fax modem speed, and a variety of other items important to someone troubleshooting a PC.

The product also includes a variety of features that enable you to track the state of your operating system, such as a utility that reports on changes made to important system files and a backup and restore application for the Windows 9x Registry. Although the package centers around the Windows 9x version of the program, the inclusion of the DOS version is a thoughtful addition, in case a system problem prevents you from loading the Windows interface.

Micro-Scope. Micro-Scope by Micro 2000 is a full-featured, general purpose diagnostic program for PC systems. It has many features and capabilities that can be very helpful in troubleshooting or diagnosing hardware problems.

Micro-Scope has a hardware interrupt and I/O port address check feature that is more accurate than the same feature in most other diagnostic software products. It enables you to accurately identify the interrupt or I/O port address that a certain adapter or hardware device in your system is using—a valuable capability in solving conflicts between adapters. Some user-level diagnostics programs have this feature, but the information they report can be grossly inaccurate, and they often miss items installed in the system.

Micro-Scope is particularly useful because the program has its own proprietary operating system, bypassing DOS, and its tests can bypass the ROM BIOS when necessary. This eliminates the masking that occurs when these elements operate in between the system hardware and a diagnostics program. For this reason, the program is also useful for PCs that run other operating systems, such as UNIX or Novell NetWare. For convenience, you can also install Micro-Scope on a hard disk and run it under regular DOS.

Like other diagnostics packages, Micro-Scope is updated regularly to accommodate new hardware as it is released. The current version detects and tests the latest processors by Intel, AMD, and Cyrix, and the latest motherboard and video BIOS releases. It also provides support for hardware peripherals such as CD-ROM and DVD-ROM drives and audio adapters. Micro-Scope includes disk repair tools, such as a sector editor that can edit and repair the master and volume boot sectors on a hard disk drive.

Micro-Scope comes complete with the serial and parallel port loopback plugs that you need to completely and accurately test these devices. A loopback plug is a wireless module that attaches to the port and diverts all the signals transmitted through the port's outputs right back to its inputs. With testing software like that included in Micro-Scope, you can verify that every element of a parallel or serial port is operating properly.

Finally, Micro 2000 offers excellent telephone technical support. Its operators do much more than explain how to operate the software—they help you with real troubleshooting problems. This information is augmented by good documentation and online help built in to the software so that, in many cases, you don't have to refer to the manual.

Norton Utilities Diagnostics. When you consider that Norton Diagnostics (NDIAGS) comes with the Norton Utilities, and that Norton Utilities is already an essential collection of system data safeguarding, troubleshooting, testing, and repairing utilities, NDIAGS probably is one of the best values in diagnostic programs.

The current versions of Norton Utilities are 8.0 for the DOS/Windows version and 3.0 for the Windows 95 version. If you don't already have Norton Utilities, you'll want to strongly consider this package, not only for NDIAGS, but also for the other utilities such as Speedisk, Disk Doctor, and Calibrate. These three hard drive utilities basically represent the state of the art in hard drive diagnostics and software-level repair. SYSINFO still handles benchmarking for the Norton Utilities, and it does as good a job as any other diagnostic package on the market.

NDIAGS adds diagnostic capabilities that previously were not provided by the Norton Utilities, including comprehensive information about the overall hardware configuration of your system—the CPU, system BIOS, math coprocessor, video adapter, keyboard and mouse type, hard and floppy drive types, amount of installed memory, bus type, and the number of serial and parallel ports. Unlike some other programs, loopback plugs do not come in the box for NDIAGS, but a coupon is included that entitles you to free plugs by mail. Note that this program uses loopback plugs that are wired slightly differently from those used by most other programs. The different wiring enables you to run some additional tests. Fortunately, the documentation includes a diagram for these plugs, which you can use to make your own if you desire.

NDIAGS thoroughly tests the major system components and enables you to check minor details such as the NumLock, CapsLock, and ScrollLock LEDs on your keyboard. NDIAGS also provides an onscreen grid you can use to center the image on your monitor and test for various kinds of distortion that may indicate a faulty monitor.

PC Technician. PC Technician by Windsor Technologies was one of the first PC diagnostics products on the market in 1984, and since then, it has been highly refined and continuously updated to reflect the changing PC market.

PC Technician is a full-featured comprehensive hardware diagnostic and troubleshooting tool, and tests all major areas of a system. Like several of the other more capable programs, PC Technician has its own operating system that isolates it from problems caused by software conflicts. The program is written in assembly language and has direct access to the hardware in the system for testing. This program also includes all the loopback plugs needed for testing serial and parallel ports.

PC Technician has long been a favorite with field service companies who equip their technicians with the product for troubleshooting. This program was designed for the professional service technician; however, it is easy for the amateur to use. As a bonus, PC Technician costs much less than many of the other programs in its class.

PC Technician is deliberately designed to concentrate on the basic PC hardware, and includes a large battery of diagnostic tests for processors, memory, disk drives, I/O ports, and video adapters. You will not find tests for multimedia devices and other peripherals in PC Technician, but you will find core system testing capabilities that meet or exceed the other products described in this section, in most areas.

Although PC Technician is designed for the PC hardware professional, Windsor also has a product called PC-Diagnosys that is geared more toward the end user. PC-Diagnosys includes many of the same tests and features as PC Technician, but lacks the loopback testing and some of the more advanced features of the larger product. Windsor also has a low-end diagnostic product called #1-TuffTEST in both end-user and professional versions that you can download from the company's Web site for a low fee.

QAPlus/FE. QAPlus/FE by Diagsoft is an advanced diagnostic program for Intel-based computers. Its testing is thorough, and its menu-based interface makes it easy to use, even for someone who is not particularly experienced with diagnosing problems with personal computers. QAPlus/FE also includes some of the most accurate system benchmarks you can get, which can be used to find out if that new system you are thinking of buying is really that much faster than the one you already have. More importantly, QAPlus/FE comes on bootable 3 1/2- and 5 1/4-inch disks that (regardless of your operating system) can start the computer system when problems are so severe that your system hardware cannot even find the hard drive.

Many people already have a less comprehensive version of this program called QAPlus, which is oriented toward end users. The basic QAPlus version is often included with systems sold by a number of different PC system vendors. Although the simple QAPlus program is okay, the full-blown QAPlus/FE (Field Engineer) version is much better for serious troubleshooting.

QAPlus/FE can test your motherboard, system RAM, video adapter, hard drive, floppy drives, CD-ROM drive, mouse, keyboard, printer, and parallel and serial ports (the QAPlus/FE package includes loopback plugs for full testing of these ports). QAPlus/FE also provides exhaustive information on your system configuration, including the hardware installed on your system, its CPU, and the total amount of RAM installed on your system. It provides full interrupt mapping—crucial when installing new adapter boards and other hardware devices—and gives you a full picture of the device drivers and other programs loaded in memory, as well as other information about DOS and system memory use.

QAPlus/FE also includes various other utilities that are more likely to appeal to the serious PC troubleshooter than to the average PC user. These special capabilities include a CMOS editor that can be used to change system date and time, the hard drive type, installed memory size, and other CMOS information; a COM port debugger; a hard drive test and low-level formatting utility; a floppy drive test utility; and a configuration file editor. The product also includes a remote system communication host program that enables service people with the full remote package to operate your computer via modem.

Unlike some diagnostics programs, QAPlus/FE has a system burn-in capability, meaning it can be used to run your system non-stop under a full load of computations and hardware activity for the purpose of determining whether any system component is likely to fail in real life use. Many people use a burn-in utility when they receive a new system, and then again just before the warranty runs out. A true system burn-in usually lasts 48–72 hours, or even longer. You can configure the amount of time that QAPlus/FE will burn in a system by setting the number of times that the selected tests are to run.

Operating System Diagnostics

In many cases, it may not be necessary to purchase third-party diagnostic software, because your operating system has all the diagnostic tools you need. Windows 95, 98, and NT include a large selection of programs that enable you to view, monitor, and troubleshoot the hardware in your system. The following sections examine some of these tools and their functions.

Microsoft Diagnostics (MSD). MS-DOS 6.x, Windows 3.1, and Windows for Workgroups all include a basic tool called Microsoft Diagnostics (MSD). MSD is a simple, DOS-based program that displays information about your system hardware. Designed in 1993 for use with these older operating systems, however, MSD does not recognize much of the new hardware in use today, such as Pentium processors.

Although MSD has garnered a reputation for incorrectly identifying certain hardware, such as the UART chips in PC serial ports and the interrupt usage listing, it is one of the best tools for identifying memory usage in the Upper Memory Area—a common source of conflicts between add-on adapter cards. It is also quite useful for documenting the version numbers of the system BIOS, Video BIOS, and other drivers.

MSD also ships on the Windows 9x CD-ROM, although it is somewhat hidden and is not automatically installed during the Windows setup procedure. You can copy MSD from the CD-ROM directly to your hard drive and run it from any DOS prompt. It does provide better information, however, if you first shut down Windows and choose Restart the computer in MS-DOS Mode.

Windows 9x Device Manager. Windows 9x's Device Manager is a far more useful hardware inventory tool than MSD. When you select the Device Manager page from the System Control Panel, you see an expandable list of the types of devices found in the system (see Figure 17.1). Expanding each type displays the actual hardware installed in the computer. Each entry has a Properties dialog box that enables you to configure the device, view the hardware resources that it is using, and update its driver.

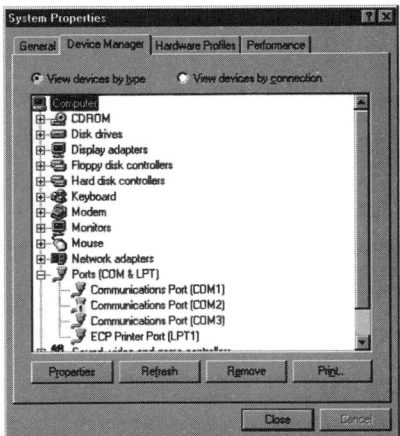

FIG. 17.1 The Windows 9x Device Manager.

By clicking the View Devices By Connection option button, the display is sorted by the computer's various ports and interfaces.

Another lesser-known feature of the Device Manager is that when you double-click the Computer entry at the top of the list, you see the Computer Properties dialog box, shown in Figure 17.2. From this dialog box, you can examine all the IRQs, I/O ports, DMA channels, and memory addresses in your system, and the devices that are using them.

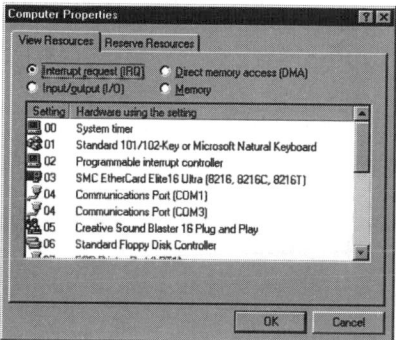

FIG. 17.2   The Computer Properties dialog box.

In cases where Windows 9x's Plug-and-Play feature cannot assign system resources for you, the Device Manager is an excellent tool for resolving device conflicts. The Properties dialog box for each device displays the resources supported by that particular device and indicates whether other devices are already using those resources, and which resources the device hardware is configured to use.

Windows 9x Resource Meter. The Windows 9x Resource Meter launches as an icon in the tray area of the toolbar. This application continuously monitors the Windows 9x system, user, and GDI (graphics device interface) resources. As you load more programs and open more windows, the icon in the tray indicates the diminishing available resources in the system by growing smaller. When you double-click the tray icon, you see a more detailed presentation, as shown in Figure 17.3.

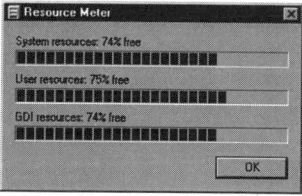

FIG. 17.3   The Windows 9x Resource Meter.

System Monitor/Performance Monitor. The Windows 9x System Monitor and the Windows NT Performance Monitor perform roughly the same function. Both programs track specific elements of a system's performance and display them in a graphical format, as shown in Figure 17.4. By default, you can choose to display various statistics pertaining to the computer's kernel, memory manager, file system, and other core functions.

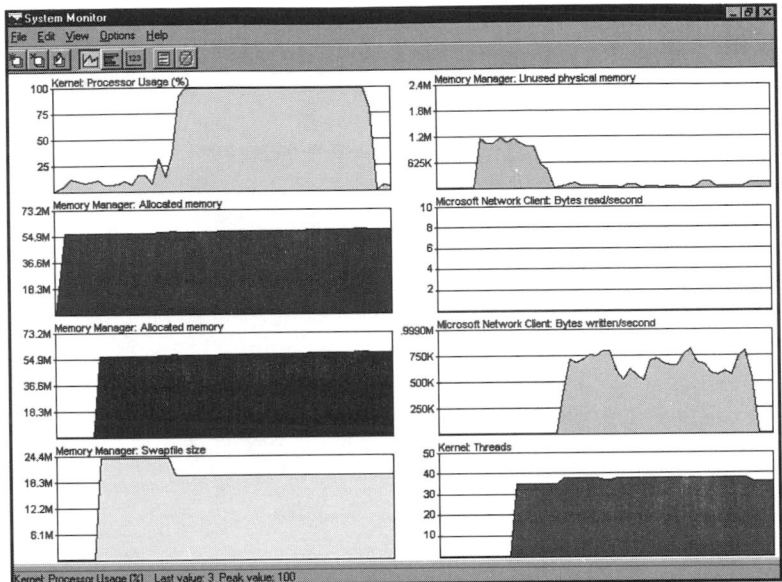

FIG. 17.4 The Windows 9x System Monitor.

Both of these programs, however, are extensible. Installing additional applications and services on the computer can add new categories of statistics. For example, installing a NetWare client on the system adds a collection of statistics regarding incoming and outgoing traffic generated by that client.

System Information and Diagnostics. Windows 98's System Information program is an excellent addition to the operating system that provides an extensive profile of the computer's hardware and software, rivaling some of the best third-party products on the market (see Figure 17.5). And, although it uses a different display format, Windows NT Diagnostics provides much of the same information.

These programs enable you to save, export, or print the information they discover, making it a simple matter to document the entire configuration of a Windows 98 or Windows NT system in great detail. If you should ever have to reinstall the operating system due to a disk failure or other malfunction, having this information handy can simplify the process considerably.

Windows NT Event Viewer. The Event Viewer is Windows NT's primary system message and logging tool. Whenever a significant event occurs in one of three areas—system operation, security, or application execution—it is entered into one of three separate logs.

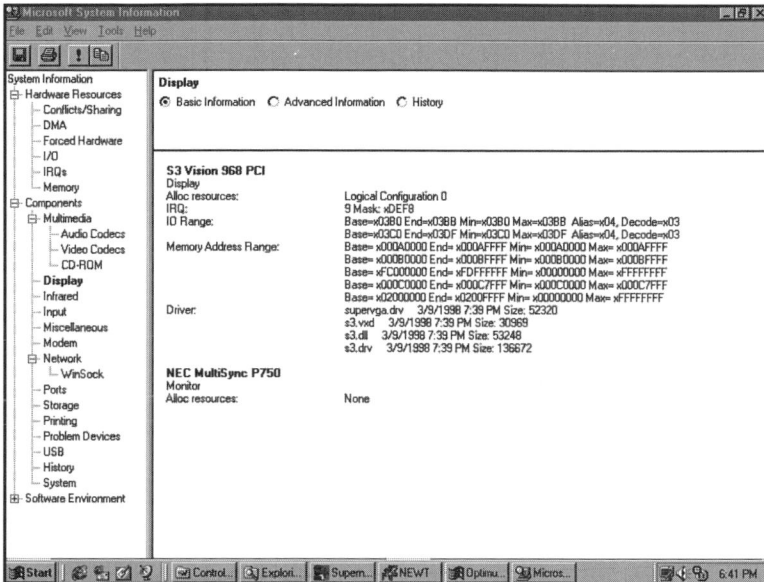

FIG. 17.5 Windows 98 System Information.

PC Maintenance Tools

To troubleshoot and repair PC systems properly, you need a few basic tools. If you intend to troubleshoot and repair PCs professionally, there are many more specialized tools you will want to purchase. These advanced tools enable you to more accurately diagnose problems and make jobs easier and faster. The basic tools that should be in every troubleshooter's toolbox are

- Simple hand tools for basic disassembly and reassembly procedures, including a flat blade and Phillips screwdrivers (both medium and small sizes), tweezers, an IC extraction tool, and a parts grabber or *hemostat*

- Diagnostics software and hardware for testing components in a system

- A multimeter that provides accurate measurements of voltage and resistance

- Chemicals, such as contact cleaners, component freeze sprays, and compressed air for cleaning the system

- Foam swabs, or lint-free cotton swabs if foam isn't available

- Small wire ties for "dressing" or organizing wires

Some environments may also have the resources to purchase the following devices, although they're not required for most work:

- Memory testing machines, used to evaluate the operation of SIMMs (Single Inline Memory Modules), DIMMs (Dual Inline Memory Modules), DIP (Dual Inline Pin) chips, and other memory modules

- Serial and parallel loopback (or wrap) plugs to test serial and parallel ports

- A network cable scanner (if you work with networked PCs)

- A serial breakout box (if you use systems that operate over serial cables, such as UNIX dumb terminals)

In addition, an experienced troubleshooter will probably want to have soldering and desoldering tools to fix bad serial cables. These tools are discussed in more detail in the following sections.

Hand Tools

When you work with PC systems, the tools required for nearly all service operations are simple and inexpensive. You can carry most of the required tools in a small pouch. Even a top-of-the-line "master mechanics" set fits inside a briefcase-size container. The cost of these tool kits ranges from about $20 for a small service kit to $500 for one of the briefcase-size deluxe kits. Compare these costs with what might be necessary for an automotive technician. An automotive service technician would have to spend $5,000 to $10,000 or more for a complete set of tools. Not only are PC tools much less expensive, but I can tell you from experience that you don't get nearly as dirty working on computers as you do working on cars.

In this section, you learn about the tools required to assemble a kit that is capable of performing basic, board-level service on PC systems. One of the best ways to start such a set of tools is to purchase a small kit sold especially for servicing PCs.

The following list shows the basic tools that you can find in one of the small PC tool kits that sell for about $20.

- 3/16-inch nut driver
- 1/4-inch nut driver
- Small Phillips screwdriver
- Small flat-blade screwdriver
- Medium Phillips screwdriver
- Medium flat-blade screwdriver
- Chip extractor

- Chip inserter

- Tweezers

- Claw-type parts grabber

- T10 and T15 Torx drivers

> **Note**
>
> Some tools aren't recommended because they are of limited use. However, they normally come with these types of kits.

You use nut drivers to remove the hexagonal-headed screws that secure the system-unit covers, adapter boards, disk drives, and power supplies in most systems. The nut drivers work much better than conventional screwdrivers.

Because some manufacturers have substituted slotted or Phillips-head screws for the more standard hexagonal-head screws, standard screwdrivers can be used for those systems.

> **Caution**
>
> When working in a cramped environment such as the inside of a computer case, screwdrivers with magnetic tips can be a real convenience, especially for retrieving that screw you dropped into the case. However, although I have used these types of screwdrivers many times with no problems, you must be aware of the damage that a magnetic field can cause to memory chips and magnetic storage devices such as hard drives and floppy disks. Laying the screwdriver down on or near a floppy or working too close to a hard drive can damage the data on the disk.

Chip-extraction and insertion tools are rarely needed these days, because memory chips are mounted on SIMMs or DIMMs and processors use *ZIF (Zero Insertion Force)* sockets or other user-friendly connectors. The ZIF socket has a lever that, when raised, releases the grip on the pins of the chip, allowing you to easily lift it out with your fingers.

However, if you work with older systems, you must use a chip extractor (see Figure 17.6) to install or remove memory chips (or other smaller chips) without bending any pins on the chip. Usually, you pry out larger chips, such as microprocessors or ROMs, with the small screwdriver. Larger processors require a chip extractor if they are mounted in the older *LIF (Low Insertion Force)* socket. These chips have so many pins on them that a large amount of force is required to remove them, despite the fact that they call the socket "low insertion force." If you use a screwdriver on a large physical size chip such as a 486, you risk cracking the case of the chip and permanently damaging it. The chip extractor tool for removing these chips has a very wide end with tines that fit between the pins on the chip to distribute the force evenly along the chip's underside. This will minimize the likelihood of breakage. Most of these types of extraction tools must be purchased specially for the chip you're trying to remove.

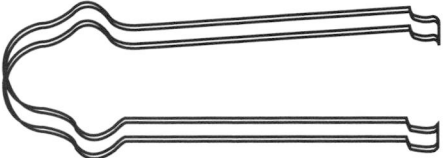

FIG. 17.6   The chip extractor would be used to remove an individual RAM or ROM chip from a socket but it would not be useful for a larger processor.

The tweezers and parts grabber can be used to hold any small screws or jumper blocks that are difficult to hold in your hand. The parts grabber (see Figure 17.7) is especially useful when you drop a small part into the interior of a system; usually, you can remove the part without completely disassembling the system.

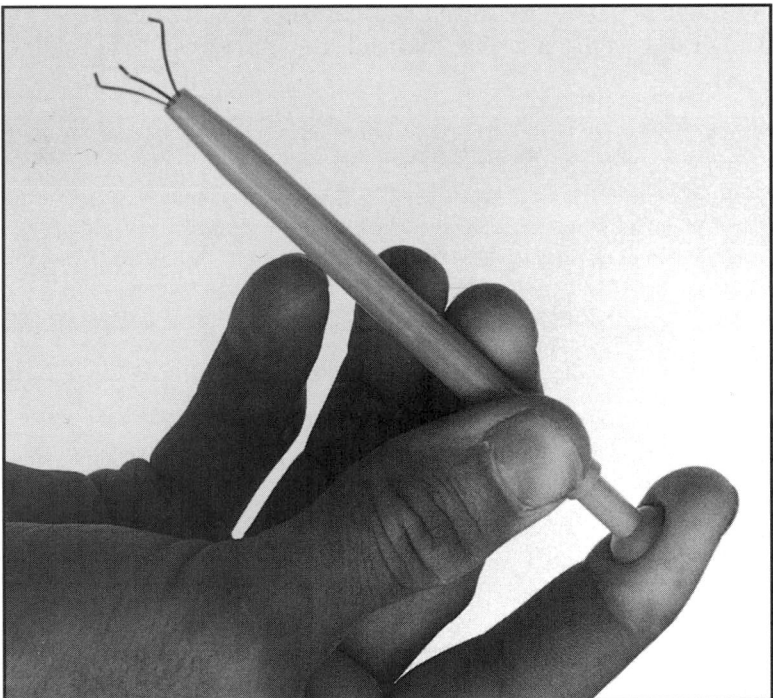

FIG. 17.7   The parts grabber has three small metal prongs that can be extended to grab a part.

Finally, the Torx driver is a special, star-shaped driver that matches the special screws found in most Compaq systems and in many other systems as well. You can also purchase tamperproof Torx drivers that can remove Torx screws with the tamper-resistant pin in the center of the screw. A tamperproof Torx driver has a hole drilled in it to allow clearance for the pin.

Although this basic set is useful, you should supplement it with some other small hand tools, such as:

- Needlenose pliers
- Vise or clamp
- Hemostat
- File
- Wire cutter or wire stripper
- Small flashlight

Pliers are useful for straightening pins on chips, applying or removing jumpers, crimping cables, or grabbing small parts.

Hemostats are especially useful for grabbing small components, such as jumpers.

The wire cutter or stripper, obviously, is useful for making or repairing cables or wiring.

You can use a vise to install connectors on cables, to crimp cables to the shape you want, and to hold parts during delicate operations. In addition to the vise, Radio Shack sells a nifty "extra hands" device that has two movable arms with alligator clips on the end. This type of device is very useful for making cables or for other delicate operations where an extra set of hands to hold something might be useful.

You can use the file to smooth rough metal edges on cases and chassis and to trim the faceplates on disk drives for a perfect fit.

You may often need a flashlight to illuminate system interiors, especially when the system is cramped and the room lighting is not good, or when you are working on a system underneath a user's desk. I consider this tool to be essential.

Another consideration for your tool kit is an *ESD (electrostatic discharge) protection kit*. This kit consists of a wrist strap with a ground wire and a specially conductive mat with its own ground wire. Using a kit like this when working on a system will help ensure that you never accidentally damage any of the components with a static discharge.

Note

You can work without an ESD protection kit, if you're disciplined and careful about working on systems. If you don't have an ESD kit available, you should discharge yourself by touching some metallic part of the case while the computer is still plugged in to the AC power source, and then unplug the computer. Many systems today continue to feed power to the motherboard through the soft off connection whenever the computer is plugged in, even when the power switch is turned off. It can be very dangerous to work inside a PC that is still connected to a power source.

The ESD kits, as well as all the other tools and much more, are available from a variety of tool vendors. Specialized Products Company and Jensen Tools are two of the most popular vendors of computer and electronic tools and of service equipment. Their catalogs show an extensive selection of very high-quality tools. (These companies and several others are listed in Appendix A, "Vendor List.") With a simple set of hand tools, you will be equipped for nearly every PC repair or installation situation. The total cost of these tools should be less than $150, which is not much considering the capabilities they give you.

A Word About Hardware

This section discusses some problems that you may encounter with the hardware (screws, nuts, bolts, and so on) used in assembling a system.

Types of Hardware. One of the biggest aggravations that you encounter in dealing with various systems is the different hardware types and designs that hold the units together.

For example, most systems use screws that fit 1/4-inch or 3/16-inch hexagonal nut drivers. IBM used these screws in all its original PC, XT, and AT systems, and most other system manufacturers use this standard hardware as well. Some manufacturers use different hardware, however. Compaq, for example, uses Torx screws extensively in many of its systems. A Torx screw has a star-shape hole driven by the correct-size Torx driver. These drivers carry size designations such as T-8, T-9, T-10, T-15, T-20, T-25, T-30, and T-40.

A variation on the Torx screw is the tamperproof Torx screw found in power supplies and other assemblies. These screws are identical to the regular Torx screws, except that a pin sticks up from the middle of the star-shape hole in the screw. This pin prevents the standard Torx driver from entering the hole to grip the screw; a special tamperproof driver with a corresponding hole for the pin is required. An alternative is to use a small chisel to knock out the pin in the screw. Usually, a device that is sealed with these types of screws is considered to be a replaceable unit that rarely, if ever, needs to be opened.

Many manufacturers also use the more standard slotted-head and Phillips-head screws. Using tools on these screws is relatively easy, but tools do not grip these fasteners as well as hexagonal head or Torx screws do, and the heads can be stripped more easily than the other types. Extremely cheap versions tend to lose bits of metal as they're turned with a driver, and the metal bits can fall onto the motherboard. Stay away from cheap fasteners whenever possible; the headaches of dealing with stripped screws aren't worth it.

Some system manufacturers now use cases that snap together or use thumb screws. These are usually advertised as "no-tool" cases because you literally do not need any tools to take off the cover and access the major assemblies.

A company called Curtis sells special nylon plastic thumb screws that fit most normal cases and can be used to replace the existing screws to make opening the case a no-tool proposition. However, you should still always use metal screws to install internal components such as adapter cards, disk drives, power supplies, and the motherboard because the metal screws provide a ground point for these devices.

English Versus Metric. Another area of aggravation with hardware is the fact that there are two types of thread systems: English and metric. IBM used mostly English-threaded fasteners in its original line of systems—but many other manufacturers used metric-threaded fasteners.

The difference between the two becomes especially apparent with disk drives. American-manufactured drives typically use English fasteners, whereas drives made in Japan or Taiwan usually use metric. Whenever you replace a floppy drive in an older PC, you encounter this problem. Try to buy the correct screws and any other hardware, such as brackets, with the drive, because they may be difficult to find as separate items. Many drive manufacturers offer retail drive kits that include all the required mounting components. The OEM's drive manual lists the correct data about a specific drive's hole locations and thread size.

Hard disks can use either English or metric fasteners; check your particular drive to see which type it uses. Most drives today use metric hardware.

Caution

Some screws in a system may be length-critical, especially screws that are used to retain hard disk drives. You can destroy some hard disks by using a mounting screw that's too long; the screw can puncture or dent the sealed disk chamber when you install the drive and fully tighten the screw. When you install a new drive in a system, always make a trial fit of the hardware to see how far the screws can be inserted into the drive before they interfere with its internal components. When you're in doubt, the drive manufacturer's OEM documentation will tell you precisely what screws are required and how long they should be.

Soldering and Desoldering Tools

In certain situations—such as repairing a broken wire, making cables, reattaching a component to a circuit board, removing and installing chips that are not in a socket, or adding jumper wires or pins to a board—you must use a soldering iron to make the repair.

Although virtually all repairs these days are done by simply replacing the entire failed board, and many PC technicians never touch a soldering iron, you may find one useful in some situations. The most common case would be where there was physical damage to a system, such as when someone rips the keyboard connector off of a motherboard by pulling on the cable improperly. Simple soldering skills can save the motherboard in this case.

Most motherboards these days include I/O components such as serial and parallel ports. Many of these ports are fuse-protected on the board; however, the fuse is usually a small soldered-in component. These fuses are designed to protect the motherboard circuits from being damaged by an external source. If a short circuit or static charge from an external device blows these fuses, the motherboard can be saved if you can replace them.

To perform minor repairs such as these, you need a low-wattage soldering iron—usually, about 25 watts. More than 30 watts generates too much heat and can damage the components on the board. Even with a low-wattage unit, you must limit the amount of heat to which you subject the board and its components. You can do this with quick and efficient use of the soldering iron and with the use of heat-sinking devices clipped to the leads of the device being soldered. A *heat sink* is a small metal clip-on device designed to absorb excessive heat before it reaches the component that the heat sink is protecting. In some cases, you can use a pair of hemostats as an effective heat sink when you solder a component.

To remove components that are soldered into place on a printed circuit board, you can use a soldering iron with a *solder sucker*. This device normally takes the form of a small tube with an air chamber and a plunger-and-spring arrangement. (I do not recommend the squeeze-bulb type of solder sucker.) The unit is "cocked" when you press the spring-loaded plunger into the air chamber. When you want to remove a device from a board, you use the soldering iron from the underside of the board, and heat the point at which one of the component leads joins the circuit board until the solder melts. As soon as melting occurs, move the solder-sucker nozzle into position, and press the actuator. When the plunger retracts, it creates a momentary suction that draws the liquid solder away from the connection and leaves the component lead dry in the hole.

Always do the heating and suctioning from the underside of a board, not from the component side. Repeat this action for every component lead joined to the circuit board. When you master this technique, you can remove a small component in a minute or two with only a small likelihood of damage to the board or other components. Larger chips that have many pins can be more difficult to remove and resolder without damaging other components or the circuit board.

> **Tip**
>
> These procedures are intended for Through-Hole devices only. These are components whose pins extend all the way through holes in the board to the underside. Surface mount devices are removed with a completely different procedure, using much more expensive tools. Working on surface-mounted components is beyond the capabilities of all but the most well-equipped shops.

If you intend to add soldering and desoldering skills to your arsenal of abilities, you should practice. Take a useless circuit board and practice removing various components from the board; then, reinstall the components. Try to remove the components from the board by using the least amount of heat possible. Also, perform the solder-melting operations as quickly as possible, limiting the time that the iron is applied to the joint. Before you install any components, clean out the holes through which the leads must project and mount the component in place. Then, apply the solder from the underside of the board, using as little heat and solder as possible.

Attempt to produce joints as clean as the joints that the board manufacturer produced by machine. Soldered joints that do not look clean may keep the component from making a good connection with the rest of the circuit. This "cold-solder joint" is normally created because you have not used enough heat. *Remember that you should not practice your new soldering skills on the motherboard of a system that you are attempting to repair!* Don't attempt to work on real boards until you are sure of your skills. I always keep a few junk boards around for soldering practice and experimentation.

> **Tip**
>
> When first learning to solder, you may be tempted to set the iron on the solder and leave it there until the solder melts. If the solder doesn't melt immediately when applying the iron to it, you're not transferring the heat from the iron to the solder efficiently. This means that either the iron is dirty, or there is debris between it and the solder. To clean the iron, take a wet sponge and drag it across the tip of the iron.
>
> If after cleaning the iron there's still some resistance, try to scratch the solder with the iron when it's hot. Generally, this removes any barriers to heat flow and will instantly melt the solder.

No matter how good you get at soldering and desoldering, some jobs are best left to professionals. Components that are surface-mounted to a circuit board, for example, require special tools for soldering and desoldering, as do other components that have high pin densities.

Test Equipment

In some cases, you must use specialized devices to test a system board or component. This test equipment is not expensive or difficult to use, but it can add much to your troubleshooting abilities.

Electrical Testing Equipment. I consider a voltmeter to be required gear for proper system testing. A *multimeter* can serve many purposes, including checking for voltage signals at different points in a system, testing the output of the power supply, and checking for continuity in a circuit or cable. An outlet tester is an invaluable accessory that can check the electrical outlet for proper wiring. This capability is useful if you believe that the problem lies outside the computer system.

Loopback Connectors (Wrap Plugs). For diagnosing serial- and parallel-port problems, you need loopback connectors (also called *wrap plugs)*, which are used to circulate, or wrap, signals. The plugs enable the serial or parallel port to send data to itself for diagnostic purposes.

Different types of loopback connectors are available. To accommodate all the ports you might encounter, you will need one for the 25-pin serial port, one for the 9-pin serial port, and one for the 25-pin parallel port. Many companies, including IBM, sell the plugs separately, but be aware that you also need diagnostic software that can make use of them. Some diagnostic software products, such as Micro 2000's Micro-Scope, include loopback connectors with the product.

IBM sells a special combination plug that includes all three connector types in one compact unit. The device costs approximately $30 from IBM. If you're handy, you can even make your own wrap plugs for testing. I include wiring diagrams for the three types of wrap plugs in Chapter 10, "I/O Interfaces." In that chapter, you also will find a detailed discussion of serial and parallel ports.

Besides simple loopback connectors, you may also want to have a *breakout box* for your toolkit. A breakout box is a DB25 connector device that enables you to make custom temporary cables or even to monitor signals on a cable. For most PC troubleshooting uses, a "mini" breakout box works well and is inexpensive.

Meters. Some troubleshooting procedures require that you measure voltage and resistance. You take these measurements by using a handheld Digital Multi-Meter (DMM). The meter can be an analog device (using an actual meter) or a digital-readout device. The DMM has a pair of wires called *test leads* or *probes*. The test leads make the connections so that you can take readings. Depending on the meter's setting, the probes measure electrical resistance, direct-current (DC) voltage, or alternating-current (AC) voltage.

Usually, each system-unit measurement setting has several ranges of operation. DC voltage, for example, usually can be read in several scales, to a maximum of 200 millivolts (mv), 2v, 20v, 200v, and 1,000v. Because computers use both +5v and +12v for various operations, you should use the 20v maximum scale for making your measurements. Making these measurements on the 200mv or 2v scale could "peg the meter" and possibly damage it, because the voltage would be much higher than expected. Using the 200v or 1,000v scale works, but the readings at 5v and 12v are so small in proportion to the maximum that accuracy is low.

If you are taking a measurement and are unsure of the actual voltage, start at the highest scale and work your way down. Most of the better meters have autoranging capability—the meter automatically selects the best range for any measurement. This type of meter is much easier to operate. You just set the meter to the type of reading you want, such as DC volts, and attach the probes to the signal source. The meter selects the correct voltage range and displays the value. Because of their design, these types of meters always have a digital display rather than a meter needle.

> ### Caution
>
> Whenever using a multimeter to test any voltage that could potentially be 110v or above, always use one hand to do the testing, not two. Either clip one lead to one of the sources and probe with the other, or hold both leads in one hand.
>
> If you are holding a lead in each hand and accidentally slip, you can very easily become a circuit, allowing power to conduct or flow through you. When the power is flowing from arm to arm, the path of the current is directly across the heart. Hearts have a tendency to quit working when subjected to high voltages. They're funny that way.

I prefer the small digital meters; you can buy them for only slightly more than the analog style, and they're extremely accurate and much safer for digital circuits. Some of these meters are not much bigger than a cassette tape; they fit in a shirt pocket. Radio Shack sells a good unit (made for Radio Shack by Beckman) in the $25 price range; the meter is a half-inch thick, weighs 3 1/2 ounces, and is digital and autoranging, as well. This type of meter works well for most, if not all, PC troubleshooting and test uses.

Caution

You should be aware that many analog meters can be dangerous to digital circuits. These meters use a 9v battery to power the meter for resistance measurements. If you use this type of meter to measure resistance on some digital circuits, you can damage the electronics, because you essentially are injecting 9v into the circuit. The digital meters universally run on 3–5v or less.

Logic Probes and Logic Pulsers. A *logic probe* can be useful for diagnosing problems in digital circuits. In a *digital circuit*, a signal is represented as either high (+5v) or low (0v). Because these signals are present for only a short time (measured in millionths of a second) or oscillate (switch on and off) rapidly, a simple voltmeter is useless. A logic probe is designed to display these signal conditions easily.

Logic probes are especially useful for troubleshooting a dead system. By using the probe, you can determine whether the basic clock circuitry is operating and whether other signals necessary for system operation are present. In some cases, a probe can help you cross-check the signals at each pin on an Integrated Circuit chip. You can compare the signals present at each pin with the signals that a known-good chip of the same type would show—a comparison that is helpful in isolating a failed component. Logic probes can also be useful for troubleshooting some disk drive problems by enabling you to test the signals present on the interface cable or drive-logic board.

A companion tool to the probe is the logic pulser. A *pulser* is designed to test circuit reaction by delivering a logical high (+5v) pulse into a circuit, usually lasting 1 1/2–10 millionths of a second. Compare the reaction with that of a *known-functional circuit*. This type of device normally is used much less frequently than a logic probe, but in some cases, it can be helpful for testing a circuit.

Outlet Testers. *Outlet testers* are very useful test tools. These simple, inexpensive devices, sold in hardware stores, are used to test electrical outlets. You simply plug the device in, and three LEDs light in various combinations, indicating whether the outlet is wired correctly.

Although you may think that badly wired outlets would be a rare problem, I have seen a large number of installations in which the outlets were wired incorrectly. Most of the time, the problem is in the ground wire. An improperly wired outlet can result in unstable system operation, such as random parity checks and lockups. With an improper ground circuit, currents can begin flowing on the electrical ground circuits in the system. Because the system uses the voltage on the ground circuits as a comparative signal to determine whether bits are 0 or 1, a floating ground can cause data errors in the system.

Once, while running one of my PC troubleshooting seminars, I was using a system that I literally could not approach without locking it up. Whenever I walked past the system, the electrostatic field generated by my body interfered with the system, and the PC locked up, displaying a parity-check error message. The problem was that the hotel at which I was giving the seminar was very old and had no grounded outlets in the room. The only way I could prevent the system from locking up was to run the class in my stocking feet, because my leather-soled shoes were generating the static charge.

Other symptoms of bad ground wiring in electrical outlets are continuous electrical shocks when you touch the case or chassis of the system. These shocks indicate that voltages are flowing where they should not be. This problem can also be caused by bad or improper grounds within the system. By using the simple outlet tester, you can quickly determine whether the outlet is at fault.

If you just walk up to a system and receive an initial shock, it's probably just static electricity. Touch the chassis again without moving your feet. If you receive another shock, there is something *very* wrong. In this case, the ground wire actually has voltage applied to it. You should have a professional electrician check the outlet immediately.

If you don't like being a human rat in an electrical experiment, you can test the outlets with your multimeter. First, remember to hold both leads in one hand. Test from one blade hole to another. This should read between 110–125v depending upon the electrical service in the area. Then check from each blade to the ground (the round hole). One blade hole, the smaller one, should show a voltage almost identical to the one that you got from the blade hole to blade hole test. The larger blade hole when measured to ground should show less than 0.5v.

Because ground and neutral are supposed to be tied together at the electrical panel, a large difference in these readings indicates that they are not tied together. However, small differences can be accounted for by current from other outlets down the line flowing on the neutral, when there isn't any on the ground.

If you don't get the results you expect, call an electrician to test the outlets for you. More weird computer problems are caused by improper grounding and other power problems than people like to believe.

Memory Testers. I now consider a memory test machine an all but mandatory piece of equipment for anyone serious about performing PC troubleshooting and repair as a profession. The tester is a small device designed to evaluate SIMMs, DIMMs, and other types of memory modules, including individual chips such as those used as cache memory. These testers can be somewhat expensive, costing upwards of $1,000 to $2,500, but these machines are the only truly accurate way to test memory.

Without one of these testers, you are reduced to testing memory by running a diagnostic program on the PC and testing the memory as it is installed. This can be very problematic, as the memory diagnostic program can only do two things to the memory—write and read. A SIMM tester can do many things that a memory diagnostic running in a PC cannot do, such as:

■ Identify the type of memory

■ Identify the memory speed

■ Identify whether the memory has parity, or is using bogus parity emulation

■ Vary the refresh timing and access speed timing

■ Locate single bit failures

■ Detect power- and noise-related failures

■ Detect solder opens and shorts

■ Isolate timing-related failures

■ Detect data retention errors

No conventional memory diagnostic software can do these things because it has to rely on the fixed access parameters set up by the memory controller hardware in the motherboard chipset. This prevents the software from being able to alter the timing and methods used to access the memory. You may have memory that fails in one system and works in another when the chips are actually bad. This type of intermittent problem is almost impossible to detect with diagnostic software.

The bottom line is that there is no way that you can test memory with true accuracy while it is installed in a PC; a memory tester is required for comprehensive and accurate testing. Although the price of a typical 32M memory module may be less than $50, the price of a memory tester can be justified very easily in a shop environment where a lot of PCs are tested, as many software and hardware upgrades today require the addition of new memory. With the large increases in the amount of memory in today's systems and stricter timing requirements of newer motherboard designs, it has become even more important to be able to identify or rule out memory as a cause of system failure. One of the memory testers I recommend the most is the SIGMA LC by Darkhorse Systems. See the vendor list in Appendix A for more information. Also see Chapter 5, "Memory," for more information on memory in general.

Preventive Maintenance

Preventive maintenance is the key to obtaining years of trouble-free service from your computer system. A properly administered preventive maintenance program pays for itself by reducing problem behavior, data loss, component failure, and by ensuring a long life for your system. In several cases, I have "repaired" an ailing system with nothing more than a preventive maintenance session. Preventive maintenance can also increase your system's resale value because it will look and run better.

Developing a preventive maintenance program is important to everyone who uses or manages personal computer systems. There are two types of preventive maintenance procedures: active and passive.

An *active* preventive maintenance program includes procedures that promote a longer, trouble-free life for your PC. This type of preventive maintenance primarily involves the periodic cleaning of the system and its components. The following sections describe several active preventive maintenance procedures, including cleaning and lubricating all major components, reseating chips and connectors, and reformatting hard disks.

Passive preventive maintenance includes steps you can take to protect a system from the environment, such as using power-protection devices; ensuring a clean, temperature-controlled environment; and preventing excessive vibration. In other words, passive preventive maintenance means treating your system well!

Active Preventive Maintenance Procedures

How often you should perform active preventive maintenance procedures depends on the system's environment and the quality of the system's components. If your system is in a dirty environment, such as a machine shop floor or a gas station service area, you might need to clean your system every three months or less. For normal office environments, cleaning a system every one to two years is usually fine. However, if you open your system after one year and find dust bunnies inside, you should probably shorten the cleaning interval.

Other hard disk preventive maintenance procedures include making periodic backups of your data and critical areas such as boot sectors, file allocation tables (FATs), and directory structures on the disk. Also, hard disk defragmentations should be performed periodically, to maintain disk efficiency and speed.

System Backups. One of the most important preventive maintenance procedures is the performance of regular system backups. A sad reality in the computer repair and servicing world is that hardware can always be repaired or replaced, but data cannot. Many hard disk troubleshooting and service procedures, for example, require that you repartition or reformat the disk, which overwrites all existing data.

The hard disk drive capacity in a typical PC has grown far beyond the point at which floppy disks are a viable backup solution. Backup solutions that employ floppy disk drives, such as the DOS backup software, are insufficient and too costly for hard disk backups in today's systems. It would take 2,867 1.44M floppy disks, for example, to back up the 4G hard disk in my portable system! That would cost more than $1,000 in disks, not to mention the time involved.

The traditional alternative to floppies is magnetic tape. A DAT (Digital Audio Tape) or Travan tape system can store 4G to 8G or more on a single tape costing less than $30. The increasing popularity of removable cartridge (such as Iomega Zip and Jaz drives) and writable CD-ROM drives presents even more alternatives.

Although a tape drive may cost up to $500 or more, the media costs are really far more significant than the cost of the drive. If you are doing responsible backups, you should have at least three sets of media for each system you are backing up. You should use each media set on a rotating basis, and store one of them offsite at all times, in case of fire or theft. You should also introduce new media to the rotation after approximately a year to prevent excessive wear. If you are backing up multiple systems, these media costs can add up quickly.

You should also factor in the cost of your time. If a backup requires manual intervention to change the media during the job, then I don't recommend it. A backup system should be able to fit a complete backup on a single tape so you can schedule the job to run unattended. If someone has to hang around to switch tapes every so often, backups become a real chore and are more likely to be overlooked. Also, every time a media change occurs, there is a substantial increase in the likelihood of errors and problems that you may not see until you attempt to perform a restore operation. Backups are far more important than most people realize, and spending a little more on a quality piece of hardware such as a Travan or DAT drive will pay off in the long run with greater reliability, lower media costs, higher performance, and unattended backups that contain the entire system file structure.

With the increasing popularity of removable bulk storage media like cartridge drives, such as Iomega's Zip and Jaz drives, and rewritable CD-ROMs (CD-RWs), many people are using these devices to perform system backups. In most cases, however, although these drives are excellent for storing backup copies of selected data, they are impractical solutions for regular system backups. This can be due both to the capacity of the media in relation to today's hard disk drives, and to the cost of the media.

Although the media for a CD-RW drive are quite inexpensive, it would take several discs to back up a multi-gigabyte hard drive, adding a measure of inconvenience to the backup process that makes it far less likely to be performed on a regular basis. Even the Iomega Jaz drive that can store up to 2G on a single cartridge, can require several media changes to complete a single system backup. Add this to the fact that the Jaz cartridges can cost $150 or more each, and you have a backup solution that is both inconvenient and expensive.

> **Tip**
>
> No matter what backup solution you use, the entire exercise is pointless if you cannot restore your data from the storage medium. You should test your backup system by performing random file restores at regular intervals, to ensure the viability of your data.

Cleaning a System. One of the most important operations in a good preventive maintenance program is regular and thorough cleaning of the system. Dust buildup on the internal components can lead to several problems. One is that the dust acts as a thermal insulator, which prevents proper system cooling. Excessive heat shortens the life of system components and adds to the thermal stress problem caused by greater temperature changes between the system's power-on and power-off states. Additionally, the dust may contain conductive elements that can cause partial short circuits in a system. Other elements in dust and dirt can accelerate corrosion of electrical contacts, resulting in improper connections. In all, the regular removal of any layer of dust and debris from within a computer system benefits that system in the long run.

Most non-ATX and some ATX PCs use a forced-air cooling system that provides even cooling inside the case. A fan is mounted in, on, or near the power supply and pushes air outside. This depressurizes the interior of the system relative to the outside environment. The lower pressure inside the system causes outside air to be drawn in through openings in the system chassis and cover. This draw-through, or depressurization, is the most efficient cooling system that can be designed without an air filter. Air filters typically are not used with depressurization systems because there is no easy way to limit the air intake to a single port that can be covered by a filter.

Some industrial computers and ATX (as well as NLX) systems use a forced-air system that uses the fan to pressurize, rather than to depressurize, the case. This system forces air to exhaust from any holes in the chassis and case or cover. The key to the pressurization system is that all air intake for the system is at a single location—the fan. You can therefore filter the air flowing into the system by integrating a filter assembly into the fan housing. The filter must be cleaned or changed periodically, however, to prevent it from becoming clogged with dust.

Because the interior of the case is pressurized relative to the outside air, airborne contaminants are not drawn into the system even though it may not be completely sealed. Any air entering the system must pass through the fan and filter housing, which removes the contaminants. Pressurization cooling systems were originally designed for use in industrial computer models intended for extremely harsh environments. However, with the growing popularity of the ATX and NLX architectures, pressurization systems are more common.

A recent trend in ATX case and power supply design, however, has reverted to the negative-pressurization design. It is claimed that using the fan in the power supply to cool the CPU directly is not effective since the air is preheated by the power supply, especially if it is heavily loaded. Another important reason is that the single biggest advantage of the positive-pressure system, the capability to filter the incoming air, is either not included in the system design or not maintained properly.

Most of the PCs now in use are depressurization systems. Mounting any sort of air filter on these types of systems is impossible because air enters the system from too many sources. With any cooling system in which incoming air is not filtered, dust and other chemical matter in the environment is drawn in and builds up inside the computer. This buildup can cause severe problems if left unchecked.

> **Tip**
>
> Cigarette smoke contains chemicals that can conduct electricity and cause corrosion of computer parts. The smoke residue can infiltrate the entire system, causing corrosion and contamination of electrical contacts and sensitive components such as floppy drive read/write heads and optical drive lens assemblies. You should avoid smoking near computer equipment and encourage your company to develop and enforce a similar policy.

Floppy disk drives are particularly vulnerable to the effects of dirt and dust. A floppy drive is essentially a large "hole" in the system case through which air continuously flows. Therefore, they accumulate a large amount of dust and chemical buildup within a short time. Hard disk drives do not present quite the same problem. Because the head disk assembly (HDA) in a hard disk is a sealed unit with a single barometric vent, no dust or dirt can enter without passing through the barometric vent filter. This filter ensures that contaminating dust or particles cannot enter the interior of the HDA. Thus, cleaning a hard disk requires simply blowing the dust and dirt off from outside the drive. No internal cleaning is required.

Disassembly and Cleaning Tools. To properly clean the system and all the boards inside requires certain supplies and tools. In addition to the tools required to disassemble the unit, you should have these items:

- Contact cleaning solution
- Canned air
- A small brush
- Lint-free foam cleaning swabs
- Anti-static wrist-grounding strap

You also might want to acquire these optional items:

- Foam tape
- Low-volatile room-temperature vulcanizing (RTV) sealer
- Silicone type lubricant
- Computer vacuum cleaner

These simple cleaning tools and chemical solutions will allow you to perform most common preventive maintenance tasks.

Chemicals. Chemicals can be used to help clean, troubleshoot, and even repair a system. You can use several different types of cleaning solutions with computers and electronic assemblies. Most fall into the following categories:

- Standard cleaners
- Contact cleaner/lubricants
- Dusters

Tip

The makeup of many of the chemicals used for cleaning electronic components has been changing because many of the chemicals originally used are now considered environmentally unsafe. They have been attributed to damaging the earth's ozone layer. Chlorine atoms from chlorofluorocarbons (CFCs) and chlorinated solvents attach themselves to ozone molecules and destroy them. Many of these chemicals are now strictly regulated by federal and international agencies in an effort to preserve the ozone layer. Most of the companies that produce chemicals used for system cleaning and maintenance have had to introduce environmentally safe replacements. The only drawback is that many of these safer chemicals cost more and usually do not work as well as those they replace.

Standard Cleaners. For the most basic function—cleaning components, electrical connectors, and contacts—one of the most useful chemicals is 1,1,1 trichloroethane. This substance is a very effective cleaner that was at one time used to clean electrical contacts and components, because it does not damage most plastics and board materials.

In fact, trichloroethane could be very useful for cleaning stains on the system case and keyboard as well. Unfortunately, trichloroethane is now being regulated as a chlorinated solvent, along with CFCs (chlorofluorocarbons) such as freon, but electronic chemical-supply companies are offering several replacements.

Alternative cleaning solutions are available in a variety of types and configurations. You can use pure isopropyl alcohol, acetone, freon, trichloroethane, or a variety of other chemicals. Most board manufacturers and service shops are now leaning toward the alcohol, acetone, or other chemicals that do not cause ozone depletion and comply with government regulations and environmental safety.

Recently, new biodegradable cleaners described as "citrus-based cleaners" have become popular in the industry, and in many cases are more effective and more economical for circuit board and contact cleaning. These cleaners are commonly known as *d-limonene* or *citrus terpenes* and are derived from orange peels, which gives it a strong (but pleasant) citric odor. Another type of terpene is called *a-pinene*, and is derived from pine trees. You must exercise care when using these cleaners, however, as they can cause swelling of some plastics, especially silicone rubber and PVC.

You should be sure that your cleaning solution is designed to clean computers or electronic assemblies. In most cases, this means that the solution should be chemically pure and free from contaminants or other unwanted substances. You should not, for example, use drugstore rubbing alcohol for cleaning electronic parts or contacts because it is not pure and could contain water or perfumes. The material must be moisture-free and residue-free. The solutions should be in liquid form, not a spray. Sprays can be wasteful, and you almost never spray the solution directly on components. Instead, wet a foam or chamois swab used for wiping the component. These electronic-component cleaning solutions are available at any good electronics parts store.

Contact Cleaner/Lubricants. These chemicals are similar to the standard cleaners but include a lubricating component. The lubricant eases the force required when plugging and unplugging cables and connectors, reducing strain on the devices. The lubricant coating also acts as a conductive protectant that insulates the contacts from corrosion. These chemicals can greatly prolong the life of a system by preventing intermittent contacts in the future.

A unique type of contact enhancer and lubricant called *Stabilant 22* is currently on the market. This chemical, which you apply to electrical contacts, greatly enhances the connection and lubricates the contact point; it is much more effective than conventional contact cleaners or lubricants.

Stabilant 22 is a liquid-polymer semiconductor; it behaves like liquid metal and conducts electricity in the presence of an electric current. The substance also fills the air gaps between the mating surfaces of two items that are in contact, making the surface area of the contact larger and also keeping out oxygen and other contaminants that can corrode the contact point.

This chemical is available in several forms. Stabilant 22 is the concentrated version, whereas Stabilant 22a is a version diluted with isopropanol in a 4:1 ratio. An even more diluted 8:1-ratio version is sold in many high-end stereo and audio shops under the name Tweek. Just 15ml of Stabilant 22a sells for about $40; a liter of the concentrate costs about $4,000!

As you can plainly see, Stabilant 22 is fairly expensive, but very little is required in an application, and nothing else has been found to be as effective in preserving electrical contacts. (NASA uses the chemical on spacecraft electronics.) An application of Stabilant can provide protection for up to 16 years, according to its manufacturer, D.W. Electrochemicals. You will find the company's address and phone number in the vendor list in Appendix A.

Stabilant is especially effective on I/O slot connectors, adapter-card edge and pin connectors, disk drive connectors, power-supply connectors, and virtually any connector in the PC. In addition to enhancing the contact and preventing corrosion, an application of Stabilant lubricates the contacts, making insertion and removal of the connector easier.

Dusters. Compressed gas often is used as an aid in system cleaning. You use the compressed gas as a blower to remove dust and debris from a system or component. Originally, these dusters used CFCs such as freon, whereas modern dusters now use HFCs (such as difluoroethane) or carbon dioxide, neither of which is damaging to the ozone layer. Be careful when you use these devices because some of them can generate a static charge when the compressed gas leaves the nozzle of the can. Be sure that you are using the kind approved for cleaning or dusting off computer equipment, and consider wearing a static grounding strap as a precaution. The type of compressed-air cans used for cleaning camera equipment can sometimes differ from the type used for cleaning static-sensitive computer components.

When using these compressed air products, make sure you hold the can upright so that only gas is ejected from the nozzle. If you tip the can, the raw propellant will come out as a cold liquid, which is not only wasteful, but can damage or discolor plastics. You should only use compressed gas on equipment that is powered off, to minimize any chance of damage through short circuits.

Closely related to compressed-air products are *chemical-freeze sprays*. These sprays are used to quickly cool down a suspected failing component, which often temporarily restores it to normal operation. These substances are not used to repair a device, but to confirm that you have found a failed device. Often, a component's failure is heat-related and cooling it temporarily restores it to normal operation. If the circuit begins operating normally, the device you are cooling is the suspect device.

Vacuum Cleaners. Some people prefer to use a vacuum cleaner instead of canned gas dusters for cleaning a system. Canned gas is usually better for cleaning in small areas. A vacuum cleaner is more useful when you are cleaning a system loaded with dust and dirt. You can use the vacuum cleaner to suck out the dust and debris instead of just blowing it around on the other components, which sometimes happens with canned air. For on-site servicing (when you are going to the location of the equipment instead of the equipment coming to you), canned air is easier to carry in a tool kit than a small vacuum cleaner. There are also tiny vacuum cleaners available for system cleaning. These small units are easy to carry and may serve as an alternative to compressed air cans.

There are special vacuum cleaners specifically designed for use on and around electronic components. They are designed to minimize ESD while in use. If you are using a regular vacuum cleaner and not one specifically designed with ESD protection, then you should take precautions such as wearing a grounding wrist strap. Also, if the cleaner has a metal nozzle, be careful not to touch it to the circuit boards or components you are cleaning.

Brushes and Swabs. You can use a small makeup, photographic, or paint brush to carefully loosen the accumulated dirt and dust inside a PC before spraying it with canned air or using the vacuum cleaner. Be careful about generating static electricity, however. In most cases, you should not use a brush directly on circuit boards, but only on the case interior and other parts such as fan blades, air vents, and keyboards. Wear a grounded wrist strap if you are brushing on or near any circuit boards, and brush slowly and lightly to prevent static discharges from occurring.

Use cleaning swabs to wipe off electrical contacts and connectors, disk drive heads, and other sensitive areas. The swabs should be made of foam or synthetic chamois material that does not leave lint or dust residue. Unfortunately, proper foam or chamois cleaning swabs are more expensive than the typical cotton swabs. Do not use cotton swabs because they leave cotton fibers on everything they touch. Cotton fibers are conductive in some situations and can remain on drive heads, which can scratch disks. Foam or chamois swabs can be purchased at most electronics supply stores.

One item to avoid is an eraser for cleaning contacts. Many people (including myself) have recommended using a soft pencil-type eraser for cleaning circuit-board contacts. Testing has proven this to be bad advice for several reasons. One reason is that any such abrasive wiping on electrical contacts generates friction and an ESD. This ESD can be damaging to boards and components, especially the newer low-voltage devices. These devices are especially static-sensitive, and cleaning the contacts without a proper liquid solution is not recommended. Also, the eraser will wear off the gold coating on many contacts, exposing the tin contact underneath, which will rapidly corrode when exposed to air. Some companies sell premoistened contact cleaning pads that are soaked in a proper contact cleaner and lubricant. These pads are safe to wipe on conductor and contacts with no likelihood of ESD damage or abrasion of the gold plating.

Silicone Lubricants. You can use a silicone lubricant such as WD40 to lubricate the door mechanisms on floppy disk drives and any other part of the system that may require clean, non-oily lubrication. Other items that you can lubricate are the disk drive head slider rails and even printer-head slider rails, to provide smoother operation.

Using silicone instead of conventional oils is important because silicone does not gum up and collect dust and other debris. Always use the silicone sparingly. Do not spray it anywhere near the equipment as it tends to migrate and will end up where it doesn't belong (such as on drive heads). Instead, apply a small amount to a toothpick or foam swab and dab the silicone lubricant on the components where needed. You can use a lint-free cleaning stick soaked in silicone to lubricate the metal print-head rails in a printer.

Obtaining Required Tools and Accessories. You can obtain most of the cleaning chemicals and tools discussed in this chapter from an electronics supply house, or even your local Radio Shack. A company called Chemtronics specializes in chemicals for the computer and electronics industry. These and other companies that supply tools, chemicals, and other computer and electronic cleaning supplies are listed in the vendor list in Appendix A. With all these items on hand, you should be equipped for most preventive maintenance operations.

Disassembling and Cleaning Procedures. To properly clean your system, you must at least partially disassemble it. Some people go as far as to remove the motherboard. Removing the motherboard results in the best possible access to other areas of the system; but in the interest of saving time, you probably need to disassemble the system only to the point at which the motherboard is completely visible.

To do this, remove all the system's plug-in adapter cards and the disk drives. Although you can clean the heads of a floppy drive with a cleaning disk without opening the system unit's cover, you probably will want to do more thorough cleaning. In addition to the drive heads, you also should clean and lubricate the door mechanism and clean any logic boards and connectors on the drive. This procedure usually requires removing the drive.

Next, do the same thing with the hard disk drives: Clean the logic boards and connectors, and lubricate the grounding strap. To do this, you must remove the hard disk assembly. As a precaution, be sure your data is backed up first.

Reseating Socketed Chips. Another primary preventive maintenance function is to undo the effects of chip creep. As your system heats and cools, it expands and contracts, and the physical expansion and contraction can cause components that are plugged into sockets to gradually work their way out of those sockets. This process is called *chip creep*. To correct its effects, you must find all socketed components in the system and make sure that they are properly reseated.

In most of today's systems, the memory chips are installed in socketed SIMMs or DIMMs. SIMM/DIMM devices are retained securely in their sockets by a positive latching mechanism and cannot creep out. The *Memory SIPP (Single Inline Pin Package) devices* (SIMMs with pins rather than contacts) used in older systems are not retained by a latching mechanism, however, and therefore can creep out of their sockets. Standard socketed memory chips are prime candidates for chip creep. Most other logic components are soldered in. On an older system, you may also find the ROM chips, a math coprocessor, and even the main system processor in sockets. Newer systems place the CPU in a ZIF socket, which has a lever that releases the grip of the socket on the chip. In most cases, there is very little creep with a ZIF socket. In most current systems, the memory (in SIMMs or DIMMs) and the processor are the only components that you will find in sockets; all others are soldered in.

Exceptions, however, might exist. A socketed component in one system might not be socketed in another—even if both are from the same manufacturer. Sometimes this difference results from a parts-availability problem when the boards are manufactured. Rather than halt the assembly line when a part is not available, the manufacturer adds a socket instead of the component. When the component becomes available, it is plugged in and the board is finished.

To make sure that all components are fully seated in their sockets, place your hand on the underside of the board and then apply downward pressure with the thumb of your other hand (from the top) on the chip to be seated. For larger chips, seat the chip carefully in the socket, and press separately on each end of the chip with your thumb to be sure that the chip is fully seated. (The processor and math coprocessor chips can usually be seated in this manner.) In most cases, you should hear a crunching sound as the chip makes its way back into the socket. Because of the great force that is sometimes required to reseat the chips, this operation is difficult if you do not remove the board.

For motherboards, forcibly seating chips can be dangerous if you do not directly support the board from the underside with your hand. Too much pressure on the board can cause it to bow or bend in the chassis, and the pressure can crack it before the chip is fully seated. The plastic standoffs that hold the board up off the metal chassis are spaced too far apart to properly support the board under this kind of stress. Try this operation only if you can remove and support the board adequately from underneath.

You may be surprised to know that, even if you fully seat each chip, they might need reseating again within a year. The creep usually is noticeable within a year or less.

Cleaning Boards. After reseating any socketed devices that may have crept out of their sockets, the next step is to clean the boards and all connectors in the system. For this step, use the cleaning solutions and the lint-free swabs mentioned earlier.

First, clean the dust and debris off the board and then clean any connectors on the board. To clean the boards, it is usually best to use a vacuum cleaner designed for electronic assemblies and circuit boards or a duster can of compressed gas. The dusters are especially effective at blasting any dust and dirt off the boards.

Also, blow any dust out of the power supply, especially around the fan intake and exhaust areas. You do not need to disassemble the power supply to do this; just use a duster can and blast the compressed air into the supply through the fan exhaust port. This will blow the dust out of the supply and clean off the fan blades and grill, which will help with system airflow.

Caution

Be careful with ESD, which can cause damage when you are cleaning electronic components. Take extra precautions in the dead of winter or in extremely dry, high-static environments. You can apply anti-static sprays and treatments to the work area to reduce the likelihood of ESD damage.

An anti-static wrist-grounding strap is recommended. This should be connected to a ground on the card or board you are wiping. This strap ensures that no electrical discharge occurs between you and the board. An alternative method is to keep a finger or thumb on the ground of the motherboard or card as you wipe it off.

Cleaning Connectors and Contacts. Cleaning the connectors and contacts in a system promotes reliable connections between devices. On a motherboard, you will want to clean the slot connectors, power supply connectors, keyboard and mouse connectors, and the speaker connector. For most plug-in cards, you will want to clean the edge connectors that plug in to slots on the motherboard and any other connectors, such as external ones mounted on the card bracket.

Submerge the lint-free swabs in the liquid cleaning solution. If you are using the spray, hold the swab away from the system and spray a small amount on the foam end until the solution starts to drip. Then, use the soaked foam swab to wipe the connectors on the boards. Pre-soaked wipes are the easiest to use. Simply wipe them along the contacts to remove any accumulated dirt and leave a protective coating behind.

On the motherboard, pay special attention to the slot connectors. Be liberal with the liquid; resoak the foam swab repeatedly, and vigorously clean the connectors. Don't worry if some of the liquid drips on the surface of the motherboard. These solutions are entirely safe for the whole board and will not damage the components.

Use the solution to wash the dirt off the gold contacts in the slot connectors, and then clean any other connectors on the board. Clean the keyboard and mouse connectors, the grounding positions where screws ground the board to the system chassis, power-supply connectors, speaker connectors, and the battery connectors.

If you are cleaning a plug-in board, pay special attention to the edge connector that mates with the slot connector on the motherboard. When people handle plug-in cards, they often touch the gold contacts on these connectors. Touching the gold contacts coats them with oils and debris, which prevents proper contact with the slot connector when the board is installed. Make sure these gold contacts are free of all finger oils and residue. It is a good idea to use one of the contact cleaners that has a conductive lubricant, which makes it easier to push the adapter into the slot and also protects the contacts from corrosion.

You will also want to use the swab and solution to clean the ends of ribbon cables or other types of cables or connectors in a system. Clean the floppy drive cables and connectors, the hard disk cables and connectors, and any others you find. Don't forget to clean the edge connectors that are on the disk drive logic boards, as well as the power connectors to the drives.

Cleaning the Keyboard and Mouse. Keyboards and mice are notorious for picking up dirt and garbage. If you have ever opened up an older keyboard, you often will be amazed at the junk you will find in there.

To prevent problems, it is a good idea to periodically clean the keyboard with a vacuum cleaner. An alternative method is to turn the keyboard upside down and shoot it with a can of compressed air. This will blow out the dirt and debris that has accumulated inside the keyboard and possibly prevent future problems with sticking keys or dirty key-switches.

If a particular key is stuck or making intermittent contact, you can soak or spray that switch with contact cleaner. The best way to do this is to first remove the keycap and then spray the cleaner into the switch. This usually does not require complete disassembly of the keyboard. Periodic vacuuming or compressed gas cleaning will prevent more serious problems with sticking keys and keyswitches.

Most mice are easy to clean. In most cases, there is a twist-off locking retainer that keeps the mouse ball retained in the body of the mouse. By removing the retainer, the ball will drop out. After removing the ball, you should clean it with one of the electronic cleaners. I would recommend a pure cleaner instead of a contact cleaner with lubricant because you do not want any lubricant on the mouse ball. Then you should wipe off the rollers in the body of the mouse with the cleaner and some swabs.

Periodic cleaning of a mouse in this manner will eliminate or prevent skipping or erratic movement. I also recommend a mouse pad for most ball-type mice because the pad will prevent the mouse ball from picking up debris from your desk.

Other pointing devices requiring little or no maintenance are the IBM-designed Trackpoint and similar systems introduced by other manufacturers, such as the Glidepoint by Alps. These devices are totally sealed, and use pressure transducers to control pointer movement. Because they are sealed, cleaning need only be performed externally, and is as simple as wiping the device off with a mild cleaning solution to remove oils and other deposits that have accumulated from handling them.

Hard Disk Maintenance. Certain preventive maintenance procedures protect your data and ensure that your hard disk works efficiently. Some of these procedures actually minimize wear and tear on your drive, which will prolong its life. Additionally, a high level of data protection can be implemented by performing some simple commands periodically. These commands provide methods for backing up (and possibly later restoring) critical areas of the hard disk that, if damaged, would disable access to all your files.

Defragmenting Files. Over time, as you delete and save files to a hard disk, the files become *fragmented*. This means that they are split into many noncontiguous areas on the disk. One of the best ways to protect both your hard disk and the data on it is to periodically defragment the files on the disk. This serves two purposes. One is that by ensuring that all the files are stored in contiguous sectors on the disk, head movement and drive wear and tear will be minimized. This has the added benefit of improving the speed at which the drive retrieves files by reducing the head thrashing that occurs every time it accesses a fragmented file.

The second major benefit, and in my estimation the more important of the two, is that in the case of a disaster where the FATs and root directory are severely damaged, the data on the drive can usually be recovered easily if the files are contiguous. On the other hand, if the files are split up in many pieces across the drive, it is virtually impossible to figure out which pieces belong to which files without an intact FAT and directory system. For the purposes of data integrity and protection, I recommend defragmenting your hard disk drives on a monthly basis.

There are three main functions in most defragmentation programs:

- File defragmentation
- File packing (Free Space Consolidation)
- File sorting

Defragmentation is the basic function, but most other programs also add file packing. Packing the files is optional on some programs because it usually takes additional time to perform. This function packs the files at the beginning of the disk so that all free space is consolidated at the end of the disk. This feature minimizes future file fragmentation by eliminating any empty holes on the disk. Because all free space is consolidated into one large area, any new files written to the disk will be able to be written in a contiguous manner with no fragmentation.

The last function, file sorting (sometimes called *disk optimizing*), is not usually necessary and is performed as an option by many defragmenting programs. This function adds a tremendous amount of time to the operation, and has little or no effect on the speed at which information is accessed. It can be somewhat beneficial for disaster recovery purposes because you will have an idea of which files came before or after other files if a disaster occurs. Not all defragmenting programs offer file sorting, and the extra time it takes is probably not worth any benefits you will receive. Other programs can sort the order that files are listed in directories, which is a quick and easy operation compared to sorting the file ordering the disk.

Windows 9x includes a disk defragmentation program with the operating system that you can use on both the FAT16 and FAT32 file systems that the OS supports. For DOS and Windows systems, you must purchase a third-party defragmentation program. Norton Utilities includes a disk defragmenter, as do many other utility packages. If you elect to use a third-party product on a Windows 9x system, be certain that it supports the file system you use on your drives. Running a FAT16 defragmentation program on a FAT32 drive can cause severe problems.

Before you defragment your disks, it is a good idea to run a disk repair program such as Windows 9x's ScanDisk or Norton Disk Doctor, even if you are not experiencing any problems. This ensures that your drives are in good working order before you begin the defragmentation process.

Windows 98 Maintenance Wizard

Windows 98 includes a Task Scheduler program that enables you to schedule programs for automatic execution at specified times. The Windows 98 Maintenance Wizard walks you through the steps of scheduling regular disk defragmentations, disk error scans, and deletions of unnecessary files. You can schedule these processes to execute during non-working hours, so regular system activities are not disturbed.

Virus Checking. Viruses are a danger to any system, and it's a good idea to make scans with an anti-virus program a regular part of your preventive maintenance program. Although both Microsoft and IBM provide anti-virus software in MS- and PC-DOS, respectively, if you run Windows 9x or Windows NT, you must obtain a third-party program to scan your system. There are many aftermarket utility packages available that will scan for and remove viruses. No matter which of these programs you use, you should perform a scan for virus programs periodically, especially before making hard disk backups. This will help ensure that you catch any potential virus problem before it spreads and becomes a major catastrophe. In addition, it is important to select an anti-virus product from a vendor that provides regular updates to the program's virus signatures. The signatures determine which viruses the software can detect and cure, and because there are new viruses constantly being introduced, these updates are essential.

Passive Preventive Maintenance Procedures

Passive preventive maintenance involves taking care of the system by providing the best possible environment—both physical and electrical—for the system. Physical concerns are conditions such as ambient temperature, thermal stress from power cycling, dust and smoke contamination, and disturbances such as shock and vibration. Electrical concerns are items such as ESD, power-line noise, and radio-frequency interference. Each of these environmental concerns is discussed in the following sections.

Examining the Operating Environment. Oddly enough, one of the most overlooked aspects of microcomputer preventive maintenance is protecting the hardware—and the sizable financial investment it represents—from environmental abuse. Computers are relatively forgiving, and they are generally safe in an environment that is comfortable for people. Computers, however, are often treated with no more respect than desktop calculators. The result of this type of abuse is many system failures.

Before you set up a new PC, prepare a proper location for it that is free of airborne contaminants such as smoke or other pollution. Do not place your system in front of a window; the computer should not be exposed to direct sunlight or temperature variations. The environmental temperature should be as constant as possible. Power should be provided through properly grounded outlets and should be stable and free from electrical noise and interference. Keep your system away from radio transmitters or other sources of radio frequency energy.

Heating and Cooling. Thermal expansion and contraction from ambient temperature changes places stress on a computer system. Therefore, keeping the temperature in your office or room relatively constant is important to the successful operation of your computer system.

Temperature variations can lead to serious problems. You might encounter excessive chip creep, for example. If extreme variations occur over a short period, signal traces on circuit boards can crack and separate, solder joints can break, and contacts in the system can undergo accelerated corrosion. Solid-state components such as chips can be damaged also, and a host of other problems can develop.

Temperature variations can play havoc with hard disk drives. Writing to a disk at different ambient temperatures can, on some drives, cause data to be written at different locations relative to the track centers. This can cause read and write problems at a later time.

To ensure that your system operates in the correct ambient temperature, you must first determine your system's specified functional range. Most manufacturers provide data about the correct operating temperature range for their systems. Two temperature specifications might be available, one indicating allowable temperatures during operation and another indicating allowable temperatures under non-operating conditions. IBM, for example, indicates the following temperature ranges as acceptable for most of its systems:

System on: 60 to 90° Fahrenheit

System off: 50 to 110° Fahrenheit

For the safety of the disk and the data it contains, avoid rapid changes in ambient temperatures. If rapid temperature changes occur—for example, when a new drive is shipped to a location during the winter and then brought indoors—let the drive acclimate to room temperature before turning it on. In extreme cases, condensation can form on the platters inside the drive HDA—disastrous for the drive if you turn it on before the condensation has a chance to evaporate. Most drive manufacturers specify a timetable to use as a guide in acclimating a drive to room temperature before operating it. You usually must wait several hours to a day before a drive is ready to use after it has been shipped or stored in a cold environment. They normally advise that you leave the drive in its packing until it is acclimated. Removing the drive from a shipping carton when extremely cold will increase the likelihood of condensation forming as the drive warms up.

Most office environments provide a stable temperature in which to operate a computer system, but some do not. Be sure to give some consideration to the placement of your equipment.

Power Cycling (On/Off). As you have just learned, the temperature variations that a system encounters greatly stress the system's physical components. The largest temperature variations a system encounters, however, are those that occur during the warmup period right after you turn the computer on. Powering on a cold system subjects it to the greatest possible internal temperature variations. If you want a system to have the longest and most trouble-free life possible, you should limit the temperature variations in its environment. You can limit the extreme temperature cycling in two simple ways during a cold startup—leave the system off all the time or leave it on all the time. Of these two possibilities, of course, you will probably want to choose the latter option. Leaving the power on is the best way I know to promote system reliability. If your only concern is system longevity, the simple recommendation would be to keep the system unit powered on (or off!) continuously. In the real world, however, there are more variables to consider, such as the cost of electricity, the potential fire hazard of unattended running equipment, and other concerns, as well.

If you think about the way light bulbs typically fail, you can begin to understand how thermal cycling can be dangerous. Light bulbs burn out most often when you first turn them on, because the filament must endure incredible thermal stress as it changes temperature—in less than one second—from ambient to several thousands of degrees. A bulb that remains on continuously lasts longer than one that is turned on and off repeatedly.

The place where problems are most likely to occur immediately at power-on is in the power supply. The start-up current draw for the system during the first few seconds of operation is very high compared to the normal operating-current draw. Because the current must come from the power supply, the supply has an extremely demanding load to carry for the first few seconds of operation, especially if several disk drives must be started. Motors have an extremely high power-on current draw. This demand often overloads a marginal circuit or component in the supply and causes it to burn or break with a "snap." I have seen several power supplies die the instant a system was powered up. To enable your equipment to have the longest possible life, try to keep the temperature of solid-state components relatively constant, and limit the number of startups on the power supply. The only way I know to do this is to leave the system on.

Although it sounds like I am telling you to leave all your computer equipment on 24 hours a day, seven days a week, I no longer recommend this type of operation. A couple of concerns have tempered my urge to leave everything running continuously. One is that an unattended system that is powered on represents a fire hazard. I have seen monitors catch fire after internally shorting, and systems whose cooling fans have frozen, causing the power supply and the entire system to overheat. I do not leave any system running in an unattended building. Another problem is wasted electrical power. Many companies have adopted austerity programs that involve turning lights and other items off when not in use. The power consumption of some of today's high-powered systems and accessories is not trivial. Also, an unattended operating system is more of a security risk than one that is powered off and locked.

Realities—such as the fire hazard of unattended systems running during night or weekend hours, security problems, and power-consumption issues—might prevent you from leaving your system on all the time. Therefore, you must compromise. Power on the system only one time daily. Don't power the system on and off several times every day. This good advice is often ignored, especially when several users share systems. Each user powers on the system to perform work on the PC and then powers off the system. These systems tend to have many more problems with component failures.

If you are in a building with a programmable thermostat, you have another reason to be concerned about temperatures and disk drives. Some buildings have thermostats programmed to turn off the heat overnight or over the weekend. These thermostats are programmed also to quickly raise the temperature just before business hours every day. In Chicago, for example, outside temperatures in the winter can dip to –20° (not including the wind-chill factor). An office building's interior temperature can drop as low as 50° during the weekend. When you arrive Monday morning, the heat has been on for only an hour or so, but the hard disk platters might not yet have reached even 60° when you turn on the system. During the first 20 minutes of operation, the disk platters rapidly rise in temperature to 120° or more. If you have an inexpensive stepper motor hard disk and begin writing to the disk at these low temperatures, you are setting yourself up for trouble.

Tip

If you do not leave a system on continuously; at least give it 15 minutes or more to warm up after a cold start before writing to the hard disk. This practice does wonders for the reliability of the data on your disk.

If you do leave your system on for long periods of time, make sure that the screen is blank or displays a random image if the system is not in use. The phosphor on the picture tube can burn if a stationary image is left onscreen continuously. Higher-persistence phosphor monochrome screens are most susceptible, and the color displays with low-persistence phosphors are the least susceptible. Most of the monitors used with today's PCs will not show the effect of a screen burn. If you ever have seen a monochrome display with the image of some program permanently burned in—even with the display off—you know what I mean. Look at the monitors that display flight information at the airport—they usually show some of the effects of phosphor burn.

Most modern displays that have power-saving features can automatically enter a standby mode on command by the system. If your system has these power-saving functions, enable them, as they will help to reduce energy costs and preserve the monitor.

Static Electricity. Static electricity can cause numerous problems within a system. The problems usually appear during the winter months when humidity is low or in extremely dry climates where the humidity is low year-round. In these cases, you might need to take special precautions to ensure that your PC is not damaged.

Static discharges outside a system-unit chassis are rarely a source of permanent problems within the system. Usually, the worst possible effect of a static discharge to the case, keyboard, or even a location near the computer, is a parity check (memory) error or a system lockup. In some cases, I have been able to cause parity checks or system lockups by simply walking past a PC. Most static-sensitivity problems such as this are caused by improper grounding of the system power. Be sure that you always use a three-prong, grounded power cord plugged into a properly grounded outlet. If you are unsure about the outlet, you can buy an outlet tester like those described earlier in this chapter at most electronics supply or hardware stores for only a few dollars.

Whenever you open a system unit or handle circuits removed from the system, you must be much more careful with static. You can permanently damage a component with a static discharge if the charge is not routed to a ground. I usually recommend handling boards and adapters first by a grounding point such as the bracket to minimize the potential for static damage.

An easy way to prevent static problems is with good power-line grounding, which is extremely important for computer equipment. A poorly designed power-line grounding system is one of the primary causes of poor computer design. The best way to prevent static damage is to prevent the static charge from getting into the computer in the first place. The chassis ground in a properly designed system serves as a static guard for the computer that redirects the static charge safely to the ground. For this ground to be complete, therefore, the system must be plugged into a properly grounded three-wire outlet.

If the static problem is extreme, you can resort to other measures. One is to use a grounded static mat underneath the computer. Touch the mat first before you touch the computer to ensure that any static charges are routed to ground and away from the system unit's internal parts. If problems still persist, you might want to check out the building's electrical ground. I have seen installations that had three-wire outlets that were rendered useless by the building's ungrounded electrical service.

Power-Line Noise. To run properly, a computer system requires a steady supply of clean noise-free power. In some installations, however, the power line serving the computer serves heavy equipment also, and the voltage variations resulting from the on-off cycling of this equipment can cause problems for the computer. Certain types of equipment on the same power line also can cause *voltage spikes*—short transient signals of sometimes 1,000v or more—that can physically damage a computer. Although these spikes are rare, they can be crippling. Even a dedicated electrical circuit used only by a single computer can experience spikes and transients, depending on the quality of the power supplied to the building or circuit.

During the site-preparation phase of a system installation, you should be aware of these factors to ensure a steady supply of clean power:

- If possible, the computer system should be on its own circuit with its own circuit breaker. This setup does not guarantee freedom from interference, but it helps.

- The circuit should be checked for a good, low-resistance ground, proper line voltage, freedom from interference, and freedom from *brownouts* (voltage dips).

- A three-wire circuit is a must, but some people substitute grounding-plug adapters to adapt a grounded plug to a two-wire socket. This setup is not recommended; the ground is there for a reason.

- Power-line noise problems increase with the resistance of the circuit, which is a function of wire size and length. To decrease resistance, therefore, avoid extension cords unless absolutely necessary, and then use only heavy-duty extension cords.

- Inevitably, you will want to plug in other equipment later. Plan ahead to avoid the temptation to connect too many items to a single outlet. If possible, provide a separate power circuit for noncomputer-related devices.

Air conditioners, coffee makers, copy machines, laser printers, space heaters, vacuum cleaners, and power tools are some of the worst corrupters of a PC system's power. Any of these items can draw an excessive amount of current and play havoc with a PC system on the same electrical circuit. I've seen offices in which all the computers begin to crash at about 9:05 a.m. daily, which is when all the coffee makers are turned on!

Also, try to ensure that copy machines and laser printers do not share a circuit with other computer equipment. These devices draw a large amount of power.

Another major problem in some companies is partitioned offices. Many of these partitions are prewired with their own electrical outlets and are plugged into one another in a sort of power-line daisy chain, similar to chaining power strips together. I pity the person in the cubicle at the end of the electrical daisy chain, who is likely to have very erratic power!

As a real-world example of too many devices sharing a single circuit, I can describe several instances in which a personal computer had a repeating parity check problem. All efforts to repair the system had been unsuccessful. The reported error locations from the parity check message were inconsistent, which normally indicates a problem with power. The problem could have been the power supply in the system unit or the external power supplied from the wall outlet. This problem was solved one day as I stood watching the system. The parity check message was displayed at the same instant someone two cubicles away turned on a copy machine. Placing the computers on a separate line solved the problem.

By following the guidelines in this section, you can create the proper power environment for your systems and help to ensure trouble-free operation.

Radio-Frequency Interference. *Radio-frequency interference (RFI)* is easily overlooked as a problem factor. The interference is caused by any source of radio transmissions near a computer system. Living next door to a 50,000-watt commercial radio station is one sure way to get RFI problems, but less powerful transmitters can cause problems, too. I know of many instances in which cordless telephones have caused sporadic random keystrokes to appear, as though an invisible entity were typing on the keyboard. I also have seen RFI cause a system to lock up. Solutions to RFI problems are more difficult to state because every case must be handled differently. Sometimes, simply moving the system eliminates the problem because radio signals can be directional in nature. At other times, you must invest in specially shielded cables for external devices such as the keyboard and the monitor.

One type of solution to an RFI noise problem with cables is to pass the cable through a *toroidal iron core*, a doughnut-shaped piece of iron placed around a cable to suppress both the reception and transmission of electromagnetic interference (EMI). Many monitors include a toroid on the cable that connects to the computer. If you can isolate an RFI noise problem in a particular cable, you often can solve the problem by passing the cable through a toroidal core. Because the cable must pass through the center hole of the core, it often is difficult, if not impossible, to add a toroid to a cable that already has end connectors installed.

Radio Shack sells a special snap-together toroid designed specifically to be added to cables already in use. This toroid looks like a thick-walled tube that has been sliced in half. You just lay the cable in the center of one of the halves, and snap the other half over the first. This type of construction makes it easy to add the noise-suppression features of a toroid to virtually any existing cable.

The best, if not the easiest, way to eliminate an RFI problem is to correct it at the source. It is not likely that you'll be able to convince the commercial radio station near your office to shut down, but if you are dealing with a small radio transmitter that is generating RFI, sometimes you can add a filter to the transmitter that suppresses spurious emissions. Unfortunately, problems sometimes persist until the transmitter is either switched off or moved some distance away from the affected computer.

Dust and Pollutants. Dirt, smoke, dust, and other pollutants are bad for your system. The power-supply fan carries airborne particles through your system, and they collect inside. If your system is used in an extremely harsh environment, you might want to investigate some of the industrial systems on the market designed for harsh conditions.

Many companies make special hardened versions of their systems for harsh environments. Industrial systems usually use a different cooling system from the one used in a regular PC. A large cooling fan is used to pressurize the case rather than depressurize it. The air pumped into the case passes through a filter unit that must be cleaned and changed periodically. The system is pressurized so that no contaminated air can flow into it; air flows only outward. The only way air can enter is through the fan and filter system.

These systems also might have special keyboards impervious to liquids and dirt. Some flat-membrane keyboards are difficult to type on, but are extremely rugged; others resemble the standard types of keyboards but have a thin, plastic membrane that covers all the keys. You can add this membrane to normal types of keyboards to seal them from the environment.

A new breed of humidifier can cause problems with computer equipment. This type of humidifier uses ultrasonics to generate a mist of water sprayed into the air. The extra humidity helps cure problems with static electricity resulting from a dry climate, but the airborne water contaminants can cause many problems. If you use one of these systems, you might notice a white ash-like deposit forming on components. The deposit is the result of abrasive and corrosive minerals suspended in the vaporized water. If these deposits collect on the system components, they can cause all kinds of problems. The only safe way to run one of these ultrasonic humidifiers is to use distilled water. If you use a humidifier, be sure it does not generate these deposits.

If you do your best to keep the environment for your computer equipment clean, your system will run better and last longer. Also, you will not have to open your unit as often for complete preventive maintenance cleaning.

Chapter 18

Operating Systems Software and Troubleshooting

This chapter focuses on the operating systems used most commonly on PCs today, and their relationships to the PC hardware. Information about operating systems may seem out of place in a book about hardware upgrade and repair, but if you ignore the operating system and other software when you troubleshoot a system, you can miss a number of problems. The best system troubleshooters and diagnosticians know the entire system—hardware and software.

Most of the PCs in use today run either DOS (usually in combination with Windows 3.1 or Windows for Workgroups) or Windows 9x. Windows NT is a more advanced alternative that is constantly growing in popularity, mostly in network environments. This chapter examines the basic structure of these operating systems, their components, the system boot process, and how to distinguish a software problem from a hardware problem.

Disk Operating System (DOS)

DOS is the original and most basic of PC operating systems. By itself, it is considered to be underpowered and unable to support the full capabilities of much of today's hardware. However, the underlying concepts of DOS form the basis for the more advanced operating systems used today, like Windows 95 and Windows 98. With the exception of Windows NT, all the operating systems discussed in this chapter rely on DOS structures for their basic functions.

Operating System Basics

DOS is just one component in a total system architecture. A PC system has a distinct hierarchy of software that controls the system at all times. Even when you are working in an application such as a word processor or spreadsheet, there are several other programming layers always executing underneath the application. Ultimately, these software layers provide access to the hardware, such as storage media, memory, and the system processor. Usually the layers can be defined distinctly, but sometimes the boundaries are vague.

In most cases, communications occur only between adjoining layers in the system architecture, but this rule is not absolute. Some programs ignore the services provided by the layer directly beneath them and eliminate the middleman by skipping one or more layers. An example of this is when a program ignores the DOS and ROM BIOS video routines and communicates directly with the video display hardware in the interest of the highest possible screen performance. Although the high performance goal is admirable, some operating systems (such as OS/2 and Windows NT) no longer permit direct access to the hardware. This generally results in a more stable operating environment with fewer crashes and system conflicts. Programs that do not play by the rules must be rewritten to run in these new environments.

The hardware is at the lowest level of the system hierarchy. By placing various bytes of information at certain ports or locations within a system's memory structure, you can control virtually any device connected to the CPU. Maintaining control at the hardware level is difficult; doing so requires a complete and accurate knowledge of the system architecture. The attention to detail required to write software operating at this level is most intense. To issue commands to the system at this level, you must use *machine language*, which consists of binary groups of information applied directly to the microprocessor. Machine language instructions are limited in their function; a great many of them are required to perform even the smallest amount of useful work. However, the large number of instructions required is not a great burden on the system because these instructions are executed extremely rapidly, wasting few system resources.

Programmers can write code consisting of machine language instructions, but generally they use a tool—an *assembler*—to ease the process. They write programs using an *editor* and then use the assembler to convert the editor's output to pure machine language. Assembler commands are still very low-level, and using them effectively requires that the programmer be extremely knowledgeable. No one (in their right mind) writes directly in machine code anymore; assembly language is the lowest-level programming environment typically used today. Even assembly language, however, is losing favor among programmers because of the amount of knowledge and work required to complete even simple tasks, and because of the difficulty in translating (or *porting*) the code to work with another system.

When you start a PC system, a series of machine code programs, the ROM BIOS, assumes control. This set of programs, always present in a system, communicates directly (using machine code) to the hardware. The BIOS accepts or interprets commands generated by programs above it in the system hierarchy. It then translates them to machine code commands that are passed on to the microprocessor. Commands at this level typically are called *interrupts* or *services*. A programmer can use nearly any language to supply these instructions to the BIOS.

DOS is made up of several components. It attaches to the BIOS so that part of DOS actually becomes an extension of the BIOS, providing more interrupts and services for other programs to use. DOS provides a communication buffer between the ROM BIOS and software running at higher layers in the system hierarchy (such as applications). Because DOS provides the application programmer with interrupts and services they can use in addition to those provided by the ROM BIOS, a lot of "reinventing the wheel" in programming routines is eliminated. For example, DOS provides a rich set of functions that can open, close, find, delete, create, and rename files, and can perform other file-handling tasks. When programmers want to include these functions in their programs, they can rely on DOS to do most of the work, rather than have to develop routines that perform these functions themselves.

> **Note**
>
> This integration of hardware functions into the operating system has been one of the basic tenets of operating system development over the years. Successive versions of Windows have built on the DOS model by adding more hardware functions to the OS, thus preventing applications from having to address the hardware directly.

This standard set of functions that applications use to read data from and write it to disks makes data recovery operations possible. Imagine how tough writing programs and using computers would be if every application program had to implement its own custom disk interface, with a proprietary directory and file retrieval system. Every application would require its own special disks. Fortunately, DOS provides a standard set of documented file storage and retrieval routines that all software applications can use.

Another primary function of DOS is to load and run other programs. As it performs that function, DOS is the *shell*, or command processor interface, within which the other program is executed. DOS provides the functions and environment required by other software—including operating environments such as Windows 3.x—to run on PC systems in a standard way. Windows 9x finally marry DOS and the Windows environment into a more seamless operating system. However, while the graphical interface is now the operational standard in Windows 9x, you can still boot the operating system to a DOS command prompt.

The System ROM BIOS

Think of the ROM BIOS in a system as a form of compatibility glue that sits between the PC hardware and the operating system. Why is it that the same DOS operating system can run on the original IBM PC and on the latest Pentium II systems—two very different hardware platforms? If DOS were written to communicate directly with the hardware on all systems, it would be a very hardware-specific program and would require extensive modifications for different hardware configurations. Instead, IBM developed a set of standard services and functions that each system should be capable of performing, and coded them as programs in the ROM BIOS. Each system then gets a completely customized ROM BIOS that can talk directly to the hardware in the system and knows exactly how to perform each specific function on that hardware only.

◄◄ See "BIOS," p. 208

This convention enables the operating system to be written to what is essentially a standard interface that can support many different types of hardware. Any applications written to the operating system can use that standard interface to access the system hardware. Figure 18.1 shows that two very different hardware platforms can each have a custom ROM BIOS that can talk directly to the hardware and still provide a standard interface to an operating system.

The two different hardware platforms described in Figure 18.1 can run not only the exact same version of DOS, but also the same application programs, because of the standard interfaces provided by the ROM BIOS and DOS. Keep in mind, however, that the actual ROM BIOS code differs among the specific machines and that it is usually not possible to run a ROM BIOS designed for one system in a different system. ROM BIOS upgrades must come from a source that has an intimate understanding of the specific motherboard on which the chip will be installed, because the ROM must be custom written for that particular hardware.

◄◄ See "Upgrading the ROM BIOS," p. 215

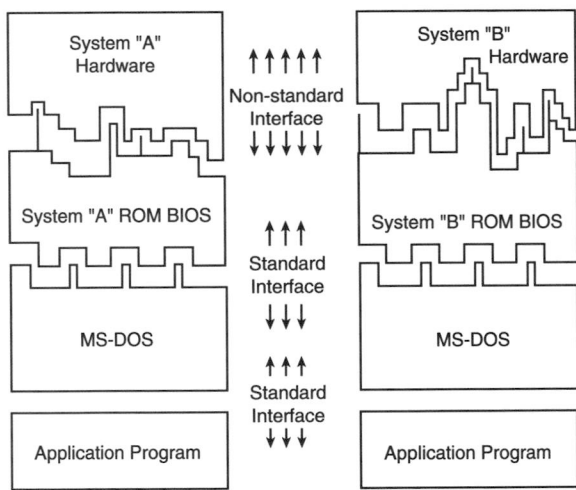

FIG. 18.1 A representation of the software layers in a PC system.

The portion of DOS shown in Figure 18.1 is the system portion, or core, of DOS. This core is physically manifested as the two system files on any bootable DOS disk. These hidden system files are called IO.SYS and MSDOS.SYS in MS-DOS and all versions of DOS licensed from Microsoft by original equipment manufacturers (OEMs). In IBM DOS, the files are called IBMBIO.COM and IBMDOS.COM.

Figure 18.1 represents a simplified view of the system; some subtle but important differences exist. Ideally, application programs are insulated from the hardware by the ROM BIOS and by DOS, but in reality many programmers write portions of their programs to communicate directly with the hardware, circumventing both DOS and the ROM BIOS. A program may therefore work only with specific hardware, even if the proper DOS and ROM BIOS interfaces for the hardware in the machine are present.

Programs designed to communicate directly with the hardware usually are written that way to increase performance. For example, some DOS programs access the video hardware directly to improve screen update performance. Applications like these typically have installation programs that require you to specify exactly what hardware is present in the system so the program can load the correct hardware-dependent routines into the application.

Some utility programs absolutely must communicate directly with the system hardware to perform their function. Another type of system-specific utility, called a *memory manager*, enables extended memory in a DOS system to function as expanded memory. These drivers work by accessing the system processor directly and using specific features of the chip.

Another way that reality might differ from the simple view is that DOS sometimes communicates directly with the hardware. The DOS system files can contain low-level drivers designed to supplant and supersede parts of the ROM BIOS code in the system. When DOS loads, it ascertains the system type and ID information by querying the ROM. It then loads different routines depending on which version of ROM it finds. For example, there are at least four different hard disk code sections in PC-DOS, but only one is loaded for a specific system.

DOS Components

DOS consists of two primary components: the input/output (I/O) system and the shell. The I/O system consists of the underlying programs that reside in memory while the system is running; these programs load when DOS first boots. The I/O system is stored in the IO.SYS and MSDOS.SYS (or IBMBIO.COM and IBMDOS.COM) files that are flagged with the hidden attribute on a bootable DOS disk. No matter what the exact names are, the function of these two files is basically the same for all versions of DOS.

The user interface program, or shell, is stored in the COMMAND.COM file, which also loads during a normal DOS boot sequence. The shell is the portion of DOS that the user employs to communicate with the system, providing the DOS prompt and internal commands like COPY and DIR.

The following sections examine the DOS I/O system and shell in more detail to help you properly identify and solve problems that are related to DOS rather than to hardware. Also included is a discussion on how DOS allocates disk file space.

IO.SYS (or IBMBIO.COM)

IO.SYS is one of the hidden files found on any DOS system (bootable) disk. This file contains the low-level programs that interact directly with devices on the system and the

ROM BIOS. During bootup, the DOS volume boot sector loads the file into low memory and gives it control of the system. The entire file, except for the system initializer portion, remains in memory during normal system operation.

For a disk to be bootable, IO.SYS or its equivalent must be listed as the first file in the directory of the disk and must occupy at least the first cluster on the disk (cluster number 2). The remainder of the file might be placed in clusters anywhere across the rest of the disk. The file normally is marked with hidden, system, and read-only attributes, and placed on a disk by the FORMAT utility (with the /S switch) or by the SYS utility.

Creating a Boot Disk

Writing the DOS system boot files to a hard or floppy disk is a process that involves more than simply copying the files. To create a bootable disk, you must use either the DOS FORMAT.COM program or the SYS.COM program. When you run FORMAT with the /S switch, as in FORMAT A: /S, the program proceeds to format the disk in the usual manner. It then copies the IO.SYS, MSDOS.SYS, and COMMAND.COM files from the drive used to boot the computer, setting the appropriate attributes.

The SYS.COM program copies the same files and sets the same attributes, but without formatting the disk first. You must have sufficient space on the disk for SYS.COM to store the boot files.

Windows 9x includes the FORMAT.COM and SYS.COM utilities as well, but also provides a GUI alternative for creating boot disks. When you select a drive in Windows 9x Explorer and choose Format from the context menu, you are given the option to copy the system files to the disk as part of the formatting process. You can also create a boot disk by launching the Add/Remove Programs Control Panel and following the instructions on the Startup Disk page.

MSDOS.SYS (or IBMDOS.COM)

MSDOS.SYS, the core of DOS, contains the DOS disk- and device-handling programs. MSDOS.SYS is loaded into low memory at system bootup by the DOS volume boot sector and remains resident in memory during normal system operation.

MSDOS.SYS or its equivalent originally had to be listed as the second entry in the root directory of any bootable disk. Most file management utilities list the files in a given directory in alphabetical order, but this is not necessarily the order in which they are stored on the drive. At one time, the only way for the IO.SYS and MSDOS.SYS files to be read sequentially was for them to be the first two physical files on the disk. The MSDOS.SYS file is flagged with the hidden, system, and read-only attributes, and like IO.SYS is placed on a disk by the FORMAT /S command or the SYS command. There are now no special requirements for the physical positioning of this file on a disk.

The Shell or Command Processor (COMMAND.COM)

The DOS command processor COMMAND.COM is the portion of DOS with which users normally interact. This file is also written to a system disk by the FORMAT /S and SYS commands, but the file is left visible, unlike IO.SYS and MSDOS.SYS. DOS loads COMMAND.COM into memory after the two system files, providing the command prompt and access to DOS system commands. These commands can be categorized into two types according to how they are made available: *resident* or *transient*.

Resident commands are built into COMMAND.COM and are available whenever the DOS prompt is present. They are generally the simpler, frequently used commands such as COPY, CLS, and DIR. Resident commands execute rapidly because the instructions for them are already loaded into memory; they are *memory-resident*.

When you look up a command in a DOS manual, you generally find some indication of whether the command is resident or transient. You can then determine what is required to execute that command. A simple rule is that, at a DOS prompt, all resident commands are instantly available for execution, with no loading of additional files required. Resident commands are also sometimes called *internal* commands. Commands that run from a separate program on disk are termed *external*, or *transient* commands, and are also often called *utilities*.

Transient commands are not resident in the computer's memory; the instructions to execute these commands must be located on a disk. Because the instructions are loaded into memory only for the execution of the command and then are overwritten in memory after they are used, they are called transient commands. Most DOS commands are transient; otherwise, the memory requirements for DOS would be much larger than they are. Transient commands are used less frequently than resident commands and take longer to execute, because their disk files must be found and loaded before they can run. DOS' transient commands take the form of individual executable files, such as FORMAT.COM and XCOPY.COM, that are located in the DOS home directory (typically C:\DOS, or C:\WINDOWS\COMMAND in Windows 9x).

Most executable files operate like transient DOS commands. The instructions to execute the command must be located on a disk. The instructions are loaded into memory only for execution and are overwritten in memory after the program is no longer being used.

DOS Command File Search Procedure

One of the most common DOS errors is the Bad command or filename message that appears when you attempt to issue a command that DOS cannot process. This can happen for a number of reasons, and your troubleshooting efforts should begin at the highest level, the software, before you begin to suspect that a hardware problem may be at fault.

Whenever you issue a transient command or run a software application's executable file, DOS attempts to find the instructions needed to execute that command by looking in several places, in a specific order. The instructions that represent the command or program are located in files on one or more disk drives. Files that contain execution instructions have an extension of either COM (command files), EXE (executable files), or BAT (batch files). COM and EXE files are machine code programs; BAT files contain ASCII text specifying a series of commands and instructions using the DOS batch facilities. DOS attempts to locate these executable files by searching the current directory and the directories specified in the PATH command.

In other words, if you type several characters, like **WIN**, at the DOS prompt and press the Enter key, DOS attempts to find and run a program named WIN by performing a two- or three-level search for the program instructions (the file). The first step in looking for command instructions is to see whether the command is resident in COMMAND.COM and, if so, to run it from the program code already loaded in memory. If the command is not resident, DOS looks in the current directory for a file called WIN with a COM, EXE, or BAT extension (in that order), and loads and executes the first file it finds with the specified name. Therefore, if two files in that directory are called WIN.COM and WIN.BAT, the WIN.COM file will always be executed in response to the WIN command.

If the command is not resident and no file by that name is found in the current directory, DOS looks in each of the directories specified in the DOS PATH environment variable in turn, searching for the file using the same extension order just indicated. (You specify the directories for the PATH environment variable using the PATH command, usually from the AUTOEXEC.BAT file.) Finally, if DOS still fails to locate the required instructions, it displays the error message Bad command or filename. As you can see, this error message can be misleading. You may puzzle at the inability of DOS to run a command file that clearly is on the disk. This might lead you to suspect a hardware problem concerning the disk drive itself, when the problem actually stems from the fact that the command instructions are simply missing from the search areas.

A common practice is to place all simple command files or utility programs (transient commands) in one directory and set the PATH to point to that directory. Each of those programs (or commands) is then instantly available simply by typing its name from any DOS prompt, just as though it were resident in memory.

This practice works well only for single-load programs such as DOS transient commands and other utilities. Major applications often consist of many individual files and might have problems if they are called up from a remote directory or drive using the DOS PATH. This is because the PATH variable has no effect when the application looks for its overlay and accessory files.

On a hard disk system, users typically install all transient commands and utilities in subdirectories and ensure that the PATH points to those directories. The path literally is a list of directories and subdirectories specified in the AUTOEXEC.BAT file that tells DOS where to search for files when the command cannot be found in the current directory. A path on such a hard drive may look like this:

```
PATH=C:\DOS;C:\BAT;C:\UTILS;
```

In the previous example, all the ancillary programs included with the DOS operating system will be immediately locatable because of the inclusion of C:\DOS in the PATH command.

The PATH normally cannot exceed 128 characters in length (including spaces, colons, semicolons, and backslashes). As a result of this limitation, you cannot have a PATH that contains all your directories if the directory names exceed 128 characters.

> **Note**
>
> On Windows 9x systems, directories can have names up to 255 characters in length and can contain spaces and other characters that DOS directories cannot. However, since the file system always maintains a truncated directory name using the standard DOS 8.3 naming convention, you can use these short names in the PATH command. To include directory names containing spaces in the PATH command, you must enclose the name in quotes, as in "C:\Program Files".

You can also completely short circuit the DOS command search procedure simply by entering the complete path to the file at the command prompt. For example, rather than include C:\DOS in the PATH and enter this command:

CHKDSK

you can enter the full name of the program:

C:\DOS\CHKDSK.COM

The latter command immediately locates and loads the CHKDSK program with no search through the current directory or PATH setting. This method of calling up a program speeds the location and execution of the program and works especially well to increase the speed of DOS batch file execution. It also enables you to immediately eliminate path problems as the source of the Bad command message.

DOS Versions

In more than a decade and a half of development, a great many DOS versions have been released. IBM released version 1.0 of the operating system in 1981, but by version 3.x Microsoft too began releasing its own DOS, using the same version numbers as IBM in most cases. Early versions of DOS were frequently designed for the hardware configurations of specific machines. At one time, IBM, Compaq, and other original equipment manufacturers would have their own versions of DOS (created by IBM or Microsoft), designed to support only their hardware. You could not, in many cases, boot an IBM computer using a Compaq DOS boot disk and still gain full functionality.

DOS 5.x. By the time that DOS 5.0 was released by Microsoft, however, this situation was all but eliminated. DOS 5.0 was the first version of the operating system to be marketed on a retail level, and users turned out in droves to upgrade their systems. Both the IBM and Microsoft versions of DOS 5.0 and later can be used on almost any system, although later versions may be required to use some of the latest hardware available.

DOS 5.0 offered vastly improved memory management and incorporated many of the features into the operating system that users had grown used to finding in third-party utilities. At this time, there are some people who still swear by DOS 5.0 and resist upgrading to DOS 6 (or higher), which, truth to tell, is more of an enhancement than a major overhaul. However, there is no reason any DOS version below 5.0 should still be in use on any computer (except for museum pieces that can handle nothing but their native versions).

The Boot Process

The term *boot* comes from the word bootstrap and describes the method by which the PC becomes operational. Just as you pull on a large boot by the small strap attached to the back, a PC loads a large operating system by first loading a small program that can then pull the operating system into memory. The chain of events begins with the application of power, and finally results in a fully functional computer system with software loaded and running. Each event is triggered by the event before it and initiates the event after it.

Tracing the system boot process might help you find the location of a problem if you examine the error messages that the system displays when the problem occurs. If you see an error message that is displayed only by a particular program, you can be sure that the program in question was at least loaded and partially running. Combine this information with the knowledge of the boot sequence, and you can at least tell how far along the system's startup procedure has progressed before the problem occurred. You usually want to look at whatever files or disk areas were being accessed during the failure in the boot process. Error messages displayed during the boot process and those displayed during normal system operation can be hard to decipher. However, the first step in decoding an error message is to know where the message came from—what program actually generated or displayed it. The following programs are capable of displaying error messages during the boot process:

- Motherboard ROM BIOS

- Adapter card ROM BIOS extensions

- Master partition boot sector

- DOS volume boot sector

- System files (IO.SYS./IBMBIO.COM and MSDOS.SYS/IBMDOS.COM)

- Device drivers (loaded through CONFIG.SYS or the Win 9x Registry SYSTEM.DAT)

- Shell program (COMMAND.COM in DOS)

- Programs run by AUTOEXEC.BAT, the Windows 9x Startup group, and the Registry

- Windows (WIN.COM)

The following section examines the system startup sequence and provides a detailed account of many of the error messages that might occur during this process.

How DOS Loads and Starts

If you have a problem with your system during startup and you can determine where in this sequence of events your system has stalled, you know what events have occurred and you probably can eliminate each of them as a cause of the problem. The following steps occur in a typical system startup:

1. You switch on electrical power to the system.

2. The power supply performs a self-test (known as the POST—Power On Self Test). When all voltages and current levels are acceptable, the supply indicates that the power is stable and sends the Power_Good signal to the motherboard. The time from switch-on to Power_Good is normally between .1 and .5 seconds.

3. The microprocessor timer chip receives the Power_Good signal, which causes it to stop generating a reset signal to the microprocessor.

◀◀ See "The Power_Good Signal," p. 409

4. The microprocessor begins executing the ROM BIOS code, starting at memory address FFFF:0000. Because this location is only 16 bytes from the very end of the available ROM space, it contains a JMP (jump) instruction to the actual ROM BIOS starting address.

◀◀ See "ROM," p. 304

5. The ROM BIOS performs a test of the central hardware to verify basic system functionality. Any errors that occur are indicated by audio "beep" codes because the video system has not yet been initialized.

6. The BIOS performs a video ROM scan of memory locations C000:0000 through C780:0000, looking for video adapter ROM BIOS programs contained on a video adapter found either on a card plugged into a slot or integrated into the motherboard. If the scan locates a video ROM BIOS, it is tested by a checksum procedure. If the video BIOS passes the checksum test, the ROM is executed; the video ROM code initializes the video adapter and a cursor appears on-screen. If the checksum test fails, the following message appears:

   `C000 ROM Error`

7. If the BIOS finds no video adapter ROM, it uses the motherboard ROM video drivers to initialize the video display hardware, and a cursor appears on-screen.

8. The motherboard ROM BIOS scans memory locations C800:0000 through DF80:0000 in 2K increments for any other ROMs located on any other adapter cards (such as SCSI adapters). If any ROMs are found, they are checksum-tested and executed. These adapter ROMs can alter existing BIOS routines and establish new ones.

9. Failure of a checksum test for any of these ROM modules causes this message to appear:

   `XXXX ROM Error`

   where the address XXXX indicates the segment address of the failed ROM module.

10. The ROM BIOS checks the word value at memory location 0000:0472 to see whether this start is a cold start or a warm start. A word value of 1234h in this location is a flag that indicates a warm start, which causes the BIOS to skip the memory test portion of the POST (Power On Self Test). Any other word value in this location indicates a cold start and the BIOS performs the full POST procedure. Some system BIOSs let you control various aspects of the POST procedure, making it possible to skip the memory test, for example, which can be lengthy on a system with a lot of RAM.

◀◀ See "POST Audio Error Codes," p. 985

11. If this is a cold start, the POST executes. Any errors found during the POST are reported by a combination of audio and displayed error messages. Successful completion of the POST is indicated by a single beep.

12. The ROM BIOS searches for a DOS volume boot sector at cylinder 0, head 0, sector 1 (the very first sector) on the default boot drive. At one time, the default boot drive was always the first floppy disk, or A: drive. However, the BIOSs on today's systems often enable you to select the default boot device and the order that the BIOS will look for other devices to boot from if needed, using either a floppy disk, hard disk, or even a CD-ROM drive in any order you choose. This sector is loaded into memory at 0000:7C00 and tested. If a disk is in the drive but the sector cannot be read, or if no disk is present, the BIOS continues with the next step.

13. If the first byte of the DOS volume boot sector loaded from the disk in the default boot drive is less than 06h, or if the first byte is greater than or equal to 06h and the first nine words contain the same data pattern, this error message appears and the system stops:

```
602-Diskette Boot Record Error
```

14. If the disk was prepared with FORMAT or SYS using DOS 3.3 or an earlier version and the specified system files are not the first two files in the directory, or if a problem was encountered loading them, the following message appears:

```
Non-System disk or disk error
Replace and strike any key when ready
```

15. If the disk was prepared with FORMAT or SYS using DOS 3.3 or an earlier version and the boot sector is corrupt, you might see this message:

```
Disk Boot failure
```

16. If the disk was prepared with FORMAT or SYS using DOS 4.0 and later versions, and the specified system files are not the first two files in the directory, or if a problem was encountered loading them, or the boot sector is corrupt, this message appears:

```
Non-System disk or disk error
Replace and press any key when ready
```

17. If no DOS volume boot sector can be read from drive A:, the BIOS looks for a master partition boot sector at cylinder 0, head 0, sector 1 (the very first sector) of the first fixed disk. If this sector is found, it is loaded into memory address 0000:7C00 and tested for a signature.

18. If the last two (signature) bytes of the master partition boot sector are not equal to 55AAh, software interrupt 18h (Int 18h) is invoked on most systems.

This causes the BIOS to display an error message that can vary for different BIOS manufacturers, but which is often something like one of the following four messages:

```
Non-System disk or disk error
replace and strike any key when ready

DISK BOOT FAILURE, INSERT SYSTEM DISK AND PRESS ENTER

No boot device available -
strike F1 to retry boot, F2 for setup utility

No boot sector on fixed disk -
strike F1 to retry boot, F2 for setup utility
```

Although the messages vary from BIOS to BIOS, the cause for each relates to specific bytes in the Master Boot Record, which is the first sector of a hard disk at the physical location Cylinder 0, Head 0, Sector 1.

The problem involves a disk that has either never been partitioned or has had the Master Boot Sector corrupted. During the boot process, the BIOS checks the last two bytes in the Master Boot Record (first sector of the drive) for a "signature" value of 55AAh. If the last two bytes are not 55AAh, an Interrupt 18h is invoked, which calls the subroutine that displays one of the error messages just shown.

The Master Boot Sector (including the signature bytes) is written to the hard disk by the DOS FDISK program. Immediately after a hard disk is low-level formatted, all the sectors are initialized with a pattern of bytes, and the first sector does *not* contain the 55AAh signature. In other words, these ROM error messages are exactly what you see if you attempt to boot from a hard disk that has been low-level formatted, but has not yet been partitioned.

19. The master partition boot sector program searches its partition table for an entry with a system indicator byte indicating an extended partition. If the program finds such an entry, it loads the extended partition boot sector at the location indicated. The extended partition boot sector also has a table that is searched for another extended partition. If another extended partition entry is found, that extended partition boot sector is loaded from the location indicated. The search continues until either no more extended partitions are indicated or the maximum number of 24 total partitions has been reached.

20. The master partition boot sector searches its partition table for a boot indicator byte marking an active partition.

21. If none of the partitions is marked active (bootable), the BIOS displays a disk error message.

22. If any boot indicator in the master partition boot record table is invalid, or if more than one indicates an active partition, the following message is displayed, and the system stops:

```
Invalid partition table
```

23. If an active partition is found in the master partition boot sector, the volume boot sector from the active partition is loaded and tested.

24. If the DOS volume boot sector cannot be read successfully from the active partition within five retries because of read errors, this message appears and the system stops:

```
Error loading operating system
```

25. The hard disk's DOS volume boot sector is tested for a signature. If the DOS volume boot sector does not contain a valid signature of 55AAh as the last two bytes in the sector, this message appears and the system stops:

```
Missing operating system
```

26. The volume boot sector is executed as a program. This program checks the root directory to ensure that the first two files are IO.SYS (or IBMBIO.COM) and MSDOS.SYS (or IBMDOS.COM). If these files are present, they are loaded.

27. If the disk was prepared with FORMAT or SYS using DOS 3.3 or an earlier version and the specified system files are not the first two files in the directory, or if a problem is encountered loading them, the following message appears:

```
Non-System disk or disk error
Replace and strike any key when ready
```

28. If the disk was prepared with FORMAT or SYS using DOS 3.3 or an earlier version and the boot sector is corrupt, you might see this message:

```
Disk Boot failure
```

29. If the disk was prepared with FORMAT or SYS using DOS 4.0 or a later version and the specified system files are not the first two files in the directory, or if a problem is encountered loading them, or the boot sector is corrupt, the following message appears:

```
Non-System disk or disk error
Replace and press any key when ready
```

30. If no problems occur, the DOS volume boot sector executes IO.SYS/IBMBIO.COM. On a Windows 9x system, if you activate the boot menu by pressing the F8 key at this time, you can select the operating system files that you want to load.

31. The initialization code in IO.SYS/IBMBIO.COM copies itself into the highest region of contiguous DOS memory and transfers control to the copy. The initialization code copy then relocates MSDOS.SYS over the portion of IO.SYS in low memory that contains the initialization code, because the initialization code no longer needs to be in that location. Windows 9x's IO.SYS combines the functions of DOS's IO.SYS and MSDOS.SYS.

32. The initialization code executes MSDOS.SYS (or IBMDOS.COM), which initializes the base device drivers, determines equipment status, resets the disk system, resets and initializes attached devices, and sets the system default parameters.

33. The full DOS file system is active, and control is returned to the IO.SYS initialization code.

34. The IO.SYS initialization code reads the CONFIG.SYS file multiple times. In Windows 9x, IO.SYS also looks for the SYSTEM.DAT Registry file.

35. When loading CONFIG.SYS, the DEVICE statements are first processed in the order in which they appear. Any device driver files named in those DEVICE statements are loaded and executed. Then any INSTALL statements are processed in the order in which they appear; the programs named are loaded and executed. The SHELL statement is processed and loads the specified command processor with the specified parameters. If the CONFIG.SYS file contains no SHELL statement, the default \COMMAND.COM processor is loaded with default parameters. Loading the command processor overwrites the initialization code in memory (because the job of the initialization code is finished).

In Windows 9x, the system looks in the Registry's Hkey_Local_Machine\ System\CurrentControlSet key to load the device drivers and other parameters specified there before executing the CONFIG.SYS file. The COMMAND.COM program is loaded at this time only if an AUTOEXEC.BAT file exists, so it can process the commands contained within it. The Windows 9x boot menu also provides a *safe mode* option. This option bypasses the loading of the drivers for the specific hardware in the system and instead loads a set of generic drivers designed to get the system up and running with only minimal functionality. This enables the computer to boot the Windows GUI in situations where a malfunctioning driver or device would otherwise prevent access to the system.

During the final reads of CONFIG.SYS, all of the remaining statements are read and processed in a predetermined order. Thus, the order of appearance for statements other than DEVICE, INSTALL, and SHELL in CONFIG.SYS is of no significance.

36. If AUTOEXEC.BAT is present, COMMAND.COM loads and runs AUTOEXEC.BAT. After the commands in AUTOEXEC.BAT have been executed, the DOS prompt appears (unless the AUTOEXEC.BAT calls an application program or shell of some kind, in which case the user might operate the system without ever seeing a DOS prompt).

37. If no AUTOEXEC.BAT file is present, COMMAND.COM executes the internal DATE and TIME commands, displays a copyright message, and displays the DOS prompt.

In Windows 9x, IO.SYS automatically loads HIMEM.SYS, IFSHLP.SYS, and SETVER.EXE. Finally, it loads WIN.COM and Windows 9x is officially started.

Some minor variations from this scenario are possible, such as those introduced by other ROM programs in the various adapters that might be plugged into an expansion slot. Also, depending on the exact ROM BIOS programs involved, some of the error messages and sequences might vary. Generally, however, a computer follows this chain of events while "coming to life."

You can modify the system startup procedures by altering the CONFIG.SYS and AUTOEXEC.BAT files, or the Windows 9x Registry. These files control the configuration of DOS or Windows 9x and allow special startup programs to be executed every time the system starts.

File Management

DOS uses several elements and structures to store and retrieve information on a disk. These elements and structures enable DOS to communicate properly with both the ROM BIOS and with application programs to process file storage and retrieval requests. Understanding these structures and how they interact help you to troubleshoot and even repair these structures.

On demand DOS allocates disk space for a file (space is not preallocated). The space is allocated one *cluster* (or allocation unit) at a time. A cluster always consists of one or more sectors.

◀◀ See "Sectors," p. 724

The clusters are arranged on a disk to minimize head movement for multisided media. DOS allocates all the space on a disk cylinder before moving to the next cylinder. It does this by using the sectors under the first head and then all the sectors under each successive head, until all sectors of all heads of the cylinder are used. The next sector DOS uses is sector 1 of head 0 on the next cylinder.

The algorithm that DOS 3.0 and later versions use for file allocation is called the *Next Available Cluster algorithm.* In this algorithm, the search for available clusters in which to write a file starts not at the beginning of the disk, as in previous DOS versions, but rather from where the last write occurred. Therefore, the disk space freed by erasing a file is not necessarily reused immediately. Rather, DOS maintains a *Last Written Cluster pointer* and begins its search from that point. This pointer is maintained in system RAM and is lost when the system is reset or rebooted, or when a disk is changed in a floppy drive.

The Next Available Cluster algorithm is faster than the First Available Cluster algorithm of earlier DOS versions and helps to minimize fragmentation. Sometimes this type of algorithm is called *elevator seeking* because write operations occur at higher and higher clusters until the heads reach the end of the disk area. At that time, the pointer is reset, and write operations work their way from the beginning of the disk again.

Files still end up becoming fragmented using the Next Available Cluster algorithm, because the pointer is reset after a reboot, a disk change operation, or when the end of the disk is reached. Nevertheless, a great benefit of the method is that it makes unerasing files more likely to succeed even if the disk has been written to since the erasure, because the file just erased is not likely to be the target of the next write operation. In fact, it might be some time before the clusters occupied by the erased file are reused.

Even when DOS overwrites a file, it does not reuse the clusters occupied by the original file during the overwrite. For example, if you accidentally save a file using the same name as an important file that already exists, DOS marks the existing file clusters as available, and writes the new file (with the same name) to the disk in other clusters. It is often possible, therefore, to recover the original copy of the file.

This is often how undelete utilities such as the UNDELETE command in DOS and other third party products are able to recover deleted files. Safety utilities like the Windows 9x Recycle Bin, however, do not work in the same way. The Recycle Bin is actually just a directory to which the system moves deleted files. The file system continues to register the space occupied by the "deleted" files as in use. The Recycle Bin directory is configured with a maximum possible size that, when reached, causes the system to delete the oldest files stored there.

Interfacing to Disk Drives

DOS uses a combination of disk management components to make files accessible. These components differ slightly between floppies and hard disks and between disks of different sizes. They determine how a disk appears to DOS and to applications. Each component used to describe the disk system fits as a layer into the complete system. Each layer communicates with the layer above and below it. When all the components work together, an application can access the disk to find and store data.

There are four primary interface layers between an application program running on a system and the disk drives attached to the system. They consist of software routines that can perform various functions, usually to communicate with the adjacent layers. These layers are as follows:

- DOS Interrupt 21h (Int 21h) routines
- DOS Interrupt 25/26h (Int 25/26h) routines
- ROM BIOS disk Interrupt 13h (Int 13h) routines
- Disk controller I/O port commands

Each layer accepts various commands, performs different functions, and generates results. These interfaces are available for both floppy disk drives and hard disks, although the floppy disk and hard disk Int 13h routines differ widely. The floppy disk controllers and hard disk controllers are very different as well, but all the layers perform the same functions for both floppy disks and hard disks.

Interrupt 21h. The DOS Int 21h routines exist at the highest level and provide the most functionality with the least amount of work. For example, if an application program needs to create a subdirectory on a disk, it can call Int 21h, Function 39h. This function performs all the operations necessary to create the subdirectory, including updating the appropriate directory and FAT sectors. The only information this function needs is the name of the subdirectory to create. DOS Int 21h would do much more work by using one of the lower-level access methods to create a subdirectory. Most applications access the disk through this level of interface.

Interrupt 25h and 26h. The DOS Int 25h and Int 26h routines provide much lower-level access to the disk than the Int 21h routines. Int 25h reads only specified sectors from a disk, and Int 26h only writes specified sectors to a disk. If you were to write a program that used these functions to create a subdirectory on a disk, the amount of work would be much greater than that required by the Int 21h method. For example, your program would have to perform all of these tasks:

- Calculate exactly which directory and FAT sectors need to be updated.

- Use Int 25h to read these sectors.

- Modify the sectors appropriately to add the new subdirectory information.

- Use Int 26h to write the sectors back to the disk.

The number of steps is even greater when you factor in the difficulty in determining exactly what sectors have to be modified. According to Int 25/26h, the entire DOS-addressable area of the disk consists of sectors numbered sequentially from 0. A program designed to access the disk using Int 25h and Int 26h must know the correct disk locations by sector number. A program designed this way might have to be modified to handle disks with different numbers of sectors or different directory and FAT sizes and locations. Because of all the overhead required to get the job done, most programmers do not choose to access the disk in this manner and instead use the higher-level Int 21h—which does all the work automatically.

Typically, only disk- and sector-editing programs that access disk drives at the Int 25h and Int 26h level. Programs that work at this level of access can edit only areas of a disk that have been defined to DOS as a logical volume (drive letter). For example, the DOS DEBUG program can read sectors from and write sectors to disks with this level of access.

Interrupt 13h. The next lower level of communications with drives, the ROM BIOS Int 13h routines, usually are found in ROM chips on the motherboard or on an adapter card in an expansion slot. However, an Int 13h handler also can be implemented by using a device driver loaded at boot time. Because DOS requires Int 13h access to boot from a drive (and a device driver cannot be loaded until after boot-up), only drives with ROM BIOS-based Int 13h support can be bootable. Int 13h routines communicate directly with the controller using the I/O ports on the controller.

Table 18.1 lists the different functions available at the Interrupt 13h BIOS interface. Some functions are available to floppy drives or hard drives only, whereas others are available to both types of drives.

Table 18.1   Int 13h BIOS Disk Functions

Function	Floppy Disk	Hard Disk	Description
00h	X	X	Reset disk system
01h	X	X	Get status of last operation
02h	X	X	Read sectors
03h	X	X	Write sectors
04h	X	X	Verify sectors
05h	X	X	Format track
06h		X	Format bad track
07h		X	Format drive
08h	X	X	Read drive parameters
09h		X	Initialize drive characteristics
0Ah		X	Read long
0Bh		X	Write long
0Ch		X	Seek
0Dh		X	Alternate hard disk reset
0Eh		X	Read sector buffer
0Fh		X	Write sector buffer
10h		X	Test for drive ready
11h		X	Recalibrate drive
12h		X	Controller RAM diagnostic
13h		X	Controller drive diagnostic
14h		X	Controller internal diagnostic
15h	X	X	Get disk type
16h	X		Get floppy disk change status
17h	X		Set floppy disk type for format
18h	X		Set media type for format
19h		X	Park hard disk heads
1Ah		X	ESDI—Low-level format
1Bh		X	ESDI—Get manufacturing header
1Ch		X	ESDI—Get configuration

Table 18.2 shows the error codes that may be returned by the BIOS INT 13h routines. In some cases, you may see these codes when running a low-level format program, disk editor, or other program that can directly access a disk drive through the BIOS.

Table 18.2	BIOS INT 13h Error Codes
Code	**Description**
00h	No error
01h	Bad command
02h	Address mark not found
03h	Write protect
04h	Request sector not found
05h	Reset failed
06h	Media change error
07h	Initialization failed
09h	Cross 64K DMA boundary
0Ah	Bad sector flag detected
0Bh	Bad track flag detected
10h	Bad ECC on disk read
11h	ECC corrected data error
20h	Controller has failed
40h	Seek operation failed
80h	Drive failed to respond
AAh	Drive not ready
BBh	Undefined error
CCh	Write fault
0Eh	Register error
FFh	Sense operation failed

Few high-powered disk utility programs, other than some basic disk formatting applications, can talk to the disk at the Int 13h level. The DOS FDISK program communicates at the Int 13h level, as does the Norton Utilities' DISKEDIT program when it is in its absolute sector mode; these are some of the few disk-repair utilities that can do so. These programs are important because you can use them for the worst data recovery situations, in which the partition tables have been corrupted. Because the partition tables, and any non-DOS partitions, exist outside the area of a disk that is defined by DOS, only programs that work at the Int 13h level can access them. Most utility programs for data recovery work only at the DOS Int 25/26h level, which makes them useless for accessing areas of a disk outside of DOS' domain.

Disk Controller I/O Port Commands. At the lowest interface level, programs communicate directly with the disk controller in the controller's own specific native language. To do this, a program must send controller commands through the I/O ports to which the controller responds.

◄◄ See "IDE Origins," p. 612

Figure 18.2 shows that most application programs work through the Int 21h interface. This interface passes commands to the ROM BIOS as Int 13h commands; the ROM BIOS then converts these commands into direct controller commands. The controller executes the commands and returns the results through the layers until the desired information reaches the application. This process enables developers to write applications without worrying about such low-level system details, leaving them instead up to DOS and the ROM BIOS. This also enables applications to run on widely different types of hardware, as long as the correct ROM BIOS and DOS support is in place.

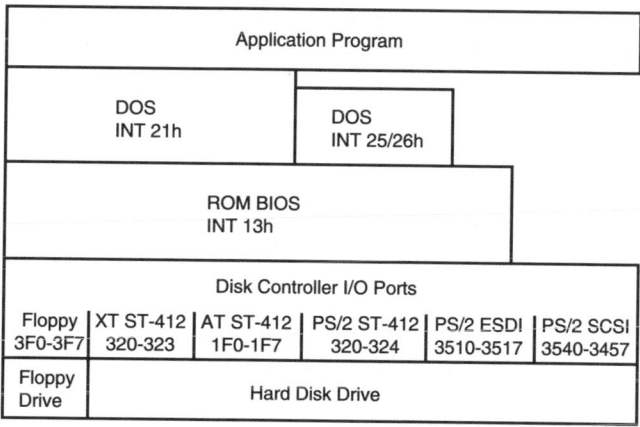

FIG. 18.2   Relationships between various interface levels.

Any software can bypass any level of interface and communicate with the level below it, but doing so requires much more work. The lowest level of interface available is direct communication with the controller using I/O port commands. As Figure 18.2 shows, each type of controller has different I/O port locations. With different controllers there are also differences among the commands presented at the ports. Only the controller can talk directly to the disk drive.

If not for the ROM BIOS Int 13h interface, a unique DOS would have to be written for each available type of hard and floppy disk drive. Instead, DOS communicates with the ROM BIOS using standard Int 13h function calls translated by the Int 13h interface into commands for the specific hardware. Because of the standard ROM BIOS interface, DOS is relatively independent from the disk hardware and can support many different types of drives and controllers.

Windows 3.1

The 16-bit Windows platforms—Windows 3.1, Windows 3.11, and Windows for Workgroups—cannot strictly be called operating systems. They are instead graphical environments that operate on top of DOS, using much of the same disk access technology described earlier in this chapter. Windows, however, takes advantage of microprocessor capabilities first introduced in the Intel 80386 chip in ways that DOS cannot.

◄◄ See "Processor Modes," p. 43

Windows also expands upon some of the basic concepts introduced in DOS to make the application programmer's job easier. You read earlier how DOS, in combination with the system ROM BIOS, provides an interface to the PC disk storage devices. This interface enables programmers to use general function calls for disk access that can be applied to any type of hardware by the operating system. However, when you install a DOS application, you often have to select drivers for components like your video display adapter, audio adapter, and printer, because DOS does not provide anything but the most rudimentary access to these devices.

Windows, on the other hand, does support the unique capabilities of your system hardware. When you install Windows, you select drivers for your specific video, audio, and printer hardware that support all the capabilities of these devices. As a result, Windows applications do not need their own drivers for these devices, because the environment provides a standard set of function calls that provides a universal interface to whatever hardware you have installed in the system.

16-bit Windows Versions

The environment that is commonly referred to as 16-bit Windows or Windows 3.1 can actually be any one of three products. The differences between the versions are rather slight, and the three are largely indistinguishable in terms of the user interface. In general, when this chapter refers to Windows 3.1, any one of the three products can be inferred.

Windows 3.1 was released in 1992, and is the standard graphical 16-bit platform for Intel-based systems. Windows 3.11 was released in 1994, and consisted of updates to the following key Windows files:

- COMMDLG.DLL
- GDI.EXE
- KRNL386.EXE
- PSCRIPT.DRV
- SHELL.DLL
- UNIDRV.DLL
- USER.EXE

The Windows 3.11 upgrade did not result in significant improvements in system performance, and was therefore ignored by many users and administrators responsible for the maintenance of Windows systems.

Both Windows 3.1 and 3.11 contain no networking support whatsoever. At the time they were released, NetWare was the dominant networking platform in the business world, and supplied the client software needed to connect a DOS or Windows system to NetWare servers. At the same time, however, Microsoft began to promote their own networking environment, culminating in the initial release of Windows NT in 1993.

Windows for Workgroups is an environment almost identical to Windows 3.1, except that it includes a Windows network client that enables the system to connect either to Windows NT servers or to other Windows for Workgroup systems on a peer-to-peer basis. Windows for Workgroups also supports external clients like those for NetWare, making it possible to run a heterogeneous network containing both Microsoft and Novell network resources.

At the time of its initial release, Windows for Workgroups and other Microsoft networking products relied on the NetBEUI protocol for network communications. As time passed, however, TCP/IP grew to be the industry standard protocol suite, and Microsoft released a TCP/IP client add-in for Windows for Workgroups called TCP/IP-32. There are still a great many PCs today that use this combination of products for business networking.

Loading Windows 3.1

As mentioned earlier, Windows 3.1 is not an operating system in itself. You must always boot the PC to a standard DOS prompt before loading the Windows environment. The system boot process, therefore, is identical to that outlined earlier in this chapter. However, as Windows loads, it changes the operating mode of the system processor and provides an additional interface layer between the system hardware and your applications.

When you load Windows 3.1 by typing **WIN** at the DOS prompt, the system executes the WIN.COM program that examines the capabilities of the hardware in the system and loads Windows in the appropriate mode to support that hardware. At the time Windows 3.1 was first released, the PC world was on the cusp between the eras of the 80286 processor and the 80386. If you had a 286-based system, Windows loaded in standard mode; 386-based and higher systems loaded in 386 enhanced mode. Today, of course, the 286 is all but extinct and nearly all systems run Windows in 386 enhanced mode.

Both Windows modes require access to XMS (extended memory specification) memory, as provided by an extended memory manager like HIMEM.SYS, that is loaded by the CONFIG.SYS file during the system boot sequence. To access XMS, WIN.COM shifts the processor from real mode to protected mode, something that DOS cannot do. In *protected mode*, a program can be allotted a specific area of memory that is protected from interference by other programs.

> **Note**
>
> Note that real mode and protected mode are attributes of the system processor and should be distinguished from the terms standard mode and 386 enhanced mode, which are Windows software states.

When WIN.COM detects a 286 processor or less, it loads Windows in standard mode by executing a file called DOSX.EXE (the MS-DOS Extended for Windows). In *standard mode*, a Windows system is capable of accessing extended memory for the purpose of task swapping. Task swapping is when the system is running two or more applications, but only the active window actually has access to the system processor. The system executes two files, WSWAP.EXE and DSWAP.EXE, to support the task swapping of Windows applications and DOS applications, respectively.

When Windows loads in *386 enhanced mode*, WIN.COM executes a file called WIN386.EXE that in turn loads the drivers specified in the [386enh] section of the SYSTEM.INI file. 386 enhanced mode makes it possible for Windows to use *virtual memory*, that is, disk space on a local hard drive that emulates RAM to provide a greater memory address space in which to run applications. With the aid of this virtual memory, a Windows system in 386 enhanced mode can *multitask*, that is, run multiple programs at the same time with each program receiving regular access to the processor.

> **Note**
>
> Although true multitasking requires a separate processor for each task, the term has come to be used to refer to the sharing of a single processor's clock cycles, as in a typical Windows PC.

Disk access times are obviously far slower than memory access times (the two being measured in milliseconds, thousandths of a second, versus nanoseconds, billionths of a second), so virtual memory is nowhere near as efficient as actual RAM. However, the capability to swap data from active memory to virtual memory at will gives the system the capability to run more code than it would with RAM alone.

Core Windows Files

After loading the files to support the appropriate mode, Windows loads the core components that provide the basic functions of the environment. These components are as follows:

- *KRNL286.EXE or KRNL386.EXE.* The kernel file (appropriate to the processor in the system) is responsible for managing system resources like memory and processor cycles, as well as loading applications and scheduling system events.

- *USER.EXE.* User is responsible for the manipulation of the windows, icons, and other elements that make up the Windows user interface. When you use the mouse or the keyboard to open, close, move, or resize a window, USER.EXE passes the input to the application associated with the window.

■ *GDI.EXE.* GDI is the graphical device interface, responsible for the generation of screen images and other graphics operations.

After the core files execute, Windows loads an array of device drivers to support the hardware installed in the system. These drivers provide the interface that Windows applications use to access the system hardware. Unlike DOS, few Windows applications access the system hardware directly. The exceptions, again like DOS, tend to be disk utilities that require lower level access than the Windows disk drivers provide.

32-bit Disk Access

Under normal conditions, the hardware interface provided by the Windows device drivers operates in addition to the other interfaces provided by DOS and the system BIOS. When a Windows application needs access to the video display, for example, it makes a function call to the Windows video driver. However, for access to a hard disk drive, the same application would typically use a standard Int 21h request, just like a DOS application. DOS then generates an Int 13h request to the system BIOS, which then communicates with the hard drive controller.

The problem with this arrangement is that although Windows and its applications run the system processor in protected mode, DOS and the BIOS require that the processor run in real mode (called *virtual 8086* mode in Windows). Thus, during the disk access procedure, the processor that is operating in protected mode to run the application must switch to virtual mode to process the Int 21h request, then revert back to protected mode. When DOS finishes processing the Int 21h request, it generates the Int 13h request for the BIOS, and again the processor must switch to virtual mode and back again to trap that interrupt. Once the request reaches the disk controller, the hard drive reads the desired information from the disk and the whole process begins again in reverse to return the requested disk data to the application.

All this mode switching by the processor slows down the disk access routine, as does the relatively slow speed of most system BIOS implementations. Windows 3.1 includes a feature called 32-bit disk access (or *fastdisk*) that speeds up the process by eliminating the calls to the system BIOS and some of the processor mode shifts.

Fastdisk is essentially a protected mode device driver that communicates directly with the hard disk drive controller, replacing the system BIOS. Applications operate as they normally do, by generating DOS Int 21h requests, forcing the processor to switch to virtual mode. However, when the processor switches back to protected mode to trap the Int 13h request generated by DOS, it does not pass this request to the system BIOS. Instead, the fastdisk driver processes the Int 13h request and communicates directly with the disk controller, all the time in protected mode.

Because the fastdisk driver communicates directly with the disk controller, it only supports hardware that conforms to the Western Digital 1003 controller model, which is used by all manufacturers of IDE drives. You cannot use fastdisk with SCSI drives.

◄◄ See "ATA Commands," p. 617

Many systems show a distinct improvement in their Windows disk access times as a result of using fastdisk. Fastdisk also makes it possible to run more non-Windows programs in the same amount of memory. Because DOS is not occupied by communications with the BIOS, it is more readily available for use by the virtual machines.

Hardware Problems Versus Software Problems

One of the most aggravating situations in computer repair is opening up a system and troubleshooting all the hardware, just to find that the cause of the problem is a software program, not the hardware. Many people have spent large sums of money on replacement hardware, all on the assumption that the hardware was causing problems, when software was actually the culprit. To eliminate these aggravating, sometimes embarrassing, and often expensive situations, you should be able to distinguish a hardware problem from a software problem.

Fortunately, making this distinction can be relatively simple. Software problems often are caused by the device drivers and memory-resident programs loaded from the CONFIG.SYS and AUTOEXEC.BAT files on many systems. One of the first things to do when you begin having problems with your system is to boot the system from a DOS disk that has no CONFIG.SYS or AUTOEXEC.BAT configuration files on it. Then test for the problem. If it has disappeared, the cause was probably something in one or both of those files.

To find the problem, begin restoring device drivers and memory-resident programs to CONFIG.SYS and AUTOEXEC.BAT one at a time (starting with CONFIG.SYS). For example, add one program back to CONFIG.SYS, reboot your system, and then determine if the problem has reappeared. When you discover the device driver or memory-resident program causing the problem, you might be able to solve the problem by editing CONFIG.SYS and AUTOEXEC.BAT to change the order in which device drivers and memory-resident programs are loaded. Or, you might have to upgrade or even eliminate the problem device driver or memory-resident program.

Windows 9x

Windows 9x is the next step in the evolution of the operating systems that began with DOS. Although it is a fully 32-bit operating system and improves on Windows 3.1 in many ways, Windows 9x is not the radical innovation that it was purported to be before its release. In fact, Windows 95 is actually a combination of a new version of MS-DOS (called DOS 7.00, according to the VER command) and a new Windows interface (called the *Explorer*).

As such, Windows 9x can indeed be called an operating system, as it marries DOS and the Windows environment into a more cohesive environment than the DOS/Windows 3.1 combination. Booting a Windows 9x system automatically loads the GUI, but changing one character of the MSDOS.SYS text file causes the computer to boot to a DOS prompt, after which you must type **WIN** to load the Windows interface. Sound familiar?

Windows 9x and DOS Compared

Much of Windows 9x is based on the same concepts as DOS and Windows 3.1, but developed to the next logical stage. The same two system files, IO.SYS and MSDOS.SYS, still exist in Windows 9x, except that all of the system file code is now located in IO.SYS.

The MSDOS.SYS file is now an ASCII text file that contains configuration settings for the system's boot behavior.

During the system startup process, the initial procedures are very like those of a DOS system, as outlined earlier in this chapter. In Windows 9x, however, IO.SYS automatically loads the equivalents of HIMEM.SYS, IFSHLP.SYS, and SETVER.EXE into memory. You can still use CONFIG.SYS and AUTOEXEC.BAT files to load real mode device drivers and memory-resident programs, but the 32-bit device drivers designed specifically for use with Windows 9x, as well as most of its configuration settings, are loaded from entries in the Windows 9x Registry. Finally, the WIN.COM file is executed and Windows 9x is officially started.

The Registry is a database of reference information, configuration settings, and application parameters that is continuously available to all Windows 9x modules. It replaces not only the functionality of the CONFIG.SYS and AUTOEXEC.BAT files, but the Windows 3.1 INI files as well.

> **Note**
>
> Be aware that when upgrading a Windows 3.1 computer to Windows 9x, many of the application and operating system settings located in configuration files like SYSTEM.INI and WIN.INI are copied to the Windows 9x Registry. Once this has occurred, changing those settings in these INI files has no effect on the system, because the actual operative setting is located in the Registry.

The Registry takes the form of two disk files called SYSTEM.DAT and USER.DAT. SYSTEM.DAT contains machine-specific settings, while USER.DAT contains the settings specific to the user who logs into the system. By maintaining multiple USER.DAT files, different people can share the same computer, with each user maintaining his or her own system configuration and desktop preferences. Registry files can be imported, exported, modified, backed up, and restored to maintain, modify, and protect the settings for a particular user or machine.

As far as disk storage is concerned, Windows 9x by default still uses the same FAT file system that DOS does, maintaining familiar structures such as the Master Boot Record (MBR), DOS Boot Record (DBR), FATs, and directories. The primary enhancement to the file system is the capability to use file and directory names that are up to 255 characters in length, while retaining backward compatibility with existing FAT file systems and utilities.

Windows 9x does this by maintaining two names for every file and directory—a long name and a truncated name that fits the standard DOS 8.3 format. This way, you can open a Windows 9x file with any DOS or Windows 3.1 application, although saving the file again will strip away the long file name. If, for example, you ran an older version of a disk repair utility like Norton Disk Doctor on a Windows 9x FAT volume, you could effectively lose the long names of all the files and directories on your system.

Versions

Since the initial release of Windows 95, quite a few patches and feature updates have been released by Microsoft, as well as two major releases. The Windows 95 OEM Service Release 2 (OSR2) is currently available only with the purchase of a new computer or hard drive from an authorized Microsoft OEM (original equipment manufacturer). This is largely due to the fact that the most important feature in the upgrade is a new file system called FAT32 that is designed to support with greater efficiency the larger hard disk drives now being found in PCs.

The OSR2 version of Windows 95 was released in this way not to thwart and irritate millions of users (which it has), but to prevent a backlash of incompatibilities that may occur when the operating system is installed on older hardware. Most of the other patches and improvements to the operating system that are included in the OSR2 release can be applied to Windows 95 installations and are freely available from Microsoft's Web site.

The Windows 98 release adds FAT32 as part of a retail product for the first time, and makes it possible to convert existing FAT16 partitions to FAT32. There are also numerous other new features and accessories in Windows 98, but very little else about the operating system's relationship to the PC hardware is changed from the OSR2 product.

Windows 9x Architecture

Much of the Windows 9x system architecture is similar to that of Windows 3.1, but re-written in 32-bit code. The core elements of the operating system are still the Kernel, the User, and the GDI, but all three now exist in both 32-bit and 16-bit versions. The 32-bit versions generally provide better performance and support for 32-bit applications, while the 16-bit versions are retained for backward compatibility.

Virtual Machine Manager. Windows 9x runs applications in separate, isolated environments called *virtual machines*. Created by the Virtual Machine Manager (which replaces the Windows 3.1 WIN386.EXE module), each virtual machine contains all the services needed for an application to run. By isolating each application in its own environment, Windows 9x is able to prevent the rest of the system from being affected by a single malfunctioning application.

Plug and Play. Perhaps the largest improvement in Windows 9x from a hardware standpoint is the introduction of support for Plug and Play (PnP). Plug and Play is a standard that enables the operating system to automatically negotiate for the system resources needed by a particular device and configure the hardware to use them. Most of the PC peripherals manufactured today support PnP, making the installation of new hardware as simple as inserting an expansion card into a slot or plugging it into a port.

To implement this functionality, Windows 9x uses a module called the Configuration Manager. The Configuration Manager consists of multiple *bus enumerators* that are responsible for scanning the system's various expansion buses for the devices connected to them. The enumerators then build a hardware tree containing all the buses and devices in the system.

Once this inventory of the system hardware is completed, the Configuration Manager loads a driver for each device in the hardware tree. The Windows 9x drivers are all 32-bit, protected mode modules, permitting them to be loaded into system memory much more easily than their real mode counterparts from Windows 3.1, which require conventional memory (memory below 640K) to load.

With the drivers loaded, the Configuration Manager then uses *resource arbitrators* to negotiate the hardware resources that are to be allocated to each device. These arbitrators reconcile any resource conflicts that may exist between devices and determine the best combination of operational settings for the hardware.

FAT32

The primary advantage of the FAT32 file system is its capability to support larger hard drives. Surely no one involved in the development of the original FAT file system could ever have dreamed that a modest home computer would come with a 2G hard drive, but that is now the minimum. The largest disk partition supported by the FAT file system is also 2G. The other problem with FAT is that the larger cluster sizes used with high-capacity hard drives are extremely wasteful in terms of the disk space lost to the slack caused by unused bits in allocated clusters.

FAT32 addresses both of these problems, by supporting drives up to 2T (2 terabytes, or 2,000G) in size, and with much smaller clusters. A 2G FAT16 partition uses 32K clusters, while the clusters on the same size FAT32 partition are only 4K. This results in a file system that is more efficient, by a factor of 10 to 15 percent when it comes to storing the maximum possible amount of data on a hard drive.

> **Note**
>
> Although 2T may seem to be an outrageously large amount of data, consider that a typical PC hard drive has gone from 10M to 2G in less than 15 years, an increase of 20,000 percent. At this rate of growth, your home computer in the year 2010 should be equipped with a 400T hard drive (probably running the FAT256 file system).

FAT32 also overcomes some of the other obvious limitations of the FAT system. For example, FAT32 still has two file allocation tables, but it can now make use of either one, switching to the backup if the first table is corrupted. Also, the root directory of a drive is no longer restricted to a specific size. It is composed of cluster chains like any other directory, and can be located anywhere on the disk. FAT32 volumes are implemented by the FDISK program included with the OSR2 Windows 95 and Windows 98 releases. When you attempt to create a partition larger than 512M, the program asks if you want to enable large disk support. Answering yes causes all partitions larger than 512M to use the FAT32 file system.

FAT32, like Windows 9x, is designed to provide the greatest possible backward compatibility, along with its advanced features. It will continue to support real mode DOS programs and today's protected mode applications. This means that you will be able to boot from any DOS disk and still access FAT32 drives. However, applications designed for use on FAT16 drives that address the hardware directly, such as disk repair programs, will not function on (and may damage) FAT32 volumes.

Windows NT

Whereas DOS, Windows 3.1, and Windows 9x can be seen as successive steps in the continuing evolution of an operating system, Windows NT is a wholly new concept Windows NT is a 32-bit operating system that was designed from the ground up to point toward the future of both network and desktop computing. The primary problem that consistently holds back the advancement of computing technology is backward compatibility. It is difficult to sell a product that forces users to junk the investment that they have already made in software or hardware.

Windows 9x is much closer to DOS/Windows 3.1 than it is to Windows NT for this very reason. Corporations hesitate to convert to a new operating system on a large scale if it forces them to waste millions of dollars spent on 16-bit software and user training. Windows NT is just such a product, and its acceptance in the marketplace since its original release in 1993 has been gradual but steady. Windows NT 4.0 is now a viable competitor to Windows 9x in the desktop marketplace, largely because of the Windows 9x marketing program that led to a massive 32-bit software development effort. Most 32-bit Windows applications can run on either Windows 9x or Windows NT, and the backward compatibility issue is fading steadily as 16-bit applications are phased out.

Windows NT is a completely different operating system from DOS. Although you can open a DOS session window from within the GUI, it is not a shell in the traditional sense. It is rather a DOS emulation that is designed to provide a familiar command line interface to users who want it. Many DOS programs will not run in a Windows NT DOS session, nor is it possible to boot the Windows NT operating system to a character-based state that precedes the loading of the graphical interface, as with Windows 9x.

Like Windows 9x, Windows NT uses a Registry to load device drivers and store its configuration settings. There are no CONFIG.SYS, AUTOEXEC.BAT, or INI files. Windows NT can use the FAT16 file system, which enables you to boot the computer using a DOS disk and still access its drives. Some of Windows NT's most advanced features, however, are provided by the NT File System (NTFS). NTFS (like FAT32) allows you to create partitions up to 2T in size, but it also provides the file compression, security, and auditing features that are important to Windows NT computers in network environments. Beginning in Windows NT 5.0, support will be provided for the FAT32 file system as well.

During the Windows NT installation process, the initial setup is performed on a FAT drive, which can be converted to NTFS at the end of the installation process, if you so desire. You can also convert the drives later, using a CONVERT.EXE utility provided with the operating system. From the time that a partition is converted to NTFS, however, it is not accessible by any other operating system. If you use a DOS disk to boot a system with NTFS partitions, you will have access to the floppy drive only, just as if there were no hard drives installed in the computer. To switch the machine back to Windows 9x,

Windows 3.1, or DOS, you must delete the NTFS partitions (and their data) and create new FAT partitions from scratch.

Versions

The first version of Windows NT was called 3.1, because it was released in 1993 when Windows 3.1 was the current 16-bit Windows product. The graphical interface was identical to that of Windows 3.1, even if the underlying infrastructure was completely different.

Subsequent versions (3.5 and 3.51) drew greater distinctions between the Server and Workstation versions of the operating system by adding the capability to create groupings of Windows NT machines called domains. These versions also provided bug fixes, implemented some architectural changes, such as making TCP/IP the default networking protocol, and added new services like DHCP and WINS.

Windows NT 4.0 was the first release to make substantial changes to the appearance of the operating system, by adding the same Explorer interface used by Windows 9x.

Windows NT Startup

When you start a Windows NT system, the boot process is identical to that of a DOS system, up until the time when the system reads the volume boot sector from the active partition. Instead of the IO.SYS and MSDOS.SYS files, Windows NT uses an OS loader program called NTLDR that begins the hardware detection process and enables you to select the operating system to load. If, for example, you have installed Windows NT on a system already running another OS, you have the option of booting either operating system. The boot options are stored in a file called BOOT.INI.

Once you elect to load the Windows NT operating system, a file called NTDETECT.COM loads and detects the hardware in the computer. After this, the Windows NT Kernel (NTOSKRNL.EXE) and the hardware abstraction layer (HAL.DLL) are loaded into memory. The kernel is responsible for initializing most of the operating system, including the device drivers, the Windows NT subsystems and services, and the memory paging file. It isn't until you press the Ctrl+Alt+Delete key combination and log on to the system that the startup process is considered to be complete.

Windows NT Components

The Windows NT *kernel* is responsible for scheduling tasks and managing threads. The thread is the smallest unit of processor activity Windows NT can handle. Because Windows NT is a multithreaded operating system, the kernel is responsible for seeing to it that the threads of the various processes running on the system at any one time receive the appropriate access to the processor, based on their priorities.

Windows NT was designed to be a modular operating system and to be portable to different hardware (that is, processor) platforms. To make this possible, a module called the *hardware abstraction layer* (HAL) creates a virtual interface to the system hardware. The operating system kernel and the device drivers then use this interface to communicate with the hardware, rather than accessing it directly. Because the interface is machine-independent, it is a relatively simple matter to port the kernel, drivers, and other components to other platforms, such as Digital's Alpha processor.

Windows NT has two operational modes: kernel mode and user mode. Kernel mode provides access to all system resources and processor instructions. The OS kernel and the HAL both run in kernel mode, as does the Windows NT Executive. The Executive consists of the following operating system components:

- *Object Manager.* All Windows NT resources, including files and directories, threads and processes, and memory segments and sections, are represented by abstract formations known as objects. The Object Manager provides an hierarchical naming system for these objects, which makes it possible to track their creation and use.

- *I/O Manager.* The I/O Manager is responsible for all of Windows NT's input and output functions and maintains communications with the various device drivers for the system hardware to make this possible.

- *Security Reference Monitor.* The Security Reference Monitor (SRM) works together with the user mode security subsystem to control access to Windows NT objects. All requests for access to an object pass through the SRM, which checks its access control list for the appropriate rights.

- *Process Manager.* The Process Manager controls the creation and deletion of process objects and the threads that make up the processes.

- *Virtual Memory Manager.* The Virtual Memory Manager is responsible for allocating a protected memory address space to each process running on the system. As with Windows 9x, Windows NT can use disk space as virtual memory, and allocate a total amount of memory that is larger than the RAM installed in the system.

- *Local Procedure Call.* The Local Procedure Call facility provides communications between client and server processes on the same system, just as Remote Procedure Calls are used for client/server communications between different systems.

User mode is a less priveledged mode that keeps the processes running in it isolated from parts of the OS that could be crashed, User mode interacts with the user and the user applications. This split in modes allows applications designed for Windows as well as some native OS/2 and POSIX applications to run without giving these other applications direct access to the kernel.

Chapter 19

File Systems and Data Recovery

Hard disks and other media provide the basic technology for storing data. However, it is the file system that provides the hierarchical structure of volumes and directories in which you store individual files and the organizational model that makes it possible for the system to locate data anywhere on the disk. File systems are usually integrated into an operating system (OS), although some OSs provide support for several file systems from which you can choose.

The most commonly used file system today is based on a file allocation table, or FAT, that keeps track of the data stored in each cluster on a disk. This is the file system originally used by DOS and it is still supported by virtually every other PC operating system in use today. This chapter examines the disk structures that DOS uses to implement the FAT file system, and then discusses the additional capabilities provided by newer file systems such as FAT32 and Windows NT's NTFS.

FAT Disk Structures

To manage files on a disk and enable all application programs to see a consistent interface to the file system no matter what type of storage hardware is being used, DOS creates several structures on the disk. These structures are the same for any OS that supports the FAT file system, including Windows 9x and Windows NT. The following list shows all the structures and areas that DOS defines and uses to manage a disk, in roughly the same order that they appear:

- Master and extended partition boot sectors
- Volume boot sector
- Root directory
- File allocation tables (FAT)
- Clusters (allocation units)

■ Data area

■ Diagnostic read-and-write cylinder

A hard disk has all these disk-management structures, and a floppy disk has all but the master and extended partition boot sectors and the diagnostic cylinder. These structures are created on hard disk drives by the FDISK program included with all versions of DOS and Windows 9x. You cannot use FDISK on a floppy disk because floppy disks cannot be partitioned. Figure 19.1 is a simple diagram showing the relative locations of these DOS disk-management structures on a 2111M Western Digital hard disk.

Note

Some removable cartridge drives, such as the Iomega Zip drive, function like high-capacity floppy disk drives. They lack a master boot sector and diagnostic cylinder and cannot be partitioned like hard disk drives. Other higher-capacity drives, such as the Iomega Jaz, can be partitioned like a hard disk drive.

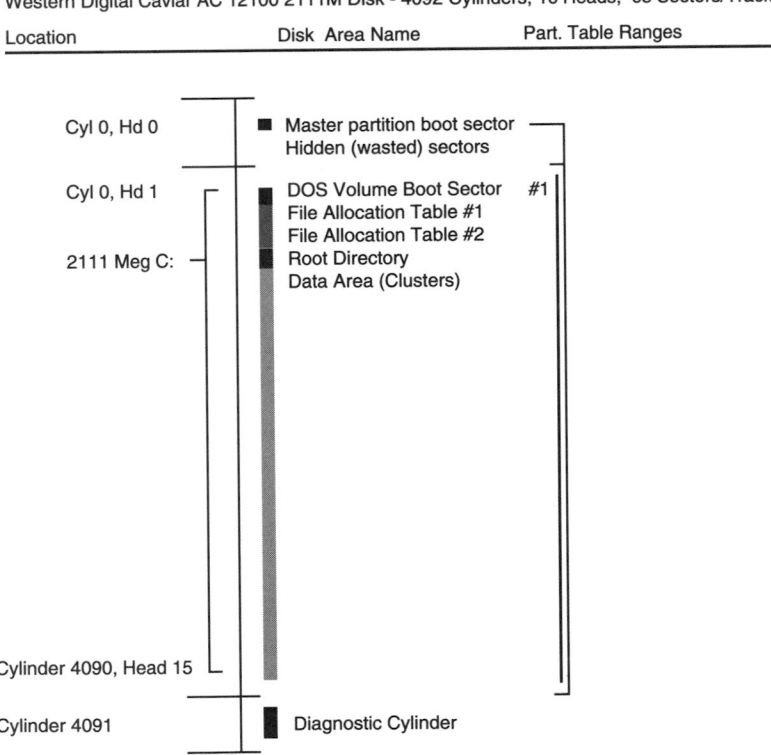

FIG. 19.1   DOS disk management structures on a Western Digital Caviar AC12100.

Each disk area has a purpose and function. If one of these special areas is damaged, serious consequences can result. Damage to one of these sensitive structures usually causes a domino effect, limiting access to other areas of the disk or causing further problems in using the disk. For example, DOS cannot read and write files if the FAT is damaged or corrupted. Therefore, you should understand these data structures well enough to be able to repair them when necessary. Rebuilding these special tables and areas of the disk is essential to the art of data recovery.

Master Partition Boot Sector

To use a hard disk with different operating systems, you can logically divide the disk by creating up to four partitions. You can, for example, use FDISK to create one or more FAT partitions for use with DOS or Windows 9x, and leave the rest of the disk storage area for use by another OS's file system. Each of the FAT partitions will appear to the OS as a separate drive letter. Information about each of the partitions on the disk is stored in a partition (or volume) boot sector at the beginning of each partition. There is also a main table listing the partitions embedded in the master partition boot sector.

The *master partition boot sector* (or master boot record) is always located in the first sector of the entire disk (cylinder 0, head 0, sector 1) and consists of the following structures:

- *Master partition table*. Contains a list of the partitions on the disk and the locations of their volume boot sectors. This table is very small and can contain only four entries at the most. Therefore, to accommodate more partitions, operating systems such as DOS can divide a single extended partition into multiple logical volumes.

- *Master boot code*. A small program that is executed by the system BIOS, the main function of which is to pass control of the system to the partition that has been designated as active (or bootable).

Primary and Extended DOS Partitions

DOS is designed to support up to 24 partitions on a single hard disk drive (represented by the drive letters C: through Z:), but the partition table in the master partition boot sector can have a maximum of only four entries. To resolve this discrepancy, the FDISK program enables you to create two types of FAT partitions: a primary DOS partition and an extended DOS partition. The first FAT partition that you create on a disk should be the primary, which is listed in the master partition table and appears to the operating system as a single drive letter.

An extended DOS partition is listed in the master partition table like the primary, but it differs in that you can use its disk space to create multiple logical partitions, or volumes. You can create only one extended DOS partition on a single drive, meaning that there will never be more than two entries in the master partition table devoted to FAT drives.

The logical volumes that you create in the extended DOS partition appear as separate drive letters to the operating system, but they are not listed in the master partition table. Logical volumes also cannot be active partitions, and are therefore not bootable. You can create up to 23 volumes out of a single extended DOS partition (assuming that you have already created a primary DOS partition, which brings the total to 24).

(continues)

(continued)

Each of the logical partitions (or volumes) in an extended DOS partition includes an *extended partition table* that contains information about that volume. The master partition table's entry for the extended DOS partition contains a reference to the first volume's extended partition table. This table in turn contains a reference detailing the location of the second volume's table. This chain of references continues, linking all the volumes in the extended DOS partition to the master partition table.

Of course, few people have any reason to create 24 FAT partitions on a single disk drive, but the extended DOS partition makes it possible to exceed the four-entry limitation of the master partition table.

Because the master boot sector contains the first program that the system executes when you boot a PC, it is frequently a target for creators of computer viruses. A virus that infects or destroys the master boot sector can make it impossible for the BIOS to find the active partition, thus preventing the operating system from loading. Because the master boot sector contains the first program executed by the system, a virus stored there loads before any anti-virus code can detect it. To remove a master boot sector virus, you must first boot the system from a clean, uninfected floppy disk and then run an anti-virus program.

Each partition on a disk contains a volume boot sector as its first sector, which is listed in the master partition table. With the FDISK utility, you can designate a single partition as active (or bootable). The master partition boot sector causes the active partition's volume boot sector to receive control whenever the system is started or reset. You can also create additional disk partitions for Novell NetWare, Windows NT's NTFS, OS/2's HPFS, AIX (UNIX), XENIX, or other file systems, using disk utilities provided with the operating systems that support them. These partitions are listed in the master partition table, even though they may use different structures within the partition.

However, you cannot access the data stored on these foreign operating system partitions with DOS. In some cases, you cannot access FAT partitions using other operating systems either, although OS/2 and Windows NT do support FAT in addition to their own file systems: HPFS and NTFS. You must create at least one partition on a hard disk for it to be accessible by an operating system. Creating a partition adds an entry to the master partition table.

Table 19.1 shows the format of the Master Boot Record (MBR) and its partition tables. The table lists the fields in each of the master partition table's four entries, the location on the disk where each field begins (the offset), and its length.

Table 19.1   Master Boot Record (Partition Table)

Master Partition Table Entry #1

Offset	Length	Description
1BEh 446	1 byte	Boot Indicator Byte (80h = Active, else 00h)
1BFh 447	1 byte	Starting Head (or Side) of Partition
1C0h 448	16 bits	Starting Cylinder (10 bits) and Sector (6 bits)

Offset	Length	Description
1C2h 450	1 byte	System Indicator Byte (see Table 19.2)
1C3h 451	1 byte	Ending Head (or Side) of Partition
1C4h 452	16 bits	Ending Cylinder (10 bits) and Sector (6 bits)
1C6h 454	1 dword	Relative Sector Offset of Partition
1CAh 458	1 dword	Total Number of Sectors in Partition

Partition Table Entry #2

Offset	Length	Description
1CEh 462	1 byte	Boot Indicator Byte (80h = Active, else 00h)
1CFh 463	1 byte	Starting Head (or Side) of Partition
1D0h 464	16 bits	Starting Cylinder (10 bits) and Sector (6 bits)
1D2h 466	1 byte	System Indicator Byte (see Table 19.2)
1D3h 467	1 byte	Ending Head (or Side) of Partition
1D4h 468	16 bits	Ending Cylinder (10 bits) and Sector (6 bits)
1D6h 470	1 dword	Relative Sector Offset of Partition
1DAh 474	1 dword	Total Number of Sectors in Partition

Partition Table Entry #3

Offset	Length	Description
1DEh 478	1 byte	Boot Indicator Byte (80h = Active, else 00h)
1DFh 479	1 byte	Starting Head (or Side) of Partition
1E0h 480	16 bits	Starting Cylinder (10 bits) and Sector (6 bits)
1E2h 482	1 byte	System Indicator Byte (see Table 19.2)
1E3h 483	1 byte	Ending Head (or Side) of Partition
1E4h 484	16 bits	Ending Cylinder (10 bits) and Sector (6 bits)
1E6h 486	1 dword	Relative Sector Offset of Partition
1EAh 490	1 dword	Total Number of Sectors in Partition

Partition Table Entry #4

Offset	Length	Description
1EEh 494	1 byte	Boot Indicator Byte (80h = Active, else 00h)
1EFh 495	1 byte	Starting Head (or Side) of Partition
1F0h 496	16 bits	Starting Cylinder (10 bits) and Sector (6 bits)
1F2h 498	1 byte	System Indicator Byte (see Table 19.2)
1F3h 499	1 byte	Ending Head (or Side) of Partition
1F4h 500	16 bits	Ending Cylinder (10 bits) and Sector (6 bits)
1F6h 502	1 dword	Relative Sector Offset of Partition
1FAh 506	1 dword	Total Number of Sectors in Partition

(continues)

Table 19.1 Master Boot Record (Partition Table) Continued		
Signature Bytes		
Offset	**Length**	**Description**
1FEh 510	2 bytes	Boot Sector Signature (55AAh)

A WORD equals 2 bytes read in reverse order, and a DWORD equals two WORDs read in reverse order.

Each entry in the Master Partition Table contains a System Indicator Byte that identifies the type of partition referenced by that entry. Table 19.2 shows the standard values and meanings of the System Indicator Byte.

Table 19.2 Partition Table System Indicator Byte Values	
Value	**Description**
00h	No allocated partition in this entry
01h	Primary DOS, 12-bit FAT (Partition < 16M)
04h	Primary DOS, 16-bit FAT (16M <= Partition <= 32M)
05h	Extended DOS (Points to next Primary Partition)
06h	Primary DOS, 16-bit FAT (Partition > 32M)
07h	OS/2 HPFS Partition
02h	MS-XENIX Root Partition
03h	MS-XENIX usr Partition
08h	AIX File System Partition
09h	AIX boot Partition
50h	Ontrack Disk Manager READ-ONLY Partition
51h	Ontrack Disk Manager READ/WRITE Partition
56h	Golden Bow Vfeature Partition
61h	Storage Dimensions Speedstor Partition
63h	IBM 386/ix or UNIX System V/386 Partition
64h	Novell NetWare Partition
75h	IBM PCIX Partition
DBh	Digital Research Concurrent DOS/CPM-86 Partition
F2h	Some OEM's DOS 3.2+ second partition
FFh	UNIX Bad Block Table Partition

Undocumented FDISK

FDISK is a very powerful program, and in DOS 5 and later versions, it gained some additional capabilities. Unfortunately, these capabilities were never documented in the DOS manual and remain undocumented even in DOS 7. The most important undocumented parameter in FDISK is the /MBR (Master Boot Record) parameter, which causes FDISK to rewrite the `Master Boot Sector` code area, leaving the partition tables intact.

The /MBR parameter is tailor-made for eliminating boot-sector virus programs that infect the Master Partition Boot Sector (Cylinder 0, Head 0, Sector 1) of a hard disk. To use this feature, you simply enter

```
FDISK /MBR
```

FDISK then rewrites the boot sector code, leaving the partition tables intact. This should not cause any problems on a normally functioning system, but just in case, I recommend backing up the partition table information to floppy disk before trying it. You can do this by using a third-party product like Norton Utilities.

Be aware that using FDISK with the /MBR switch will overwrite the partition tables if the two signature bytes at the end of the sector (55AAh) are damaged. This situation is highly unlikely, however. In fact, if these signature bytes were damaged, you would know; the system would not boot and would act as though there were no partitions at all.

Volume Boot Sectors

The *volume boot sector* is the first sector on any area of a drive addressed as a partition or volume (or logical DOS disk). On a floppy disk or a removable cartridge (such as a Zip disk), for example, this sector is the first one on the disk because DOS recognizes the disk as a volume without the need for partitioning. On a hard disk, the volume boot sector or sectors are located as the first sector within any disk area allocated as a nonextended partition, or any area recognizable as a DOS volume.

The volume boot sector resembles the master partition boot sector in that it contains two elements, which are as follows:

- *Disk parameter block*. Sometimes called the *media parameter block*, the disk parameter block contains specific information about the volume, such as its size, the number of disk sectors it uses, the size of its clusters, and the volume label name.

- *Volume boot code*. The program that begins the process of loading the operating system. For DOS and Windows 9x systems, this is the IO.SYS file.

◀◀ See "IO.SYS (or IBMBIO.COM)," p. 1035

The volume boot sector of the active partition on a disk is loaded by the system ROM BIOS for floppy disks or by the master partition boot sector on a hard disk. The program code in the volume boot sector is given control of the system; it performs some tests and then attempts to load the first system file (in DOS, this is IO.SYS). The volume boot sector, such as the master boot sector, is transparent to the running system; it is outside the data area of the disk on which files are stored.

Note

Many of the systems today are capable of booting from drives other than standard floppy disk and hard disk drives. In these cases, the boot drive must be specifically supported by system BIOS. For

(continues)

> (continued)
>
> example, some BIOS products enable you to select an ATAPI CD-ROM as a boot device, in addition to the floppy and hard disk drives.
>
> Other types of removable media, such as Zip cartridges and LS-120 disks, can also be made bootable. When properly supported by the BIOS, an LS-120 drive can replace the existing floppy disk drive as drive A:.

On a FAT partition, you create a volume boot sector with the FORMAT command (high-level format) included with DOS and Windows 9x. Hard disks on FAT systems have a volume boot sector at the beginning of every DOS logical drive area allocated on the disk, in both the primary and extended partitions. Although all the logical drives contain the program area as well as a data table area, only the program code from the volume boot sector in the active partition on a hard disk is executed. The others are simply read by the operating system files during bootup to obtain their data tables and determine the volume parameters.

The volume boot sector contains program code and data. The single data table in this sector is called the *media parameter block* or *disk parameter block*. The operating system needs the information this table contains to verify the capacity of the disk volume as well as the location of important structures such as the FAT. The format of this data is very specific.

Table 19.3 shows the format and layout of the DOS Boot Record (DBR), including the location of each field within the record (the offset) in both hexadecimal and decimal notation, and the length of each field.

Table 19.3   DOS Boot Record (DBR) Format

Offset			
Hex	**Dec**	**Field Length**	**Description**
00h	0	3 bytes	Jump Instruction to Boot Program Code
03h	3	8 bytes	OEM Name and DOS Version (IBM 5.0)
0Bh	11	1 word	Bytes/Sector (usually 512)
0Dh	13	1 byte	Sectors/Cluster (Must be a power of 2)
0Eh	14	1 word	Reserved Sectors (Boot Sectors, usually 1)
10h	16	1 byte	FAT Copies (usually 2)
11h	17	1 word	Maximum Root Directory Entries (usually 512)
13h	19	1 word	Total Sectors (If Partition <= 32M, else 0)
15h	21	1 byte	Media Descriptor Byte (F8h for Hard Disks)
16h	22	1 word	Sectors/FAT
18h	24	1 word	Sectors/Track
1Ah	26	1 word	Number of Heads
1Ch	28	1 dword	Hidden Sectors (If Partition <= 32M, 1 word only)

For DOS 4.0 or Higher Only, Else 00h

Hex	Dec	Field Length	Description
20h	32	1 dword	Total Sectors (If Partition > 32M, else 0)
24h	36	1 byte	Physical Drive No. (00h=floppy, 80h=hard disk)
25h	37	1 byte	Reserved (00h)
26h	38	1 byte	Extended Boot Record Signature (29h)
27h	39	1 dword	Volume Serial Number (32-bit random number)
2Bh	43	11 bytes	Volume Label ("NO NAME " stored if no label)
36h	54	8 bytes	File System ID ("FAT12 " or "FAT16 ")

For All Versions of DOS

Hex	Dec	Field Length	Description
3Eh	62	448 bytes	Boot Program Code
1FEh	510	2 bytes	Signature Bytes (55AAh)

A WORD is 2 bytes read in reverse order, and a DWORD is two WORDs read in reverse order.

Root Directory

A *directory* is a simple database containing information about the files stored on a FAT partition. Each record in this database is 32 bytes long, with no delimiters or separating characters between the fields or records. A directory stores almost all the information that the operating system knows about a file, including the following:

- *File name and extension.* The 8-character name and 3-character extension of the file. The dot between the name and the extension is implied, but not included in the entry. (To see how Windows 9x extends file names to allow 255 characters within the 8.3 directory structure, see "VFAT and Long File Names" later in this chapter.)

- *File attribute byte.* The byte containing the flags representing the standard DOS file attributes, using the format shown in Table 19.5.

- *Date/Time of last change.* The date and time that the file was created or last modified.

- *File size.* The size of the file, in bytes.

- *Link to start cluster.* The number of the cluster in the partition where the beginning of the file is stored. To learn more about clusters, see "Clusters (Allocation Units)" later in this chapter.

There is information that a directory does not contain about a file. This includes where the rest of its clusters in the partition are located and whether the file is contiguous or fragmented. This information is contained in the FAT.

There are two basic types of directories: the *root directory* and *subdirectories*. Any given volume can have only one root directory. The root directory is always stored on a disk in a fixed location immediately following the two copies of the FAT. Root directories vary in size because of the different types and capacities of disks, but the root directory of a given disk is fixed. After a root directory is created by the FORMAT command, it has a fixed length and cannot be extended to hold more entries. The root directory entry limits are shown in Table 19.4. Subdirectories are stored as files in the data area of the disk and therefore have no fixed length limits.

Table 19.4   Root Directory Entry Limits

Drive Type	Maximum Root Directory Entries
Hard disk	512
1.44M floppy disk	224
2.88M floppy disk	448
Jaz and Zip	512
LS-120	512
Sparq	512

Note

One of the advantages of the FAT32 file system is that the root directory can be located anywhere on the disk and it can have an unlimited number of entries.

Every directory, whether it is the root directory or a subdirectory, is organized in the same way. Entries in the directory database store important information about individual files and how files are named on the disk. The directory information is linked to the FAT by the starting cluster entry. In fact, if no file on a disk were longer than one single cluster, the FAT would be unnecessary. The directory stores all the information needed by DOS to manage the file, with the exception of the list of clusters that the file occupies other than the first one. The FAT stores the remaining information about the other clusters that the file occupies.

To trace a file on a disk, you start with the directory entry to get the information about the starting cluster of the file and its size. Then you go to the file allocation table, where you can follow the chain of clusters that the file occupies until you reach the end of the file.

DOS directory entries are 32 bytes long and are in the format shown in Table 19.5, which shows the location (or offset) of each field within the entry (in both hexadecimal and decimal form) and the length of each field.

Table 19.5   DOS Directory Format

Offset Hex	Dec	Field Length	Description
00h	0	8 bytes	File name
08h	8	3 bytes	File extension
0Bh	11	1 byte	File attributes

Offset			
Hex	**Dec**	**Field Length**	**Description**
0Ch	12	10 bytes	Reserved (00h)
16h	22	1 word	Time of creation
18h	24	1 word	Date of creation
1Ah	26	1 word	Starting cluster
1Ch	28	1 dword	Size in bytes

Note

File names and extensions are left-justified and padded with spaces (32h). The first byte of the file name indicates the file status as follows:

Hex	File Status
00h	Entry never used; entries past this point not searched
05h	Indicates that the first character of the file name is actually E5h
E5h	σ (lowercase sigma) indicates that the file has been erased
2Eh	. (period) indicates that this entry is a directory. If the second byte is also 2Eh, the cluster field contains the cluster number of the parent directory (0000h, if the parent is the root).

A WORD is 2 bytes read in reverse order, and a DWORD is two WORDs read in reverse order.

Table 19.6 describes the DOS directory file attribute byte. Attributes are one-bit flags that control specific properties of a file, such as whether it is hidden or designated as read-only. Each flag is individually activated (1) or deactivated (0) by changing the bit value. The combination of the eight bit values can be expressed as a single hexadecimal byte value.

Table 19.6   DOS Directory File Attribute Byte

Bit Positions 7 6 5 4 3 2 1 0	Hex Value	Description
0 0 0 0 0 0 0 1	01h	Read-only file
0 0 0 0 0 0 1 0	02h	Hidden file
0 0 0 0 0 1 0 0	04h	System file
0 0 0 0 1 0 0 0	08h	Volume label
0 0 0 1 0 0 0 0	10h	Subdirectory
0 0 1 0 0 0 0 0	20h	Archive (updated since backup)
0 1 0 0 0 0 0 0	40h	Reserved
1 0 0 0 0 0 0 0	80h	Reserved
Examples		
0 0 1 0 0 0 0 1	21h	Read-only, archive
0 0 1 1 0 0 1 0	32h	Hidden, subdirectory, archive
0 0 1 0 0 1 1 1	27h	Read-only, hidden, system, archive

File Allocation Tables (FATs)

The *file allocation table (FAT)* is a list of numerical entries describing how each cluster in the partition is allocated. The data area of the partition has a single entry in the table for each of its clusters. Sectors in the nondata area of the partition are outside the range of the disk controlled by the FAT. Thus, the sectors that comprise the boot sectors, file allocation tables, and the root directory are outside the range of sectors controlled by the FAT.

The FAT does not manage every data sector specifically, but rather allocates space in groups of sectors called *clusters* or *allocation units*. A cluster is a unit of storage consisting of one or more sectors. The size of a cluster is determined by the FDISK program during the creation of the partition, based on the partition's size. The smallest space that a file can occupy in a partition is one cluster; all files use space in integer cluster units. If a file is one byte larger than one cluster, two whole clusters are used.

You can think of the FAT as a type of spreadsheet that tracks the allocation of the disk's clusters. Each cell in the spreadsheet corresponds to a single cluster on the disk. The number stored in that cell is a code indicating whether the cluster is used by a file and, if so, where the next cluster of the file is located. Thus, to determine which clusters a particular file is using, you would start by looking at the first FAT reference in the file's directory entry. When you look up the referenced cluster in the FAT, the table contains a reference to the file's next cluster. Each FAT reference therefore points to the next cluster in what is called a *FAT chain*, until you reach the cluster containing the end of the file. Numbers stored in the FAT are hexadecimal numbers that are either 12 or 16 bits long. The 16-bit FAT numbers are easy to follow in a disk sector editor because they take an even two bytes of space. The 12-bit numbers are 1 1/2 bytes long, which presents a problem because most disk sector editors show data in byte units. To edit a 12-bit FAT, you must do some hex/binary math to convert the displayed byte units to FAT numbers. Fortunately (unless you are using the DOS DEBUG program), most of the available tools and utility programs have a FAT-editing mode that automatically converts the numbers for you. Most of them also show the FAT numbers in decimal form, which most people find easier to handle.

The first two entries in the FAT contain information about the table. The entries corresponding to the clusters in the partition begin after these two. Most FAT entries consist of a reference to another cluster, containing the next part of a particular file. However, some FAT entries contain hexadecimal values with special meanings, as follows:

- *0000.* Indicates that the cluster is not in use by a file.

- *FFF7.* Indicates that at least one sector in the cluster is damaged and that it should not be used to store data.

- *FFFF8-FFFF.* Indicates that the cluster contains the end of a file and that no reference to another cluster is needed.

The FDISK program determines whether a 12-bit or 16-bit FAT is placed on a disk, even though the FAT isn't written until you perform a high-level format (using the FORMAT utility). On today's systems, usually only floppy disks use 12-bit FATs, but FDISK also creates a 12-bit FAT if you create a hard disk volume that is smaller than 16M (32,756 sectors). On hard disk volumes of more than 16M, FDISK creates a 16-bit FAT. On drives larger than 512M, the FDISK program included in Windows 95 OSR2 and Windows 98 enables you to create 32-bit FATs.

FDISK creates two copies of the FAT. Each one occupies contiguous sectors on the disk, and the second FAT copy immediately follows the first. Unfortunately, DOS uses the second FAT copy only if sectors in the first FAT copy become unreadable. If the first FAT copy is corrupted, which is a much more common problem, DOS does not use the second FAT copy. Even the DOS CHKDSK command does not check or verify the second FAT copy. Moreover, whenever DOS updates the first FAT, it automatically copies large portions of the first FAT to the second FAT. If the first copy was corrupted and then subsequently updated by DOS, a large portion of the first FAT would be copied over to the second FAT copy, damaging it in the process. After the update, the second copy is usually a mirror image of the first one, complete with any corruption. Two FATs rarely stay out of sync for very long. When they are out of sync and DOS writes to the disk, it updates the first FAT and also overwrites the second FAT with the first. This is why disk repair and recovery utilities warn you to stop working as soon as you detect a FAT problem. Programs such as Norton Disk Doctor use the second copy of the FAT as a reference to repair the first one, but if DOS has already updated the second FAT, repair may be impossible.

Clusters (Allocation Units)

The term *cluster* was changed to *allocation unit* in DOS 4.0 (although many people continue to use the old term). Allocation unit is appropriate because a single cluster is the smallest unit of the disk that the operating system can handle when it writes or reads a file. A cluster is equal to one or more 512-byte sectors, in a power of two. Although a cluster can be a single disk sector, it is usually more than one. Having more than one sector per cluster reduces the size and processing overhead of the FAT and enables the operating system to run faster because it has fewer individual units to manage. The trade-off is in wasted disk space. Because operating systems manage space only in full-cluster units, every file consumes space on the disk in increments of one cluster.

Table 19.7 shows the default cluster (or allocation unit) sizes for the various floppy disk formats used over the years.

Table 19.7 Default Floppy Disk Cluster (Allocation Unit) Sizes		
Drive Type	**Cluster (Allocation Unit) Size**	**Density**
5 1/4-inch 360K	2 sectors (1,024 bytes)	Low
5 1/4-inch 1.2M	1 sector (512 bytes)	High
3 1/2-inch 720K	2 sectors (1,024 bytes)	Low
3 1/2-inch 1.44M	1 sector (512 bytes)	High
3 1/2-inch 2.88M	2 sectors (1,024 bytes)	Extra

It seems strange that the high-density disks, which have many more individual sectors than low-density disks, sometimes have smaller cluster sizes. The larger the FAT, the more entries the operating system must manage, and the slower it seems to function. This sluggishness is due to the excessive overhead required to manage all the individual clusters; the more clusters to be managed, the slower things become. The trade-off is in the minimum cluster size. High-density floppy disk drives are faster than their low-density counterparts, so perhaps IBM and Microsoft determined that the decrease in cluster size balances the drive's faster operation and offsets the use of a larger FAT.

Because the operating system can allocate only whole clusters, there is inevitably a certain amount of wasted storage space. File sizes rarely fall on cluster boundaries, so the last cluster allocated to a particular file is rarely filled completely. The extra space left over between the actual end of the file and the end of the cluster is called *slack*. A partition with large clusters has more slack space, while smaller clusters generate less slack.

For hard disks, the cluster size varies greatly among different partition sizes. The field in the disk parameter block that specifies the cluster size is two bytes long, meaning that its maximum possible value is 65,535. Thus, the largest possible cluster is 32K, because a 64K cluster would require a value of 65,536 in this field. Table 19.8 shows the cluster sizes that FDISK selects for a particular volume size.

Table 19.8 Default Hard Disk Cluster (Allocation Unit) Sizes		
Hard Disk Volume Size	**Cluster (Allocation Unit) Size**	**FAT Type**
0M to less than 16M	8 sectors or 4,096 bytes	12-bit
16M through 128M	4 sectors or 2,048 bytes	16-bit
More than 128–256M	8 sectors or 4,096 bytes	16-bit
More than 256–512M	16 sectors or 8,192 bytes	16-bit
More than 512–1,024M	32 sectors or 16,384 bytes	16-bit
More than 1,024–2,048M	64 sectors or 32,768 bytes	16-bit

The effect of larger cluster sizes on disk utilization can be substantial. A 2G partition containing about 5,000 files, with average slack of one-half of the last 32K cluster used for each file, wastes over 78M [5000*(.5*32)K] of file space.

The cluster size, in combination with the structure of the FAT, also dictates the maximum possible FAT partition size. Because the FAT uses 16-byte entries to reference the clusters in the partition, there can be a maximum of only 65,536 (2^{16}) clusters. At 32K per cluster, this means that the largest possible FAT partition is 2,096,832K or 2,047.6875M in size.

Even if the 2-byte cluster size field could contain the value indicating 64K clusters, the maximum partition size would still be constrained. The maximum partition size would be limited by the field in the disk parameter block that specifies the number of sectors per cluster. This field is only one byte long and its value must be a power of two. This makes its highest possible value 128 sectors, which equates to a maximum cluster size of 64K. 65,536 clusters at 64K each equals a maximum partition size of 4G.

> **Note**
>
> Windows NT does support the use of 64K clusters on FAT16 partitions, enabling you to create partitions up to 4G in size. However, the huge amount of slack that generally results from clusters this large makes this practice undesirable.

The Data Area

The *data area* of a partition is the place where the actual files are stored. It is located following the boot sector, file allocation tables, and root directory. This is the area of the disk that is divided into clusters and managed by the FAT and the root directory.

Diagnostic Read-and-Write Cylinder

The FDISK partitioning program always reserves the last cylinder of a hard disk for use as a special diagnostic read-and-write test cylinder. That this cylinder is reserved is one reason FDISK always reports fewer total cylinders than the drive manufacturer states are available. Operating systems do not use this cylinder for any normal purpose because it lies outside the partitioned area of the disk.

◀◀ See "Disk Formatting," p. 728

On systems with IDE or SCSI disk interfaces, the drive and controller might also allocate an additional area past the logical end of the drive for a bad-track table and spare sectors. This situation may account for additional discrepancies between the FDISK and the drive manufacturer's reported sizes.

The diagnostics area enables software such as a manufacturer-supplied diagnostics disk to perform read-and-write tests on a hard disk without corrupting any user data.

VFAT and Long File Names

The original Windows 95 release uses what is essentially the same FAT file system as DOS, except for a few important enhancements. Like much of the rest of Windows 95, the operating system support for the FAT file system was rewritten using 32-bit code and called VFAT, or *Virtual File Allocation Table*. VFAT works in combination with the 32-bit protected mode VCACHE (that replaces the 16-bit real mode SMARTDrive cache used in DOS and Windows 3.1) to provide better file system performance. However, the most obvious improvement in VFAT is its support for long file names. DOS and Windows 3.1 had been encumbered by the standard 8.3 file naming convention for many years and adding long file name support was a high priority in Windows 95, particularly in light of the fact that Macintosh and OS/2 users had long enjoyed this capability.

The problem for the Windows 95 designers, as is often the case in the PC industry, was backward compatibility. It is no great feat to make long file names possible when you are designing a new file system from scratch, as Microsoft did years before with Windows NT's NTFS. However, the Windows 95 developers wanted to add long file names to the existing FAT file system, while still making it possible to store those names on existing DOS volumes and for previous versions of DOS and Windows to access the files.

VFAT provides the capability to assign file and directory names that are up to 255 characters in length (including the length of the path). The 3-character extension is maintained because, like previous Windows versions, Windows 95 relies on the extensions to associate file types with specific applications. VFAT's long file names can also include spaces, as well as the following characters, which standard DOS 8.3 names cannot: +,;=[].

The first problem when implementing the long file names was how to make them usable to previous versions of DOS and 16-bit Windows applications that support only 8.3 names. The resolution to this problem is to give each file two names: a long file name and an alias that uses the traditional 8.3 naming convention. When you create a file with a long file name in Windows 9x, VFAT uses the following process to create an equivalent 8.3 alias name:

1. The first three characters after the last dot in the long file name become the extension of the alias.

2. The first six characters of the long file name (excluding spaces, which are ignored) are converted into uppercase, and become the first six characters of the alias file name. If any of these six characters are illegal under the standard 8.3 naming rules (that is, +,;=[or]), VFAT converts those characters into underscores.

3. VFAT adds the two characters ~1 as the seventh and eighth characters of the alias file name, unless this will result in a name conflict, in which case it uses ~2, ~3, and so on, as needed.

> **Tip**
>
> You can modify the behavior of the VFAT file name truncation mechanism to make it use the first eight characters of the long file name instead of the first six characters plus ~1. To do this, you must add a new binary value to the HKEY_LOCAL_MACHINE\System\CurrentControlSet\control\FileSystem Registry key called *NameNumericTail*, with a value of 0. Changing the value to 1 returns the truncation process to its original state.

VFAT stores this alias file name in the standard name field of the file's directory entry. Any version of DOS or 16-bit Windows can therefore access the file using the alias name. The big problem that still remains, however, is where to store the long file names. Clearly, it is not possible to store a 255-character file name in a 32-byte directory entry (because each character requires one byte). However, modifying the structure of the directory entry would make the files unusable by previous DOS versions.

The developers of VFAT resolved this problem by using additional directory entries to store the long file names. Each of the directory entries is still 32 bytes long, so up to eight may be required for each long name, depending on its length. To ensure that these additional directory entries are not misinterpreted by earlier DOS versions, VFAT flags them with a combination of attributes that is not possible for a normal file: read-only, hidden, system, and volume label. These attributes cause DOS to ignore the long file name entries, while preventing them from being mistakenly overwritten.

This solution for implementing backward-compatible long file names in Windows 9x is ingenious, but it is not without its problems. Most of these problems stem from the use of applications that can access only the 8.3 alias names assigned to files. In some cases, if you open a file with a long name using one of these programs and then save it again, the connection to the additional directory entries containing the long name is severed and the long name is lost.

This is especially true for older versions of disk utilities, such as Norton Disk Doctor, that are not designed to support VFAT. Most older applications ignore the additional directory entries because of the combination of attributes assigned to them, but disk repair utilities are usually designed to detect and "correct" discrepancies of this type. The result is that running an old version of Norton Disk Doctor on a partition with long file names will result in the loss of all the long names. In the same way, backup utilities not designed for use with VFAT can strip off the long file names from a partition.

Another problem with VFAT's long file names involves the process by which the file system creates the 8.3 alias names. VFAT creates a new alias every time you create or copy a file into a new directory, meaning that it is possible for the alias to change. For example, you may have a file called Expenses-January98.doc stored in a directory with the alias EXPENS~1.DOC. If you use Windows 9x Explorer to copy this file to another directory that already contains a file called Expenses-December97.doc, you are likely to find that this existing file is already using the alias EXPENS~1.DOC. In this case, VFAT will assign EXPENS~2.DOC as the alias of the newly copied file, with no warning to the user. This is not a problem for applications that support VFAT because the long file names are unchanged, but a user running an older application may open the EXPENS~1.DOC file expecting to find the list of January 1998 expenses, and see the December 1997 expenses list instead.

FAT32

When the FAT file system was being developed, 2G hard disk drives were a fantasy, and no one expected the partition size limitation imposed by the combination of 16-bit FAT entries and 32K cluster sizes to be a problem. Today, however, even low-end PCs come equipped with hard drives holding at least 2G, and 6 or 8G drives are common. When you use the standard FAT file system with these larger drives, you have to create several partitions, each no larger than approximately 2G. To many users, having multiple drive letters representing a single disk is confusing, making it difficult to organize and locate files.

To address this problem, Microsoft has released an enhanced version of the FAT file system, called FAT32. Unlike VFAT, which is a Windows 9x innovation that makes use of existing file system structures, FAT32 is an enhancement of the FAT file system itself. In other words, while VFAT is implemented as part of the Windows 9x Virtual Machine Manager (Vmm.vxd), FAT32 is implemented by the FDISK program, before the Windows GUI is even loaded. FAT32 was first included in the Windows 95 OEM Service Release 2 (OSR2), and is also part of Windows 98. Windows NT 5.0 will also provide support for FAT32.

Note

Because the FAT32 file system is implemented by the FDISK utility when you partition the drive, you cannot use it on a floppy disk or any removable cartridge that does not have a partition table. However, any medium that you can partition with FDISK, such as an Iomega Jaz cartridge, can use FAT32.

The most obvious improvement in FAT32 is that by using 32-bit values for FAT entries instead of 16-bit ones, the maximum number of clusters allowed in a single partition jumps from 65,536 (2^{16}) to 268,435,456. This value is equivalent to 2^{28}, not 2^{32}, because four bits out of the 32 are reserved for other uses. FAT32 also uses 32-bit values for the low-level operating system calls used to retrieve a specific disk sector.

These expanded values blow the top off of the 2G limit on partition sizes; FAT32 partitions can theoretically be up to 2T in size (1 terabyte = 1,024 gigabytes). This figure that is derived from a new maximum of 4,294,967,296 (2^{32}) possible 512-byte sectors. Individual files can be up to 4G in size, as limited by the size field in the directory entry, which is 4 bytes long. Because the clusters are numbered using 32-bit values instead of 16-bit ones, the format of the directory entries on a FAT32 partition must be changed slightly. The 2-byte link to start cluster field is increased to 4 bytes, using two of the ten bytes (bytes 12 to 21) in the directory entry that were reserved for future use.

Another important difference in FAT32 partitions is the nature of the root directory. In a FAT32 partition, the root directory does not occupy a fixed position on the disk as in a FAT16 partition. Instead, it can be located anywhere in the partition and expand to any size. This eliminates the preset limit on root directory entries and provides the infrastructure needed to make FAT32 partitions dynamically resizable. Microsoft has not yet implemented this feature in Windows 9x, but there are third-party products such as PowerQuest's Partition Magic that take advantage of this capability.

The primary drawback of FAT32 is that it is not compatible with previous versions of DOS and Windows 95. You cannot boot to a previous version of DOS or (pre-OSR2) Windows 95 from a FAT32 drive, nor will a system started with an old DOS or Windows 95 boot disk be able to see FAT32 partitions. Apart from Windows 95 OSR2 and Windows 98, the only operating system that natively supports FAT32 is Linux.

FAT32 Cluster Sizes

Because FAT32 partitions can have so many more clusters than FAT16 partitions, the clusters themselves can be smaller. Using smaller clusters reduces the wasted disk space caused by slack. For example, the same 2G partition with 5,000 files on it mentioned earlier would use 4K clusters with FAT32 instead of 32K clusters with FAT16. Assuming the same amount of slack for each file, the smaller cluster size reduces the wasted space on that partition from over 78M to under 10M.

> **Note**
>
> *PC Magazine* has released a free DOS utility called CHKDRV that calculates the slack on a FAT16 or FAT32 partition. You can download this program from **ftp://ftp.zdnet.com/pcmag/1995/ 0627/chkdrv.zip**.

Table 19.9 lists the cluster sizes for various FAT32 partition sizes.

Table 19.9   FAT32 Cluster Sizes

Partition Size	Cluster Size
0M to less than 260M	512 bytes
260M–8G	4,096 bytes
6–16G	8,192 bytes
16–32G	16,384 bytes
32G–2T	32,768 bytes

Of course, using smaller clusters means that there must be many more of them, and more entries in the FAT as well. A 2G partition using FAT32 requires 524,288 FAT entries, while the same drive needs only 65,536 entries using FAT16. Thus, the size of one copy of the FAT16 table is 128K (65,536 entries * 16 bits = 1,048,576 bits/8 = 131,072 bytes/ 1,024 = 128K), while the FAT32 table is 2M in size.

The size of the FAT has a definite impact on the performance of the file system. Windows 9x uses its VCACHE to try to keep the FAT in memory at all times to improve file system performance. The use of 4K clusters for drives up to 8G in size is therefore a reasonable compromise for the average PC's memory capacity. Were the file system to use clusters that are equal to one disk sector (1 sector = 512K) in an attempt to minimize slack as much as possible, the FAT table for a 2G drive would contain 4,194,304 entries and be 16M in size.

This would monopolize a substantial portion of the memory in the average system, probably resulting in noticeably degraded performance. Although it may at first seem as though even a 2M FAT is quite large when compared to 128K, keep in mind that hard disk drives are a great deal faster now than they were when the FAT file system was originally designed. In practice, implementing FAT32 on a Windows 9x system typically results in a minor (less than 5%) improvement in file system performance. However, systems that perform a great many sequential disk writes may see an equally minor degradation in performance.

FAT Mirroring

FAT32 also takes greater advantage of the two copies of the FAT stored on a disk partition. On a FAT16 partition, the first copy of the FAT is always the primary copy and replicates its data to the secondary FAT, sometimes corrupting it in the process. On a FAT32 partition, when the system detects a problem with the primary copy of the FAT, it can switch to the other copy, which then becomes the primary. The system can also disable the FAT mirroring process, to prevent the viable FAT from being corrupted by the other copy. This provides a greater degree of fault tolerance to FAT32 partitions, often making it possible to repair a damaged FAT without an immediate system interruption or a loss of table data.

Creating FAT32 Partitions

Despite the substantial changes provided by FAT32, the new file system does have a large effect on the procedures you use to create and manage partitions. You create new FAT32 partitions in Windows 9x using the FDISK utility from the command prompt, just like you would create FAT16 partitions. When you launch FDISK, the program examines your hard disk drives and, if they have a capacity larger than 512M, presents the following message:

```
Your computer has a disk larger than 512 MB. This version of Windows
includes improved support for large disks, resulting in more efficient
use of disk space on large drives, and allowing disks over 2 GB to be
formatted as a single drive.

IMPORTANT: If you enable large disk support and create any new drives on this
disk, you will not be able to access the new drive(s) using other operating
systems, including some versions of Windows 95 and Windows NT, as well as
earlier versions of Windows and MS-DOS. In addition, disk utilities that
were not designed explicitly for the FAT32 file system will not be able
to work with this disk. If you need to access this disk with other operating
systems or older disk utilities, do not enable large drive support.

Do you wish to enable large disk support (Y/N)...........? [N]
```

If you answer yes to this question, then any partitions you create that are larger than 512M will be FAT32 partitions. If you want to create partitions larger than 2G, then you must use FAT32. Otherwise, you can choose which file system you prefer. All the screens following this one are the same as those in previous versions of FDISK.

Normally, the FDISK utility determines the cluster size that will be used when you format the partition, based on the partition's size and the file system used. However, you can override FDISK using an undocumented switch for the FORMAT utility. If you use the command

```
FORMAT /Z:n
```

where *n* multiplied by 512 equals the desired cluster size in bytes, you can create a partition that uses cluster sizes that are larger or smaller than the defaults for the file system.

> **Caution**
>
> The /Z switch does not override the 65,536 cluster limit on FAT16 partitions, so it is recommended that you use it only with FAT32. In addition, you should not use this switch on a production system without extensive testing first. Modifying the cluster size may increase or reduce the amount of slack on the partition, but it also may have a pronounced effect on the performance of the drive.

Converting FAT16 to FAT32

The Windows 95 OSR2 release can create FAT32 partitions only out of empty disk space. If you want to convert an existing FAT16 partition to FAT32, you have to back up the data, destroy the FAT16 partition, create a new FAT32 partition, and then restore the data. Windows 98, on the other hand, includes a FAT32 conversion wizard that enables you to migrate existing partitions in place.

The wizard gathers the information needed to perform the conversion, informs you of the consequences of implementing FAT32, and attempts to prevent data loss and other problems. After you have selected the drive that you want to convert (see Figure 19.2), the wizard performs a scan for applications (such as disk utilities) that might not function properly on the converted partition. The wizard gives you the opportunity to remove these. The wizard also warns you to back up the data on the partition before proceeding with the conversion. Even if you don't use the Microsoft Backup utility that the wizard offers, backing up your data is a strongly recommended precaution.

After you answer all the wizard's prompts and confirm that you want to continue with the conversion, the system reboots to a DOS prompt. The actual conversion is a DOS process, making it possible to convert even the partition on which Windows 98 is installed. Because the conversion must deal with the existing partition data in addition to creating new volume boot sector information, FATs, and clusters, the process can take far longer than partitioning and formatting an empty drive. Depending on the amount of data involved and the new cluster size, the conversion may take several hours to complete.

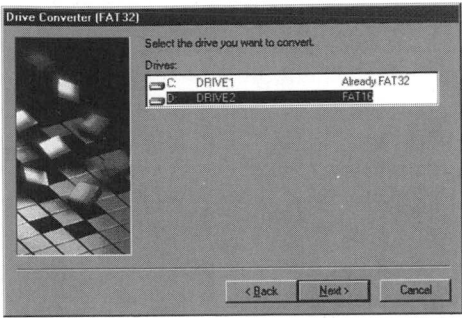

FIG. 19.2 The FAT32 Conversion Wizard enables Windows 98 users to convert existing FAT16 partitions to FAT32.

After you convert a FAT16 partition to FAT32, you cannot convert it back with Windows 98's tools, except by destroying the partition and using FDISK to create a new one. Therefore, be sure to carefully consider your actions before proceeding. It is also a good idea to take other precautions before beginning the conversion process, such as connecting the system to a UPS. A power failure during the conversion could result in a loss of data.

FAT32 and Partition Magic

Windows 95 OSR2 and Windows 98 include only basic tools for creating FAT32 partitions, but there is a product called Partition Magic, from PowerQuest, that provides many other partition manipulation features. Partition Magic can convert FAT16 partitions to FAT32 in place, as the Windows 98 FAT32 Conversion Wizard can, but unlike Windows 98, it can also convert FAT32 partitioned back to FAT16.

Among many other things, this product can also resize FAT16 and FAT32 partitions without destroying the data they contain, shrink and expand FAT clusters, and tell you how much disk space you will save as the result of changing the cluster size. Partition Magic takes advantage of the inherent capabilities of the FAT16 and FAT32 file systems to provide features that will probably be added to Windows 9x at some future time.

FAT File System Errors

File system errors can, of course, occur because of hardware problems, but you are more likely to see them result from software crashes and improper system handling. Turning off a system without shutting down Windows properly, for example, can result in errors that cause clusters to be incorrectly listed as in use when they are not. Some of the most common file system errors that occur on FAT partitions are described in the following sections.

Lost Clusters

Probably the most common file system error, lost clusters are clusters that the FAT designates as being in use when they actually are not. Most often caused by an interruption of a file system process, due to an application crash or a system shutdown, for example, the FAT entry of a lost cluster may contain a reference to a subsequent cluster. However, the FAT chain stemming from the directory entry has been broken somewhere along the line.

Disk repair programs check for lost clusters by tracing the FAT chain for each file and subdirectory in the partition, and building a facsimile of the FAT in memory. After compiling a list of all the FAT entries that indicate properly allocated clusters, the program compares this facsimile with the actual FAT. Any entries denoting allocated clusters in the real FAT that do not appear in the facsimile are lost clusters because they are not part of a valid FAT chain.

The utility typically gives you the opportunity to save the data in the lost clusters as a file before it changes the FAT entries to show them as unallocated clusters. If your system crashed or lost power while you were working with a word processor data file, for example, you may be able to retrieve text from the lost clusters in this way. When left unrepaired, lost clusters are unavailable for use by the system, reducing the storage capacity of your drive.

Cross-Linked Files

Cross-linked files occur when two directory entries improperly reference the same cluster in their Link to Start Cluster fields. The result of this is that each file utilizes the same FAT chain. Because the clusters can store data from only one file, working with one of the two files can inadvertently overwrite the other file's data.

Detecting cross-linked files is a relatively easy task for a disk repair utility because it has to examine only the partition's directory entries, and not the file clusters themselves. However, by the time that the utility detects the error, the data from one of the two files is probably already lost, although you may be able to recover parts of it from lost clusters.

Invalid Files or Directories

Sometimes the information in a directory entry for a file or subdirectory can be corrupted to the point at which the entry is not just erroneous (as in cross-linked files) but invalid. The entry may have a cluster or date reference that is invalid or may violate the rules for the entry format in some other way. In most cases, disk repair software can correct these problems, permitting access to the file.

FAT Errors

As discussed earlier, corruption of the FAT can sometimes be repaired by accessing its duplicate copy. Disk repair utilities typically rely on this technique to restore a damaged FAT to its original state, as long as the copy has not been corrupted by the mirroring process. FAT32 tables are more likely to be repairable, because their more advanced mirroring capabilities make it less likely for the copy to be corrupted.

FAT File System Utilities

The CHKDSK, RECOVER, and SCANDISK commands are the DOS damaged disk recovery team. These commands are crude, and their actions sometimes are drastic, but at times they are all that is available or needed. RECOVER is best known for its function as a data recovery program. CHKDSK usually is used for inspection of the file structure. Many users are unaware that CHKDSK can implement repairs to a damaged file structure. DEBUG, a crude, manually controlled program, can help in the case of a disk disaster, if you know exactly what you are doing.

SCANDISK is a safer, more automated, more powerful replacement for CHKDSK and RECOVER. It should be used in their place if you are running DOS 6 or higher or Windows 9x.

The *CHKDSK* Command

The useful and powerful DOS CHKDSK command is frequently misunderstood. To casual users, the primary function of CHKDSK seems to be providing a disk space allocation report for a given volume as well as a memory allocation report. CHKDSK does those things, but its primary value is in discovering, defining, and repairing problems with the DOS directory and FAT system on a disk volume. In handling data recovery problems, CHKDSK is a valuable tool, although it is crude and simplistic compared to some of the aftermarket utilities that perform similar functions.

The output of the CHKDSK command when it runs on a typical hard disk is as follows:

```
Volume 4GB_SCSI    created 01-31-1998 5:05p
Volume Serial Number is 1882-18CF

2,146,631,680 bytes total disk space
      163,840 bytes in 3 hidden files
   16,220,160 bytes in 495 directories
  861,634,560 bytes in 10,355 user files
1,268,613,120 bytes available on disk

       32,768 bytes in each allocation unit
       65,510 total allocation units on disk
       38,715 available allocation units on disk

      655,360 total bytes memory
      632,736 bytes free
```

A little-known CHKDSK function is its capability to report on a specified file's (or group of files') level of fragmentation. CHKDSK can also produce a list of all files (including hidden and system files) on a particular volume, such as a super DIR command. By far, the most important CHKDSK capabilities are its detection and correction of problems in the FAT file system.

The name of the CHKDSK program is misleading: It seems to be a contraction of CHECK DISK. The program does not actually check a disk, or even the files on a disk, for integrity. CHKDSK cannot even truly show how many bad sectors are on a disk, much less locate and mark them. The real function of CHKDSK is to inspect the directories and FATs to see whether they correspond with each other or contain discrepancies. CHKDSK does not detect (and does not report on) damage in a file; it checks only the FAT and directory areas of a disk.

CHKDSK also can test files for contiguity. Files loaded into contiguous tracks and sectors of a disk or floppy disk naturally are more efficient. Files spread over wide areas of the disk make access operations take longer. DOS always knows the location of all a file's fragments by using the cluster references in the FAT. Sometimes, for various reasons, these references might be lost or corrupted and leave DOS incapable of locating some portion of a file. Using CHKDSK can alert you to this condition and even enable you to reclaim the unused file space.

***CHKDSK* Command Syntax.** The syntax of the CHKDSK command is as follows:

    CHKDSK [*d:\path*] [*filename*] [/F] [/V]

The *d:* switch specifies the disk volume to analyze. The *\path* and *filename* options specify files to check for fragmentation in addition to the volume analysis. Wild cards are permitted in the file name specification, to specify multiple files in a specified directory for fragmentation analysis. One limitation of the fragmentation analysis is that it does not check for fragmentation across directory boundaries, only within a specified directory.

The /F (Fix) switch enables CHKDSK to perform repairs if it finds problems with the directories and FATs. If /F is not specified, the program cannot write to the disk and no repairs are performed.

The /V (Verbose) switch causes the program to list all the entries in all the directories on a disk and give detailed information in cases where it encounters errors.

The drive, path, and file specifiers are optional. If you add no parameters for the command, CHKDSK processes the default volume or drive and does not check files for contiguity. If you specify [*path*] and [*filename*] parameters, CHKDSK checks all specified files to see whether they are stored contiguously on the disk. The program displays one of two messages as a result:

    All specified file(s) are contiguous

or

    [*filename*] Contains xxx non-contiguous blocks

CHKDSK displays the second message for each file on the disk that it finds to be fragmented and displays the number of fragments that compose the file. A *fragmented file* is one that is scattered around the disk in pieces rather than existing in one contiguous area of the disk. Fragmented files are slower to load than contiguous files, which reduces disk performance. Fragmented files are also much more difficult to recover if a problem with the FAT or directory on the disk occurs.

If you have only DOS, there are several ways to accomplish a full defragmentation. To defragment files on a floppy disk, you can format a new floppy disk and use COPY or XCOPY to copy all the files from the fragmented disk to the replacement. For a hard disk, you must completely back up, format, and then restore the disk. This procedure is time-consuming and dangerous, which is why there are so many third-party defragmenting utilities available.

CHKDSK Operation

CHKDSK reports problems found in a disk volume's FAT or directory system with one of several descriptive messages that vary to fit the specific error. Sometimes the messages are cryptic or misleading. CHKDSK does not specify how an error should be handled. It does not tell you whether CHKDSK can repair the problem, whether you must use some other utility, or what the consequences of the error and the repair will be. Neither does CHKDSK tell you what caused the problem nor how to avoid repeating the problem.

The primary function of CHKDSK is to compare the directory and FAT to determine whether they agree with each other—whether all the data in the directory entries for the files (such as the starting cluster and size information) corresponds to what is in the FAT (such as chains of clusters with end-of-chain indicators). CHKDSK also checks subdirectory file entries, as well as the special "dot" (.) and "double dot" (..) entries that tie the subdirectory system together.

The second function of CHKDSK is to implement repairs to the disk structure. CHKDSK patches the disk so that the directory and FAT are in alignment and agreement. From a repair standpoint, understanding CHKDSK is relatively easy. CHKDSK almost always modifies the directories on a disk to correspond to what it finds in the FAT. There are only a few special cases in which CHKDSK modifies the FAT. When it does, the FAT modifications are always the same type of simple change.

Think of CHKDSK's repair capability as a directory patcher. Because CHKDSK cannot repair most types of FAT damage effectively, it simply modifies the disk directories to match whatever problems it finds in the FAT.

CHKDSK is not a very smart repair program and often can do more damage repairing the disk than if it had left the disk alone. In many cases, the information in the directories is correct and can be used (by some other utility) to help repair the FAT tables. If you have run CHKDSK with the /F parameter, however, the original directory information no longer exists, and a good FAT repair is impossible.

> **Caution**
>
> You should never run CHKDSK with the /F parameter without first running it in read-only mode (without the /F parameter) to determine whether and to what extent damage exists.

Only after carefully examining the disk damage and determining how CHKDSK would fix the problems should you run CHKDSK with the /F parameter. If you do not specify the /F parameter when you run CHKDSK, the program does not make corrections to the disk. Rather, it performs repairs in a mock fashion. This limitation is a safety feature because you do not want CHKDSK to take action until you have examined the problem. After deciding whether CHKDSK will make the correct assumptions about the damage, you might want to run it with the /F parameter.

Caution

Sometimes people place a CHKDSK /F command in their AUTOEXEC.BAT file—this is *a very dangerous practice*. If a system's disk directories and FAT system become damaged, attempting to load a program whose directory and FAT entries are damaged might lock the system. If, after you reboot, CHKDSK is fixing the problem because it is in the AUTOEXEC.BAT, it can irreparably damage the file structure of the disk. In many cases, CHKDSK ends up causing more damage than originally existed, and no easy way exists to undo the CHKDSK repair. Because CHKDSK is a simple utility that often makes faulty assumptions in repairing a disk, you must run it with great care when you specify the /F parameter.

Problems reported by CHKDSK are usually problems with the software and not the hardware. You rarely see a case in which lost clusters, allocation errors, or cross-linked files reported by CHKDSK were caused directly by a hardware fault, although it is certainly possible. The cause is usually a defective program or a program that was stopped before it could close files or purge buffers. A hardware fault certainly can stop a program before it can close files, but many people think that these error messages signify fault with the disk hardware, which is almost never the case.

The *RECOVER* Command

The DOS RECOVER command is designed to mark clusters as bad in the FAT when the clusters cannot be read properly. When the system cannot read a file because of a problem with a sector on the disk going bad, the RECOVER command can mark the FAT so that those clusters are not used by another file. When used improperly, this program is highly dangerous. The RECOVER utility has not been included in DOS since version 5 and is not supplied in Windows 9x, as its functionality has been replaced by SCANDISK.

Caution

Be very careful when you use RECOVER. Used improperly, it can do severe damage to your files and the FAT. If you enter the RECOVER command without a file name for it to work on, the program assumes that you want every file on the disk recovered, and operates on every file and subdirectory on the disk. It converts all subdirectories to files, places all file names in the root directory, and gives them new names (FILE0000.REC, FILE0001.REC, and so on). This process essentially wipes out the file system on the entire disk. *Do not use RECOVER without providing a file name for it to work on*. This program should be considered as dangerous as the FORMAT command.

SCANDISK

It's a good idea to check your FAT partitions regularly for the problems discussed in this chapter and any other difficulties that may arise. By far an easier and more effective solution for disk diagnosis and repair than CHKDSK and RECOVER is the SCANDISK utility, included with DOS 6 and higher versions as well as with Windows 9x. This program is more thorough and comprehensive than CHKDSK or RECOVER, and can perform the functions of both of them, and a great deal more. Windows 95 OSR2 and Windows 98 include SCANDISK versions that support FAT32 partitions.

SCANDISK is like a scaled-down version of third-party disk repair programs such as Norton Disk Doctor, and it can verify both file structure and disk sector integrity. If SCANDISK finds problems, it can repair directories and FATs. If the program finds bad sectors in the middle of a file, it marks the clusters (allocation units) containing the bad sectors as bad in the FAT, and attempts to read the file data by rerouting around the defect.

Windows 9x includes both DOS and Windows versions of SCANDISK, which are named SCANDISK.EXE and SCANDSKW.EXE, respectively. Windows 9x scans your drives at the beginning of the operating system installation process and automatically loads the DOS version of SCANDISK whenever you restart your system after turning it off without completing the proper shutdown procedure. You can also launch SCANDISK.EXE from a DOS prompt or from a batch file, using the following syntax.

```
Scandisk x: [/a] [/n] [/p] [dblspace.nnn/drvspace.nnn]
        x: - designator of the drive that you want to scan
        /a - scans all local fixed hard disks
        /n - noninteractive mode; requires no user input
        /p - scans only, without correcting errors
        /custom - runs Scandisk with the options configured in the [CUSTOM]
section of the Scandisk.ini file
dblspace.nnn or drvspace.nnn - scans a compressed volume file, where nnn is
replaced by the file extension (such as 001)
```

The SCANDISK.INI file, located in the C:\WINDOWS\COMMAND directory on a Windows 9x system by default, contains extensive and well-documented parameters that you can use to control the behavior of SCANDISK.EXE. Note that the options in the SCANDISK.INI file are applied only to the DOS version of the utility, and have no effect on the Windows GUI version.

You can also run the GUI version of the utility by opening the Start menu and choosing Programs, Accessories, System Tools. Both versions scan and repair the FAT and the directory and file structures, repair problems with long file names, and scan volumes that have been compressed with DriveSpace or DoubleSpace.

SCANDISK provides two basic testing options: Standard and Thorough. The difference between the two is that the Thorough option causes the program to scan the entire surface of the disk for errors in addition to the items just mentioned. You can also select whether to run the program interactively, or let it automatically repair any errors that it finds.

The DOS and Windows 9x versions of SCANDISK also test the FAT in different ways. The DOS version scans and, if necessary, repairs the primary copy of the file allocation table. After this it copies the repaired version of the primary to the backup copy. The Windows version, on the other hand, scans both copies of the FAT. If the program finds discrepancies between the two copies, it uses the data from the copy that it judges to be correct and reassembles the primary FAT using the best data from both copies.

SCANDISK also has an Advanced Options dialog box that enables you to set the following parameters:

- Whether the program should display a summary of its findings

- Whether the program should log its findings

- How the program should repair cross-linked files (two directory entries pointing to the same cluster)

- How the program should repair lost file fragments

- Whether to check files for invalid names, dates, and times

Although SCANDISK is good, and is certainly a vast improvement over CHKDSK, I would recommend using one of the commercial packages, such as the Norton Utilities, for any major disk problems. These utilities go far beyond what is included in DOS or Windows 9x.

Disk Defragmentation

The entire premise of the FAT file systems is based on the storage of data in clusters that can be located anywhere on the disk. This enables the computer to store a file of nearly any size, at any time. The process of following a FAT chain to locate all the clusters holding the data for a particular file can force the hard disk drive to access many different locations on the disk. Because of the physical work involved in moving the disk drive heads, reading a file that is heavily fragmented in this way is necessarily slower than reading one that is stored on consecutive clusters.

As you regularly add, move, and delete files on a disk over a period of time, the files become increasingly fragmented, which can slow down disk performance. You can relieve this problem by periodically running a disk defragmentation utility on your drives, such as the one included with Windows 9x. When you run Disk Defragmenter, the program reads each of the files in the disk, using the FAT table to access its clusters, wherever they may be located.

The program then writes the file to a series of contiguous clusters and deletes the original. By progressively reading, erasing, and writing files, the program eventually leaves the disk in a state where all its files exist on contiguous clusters. As a result, the drive is able to read any file on the disk with a minimum of head movement, thus providing what is often a noticeable performance increase.

The Windows 95 Disk Defragmentation utility provides this basic defragmenting function. It also enables you to select whether you want to arrange the files on the disk to consolidate the empty clusters into one contiguous free space (which takes longer). The Windows 98 version adds a feature that examines the files on the disk and arranges them with the most often used program files grouped together at the front of the disk, which can make programs load faster.

Third-party defragmentation utilities such as the Speed Disk program included in the Norton Utilities provide additional features, such as the capability to select specific files that should be moved to the front of the disk. Speed Disk can also defragment the Windows 9x swap file and files that are flagged with the System and Hidden attributes, which Disk Defragmenter will not touch.

> **Caution**
>
> Although the Disk Defragmentation utilities included with Windows 9x and third-party products are usually quite safe, you should always be aware that defragmenting a disk is an inherently dangerous procedure. The program reads, erases, and rewrites every file on the disk and has the potential to cause damage to your data when interrupted improperly. Although I have never seen a problem result from the process, an unforeseen event such as a power failure during a defragmentation procedure can conceivably be disastrous. I strongly recommend that you always run a disk repair utility such as SCANDISK on your drives before defragmenting them, and have a current backup ready.

Third-Party Programs

When you get a Sector not found error reading drive C:, by far the best course of action is to use one of the third-party disk repair utilities on the market, rather than DOS' RECOVER or even SCANDISK. The Norton Utilities by Symantec stands as perhaps the premier data recovery package on the market today. This package is comprehensive and automatically repairs most types of disk problems.

Programs such as the Norton Disk Doctor can perform much more detailed repairs, with a greater amount of safety. If the error is on a floppy disk, use Norton's DiskTool before you use Disk Doctor. DiskTool is specially designed to help you recover data from floppy disks. Disk Doctor and DiskTool preserve as much of the data in the file as possible, and can mark the FAT so the bad sectors or clusters of the disk are not used again. These programs also save Undo information, making it possible for you to reverse any data recovery operation.

Disk Doctor and DiskTool are part of Symantec's Norton Utilities package, which includes a great many other useful tools. For example, Norton Utilities has an excellent sector editor that enables you to view and edit any part of a disk, including the master and volume boot records, FATs, and other areas that fall outside of the disk's normal data area. Currently, there is no other program as comprehensive or as capable of editing disks at the sector level. The Disk Editor included with the Norton Utilities can give the professional PC troubleshooter or repairperson the ability to work directly with any sector on the disk, but this does require extensive knowledge of sector formats and disk structures. The documentation with the package is excellent and can be very helpful if you are learning data recovery on your own.

> **Note**
>
> Data recovery is a lucrative service that the more advanced technician can provide. People are willing to pay much more to get their data back than to replace a hard drive.

For more automatic recovery that anybody can perform, Norton Utilities has several other useful modules. Disk Doctor and Calibrate are two of the modules included with the Norton Utilities (both version 8.0 for DOS/Windows and version 3.0 for Windows 95). Together, these two utilities provide exhaustive testing of the data structures and sectors of a hard drive. Disk Doctor works with both hard disks and floppy disks. It tests the capability of the drive to work with the system in which it is installed, including the drive's boot sector, file allocation tables (FAT), file structure, and data areas. Calibrate, which is used for the most intensive testing of the data area of a drive, also tests the hard drive controller electronics.

You can also use Calibrate to perform deep-pattern testing of IDE and SCSI drives. This process writes millions of bytes of data to every sector of the drive to see whether it can properly retain data. It moves data if the sector where the data is stored is flawed. Bad sectors are then marked as bad in the FAT.

Due to the excellent Disk Editor, anybody serious about data recovery needs a copy of Norton Utilities. The many other modules that are included are excellent as well. The latest versions now include NDIAGS, which is a comprehensive PC hardware diagnostic.

The most important consideration when you purchase third-party disk utilities is to choose products that support your file system. Norton Utilities, for example, is available in a DOS version and a Windows 9x version, and only the latter supports FAT32 partitions.

NTFS

NTFS is Windows NT's native file system. Although NT supports FAT partitions, NTFS provides many advantages over FAT, including long file names, support for larger files and partitions, extended attributes, and increased security. NTFS, like all of Windows NT, was newly designed from the ground up. Backward compatibility with previous Microsoft operating systems was not a concern, as the developers were intent on creating an entirely new 32-bit platform. As a result, no operating systems other than Windows NT can read NTFS partitions.

This is an important consideration. All the other Windows operating systems are fundamentally based on DOS and leave you the alternative of booting to a DOS prompt in special situations. Whether you have to run a special DOS utility to configure a piece of hardware or perform an emergency disk repair, the DOS option is always there.

Windows NT is not DOS-based. You can open a window that provides a DOS-like command prompt in Windows NT, but this is actually a DOS emulation, not a true shell. You cannot boot the system to a command prompt, avoiding the GUI, as you can with Windows 9x. You can, of course, bypass NT entirely by starting the system with a DOS boot disk, but if you have NTFS partitions on your drives, you will not be able to access them from the DOS prompt.

NTFS supports file names of up to 255 characters, using spaces, multiple periods, and any other standard characters except the following: *?/\;<>|. Because NTFS file offsets are 64 bits long, files and partitions can be truly enormous: up to 16E (*exabytes*) in size (1 exabyte = 2^{64} bytes = 17,179,869,184 terabytes)! To give you an idea of just how much data this is, it is estimated that all the words ever spoken by human beings throughout history would occupy 5E of storage.

NTFS Architecture

Although NTFS partitions are very different from FAT partitions internally, they do comply with the extra-partitional disk structures described earlier in this chapter. NTFS partitions are listed in the master partition table of a disk drive's master boot record, just like FAT partitions, and they have a volume boot sector as well, although it is formatted somewhat differently.

An NTFS partition is based on a structure called the Master File Table, or MFT. The MFT concept expands on that of the FAT. Instead of using a table of cluster references, the MFT contains much more detailed information about the files and directories in the partition. In some cases, it even contains the files and directories themselves.

The first record in the MFT is called the *descriptor*, which contains information about the MFT itself. The volume boot sector for an NTFS partition contains a reference that points to the location of this descriptor record. The second record in the MFT is a mirror copy of the descriptor, which copy provides fault tolerance, should the first copy be damaged.

The third record is the log file record. All NTFS transactions are logged to a file that can be used to restore data in the event of a disk problem. The bulk of the MFT consists of records for the files and directories that are stored on the partition. NTFS files take the form of objects that have both user- and system-defined attributes. Attributes on NTFS partitions are more comprehensive than the few simple flags used on FAT partitions. All the information on an NTFS file is stored as attributes of that file. In fact, even the file data itself is an attribute. Unlike FAT files, the attributes of NTFS files are part of the file itself; they are not listed separately in a directory entry. Directories exist as MFT records as well, but they consist mainly of indexes listing the files in the directory; they do not contain the size, date, time, and other information about the individual files.

Thus, an NTFS drive's MFT is much more than a cluster list, like a FAT; it is actually the primary data storage structure on the partition. If a file or directory is relatively small (less than approximately 1,500 bytes), the entire thing may even be stored in the MFT. For larger amounts of storage, the MFT record for a file or directory contains pointers to external clusters in the partition. These external clusters are called *extents*. All the records in the MFT, including the descriptors and the log file, are capable of using extents for storage of additional attributes. The attributes of a file that are part of the MFT record are called *resident* attributes. Those stored in extents are called *nonresident* attributes.

NTFS Compatibility

Although NTFS partitions are not directly accessible by DOS and other operating systems, Windows NT is designed for network use, and NTFS files are expected to be accessed by other operating systems. For this reason, NTFS continues to support the standard DOS file attributes and the 8.3 FAT naming convention.

One of the main reasons for using NTFS is the security that it provides for its files and directories. NTFS security attributes are called *permissions*, and are designed to enable system administrators to control access to files and directories by granting specific rights to users and groups. This is a much more granular approach than the FAT file system attributes, which apply to all users.

However, you can still set the FAT-style attributes on NTFS files using the standard Windows NT file management tools, including Windows NT Explorer and even the DOS ATTRIB command. When you copy FAT files to an NTFS drive over the network, the FAT-style attributes remain in place until you explicitly remove them. This can be an important consideration, because the FAT-style attributes take precedence over the NTFS permissions. A file on an NTFS drive that is flagged with the FAT read-only attribute, for example, cannot be deleted by a Windows NT user, even if that user has NTFS permissions that grant them full access.

To enable DOS and 16-bit Windows systems to access files on NTFS partitions over a network, the file system maintains an 8.3 alias name for every file and directory on the partition. The algorithm for deriving the alias from the long file name is the same as that used by Windows 95's VFAT. Windows NT also provides its FAT partitions with the same type of long file name support used by VFAT, allocating additional directory entries to store the long file names as needed.

Creating NTFS Drives

NTFS is for use on hard disk drives. You cannot create an NTFS floppy disk (although you can format removable media such as Iomega Zip and Jaz cartridges to use NTFS). Three basic ways to create an NTFS disk partition are

- Create a new NTFS volume out of unpartitioned disk space during the Windows NT installation process or after the installation with the Disk Administrator utility.

- Format an existing partition to NTFS (destroying its data in the process) using the Windows NT Format dialog box (accessible from Windows NT Explorer or Disk Administrator) or the FORMAT command (with the /fs:ntfs switch) from the command prompt.

- Convert an existing FAT partition to NTFS (preserving its data) during the Windows NT installation process or after the installation with the command-line CONVERT utility.

NTFS Tools

Because it uses a fundamentally different architecture, virtually none of the trouble-shooting techniques outlined earlier in this chapter are applicable when dealing with NTFS partitions, nor can the disk utilities intended for use on FAT partitions address them. Windows NT has a rudimentary capability to check a disk for file system errors and bad sectors, but apart from that, the operating system contains no other disk repair or defragmentation utilities.

The NTFS file system, however, does have its own automatic disk repair capabilities. In addition to Windows NT's fault-tolerance features, such as disk mirroring (maintaining the same data on two separate drives) and disk striping with parity (splitting data across several drives with parity information for data reconstruction), the OS also uses a disk error recover technique called *cluster remapping*.

With cluster remapping, when Windows NT detects a bad sector on an NTFS partition, it automatically remaps to another cluster the data in the cluster containing that sector. If the drive is part of a fault-tolerant drive array, any lost data is reconstructed from the duplicate data on the other drive(s).

Despite these features, however, there is still a real need for disk repair and defragmentation utilities for Windows NT. They have been a long time in coming, but there are now finally third-party utilities that can repair and defragment NTFS drives.

Chapter 20

IBM Personal Computer Family Hardware

Although IBM no longer seems in a position to dictate the majority of PC standards (Intel and Microsoft seem to have taken on that role), all the original PC specifications and standards were determined by IBM and set forth in its original line of personal computers. From these original IBM PC, XT, and AT systems came many of the standards to which even new systems today must still conform. This includes motherboard form factors, case and power supply designs, ISA bus architecture, system resource usage, memory mapping and architecture, system interfaces, connectors, pinouts, and more. As such, nearly every PC-compatible system on the market today is based in some form on one or more of the original IBM products. The original lines of systems are often called *Industry Standard Architecture (ISA) systems*, or *Classic PCs*. IBM calls them *Family/1 systems*.

This chapter serves as a technical reference for IBM's original family of personal computer systems. Much of the information in this chapter serves as a sort of history lesson; it is easy to see how far IBM-compatible computing has come when you look over the specifications of the original systems the PC standard is based on. I find the information valuable to teach others the origins of what we call a PC-compatible system.

Because the PC compatibles are mostly based on the IBM XT and especially AT systems, you can see where things such as the motherboard, case, and power supply shapes came from, the positions of slots, connectors, and other components on the boards, and the levels of performance these systems originally offered.

Although these systems have long since been discontinued, I am amazed that I still find many of these systems in use. From individuals to large corporations, to the government and military, I still occasionally encounter these old systems in my training and consulting practice. Often the only part that remains of the original system is the case and power supply, because newer Baby-AT form factor motherboards easily fit in most of the original IBM machines. In fact, I still have several of the original IBM XT and AT cases around that now sport modern Pentium motherboards, large hard drives, and all-new components!

System-Unit Features by Model

The following sections discuss the makeup of all the various versions or models of the original IBM systems, and also include technical details and specifications of each system. Every system unit has a few standard parts. The primary component is the *motherboard*, which has the CPU (central processing unit, or microprocessor) and other primary computer circuitry. Each unit also includes a case with an internal power supply, a keyboard, certain standard adapters or plug-in cards, and usually some form of disk drive.

There is an explanation of each system's various submodels and details about the differences between and features of each model. The changes from model to model and version to version of each system are also shown.

Included for your reference is part-number information for some of the systems and options. This information is for comparison and reference purposes only; all these systems have been discontinued and generally are no longer available. However, it is interesting to note that IBM still stocks and sells component parts and assemblies for even these discontinued units—including the original PC, XT, and AT systems.

The original IBM systems can be identified not only by their name, but by a number assigned to each system. IBM normally put the name of the computer on a small 1×1-inch-square brushed-metal plate on the front cover, and the system number on a similar metal plate on the rear of the chassis. The system names and numbers correspond as follows:

System Number	System Name
4860	PCjr
5140	PC Convertible (laptop)
5150	PC
5155	Portable PC (really a portable XT)
5160	XT
5162	XT-286 (really an AT)
5170	AT

Note that because modern PC components are often designed to be physically compatible with the original IBM systems, you can (and usually should) replace any failed or obsolete components in the older IBM systems with non-IBM replacement parts. Invariably you will be able to obtain upgraded or improved components compared to the originals, and at a greatly reduced price. An example is one original 286 IBM AT that I have that now sports a Pentium MMX motherboard, 64M of RAM, 9G SCSI drive, 12x CD-ROM, and a host of other options. Of course, the only original IBM parts left in the system are the case and power supply, which are both more than 14 years old!

An Introduction to the PC (5150)

IBM introduced the IBM Personal Computer on August 12, 1981, and officially withdrew the machine from the market on April 2, 1987. During the nearly six-year life of the PC, IBM made only a few basic changes to the system. The basic motherboard circuit design was changed in April 1983 to accommodate 64K RAM chips. Three different ROM BIOS versions were used during the life of the system; most other specifications, however, remained unchanged. Because IBM no longer markets the PC system, and because of the PC's relatively limited expansion capability and power, the standard PC is obsolete by most standards.

The system unit supports only floppy disk drives unless the power supply is upgraded or an expansion chassis is used to house the hard disk externally. IBM never offered an internal hard disk for the PC, but many third-party companies stepped in to fill this void with upgrades. The system unit included many configurations with single or dual floppy disk drives. Early on, one version was even available with no disk drives, and others used single-sided floppy drives.

The PC motherboard was based on the 16-bit Intel 8088 microprocessor and included the Microsoft Cassette BASIC language built into ROM. For standard memory, the PC offered configurations with as little as 16K of RAM (when the system was first announced) and as much as 256K on the motherboard. Two motherboard designs were used. Systems sold before March 1983 had a motherboard that supported a maximum of only 64K of RAM, and later systems supported a maximum of 256K on the motherboard. In either case, you added more memory (as much as 640K) by installing memory cards in the expansion slots.

The first bank of memory chips in every PC is soldered to the motherboard. Soldered memory is reliable but not conducive to easy servicing because it prevents you from easily exchanging failing memory chips located in the first bank. The chips must be unsoldered and the defective chip replaced with a socket so that a replacement can be plugged in. When IBM services the defective memory, IBM advises you to exchange the entire motherboard. Considering today's value of these systems, replacing the motherboard with one of the many compatible motherboards on the market may be a better idea. Repairing the same defective memory chip in the XT system is much easier because all memory in an XT is socketed.

The only disk drive available from IBM for the PC is a double-sided (320 or 360K) floppy disk drive. You can install a maximum of two drives in the system unit by using IBM-supplied drives, or four using half-height third-party drives and mounting brackets.

The system unit has five slots that support expansion cards for additional devices, features, or memory. All these slots support full-length adapter cards. In most configurations, the PC included at least a floppy disk controller card. You need a second slot for a monitor adapter, which leaves three slots for adapter cards.

All models of the PC have a fan-cooled 63.5-watt power supply. This low-output power supply doesn't support much in the way of system expansion, especially power-hungry items such as hard disks. Usually, this low-output supply must be replaced by a higher-output unit, such as the one used in the XT. Figure 20.1 shows an interior view of a PC system unit.

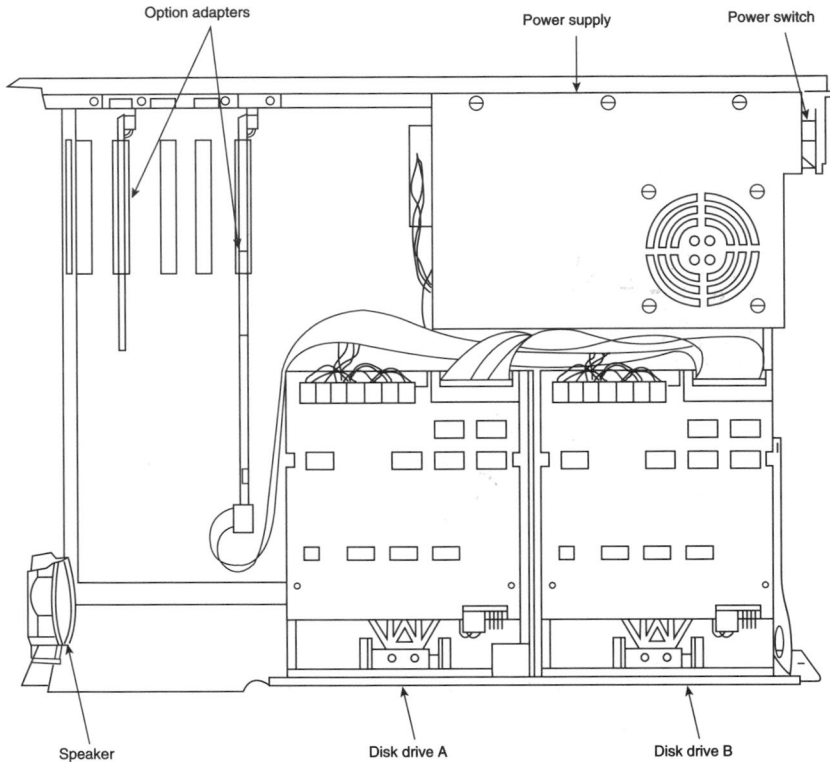

FIG. 20.1 The IBM PC interior view.

An 83-key keyboard with an adjustable typing angle is standard equipment on the PC. The keyboard is attached to the rear of the system unit by a six-foot coiled cable. Figure 20.2 shows the back panel of the PC.

Most model configurations of the PC system unit included these major functional components:

■ Intel 8088 microprocessor

■ ROM-based diagnostics (POST)

■ BASIC language interpreter in ROM

■ 256K of dynamic RAM

■ Floppy disk controller

■ One or two 360K floppy drives

- A 63.5-watt power supply
- Five I/O expansion slots
- Socket for the 8087 math coprocessor

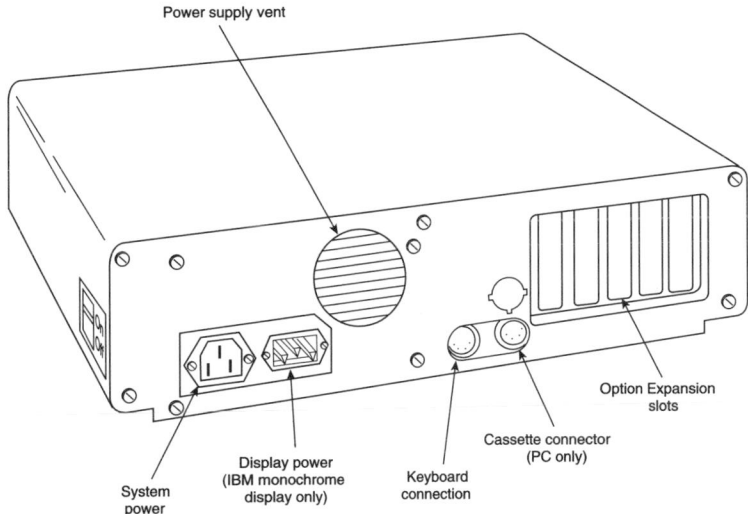

FIG. 20.2 The IBM PC rear view.

PC Models and Features

Although several configurations of the IBM PC were available before March 1983, only two models were available after that time. The later models differ only in the number of floppy drives. IBM designated these models as follows:

- *IBM PC 5150 Model 166.* 256K RAM, one 360K drive.
- *IBM PC 5150 Model 176.* 256K RAM, two 360K drives.

The IBM PC was never available with a factory-installed hard disk (XT systems came with hard disks), primarily because the system unit had limited room for expansion and offered few resources with which to work. After IBM started selling XTs with only floppy disk drives (on April 2, 1985), the PC essentially became obsolete. The XT offered much more for virtually the same price, so investing in a PC after the XT introduction was questionable.

IBM finally officially withdrew the PC from the market on April 2, 1987. IBM's plans for the system became obvious when the company didn't announce a new model with the enhanced keyboard, as it did with other IBM systems. In retrospect, it is amazing that the system was sold over a period of nearly six years with few changes!

Table 20.1 shows the part numbers for the IBM PC system units and options.

Table 20.1 IBM PC Models and Part Numbers	
Description	**Number**
PC system unit, 256K, one double-sided drive	5150166
PC system unit, 256K, two double-sided drives	5150176
Options	**Number**
PC expansion-unit Model 001 with 10M hard disk	5161001
Double-sided disk drive	1503810
8087 math coprocessor option	1501002
BIOS update kit (10/27/82 BIOS)	1501005

With some creative purchasing, you could make a usable system of a base PC by adding the requisite components, such as a full 640K of memory as well as hard disk and floppy drives. Only you can decide when your money is better invested in a new system.

Before you can think of expanding a PC beyond even a simple configuration, and to allow for compatibility and reliability, you must address the following two major areas:

- ROM BIOS level (version)

- 63.5-watt power supply

In most cases, the low-output power supply is the most critical issue, because all PCs sold after March 1983 already had the latest ROM BIOS. If you have an earlier PC system, you also must upgrade the ROM, because the early versions lack some required capabilities—in particular, the capability to scan the memory range C0000-DFFFF in the Upper Memory Area (UMA) for adapter card ROMs.

PC BIOS Versions

Three different BIOS versions have been used in the IBM PC. They can be identified by their date and summarized as follows:

- April 24, 1981: The first PC BIOS version would only support a maximum of 544K of RAM. In addition, it would not scan the UMA for adapter card ROMs, such as those found on EGA/VGA video adapters, hard disk controllers, and SCSI adapters. This BIOS is very rare, and any such machine is almost a collector's item because it represents one of the first PCs ever made.

- October 19, 1981: The second PC BIOS has the same 544K RAM and UMA scan limitations as the first BIOS, but it does fix a couple of minor display bugs. Even this BIOS is not very common.

- October 27, 1982: The third and final PC BIOS has support for a full 640K of base RAM plus the necessary UMA scan to support adapter cards with ROMs on them. To be useful at all, a PC must have this BIOS revision. If your PC BIOS is one of the older two versions, note that IBM sells a BIOS update kit under part number 1501005.

Table 20.2 lists the different IBM Family/1 (PC, XT, and AT) BIOS versions. It also shows the ID, submodel, and revision bytes that can be determined by a software function call

```
Int 15h, C0 = Return System Configuration Parameters
```

Some of the systems, such as the PC and earlier XT and AT systems, only support the ID byte; the submodel and revision bytes had not been established when those systems were developed. The table also shows the number of drive types supported in the AT and XT-286 systems BIOS.

System	CPU	Speed	BIOS Date	ID, Submodel, Revision	BIOS Drive Types
PC	8088	4.77MHz	04/24/81	FF - -	-
PC	8088	4.77MHz	10/19/81	FF - -	-
PC	8088	4.77MHz	10/27/82	FF - -	-
PCjr	8088	4.77MHz	06/01/83	FD - -	-
PC-XT, PPC	8088	4.77MHz	11/08/82	FE - -	-
PC-XT	8088	4.77MHz	01/10/86	FB 00 01	-
PC-XT	8088	4.77MHz	05/09/86	FB 00 02	-
PC Convertible	80C88	4.77MHz	09/13/85	F9 00 00	-
PC-AT	286	6MHz	01/10/84	FC - -	15
PC-AT	286	6MHz	06/10/85	FC 00 01	23
PC-AT	286	8MHz	11/15/85	FC 01 00	23
PC-XT 286	286	6MHz	04/21/86	FC 02 00	24

Table 20.2   IBM Family/1 (PC, XT, AT) System BIOS Dates

The ID, submodel, and revision byte numbers are in hexadecimal.
- means this feature is not supported.

The BIOS date is stored in all PC-compatible systems at memory address FFFF5h. To display the date of your BIOS, a simple DEBUG command can be used to view this address. DEBUG is a command program supplied with MS-DOS. At the DOS prompt, execute the following commands to run DEBUG, display the date stored in your BIOS, and then exit back to DOS:

```
C:\>DEBUG
-D FFFF:5 L 8
FFFF:0000          30 31 2F-32 32 2F 39 37          01/22/97
-Q
```

In this example, the system queried shows a BIOS date of 01/22/97.

PC Technical Specifications

Technical information for the personal computer system and keyboard is described in this section. Here, you find information about the system architecture, memory configurations and capacities, standard system features, disk storage, expansion slots, keyboard specifications, and physical and environmental specifications. This kind of information may be useful in determining what parts you need when you are upgrading or repairing these systems. Figure 20.3 shows the layout and components on the PC motherboard.

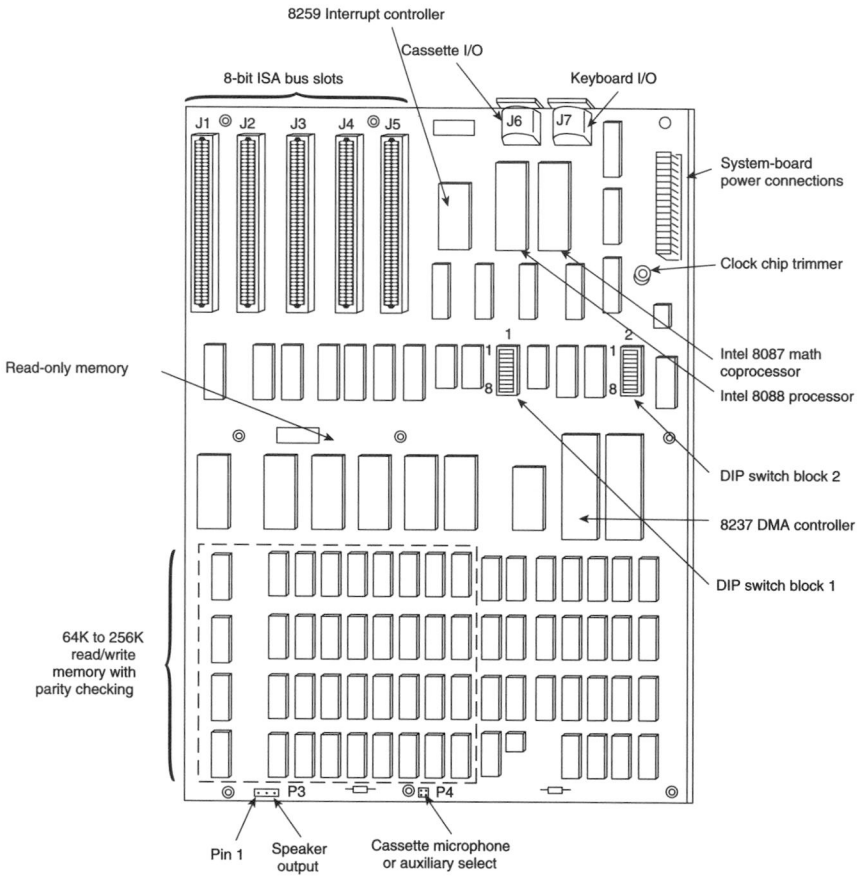

FIG. 20.3   The IBM PC motherboard.

System Architecture

Microprocessor	8088
Clock speed	4.77MHz
Bus type	ISA (Industry Standard Architecture)
Bus width	8-bit
Interrupt levels	8 (6 usable)
Type	Edge-triggered
Shareable	No
DMA channels	4 (3 usable)
Bus masters supported	No
Upgradable processor complex	No

Memory

Standard on system board	16K, 64K, or 256K
Maximum on system board	256K
Maximum total memory	640K
Memory speed (ns) and type	200ns dynamic RAM chips
System board memory-socket type	16-pin DIP
Number of memory-module sockets	27 (3 banks of 9 chips)
Memory used on system board	27 16K×1-bit or 64K×1-bit DRAM chips in 3 banks of 9, one soldered bank of 9 16K×1-bit or 64K×1-bit chips
Memory cache controller	No
Wait states:	
System board	1
Adapter	1

Standard Features

ROM size	40K
ROM shadowing	No
Optional math coprocessor	8087
Coprocessor speed	4.77MHz
Standard graphics	None standard
RS232C serial ports	None standard
UART chip used	NS8250B
Maximum speed (bits per second)	9,600bps
Maximum number of ports supported	2
Pointing device (mouse) ports	None standard
Parallel printer ports	None standard
Bidirectional	No
Maximum number of ports supported	3
CMOS real-time clock (RTC)	No
CMOS RAM	None

Disk Storage

Internal disk and tape drive bays	2 full-height
Number of 3 1/2-inch and 5 1/4-inch bays	0/2
Standard floppy drives	1×360K
Optional floppy drives:	
5 1/4-inch 360K	Optional
5 1/4-inch 1.2M	No
3 1/2-inch 720K	Optional
3 1/2-inch 1.44M	No
3 1/2-inch 2.88M	No
Hard disk controller included	None

(continues)

(continued)

Expansion Slots

Total adapter slots	5
Number of long/short slots	5/0
Number of 8-/16-/32-bit slots	5/0/0
Available slots (with video)	3

Keyboard Specifications

101-key Enhanced keyboard	No, 83-key
Fast keyboard speed setting	No
Keyboard cable length	6 feet

Physical Specifications

Footprint type	Desktop
Dimensions:	
Height	5.5 inches
Width	19.5 inches
Depth	16.0 inches
Weight	25 pounds

Environmental Specifications

Power-supply output	63.5 watts
Worldwide (110/60,220/50)	No
Auto-sensing/switching	No
Maximum current:	
104-127 VAC	2.5 amps
Operating range:	
Temperature	60–90 degrees F
Relative humidity	8–80 percent
Maximum operating altitude	7,000 feet
Heat (BTUs/hour)	505
Noise (Average db, operating, 1m)	43
FCC classification	Class B

Tables 20.3 and 20.4 show the switch settings for the PC (and XT) motherboard. The PC has two eight-position switch blocks (Switch Block 1 and Switch Block 2), whereas the XT has only a single Switch Block 1. The PC used the additional switch block to control the amount of memory the system would recognize, and the XT automatically counted up the memory amount.

Table 20.3   IBM PC/XT Motherboard Switch Settings

Switch Block 1 (PC and XT)

Switch 1	IBM PC Function (PC Only)
Off	Boot From Floppy Drives

Switch Block 1 (PC and XT)

	On	Do Not Boot From Floppy Drives
	Switch 1	**IBM XT Function (XT Only)**
	Off	Normal POST (Power-On Self Test)
	On	Continuous Looping POST
	Switch 2	**Math Coprocessor (PC/XT)**
	Off	Installed
	On	Not Installed
Switch 3	**Switch 4**	**Installed Motherboard Memory (PC/XT)**
On	On	Bank 0 Only
Off	On	Banks 0 and 1
On	Off	Banks 0, 1, and 2
Off	Off	All 4 Banks
Switch 5	**Switch 6**	**Video Adapter Type (PC/XT)**
Off	Off	Monochrome (MDA)
Off	On	Color (CGA) - 40×25 mode
On	Off	Color (CGA) - 80×25 mode
On	On	Any Video Card w/onboard BIOS (EGA/VGA)
Switch 7	**Switch 8**	**Number of Floppy Drives (PC/XT)**
On	On	1 floppy drive
Off	On	2 floppy drives
On	Off	3 floppy drives
Off	Off	4 floppy drives

Table 20.4 Switch Block 2 (PC Only) Memory Settings

Memory	Switch Number (Switch Block 2, PC Only)							
	1	**2**	**3**	**4**	**5**	**6**	**7**	**8**
16K	On	On	On	On	On	Off	Off	Off
32K	On	On	On	On	On	Off	Off	Off
48K	On	On	On	On	On	Off	Off	Off
64K	On	On	On	On	On	Off	Off	Off
96K	Off	On	On	On	On	Off	Off	Off
128K	On	Off	On	On	On	Off	Off	Off
160K	Off	Off	On	On	On	Off	Off	Off
192K	On	On	Off	On	On	Off	Off	Off
224K	Off	On	Off	On	On	Off	Off	Off
256K	On	Off	Off	On	On	Off	Off	Off
288K	Off	Off	Off	On	On	Off	Off	Off
320K	On	On	On	Off	On	Off	Off	Off
352K	Off	On	On	Off	On	Off	Off	Off
384K	On	Off	On	Off	On	Off	Off	Off

(continues)

Table 20.4 Switch Block 2 (PC Only) Memory Settings Continued								
	Switch Number (Switch Block 2, PC Only)							
Memory	**1**	**2**	**3**	**4**	**5**	**6**	**7**	**8**
416K	Off	Off	On	Off	On	Off	Off	Off
448K	On	On	Off	Off	On	Off	Off	Off
480K	Off	On	Off	Off	On	Off	Off	Off
512K	On	Off	Off	Off	On	Off	Off	Off
544K	Off	Off	Off	Off	On	Off	Off	Off
576K	On	On	On	On	Off	Off	Off	Off
608K	Off	On	On	On	Off	Off	Off	Off
640K	On	Off	On	On	Off	Off	Off	Off

An Introduction to the PC Convertible (5140)

IBM marked its entry into the laptop computer market on April 2, 1986, by introducing the IBM 5140 PC Convertible. The system superseded the 5155 Portable PC (IBM's transportable system), which was discontinued. The IBM 5140 system wasn't a very successful laptop system. Other laptops offered more disk storage, higher processor speeds, more-readable screens, lower cost, and more-compact cases, which pressured IBM to improve the Convertible. Because the improvements were limited to the display, however, this system never gained respect in the marketplace. It is significant in two respects. The first is that it marked IBM's entry into the laptop and notebook portable system market—a market they have tremendous success in today with the ThinkPad systems. The second is that the Convertible was the first IBM PC system supplied with 3 1/2-inch floppy drives.

The PC Convertible was available in two models. The Model 2 had a CMOS 80C88 4.77MHz microprocessor, 64K of ROM, 256K of Static RAM, an 80-column×25-line detachable liquid crystal display (LCD), two 3 1/2-inch floppy disk drives, a 78-key keyboard, an AC adapter, and a battery pack. Also included were software programs called Application Selector, SystemApps, Tools, Exploring the IBM PC Convertible, and Diagnostics. The Model 22 is the same basic computer as the Model 2 but with the diagnostics software only. You can expand either system to 512K of RAM by using 128K RAM memory cards, and you can include an internal 1,200bps modem in the system unit. With aftermarket memory expansion, the computers can reach 640K.

Although the unit was painfully slow at 4.77MHz, one notable feature is the use of Static memory chips for the system's RAM. Static RAM does not require the refresh signal that normal Dynamic RAM (DRAM) requires, which would normally require about 7 percent of the processor's time in a standard PC or XT system. This means that the Convertible is about 7 percent faster than an IBM PC or XT, even though they all operate at the same clock speed of 4.77MHz. Because of the increased reliability of the Static RAM (compared to DRAM) used in the Convertible, as well as the desire to minimize power consumption, none of the RAM in the Convertible is parity checked.

At the back of each system unit is an extendable bus interface. This 72-pin connector enables you to attach the following options to the base unit: a printer, a serial or parallel adapter, and a CRT display adapter. Each feature is powered from the system unit. The CRT display adapter operates only when the system is powered from a standard AC adapter. A separate CRT display or a television set attached through the CRT display adapter requires a separate AC power source.

Each system unit includes a detachable LCD. When the computer is not mobile, the LCD screen can be replaced by an external monitor. When the LCD is latched in the closed position, it forms the cover for the keyboard and floppy disk drives. Because the LCD is attached with a quick-disconnect connector, you can remove it easily to place the 5140 system unit below an optional IBM 5144 PC Convertible monochrome or IBM 5145 PC Convertible color display. During the life of the Convertible, IBM offered three different LCD displays. The first display was a standard LCD, which suffered from problems with contrast and readability. Due to complaints, IBM then changed the LCD to a super-twisted-type LCD display, which had much greater contrast. Finally, in the third LCD, IBM added a fluorescent backlight to the super-twisted LCD display, which not only offered greater contrast, but also made the unit usable in low-light situations.

The PC Convertible system unit has these standard features:

- Complementary Metal-Oxide Semiconductor (CMOS) 80C88 4.77 MHz microprocessor

- Two 32K CMOS ROMs containing these items:

    POST (Power-On Self Test) of system components
    BIOS (basic input-output system) support
    BASIC language interpreter

- 256K CMOS Static RAM (expandable to 512K)

- Two 3 1/2-inch, 720K (formatted) floppy drives

- An 80-column×25-line detachable LCD panel (graphics modes: 640×200 resolution and 320×200 resolution)

- LCD controller

- 16K RAM display buffer

- 8K LCD font RAM

- Adapter for optional printer (#4010)

- Professional keyboard (78 keys)

- AC adapter

- Battery pack

The system-unit options for the 5140 are shown in this list:

- 128K Static RAM memory card (#4005)
- Printer (#4010)
- Serial/parallel adapter (#4015)
- CRT display adapter (#4020)
- Internal modem (#4025)
- Printer cable (#4055)
- Battery charger (#4060)
- Automobile power adapter (#4065)

The following two optional displays were available for the PC Convertible:

- IBM 5144 PC Convertible Monochrome Display Model 1
- IBM 5145 PC Convertible Color Display Model 1

PC Convertible Specifications and Highlights

This section lists some technical specifications for the IBM 5140 PC Convertible system. The weights of the unit and options are listed because weight is an important consideration when you carry a laptop system. Figure 20.4 shows the PC Convertible motherboard components and layout.

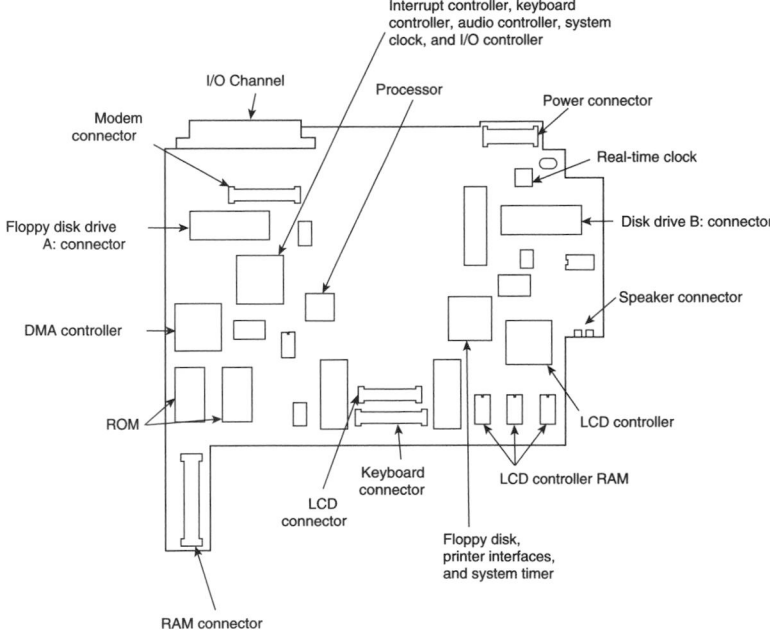

FIG. 20.4 The PC Convertible motherboard.

Dimensions	
Depth	360mm (14.17 inches) 374mm (14.72 inches) including handle
Width	309.6mm (12.19 inches) 312mm (12.28 inches) including handle
Height	67mm (2.64 inches) 68mm (2.68 inches) including footpads

Weight	
Models 2 and 22 (including battery)	5.5kg (12.17 pounds)
128K/256K memory card	40g (1.41 ounces)
Printer	1.6kg (3.50 pounds)
Serial/parallel adapter	470g (1.04 pounds)
CRT display adapter	630g (1.40 pounds)
Internal modem	170g (6 ounces)
Printer cable	227g (8 ounces)
Battery charger	340g (12 ounces)
Automobile power adapter	113g (4 ounces)
5144 PC Convertible monochrome display	7.3kg (16 pounds)
5145 PC Convertible color display	16.9kg (37.04 pounds)

To operate the IBM 5140 PC Convertible properly, you must have PC DOS version 3.2 or later. Previous DOS versions aren't supported because they don't support the 720K floppy drive.

PC Convertible Models and Features

This section covers the options and special features available for the PC Convertible. Several kinds of options were available, from additional memory to external display adapters, serial/parallel ports, modems, and even printers.

Memory Cards. A 128K or 256K memory card expands the base memory in the system unit. You can add two of these cards, for a system-unit total of 640K with one 256K card and one 128K card.

Optional Printer. A special printer is available that attaches to the back of the system unit or to an optional printer-attachment cable for adjacent printer operation. The printer's intelligent, microprocessor-based, 40cps, non-impact dot-matrix design makes it capable of low-power operation. The printer draws power from and is controlled by the system unit. Standard ASCII 96-character upper- and lowercase character sets were printed with a high-resolution 24-element print head. A mode for graphics capability is also provided. You can achieve near-letter-quality printing by using either a thermal transfer ribbon on smooth paper or no ribbon on heat-sensitive thermal paper.

A special printer cable is available that is 22 inches (0.6 meters) long with a custom 72-pin connector attached to each end. With this cable, you can operate the Convertible printer when it is detached from the system unit and place the unit for ease of use and visibility.

Serial/Parallel Adapter. A serial/parallel adapter attaches to the back of the system unit, to a printer, or to another feature module attached to the back of the system unit. The adapter provides an RS-232C asynchronous communications interface and a parallel printer interface, both compatible with the IBM personal computer asynchronous communications adapter and the IBM personal computer parallel printer adapter.

CRT Display Adapter. A CRT display adapter attaches to the back of the system unit, printer, or other feature module attached to the back of the system unit. This adapter enables you to connect to the system a separate CRT display, such as the PC Convertible monochrome display or PC Convertible color display. By using optional connectors or cables, you can use the CRT display adapter to attach a standard Color Graphics Adapter (CGA) monitor. Because composite video output is available, you can use a standard television set.

Internal Modems. IBM offered two different internal modems for the Convertible. Both run Bell 212A (1,200bps) or Bell 103A (300bps) protocols. The modems came as a complete assembly, consisting of two cards connected by a cable. The entire assembly is installed inside the system unit. The original first design modem was made for IBM by Novation and did not follow the Hayes standard for commands and protocols. This rendered the modem largely incompatible with popular software designed to use the Hayes-command set. Later, IBM changed the modem to one that was fully Hayes compatible, and this resolved the problems with software. IBM never introduced a modem faster than 1,200bps for the Convertible. Fortunately, you can operate a standard external modem through the serial port, although you lose the convenience of having it built in.

Battery Charger/Auto Power Adapter. The battery charger is a 110-volt input device that charges the system's internal batteries. It does not provide sufficient power output for the system to operate while the batteries are being charged.

An available automobile power adapter plugs into the cigarette-lighter outlet in a vehicle with a 12-volt negative-ground electrical system. You can use the system while the adapter also charges the Convertible's battery.

Optional Displays. The 5144 PC Convertible monochrome display is a 9-inch (measured diagonally) composite video display attached to the system unit through the CRT display adapter. It comes with a display stand, an AC power cord, and a signal cable that connects the 5144 to the CRT display adapter. This display does not resemble—and is not compatible with—the IBM monochrome display for larger PC systems. The CRT adapter emits the same signal as the one supplied by the Color Graphics Adapter for a regular PC. This display is functionally equivalent to the display on the IBM Portable PC.

The 5145 PC Convertible color display is a 13-inch color display attached to the system unit through the CRT display adapter. It comes with a display stand, an AC power cord, a signal cable that connects the 5145 to the CRT display adapter, and a speaker for external audio output. The monitor is a low-cost unit compatible with the standard IBM CGA display.

Table 20.5 shows the part numbers of the IBM Convertible system units.

Table 20.5 IBM Convertible Part Numbers	
5140 PC Convertible System Units	**Number**
Two drives, 256K with system applications	5140002
Two drives, 256K without system applications	5140022

An Introduction to the XT (5160)

Introduced on March 8, 1983, the PC XT with a built-in 10M hard disk (originally standard, later optional) caused a revolution in personal computer configurations. At the time, having even a 10M hard disk was something very special. *XT* stands for *eXTended*. IBM chose this name because the IBM PC XT system includes many features not available in the standard PC. The XT has eight slots, allowing increased expansion capabilities, greater power-supply capacity, completely socketed memory, motherboards that support memory expansion to 640K without using an expansion slot, and optional hard disk drives. To obtain these advantages, the XT uses a different motherboard circuit design than the PC.

The system unit was available in several models, with a variety of disk drive configurations: one 360K floppy disk drive, two 360K floppy disk drives, one floppy disk and one hard disk drive, or two floppy disk drives and one hard disk drive. The floppy disk drives were full-height drives in the earlier models, and half-height drives in more recent models. With the four available drive bays, IBM had standard configurations with two floppy drives and a single hard disk, with room for a second hard disk provided all half-height units were used.

IBM offered only 10M and 20M full-height hard disks. In some cases, they also installed half-height hard disks, but they were always installed in a bracket-and-cradle assembly that took up the equivalent space of a full-height drive. If you wanted half-height hard disks (to install two of them stacked, for example), you had to use non-IBM-supplied drives or modify the mounting of the IBM-supplied half-height unit so that two could fit. Most aftermarket sources for hard disks had mounting kits that would work.

IBM also used double-sided (320/360K) floppy disk drives in full- or half-height configurations. A 3 1/2-inch 720K floppy disk drive was available in more recent models. The 3 1/2-inch drives were available in a normal internal configuration or as an external device. You could install a maximum of two floppy disk drives and one hard disk drive in the system unit, using IBM-supplied drives. With half-height hard disks, you could install two hard drives in the system unit.

The XT is based on the same 8- and 16-bit Intel 8088 microprocessor (the CPU has 16-bit registers but only an 8-bit data bus) as the PC and runs at the same clock speed. Operationally, the XT systems are identical to the PC systems except for the hard disk. All models have at least one 360K floppy disk drive and a keyboard. For standard memory, the XT offers 256K or 640K on the main board. The hard disk models also include a serial adapter.

The system unit has eight slots that support cards for additional devices, features, or memory. Two of the slots support only short option cards because of physical interference from the disk drives. The XT has at least a disk drive adapter card in the floppy-disk-only models, and a hard disk controller card and serial adapter in the hard disk models. Either five or seven expansion slots (depending on the model) are available. Figure 20.5 shows the interior of an XT.

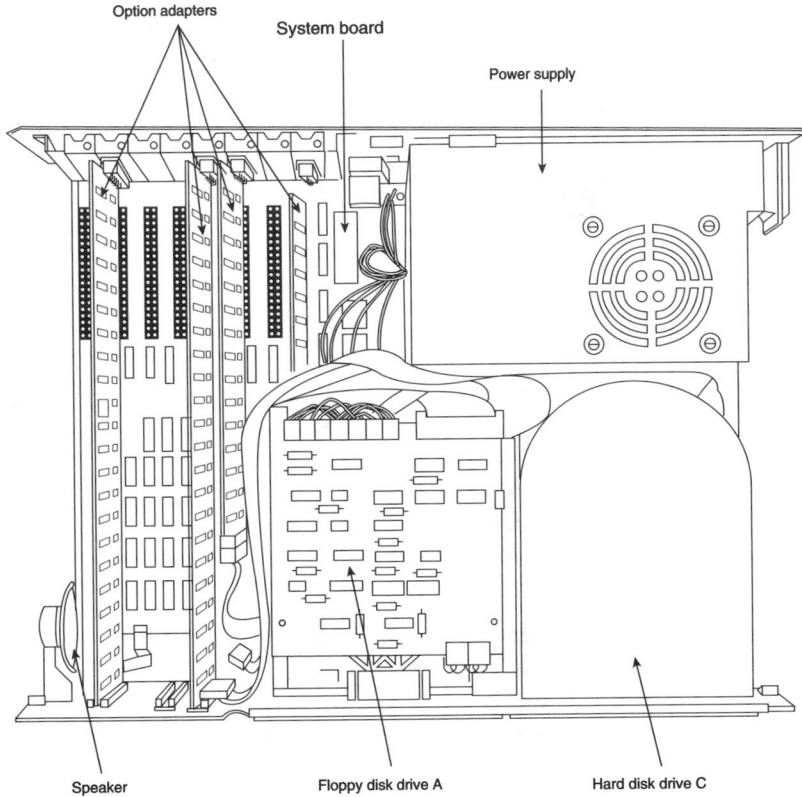

FIG. 20.5 The IBM PC XT interior.

All XT models include a heavy-duty, fan-cooled, 130-watt power supply to support the greater expansion capabilities and disk drive options. The power supply has more than double the capacity of the PC's supply and can easily support hard disk drives and the full complement of expansion cards.

An 83-key keyboard was standard equipment with the early XT models but was changed to an enhanced 101-key unit in the more recent models. The keyboard is attached to the system unit by a six-foot coiled cable.

All models of the PC XT system unit contain these major functional components:

- Intel 8088 microprocessor

- ROM-based diagnostics (POST)

- BASIC language interpreter in ROM

- 256K or 640K of dynamic RAM

- Floppy disk controller

- One 360K floppy drive (full- or half-height)

- 10M or 20M hard disk drive with interface (enhanced models)

- Serial interface (enhanced models)

- Heavy-duty, 135-watt power supply

- Eight I/O expansion slots

- Socket for 8087 math coprocessor

XT Models and Features

The XT was available in many different model configurations, but originally only one model was available. This model included a 10M hard disk, marking the first time that a hard disk was standard equipment in a personal computer and was properly supported by the operating system and peripherals. This computer helped change the industry standard for personal computers from normally having only one or two floppy disk drives to now including one or more hard disks.

Today, most people wouldn't consider a PC to be even remotely usable without a hard disk. The original XT was expensive, however, and buyers couldn't unbundle, or delete, the hard disk from the system at purchase time for credit and add it later. This fact distinguished the XT from the PC and misled many people to believe that the only difference between the two computers was the hard disk. People who recognized and wanted the greater capabilities of the XT without the standard IBM hard disk unfortunately had to wait for IBM to sell versions of the XT without the hard disk drive.

The original Model 087 of the XT included a 10M hard disk, 128K of RAM, and a standard serial interface. IBM later increased the standard memory in all PC systems to 256K. The XT reflected the change in Model 086, which was the same as the preceding 087 except for a standard 256K of RAM.

On April 2, 1985, IBM finally introduced new models of the XT without the standard hard disk. Designed for expansion and configuration flexibility, the new models enabled you to buy the system initially at a lower cost and add your own hard disk later. The XT therefore could be considered in configurations that previously only the original PC could fill. The primary difference between the PC and the XT is the XT's expansion capability, provided by the larger power supply, eight slots, and better memory layout. These models cost only $300 more than equivalent PCs, rendering the original PC no longer a viable option.

The extra expense of the XT can be justified with the first power-supply replacement you make with an overworked PC. The IBM PC XT is available in two floppy disk models:

- 5160068 XT with one full-height 360K disk drive

- 5160078 XT with two full-height 360K disk drives

Both these models have 256K of memory and use the IBM PC XT motherboard, power supply, frame, and cover. The serial (asynchronous communications) port adapter isn't included as a standard feature with these models.

IBM introduced several more models of the PC XT on April 2, 1986. These models were significantly different from previous models. The most obvious difference, the 101-key enhanced keyboard, was standard with these newer computers. A 20M (rather than 10M) hard disk and one or two half-height floppy disk drives were included. The new half-height floppy disk drives allow for two drives in the space that previously held only one floppy drive. With two drives, backing up floppy disks became easy. A new 3 1/2-inch floppy disk drive, storing 720K for compatibility with the PC Convertible laptop computer, was released also. These newer XT system units were configured with a slightly different memory layout, allowing for 640K of RAM on the motherboard without an expansion slot. This feature conserves power, improves reliability, and lowers the cost of the system.

One 5 1/4-inch, half-height, 360K floppy disk drive and 256K of system-board memory was standard with the XT Models 267 and 268. Models 277 and 278 have a second 5 1/4-inch floppy disk drive. Models 088 and 089 were expanded PC XTs with all the standard features of the Models 267 and 268, a 20M hard disk, a 20M fixed disk drive adapter, a serial port adapter, and an additional 256K of system-board memory—a total of 512K.

The following list shows the highlights of these new models:

- Enhanced keyboard standard on Models 268, 278, and 089; 101 keys, and no status LEDs (XT interface cannot drive LEDs)

- Standard PC XT keyboard on Models 267, 277, and 088

- More disk capacity (20M)

- Standard 5 1/4-inch, half-height, 360K floppy drive

- Available 3 1/2-inch, half-height, 720K floppy drive

- Capacity for four half-height storage devices within the system unit

- Capacity to expand to 640K memory on system board without using expansion slots

These newest XT models have an extensively changed ROM BIOS. The new BIOS is 64K and is internally similar to the BIOS found in ATs. The ROM includes support for the new keyboard and 3 1/2-inch floppy disk drives. The POST also is enhanced.

The new XTs were originally incompatible in some respects with some software programs. These problems centered on the new 101-key enhanced keyboard and the way the new ROM addressed the keys. These problems weren't major and were solved quickly by the software companies.

Seeing how much IBM changed the computer without changing the basic motherboard design is interesting. The ROM is different, and the board now could hold 640K of memory without a card in a slot. The memory trick is a simple one. IBM designed this feature into the board originally and chose to unleash it with these models of the XT.

During the past several years, I have modified many XTs to have 640K on the motherboard, using a simple technique designed into the system by IBM. A jumper and chip added to the motherboard can alter the memory addressing in the board to enable the system to recognize 640K. The new addressing is set up for 256K chips, installed in two of the four banks. The other two banks of memory contain 64K chips—a total of 640K.

Complete instructions for how to install 640K of memory on the XT motherboard can be found on the CD that accompanies this book.

XT BIOS Versions

Three different BIOS versions have been used in the IBM PC-XT. They can be identified by their date and summarized as follows:

- November 8, 1982: The original XT BIOS had all the features of the latest 10/27/82 PC BIOS, including 640K base memory and UMA scan support. This BIOS version was also used in the XT motherboards found in the IBM Portable PC (PPC).

- January 10, 1986: The second revision XT BIOS added support for the 101-key Enhanced keyboard, plus full support for 3 1/2-inch 720K floppy drives.

- May 9, 1986: This final revision contained some fixes for minor keyboard bugs related mainly to the enhanced keyboard.

Table 20.2 lists the different IBM Family/1 (PC, XT, and AT) BIOS versions. It also shows the ID, submodel, and revision bytes that can be determined by the software function call

```
Int 15h, C0 = Return System Configuration Parameters
```

Some of the systems such as the PC and earlier XT and AT systems only support the ID byte; the submodel and revision bytes had not been established when those systems were developed. Table 20.2 also shows the number of drive types supported in the AT and XT-286 systems BIOS.

The BIOS date is stored in all PC-compatible systems at memory address FFFF5h. To display the date of your BIOS, a simple DEBUG command can be used to view this address. DEBUG is a command program supplied with MS-DOS. At the DOS prompt, execute the following commands to run DEBUG, display the date stored in your BIOS, and then exit back to DOS:

```
C:\>DEBUG
-D FFFF:5 L 8
FFFF:0000                     30 31 2F-32 32 2F 39 37              01/22/97
-Q
```

In this example, the system queried shows a BIOS date of 01/22/97.

XT Technical Specifications

Technical information for the XT system, described in this section, provides information about the system architecture, memory configurations and capacities, standard system features, disk storage, expansion slots, keyboard specifications, and also physical and environmental specifications. Figure 20.6 shows the layout and components on the XT motherboard.

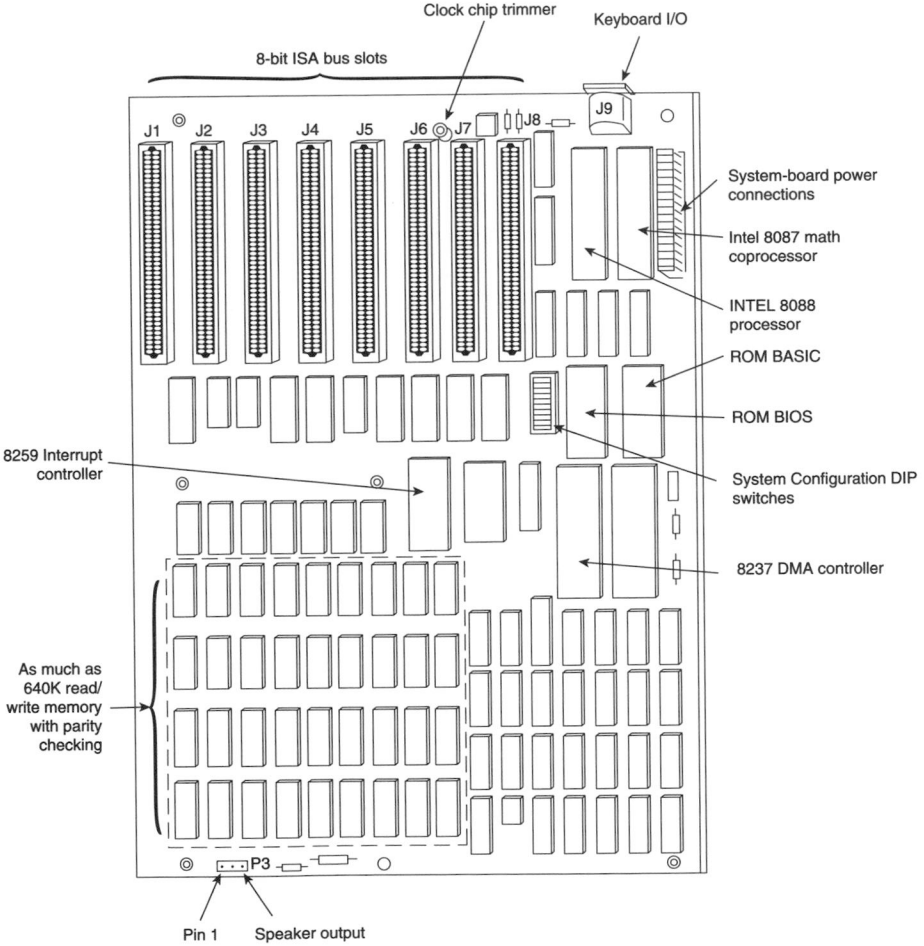

FIG. 20.6 The XT motherboard.

System Architecture

Microprocessor	8088
Clock speed	4.77MHz
Bus type	ISA (Industry Standard Architecture)
Bus width	8-bit
Interrupt levels	8 (6 usable)
Type	Edge-triggered
Shareable	No
DMA channels	4 (3 usable)
Bus masters supported	No
Upgradable processor complex	No

Memory

Standard on system board	256K or 640K
Maximum on system board	256K or 640K
Maximum total memory	640K
Memory speed (ns) and type	200ns dynamic RAM chips
System board memory-socket type	16-pin DIP
Number of memory-module sockets	36 (4 banks of 9)
Memory used on system board	36 64K×1-bit DRAM chips in 4 banks of 9, or 2 banks of 9 256K×1-bit and 2 banks of 9 64K×1-bit chips
Memory cache controller	No
Wait states:	
System board	1
Adapter	1

Standard Features

ROM size	40K or 64K
ROM shadowing	No
Optional math coprocessor	8087
Coprocessor speed	4.77MHz
Standard graphics	None standard
RS232C serial ports	1 (some models)
UART chip used	NS8250B
Maximum speed (bits per second)	9,600bps
Maximum number of ports supported	2
Pointing device (mouse) ports	None standard
Parallel printer ports	1 (some models)
Bidirectional	No
Maximum number of ports supported	3
CMOS real-time clock (RTC)	No
CMOS RAM	None

(continues)

(continued)

Disk Storage

Internal disk and tape drive bays	2 full-height or 4 half-height	
Number of 3 1/2-inch or 5 1/4-inch bays	0/2 or 0/4	
Standard floppy drives	1×360K	
Optional floppy drives:		
5 1/4-inch 360K	Optional	
5 1/4-inch 1.2M	No	
3 1/2-inch 720K	Optional	
3 1/2-inch 1.44M	No	
3 1/2-inch 2.88M	No	
Hard disk controller included	ST-506/412 (Xebec Model 1210)	
ST-506/412 hard disks available	10/20M	
Drive form factor	5 1/4-inch	
Drive interface	ST-506/412	
Drive capacity	10M	20M
Average access rate (ms)	85	65
Encoding scheme	MFM	MFM
BIOS drive type number	1	2
Cylinders	306	615
Heads	4	4
Sectors per track	17	17
Rotational speed (RPMs)	3600	3600
Interleave factor	6:1	6:1
Data transfer rate (kilobytes/ second)	85	85
Automatic head parking	No	No

Expansion Slots

Total adapter slots	8
Number of long/short slots	6/2
Number of 8-/16-/32-bit slots	8/0/0
Available slots (with video)	4

Keyboard Specifications

101-key Enhanced keyboard	Yes
Fast keyboard speed setting	No
Keyboard cable length	6 feet

Physical Specifications

Footprint type	Desktop
Dimensions:	
Height	5.5 inches
Width	19.5 inches
Depth	16.0 inches
Weight	32 pounds

Environmental Specifications

Power-supply output	130 watts
Worldwide (110v/60Hz, 220v/50Hz)	No
Auto-sensing/switching	No
Maximum current:	
90-137 VAC	4.2 amps
Operating range:	
Temperature	60–90 degrees F
Relative humidity	8–80 percent
Maximum operating altitude	7,000 feet
Heat (BTUs/hour)	717
Noise (Average db, operating, 1m)	56
FCC classification	Class B

Table 20.6 shows the XT motherboard switch settings. The XT motherboard uses a single eight-position switch block to control various functions, as detailed in the table.

Table 20.6   IBM PC/XT Motherboard Switch Settings

Switch Block 1 (PC and XT)

Switch 3	Switch 4	
	Switch 1	**IBM PC Function (PC Only)**
	Off	Boot From Floppy Drives
	On	Do Not Boot From Floppy Drives
	Switch 1	**IBM XT Function (XT Only)**
	Off	Normal POST (Power-On Self Test)
	On	Continuous Looping POST
	Switch 2	**Math Coprocessor (PC/XT)**
	Off	Installed
	On	Not Installed
Switch 3	**Switch 4**	**Installed Motherboard Memory (PC/XT)**
On	On	Bank 0 Only
Off	On	Banks 0 and 1
On	Off	Banks 0, 1, and 2
Off	Off	All 4 Banks

(continues)

Table 20.6   IBM PC/XT Motherboard Switch Settings Continued

Switch Block 1 (PC and XT)

Switch 5	Switch 6	Video Adapter Type (PC/XT):
Off	Off	Monochrome (MDA)
Off	On	Color (CGA); 40×25 mode
On	Off	Color (CGA); 80×25 mode
On	On	Any Video Card w/onboard BIOS (EGA/VGA)
Switch 7	**Switch 8**	**Number of Floppy Drives (PC/XT):**
On	On	1 floppy drive
Off	On	2 floppy drives
On	Off	3 floppy drives
Off	Off	4 floppy drives

Table 20.7 shows the part numbers of the XT system units.

Table 20.7   IBM XT Model Part Numbers

Description	Number
XT system unit/83-key keyboard, 256K:	
One full-height 360K drive	5160068
One half-height 360K drive	5160267
Two full-height 360K drives	5160078
Two half-height 360K drives	5160277
XT system unit/101-key keyboard, 256K:	
One half-height 360K drive	5160268
Two half-height 360K drives	5160278
XT system unit/83-key keyboard, 256K, one serial, one full-height 360K drive, 10M hard disk	5160086
XT system unit/83-key keyboard, 640K, one serial, one half-height 360K drive, 20M fixed disk	5160088
XT system unit/101-key keyboard, 640K, one serial, one half-height 360K drive, 20M fixed disk	5160089

Option Numbers

PC expansion-unit Model 002, 20M fixed disk	5161002
20M fixed disk drive	6450326
20M fixed disk adapter	6450327
10M fixed disk drive	1602500
10M fixed disk adapter	1602501
5 1/4-inch, half-height, 360K drive	6450325
5 1/4-inch, full-height, 360K drive	1503810
3 1/2-inch, half-height, 720K internal drive	6450258
3 1/2-inch, half-height, 720K external drive	2683190

Option Numbers

8087 math coprocessor option	1501002
Asynchronous serial adapter	1502074

Enhanced Keyboard Accessories

Clear keycaps (60) with paper inserts	6341707
Blank light keycaps	1351710
Blank dark keycaps	1351728
Paper inserts (300)	6341704
Keycap-removal tools (6)	1351717

An Introduction to the Portable PC

IBM introduced the Portable PC on February 16, 1984. The IBM Portable PC, a "transportable" personal computer, is a small suitcase-sized system that has a built-in 9-inch amber composite video monitor; one 5 1/4-inch half-height floppy disk drive (with space for an optional second drive); an 83-key keyboard; two adapter cards; a floppy disk controller; and a CGA. The unit also has a universal-voltage power supply capable of overseas operation on 220-volt power. Figure 20.7 shows the Portable PC exterior.

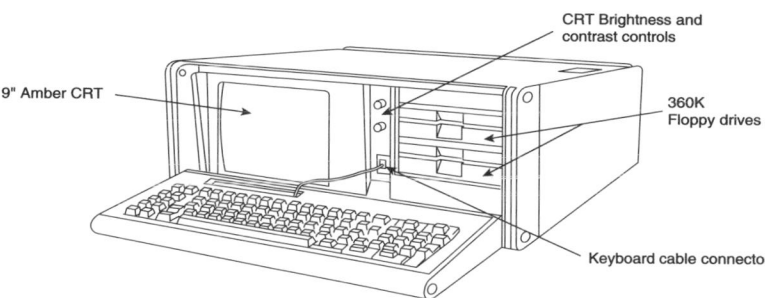

FIG. 20.7   The IBM Portable PC.

The system board used in the IBM Portable PC is the same board used in the original IBM XTs, with 256K of memory. Because the XT motherboard was used, eight expansion slots are available for the connection of adapter boards, although only two slots can accept a full-length adapter card due to internal space restrictions. The power supply is basically the same as an XT's, with physical changes for portability and a small amount of power drawn to run the built-in monitor. In function and performance, the Portable PC system unit has identical characteristics to an equivalently configured IBM PC XT system unit. Figure 20.8 shows the Portable PC interior view.

IBM withdrew the Portable PC from the market on April 2, 1986, a date that coincides with the introduction of the IBM Convertible laptop PC. The Portable PC is rare because not many were sold, although it compared to, and in many ways was better than, the highly successful Compaq Portable that was available at the time. The system was largely misunderstood by the trade press and user community. Most did not understand that the system was really a portable XT and had more to offer than the standard IBM PC. Maybe if IBM had called the system the Portable XT, it would have sold better!

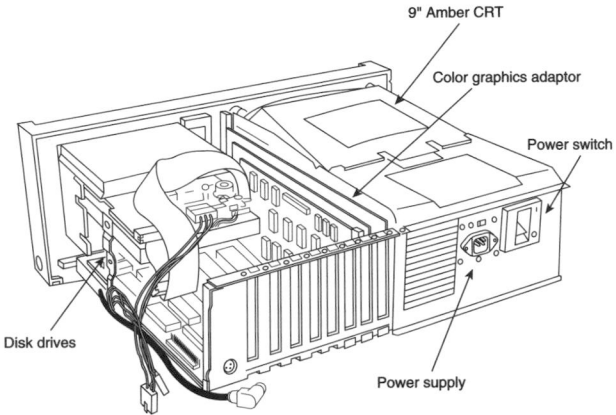

FIG. 20.8   The IBM Portable PC interior.

The Portable PC system unit has these major functional components:

- Intel 8088 4.77MHz microprocessor
- ROM-based diagnostics (POST)
- BASIC language interpreter in ROM
- 256K of dynamic RAM
- Eight expansion slots (two long slots, one 3/4-length slot, and five short slots)
- Socket for 8087 math coprocessor
- Color/Graphics Monitor Adapter
- 9-inch amber composite video monitor
- Floppy disk interface
- One or two half-height 360K floppy drives
- 114-watt universal power supply (115–230V, 50–60Hz)
- Lightweight 83-key keyboard
- Enclosure with carrying handle
- Carrying bag for the system unit

Figure 20.6 showed the XT motherboard, which is also used in the Portable PC. The following is the technical data for the Portable PC system:

System Architecture

Microprocessor	8088
Clock speed	4.77MHz
Bus type	ISA (Industry Standard Architecture)
Bus width	8-bit
Interrupt levels	8 (6 usable)
Type	Edge-triggered
Shareable	No
DMA channels	4 (3 usable)
Bus masters supported	No
Upgradable processor complex	No

Memory

Standard on system board	256K
Maximum on system board	256K
Maximum total memory	640K
Memory speed (ns) and type	200ns dynamic RAM chips
System board memory-socket type	16-pin DIP
Number of memory-module sockets	36 (4 banks of 9)
Memory used on system board	36 64K×1-bit DRAM chips in 4 banks of 9 chips
Memory cache controller	No
Wait states:	
System board	1
Adapter	1

Standard Features

ROM size	40K
ROM shadowing	No
Optional math coprocessor	8087
Coprocessor speed	4.77MHz
Standard graphics	CGA adapter with built-in 9-inch amber CRT
RS232C serial ports	None standard
UART chip used	NS8250B
Maximum speed (bits per second)	9,600bps
Maximum number of ports supported	2
Pointing device (mouse) ports	None standard
Parallel printer ports	None standard
Bidirectional	No
Maximum number of ports supported	3
CMOS real-time clock (RTC)	No
CMOS RAM	None

(continues)

(continued)

Disk Storage

Internal disk and tape drive bays	2 half-height
Number of 3 1/2-inch /5 1/4-inch bays	0/2
Standard floppy drives	1 or 2×360K
Optional floppy drives:	
5 1/4-inch 360K	Optional
5 1/4-inch 1.2M	No
3 1/2-inch 720K	Optional
3 1/2-inch 1.44M	No
3 1/2-inch 2.88M	No
Hard disk controller included	None

Expansion Slots

Total adapter slots	8
Number of long/short slots	2/6
Number of 8-/16-/32-bit slots	8/0/0
Available slots (with video)	6

Keyboard Specifications

101-key Enhanced keyboard	No
Fast keyboard speed setting	No
Keyboard cable length	6 feet

Physical Specifications

Footprint type	Desktop
Dimensions:	
Height	8.0 inches
Width	20.0 inches
Depth	17.0 inches
Weight	31 pounds

Environmental Specifications

Power-supply output	114 watts
Worldwide (110/60,220/50)	Yes
Auto-sensing/switching	No
Maximum current:	
90-137 VAC	4.0 amps
Operating range:	
Temperature	60–90 degrees F
Relative humidity	8–80 percent
Maximum operating altitude	7,000 feet

Environmental Specifications	
Heat (BTUs/hour)	650
Noise (Average db, operating, 1m)	42
FCC classification	Class B

Table 20.8 shows the part numbers for the Portable PC.

Table 20.8 IBM Portable PC Model Part Numbers	
Description	**Number**
256K, one 360K half-height drive	5155068
256K, two 360K half-height drives	5155076
Half-height 360K floppy disk drive	6450300

The disk drive used in the Portable PC was a half-height drive, the same unit specified for use in the PCjr. When the Portable PC was introduced, PCjr was the only other IBM sold with the same half-height drive.

An Introduction to the AT

IBM introduced the *Personal Computer AT (Advanced Technology)* on August 14, 1984. The IBM AT system included many features previously unavailable in IBM's PC systems, such as increased performance, an advanced 16-bit microprocessor, high-density floppy disk and hard disk drives, larger memory space, and an advanced coprocessor. Despite its new design, the IBM AT incredibly retained compatibility with most existing hardware and software products for the earlier systems.

In most cases, IBM AT system performance was from three to five times faster than the IBM XT for single applications running DOS on both computers. The performance increase was due to the combination of a reduced cycle count for most instructions by the 80286 processor, an increased system clock rate, 16-bit memory, and a faster hard disk and controller.

The AT system unit has been available in several models: a floppy-disk-equipped base model (068) and several hard-disk-enhanced models. Based on a high-performance 16-bit Intel 80286 microprocessor, each computer includes Cassette BASIC language in ROM and a CMOS (Complementary Metal Oxide Semiconductor) clock and calendar with battery backup. All models are equipped with a high-density (1.2M) floppy disk drive, a keyboard, and a lock. For standard memory, the base model offers 256K, and the enhanced models offer 512K. In addition, the enhanced models have a 20M or a 30M hard disk drive and a serial/parallel adapter. Each system can be expanded through customer-installable options. You can add memory (up to 512K) for the base model by adding chips to the system board. You can expand all models to 16M by installing memory cards.

Besides the standard drives included with the system, IBM only offered two different hard disks as upgrades for the AT:

- 30M hard disk drive

- 20M hard disk drive

IBM also offered only three different types of floppy drives for the AT:

- A second, high-density (1.2M) floppy disk drive

- A double-density (320/360K) floppy disk drive

- A new 3 1/2-inch 720K drive

The original 068 and 099 models of the AT did not support the 720K drive in the BIOS; you had to add a special driver (DRIVER.SYS—supplied with DOS) for the drive to work properly. The later-model ATs supported the 720K drive directly in the BIOS, and also added support for the 1.44M high-density 3 1/2-inch floppy drive, although IBM never sold or officially supported such a drive in the AT.

You can install as many as two floppy disk drives and one hard disk drive or one floppy disk drive and two hard disk drives in the system unit. To use the high-density 5 1/4-inch floppy disk drives properly, you must have special floppy disks—5 1/4-inch, high-coercivity, double-sided, soft-sectored disks. Due to track width problems between the high-density (1.2M) drives and the double-density (360K) drives, a double-density floppy disk drive (320/360K) was available for compatibility with the standard PC or XT systems. You can exchange disks reliably between the 1.2M and the standard 360K drives if you use the proper method and understand the recording process. For transferring data between a system with a 1.2M drive to a system with a 360K drive, you must start with a blank (never previously formatted) 360K disk, which must be formatted and written only by the 1.2M drive. No special precautions are needed to transfer the data the other way. This information is covered in Chapter 13, "Optical Storage." For complete interchange reliability and to simplify the process, however, IBM recommends that you purchase the 360K drive.

The AT motherboard has eight slots that support cards for additional devices, features, or memory. Six slots support the advanced 16-bit or 8-bit cards. Two slots support only 8-bit cards. All system-unit models use one 16-bit slot for the fixed disk and floppy disk drive adapter. The enhanced models use an additional 8-bit slot for the serial/parallel adapter. The result is seven available expansion slots for the base model and six available expansion slots for enhanced models. Figure 20.9 shows the interior of an AT system unit.

All AT models include a 192-watt universal power supply; a temperature-controlled, variable-speed cooling fan; and a security lock with key. The user selects the power supply for a country's voltage range. The cooling fan significantly reduces the noise in most environments; the fan runs slower when the system unit is cool and faster when the system unit is hot. When the system is locked, no one can remove the system-unit cover, boot the system, or enter commands or data from the keyboard, thereby enhancing the system's security.

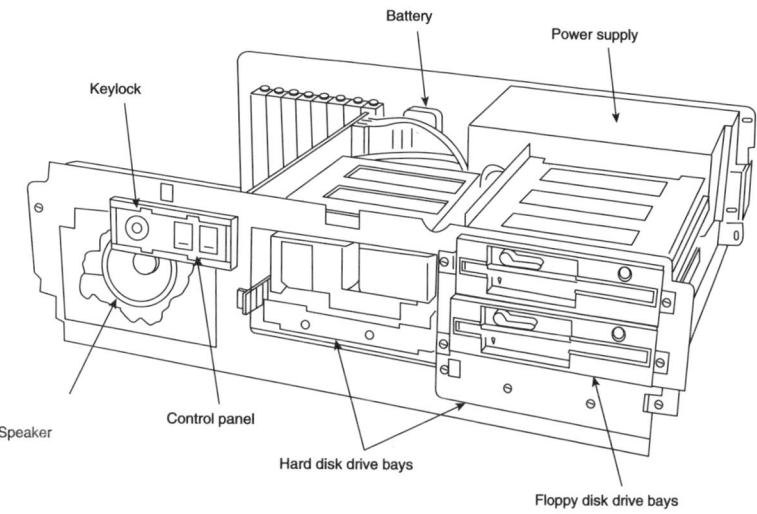

FIG. 20.9   The IBM AT unit interior.

The keyboard is attached to the system unit by a 9-foot coiled cable that enables the AT to adapt to a variety of workspace configurations. The keyboard includes key-location enhancements and mode indicators for improved keyboard usability. Figure 20.10 shows the rear panel of an AT.

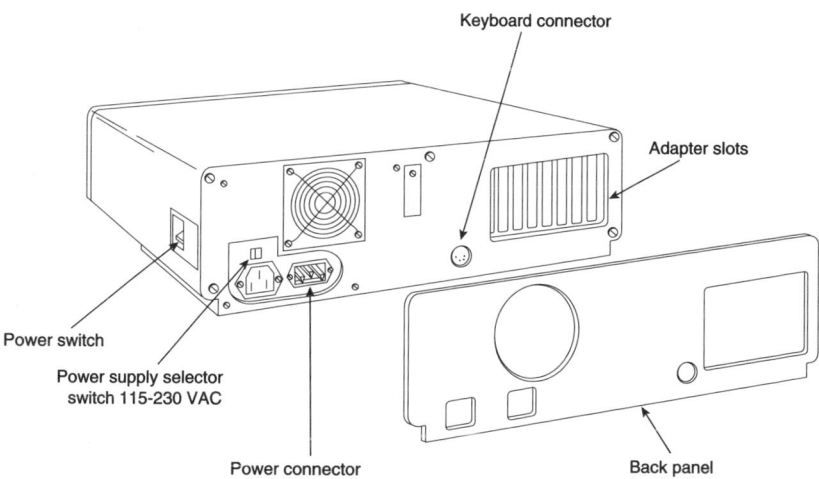

FIG. 20.10   The IBM AT rear panel.

Every system unit for the AT models has these major functional components:

■ Intel 80286 (6MHz or 8MHz) microprocessor

■ Socket for 80287 math coprocessor

- Eight I/O expansion slots (six 16-bit, two 8-bit)

- 256K of dynamic RAM (base model)

- 512K of dynamic RAM (enhanced models)

- ROM-based diagnostics (POST)

- BASIC language interpreter in ROM

- Hard/floppy disk controller

- 1.2M hard disk floppy drive

- 20M or 30M hard disk drive (enhanced models)

- Serial/parallel interface (enhanced models)

- CMOS clock-calendar and configuration with battery backup

- Keylock

- 84-key keyboard or Enhanced 101-key keyboard (standard on newer models)

- Switchable worldwide power supply

AT Models and Features

Since the introduction of the AT, several models have become available. First, IBM announced two systems: a *base model (068)* and an *enhanced model (099)*. The primary difference between the two systems is the standard hard disk that came with the enhanced model. IBM has introduced two other AT systems since the first systems, each offering new features.

The first generation of AT systems has a 6MHz system clock that dictates the processor cycle time. The *cycle time*, the system's smallest interval of time, represents the speed at which operations occur. Every operation in a computer takes at least one or (usually) several cycles to complete. Therefore, if two computers are the same in every way except for the clock speed, the system with the faster clock rate executes the same operations in a shorter time proportional to the difference in clock speed. Cycle time and clock speed are two different ways of describing the same thing. Discussions of clock speed are significant when you're considering buying the AT, because not all models have the same clock speed.

All models of the AT include a combination hard/floppy disk controller that is really two separate controllers on the same circuit board. The board was designed by IBM and Western Digital (WD) and manufactured for IBM by WD. This controller has no onboard ROM BIOS like the Xebec hard disk controller used in the XT. In the AT, IBM built full support for the hard disk controller directly into the motherboard ROM BIOS. To support different types of hard disks, IBM encoded a table into the motherboard ROM that listed the parameters of various drives that could be installed. In the first version of the AT, with a ROM BIOS dated 01/10/84, only the first 14 types in the table were filled in. Type 15 was reserved for internal reasons, and was not usable. Other table entries from 16 through 47 were left unused and were actually filled with zeros. Later versions of the AT added new drive types to the tables, starting from Type 16 and up.

The first two AT models were the 068 (base) model, which had 256K on the motherboard and a single 1.2M floppy disk drive; and the model 099 (enhanced), which had a 20M hard disk drive, a serial/parallel adapter, and 512K on the motherboard. IBM designated the motherboard on these computers as Type 1, which is larger than the later Type 2 board and used an unusual memory layout. The memory is configured as four banks of 128K chips—a total of 512K on the board. This configuration sounds reasonable until you realize that a 128K chip does not really exist in the physical form factor that IBM used. IBM actually created this type of memory device by stacking a 64K chip on top of another one and soldering the two together. My guess is that IBM had many 64K chips to use, and the AT was available to take them.

On October 2, 1985, IBM announced a new model of the AT, the Personal Computer AT Model 239. The system has all the standard features of the AT Model 099, but also has a 30M hard disk rather than a 20M hard disk. A second, optional 30M hard disk drive expands the Model 239's hard disk storage to 60M. This unit's motherboard, a second-generation design IBM calls Type 2, is about 25 percent smaller than the Type 1 but uses the same mounting locations, for physical compatibility. All important items, such as the slots and connectors, remain in the same locations. Other major improvements in this board are in the memory. The 128K memory chips have been replaced by 256K devices. Now only two banks of chips were needed to get the same 512K on the board.

The AT Model 239 includes these items:

- 512K of RAM (standard)
- 6MHz Type 2 motherboard with 256K memory chips
- Serial/parallel adapter (standard)
- 30M hard disk (standard)
- New ROM BIOS (dated 06/10/85). ROM supports 3 1/2-inch 720K floppy drives without using external driver programs, and 22 usable hard disk types (up to Type 23), including the supplied 30M disk. POST "fixes" clock rate to 6MHz.

The Type 2 motherboard's design is much improved over Type 1's; the Type 2 motherboard improved internal-circuit timing and layout. Improvements in the motherboard indicated that the system would be pushed to higher speeds—exactly what happened with the next round of introductions.

In addition to obvious physical differences, the Model 239 includes significantly different ROM software from the previous models. The new ROM supports more types of hard and floppy disks, and its new POST prevents alteration of the clock rate from the standard 6MHz models. Because support for the 30M hard disk is built into the new ROM, IBM sold a 30M hard disk upgrade kit that included the new ROM for the original AT systems. This $1,795 kit represented the only legal way to obtain the newer ROM.

The 30M hard disk drive upgrade kit for the Personal Computer AT Models 068 and 099 included all the features in the 30M hard disk drive announced for the AT Model 239. The upgrade kit also had a new basic input-output subsystem (BIOS), essential to AT operation. The new ROM BIOS supports 22 drive types (compared to the original 14 in earlier ATs), including the new 30M drive. To support the 30M hard disk drive, a new diagnostics floppy disk and an updated guide-to-operations manual were shipped with this kit.

The 30M update kit included these items:

- 30M hard disk drive

- Two new ROM BIOS modules

- Channel keeper bar (a bracket for the fixed disk)

- Data cable for the hard disk

- Diagnostics and Setup disk

- An insert to the AT guide-to-operations manual

Some people were upset initially that IBM had "fixed" the microprocessor clock to 6MHz in the new model, thereby disallowing any possible "hot rod" or overclocking modifications. Many people realized that the clock crystal on the AT models was socketed so that the crystal could be replaced easily by a faster one. More importantly, because the AT circuit design is modular, changing the clock crystal does not have repercussions throughout the rest of the system, as is the case in the PC and PC XT. For the price of a new crystal (from $1 to $30) and the time needed to plug it in, someone easily could increase an AT's speed by 30 percent, and sometimes more. Unfortunately, due to the POST in the newer model's BIOS, you no longer can implement a simple speedup alteration without also changing the ROM BIOS as well.

Many people believed that this change was made to prevent the AT from being "too fast" and therefore competing with IBM's minicomputers. In reality, the earlier motherboard was intentionally run at 6MHz because IBM did not believe that the ROM BIOS software and critical system timing was fully operational at a higher speed. Also, IBM used some components that were rated only for 6MHz operation, starting, of course, with the CPU. Users who increased the speed of their early computers often received DOS error messages from timing problems, and in some cases, total system lockups due to components not functioning properly at the higher speeds.

Many companies selling speedup kits sold software to help smooth over some of these problems, but IBM's official solution was to improve the ROM BIOS software and motherboard circuitry, and to introduce a complete new system running at the faster speed. If you want increased speed no matter what model you have, several companies used to sell clock-crystal replacements that are frequency synthesizers rather than a fixed type of crystal. The units can wait until the POST is finished and change midstream to an increased operating speed. Unfortunately, I don't know of anyone who is still making or selling these upgrades.

If you really want to speed up your AT by installing a faster clock crystal, instructions can be found on the CD accompanying this book on how to burn your own set of BIOS without the check. However, it requires the use of a specialized PROM or EPROM burner, or access to one.

On April 2, 1986, IBM introduced the Personal Computer AT Models 319 and 339. These were the last and best AT models, and were an enhancement of the earlier Model 239. The primary difference from the Model 239 is a faster clock crystal that provides 8MHz operation. The Model 339 has a new keyboard—the Enhanced keyboard—with 101 keys rather than the usual 84. Model 319 is the same as Model 339, but includes the original keyboard.

Highlights of the Models 319 and 339 are shown in this list:

- Faster processor speed (8MHz)

- Type 2 motherboard, with 256K chips

- 512K of RAM (standard)

- Serial/parallel adapter (standard)

- 30M hard disk (standard)

- New ROM BIOS (dated 11/15/85). ROM support for 22 usable types (up to type 23) of hard disks, and 3 1/2-inch drives, at both 720K and 1.44M capacities. POST "fixes" clock rate to 8MHz.

- 101-key Enhanced keyboard (standard on Model 339)

The most significant physical difference in these new systems is the Enhanced keyboard on the Model 339. This keyboard, similar to a 3270 keyboard, has 101 keys. It could be called the IBM "corporate" keyboard because it is standard on all new desktop systems. The 84-key PC keyboard still was available, with a new 8MHz model, as the Model 319.

These new 8MHz systems were available only in an enhanced configuration with a standard 30M hard drive. If you wanted a hard disk larger than IBM's 30M, you could either add a second drive or simply replace the 30M unit with something larger.

ROM support for 3 1/2-inch disk drives at both 720K and 1.44M exists only in Models 339 and 319. In particular, the 1.44M drive, although definitely supported by the ROM BIOS and controller, was never offered as an option by IBM. This means that the IBM Setup program found on the Diagnostics and Setup disk did not offer the 1.44M floppy drive as a choice when configuring the system. Anybody adding such a drive had to use one of the many Setup replacement programs available in the public domain, or "borrow" one from an IBM-compatible system that used a floppy disk–based setup program. Adding the 1.44M drive became one of the most popular upgrades for the AT systems because many newer systems came with that type of drive as standard equipment. Earlier AT systems still can use the 720K and 1.44M drives, but they need to either upgrade the ROM to support them (recommended) or possibly use software drivers to make them work.

AT BIOS Versions

Three different BIOS versions have been used in the IBM AT. They can be identified by their date and summarized as follows:

- January 1, 1984: The first AT BIOS version supported only 1.2M and 360K floppy drives directly. Only 14 hard disk types were supported. It came on the Model 068 and 099 systems with the Type 1 motherboard.

- June 10, 1985: The second AT BIOS added support for 720K 3 1/2-inch drives directly (no drivers were required). Also, more hard disk drive types were added, for a total of 22 usable types. A new test was added to the POST that caused the POST to fail if the clock speed was altered from 6MHz. This BIOS was used on the Model 239 with a Type 2 motherboard.

- November 15, 1985: The third and final AT BIOS added support for 1.44M 3 1/2-inch drives (no drivers required). Enhanced 101-key keyboard support was added. The POST test checked for 8MHz operation, and failed if the system was running at any other speed. This BIOS was used on Model 319 and 339 systems, and came on a Type 2 motherboard.

Table 20.2 lists the different IBM Family/1 (PC, XT, and AT) BIOS versions. It also shows the ID, submodel, and revision bytes that can be determined by a software function call

```
Int 15h, C0 = Return System Configuration Parameters
```

Some of the systems such as the PC and earlier XT and AT systems only support the ID byte; the submodel and revision bytes had not been established when those systems were developed. The table also shows the number of drive types supported in the AT and XT-286 systems BIOS.

The BIOS date is stored in all PC-compatible systems at memory address FFFF5h. To display the date of your BIOS, a simple DEBUG command can be used to view this address. DEBUG is a command program supplied with MS-DOS. At the DOS prompt, execute the following commands to run DEBUG, display the date stored in your BIOS, and then exit back to DOS:

```
C:\>DEBUG
-D FFFF:5 L 8
FFFF:0000                 30 31 2F-32 32 2F 39 37              01/22/97
-Q
```

In this example, the system queried shows a BIOS date of 01/22/97.

AT Motherboard BIOS Hard Drive Tables. The AT BIOS contains a special table that is used by the hard disk controller driver to determine the hard drive parameters. When a hard disk is installed into this type of system, the "type" of drive is entered into the CMOS RAM by whoever has installed the drive. Then, every time the system boots, it looks up the parameters by consulting the CMOS RAM for the particular type that has been selected.

Older systems were therefore limited to what different drives they could support or recognize by the entries burned into their BIOS table. The table used in IBM AT and PS/2 systems is shown in this section.

The various IBM AT and PS/2 systems that use a BIOS drive table do not necessarily have all of the entries shown here. The number of table entries contained in a particular system BIOS can vary from one version to the next. For example, the original AT BIOS (01/10/84) only had Types 1–14 usable, while the later AT BIOS versions (06/10/85 and 11/15/85) had 1–14 and 16–23 usable. The XT-286 had 1–14 and 16–24 as usable types. Some of the PS/1 and PS/2 systems had the table filled in as far as Type 44.

Non-IBM systems quickly adopted special "User Definable" or even "Auto-Detect" types where you could either manually enter the complete table entry (rather than selecting a predetermined "type"), or the system would automatically read the type information directly from the drive.

Note

If you have a non-IBM PC-compatible system, note that the IBM table may be inaccurate for many of the entries past Type 15. Instead, you should consult your CMOS Setup program; most will show the available types as you scroll through them. Another option is to consult your system, motherboard, or BIOS documentation to see if it shows the correct table entries. A final alternative is a program such as the Seagate FINDTYPE program that will scan your BIOS, locate the table, and display or print it for viewing. This program can be downloaded from the Seagate Web site or BBS. Most compatibles follow the IBM table for at least the first 15 entries.

Most PS/2 systems have the drive's defect map written as data on the drive one cylinder beyond the highest reported cylinder. This special data is read by the IBM PS/2 Advanced Diagnostics low-level format program. This process automates the entry of the defect list and eliminates the chance of human error, as long as you use only the IBM PS/2 Advanced Diagnostics for hard disk low-level formatting on those systems.

This type of table does not apply to IBM Enhanced Small Device Interface (ESDI) or SCSI hard disk controllers, host adapters, and drives. Because the ESDI and SCSI controllers or host adapters query the drive directly for the required parameters, no table-entry selection is necessary. Note, however, that the table for the ST-506/412 drives can still be found currently in the ROM BIOS of most of the PS/2 systems, even if the model came standard with an ESDI or SCSI disk subsystem.

Table 20.9 shows the IBM motherboard ROM BIOS hard disk parameters for AT or PS/2 systems using ST-506/412 (standard or IDE) controllers.

Table 20.9 IBM AT and PS/2 BIOS Hard Disk Table

Type	Cylinders	Heads	WPC	Ctrl	LZ	S/T	M	Bytes
1	306	4	128	00h	305	17	10.16	10.65
2	615	4	300	00h	615	17	20.42	21.41
3	615	6	300	00h	615	17	30.63	32.12
4	940	8	512	00h	940	17	62.42	65.45
5	940	6	512	00h	940	17	46.82	49.09
6	615	4	65535	00h	615	17	20.42	21.41
7	462	8	256	00h	511	17	30.68	32.17
8	733	5	65535	00h	733	17	30.42	31.90
9	900	15	65535	08h	901	17	112.06	117.50
10	820	3	65535	00h	820	17	20.42	21.41
11	855	5	65535	00h	855	17	35.49	37.21
12	855	7	65535	00h	855	17	49.68	52.09
13	306	8	128	00h	319	17	20.32	21.31
14	733	7	65535	00h	733	17	42.59	44.66
15*	0	0	0	00h	0	0	0	0
16	612	4	0	00h	663	17	20.32	21.31
17	977	5	300	00h	977	17	40.55	42.52
18	977	7	65535	00h	977	17	56.77	59.53
19	1024	7	512	00h	1023	17	59.50	62.39
20	733	5	300	00h	732	17	30.42	31.90
21	733	7	300	00h	732	17	42.59	44.66
22	733	5	300	00h	733	17	30.42	31.90
23	306	4	0	00h	336	17	10.16	10.65
24	612	4	305	00h	663	17	20.32	21.31
25	306	4	65535	00h	340	17	10.16	10.65
26	612	4	65535	00h	670	17	20.32	21.31
27	698	7	300	20h	732	17	40.56	42.53
28	976	5	488	20h	977	17	40.51	42.48
29	306	4	0	00h	340	17	10.16	10.65
30	611	4	306	20h	663	17	20.29	21.27
31	732	7	300	20h	732	17	42.53	44.60
32	1023	5	65535	20h	1023	17	42.46	44.52
33	614	4	65535	20h	663	25	29.98	31.44
34	775	2	65535	20h	900	27	20.43	21.43
35	921	2	65535	20h	1000	33	29.68	31.12
36	402	4	65535	20h	460	26	20.41	21.41
37	580	6	65535	20h	640	26	44.18	46.33
38	845	2	65535	20h	1023	36	29.71	31.15
39	769	3	65535	20h	1023	36	40.55	42.52

Type	Cylinders	Heads	WPC	Ctrl	LZ	S/T	M	Bytes
40	531	4	65535	20h	532	39	40.45	42.41
41	577	2	65535	20h	1023	36	20.29	21.27
42	654	2	65535	20h	674	32	20.44	21.43
43	923	5	65535	20h	1023	36	81.12	85.06
44	531	8	65535	20h	532	39	80.89	84.82
45	0	0	0	00h	0	0	0.00	0.00
46	0	0	0	00h	0	0	0.00	0.00
47	0	0	0	00h	0	0	0.00	0.00

*Table entry 15 is reserved to act as a pointer to indicate that the type is greater than 15.
Type = Table entry number
Cylinders = Total number of cylinders
Heads = Total number of heads
WPC = Write Pre-Compensation starting cylinder
      65535 = No Write Pre-Compensation (also shown as –1)
      0 = Write Pre-Compensation on all cylinders
Ctrl = Control byte, with values according to the following table

Bit Number	Hex	Meaning
Bit 0	01h	Not used (XT = drive step rate)
Bit 1	02h	Not used (XT = drive step rate)
Bit 2	04h	Not used (XT = drive step rate)
Bit 3	08h	More than eight heads
Bit 4	10h	Not used (XT = imbedded servo drive)
Bit 5	20h	OEM defect map at (cylinders + 1)
Bit 6	40h	Disable ECC retries
Bit 7	80h	Disable disk access retries

LZ = Landing-Zone cylinder used for head parking
S/T = Number of Sectors per Track
M = Drive capacity in Megabytes
Bytes = in Millions

Modifying ROM BIOS Hard Disk Drive Parameter Tables. Because the IBM tables in the AT and XT-286 systems (as well as many of the compatibles of the day) were fixed, technicians back then often found it necessary to modify the BIOS in those systems to add drive types for new drives they wanted to install. For example, I added two new drive types to one of my old AT systems. Those types—25 and 26—have these parameters:

Type	Cylinders	Heads	WPC	Ctrl	LZ	S/T	M	Bytes
25	918	15	65535	08h	918	17	114.30	119.85
26	918	15	65535	08h	918	26	174.81	183.31

WPC = Write Pre-Compensation start cylinder
Ctrl = Control byte, 08h = More than 8 heads, else 00h
LZ = Landing Zone or head-parking cylinder
S/T = Sectors per Track
M = Megabytes
Bytes = in Millions

In my old AT system, these table entries originally were unused (zeros), as are the remainder of types from 27–47. By burning a new set of ROMs with these two new completed entries, I was able to use a Maxtor XT-1140 drive to maximum capacity with an MFM 17-sector-per-track controller (as Type 25) or an RLL 26-sector-per-track controller (as Type 26). This method precluded the need for a controller with its own separate onboard BIOS to override the motherboard table values. It also saved memory in the C000 or D000 UMA segments, where such a hard disk controller ROM normally would reside.

> **Tip**
>
> If you are interested in performing this modification, get the *IBM AT Technical Reference Manual* (sold by IBM or Annabooks), which documents the position and format of the drive tables in the BIOS.

Changing the Hard Disk Controller Head Step Rate. Another more complicated modification that you can perform to the AT BIOS is to increase the stepping rate of the hard disk controller. The first edition of this book briefly mentioned this modification, and a reader wrote to me to express interest in it. Details of the modification can be found on the CD. However, the performance increase is relatively slight.

AT Technical Specifications

Technical information for the AT system is described in this section. You will find information about the system architecture, memory configurations and capacities, standard system features, disk storage, expansion slots, and keyboard specifications, as well as physical and environmental specifications. This type of information can be useful in determining what types of parts are needed when you are upgrading or repairing these systems. Figures 20.11 and 20.12 show the layout and components on the two different AT motherboards.

System Architecture	
Microprocessor	80286
Clock speed	6MHz or 8MHz
Bus type	ISA (Industry Standard Architecture)
Bus width	16-bit
Interrupt levels	16 (11 usable)
Type	Edge-triggered
Shareable	No
DMA channels	8 (7 usable)
Bus masters supported	Yes
Upgradable processor complex	No

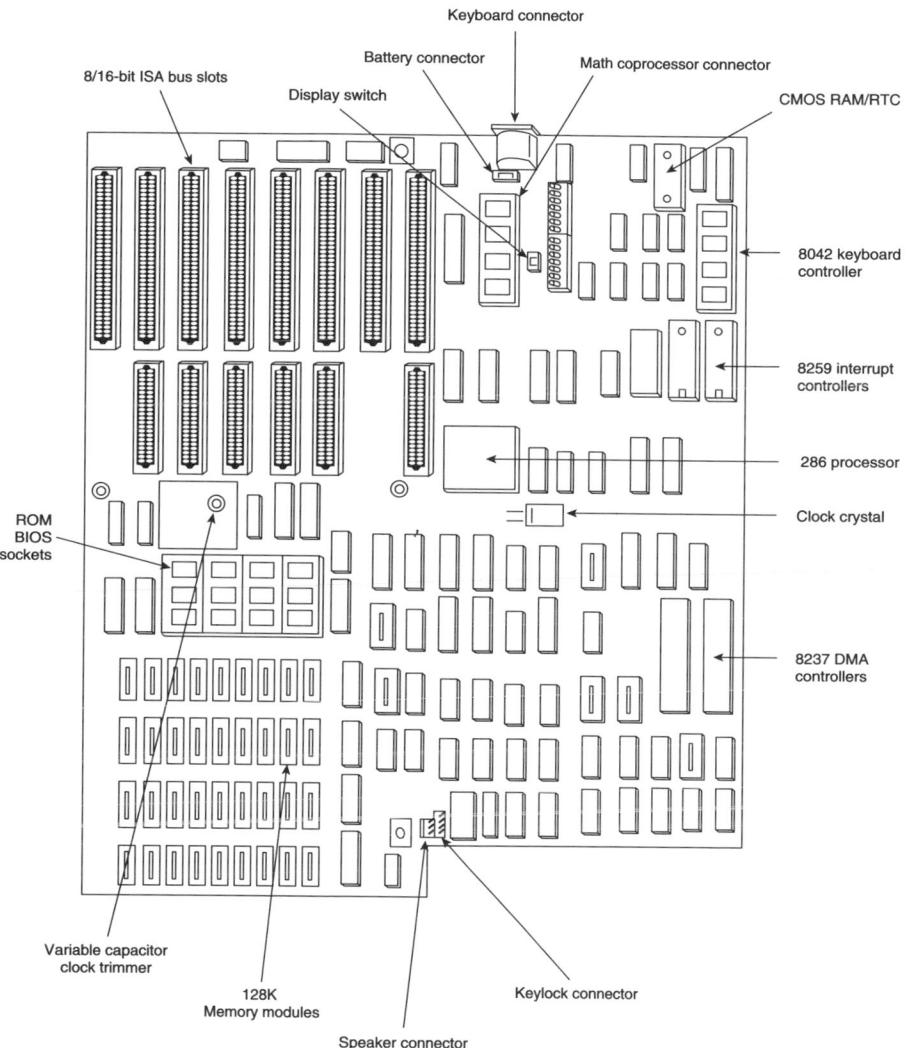

FIG. 20.11 The IBM AT Type 1 motherboard.

Memory

Standard on system board	512K
Maximum on system board	512K
Maximum total memory	16M
Memory speed (ns) and type	150ns dynamic RAM chips
System board memory-socket type	16-pin DIP
Number of memory-module sockets	18 or 36 (2 or 4 banks of 18)
Memory used on system board	36 128K×1-bit DRAM chips in 2 banks of 18, or 18 256K×1-bit chips in one bank

(continues)

(continued)

Memory

Memory cache controller	No
Wait states:	
System board	1
Adapter	1

Standard Features

ROM size	64K
ROM shadowing	No
Optional math coprocessor	80287
Coprocessor speed	4 or 5.33MHz
Standard graphics	None standard
RS232C serial ports	1 (some models)
UART chip used	NS16450
Maximum speed (bits per second)	9,600bps
Maximum number of ports supported	2
Pointing device (mouse) ports	None standard
Parallel printer ports	1 (some models)
Bidirectional	Yes
Maximum number of ports supported	3
CMOS real-time clock (RTC)	Yes
CMOS RAM	64 bytes
Battery life	5 years

Disk Storage

Internal disk and tape drive bays	1 full-height and 2 half-height	
Number of 3 1/2-inch and 5 1/4-inch bays	0/3	
Standard floppy drives	1×1.2M	
Optional floppy drives:		
5 1/4-inch 360K	Optional	
5 1/4-inch 1.2M	Standard	
3 1/2-inch 720K	Optional	
3 1/2-inch 1.44M	Optional (8MHz models)	
3 1/2-inch 2.88M	No	
Hard disk controller included	ST-506/412 (Western Digital WD1002-WA2 or WD1003-WA2)	
ST-506/412 hard disks available	20/30M	
Drive form factor	5 1/4-inch	
Drive interface	ST-506/412	
Drive capacity	20M	30M
Average access rate (ms)	40	40
Encoding scheme	MFM	MFM

Disk Storage

BIOS drive type number	2	20
Cylinders	615	733
Heads	4	5
Sectors per track	17	17
Rotational speed (RPMs)	3600	3600
Interleave factor	3:1	3:1
Data transfer rate (kilobytes/ second)	170	170
Automatic head parking	Yes	Yes

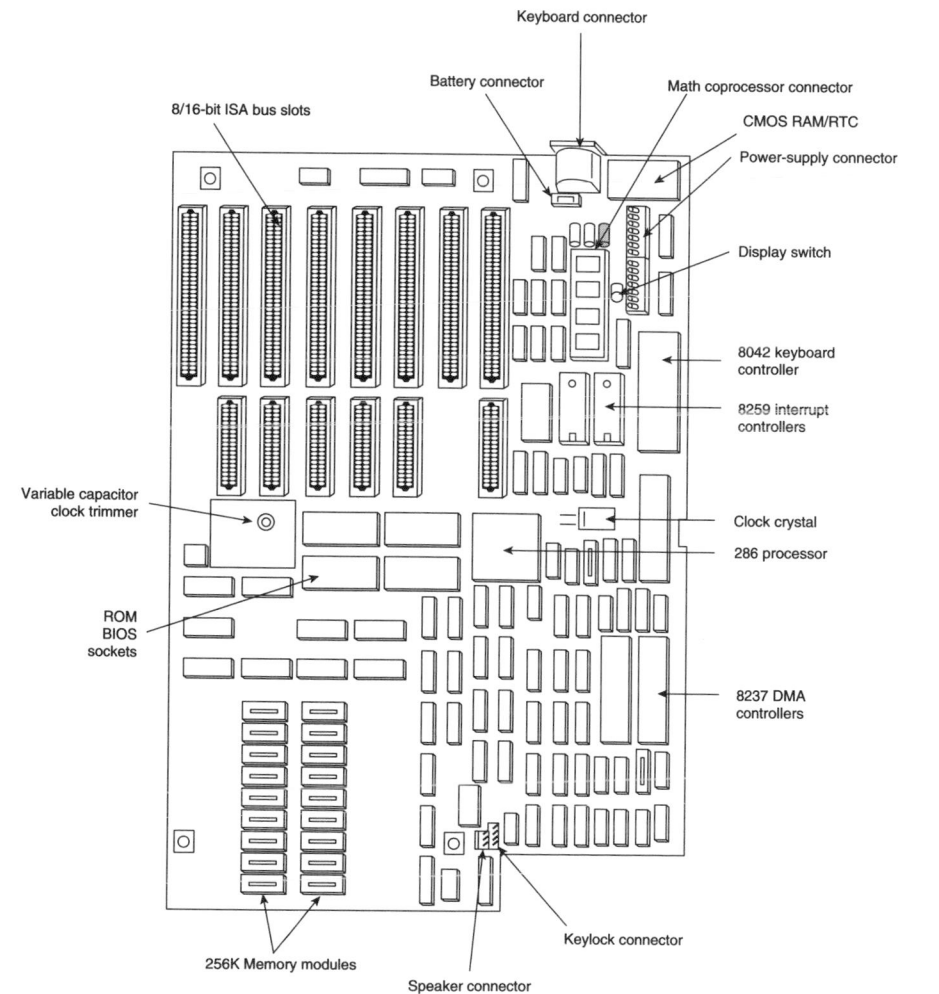

FIG. 20.12 The IBM AT Type 2 motherboard.

Expansion Slots

Total adapter slots	8
Number of long and short slots	8/0
Number of 8-/16-/32-bit slots	2/6/0
Available slots (with video)	5

Keyboard Specifications

101-key Enhanced keyboard	Yes (8MHz models)
Fast keyboard speed setting	Yes
Keyboard cable length	6 feet

Physical Specifications

Footprint type	Desktop
Dimensions:	
Height	6.4 inches
Width	21.3 inches
Depth	17.3 inches
Weight	43 pounds

Environmental Specifications

Power-supply output	192 watts
Worldwide (110/60,220/50)	Yes
Auto-sensing/switching	No
Maximum current:	
90-137 VAC	5.0 amps
Operating range:	
Temperature	60–90 degrees F
Relative humidity	8–80 percent
Maximum operating altitude	7,000 feet
Heat (BTUs/hour)	1229
Noise (Average db, operating, 1m)	42
FCC classification	Class B

Table 20.12 shows the AT system-unit part-number information.

Table 20.12   IBM AT Model Part Numbers

Description	Number
AT 6MHz/84-key keyboard, 256K	
One 1.2M floppy drive	5170068
AT 6MHz/84-key keyboard, 512K, serial/parallel	
One 1.2M floppy drive, 20M hard disk	5170099
One 1.2M floppy drive, 30M hard disk	5170239

Description	Number
AT 8MHz/84-key keyboard, 512K, serial/parallel	
One 1.2M floppy drive, 30M hard disk	5170319
AT 8MHz/101-key, 512K, serial/parallel	
One 1.2M floppy drive, 30M hard disk	5170339
System Options	
20M fixed disk drive	6450205
30M fixed disk	6450210
30M fixed disk drive upgrade kit	6450468
360K half-height floppy disk drive (AT)	6450207
1.2M high-density drive	6450206
3 1/2-inch, half-height, 720K external drive (AT)	2683191
Serial/parallel adapter	6450215
80287 math coprocessor option	6450211
Floor-standing enclosure	6450218
Enhanced Keyboard Accessories	
Clear keycaps (60) with paper inserts	6341707
Blank light keycaps	1351710
Blank dark keycaps	1351728
Paper keycap inserts (300)	6341704
Keycap-removal tools (6)	1351717

An Introduction to the XT Model 286

On September 9, 1986, IBM introduced a new AT-type system disguised inside the chassis and case of an XT. This XT Model 286 system featured increased memory, an Intel 80286 microprocessor, and as many as three internal drives standard. The computer combined an XT's cost-effectiveness, flexibility, and appearance with the high-speed, high-performance technology of the Intel 80286 microprocessor. This model looked like an XT, but underneath the cover, it was all AT.

The IBM XT Model 286 can operate as much as three times faster than earlier models of the XT in most applications. It has a standard 640K of memory. Various memory-expansion options enable users to increase its memory to 16M.

Standard features in this system include a half-height, 1.2M, 5 1/4-inch, high-density floppy disk drive; a 20M hard disk drive; a serial/parallel adapter card; and the IBM Enhanced keyboard. You can select an optional, internal, second floppy disk drive from the following list:

- Half-height, 3 1/2-inch, 720K floppy drive

- Half-height, 3 1/2-inch, 1.44M floppy drive

- Half-height, 5 1/4-inch, 1.2M floppy drive

- Half-height, 5 1/4-inch, 360K floppy drive

The IBM XT Model 286's performance stems primarily from the AT motherboard design, with 16-bit I/O slots and an Intel 80286 processor running at 6MHz. In addition to the type of processor used, clock speed and memory architecture are the primary factors in determining system performance. Depending on the model, the IBM AT's clock speed is 6MHz or 8MHz, with one wait state; the XT Model 286 processes data at 6MHz, with zero wait states. The elimination of a wait state improves performance by increasing processing speed for system memory access. The zero-wait-state design makes the XT Model 286 definitely faster than the original AT models that ran at 6MHz and about equal in speed to the 8MHz AT systems. Based on tests, the XT Model 286 also is about three times faster than an actual XT.

Because the XT Model 286 is an AT-class system, the processor supports both real and protected modes. Operating in real address mode, the 80286 is 8088-compatible; therefore, you can use most software that runs on the standard PC systems. In real address mode, the system can address as much as 1M of RAM. Protected mode provides a number of advanced features to facilitate multitasking operations. Protected mode provides separation and protection of programs and data in multitasking environments. In protected mode, the 80286 can address as much as 16M of real memory and 1G of virtual memory. In this mode, the XT Model 286 can run advanced operating systems such as OS/2 and UNIX. When the XT Model 286 was introduced, it was the least-expensive IBM system capable of running a true multitasking operating system.

The IBM XT Model 286 has a standard 640K of RAM. Memory options enable the system to grow to 15 1/2M, much higher than the 640K limit in other PC XTs. If you add an operating system such as OS/2 or Windows, you can take advantage of the larger memory capacities that the XT Model 286 provides.

A 20M hard disk drive is a standard feature in the XT Model 286, as is a 5 1/4-inch, 1.2M, high-density floppy disk drive. A similar floppy disk drive is standard on all models of the AT. Floppy disks formatted on a 1.2M floppy disk drive therefore can be read by an AT or an XT Model 286. The 1.2M floppy disk drive also can read floppy disks formatted with PC-family members that use a 360K floppy disk drive. Figure 20.13 shows the interior of an XT-286 system unit.

The XT Model 286 features the IBM Enhanced keyboard with indicator lights. Many IBM personal computers use the Enhanced keyboard, but the XT Model 286 was the first PC XT to feature keyboard indicator lights.

Five slots support the advanced 16-bit cards or 8-bit cards; three support only 8-bit cards. Two of the three 8-bit slots support only short cards.

A hard disk and floppy drive adapter card are standard features in the XT Model 286. This multifunction card takes only one 16-bit slot and supports as many as four disk drives (two floppy disk drives and two hard disk drives).

The serial/parallel adapter, another standard feature, is a combination card that requires only one slot (either type) and provides a serial and a parallel port. The parallel portion of the adapter has the capacity to attach devices, such as a parallel printer, that accept eight bits of parallel data. The fully programmable serial portion supports asynchronous communications from 50bps to 9,600bps, although even higher speeds are possible with the right software. The serial portion requires an optional serial-adapter cable or a serial-adapter connector. When one of these options is connected to the adapter, all the signals in a standard EIA RS-232C interface are available. You can use the serial port for interfacing a modem, a remote display terminal, a mouse, or other serial device. The XT Model 286 supports up to two serial/parallel adapters.

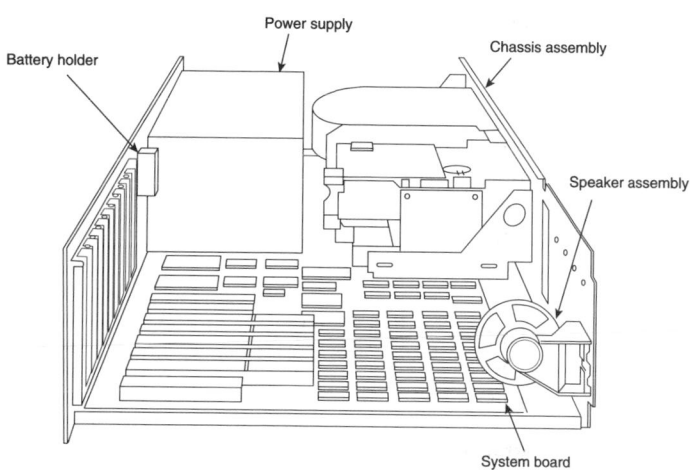

FIG. 20.13 The IBM XT-286 interior.

A standard IBM XT Model 286 offers these features:

- 80286 processor at 6MHz with 0 wait states
- 640K of motherboard memory
- 1.2M floppy drive
- 20M hard disk
- Five 16-bit and three 8-bit expansion slots
- Fixed disk/floppy disk drive adapter (occupies one 16-bit expansion slot)
- Serial/parallel adapter (occupies one 16-bit expansion slot)
- Enhanced 101-key keyboard with indicator lights
- CMOS time-and-date clock with battery backup

XT Model 286 Models and Features

The XT Model 286 processor is as much as three times faster internally than the preceding XT family and as much as 25 percent faster than the AT Model 239, depending on specific applications. A 20M fixed disk and a 1.2M 5 1/4-inch floppy disk drive were standard on the XT Model 286. One additional floppy disk drive can be installed internally as drive B. You can add as a second half-height floppy drive any type of floppy drive, including both the double and high-density versions of the 5 1/4- and 3 1/2-inch drives.

If you want to be able to read standard 5 1/4-inch data or program floppy disks created by the XT Model 286 on other PC systems, you might want to add a 5 1/4-inch 360K floppy disk drive, which provides full read/write compatibility with those systems. This is due to the fact that the 1.2M drives write a narrower track than the 360K drives and are unable to properly overwrite a floppy disk written on first by a 360K drive. If full read/write compatibility with 360K drives is not important, you can add a second 1.2M high-density floppy disk drive.

You can add any 3 1/2-inch drive, including the 720K and 1.44M versions. Because the 1.44M does not have any read/write compatibility problems with the 720K drives, however, and the 1.44M drives always can operate in 720K mode, I suggest adding only the 1.44M 3 1/2-inch drives rather than the 720K versions. The higher-density drive is only a small extra expense compared to the double-density version. Most people do not know that full ROM BIOS support for these 1.44M drives is provided in the XT Model 286. Unfortunately, because IBM never offered the 1.44M drive as an option, the supplied Setup program does not offer the 1.44M drive as a choice in the Setup routine. Instead, you have to use one of the many available public domain AT type setup programs, or "borrow" such a program from an AT-compatible system.

XT Model 286 Technical Specifications

The technical information for the XT-286 system described in this section covers the system architecture, memory configurations and capacities, standard system features, disk storage, expansion slots, keyboard specifications, and also physical and environmental specifications. You can use this information to determine the parts you need when you are upgrading or repairing these systems. Figure 20.14 shows the layout and components on the XT-286 motherboard.

System Architecture	
Microprocessor	80286
Clock speed	6MHz
Bus type	ISA (Industry Standard Architecture)
Bus width	16-bit
Interrupt levels	16 (11 usable)
Type	Edge-triggered
Shareable	No
DMA channels	8 (7 usable)
Bus masters supported	Yes
Upgradable processor complex	No
Memory	
Standard on system board	640K
Maximum on system board	640K

Memory

Maximum total memory	16M
Memory speed (ns) and type	150ns dynamic RAM chips/SIMMs
System board memory-socket type	30-pin (9-bit) SIMM
Number of memory-module sockets	2
Memory used on system board	One bank of 4 64K×4-bit and 2 64K×1-bit DRAM parity chips, and one bank of 2 9-bit SIMMs
Memory cache controller	No
Wait states:	
System board	0
Adapter	1

Standard Features

ROM size	64K
ROM shadowing	No
Optional math coprocessor	80287
Coprocessor speed	4.77MHz
Standard graphics	None standard
RS232C serial ports	1
UART chip used	NS16450
Maximum speed (bits per second)	9,600bps
Maximum number of ports supported	2
Pointing device (mouse) ports	None standard
Parallel printer ports	1
Bidirectional	Yes
Maximum number of ports supported	3
CMOS real-time clock (RTC)	Yes
CMOS RAM	64 bytes
Battery life	5 years

Disk Storage

Internal disk and tape drive bays	1 full-height and 2 half-height
Number of 3 1/2-inch and 5 1/4-inch bays	0/3
Standard floppy drives	1×1.2M
Optional floppy drives:	
5 1/4-inch 360K	Optional
5 1/4-inch 1.2M	Standard
3 1/2-inch 720K	Optional
3 1/2-inch 1.44M	Optional
3 1/2-inch 2.88M	No
Hard disk controller included	ST-506/412 (Western Digital WD1003-WA2)
ST-506/412 hard disks available	20M
Drive form factor	5 1/4-inch

(continues)

(continued)

Disk Storage

Drive interface	ST-506/412
Drive capacity	20M
Average access rate (ms)	65
Encoding scheme	MFM
BIOS drive type number	2
Cylinders	615
Heads	4
Sectors per track	17
Rotational speed (RPMs)	3600
Interleave factor	3:1
Data transfer rate (kilobytes/second)	170
Automatic head parking	No

Expansion Slots

Total adapter slots	8
Number of long and short slots	6/2
Number of 8-/16-/32-bit slots	3/5/0
Available slots (with video)	5

Keyboard Specifications

101-key Enhanced keyboard	Yes
Fast keyboard speed setting	Yes
Keyboard cable length	6 feet

Physical Specifications

Footprint type	Desktop
Dimensions:	
Height	5.5 inches
Width	19.5 inches
Depth	16.0 inches
Weight	28 pounds

Environmental Specifications

Power-supply output	157 watts
Worldwide (110v/60Hz, 220v/50Hz)	Yes
Auto-sensing/switching	Yes
Maximum current:	
90-137 VAC	4.5 amps
Operating range:	
Temperature	60–90 degrees F
Relative humidity	8–80 percent

Environmental Specifications

Maximum operating altitude	7,000 feet
Heat (BTUs/hour)	824
Noise (Average db, operating, 1m)	42
FCC classification	Class B

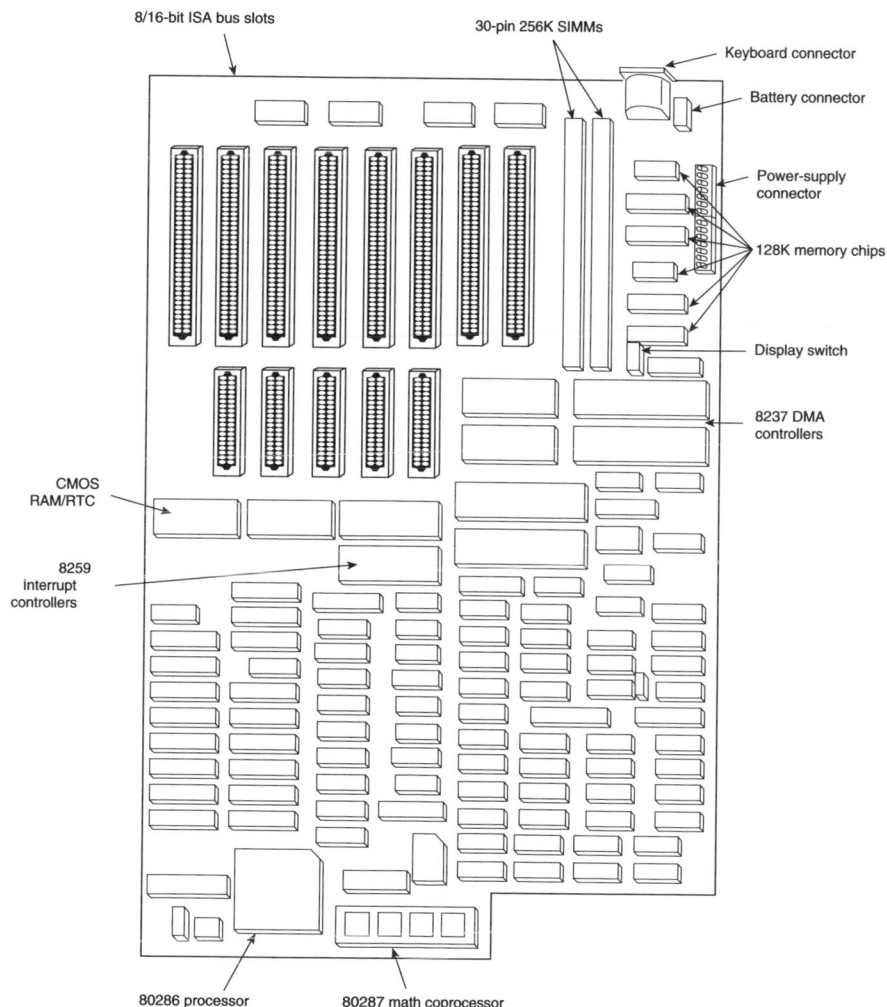

FIG. 20.14 The IBM XT-286 motherboard.

Table 20.13 lists the XT Model 286 system-unit part numbers.

Table 20.13   IBM XT-286 Model Part Numbers

Description	Number
XT Model 286 system unit, 6MHz 0 wait state, 640K, serial/parallel, 1.2M floppy drive, one 20M hard disk	5162286
Optional Accessories	
5 1/4-inch, half-height 360K drive	6450325
3 1/2-inch, half-height 720K internal drive	6450258
3 1/2-inch, half-height 720K external drive	2683190
80287 math coprocessor option	6450211
Enhanced Keyboard Accessories	
Clear keycaps (60) with paper inserts	6341707
Blank light keycaps	1351710
Blank dark keycaps	1351728
Paper keycap inserts (300)	6341704
Keycap removal tools (6)	1351717

Chapter 21

A Final Word

The contents of this book cover the components of a PC-compatible system. In this book, you have discovered how all the components operate and interact, and how they should be set up and installed. You have seen the ways that components fail and learned the symptoms of these failures. You reviewed steps in diagnosing and troubleshooting the major components in a system so you can locate and replace a failing component. You also learned about upgrades for components, including what upgrades are available, the benefits of an upgrade, and how to obtain and perform the actual upgrade. Because failing components so often are technically obsolete, it is often desirable to combine repair and upgrade procedures to replace a failing part with an upgraded or higher-performance part.

The information I have presented in this book represents many years of research, along with years of hands-on, practical experience with PC-compatible systems. A great deal of research and investigation have gone into each section. This information and knowledge have saved many companies and even individuals many thousands of dollars. By reading this book, you can also take advantage of this wealth of information; the information presented may save you and your company time, energy, and, most importantly, money!

Bringing PC service and support in-house is one of the best ways to save money. Eliminating service contracts for most systems and reducing downtime are just two of the benefits of applying the information presented in this book. As I have indicated many times in this book, you can also save a lot of money on component purchases by eliminating the middleman and purchasing the components directly from distributors or manufacturers.

Appendix A, "Vendor List," provides the best of these sources for you to contact. If you intend to build your own systems, the vendor list will be extremely useful, as I have listed sources for all the components needed to assemble a complete system—from the screws and brackets all the way to the cases, power supplies, and motherboards. I have found that this list is one of the most frequently used parts of this book; I use it myself all the time. In the past, people have been unable to make direct purchases because doing so required a new level of understanding of the components involved. Also, many of the manufacturers and direct distributors of products are unable to provide support for beginning users; this is why they often rely on the middlemen to sell and support their products. Of course, armed with this knowledge, you can now purchase products from more direct sources, eliminating the middleman and paying less for the products in the process. This book can give you the deeper level of knowledge and understanding you need so you can purchase the components you want directly from the vendors who manufacture and distribute them, saving a great deal of money in the long run.

Not only can you use this book to save money, but the information contained within will allow you to have the knowledge and confidence to select exactly the components you need to build a custom and yet nonproprietary system to your own specifications. Such a system would be fully upgradable and maintainable using inexpensive industry-standard components.

I used many sources to gather the information in this book, starting with my own real-world experiences. I have also taught this information to thousands of people in the hundreds of seminars presented over the last 17 years by my company, Mueller Technical Research. In fact, my PC Hardware seminars are the longest-running seminars on the subject. During these seminars, I am often asked where more technical information can be obtained and whether I have any "secrets" for acquiring this knowledge. Well, I won't keep any secrets! I can freely share the following five key sources of information that can help you become a verifiable expert in PC upgrading and repairing:

- Manuals (documentation)
- Magazines

- Modems (online resources such as the Internet)
- Meetings (seminars)

- Machines (hands-on work with actual systems)

The last thing I'll show you in this chapter is how this book can be a great resource to prepare for the CompTIA A+ certification exam. Thousands of A+-certified PC Technicians have used this book as part of their training (and continue to use it in their jobs).

Manuals (Documentation)

Manuals and documentation are the single most important sources of computer information. Unfortunately, these also are the most frequently overlooked sources of information. Much of my knowledge has come from poring over technical-reference manuals and other original equipment manufacturers' (OEM) manuals.

One of the biggest problems in troubleshooting, servicing, or upgrading a system is having proper documentation. I believe that good documentation is critical for system support and future upgrade capability. Because it can be a problem getting documentation on older systems or components, the best time to acquire documentation is when the system or components are new.

Oftentimes, these manuals must be obtained from the OEM of the equipment you purchase, meaning the vendor or reseller will not supply them. Wherever possible, you should make an effort to discover who the real OEM of each component in your system is, so you can obtain documentation on the product or component.

A simple analogy explains the importance of manuals and other issues concerning repair and maintenance of a system. Compare your business use of computers to a taxicab company. The company has to purchase automobiles to use as cabs. The owners purchase not one car but an entire fleet of cars. Do you think that they would purchase a fleet of automobiles based solely on reliability, performance, or even gas-mileage statistics? Would they neglect to consider ongoing maintenance and service of these automobiles? Would they purchase a fleet of cars that could be serviced only by the original manufacturer and for which parts could not be obtained easily or inexpensively? Do you think that they would buy a car that did not have available a detailed service and repair manual? Would they buy an automobile for which parts were scarce and that was supported by a sparse dealer network with few service and parts outlets, making long waits for parts and service inevitable? The answer (of course) to all these questions is no, no, no!

You can see why most taxicab companies and police departments use "standard" automobiles such as the Chevrolet Caprice or Ford Crown Victoria. If ever there were "generic" cars, these models would qualify! Dealers, parts, and documentation for these particular models are everywhere. These cars share parts with many other automobiles as well, which makes them easy to service and maintain.

Your business (especially if it is large) also amounts to a "fleet" of computers. Think of this fleet as being similar to the cars of a cab company, which would go out of business quickly if these cars could not be kept running smoothly and inexpensively. Now you know why the old Checker Marathon automobile used to be so popular with cab companies: Its design barely changed from the time it was introduced in 1956 until it was discontinued in July 1982. This meant that parts interchanged and service procedures remained largely the same over the entire 26-year life of the product.

In many ways, the industry-standard PC-compatible systems are like the venerable Checker Marathon. You can get technical information by the shelfful for these systems. You can get parts and upgrade material from so many sources that anything you need is always immediately available and at a discounted price. These are the benefits of purchasing industry-standard systems using standard motherboard and chassis form factors. This results in systems that are easily supported, repaired, and upgraded. An additional benefit is that when these standards are followed, the systems in a company can be easily maintained using largely interchangeable parts.

Several types of documentation are available to cover a given system:

- *System-level documentation.* The system-specific manual(s) put together by the system manufacturer or assembler. Some companies break this down further into Operations, Technical Reference, and Service manuals.

- *Component-level documentation.* The specific OEM (Original Equipment Manufacturer) manuals for each major component, such as the motherboard, video card, hard disk, floppy disk drive, CD-ROM drive, modem, network card, SCSI adapter, and so on.

- *Chip- and chipset-level documentation.* The most specific and technical manuals that cover items such as the processor, motherboard chipset, Super I/O chip, BIOS, memory modules, video chipset, and various disk controller, SCSI bus interface, network interface, and other chips used throughout the system.

The system- and component-level documentation is essential for even the most basic troubleshooting and upgrading tasks. More technical literature, such as the chip- and chipset-level documentation, is probably necessary only for software and hardware developers who have more special requirements. However, if you are like me and really want to know as much about a system as possible, you will find that having the chip- and chipset-level documentation can give you insights and information about a system you simply can't get otherwise. This section will examine all this documentation and, most importantly, explain how to get it!

Basic System Documentation

When you purchase a complete system, it should include a basic set of documentation. What you actually get will vary widely, depending on what type of system you get and who put it together.

Name-brand manufacturers such as IBM, Compaq, Hewlett-Packard, Toshiba, Packard Bell, and others will almost certainly include custom user-level manuals they have developed specifically for each system they sell. These manuals are often very basic and contain only enough information for basic system setup, installation, and minor troubleshooting. Most of the bigger name manufacturers who design and manufacture their own motherboards have much more technical documentation available. For example, IBM, HP, Toshiba, and Compaq have available technical reference and service manuals for their systems that contain much more information than the books that come free with their systems.

These technical reference manuals contain detailed information about the components used in the system—information that would be useful to technicians or sophisticated users wishing to know more details. Service manuals contain detailed instructions on system disassembly and reassembly, and troubleshooting flowcharts, problem-solving guides, and a complete parts listing. Service manuals are particularly useful for laptop and notebook computers, where the disassembly and reassembly is often not intuitive and where virtually all the parts are custom. You should contact the manufacturer or a manufacturer-authorized service center to find out about any service or technical reference documentation that might be available.

Companies who assemble or build systems out of industry-standard components such as most of the well-known mail-order brands may either produce their own documentation or simply include the documentation that is supplied with the components they install in their systems. Most of the larger system assemblers, such as Gateway, Dell, Micron, Midwest Micro, Quantex, and others, will also have their own custom-produced documentation for the main system unit, and may even have custom manuals for many of the individual system components.

This type of documentation is useful for people setting up a system for the first time or for performing simple upgrades, but it often lacks the detailed technical reference information needed by somebody who might be troubleshooting the system or upgrading it beyond what the manufacturer or assembler had originally intended. In that case, you are better off with any of the OEM component manuals that are available directly from the component or peripheral manufacturers themselves.

Most of the smaller system assemblers will forego any custom-produced system documentation and simply include the component-level manuals for the components they are including in the assembled system. For example, if an Asus motherboard and STB video card were included in a particular system, the manuals from Asus and STB that originally came with those products would be included with the assembled system.

Getting Documentation from an Assembler

Some system assemblers like to keep the component documentation and not include it with the systems they build. This forces the purchaser of the systems to go back to the assembler for any support or technical information. It also tends to make the purchaser believe that the assembler actually manufactured the system rather than simply assembling it using off-the-shelf components. In other cases, system assemblers use special OEM versions of products that come in plain white boxes with little or no documentation. In that case, the system assembler is expected to provide the documentation in their custom manual. If you get the generic OEM product versions with your system, I would recommend contacting the actual OEM component manufacturer for more detailed and specific documentation.

The standard manuals included with most system components and peripherals contain basic instructions for system setup, operation, testing, relocation, and option installation. Some sort of basic diagnostics disk (sometimes called a *Diagnostics and Setup* or *Reference Disk*) normally is included with a system as well. Often the diagnostics are simply a custom-labeled version of a commonly available commercial diagnostic program.

Tip

Most system vendors and equipment manufacturers have jumper settings and manuals available on their Web sites in downloadable form. Appendix B, "Useful Hardware Web Sites," contains a list of vendors and their Web sites.

Component and Peripheral Documentation

It is a well-known fact that many systems sold today are not really manufactured as a custom unit by a single company but instead are assembled out of standard off-the-shelf components that are available on the open market. In fact, I normally recommend that people purchase exactly that type of system, because all the components conform to known standards and can easily be replaced or upgraded later.

Even proprietary manufactured systems such as IBM, Compaq, Hewlett-Packard, Packard Bell, and others use at least some off-the-shelf standard components (disk drives, for example). To fully document a system, I recommend you take an inventory of the standard components used and then collect all the OEM documentation or product manuals for them.

This process is simple; when I am supporting a given system, I first disassemble it and write down all the information on each of the components inside. Sometimes, you will need to do a little more investigating or even ask the company that assembled the system exactly what components they included. Most components, such as hard disks, CD-ROM drives, video cards, sound cards, network cards, and more, are pretty easy to identify. Somewhere on the device or card there should be a label indicating at least the manufacturer and usually also the model number. From this, you can look up the manufacturer in the vendor listing in Appendix A of this book. Using that information, you can contact the company via telephone, fax, or Internet Web site to obtain the complete documentation on their products.

If you are running a fully Plug-and-Play-compatible operating system such as Windows 95/98 or Windows NT 5.0, you can find out the manufacturers and model numbers of many of the devices in your system by using the Device Manager program.

Motherboards can be tricky to identify because not all manufacturers mark them clearly. In fact, the largest manufacturer of motherboards, Intel, does not mark its boards with either the name or the model number! This is because the major system assemblers who use the boards (Gateway, Dell, Micron, and many others) don't really want people to know where the board originally came from. In some cases, the system assembler will even stamp their own name on the board, even though they did not manufacture it.

If there are no motherboard manufacturer markings, you should contact the company that sold you the computer to ask them exactly what motherboard you have. I would not even consider purchasing a new system unless I knew exactly whose motherboard was being included and exactly what model it was. Don't be afraid to ask the system assembler company exactly what motherboard or other components they are installing in the systems they sell. If they can't or won't answer, you may be better off purchasing from a different company in the future. If the company who sold the system is no longer available or cannot help, check the paperwork that came with the system. Sometimes there are clues in the original paperwork that might indicate what mother-board your system includes. Most of the popular motherboard manufacturers are listed in the vendor list in Appendix A.

The Micro House CD included with this book has a very useful reference to over 150 common PC motherboards. Part of the Micro House Support Source for Hardware product, this reference has specifications, jumper settings, memory configurations, and schematics for some of the most popular 486, Pentium, Pentium Pro, and Pentium II motherboards available. These 150 motherboards cover many of the systems in use today. Many of the motherboards are from Intel, and many more are from major system vendors such as IMB, Hewlett-Packard, and Compaq. As a last resort, you might be able to identify your board by comparing it to those shown in this reference. The version of Support Source for Hardware included on the CD also includes documentation on hundreds of drives, drive controllers, NICs, and modems.

> **Note**
>
> Every electronic component in your computer is required to have an FCC ID number. If you are having trouble determining the original manufacturer of a component, use the FCC ID locator function of the Micro House Support Source product on the CD to look up the FCC ID number and find the name of the manufacturer.

As an example, one system I worked on is a Gateway P6 (Pentium Pro) 200MHz system that included the following industry-standard components:

Motherboard:	Intel VS440FX "Venus"
Video Card:	STB Velocity 3D
Hard Disk:	Quantum Fireball TM3840A
Floppy Disk Drive:	Panasonic JU-256
CD-ROM Drive:	Mitsumi FX120

Most of the larger system assemblers like Gateway, Dell, Micron, and others have been using Intel motherboards. Most motherboards today use Intel processors and chipsets, but some people may not be aware that Intel makes complete PC motherboards, as well. Even so, Gateway did not include the actual Intel motherboard or other component manuals but instead included their own custom manuals for the motherboard, video card, hard disk, and CD-ROM drive. By contacting the individual companies directly over the Internet and via the telephone, I was able to obtain more detailed documentation on all these products. Many times, the OEM documentation or product manuals can be downloaded directly from the respective companies' Web sites, often in the form of Adobe Acrobat .PDF files, which you can read with the Acrobat reader available for free downloading from Adobe.

> **Note**
>
> Not all these manuals are available online, and even if they are, it is still nice to have the printed manuals or datasheets in your documentation library for future reference.

Chip and Chipset Documentation

If you really want the ultimate in documentation for your system, I highly recommend getting the documentation for the various chips and chipsets in your system. This would include specific manuals for each of the major chip-level components in the system—such as the processor, motherboard chipset, BIOS, Super I/O chipset, and so on. Before you can get this documentation, you must first identify all the relevant chips and chipsets in your system.

The process is relatively simple. Look at the documentation for each major component, especially the motherboard. The OEM motherboard documentation should tell you which chipset is used on the board, which processors are supported, and which Super I/O chip is used. From the OEM documentation you have on your system components, you should be able to find out what the following major chip and chipsets are:

> Processor
>
> Motherboard Chipset
>
> ROM BIOS
>
> Super I/O Chip
>
> Video Chipset

If your motherboard has an integrated video card, the video chipset type will be listed there also. If you have a separate video card, look in the video card manual, which should clearly identify the video chipset used.

The most important chips you will want to identify are on the motherboard. The first thing you would want to identify is the processor. This should be relatively easy; most PC systems use Intel processors. A small percentage of systems use AMD or Cyrix processors, or versions of these processors sold under other names. The documentation that comes with the system will normally identify which brand of processor you have and which model and speed it is.

If you aren't sure what processor is in the system, software programs such as the MSD (Microsoft Diagnostics) program can tell you. It's included with Windows 3.1, the System Control Panel in Windows 9x, or a system diagnostic you purchase, such as the Norton Utilities. Commercial utilities like the Norton Utilities can give you more detailed information about your processor, often including the speed it is running at and other pertinent info, such as whether it supports MMX instructions or not.

Normally, the processor is the largest chip on the motherboard, and can often be identified by simply reading the information stamped on it. In some cases, the processor will have a heat sink or fan attached to the top. In this case, you may have to either remove the heat sink or fan to read the information stamped on top of the chip, or simply remove the entire processor and heat sink or fan assembly to read the information stamped on the bottom of the chip.

> **Note**
>
> You should check to see that the processor in your system is really rated to run at the speed your system is set for. Many of the smaller system assemblers have been installing overclocked CPUs in their systems. For example, they might have sold you a 266MHz system but only have a 233MHz processor installed. The only way to verify the actual chip rating is to check the chip manufacturer markings stamped or printed on the chip. Some vendors have even resorted to wiping off the original markings and remarking the chips at a higher speed, or carefully placing an official-looking sticker over the original marks. Unfortunately, these remarked chips can be difficult to spot for the less experienced. These types of scams are one reason for recommending the bigger name-brand system assemblers. Intel has more recently been building overclock protection circuitry into their chips that is designed to prevent this.

The motherboard chipset type can be difficult for software to determine, so you will normally have to find out which chipset you have from the motherboard documentation or by firsthand inspection. The motherboard chipset usually consists of two or more large chips on the board; however, there are chipsets that use anywhere from one to six chips. Generally, each chip in the set will have a part number stamped on it, but the chipset will be named after the main chip. The Pentium Pro board I mentioned had two chips labeled 82441FX and 82442FX; these two chips are called the *North Bridge* or primary components of the chipset. There was also an 82371SB *South Bridge* chip that is also called the PIIX3 (PCI/IDE/ISA eXcelerator). All three chips are a part of what Intel calls the *440FX chipset.* Most of their newer chipsets such as the 440LX and 440BX, consist of only two chips—one for the North Bridge and one for the South Bridge.

◀◀ See "Chipsets," p. 183

Finding out the manufacturer of the motherboard BIOS is easy; that is normally found in the motherboard manual. It is also normally displayed, along with the exact version number you have, every time you power the system on. Most systems today use an AMI, Award, or Phoenix BIOS, but there are several other manufacturers as well.

Virtually all motherboards built in the '90s and later include a special interface chip called a Super I/O chip. This is a single-chip device that normally includes the following components:

- Primary and secondary IDE host adapters
- Floppy disk drive controller
- Two serial ports
- One parallel port

Many of the more recent Super I/O chips do not include the IDE host adapters, such as the National Semiconductor 87308 or 87309 used in the Intel Pentium Pro and Pentium II motherboards. That is because the IDE ports are already built into the various Intel 82371 South Bridge chips. The National Semiconductor Super I/O chips also include an

8042-style keyboard and mouse controller. Some Super I/O chips include an MC146818-style real-time clock with nonvolatile CMOS RAM, although that is also normally a part of the Intel chipset South Bridge. Other Super I/O chips may include a game (joystick) interface as well. Obtaining the documentation for your particular Super I/O chip will, of course, tell you exactly what its capabilities are.

Another important chipset in a system is the *video chipset*. This is normally found on the video card, or on the motherboard if the motherboard has built-in video. The OEM video card or motherboard documentation should tell you exactly which video chipset you have. If not, you can use free software such as MSD or commercial programs such as Norton Utilities to identify which chipset you have without even opening up the case. A last resort would be to open the system and read the part number right off of the video chipset, which is usually the largest chip on the video card.

Using a Pentium Pro 200MHz system as an example, I found it contained the following main chip and chipset components:

Processor:	Intel Pentium Pro
Motherboard Chipset:	Intel 440FX "Natoma"
ROM BIOS:	AMI
Super I/O Chip:	National Semiconductor PC87308
Video Chipset:	S3 Inc. ViRGE/VX

Note that this particular motherboard did not have the video integrated, so the video chipset was on the video card.

From this documentation, I learned about the capability to increase the clock multiplier setting on the motherboard to an otherwise undocumented 3.5x, which resulted in running the Pentium Pro 200 chip at 233MHz! I was also able to get more information on the various serial, parallel, and disk controllers contained in the Super I/O chip, and I learned more about the advanced CMOS settings in the BIOS Setup routines.

For example, I often get questions about the Advanced CMOS settings. Most people assume that these settings are described in their ROM BIOS documentation, because the ROM-based CMOS Setup program in their system controls these settings. If you contact the BIOS manufacturer or read the BIOS documentation, you will quickly find out that the ROM BIOS manufacturer knows little or nothing about these settings. In fact, these settings actually have little or nothing to do with the particular ROM BIOS used and everything to do with the particular motherboard *chipset* used. You can find descriptions of all these settings in the documentation for your motherboard chipset, which can be obtained from the chipset manufacturer.

Manufacturer System-Specific Documentation

If your system is from a name-brand manufacturer—such as IBM, Compaq, Hewlett-Packard, Toshiba, and others—there may be a wealth of information available in manufacturer-specific manuals and documentation. Because of the specific nature of the information in these types of manuals, you most likely will have to obtain it from the manufacturer of the system.

Large manufacturers such as Intel, IBM, Compaq, Hewlett-Packard, and others both manufacture their own components and purchase components from other sources. Many of these manufacturers also make available complete libraries of technical documentation for their systems. IBM, HP, and Compaq also make their technical libraries available in CD-ROM versions, which are not only very comprehensive but also very convenient and easy to search. These CD-ROMs contain detailed information about PC systems and peripherals from these companies. If you have an IBM, Compaq, or HP system, contact the manufacturer to see about ordering their CD-ROM reference library. Normally, these are offered as subscriptions for $250 or so annually.

The process of obtaining other manufacturers' manuals may (or may not) be easy. Most large companies run responsible service and support operations that provide technical documentation. Other companies either do not have or are unwilling to part with such documentation, in an effort to protect their service departments (and their dealers' service departments) from competition. Contact the manufacturer directly; the manufacturer can direct you to the correct department so that you can inquire about this information. Information on how to contact most PC manufacturers can be found in the vendor listing in Appendix A of this book.

Magazines

The next source of information, magazines, is one of the best sources of up-to-date reviews and technical data. Featured are "bug fixes," problem alerts, and general industry news. Keeping a printed book up-to-date with the latest events in the computer industry is extremely difficult or even impossible. Things move so fast that the magazines themselves barely keep pace. I subscribe to most of the major computer magazines and am hard-pressed to pick one as the best. They all are important to me, and each one provides different information or the same information with a different angle or twist. Although the reviews usually leave me wanting, the magazines still are a valuable way to at least hear about products, most of which I never would have known about without the magazines' reports and advertisements. Most computer magazines are also available on CD-ROM, which can ease the frantic search for a specific piece of information you remember reading about. If CD-ROM versions are too much for your needs, be aware that you can access and search most major magazines on the Internet. This capability is valuable when you want to research everything you can about a specific subject.

One of the best kept secrets in the computer industry is the excellent trade magazines that offer free subscriptions. Although many of these magazines are directed toward the wholesale or technical end of the industry, I like to subscribe to them. Some of my favorite magazines in this category include the following:

- *Computer Design*
- *Computer Hotline*
- *Computer Reseller News*
- *Electronic Design News*
- *Electronic Buyer's News*
- *Electronic Engineering Times*
- *Electronic News*
- *Electronic Products*
- *Processor*
- *Service News*
- *Test and Measurement World*

Most of these magazines offer free subscriptions to anyone who qualifies. Aimed at people in the computer and electronics industries, these magazines offer a much greater depth and breadth of technical and industry information than the more "public" magazines that most people are familiar with. You'll find these and other recommended magazines in the vendor list in Appendix A.

Online Resources

With a modem, you can tie into everything from the Internet (World Wide Web) to local electronic bulletin board systems (BBSs) to major information networks such as CompuServe and AOL. Many hardware and software companies offer technical support and even software upgrades over the Internet. Through the Internet and other online resources, you can reach computer enthusiasts and technical-support people from various organizations, and experts in virtually all areas of computer hardware and software. You can also collect useful utility and help programs that can make your job much easier. The world of public-domain and user-supported software awaits, as do more technical information and related experiences than you can imagine.

Appendix A includes not only the name, address, and voice phone number for the company, but also the Internet addresses (Web sites) or BBS numbers, where available. If you need more information on a vendor's products, or need technical support, try using the vendor's online connection. Many companies today provide online services to facilitate obtaining updated software or driver files that you can download quickly and easily. When a vendor provides an online connection, I consider that service a major advantage in comparison to other vendors who do not provide such a service. Using vendor-provided online connections either through the Internet or via a private BBS or even CompuServe has saved me money and countless hours of time.

In fact, the Internet is probably the most efficient method of reaching me. My e-mail address is **scottmueller@compuserve.com**. If you have questions or just a comment or useful information you think I might be interested in, send me a message. Because of the extra steps in processing, my standard mail can get backed up, and it can take me quite a while to answer a regular postal letter. Electronic mail, however, involves fewer steps for me to send, and always seems to have a higher priority. If you do send a regular letter, be sure to include a SASE (Self-Addressed, Stamped Envelope) so I will be able to reply.

Seminars

Public and private seminars are a very valuable resource. This is, in fact, how I got my start writing; I teach PC hardware seminars, and I had to write a course book to go along with the seminars! Seminars are an excellent way to have information explained in person, often filling in gaps and adding visual information that isn't nearly as easy to present in a printed book alone.

Seminars come in two main types, public and on-site. A public course is just that, offered to the general public so anybody can sign up and attend. These are most often conducted in hotels or at specific training facilities around the country. On-site seminars are conducted at a particular company's location and only for employees of that company. These seminars are often customized with that company's individual needs in mind.

Machines

The term *machines* refers to the systems themselves—that is, hands-on experience. Actual experience on live systems is one of my best sources of information. For example, suppose that I need to answer the question "Will the XYZ SCSI host adapter work with the ABC tape drive?" The answer is as simple as plugging everything in and flipping the switch. (Simple to talk about, that is; actual testing can take quite a bit of time!)

Seriously, experimenting with and observing running systems are some of the best learning tools at your disposal. I recommend that you try everything; rarely will anything you try harm the equipment. Harming valuable data is definitely possible, if not likely, however, so make regular backups as insurance. You should not use a system you depend on for day-to-day operations as an experimental system; if possible, use a secondary machine. People sometimes are reluctant to experiment with systems that cost a lot of money, but much can be learned through direct tests and studies of the system. I often find that vendor claims about a product are somewhat misleading when I actually install it and run some tests. If you are unsure that something will really work, make sure that the company has a return policy that allows you to return the item for a refund if it does not meet your expectations.

Support people in larger companies have access to quantities of hardware and software I can only dream about. Some larger companies have *toy stores*, where they regularly purchase equipment solely for evaluation and testing. Dealers and manufacturers also have access to an enormous variety of equipment. If you are in this position, take advantage of this access to equipment, and learn from this resource. When new systems are purchased, take notes on their construction and components.

Every time I encounter a system I have not previously worked with, I immediately open it up and start taking notes. I want to know the make and model of all the internal components, such as disk drives, power supplies, and motherboards. As far as motherboards are concerned, I like to record the numbers of the primary IC chips on the board, such as the processor (of course), integrated chipsets, floppy drive controller chips, keyboard controller chips, video chipsets, and any other major chips on the board. By knowing which chipset your system uses, you can often infer other capabilities of the system, such as enhanced setup or configuration capabilities.

I like to know which BIOS version is in the system, and I even make a copy of the BIOS on disk for backup and further study purposes. I want to know the hard drive tables from the BIOS, and any other particulars involved in setting up and installing a system. Write down the type of battery a system uses so that you can obtain spares. Note any unique brackets or construction techniques such as specialized hardware (Torx screws, for example) so that you can be prepared for servicing the system later. Some programs have been designed to help you maintain an inventory of systems and components, but I find that these fall far short of the detail I am talking about here.

This discussion brings up a pet peeve of mine. Nothing burns me up as much as reading a review of computer systems in a major magazine, in which reviewers test systems and produce benchmark and performance results for, let's say, the hard disks or video displays in a system. Then, they do not open up the machines and tell me (and the world) exactly which components the manufacturer of the system is using! I want to know exactly which disk controller, hard drive, BIOS, motherboard, video adapter, and so on are found in each system. Without this information, their review and benchmark tests are useless to me.

Then these reviewers run a test of disk performance between two systems with the same disk controller and drives and say (with a straight face) that the one that came out a few milliseconds ahead of the other wins the test. With the statistical variation that normally occurs in any manufactured components, these results are meaningless. The point is perhaps to be very careful of whom you trust in a normal magazine review. If it tells me exactly which components were tested, I can draw my own conclusions and even make comparisons to other systems not included in that review.

You can always search the Net for unbiased reviews written by individuals about a given product. Some products with poor support or reliability problems often have anti-product Web sites put up by disgruntled individuals. Although one person's experience with a product may not be indicative of the normal performance, when you see hundreds of messages or sites complaining about something, you usually get the idea. Similarly, you may also find great praise for a product, or messages indicating how people have found uses that are out of the ordinary.

The Appendixes

The appendixes provide a collection of technical information, tables, charts, and lists especially useful to people in a computer support, troubleshooting, service, or upgrading role. Whether you're looking for the meaning of a word in the glossary, seeking the address and phone number of a company or vendor in the vendor list, or searching for an arcane table not found in the normal chapter text, you'll most likely find the information in the appendixes.

The appendixes started out as a brief collection of essential information but have grown into a reference resource of their own.

CompTIA A+ Core Examination Objective Map

CompTIA is the organization that sets the objectives for the A+ certification. As with many computing fields, earning your certification can increase your job security or increase your value to prospective employers.

CompTIA released a new set of exam objectives and a new exam in July '98. This new exam is updated to slant the coverage more toward newer hardware and newer operating systems. If you aren't yet A+ certified, now is the perfect time to study for and pass the tests, as the objectives are more relevant than ever before. Even if you are certified, any employer or prospective employer would be impressed to see you recertify on the new objectives.

The A+ exam consists of two parts. The part that is most closely related to the topics in this book is the Core exam, which mostly covers hardware.

To become A+ certified, you must also pass the DOS/Windows Module Examination. Although this book does cover many of the topics tested by the DOS/Windows module in the course of discussing hardware, this book does not pretend to be a thorough reference to DOS or Windows, so those objectives are not listed here. I highly recommend the *A+ Certification Training Guide* published by New Riders Publishing (ISBN: 1-56205-896-7).

> **Tip**
>
> The CD-ROM that comes with this book includes test preparation software with 150 questions to help you prepare for the A+ Core exam. These 150 questions are part of a larger test prep program from Marcraft. Their complete program covers both components of the A+ exam and contains over 900 sample questions. For more information about this program and a special discount offer for purchasers of this book, see the page describing it near the end of the book.

The CompTIA organization has established the following objectives for the Core portion of the A+ Certification examination.

1.0 Installation, Configuration, and Upgrading

This section challenges the test taker to identify, install, configure, and upgrade microcomputer modules and peripherals. Established procedures for system assembly and disassembly must be followed. Test elements include the ability to identify and configure IRQs, DMAs, and I/O addresses, and to properly set configuration switches and jumpers.

1.1 Identify basic terms, concepts, and functions of system modules, including how each module should work during normal operation. Examples of concepts and modules include the following:

- System board
- Power supply
- CPU/microprocessor
- Memory
- Storage devices
- Monitor
- Modem
- Firmware
- Boot process
- BIOS
- CMOS

1.2 Identify basic procedures for adding and removing field-replaceable modules. Examples of modules include

- System board
- Power supply
- CPU/microprocessor
- Memory
- Storage devices
- Input devices

1.3 Identify available IRQs, DMAs, and I/O addresses with procedures for configuring them for device installation. Examples include

- Standard IRQ settings
- Modems
- Floppy disk drives
- Hard drives

1.4 Identify common peripheral ports, associated cables, and their connectors. Examples include

- Cable types
- Cable orientation
- Serial versus parallel
- Pin connections

Examples of connector types include

- DB-9
- DB-25
- RJ-11
- BNC
- RJ-45
- PS2/Mini-DIN

1.5 Identify proper procedures for installing and configuring IDE/EIDE devices. Examples include

- Master/slave
- Devices per channel

1.6 Identify proper procedures for installing and configuring SCSI devices. Topics include

- Address/termination conflicts
- Cabling
- Types (standard, wide, fast, ultra wide)
- Internal versus external
- Switch and jumper settings

1.7 Identify proper procedures for installing and configuring peripheral devices. Topics include

- Monitor/video card
- Modem
- Storage devices

1.8 Identify procedures for upgrading BIOS. Topics include

- Methods for upgrading
- When to upgrade

1.9 Identify hardware methods of system optimization and when to use them. Examples include

- Memory
- Hard drives
- CPU/microprocessors
- Cache memory

2.0 Diagnosing and Troubleshooting

This item requires the test taker to apply knowledge relating to diagnosing and troubleshooting common module problems and system malfunctions. This includes knowledge of the symptoms relating to common problems.

2.1 Identify common symptoms and problems associated with each module and how to troubleshoot and isolate the problems. Contents may include

- Processor/memory symptoms
- Keyboards/mouse/trackball/pen/microphones/touch pad
- Floppy drive failures
- Parallel ports/scanners/tape drives
- Hard drives
- Sounds card/audio
- Monitor/video
- Motherboards
- Modems
- BIOS
- CMOS
- Power supply
- Slot covers
- POST audible/visual error codes
- Troubleshooting tools; for example, multimeter

2.2 Identify basic troubleshooting procedures and good practices for eliciting problem symptoms from customers. Topics include

- Troubleshooting/isolation/problem determination
- Determine whether hardware or software problem

Gather information from the user regarding

- Customer environment
- Symptoms/error codes
- Situation when the problem occurred

3.0 Safety and Preventive Maintenance

This section requires the test taker to show knowledge of safety and preventive maintenance. With regard to safety, it includes the potential hazards to personnel and equipment when working with lasers, high-voltage equipment, ESD (Electrostatic Discharge), and items that require special disposal procedures that comply with environmental guidelines. With regard to preventive maintenance, this includes knowledge of preventive maintenance products, procedures, environmental hazards, and precautions when working on microcomputer systems.

3.1 Identify the purpose of various types of preventive maintenance products and procedures, and when to use or perform them. Examples include

- Liquid cleaning compounds
- Types of materials to clean contacts and connections
- Vacuum-out systems, power supplies, fans

3.2 Identify procedures and devices for protecting against environmental hazards. Examples include

- UPS (uninterruptible power supply)/suppressors/noise filters/plug strips
- Determining the signs of power issues
- Proper methods of component storage for future use

3.3 Identify the potential hazards and proper safety procedures relating to lasers and high-voltage equipment. Examples include

- Lasers can cause blindness.
- High-voltage equipment can cause electrocution; for example, power supply/CRT.

3.4 Identify items that require special disposal procedures that comply with environmental guidelines. Examples include

- Batteries
- Toner kits/cartridges
- Chemical solvents and cans
- CRTs
- MSDS (Material Safety Data Sheet)

3.5 Identify ESD (Electrostatic Discharge) precautions and procedures, including the use of ESD protection devices. Examples include

- What ESD can do, and how it may be apparent or hidden
- Common ESD protection devices
- Situations that could present a danger or hazard

4.0 Motherboard/Processors/Memory

This section requires the test taker to demonstrate knowledge of specific terminology, and facts, ways, and means of dealing with classifications, categories, and principles of motherboards, processors, and memory in microcomputer systems.

4.1 Distinguish between the popular CPU chips in terms of their basic characteristics. Popular CPU chips include

- Popular CPU chips

Characteristics include

- Physical size
- Voltage
- Speeds
- Onboard cache or not
- Sockets
- Number of pins

4.2 Identify the categories of RAM (Random Access Memory) terminology, their locations, and physical characteristics. Terminology includes

- EDO RAM (Extended Data Output RAM)
- DRAM (Dynamic Random Access Memory)
- SRAM (Static RAM)
- VRAM (Video RAM)
- WRAM (Windows Accelerator Card RAM)

Locations and physical characteristics include

- Memory bank
- Memory chips (8-bit, 16-bit, and 32-bit)
- SIMMS (Single Inline Memory Module)
- DIMMS (Dual Inline Memory Module)
- Parity chips versus non-parity chips

4.3 Identify the most popular type of motherboards, their components, and their architecture (for example, bus structures and power supplies).

Types of motherboards include

- AT (Full and Baby)
- ATX

Motherboard components include

- Communication ports
- SIMM and DIMM

- Processor sockets
- External cache memory (Level 2)

Bus architecture includes

- ISA
- EISA
- PCI
- USB (Universal Serial Bus)
- VESA local bus (VL-BUS)
- PC Card (PCMCIA)

Basic compatibility guidelines

4.4 Identify the purpose of CMOS (Complementary Metal-Oxide Semiconductor), what it contains, and how to change its basic parameters. Examples include

- Printer parallel port: Unidirectional/bidirectional, disable/enable, ECP/EPP
- COM/serial port: memory address, interrupt request, disable
- Hard drive: size and drive type
- Floppy drive: enable/disable drive or boot, speed, density
- Boot sequence
- Memory: parity, non-parity
- Date/time
- Passwords

5.0 Printers

This domain requires knowledge of basic types of printers, basic concepts, printer components, how they work, how they print onto a page, paper path, care and service techniques, and common problems.

5.1 Identify basic concepts, printer operations, printer components, and field-replaceable units in primary printer types.

Types of printers include

- Laser
- Inkjet
- Dot matrix

Paper feeder mechanisms

5.2 Identify care and service techniques and common problems with primary printer types. Examples include

- Feed and output

- Errors

- Paper jam

- Print quality

- Safety precautions

- Preventive maintenance

5.3 Identify the types of printer connections and configurations. Topics include

- Parallel

- Serial

- Network

6.0 Portable Systems

This section requires the test taker to demonstrate knowledge of portable computers and their unique components and problems.

6.1 Identify the unique components of portable systems and their unique problems. Examples include

- Battery

- LCD

- AC adapter

- Docking stations

- Hard drive

- Types I, II, III cards

- Network cards

- Memory

7.0 Basic Networking

This section requires the test taker to demonstrate knowledge of basic network concepts and terminology, ability to determine whether a computer is networked, knowledge of procedures for swapping and configuring network interface cards, and knowledge of the ramifications of repairs when a computer is networked.

7.1 Identify basic networking concepts, including how a network works. Examples include the following:

- Network access

- Protocol

- Network Interface Cards

- Full duplexing

- Cabling/Twisted-Pair, Coaxial, Fiber-Optic

- Ways to network a PC

7.2 Identify procedures for swapping and configuring network interface cards.

7.3 Identify ramifications of repairs on the network. Examples include

- Reduced bandwidth

- Loss of data

- Network slowdown

8.0 Customer Satisfaction

No one can underestimate the value and importance of customer satisfaction, especially personal computer repair technicians who must deal with customers who are often under stress because their computer has crashed. The CompTIA A+ Core Exam has several objectives dealing with customer service. As important as this topic is, it is not covered in this book, which is really about the nuts and bolts of PC repair.

In Conclusion

This edition marks a milestone in computer book publishing. This year marks the 10th anniversary of this book! This was the first book of its kind on the market, and it has since spawned an entire series of clone books from other competitors, many with surprisingly similar names. Despite the similar competitor books, this is still the longest-running, best-selling, most popular book of its kind. Actually, this book was previously published as my seminar manual for several years prior to this incarnation, so it has been around in one form or another even longer than this anniversary edition indicates.

No other book currently on the market contains such a complete and informative technical reference, which is one reason why so many large companies and educational institutions have standardized on this book for their technicians and students. This book is currently being used as an official textbook for many corporate and college-level computer training courses, as well as for my own PC training seminars, for which the book was originally designed.

I'd like to personally thank all the people who have supported the book over the years, especially those who have written with comments and suggestions.

I hope that *Upgrading and Repairing PCs, Tenth Anniversary Edition,* is beneficial to you, and I hope that you have enjoyed reading it as much as I have enjoyed writing it over the last 10 years. If you have questions about this book, or if you have ideas for future versions, I can be reached at the following address:

Scott Mueller
Mueller Technical Research
21 Spring Lane
Barrington Hills, IL 60010-9009
Phone: (847) 854-6794
Fax: (847) 854-6795
E-mail: **scottmueller@compuserve.com**
Web Address: **http://www.m-tr.com**

Remember that the best way to contact me is through e-mail; time constraints normally prevent me from responding to regular mail. If you do need a response through the mail, please include a self-addressed, stamped envelope so that I can reply to you. If you are interested in one of my many intensive PC training seminars or videotapes, please call my office.

Thank you again for reading this book, and a special thanks to those people who have been loyal readers since the first edition came out in December 1988.

Sincerely,

Scott Mueller

Appendix A

Vendor List

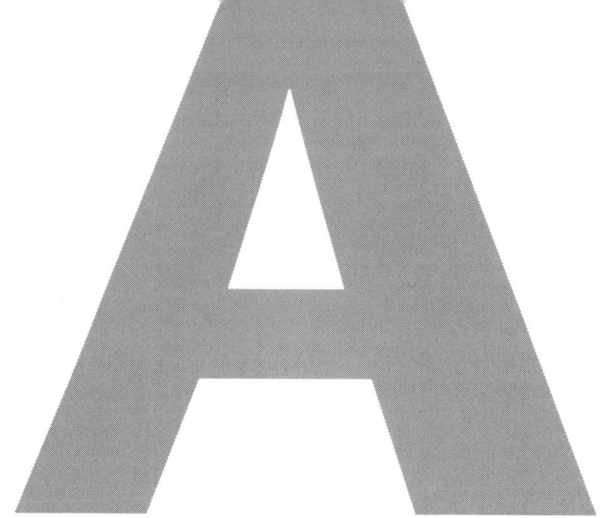

One of the most frustrating things about supporting PCs is finding a specific adapter board, part, driver program, or whatever you need to make a system work. If you are supporting or installing products, you will need access to technical support or documentation for products you may not have purchased. Over the years, I have compiled a list of companies whose products are popular or whose products I have found to work exceptionally well. I use these contacts regularly to provide information and components that enable me to support PC systems effectively.

Many of these companies have been mentioned in this book, but others not specifically mentioned have been added here. These companies carry many computer products you will have contact with or that I simply recommend. I have tried to list as many vendors as possible. These vendors are important in day-to-day work with PC systems and can supply documentation for your components, provide parts and service, and be used as a source for new equipment and software. This list is as up-to-date as possible, but companies move or go out of business all the time. If you find any information in this list that is no longer accurate, please call me or leave me a message on CompuServe at **scottmueller@compuserve.com**.

Many of the companies listed also provide support via electronic bulletin board systems (BBSes) and the World Wide Web (WWW).

Although originally exclusively the domain of computer enthusiasts, today many companies use Internet Web sites and BBS systems to provide a high level of technical support. Through a company-run Web site or BBS, you can receive detailed technical support on that company's products and download product literature and reference materials. I usually find the level of support I can obtain online is superior to traditional phone support, especially because I don't have to wait on hold!

With each company listing, I have included both standard phone numbers and 800 numbers where possible, so U.S. and international readers can easily contact these companies. Also included are fax numbers, Internet addresses, and BBS numbers, where available. I have not included any communications parameter settings, but virtually all BBS systems support 28.8K (V.34) connections.

Some companies run a *FAXback system*, an automated system through which you can request product and technical information to be sent directly to your own fax machine. FAXback systems are an excellent way to get immediate documentation or technical support to solve tough problems.

I have tried to include Net and WWW addresses for any companies that offer this access. Companies are adding this type of access rapidly these days, so many companies may have added Internet sites after this book was printed. If you discover any such information that I have not included, please e-mail me detailing what you have found.

Finally, each listing includes a short description of the products or services the company provides. I use this vendor list constantly myself; I hope you find this list as useful as I do!

As an improvement to this *Tenth Anniversary Edition*, I've added a categorical listing of products and services at the end of the vendor list. This way, if you need to find a product but you don't know what companies make them, look up the category at the end of the vendor list, find the vendors there that make or sell this type of product, and then look up the contact information for those vendors.

#1-PC Diagnostics Company (The ESD Division of Windsor Technologies, Inc.)

130 Alto St.
San Rafael, CA 94901

Phone	(415) 456-2200
Fax	(415) 456-2244
Web	**www.tufftest.com**
E-mail	**sales@tufftest.com**

Manufactures TuffTEST-Pro™, an excellent high-end service technician-level, PC diagnostics, and troubleshooting program that can be downloaded from their Web site.

3Com Corp.

5400 Bayfront Plaza
P.O. Box 58145
Santa Clara, CA 95052-8145

Phone	(408) 764-5000
Sales	(800) 638-3266
Fax	(408) 764-5001
Web	**www.3com.com**

Manufactures network adapters, servers, modems, and other networking equipment.

3D Labs

181 Metro Drive, Suite 520
San Jose, CA 95110

Phone	(408) 436-3455
Fax	(408) 436-3458
Web	**www.3dlabs.com**
E-mail	**support@3Dlabs.com**

Creates 3D graphics accelerators including a popular line called "Glint," included in many OEM graphics cards.

3Dfx

4435 Fortran Drive
San Jose, CA 95134

Phone	(408) 935-4400
Fax	(408) 262-8874
Web	**www.3dfx.com**

Creates 3D graphics accelerators including a popular line called "Voodoo," included in many OEM graphics cards.

3M Data Storage Products Division
1 Imation Place
Oakdale, MN 55128

Sales	(612) 704-4000
Tech Support	(800) 328-9438
Web	**www.Imation.com**

Manufactures magnetic disk and tape media.

Aavid Thermal Technologies, Inc.
One Kool Path
P.O. Box 400
Laconia, NH 03247-0400

Phone	(603) 528-3400
Fax	(603) 528-1478
Web	**www.aavid.com**

Manufactures a line of heat sinks and thermal management materials.

ABIT Computer (USA) Corporation
46808 Lakeview Blvd.
Fremont, CA 94538

Phone	(510) 623-0500
Fax	(510) 623-1092
Web	**www.abit-usa.com**
E-mail	**sales@abit-usa.com**

Manufactures an excellent line of PC motherboards in ATX and Baby-AT form factors. Their motherboards are known for having jumper and switchless software configuration.

Accurite Technologies, Inc.
48460 Lakeview Blvd.
Fremont, CA 94538-6532

Phone	(510) 668-4900
Fax	(510) 668-4905
Web	**www.accurite.com**
E-mail	**sales@accurite.com**

Manufactures floppy drive diagnostic products, PCMCIA diagnostic products, and PCMCIA floppy drive subsystems. Floppy drive diagnostic products include the Accurite Drive Probe floppy drive diagnostics program and HRD, DDD, and AAD industry standard test disks. PCMCIA products include the PC ExtenderCard, the PC ReportCard (a PCMCIA diagnostic card), the HeadstartCard (a PCMCIA developers' kit) and the Travel Floppy 144 (a PCMCIA interfaced floppy drive subsystem).

Acer America Corp.
2641 Orchard Pkwy.
San Jose, CA 95134-2073

Phone	(408) 432-6200
Tech Support	(800) 445-6495
Fax	(408) 922-2933
Web	**www.acer.com/AAC/**

The second-largest worldwide motherboard and PC system component manufacturer. Manufactures everything from components to complete desktop and notebook systems, as well as monitors and printers.

Acer Laboratories, Inc. (ALi)
Pacific Technology Group
4701 Patrick Henry Dr., Ste. 2101
Santa Clara, CA 95054

Phone	(408) 764-0644
Fax	(408) 496-6142
Web	**www.ali.com.tw**

Manufactures chipsets including PC motherboard, Super I/O, disk controller, and others. They make the Aladdin series chips for Pentium systems.

Acme Electric/Electronics Division
9962 Route 446
Cuba, NY 14727

Phone	(716) 968-2400
Live Wire Express (Repairs)	(800) 325-5848
Fax	(716) 968-3948

Manufactures uninterruptible power supplies (UPS) systems and power conditioners.

Adaptec
691 S. Milpitas Blvd.
Milpitas, CA 95035

Phone	(408) 945-8600
FaxBack	(800) 934-2766
Fax	(408) 262-2533
Tech Support	(408) 945-2550
Web	**www.adaptec.com**

A leading supplier of high-performance input/output solutions, including a broad array of SCSI host adapters and software solutions. Their SCSI host adapters have become a *de facto* standard and have an enormous amount of third-party support. Acquired Trantor Systems, Ltd. company, and now manufactures the MiniSCSI Parallel Port SCSI adapters, including hard disk and CD-ROM drivers for a variety of devices. Also acquired Future Domain.

Adobe Systems, Inc.
345 Park Ave.
San Jose, CA 95110-2704

Phone	(408) 536-6000
Fax	(408) 537-6000
Tech Support	(800) 833-6687
Web	**www.adobe.com**

Manufactures (and created) the PostScript language and a variety of graphics software. Publisher of PageMaker, Pagemill, Illustrator, and PostScript fonts (for DOS and Macintosh systems).

ADP Hollander Company
14800 28th Avenue North, Ste. 190
Plymouth, MN 55447

Phone	(800) 825-0644
Fax	(612) 553-0270

Publishes automotive parts interchange manuals.

Advanced Digital Information Corporation
11431 Willows Rd.
Redmond, WA 98052

Phone	(800) 336-1233
Fax	(206) 881-2296
Web	**www.adic.com**

Manufactures high-capacity tape-backup subsystems.

Advanced Integration Research (AIR)
2188 Del Franco St.
San Jose, CA 95131

Phone	(408) 428-0800
Fax	(408) 428-0950
BBS	(408) 428-1735
Web	**www.airwebs.com**

Manufactures a line of Pentium, Pentium Pro, and Pentium II-class high-performance motherboards.

Advanced Logic Research (ALR)
9401 Jeronimo St.
Irvine, CA 92618

Phone	(714) 581-6770
Sales	(800) 444-4257
Tech Support	(800) 257-1230
BBS	(714) 458-6834
Fax	(714) 581-9240
Web	**www.alr.com**

Manufactures high-performance business desktops, workstations, and server systems.

Advanced Micro Devices (AMD)

One AMD Place
P.O. Box 3453
Sunnyvale, CA 94088-3453

Phone	(408) 732-2400
Toll Free	(800) 538-8450
Tech Support	(800) 222-9323
Fax	(408) 749-4753
Web	**www.amd.com**

Manufactures Intel-compatible chips and math coprocessors. They have high-end processors including a Pentium-class chip called the K5 and their K6 technology rivals Pentium II in speed and performance.

Advanced Personal Systems

105 Serra Way, Ste. 418
Milpitas, CA 95035

Phone	(408) 298-3703
Fax	(408) 945-0242
Web	**www.syschk.com**

Manufactures the excellent SysChk diagnostics program, which provides valuable information about devices installed in your system.

Aeronics, Inc.

12741 Research Blvd., Ste. #500
Austin, TX 78759

Phone	(512) 258-2303
Fax	(512) 258-4392

Manufactures the highest-quality active and forced-perfect terminators for use in SCSI-bus systems. They are known for solving problems with longer distances or multiple-SCSI devices.

AIWA America, Inc. Computer Systems Division

16969 Von Karman, Ste. 260
Irvine, CA 92612

Phone	(949) 862-0200
Fax	(949) 862-0213
Web	**www.aiwa.com/csd**

Markets and sells mass storage solutions for network systems and personal workstations.

AllMicro, Inc. (Purchased by ForeFront Direct)

25400 US Hwy 19 N., Ste. 285
Clearwater, FL 33763

Phone	(813) 539-7283
Fax	(813) 531-0200
Sales	(800) 653-4933
BBS	(813) 535-9042
Web	**www.allmicro.com**
E-mail	**allmicro@allmicro.com**

Manufacturer and distributor of the Rescue data recovery software, the Post Plus, Discovery Card, Alert Card, and other various hardware and software diagnostic utilities and troubleshooting tools.

Alloy Computer Products

165 Forest St.
Marlborough, MA 01752

Phone	(978) 486-0001
Tech Support	(900) 680-2556
Fax	(978) 481-7711
BBS	(978) 486-4044

Manufactures tape-backup subsystems.

ALPS Electric

3553 N. First St.
San Jose, CA 95134

Phone	(408) 432-6000
Sales	(800) 950-ALPS (2577)
Tech Support	(800) 449-ALPS (2577)
Customer Service	(800) 825-ALPS (2577)
Fax	(408) 432-6035
BBS	(408) 432-6424
Web	**www.alpsusa.com**

Manufactures high-quality keyboards and keyboard switches. They have an excellent mechanical keyswitch design with a quality tactile feedback. Also makes printers, floppy drives, mice, and keypads.

Altex Electronics, Inc.
11342 IH 35 North
San Antonio, TX 78233

Phone	(210) 655-8882
Fax	(210) 637-3264 or
	(210) 637-3276
	(Attn: Jim Mundt)
Web	**www.altex.com**

Supplies mail-order computer/electronics parts.

Amdek Corporation (A Division of Wyse Technology)
1901 Zanker Rd.
San Jose, CA 95112

Phone	(408) 473-1200
Sales	(800) 722-WYSE (9973)
Tech Support	(408) 435-2770
Fax	(408) 473-1972
BBS	(408) 922-4400
Web	**www.wyse.com**

Manufactures monitors.

America Online
2200 AOL Way
Dulles, VA 20166

Phone	(703) 448-8700
Headquarters	(703) 265-2120
Web	**www.aol.com**

Provides a popular online service that allows access to their own network and the Internet.

American Megatrends, Inc. (AMI)
6145-F Northbelt Pkwy.
Norcross, GA 30071

Phone	(770) 246-8600
Sales	(800) 828-9264
BBS	(770) 246-8780
Web	**www.ami.com**

As a core technology provider, American Megatrends develops and provides superior system-level technologies including RAID products, BIOS, motherboards, and utilities.

American National Standards Institute (ANSI)
11 West 42nd St.
13th Floor
New York, NY 10036

Phone	(212) 642-4900
Fax	(212) 398-0023
Web	**www.ansi.org**

ANSI committees set standards throughout the computer industry. Copies of any ANSI-approved standard can be ordered here.

American Power Conversion (APC)
132 Fairgrounds Rd.
West Kingston, RI 02892

Phone	(401) 789-5735
Tech Support	(800) 800-4272
Fax	(401) 789-3710
Web	**www.apcc.com**

Manufactures a line of power protection equipment.

AMP, Inc.
AMP Building
P.O. Box 3608
Harrisburg, PA 17105

Phone	(717) 564-0100
Sales	(800) 522-6752
Fax	(717) 986-7605
Web	**www.amp.com**

Manufactures a variety of computer connectors, sockets, voltage adapters, and cables used by many OEMs.

Andromeda Research

P.O. Box 222
Milford, OH 45150

Phone	(513) 831-9708
Fax	(513) 831-7562
Web	**www.arlabs.com**

Manufactures an excellent EPROM programmer that runs from a PC parallel port. The device can program up to 16M UV and FLASH EPROMS, plus more. The included software runs under DOS, Win 3.1 and WINGS on any PC-compatible computer.

Annabooks/Annasoft Systems

11838 Bernardo Plaza Ct., Ste. 102
San Diego, CA 92128-2417

Phone	(619) 673-0870
Sales	(800) 462-1042
Fax	(619) 673-1432
Web	**www.annabooks.com**
E-mail	**info@annabooks.com**

Publishes and sells an excellent line of technical books and information on PC hardware and software design. Teaches workshops on PCI, Cardbus, and USB design.

Anvil Cases

15650 Salt Lake Ave.
Industry, CA 91745

Phone	(626) 968-4100
Sales	(800) 359-2684
Fax	(626) 968-1703
Web	**www.anvildealer.com**

Manufactures heavy-duty equipment cases.

Apple Computer, Inc.

1 Infinite Loop
Cupertino, CA 95014

Phone	(408) 996-1010
Sales	(800) 538-9696

Fax	(800) 505-0171
Web	**www.apple.com**

Manufactures a line of personal computers under the Macintosh (Mac) brand name, peripherals, and software.

Arco Computer Products, Inc.

2750 N. 29th Ave., Ste. 316
Hollywood, FL 33020

Phone	(954) 925-2688
Fax	(954) 925-2889
BBS	(954) 925-2791
Web	**www.arcoide.com**
E-mail	**arco@arcoide.com**

Specializes in IDE RAID 1 disk mirroring adapters for the PC.

Arrow Electronic

1350 McCandless Drive, Bldg. 3
Milpitas, CA 95035

Phone	(408) 441-4050
Toll Free	(888) 263-7720
Fax	(408) 441-4451
Web	**www.arrowamericas.com**

A large distributor of Hewlett-Packard DAT tape and hard disk drives. They also distribute other hard disk and storage products.

Arrowfield International, Inc.

2812-A Walnut Ave.
Tustin, CA 92780

Sales	(800) 227-9628
Phone	(714) 669-0101
Fax	(714) 669-0526
Web	**www.arrowfieldinc.com**
E-mail	**arowfld@ix.netcom.com**

Manufactures an incredible array of disk drive brackets, rails, slides, cable adapters, bezels, cabinets, and complete drive upgrade and repair assemblies for PC-compatible and Compaq proprietary systems.

**Association of Shareware
Professionals (ASP)**
157-F Love Ave.
Greenwood, IN 46142

Phone	(317) 888-2194
Fax	(317) 888-2195
Web	**www.asp-shareware.org**
E-mail	**execdir@asp-shareware.org**

The ASP sets standards for shareware products and provides an ombudsman for disputes between users and authors as well as marketing information for shareware authors.

AST Research, Inc.
16225 Alton Pkwy.
Irvine, CA 92618

Phone	(714) 727-4141
Sales	(800) 876-4278
Fax	(714) 727-9355
BBS	(817) 230-6850
Web	**www.ast.com**

Manufactures an extensive line of adapter boards and peripherals for PC systems, and a line of PC systems.

Astec America, Inc.
6339 Paseo Del Lago
Carlsbad, CA 92009

Phone	(760) 930-4600
Fax	(760) 930-4700
Web	**www.astec.com**

Manufactures high-end power supplies for PC systems and many other applications. Astec power supplies are used as OEM equipment in many of the top manufacturers' systems, including IBM and others.

**Asus Computer International
(ASUStek)**
721 Charcot Ave.
San Jose, CA 95013

Phone	(510) 739-3777
Web	**www.asus.com.tw**

Manufactures a line of PC-compatible motherboards, including Pentium- and Pentium II-class motherboards.

**AT&T National Parts Sales Center/
Lucent Technologies**
7424 Scott Hamilton Dr.
Little Rock, AR 72209

Phone	(800) 222-7278
Tech Support	(800) 628-2888
Fax	(800) 527-4360

Supplies parts and components for AT&T computer systems. Call and ask for the free AT&T parts catalog.

ATI Technologies, Inc.
33 Commerce Valley Dr. East
Thornhill, ONT L3T 7N6 Canada

Phone	(905) 882-2600
Tech Support	(905) 882-2626
Fax	(905) 882-2620
BBS	(905) 764-9404
Web	**www.atitech.ca**

Manufactures a popular line of high-performance PC video adapters and chipsets.

Autodesk, Inc.
111 McInnis Pkwy.
San Rafael, CA 94903

Phone	(415) 507-5000
Sales	(800) 445-5415
Fax	(415) 507-5100
Web	**www.autodesk.com**

Manufactures AutoCAD software.

Autotime Corporation

6605 SW Macadam Ave.
Portland, OR 97201

Phone	(503) 452-8577
Fax	(503) 452-8495
Web	**www.autotime.com**
E-mail	**info@autotime.com**

Manufactures the Hypercable, which transmits high-speed parallel data up to 200 feet. The new bidirectional cable supports parallel-ported CD-ROM and tape backup peripherals. They also convert DIP chips to SIMMs and sell 30-pin to 72-pin SIMM adapters.

Award Software International, Inc.

777 E. Middlefield Rd.
Mountain View, CA 94043

Phone	(650) 237-6800
Fax	(650) 968-0274
BBS	(415) 968-0249
Web	**www.award.com**

Manufactures a line of PC ROM BIOS software. Recently merged with Phoenix.

AZ-COM, Inc.

3343 Vincent Rd., Ste. D
Pleasant Hills, CA 94523

Phone	(800) 209-2418
Tech Support	(510) 947-1000
Fax	(510) 947-1900
Web	**www.az-com.com**
E-mail	**sales@az-com.com**

Manufactures a complete line of Bus-Extender cards for ISA, EISA, MCA, VL-Bus, PCI, and others. These extenders allow you to easily insert and remove adapter cards for testing with the power on.

Belden Wire and Cable

P.O. Box 1980
Richmond, IN 47375

Phone	(317) 983-5200
Sales	(800) 235-3362
Fax	(317) 983-5656
Web	**www.belden.com**
E-mail	**info@belden.com**

Manufactures cable and wire products.

Berkshire Products

P.O. Box 1015
Suwanee, GA 30024

Phone	(770) 271-0088
Fax	(770) 932-0082
Web	**www.berkprod.com**

Manufactures the PC Watchdog system monitor, including an optional temperature alarm. This board can automatically restart a server or other system that has locked up.

Best Power (A Division of General Signal Power)

P.O. Box 280
Necedah, WI 54646

Phone	(608) 565-7200
Sales	(800) 356-5794
Fax	(608) 565-2221
Web	**www.bestpower.com**

Manufactures an excellent line of computer power protection equipment from high-end ferroresonant UPS systems to line conditioners and standby power protection systems.

Bitstream, Inc.

215 First St.
Cambridge, MA 02142

Phone	(617) 497-6222
Sales	(800) 522-3668
Fax	(617) 868-0784
Web	**www.bitstream.com**
E-mail	**sales@bitstream.com**

Manufactures fonts and font software.

Black Box Corporation
1000 Park Drive
Lawrence, PA 15055

Phone	(724) 746-5500
Fax	(724) 746-0746
Web	**www.blackbox.com**
E-mail	**info@blackbox.com**

A leading direct marketer of computer communications and networking products and services, including network equipment, cables, and connectors for a variety of applications.

Boca Research, Inc.
1377 Clint Moore
Boca Raton, FL 33487

Phone	(561) 997-6227
Tech Support	(561) 241-8088
Fax	(561) 994-5848
BBS	(561) 241-1601
Web	**www.bocaresearch.com**

Manufactures a low-cost line of adapter card products for PCs.

Borland International (Now Inprise)
100 Enterprise Way
Scotts Valley, CA 95066-3249

Phone	(408) 431-1000
Sales	(800) 331-0877
Tech Support	(800) 523-7070
BBS	(408) 431-5096
Web	**www.inprise.com**

Software manufacturer that features Turbo language products, Paradox, and dBASE. Also the software manufacturer of Delphi.

Bose Corp.
The Mountain
Framingham, MA 01701-9168

Phone	(508) 879-7330
Fax	(508) 879-1157
Web	**www.bose.com**

Manufactures speakers and integrated amplifiers.

Boston Computer Exchange
210 South Street
Boston, MA 02111

Phone	(617) 542-4414
Fax	(617) 542-8849
Web	**www.bocoex.com**

A broker for used PC computers.

Brooktree Corporation (Purchased by Rockwell)
9868 Scranton Rd.
San Diego, CA 92121-3707

Phone	(619) 452-7580
Sales	(800) 228-2777
Fax	(619) 452-2104
Web	**www.nb.rockwell.com**

Manufactures a line of digital-to-analog converter (DAC) chips and multimedia chipsets.

Buerg, Vernon D.
850 Petaluma Blvd. North
Petaluma, CA 94952

Phone	(707) 778-1811
Fax	(707) 769-5479
BBS	(707) 778-8944
Web	**www.buerg.com**

Manufactures an excellent line of utility programs, including the popular LIST program. Buerg software is distributed online through BBSes and the Internet.

Byte Information Exchange (BIX)
1030 Massachusetts Ave.
Cambridge, MA 02138

Phone	(800) 695-4775
Fax	(617) 491-6642
Web	**www.bix.com**
E-mail	**info@bix.com**

An online computer information and messaging system.

Byte Magazine/McGraw-Hill
One Phoenix Mill Ln.
Peterborough, NH 03458

Phone	(603) 924-9281
Customer Service	(603) 924-7507
BBS	(617) 861-9764
E-mail	**editors@bix.com**

A monthly magazine covering all lines of microcomputers.

Byte Runner Technologies
1316 Willow Grove Drive
Knoxville, TN 37922

Phone	(423) 470-4938
Sales	(800) 274-7897
Tech Support	(423) 693-5560
Fax	(423) 693-6785
Web	**www.byterunner.com**
E-mail	**sdudley@byterunner.com**

Carries a line of high-performance I/O cards featuring FIFO (16550/16650/16750 type) serial port UART chips, and EPP/ECP parallel ports. They also carry adapters that allow any IRQ setting (including IRQs 9–15) to prevent conflicts with other existing ports, and many cards that allow IRQ sharing.

Cables to Go (CTG)
1501 Webster St.
Dayton, OH 45404

Phone	(513) 224-8646
Sales	(800) 826-7904
Fax	(800) 331-2841
Web	**www.cablestogo.com**

Manufactures a variety of cable, connector, and switch products.

CAIG Laboratories
16744 W. Bernardo Dr.
San Diego, CA 92127-1904

Phone	(619) 451-1799
Sales	(800) CAIG-123 (224-4123)
Fax	(619) 451-2799
Web	**www.caig.com**
E-mail	**caig123@aol.com**

Manufactures and sells cleaners and lubricants for electronic applications, featuring ProGold contact enhancer for plated contacts and connectors.

Cal-Abco
6041 Variel Ave.
Woodland Hills, CA 91367

Phone	(800) 669-2226
Fax	(818) 704-7733

Distributes computer systems and peripherals.

Canon USA, Inc.
One Canon Plaza
Lake Success, NY 11042

Phone	(516) 488-6700
Fax	(516) 354-5805
BBS	(516) 488-6528

Manufactures a line of printer and video equipment as well as floppy drives.

Casio, Inc.
570 Mt. Pleasant Ave.
Dover, NJ 07801

Phone	(973) 361-5400
Sales	(800) 962-2746
Fax	(201) 361-3819
Web	**www.casio-usa.com**

Manufactures digital cameras, personal data systems, and digital watches.

Centon Electronics, Inc.
20 Morgan
Irvine, CA 92718

Phone	(714) 855-9111
Fax	(714) 855-3132
Web	**www.centon.com**

Manufactures memory enhancement kits, SIMM and DIMM modules, expansion boards, credit cards, and PCMCIA cards.

Chemtronics, Inc.
8125 Cobb Center Dr.
Kennesaw, GA 30152

Phone	(770) 424-4888
Sales	(800) 645-5244
Fax	(770) 424-4267
Web	**www.chemtronics.com**

Manufactures and sells a complete line of computer and electronic grade chemicals, materials, and supplies, as well as solder wick and clean room items.

Cherry Electrical Products
3600 Sunset Ave.
Waukegan, IL 60087

Phone	(847) 662-9200
Fax	(847) 360-3498
Web	**www.industry.net/ cherry.electrical**

Manufactures a line of high-quality keyboards for PC systems. Also produces a line of industrial Gas Plasma displays.

Chicago Case Company
4446 S. Ashland Ave.
Chicago, IL 60609

Phone	(312) 927-1600
Fax	(800) 333-8172

Manufactures equipment-shipping and travel cases.

Chilton Book Company
Chilton Way
Radnor, PA 19089-0230

Phone	(610) 964-4743

Manufactures a number of excellent automotive service manuals and documentation.

Chinon America, Inc.
615 Hawaii
Torrance, CA 90503

Phone	(310) 533-0274
Sales	(800) 441-0222

Fax	(310) 533-1727
BBS	(310) 320-4160

Manufactures a line of floppy disk and CD-ROM drives.

Chips and Technologies, Inc.
2950 Zanker Rd.
San Jose, CA 95134

Phone	(408) 434-0600
Fax	(408) 894-2079
BBS	(408) 456-0721
Web	**www.chips.com**

A wholly owned subsidiary of Intel Corporation that develops semiconductor and software solutions for leading manufacturers of personal computers. Integrated solutions product line provides enhanced graphics, full-motion video, and other advanced display capabilities for both notebook and desktop computers. Chips and Technologies is a supplier of flat-panel video graphics controllers and accelerators to the portable computer market.

Chrysler Motors Service Publications
Service Publications
P.O Box 360450
Strongsville, OH 44136

Phone	(800) 890-4038
	(216) 572-0725
Fax	(216) 572-0815

Publishes Chrysler service manuals and documentation.

CI Design Company
1695 W. McCarther Blvd.
Costa Mesa, CA 92626

Phone	(714) 556-0888
Fax	(714) 556-0890

Manufactures custom-made 3 1/2-inch drive mounting kits used by Toshiba, Panasonic, and NEC for their drive products. Also makes drive faceplates, enclosures, and custom cable assemblies.

CIE America
2701 Dow Ave.
Tustin, CA 92680

Phone	(714) 573-2942
Sales	(800) 877-1421
Fax	(714) 757-4488
BBS	(714) 573-2645
Web	**www.citoh.com**

Manufactures PC printers and other peripherals.

Cirrus Logic, Inc.
3100 W. Warren Ave.
Fremont, CA 94538

Phone	(510) 623-8300
Fax	(510) 252-6020
FAXBack	(800) 359-6414
BBS	(510) 440-9080
Web	**www.cirrus.com**

Manufactures PC motherboard chipsets for mobile and desktop systems and a line of chipsets for disk controller, video, and communications circuits.

Citizen America Corporation
2450 Broadway, Ste. 600
Santa Monica, CA 90404

Phone	(310) 453-0614
Fax	(310) 453-2814
Web	**www.citizen-america.com**

Manufactures a line of printers and floppy disk drives.

CMD Technology, Inc.
1 Vanderbilt
Irvine, CA 92618

Phone	(714) 454-0800
Sales	(800) 426-3832
Fax	(714) 455-1656
BBS	(714) 454-0795
Web	**www.cmd.com**

Manufactures EISA adapters, PCI and VL-Bus IDE, and SCSI disk adapters.

Colorado Memory Systems, Inc.
See Hewlett-Packard (Storage Division)

Columbia Data Products
1070B Rainer Dr.
Altamonte Springs, FL 32714

Phone	(407) 869-6700
Fax	(407) 862-4725
BBS	(407) 862-4724
Web	**www.cdp.com**

Manufactures image backup software for all PC platforms and tools for quick replication of servers and workstations.

Compaq Computer Corporation
P.O. Box 692000
Houston, TX 77269-2000

Phone	(281) 370-0670
Sales	(800) 231-0900
Tech Support	(800) 652-6672
Product Info	(800) 345-1518
Fax	(281) 378-8754
BBS	(281) 378-1418
Web	**www.compaq.com**
E-mail	**support@compaq.com**

Manufactures desktop, notebook, and server PC computer systems.

CompTIA (Computing Technology Industry Association)
450 E. 22nd St., Ste. 230
Lombard, IL 60148-6158

Phone	(630) 268-1818
Fax	(630) 268-1384
Web	**www.comptia.org**
E-mail	**info@comptia.org**

A nonprofit trade association who sponsors the A+ Certification program.

Compton's New Media, Inc. (A Division of Softkey International, Inc.)
1 Athenaeum St.
Cambridge, MA 02142

Phone	(617) 494-1200
Fax	(617) 494-1279
Web	**www.softkey.com**

Produces entertainment, multimedia, and edutainment software for floppy and CD-ROM users. CD-ROM titles include *Compton's Interactive Encyclopedia*.

CompUSA, Inc.
14951 N. Dallas Pkwy.
Dallas, TX 75240

Phone	(972) 982-4000
Sales	(800) 266-7872
Fax	(800) 329-2212

Computer retail superstore and mail-order outlet.

CompuServe Information Service (CIS)
5000 Arlington Centre Blvd.
Columbus, OH 43220

Phone	(614) 457-8600
Customer Service	(800) 848-8990
Fax	(614) 529-1610

Largest online information and messaging service; offers Internet access and manufacturer- and vendor-sponsored forums for technical support. Recently purchased by America Online.

Computer Component Source, Inc.
7 Oser Avenue
Hauppauge, NY 11788

Phone	(516) 496-8727
Sales	(800) 356-1227
Fax	(800) 926-2062

Distributes a large number of computer components for repair. Specializes in display parts such as flyback transformers and other components.

Computer Design Magazine
PennWell Publishing Co.
Advanced Technology Division
10 Tara Blvd., 5th Floor
Nashua, NH 03062-2801

Phone	(603) 891-0123
Fax	(603) 891-0539
Web	**atd.pennwell.com**

An excellent industry magazine for electronic engineers and engineering managers, featuring articles on all types of computer components and hardware.

Computer Discount Warehouse (CDW)
200 N. Milwaukee Avenue
Vernon Hills, IL 60061

Phone	(708) 465-6000
Sales	(800) 726-4239
Tech Support	(800) 383-4239
Fax	(708) 465-6800
BBS	(708) 465-6899
Web	**www.cdw.com**

Computer retail superstore and mail-order catalog outlet.

Computer Graphics World Magazine
PennWell Publishing Co.
Advanced Technology Group
10 Tara Blvd., 5th Floor
Nashua, NH 03062-2801

Phone	(603) 891-0123
Fax	(603) 891-0539
Web	**www.cgw.com**

An industry magazine covering graphics hardware, software, and applications.

Computer Hotline Magazine
15400 Knoll Trail Ste. #500
Dallas, TX 75248

Phone	(214) 233-5131
Sales	(800) 999-5131
Fax	(214) 233-5514

A publication that features advertisers offering excellent sources of replacement and repair parts and new and used equipment at wholesale prices.

Computer Library
1 Park Ave.
New York, NY 10016

Phone	(212) 503-4400
Sales	(800) 419-0313
Fax	(212) 503-4414
Web	**www.iacnet.com**

Manufactures the Computer Select CD-ROM database including full text and abstracts from more than 120 computer publications. This is a valuable research tool.

Computer Reseller News
CMP Media, Inc.
1 Jericho Plaza
Jericho, NY 11753

Phone	(516) 733-6700
Editorial Dept. Fax	(516) 733-8636
Web	**www.crn.com**

An excellent industry trade weekly news magazine featuring news for computer professionals involved in value-added reselling of computer equipment. Subscriptions are free to those who qualify.

Computer Retail Week Magazine
CMP Publications, Inc.
1 Jericho Plaza
Jericho, NY 11753

Phone	(516) 733-6700
Fax	(516) 733-8577
Web	**www.crw.com**

An excellent industry trade weekly news magazine featuring news for computer superstores, mass merchants, and retailers. Subscriptions are free to those who qualify.

Computer Shopper Magazine
Ziff-Davis Publishing
One Park Ave.
New York, NY 10016

Phone	(212) 503-3500
Web	**www.zdnet.com/cshopper**

Monthly magazine for experimenters and bargain hunters; features a large number of advertisements.

Computer Technology Review Magazine
West World Productions, Inc.
924 Westwood Blvd., Ste. 650
Los Angeles, CA 90024-2910

Phone	(310) 208-1335
Fax	(310) 208-1054

An excellent monthly technical magazine for systems integrators, value-added resellers, and original equipment manufacturers. Subscriptions are free to those who qualify.

Comtech Publishing Ltd.
P.O. Box 12340
Reno, NV 89510

Phone	(702) 825-9000
Sales	(800) 456-7005
Fax	(702) 825-1818
Web	**www.accutek.com/comtech**

Manufactures dSalvage Professional, the best and most comprehensive Xbase data-recovery and file repair software available.

Connector Resources Unlimited (CRU)
1005 Ames Ave.
Milpitas, CA 95035

Phone	(408) 957-5757
Sales	(800) 260-9800
Fax	(408) 942-0862
Web	**www.cruinc.com**

Manufactures removable hard drive modules. The original patented American-made Dataport. Dataport supports all hard-drive interfaces and has special cooling for complex, high-RPM drives.

Conner Peripherals, Inc.
See Seagate Technology

Corel Systems, Inc.
1600 Carling Ave.
Ottawa, ONT K1Z 8R7 Canada

Phone	(613) 728-8200
Fax	(613) 728-9790
BBS	(613) 728-4752
Web	**www.corel.com**

Manufactures the CorelDRAW! graphics program and Corel SCSI, a SCSI driver kit featuring drivers for a variety of SCSI host adapters and devices. Also manufactures the WordPerfect Suite.

Creative Labs, Inc.
1901 McCarthy Blvd.
Milpitas, CA 95035

Phone	(408) 428-6600
Sales	(800) 544-6146
Customer Service	(800) 998-1000
Tech Support	(408) 742-6600
Fax	(408) 428-6611
BBS	(405) 742-6660
Web	**www.creaf.com**

Manufactures the Sound Blaster series of audio cards for multimedia and sound applications.

CS Electronics
1342 Bell Ave.
Tustin, CA 92780

Phone	(714) 259-9100
Fax	(714) 259-0911
Web	**www.scsi-cables.com/scsi**
E-mail	**cablescs@aol.com**

Manufactures a very high-quality line of disk and tape drive cables, specializing in SCSI-1, SCSI-2, and SCSI-3 applications. They offer custom lengths, connectors, and impedances for a proper match with an existing installation, and use the highest-quality raw cable available.

CST
2336 Lu Field Rd.
Dallas, TX 75229

Phone	(972) 241-2662
Fax	(972) 241-2661
BBS	(972) 241-3782
Web	**www.simmtester.com**

Manufacturer of memory/SIMMs testers.

CTX International, Inc.
20470 Walnut Dr.
Walnut, CA 91789

Phone	(909) 595-6146
Sales	(800) 888-9052
Fax	(909) 595-6293
Web	**www.ctxintl.com**

Manufactures a line of high-performance notebook computers.

Curtis Computer Products

492 Heller Park Court
Dayton, NJ 08810

Phone	(732) 438-9436
Fax	(732) 438-9437

Manufactures a complete line of computer accessories, including copy holders, glare filters, keyboard drawers, media storage, printer stands, data switches, cleaning and toolkits, notebook cases, travel accessories, and surge protectors.

CyberMedia

3000 Ocean Park Blvd., Ste. 2001
Santa Monica, CA 90405

Phone	(800) 721-7824
Fax	(800) 833-120 or (310) 581-4700
Web	**www.cybermedia.com**

Manufactures diagnostic software for Windows, including First Aid 9X.

Cypress Semiconductor Corporation

3901 N. First St.
San Jose, CA 95134

Phone	(408) 943-2600
Web	**www.cypress.com**

Manufactures PC chipsets and other semiconductor devices.

Cyrix Corporation

2703 N. Central Expressway
Richardson, TX 75080

Phone	(972) 968-8388
Sales	(800) 462-9749
Fax	(972) 699-9857
FAXBack	(800) GO-CYRIX (462-9749)
Web	**www.cyrix.com**

Manufactures the 6x86MX and MII line of Pentium-compatible processors.

D.W. Electrochemicals, Ltd.

97 Newkirk Rd. North, Unit 3
Richmond Hill, ONT L4C 3G4 Canada

Phone	(905) 508-7500
Fax	(905) 508-7502
E-mail	**dwel@stabilant.com**
Web	**www.stabilant.com**

Manufactures and sells Stabilant 22 contact enhancer and treatment. Stabilant 22 is the gel concentrate, and Stabilant 22a is a 4-to-1 isopropanol diluted form.

DakTech

4900 Ritter Rd.
Mechanicsburg, PA 17055

Phone	(717) 795-9544
Sales	(800) 325-3238
Fax	(717) 795-9420
Web	**www.daktech.com**
E-mail	**daktech@ix.netcom.com**

Distributor of new and used original equipment IBM and Compaq parts.

Da-Lite Screen Co.

3100 N. Detroit St.
P.O. Box 137
Warsaw, IN 46581-0137

Phone	(219) 267-8101
Sales	(800) 622-3737
Web	**www.da-lite.com**

Manufactures a line of projection screens and computer furniture.

Dallas Semiconductor

4401 S. Beltwood Pkwy.
Dallas, TX 75244-3292

Phone	(972) 371-4000
Customer Service	(972) 371-4969
Fax	(972) 371-4470
Web	**www.dalsemi.com**

Manufactures real-time clock and non-volatile RAM modules used by a number of OEMs.

Damark International, Inc.
7101 Winnetka Ave. North
Minneapolis, MN 55428

Phone	(612) 531-0066
Sales	(800) 729-9000
Fax	(612) 549-2098
Web	**www.damark.com**

Liquidates and distributes a variety of discontinued products, including PC-compatible systems and peripherals.

Darkhorse Systems, Inc.
12201 Technology Blvd., Ste. 130
Austin, TX 78727

Phone	(512) 335-4440
	(800) 533-1744
Tech Support	(888) 255-2210
Fax	(512) 257-0296
BBS	(512) 257-5087

Manufactures the SIGMA.LC memory test system. This is a high-quality memory test device that can accurately test SIMMs, individual chips, and other types of memory modules.

Data Base Advisor Magazine
Advisor Publications
4010 Morena Blvd., Ste. 200
San Diego, CA 92117

Phone	(619) 483-6400
Fax	(619) 483-9851
Subscriptions	(800) 336-6060
Web	**www.advisor.com**
E-mail	**70007.1614@compuserve.com**

An excellent magazine featuring articles on database applications software and programming routines. They also publish *Access Visual Basic Advisor*, *Internet Advisor*, *FoxPro Advisor*, *Lotus Notes Advisor*, and *Power Builder Advisor*.

Data Communications Magazine
McGraw-Hill Companies
1221 Avenue of the Americas
New York, NY 10020

Phone	(212) 512-2000
Subscriptions	(800) 525-5003
Fax	(212) 512-6833
Web	**www.data.com**

An excellent industry publication featuring articles on networking and communications.

Data Depot
1710 Drew St.
Clearwater, FL 33755

Phone	(813) 446-3402
Sales	(800) SOS-DIAG (767-3424)
Fax	(813) 443-4377
Web	**www.datadepo.com/datadepo.htm**
E-mail	**datadepo@ix.net_com.com**

Manufactures the PocketPOST diagnostic card for ISA and EISA systems, and several other excellent diagnostics hardware and software products.

Data Exchange Corporation
3600 Via Pescador
Camarillo, CA 93012

Phone	(805) 388-1711
Sales	(800) 237-7911
Fax	(805) 482-4856
Web	**www.dex.com**
E-mail	**sales@dex.com**

Specializes in contract manufacturing, end-of-life support, depot repair, logistic services, and spare parts and unit sales. A complete repair and refurbishment facility providing ISO 9002 certified depot repair of high-tech electronics and computer-related products from all major manufacturers.

Data Retrieval Services, Inc.
1040 Kapp Dr.
Clearwater, FL 34625

Phone	(813) 461-5900
Fax	(813) 461-5668

Specialists in data retrieval from head-crashed disk packs, damaged disk drives, floppies, and tapes.

Data Technology Corporation (DTC)
1515 Centre Pointe Dr.
Milpitas, CA 95035-8010

Phone	(408) 942-4000
Tech Support	(408) 262-7700
Fax	(408) 942-4027
FAXBack	(408) 942-4005
BBS	(408) 942-4197
Web	**www.datatechnology.com**

Manufactures a complete line of PC peripherals and multimedia products.

Datastorm Technologies, Inc. (Purchased by Quarterdeck Corporation)
2401 Lemone Blvd.
Columbia, MO 65205

Phone	(573) 443-3282
Sales	(800) 474-1573
Tech Support	(573) 875-0530
Fax	(573) 875-0595
BBS	(573) 875-0503
Web	**www.datastorm.com**

Manufactures ProCOMM, ProCOMM Plus, and ProCOMM Plus for Windows Internet, fax, and data communications software. Datastorm has been purchased by Quarterdeck Corporation, which has integrated Datastorm's product line into Quarterdeck's.

Dell Computer Corporation
1 Dellway
Round Rock, TX 78682

Phone	(512) 338-4400
Sales	(800) 426-5150
Tech Support	(800) 624-9896
Fax	(800) 727-8320
BBS	(512) 338-8528
Web	**www.dell.com**

Manufactures a line of low-cost, high-performance PC computer systems.

DiagSoft, Inc.
5615 Scotts Valley Dr., Ste. 140
Scotts Valley, CA 95066

Phone	(408) 438-8247
Sales	(800) 342-4763
Fax	(408) 438-7113
Web	**www.diagsoft.com**

Tampa Office
6200 Courtney Campbell Causeway, Ste. 320
Tampa, FL 33607

Phone	(813) 207-7000
Fax	(813) 207-7001

Manufactures the QAPlus user-level PC diagnostics software and the high-end QAPlus/FE (Field Engineer) software, which is an excellent program that includes complete high-resolution floppy drive testing and the Power Meter benchmarking utility.

Diamond Flower, Inc. (DFI)
135 Main Ave.
Sacramento, CA 95838

Phone	(916) 568-1234
Fax	(916) 568-1233
Web	**www.dfiusa.com**

Manufactures a line of PC-compatible systems, motherboards, adapter cards, and other products.

Diamond Multimedia Systems, Inc.
2880 Junction Ave.
San Jose, CA 95134-1922

Phone   (408) 325-7000
Sales   (800) 468-5846
Fax   (408) 325-7070
Web   **www.diamondmm.com**

Manufactures a line of high-performance
video and multimedia adapters. Also
makes and sells the Supra line of modem
and telephony products.

Digi-Key Corporation
701 Brooks Ave. South
P.O. Box 677
Thief River Falls, MN 56701-0677

Phone   (218) 681-6674
Sales   (800) 344-4539
Fax   (218) 681-3380
Web   **www.digikey.com**

Sells an enormous variety of electronic and
computer components, tools, and test
equipment. Publishes a complete catalog
listing all items.

Distributed Processing Tech. (DPT)
140 Candace Dr.
Maitland, FL 32751

Phone   (407) 830-5522
Sales   (800) 322-4378
Fax   (407) 260-6690
BBS   (407) 831-6432
Web   **www.dpt.com**

Manufactures high-performance caching
SCSI host adapters and disk array (RAID)
controllers.

Diversified Technology
P.O. Box 748
Ridgeland, MS 39158

Phone   (601) 856-4121
Sales   (800) 443-2667
Fax   (601) 856-2888

Manufactures industrial and rack-mount
PC-compatible systems and a variety of
backplane-design CPU boards and multi-
function adapters.

Dolch Computer Systems
3178 Laurelview Ct.
Fremont, CA 94538

Phone   (510) 661-2220
Fax   (510) 490-2360
Web   **www.dolch.com**

Manufactures a series of very powerful
portable computers that are also very expandable and rugged. If you need something more powerful than a laptop, they
have lunchbox-sized portables with large
hard disks and high-end video displays.

DTK Computer, Inc.
770 Epperson Dr.
City of Industry, CA 91748

Phone   (818) 810-0098
Fax   (818) 810-0090
BBS   (818) 854-0797
Web   **www.dtk.com**

Manufactures PC-compatible systems and
BIOS software.

Dukane Corporation
2900 Dukane Dr.
St. Charles, IL 60174

Phone   (630) 584-2300
Sales   (800) 676-2485
Fax   (630) 584-5156
Web   **www.industry.net/dukane.av**

Manufactures a complete line of high-
intensity overhead projectors, LCD panels,
and LCD data/video projectors. They specialize in portable high-brightness overhead projector units designed for
LCD-panel projection applications.

Duracell, Inc.
Berkshire Industrial Park
Bethel, CT 06801

Phone	(203) 796-4000
Fax	(203) 791-3386
Sales	(203) 791-3257
Web	**www.duracell.com**

Manufactures high-performance consumer application batteries including alkaline, lithium, and standard-sized nickel-metal hydride rechargeable batteries.

Edmund Scientific
101 E. Gloucester Pike
Barrington, NJ 08007-1380

Phone	(609) 573-6280
Fax	(609) 573-6233
Sales	(609) 573-6250
Web	**www.edsci.com**

They offer a wide range of optical components and scientific equipment for industry and research. Volume discounts offered. Free catalog offered to those who qualify.

Electrocution
P.O. Box 52083
Winnipeg MB R2M 5P9 Canada

Phone	(204) 889-8430
Web	**www.electrocution.com**

Publishes *The BIOS Companion*, an invaluable book covering in detail the different BIOS versions on the market including detailed setup, configuration, and diagnostics information.

Electronic Buyers' News
CMP Publications, Inc.
600 Community Dr.
Manhasset, NY 11030-3875

Phone	(516) 562-5899
Subscriptions	(800) 291-5215
Fax	(516) 562-5123
Web	**techweb.cmp.com/ebn**

An excellent industry trade weekly magazine featuring news and information for those involved in electronics purchasing, materials, and management. Subscriptions are free to those who qualify.

Electronic Engineering Times Magazine
CMP Publications, Inc.
600 Community Dr.
Manhasset, NY 11030-3875

Phone	(516) 562-5000
Subscriptions	(800) 291-5215
Fax	(516) 562-5325
Web	**www.eetimes.com**

An excellent industry trade weekly news magazine featuring news for engineers and technical management. Subscriptions are free to those who qualify.

Electronic Products Magazine
Hearst Business Publications, Inc.
645 Stewart Ave.
Garden City, NY 11530

Phone	(516) 227-1300
Fax	(516) 227-1444
Web	**www.electronicproducts.com**

An excellent industry trade magazine featuring engineering-type information on electronic and computer components and in-depth technical articles. Subscriptions are free to those who qualify.

Electroservice Laboratories
6085 Sikorsky St.
Ventura, CA 93003

Phone	(805) 644-2944
Fax	(805) 644-5006
BBS	(805) 644-7810
Web	**www.esl.com**

Provides repair parts for most major computer OEMs, including all major PC components.

Elitegroup Computer Systems, Inc.
45401 Research Ave.
Fremont, CA 94539

Phone	(510) 226-7333
Sales	(800) 829-8890
Fax	(510) 226-7350
Web	**www.ecsusa.com**
E-mail	**info@ecsusa.com**

One of the largest Taiwan-based PC
motherboard manufacturers.

Endl Publications
14426 Black Walnut Ct.
Saratoga, CA 95070

Phone	(408) 867-6642
Fax	(408) 867-2115
FAXBack	(408) 741-1600
E-mail	**2501752@mclmail.com**

Publishes the *SSF Reflector*, containing
specs for local bus disk drive attachments.
Also publishes SCSI technical documentation such as *The SCSI Bench Reference* and
The SCSI Encyclopedia.

Epson America, Inc. (OEM Division)
20770 Madrona Ave.
Torrance, CA 90509-2842

Phone	(310) 787-6300
Fax	(310) 782-5350
FAXBack	(800) 922-8911
BBS	(408) 782-4531
Web	**www.epson.com**

Manufactures printers and complete PC-
compatible systems.

Everex Systems, Inc.
5020 Brandin Ct.
Fremont, CA 94538

Phone	(510) 498-1111
Sales	(800) 821-0806
Tech Support	(510) 498-4411
Fax	(510) 683-2062
BBS	(510) 226-9694
Web	**www.everex.com**

Manufactures PC-compatible systems and
peripherals.

Exabyte Corporation
1685 38th St.
Boulder, CO 80301

Phone	(303) 442-4333
Fax	(303) 417-7170
Web	**www.exabyte.com**

Manufactures high-performance 8mm and
minicartridge tape-backup systems and
8mm and 4mm tape libraries. Also produces the Eagle Nest modular storage systems.

Extron Electronics
1230 S. Lewis St.
Anaheim, CA 92805

Phone	(714) 491-1500
Sales	(800) 633-9876
Fax	(714) 491-1517
Web	**www.extron.com**

Manufactures computer-video interface
products used to connect PCs to large-
screen video projectors and monitors. The
company also manufactures VGA, Mac,
and RGB distribution amplifiers and
switchers used to connect multimedia
classroom and boardroom equipment, and
VGA- and Mac-to-NTSC/PAL converters for
recording computer information and
graphics on videotape.

**Fantasy Productions (A Division of
Fortner & Associates)**
1305 Bert St.
Claremore, OK 74017

Phone	(918) 341-4577
Sales	(800) 358-5887
Tech Support	(918) 341-4577

The source for discontinued IBM reference
manuals and technical support. Call for a
complete listing.

FCI Electronics - America
50 Grumbacher Road
York, PA 17402

Phone	(717) 767-8492
Fax	(717) 767-8056
	(Attn: Scott Roland)

Manufactures electronic connector products for portable and desktop PCs and workstations.

Fedco Electronics, Inc.
1363 Capital Drive
Fond du Lac, WI 54937

Phone	(414) 922-6490
Sales	(800) 542-9761
Fax	(414) 922-6750

Manufactures and supplies a large variety of computer batteries.

Fessenden Technologies
116 N. 3rd St.
Ozark, MO 65721

Phone	(417) 485-2501
Fax	(417) 485-3133
Web	**www.oznet.com/fessenden/**
E-mail	**76660.1035@Compuserve.com**

Service company that offers monitor and terminal depot repair. They also repair hard drives for older Seagate and Miniscribe MFM/RLL drives.

First International Computer, Inc. (FIC)
980-A Mission Ct.
Fremont, CA 94539

Phone	(510) 252-7777
Sales	(800) FICA-OEM
	(342-2636)
Fax	(510) 252-8888
Web	**www.fica.com**

The largest Taiwan-based manufacturer of PC-compatible motherboards.

Fluke, John Manufacturing Company, Inc.
6920 Seaway Blvd.
P.O. Box 9090
Everett, WA 98206-9090

Phone	(206) 347-6100
Sales	(800) 443-5853
Fax	(206) 356-5019
Web	**www.fluke.com**

Manufactures a line of high-end digital troubleshooting tools, including the Scopemeter handheld scope.

Folio Corporation
5072 N. 300 W.
Provo, UT 84604

Phone	(801) 229-6700
Fax	(801) 229-6787
Sales	(800) 543-6546
Web	**www.folio.com**

Manufactures the Folio VIEWS infobase software. Also publishes the annual COMDEX exhibitors' list on disk.

ForeFront Direct
25400 U.S. Highway 19 North
Suite 285
Clearwater, FL 33763

Sales	(800) 475-5831
Support	(813) 725-2755
Web	**www.ffg.com**

Makers of training software and videos for PC technicians and diagnostic and troubleshooting hardware and software.

**Fujitsu Computer Products
of America, Inc.**
2904 Orchard Dr.
San Jose, CA 95134-2009

Phone	(800) 626-4686
Fax	(408) 432-6333
Web	**www.fcpa.com**

Manufactures a line of high-capacity hard
disk drives. Also manufactures scanners,
laser and dot-matrix printers, rewritable
optical drives, and high-end tape drives.

**Future Domain Corporation (Purchased
by Adaptec)**
691 South Milpitas Blvd.
Milpitas, CA 95035

Sales	(800) 959-7274
Tech Support	(408) 934-7274
CD Recordable Software Tech Support	(408) 934-7283
Fax	(408) 957-6776
BBS	(408) 945-7727
Web	**www.adaptec.com**

Manufactures a line of high-performance
SCSI host adapters and software. Acquired
by Adaptec.

Gateway 2000
P.O. Box 2000
610 Gateway Dr.
North Sioux City, SD 57049

Phone	(605) 232-2000
Sales	(800) 523-2000
Tech Support	(800) 846-2000
Fax	(605) 232-2023
BBS	(605) 232-2224
Web	**www.gw2k.com**

Manufactures a popular line of PC systems
sold by mail-order and new outlet stores in
some cities.

Gazelle/GTM Software
P.O. Box 1930
Orem, UT 84059

Phone	(801) 235-7000
Fax	(801) 235-7099
Web	**www.gtmsoftware.com**

Manufactures the Optune disk
defragmenter and disk performance utility
program.

Giga-Byte Technology Co., Ltd.
18305 Valley Blvd., Ste. A
LaPuente, CA 91744

Phone	(626) 854-9338
Fax	(626) 854-9339
Web	**www.giga-byte.com**

One of the top 10 largest Taiwan-based
motherboard manufacturers.

GigaTrend, Inc.
2234 Rutherford Rd.
Carlsbad, CA 92008

Phone	(760) 931-9122
Sales	(800) 743-4442
Fax	(760) 931-9959
BBS	(760) 931-9469
Web	**www.gigatrend.com**

Manufactures high-capacity tape drives.

Global Engineering Documents
15 Inverness Way East
Englewood, CO 80112-5704

Phone	(303) 792-2181
Sales	(800) 854-7179
Fax	(303) 792-2192
Web	**global.ihs.com**

A source for various ANSI and other industry standard documents, including SCSI-1,
2, and 3, ATA IDE, ESDI, and many others.
Unlike ANSI, they sell draft documents of
standards that are not yet fully ANSI approved.

Globe Manufacturing, Inc.
1159 Route 22
Mountainside, NJ 07092

Phone	(908) 232-7301
Sales	(800) 227-3258
Fax	(908) 232-4729
Web	**www.akstamping.com**

Manufactures assorted PC adapter card brackets.

Golden Bow Systems
P.O. Box 3039
San Diego, CA 92163-1039

Phone	(619) 298-9349
Sales	(800) 284-3269
Fax	(619) 298-9950
Web	**www.goldenbow.com**

Manufactures VOPT, the best and fastest disk optimizer software available. They also offer Vcache, VQ, and VLock.

GoldStar Technology, Inc.
1000 Sylvan Ave.
Englewood Cliffs, NJ 07632

Phone	(201) 816-2000
Fax	(201) 816-0636

Manufactures a line of color monitors and a full line of computer and electronics products.

GRACE Specialty Polymers/WR GRACE, Emerson & Cuming, Inc.
869 Washington St.
Canton, MA 02021

Phone	(617) 828-3300
Sales	(800) 472-2391
Tech Support	(800) 832-4929
Orders	(800) 225-9936
Fax	(617) 828-3104

Manufactures structurally, thermally, and electronically conductive epoxy and silicone adhesives, coatings, and encapsulates. They also manufacture room temperature, heat-cured, UV-cured systems, and circuit board fabrication materials. These include solder mask, solder resist, and polymer thick films.

GSI, Inc.
17951-H Skypark Circle
Irvine, CA 92614-6343

Phone	(714) 261-7949
Sales	(800) 486-7800
Support	(714) 757-9744
Fax	(714) 757-1778
Web	**www.gsi-inc.com** or **www.hotport.com**

Develops and manufactures internal and external EIDE solutions. Also manufactures floppy, tape, and I/O adapters for upgrading older PCs. New products are cable select (CSEL) cables and Hotport external IDE connectivity solutions.

Hauppauge Computer Works, Inc.
91 Cabot Ct.
Hauppauge, NY 11788

Phone	(516) 434-1600
Sales	(800) 443-6284
Customer Service	(516) 434-3197
Fax	(516) 434-3198
BBS	(516) 434-8454
Web	**www.hauppauge. com/hcw/index.htm**

Manufactures video capture cards.

Hayes Microcomputer Products
5835 Peachtree Corners East
Norcross, GA 30092-3405

Phone	(770) 840-9200
Sales	(800) 874-3734
Fax	(770) 441-1213
FAXBack	(800) 429-3739
BBS	(770) 429-3734
Web	**www.hayes.com**

Manufactures a complete line of modems.

Heathkit Education Systems
Heath Company
455 Riverview Dr.
Benton Harbor, MI 49023

Phone	(616) 925-6000
Sales	(800) 253-0570
Fax	(616) 925-2982
Web	**www.heathkit.com**

Sells courses and training materials for
learning electronics and computer design
including A+ Certification for Computer
Technicians.

Helm, Inc.
Publications Division
P.O. Box 07130
Detroit, MI 48207

Phone	(313) 865-5000
Fax	(313) 865-5927

Publishes General Motors service manuals
and documentation.

Hewlett-Packard Company
800 South Taft
Loveland, CO 80537

Phone	(970) 635-1500
Fax	(970) 667-0997
Web	**www.hp.com/storage/**

Manufactures tape-backup subsystems,
specializing in Travan, SCSI, IDE, and
floppy-based systems that attach via an
interface card, floppy controller, or parallel
port connection.

**Hewlett-Packard (Disk Memory
Division)**
1311 Chinden Blvd.
Boise, ID 83714

Sales	(800) 826-4111
Phone	(208) 396-6000
Fax	(208) 396-2896
Web	**www.hp.com**

Manufactures high-capacity 3 1/2-inch
hard disk drives.

Hewlett-Packard (Storage Division)
800 S. Taft Ave.
Loveland, CO 80537

Phone	(970) 635-1500
Fax	(970) 667-0997

Manufactures tape-backup subsystems
specializing in Travan, SCSI, and floppy
systems that attach through an interface
card, floppy controller, or parallel port
connection.

**Hitachi America, Ltd. (Semiconductor
& IC Division)**
2000 Sierra Point Pkwy.
Brisbane, CA 94005

Phone	(650) 589-8300
Fax	(650) 583-4207
Web	**www.hitachi.com**

Manufactures a variety of memory and
other semiconductor devices. Also manufactures computer peripherals, including
Office automation, digital graphics products, and LCD devices.

Hypertech
1910 Thomas Rd.
Memphis, TN 38134

Phone	(901) 382-8888
Fax	(901) 373-5290

Manufactures and sells a wide variety of
well-engineered, high-performance automotive computer EPROM replacements for
many different types of vehicles. Also
makes the Power Programmer for reprogramming vehicle PCMs with EEPROMs
(Flash ROMs).

Hyundai Electronics America

3101 N. 1st St.
San Jose, CA 95134

Phone	(408) 232-8000
Web	**www.hea.com**

Manufactures PC-compatible systems. Hyundai also makes monitors, memory, chips, and other peripherals.

IBM Fullfilment Center

P.O. Box 1900
Dept EZE/010J
Boulder, CO 80303

Phone	(800) 426-7282
Developer Connection	(800) 633-8266

The source for OS/2 software developer kits, reseller literature, and orders for server guides.

IBM Microelectronics

3605 Hwy. 52 North
Rochester, MN 55901

Phone	(507) 253-4011
Fax	(507) 253-3256
Web	**www.chips.ibm.com**

The IBM division responsible for development, manufacturing, and marketing of semiconductor and electronic packaging products, services, and solutions.

IBM National Publications

4800 Falls of The Neause
Raleigh, NC 27609

Phone	(800) 879-2755
Fax	(800) 445-9269

The source for current books, reference manuals, documentation, software toolkits, and language products for IBM systems. For discontinued publications, contact Fantasy Productions or Annabooks.

IBM OEM Division

44 S. Broadway Rd.
White Plains, NY 10601

Phone	(914) 288-3000

Manufactures and distributes IBM products such as high-capacity 3 1/2-inch hard disk drives, networking, and chipset products.

IBM Parts Order Center

6300 Diagonal Highway
Boulder, CO 80301

Phone	(303) 924-6300 (Orders)

IBM's nationwide service parts ordering center.

IBM PC Company

11400 Burnet Rd.
Austin, TX 78758

Phone	(512) 823-0000
Sales	(800) IBM-3333
FAXBack	(800) 426-4329
BBS	(919) 517-0001
Web	**www.ibm.com**

Manufactures and supports IBM personal computers.

IBM PC Direct

3039 Cornwallis Rd.
Building 203
Research Triangle Park, NC 27709-9766

Sales	(800) IBM-2YOU
	(426-2968)
Canada Sales	(800) 465-7999
Fax	(800) 426-4182
General Information	(800) 426-3332
Tech Support	(800) 772-2227
Orders	(800) 426-2968
Web	**www.pc.ibm.com**

IBM PC Company's direct mail-order catalog sales division. They sell IBM and approved third-party systems and peripherals at a discount from list price, and publish a catalog listing all items.

IBM Personal Systems Technical Solutions
Magazine
NCM
P.O. Box 165447
Irving, TX 75016

Sales	(800) 678-8014
Phone	(972) 550-0433
Fax	(972) 518-2507

Publishes an excellent bimonthly magazine covering IBM personal computer systems and software.

Illinois Lock
301 West Hintz Rd.
Wheeling, IL 60090-5754

Phone	(847) 537-1800
Fax	(847) 537-1881
E-mail	**iillock@aol.com**

Manufactures keylocks used in many different PC systems.

Information Access Company
One Park Ave.
New York, NY 10016

Phone	(212) 503-4400
Web	**www.iacnet.com**

Manufactures the Computer Library and Computer Select CD-ROM information databases.

***InfoWorld* Magazine**
375 Cochituate Rd.
Framingham, MA 01701

Phone	(508) 879-0700
Sales	(800) 227-8365
Fax	(508) 879-0446
Web	**www.infoworld.com**

Features excellent product reviews.

Inline, Inc.
22860 Savi Ranch Pkwy.
Yorba Linda, CA 92887

Phone	(714) 921-4100
Sales	(800) 882-7117
Fax	(714) 921-4160

Manufactures a complete line of video-connection accessories, including distribution amplifiers, scan converters, line drivers, projector interfaces, and cables. They also offer interactive training systems for computer-based training facilities.

Innerworks Technology, Inc.
319 Sundance Dr.
Bartlett, IL 60103

Manufactures an excellent PC diagnostic program called the Third Degree.

Integrated Device Technology, Inc.
2975 Stender Way
Santa Clara, CA 95054-3090

Phone	(408) 727-6116
Sales	(800) 345-7015
Web	**www.idt.com**

Manufactures chipsets and other semiconductor devices.

Intel Corporation
2200 Mission College Blvd.
Santa Clara, CA 95054-1537

Phone	(408) 765-8080
Customer Service	(800) 468-3548
Tech Support	(800) 321-4044
Fax	(408) 765-9904
Web	**www.intel.com**

Manufactures microprocessors used in PC systems. Also makes a line of memory and accelerator boards, and one of the most popular lines of PC-compatible Pentium, Pentium Pro, and Pentium II motherboards and chipsets.

Intel PC and LAN Enhancement Product Division

5200 N.E. Elam Young Pkwy.
Hillsboro, OR 97124-6427

Phone	(503) 629-7354
Sales	(800) 538-3373
Customer Service	(800) 321-4044
Tech Support	(800) 628-8686
Fax	(503) 264-7969
BBS	(503) 264-7999

Manufactures OverDrive CPU upgrades and networking devices.

International Electronic Research Corp. (IERC)

135 W. Magnolia Blvd.
Burbank, CA 91502

Phone	(818) 842-7277
Fax	(818) 848-8872
Web	**www.iercdya.com**

Manufactures a line of excellent CPU heat sink products, including clip-on, low-profile models especially for 486 and Pentium processors that do not require a special socket.

Iomega Corporation

1821 West Iomega Way
Roy, UT 84067

Phone	(801) 778-1000
Sales	(800) 777-6654
Fax	(801) 778-3461
BBS	(801) 778-5888
Web	**www.iomega.com**

Manufactures the Jaz, Ditto, and Zip drive removable-cartridge drives.

IX Micro Solutions, Inc.

2085 Hamilton Ave, 3rd Floor
San Jose, CA 95125

Phone	(408) 369-8282
Sales Fax	(408) 369-0128
Web	**users.aol.com\imsteksup**

Manufactures graphic accelerator chips and boards, and ATM network products.

J. Bond Computer Systems

93 W. Montague Expressway
Milpitas, CA 95035

Phone	(408) 946-9622
Fax	(408) 946-2898
Web	**www.jbond.com**

Manufactures PC motherboards.

Jameco Computer Products

1355 Shoreway Rd.
Belmont, CA 94002

Phone	(415) 592-8097
Sales	(800) 831-4242
Fax	(415) 592-2503
BBS	(415) 637-9025
Web	**www.jameco.com**

Supplies computer components, parts, and peripherals by mail order.

JC Whitney & Company

1104 S. Wabash Street
Chicago, IL 60605

Phone	(312) 431-6100
Fax	(312) 431-5625
Web	**www.jcwhitneyusa.com**

Distributes an enormous collection of bargain-priced tools and equipment. Its products are primarily for automotive applications, but many of the tools have universal uses.

JDR Microdevices

1850 S. 10th
San Jose, CA 95112

Phone	(408) 494-1400
Sales	(800) 538-5000
BBS	(408) 494-1430
Web	**www.jdr.com**

A vendor for chips, disk drives, and various computer and electronic parts and components.

Jensen Tools, Inc.
7815 S. 46th St.
Phoenix, AZ 85044

Phone	(602) 968-6231
Sales	(800) 426-1194
Fax	(800) 366-9662
Web	**www.jensentools.com**

Catalog distributor of networking tools and PC test equipment.

JTS Corporation
166 Baypoint Pkwy.
San Jose, CA 95134

Phone	(408) 468-1800
Fax	(408) 468-1801
Web	**www.jtscorp.com**

Manufactures a line of low-cost 3 1/2-inch hard disk drives.

JVC Information Products
5665 Corporate Drive
Cypress, CA 90630

Phone	(714) 816-6500
Sales Fax	(714) 816-6519

Manufactures CD-Recordable and CD-ROM drives.

Kensington Technology Group
2855 Campus Dr.
San Mateo, CA 94403

Phone	(650) 572-2700
Tech Support	(800) 535-4242
Reseller Support	(800) 280-8318
Fax	(650) 572-9675
Web	**www.kensington.com**

Manufactures and supplies computer accessories.

Key Tronic Corporation
P.O. Box 14687
Spokane, WA 99214

Phone	(509) 928-8000
Sales	(800) 262-6006

Fax	(509) 927-5248
BBS	(509) 927-5288
Web	**www.keytronic.com**

Manufactures a variety of high-quality keyboards and mice for PC-compatible systems. Acquired the Honeywell Keyboard division. The Honeywell mouse uses revolutionary new technology that never needs cleaning and works on any surface, unlike traditional ball and roller mice. Supplies Compaq and Microsoft with keyboards.

Kingston Technology Corporation
17600 Newhope St.
Fountain Valley, CA 92708

Phone	(714) 435-2600
Sales	(800) 835-6575
Fax	(714) 435-2699
Web	**www.kingston.com**

They are the world's largest vendor of memory modules. They also manufacture an excellent line of direct processor upgrade modules.

Labconco Corporation
8811 Prospect
Kansas City, MO 64132

Phone	(816) 333-8811
Sales	(800) 821-5525
Fax	(816) 363-0130

Manufactures a variety of clean room cabinets and clean benches for use in hard disk drive and other sensitive component repair.

Labtec Enterprises, Inc.
1499 SE Tech Center Place, Ste. 350
Vancouver, WA 98683

Phone	(360) 896-2000
Fax	(360) 896-2020
Web	**www.labtec.com**

Imports amplified speakers for multimedia applications.

Lantronix
15353 Barranca Pkwy.
Irvine, CA 92718-2216

Phone	(714) 453-3990
Sales	(800) 422-7055
Fax	(714) 453-3995
Web	**www.lantronix.com**

Manufactures a variety of network hardware including servers, bridges, repeaters, hubs, converters, and transceivers.

Laser Magnetic Storage
4425 Arrowswest Dr.
Colorado Springs, CO 80907

Phone	(719) 593-7900
Fax	(719) 599-8713
BBS	(719) 593-4081

Division of DPMG that manufactures a variety of optical and tape disk products.

LearnKey, Inc.
1845 W. Sunset Blvd.
St George, UT 84770

Phone	(801) 674-9733
Sales	(800) 937-3279
Fax	(801) 674-9734
Web	**www.learnkey.com**

Produces and distributes the highest quality computer training videos.

Lexmark
740 New Circle Rd.
Lexington, KY 40511

Phone	(606) 232-2000
Fax	(606) 232-3557
BBS	(606) 232-5238
Web	**www.lexmark.com**

Manufactures IBM keyboards and printers for retail distribution. Spun off from IBM in 1991, now sells to other OEMs and distributors.

Libi Industries, Ltd.
1983 Marcus Ave.
Lake Success, NY 11042

Phone	(516) 326-2000
Fax	(516) 326-1100
Web	**www.libi.com**

Distributes a complete line of hardware and software diagnostics, memory upgrades, and the Multimedia CPU Upgrade Kit.

Liebert
1050 Dearborn Dr.
Columbus, OH 43229

Phone	(614) 888-0246
Sales	(800) 877-9222
Fax	(614) 841-6022
Web	**www.liebert.com**

Manufactures a line of computer power-protection devices.

Liuski International
6585 Crescent Dr.
Norcross, GA 30071

Phone	(770) 447-9454
Web	**www.liuski.com**

Hardware distributor that carries a variety of peripherals and systems. They are the exclusive distributor of Magitronic PC systems and motherboards.

Longshine Microsystems, Inc.
10400-9 Pioneer Blvd.
Santa Fe Springs, CA 90670

Phone	(310) 903-0899
Fax	(310) 944-2201

Manufactures PC interface boards including disk controllers, Super I/O adapters, network cards, and more.

**Lotus Development Corporation
(A Division of IBM)**
55 Cambridge Pkwy.
Cambridge, MA 02142

Phone	(617) 577-8500
Customer Service	(800) 343-5414
Fax	(617) 693-3899
BBS	(617) 693-7000
Web	**www.lotus.com**

Manufactures Lotus 1-2-3, Symphony, and Magellan software. Acquired by IBM.

LSI Logic, Inc.
1551 McCarthy Blvd.
Milpitas, CA 95035

Phone	(408) 433-8000
Sales	(800) 433-8778
Fax	(408) 433-2882
Web	**www.lsilogic.com**

Manufactures motherboard logic and chipsets.

Ma Laboratories, Inc.
1972 Concourse Dr.
San Jose, CA 95131

Phone	(408) 954-8188
Fax	(408) 954-0944
Web	**www.malabs.com**

Manufactures and supplies CPUs and SIMMs, PC boards, hard disk drives, floppy drives, motherboards, and math coprocessors. They also manufacture a dummy parity chip that allows fake parity SIMMs to be constructed, which they also sell.

Macworld Communications, Inc.
501 Second St.
San Francisco, CA 94107

Phone	(415) 243-0505
Fax	(415) 442-1891
Web	**macworld.zdnet.com**

Produces an excellent publication covering news in the Macintosh universe.

MAG InnoVision
2801 S. Yale St.
Santa Ana, CA 92704

Phone	(714) 751-2008
Sales	(800) 827-3998
Fax	(714) 751-5522
Web	**www.maginnovision.com**

Manufactures Flat Square Technology monitors with advanced performance features.

MAGNI Systems, Inc.
22965 NW Evergreen Pkwy.
Hillsboro, OR 97124

Phone	(503) 615-1900
Sales	(800) 624-6465
Fax	(503) 615-1999
Web	**www.magnisystems.com**

Manufactures a line of products for converting VGA graphics screens to either NTSC (VHS) or S-video (S-VHS).

MapInfo Corporation
One Global View
Troy, NY 12180

Phone	(518) 285-6000
Fax	(518) 285-6070
Sales	(800) 552-2511
Web	**www.mapinfo.com**

Produces desktop, embedded object, and Internet/intranet mapping software and data for public and private sector information discovery.

Matrox Graphics, Inc.
1025 St. Regis Blvd.
Dorval, PQ H9P 2T4 Canada

Phone	(514) 969-6300
Fax	(514) 969-6363
Sales	(514) 969-6330
Web	**www.matrox.com**

Manufactures a line of high-performance PC graphics chipsets and adapters.

Maxell Corporation of America

22-08 Route 208
Fair Lawn, NJ 07410

Phone	(800) 533-2836
Fax	(201) 796-8790

Manufactures magnetic media products, including disks and tape cartridges, as well as optical products, including CD-R media.

Maxi Switch, Inc.

2901 East Elvira Rd.
Tucson, AZ 85706

Phone	(602) 294-5450
Fax	(602) 294-6890
BBS	(602) 741-9230
Web	**www.maxiswitch.com**

Manufactures a line of high-quality PC keyboards, including some designed for harsh or industrial environments and programmable keyboards. Maxi Switch keyboards are used by many compatible system manufacturers, including Gateway 2000.

Maxoptix Corporation

3342 Gateway Blvd.
Fremont, CA 94538

Phone	(510) 353-9700
Toll Free	(800) 848-3092
Fax	(510) 353-1845
BBS	(510) 353-1448
Web	**www.maxoptix.com**
E-mail	**maxsales@maxoptix.com**

A leading supplier of high-performance 5.25-inch magneto-optical drives, jukeboxes, and media. Joint venture with Maxtor and Kubota Corporations.

Maxtor Corporation

211 River Oaks Pkwy.
San Jose, CA 95134

Phone	(408) 432-1700
Sales	(800) 262-9867
Fax	(408) 432-4510
BBS	(303) 678-2222
Web	**www.maxtor.com**

Manufactures a line of large-capacity, high-quality hard disk drives.

McAfee Associates

2710 Walsh Ave.
Santa Clara, CA 95051

Phone	(408) 988-3832
Sales	(800) 707-1274
Fax	(408) 970-9727
BBS	(408) 988-4044
Web	**www.mcafee.com**

Manufactures the famous McAfee anti-virus software and a diagnostic program called PC Medic 97.

McKenzie Technology

910 Page Ave.
Fremont, CA 94538

Phone	(510) 651-2700
Fax	(510) 651-1020

Manufactures sockets for processors and IC chips.

Megahertz Corporation (A Division of 3Com)

605 N 5600 W
Salt Lake City, UT 84116

Phone	(801) 320-7000
Sales	(800) 527-8677
FAXBack	(800) 856-1045
Fax	(801) 320-6022
Web	**www.megahertz.com**

Manufactures laptop modems and external network adapters. Also makes AT-speedup products.

Merisel
200 N. Continental Blvd.
El Segundo, CA 90245

Phone	(310) 615-3080
Sales	(800) 542-9955
Customer Service	(800) 462-5241
Fax	(800) 845-3744
Web	**www.merisel.com**

World's largest distributor of PC hardware and software products from many manufacturers.

Meritec
1359 West Jackson St.
P.O. Box 8003
Painesville, OH 44077

Phone	(440) 354-3148
Fax	(440) 354-0509
Sales	(800) 627-7752
Web	**www.meritec.com**

Manufactures a line of SCSI 8-bit to 16-bit (Wide SCSI) adapters in a variety of configurations. These adapters allow Wide SCSI devices to be installed in a standard 8-bit SCSI bus and vice versa.

Merritt Computer Products, Inc.
5565 Red Bird Center Dr., #150
Dallas, TX 75237

Phone	(214) 339-0753
Fax	(214) 339-1313

Manufactures the SafeSkin keyboard protector.

Methode Electronics, Inc.
DataMate Division
7444 W. Wilson Ave.
Chicago, IL 60656

Phone	(708) 867-9600
Fax	(708) 867-3149
web	**www.methode.com**

Manufactures and sells a complete line of SCSI terminators.

Micro 2000, Inc.
1100 E. Broadway, 3rd Floor
Glendale, CA 91205

Phone	(818) 547-0125
Fax	(818) 547-0397
Web	**www.micro2000.com**

Manufactures the MicroScope PC diagnostics program and the POSTProbe ISA, EISA, and MCA POST diagnostics card.

Micro Accessories, Inc.
6036 Stewart Ave.
Fremont, CA 94538

Phone	(510) 226-6310
Sales	(800) 777-6687
Fax	(510) 226-6316
Web	**www.micro-a.com**

Manufactures a variety of cables and disk drive mounting brackets and accessories, including PS/2 adapter kits.

Micro Channel Developers Association
169 Hartnell Ave., Ste. 200
Redding, CA 96002

Phone	(916) 222-2262
Sales	(800) GET-MCDA (438-6232)
Fax	(916) 222-2528
Web	**www.microchannel.inter .net/microchannel**

An independent organization established to facilitate the evolution and support of the Micro Channel Architecture (MCA). The association also provides microchannel products direct to end users. They publish the *International Catalog of Micro Channel Products and Services*.

Micro Computer Cable Company, Inc.
12200 Delta Dr.
Taylor, MI 48180

Phone	(313) 946-9700
Fax	(313) 946-9645
Web	**www.microccc.com**

Manufactures and sells a complete line of computer cables, connectors, switchboxes, and cabling accessories.

Micro Design International (MDI)
6985 University Blvd.
Winter Park, FL 32792

Phone	(407) 677-8333
Sales	(800) 228-0891
Fax	(407) 677-8365
BBS	(407) 677-4854
Web	**www.mdi.com**

Manufactures the SCSI Express driver software for integration of SCSI peripherals in a variety of environments. Recently acquired PC-Kwik Corporation.

Micro Firmware, Inc.
330 West Gray St., Ste. 170
Norman, OK 73069-7111

Sales	(800) 767-5465
Fax	(405) 573-5535
BBS	(405) 573-5538
Web	**www.firmware.com**

The largest distributor of Phoenix ROM BIOS upgrades. Develops custom versions for specific motherboards and supplies many other BIOS vendors with products.

Micro House International
2477 N. 55th St.
Boulder, CO 80301

Phone	(303) 443-3388
Sales	(800) 926-8299
Fax	(303) 443-3323
BBS	(303) 443-9957
Web	**www.microhouse.com**

Publishes the Micro House Technical Library on CD-ROM. The technical library is a Windows-compatible reference tool designed for PC service technicians that covers adapter cards, network cards, motherboards, and disk drives. Also produces DrivePro, EZ Drive, EZ Copy, and many other hard-drive formatting and protection products. EZ Drive is the utility shipped with many of the new large IDE hard drives (allows bypass of the BIOS).

Micro Industries Corporation
8399 Green Meadows Dr. North
North Westerville, OH 43081-9486

Phone	(614) 548-7878
Fax	(614) 548-6184
Web	**www.microindustries.com**

Manufactures PC-compatible motherboards.

Micro Solutions, inc.
132 W. Lincoln Hwy.
DeKalb, IL 60115

Phone	(815) 756-3411
Sales	(800) 890-7227
Fax	(815) 756-9100
Web	**www.micro-solutions.com**

Manufactures a complete line of floppy controllers and subsystems, including 2.88M versions. Also offers floppy drive and tape-backup systems that run from a standard parallel port, using no expansion slots. Also makes the backpack line of hard drives, CD-ROMS, disk drives, and tape drives.

Micro Solutions, Inc.
40 Old Ridgebury Rd., Ste. 106
Danbury, CT 06810

Phone	(203) 748-4633
Fax	(203) 797-9849
Web	**www.micsol.com**

A Premier Service center for Toshiba
America, specializing in sales, service, and
upgrades for laptop and portable computers.

Micro Warehouse
535 Connecticut Ave.
Norwalk, CT 06854

Phone	(203) 899-4000
Fax	(203) 853-2267
Sales	(800) 547-5444
Web	**www.warehouse.com**

Distributes a large variety of computers,
computer supplies, floppy disks, cables,
and so on.

Microcom, Inc.
500 River Ridge Dr.
Norwood, MA 02062

Phone	(781) 551-1000
Sales	(800) 822-8224
Fax	(781) 255-1125
Web	**www.microcom.com**

Manufactures error-correcting modems and
remote access products; created and develops the MNP communications protocols.

MicroData Corporation
2727 Ulmerton Road, Ste. 300
Clearwater, FL 33762

Phone	(800) 539-0123
	(813) 573-5900
Fax	(813) 572-5085
Web	**www.quicktech.com**

Manufactures and distributes a complete
line of hardware and software diagnostic
tools including Ultra-X, QuickTech PRO,
QuickTech 98, P.H.D. Plus, The Examiner,
and P.C. Inspector.

Micrografx, Inc.
1303 E. Arapaho Rd.
Richardson, TX 75081

Phone	(972) 234-1769
Sales and	(800) 733-3729
Customer Service	
Tech Support	(972) 234-2694
Fax	(972) 994-6476
BBS	(972) 644-4194
Web	**www.micrografx.com**

Manufactures the Micrografx Designer,
Windows Draw, ABC Toolkit, Photomagic,
and Charisma software. Specializes in Windows and OS/2 development.

**Micron Technologies (Parent Company
of Micron Electronics and Micron Custom Manufacturing)**
8000 S. Federal Way
Boise, ID 83707

Phone	(208) 368-3900
Sales	(800) 388-6334
Fax	(208) 368-3809
BBS	(208) 368-4530
Web	**www.micron.com**

Manufactures various memory boards,
memory chips, SIMMs, DRAM, SRAM, and
other semiconductors, and a line of PC
systems.

Micronics Computers, Inc.
45365 Northport Loop West
Fremont, CA 94538

Phone	(510) 651-2300
Fax	(510) 651-6692
Sales	(800) 577-0977
Tech Support	(510) 661-3000
FAXBack	(510) 661-3199
BBS	(510) 651-6837
Web	**www.micronics.com**

Manufactures PC motherboards.

Micropolis Corporation

21211 Nordhoff St.
Chatsworth, CA 91311

Phone	(818) 709-3300
Sales	(800) 395-DRIV (3748)
Fax	(818) 709-3396
BBS	(818) 709-3310

Manufactured a line of high-capacity
5 1/4- and 3 1/2-inch hard disk drives.
Recently acquired by Singapore Technologies and since liquidated.

Microprocessors Unlimited, Inc.

24000 S. Peoria Ave.
Beggs, OK 74421

Phone	(918) 267-4961
Fax	(918) 267-3879

Distributes memory chips, SIMMs, math
coprocessors, UART chips, and other integrated circuits.

Microsoft Corporation

One Microsoft Way
Redmond, WA 98052-6399

Phone	(425) 882-8080
Sales	(800) 426-9400
Fax	(425) 936-7329
BBS	(425) 936-6735
Web	**www.microsoft.com**

Manufactures MS-DOS, Windows 9x, Windows NT, and a variety of applications
software.

Micro-Star International

4059 Clipper Ct.
Fremont, CA 94538

Phone	(510) 623-8818
Fax	(510) 623-8585
BBS	(510) 623-7398
Web	**www.achme.com**

One of the top 10 largest Taiwan-based
motherboard manufacturers.

MicroSystems Development, Inc.

4100 Moorpark Ave. #104
San Jose, CA 95117

Phone	(408) 296-4000
Fax	(408) 296-5877
BBS	(408) 296-4200
Web	**www.msd.com/diags**

Manufactures a line of excellent hardware
diagnostics products including Post Code
Master, Port Test, and Test Drive.

Microtest Enterprises

22 Cotton Rd.
Nashua, NH 03063

Phone	(603) 880-0300
Sales	(800) 880-5644
Fax	(603) 880-7229
Web	**www.microtest.com**

Manufacturer of CD-ROM networking and
optical storage solutions for the DOS, Windows, Window 95, Windows NT, and
Macintosh environments. The company's
products provide fast access to CD-ROM
databases over a wide range of networks
and technologies in the industry, featuring
the FastCD PersonalEdition. FastCD has
been renamed Virtual CD, which also allows CD-based programs to be run from
any local or network disk.

MicroWay, Inc.

Research Park
Box 79
Kingston, MA 02364

Phone	(508) 746-7341
BBS	(508) 746-7946
Web	**www.microway.com**

Manufactures a line of Digital Alpha Based
Screamer workstations, and NDP Fortran
and C compilers.

Mini Micro Supply
4900 Patrick Henry Dr., Bldg. B
Santa Clara, CA 95054

Phone	(408) 327-0388
Sales	(800) 275-4642
Fax	(408) 327-0389
BBS	(408) 434-9319
Web	**www.mini-micro.com**

Partly owned by Greenleaf Corporation, a wholesale distributor of Conner Peripherals, Inc.

Mitsubishi Computers, Ltd.
3500 Parkside
Birmingham Business Park
Birmingham, B37 7YS England

Phone	+44 (121) 717-7171
Fax	+44 (021) 717-7799
Web	**www.mitsubishi-computers.com**

Manufactures a popular line of PC systems sold primarily in Europe. Acquired by Mitsubishi Electric in 1990.

Mitsubishi Electronics America, Inc.
Electronic Device Group
1050 E. Arques Ave.
Sunnyvale, CA 94086

Phone	(408) 730-5900
Sales	(800) 843-2515
Tech Support	(800) 344-6352
Web	**www.mitsubishichips.com**

Manufactures monitors, printers, and consumables. For hard disks and floppy disk storage products, contact the Electronic Device Group.

Mitsumi Electronics Corporation
5808 W. Campus Circle Drive
Irving, TX 75063

Phone	(214) 550-7300
Fax	(214) 550-7424
Web	**www.mitsumi.com**

Manufactures a line of CD-ROM and floppy drives and keyboards and mice.

Molex, Inc.
2222 Wellington Ct.
Lisle, IL 60532

Phone	(630) 969-4550
Sales	(800) 78MOLEX (786-6539)
Fax	(630) 969-2321
Web	**www.molex.com**

Manufactures a variety of connectors used in PC systems.

Mosel Vitelic
3910 N. First St.
San Jose, CA 95134

Phone	(408) 433-6000
Fax	(408) 433-0331
Web	**www.moselvitelic.com**

Manufactures memory modules.

Motor Magazine
Hearst Corporation
645 Stewart Ave.
Garden City, NY 11530

Phone	(516) 227-1300
Sales	(800) 426-6867
Fax	(516) 227-1444

The essential trade magazine for the automotive technician, including troubleshooting tips and service product information. Subscriptions are free to those who qualify.

Motorola, Inc.

Microprocessor and Memory Technology Group
3501 Ed Bluestein Blvd.
Austin, TX 78762

Phone	(512) 895-2000
Sales	(800) 521-6274
Fax	(512) 895-2652
Web	**www.mot.com**

Manufactures PC memory including fast static RAM for cache. Also makes the Macintosh, Power PC, and Motorola processors.

Mountain Network Solutions, Inc. (Subsidiary of NCE Star Solutions)

9717 Pacific Heights Blvd.
San Diego, CA 92121

Phone	(800) 458-0300
Fax	(408) 438-7623
BBS	(408) 438-2665

Manufactures tape drives and backup subsystems, including hardware and software.

Mueller Technical Research

21 Spring Lane
Barrington Hills, IL 60010

Phone	(847) 854-6794
Fax	(847) 854-6795
Web	**www.m-tr.com**
E-mail	**scottmueller@compuserve.com**

You found me! I run a service company that offers the best in custom onsite PC hardware and software technical seminars and training, specializing in all aspects of PC hardware, software, and data recovery. We can present a custom seminar for your organization. *Scott Mueller.*

Mustang Software

P.O. Box 2264
Bakersfield, CA 93303

Phone	(805) 873-2500
Sales	(800) 999-9619
Technical Support	(805) 873-2550
Fax	(805) 873-2599
BBS	(805) 873-2400
Web	**www.mustang.com**

Manufactures Wildcat! BBS software.

Mylex Corporation

34551 Ardenwood Blvd.
Fremont, CA 94555-3067

Phone	(510) 796-6100
Sales	(800) 776-9539
Fax	(510) 745-8016
Web	**www.mylex.com**

Manufactures high-performance motherboards, SCSI RAID, and SCSI host adapters.

Myoda Computer Centers

1070 N Roselle Rd.
Hoffman Estates, IL 60195

Phone	(847) 885-7600
Fax	(847) 885-7661
Web	**www.myoda.com**

Assembles PC systems for retail sale.

National Semiconductor Corporation

2900 Semiconductor Dr.
Santa Clara, CA 95051

Phone	(408) 721-5000
BBS	(408) 245-0671
Web	**www.nsc.com**

Manufactures a variety of chips for PC circuit applications. Known especially for its UART and Super I/O chips.

NCR Microelectronics
1635 Aeroplaza
Colorado Springs, CO 80916

Phone	(719) 596-5795
Sales	(800) 334-5454
Fax	(719) 573-3286
BBS	(719) 574-0424
Web	**www.ncr.com**

Manufactures a variety of integrated circuits for PC systems, including SCSI protocol chips used by many OEMs. They also sponsor the SCSI BBS, an excellent source for standard documents covering SCSI, IDE, and other interfaces.

NEC Electronics, Inc.
2880 Scott Blvd.
Santa Clara, CA 95052

Phone	(408) 588-6000
Web	**www.nec.com**

Manufactures memory and other semiconductor devices.

NEC Technologies, Inc.
1414 Massachusetts Ave.
Boxborough, MA 01719

Phone	(978) 264-8000
Sales	(800) 632-4636
Fax	(978) 264-8245
BBS	(708) 860-2602
Web	**www.nec.com**

Manufactures multisync monitors, CD-ROM drives, video adapters, printers, and other peripherals as well as complete PC-compatible systems.

Newark Electronics
4801 N. Ravenswood
Chicago, IL 60640-4496

Phone	(773) 784-5100
Fax	(773) 907-5217
Web	**www.newark.com**

An electronic component and product supplier with a huge catalog of products. Its 1500+ page catalog is an excellent source of components and information.

NexGen, Inc. (A Division of AMD)
1623 Buckeye Dr.
Milpitas, CA 95035

Phone	(408) 260-0117
Web	**www.amd.com**

Manufactured the Nx586 family of processors, which were marketed as alternatives to the Intel Pentium family. NexGen features are now incorporated into some lines of AMD processors.

Novell, Inc.
122 E. 1700 South
Provo, UT 84606

Phone	(801) 379-5588
Sales	(800) 526-7937
Tech Support	(800) 858-4000
BBS	(801) 429-3030
Web	**www.novell.com**

Manufactures the NetWare LAN operating system.

Number Nine Visual Technology Corporation
18 Hartwell Ave.
Lexington, MA 02173

Phone	(781) 674-0009
Fax	(781) 674-2919
BBS	(781) 862-7502
Web	**www.numbernine.com**

Manufactures a line of high-end PC video graphics accelerator cards.

nVidia Corporation
1226 Tiros Way
Sunnyvale, CA 94086

Phone	(408) 617-4000
Fax	(408) 617-4100
Web	**www.nvidia.com**
E-mail	**info@nvidia.com**

A leading provider of 3D graphics processors used in many OEM branded graphics adapters.

Oak Technology, Inc.
139 Kifer Ct.
Sunnyvale, CA 94086

Phone	(408) 737-0888
Fax	(408) 737-3838
BBS	(408) 774-5308
Web	**www.oaktech.com**

Manufactures semiconductors.

Ocean Information Systems
688 Arrow Grand Circle
Covina, CA 91722

Phone	(626) 339-8888
Fax	(626) 859-7668
Web	**www.ocean-usa.com/ocean**

Manufactures high-performance PC motherboards.

OEM Magazine
CMP Publications
600 Community Dr.
Manhasset, NY 11030

Phone	(516) 562-5000
Web	**techweb.cmp.com/oem**

An excellent magazine for the systems integrator or systems assembler. Free subscription for those who qualify.

Okidata
532 Fellowship Rd.
Mount Laurel, NJ 08054

Phone	(609) 235-2600
Sales	(800) OKIDATA (654-3282)
Fax	(609) 222-5010
BBS	(800) 283-5474
Web	**www.okidata.com**

Manufacturer of printers, faxes, and multi-function peripherals.

Olivetti
765 U.S. Hwy. 202
Bridgewater, NJ 08807

Phone	(908) 526-8200
Fax	(908) 526-8405
Web	**www.olivetti.com**

Manufactures Olivetti and many AT&T PC systems.

Ontrack Data International, Inc. (Formerly Ontrack Computer Systems)
6321 Bury Dr., Ste. 13-21
Eden Prairie, MN 55346

Phone	(612) 937-5161
Fax	(612) 937-5750
Sales	(800) 872-2599
Tech Support	(612) 937-2121
BBS	(612) 937-8567
Web	**www.ontrack.com**

Manufactures the Disk Manager hard disk utilities for PC, PS/2, and Macintosh. Disk Manager is the most comprehensive and flexible low-level format program available, supporting even IDE drives. Also provides extensive data recovery services.

Opti, Inc.
888 Tasman Dr.
Milpitas, CA 95035

Phone	(408) 486-8000
Sales	(800) 398-6784
Fax	(408) 486-8001
BBS	(408) 486-8051
Web	**www.opti.com**

Manufactures PC motherboard chipsets including the Viper series for Pentium systems.

Orchid Technology (A Division of Micronics)
45365 Northport Loop West
Fremont, CA 94538

Phone	(510) 683-0300
Customer Service	(800) 767-2443
Sales	(510) 651-2300
Tech Support	(510) 661-3000
Fax	(510) 651-5612
FAXBack	(510) 661-3199
BBS	(510) 651-6837
Web	**www.orchid.com**

Manufactures a line of video and memory board products for PC systems. Also produces 32-bit sound cards.

Pacific Data Products
9855 Scranton Rd.
San Diego, CA 92121

Phone	(619) 229-9900
Fax	(619) 552-0889
BBS	(619) 452-6329

Manufactures the Pacific Page XL and Pacific Page PE PostScript-compatible enhancement products for HP LaserJet printers.

Packard Bell
6041 Variel Avenue
Woodland Hills, CA 91367

Phone	(818) 673-4800
Service	(800) 733-4411
Sales Fax	(818) 673-4883
Customer Service	(800) 244-0049
Web	**www.packardbell.com**

Manufactures a popular line of low-cost PC-compatible computer systems.

Palo Alto Design Group
567 University Ave.
Palo Alto, CA 94301

Phone	(650) 327-9444
Web	**www.padg.com**

Manufactures enclosures that accept Intel ATX motherboards. For OEMs.

Panasonic Communications & Systems
2 Panasonic Way
Secaucus, NJ 07094

Phone	(201) 348-7000
Web	**www.panasonic.com**

Manufactures monitors, optical drive products, floppy drives, printers, and PC-compatible laptop systems.

Panasonic Industrial Co.
2 Panasonic Way
Secaucus, NJ 07094

Phone	(201) 348-7000

Manufactures IC memory cards; batteries (nickel metal hydride); cellular components (planar filters and resonators); optical and floppy disk drives; CD-ROM drives; printer mechanisms; power supplies (custom AC adapters); semiconductors (video digital signal processors, CCD card cameras); microphones; speakers; high-resolution color monitors; TV tuners; ceramic receivers; and video camera modules.

Parallel Technologies, Inc.
4240 B Street NW
Auburn, WA 98001

Phone	(253) 813-8728
Fax	(253) 813-3730
Web	**www.lpt.com**

Manufactures the Parallel Port Information Utility and a line of cables and software supporting the Windows 95 Direct Cable Connection (DCC). It sells a special Universal Cable offering the highest possible speed connection using DCC.

PARTS NOW!, Inc.

3517 West Beltline Hwy.
Madison, WI 53713

Phone (608) 276-8688
Fax (608) 276-9134

Sells a large variety of laser printer parts for HP, Canon, Apple, and other laser printers using Canon engines.

PC & MAC Connection

528 Rt 13 South
Milford, NH 03055

Phone (603) 446-7721
Sales (800) 800-5555
Fax (603) 446-7791
Web **www.pcconnection.com**

Distributes many different hardware and software packages by way of mail order.

PC Magazine

Ziff-Davis Communications Co.
One Park Ave.
New York, NY 10016

Phone (212) 503-3500
Fax (212) 503-5799
Web **www.zdnet.com/pcmag**

Magazine featuring product reviews and comparisons.

PC Portable Manufacturer, Inc.

1431 Potrero Ave., Unit E
El Monte, CA 91733

Phone (616) 444-3585
Sales (800) 966-7237
Fax (616) 444-1027

Manufactures a line of portable cases that accept standard Baby-AT and ATX motherboards, which are ideal for building your own portable systems.

PC Power & Cooling, Inc.

5995 Avenida Encinas
Carlsbad, CA 92008

Phone (760) 931-5700
Sales (800) 722-6555
Fax (760) 931-6988
Web **www.pcpowercooling.com**

Manufactures a line of high-quality, high-output power supplies and cooling fans for PC systems. Known for high-power output and quiet fan operation.

PC Week Magazine

10 Presidents Landing
Medford, MA 02155

Phone (781) 393-3700
Fax (781) 393-3859
Web **www.zdnet.com/pcweek**

Weekly magazine featuring industry news and information.

PC World Magazine

P.O. Box 9208
Framingham, MA 01701

Phone (508) 820-0440
Fax (508) 620-7739
Web **www.pcworld.com**

A monthly magazine featuring product reviews and comparisons.

PCI Special Interest Group

2575 NE Kathryn #17
Hillsboro, OR 97124

Phone	(503) 693-6232
Sales	(800) 433-5177
Fax	(503) 693-8344
Web	**www.pcisig.com**

Formed in June 1992, the PCI SIG (Peripheral Component Interconnect Special Interest Group) is the industry organization that owns and manages the PCI Local Bus Specification. More than 500 industry-leading companies are active PCI SIG members. The organization is chartered to support new requirements, while maintaining backward compatibility for all PCI revisions; maintain the specification as an easy-to-implement, stable technology; and contribute to the technical longevity of PCI and its establishment as an industry-wide standard.

PCMCIA—Personal Computer Memory Card International Association

2635 N. First St., Ste. 209
San Jose, CA 95134

Phone	(408) 433-2273
Fax	(408) 433-9558
BBS	(408) 433-2270
Web	**www.pc-card.com**

An independent organization that maintains the PC card standard for credit card-sized expansion adapters.

Philips Consumer Electronics

P.O. Box 14810
One Philips Dr.
Knoxville, TN 37914

Phone	(423) 521-4316
Fax	(423) 521-4586
Web	**www.magvavox.com**

Manufactures Magnavox PCs, monitors, and CD-ROM drives.

Phoenix Technologies, Ltd.

411 East Plumeria Drive
San Jose, CA 95134

Phone	(408) 570-1000
Fax	(408) 570-1001
BBS	(714) 440-8026
Web	**www.phoenix.com**

Designs PC BIOS software for all types of PC systems and processors. Recently merged with Award.

Pivar Computing Services, Inc.

165 Arlington Heights Rd.
Buffalo Grove, IL 60089

Phone	(847) 459-6010
Sales	(800) Convert (266-8378)
Fax	(847) 459-6095
Web	**www.convert.com**

Service company that specializes in data and media conversion.

PKWare, Inc.

9025 N. Deerwood Dr.
Brown Deer, WI 53223

Phone	(414) 354-8699
Fax	(414) 354-8559
BBS	(414) 354-8670
Web	**www.pkware.com**

Originated and introduced the Zip file compression format. PKWare manufactures data compression products such as PKZip, PKLite, and the PKWare Data Compression Library, which are all available for multiple operating systems and processors. Widely used on the Internet and BBS Systems, and by manufacturers for software distribution.

Plextor

4255 Burton Dr.
Santa Clara, CA 95054

Phone	(408) 980-1838
Sales	(800) 886-3935
Fax	(408) 986-1010
BBS	(408) 986-1569
Web	**www.plextor.com**

Manufactures a line of high-performance CD-ROM drives.

PlugIn Datamation

Cahners Business Information
275 Washington St.
Newton, MA 02158-1630

Phone	(617) 964-3030
Fax	(617) 558-4506
Web	**www.datamation.com**
E-mail	**rtwiss@cahners.com**

An excellent industry publication, featuring articles on networking and communications.

PowerQuest Corporation

1359 N. Research Way, Bldg. K
Orem, UT 84097

Phone	(801) 437-8900
Sales	(800) 379-2566
Fax	(801) 226-8941
Web	**www.powerquest.com**

Leading developer of hard disk management software for network servers and desktop computers. PowerQuest is the maker of Partition Magic Drive Copy, Drive Image Drive, Image Professional, Guardian Angel, Server Max, and Server Magic for Netware.

Practical Enhanced Logic

22695 Old Canal Rd.
Yorba Linda, CA 92887

Phone	(714) 282-6188
Fax	(714) 282-6199
Sales	(800) 345-7274
Web	**www.pelogic.com**

Manufactures the Systo Tek CPU fan failure alarm, as well as the SCSI-Link parallel-to-SCSI converter and other high-performance SCSI adapters.

Precision Plastics

340 Roebling Rd.
San Francisco, CA 94080

Phone	(415) 588-4450
Fax	(415) 588-5336

A supplier of test and emulation PC cards.

Processor Magazine

P.O. Box 85518
Lincoln, NE 68501

Sales	(800) 247-4880
Fax	(402) 479-2120
Web	**www.processor.com**

Publication that offers excellent sources of replacement and repair parts and new equipment at discount prices.

Public Software Library

P.O. Box 35705
Houston, TX 77235

Phone	(713) 524-6394
Sales	(800) 242-4775
Fax	(713) 524-6398
Web	**www.pslweb.com**

Distributor of high-quality public domain and shareware software. Its library is the most well-researched and well-tested available. Also offers an excellent newsletter that reviews the software.

Qlogic Corporation
3545 Harbor Blvd.
P.O. Box 5001
Costa Mesa, CA 92626

Phone	(714) 438-2200
Tech Support	(714) 668-5037
Fax	(714) 668-5324
Web	**www.qlc.com**

Manufactures a line of high-end PCI SCSI adapters.

Qualitas, Inc.
8601 Georgia Ave. #908
Silver Spring, MD 20910

Web	**www.qualitas.com**

Manufactures the Qualitas Max 8 memory-manager utility programs.

Quantum Corporation
500 McCarthy Blvd.
Milpitas, CA 95035

Phone	(408) 894-4000
Sales	(800) 624-5545
Tech Support	(800) 826-8022
FAXBack	(800) 434-7532
BBS	(800) 894-3214
Web	**www.quantum.com**

Manufactures a line of 5.25- and 3.5-inch hard disk drives. Supplies drives to Apple Computer, Compaq, IBM, Dell, and HP. Also produces DLT and SSD (solid state disk).

Quarterdeck Corporation
13160 Mindanao
Marina Del Rey, CA 90292

Phone	(310) 309-3700
Fax	(310) 314-4218
BBS	(310) 309-3227
Web	**www.quarterdeck.com**

Manufactures the popular ProComm Plus/ Rapid Remote, CleanSweep, Iware Connect, QEMM, HiJaak Pro, Winprobe, Zip It, Fix It, Partition It, and Remove It utility and diagnostics software.

Quarter-Inch Cartridge Drive Standards, Inc. (QIC)
311 E. Carrillo St.
Santa Barbara, CA 93101

Phone	(805) 963-3853
Fax	(805) 962-1541
Web	**www.qic.org**

An independent industry group that sets and maintains Quarter-Inch Cartridge (QIC) tape drive standards for backup and archiving purposes.

Que Corporation
201 W. 103rd St.
Indianapolis, IN 46290

Phone	(317) 581-3500
Sales	(800) 428-5331
Fax	(800) 448-3804
Web	**www.mcp.com**

Publishes the highest-quality computer software and hardware books in the industry.

Radio Shack (A Division of Tandy Corporation)
100 G Throckmorton Street #1700
Fort Worth, TX 76102

Phone	(817) 390-3011
Fax	(817) 390-2774
Web	**www.radioshack.com**

Manages the Radio Shack electronics stores, which sell numerous electronics devices, parts, and supplies. Also manufactures a line of PC-compatible computers and computer accessories and supplies.

Ramtron International Corporation
1850 Ramtron Dr.
Colorado Springs, CO 80921

Phone	(719) 481-7000
Web	**www.ramtron.com**

Manufactures special memory components including EDRAM dynamic RAM products that combine high-speed DRAM with an even faster SRAM cache on a single chip.

Rancho Technology, Inc.
10783 Bell Ct.
Rancho Cucamonga, CA 91730

Phone	(909) 987-3966
Fax	(909) 989-2365
BBS	(909) 980-7699
Web	**www.rancho.com**
E-mail	**scsi@rancho.com**

Designs and manufactures SCSI expander products, such as Single to Differential-Ended Converters, Extenders, LVD SCSI, ASIC, and others. Also specializes in Custom (OEM) Solutions.

Rendition
999 East Arques Avenue
Sunnyvale, CA 94086

Phone	(408) 822-0100
Fax	(408) 822-0199
Web	**www.rendition.com**
E-mail	**info@rendition.com**

Manufactures low-cost, high-performance 2D/3D graphics acceleration chips for the mainstream personal computer market.

Rip-Tie Company
P.O. Box 77394
San Francisco, CA 94107

Phone	(415) 543-0170
Fax	(415) 777-9868
Web	**www.riptie.com**

Manufactures cable management products made from velcro.

Rockwell Semiconductor Systems
4311 Jamboree Rd.
Newport Beach, CA 92660-3095

Phone	(714) 221-4600
Fax	(714) 221-4078
Web	**www.rockwell.com/ semi.html**

Manufactures communications chipsets used in many PC-compatible modems and high-speed data, fax, business audio, voice-mail and mobile-communication applications.

Roland Corporation U.S.
7200 Dominion Circle
Los Angeles, CA 90040

Phone	(213) 685-5141
Fax	(213) 722-0911
Web	**www.rolandus.com**

Manufactures a variety of musical equipment and MIDI interfaces for computers.

Rosenthal Engineering
P.O. Box 1650
San Luis Obispo, CA 93406

Phone	(805) 541-0910
Fax	(805) 541-2676
Web	**slonet.org/~doren/**

Manufactures a unique line of system and disk utilities including The Disk Drive Cleaner, Conflict Resolver, System Workout, R-Format, Year 2000 Fix, and Uninstall.

Rupp Technology Corporation (Retail Locations – Mobilscape)
2240 N. Scottsdale Road
Tempe, AZ 85281

Phone	(602) 941-4789
Sales	(800) 852-7877
Tech Support	(800) 941-5602
Fax	(602) 224-0898
Web	**www.rupp.com**

Developer of the DOS Interlink software used in MS- and PC-DOS. Also sells a commercial version called Fastlynx Lite for DOS that offers many enhancements over Interlink. WinLynx is a full windows file transfer and management program. Also makes custom-length parallel transfer cables using a high-speed, 18-wire design supported by virtually all parallel transfer programs.

S3, Inc.
2841 Mission College Blvd.
P.O. Box 58058
Santa Clara, CA 95052-8058

Phone	(408) 588-8000
Fax	(408) 980-5444
Web	**www.s3.com**

Manufactures a line of very popular high-performance video chipsets.

Safeware Insurance Agency, Inc.
P.O. Box 656
5760 N. High St.
Columbus, OH 43085

Phone	(614) 781-1492
Sales	(800) 848-3469
Fax	(614) 781-0559
Web	**www.safeware-ins.com**

Insurance company that specializes in insurance for computer equipment.

Sams
201 W. 103rd St.
Indianapolis, IN 46290

Phone	(317) 581-3500
Web	**www.mcp.com**

Publishes technical books on computers and electronic equipment.

Samsung Semiconductor, Inc.
3655 N. First St.
San Jose, CA 95134

Phone	(408) 544-4000
Web	**www.samsungsemi.com** or **www.sec.samsung.com**

Manufactures memory and semiconductor devices.

Seagate Software
400 International Pkwy.
Heathrow, FL 32746

Phone	(407) 333-7500
Automated Tech Support	(800) 821-8782
FAXBack	(800) 732-4283
Fax	(407) 262-4225
BBS	(407) 263-3662
TDD	(408) 438-5382
Web	**www.seagate.com**

Manufactures a line of tape-backup products. Acquired by Seagate Technologies.

Seagate Software Storage Management Group (Formerly Sytron)
400 International Pkwy.
Heathrow, FL 32746

Phone	(407) 333-7500
Fax	(407) 531-7770
Sales	(800) 327-2232
Web	**www.seagatesoftware.com**

Manufactures the SyTOS tape-backup software for DOS and OS/2, the most widely used tape software in the industry.

Seagate Technology
920 Disc Dr.
Scotts Valley, CA 95066

Phone	(714) 641-2500
Fax	(408) 429-6356
Customer Service	(800) 468-3472
FAXBack	(408) 438-2620
BBS	(408) 438-8771
Web	**www.seagate.com**

The largest hard disk manufacturer in the world. Offers the most extensive product line of any disk manufacturer, ranging from low-cost units to the highest-performance, -capacity, and -quality drives available. Also a complete line of backup software including Backup Exec for Windows 95.

Sencore
3200 Sencore Dr.
Sioux Falls, SD 57107

Phone	(605) 339-0100
Sales	(800) 736-2673
Fax	(605) 335-6379
Web	**www.sencore.com**

Manufactures a line of computer monitor signal generators and repair equipment.

Service News Magazine
106 Lafayette Street
Yarmouth, ME 04096

Phone	(207) 846-0600
Fax	(207) 846-0657
Web	**www.servicenews.com**

An excellent monthly newspaper for computer service and support personnel featuring articles covering PC service and repair products. Service news boasts a circulation of 45,000 IT support professionals across the United States.

SGS-Thomson Microelectronics, Inc.
55 Old Bedford Rd.
Lincoln, MA 01773

Phone	(617) 259-0300
Fax	(617) 259-4421
Web	**www.st.com**

Manufactures a variety of memory and semiconductor devices.

Sharp Electronics Corporation
Sharp Plaza
Mahwah, NJ 07430-2135

Phone	(201) 529-8200
Fax	(201) 529-8413
Sales	(800) BE SHARP (237-4277)
Web	**www.sharp-usa.com**

Manufactures a wide variety of electronic and computer equipment, including the best LCD monochrome and active matrix color displays and panels, as well as scanners, printers, and complete laptop and notebook systems.

Sharp Microelectronics Group
5700 NW Pacific Rim Blvd.
Camas, WA 98607

Phone	(800) 642-0261
Web	**www.sharpmeg.com**

Manufactures memory and semiconductor devices.

Sigma Data
26 Newport Rd.
New London, NH 03257-4565

Phone	(603) 526-6909
Sales	(800) 446-4525
Fax	(603) 526-6915
Web	**www.sigmadata.com**

Manufacturer/distributor of personal computer add-on and peripheral products specializing in easy-to-install hard drives, processors, and memory upgrades. It offers a unique line of "Quick Easy" upgrades including the QED (Quick Easy Disk) and QEP (Quick Easy Processor). Its product line also includes high-speed, high-capacity drives for a variety of popular portable, laptop, and notebook computers.

Silicon Integrated Systems Corp. (SiS)
240 N. Wolfe Rd.
Sunnyvale, CA 94086

Phone	(408) 730-5600
Fax	(408) 730-5639
Web	**www.sis.com.tw**

Manufactures PC motherboard chipsets.

Silicon Valley Research
6360 San Ignacio Ave.
San Jose, CA 95119

Phone	(408) 361-0333
Fax	(408) 361-0330
Web	**www.svri.com**

Manufactures a complete line of IDE interface adapters, including a unique model that supports 16-bit IDE (ATA) drives on PC and XT systems (8-bit ISA bus) and models, including floppy drive support and serial and parallel ports.

Simple Technology
3001 Daimler St.
Santa Ana, CA 92705

Phone	(714) 476-1180
Sales	(800) 854-3900
Fax	(714) 476-1209
Web	**www.simpletech.com**

Manufactures the SIMMswitch, which replaces the soldered resistors on a SIMM, allowing it to be easily reconfigured. It also sells SIMMs with the switch already installed.

SL Waber
520 Fellowship Rd. #306
Mt. Laurel, NJ 08054

Phone	(609) 866-8888
Web	**www.waber.com**

Manufactures a complete line of power protection equipment for PC computers.

Smart Cable Inc.
13625 NE 126th Place, Ste. 400
Kirkland, WA 98034

Phone	(206) 823-2273
Sales	(800) 752-6526
Fax	(206) 821-3961

Manufactures the SmartCable universal serial RS-232 cable.

SofTouch Systems, Inc.
1300 S. Meridian, Ste. 600
Oklahoma City, OK 73108-1751

Phone	(405) 947-8080
Fax	(405) 947-8169
Web	**www.softouch.com**

Manufactures GammaTech Utilities for OS/2 that can undelete and recover files running under OS/2 even on an OS/2 HPFS partition, and UniMaint, a desktop repair and recovery program.

Stac Incorporated **1227**

Sola Heavy Duty Electric (Acquired by Best Power, a Division of General Signal Power)
P.O. Box 280
Necedah, WI 54646

Phone	(800) 289-7652
Sales	(800) 356-5794
Fax	(608) 565-2221
Web	**www.bestpower.com**

Manufactures a line of computer power-protection devices.

SONERA Technologies
P.O. Box 565
Rumson, NJ 07760

Phone	(732) 747-6886
Sales	(800) 932-6323
Fax	(732)747-4523
Web	**www.displaymate.com**

Manufactures the DisplayMate video display utility and diagnostic program. DisplayMate exercises, troubleshoots, and diagnoses video display adapter and monitor problems.

Sony Corporation of America
Sony Drive
Park Ridge, NJ 07656

Phone	(800) 326-9551
Fax	(408) 955-5171
BBS	(408) 955-5107
Web	**www.sony.com**

Manufactures all types of high-quality electronic and computer equipment, including displays and magnetic- and optical-storage devices.

SOYO Tek, Inc.
1209 John Reed Ct.
City of Industry, CA 91745

Phone	(818) 330-1712
Fax	(818) 968-4164
Web	**www.soyo.com**

One of the top 10 largest Taiwan-based motherboard manufacturers.

Specialized Products Company
1100 S. Kimball Avenue
Southlake, TX 76092

Phone	(817) 329-6647
Sales	(800) 866-5353
Fax	(800) 234-8286
Web	**www.specializedproducts. com**

Distributes a variety of tools and test equipment.

Sprague Magnetics, Inc.
12806 Bradley Ave.
Sylmar, CA 91342

Phone	(818) 364-1800
Fax	(818) 364-1810
Sales	(800) 553-8712
Web	**www.sprague-magnetics.com**

Distributes a unique and interesting magnetic developer fluid that can be used to view sectors and tracks on a magnetic disk or tape. Also repairs computer tape drives.

Stac Incorporated
12636 High Bluff Dr.
San Diego, CA 92130

Phone	(619) 794-4300
Sales	(800) 522-7822
Fax	(619) 794-3715
BBS	(619) 794-3711
Web	**www.stac.com**

Products include Replica and Reach Out Enterprise remote/control access for centrally managed Windows networks. They also offer Replica 3, backup and disaster recovery for distributed Windows NT and Netware servers (to tape).

Standard Microsystems Corporation (SMSC)
80 Arkay Dr.
Hauppauge, NY 11788

Phone	(516) 273-3100
Fax	(516) 273-1803
FAXBack	(800) 762-8329
BBS	(516) 434-3162
Web	**www.smc.com**

Manufactures component-based products. (Sold their system-based products division, SMC Networks, Inc.)

SMC Networks, Inc. (Formerly a Division Within Standard Microsystems Corp.)
350 Kennedy Drive
Hauppauge, NY 11788

Phone	(516) 435-6000

Manufactures various system-based products such as Ethernet and ARCnet network adapters, as well as hubs, boards, and PC cards.

Star Micronics America, Inc.
70-D Ethel Rd. West
Piscataway, NJ 08854

Phone	(732) 572-6597
Fax	(732) 572-5095
Web	**www.starmicronics.com**

Manufactures a line of low-cost printers, receipt printers, and visual card systems.

STB Systems, Inc.
1651 N. Glenville
Suite 210
Richardson, TX 75085-0957

Phone	(972) 234-8750
Fax	(972) 234-1306
BBS	(214) 437-9615
Web	**www.stb.com**

Manufactures various adapter boards, and specializes in a line of high-resolution VGA video adapters.

Storage Dimensions, Inc.
1656 McCarthy Blvd.
Milpitas, CA 95035

Phone	(408) 954-0710
Fax	(408) 944-1200
BBS	(408) 944-1221
Web	**www.artecom.com**

Manufactures high-performance disk and tape storage solutions for open system environments. Distributes Maxtor hard disk and optical drives as complete subsystems.

Sun Moon Star
1941 Ringwood Ave.
San Jose, CA 95131

Phone	(408) 452-7811
Web	**www.sun-moon-star.com**

Manufactures CD-ROM, multimedia kits, and power supplies for PC compatibles.

Supermicro Computer, Inc.
2051 Junction Ave.
San Jose, CA 95131

Phone	(408) 895-2000
Fax	(408) 895-2008
BBS	(408) 895-2022
Web	**www.supermicro.com**

Manufactures a high-quality line of Pentium-class motherboards.

Superpower Supply, Inc.
990 Norcross Industrial Ct.
Norcross, GA 30071

Phone	(770) 263-9647
Web	**www.spower.com**

Manufactures a line of PC-compatible power supplies and cases. They also distribute PC components.

Symantec Corporation

World Headquarters
10201 Torre Avenue
Cupertino, CA 95014

Phone	(800) 441-7234
Fax	(541) 984-8020
BBS	(541) 484-6669
Web	**www.symantec.com**

Manufactures a line of utility and applications software featuring the Norton Utilities for PC systems and PC Tools. Also distributes Winfax Pro.

SyQuest Technology

47071 Bayside Pkwy.
Fremont, CA 94538

Phone	(510) 226-4000
Sales	(800) 245-2278
Tech Support	(510) 226-5400
Fax	(510) 226-4102
BBS	(510) 226-4120
Web	**www.syquest.com**

Manufactures removable-cartridge hard disk drives.

Tadiran

2 Seaview Blvd. #102
Port Washington, NY 11050

Phone	(516) 621-4980
Sales	(800) 537-1368
Fax	(516) 621-4517
Web	**www.tadrianbat.com**

Manufactures a variety of lithium batteries for computer and other applications.

Tandy Corporation

100 Throckmorton Street
Fort Worth, TX 76102

Phone	(817) 390-3700
Fax	(817) 390-2647
Web	**www.tandy.com**

Manufactures a line of PC systems, peripherals, and accessories.

Tatung Company of America, Inc.

2850 El Presidio St.
Long Beach, CA 90810

Phone	(310) 637-2105
Sales	(800) 827-2850
Fax	(310) 637-8484
Web	**www.tatungusa.com**

Manufactures monitors and complete compatible systems.

TDK Corporation of America

12 Harbor Park Dr.
Port Washington, NY 11050

Phone	(516) 625-0100
Fax	(516) 625-0651
Web	**www.tdk.com**

Manufactures a line of magnetic and optical media, including disk and tape cartridges. Also produces modems, ICs, semiconductors, and power supply products.

Teac America, Inc.

7733 Telegraph Rd.
Montebello, CA 90640

Phone	(213) 726-0303
Fax	(213) 727-7656
BBS	(213) 727-7660
FAXBack	(213) 727-7629
Web	**www.teac.com**

Manufactures a line of floppy and tape drives, including a unit that combines both 3 1/2-inch and 5 1/4-inch drives in one half-height package.

Tech Data Corporation
5350 Tech Data Dr.
Clearwater, FL 34620

Phone	(813) 539-7429
Sales	(800) 237-8931
Fax	(813) 538-7876
BBS	(813) 538-7090
Web	**www.techdata.com**

Distributes computer equipment and supplies.

Tech Spray, Inc.
P.O. Box 949
Amarillo, TX 79105-0949

Phone	(806) 372-8523
Fax	(806) 372-8750
Web	**www.techspray.com**

Manufactures a complete line of computer and electronic cleaning chemicals and products.

Tecmar Technologies, Inc.
1900 Pike Rd.
Longmont, CO 80501

Phone	(303) 682-3700
Sales	(800) 4-BACKUP
	(422-2587)
Tech Support	(800) 344-4463
Customer Service	(800) 992-9916
Fax	(303) 776-7706
Web	**www.tecmar.com**

Manufactures Wangtech, WangDAT, and Proline tape back up drives.

Tekram Technologies
11500 Metric Blvd., Ste. 190
Austin, TX 78758

Phone	(512) 833-6550
Fax	(512) 833-7276
Web	**www.tekram.com**

Manufactures a complete line of caching and noncaching disk controllers, PCI motherboards, multimedia products, CD-ROM servers, printer servers, and video cards. Specializes in IDE and SCSI adapters that are fast and flexible.

***Test and Measurement World* Magazine**
275 Washington St.
Newton, MA 02158-1611

Phone	(617) 558-4671
Fax	(617) 558-4470
E-mail	**tmw@cahneis.com**

A magazine for quality control and testing in the electronics industry. Free for those who qualify.

Texas Instruments, Inc.
Box 14149
12501 Research Blvd.
Austin, TX 78714-9149

Phone	(512) 250-7111
Sales	(800) TI-TEXAS (848-3927)
Web	**www.ti.com**

Manufactures memory and other semiconductor devices.

The Learning Company
1 Athenaeum St.
Cambridge, MA 02142

Phone	(617) 494-1200
Fax	(617) 494-5898
BBS	(423) 670-2023
Web	**www.learningco.com**

Manufactures WordStar 7, and distributes more than 500 other software programs including *Compton's Encyclopedia* and various educational titles.

Thermalloy, Inc.
2021 W. Valley View Ln.
P.O. Box 810839
Dallas, TX 75234

Phone	(972) 243-4321
Fax	(972) 241-4656
Web	**www.thermalloy.com**

Manufactures a line of excellent CPU heat-sink products, including versions with built-in fan modules.

Toshiba America, Inc.
9740 Irvine Blvd.
Irvine, CA 92718

Phone	(714) 583-3926
Sales	(800) 999-4273
Fax	(800) 950-4373
BBS	(714) 837-2116
Web	**www.computers.toshiba.com**

Manufactures a complete line of 5 1/4- and 3 1/2-inch floppy and hard disk drives, CD-ROM drives, display products, printers, and a popular line of laptop and notebook PC systems.

TouchStone Software Corporation
2124 Main St.
Huntington Beach, CA 92648

Phone	(714) 969-7746
Sales	(800) 531-0450
Fax	(714) 959-1886
Web	**www.touchstonesoftware.com**

Manufactures the CheckIt line of products including CheckIt v5.0 for Windows 95 and CheckIt Professional Edition, which provides repair technicians with CheckIt v5.0, CheckIt DOS, PC-Cillan Anti-Virus, and toolkit.

Trace Research and Development Center
University of Wisconsin
S-151 Waisman Center
1500 Highland Ave.
Madison, WI 53705

Phone	(608) 263-2309
TDD	(608) 263-5408
E-mail	**info@trace.wisc.edu**

An interdisciplinary research, development, and resource center on technology and disability.

Traveling Software, Inc.
18702 N. Creek Pkwy. #102
Bothell, WA 98011

Phone	(425) 483-8088
Sales	(800) 662-2652
Fax	(425) 485-6786
BBS	(425) 485-1736
Web	**www.travsoft.com**

Manufactures the LapLink file-transfer program for PC and Mac systems as well as several other utility programs.

Trident Microsystems
189 N. Bernado Ave.
Mountain View, CA 94043

Phone	(650) 691-9211
Fax	(650) 691-9260
BBS	(650) 961-1016
Web	**www.tridentmicro.com**

Manufactures a line of high-end video chipsets and multimedia video adapters.

TriniTech, Inc.
8751 Ulmerton, Bldg. 101
Largo, FL 33771

Phone	(813) 532-4151
Sales	(800) 909-3424
Fax	(813) 532-0457
Web	**www.pcanalyzer.com**

Manufactures a complete line of PC diagnostics products including the OmniPOST, IRQuest Plus PC Power Sentry diagnostics cards, Omni Analyzer, PC Check, virus Web MCSC, A+ Certification Software, CNE Certificate Course, and Expertrace diagnostics software.

Tripp Lite Manufacturing
11 West 35th Street
Chicago, IL 60609

Phone	(773) 329-1777
Fax	(773) 869-1329
Web	**www.tripplite.com**

Manufactures a complete line of computer power-protection devices.

TTI Technologies
2101 Auto Center Drive, #150
Oxnard, CA 93030

Phone	(805) 988-4711
Sales	(800) 541-1943
Fax	(805) 988-2437

Distributes AMI, Award, Phoenix MR BIOS upgrades, and microid research.

Twinhead Corporation
48295 Fremont Blvd.
Fremont, CA 94538

Phone	(510) 492-0828
Sales	(800) 552-8946
Web	**www.twinhead.com**

Manufactures notebook, subnotebook, and desktop computer systems.

Tyan Computer Corporation
1753 S. Main St.
Milpitas, CA 95035

Phone	(408) 956-8000
Fax	(408) 956-8044
Tech Support	(408) 942-5526
BBS	(408) 956-8171
Web	**www.tyan.com**

Manufactures an excellent line of PC motherboards in ATX and Baby-AT form factors.

Ultra-X, Inc.
1765 Scott Blvd., Ste. 101
Santa Clara, CA 95050

Phone	(408) 261-7090
Sales	(800) 722-3789
Fax	(408) 261-7077
Web	**www.uxd.com**

Manufactures the excellent QuickPost PC, QuickPost PCIS/2, QuickPost PRO, PhD+ PC Inspector, and Racer II diagnostic cards, as well as the QuickTech PRO, QuickTech 98, Ramstress Test (RST), and Diagnostic Reference diagnostic software packages. The Racer II is one of the most complete troubleshooting hardware cards on the market.

Underwriters Laboratories, Inc.
Corporate Headquarters
333 Pfingsten Rd.
Northbrook, IL 60062-2096

Phone	(847) 272-8800
Fax	(847) 272-8129
Web	**www.ul.com**

The leading third-party product safety certification organization in the United States, and the largest in North America. Established in 1894.

Unicomp, Inc.
2501 W. Fifth St.
Santa Ana, CA 92703

Phone	(800) 359-5092
Fax	(714) 571-1909

Distributes new and refurbished printer repair parts for all types of printers.

Unicore Software, Inc.
1538 Turnpike St.
North Andover, MA 01845

Phone	(978) 685-6468
Fax	(978) 683-1630
Web	**www.mrbios.com**

Manufactures the MR BIOS, one of the most flexible and configurable BIOS versions available. They have versions available for a variety of different chipsets and motherboards.

UNISYS
Township Line and Union Meeting Rd.
Blue Bell, PA 19424

Phone	(800) 448-1424
Fax	(716) 742-6671
Web	**www.unisys.com**

Manufactures PC-compatible systems that are part of the government Desktop IV contract. Also offers a complete line of information management software solutions.

U.S. Robotics, Inc. (Merged with 3Com)
8100 N. McCormick Blvd.
Skokie, IL 60076

Phone	(847) 982-5010
Sales	(800) 550-7800
Fax	(847) 933-5300
FAXBack	(800) 762-6163
BBS	(847) 982-5092
Web	**www.3com.com**

Manufactures a complete line of modems and ISDN communications products.

V Communications, Inc.
2290 N. 1st Street #101
San Jose, CA 95131

Phone	(408) 296-4224
Fax	(408) 965-4014
Tech Support	(408) 965-4018
Web	**www.v-com.com**

Manufactures the Sourcer disassembler and other programming tools.

Varta Batteries, Inc.
300 Executive Blvd.
Elmsford, NY 10523

Phone	(914) 592-2500
Fax	(914) 592-2667
Web	**www.varta.com**

Manufactures a complete line of computer batteries.

Verbatim Corporation
1200 WT Harris Blvd.
Charlotte, NC 28262

Phone	(704)547-6500
Web	**www.verbatimcorp.com**

Manufactures a line of storage media, including optical and magnetic disks and tapes.

VESA Standards
2150 N. First St., Ste. 440
San Jose, CA 95131-2029

Phone	(408) 435-0333
Fax	(408) 435-8225
Web	**www.vesa.org**
E-mail	**marketing@vesa.org**

Leading worldwide open trade association with more than 360 member companies. VESA's mission is to promote and develop timely, relevant, open display and display interface standards ensuring inter-operability and encouraging innovation and market growth. Membership includes hardware, software, PC display and component manufacturers, cable and telephone companies, and service providers.

VIA Technologies, Inc.
1045 Mission Court
Fremont, CA 94539

Phone	(510) 683-3300
Fax	(510) 683-3301
Web	**www.viatech.com**

Manufactures PC motherboard chipsets.

ViewSonic
381 Brea Canyon Road
Walnut, CA 91789

Phone	(909) 869-7976
Fax	(909) 869-7958
BBS	(909) 444-5219
Web	**www.viewsonic.com**

Manufactures a line of high-quality monitors and displays with Plug and Play and energy star compliance. Also produces network-level power backup systems.

Visiflex Seals
16 E. Lafayette St.
Hackensack, NJ 07601

Phone	(201) 487-8080

Manufactures form-fitting clear keyboard covers and other computer accessories.

VLSI Technology, Inc.
1109 McKay Dr.
San Jose, CA 95131

Phone	(408)434-3000
Web	**www.vlsi.com**

Manufactures chipsets and circuits for PC-compatible motherboards and adapters.

Volpe, Hank
P.O. Box 43214
Baltimore, MD 21236

Phone	(410) 256-5767
BBS	(410) 256-3631
Web	**www.modemdoctor.com**

Manufactures the Modem Doctor Version 6 serial port and modem diagnostics program.

Walling Company
4401 Juniper St.
Tempe, AZ 85282

Phone/Fax	(602) 838-1277

Manufactures the DataRase EPROM eraser, which can erase as many as four EPROM chips simultaneously using ultraviolet light.

Wang Laboratories, Inc.
600 Technology Park Dr.
Billerica, MA 01821-4130

Phone	(800) 225-0654

Manufactures a variety of PC-compatible systems, including some with MCA bus slots.

Watergate Software
2000 Powell St. #1200
Emeryville, CA 94608

Phone	(510) 596-2080
Fax	(510) 596-2092
Web	**www.ws.com**

Manufactures the excellent PC-Doctor diagnostic program for PC troubleshooting and repair.

Wave Tech
9145 Balboa Ave.
San Diego, CA 92123

Phone	(619) 279-2200
Sales	(800) 854-2708
Fax	(619) 627-0132
BBS	(619) 278-5034
Web	**www.wavetech.com**

Manufactures diagnostics and test equipment.

Western Digital Corporation
8105 Irvine Center Dr.
Irvine, CA 92618

Phone	(714) 932-5000
Sales	(800) 832-4778
Fax	(714) 932-4012
FAXBack	(714) 932-4300
BBS	(714) 753-1068
Web	**www.westerndigital.com**

Leader in information storage management, providing a broad array of hard drive products for both personal and enterprisewide computing.

Winbond (Formerly Symphony Laboratories)
2730 Orchard Pkwy.
San Jose, CA 95134

Phone	(408) 943-6666
Fax	(408) 474-1600
Web	**www.winbond.com.tw**

Manufactures PC motherboard chipsets.

WordPerfect (A Division of Corel Software)
P.O. Box 1036
Buffalo, NY 14240

Phone	(800) 772-6735
Web	**www.corel.com**

Manufactures the popular WordPerfect word processing program. Acquired by Novell, then sold to Corel.

Wyse Technology
3471 N. 1st St.
San Jose, CA 95134

Phone	(408) 473-1200
Sales	(800) 438-9973
Fax	(408) 473-1972
BBS	(408) 922-4400
Web	**www.wyse.com**

Manufactures general purpose terminals and WIN TERM Windows-based terminals.

Xerox Corporation
Xerox Square
Rochester, NY 14644

Phone	(203) 968-3000
Fax	(203) 968-3368

Manufactures an extensive line of computer equipment, copiers, and printers.

Xircom
2300 Corporate Center Dr.
Thousand Oaks, CA 91320

Phone	(805) 376-9300
Sales	(800) 438-4562
Tech Support	(805) 376-9220
Fax	(805) 376-9311
BBS	(805) 376-9130
Web	**www.xircom.com**

Manufactures external Token Ring and Ethernet adapters that attach to a parallel port, and PCMCIA cards for laptops.

Y-E Data America, Inc.
5824 Peachtree Corners East, Ste. A
Norcross, GA 30092

Phone   (404) 237-5615

Manufactures a line of floppy disk drives, tape drives, and printers. Supplied 5 1/4-inch floppy drives to IBM for use in XT, AT, and PS/2 systems.

ZD Comdex and Forums
300 First Ave.
Needham, MA 02194-2722

Phone   (781) 433-1500
Fax   (781) 449-2674
Web   **www.comdex.com**

Producer of the world's leading computer tradeshows.

Zenith Data Systems
P.O. Box 36
Magna, UT 84044

Phone   (916) 388-0101
Web   **www.zds.com**

Manufactures a line of PC systems.

Zeos International, Ltd. (Purchased by Micron Electronics)
900 E. Karcher Rd.
Napa, ID 83687

Phone   (208) 893-3434
Sales   (800) 438-3343
Fax   (208) 893-3424
BBS   (208) 893-8982
Web   **www.mei.micron.com**

Manufactured a line of good, low-cost, PC systems sold by way of mail order.

Vendors by Product or Service Category

If you are looking for a product or service but don't know a specific vendor that provides it, use this part of the vendor list to find a vendor that provides what you need. Then look up the vendor's contact information in the earlier part of this appendix.

Audio Adapters (Sound Cards)
Creative Labs, Inc.

Orchid Technology (A Division of Micronics)

Roland Corporation U.S.

Batteries
Duracell, Inc.

Fedco Electronics, Inc.

Panasonic Industrial Co.

Tadiran

Varta Batteries, Inc.

BIOS
American Megatrends, Inc. (AMI)

Award Software International, Inc.

DTK Computer, Inc.

Micro Firmware, Inc.

Phoenix Technologies, Ltd.

TTI Technologies

Unicore Software, Inc.

Books, Magazines, Documentation
Annabooks

Byte Magazine/McGraw-Hill

Computer Design Magazine

Computer Graphics World Magazine

Computer Hotline Magazine

Computer Reseller News

Computer Retail Week Magazine

Computer Shopper Magazine

Computer Technology Review Magazine

Comtech Publishing, Ltd.

Data Base Advisor Magazine

Data Communications Magazine

Electrocution

Electronic Buyers' News

Electronic Engineering Times Magazine

Electronic Products Magazine

Endl Publications

Fantasy Productions (A Division of Fortner & Associates)

Global Engineering Documents

IBM Fullfilment Center

IBM National Publications

IBM Personal Systems Technical Solutions Magazine

InfoWorld Magazine

Macworld Communications Inc.

Motor Magazine

OEM Magazine

PC Magazine

PC Week Magazine

PC World Magazine

PlugIn Datamation

Processor Magazine

Que Corporation

Sams

Service News Magazine

Test and Measurement World Magazine

Cables and Connectors

AMP, Inc.

Autotime Corporation

Belden Wire and Cable

Cables to Go (CTG)

CS Electronics

FCI Electronics - Americas

Micro Accessories, Inc.

Micro Computer Cable Company, Inc.

Smart Cable Inc.

Cases

Palo Alto Design Group

PC Portable Manufacturer, Inc.

Superpower Supply, Inc.

CD-ROM Drives and Media

Chinon America, Inc.

Creative Labs, Inc.

JVC Information Products

Maxell Corporation of America

Microtest Enterprises

Mitsumi Electronics Corporation

NEC Technologies, Inc.

Panasonic Industrial Co.

Philips Consumer Electronics

Plextor

Sun Moon Star

Toshiba America, Inc.

Chipsets

Acer Laboratories, Inc. (ALi)

Auctor Corporation

Cirrus Logic, Inc.

Cypress Semiconductor Corporation

Integrated Device Technology, Inc.

Intel Corporation

LSI Logic, Inc.

National Semiconductor Corporation

Oak Technology, Inc.

Opti, Inc.

Rockwell Semiconductor Systems

Silicon Integrated Systems Corp. (SiS)

VIA Technologies, Inc.

VLSI Technology, Inc.

Winbond (Formerly Symphony Laboratories)

Diagnostics Software and Hardware

#1-PC Diagnostics Company (The ESD Division of Windsor Technologies, Inc.)

Accurite Technologies Inc.

Advanced Personal Systems

AllMicro, Inc. (Purchased by ForeFront Direct)

American Megatrends, Inc. (AMI)

Buerg, Vernon D.

CST

CyberMedia

Darkhorse Systems

Data Depot

DiagSoft, Inc.

Fluke, John Manufacturing Company, Inc.

Gazelle/GTM Software

Golden Bow Systems

Innerworks Technology, Inc.

Micro 2000, Inc.

MicroSystems Development, Inc.

Ontrack Data International, Inc. (Formerly Ontrack Computer Systems)

Parallel Technologies, Inc.

Precision Plastics

Quarterdeck Corporation

Rosenthal Engineering

Sencore

SONERA Technologies

TouchStone Software Corporation

TriniTech, Inc.

Ultra-X, Inc.

Volpe, Hank

Walling Company

Watergate Software

Wave Tech

Distributors

Arrow Electronic

Cal-Abco

Computer Component Source, Inc.

DakTech

Liuski International

Merisel

Mini Micro Supply

Tech Data Corporation

Floppy Drives

ALPS Electric

Canon USA, Inc.

Chinon America, Inc.

Citizen America Corporation

Ma Laboratories, Inc.

Micro Solutions, Inc.

Mitsumi Electronics Corporation

Panasonic Communications & Systems

Teac America, Inc.

Toshiba America, Inc.

Y-E Data America, Inc.

Graphics Adapters

3D Labs

3Dfx

Alaris

ATI Technologies, Inc.

Boca Research, Inc.

Chips and Technologies, Inc.

Cirrus Logic, Inc.

Creative Labs, Inc.

Diamond Multimedia Systems, Inc.

Hauppauge Computer Works, Inc.

IX Micro Solutions, Inc.

Matrox Graphics, Inc.

Number Nine Visual Technology Corporation

nVidia Corporation

Orchid Technology (A Division of Micronics)

Rendition

S3 Inc.

STB Systems, Inc.

Trident Microsystems

Hard Disk Drives and Drive Controllers

Adaptec

AIWA America, Inc. Computer Systems Division

Fujitsu Computer Products of America, Inc.

Hewlett-Packard (Disk Memory Division)

IBM OEM Division

Iomega Corporation

JTS Corporation

Longshine Microsystems, Inc.

Ma Laboratories, Inc.

Maxoptix Corporation

Maxtor Corporation

Quantum Corporation

Seagate Technology

Sigma Data

SyQuest Technology

Tekram Technologies

Toshiba America, Inc.

Western Digital Corporation

Hardware (Screws, Mounting Brackets, and So On)

Arrowfield International, Inc.

CI Design Company

Connector Resources Unlimited (CRU)

Globe Manufacturing, Inc.

Micro Accessories, Inc.

Radio Shack (A Division of Tandy Corporation)

Keyboards

ALPS Electric

Cherry Electrical Products

Key Tronic Corporation

Lexmark

Maxi Switch, Inc.

Microsoft Corporation ·

Mitsumi Electronics Corporation

Memory

Andromeda Research

Centon Electronics, Inc.

Dallas Semiconductor

Hitachi America, Ltd. (Semiconductor & IC Division)

IBM Microelectronics

Kingston Technology Corporation

Ma Laboratories, Inc.

Micron Technologies (Parent Company of Micron Electronics and Micron Custom Manufacturing)

Mosel Vitelic

NEC Electronics, Inc.

Panasonic Industrial Co.

Ramtron International Corporation

Samsung Semiconductor, Inc.

SGS-Thomson Microelectronics, Inc.

Sharp Microelectronics Group

Sigma Data

Simple Technology

Texas Instruments, Inc.

Mice

ALPS Electric

Key Tronic Corporation

Microsoft Corporation

Mitsumi Electronics Corporation

Miscellaneous

Aavid Thermal Technologies, Inc.

Andromeda Research

Anvil Cases

AT&T National Parts Sales Center/ Lucent Technologies

AZ-COM, Inc.

Berkshire Products

Byte Runner Technologies

Casio, Inc.

Chicago Case Company

Curtis Computer Products

Da-Lite Screen Co.

Data Exchange Corporation

Data Retrieval Services, Inc.

Data Technology Corporation (DTC)

Digi-Key Corporation

Edmund Scientific

Extron Electronics

Heathkit Education Systems

Hypertech

IBM Parts Order Center

Illinois Lock

Inline, Inc.

International Electronic Research Corp. (IERC)

JC Whitney & Company

Labconco Corporation

LearnKey, Inc.

MAGNI Systems, Inc.

McKenzie Technology

Merritt Computer Products, Inc.

Molex, Inc.

NCR Microelectronics

Pivar Computing Services, Inc.

Rip-Tie Company

Safeware Insurance Agency, Inc.

Specialized Products Company

Sprague Magnetics, Inc.

Tandy Corporation

Thermalloy Inc.

Trace Research and Development Center

Visiflex Seals

Wyse Technology

ZD Comdex and Forums

Modems

3Com Corp.

Boca Research, Inc.

Creative Labs, Inc.

Diamond Multimedia Systems, Inc.

Hayes Microcomputer Products

Megahertz Corporation (A Division of 3Com)

Microcom, Inc.

Motorola, Inc.

TDK Corporation of America

Monitors and Display Devices

Amdek Corporation (A Division of Wyse Technology)

Dukane Corporation

GoldStar Technology, Inc.

Hitachi America, Ltd. (Semiconductor & IC Division)

MAG InnoVision

Mitsubishi Electronics America, Inc.

NEC Technologies, Inc.

Panasonic Communications & Systems

Philips Consumer Electronics

Sharp Electronics Corporation

Sony Corporation of America

Tatung Company of America, Inc.

Toshiba America, Inc.

ViewSonic

Motherboards

ABIT Computer (USA) Corporation

Acer Laboratories, Inc. (ALi)

Advanced Integration Research (AIR)

American Megatrends, Inc. (AMI)

Diamond Flower, Inc (DFI)

Elitegroup Computer Systems, Inc.

First International Computer, Inc. (FIC)

Giga-Byte Technology Co., Ltd.

Intel Corporation

J. Bond Computer Systems

Ma Laboratories, Inc.

Micro Industries Corporation

Micronics Computers, Inc.

Micro-Star International

Mylex Corporation

Ocean Information Systems

SOYO Tek, Inc.

Supermicro Computer, Inc.

Tyan Computer Corporation

Networking

3Com Corp.

IBM OEM Division

Intel PC and LAN Enhancement Product Division

IX Micro Solutions, Inc.

Lantronix

Longshine Microsystems, Inc.

SMC Networks, Inc. (Formerly a Division Within Standard Microsystems Corp.)

Xircom

Online Services

America Online

Byte Information Exchange (BIX)

CompuServe Information Service (CIS)

Optical Drives and Media

Fujitsu Computer Products of America, Inc.

Laser Magnetic Storage

Maxoptix Corporation

Microtest Enterprises

Panasonic Communications & Systems

Sony Corporation of America

TDK Corporation of America

Power Protection and UPS

Acme Electric/Electronics Division

American Power Conversion (APC)

Best Power (A Division of General Signal Power)

Liebert

SL Waber

Sola Heavy Duty Electric (Acquired by Best Power, a Division of General Signal Power)

Tripp Lite Manufacturing

ViewSonic

Power Supplies

Astec America, Inc.

Panasonic Industrial Co.

PC Power & Cooling, Inc.

Sun Moon Star

Superpower Supply, Inc.

Printers, Printer Parts, and Supplies

ALPS Electric

Canon USA, Inc.

CIE America

Citizen America Corporation

Epson America, Inc. (OEM Division)

Fujitsu Computer Products of America, Inc.

Hewlett-Packard Company

Lexmark

Mitsubishi Electronics America, Inc.

NEC Technologies, Inc.

Okidata

Pacific Data Products

Panasonic Communications & Systems

PARTS NOW!, Inc.

Sharp Electronics Corporation

Star Micronics America, Inc.

Unicomp, Inc.

Y-E Data America, Inc.

Processors and Processor Upgrades

Advanced Micro Devices (AMD)

Cyrix Corporation

IBM Microelectronics

Intel Corporation

Kingston Technology Corporation

Ma Laboratories, Inc.

Motorola, Inc.

Sigma Data

Texas Instruments, Inc.

RAID

American Megatrends, Inc. (AMI)

Arco Computer Products, Inc.

Distributed Processing Tech. (DPT)

Mylex Corporation

Removable Media

3M Data Storage Products Division

Maxell Corporation of America

Sony Corporation of America

TDK Corporation of America

Verbatim Corporation

Repair Services

Electroservice Laboratories

Fessenden Technologies

Micro Solutions, Inc.

Retail and Direct Mail

Altex Electronics, Inc.

Black Box Corporation

Boston Computer Exchange

CompUSA, Inc.

Computer Discount Warehouse (CDW)

Damark International, Inc.

IBM PC Direct

Jameco Computer Products

JDR Microdevices

Jensen Tools, Inc.

Micro Warehouse

Microprocessors Unlimited, Inc.

Newark Electronics

PC & MAC Connection

SCSI Accessories

Aeronics, Inc.

Meritec

Methode Electronics, Inc.

Micro Design International (MDI)

Mylex Corporation

Practical Enhanced Logic

Qlogic Corporation

Rancho Technology, Inc.

Software

Adobe Systems, Inc.

Autodesk, Inc.

Bitstream, Inc.

Borland International (Now Inprise)

Columbia Data Products

Compton's New Media, Inc. (A Division of Softkey International, Inc.)

Computer Library

Corel Systems, Inc.

Datastorm Technologies, Inc.

Folio Corporation

Information Access Company

Lotus Development Corporation (A Division of IBM)

MapInfo Corporation

McAfee Associates

Micro House International

Micrografx, Inc.

Microsoft Corporation

Mustang Software

Novell, Inc.

PKWare, Inc.

PowerQuest Corporation

Public Software Library

Qualitas, Inc.

Quarterdeck Corporation

Rupp Technology Corporation (Retail Locations - Mobilscape)

Seagate Software

SofTouch Systems, Inc.

Stac Incorporated

Symantec Corporation

The Learning Company

Traveling Software, Inc.

V Communications, Inc.

Speakers

Bose Corp.

Labtec Enterprises, Inc.

Standards Bodies and Organizations

American National Standards Institute (ANSI)

Association of Shareware Professionals (ASP)

CompTIA (Computing Technology Industry Association)

Micro Channel Developers Association

PCI Special Interest Group

PCMCIA—Personal Computer Memory Card International Association

Quarter-Inch Cartridge Drive Standards, Inc. (QIC)

Underwriters Laboratories, Inc.

VESA Standards

Supplies (Chemicals, Cleaners, and So On)

CAIG Laboratories

Chemtronics, Inc.

D.W. Electrochemicals, Ltd.

GRACE Specialty Polymers/WR GRACE, Emerson & Cuming Inc.

Tech Spray Inc.

Systems (Desktop, Server, and Mobile)

Acer America Corp.

Advanced Logic Research (ALR)

Alaris

Apple Computer, Inc.

AST Research, Inc.

Compaq Computer Corporation

CTX International, Inc.

Dell Computer Corporation

Diamond Flower, Inc. (DFI)

Diversified Technology

Dolch Computer Systems

DTK Computer, Inc.

Epson America, Inc. (OEM Division)

Everex Systems, Inc.

Fujitsu Computer Products of America, Inc.

Gateway 2000

Hewlett-Packard Company

Hyundai Electronics America

IBM PC Company

Micron Technologies (Parent Company of Micron Electronics and Micron Custom Manufacturing)

Micronics Computers, Inc.

MicroWay, Inc.

Mitsubishi Computers, Ltd.

Mosel Vitelic

Myoda Computer Centers

NEC Technologies, Inc.

Olivetti

Packard Bell

Panasonic Communications & Systems

Philips Consumer Electronics

Radio Shack (A Division of Tandy Corporation)

Sharp Electronics Corporation

Tandy Corporation

Tatung Company of America, Inc.

Toshiba America, Inc.

Twinhead Corporation

UNISYS

Wang Laboratories, Inc.

Zenith Data Systems

Tape Drives and Media

Advanced Digital Information Corporation

Alloy Computer Products

Exabyte Corporation

GigaTrend, Inc.

Hewlett-Packard Company

Hewlett-Packard (Storage Division)

Laser Magnetic Storage

Micro Solutions, Inc.

Mountain Network Solutions, Inc. (Subsidiary of NCE Star Solutions)

Seagate Software Storage Management Group (Formerly Sytron)

Storage Dimensions, Inc.

Tecmar Technologies, Inc.

Y-E Data America, Inc.

Appendix B

Useful Hardware Web Sites

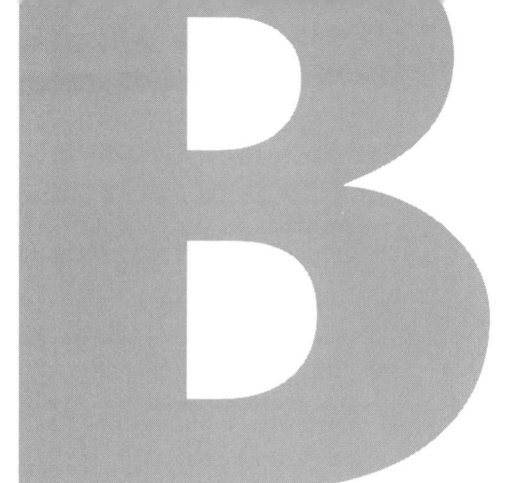

Most of the vendors listed in the vendor list in Appendix A, "Vendor List," have their own Web sites where you can find information about their specific products, services, and technologies. In addition to those, there are many Web sites not affiliated with any specific product. These range from professional standards organizations that publish documents about the hardware they write specifications for, to individuals who collect and disseminate useful hardware information as a hobby or pet project, to vendors who distribute general information that isn't supporting a specific product. And several of these are "meta-sites" that collect and index information from other sites. This appendix lists the sites in those areas that I have found most useful.

Address	Description
elaine.teleport.com/%7Ecurt/modems.html	High speed modem FAQ
hardware.pairnet.com	Links to hardware news and reviews
infopad.eecs.berkeley.edu/CIC	CPU Information
pclt.cis.yale.edu/pclt/PCHW/PLATYPUS.HTM	General overview of PC hardware technologies
tx.scitexdv.com/SCSI2/SCSI2.html	SCSI 2 Specification
Web.idirect.com/~frank/index.html	Hard drive and CD-ROM specifications
www.56k.com	News and information on KFlex, X2, and v.90 standard modems
www.agpforum.org	AGP Specifications and information
www.anandtech.com	Reviews of motherboards, processors, and more
www.atipa.com/InfoSheets/irqs.shtml	Troubleshooting COM and IRQ conflicts
www.cd-info.com	Compact disc development and production technology

(continues)

(continued)

Address	Description
www.chipanalyst.com/q/	Microprocessor design resources
www.chipset.com	Links to chipset vendor Web sites
www.cis.ohio-state.edu/hypertext/faq/usenet/scsi-faq/top.html	SCSI FAQs from USENET
www.cis.ohio-state.edu/hypertext/faq/usenet-faqs/bygroup/comp/sys/ibm/pc/hardware/top.html	Links to several hardware-related Usenet group FAQs
www.cpu-central.com	CPU specifications, information, and reviews
www.drivershq.com	Links to hardware drivers
www.driverupdate.com	Windows 95 and 3.1 hardware drivers
www.erols.com/chare/main.htm	Links to processors specifications and FAQs
www.firewire.org	FireWire specification and information
www.hardwarecentral.com	Reviews, FAQs, and more about most PC hardware components
www.heartlab.rri.uwo.ca/vidfaq/chipset.html	Video chipset FAQ
www.irda.org	Infrared technology standards
www.isdn.ocn.com	ISDN information and FAQs
www.itu.ch	International Telecommunication Union (standards body for modems and other telecommunications)
www.k56.org	Specifications on the KFlex version of 56K modems
www.lemig.umontreal.ca/bios/bios_sg.htm	The BIOS survival guide
www.motherboards.org	Motherboard reviews, tips, and performance comparisons
www.mrdriver.com	Links to hardware drivers for many operating systems
www.pc-card.com	PCCard and PCMCIA standards
www.pcengines.com/simm.htm	Memory buyer's guide
www.pcguide.com	General PC hardware information
www.pcisig.com	PCI specifications and developments
www.pcWebopedia.com	PC technology encyclopedia and search engine
www.ping.be/bios/numbers.shtml	Identifies BIOS by ID numbers
www.scsita.org	SCSI Trade Association's SCSI information
www.sig.net/~slogan/hardware.htm	Hardware advice, reviews, and links

Address	Description
www.sldram.com	Information on new SLDRAM memory technology
www.spa.org	MPC specifications
www.storagereview.com	Reviews and benchmarks of SCSI and ATA IDE hard drives
www.symbios.com/x3t10	I/O information, mainly about SCSI
www.sysopt.com	System optimization and performance with special emphasis on motherboards
www.teleport.com/~nlx/	NLX motherboard specifications
www.the-view.com	Hardware reviews and news
www.tomshardware.com	Reviews and analysis of motherboards, processors, video cards, and more
www.tweakit.com	Reviews and performance comparisons of new hardware
www.twinight.org/chipdir/	Directory of chips, manufacturers, pinouts, and so on
www.usb.org	USB specifications and information
www.vesa.org	VESA standards
www.west.net/~jay/modem	Modem initialization strings
www.windrivers.com	Hardware drivers for all Windows versions
www.winfiles.com/drivers	Windows 95 hardware drivers
www.x86.org	"Secrets" about Intel processors and technologies
wwwcsif.cs.ucdavis.edu/~wen/intel.html	Guide to Intel chipsets

Glossary

This glossary contains computer and electronics terms that are applicable to the subject matter in this book. The glossary is meant to be as comprehensive as possible on the subject of upgrading or repairing PCs. Many terms correspond to the latest technology in disk interfaces, modems, video and display equipment, and standards that govern the PC industry. Although a glossary is a resource not designed to be read from beginning to end, you should find that scanning through this one is interesting, if not enlightening, with respect to some of the newer PC technology.

The computer industry is filled with acronyms used as shorthand for a number of terms. This glossary defines many acronyms, as well as the term on which the acronym is based. The definition of an acronym usually is included under the acronym. For example, *Video Graphics Array* is defined under the acronym *VGA* rather than under *Video Graphics Array*. This organization makes it easier to look up a term—*IDE*, for example—even if you do not know in advance what it stands for (*Integrated Drive Electronics*).

For additional reference, Que's *Computer Dictionary* (ISBN: 0-7897-1670-4) is a comprehensive dictionary of computer terminology.

These Web sites can also help you with terms that are not included in this chapter:

http://zeppo.cnet.com/Resources/Info/Glossary/

http://www-edlab.ucdavis.edu/ed180/hardwarepracticum.html

10Base2   IEEE standard for baseband Ethernet at 10Mbps over RG-58 coaxial cable to a maximum distance of 185 meters. Also known as *Thin Ethernet (Thinnet)* or *IEEE 802.3*.

10Base5   IEEE standard for baseband Ethernet at 10Mbps over thick coaxial cable to a maximum distance of 500 meters. Also known as *Thick Ethernet* or *Thicknet*.

10BaseT   A 10Mbps CSMA/CD Ethernet local area network that works on Category 3 or better twisted-pair wiring that is very similar to standard telephone cabling. 10BaseT Ethernet local area networks work on a "star" configuration in which the wire from each workstation routes directly to a 10BaseT hub. Hubs may be joined together.

100BaseT   A 100Mbps CSMA/CD Ethernet local area network that works on Category 5 twisted-pair wiring. 100BaseT Ethernet local area networks work on a "star" configuration in which the wire from each workstation routes directly to a central 100BaseT hub. This is the new standard for 100Mbps Ethernet.

100BaseVG The joint Hewlett-Packard-AT&T proposal for Fast Ethernet running at 100Mbps. It uses four pairs of Category 5 cable using the 10BaseT twisted-pair wiring scheme to transmit or receive. 100BaseVG splits the signal across the four wire pairs at 25MHz each. This standard has not found favor with corporations and has been almost totally replaced by 100BaseT.

56K The generic term for modems that can receive data at 56Kbps. See also *V.90*, *X2*, *Kflex*.

286 See *80286*.

386 See *80386*.

486 See *80486*.

586 A generic term used to refer to fifth-generation processors similar to the Intel Pentium.

640K barrier The limit imposed by the PC-compatible memory model using DOS mode. DOS programs can address only 1M total memory, and PC-compatibility generally requires the top 384K to be reserved for the system, leaving only the lower 640K for DOS or other real-mode applications.

8086 An Intel microprocessor with 16-bit registers, a 16-bit data bus, and a 20-bit address bus. This processor can operate only in real mode.

8087 An Intel math coprocessor designed to perform floating-point math with much greater speed and precision than the main CPU. The 8087 can be installed in most 8086- and 8088-based systems, and adds more than 50 new instructions to those available in the primary CPU alone.

8088 An Intel microprocessor with 16-bit registers, an 8-bit data bus, and a 20-bit address bus. This processor can operate only in real mode, and was designed as a low-cost version of the 8086.

8514/A An analog video display adapter from IBM for the PS/2 line of personal computers. Compared to previous display adapters such as EGA and VGA, it provides a high resolution of 1,024×768 pixels with as many as 256 colors or 64 shades of gray. It provides a video coprocessor that performs two-dimensional graphics functions internally, thus relieving the CPU of graphics tasks. It uses an interlaced monitor; it scans every other line every time the screen is refreshed.

80286 An Intel microprocessor with 16-bit registers, a 16-bit data bus, and a 24-bit address bus. It can operate in both real and protected virtual modes.

80287 An Intel math coprocessor designed to perform floating-point math with much greater speed and precision than the main CPU. The 80287 can be installed in most 286- and some 386DX-based systems, and adds more than 50 new instructions to what is available in the primary CPU alone.

80386 See *80386DX*.

80386DX An Intel microprocessor with 32-bit registers, a 32-bit data bus, and a 32-bit address bus. This processor can operate in real, protected virtual, and virtual real modes.

80386SX An Intel microprocessor with 32-bit registers, a 16-bit data bus, and a 24-bit address bus. This processor, designed as a low-cost version of the 386DX, can operate in real, protected virtual, and virtual real modes.

80387 An Intel math coprocessor designed to perform floating-point math with much greater speed and precision than the main CPU. The 80387 can be installed in most 386DX-based systems, and adds more than 50 new instructions to those available in the primary CPU alone.

80486 See *80486DX*.

80486DX An Intel microprocessor with 32-bit registers, a 32-bit data bus, and a 32-bit address bus. The 486DX has a built-in cache controller with 8K of cache memory as well as a built-in math coprocessor equivalent to a 387DX. The 486DX can operate in real, protected virtual, and virtual real modes.

80486DX2 A version of the 486DX with an internal clock doubling circuit that causes the chip to run at twice the motherboard clock speed. If the motherboard clock is 33MHz, the DX2 chip will run at 66MHz. The DX2 designation applies to chips sold through the OEM market, while a retail version of the DX2 is sold as an over-drive processor.

80486DX4 A version of the 486DX with an internal clock tripling circuit that causes the chip to run at three times the motherboard clock speed. If the motherboard clock is 33.33MHz, the DX4 chip will run at 100MHz.

80486SX An Intel microprocessor with 32-bit registers, a 32-bit data bus, and a 32-bit address bus. The 486SX is the same as the 486DX except that it lacks the built-in math coprocessor function, and was designed as a low-cost version of the 486DX. The 486SX can operate in real, protected virtual, and virtual real modes.

abend Short for *abnormal end*. A condition occurring when the execution of a program or task is terminated unexpectedly because of a bug or crash.

absolute address An explicit identification of a memory location, device, or location within a device.

AC Alternating current. The frequency is measured in cycles per seconds (cps), or hertz (Hz). The standard value running through the wall outlet is 120 volts at 60Hz, through a fuse or circuit breaker that usually can handle about 15 or 20 amps.

accelerator board An add-in board replacing the computer's CPU with circuitry that enables the system to run faster. See *graphics accelerator*.

access light The LED on the front of a drive or other device (or on the front panel of the system) that indicates the computer is reading or writing data on the device.

access mechanism See *actuator*.

access time The time that elapses from the instant information is requested to the point that delivery is completed. Usually described in nanoseconds (ns) for memory chips, and in milliseconds (ms) for disk drives. Most manufacturers rate average access time on a hard disk as the time required for a seek across one third of the total number of cylinders plus one half of the time for a single revolution of the disk platters (latency).

accumulator   A register (temporary storage) in which the result of an operation is formed.

acoustic coupler   A device used to connect a computer modem to a phone line by connecting to the handset of a standard AT&T-style phone. The audible sounds to and from the modem are transmitted to the handset through the coupler while the handset is resting in the coupler. Although often thought of as obsolete, an acoustic coupler can be used to ensure the availability of a modem connection when traveling and access to an RJ-11 jack is unavailable.

ACPI   Advanced Configuration and Power Interface. A standard developed by Intel, Microsoft, and Toshiba that is designed to implement power management functions in the operating system. ACPI is a replacement for APM. See also *APM*.

active high   Designates a digital signal that has to go to a high value to be true. Synonymous with *positive*.

active low   Designates a digital signal that has to go to a low value to be true. Synonymous with *negative*.

active matrix   A type of LCD screen that contains at least one transistor for every pixel on the screen. Color active matrix screens use three transistors for each pixel, one each for the red, green, and blue dots. The transistors are arranged on a grid of conductive material, with each connected to a horizontal and a vertical member. See also *TFT*.

actuator   The device that moves a disk drive's read/write heads across the platter surfaces. Also known as an *access mechanism*.

adapter   The device that serves as an interface between the system unit and the devices attached to it. Often synonymous with circuit board, circuit card, or card, but may also refer to a connector or cable adapter, which changes one type of connector to another.

adapter description files (ADF)   Refers to the setup and configuration files, and drivers necessary to install an adapter card such as a network adapter card. Primarily used with Micro Channel Architecture bus cards.

add-in board   See *expansion card*.

address   Refers to where a particular piece of data or other information is found in the computer. Also can refer to the location of a set of instructions.

address bus   One or more electrical conductors used to carry the binary-coded address from the microprocessor throughout the rest of the system.

AGP   Accelerated Graphics Port. Developed by Intel, a fast dedicated interface between the video adapter or chipset and the motherboard chipset North Bridge. AGP is 32 bits wide, runs at 66MHz, and can transfer 1 or 2 bits per cycle (1x or 2x modes).

aliasing   Undesirable visual effects (sometimes called *artifacts*) in computer-generated images, caused by inadequate sampling techniques. The most common effect is jagged edges along diagonal or curved object boundaries. See also *anti-aliasing*.

allocation unit   See *cluster*.

alphanumeric characters   A character set that contains only letters (A–Z) and digits (0–9). Other characters, such as punctuation marks, may also be allowed.

ampere   The basic unit for measuring electrical current. Also called *amp*.

analog   The representation of numerical values by physical variables such as voltage, current, and so on; continuously variable quantities whose values correspond to the quantitative magnitude of the variables. See also *digital*.

analog loopback   A modem self-test in which data from the keyboard is sent to the modem's transmitter, modulated into analog form, looped back to the receiver, demodulated into digital form, and returned to the screen for verification.

analog signals   Continuously variable signals. Analog circuits are more subject to distortion and noise than are digital circuits but are capable of handling complex signals with relatively simple circuitry. See also *digital signals*.

analog-to-digital converter   An electronic device that converts analog signals to digital form.

AND   A logic operator having the property that if P is a statement, Q is a statement, R is a statement…, then the AND of P, Q, R… is true if all statements are true and is false if any statement is false.

AND gate   A logic gate in which the output is 1 only if all inputs are 1.

animation   The process of displaying a sequential series of still images to achieve a motion effect.

ANSI   American National Standards Institute. A nongovernmental organization founded in 1918 to propose, modify, approve, and publish data processing standards for voluntary use in the United States. Also the U.S. representative to the International Standards Organization (ISO) in Paris and the International Electrotechnical Commission (IEC). For more information, see Appendix A, "Vendor List." Contact ANSI, 1430 Broadway, New York, NY 10018.

answer mode   A state in which the modem transmits at the predefined high frequency of the communications channel and receives at the low frequency. The transmit/receive frequencies are the reverse of the calling modem, which is in originate mode. See also *originate mode*.

anti-aliasing   Software adjustment to make diagonal or curved lines appear smooth and continuous in computer-generated images. See also *aliasing*.

anti-static mat   A pad placed next to a computer upon which components are placed while servicing the system to prevent static damage. Also can refer to a larger sized mat below an entire computer desk and chair to discharge static from a user before he touches the computer.

anti-virus   Software that prevents files containing viruses from running on a computer or software that detects, repairs, cleans, or removes virus-infected files.

APA   All points addressable. A mode in which all points of a displayable image can be controlled by the user or a program.

aperture grille   A type of shadow mask used in CRTs. The most common is used in Sony's Trinitron monitors, which use vertical phosphor stripes and vertical slots in the mask, compared to the traditional shadow mask that uses phosphor dots and round holes in the mask. See also *shadow mask*.

API Application Program Interface. A system call (routine) that gives programmers access to the services provided by the operating system. In IBM-compatible systems, the ROM BIOS and DOS together present an API that a programmer can use to control the system hardware.

APM Advanced Power Management. A specification sponsored by Intel and Microsoft originally proposed to extend the life of batteries in battery-powered computers. It is now used in desktop computers, as well. APM allows application programs, the system BIOS, and the hardware to work together to reduce power consumption. An APM-compliant BIOS provides built-in power management services to the operating system. The application software communicates power-saving data via predefined APM interfaces. Replaced in newer systems by ACPI. See also *ACPI*.

application End-user oriented software such as a word processor, spreadsheet, database, graphics editor, game, or Web browser.

arbitration A method by which multiple devices attached to a single bus can bid or arbitrate to get control of that bus.

archive bit The bit in a file's attribute byte that sets the archive attribute. Tells whether the file has been changed since it last was backed up.

archive medium A storage medium (floppy disk, tape cartridge, or removable cartridge) to hold files that need not be accessible instantly.

ARCnet Attached Resource Computer Network. A baseband, token-passing local area network technology offering a flexible bus/star topology for connecting personal computers. Operating at 2.5Mbit/sec, it is one of the oldest LAN systems and was popular in low-cost networks. Originally developed by John Murphy of Datapoint Corporation, although ARCnet interface cards are available from a variety of vendors.

areal density A calculation of the bit density (bits per inch, or BPI) multiplied by the track density (tracks per inch, or TPI), which results in a figure indicating how many bits per square inch are present on the disk surface.

ARQ Automatic repeat request. A general term for error-control protocols that feature error detection and automatic retransmission of defective blocks of data.

ASCII American Standard Code for Information Interchange. A standard 7-bit code created in 1965 by Robert W. Bemer to achieve compatibility among various types of data processing equipment. The standard ASCII character set consists of 128 decimal numbers ranging from 0 through 127, which are assigned to letters, numbers, punctuation marks, and the most common special characters. In 1981, IBM introduced the extended ASCII character set with the IBM PC, extending the code to 8 bits and adding characters from 128 through 255 to represent additional special mathematical, graphics, and foreign characters.

ASCII character A 1-byte character from the ASCII character set, including alphabetic and numeric characters, punctuation symbols, and various graphics characters.

ASME American Society of Mechanical Engineers (**http://www.asme.org/**). ASME International has nearly 600 codes and standards in print, and its many committees involve more than 3,000 individuals, mostly engineers but not necessarily members of the society. The standards are used in more than 90 countries throughout the world.

aspect ratio   The measurement of a film or television viewing area in terms of relative height and width. The aspect ratio of most modern motion pictures varies between 3:5 to as large as 3:7, which creates a problem when a wide-format motion picture is transferred to the more square-shaped television screen, with its aspect ratio of 3:4.

assemble   The act of translating a program expressed in an assembler language into a computer machine language.

assembler language   A computer-oriented language whose instructions are usually in one-to-one correspondence with machine language instructions.

asymmetrical modulation   A duplex transmission technique that splits the communications channel into one high-speed channel and one slower channel. During a call under asymmetrical modulation, the modem with the greater amount of data to transmit is allocated the high-speed channel. The modem with less data is allocated the slow, or back, channel. The modems dynamically reverse the channels during a call if the volume of data transfer changes.

asynchronous communication   Data transmission in which the length of time between transmitted characters may vary. Timing is dependent on the actual time for the transfer to take place, as opposed to synchronous communication, which is timed rigidly by an external clock signal. Because the receiving modem must be signaled about when the data bits of a character begin and end, start and stop bits are added to each character. See also *synchronous communication*.

asynchronous memory   Memory that runs using a different timing or clock rate (usually slower) than the motherboard speed.

AT clock   Refers to the Motorola 146818 realtime clock (RTC) and CMOS RAM chip which first debuted in the IBM AT and whose function has been present in all PC-compatible systems since. Keeps track of the time of day and makes this data available to the operating system or other software.

ATA   AT Attachment interface. An IDE disk interface standard introduced in March 1989 that defines a compatible register set and a 40-pin connector and its associated signals. See also *IDE*.

ATA-2   The second generation AT Attachment interface specification. This version defines faster transfer modes and Logical Block Addressing schemes to allow high-performance large-capacity drives. Also called *Fast ATA*, *Fast ATA-2*, and *Enhanced IDE (EIDE)*.

ATAPI   AT Attachment Packet Interface. A specification that defines device-side characteristics for an IDE-connected peripheral, such as CD-ROM or tape drives. ATAPI is essentially an adaptation of the SCSI command set to the IDE interface.

ATM   Asynchronous Transfer Mode. A high-bandwidth, low-delay, packet-like switching and multiplexing technique. Usable capacity is segmented into fixed-size cells consisting of header and information fields, allocated to services on demand.

attribute byte A byte of information, held in the directory entry of any file, that describes various attributes of the file, such as whether it is read-only or has been backed up since it last was changed. Attributes can be set by the DOS ATTRIB command.

ATX A motherboard and power supply form-factor standard designed by Intel and introduced in 1995 that is characterized by a double row of rear external I/O connectors on the motherboard; a single keyed power supply connector; memory and processor locations that are designed not to interfere with the installation of adapter cards; and an improved cooling flow.

audio A signal that can be heard, such as through the speaker of the PC. Many PC diagnostics tests use both visual (onscreen) codes and audio signals.

audio frequencies Frequencies that can be heard by the human ear (approximately 20–20,000Hz).

auto answer A setting in modems enabling them to answer incoming calls over the phone lines automatically.

auto dial A feature in modems enabling them to dial phone numbers without human intervention.

auto-disconnect A modem feature that allows a modem to hang up the telephone line when the modem at the other end hangs up.

AUTOEXEC.BAT A special batch file that DOS executes at startup. Contains any number of DOS commands that are executed automatically, including the capability to start programs at startup. See also *batch file*.

automatic head parking Disk drive head parking performed whenever the drive is powered off. Found in all modern hard disk drives with a voice-coil actuator.

auto-redial A modem or software feature that automatically redials the last number dialed if the number is busy or does not answer.

available memory Memory currently not in use by the operating system, drivers, or applications that may be used to load additional software.

average access time The average time it takes a disk drive to begin reading any data placed anywhere on the drive. This includes the average seek time, which is when the heads are moved, as well as the latency, which is the average amount of time required for any given data sector to pass underneath the heads. Together, these factors make up the average access time. See also *average seek time* and *latency*.

average latency The average time required for any byte of data stored on a disk to rotate under the disk drive's read/write head. Equal to one half the time required for a single rotation of a platter.

average seek time The average amount of time it takes to move the heads from one random cylinder location to another, usually including any head settling time. In many cases, the average seek time is defined as the seek time across one third of the total number of cylinders.

AVI Audio Video Interleave. A storage technique developed by Microsoft for its Video for Windows product that combines audio and video into a single frame or track, saving valuable disk space and keeping audio in synchronization with the corresponding video.

backbone The portion of the Internet or wide area network (WAN) transmission wiring that connects the main Internet/WAN servers and routers and is responsible for carrying the bulk of the Internet/WAN data.

backplane A rarely used motherboard design in which the components normally found on a motherboard are located instead on an expansion adapter card plugged into a slot. In these systems, the board with the slots is the backplane.

backup The process of duplicating a file or library onto a separate piece of media. Good insurance against the loss of an original.

backup disk Contains information copied from another disk. Used to make sure that original information is not destroyed or altered.

backward compatibility The design of software and hardware to work with previous versions of the same software or hardware.

bad sector A disk sector that cannot hold data reliably because of a media flaw or damaged format markings.

bad track table A label affixed to the casing of a hard disk drive that tells which tracks are flawed and cannot hold data. The listing is entered into the low-level formatting program.

balanced signal Refers to signals consisting of equal currents moving in opposite directions. When balanced or nearly balanced signals pass through twisted-pair lines, the electromagnetic interference effects such as crosstalk caused by the two opposite currents largely cancel each other out. *Differential signaling* is a method that uses balanced signals.

balun Short for balanced/unbalanced. A type of transformer that enables balanced cables to be joined with unbalanced cables. Twisted-pair (balanced) cables, for example, can be joined with coaxial (unbalanced) cables if the proper balun transformer is used.

bandwidth 1) Generally, the measure of the range of frequencies within a radiation band required to transmit a particular signal. The difference between the lowest and highest signal frequencies. The bandwidth of a computer monitor is a measure of the rate that a monitor can handle information from the display adapter. The wider the bandwidth, the more information the monitor can carry, and the greater the resolution. 2) Used to describe the data-carrying capacity of a given communications circuit or pathway. The bandwidth of a circuit is a measure of the rate at which information can be passed.

bank The collection of memory chips or modules that make up a block of memory readable or writable by the processor in a single cycle. This block, therefore, must be as large as the data bus of the particular microprocessor. In PC systems, the processor data bus (and therefore the bank size) is usually 8, 16, 32, or 64 bits wide. Optionally, some systems also incorporate an additional parity or ECC bit for each 8 data bits, resulting in a total of 9, 18, 36, or 72 bits (respectively) for each bank. Memory in a PC must always be added or removed in full-bank increments.

bar code   The code used on consumer products and inventory parts for identification purposes. Consists of bars of varying thickness that represent characters and numerals that are read with an optical reader. The most common version is called the *Universal Product Code (UPC)*.

base-2   Refers to the computer numbering system that consists of two numerals: 0 and 1. Also called *binary*.

base address   Starting location for consecutive string of memory or I/O addresses/ports.

base memory   The amount of memory available to the operating system or application programs within the first megabyte, accessible in the processor's real mode.

baseband transmission   The transmission of digital signals over a limited distance. ARCnet and Ethernet local area networks use baseband signaling. Contrasts with *broadband transmission*, which refers to the transmission of analog signals over a greater distance.

BASIC   Beginner's All-purpose Symbolic Instruction Code. A popular computer programming language. Originally developed by John Kemeny and Thomas Kurtz in the mid-1960s at Dartmouth College. Normally, an interpretive language, meaning that each statement is translated and executed as it is encountered, but can be a compiled language, in which all the program statements are compiled before execution.

batch file   A set of commands stored in a disk file for execution by the operating system. A special batch file called *AUTOEXEC.BAT* is executed by DOS each time the system is started. All DOS batch files have a BAT file extension.

baud   A unit of signaling speed denoting the number of discrete signal elements that can be transmitted per second. The word *baud* is derived from the name of J.M.E. Baudot (1845-1903), a French pioneer in the field of printing telegraphy and the inventor of Baudot code. Although technically inaccurate, *baud rate* commonly is used to mean *bit rate*. Because each signal element or baud may translate into many individual bits, *bits per second (bps)* normally differs from baud rate. A rate of 2400 baud means that 2,400 frequency or signal changes per second are being sent, but each frequency change may signal several bits of information. For example, 33.6Kbps modems actually transmit at only 2,400 baud.

Baudot code   A 5-bit code used in many types of data communications, including teletype (TTY), radio teletype (RTTY), and telecommunications devices for the deaf (TDD). Baudot code has been revised and extended several times. See also *baud*.

bay   An opening in a computer case or chassis that holds disk drives.

B-channel   The two bearer channels in ISDN that run at 64Kbps each and that carry the data.

BBS   Bulletin board system. A computer that operates with a program and a modem to enable other computers with modems to communicate with it, often on a round-the-clock basis. Thousands of PC IBM- and Apple-related BBSs offer a wealth of information and public-domain software that can be downloaded.

bezel   A cosmetic panel that covers the face of a drive or some other device.

Bézier curve A mathematical method for describing a curve, often used in illustration and CAD programs to draw complex shapes.

bidirectional 1) Refers to lines over which data can move in two directions, such as a data bus or a telephone line. 2) Refers to the capability of a printer to print from right to left and from left to right alternately.

binary Refers to the computer numbering system that consists of two numerals: 0 and 1. Also called *base-2*.

BIOS Basic Input/Output System. The part of an operating system that handles the communications between the computer and its peripherals. Often burned into read-only memory (ROM) chips or rewritable flash (EEPROM) memory chips.

bipolar A category of semiconductor circuit design, which was used to create the first transistor and the first integrated circuit. Bipolar and CMOS are the two major transistor technologies. Most all personal computers use CMOS technology chips. CMOS uses far less energy than bipolar.

bisynchronous Binary synchronous control. An earlier protocol developed by IBM for software applications and communicating devices operating in synchronous environments. The protocol defines operations at the link level of communications— for example, the format of data frames exchanged between modems over a phone line.

bit Binary digit. Represented logically by 0 or 1 and electrically by 0 volts and (typically) 5 volts. Other methods are used to represent binary digits physically (tones, different voltages, lights, and so on), but the logic is always the same.

bit density Expressed as bits per inch (BPI). Defines how many bits can be written onto one linear inch of a track. Sometimes also called *linear density*.

bit depth The number of bits used to describe the color of each pixel on a computer display. For example, a bit depth of two means that the monitor can display only black and white pixels; a bit depth of four means the monitor can display 16 different colors; a bit depth of eight allows for 256 colors; and so on.

bit map A method of storing graphics information in memory in which a bit devoted to each pixel (picture element) onscreen indicates whether that pixel is on or off. A bit map contains a bit for each point or dot on a video display screen and allows for fine resolution because any point or pixel onscreen can be addressed. A greater number of bits can be used to describe each pixel's color, intensity, and other display characteristics.

blank or **blanking interval** A period in which no video signal is received by a monitor, while the videodisc or digital video player searches for the next video segment or frame to display.

block A string of records, words, or characters formed for technical or logic reasons and to be treated as an entity.

block diagram The logical structure or layout of a system in graphics form. Does not necessarily match the physical layout and does not specify all the components and their interconnections.

BMP   A Windows graphics format that may be device dependent or independent. Device-independent BMP files (DIB) are coded for translation to a wide variety of displays and printers.

BNC   Bayonet-Neill-Concelman. Also known as British-Naval-Connector, Baby-N-Connector, or Bayonet-Nut-Coupler; nobody seems to be quite sure what the actual name is. This bayonet-locking connector is noted for its excellent shielding and impedance-matching characteristics, resulting in low noise and minimal signal loss at any frequency up to 4GHz. It is used in Ethernet 10Base2 networks (also known as *IEEE 802.3*, or *Thinnet*) to terminate coaxial cables. It is also used for some high-end video monitors.

bonding   In ISDN, joining two 64Kbps B-channels to achieve 128Kbps speed.

Boolean operation   Any operation in which each of the operands and the result take one of two values.

boot   To load a program into the computer. The term comes from the phrase "pulling a boot on by the bootstrap."

boot record   The first sector on a disk or partition that contains disk parameter information for the BIOS and operating system as well as bootstrap loader code that instructs the system how to load the operating system files into memory, thus beginning the initial boot sequence to boot the machine.

boot sector   See *boot record*.

boot sector virus   A virus designed to occupy the boot sector of a disk. Any attempt to start or boot a system from this disk will transfer the virus to the hard disk, after which it will subsequently be loaded every time the system is started. Most PC viruses are boot sector viruses.

bootstrap   A technique or device designed to bring itself into a desired state by means of its own action. The term is used to describe the process by which a device such as a PC goes from its initial power-on condition to a running condition without human intervention. See also *boot*.

boule   Purified, cylindrical silicon crystals from which semiconducting electronic chips including microprocessors, memory, and other chips in a PC are manufactured.

bps   Bits per second. The number of binary digits, or bits, transmitted per second. Sometimes confused with *baud*.

branch prediction   A feature of fifth-generation (Pentium and higher) processors that attempts to predict whether a program branch will be taken or not and then fetches the appropriate following instructions.

bridge   In local area networks, an interconnection between two similar networks. Also the hardware equipment used to establish such an interconnection.

broadband transmission   A term used to describe analog transmission. Requires modems for connecting terminals and computers to the network. Using frequency division multiplexing, many different signals or sets of data can be transmitted simultaneously. The alternate transmission scheme is baseband, or digital, transmission.

brownout An AC supply voltage drop in which the power does not shut off entirely but continues to be supplied at lower than normal levels.

bubble memory A special type of nonvolatile read/write memory introduced by Intel in which magnetic regions are suspended in crystal film and data is maintained when the power is off. A typical bubble memory chip contains about 512K, or more than 4 million bubbles. Bubble memory failed to catch on because of slow access times measured in several milliseconds. It has, however, found a niche use as solid-state "disk" emulators in environments where conventional drives are unacceptable, such as in military or factory use.

buffer A block of memory used as a holding tank to store data temporarily. Often positioned between a slower peripheral device and the faster computer. All data moving between the peripheral and the computer passes through the buffer. A buffer enables the data to be read from or written to the peripheral in larger chunks, which improves performance. A buffer that is *x* bytes in size usually holds the last *x* bytes of data that moved between the peripheral and CPU. This method contrasts with that of a *cache*, which adds intelligence to the buffer so that the most often accessed data rather than the last accessed data remains in the buffer (cache). A cache can improve performance greatly over a plain buffer.

bug An error or defect in a program.

burn-in The operation of a circuit or equipment to establish that its components are stable and to screen out defective ports or assemblies.

burst mode A memory cycling technology that takes advantage of the fact that most memory accesses are consecutive in nature. After setting up the row and column addresses for a given access, using burst mode can then access the next three adjacent addresses with no additional latency.

Burst Static RAMs (BSRAMs) Short for Pipeline Burst SRAM, BSRAMs are a common type of static RAM chip used for memory caches where access to subsequent memory locations after the first byte is accessed takes fewer machine cycles.

bus A linear electrical signal pathway over which power, data, and other signals travel. It is capable of connecting to three or more attachments. A bus is generally considered to be distinct from radial or point-to-point signal connections. The term comes from the Latin "omnibus" meaning "for all." When used to describe a topology, bus always implies a linear structure.

bus mouse An obsolete type of mouse used in the '80s that plugs into a special mouse expansion board instead of a serial port or motherboard mouse port. The bus mouse connector looks like a motherboard mouse (sometimes called PS/2 mouse) connector, but the pin configurations are different and not compatible.

busmaster An intelligent device that when attached to the Micro Channel, EISA, VLB, or PCI bus can bid for and gain control of the bus to perform its specific task without processor intervention.

byte A collection of bits that makes up a character or other designation. Generally, a byte is 8 data bits. When referring to system RAM, an additional parity (error-checking) bit is also stored (see *parity*), making the total 9 bits.

C   A high-level computer programming language. A frequently used programming language on mainframes, minis, and PC computer systems. C++ is a popular variant.

cache   An intelligent buffer. By using an intelligent algorithm, a cache contains the data that is accessed most often between a slower peripheral device and the faster CPU. See also *L2 cache*, *L1 cache*, and *disk cache*.

CAM   Common Access Method. A committee formed in 1988 that consists of a number of computer peripheral suppliers and is dedicated to developing standards for a common software interface between SCSI peripherals and host adapters.

capacitor   A device consisting of two plates separated by insulating material and designed to store an electrical charge.

card   A printed circuit board containing electronic components that form an entire circuit, usually designed to plug into a connector or slot. Sometimes also called an *adapter*.

card edge connector   See *edge connector*.

CardBus   A PC Card specification for a 32-bit interface that runs at 33MHz and provides 32-bit data paths to the computer's I/O and memory systems, as well as a new shielded connector that prevents CardBus devices from being inserted into slots that do not support the latest version of the PC Card standard.

carpal tunnel syndrome   A painful hand injury that gets its name from the narrow tunnel in the wrist that connects ligament and bone. When undue pressure is put on the tendons, they can swell and compress the median nerve, which carries impulses from the brain to the hand, causing numbness, weakness, tingling, and burning in the fingers and hands. Computer users get carpal tunnel syndrome primarily from improper keyboard ergonomics that result in undue strain on the wrist and hand.

carrier   A continuous frequency signal capable of being either modulated or impressed with another information-carrying signal. The reference signal used for the transmission or reception of data. The most common use of this signal with computers involves modem communications over phone lines. The carrier is used as a signal on which the information is superimposed.

carrier detect signal   A modem interface signal that indicates to the attached data terminal equipment (DTE) that it is receiving a signal from the distant modem. Defined in the RS-232 specification. Same as the received line-signal detector.

cathode ray tube (CRT)   A device that contains electrodes surrounded by a glass sphere or cylinder and displays information by creating a beam of electrons that strike a phosphor coating inside the display unit. This device is most commonly used in computer monitors and terminals.

CAV   Constant Angular Velocity. An optical disk recording format where the data is recorded on the disk in concentric circles. CAV disks are rotated at a constant speed. This is similar to the recording technique used on floppy disk drives. CAV limits the total recorded capacity compared to CLV (Constant Linear Velocity), which is also used in optical recording.

CCITT   An acronym for the Comité Consultatif International de Télégraphique et Téléphonique (in English, the International Telegraph and Telephone Consultative

Committee or the Consultative Committee for International Telegraph and Telephone). Renamed ITU (International Telecommunications Union). See *ITU*.

CCS Common Command Set. A set of SCSI commands specified in the ANSI SCSI-1 Standard X3.131-1986 Addendum 4.B. All SCSI devices must be capable of using the CCS to be fully compatible with the ANSI SCSI-1 standard.

CD Compact Disc or compact audio disc. A 4.75-inch (12cm) optical disc that contains information encoded digitally in the constant linear velocity (CLV) format. This popular format for high-fidelity music offers 90 decibels signal/noise ratio, 74 minutes of digital sound, and no degradation of quality from playback. The standards for this format (developed by NV Philips and Sony Corporation) are known as the *Red Book*. The official (and rarely used) designation for the audio-only format is CD-DA (compact disc-digital audio). The simple audio format is also known as CD-A (compact disc-audio). A smaller (3-inch) version of the CD is known as CD-3.

CD Video A CD format introduced in 1987 that combined 20 minutes of digital audio and 6 minutes of analog video on a standard 4.75-inch CD. Upon introduction, many firms renamed 8-inch and 12-inch videodiscs as CDV, in an attempt to capitalize on the consumer popularity of the audio CD. The term fell out of use in 1990 and was replaced in some part by *laserdisc* and more recently, *DVD*.

CD+G Compact Disc-Graphics. A CD format that includes extended graphics capabilities as written into the original CD-ROM specifications. Includes limited video graphics encoded into the CD subcode area. Developed and marketed by Warner New Media.

CD+MIDI Compact Disc-Musical Instrument Digital Interface. A CD format that adds to the CD+G format digital audio, graphics information, and musical instrument digital interface (MIDI) specifications and capabilities. Developed and marketed by Warner New Media.

CD-DA Compact Disc Digital Audio. Also known as *Red Book Audio* and is the digital sound format used by audio CDs. CD-DA uses a sampling rate of 44.1KHz and stores 16 bits of information for each sample. CD audio is not played through the computer, but through a special chip in the CD-ROM drive. Fifteen minutes of CD-DA sound can require about 80M. The highest quality sound that can be used by multimedia PC is the CD-DA format at 44.1KHz sample rate. See *CD*.

CD-I Compact Disc-Interactive. A compact disc format released in October 1991 that provides audio, digital data, still graphics, and motion video. The standards for this format (developed by NV Philips and Sony Corporation) are known as the *Green Book*. CD-I did not catch on with consumers and is now considered obsolete.

CD-R Compact Disc-Recordable, sometimes also called CD-Writable. CD-R disks are compact discs that can be recorded and read as many times as desired. CD-R is part of the Orange Book Standard defined by ISO. CD-R technology is used for mass production of multimedia applications. CD-R discs can be compatible with CD-ROM, CD-ROM XA, and CD audio. Orange Book specifies multi-session capabilities, which allow data recording on the disc at different times in several recording sessions. Kodak's Photo CD is an example of CD-R technology and fits up to 100 digital photographs on a single CD. Multi-session capability allows several rolls of 35mm film to be added to a single disc on different occasions.

CD-ROM Compact Disc-Read Only Memory. A 4.75-inch laser-encoded optical memory storage medium with the same constant linear velocity (CLV) spiral format as audio CDs and some videodiscs, CD-ROMs can hold about 650M of data. CD-ROMs require more error-correction information than the standard prerecorded compact audio disc. The standards for this format (developed by NV Philips and Sony Corporation) are known as the *Yellow Book*. See also *CD-ROM XA*.

CD-ROM drive A device that retrieves data from a CD-ROM disc; differs from a standard audio CD player by the incorporation of additional error-correction circuitry. CD-ROM drives usually can also play music from audio CDs.

CD-ROM XA Compact Disc-Read Only Memory eXtended Architecture. The XA standard was developed jointly by Sony, Philips, and Microsoft in 1988 and is now part of the Yellow Book standard. XA is a built-in feature of newer CD-ROM drives, and supports simultaneous sound playback with data transfer. Non-XA drives support either sound playback or data transfer, but not both simultaneously. XA also provides for data compression right on the disk, which can also increase data transfer rates.

CD-RW Compact Disc-ReWritable A type of rewritable CD-ROM technology defined in Part III of the Orange Book Standard that uses a different type of disc that the drive can rewrite at least one thousand times. CD-RW drives can also be used to write CD-R discs, and they can read CD-ROMs. CD-RW discs have a lower reflectivity than standard CD-ROMs, and CD-ROM drives must be of the newer multiread variety to read them. CD-RW was initially known as CD-E (for CD-Erasable).

CD-WO Compact Disc-Write Once. A variant on CD-ROM that can be written to once and read many times; developed by NV Philips and Sony Corporation. Also known as *CD-WORM* (CD-write once/read many), CD-Recordable, or CD-Writable. Standards for this format are known as the *Orange Book*.

CD-WORM See *CD-WO*.

Centronics connector Refers to one of two types of cable connectors used with either parallel or SCSI devices.

ceramic substrate A thin, flat, fired ceramic part used to hold an IC chip (usually made of beryllium oxide or aluminum oxide).

CERN Conseil Européen pour la Recherche Nucléaire (The European Laboratory for Particle Physics). The site in Geneva where the World Wide Web was created in 1989.

CGA Color Graphics Adapter. A type of PC video display adapter introduced by IBM on August 12, 1981, that supports text and graphics. Text is supported at a maximum resolution of 80×25 characters in 16 colors with a character box of 8×8 pixels. Graphics is supported at a maximum resolution of 320×200 pixels in 16 colors or 640×200 pixels in two colors. The CGA outputs a TTL (digital) signal with a horizontal scanning frequency of 15.75KHz, and supports TTL color or NTSC composite displays.

channel 1) Any path along which signals can be sent. 2) In ISDN, data bandwidth is divided into two B-channels that bear data and one D-channel that carries information about the call.

character   A representation, coded in binary digits, of a letter, number, or other symbol.

character set   All the letters, numbers, and characters that a computer can use to represent data. The ASCII standard has 256 characters, each represented by a binary number from 1 to 256. The ASCII set includes all the letters in the alphabet, numbers, most punctuation marks, some mathematical symbols, and other characters.

charge coupled device   A light sensing and storage device used in scanners and digital cameras to capture the pixels.

check bit   See *parity*.

checksum   Short for *summation check*, a technique for determining whether a package of data is valid. The package, a string of binary digits, is added up and compared with the expected number.

chip   Another name for an *IC*, or *integrated circuit*. Housed in a plastic or ceramic carrier device with pins for making electrical connections.

chip carrier   A ceramic or plastic package that carries an integrated circuit.

chipset   A single chip or pair of chips that integrates into it the Clock Generator, Bus Controller, System Timer, Interrupt Controller, DMA Controller, CMOS RAM/ Clock, and Keyboard Controller. See also *North Bridge* and *South Bridge*.

CHS   Cylinder Head Sector. The term used to describe the nontranslating scheme used by the BIOS to access IDE drives that are less than or equal to 528M in capacity. See *LBA*.

CIF   Common Image Format. The standard sample structure that represents the picture information of a single frame in digital HDTV, independent of frame rate and sync/ blank structure. The uncompressed bit rate for transmitting CIF at 29.97 frames/sec is 36.45Mbps.

circuit   A complete electronic path.

circuit board   The collection of circuits gathered on a sheet of plastic, usually with all contacts made through a strip of pins. The circuit board usually is made by chemically etching metal-coated plastic.

CISC   Complex Instruction Set Computer. Refers to traditional computers that operate with large sets of processor instructions. Most modern computers, including the Intel 80*xxx* processors, are in this category. CISC processors have expanded instruction sets that are complex in nature and require several to many execution cycles to complete. This structure contrasts with *RISC (reduced instruction set computer) processors*, which have far fewer instructions that execute quickly.

clean room   1) A dust-free room in which certain electronic components (such as chips or hard disk drives) must be manufactured and serviced to prevent contamination. Rooms are rated by Class numbers. A Class 100 clean room must have fewer than 100 particles larger than 0.5 microns per cubic foot of space. 2) A legal approach to copying software or hardware where one team analyzes the product and writes a detailed description, followed by a second team who reads the description written by the first and who then develops a compatible version of the product. When done correctly, such a design methodology will survive a legal attack.

client/server   A type of network in which every computer is either a server with a defined role of sharing resources with clients or a client that can access the resources on the server.

clock   The source of a computer's timing signals. Synchronizes every operation of the CPU.

clock multiplier   A processor feature where the internal core runs at a higher speed than the motherboard or processor bus. See also *overclocking*.

clock speed   A measurement of the rate at which the clock signal for a device oscillates, usually expressed in millions of cycles per second (MHz).

clone   Originally referred to an IBM-compatible computer system that physically as well as electrically emulates the design of one of IBM's personal computer systems. More currently, it refers to any PC system running an Intel or compatible processor in the 80x86 family.

cluster   Also called *allocation unit*. A group of one or more sectors on a disk that forms a fundamental unit of storage to the operating system. Cluster or allocation unit size is determined by the operating system when the disk is formatted. Larger clusters generally offer faster system performance but waste disk space.

CLV   Constant Linear Velocity. An optical recording format where the spacing of data is consistent throughout the disk, and the rotational speed of the disk varies depending on what track is being read. Additionally, more sectors of data are placed on the outer tracks compared to the inner tracks of the disk, which is similar to Zone Recording on hard drives. CLV drives will adjust the rotational speed to maintain a constant track velocity as the diameter of the track changes. CLV drives rotate faster near the center of the disk and slower toward the edge. Rotational adjustment maximizes the amount of data that can be stored on a disk. CD audio and CD-ROM use CLV recording.

CMOS   Complementary Metal-Oxide Semiconductor. A type of chip design that requires little power to operate. In PCs, a battery-powered CMOS memory and clock chip is used to store and maintain the clock setting and system configuration information.

CMYK   Cyan Magenta Yellow Black. The standard four-color model used for printing.

coated media   Hard disk platters coated with a reddish iron-oxide medium on which data is recorded.

coaxial cable   Also called *coax cable*. A data-transmission medium noted for its wide bandwidth, immunity to interference, and high cost compared to other types of cable. Signals are transmitted inside a fully shielded environment, in which an inner conductor is surrounded by a solid insulating material and then an outer conductor or shield. Used in many local area network systems such as *Ethernet* and *ARCnet*.

COBOL   Common Business-Oriented Language. A high-level computer programming language primarily used by some larger companies. It has never achieved popularity on personal and small business computers.

code page   A table used in DOS 3.3 and later that sets up the keyboard and display characters for various foreign languages.

code page switching   A DOS feature in versions 3.3 and later that changes the characters displayed onscreen or printed on an output device. Primarily used to support foreign-language characters. Requires an EGA or better video system and an IBM-compatible graphics printer.

CODEC   CODer-DECoder. A device that converts voice signals from their analog form to digital signals acceptable to more modern digital PBXs and digital transmission systems. It then converts those digital signals back to analog so that you may hear and understand what the other party is saying.

coercivity   A measurement in units of oersteds of the amount of magnetic energy to switch or "coerce" the flux change in the magnetic recording media. High-coercivity disk media requires a stronger write current.

cold boot   Starting or restarting a computer by resetting or turning on the power supply. See also *warm boot.*

collision   In a LAN, if two computers transmit a packet of data at the same time on the network, the data may become garbled, which is known as a collision.

collision detection/avoidance   A process used on a LAN to prevent data packets from interfering with each other and to determine whether data packets have encountered a collision and initiate a resend of the affected packets.

Color Graphics Adapter   See *CGA.*

color palette   The colors available to a graphics adapter for display.

COM port   A serial port on a PC that conforms to the RS-232 standard. See also *RS-232.*

COMDEX   The largest international computer trade show and conference in the world. COMDEX/Fall is held in Las Vegas during October, and COMDEX/Spring usually is held in Chicago or Atlanta during April.

command   An instruction that tells the computer to start, stop, or continue an operation.

command interpreter   The operating system program that controls a computer's shell or user interface. The command interpreter for MS-DOS is COMMAND.COM. The command interpreter for Windows is WIN.COM.

COMMAND.COM   An operating system file that is loaded last when the computer is booted. The command interpreter or user interface and program-loader portion of DOS.

common   The ground or return path for an electrical signal. If a wire, it usually is colored black.

common mode noise   Noise or electrical disturbances that can be measured between a current- or signal-carrying line and its associated ground. Common mode noise is frequently introduced to signals between separate computer equipment components through the power distribution circuits. It can be a problem when single-ended signals are used to connect different equipment or components that are powered by different circuits.

compatible   1) In the early days of the PC industry when IBM dominated the market, a term used to refer to computers from other manufacturers that had the same features as a given IBM model. 2) In general, software or hardware that conforms to industry standards or other de facto standards so that it can be used in conjuction with or in lieu of other versions of software or hardware from other vendors in a like manner.

compiler   A program that translates a program written in a high-level language into its equivalent machine language. The output from a compiler is called an *object program*.

complete backup   A backup of all information on a hard disk, including the directory tree structure.

composite video   Television picture information and sync pulses combined. The complete wave form of the color video signal composed of chrominance and luminance picture information; blanking pedestal; field, line, and color sync pulses; and field equalizing pulses. Some video cards have an RCA jack that outputs a composite video signal. See also *RGB*.

compressed file   A file that has been reduced in size via one or more compression techniques.

computer   Device capable of accepting data, applying prescribed processes to this data, and displaying the results or information produced.

computer-based training   CBT. The use of a computer to deliver instruction or training; also known as Computer-Aided (or Assisted) Instruction (CAI), Computer-Aided Learning (CAL), Computer-Based Instruction (CBI), and Computer-Based Learning (CBL).

CONFIG.SYS   A file that can be created to tell DOS how to configure itself when the machine starts up. Can load device drivers, set the number of DOS buffers, and so on.

configuration file   A file kept by application software to record various aspects of the software's configuration, such as the printer it uses.

console   The unit, such as a terminal or a keyboard, in your system with which you communicate with the computer.

contiguous   Touching or joined at the edge or boundary, in one piece.

continuity   In electronics, an unbroken pathway. Testing for continuity normally means testing to determine whether a wire or other conductor is complete and unbroken (by measuring 0 ohms). A broken wire shows infinite resistance (or infinite ohms).

control cable   The wider of the two cables that connect an ST-506/412 or ESDI hard disk drive to a controller card. A 34-pin cable that carries commands and acknowledgments between the drive and controller.

controller   The electronics that control a device such as a hard disk drive and intermediate the passage of data between the device and the computer.

controller card   An adapter holding the control electronics for one or more devices such as hard disks. Ordinarily occupies one of the computer's slots.

conventional memory   The first megabyte or first 640K of system memory accessible by an Intel processor in real mode. Sometimes called base memory.

convergence   Describes the capability of a color monitor to focus the three colored electron beams on a single point. Poor convergence causes the characters onscreen to appear fuzzy and can cause headaches and eyestrain.

coprocessor   An additional computer processing unit designed to handle specific tasks in conjunction with the main or central processing unit.

copy protection   A hardware or software scheme to prohibit making illegal copies of a program.

core   An "old-fashioned" term for computer memory.

core speed   The internal speed of a processor. With all modern processors, this speed is faster than the system bus speed and that speed relationship is regulated by the clock multiplier in the processor.

CP/M   Control Program for Microcomputers, originally Control Program/Monitor. An operating system created by Gary Kildall, the founder of Digital Research. Created for the old 8-bit microcomputers that used the 8080, 8085, and Z-80 microprocessors. Was the dominant operating system in the late 1970s and early 1980s for small computers used in a business environment.

cps   Characters per second. A data transfer rate generally estimated from the bit rate and the character length. At 2,400bps, for example, 8-bit characters with start and stop bits (for a total of 10 bits per character) are transmitted at a rate of approximately 240cps. Some protocols, such as V.42 and MNP, employ advanced techniques such as longer transmission frames and data compression to increase characters per second.

CPU   Central Processing Unit. The computer's microprocessor chip; the brains of the outfit. Typically, an IC using VLSI (very-large-scale integration) technology to pack several different functions into a tiny area. The most common electronic device in the CPU is the transistor, of which several thousand to several million or more are found.

crash   A malfunction that brings work to a halt. A *system crash* usually is caused by a software malfunction, and ordinarily you can restart the system by rebooting the machine. A *head crash*, however, entails physical damage to a disk and probable data loss.

CRC   Cyclic Redundancy Checking. An error-detection technique consisting of a cyclic algorithm performed on each block or frame of data by both sending and receiving modems. The sending modem inserts the results of its computation in each data block in the form of a CRC code. The receiving modem compares its results with the received CRC code and responds with either a positive or negative acknowledgment. In the ARQ protocol implemented in high-speed modems, the receiving modem accepts no more data until a defective block is received correctly.

crosstalk   The electromagnetic coupling of a signal on one line with another nearby signal line. Crosstalk is caused by electromagnetic induction, where a signal traveling through a wire creates a magnetic field that induces a current in other nearby wires.

CRT   Cathode-Ray Tube. A term used to describe a television or monitor screen tube.

current   The flow of electrons, measured in amperes, or amps.

cursor   The small flashing hyphen that appears onscreen to indicate the point at which any input from the keyboard will be placed.

cycle   Time for a signal to transition from leading edge to the next leading edge.

cyclic redundancy checking   See *CRC*.

cylinder   The set of tracks on a disk that are on each side of all the disk platters in a stack and are the same distance from the center of the disk. The total number of tracks that can be read without moving the heads. A floppy drive with two heads usually has 160 tracks, which are accessible as 80 cylinders. A typical 4G hard disk has 10 platters with 20 heads (19 for data and one servo head) and 4,000 cylinders, in which each cylinder is composed of 19 tracks.

D/A Converter   DAC. A device that converts digital signals to analog form.

daisy chain   Stringing up components in such a manner that the signals move serially from one to the other. Most microcomputer multiple disk drive systems are daisy-chained. The SCSI bus system is a daisy-chain arrangement, in which the signals move from computer to disk drives to tape units, and so on.

daisywheel printer   An impact printer that prints fully formed characters one at a time by rotating a circular print element composed of a series of individual spokes, each containing two characters that radiate from a center hub. Produces letter-quality output.

DAT   Digital Audio Tape. A small cassette containing 4mm-wide tape used for storing large amounts of digital information. DAT technology emerged in Europe and Japan in 1986 as a way to produce high-quality, digital audio recordings and was modified in 1988 to conform to the DDS (Digital Data Storage) standard for storing computer data. Raw capacities for a single tape are 2G for DDS, 4G for DDS-2, and 12G for DDS-3, with double that for compressed data.

data   1) Groups of facts processed into information. A graphic or textural representation of facts, concepts, numbers, letters, symbols, or instructions used for communication or processing. 2) An android from the 24th century with a processing speed of 60 trillion operations per second and a storage capacity of 800 quadrillion bits, and who serves on the *USS Enterprise NCC-1701-D* with the rank of lieutenant commander.

data bus   The connection that transmits data between the processor and the rest of the system. The width of the data bus defines the number of data bits that can be moved into or out of the processor in one cycle.

data cable   Generically, a cable that carries data. Specific to HD connections, the narrower (20 pin) of two cables that connects an ST-506/412 or ESDI hard disk drive to a controller card.

data communications   A type of communication in which computers and terminals can exchange data over an electronic medium.

data compression   A technique where mathematical algorithms are applied to the data in a file to eliminate redundancies and therefore reduce the size of the file. See *lossy compression* and *lossless compression*.

data link layer   In networking, the layer of the OSI reference model that controls how the electrical impulses enter or leave the network cable. Ethernet and Token Ring are the two most common examples of data link layer protocols.

data separator   A device that separates data and clock signals from a single encoded signal pattern. Usually, the same device does both data separation and combination and is sometimes called an *endec*, or *encoder/decoder*.

data transfer rate   The maximum rate at which data can be transferred from one device to another.

daughterboard   Add-on board to increase functionality and/or memory. Attaches to existing board.

D-channel   In ISDN, a 16Kbps channel that is used to transmit control data about a connection.

DB-9   9-pin D-shell connector, primarily used for PC serial ports.

DB-25   25-pin D-shell connector, primarily used for PC parallel ports.

DC   Direct current, such as that provided by a power supply or batteries.

DC-600   Data Cartridge 600, a data-storage medium invented by 3M in 1971 that uses a quarter-inch-wide tape 600 feet in length.

DCE   Data Communications Equipment. The hardware that performs the communication—usually a dial-up modem that establishes and controls the data link through the telephone network. See also *DTE*.

DDE   Dynamic Data Exchange. A form of interprocess communications used by Microsoft Windows to support the exchange of commands and data between two applications running simultaneously. This capability has been enhanced further with Object Linking and Embedding (OLE).

de facto standard   A software or hardware technology that is not officially made a standard by any recognized standards organization but that is used as a reference for consumers and vendors due to its dominance in the marketplace.

DEBUG   The name of a utility program included with DOS used for specialized purposes such as altering memory locations, tracing program execution, patching programs and disk sectors, and performing other low-level tasks.

decibel (dB)   A logarithmic measure of the ratio between two powers, voltages, currents, sound intensities, and so on. Signal-to-noise ratios are expressed in decibels.

dedicated line   A user-installed telephone line that connects a specified number of computers or terminals within a limited area, such as a single building. The line is a cable rather than a public-access telephone line. The communications channel also may be referred to as nonswitched because calls do not go through telephone company switching equipment.

dedicated servo surface In voice-coil-actuated hard disk drives, one side of one platter given over to servo data that is used to guide and position the read/write heads.

default Any setting assumed at startup or reset by the computer's software and attached devices and operational until changed by the user. An assumption the computer makes when no other parameters are specified. When you type DIR without specifying the drive to search, for example, the computer assumes that you want it to search the default drive. The term is used in software to describe any action the computer or program takes on its own with embedded values.

defect map A list of unusable sectors and tracks coded onto a drive during the low-level format process.

defragmentation The process of rearranging disk sectors so files are stored on consecutive sectors in adjacent tracks.

degauss 1) To remove magnetic charges, or to erase magnetic images. Normal applications include monitors and disks or tapes. Most monitors incorporate a degaussing coil, which surrounds the CRT, and automatically energize this coil for a few seconds when powered up to remove color or image distorting magnetic fields from the metal mask inside the tube. Some monitors include a button or control that can be used for additional applications of this coil to remove more stubborn magnetic traces. 2) Also the act of erasing or demagnetizing a magnetic disk or tape using a special tool called a degaussing coil.

density The amount of data that can be packed into a certain area on a specific storage media.

desktop A personal computer that sits on a desk.

device driver A memory-resident program loaded by CONFIG.SYS that controls an unusual device, such as an expanded memory board.

Dhrystone A benchmark program used as a standard figure of merit indicating aspects of a computer system's performance in areas other than floating-point math performance. Because the program does not use any floating-point operations, performs no I/O, and makes no operating system calls, it is most useful for measuring the processor performance of a system. The original Dhrystone program was developed in 1984 and was written in Ada, although the C and Pascal versions became more popular by 1989.

diagnostics Programs used to check the operation of a computer system. These programs enable the operator to check the entire system for any problems and to indicate in what area the problems lie.

dial-up adapter In Windows 9x, a software program that uses a modem to emulate a network interface card for networking. Most commonly used to connect to an Internet service provider or a dial-up server for remote access to a LAN.

die An individual chip (processor, RAM, or other integrated circuit) cut from a finished silicon chip wafer and built into the physical package that will connect it to the rest of the PC or a circuit board.

differential   An electrical signaling method where a pair of lines are used for each signal in "push-pull" fashion. In most cases, differential signals are balanced so that the same current flows on each line in opposite directions. This is unlike single-ended signals, which use only one line per signal referenced to a single ground. Differential signals have a large tolerance for common-mode noise and little crosstalk when used with twisted-pair wires even in long cables. Differential signaling is expensive because two pins are required for each signal.

digital loopback   A test that checks the modem's RS-232 interface and the cable that connects the terminal or computer and the modem. The modem receives data (in the form of digital signals) from the computer or terminal and immediately returns the data to the screen for verification.

digital signals   Discrete, uniform signals. In this book, the term refers to the binary digits 0 and 1.

digitize   To transform an analog wave to a digital signal that a computer can store. Conversion to digital data and back is performed by a *Digital to Analog Converter (DAC)*, often a single-chip device. How closely a digitized sample represents an analog wave depends on the number of times the amplitude of a wave is measured and recorded (the rate of digitization) as well as the number of different levels that can be specified at each instance. The number of possible signal levels is dictated by the resolution in bits.

DIMM   Dual Inline Memory Module. A 64-bit wide, 168-pin memory module used in Pentium and newer PCs. They are available in several versions, including 5v or 3v, buffered or unbuffered, with FPM/EDO or SDRAM memory, and in 64-bit (non-ECC/parity) or 72-bit (ECC/parity) form. Most Pentium and newer PCs require 3.3v unbuffered SDRAM DIMMs in either non-ECC or ECC versions (ECC recommended).

DIP   Dual Inline Package. A family of rectangular, integrated-circuit flat packages that have leads on the two longer sides. Package material is plastic or ceramic.

DIP switch   A tiny switch (or group of switches) on a circuit board. Named for the form factor of the carrier device in which the switch is housed.

direct memory access (DMA)   A process by which data moves between a disk drive (or other device) and system memory without direct control of the central processing unit, thus freeing it up for other tasks.

Direct Rambus DRAM   See *RDRAM*.

directory   An area of a disk that stores the titles given to the files saved on the disk and serves as a table of contents for those files. Contains data that identifies the name of a file, the size, the attributes (system, hidden, read-only, and so on), the date and time of creation, and a pointer to the location of the file. Each entry in a directory is 32 bytes long.

disc   Flat, circular, rotating medium that can store various types of information, both analog and digital. "Disc" is often used in reference to optical storage media, while "disk" refers to magnetic storage media. Disc is often used as a short form for video-disc or compact audio disc (CD).

disk   Alternative spelling for "disc" that generally refers to magnetic storage medium on which information can be accessed at random. Floppy disks and hard disks are examples.

disk access time   See *access time*.

disk cache   A portion of memory on the PC motherboard or on a drive interface card or controller used to store frequently accessed information from the drive (such as the file allocation table (FAT) or directory structure) to speed up disk access. With a larger disk cache, additional data from the data portion of a drive can be cached as well. See also *cache, L1 cache,* and *L2 cache*.

disk partition   See *partition*.

display adapter   The interface between the computer and the monitor that transmits the signals that appear as images on the display. This can take the form of an expansion card or a chip built into the motherboard.

dithering   The process of creating more colors and shades from a given color palette. In monochrome displays or printers, dithering will vary the black and white dot patterns to simulate shades of gray. Grayscale dithering is used to produce different shades of gray when the device can only produce limited levels of black or white outputs. Color screens or printers use dithering to create additional colors by mixing and varying the dot sizing and spacing. For example, when converting from 24-bit color to 8-bit color (an 8-bit palette has only 256 colors compared to the 24-bit palette's millions), dithering adds pixels of different colors to simulate the original color. Dithering is also known as *error diffusion*.

DLL   Dynamic Link Library. An executable driver program module for Microsoft Windows that can be loaded on demand and linked in at runtime and subsequently unloaded when the driver is no longer needed.

DMA   See *direct memory access*.

DMI   Desktop Management Interface. DMI is an operating system- and protocol-independent standard developed by the Desktop Management Task Force (DMTF) for managing desktop systems and servers. DMI provides a bidirectional path to interrogate all the hardware and software components within a PC, allowing hardware and software configurations to be monitored from a central station in a network.

docking station   Equipment that allows a laptop or notebook computer to use peripherals and accessories normally associated with desktop systems.

doping   Adding chemical impurities to silicon (which is naturally a nonconductor), creating a material with semiconductor properties that is then used in the manufacturing of electronic chips.

DOS   Disk Operating System. A collection of programs stored on the DOS disk that contain routines enabling the system and user to manage information and the hardware resources of the computer. DOS must be loaded into the computer before other programs can be started.

dot pitch   A measurement of the width of the dots that make up a pixel. The smaller the dot pitch, the sharper the image.

dot-matrix printer An impact printer that prints characters composed of dots. Characters are printed one at a time by pressing the ends of selected wires against an inked ribbon and paper.

double density (DD) An indication of the storage capacity of a floppy drive or disk in which eight or nine sectors per track are recorded using MFM encoding. See *MFM*.

downtime Operating time lost because of a computer malfunction.

DPMI DOS Protected Mode Interface. An industry standard interface that allows DOS applications to execute program code in the protected mode of the 286 or later Intel processor. The DPMI specification is available from Intel.

DPMS Display Power Management Signaling. A VESA standard for signaling a monitor or display to switch into energy conservation modes. DPMS provides for two low energy modes: standby and suspend.

DRAM Dynamic Random Access Memory. The most common type of computer memory, DRAM can be made very inexpensively compared to other types of memory. DRAM chips are small and inexpensive because they normally require only one transistor and a capacitor to represent each bit. The capacitors must be energized every 15ms or so (hundreds of times per second) to maintain their charges. DRAM is volatile, meaning it will lose data with no power or without regular refresh cycles.

drive A mechanical device that manipulates data storage media.

driver A program designed to interface a particular piece of hardware to an operating system or other standard software.

drum The cylindrical photoreceptor in a laser printer that receives the document image from the laser and applies it to the page as it slowly rotates.

DSM Digital Storage Media. A digital storage or transmission device or system.

DSP Digital Signal Processor. Dedicated, limited function processor often found in modems, sound cards, cellular phones, and so on.

DTE Data Terminal (or Terminating) Equipment. The device, usually a computer or terminal, that generates or is the final destination of data. See also *DCE*.

dual cavity pin grid array Chip packaging designed by Intel for use with the Pentium Pro processor that houses the processor die in one cavity of the package and the L2 cache memory in a second cavity within the same package.

Dual Independent Bus (DIB) Architecture A processor technology with the existence of two independent buses on the processor—the L2 cache bus and the processor-to-main-memory system bus. The processor can use both buses simultaneously, thus getting as much as two times more data into and out of the processor than a single bus architecture processor. The Intel Pentium Pro, Pentium II, and newer processors have DIB architecture.

dual scan display A lower quality but economical type of LCD color display that has an array of transistors running down the x and y axes of two sides of the screen. The number of transistors determines the screen's resolution.

duplex Indicates a communications channel capable of carrying signals in both directions.

DVD Digital Versatile Disc, originally called Digital Video Disc. A new type of high-capacity CD-ROM disc and drive format with up to 28 times the capacity of standard CD-ROM. The disc is the same diameter as a CD-ROM but can be recorded on both sides and on two layers for each side. Each side holds 4.7G on a single layer disc, while dual-layer versions hold 8.5G per side, for a maximum of 17G total if both sides and both layers are used, which is the equivalent of 28 CD-ROMs. DVD drives can read standard audio CDs and CD-ROMs.

DVI Digital Video Interactive. A standard that was originally developed at RCA Laboratories and sold to Intel in 1988. DVI integrates digital motion, still video, sound, graphics, and special effects in a compressed format. DVI is a highly sophisticated hardware compression technique used in interactive multimedia applications.

Dvorak keyboard A keyboard design by August Dvorak that was patented in 1936 and approved by ANSI in 1982. Provides increased speed and comfort and reduces the rate of errors by placing the most frequently used letters in the center for use by the strongest fingers. Finger motions and awkward strokes are reduced by more than 90 percent in comparison with the familiar QWERTY keyboard. The Dvorak keyboard has the five vowel keys, AOEUI, together under the left hand in the center row and the five most frequently used consonants, DHTNS, under the fingers of the right hand.

dynamic execution A processing technique that allows the processor to dynamically predict the order of instructions and execute them out of order internally if necessary for an improvement in speed. Makes use of the three techniques Multiple Branch Prediction, Data Flow Analysis, and Speculative Execution.

EBCDIC Extended Binary Coded Decimal Interchange Code. An IBM-developed 8-bit code for the representation of characters. It allows 256 possible character combinations within a single byte. EBCDIC is the standard code on IBM mini-computers and mainframes, but not on the IBM microcomputers, where ASCII is used instead.

ECC Error Correcting Code. A type of system memory or cache that is capable of detecting and correcting some types of memory errors without interrupting processing.

ECP Enhanced Capabilities Port. A type of high-speed parallel port jointly developed by Microsoft and Hewlett-Packard that offers improved performance for the parallel port and requires special hardware logic.

edge connector The part of a circuit board containing a series of printed contacts that is inserted into an expansion slot or connector.

EDO (Extended Data Out) RAM A type of RAM chips that allow for a timing overlap between successive accesses, thus improving memory cycle time.

EEPROM Electrically Erasable Programmable Read Only Memory. A type of nonvolatile memory chip used to store semipermanent information in a computer such as the BIOS. An EEPROM can be erased and reprogrammed directly in the host system without special equipment. This is used so manufacturers can upgrade the ROM code in a system by supplying a special program that erases and reprograms the EEPROM chip with the new code. Also called a *flash ROM*.

EGA   Enhanced Graphics Adapter. A type of PC video display adapter first introduced by IBM on September 10, 1984, that supports text and graphics. Text is supported at a maximum resolution of 80×25 characters in 16 colors with a character box of 8×14 pixels. Graphics is supported at a maximum resolution of 640×350 pixels in 16 (from a palette of 64) colors. The EGA outputs a TTL (digital) signal with a horizontal scanning frequency of 15.75, 18.432, or 21.85KHz, and supports TTL color or TTL monochrome displays.

EIA   Electronic Industries Association. An organization that defines electronic standards in the United States.

EIDE   Enhanced Integrated Drive Electronics. A specific Western Digital implementation of the ATA-2 specification. See *ATA-2*.

EISA   Extended Industry Standard Architecture. An extension of the Industry Standard Architecture (ISA) bus developed by IBM for the AT. The EISA design was led by Compaq Corporation. Later, eight other manufacturers (AST, Epson, Hewlett-Packard, NEC, Olivetti, Tandy, Wyse, and Zenith) joined Compaq in a consortium founded September 13, 1988. This group became known as the "gang of nine." The EISA design was patterned largely after IBM's Micro Channel Architecture (MCA) in the PS/2 systems, but unlike MCA, EISA allows for backward compatibility with older plug-in adapters.

electronic mail (e-mail)   A method of transferring messages from one computer to another.

electrostatic discharge (ESD)   The grounding of static electricity. A sudden flow of electricity between two objects at different electrical potentials. ESD is a primary cause of integrated circuit damage or failure.

embedded controller   In disk drives, a controller built into the same physical unit that houses the drive rather than on a separate adapter card. IDE and SCSI drives both use embedded controllers.

embedded servo data   Magnetic markings embedded between or inside tracks on disk drives that use voice-coil actuators. These markings enable the actuator to fine-tune the position of the read/write heads.

EMM   Expanded Memory Manager. A driver that provides a software interface to expanded memory. EMMs were originally created for expanded memory boards, but can also use the memory management capabilities of the 386 or later processors to emulate an expanded memory board. EMM386.EXE is an example of an EMM that comes with DOS.

EMS   Expanded Memory Specification. Sometimes also called the *LIM spec* because it was developed by Lotus, Intel, and Microsoft. Provides a way for microcomputers running under DOS to access additional memory. EMS memory management provides access to a maximum of 32M of expanded memory through a small (usually 64K) window in conventional memory. EMS is a cumbersome access scheme designed primarily for pre-286 systems that could not access extended memory.

emulator   A piece of test apparatus that emulates or imitates the function of a particular chip.

encoding   The protocol by which data is carried or stored by a medium.

encryption   The translation of data into unreadable codes to maintain security.

endec (encoder/decoder)   A device that takes data and clock signals and combines or encodes them using a particular encoding scheme into a single signal for transmission or storage. The same device also later separates or decodes the data and clock signals during a receive or read operation. Sometimes called a *data separator*.

Energy Star   A certification program started by the Environmental Protection Agency. Energy Star certified computers and peripherals are designed to draw less than 30 watts of electrical energy from a standard 110-volt AC outlet during periods of inactivity. Also called *Green PCs*.

Enhanced Graphics Adapter   See *EGA*.

Enhanced Small Device Interface   See *ESDI*.

EPP   Enhanced Parallel Port. A type of parallel port developed by Intel, Xircom, and Zenith Data Systems that operates almost at ISA bus speed and offers a tenfold increase in the raw throughput capability over a conventional parallel port. EPP is especially designed for parallel port peripherals such as LAN adapters, disk drives, and tape backups.

EPROM   Erasable programmable read-only memory. A type of read-only memory (ROM) in which the data pattern can be erased to allow a new pattern. EPROM usually is erased by ultraviolet light and recorded by a higher-than-normal voltage programming signal.

equalization   A compensation circuit designed into modems to counteract certain distortions introduced by the telephone channel. Two types are used: fixed (compromise) equalizers and those that adapt to channel conditions (adaptive). Good-quality modems use adaptive equalization.

error control   Various techniques that check the reliability of characters (parity) or blocks of data. V.42, MNP, and HST error-control protocols use error detection (CRC) and retransmission of error frames (ARQ).

error message   A word or combination of words to indicate to the user that an error has occurred somewhere in the program.

ESCD   Extended System Configuration Data. Area in CMOS or Flash/NVRAM where Plug-and-Play information is stored.

ESDI   Enhanced Small Device Interface. A hardware standard developed by Maxtor and standardized by a consortium of 22 disk drive manufacturers on January 26, 1983. A group of 27 manufacturers formed the ESDI steering committee on September 15, 1986, to enhance and improve the specification. A high-performance interface used primarily with hard disks, ESDI provides for a maximum data transfer rate to and from a hard disk of between 10 and 24Mbit/sec.

Ethernet   A type of network protocol developed in the late 1970s by Bob Metcalf at Xerox Corporation and endorsed by the IEEE. One of the oldest LAN communications protocols in the personal computing industry, Ethernet networks use a collision-detection protocol to manage contention.

expanded memory   Otherwise known as *EMS memory*, memory that conforms to the EMS specification. Requires a special device driver and conforms to a standard developed by Lotus, Intel, and Microsoft.

expansion card   An integrated circuit card that plugs into an expansion slot on a motherboard to provide access to additional peripherals or features not built into the motherboard. Also referred to as an *add-in board*.

expansion slot   A slot on the motherboard that physically and electrically connects an expansion card to the motherboard and the system buses.

eXtended graphics array   See *XGA*.

extended memory   Direct processor-addressable memory that is addressed by an Intel (or compatible) 286, 386, or 486 processor in the region beyond the first megabyte. Addressable only in the processor's protected mode of operation.

extended partition   A nonbootable DOS partition containing DOS volumes. Starting with DOS v3.3, the DOS FDISK program can create two partitions that serve DOS: an ordinary, bootable partition (called the primary partition) and an extended partition, which may contain as many as 23 volumes from D: through Z:.

external device   A peripheral that is installed outside of the system case.

extra-high density (ED)   An indication of the storage capacity of a floppy drive or disk in which 36 sectors per track are recorded using a vertical recording technique with MFM encoding.

fast ATA   Fast AT Attachment interface. Also called *Fast ATA-2*, these are specific Seagate and Quantum implementations of the ATA-2 interface. See *ATA-2*.

Fast Page Mode RAM   A type of RAM that improves on standard DRAM speed by allowing for faster access to all the data within a given row of memory by keeping the row address the same and changing only the column.

FAT   File Allocation Table. A table held near the outer edge of a disk that tells which sectors are allocated to each file and in what order.

FAT 32   A disk file allocation system from Microsoft that uses 32-bit values for FAT entries instead of 16-bit values used by the original FAT system, enabling partition sizes up to 2T (terabytes). FAT32 first appeared in Windows 95B and is also found in Windows 98 and Windows NT 5.0.

fax/modem   A peripheral that integrates the capabilities of a fax machine and a modem in one expansion card or external unit.

FDISK   The name of the disk-partitioning program under several operating systems to create the master boot record and allocate partitions for the operating system's use.

feature connector   On a video adapter, a connector that allows an additional video feature card such as a separate 3D accelerator, video capture card, or MPEG decoder to be connected to the main video adapter and display.

FIFO   First-in, first-out. A method of storing and retrieving items from a list, table, or stack so that the first element stored is the first one retrieved.

file A collection of information kept somewhere other than in random-access memory.

file attribute Information held in the attribute byte of a file's directory entry.

file compression See *compressed file*.

file name The name given to the disk file. For DOS, it must be one to eight characters long and may be followed by a file name extension, which can be one to three characters long. Windows 95 eases these constraints by allowing file names of up to 255 characters.

FireWire Also called *IEEE 1394*. A serial I/O interface standard that is extremely fast, with data transfer rates up to 400M/sec, 800M/sec, or 3.2G/sec, depending on the version of standard used.

firmware Software contained in a read-only memory (ROM) device. A cross between hardware and software.

fixed disk Also called a *hard disk*, a disk that cannot be removed from its controlling hardware or housing. Made of rigid material with a magnetic coating and used for the mass storage and retrieval of data.

flash ROM A type of EEPROM developed by Intel that can be erased and reprogrammed in the host system. See *EEPROM*.

flicker A monitor condition caused by refresh rates that are too low in which the display flashes visibly. This can cause eyestrain or more severe physical problems.

floating-point unit (FPU) Sometimes called the math coprocessor; handles the more complex calculations of the processing cycle.

floppy disk A removable disk using flexible magnetic media enclosed in a semirigid or rigid plastic case.

floppy disk controller The logic and interface that connects a floppy disk drive to the system.

floppy tape A tape standard that uses drives connecting to an ordinary floppy disk controller.

floptical drive A special type of high-capacity removable disk drive that uses an optical mechanism to properly position the drive read/write heads over the data tracks on the disk, allowing for more precise control of the read/write positioning and therefore narrower track spacing and more data packed into a smaller area than traditional floppy disks.

flow control A mechanism that compensates for differences in the flow of data input to and output from a modem or other device.

FM encoding Frequency modulation encoding. An outdated method of encoding data on the disk surface that uses up half the disk space with timing signals.

FM synthesis An audio technology that uses one sine wave operator to modify another and create an artificial sound that mimics an instrument.

folder In a graphical user interface, a simulated file folder that holds documents (text, data, or graphics), applications, and other folders. A folder is like a DOS subdirectory.

form factor   The physical dimensions of a device. Two devices with the same form factor are physically interchangeable. The IBM PC, XT, and XT Model 286, for example, all use power supplies that are internally different but have exactly the same form factor.

FORMAT   The DOS format program that performs both low- and high-level formatting on floppy disks but only high-level formatting on hard disks.

formatted capacity   The total number of bytes of data that can fit on a formatted disk. The unformatted capacity is higher because space is lost defining the boundaries between sectors.

formatting   Preparing a disk so that the computer can read or write to it. Checks the disk for defects and constructs an organizational system to manage information on the disk.

FORTRAN   Formula translator. A high-level programming language developed in 1954 by John Backus at IBM, primarily for programs dealing with mathematical formulas and expressions similar to algebra and used primarily in scientific and technical applications.

fragmentation   The state of having a file scattered around a disk in pieces rather than existing in one contiguous area of the disk. Fragmented files are slower to read than files stored in contiguous areas and can be more difficult to recover if the FAT or a directory becomes damaged.

frame   1) A data communications term for a block of data with header and trailer information attached. The added information usually includes a frame number, block size data, error-check codes, and start/end indicators. 2) Also a single, complete picture in a video or film recording. A video frame consists of two interlaced fields of either 525 lines (NTSC) or 625 lines (PAL/SECAM), running at 30 frames per second (NTSC) or 25 frames per second (PAL/SECAM).

frame buffer   A memory device that stores, pixel by pixel, the contents of an image. Frame buffers are used to refresh a raster image. Sometimes they incorporate local processing capability. The "depth" of the frame buffer is the number of bits per pixel, which determines the number of colors or intensities that can be displayed.

frame rate   The speed at which video frames are scanned or displayed, 30 frames per second for NTSC, 25 frames a second for PAL/SECAM.

FTP   File Transfer Protocol. A method of transferring files over the Internet. FTP can be used to transfer files between two machines on which the user has accounts. Anonymous FTP can be used by a user to retrieve a file from a server without having an account on that server.

full duplex   Signal flow in both directions at the same time. In microcomputer communications, also may refer to the suppression of the online local echo.

full-height drive   A drive unit that is 3.25 inches high, 5.75 inches wide, and 8 inches deep.

full-motion video   A video sequence displayed at full television standard resolutions and frame rates. In the U.S., this would equate to NTSC video at 30 frames per second.

function keys   Special-purpose keys that can be programmed to perform various operations. Serve many different functions depending on the program being used.

gas-plasma display   Commonly used in portable systems, a type of display that operates by exciting a gas, usually neon or an argon-neon mixture, through the application of a voltage. When sufficient voltage is applied at the intersection of two electrodes, the gas glows an orange-red. Because gas-plasma displays generate light, they require no backlighting.

gateway   Officially, an application-to-application conversion program or system. For example, an e-mail gateway would convert between SMTP (Internet) e-mail format to MHS (Novell) e-mail format. The term gateway is also used as a slang term for router. See also *router*.

gender   When describing connectors for PCs, connectors are described as male if they have pins or female if they have receptacles designed to accept the pins of a male connector.

genlocking   The process of aligning the data rate of a video image with that of a digital device to digitize the image and enter it into computer memory. The machine that performs this function is known as a *genlock*.

GIF   Graphics Interchange Format. A popular raster graphics file format developed by CompuServe that handles 8-bit color (256 colors) and uses the LZW method to achieve compression ratios of approximately 1.5:1 to 2:1.

giga   A multiplier indicating 1 billion (1,000,000,000) of some unit. Abbreviated as g or G. When used to indicate a number of bytes of memory storage, the multiplier definition changes to 1,073,741,824. One gigabit, for example, equals 1,000,000,000 bits, and one gigabyte equals 1,073,741,824 bytes.

gigabyte (G)   A unit of information storage equal to 1,073,741,824 bytes.

graphics accelerator   A video processor or chipset specially designed to speed display and rendering of graphical objects onscreen.

graphics adapter   See *video adapter*.

Green Book   The standard for Compact Disc-Interactive (CD-I). Philips developed CD-I technology for the consumer market, to be connected to a television instead of a computer monitor. CD-I is not a computer system but a consumer device that made a small splash in the market and disappeared. CD-I disks require special code and are not compatible with standard CD-ROMs. A CD-ROM cannot be played on the CD-I machine, but Red Book audio can be played on CD-I devices.

GUI   Graphical User Interface. A type of program interface that allows users to choose commands and functions by pointing to a graphical icon using either a keyboard or pointing device such as a mouse. Windows and OS/2 are the most popular GUIs available for PC systems.

half duplex   Signal flow in both directions but only one way at a time. In microcomputer communications, half duplex may refer to activation of the online local echo, which causes the modem to send a copy of the transmitted data to the screen of the sending computer.

half-height drive   A drive unit that is 1.625 inches high, and either 5.75 or 4 inches wide and 4 or 8 inches deep.

halftoning   A process that uses dithering to simulate a continuous tone image such as a photograph or shaded drawing using various sizes of dots. Newspapers, magazines, and many books use halftoning. The human eye will merge the dots to give the impression of gray shades.

hard disk   A high-capacity disk storage unit characterized by a normally nonremovable rigid substrate medium. The platters in a hard disk normally are constructed of aluminum or glass/ceramic. Also sometimes called a *fixed disk*.

hard error   An error in reading or writing data that is caused by damaged hardware.

hardware   Physical components that make up a microcomputer, monitor, printer, and so on.

HDLC   High-Level Data Link Control. A standard protocol developed by the ISO for software applications and communicating devices operating in synchronous environments. Defines operations at the link level of communications—for example, the format of data frames exchanged between modems over a phone line.

head   A small electromagnetic device inside a drive that reads, records, and erases data on the media.

head actuator   The device that moves read/write heads across a disk drive's platters. Most drives use a stepper-motor or a voice-coil actuator.

head crash   A (usually) rare occurrence in which a read/write head strikes a platter surface with sufficient force to damage the magnetic medium.

head parking   A procedure in which a disk drive's read/write heads are moved to an unused track so that they will not damage data in the event of a head crash or other failure.

head seek   The movement of a drive's read/write heads to a particular track.

heat sink   A mass of metal attached to a chip carrier or socket for the purpose of dissipating heat.

helical scan   A type of recording technology that has vastly increased the capacity of tape drives. Invented for use in broadcast systems and now used in VCRs. Conventional longitudinal recording records a track of data straight across the width of a single-track tape. Helical scan recording packs more data on the tape by positioning the tape at an angle to the recording heads. The heads spin to record diagonal stripes of information on the tape.

hexadecimal number   A number encoded in base-16, such that digits include the letters A through F as well as the numerals 0 through 9 (for example, 8BF3, which equals 35,827 in base-10).

hidden file   A file that is not displayed in DOS directory listings because the file's attribute byte holds a special setting.

high density (HD)   An indication of the storage capacity of a floppy drive or disk in which 15 or 18 sectors per track are recorded using MFM encoding.

high sierra format   A standard format for placing files and directories on CD-ROMs, proposed by an ad hoc committee of computer vendors, software developers, and CD-ROM system integrators. (Work on the format proposal began at the High Sierra Hotel at Lake Tahoe, Nevada.) A revised version of the format was adopted by the ISO as ISO 9660.

high-definition television   HDTV. Video formats offering greater visual accuracy (or resolution) than current NTSC, PAL, or SECAM broadcast standards. HDTV formats generally range in resolution from 655 to 2,125 scanning lines, having an aspect ration of 5:3 (or 1.67:1) and a video bandwidth of 30 to 50MHz (5+ times greater than NTSC standard). Digital HDTV has a bandwidth of 300MHz. HDTV is subjectively comparable to 35mm film.

high-level formatting   Formatting performed by the DOS FORMAT program. Among other things, it creates the root directory and FATs.

history file   A file created by utility software to keep track of earlier use of the software. Many backup programs, for example, keep history files describing earlier backup sessions.

hit ratio   In describing the efficiency of a disk or memory cache, the ratio of the number of times the data is found in the cache to the total number of data requests is the hit ratio. 1:1 would be a perfect hit ratio, meaning that every data request was found in the cache. The closer to 1:1 the ratio is, the more efficient the cache.

HMA   High Memory Area. The first 64K of extended memory, which is controlled typically by the HIMEM.SYS device driver. Real-mode programs can be loaded into the HMA to conserve conventional memory. Normally, DOS 5.0 and later use the HMA exclusively to reduce the DOS conventional memory footprint.

horizontal scan rate   In monitors, the speed at which the electron beam moves laterally across the screen. Normally expressed as a frequency; typical monitors range from 31.5KHz to 90KHz, with the higher frequencies being more desirable.

HPT   High-Pressure Tin. A PLCC socket that promotes high forces between socket contacts and PLCC contacts for a good connection.

HST   High-Speed Technology. The USRobotics proprietary high-speed modem-signaling scheme, developed as an interim protocol until the V.32 protocol could be implemented in a cost-effective manner.

HTML   Hypertext Markup Language. A language used to describe and format plain-text files on the Web. HTML is based on pairs of tags that allow you to mix graphics with text, change the appearance of text, and create hypertext documents with links to other documents.

HTTP   Hypertext Transfer Protocol. The protocol that describes the rules that a browser and server use to communicate over the World Wide Web. HTTP allows a Web browser to request HTML documents from a Web server. See also *hypertext*.

Huffman coding   A technique that minimizes the average number of bytes required to represent the characters in a text. Huffman coding works for a given character distribution by assigning short codes to frequently occurring characters and longer codes to infrequently occurring characters.

hypertext A technology that allows for quick and easy navigation between and within large documents. Hypertext links are pointers to other sections within the same document, other documents, or other resources such as FTP sites, images, or sounds.

Hz An abbreviation for hertz, a frequency measurement unit used internationally to indicate one cycle per second.

I/O Input/Output. A circuit path that enables independent communications between the processor and external devices.

I/O port Input/Output port. Used to communicate to and from devices, such as a printer or disk.

IBMBIO.COM One of the DOS system files required to boot the machine. The first file loaded from disk during the boot. Contains extensions to the ROM BIOS.

IBMDOS.COM One of the DOS system files required to boot the machine. Contains the primary DOS routines. Loaded by IBMBIO.COM, it in turn loads COMMAND.COM.

IC Integrated Circuit. A complete electronic circuit contained on a single chip. May consist of only a few or thousands of transistors, capacitors, diodes, or resistors, and generally is classified according to the complexity of the circuitry and the approximate number of circuits on the chip. SSI (small-scale integration) equals 2 to 10 circuits. MSI (medium-scale integration) equals 10 to 100 circuits. LSI (large-scale integration) equals 100 to 1,000 circuits. VLSI (very-large-scale integration) equals 1,000 to 10,000 circuits. ULSI (ultra-large-scale integration) equals more than 10,000 circuits.

IEEE 802.3 See *10Base2.*

IEEE 1394 See *FireWire.*

IDE Integrated Drive Electronics. Describes a hard disk with the disk controller circuitry integrated within it. The first IDE drives commonly were called hard cards. Also refers to the *ATA interface standard*, the standard for attaching hard disk drives to ISA bus IBM-compatible computers. IDE drives typically operate as though they were standard ST-506/412 drives. See also *ATA.*

incremental backup A backup of all files that have changed since the last backup.

inductive A property where energy can be transferred from one device to another via the magnetic field generated by the device even though no direct electrical connection is established between the two.

.INF file A Windows driver and device information file used to install new drivers or services.

initiator A device attached to the SCSI bus that sends a command to another device (the target) on the SCSI bus. The SCSI host adapter plugged into the system bus is an example of a SCSI initiator.

inkjet printer A type of printer that sprays one or more colors of ink on the paper. Can produce output with quality approaching that of a laser printer at a lower cost.

input   Data sent to the computer from the keyboard, telephone, video camera, another computer, paddles, joysticks, and so on.

instruction   Program step that tells the computer what to do for a single operation.

integrated circuit   See *IC*.

interface   A communications device or protocol that enables one device to communicate with another. Matches the output of one device to the input of the other device.

interlacing   A method of scanning alternate lines of pixels on a display screen. The odd lines are scanned first from top to bottom and left to right. The electron gun goes back to the top and makes a second pass, scanning the even lines. Interlacing requires two scan passes to construct a single image. Because of this additional scanning, interlaced screens often seem to flicker unless a long persistence phosphor is used in the display.

interleave ratio   The number of sectors that pass beneath the read/write heads before the "next" numbered sector arrives. When the interleave ratio is 3:1, for example, a sector is read, two pass by, and then the next is read. A proper interleave ratio, laid down during low-level formatting, enables the disk to transfer information without excessive revolutions due to missed sectors.

interleaved memory   The process of alternating access between two banks of memory to overlap accesses, thus speeding up data retrieval.

internal command   In DOS, a command contained in COMMAND.COM so that no other file must be loaded to perform the command. DIR and COPY are two examples of internal commands.

internal device   A peripheral device that is installed inside the main system case either in an expansion slot or in a drive bay.

internal drive   A disk or tape drive mounted inside one of a computer's disk drive bays (or a hard disk card, which is installed in one of the computer's slots).

Internet   A computer network that joins many government, university, and private computers together over phone lines. The Internet traces its origins to a network set up in 1969 by the Department of Defense. You can connect to the Internet through many online services such as CompuServe and America Online, or you can connect through local Internet service providers (ISPs). Internet computers use the TCP/IP communications protocol. There are several million hosts on the Internet. A *host* is a mainframe, mini, or workstation that directly supports the Internet protocol (the IP in TCP/IP).

interpreter   A program for a high-level language that translates and executes the program at the same time. The program statements that are interpreted remain in their original source language, the way the programmer wrote them—that is, the program does not need to be compiled before execution. Interpreted programs run slower than compiled programs and always must be run with the interpreter loaded in memory.

interrupt   A suspension of a process, such as the execution of a computer program, caused by an event external to that process and performed in such a way that the process can be resumed. An interrupt can be caused by internal or external conditions such as a signal indicating that a device or program has completed a transfer of data.

interrupt vector   A pointer in a table that gives the location of a set of instructions that the computer should execute when a particular interrupt occurs.

IO.SYS   One of the DOS system files required to boot the machine. The first file loaded from disk during the boot. Contains extensions to the ROM BIOS.

IPX   Internet Packet eXchange. Novell NetWare's native LAN communications protocol used to move data between server and/or workstation programs running on different network nodes. IPX packets are encapsulated and carried by the packets used in Ethernet and the similar frames used in Token-Ring networks.

IRQ   Interrupt request. Physical connections between external hardware devices and the interrupt controllers. When a device such as a floppy controller or a printer needs the attention of the CPU, an IRQ line is used to get the attention of the system to perform a task. On PC and XT IBM-compatible systems, eight IRQ lines are included, numbered IRQ0 through IRQ7. On the AT and PS/2 systems, 16 IRQ lines are numbered IRQ0 through IRQ15. IRQ lines must be used only by a single adapter in the ISA bus systems, but Micro Channel Architecture (MCA) adapters can share interrupts.

ISA   Industry Standard Architecture. The bus architecture that was introduced as an 8-bit bus with the original IBM PC in 1981 and later expanded to 16 bits with the IBM PC/AT in 1984. ISA slots are still found in PC systems today.

ISA bus clock   Clock that operates the ISA bus at normally 8.33MHz.

ISDN   Integrated Services Digital Network. An international telecommunications standard that enables a communications channel to carry digital data simultaneously with voice and video information.

ISO   International Standards Organization. The ISO, based in Paris, develops standards for international and national data communications. The U.S. representative to the ISO is the American National Standards Institute (ANSI). See also *high sierra format.*

ISO 9660   An international standard that defines file systems for CD-ROM disks, independent of the operating system. ISO (International Standards Organization) 9660 has two levels. Level one provides for DOS file system compatibility, while Level two allows file names of up to 32 characters. See also *high sierra format.*

ITU   International Telecommunications Union. Formerly called CCITT. An international committee organized by the United Nations to set international communications recommendations, which frequently are adopted as standards, and to develop interface, modem, and data network recommendations. The Bell 212A standard for 1,200bps communication in North America, for example, is observed internationally as CCITT V.22. For 2,400bps communication, most U.S. manufacturers observe V.22bis, while V.32, V.32bis, V34 and V34+ are standards for 9,600, 14,400, 28,800, and 33,600bps, respectively. The V.90 standard recently was defined for 56Kbps modems.

J-lead   J-shaped leads on chip carriers, which can be surface-mounted on a PC board or plugged into a socket that then is mounted on a PC board, usually on .050-inch centers.

Java An object-oriented programming language and environment similar to C or C++. Java was developed by Sun Microsystems and is used to create network-based applications.

Jaz drive A proprietary type of removable media drive with a magnetic hard disk platter in a rigid plastic case. Developed by Iomega and currently available in 1G and 2G sizes.

JEDEC Joint Electronic Devices Engineering Council. A group that establishes standards for the electronics industry.

joystick An input device generally used for game software usually consisting of a central upright stick that controls horizontal and vertical motion and one or more buttons to control discrete events such as firing guns. More complex models may resemble flight yokes and steering wheels or may incorporate tactile feedback.

JPEG Joint Photographic Experts Group. The international consortium of hardware, software, and publishing interests who, under the auspices of the ISO, has defined a universal standard for digital compression and decompression of still images for use in computer systems. JPEG compresses at about a 20:1 ratio before visible image degradation occurs. A lossy data compression standard that was originally designed for still images but can also compress real-time video (30 frames per second) and animation. Lossy compression permanently discards unnecessary data, resulting in some loss of precision.

jukebox A type of CD-ROM drive that allows several CD-ROM disks to be in the drive at the same time. The drive itself determines which disk is needed by the system and loads the disks into the reading mechanism as needed.

jumper A small, plastic-covered metal clip that slips over two pins protruding from a circuit board. Sometimes also called a *shunt*. When in place, the jumper connects the pins electrically and closes the circuit. By doing so, it connects the two terminals of a switch, turning it "on."

Kermit A protocol designed for transferring files between microcomputers and mainframes. Developed by Frank DaCruz and Bill Catchings at Columbia University (and named after the talking frog on *The Muppet Show*), Kermit is widely accepted in the academic world.

kernel Operating system core component.

key disk In software copy protection, a distribution floppy disk that must be present in a floppy disk drive for an application program to run.

keyboard The primary input device for most computers consisting of keys with letters of the alphabet, digits, punctuation, and function control keys.

keyboard macro A series of keystrokes automatically input when a single key is pressed.

keylock Physical locking mechanism to preventing internal access to the system unit or peripherals.

KFlex A proprietary standard for 56Kbps modem transmissions developed by Rockwell and implemented in modems from a variety of vendors. Superseded by the official V.90 standard for 56Kbps modems. See also *X2* and *V.90.*

kilo   A multiplier indicating one thousand (1,000) of some unit. Abbreviated as k or K. When used to indicate a number of bytes of memory storage, the multiplier definition changes to 1,024. One kilobit, for example, equals 1,000 bits, and one kilobyte equals 1,024 bytes.

kilobyte (K)   A unit of information storage equal to 1,024 bytes.

L1 cache (level one)   A memory cache that is built into the CPU core of 486 and later generation processors. See *cache* and *disk cache*.

L2 cache (level two)   A second-level memory cache that is external to the processor core, usually larger and slower than L1. Normally found on the motherboard of 386, 486, and Pentium systems and inside the processor package or module in Pentium Pro and Pentium II systems. Moving the L2 cache onto the processor in the Pentium Pro and Pentium II allows it to run at speeds up to full processor speed rather than motherboard speed. See *SEC (single edge contact) cartridge, cache,* and *disk cache*.

landing zone   An unused track on a disk surface on which the read/write heads can land when power is shut off. The place that a parking program or a drive with an autopark mechanism parks the heads.

LAPM   Link-access procedure for modems. An error-control protocol incorporated in CCITT Recommendation V.42. Like the MNP and HST protocols, uses cyclic redundancy checking (CRC) and retransmission of corrupted data (ARQ) to ensure data reliability.

laptop computer   A computer system smaller than a briefcase but larger than a notebook that usually has a clamshell design in which the keyboard and display are on separate halves of the system, which are hinged together. These systems normally run on battery power.

large mode   Another name for the LBA translation scheme used by IDE drives to translate the cylinder, head, and sector specifications of the drive to those usable by an enhanced BIOS.

large scale integration   See *IC*.

laser printer   A type of printer that is a combination of an electrostatic copying machine and a computer printer. The output data from the computer is converted by an interface into a raster feed, similar to the impulses that a TV picture tube receives. The impulses cause the laser beam to scan a small drum that carries a positive electrical charge. Where the laser hits, the drum is discharged. A toner, which also carries a positive charge, is then applied to the drum. This toner, a fine black powder, sticks only to the areas of the drum that have been discharged electrically. As it rotates, the drum deposits the toner on a negatively charged sheet of paper. Another roller then heats and bonds the toner to the page.

latency   1) The amount of time required for a disk drive to rotate half of a revolution. Represents the average amount of time to locate a specific sector after the heads have arrived at a specific track. Latency is part of the average access time for a drive. 2) The initial setup time required for a memory transfer in DRAM to select the row and column addresses for the memory to be read/written.

LBA Logical Block Addressing. A method used with SCSI and IDE drives to translate the cylinder, head, and sector specifications of the drive to those usable by an enhanced BIOS. LBA is used with drives that are larger than 528M and causes the BIOS to translate the drive's logical parameters to those usable by the system BIOS.

LCC Leadless Chip Carrier. A type of integrated circuit package that has input and output pads rather than leads on its perimeter.

LCD Liquid Crystal Display. A display that uses liquid crystal sealed between two pieces of polarized glass. The polarity of the liquid crystal is changed by an electric current to vary the amount of light that can pass through. Because LCD displays do not generate light, they depend on either the reflection of ambient light or backlighting the screen. The best type of LCD, the active-matrix or thin-film transistor (TFT) LCD, offers fast screen updates and true color capability.

LED Light-Emitting Diode. A semiconductor diode that emits light when a current is passed through it.

LIF Low Insertion Force. A type of socket that requires only a minimum of force to insert a chip carrier.

light pen A handheld input device with a light-sensitive probe or stylus connected to the computer's graphics adapter board by a cable. Used for writing or sketching onscreen or as a pointing device for making selections. Unlike mice, not widely supported by software applications.

line voltage The AC voltage available at a standard wall outlet, nominally 110-120v.

Lithium Ion A portable system battery type that is longer-lived than either NiCad or NiMH technologies, cannot be overcharged, and holds a charge well when not in use. Lithium Ion batteries are also lighter weight than the either NiCad or NiMH technologies. Because of these superior features, Li-ion batteries have come to be used in all but the very low end of the portable system market.

local area network (LAN) The connection of two or more computers, usually via a network adapter card or NIC.

local bus A generic term used to describe a bus that is directly attached to a processor and which operates at the processor's speed and data transfer width.

local echo A modem feature that enables the modem to send copies of keyboard commands and transmitted data to the screen. When the modem is in command mode (not online to another system), the local echo normally is invoked through an ATE1 command, which causes the modem to display your typed commands. When the modem is online to another system, the local echo is invoked by an ATF0 command, which causes the modem to display the data it transmits to the remote system.

logical drive A drive as named by a DOS drive specifier, such as C: or D:. Under DOS 3.3 or later, a single physical drive can act as several logical drives, each with its own specifier.

logical unit number See *LUN*.

lossless compression   A compression technique that preserves all the original information in an image or other data structures.

lossy compression   A compression technique that achieves optimal data reduction by discarding redundant and unnecessary information in an image.

lost clusters   Clusters that have been marked accidentally as "unavailable" in the FAT even though they don't belong to any file listed in a directory. See also *clusters* and *allocation units.*

low-level formatting   Formatting that divides tracks into sectors on the platter surfaces. Places sector-identifying information before and after each sector and fills each sector with null data (usually hex F6). Specifies the sector interleave and marks defective tracks by placing invalid checksum figures in each sector on a defective track.

LPT port   Line Printer port, a common system abbreviation for a parallel printer port.

LPX   A semi-proprietary motherboard design used in many Low Profile or Slimline case systems. Because there is no formal standard, these are typically not interchangeable between vendors and are often difficult to find replacement parts for repair or upgrade.

luminance   Measure of brightness usually used in specifying monitor brightness.

LUN   Logical Unit Number. A number given to a device (a logical unit) attached to a SCSI physical unit and not directly to the SCSI bus. Although as many as eight logical units can be attached to a single physical unit, normally a single logical unit is a built-in part of a single physical unit. A SCSI hard disk, for example, has a built-in SCSI bus adapter that is assigned a physical unit number or SCSI ID, and the controller and drive portions of the hard disk are assigned a LUN (usually 0). Also see *PUN.*

LZH   Lempel Zev Welch. A compression scheme used in the GIF graphic format.

machine address   A hexadecimal (hex) location in memory.

machine language   Hexadecimal program code that a computer can understand and execute. It can be output from assembler or compiler.

magnetic domain   A tiny segment of a track just large enough to hold one of the magnetic flux reversals that encode data on a disk surface.

magneto-optical recording   An erasable optical disk recording technique that uses a laser beam to heat pits on the disk surface to the point at which a magnet can make flux changes.

magnetoresistive   A technology originally developed by IBM and commonly used for the read element of a read/write head on a high-density magnetic disk. Based on the principle that the resistance to electricity changes in a material when brought in contact with a magnetic field, in this case, the read element material and the magnetic bit. Such drives use a magnetoresistive read sensor for reading and a standard inductive element for writing. A magnetoresistive read head is more sensitive to magnetic fields than inductive read heads.

mask   A photographic map of the circuits for a particular layer of a semiconductor chip used in manufacturing the chip.

master partition boot sector   On hard disks, a one-sector record that gives essential information about the disk and tells the starting locations of the various partitions. Always the first physical sector of the disk.

math coprocessor   A processing chip designed to quickly handle complex arithmetic computations involving floating-point arithmetic, offloading these from the main processor. Originally contained in a separate coprocessor chip, starting with the 486 family of processors, Intel has incorporated the math coprocessor into the main processors in what is called the floating-point unit.

MCA   Micro Channel Architecture. Developed by IBM for the PS/2 line of computers and introduced on April 2, 1987. Features include a 16- or 32-bit bus width and multiple master control. By allowing several processors to arbitrate for resources on a single bus, the MCA is optimized for multitasking, multiprocessor systems. Offers switchless configuration of adapters, which eliminates one of the biggest headaches of installing older adapters.

MCGA   MultiColor Graphics Array. A type of PC video display circuit introduced by IBM on April 2, 1987, that supports text and graphics. Text is supported at a maximum resolution of 80×25 characters in 16 colors with a character box of 8×16 pixels. Graphics is supported at a maximum resolution of 320×200 pixels in 256 (from a palette of 262,144) colors or 640×480 pixels in two colors. The MCGA outputs an analog signal with a horizontal scanning frequency of 31.5KHz, and supports analog color or analog monochrome displays.

MCI   Media Control Interface. A device-independent specification for controlling multimedia devices and files. MCI is a part of the multimedia extensions and offers a standard interface set of device control commands. MCI commands are used for audio recording and playback and animation playback. Device types include CD audio, digital audio tape players, scanners, MIDI sequencers, videotape players or recorders, and audio devices that play digitized waveform files.

MDA   Monochrome Display Adapter (also, MGA—Mono Graphics Adapter). A type of PC video display adapter introduced by IBM on August 12, 1981, that supports text only. Text is supported at a maximum resolution of 80×25 characters in four colors with a character box of 9×14 pixels. Colors, in this case, indicate black, white, bright white, and underlined. Graphics modes are not supported. The MDA outputs a digital signal with a horizontal scanning frequency of 18.432KHz, and supports TTL monochrome displays. The IBM MDA also included a parallel printer port.

mean time between failure   See *MTBF*.

mean time to repair   See *MTTR*.

medium   The magnetic coating or plating that covers a disk or tape.

mega   A multiplier indicating 1 million (1,000,000) of some unit. Abbreviated as m or M. When used to indicate a number of bytes of memory storage, the multiplier definition changes to 1,048,576. One megabit, for example, equals 1,000,000 bits, and one megabyte equals 1,048,576 bytes.

megabyte (M)   A unit of information storage equal to 1,048,576 bytes.

memory   Any component in a computer system that stores information for future use.

memory caching   A service provided by extremely fast memory chips that keeps copies of the most recent memory accesses. When the CPU makes a subsequent access, the value is supplied by the fast memory rather than by relatively slow system memory.

memory-resident program   A program that remains in memory after it has been loaded, consuming memory that otherwise might be used by application software.

menu software   Utility software that makes a computer easier to use by replacing DOS commands with a series of menu selections.

MFM encoding   Modified Frequency Modulation encoding. A method of encoding data on the surface of a disk. The coding of a bit of data varies by the coding of the preceding bit to preserve clocking information.

MHz   An abbreviation for megahertz, a unit of measurement indicating the frequency of one million cycles per second. One hertz (Hz) is equal to one cycle per second. Named after Heinrich R. Hertz, a German physicist who first detected electromagnetic waves in 1883.

MI/MIC   Mode Indicate/Mode Indicate Common. Also called *forced* or *manual originate*. Provided for installations in which equipment other than the modem does the dialing. In such installations, the modem operates in dumb mode (no auto-dial capability), yet must go off-hook in originate mode to connect with answering modems.

micro (μ)   A prefix indicating one millionth (1/1,000,000 or .000001) of some unit.

Micron   A unit of measurement equaling one millionth of a meter. Often used in measuring the size of circuits in chip manufacturing processes. Current state-of-the-art chip fabrication builds chips with 0.25 micron circuits.

microprocessor   A solid-state central processing unit much like a computer on a chip. An integrated circuit that accepts coded instructions for execution.

microsecond (μs)   A unit of time equal to one millionth (1/1,000,000 or .000001) of a second.

MIDI   Musical Instrument Digital Interface. An interface and file format standard for connecting a musical instrument to a microcomputer and storing musical instrument data. Multiple musical instruments can be daisy-chained and played simultaneously with the help of the computer and related software. The various operations of the instruments can be captured, saved, edited, and played back. A MIDI file contains note information, timing (how long a note is held), volume, and instrument type for as many as 16 channels. Sequencer programs are used to control MIDI functions such as recording, playback, and editing. MIDI files store only note instructions and not actual sound data.

milli (m)   A prefix indicating one thousandth (1/1,000 or .001) of some unit.

millisecond (ms)   A unit of time equal to one thousandth (1/1,000 or .001) of a second.

MTTR   Mean Time To Repair. A measure of the probable time it will take a technician to service or repair a specific device, usually given in hours.

MultiColor Graphics Array   See *MCGA*.

multimedia   The integration of sound, graphic images, animation, motion video, and text in one environment on a computer. It is a set of hardware and software technologies that are rapidly changing and enhancing the computing environment.

multisession   A term used in CD-ROM recording to describe a recording event. Multisession capabilities allow data recording on the disk at different times in several recording sessions. Kodak's Photo CD is an example of CD-R technology. See also *session (single or multisession)*.

multitask   To run several programs simultaneously.

multithread   To concurrently process more than one message by an application program. OS/2, Windows 95, and Windows NT are examples of multithreaded operating systems. Each program can start two or more threads, which carry out various interrelated tasks with less overhead than two separate programs would require.

multiuser system   A system in which several computer terminals share the same central processing unit (CPU).

nano (n)   A prefix indicating one billionth (1/1,000,000,000 or .000000001) of some unit.

nanosecond (ns)   A unit of time equal to one billionth (1/1,000,000,000 or .000000001) of a second.

NetBEUI   NetBIOS Extended User Interface. A network protocol used primarily by Windows NT and most suitable for small peer-to-peer networks.

NetBIOS   Network Basic Input/Output System. A commonly used network protocol originally developed by IBM and Sytek for PC local area networks. NetBIOS provides session and transport services (layers 4 and 5 of the OSI model).

network   A system in which a number of independent computers are linked to share data and peripherals, such as hard disks and printers.

Network Interface Card (NIC)   An adapter that connects a PC to a network.

network layer   In the OSI reference model, the layer that switches and routes the packets as necessary to get them to their destinations. This layer is responsible for addressing and delivering message packets.

NiCad   The oldest of the three battery technologies used in portable systems, nickel cadmium batteries are rarely used in portable systems today because of their shorter life and their sensitivity to improper charging and discharging. See also *NiMH* and *Lithium Ion*.

NiMH   A battery technology used in portable systems. Nickel Metal-Hydride batteries have approximately a 30% longer life than NiCads, are less sensitive to the memory effect caused by improper charging and discharging, and do not use the environmentally dangerous substances found in NiCads. Newer Lithium Ion (Li-ion) batteries are far superior.

NLX   A new low-profile motherboard form factor standard that is basically an improved version of the semiproprietary LPX design. Designed to accommodate larger processor and memory form factors and incorporate newer bus technologies such as AGP and USB. Besides design improvements, it is fully standardized, which means you should be able to replace one NLX board with another from a different manufacturer, something that was not normally possible with LPX.

noninterlaced monitor   A desirable monitor design where the electron beam sweeps the screen in lines from top to bottom, one line after the other, completing the entire screen in one pass.

nonvolatile memory (NVRAM)   Random-access memory whose data is retained when power is turned off. Sometimes NVRAM is retained without any power whatsoever, as in EEPROM or flash memory devices. In other cases, the memory is maintained by a small battery. NVRAM that is battery maintained is sometimes also called *CMOS memory*. *CMOS NVRAM* is used in IBM-compatible systems to store configuration information. *True NVRAM* often is used in intelligent modems to store a user-defined default configuration loaded into normal modem RAM at power-up.

nonvolatile RAM disk   A RAM disk powered by a battery supply so that it continues to hold its data during a power outage.

North Bridge   The Intel term for the main portion of the motherboard chipset that incorporates the interface between the processor and the rest of the motherboard. The North Bridge contains the cache, main memory, and AGP controllers as well as the interface between the high-speed (normally 66MHz or 100MHz) processor bus and the 33MHz PCI (Peripheral Component Interconnect) or 66MHz AGP (Accelerated Graphics Port) buses. See also *chipset* and *South Bridge*.

notebook computer   A very small personal computer approximately the size of a notebook.

NTSC   The National Television Standards Committee, which governs the standard for television and video playback and recording in the United States. The NTSC was originally organized in 1941 when TV broadcasting first began on a wide scale in black and white, and the format was revised in 1953 for color. The NTSC format has 525 scan lines, a field frequency of 60Hz, a broadcast bandwidth of 4MHz, line frequency of 15.75KHz, frame frequency of 1/30 of a second, and a color subcarrier frequency of 3.58MHz. It is an interlaced signal, which means that it scans every other line each time the screen is refreshed. The signal is generated as a composite of red, green, and blue signals for color and includes an FM frequency for audio and a signal for stereo. See also *PAL* and *SECAM*, which are incompatible systems used in Europe. NTSC is also called *composite video*.

null modem   A serial cable wired so that two data terminal equipment (DTE) devices, such as personal computers, or two data communication equipment (DCE) devices, such as modems or mice, can be connected. Also sometimes called a *modem-eliminator* or a *LapLink cable*. To make a null-modem cable with DB-25 connectors, you wire these pins together: 1-1, 2-3, 3-2, 4-5, 5-4, 6-8-20, 20-8-6, and 7-7.

numeric coprocessor   See *math coprocessor*.

NVRAM   Nonvolatile Random Access Memory. Memory that retains data without power. Flash memory and battery-backed CMOS RAM are examples of NVRAM.

object hierarchy   Occurs in a graphical program when two or more objects are linked and one object's movement is dependent on the other object. This is known as a *parent-child hierarchy*. In an example using a human figure, the fingers would be child objects to the hand, which is a child object to the arm, which is a child to the shoulder, and so on. Object hierarchy provides much control for an animator in moving complex figures.

OCR   Optical Character Recognition. An information-processing technology that converts human-readable text into computer data. Usually a scanner is used to read the text on a page, and OCR software converts the images to characters.

ODI   Open Data-link Interface. A device driver standard from Novell that allows you to run multiple protocols on the same network adapter card. ODI adds functionality to Novell's NetWare and network computing environments by supporting multiple protocols and drivers.

OEM   Original Equipment Manufacturer. Any manufacturer that sells its product to a reseller. Usually refers to the original manufacturer of a particular device or component. Most Compaq hard disks, for example, are made by Conner Peripherals, who is considered the OEM.

OLE   Object Linking and Embedding. An enhancement to the original Dynamic Data Exchange (DDE) protocol that allows you to embed or link data created in one application in a document created in another application and subsequently edit that data directly from the final document.

online fallback   A feature that enables high-speed error-control modems to monitor line quality and fall back to the next lower speed if line quality degrades. Some modems fall forward as line quality improves.

open architecture   A system design in which the specifications are made public to encourage third-party vendors to develop add-on products. The PC is a true open architecture system, but the Macintosh is proprietary.

operating system (OS)   A collection of programs for operating the computer. Operating systems perform housekeeping tasks such as input and output between the computer and peripherals and accepting and interpreting information from the keyboard. DOS and OS/2 are examples of popular OSs.

optical disk   A disk that encodes data as a series of reflective pits that are read (and sometimes written) by a laser beam.

Orange Book   The standard for recordable compact discs (like CD-ROM, but recordable instead of read-only). Recordable compact discs are called *CD-R* and are becoming popular with the widespread use of multimedia. Part of the Orange Book standard defines rewritable Magneto-Optical disks and another section defines optical Write Once Read Many (WORM) disks.

originate mode   A state in which the modem transmits at the predefined low frequency of the communications channel and receives at the high frequency. The transmit/receive frequencies are the reverse of the called modem, which is in answer mode. See also *answer mode*.

OS/2   An operating system originally developed through a joint effort by IBM and Microsoft Corporation and later by IBM alone. Originally released in 1987, OS/2 is a 32-bit operating system designed to run on computers using the Intel 386 or later microprocessors. The OS/2 Workplace Shell, an integral part of the system, is a graphical interface similar to Microsoft Windows and the Apple Macintosh system.

OSI (Open Systems Interconnection) Reference Model   Developed by the International Organization for Standardization (abbreviated as the ISO) in the 1980s, the OSI model splits a computer's networking stack into seven discrete layers. Each layer provides specific services to the layers above and below it.

output   Information processed by the computer, or the act of sending that information to a mass storage device such as a video display, a printer, or a modem.

over-clocking   The process of running a processor at a speed faster than the officially marked speed by using a higher clock multiplier or faster bus speed. Not recommended or endorsed by processor manufacturers. See also *clock multiplier*.

OverDrive   An Intel trademark name for its line of upgrade processors.

overlay   Part of a program that is loaded into memory only when it is required.

overrun   A situation in which data moves from one device faster than a second device can accept it.

overscanning   A technique used in consumer display products that extends the deflection of a CRT's electron beam beyond the physical boundaries of the screen to ensure that images will always fill the display area. See also *underscanning*.

overwrite   To write data on top of existing data, thus erasing the existing data.

package   A device that includes a chip mounted on a carrier and sealed.

pairing   Combining processor instructions for optimal execution on superscalar processors.

PAL   1) Phase Alternating Line system. Invented in 1961, a system of TV broadcasting used in England and other European countries (except France). PAL's image format is 4:3, 625 lines, 50Hz, and 4MHz video bandwidth with a total 8MHz of video channel width. With its 625-line picture delivered at 25 frames per second, PAL provides a better image and an improved color transmission over the NTSC system used in North America. 2) PAL also stands for *Programmable Array Logic*, a type of chip that has logic gates specified by a device programmer.

palmtop computer   A computer system smaller than a notebook that is designed so that it can be held in one hand while being operated by the other. Many are now called *PDAs* or *personal digital assistants*.

parallel   A method of transferring data characters in which the bits travel down parallel electrical paths simultaneously—for example, eight paths for 8-bit characters. Data is stored in computers in parallel form but may be converted to serial form for certain operations.

parity   A method of error checking in which an extra bit is sent to the receiving device to indicate whether an even or odd number of binary 1 bits were transmitted. The receiving unit compares the received information with this bit and can obtain a reasonable judgment about the validity of the character. The same type of parity (even or odd) must be used by two communicating computers, or both may omit parity. When parity is used, a parity bit is added to each transmitted character. The bit's value is 0 or 1, to make the total number of 1s in the character even or odd, depending on which type of parity is used.

park program   A program that executes a seek to the highest cylinder or just past the highest cylinder of a drive so that the potential of data loss is minimized if the drive is moved.

partition   A section of a hard disk devoted to a particular operating system. Most hard disks have only one partition, devoted to DOS. A hard disk can have as many as four partitions, each occupied by a different operating system. DOS v3.3 or later can occupy two of these four partitions.

Pascal   A high-level programming language named for the French mathematician Blaise Pascal (1623-1662). Developed in the early 1970s by Niklaus Wirth for teaching programming and designed to support the concepts of structured programming.

passive matrix   Another name for *dual scan display* type LCDs.

PC Card (PCMCIA)   Personal Computer Memory Card International Association. A credit card-sized expansion adapter for notebook and laptop PCs. PC Card is the official PCMCIA trademark; however, both PC Card and PCMCIA card are used to refer to these standards. PCMCIA cards are removable modules that can hold numerous types of devices including memory, modems, fax/modems, radio transceivers, network adapters, solid state disks, and hard disks.

PCI   Peripheral Component Interconnect. A standard bus specification initially developed by Intel that bypasses the standard ISA I/O bus and uses the system bus to increase the bus clock speed and take full advantage of the CPU's data path.

PCL   Printer Control Language. Developed by Hewlett-Packard in 1984 as a language for the HP LaserJet printer. PCL is now the de facto industry standard for PC printing. PCL defines a standard set of commands, enabling applications to communicate with HP or HP-compatible printers, and is supported by virtually all printer manufacturers.

peer-to-peer   A type of network in which any computer can act as both a server (by providing access to its resources to other computers) and a client (by accessing shared resources from other computers).

PEL   See *pixel*.

Pentium   An Intel microprocessor with 32-bit registers, a 64-bit data bus, and a 32-bit address bus. The Pentium has a built-in Level 1 cache that is segmented into a separate 8K cache for code and another 8K cache for data. The Pentium includes an FPU (floating-point unit) or math coprocessor. The Pentium is backward-compatible with the 486 and can operate in real, protected virtual, and virtual real modes.

Pentium II   An Intel sixth-generation processor similar to the Pentium Pro, but with MMX capabilities and single edge contact (SEC) cartridge packaging technology.

Pentium Pro   An Intel sixth-generation processor with 32-bit registers, a 64-bit data bus, and a 36-bit address bus. The Pentium Pro has the same segmented Level 1 cache as the Pentium but also includes a 256K, 512K, or 1M of Level 2 cache on separate die(s) inside the processor package. The Pentium Pro includes a FPU (floating-point unit) or math coprocessor. The Pentium Pro is backward-compatible with the Pentium and can operate in real, protected, and virtual real modes.

peripheral   Any piece of equipment used in computer systems that is an attachment to the computer. Disk drives, terminals, and printers are all examples of peripherals.

persistence   In a monitor, the quality of the phosphor chemical that indicates how long the glow caused by the electrons striking the phosphor will remain onscreen.

PGA   1) Pin-Grid Array. A chip package that has a large number of pins on the bottom designed for socket mounting. 2) Also a Professional Graphics Adapter, a limited-production, high-resolution graphics card for XT and AT systems from IBM.

Photo CD   A technology developed by Eastman Kodak and Philips that stores photographic images on a CD-R recordable compact disc. Images stored on the Photo CD may have resolutions as high as 2,048×3,072 pixels. Up to 100 true-color images (24-bit color) can be stored on one disk. Photo CD images are created by scanning film and digitally recording the images on compact discs (CDs). The digitized images are indexed (given a 4-digit code), and thumbnails of each image on the disc are shown on the front of the case along with its index number. Multisession capability allows several rolls of film to be added to a single disk on different occasions.

photolithography   The photographic process used in electronic chip manufacturing that creates transistors and circuit and signal pathways in semiconductors by depositing different layers of various materials on the chip.

photoresist   A chemical used to coat a silicon wafer in the semiconductor manufacturing process that makes the silicon sensitive to light for photolithography.

physical drive   A single disk drive. DOS defines logical drives, which are given a specifier, such as C: or D:. A single physical drive may be divided into multiple logical drives. Conversely, special software can span a single logical drive across two physical drives.

physical unit number   See *PUN*.

PIF   Program Information File. A file that contains information about a non-Windows application specifying optimum settings for running the program under Windows 3.x. These are called *property sheets* in Windows 95.

pin   1) The lead on a connector, chip, module or device. 2) Personal Identification Number. A personal password used for identification purposes.

pin compatible   Chips having the same pinout functions.

pinout   A listing of which pins have what functions on a chip, socket, slot, or other connector.

PIO mode   Programmed Input/Output mode. The standard data transfer modes used by IDE drives that use the processor's registers for data transfer. This is in contrast with DMA modes, which transfer data directly between main memory and the device. The slowest PIO mode is 0 and the fastest current mode is mode 4.

pipeline   A path for instructions or data to follow.

pixel   A mnemonic term meaning picture element. Any of the tiny elements that form a picture on a video display screen. Also called a *pel*.

planar board   A term equivalent to *motherboard*, used by IBM in some of its literature.

plated media   Hard disk platters plated with a form of thin metal film medium on which data is recorded.

platter   A disk contained in a hard disk drive. Most drives have two or more platters, each with data recorded on both sides.

PLCC   Plastic Leaded-Chip Carrier. A popular chip-carrier package with J-leads around the perimeter of the package.

Plug and Play (PnP)   A hardware and software specification developed by Intel that allows a PnP system and PnP adapter cards to automatically configure themselves. PnP cards are free from switches and jumpers and are configured via the PnP BIOS in the host system, or via supplied programs for non-PnP systems.

polling   A communications technique that determines when a device is ready to send data. The system continually interrogates polled devices in a round-robin sequence. If a device has data to send, it sends back an acknowledgment and the transmission begins. Contrasts with interrupt-driven communications, in which the device generates a signal to interrupt the system when it has data to send.

port   Plug or socket that enables an external device such as a printer to be attached to the adapter card in the computer. Also a logical address used by a microprocessor for communications between it and various devices.

port address   One of a system of addresses used by the computer to access devices such as disk drives or printer ports. You may need to specify an unused port address when installing any adapter boards in a system unit.

port replicator   For mobile computers, a device that plugs into the laptop and provides all of the ports for connecting external devices. The advantage of using a port replicator is that the external devices can be left connected to the replicator and the mobile computer connected to them all at once by connecting to the replicator, rather than connecting to each individual device. A port replicator differs from a docking station in that the latter can provide additional drive bays and expansion slots not found in port replicators.

portable computer   A computer system smaller than a transportable system but larger than a laptop system. Most portable systems conform to the lunchbox style popularized by Compaq or the briefcase style popularized by IBM, each with a fold-down (removable) keyboard and built-in display. These systems characteristically run on AC power and not on batteries, include several expansion slots, and can be as powerful as full desktop systems.

POS Programmable Option Select. The Micro Channel Architecture's POS eliminates switches and jumpers from the system board and adapters by replacing them with programmable registers. Automatic configuration routines store the POS data in a battery-powered CMOS memory for system configuration and operations. The configuration utilities rely on adapter description files (ADF) that contain the setup data for each card.

POST Power-On Self Test. A series of tests run by the computer at power-on. Most computers scan and test many of their circuits and sound a beep from the internal speaker if this initial test indicates proper system performance.

PostScript A page-description language developed primarily by John Warnock of Adobe Systems for converting and moving data to the laser-printed page. Instead of using the standard method of transmitting graphics or character information to a printer, telling it where to place dots one-by-one on a page, PostScript provides a way for the laser printer to interpret mathematically a full page of shapes and curves.

POTS Plain Old Telephone Service. Standard analog telephone service.

power management Systems used initially in mobile computers (and now also used in desktop systems) to decrease power consumption by turning off or slowing down devices during periods of inactivity. See *APM*.

power supply An electrical/electronic circuit that supplies all operating voltage and current to the computer system.

PPGA Plastic Pin Grid Array. A chip-packaging form factor used by Intel as an alternative to traditional ceramic packaging.

PPP Point-to-Point Protocol. A protocol that allows a computer to use the Internet with a standard telephone line and a high-speed modem. PPP is a new standard that replaces SLIP. PPP is less common than SLIP; however, it is increasing in popularity.

precompensation A data write modification required by some older drives on the inner cylinders to compensate for the higher density of data on the (smaller) inner cylinders.

primary partition An ordinary, single-volume bootable partition. See also *extended partition*.

processor See *microprocessor*.

processor speed The clock rate at which a microprocessor processes data. A typical Pentium PC, for example, operates at 200MHz (200 million cycles per second).

program A set of instructions or steps telling the computer how to handle a problem or task.

PROM Programmable Read-Only Memory. A type of memory chip that can be programmed to store information permanently—information that cannot be erased.

proprietary   Anything invented by one company and that uses components only available from that one company. Especially applies to cases in which the inventing company goes to lengths to hide the specifications of the new invention or to prevent other manufacturers from making similar or compatible items. The opposite of *standard* or *open architecture*. Computers with nonstandard components that are available only from the original manufacturer, such as Apple Macintosh systems, are known as proprietary.

protected mode   A mode available in all Intel and compatible processors except the first-generation 8086 and 8088. In this mode, memory addressing is extended beyond the 1M limits of the 8088 and real mode, and restricted protection levels can be set to trap software crashes and control the system.

protocol   A system of rules and procedures governing communications between two or more devices. Protocols vary, but communicating devices must follow the same protocol to exchange data. The data format, readiness to receive or send, error detection, and error correction are some of the operations that may be defined in protocols.

PS/2 mouse   A mouse designed to plug into a dedicated mouse port (a round, 6-pin DIN connector) on the motherboard, rather than plug into a serial port. The name comes from the fact that this port was first introduced on the IBM PS/2 systems.

PUN   Physical Unit Number. A term used to describe a device attached directly to the SCSI bus. Also known as a *SCSI ID*. As many as eight SCSI devices can be attached to a single SCSI bus, and each must have a unique PUN or ID assigned from 7 to 0. Normally, the SCSI host adapter is assigned the highest-priority ID, which is 7. A bootable hard disk is assigned an ID of 0, and other nonbootable drives are assigned higher priorities.

QAM   Quadrature Amplitude Modulation. A modulation technique used by high-speed modems that combines both phase and amplitude modulation. This technique enables multiple bits to be encoded in a single time interval.

QIC   Quarter-Inch Committee. An industry association that sets hardware and software standards for tape-backup units that use quarter-inch-wide tapes.

QWERTY keyboard   The standard typewriter or computer keyboard, with the characters Q, W, E, R, T, and Y on the top row of alpha keys. Because of the haphazard placement of characters, this keyboard can hinder fast typing.

rails   Plastic strips attached to the sides of disk drives mounted in IBM ATs and compatibles so that the drives can slide into place. These rails fit into channels in the side of each disk drive bay position.

RAM   Random-Access Memory. All memory accessible at any instant (randomly) by a microprocessor.

RAM disk   A "phantom disk drive" in which a section of system memory (RAM) is set aside to hold data, just as though it were a number of disk sectors. To DOS, a RAM disk looks like and functions like any other drive.

RAMBUS Dynamic RAM   See *RDRAM*.

random-access file   A file in which all data elements (or records) are of equal length and written in the file end to end, without delimiting characters between. Any element (or record) in the file can be found directly by calculating the record's offset in the file.

random-access memory   See *RAM*.

raster   A pattern of horizontal scanning lines normally on a computer monitor. An electromagnetic field causes the beam of the monitor's tube to illuminate the correct dots to produce the required characters.

raster graphics   A technique for representing a picture image as a matrix of dots. It is the digital counterpart of the analog method used in TV. There are several raster graphics standards.

RCA jack   Also called a *phono connector*. A plug and socket for a two-wire coaxial cable used to connect audio and video components. The plug is a 1/8-inch thick prong that sticks out 5/16-inch from the middle of a cylinder.

RDRAM   Rambus DRAM. A high-speed dynamic RAM technology developed by Rambus, Inc., which will be supported by Intel's 1999 and later motherboard chipsets. RDRAM transfers data at 1G/sec or faster, which is significantly faster than SDRAM and other technologies and which will be able to keep up with future-generation high-speed processors. Memory modules with RDRAM chips are called RIMMs (Rambus Inline Memory Modules). Rambus licenses its technology to other semiconductor companies, who manufacture the chips and RIMMs.

read/write head   A tiny magnet that reads and writes data on a disk track.

read-only file   A file whose attribute setting in the file's directory entry tells DOS not to allow software to write into or over the file.

read-only memory   See *ROM*.

real mode   A mode available in all Intel 8086-compatible processors that enables compatibility with the original 8086. In this mode, memory addressing is limited to 1M.

real time   The actual time in which a program or event takes place. In computing, real time refers to an operating mode under which data is received and processed and the results returned so quickly that the process appears instantaneous to the user. The term is also used to describe the process of simultaneous digitization and compression of audio and video information.

reboot   The process of restarting a computer and reloading the operating system.

Red Book   More commonly known as Compact Disc-Digital Audio (CD-DA), and is one of four compact disc standards. Red Book got its name from the color of the manual used to describe the CD Audio specifications. The Red Book audio standard requires that digital audio be sampled at a 44.1KHz sample rate using 16 bits for each sample. This is the standard used by audio CDs and many CD-ROMs. See also *CD-A* and *CD-DA*.

refresh cycle   A cycle in which the computer accesses all memory locations stored by DRAM chips so that the information remains intact. DRAM chips must be accessed several times a second, or else the information fades.

refresh rate   Another term for the vertical scan frequency of monitors.

register   Storage area in memory having a specified storage capacity, such as a bit, a byte, or a computer word, and intended for a special purpose.

Registry   The system configuration files used by Windows 9x and Windows NT to store settings about installed hardware and drivers, user preferences, installed software, and other settings required to keep Windows running correctly. Replaces the WIN.INI and SYSTEM.INI files from Windows 3.x.

remote digital loopback   A test that checks the phone link and a remote modem's transmitter and receiver. Data entered from the keyboard is transmitted from the initiating modem, received by the remote modem's receiver, looped through its transmitter, and returned to the local screen for verification.

remote echo   A copy of the data received by the remote system, returned to the sending system, and displayed onscreen. A function of the remote system.

resolution   1) A reference to the size of the pixels used in graphics. In medium-resolution graphics, pixels are large. In high-resolution graphics, pixels are small. 2) A measure of the number of horizontal and vertical pixels that can be displayed by a video adapter and monitor.

RFI   Radio Frequency Interference. A high frequency signal radiated by improperly shielded conductors, particularly when signal path lengths are comparable to or longer than the signal wavelengths. The FCC now regulates RFI in computer equipment sold in the U.S. under FCC Regulations Part 15, Subpart J.

RGB   Red-Green-Blue. A type of computer color display output signal comprised of separately controllable red, green, and blue signals; as opposed to composite video, in which signals are combined prior to output. RGB monitors typically offer higher resolution than composite monitors.

ribbon cable   Flat cable with wires running in parallel, such as those used for internal IDE or SCSI.

RISC   Reduced Instruction Set Computer. Differentiated from CISC, Complex Instruction Set Computer. RISC processors have simple instruction sets requiring only one or a few execution cycles. These simple instructions can be used more effectively than CISC systems with appropriately designed software, resulting in faster operations. See also *CISC*.

RJ-11   The standard 2-wire connector type used for single-line telephone connections.

RJ-14   The standard 4-wire connector type used for two-line telephone connections.

RJ-45   A standard connector type used in networking with twisted-pair cabling. Resembles an RJ-11/14 telephone jack, but RJ-45 is larger with more wires.

RLL   Run-Length Limited. A type of encoding that derives its name from the fact that the techniques used limit the distance (run length) between magnetic flux reversals on the disk platter. Several types of RLL encoding techniques exist, although only two are commonly used. (1,7)RLL encoding increases storage capacity by about 30% over MFM encoding and is most popular in the very highest capacity drives due to a better window margin, while (2,7)RLL encoding increases storage capacity by 50% over MFM encoding and is used in the majority of RLL implementations. Most IDE, ESDI, and SCSI hard disks use one of these forms of RLL encoding.

RMA number Return-Merchandise Authorization Number. A number given to you by a vendor when you arrange to return an item for repairs. Used to track the item and the repair.

ROM Read-Only Memory. A type of memory that has values permanently or semi-permanently burned in. These locations are used to hold important programs or data that must be available to the computer when the power initially is turned on.

ROM BIOS Read Only Memory-Basic Input Output System. A BIOS encoded in a form of read-only memory for protection. Often applied to important startup programs that must be present in a system for it to operate.

root directory The main directory of any hard or floppy disk. Has a fixed size and location for a particular disk volume and cannot be resized dynamically the way subdirectories can.

router Hardware that routes messages from one local area network to another. It is used to internetwork similar and dissimilar networks and can select the most expe-dient route based on traffic load, line speeds, costs, and network failures.

routine Set of frequently used instructions. May be considered as a subdivision of a program with two or more instructions that are related functionally.

RS-232 An interface introduced in August 1969 by the Electronic Industries Associa-tion. The RS-232 interface standard provides an electrical description for connect-ing peripheral devices to computers.

S-Video (Y/C) Type of video signal used in the Hi8 and S-VHS videotape formats in which the luminance and chrominance (Y/C) components are kept separate, pro-viding greater control and quality of each image. S-video transmits luminance and color portions separately, thus avoiding the NTSC encoding process and its inevi-table loss of picture quality.

scan codes The hexadecimal codes actually sent by the keyboard to the motherboard when a key is pressed.

scan lines The parallel lines across a video screen, along which the scanning spot travels in painting the video information that makes up a monitor picture. NTSC systems use 525 scan lines to a screen; PAL systems use 625.

scanning frequency A monitor measurement that specifies how often the image is refreshed. See also *vertical scan frequency*.

scratch disk A disk that contains no useful information and can be used as a test disk. IBM has a routine on the Advanced Diagnostics disks that creates a specially for-matted scratch disk to be used for testing floppy drives.

SCSI Small Computer System Interface. A standard originally developed by Shugart Associates (then called SASI for Shugart Associates System Interface) and later ap-proved by ANSI in 1986. SCSI-2 was approved in 1994, and SCSI-3 is currently in the development process. Normally uses a 50-pin connector and permits multiple devices (up to eight including the host) to be connected in daisy-chain fashion.

SDLC Synchronous Data Link Control. A protocol developed by IBM for software applications and communicating devices operation in IBM's Systems Network Architecture (SNA). Defines operations at the link level of communications—for example, the format of data frames exchanged between modems over a phone line.

SDRAM Synchronous DRAM. RAM that runs at the same speed as the main system bus.

SEC (Single Edge Contact) cartridge An Intel processor packaging design in which the processor along with several L2 cache chips are mounted on a small circuit board (much like an oversized memory SIMM), which is then sealed in a metal and plastic cartridge. The cartridge is then plugged into the motherboard through an edge connector called Slot 1 or Slot 2, which looks very much like an adapter card slot.

SECAM SEquential Couleur A Mémoire (sequential color with memory), the French color TV system also adopted in Russia. The basis of operation is the sequential recording of primary colors in alternate lines. The image format is 4:3, 625 lines, 50Hz, and 6MHz video bandwidth with a total 8MHz of video channel width.

sector A section of one track defined with identification markings and an identification number. Most sectors hold 512 bytes of data.

security software Utility software that uses a system of passwords and other devices to restrict an individual's access to subdirectories and files.

seek time The amount of time required for a disk drive to move the heads across one third of the total number of cylinders. Represents the average time it takes to move the heads from one cylinder to another randomly selected cylinder. Seek time is a part of the average access time for a drive.

semiconductor A substance, such as germanium or silicon, whose conductivity is poor at low temperatures but is improved by minute additions of certain substances or by the application of heat, light, or voltage. Depending on the temperature and pressure, a semiconductor can control a flow of electricity. Semiconductors are the basis of modern electronic-circuit technology.

sequencer A software program that controls MIDI file messages and keeps track of music timing. Because MIDI files store note instructions instead of actual sounds, a sequencer is needed to play, record, and edit MIDI sounds. Sequencer programs allow for recording and playback of MIDI files by storing the instrument, note pitch (frequency), duration (in real time) that each note is held, and loudness (amplitude) of each musical or sound-effect note.

sequential file A file in which varying-length data elements are recorded end to end, with delimiting characters placed between each element. To find a particular element, you must read the whole file up to that element.

serial The transfer of data characters one bit at a time, sequentially, using a single electrical path.

serial mouse A mouse designed to connect to a computer's serial port.

serial port An I/O connector used to connect to serial devices.

servo The mechanism in a drive that enables the head positioner to adjust continuously so that it is precisely placed above a given cylinder in the drive.

servo data Magnetic markings written on disk platters to guide the read/write heads in drives that use voice-coil actuators.

session (single or multisession) A term used in CD-ROM recording to describe a recording event. In a single session, data is recorded on a CD-ROM disc and an index is created. If additional space is left on the disc, another session can be used to record additional files along with another index. Some older CD-ROM drives do not expect additional recording sessions and therefore will be unable to read the additional session data on the disk. The advent of Kodak's Photo CD propelled the desire for multisession CD-ROM XA (extended architecture) drives.

settling time The time required for read/write heads to stop vibrating after they have been moved to a new track.

shadow mask A thin screen full of holes that adheres to the inside of a color CRT. The electron beam is aimed through the holes in the mask onto the phosphor dots. See also *aperture grille*.

shadow ROM A copy of a system's slower access ROM BIOS placed in faster access RAM, usually during the startup or boot procedure. This setup enables the system to access BIOS code without the penalty of additional wait states required by the slower ROM chips. Also called *shadow RAM*.

shell The generic name of any user interface software. COMMAND.COM is the standard shell for DOS. OS/2 comes with three shells: a DOS command shell, an OS/2 command shell, and the OS/2 Presentation Manager, a graphical shell.

shielded twisted-pair (STP) Unshielded twisted-pair (UTP) network cabling with a metal sheath or braid around it to reduce interference, usually used in Token-Ring networks.

shock rating A rating (usually expressed in G force units) of how much shock a disk drive can sustain without damage. Usually two different specifications exist for a drive powered on or off.

signal-to-noise (S/N) ratio The strength of a video or audio signal in relation to interference (noise). The higher the S/N ratio, the better the quality of the signal.

SIMM Single Inline Memory Module. An array of memory chips on a small PC board with a single row of I/O contacts.

single-ended An electrical signaling method where a single line is referenced by a ground path common to other signals. In a single-ended bus intended for moderately long distances, there is commonly one ground line between groups of signal lines to provide some resistance to signal crosstalk. Single-ended signals require only one driver or receiver pin per signal, plus one ground pin per group of signals. Single-ended signals are vulnerable to common mode noise and crosstalk but are much less expensive than differential signaling methods.

SIP Single Inline Package. A DIP-like package with only one row of leads.

skinny dip Twenty-four- and twenty-eight-position DIP devices with .300-inch row-to-row centerlines.

sleep See *suspend*.

SLIP   Serial Line Internet Protocol. An Internet protocol that is used to run the Internet Protocol (IP) over serial lines such as telephone circuits. IP allows a packet to traverse multiple networks on the way to its final destination.

slot   A physical connector on a motherboard to hold an expansion card, SIMMs and DIMMs, or a processor card in place and make contact with the electrical connections.

Slot 1   The motherboard connector designed by Intel to accept its SEC cartridge processor design used by the Pentium II.

Slot 2   A motherboard connector for Pentium II Xeon processors intended mainly for fileserver applications. Slot 2 systems support up to 4-way symmetric multiprocessing.

SMBIOS   A BIOS that incorporates system management functions and reporting compatible with the Desktop Management Interface (DMI).

SMPTE time code   An 80-bit standardized edit time code adopted by SMPTE, the Society of Motion Picture and Television Engineers. The SMPTE time code is a standard used to identify individual video frames in the video-editing process. SMPTE time code controls such functions as play, record, rewind, and forward of video tapes. SMPTE time code displays video in terms of hours, minutes, seconds, and frames for accurate video editing.

snow   A flurry of bright dots that can appear anywhere onscreen on a monitor.

socket   A receptacle, usually on a motherboard although sometimes also found on expansion cards, that processors or chips can be plugged into.

Socket 1–8   The Intel specifications for eight different sockets to accept various Intel processors in the 486, Pentium, and Pentium Pro families.

soft error   An error in reading or writing data that occurs sporadically, usually because of a transient problem such as a power fluctuation.

software   A series of instructions loaded in the computer's memory that instructs the computer in how to accomplish a problem or task.

SO-J   Small Outline J-lead. A small DIP package with J-shaped leads for surface mounting or socketing.

South Bridge   The Intel term for the lower-speed component in the chipset that has always been a single individual chip. Also called the PIIX (PCI, ISA, IDE eXcelerator), the South Bridge connects to the 33MHz PCI bus and contains the IDE interface ports and the interface to the 8MHz ISA bus. It also normally contains the USB (Universal Serial Bus) interface and even the CMOS RAM and real-time clock functions. The South Bridge contains all of the components that make up the ISA bus, including the interrupt and DMA controllers. See also *chipset* and *North Bridge*.

spindle   The central post on which a disk drive's platters are mounted.

spindle count   In notebook and laptop computers with interchangeable drives, spindle count refers to how many drives can be installed and used at the same time.

SRAM   Static Random Access Memory. A form of high-speed memory. SRAM chips do not require a refresh cycle like DRAM chips and can be made to operate at very high-access speeds. SRAM chips are very expensive because they normally require six transistors per bit. This also makes the chip larger than conventional DRAM chips. SRAM is volatile, meaning it will lose data with no power.

ST-506/412   A hard disk interface invented by Seagate Technology and introduced in 1980 with the ST-506 5M hard drive.

stair-stepping   Jagged raster representation of diagonals or curves; corrected by anti-aliasing.

standby   Defines an optional operating state of minimal power reduction with the shortest recovery time.

standby power supply   A backup power supply that quickly switches into operation during a power outage.

Standoff   In a motherboard and case design, small nonconductive spacers (usually plastic or nylon) used to keep the underside of the motherboard from contacting the metallic case, therefore preventing short circuits of the motherboard.

start/stop bits   The signaling bits attached to a character before and after the character is transmitted during asynchronous transmission.

starting cluster   The number of the first cluster occupied by a file. Listed in the directory entry of every file.

stepper motor actuator   An assembly that moves disk drive read/write heads across platters by a sequence of small partial turns of a stepper motor.

stepping   The code used to identify the revision of a processor. New masks are introduced to build each successive stepping, incorporating any changes needed to fix known bugs in prior steppings.

storage   Device or medium on or in which data can be entered or held and retrieved at a later time. Synonymous with *memory*.

streaming   In tape backup, a condition in which data is transferred from the hard disk as quickly as the tape drive can record the data so that the drive does not start and stop or waste tape.

string   A sequence of characters.

subdirectory   A directory listed in another directory. Subdirectories themselves exist as files.

subroutine   A segment of a program that can be executed by a single call. Also called *program module*.

superscalar execution   The capability of a processor to execute more than one instruction at a time.

surface mount   Chip carriers and sockets designed to mount to the surface of a PC board.

surge protector   A device in the power line that feeds the computer and provides protection against voltage spikes and other transients.

suspend   Refers to a level of power management in which substantial power reduction is achieved by the display or other components. The components can have a longer recovery time from this state than from the standby state.

SVGA (Super VGA)   Originally, this referred to a video adapter or monitor capable of 800×600 resolution. However, this term is now often misused and used to refer to any video adapter or monitor that can display any resolution greater than 640×480.

SWEDAC   Swedish Board for Technical Accreditation. Regulatory agency establishing standards such as MPR1 and MPR2, which specify maximum values for both alternating electric fields and magnetic fields and provide monitor manufacturers with guidelines in creating low-emission monitors.

synchronous communication   A form of communication in which blocks of data are sent at strictly timed intervals. Because the timing is uniform, no start or stop bits are required. Compare with asynchronous communication. Some mainframes support only synchronous communications unless a synchronous adapter and appropriate software have been installed. See also *asynchronous communication*.

system crash   A situation in which the computer freezes up and refuses to proceed without rebooting. Usually caused by faulty software. Unlike a hard disk crash, no permanent physical damage occurs.

system files   Files with the system attribute. Normally, the hidden files that are used to boot the operating system. The MS-DOS and Windows 9x system files include IO.SYS and MSDOS.SYS; the IBM DOS system files are IBMBIO.COM and IBMDOS.COM.

System Management Mode (SMM)   Circuitry integrated into Intel processors that operates independently to control the processor's power use based on its activity level. It allows the user to specify time intervals after which the CPU will be powered down partially or fully and also supports the suspend/resume feature that allows for instant power on and power off.

target   A device attached to a SCSI bus that receives and processes commands sent from another device (the initiator) on the SCSI bus. A SCSI hard disk is an example of a target.

TCM   Trellis-coded modulation. An error-detection and correction technique employed by high-speed modems to enable higher-speed transmissions that are more resistant to line impairments.

TCO   1) Refers to the Swedish Confederation of Professional Employees, which has set stringent standards for devices that emit radiation. See *MPR II*. 2) Total Cost of Ownership. The cost of using a computer. It includes the cost of the hardware, software, and upgrades as well as the cost of the in-house staff and consultants that provide training and technical support.

TCP   Tape Carrier Package. A method of packaging processors for use in portable systems that reduces the size, the power consumed, and the heat generated by the chip. A processor in the TCP form factor is essentially a raw die encased in an oversized piece of polyamide film. The film is laminated with copper foil that is etched to form the leads that will connect the processor to the motherboard.

TCP/IP   Transmission Control Protocol/Internet Protocol. A set of protocols developed by the U.S. Department of Defense (DoD) to link dissimilar computers across many kinds of networks. This is the primary protocol used by the Internet.

temporary backup   A second copy of a work file, usually having the extension BAK. Created by application software so that you easily can return to a previous version of your work.

temporary file   A file temporarily (and usually invisibly) created by a program for its own use.

tera   A multiplier indicating 1 trillion (1,000,000,000,000) of some unit. Abbreviated as t or T. When used to indicate a number of bytes of memory storage, the multiplier definition changes to 1,099,511,627,776. One terabit, for example, equals 1,000,000,000,000 bits, and one terabyte equals 1,099,511,627,776 bytes.

terabyte (T)   A unit of information storage equal to 1,099,511,627,776 bytes.

terminal   A device whose keyboard and display are used for sending and receiving data over a communications link. Differs from a microcomputer in that it has no internal processing capabilities. Used to enter data into or retrieve processed data from a system or network.

terminal mode   An operational mode required for microcomputers to transmit data. In terminal mode, the computer acts as though it were a standard terminal such as a teletypewriter rather than a data processor. Keyboard entries go directly to the modem, whether the entry is a modem command or data to be transmitted over the phone lines. Received data is output directly to the screen. The more popular communications software products control terminal mode and enable more complex operations, including file transmission and saving received files.

terminator   Hardware or circuits that must be attached to or enabled at both ends of an electrical bus. Functions to prevent the reflection or echoing of signals that reach the ends of the bus and to ensure that the correct impedance load is placed on the driver circuits on the bus. Most commonly used with the SCSI bus.

TFT   Thin Film Transistor. The highest quality and brightest LCD color display type. A method for packaging one to four transistors per pixel within a flexible material that is the same size and shape as the LCD display, so that the transistors for each pixel lie directly behind the liquid crystal cells that they control.

thin Ethernet   See *10base2* or *IEEE 802.3*.

thin-film media   Hard disk platters that have a thin film (usually three-millionths of an inch) of medium deposited on the aluminum substrate through a sputtering or plating process.

Thinnet   See *10base2* or *IEEE 802.3*.

through-hole   Chip carriers and sockets equipped with leads that extend through holes in a PC board.

throughput   The amount of user data transmitted per second without the overhead of protocol information such as start and stop bits or frame headers and trailers.

TIFF Tagged Image File Format. A way of storing and exchanging digital image data. Developed by Aldus Corporation, Microsoft Corporation, and major scanner vendors to help link scanned images with the popular desktop publishing applications. Supports three main types of image data: black-and-white data, halftones or dithered data, and grayscale data.

time code A frame-by-frame address code time reference recorded on the spare track of a videotape or inserted in the vertical blanking interval. The time code is an eight-digit number encoding time in hours, minutes, seconds, and video frames.

Token Ring A type of local area network in which the workstations relay a packet of data called a *token* in a logical ring configuration. When a station wants to transmit, it takes possession of the token, attaches its data, and then frees the token after the data has made a complete circuit of the electrical ring. Transmits at speeds of 16Mbps. Because of the token-passing scheme, access to the network is controlled, unlike the slower 10BaseX Ethernet system in which collisions of data can occur, which wastes time. The Token-Ring network uses shielded twisted-pair wiring, which is cheaper than the coaxial cable used by 10Base2 and 10Base5 Ethernet and ARCnet.

toner The ultrafine colored plastic powder used in laser printers and photocopiers to produce the image on paper.

tower A personal computer that normally sits on the floor and that is mounted vertically rather than horizontally.

TPI Tracks Per Inch. Used as a measurement of magnetic track density. Standard 5 1/4-inch 360K floppy disks have a density of 48 TPI, and the 1.2M disks have a 96 TPI density. All 3 1/2-inch disks have a 135.4667 TPI density, and hard disks can have densities greater than 3,000 TPI.

track One of the many concentric circles that holds data on a disk surface. Consists of a single line of magnetic flux changes and is divided into some number of 512-byte sectors.

track density Expressed as tracks per inch (TPI); defines how many tracks are recorded in 1 inch of space measured radially from the center of the disk. Sometimes also called *radial density*.

track-to-track seek time The time required for read/write heads to move between adjacent tracks.

transport layer In the OSI reference model, when more than one packet is in process at any time, such as when a large file must be split into multiple packets for transmission, this is the layer that controls the sequencing of the message components and regulates inbound traffic flow.

transportable computer A computer system larger than a portable system and similar in size and shape to a portable sewing machine. Most transportables conform to a design similar to the original Compaq portable, with a built-in CRT display. These systems are characteristically very heavy and run only on AC power. Because of advances primarily in LCD and plasma-display technology, these systems are largely obsolete and have been replaced by portable systems.

troubleshooting   The task of determining the cause of a problem.

true-color images   True-color images are also called 24-bit color images because each pixel is represented by 24 bits of data, allowing for 16.7 million colors. The number of colors possible is based on the number of bits used to represent the color. If 8 bits are used, there are 256 possible color values (2 to the 8th power). To obtain 16.7 million colors, each of the primary colors (red, green, and blue) is represented by 8 bits per pixel, which allows for 256 possible shades for each of the primary red, green, and blue colors or 256×256×256 = 16.7 million total colors.

TSR   Terminate-and-Stay-Resident. A program that remains in memory after being loaded. Because they remain in memory, TSR programs can be reactivated by a predefined keystroke sequence or other operation while another program is active. Usually called *resident programs*.

TTL   Transistor-to-Transistor Logic. Digital signals often are called TTL signals. A TTL display is a monitor that accepts digital input at standardized signal voltage levels.

twisted pair   A type of wire in which two small, insulated copper wires are wrapped or twisted around each other to minimize interference from other wires in the cable. Two types of twisted-pair cables are available: unshielded and shielded. Unshielded twisted-pair (UTP) wiring commonly is used in telephone cables and provides little protection against interference. Shielded twisted-pair (STP) wiring is used in some networks or any application in which immunity from electrical interference is more important. Twisted-pair wire is much easier to work with than coaxial cable and is cheaper as well.

typematic   The keyboard repeatedly sending the keypress code to the motherboard for a key that is held down. The delay before the code begins to repeat and the speed at which it repeats are user adjustable.

UART   Universal Asynchronous Receiver Transmitter. A chip device that controls the RS-232 serial port in a PC-compatible system. Originally developed by National Semiconductor, several UART versions are in PC-compatible systems: The 8250B is used in PC- or XT-class systems, and the 16450 and 16550A are used in AT-class systems.

unformatted capacity   The total number of bytes of data that can fit on a disk. The formatted capacity is lower because space is lost defining the boundaries between sectors.

uninterruptible power supply (UPS)   A device that supplies power to the computer from batteries so that power will not stop, even momentarily, during a power outage. The batteries are recharged constantly from a wall socket.

Universal Asynchronous Receiver Transmitter   See *UART*.

UPC   Universal Product Code. A 10-digit computer-readable bar code used in labeling retail products. The code in the form of vertical bars includes a five-digit manufacturer identification number and a five-digit product code number.

update   To modify information already contained in a file or program with current information.

Upper Memory Area (UMA) The 384K of memory between 640K and 1M.

URL Uniform Resource Locator. The primary naming scheme used to identify a particular site or file on the World Wide Web. URLs combine information about the protocol being used, the address of the site where the resource is located, the subdirectory location at the site, and the name of the particular file (or page) in question.

USB Universal Serial Bus. A 12Mbit/sec (1.5M/sec) interface over a simple 4-wire connection. The bus supports up to 127 devices and uses a tiered star topology built on expansion hubs that can reside in the PC, any USB peripheral, or even standalone hub boxes.

utility Programs that carry out routine procedures to make computer use easier.

UTP Unshielded Twisted Pair. A type of wire often used indoors to connect telephones or computer devices. Comes with two or four wires twisted inside a flexible plastic sheath or conduit and uses modular plugs and phone jacks.

V.21 An ITU standard for modem communications at 300bps. Modems made in the U.S. or Canada follow the Bell 103 standard but can be set to answer V.21 calls from overseas. The actual transmission rate is 300 baud and employs FSK (frequency shift keying) modulation, which encodes a single bit per baud.

V.22 An ITU standard for modem communications at 1,200bps, with an optional fallback to 600bps. V.22 is partially compatible with the Bell 212A standard observed in the U.S. and Canada. The actual transmission rate is 600 baud, using DPSK (differential-phase shift keying) to encode as much as 2 bits per baud.

V.22bis An ITU standard for modem communications at 2,400bps. Includes an automatic link-negotiation fallback to 1,200bps and compatibility with Bell 212A/V.22 modems. The actual transmission rate is 600 baud, using QAM (quadrature amplitude modulation) to encode as much as 4 bits per baud.

V.23 An ITU standard for modem communications at 1,200 or 600bps with a 75bps back channel. Used in the United Kingdom for some videotext systems.

V.25 An ITU standard for modem communications that specifies an answer tone different from the Bell answer tone used in the U.S. and Canada. Most intelligent modems can be set with an ATB0 command so that they use the V.25 2,100Hz tone when answering overseas calls.

V.32 An ITU standard for modem communications at 9,600bps and 4,800bps. V.32 modems fall back to 4,800bps when line quality is impaired and fall forward again to 9,600bps when line quality improves. The actual transmission rate is 2,400 baud using QAM (quadrature amplitude modulation) and optional TCM (trellis-coded modulation) to encode as much as 4 data bits per baud.

V.32bis An ITU standard that extends the standard V.32 connection range and supports 4,800; 7,200; 9,600; 12,000; and 14,400bps transmission rates. V.32bis modems fall back to the next lower speed when line quality is impaired, fall back further as necessary, and fall forward to the next higher speed when line quality improves. The actual transmission rate is 2,400 baud using QAM (quadrature amplitude modulation) and TCM (trellis-coded modulation) to encode as much as 6 data bits per baud.

V.32terbo   A proprietary standard proposed by several modem manufacturers that will be cheaper to implement than the standard V.32 fast protocol but that will only support transmission speeds of up to 18,800bps. Because it is not an industry standard, it is not likely to have widespread industry support.

V.34   An ITU standard that extends the standard V.32bis connection range, supporting 28,800bps transmission rates as well as all the functions and rates of V.32bis. This was called V.32fast or V.fast while under development.

V.34+   An ITU standard that extends the standard V.34 connection range, supporting 33,600bps transmission rates as well as all the functions and rates of V.34.

V.42   An ITU standard for modem communications that defines a two-stage process of detection and negotiation for LAPM error control. Also supports MNP error-control protocol, Levels 1 through 4.

V.42bis   An extension of CCITT V.42 that defines a specific data-compression scheme for use with V.42 and MNP error control.

V.90   ITU-T designation for a defining the standard for 56Kbps communication. Supercedes the proprietary X2 schemes from U.S. Robotics (3Com) and K56Flex from Rockwell.

vaccine   A type of program used to locate and eradicate virus code from infected programs or systems.

VCPI   Virtual Control Program Interface. A 386 and later processor memory management standard created by Phar Lap software in conjunction with other software developers. VCPI provides an interface between applications using DOS extenders and 386 memory managers.

Vertical Blanking Interval (VBI)   The top and bottom lines in the video field, in which frame numbers, picture stops, chapter stops, white flags, closed captions, and more may be encoded. These lines do not appear on the display screen but maintain image stability and enhance image access.

vertical scan frequency   The rate at which the electron gun in a monitor scans or refreshes the entire screen each second.

Very Large Scale Integration   See *IC*.

VESA   Video Electronics Standards Association. Founded in the late 1980s by NEC Home Electronics and eight other leading video board manufacturers, with the main goal to standardize the electrical, timing, and programming issues surrounding 800×600 resolution video displays, commonly known as *Super VGA*. VESA has also developed the Video Local Bus (VL-Bus) standard for connecting high-speed adapters directly to the local processor bus.

VGA   Video Graphics Array. A type of PC video display circuit (and adapter) first introduced by IBM on April 2, 1987, that supports text and graphics. Text is supported at a maximum resolution of 80×25 characters in 16 colors with a character box of 9×16 pixels. Graphics is supported at a maximum resolution of 320×200 pixels in 256 (from a palette of 262,144) colors or 640×480 pixels in 16 colors. The VGA outputs an analog signal with a horizontal scanning frequency of 31.5KHz and supports analog color or analog monochrome displays.

VHS   Video Home System. A popular consumer videotape format developed by Matsushita and JVC.

video   A system of recording and transmitting primarily visual information by translating moving or still images into electrical signals. The term video properly refers only to the picture, but as a generic term, video usually embraces audio and other signals that are part of a complete program. Video now includes not only broadcast television but many nonbroadcast applications such as corporate communications, marketing, home entertainment, games, teletext, security, and even the visual display units of computer-based technology.

Video 8 or 8mm Video   Video format based on the 8mm videotapes popularized by Sony for camcorders.

video adapter   An expansion card or chipset built into a motherboard that provides the capability to display text and graphics onscreen. If the adapter is part of an expansion card, it also includes the physical connector for the monitor cable. If the chipset is on the motherboard, the video connector will be on the motherboard as well.

video graphics array   See *VGA*.

video-on-CD or video CD   A full-motion digital video format using MPEG video compression and incorporating a variety of VCR-like control capabilities. See also *White Book*.

virtual disk   A RAM disk or "phantom disk drive" in which a section of system memory (usually RAM) is set aside to hold data, just as though it were a number of disk sectors. To DOS, a virtual disk looks like and functions like any other "real" drive.

virtual memory   A technique by which operating systems (including OS/2) load more programs and data into memory than they can hold. Parts of the programs and data are kept on disk and constantly swapped back and forth into system memory. The applications' software programs are unaware of this setup and act as though a large amount of memory is available.

virtual real mode   A mode available in all Intel 80386-compatible processors. In this mode, memory addressing is limited to 4,096M, restricted protection levels can be set to trap software crashes and control the system, and individual real-mode compatible sessions can be set up and maintained separately from one another.

virus   A type of resident program designed to replicate itself. Usually at some later time when the virus is running, it causes an undesirable action to take place.

VL-Bus   VESA Local Bus. A standard 32-bit expansion slot bus specification used in 486 PCs. Now replaced by PCI bus.

VMM   Virtual Memory Manager. A facility in Windows enhanced mode that manages the task of swapping data in and out of 386 and later processor virtual real-mode memory space for multiple non-Windows applications running in virtual real mode.

voice-coil actuator   A device that moves read/write heads across hard disk platters by magnetic interaction between coils of wire and a magnet. Functions somewhat like an audio speaker, from which the name originated.

voltage reduction technology   An Intel processor technology that allows a processor to draw the standard voltage from the motherboard but run the internal processor core at a lower voltage.

voltage regulator   A device that smoothes out voltage irregularities in the power fed to the computer.

volume   A portion of a disk signified by a single drive specifier. Under DOS v3.3 and later, a single hard disk can be partitioned into several volumes, each with its own logical drive specifier (C:, D:, E:, and so on).

volume label   An identifier or name of up to 11 characters that names a disk.

VRAM   Video Random-Access Memory. VRAM chips are modified DRAMs on video boards that enable simultaneous access by the host system's processor and the processor on the video board. A large amount of information thus can be transferred quickly between the video board and the system processor. Sometimes also called *dual-ported RAM*.

VxD   Virtual Device Driver. A special type of Windows driver. VxDs run at the most privileged CPU mode (ring 0) and allow low-level interaction with the hardware and internal Windows functions.

wafer   A thin circular piece of silicon from which processors, memory, and other semiconductor electronics are manufactured.

wait states   Pause cycles during system operation that require the processor to wait one or more clock cycles until memory can respond to the processor's request. Enables the microprocessor to synchronize with lower-cost, slower memory. A system that runs with "zero wait states" requires none of these cycles because of the use of faster memory or a memory cache system.

warm boot   Rebooting a system by means of a software command rather than turning the power off and back on. See also *cold boot*.

wave table synthesis   A method of creating synthetic sound on a sound card that uses actual musical instrument sounds sampled and stored on ROM (or RAM) on the sound card. The sound card then modifies this sample to create any note needed for that instrument. Produces much better sound quality than FM synthesis.

Whetstone   A benchmark program developed in 1976 and designed to simulate arithmetic-intensive programs used in scientific computing. Remains completely CPU-bound and performs no I/O or system calls. Originally written in ALGOL, although the C and Pascal versions became more popular by the late 1980s. The speed at which a system performs floating-point operations often is measured in units of Whetstones.

White Book   A standard specification developed by Philips and JVC in 1993 for storing MPEG standard video on CDs. An extension of the Red Book standard for digital audio, Yellow Book standard for CD-ROM, Green Book standard for CD-I, and Orange Book standard for CD Write Once.

Whitney technology   A term referring to a magnetic disk design that usually has oxide or thin film media, thin film read/write heads, low floating-height sliders, and low-mass actuator arms that together allow higher-bit densities than the older

Winchester technology. Whitney technology was first introduced with the IBM 3370 disk drive, circa 1979.

wide area network (WAN)   A LAN that extends beyond the boundaries of a single building.

Winchester drive   Any ordinary, nonremovable (or fixed) hard disk drive. The name originates from a particular IBM drive in the 1960s that had 30M of fixed and 30M of removable storage. This 30-30 drive matched the caliber figure for a popular series of rifles made by Winchester, so the slang term *Winchester* was applied to any fixed-platter hard disk.

Winchester technology   The term *Winchester* is loosely applied to mean any disk with a fixed or nonremovable recording medium. More precisely, the term applies to a ferrite read/write head and slider design with oxide media that was first employed in the IBM 3340 disk drive, circa 1973. Most drives today actually use Whitney technology.

Wintel   The common name given to computers running Microsoft Windows using Intel processors. A slang term for the PC standard.

wire frames   The most common technique used to construct a three-dimensional object for animation. A wire frame is given coordinates of length, height, and width. Wire frames are then filled with textures, colors, and movement. Transforming a wire frame into a textured object is called *rendering*.

word length   The number of bits in a data character without parity, start, or stop bits.

World Wide Web   Also called simply the Web. A graphical information system based on hypertext that enables a user to easily access documents located on the Internet.

WORM   Write Once, Read Many (or Multiple). An optical mass-storage device capable of storing many megabytes of information but that can be written to only once on any given area of the disk. A WORM disk typically holds more than 200M of data. Because a WORM drive cannot write over an old version of a file, new copies of files are made and stored on other parts of the disk whenever a file is revised. WORM disks are used to store information when a history of older versions must be maintained. Recording on a WORM disk is performed by a laser writer that burns pits in a thin metallic film (usually tellurium) embedded in the disk. This burning process is called *ablation*. WORM drives are frequently used for archiving data.

write precompensation   A modification applied to write data by a controller to alleviate partially the problem of bit shift, which causes adjacent 1s written on magnetic media to read as though they were farther apart. When adjacent 1s are sensed by the controller, precompensation is used to write them closer together on the disk, thus enabling them to be read in the proper bit cell window. Drives with built-in controllers normally handle precompensation automatically. Precompensation normally is required for the inner cylinders of oxide media drives.

write protect   Preventing a removable disk from being overwritten by means of covering a notch or repositioning a sliding switch, depending on the type of media.

X2 A proprietary modem standard developed by U.S. Robotics (since acquired by 3Com) that allows modems to receive data at up to 56Kbps. This has been superseded by the V.90 standard. See also *X2* and *V.90*.

x86 A generic term referring to Intel and Intel-compatible PC microprocessors. Although the Pentium, Pentium Pro, and Pentium II do not have a numeric designation due to trademark law, they are later generations of this family.

XGA eXtended Graphics Array. A type of PC video display circuit (and adapter) first introduced by IBM on October 30, 1990, that supports text and graphics. Text is supported at a maximum resolution of 132×60 characters in 16 colors with a character box of 8×6 pixels. Graphics is supported at a maximum resolution of 1024×768 pixels in 256 (from a palette of 262,144) colors or 640×480 pixels in 65,536 colors. The XGA outputs an analog signal with a horizontal scanning frequency of 31.5 or 35.52KHz and supports analog color or analog monochrome displays.

XMM eXtended Memory Manager. A driver that controls access to extended memory on 286 and later processor systems. HIMEM.SYS is an example of an XMM that comes with DOS.

Xmodem A file-transfer protocol—with error checking—developed by Ward Christensen in the mid-1970s and placed in the public domain. Designed to transfer files between machines running the CP/M operating system and using 300 or 1,200 bps modems. Until the late 1980s, because of its simplicity and public-domain status, Xmodem remained the most widely used microcomputer file-transfer protocol. In standard Xmodem, the transmitted blocks are 128 bytes. 1K-Xmodem is an extension to Xmodem that increases the block size to 1,024 bytes. Many newer file-transfer protocols that are much faster and more accurate than Xmodem have been developed, such as Ymodem and Zmodem.

XMS eXtended Memory Specification. A Microsoft-developed standard that provides a way for real-mode applications to access extended memory in a controlled fashion. The XMS standard is available from Microsoft.

XON/XOFF Standard ASCII control characters used to tell an intelligent device to stop or resume transmitting data. In most systems, typing Ctrl+S sends the XOFF character. Most devices understand Ctrl+Q as XON; others interpret the pressing of any key after Ctrl+S as XON.

Y-connector A Y-shaped splitter cable that divides a source input into two output signals.

Yellow Book The standard used by Compact Disc-Read Only Memory (CD-ROM). Multimedia applications most commonly use the Yellow Book standard, which specifies how digital information is to be stored on the CD-ROM and read by a computer. EXtended Architecture (XA) is currently an extension of the Yellow Book that allows for the combination of different data types (audio and video, for example) onto one track in a CD-ROM. Without XA, a CD-ROM can access only one data type at a time. Many CD-ROM drives are now XA capable.

Yellow Book standards See *CD-ROM*.

Ymodem   A file-transfer protocol first released as part of Chuck Forsberg's YAM (yet another modem) program. An extension to Xmodem designed to overcome some of the limitations of the original. Enables information about the transmitted file, such as the file name and length, to be sent along with the file data and increases the size of a block from 128 to 1,024 bytes. Ymodem-batch adds the capability to transmit "batches" or groups of files without operator interruption. YmodemG is a variation that sends the entire file before waiting for an acknowledgment. If the receiving side detects an error in midstream, the transfer is aborted. YmodemG is designed for use with modems that have built-in error-correcting capabilities.

ZIF   Zero Insertion Force. Sockets that require no force for the insertion of a chip carrier. Usually accomplished through movable contacts and uses primarily 486, Pentium, and Pentium Pro processor systems.

ZIP   Zigzag Inline Package. A DIP package that has all leads on one edge in a zigzag pattern and mounts in a vertical plane.

zip drive   An external drive manufactured by Iomega that supports 100M magnetic media on a 3 1/2-inch removable drive.

Zmodem   A file-transfer protocol commissioned by Telenet and placed in the public domain. Like Ymodem, it was designed by Chuck Forsberg and developed as an extension to Xmodem to overcome the inherent latency when using Send/Ack-based protocols such as XModem and YModem. It is a streaming, sliding-window protocol.

zoned recording   In hard drives, a way to increase the capacity of a hard drive is to format more sectors on the outer cylinders than on the inner ones. Zoned recording splits the cylinders into groups called zones, with each successive zone having more and more sectors per track as you move out from the inner radius of the disk. All the cylinders in a particular zone have the same number of sectors per track.

zoomed video   A direct video bus connection between the PC Card adapter and a mobile system's VGA controller, allowing high-speed video displays for videoconferencing applications and MPEG decoders.

Appendix D

Technical Reference

General Information

ASCII Character Code Charts

Figure D.1 lists ASCII control character values. Figure D.2 shows the IBM extended ASCII line-drawing characters in an easy-to-use format. I frequently use these extended ASCII line-drawing characters for visual enhancement in documents I create.

DEC	HEX	CHAR	NAME		CONTROL CODE
0	00		Ctrl-@	NUL	Null
1	01	☺	Ctrl-A	SOH	Start of Heading
2	02	●	Ctrl-B	STX	Start of Text
3	03	♥	Ctrl-C	ETX	End of Text
4	04	♦	Ctrl-D	EOT	End of Transit
5	05	♣	Ctrl-E	ENQ	Enquiry
6	06	♠	Ctrl-F	ACK	Acknowledge
7	07	•	Ctrl-G	BEL	Bell
8	08	◘	Ctrl-H	BS	Back Space
9	09	○	Ctrl-I	HT	Horizontal Tab
10	0A	◙	Ctrl-J	LF	Line Feed
11	0B	♂	Ctrl-K	VT	Vertical Tab
12	0C	♀	Ctrl-L	FF	Form Feed
13	0D	♪	Ctrl-M	CR	Carriage Return
14	0E	♫	Ctrl-N	SO	Shift Out
15	0F	☼	Ctrl-O	SI	Shift In
16	10	►	Ctrl-P	DLE	Data Line Escape
17	11	◄	Ctrl-Q	DC1	Device Control 1
18	12	↕	Ctrl-R	DC2	Device Control 2
19	13	‼	Ctrl-S	DC3	Device Control 3
20	14	¶	Ctrl-T	DC4	Device Control 4
21	15	§	Ctrl-U	NAK	Negative Acknowledge
22	16	▬	Ctrl-V	SYN	Synchronous Idle
23	17	↨	Ctrl-W	ETB	End of Transmit Block
24	18	↑	Ctrl-X	CAN	Cancel
25	19	↓	Ctrl-Y	EM	End of Medium
26	1A	←	Ctrl-Z	SUB	Substitute
27	1B	→	Ctrl-[	ESC	Escape
28	1C	∟	Ctrl-\	FS	File Separator
29	1D	↔	Ctrl-]	GS	Group Separator
30	1E	▲	Ctrl-^	RS	Record Separator
31	1FA	▼	Ctrl-_	US	Unit Separator

FIG. D.1 ASCII control codes.

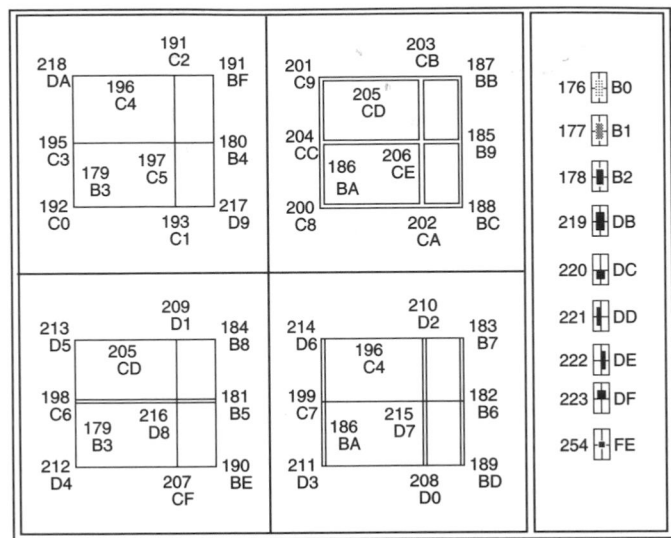

FIG. D.2 Extended ASCII line-drawing characters.

Hexadecimal/ASCII Conversions

Dec	Hex	Octal	Binary	Name	Character
Table D.1		**Hexadecimal/ASCII Conversions**			
0	00	000	0000 0000	blank	
1	01	001	0000 0001	happy face	☺
2	02	002	0000 0010	inverse happy face	☻
3	03	003	0000 0011	heart	♥
4	04	004	0000 0100	diamond	♦
5	05	005	0000 0101	club	♣
6	06	006	0000 0110	spade	♠
7	07	007	0000 0111	bullet	•
8	08	010	0000 1000	inverse bullet	◘
9	09	011	0000 1001	circle	o
10	0A	012	0000 1010	inverse circle	○
11	0B	013	0000 1011	male sign	♂
12	0C	014	0000 1100	female sign	♀
13	0D	015	0000 1101	single note	♪
14	0E	016	0000 1110	double note	♫
15	0F	017	0000 1111	sun	☼
16	10	020	0001 0000	right triangle	►
17	11	021	0001 0001	left triangle	◄
18	12	022	0001 0010	up/down arrow	↕
19	13	023	0001 0011	double exclamation	‼
20	14	024	0001 0100	paragraph sign	¶

Dec	Hex	Octal	Binary	Name	Character
21	15	025	0001 0101	section sign	§
22	16	026	0001 0110	rectangular bullet	■
23	17	027	0001 0111	up/down to line	↕
24	18	030	0001 1000	up arrow	↑
25	19	031	0001 1001	down arrow	↓
26	1A	032	0001 1010	right arrow	→
27	1B	033	0001 1011	left arrow	←
28	1C	034	0001 1100	lower left box	∟
29	1D	035	0001 1101	left/right arrow	↔
30	1E	036	0001 1110	up triangle	▲
31	1F	037	0001 1111	down triangle	▼
32	20	040	0010 0000	space	Space
33	21	041	0010 0001	exclamation point	!
34	22	042	0010 0010	quotation mark	"
35	23	043	0010 0011	number sign	#
36	24	044	0010 0100	dollar sign	$
37	25	045	0010 0101	percent sign	%
38	26	046	0010 0110	ampersand	&
39	27	047	0010 0111	apostrophe	'
40	28	050	0010 1000	opening parenthesis	(
41	29	051	0010 1001	closing parenthesis	)
42	2A	052	0010 1010	asterisk	*
43	2B	053	0010 1011	plus sign	+
44	2C	054	0010 1100	comma	,
45	2D	055	0010 1101	hyphen or minus sign	-
46	2E	056	0010 1110	period	.
47	2F	057	0010 1111	slash	/
48	30	060	0011 0000	zero	0
49	31	061	0011 0001	one	1
50	32	062	0011 0010	two	2
51	33	063	0011 0011	three	3
52	34	064	0011 0100	four	4
53	35	065	0011 0101	five	5
54	36	066	0011 0110	six	6
55	37	067	0011 0111	seven	7
56	38	070	0011 1000	eight	8
57	39	071	0011 1001	nine	9
58	3A	072	0011 1010	colon	:
59	3B	073	0011 1011	semicolon	;
60	3C	074	0011 1100	less-than sign	<

(continues)

	Table D.1		Hexadecimal/ASCII Conversions Continued		
Dec	**Hex**	**Octal**	**Binary**	**Name**	**Character**
61	3D	075	0011 1101	equal sign	=
62	3E	076	0011 1110	greater-than sign	>
63	3F	077	0011 1111	question mark	?
64	40	100	0100 0000	at sign	@
65	41	101	0100 0001	capital A	A
66	42	102	0100 0010	capital B	B
67	43	103	0100 0011	capital C	C
68	44	104	0100 0100	capital D	D
69	45	105	0100 0101	capital E	E
70	46	106	0100 0110	capital F	F
71	47	107	0100 0111	capital G	G
72	48	110	0100 1000	capital H	H
73	49	111	0100 1001	capital I	I
74	4A	112	0100 1010	capital J	J
75	4B	113	0100 1011	capital K	K
76	4C	114	0100 1100	capital L	L
77	4D	115	0100 1101	capital M	M
78	4E	116	0100 1110	capital N	N
79	4F	117	0100 1111	capital O	O
80	50	120	0101 0000	capital P	P
81	51	121	0101 0001	capital Q	Q
82	52	122	0101 0010	capital R	R
83	53	123	0101 0011	capital S	S
84	54	124	0101 0100	capital T	T
85	55	125	0101 0101	capital U	U
86	56	126	0101 0110	capital V	V
87	57	127	0101 0111	capital W	W
88	58	130	0101 1000	capital X	X
89	59	131	0101 1001	capital Y	Y
90	5A	132	0101 1010	capital Z	Z
91	5B	133	0101 1011	opening bracket	[
92	5C	134	0101 1100	backward slash	\
93	5D	135	0101 1101	closing bracket	]
94	5E	136	0101 1110	caret	^
95	5F	137	0101 1111	underscore	_
96	60	140	0110 0000	grave	`
97	61	141	0110 0001	lowercase A	a
98	62	142	0110 0010	lowercase B	b
99	63	143	0110 0011	lowercase C	c

Dec	Hex	Octal	Binary	Name	Character
100	64	144	0110 0100	lowercase D	d
101	65	145	0110 0101	lowercase E	e
102	66	146	0110 0110	lowercase F	f
103	67	147	0110 0111	lowercase G	g
104	68	150	0110 1000	lowercase H	h
105	69	151	0110 1001	lowercase I	i
106	6A	152	0110 1010	lowercase J	j
107	6B	153	0110 1011	lowercase K	k
108	6C	154	0110 1100	lowercase L	l
109	6D	155	0110 1101	lowercase M	m
110	6E	156	0110 1110	lowercase N	n
111	6F	157	0110 1111	lowercase O	o
112	70	160	0111 0000	lowercase P	p
113	71	161	0111 0001	lowercase Q	q
114	72	162	0111 0010	lowercase R	r
115	73	163	0111 0011	lowercase S	s
116	74	164	0111 0100	lowercase T	t
117	75	165	0111 0101	lowercase U	u
118	76	166	0111 0110	lowercase V	v
119	77	167	0111 0111	lowercase W	w
120	78	170	0111 1000	lowercase X	x
121	79	171	0111 1001	lowercase Y	y
122	7A	172	0111 1010	lowercase Z	z
123	7B	173	0111 1011	opening brace	{
124	7C	174	0111 1100	vertical line	|
125	7D	175	0111 1101	closing brace	}
126	7E	176	0111 1110	tilde	~
127	7F	177	0111 1111	small house	Δ
128	80	200	1000 0000	C cedilla	Ç
129	81	201	1000 0001	u umlaut	ü
130	82	202	1000 0010	e acute	é
131	83	203	1000 0011	a circumflex	â
132	84	204	1000 0100	a umlaut	ä
133	85	205	1000 0101	a grave	à
134	86	206	1000 0110	a ring	å
135	87	207	1000 0111	c cedilla	ç
136	88	210	1000 1000	e circumflex	ê
137	89	211	1000 1001	e umlaut	ë
138	8A	212	1000 1010	e grave	è
139	8B	213	1000 1011	I umlaut	ï

(continues)

Table D.1 Hexadecimal/ASCII Conversions Continued

Dec	Hex	Octal	Binary	Name	Character
140	8C	214	1000 1100	I circumflex	Î
141	8D	215	1000 1101	I grave	Ì
142	8E	216	1000 1110	A umlaut	Ä
143	8F	217	1000 1111	A ring	Å
144	90	220	1001 0000	E acute	É
145	91	221	1001 0001	ae ligature	æ
146	92	222	1001 0010	AE ligature	Æ
147	93	223	1001 0011	o circumflex	ô
148	94	224	1001 0100	o umlaut	ö
149	95	225	1001 0101	o grave	ò
150	96	226	1001 0110	u circumflex	û
151	97	227	1001 0111	u grave	ù
152	98	230	1001 1000	y umlaut	ÿ
153	99	231	1001 1001	O umlaut	Ö
154	9A	232	1001 1010	U umlaut	Ü
155	9B	233	1001 1011	cent sign	¢
156	9C	234	1001 1100	pound sign	£
157	9D	235	1001 1101	yen sign	¥
158	9E	236	1001 1110	Pt	₧
159	9F	237	1001 1111	function	ƒ
160	A0	240	1010 0000	a acute	á
161	A1	241	1010 0001	I acute	Í
162	A2	242	1010 0010	o acute	ó
163	A3	243	1010 0011	u acute	ú
164	A4	244	1010 0100	n tilde	ñ
165	A5	245	1010 0101	N tilde	Ñ
166	A6	246	1010 0110	a macron	ā
167	A7	247	1010 0111	o macron	ō
168	A8	250	1010 1000	opening question mark	¿
169	A9	251	1010 1001	upper-left box	⌐
170	AA	252	1010 1010	upper-right box	¬
171	AB	253	1010 1011	1/2	½
172	AC	254	1010 1100	1/4	¼
173	AD	255	1010 1101	opening exclamation	¡
174	AE	256	1010 1110	opening guillemets	«
175	AF	257	1010 1111	closing guillemets	»
176	B0	260	1011 0000	light block	
177	B1	261	1011 0001	medium block	▪
178	B2	262	1011 0010	dark block	▪
179	B3	263	1011 0011	single vertical	│

Dec	Hex	Octal	Binary	Name	Character
180	B4	264	1011 0100	single right junction	┤
181	B5	265	1011 0101	2 to 1 right junction	╡
182	B6	266	1011 0110	1 to 2 right junction	╢
183	B7	267	1011 0111	1 to 2 upper-right	╖
184	B8	270	1011 1000	2 to 1 upper-right	╕
185	B9	271	1011 1001	double right junction	╣
186	BA	272	1011 1010	double vertical	║
187	BB	273	1011 1011	double upper-right	╗
188	BC	274	1011 1100	double lower-right	╝
189	BD	275	1011 1101	1 to 2 lower-right	╜
190	BE	276	1011 1110	2 to 1 lower-right	╛
191	BF	277	1011 1111	single upper-right	┐
192	C0	300	1100 0000	single lower-left	└
193	C1	301	1100 0001	single lower junction	┴
194	C2	302	1100 0010	single upper junction	┬
195	C3	303	1100 0011	single left junction	├
196	C4	304	1100 0100	single horizontal	─
197	C5	305	1100 0101	single intersection	┼
198	C6	306	1100 0110	2 to 1 left junction	╞
199	C7	307	1100 0111	1 to 2 left junction	╟
200	C8	310	1100 1000	double lower-left	╚
201	C9	311	1100 1001	double upper-left	╔
202	CA	312	1100 1010	double lower junction	╩
203	CB	313	1100 1011	double upper junction	╦
204	CC	314	1100 1100	double left junction	╠
205	CD	315	1100 1101	double horizontal	═
206	CE	316	1100 1110	double intersection	╬
207	CF	317	1100 1111	1 to 2 lower junction	╧
208	D0	320	1101 0000	2 to 1 lower junction	╨
209	D1	321	1101 0001	1 to 2 upper junction	╤
210	D2	322	1101 0010	2 to 1 upper junction	╥
211	D3	323	1101 0011	1 to 2 lower-left	╙
212	D4	324	1101 0100	2 to 1 lower-left	╘
213	D5	325	1101 0101	2 to 1 upper-left	╒
214	D6	326	1101 0110	1 to 2 upper-left	╓
215	D7	327	1101 0111	2 to 1 intersection	╫
216	D8	330	1101 1000	1 to 2 intersection	╪
217	D9	331	1101 1001	single lower-right	┘
218	DA	332	1101 1010	single upper-right	┌
219	DB	333	1101 1011	inverse space	█

(continues)

Table D.1		Hexadecimal/ASCII Conversions Continued			
Dec	**Hex**	**Octal**	**Binary**	**Name**	**Character**
220	DC	334	1101 1100	lower inverse	■
221	DD	335	1101 1101	left inverse	▌
222	DE	336	1101 1110	right inverse	▐
223	DF	337	1101 1111	upper inverse	▬
224	E0	340	1110 0000	alpha	α
225	E1	341	1110 0001	beta	β
226	E2	342	1110 0010	Gamma	Γ
227	E3	343	1110 0011	pi	π
228	E4	344	1110 0100	Sigma	Σ
229	E5	345	1110 0101	sigma	σ
230	E6	346	1110 0110	mu	μ
231	E7	347	1110 0111	tau	τ
232	E8	350	1110 1000	Phi	Φ
233	E9	351	1110 1001	theta	θ
234	EA	352	1110 1010	Omega	Ω
235	EB	353	1110 1011	delta	δ
236	EC	354	1110 1100	infinity	∞
237	ED	355	1110 1101	phi	ϕ
238	EE	356	1110 1110	epsilon	ε
239	EF	357	1110 1111	intersection of sets	$\cap$
240	F0	360	1111 0000	is identical to	$\equiv$
241	F1	361	1111 0001	plus/minus sign	$\pm$
242	F2	362	1111 0010	greater/equal sign	$\geq$
243	F3	363	1111 0011	less/equal sign	$\leq$
244	F4	364	1111 0100	top half integral	$\lceil$
245	F5	365	1111 0101	lower half integral	$\rfloor$
246	F6	366	1111 0110	division sign	$\div$
247	F7	367	1111 0111	approximately	$\approx$
248	F8	370	1111 1000	degree	$^\circ$
249	F9	371	1111 1001	filled-in degree	•
250	FA	372	1111 1010	small bullet	·
251	FB	373	1111 1011	square root	$\sqrt{\ }$
252	FC	374	1111 1100	superscript n	^{n}
253	FD	375	1111 1101	superscript 2	^{2}
254	FE	376	1111 1110	box	■
255	FF	377	1111 1111	phantom space	˘

Extended ASCII Keycodes for ANSI.SYS

Table D.2 Extended ASCII Keycodes for ANSI.SYS					
Code	**Keystroke**	**Code**	**Keystroke**	**Code**	**Keystroke**
0;1	<Alt> Esc	0;53	<Alt> /	0;98	<Ctrl> F5
0;3	Null Character	0;55	<Alt> Keypad *	0;99	<Ctrl> F6
0;14	<Alt> Backspace	0;59	F1	0;100	<Ctrl> F7
0;15	<Shift> Tab	0;60	F2	0;101	<Ctrl> F8
0;16	<Alt> Q	0;61	F3	0;102	<Ctrl> F9
0;17	<Alt> W	0;62	F4	0;103	<Ctrl> F10
0;18	<Alt> E	0;63	F5	0;104	<Alt> F1
0;19	<Alt> R	0;64	F6	0;105	<Alt> F2
0;20	<Alt> T	0;65	F7	0;106	<Alt> F3
0;21	<Alt> Y	0;66	F8	0;107	<Alt> F4
0;22	<Alt> U	0;67	F9	0;108	<Alt> F5
0;23	<Alt> I	0;68	F10	0;109	<Alt> F6
0;24	<Alt> O	0;71	Home	0;110	<Alt> F7
0;25	<Alt> P	0;72	Up Arrow	0;111	<Alt> F8
0;26	<Alt> [	0;73	Page Up	0;112	<Alt> F9
0;27	<Alt>]	0;74	<Alt> Keypad -	0;113	<Alt> F10
0;28	<Alt> Enter	0;75	Left Arrow	0;114	<Ctrl> Print Screen
0;30	<Alt> A	0;76	Keypad 5	0;115	<Ctrl> Left Arrow
0;31	<Alt> S	0;77	Right Arrow	0;116	<Ctrl> Right Arrow
0;32	<Alt> D	0;78	<Alt> Keypad +	0;117	<Ctrl> End
0;33	<Alt> F	0;79	End	0;118	<Ctrl> Page Down
0;34	<Alt> G	0;80	Down Arrow	0;119	<Ctrl> Home
0;35	<Alt> H	0;81	Page Down	0;120	<Alt> 1
0;36	<Alt> J	0;82	Insert	0;121	<Alt> 2
0;37	<Alt> K	0;83	Delete	0;122	<Alt> 3
0;38	<Alt> L	0;84	<Shift> F1	0;123	<Alt> 4
0;39	<Alt> ;	0;85	<Shift> F2	0;124	<Alt> 5
0;40	<Alt> '	0;86	<Shift> F3	0;125	<Alt> 6
0;41	<Alt> '	0;87	<Shift> F4	0;126	<Alt> 7
0;43	<Alt> \	0;88	<Shift> F5	0;127	<Alt> 8
0;44	<Alt> Z	0;89	<Shift> F6	0;128	<Alt> 9
0;45	<Alt> X	0;90	<Shift> F7	0;129	<Alt> 0
0;46	<Alt> C	0;91	<Shift> F8	0;130	<Alt> -
0;47	<Alt> V	0;92	<Shift> F9	0;131	<Alt> =
0;48	<Alt> B	0;93	<Shift> F10	0;132	<Ctrl> Page Up
0;49	<Alt> N	0;94	<Ctrl> F1	0;133	F11
0;50	<Alt> M	0;95	<Ctrl> F2	0;134	F12
0;51	<Alt> ,	0;96	<Ctrl> F3	0;135	<Shift> F11
0;52	<Alt> .	0;97	<Ctrl> F4	0;136	<Shift> F12

(continues)

Table D.2	Extended ASCII Keycodes for ANSI.SYS Continued				
Code	**Keystroke**	**Code**	**Keystroke**	**Code**	**Keystroke**
0;137	<Ctrl> F11	0;146	<Ctrl> Insert	0;157	<Alt> Right Arrow
0;138	<Ctrl> F12	0;147	<Ctrl> Delete	0;159	<Alt> End
0;139	<Alt> F11	0;148	<Ctrl> Tab	0;160	<Alt> Down Arrow
0;140	<Alt> F12	0;149	<Ctrl> Keypad /	0;161	<Alt> Page Down
0;141	<Ctrl> Up Arrow	0;150	<Ctrl> Keypad *	0;162	<Alt> Insert
0;142	<Ctrl> Keypad -	0;151	<Alt> Home	0;163	<Alt> Delete
0;143	<Ctrl> Keypad 5	0;152	<Alt> Up Arrow	0;164	<Alt> Keypad /
0;144	<Ctrl> Keypad +	0;153	<Alt> Page Up	0;165	<Alt> Tab
0;145	<Ctrl> Down Arrow	0;155	<Alt> Left Arrow	0;166	<Alt> Keypad Enter

EBCDIC Character Codes

Table D.3	EBCDIC Character Codes				
Dec	**Hex**	**Octal**	**Binary**	**Name**	**Character**
0	00	000	0000 0000	NUL	
1	01	001	0000 0001	SOH	
2	02	002	0000 0010	STX	
3	03	003	0000 0011	ETX	
4	04	004	0000 0100	SEL	
5	05	005	0000 0101	HT	
6	06	006	0000 0110	RNL	
7	07	007	0000 0111	DEL	
8	08	010	0000 1000	GE	
9	09	011	0000 1001	SPS	
10	0A	012	0000 1010	RPT	
11	0B	013	0000 1011	VT	
12	0C	014	0000 1100	FF	
13	0D	015	0000 1101	CR	
14	0E	016	0000 1110	SO	
15	0F	017	0000 1111	SI	
16	10	020	0001 0000	DLE	
17	11	021	0001 0001	DC1	
18	12	022	0001 0010	DC2	
19	13	023	0001 0011	DC3	
20	14	024	0001 0100	RES/ENP	
21	15	025	0001 0101	NL	
22	16	026	0001 0110	BS	
23	17	027	0001 0111	POC	
24	18	030	0001 1000	CAN	

Dec	Hex	Octal	Binary	Name	Character
25	19	031	0001 1001	EM	
26	1A	032	0001 1010	UBS	
27	1B	033	0001 1011	CU1	
28	1C	034	0001 1100	IFS	
29	1D	035	0001 1101	IGS	
30	1E	036	0001 1110	IRS	
31	1F	037	0001 1111	IUS/ITB	
32	20	040	0010 0000	DS	
33	21	041	0010 0001	SOS	
34	22	042	0010 0010	FS	
35	23	043	0010 0011	WUS	
36	24	044	0010 0100	BYP/INP	
37	25	045	0010 0101	LF	
38	26	046	0010 0110	ETB	
39	27	047	0010 0111	ESC	
40	28	050	0010 1000	SA	
41	29	051	0010 1001	SFE	
42	2A	052	0010 1010	SM/SW	
43	2B	053	0010 1011	CSP	
44	2C	054	0010 1100	MFA	
45	2D	055	0010 1101	ENQ	
46	2E	056	0010 1110	ACK	
47	2F	057	0010 1111	BEL	
48	30	060	0011 0000		
49	31	061	0011 0001		
50	32	062	0011 0010	SYN	
51	33	063	0011 0011	IR	
52	34	064	0011 0100	PP	
53	35	065	0011 0101	TRN	
54	36	066	0011 0110	NBS	
55	37	067	0011 0111	EOT	
56	38	070	0011 1000	SBS	
57	39	071	0011 1001	IT	
58	3A	072	0011 1010	RFF	
59	3B	073	0011 1011	CU3	
60	3C	074	0011 1100	DC4	
61	3D	075	0011 1101	NAK	
62	3E	076	0011 1110		
63	3F	077	0011 1111	SUB	

(continues)

Table D.3		EBCDIC Character Codes Continued			
Dec	**Hex**	**Octal**	**Binary**	**Name**	**Character**
64	40	100	0100 0000	SP	
65	41	101	0100 0001	RSP	
66	42	102	0100 0010		
67	43	103	0100 0011		
68	44	104	0100 0100		
69	45	105	0100 0101		
70	46	106	0100 0110		
71	47	107	0100 0111		
72	48	110	0100 1000		
73	49	111	0100 1001		
74	4A	112	0100 1010		¢
75	4B	113	0100 1011		.
76	4C	114	0100 1100		<
77	4D	115	0100 1101		(
78	4E	116	0100 1110		+
79	4F	117	0100 1111		|
80	50	120	0101 0000		&
81	51	121	0101 0001		
82	52	122	0101 0010		
83	53	123	0101 0011		
84	54	124	0101 0100		
85	55	125	0101 0101		
86	56	126	0101 0110		
87	57	127	0101 0111		
88	58	130	0101 1000		
89	59	131	0101 1001		
90	5A	132	0101 1010		!
91	5B	133	0101 1011		$
92	5C	134	0101 1100		*
93	5D	135	0101 1101		)
94	5E	136	0101 1110		;
95	5F	137	0101 1111		¬
96	60	140	0110 0000		–
97	61	141	0110 0001		/
98	62	142	0110 0010		
99	63	143	0110 0011		
100	64	144	0110 0100		
101	65	145	0110 0101		
102	66	146	0110 0110		

Dec	Hex	Octal	Binary	Name	Character
103	67	147	0110 0111		
104	68	150	0110 1000		
105	69	151	0110 1001		
106	6A	152	0110 1010		|
107	6B	153	0110 1011		,
108	6C	154	0110 1100		%
109	6D	155	0110 1101		-
110	6E	156	0110 1110		>
111	6F	157	0110 1111		?
112	70	160	0111 0000		
113	71	161	0111 0001		
114	72	162	0111 0010		
115	73	163	0111 0011		
116	74	164	0111 0100		
117	75	165	0111 0101		
118	76	166	0111 0110		
119	77	167	0111 0111		
120	78	170	0111 1000		
121	79	171	0111 1001		`
122	7A	172	0111 1010		:
123	7B	173	0111 1011		#
124	7C	174	0111 1100		@
125	7D	175	0111 1101		'
126	7E	176	0111 1110		=
127	7F	177	0111 1111		"
128	80	200	1000 0000		
129	81	201	1000 0001		a
130	82	202	1000 0010		b
131	83	203	1000 0011		c
132	84	204	1000 0100		d
133	85	205	1000 0101		e
134	86	206	1000 0110		f
135	87	207	1000 0111		g
136	88	210	1000 1000		h
137	89	211	1000 1001		i
138	8A	212	1000 1010		
139	8B	213	1000 1011		
140	8C	214	1000 1100		
141	8D	215	1000 1101		
142	8E	216	1000 1110		

(continues)

Table D.3   EBCDIC Character Codes Continued

Dec	Hex	Octal	Binary	Name	Character
143	8F	217	1000 1111		
144	90	220	1001 0000		
145	91	221	1001 0001		j
146	92	222	1001 0010		k
147	93	223	1001 0011		l
148	94	224	1001 0100		m
149	95	225	1001 0101		n
150	96	226	1001 0110		o
151	97	227	1001 0111		p
152	98	230	1001 1000		q
153	99	231	1001 1001		r
154	9A	232	1001 1010		
155	9B	233	1001 1011		
156	9C	234	1001 1100		
157	9D	235	1001 1101		
158	9E	236	1001 1110		
159	9F	237	1001 1111		
160	A0	240	1010 0000		
161	A1	241	1010 0001		~
162	A2	242	1010 0010		s
163	A3	243	1010 0011		t
164	A4	244	1010 0100		u
165	A5	245	1010 0101		v
166	A6	246	1010 0110		w
167	A7	247	1010 0111		x
168	A8	250	1010 1000		y
169	A9	251	1010 1001		z
170	AA	252	1010 1010		
171	AB	253	1010 1011		
172	AC	254	1010 1100		
173	AD	255	1010 1101		
174	AE	256	1010 1110		
175	AF	257	1010 1111		
176	B0	260	1011 0000		
177	B1	261	1011 0001		
178	B2	262	1011 0010		
179	B3	263	1011 0011		
180	B4	264	1011 0100		
181	B5	265	1011 0101		

Dec	Hex	Octal	Binary	Name	Character
182	B6	266	1011 0110		
183	B7	267	1011 0111		
184	B8	270	1011 1000		
185	B9	271	1011 1001		
186	BA	272	1011 1010		
187	BB	273	1011 1011		
188	BC	274	1011 1100		
189	BD	275	1011 1101		
190	BE	276	1011 1110		
191	BF	277	1011 1111		
192	C0	300	1100 0000		{
193	C1	301	1100 0001		A
194	C2	302	1100 0010		B
195	C3	303	1100 0011		C
196	C4	304	1100 0100		D
197	C5	305	1100 0101		E
198	C6	306	1100 0110		F
199	C7	307	1100 0111		G
200	C8	310	1100 1000		H
201	C9	311	1100 1001		I
202	CA	312	1100 1010	SHY	
203	CB	313	1100 1011		
204	CC	314	1100 1100		
205	CD	315	1100 1101		
206	CE	316	1100 1110		
207	CF	317	1100 1111		
208	D0	320	1101 0000		}
209	D1	321	1101 0001		J
210	D2	322	1101 0010		K
211	D3	323	1101 0011		L
212	D4	324	1101 0100		M
213	D5	325	1101 0101		N
214	D6	326	1101 0110		O
215	D7	327	1101 0111		P
216	D8	330	1101 1000		Q
217	D9	331	1101 1001		R
218	DA	332	1101 1010		
219	DB	333	1101 1011		
220	DC	334	1101 1100		
221	DD	335	1101 1101		

(continues)

Table D.3	EBCDIC Character Codes Continued				
Dec	**Hex**	**Octal**	**Binary**	**Name**	**Character**
222	DE	336	1101 1110		
223	DF	337	1101 1111		
224	E0	340	1110 0000		\
225	E1	341	1110 0001	NSP	
226	E2	342	1110 0010		S
227	E3	343	1110 0011		T
228	E4	344	1110 0100		U
229	E5	345	1110 0101		V
230	E6	346	1110 0110		W
231	E7	347	1110 0111		X
232	E8	350	1110 1000		Y
233	E9	351	1110 1001		Z
234	EA	352	1110 1010		
235	EB	353	1110 1011		
236	EC	354	1110 1100		
237	ED	355	1110 1101		
238	EE	356	1110 1110		
239	EF	357	1110 1111		
240	F0	360	1111 0000		0
241	F1	361	1111 0001		1
242	F2	362	1111 0010		2
243	F3	363	1111 0011		3
244	F4	364	1111 0100		4
245	F5	365	1111 0101		5
246	F6	366	1111 0110		6
247	F7	367	1111 0111		7
248	F8	370	1111 1000		8
249	F9	371	1111 1001		9
250	FA	372	1111 1010		
251	FB	373	1111 1011		
252	FC	374	1111 1100		
253	FD	375	1111 1101		
254	FE	376	1111 1110		
255	FF	377	1111 1111	EO	

Metric System (SI) Prefixes

Table D.4   Metric System Prefixes

Multiplier	Exponent Form	Prefix	SI Symbol
1 000 000 000 000 000 000 000 000	10^{24}	yotta	Y
1 000 000 000 000 000 000 000	10^{21}	zetta	Z
1 000 000 000 000 000 000	10^{18}	exa	E
1 000 000 000 000 000	10^{15}	peta	P
1 000 000 000 000	10^{12}	tera	T
1 000 000 000	10^{9}	giga	G
1 000 000	10^{6}	mega	M
1 000	10^{3}	Kilo	k
100	10^{2}	hecto	h
10	10^{1}	deca	da
0.1	10^{-1}	deci	d
0.01	10^{-2}	centi	c
0.001	10^{-3}	milli	m
0.000 001	10^{-6}	micro	μ
0.000 000 001	10^{-9}	nano	n
0.000 000 000 001	10^{-12}	pico	p
0.000 000 000 000 001	10^{-15}	femto	f
0.000 000 000 000 000 001	10^{-18}	atto	a
0.000 000 000 000 000 000 001	10^{-21}	zepto	z
0.000 000 000 000 000 000 000 001	10^{-24}	yocto	y

U.S.—Metric Units of Length Conversions

Table D.5   Conversions from U.S. to Metric

1 Inch = 2.54 centimeters = 25.4 millimeters

1 foot = 30.48 centimeters = .3048 meter

1 yard = .914 meter

1 mile = 1.609 kilometers

Table D.6   Conversions from Metric to U.S.

1 millimeter = .03937 inch

1 centimeter = .3937 inch

1 meter = 3.2808 feet = 1.0936 yards = 39.37 inches

1 kilometer = .621 mile

Powers of 2

n	2^n	Hexadecimal
0	1	1
1	2	2
2	4	4
3	8	8
4	16	10
5	32	20
6	64	40
7	128	80
8	256	100
9	512	200
10	1,024	400
11	2,048	800
12	4,096	1000
13	8,192	2000
14	16,384	4000
15	32,768	8000
16	65,536	10000
17	131,072	20000
18	262,144	40000
19	524,288	80000
20	1,048,576	100000
21	2,097,152	200000
22	4,194,304	400000
23	8,388,608	800000
24	16,777,216	1000000
25	33,554,432	2000000
26	67,108,864	4000000
27	134,217,728	8000000
28	268,435,456	10000000
29	536,870,912	20000000
30	1,073,741,824	40000000
31	2,147,483,648	80000000
32	4,294,967,296	100000000
33	8,589,934,592	200000000
34	17,179,869,184	400000000
35	34,359,738,368	800000000
36	68,719,476,736	1000000000
37	137,438,953,472	2000000000

Table D.7 Powers of 2

n	2ⁿ	Hexadecimal
38	274,877,906,944	4000000000
39	549,755,813,888	8000000000
40	1,099,511,627,776	10000000000
41	2,199,023,255,552	20000000000
42	4,398,046,511,104	40000000000
43	8,796,093,022,208	80000000000
44	17,592,186,044,416	100000000000
45	35,184,372,088,832	200000000000
46	70,368,744,177,664	400000000000
47	140,737,488,355,328	800000000000
48	281,474,976,710,656	1000000000000
49	562,949,953,421,312	2000000000000
50	1,125,899,906,842,624	4000000000000
51	2,251,799,813,685,248	8000000000000
52	4,503,599,627,370,496	10000000000000
53	9,007,199,254,740,992	20000000000000
54	18,014,398,509,481,984	40000000000000
55	36,028,797,018,963,968	80000000000000
56	72,057,594,037,927,936	100000000000000
57	144,115,188,075,855,872	200000000000000
58	288,230,376,151,711,744	400000000000000
59	576,460,752,303,423,488	800000000000000
60	1,152,921,504,606,846,976	1000000000000000
61	2,305,843,009,213,693,952	2000000000000000
62	4,611,686,018,427,387,904	4000000000000000
63	9,223,372,036,854,775,808	8000000000000000
64	18,446,744,073,709,551,616	10000000000000000

Electromagnetic Spectrum

The electromagnetic spectrum plays a crucial role in most computer technologies. An obvious application is the light in the visible spectrum produced by a monitor. In addition, CD-ROM drives use light in the infrared region to read CDs; wireless keyboards and mice use infrared to communicate with the PC; wireless networks commonly use a portion of the UHF band at 2.4GHz; and ultraviolet light is used in photolithography to create chips on silicon wafers. Table D.8 lists all the broad regions of the electromagnetic spectrum and breaks them down into their commonly named bands. There is some overlap in these defined regions.

Table D.8 Regions of the Electromagnetic Spectrum

Broad Region	Band	Frequency (Hz)	Wavelength (cm, mm, μm, nm)
Radio Waves			
	ultra-low (ULF)	3–30Hz	10^7–10^8 m
	extremely low (ELF)	30–300Hz	10^6–10^7 m
	voice frequencies (VF)	300Hz–3KHz	10^5–10^6 m
	very low (VLF)	3–30KHz	10^4–10^5 m
	low (LF)	30–300KHz	10^3–10^4 m
	medium (MF) (shortwave radio and AM radio)	300KHz–3MHz	10^2–10^3 m
	high (HF) (shortwave radio)	3–30MHz	10–100 m
	very high (VHF) (television and FM radio)	30–300MHz	1–10 m
	ultra high (UHF) (television)	300MHz–3GHz	100 cm–1 m
	super high (SHF)	3–30GHz	10–100 cm
	extremely high (EHF)	30–300GHz	1- 10 cm
	microwave	1–300GHz	1 mm–30 cm
Infrared Visible		3×10^{11} –4×10^{14}Hz	0.75–1000 μm
	red	3.9×10^{14} –4.8×10^{14}Hz	622–770 nm
	orange	4.8×10^{14} –5×10^{14}Hz	597–622 nm
	yellow	5×10^{14} –5.2×10^{14}Hz	577–597 nm
	green	5.2×10^{14} –6.1×10^{14}Hz	492–577 nm
	blue	6.1×10^{14} –6.6×10^{14}Hz	455–492 nm
	violet	6.6×10^{14} –7.7×10^{14}Hz	390–455 nm
Ultraviolet	UV	7.5×10^{14} –3×10^{16}Hz	10–400 nm
	UV-A	7.5×10^{14} –9.4×10^{14}Hz	320–400 nm
	UV-B	9.4×10^{14} –1.1×10^{15}Hz	280–320 nm
X ray		10^{16}–10^{21}Hz	3×10^{-8}–3×10^{-13} m
Gamma ray		10^{18}–10^{23}Hz	3×10^{-10}–3×10^{-15} m

Modem Control Codes

This section lists the command and control codes for popular modems. Most modems use a standard AT command set that was developed by Hayes and augmented by U.S. Robotics. Table D.9 comes in handy when you need to reconfigure a modem without the original manual. Even if your modem is not Hayes or U.S. Robotics, it probably follows most of these commands because this command set has become somewhat of a standard. S-register values listed at the end of the table are also somewhat standard but are more subject to variation in the defaults by brand and model.

Table D.9   Modem AT Commands and S-Register Features

Command	Modem Functions and Options	
&	See Extended Command Set	
%	See Extended Command Set	
A	Force Answer mode when modem has not received an incoming call	
A/	Reexecute last command once	
A>	Repeat last command continuously	
Any key	Terminate current connection attempt; exit Repeat mode	
AT	Attention: must precede all other commands, except A/, A>, and +++	
Bn	Handshake options	
	B0	CCITT answer sequence
	B1	Bell answer tone
Cn	Transmitter On/Off	
	C0	Transmitter Off
	C1	Transmitter On—Default
Dn	Dial number n and go into originate mode	
	Use any of these options:	
	P	Pulse dial—Default
	T	Touch-Tone dial
	,	(Comma) Pause for 2 seconds
	;	Return to command state after dialing
	"…	Dial the letters that follow
	!	Flash switch-hook to transfer call
	W	Wait for 2nd dial tone (if X3 or higher is set)
	@	Wait for an answer (if X3 or higher is set)
	R	Reverse frequencies
	S	Dial stored number
DL	Dial the last-dialed number	
DSn	Dial number stored in NVRAM at position n	
En	Command mode local echo; not applicable after a connection has been made	
	E0	Echo Off
	E1	Echo On
Fn	Local echo On/Off when a connection has been made	

(continues)

Table D.9 Modem AT Commands and S-Register Features Continued

Command	Modem Functions and Options
	F0 Echo On (Half duplex)
	F1 Echo Off (Full duplex)—Default
Hn	On/Off hook control
	H0 Hang up (go on hook)—Default
	H1 Go off hook
In	Inquiry
	I0 Return product code
	I1 Return memory (ROM) checksum
	I2 Run memory (RAM) test
	I3 Return call duration/real time
	I4 Return current modem settings
	I5 Return NVRAM settings
	I6 Return link diagnostics
	I7 Return product configuration
Kn	Modem clock operation
	K0 ATI3 displays call duration—Default
	K1 ATI3 displays real time; set with ATI3=HH:MM:SSK1
Ln	Loudness of speaker volume
	L0 Low
	L1 Low
	L2 Medium
	L3 High
Mn	Monitor (speaker) control
	M0 Speaker always Off
	M1 Speaker On until carrier is established—Default
	M2 Speaker always On
	M3 Speaker On after last digit dialed, Off at carrier detect
O	Return on-line after command execution
	O0 Return on-line, normal
	O1 Return on-line, retrain
P	Pulse dial
Qn	Result codes display
	Q0 Result codes displayed
	Q1 Result codes suppressed (quiet mode)
	Q2 Quiet in answer mode only
Sr=n	Set Register commands: r is any S-register; n must be a decimal number between 0 and 255.
Sr.b=n	Set bit .b of register r to n (0/Off or 1/On)
Sr?	Query register r

Command	Modem Functions and Options	
T	Tone dial	
Vn	Verbal/Numeric result codes	
	V0	Numeric mode
	V1	Verbal mode
Xn	Result code options	
Yn	Long space disconnect	
	Y0	Disabled
	Y1	Enabled; disconnects after 1.5-second
break		
Z	Software reset	
+++	Escape code sequence, preceded and followed by at least one second of no data transmission	
/(Slash)	Pause for 125 msec	
>	Repeat command continuously or up to 10 dial attempts Cancel by pressing any key	
$	Online Help—Basic command summary	
&$	Online Help—Ampersand command summary	
%$	Online Help—Percent command summary	
D$	Online Help—Dial command summary	
S$	Online Help—S-register summary	
<Ctrl>-S	Stop/restart display of HELP screens	
<Ctrl>-C	Cancel display HELP screens	
<Ctrl>-K	Cancel display HELP screens	

Extended Command Set

Command	Modem Functions and Options	
&An	ARQ result codes 14–17, 19	
	&A0	Suppress ARQ result codes
	&A1	Display ARQ result codes —Default
	&A2	Display HST and V.32 result codes
	&A3	Display protocol result codes
&Bn	Data Rate, terminal-to-modem (DTE/DCE)	
	&B0	DTE rate follows connection rate—Default
	&B1	Fixed DTE rate
	&B2	Fixed DTE rate in ARQ mode; variable DTE rate in non-ARQ mode
&Cn	Carrier Detect (CD) operations	
	&C0	CD override
	&C1	Normal CD operations
&Dn	Data Terminal Ready (DTR) operations	
	&D0	DTR override
	&D1	DTR Off; goes to command state
	&D2	DTR Off; goes to command state and on hook
	&D3	DTR Off; resets modem

(continues)

Table D.9 Modem AT Commands and S-Register Features Continued

Command	Modem Functions and Options
&F	Load factory settings into RAM
&Gn	Guard tone
	&G0 No guard tone; U.S., Canada—Default
	&G1 Guard tone; some European countries
	&G2 Guard tone; U.K., requires B0
&Hn	Transmit Data flow control
	&H0 Flow control disabled—Default
	&H1 Hardware (CTS) flow control
	&H2 Software (XON/XOFF) flow control
	&H3 Hardware and software control
&In	Received Data software flow control
	&I0 Flow control disabled—Default
	&I1 XON/XOFF to local modem and remote computer
	&I2 XON/XOFF to local modem only
	&I3 Host mode, Hewlett-Packard protocol
	&I4 Terminal mode, Hewlett-Packard protocol
	&I5 ARQ mode-same as &I2; non-ARQ mode; look for incoming XON/XOFF
&Jn	Telephone jack selection
	&J0 RJ-11/ RJ-41S/ RJ-45S
	&J1 RJ-12/ RJ-13
&Kn	Data compression
	&K0 Disabled
	&K1 Auto enable/disable—Default
	&K2 Enabled
	&K3 V.42bis only
&Ln	Normal/Leased line operation
	&L0 Normal phone line—Default
	&L1 Leased line
&Mn	Error Control/Synchronous Options
	&M0 Normal mode, no error control
	&M1 Synch mode
	&M2 Synch mode 2—stored number dialing
	&M3 Synch mode 3—manual dialing
	&M4 Normal/ARQ mode-Normal if ARQ connection cannot be made-Default
	&M5 ARQ mode-hang up if ARQ connection cannot be made
&Nn	Data Rate, data link (DCE/DCE)
	&N0 Normal link operations—Default
	&N1 300 bps
	&N2 1200 bps

Command	Modem Functions and Options	
	&N3	2400 bps
	&N4	4800 bps
	&N5	7200 bps
	&N6	9600 bps
	&N7	12K bps
	&N8	14.4K bps
&Pn	Pulse dial make/break ratio	
&P0	North America—Default	
&P1	British Commonwealth	
&Rn	Received Data hardware (RTS) flow control	
	&R0	CTS tracks RTS
	&R1	Ignore RTS—Default
	&R2	Pass received data on RTS high; used Pass received data on RTS high

Extended Command Set

Command	Modem Functions and Options	
&Sn	Data Set Ready (DSR) override	
	&S0	DSR override (always On—Default)
	&S1	Modem controls DSR
	&S2	Pulsed DSR; CTS follows CD
	&S3	Pulsed DSR
&Tn	Modem Testing	
	&T0	End testing
	&T1	Analog loopback
	&T2	Reserved
	&T3	Digital loopback
	&T4	Grant remote digital loopback
	&T5	Deny remote digital loopback
	&T6	Initiate remote digital loopback
	&T7	Remote digital loopback with self-test
	&T8	Analog loopback with self-test
&W	Write current settings to NVRAM	
&Xn	Synchronous timing source	
	&X0	Modem's transmit clock—Default
	&X1	Terminal equipment
	&X2	Modem's receiver clock
&Yn	Break handling. Destructive breaks clear the buffer; expedited Breaks are sent immediately to remote system.	
	&Y0	Destructive, but don't send break
	&Y1	Destructive, expedited—Default
	&Y2	Nondestructive, expedited
	&Y3	Nondestructive, unexpedited

(continues)

Table D.9 Modem AT Commands and S-Register Features Continued

Command	Modem Functions and Options
&Zn=L	Store last-dialed phone number in NVRAM at position n
&Zn=s	Write phone number(s) to NVRAM at position n (0–3); 36 characters maximum
&Zn?	Display phone number in NVRAM at position n (n=0–3)
%Rn	Remote access to Rack Controller Unit (RCU)
	%R0 Disabled
	%R1 Enabled
%T	Enable Touch-Tone recognition

Modem S-Register Functions and Defaults

S0	Number of rings before automatic answering when DIP switch 5 is UP. Default = 1. S0 = 0 disables Auto Answer, equivalent to DIP switch 5 Down
S1	Counts and stores number of rings from incoming call
S2	Define escape code character. Default = +
S3	Define ASCII carriage return
S4	Define ASCII line feed
S5	Define ASCII Backspace
S6	Number of seconds modem waits before dialing
S7	Number of seconds modem waits for a carrier
S8	Duration (sec) for pause (,) option in Dial command and pause between command reexecutions for Repeat (>) command
S9	Duration (.1 sec units) of remote carrier signal before recognition
S10	Duration (.1 sec units) modem waits after loss of carrier before hanging up
S11	Duration and spacing (ms) of dialed Touch-Tones
S12	Guard time (in .02 sec units) for escape code sequence (+++)
S13	Bit-mapped register:
	1 Reset when DTR drops
	2 Auto answer in originate mode
	4 Disable result code pause
	8 DS0 on DTR low-to-high
	16 DS0 on power up, ATZ
	32 Disable HST modulation
	64 Disable MNP Level 3
	128 Watchdog hardware reset
S15	Bit-mapped register:
	1 Disable high-frequency equalization
	2 Disable on-line fallback
	4 Force 300-bps back channel
	8 Set non-ARQ transmit buffer to 128 bytes
	16 Disable MNP Level 4
	32 Set Del as Backspace key

Command	Modem Functions and Options		
	64 Unusual MNP incompatibility		
	128 Custom applications only		
S16	Bit-mapped register:		
	1 Analog loopback		
	2 Dial test		
	4 Test pattern		
	8 Initiate remote digital loopback		
	16 Reserved		
	32 Reserved		
	64 Reserved		
	128 Reserved		
S18	&Tn Test timer, disabled when set to 0		
S19	Set inactivity timer in minutes		
S21	Length of Break, DCE to DTE, in 10ms units		
S22	Define ASCII XON	17	17
S23	Define ASCII XOFF	19	19

Modem S-Register Functions and Defaults

Command	Modem Functions and Options	
S24	Duration (20ms units) of pulsed DSR when modem is set to &S2 or &S3	
S25	Delay to DTR in 10ms units	
S26	Duration (10ms units) of delay between RTS and CTS, synchronous mode	
S27	Bit-mapped register:	
	1 Enable V.21 modulation, 300 bps	
	2 Enable unencoded V.32 modulation	
	4 Disable V.32 modulation	
	8 Disable 2100 Hz answer tone	
	16 Disable MNP handshake	
	32 Disable V.42 Detect phase	
	64 Reserved	
	128 Unusual software incompatibility	
S28	Duration (.1 sec units) of V.21/V.23 handshake delay	
S32	Voice/Data switch options:	1
	0 Disabled	
	1 Go off hook in originate mode	
	2 Go off hook in answer mode	
	3 Redial last-dialed number	
	4 Dial number stored at position 0	
	5 Auto answer toggle On/Off	
	6 Reset modem	
	7 Initiate remote digital loopback	

(continues)

Table D.9 Modem AT Commands and S-Register Features Continued	
Command	**Modem Functions and Options**
S34	Bit-mapped register:
	1 Disable V.32bis
	2 Disable enhanced V.32 mode
	4 Disable quick V.32 retrain
	8 Enable V.23 modulation
	16 Change MR LED to DSR
	32 Enable MI/MIC
	64 Reserved
	128 Reserved
S38	Duration (sec) before disconnect when DTR drops during an ARQ call

ARQ = Automatic repeat request
ASCII = American Standard Code for Information Interchange
BPS = Bits per second
CCITT = Consultative Committee for International Telephone and Telegraph
CD = Carrier detect
CRC = Cyclic redundancy check
DCE = Data communications equipment
DTE = Data terminal equipment
EIA = Electronic Industries Association
HDLC = High-level data link control
HST = High-speed technology
Hz = Hertz
LAPM = Link access procedure for modems
MI/MIC = Mode indicate/Mode indicate common
MNP = Microcom networking protocol
NVRAM = Non-volatile memory
RAM = Random-access memory
ROM = Read-only memory
SDLC = Synchronous Data Link Control
MR = Modem ready
LED = Light-emitting diode
DTR = Data terminal ready
CTS = Clear to send
RTS = Ready to send
DSR = Data set ready

Hard Disk Drives

This section has a great deal of information concerning all aspects of hard disk drives, including several tables that list a large number of different drive parameters, organized by manufacturer. This section also shows BIOS hard drive parameter tables for a number of ROM BIOS versions, including those from IBM, Compaq, AMI, Award, and Phoenix. Note that these ROM BIOS parameter tables are representative of the tables that were used by these manufacturers before IDE drives and user-definable drive types were common in all systems. Therefore, the ROM BIOS tables are mostly useful for supporting legacy hardware.

Hard Drive Parameters

Tables D.10–D.16 contain the specifications for drives from several of the major manufacturers*. The manufacturers represented are:

Conner—Table D.10

IBM—Table D.11

Maxtor—Table D.12

Quantum—Table D.13

Seagate—Table D.14

Toshiba—Table D.15

Western Digital—Table D.16

Note that Conner is now part of Seagate but Conner model drives are listed separately here for convenience.

The following list defines the abbreviations used in the table column headings that follow.

- *INT*. Interface type.
- *CAP*. Capacity in megabytes.
- *FF*. Form Factor denotes the diameter of the drive platter(s) in inches.
- *HGT*. The drive's height.
- *CODE*. Encoding scheme.
- *LZ*. Landing zone (or parking, shipping) cylinder. Not used on most of the newer drives.
- *WP*. Write Precompensation cylinder. Not used on most of the newer drives.
- *RWC*. Reduced Write Current cylinder. Not used on most of the newer drives.
- *MTBF*. Mean Time Between Failures, in thousands of hours.
- *PHDS*. Number of *physical* data heads. Servo heads are not included in this figure.
- *PCYL*. Number of *physical* user-accessible cylinders. *If the drive is an IDE drive and this number exceeds 1,024, a translation must be used.*
- *PSPT*. Number of *physical* sectors per track.
- *LHDS*. Number of *logical* data heads. Servo heads are not included in this figure.
- *LCYL*. Number of *logical* user-accessible cylinders.
- *LSPT*. Number of *logical* sectors per track.

* *Tables D.10–D.16 are reprinted from* The Micro House PC Hardware Library, *Copyright © Que Corporation and Micro House International, Inc. 1998.*

In addition, the following abbreviations are used to save space within the table rows:

- *INT.* COMM=COMMODORE

  IDE-CPQ=IDE-COMPAQ

  U-SCSI=ULTRA-SCSI

  PCM=PCMCIA

  U=UNIDEN

- *FF.* FH=Full

  HH=Half

  3H=1 inch

  4H=less than 1 inch

- *CODE.* RLL 1=RLL 1,7

  RLL 2=RLL 2,7

  RLL 3=RLL 3,9

- *PSPT.* VAR=Variable sectors per track

For IDE drives, LHDS, LCYL, and LSPT are the figures you should enter in a user-definable BIOS Drive Type (usually Type 46 or Type 47). If these figures aren't listed for an IDE drive and the actual physical parameters cannot be used, you can use the values from the IDE Quick Reference Chart (see Table D.17). Alternatively, you may need to upgrade the BIOS to a newer version that supports the IDE Identify Drive command if the drive supports that command. Table D.11 shows the IBM motherboard ROM BIOS hard disk parameters for AT or PS/2 systems using ST-506/412 (standard or IDE) controllers.

Table D.10	CONNER PERIPHERALS, INC.														
MODEL	**INT**	**CAP**	**FF**	**HGT**	**CODE**	**LZ**	**WP**	**RWC**	**MTBF**	**PHDS**	**PCYL**	**PSPT**	**LHDS**	**LCYL**	**LSPT**
CFA-1080A	IDE(AT)	1000	3.50	3H	RLL 1	AUTO	N/A	N/A	250	0	0	0	16	2100	63
CFA-1275A	IDE(AT)	1278	3.50	3H	U	2480	N/A	N/A	300	6	2479	0	16	2479	63
CFA-1275S	SCSI-2	1278	3.50	3H	RLL 1	AUTO	N/A	N/A	300	6	0	0			
CFA-170A	IDE(AT)	163.4	3.50	3H	RLL 1	AUTO	N/A	N/A		0	0	0	16	332	63
CFA-170S	SCSI	170.13	3.50	3H	RLL 1	AUTO	N/A	N/A	150	4	1806	46			
CFA-2161A	IDE(AT)	2147	3.50	3H	RLL 1	AUTO	N/A	N/A	500	8	4474	0	16	4095	63
CFA-270A	IDE(AT)	270.5	3.50	3H	RLL 1	AUTO			0	2	2805	0	16	524	63
CFA-270S	SCSI-2	270.5	3.50	3H	RLL 1	AUTO			0	2	2805	0			
CFA-340A	IDE(AT)	343	3.50	3H	RLL 1	AUTO	N/A	N/A	250	4	2111	0	16	665	63
CFA-340S	SCSI-2	343	3.50	3H	RLL 1	AUTO	N/A	N/A	250	4	0	0			
CFA-425A	IDE(AT)	426	3.50	3H	U	863	N/A	N/A	300	2	862	0	16	826	63

MODEL	INT	CAP	FF	HGT	CODE	LZ	WP	RWC	MTBF	PHDS	PCYL	PSPT	LHDS	LCYL	LSPT
CFA-540A	IDE(AT)	540.86	3.50	3H	RLL 1	AUTO	N/A	N/A	250	4	2111	0	16	1048	63
CFA-540S	SCSI-2	541	3.50	3H	RLL 1	AUTO	N/A	N/A	300	4	2805	0			
CFA-810A	IDE(AT)	810	3.50	3H	RLL 1	1572	N/A	N/A	300	0	0	0	16	1572	63
CFA-850A	IDE(AT)	850	3.50	3H	RLL 1	N/A	N/A	N/A	250	4	3640	111	16	1652	63
CFA-850S	SCSI-2	852	3.50	3H	RLL 1	AUTO	N/A	N/A	300	4	0	0			
CFL-350A	IDE(AT)	350	2.50	FH	RLL 1	905	N/A	N/A	300	4	2225	0	12	905	63
CFL-420A	IDE(AT)	422	2.50	5H	RLL 1	818	N/A	N/A	300	4	2393	0	16	818	63
CFN-170A	IDE(AT)	168.2	2.50	4H	RLL 1	AUTO	N/A	N/A	250	4	1339	0	16	326	63
CFN-170S	SCSI-2	168.2	2.50	4H	RLL 1	AUTO	N/A	N/A	250	4	1339	0			
CFN-250A	IDE(AT)	252.7	2.50	4H	RLL 1	AUTO			0	6	1339	0	16	489	63
CFN-250S	SCSI-2	252.7	2.50	4H	RLL 1	AUTO			0	6	1339	0			
CFN-340A	IDE(AT)	344.5	2.50	4H	RLL 1	AUTO	N/A	N/A	250	6	1598	0	16	667	63
CFN-340S	SCSI-2	344.5	2.50	4H	RLL 1	AUTO	N/A	N/A	250	6	1598	0			
CFP-1060B	SCSI-2 D	1062.44	3.50	3H	RLL 1				500	8	2757	0			
CFP-1060E	SCSI	1062.44	3.50	3H	RLL 1				500	8	2757	0			
CFP-1060S	SCSI-2	1062.44	3.50	3H	RLL 1				500	8	2757	0			
CFP-1060W	SCSI-2 W	1062.44	3.50	3H	RLL 1				500	8	2757	0			
CFP-1080S	SCSI-2 F	1080	3.50	3H	RLL 1	AUTO	N/A	N/A	500	6	0	0			
CFP-2105S	SCSI-2 W	2147	3.50	3H	U	AUTO	N/A	N/A	999	10	3892	0			
CFP-2105W	SCSI-2	2147	3.50	3H	U	AUTO	N/A	N/A	999	10	3892	0			
CFP-2107E	SCSI-2 FW	2110	3.50	3H	RLL 1	AUTO	N/A	N/A	999	10	3924	91			
CFP-2107S	SCSI-2 F	2110	3.50	3H	RLL 1	AUTO	N/A	N/A	999	10	3924	91			
CFP-2107W	SCSI-2 FW	2110	3.50	3H	RLL 1	AUTO	N/A	N/A	999	10	3924	91			
CFP-4207E	SCSI-2 FW	4295	3.50	3H	RLL 1	AUTO	N/A	N/A	999	20	3924	96			
CFP-4207S	SCSI-2 W	4295	3.50	3H	RLL 1	AUTO	N/A	N/A	999	20	3924	96			
CFP-4207W	SCSI-2 FW	4295	3.50	3H	RLL 1		N/A	N/A	999	20	3924	96			
CFS-1081A	IDE(AT)	1080	3.50	3H	U	2097	N/A	N/A	300	4	3924	0	16	2097	63
CFS-1275A	IDE(AT)	1278	3.50	HH	RLL 1	2479	0		250	0	0	0	16	2479	63
CFS-1275A (REV. A)	IDE(AT)	1275	3.50	HH	RLL 1	AUTO	N/A	N/A	250	6	3640	0	16	2477	63
CFS-1621A	IDE(AT)	1620	3.50	3H	U	3146	N/A	N/A	300	6	3924	0	16	3146	63
CFS-210A	IDE(AT)	213.23	3.50	3H	RLL 1	AUTO	N/A	N/A	250	0	0	0	16	685	38
CFS-270A	IDE(AT)	270.9	3.50	3H	RLL 1	AUTO	N/A	N/A	250	2	0	0	16	525	63
CFS-420A	IDE(AT)	426.8	3.50	3H	RLL 1	AUTO			250	4	2388	0	16	826	63
CFS-425A	IDE(AT)	425	3.50	3H	RLL 1	AUTO	N/A	N/A	250	2	0	0	16	826	63
CFS-540A	IDE(AT)	540	3.50	3H	RLL 1	AUTO	N/A	N/A	250	4	0	0	16	1050	63
CFS-541A	IDE(AT)	540	3.50	3H	RLL 1	1048	N/A	N/A	300	2	3924	0	16	1048	63
CFS-635A	IDE(AT)	635	3.50	3H	RLL 1	AUTO	N/A	N/A	300	3	3640	0	16	1238	63
CFS-850A	IDE(AT)	850	3.50	3H	RLL 1	AUTO	N/A	N/A	300	4	3640	0	16	1651	63

(continues)

Table D.10 CONNER PERIPHERALS, INC. Continued

MODEL	INT	CAP	FF	HGT	CODE	LZ	WP	RWC	MTBF	PHDS	PCYL	PSPT	LHDS	LCYL	LSPT
CP-2020 KATO	SCSI	21.39	2.50	4H	RLL 2	AUTO	N/A	N/A	150	2	653	32			
CP-2022	IDE(AT)	21.39	2.50	4H	RLL 2	AUTO	N/A	N/A	0	2	653	32	2	653	32
CP-2024	IDE(XT/AT)	21.39	2.50	4H	RLL 2	AUTO	N/A	N/A	150	2	653	32	2	653	32
CP-2034	IDE(AT)	32.02	2.50	4H	RLL 2	AUTO	N/A	N/A	150	2	823	38	2	823	38
CP-2044	IDE(44PIN)	42.6	2.50	4H	RLL 2	980	N/A	N/A	150	4	548	38	5	980	17
CP-2044PK	IDE(44PIN)	42.6	2.50	4H	RLL 2	980	N/A	N/A	150	4	548	38	5	980	17
CP-2064	IDE(AT)	64.04	2.50	4H	RLL 2	AUTO	N/A	N/A	150	4	823	38	4	823	38
CP-2084	IDE(AT)	85.37	2.50	4H	RLL 1	AUTO	N/A	N/A	150	4	1097	38	8	548	38
CP-2124	IDE(AT)	121.6	2.50	4H	RLL 1	762	0		150	4	0	53	8	762	39
CP-2304	IDE(AT)	215.33	3.50	4H	RLL	AUTO	N/A	N/A	0	8	1348	39			
CP-3000	IDE(AT)	42.8	3.50	3H	RLL 2	AUTO	N/A	N/A	150	2	1045	40	5	980	17
CP-30060	SCSI	60.86	3.50	3H	RLL 1	AUTO	N/A	N/A	150	2	1524	39			
CP-30064	IDE(AT)	60.86	3.50	3H	RLL 1	AUTO	N/A	N/A	150	2	1524	39	4	762	39
CP-30064H	IDE(AT)	60.86	3.50	3H	RLL 1	AUTO	N/A	N/A	150	2	1524	39	4	762	39
CP-30069	MCA	60.86	3.50	3H	RLL 1	AUTO	N/A	N/A	150	2	1524	39			
CP-30080	SCSI	84.5	3.50	3H	RLL 2	AUTO	N/A	N/A	150	4	1058	39			
CP-30080E	SCSI	85.06	3.50	4H	RLL 1	AUTO	N/A	N/A	150	2	1806	46			
CP-30084	IDE(AT)	84.5	3.50	3H	RLL 2	AUTO	N/A	N/A	150	4	1058	39	8	526	39
CP-30084E	IDE(AT)	85.06	3.50	3H	RLL 1	AUTO	N/A	N/A	150	2	1806	46	4	903	46
CP-30100	SCSI	121.72	3.50	3H	RLL 1	AUTO	N/A	N/A	150	4	1524	39			
CP-30104	IDE(AT)	121.56	3.50	3H	RLL 1	AUTO	N/A	N/A	150	4	1522	39	8	762	39
CP-30104H	IDE(AT)	121.56	3.50	3H	RLL 1	AUTO	N/A	N/A	150	4	1522	39	8	762	39
CP-30109	MCA	121.56	3.50	3H	RLL 1	AUTO	N/A	N/A	150	4	1522	39			
CP-30124	IDE(AT)	125.02	3.50	3H	RLL 1	AUTO	N/A	N/A	250	2	1985	62	5	895	55
CP-30170	SCSI	170.13	3.50	3H	RLL 1	AUTO	N/A	N/A	150	4	1806	46			
CP-30170E	SCSI	170	3.50	3H	RLL 1	AUTO	N/A	N/A	150	4	1806	46			
CP-30174	IDE(AT)	171.6	3.50	3H	RLL 1	AUTO	N/A	N/A	250	0	0	0	16	332	63
CP-30174E	IDE(AT)	170.13	3.50	3H	RLL 1	AUTO	N/A	N/A	150	4	1806	46	8	903	46
CP-3020	SCSI	21.01	3.50	3H	RLL 2	AUTO	N/A	N/A	150	2	622	33			
CP-30200	SCSI-2	212.64	3.50	3H	RLL 2	AUTO	N/A	N/A	150	4	2119	49			
CP-30204	IDE(AT)	212.64	3.50	3H	RLL 2	AUTO	N/A	N/A	150	4	2119	49	16	683	38
CP-3022	IDE(AT)	21.49	3.50	3H	RLL 2	AUTO	N/A	N/A	150	2	636	33	2	636	33
CP-3024	IDE(AT)	21.49	3.50	3H	RLL 2	AUTO	N/A	N/A	150	2	636	33	2	636	33
CP-30254	IDE(AT)	251	3.50	3H	RLL 1	895	N/A	N/A	250	0	0	0	10	895	55
CP-30254H	IDE(AT)	251	3.50	3H	RLL 1	895	N/A	N/A	250	0	0	0	10	895	55
CP-30340	SCSI-2	343	3.50	3H	RLL 1	AUTO	N/A	N/A	250	4	0	0			
CP-30344	IDE(AT)	343	3.50	3H	RLL 1	665	N/A	N/A	300	0	0	0	16	665	63

MODEL	INT	CAP	FF	HGT	CODE	LZ	WP	RWC	MTBF	PHDS	PCYL	PSPT	LHDS	LCYL	LSPT
CP-3040	SCSI	42.02	3.50	3H	RLL 2	AUTO	N/A	N/A	150	2	1026	40			
CP-3044	IDE(AT)	42.88	3.50	3H	RLL 2	AUTO	N/A	N/A	150	2	1047	40	5	980	17
CP-3046F	IDE(AT)	42.8	3.50	3H	U	977	300	N/A	100	2	1045	40	5	977	17
CP-30540	SCSI	0	3.50	3H	RLL 1				0	0	0	0			
CP-30544	IDE(AT)	545.51	3.50	3H	RLL 2	AUTO	N/A	N/A	150	12	1806	49	16	1057	63
CP-3100	SCSI	104.89	3.50	3H	RLL 2	AUTO	N/A	N/A	150	8	776	33			
CP-3102	IDE(AT)	104.89	3.50	HH	RLL 2	AUTO	N/A	N/A	150	8	776	33	8	776	33
CP-3104	IDE(AT)	104.89	3.50	HH	RLL 2	AUTO	N/A	N/A	150	8	776	33	8	776	33
CP-3114	IDE(AT)	112.45	3.50	HH	RLL	AUTO	N/A	N/A	0	8	832	33	8	832	33
CP-31370	SCSI-2	1300	3.50	3H	RLL	AUTO	N/A	N/A	0	14	2386	0			
CP-3150	SCSI	52.44	3.50	HH	RLL 2	AUTO	N/A	N/A	150	4	776	33			
CP-3180	SCSI	84.34	3.50	HH	RLL 2	AUTO	N/A	N/A	150	6	832	33			
CP-3184	IDE(AT)	84.34	3.50	HH	RLL 2	AUTO	N/A	N/A	150	6	832	33	6	832	33
CP-3200	SCSI	212.61	3.50	HH	RLL	AUTO	N/A	N/A	150	8	1366	38			
CP-3200F	SCSI	212.61	3.50	HH	RLL 2	AUTO	N/A	N/A	150	8	1366	38			
CP-3204	IDE(AT)	215.33	3.50	HH	RLL 2	AUTO	N/A	N/A	150	8	1348	39	16	683	38
CP-3204F	IDE(AT)	212.61	3.50	HH	RLL 2	AUTO	N/A	N/A	50	8	1366	38	16	683	38
CP-3209F	MCA	212.61	3.50	HH	RLL 2	AUTO	N/A	N/A	50	8	1366	38			
CP-3304	IDE(AT)	340.27	3.50	HH	RLL 1	AUTO	N/A	N/A	150	8	1806	46	16	659	63
CP-3360	SCSI-2	362.47	3.50	3H	RLL 2	AUTO	N/A	N/A	150	8	1806	49			
CP-3364	IDE(AT)	362.47	3.50	3H	RLL 2	AUTO	N/A	N/A	150	8	1806	49	16	702	63
CP-340	SCSI	41.95	3.50	HH	RLL 2	AUTO	N/A	N/A	20	4	788	26			
CP-341	IDE(AT)	0	3.50	HH	U	AUTO	N/A	N/A		0	0	0			
CP-3411	IDE(AT)	0	3.50	HH	U	AUTO	N/A	N/A		0	0	0			
CP-342	IDE(AT)	42.86	3.50	HH	RLL 2	AUTO	N/A	N/A	0	4	805	26	4	805	26
CP-344	IDE(AT)	42.86	3.50	HH	RLL 2	AUTO	N/A	N/A	20	4	805	26	4	805	26
CP-346	IDE(AT)	42.86	3.50	HH	RLL 2	AUTO	N/A	N/A	20	4	805	26	4	805	26
CP-3500	SCSI-2	510.41	3.50	HH	RLL 2	AUTO	N/A	N/A	150	12	1806	46			
CP-3504	IDE(AT)	509.38	3.50	HH	RLL 2	AUTO	N/A	N/A	150	12	1806	46	16	987	63
CP-3540	SCSI-2	543.7	3.50	3H	RLL 2	AUTO	N/A	N/A	150	12	1806	49			
CP-3544 SUMMIT	IDE(AT)	544.3	3.50	HH	RLL 2	AUTO	N/A	N/A	150	12	1808	49	16	1023	63
CP-4024	IDE (XT/AT)	21.58	3.50	4H	RLL 2	AUTO	N/A	N/A	150	2	620	34	2	620	34
CP-4044	IDE (XT/AT)	42.64	3.50	4H	RLL 2	AUTO	N/A	N/A	150	2	1096	38	5	980	17

Table D.11   IBM CORPORATION

MODEL	INT	CAP	FF	HGT	CODE	LZ	WP	RWC	MTBF	PHDS	PCYL	PSPT	LHDS	LCYL	LSPT
0664-CSH	SCSI-2	4000	5.25	FH		AUTO	N/A	N/A	0	0	0				
0664-ESH	SCSI-2 W	4000	5.25	FH		AUTO	N/A	N/A	0	0	0				

(continues)

Table D.11 IBM CORPORATION Continued

MODEL	INT	CAP	FF	HGT	CODE	LZ	WP	RWC	MTBF	PHDS	PCYL	PSPT	LHDS	LCYL	LSPT
115MB	ESDI-10MHZ	118.05	5.25	—	RLL	AUTO			0	7	915	36			
120MB	ST-506/412	120.58	5.25	FH	MFM				0	8	920	32			
20MB	ST-506/412	21.3	5.25	FH	MFM	663	306		0	4	612	17			
20MB PS/2	ST-506/412	21.3	3.50	HH	MFM		128		0	4	612	17			
30MB	ST-506/412	31.48	5.25	FH	MFM	663	300		0	4	615	25			
314MB	ESDI-10MHZ	319.87	5.25	FH	RLL	AUTO	N/A	N/A	0	15	1225	34			
44MB	ST-506/412	44.66	5.25	FH	MFM	733	300		0	7	733	17			
60MB	ST-506/412	60.86	5.25	FH	MFM				0	6	762	26			
70MB	ESDI-10MHZ	75.22	5.25	FH	RLL	AUTO	N/A	N/A	0	7	583	36			
DALA-3540	IDE(AT)	540	3.50			AUTO	N/A	N/A	300	0	0	0			
DALS-3540		0							0	0	0	0			
DAQA-32160	IDE(AT)	2160	3.50	3H		AUTO	N/A	N/A		4	0	0	16	4200	63
DAQA-33240	IDE(AT)	2160	3.50	3H		AUTO	N/A	N/A		6	0	0	16	6296	63
DBOA-2360	IDE(AT)	360	2.50	4H		AUTO	N/A	N/A	300	0	0	0			
DBOA-2528	IDE(AT)	528	2.50	4H		AUTO	N/A	N/A	300	0	0	0			
DBOA-2540	IDE(AT)	540	2.50	4H		AUTO	N/A	N/A	300	0	0	0			
DBOA-2720	IDE(AT)	720	2.50	4H		AUTO	N/A	N/A	300	0	0	0			
DCAA-33610	IDE(AT)	3610	3.50	3H	PRML	AUTO	N/A	N/A		5	0	0	16	7000	63
DCAA-34330	IDE(AT)	4330	3.50	3H	PRML	AUTO	N/A	N/A		6	0	0	16	8400	63
DCAS-32160 (50-PIN)	U-SCSI	2160	3.50	3H		AUTO	N/A	N/A		0	0	0			
DCAS-32160 (68-PIN)	U-SCSI W	2160	3.50	3H		AUTO	N/A	N/A		0	0	0			
DCAS-32160 (80-PIN)	U-SCSI W	2160	3.50	3H		AUTO	N/A	N/A		0	0	0			
DCAS-34330 (50-PIN)	U-SCSI	4330	3.50	3H		AUTO	N/A	N/A		0	0	0			
DCAS-34330 (68-PIN)	U-SCSI W	4330	3.50	3H		AUTO	N/A	N/A		0	0	0			
DCAS-34330 (80-PIN)	U-SCSI W	4330	3.50	3H		AUTO	N/A	N/A		0	0	0			
DCHS-34550 (50-PIN)	SCSI-2 F	4550	3.50	3H	PRML	AUTO	N/A	N/A		0	0	0			
DCHS-34550 (68-PIN)	SCSI-2 FW	4550	3.50	3H	PRML	AUTO	N/A	N/A		0	0	0			
DCHS-34550 (80-PIN)	U-SCSI	4550	3.50	3H	PRML	AUTO	N/A	N/A		0	0	0			
DCHS-39100 (50-PIN)	SCSI-2 F	9111	3.50	3H	PRML	AUTO	N/A	N/A		0	0	0			
DCHS-39100 (68-PIN)	SCSI-2 FW	9111	3.50	3H	PRML	AUTO	N/A	N/A		0	0	0			
DCHS-39100 (80-PIN)	U-SCSI	9111	3.50	3H	PRML	AUTO	N/A	N/A		0	0	0			

MODEL	INT	CAP	FF	HGT	CODE	LZ	WP	RWC	MTBF	PHDS	PCYL	PSPT	LHDS	LCYL	LSPT
DCRA-22160	IDE(AT)	2160	2.50	5H	U	AUTO	N/A	N/A		0	0	0	16	4200	63
DDLA-21215	IDE(AT)	1215	2.50	5H						0	0	0			
DDLA-21620	IDE(AT)	1620	2.50	5H						0	0	0			
DESKSTAR (VER. 2)	IDE(AT)	0	3.50	3H		AUTO	N/A	N/A	300	0	0	0	16	954	36
DESKSTAR (VER. 3)	IDE(AT)	540	3.50			AUTO	N/A	N/A	300	0	0	0			
DESKSTAR (VER. 4)	IDE(AT)	0	3.50	3H		AUTO	N/A	N/A		3	0	0	16	2480	63
DESKSTAR (VER. 1)	SCSI-2 F	281	3.50	3H					300	2	0	0			
DESKSTAR (VER. 2)		0								0	0	0			
DESKSTAR 540MB (06H8558,9)	SCSI-2 F	540	3.50	3H	PRML	AUTO	N/A	N/A	350	2	4899	0			
DESKSTAR-3	IDE(AT)	0	3.50	3H		AUTO	N/A	N/A		4	0	0	16	4200	63
DESKSTAR-4	IDE(AT)	0	3.50	3H	PRML	AUTO	N/A	N/A		5	0	0	16	7000	63
DESKSTAR-5	IDE(AT)	6480	3.50	FH						8	0	0			
DESKSTAR-5	IDE(AT)	6480	3.50	FH						8	0	0			
DESKSTAR-8	IDE(AT)	8041	3.50	FH						16	16351	63			
DESKSTAR-XP	IDE(AT)	0	3.50			AUTO	N/A	N/A	300	0	0	0			
DESKSTAR-XP	SCSI-2 F	0	3.50	3H	U	AUTO	N/A	N/A	0	2	0	0			
DFHS-31080	SCSI-2 F	1120	3.50	3H		AUTO	N/A	N/A		0	0	0			
DFHS-31080	U-SCSI FW	1120	3.50	3H	PRML	AUTO	N/A	N/A	100	0	0	0			
DFHS-31080	U-SCSI FWD	1120	3.50	3H	PRML	AUTO	N/A	N/A	100	0	0	0			
DFHS-31080 (80-PIN)	SCSI SCA	1120	3.50	3H	PRML				100	0	0	0			
DFHS-32160	SCSI-2 F	2250	3.50	3H		AUTO	N/A	N/A	1000	0	0	0			
DFHS-32160	U-SCSI FW	2250	3.50	3H	PRML	AUTO	N/A	N/A	100	0	0	0			
DFHS-32160	U-SCSI FWD	2250	3.50	3H	PRML	AUTO	N/A	N/A	100	0	0	0			
DFHS-32160 (80-PIN)	SCSI SCA	2250	3.50	3H	PRML				100	0	0	0			
DFHS-34320	SCSI-2 F	4510	3.50	3H		AUTO	N/A	N/A		0	0	0			
DFHS-34320	U-SCSI FW	4510	3.50	3H		AUTO	N/A	N/A		0	0	0			
DFHS-34320	U-SCSI FWD	4510	3.50	3H		AUTO	N/A	N/A		0	0	0			
DFHS-34320 (80-PIN)	SCSI SCA	4510	3.50	3H	PRML				100	0	0	0			
DFMS-31080	SCSI-2 F	1320	3.50	3H		AUTO	N/A	N/A		0	0	0			
DFMS-31080	U-SCSI FW	1320	3.50	3H	PRML	AUTO	N/A	N/A	100	0	0	0			
DFMS-31080	U-SCSI FWD	1320	3.50	3H	PRML	AUTO	N/A	N/A	100	0	0	0			
DFMS-31080 (80-PIN)	SCSI SCA	1120	3.50	3H	PRML				100	0	0	0			

(continues)

Table D.11 IBM CORPORATION Continued

MODEL	INT	CAP	FF	HGT	CODE	LZ	WP	RWC	MTBF	PHDS	PCYL	PSPT	LHDS	LCYL	LSPT
DFMS-32160	SCSI-2 F	2320	3.50	3H		AUTO	N/A	N/A		0	0	0			
DFMS-32160	U-SCSI FW	2320	3.50	3H	PRML	AUTO	N/A	N/A	100	0	0	0			
DFMS-32160	U-SCSI FWD	2320	3.50	3H	PRML	AUTO	N/A	N/A	100	0	0	0			
DFMS-32160 (80-PIN)	SCSI SCA	2320	3.50	3H	PRML	AUTO	N/A	N/A	100	0	0	0			
DFMS-32600	SCSI-2 F	2650	3.50	3H						0	0	0			
DFMS-32600	U-SCSI FW	2650	3.50	3H	PRML				100	0	0	0			
DFMS-32600 (80-PIN)	SCSI SCA	2650	3.50	3H	PRML				100	0	0	0			
DFMS-32600	U-SCSI FWD	2650	3.50	3H	PRML				100	0	0	0			
DFMS-34320	SCSI-2 F	4320	3.50	3H		AUTO	N/A	N/A		0	0	0			
DFMS-34320	U-SCSI FW	4320	3.50	3H	PRML	AUTO	N/A	N/A	100	0	0	0			
DFMS-34320	U-SCSI FWD	4320	3.50	3H	PRML	AUTO	N/A	N/A	100	0	0	0			
DFMS-34320 (80-PIN)	SCSI SCA	4510	3.50	3H	PRML				100	0	0	0			
DFMS-35250	SCSI-2 F	5310	3.50	3H		AUTO	N/A	N/A		0	0	0			
DFMS-35250	U-SCSI FW	5310	3.50	3H	PRML	AUTO	N/A	N/A	100	0	0	0			
DFMS-35250	U-SCSI FWD	5310	3.50	3H	PRML	AUTO	N/A	N/A		0	0	0			
DFMS-35250 (80-PIN)	SCSI SCA	5310	3.50	3H	PRML				100	0	0	0			
DHAA-2270		0								0	0	0			
DHAA-2405	IDE(44PIN)	405.13	2.50	4H		AUTO	N/A	N/A	300	0	0	0	16	785	63
DHAA-2540	IDE(44PIN)	540.35	2.50	4H		AUTO	N/A	N/A	300	0	0	0	16	1047	63
DHAA-2810	IDE(AT)	810	2.50	4H		AUTO	N/A	N/A	300	0	0	0			
DHAS-2270	SCSI-2	270	2.50	5H						0	0	0			
DHAS-2405	SCSI-2	405	2.50	5H						0	0	0			
DHAS-2540	SCSI-2	540	2.50	5H						0	0	0			
DHEA-34330 (VER. 1.7)	IDE(AT)	4033	2.50		U	AUTO	N/A	N/A	250	16	8400	63			
DHEA-34331	IDE(AT)	4026	3.50	FH						16	8184	63			
DHEA-34860 (VER. 1.7)	IDE(AT)	4086	2.50		U	AUTO	N/A	N/A	250	16	8400	63			
DHEA-36480	IDE(AT)	6480	3.50	FH						8	0	0			
DHEA-36480 (VER. 1.7)	IDE(AT)	6480	3.50	FH						8	0	0			
DHEA-36481	IDE(AT)	6041	3.50	FH						16	12592	63			
DHEA-38451	IDE(AT)	8041	3.50	FH						16	16351	63			
DJAA-31270	IDE(AT)	1270	3.50	3H		AUTO	N/A	N/A		3	0	0	16	2480	63
DJAA-31700	IDE(AT)	1700	3.50	3H		AUTO	N/A	N/A		4	0	0	16	3308	63
DLGA-22690	IDE(AT)	2690	2.50	5H		AUTO	N/A	N/A		0	0	0	16	5216	63

MODEL	INT	CAP	FF	HGT	CODE	LZ	WP	RWC	MTBF	PHDS	PCYL	PSPT	LHDS	LCYL	LSPT
DLGA-23080	IDE(AT)	3080	2.50	5H		AUTO	N/A	N/A		0	0	0	16	5968	63
DMCA-21080	IDE(AT)	1080	2.50	5H						0	0	0	16	2100	63
DMCA-21440	IDE(AT)	1440	2.50	5H						0	0	0	16	2800	63
DMCA-22160	IDE(AT)	2160	2.50	5H					300	6	4928	0	16	4200	
DORS-32160 (50-PIN)	U-SCSI	2160	3.50	3H		AUTO	N/A	N/A	800	0	0	0	5		
DORS-32160 (68-PIN)	U-SCSI W	2160	3.50	3H		AUTO	N/A	N/A	800	0	0	0	5		
DORS-32160 (80-PIN)	U-SCSI W	2160	3.50	3H		AUTO	N/A	N/A	800	0	0	0	5		
DPEA-30540	IDE(AT)	540	3.50			AUTO	N/A	N/A	300	0	0	0			
DPEA-30810	IDE(AT)	810	3.50	3H		AUTO	N/A	N/A	300	0	0	0			
DPEA-31080	IDE(AT)	1080	3.50			AUTO	N/A	N/A	300	0	0	0			
DPES-30540	SCSI-2 F	540	3.50	3H	U	AUTO	N/A	N/A	0	2	0	0			
DPES-30810	SCSI-2 F	810	3.50	3H	U	AUTO	N/A	N/A	0	3	0	0			
DPES-31080	SCSI-2 F	1080	3.50	3H	U	AUTO	N/A	N/A	0	4	0	0			
DPLA-24480	IDE(AT)	4480	2.50	FH						15	9264	63			
DPLA-25120	IDE(AT)	4480	2.50	FH						15	10592	63			
DPRA-20810	IDE(AT)	810	2.50	4H		AUTO	N/A	N/A	300	0	0	0			
DPRA-21215	IDE(AT)	1215	2.50	4H		AUTO	N/A	N/A	300	0	0	0			
DPRS-20810	SCSI-2	810	2.50	5H	·	AUTO	N/A	N/A		6	3481	0	0		0
DPRS-21215	SCSI-2	1215	2.50	5H		AUTO	N/A	N/A		6	3481	0	0		0
DSAA-3270	IDE(AT)	281.34	3.50	3H		AUTO	N/A	N/A	300	0	0	0	16	954	36
DSAA-3360	IDE(AT)	365.29	3.50	3H		AUTO	N/A	N/A	300	0	0	0	16	929	48
DSAA-3540 VER. 1	IDE(AT)	548.09	3.50	3H		AUTO	N/A	N/A	300	0	0	0	16	1062	63
DSAA-3540 VER. 2	IDE(AT)	528.48	3.50	3H		AUTO	N/A	N/A	300	0	0	0	16	1024	63
DSAA-3720	IDE(AT)	730.79	3.50	3H		AUTO	N/A	N/A	300	0	0	0	16	1416	63
DSAS-3270	SCSI-2 F	281	3.50	3H					300	2	0	0			
DSAS-3360	SCSI-2 F	365	3.50	3H					300	2	0	0			
DSAS-3540	SCSI-2 F	548	3.50	3H					300	3	0	0			
DSAS-3720	SCSI-2 F	730	3.50	3H					300	4	0	0			
DSOA-20540	IDE(44PIN)	540	2.50	5H		AUTO	N/A	N/A	0	0	0	0	16	1050	63
DSOA-20810	IDE(44PIN)	810	2.50	5H		AUTO	N/A	N/A	0	0	0	0	16	1575	63
DSOA-21080	IDE(44PIN)	1080	2.50	5H		AUTO	N/A	N/A	0	0	0	0	16	2100	63
DTCA-23240	IDE(AT)	3240	2.50	FH						16	6304	63			
DTCA-24090	IDE(AT)	4090	2.50	FH						16	7944	63			
DTNA-21800	IDE(AT)	1800	2.50	5H	PRML	AUTO	N/A	N/A		0	0	0	16	3500	63
DTNA-22160	IDE(AT)	2160	2.50	5H	PRML	AUTO	N/A	N/A		0	0	0	16	4200	63

(continues)

Table D.11 IBM CORPORATION Continued

MODEL	INT	CAP	FF	HGT	CODE	LZ	WP	RWC	MTBF	PHDS	PCYL	PSPT	LHDS	LCYL	LSPT
DVAA-2810	IDE(AT)	810	2.50	5H	U	AUTO	N/A	N/A	300	16	1571	63			
DVAS-2810	SCSI-2	810	2.50	5H		AUTO	N/A	N/A		6	2788	0	0		0
DYKA-22160	IDE(AT)	2130	2.50	FH						16	4200	63			
DYKA-23240	IDE(AT)	3240	2.50	FH						16	6304	63			
DYLA-26480	IDE(AT)	6480	2.50	FH						15	16944	63			
DYLA-28100	IDE(AT)	8100	2.50	FH						15	16944	63			
H2172-A2	IDE(44PIN)	172.16	2.50	4H		AUTO	N/A	N/A	0	0	0	0	10	989	34
H2172-S2	SCSI-2	172	2.50	3H		AUTO	N/A	N/A	300	0	0	0			
H2258-A3	IDE(44PIN)	258.24	2.50	4H		AUTO	N/A	N/A	0	0	0	0	15	989	34
H2258-S3	SCSI-2	258	2.50	3H		AUTO	N/A	N/A	300	0	0	0			
H2344-A4	IDE(44PIN)	344.33	2.50	4H		AUTO	N/A	N/A	0	0	0	0	15	915	49
H2344-S4	SCSI-2	344	2.50	3H		AUTO	N/A	N/A	300	0	0	0			
H3133-A2	IDE(AT)	133.56	3.50	3H		AUTO	N/A	N/A	250	0	0	0	15	1023	17
H3171-A2	IDE(AT)	171.29	3.50	3H		AUTO	N/A	N/A	250	0	0	0	10	984	34
H3256-A3	IDE(AT)	257.16	3.50	3H		AUTO	N/A	N/A	250	0	0	0	16	872	36
H3342-A4	IDE(AT)	342.88	3.50	3H		AUTO	N/A	N/A	250	0	0	0	16	872	48
PS/2 MODEL 25 20MB	ST-506/412	20	5.25	—					0	0	0	0			
TRAVELSTAR (VER. 2)	IDE(AT)	810	2.50	5H	U	AUTO	N/A	N/A	300	16	1571	63			
TRAVELSTAR		0								0	0	0			
TRAVELSTAR (VER. 2)	SCSI-2	810	2.50	5H		AUTO	N/A	N/A		6	2788	0	0		0
TRAVELSTAR	SCSI-2	0	2.50	5H						0	0	0			
TRAVELSTAR-2LP	IDE(44PIN)	0	2.50	5H		AUTO	N/A	N/A		0	0	0	16	1575	63
TRAVELSTAR-2XP	IDE(AT)	0	2.50	5H	U	AUTO	N/A	N/A		0	0	0	16	4200	63
TRAVELSTAR-3GN	IDE(AT)	8100	2.50	FH						15	16944	63			
TRAVELSTAR-3LP	IDE(AT)	0	2.50	5H						0	0	0	16	2100	63
TRAVELSTAR-3XP	IDE(AT)	0	2.50	5H		AUTO	N/A	N/A		0	0	0	16	5216	63
TRAVELSTAR-4GT	IDE(AT)	4480	2.50	FH						15	10592	63			
TRAVELSTAR-4LP	IDE(AT)	0	2.50	5H	PRML	AUTO	N/A	N/A		0	0	0	16	3500	63
TRAVELSTAR-5GS	IDE(AT)	4480	2.50	FH						15	10592	63			
TRAVELSTAR-8GS	IDE(AT)	8100	2.50	FH						15	16944	63			
TRAVELSTAR-LP	IDE(AT)	0	2.50	4H		AUTO	N/A	N/A	300	0	0	0			
TRAVELSTAR-VP	IDE(AT)	0	2.50	5H						0	0	0			
TRAVELSTAR-XP	IDE(AT)	0	2.50	4H		AUTO	N/A	N/A	300	0	0	0			
TRAVELSTAR-XP	SCSI-2	0	2.50	5H		AUTO	N/A	N/A		6	3481	0	0		0
TYPE 0661 MODEL 371	SCSI-2	326.51	3.50	HH	RLL	AUTO	N/A	N/A	300	14	949	48			

MODEL	INT	CAP	FF	HGT	CODE	LZ	WP	RWC	MTBF	PHDS	PCYL	PSPT	LHDS	LCYL	LSPT
TYPE 0661 MODEL 467	SCSI-2	412.53	3.50	HH	RLL	AUTO	N/A	N/A	300	14	1199	48			
TYPE 0662 (SPITFIRE) MODEL A10	IDE(AT)	1051.8	3.50	3H		AUTO	N/A	N/A	500	0	0	0	16	2038	63
TYPE 0662 (SPITFIRE) MODEL S12	SCSI-2 F	1050	3.50	FH	U	AUTO	N/A	N/A	800	16	2038	63			
TYPE 0662 (SPITFIRE) MODEL S1D	SCSI-2 F	1050	3.50	FH	U	AUTO	N/A	N/A	800	16	2038	63			
TYPE 0662 (SPITFIRE) MODEL SW1	SCSI-2 W	1050	3.50	FH	U	AUTO	N/A	N/A	800	16	2038	63			
TYPE 0662 (SPITFIRE) MODEL SWD	SCSI-2 W	1050	3.50	FH	U	AUTO	N/A	N/A	800	16	2038	63			
TYPE 0663 MODEL E12	SCSI	1044	3.50	HH	RLL	AUTO	N/A	N/A	500	13	2469	0			
TYPE 0663 MODEL E15	SCSI	1206	3.50	HH	RLL	AUTO	N/A	N/A	500	15	2469	0			
TYPE 0663 MODEL H11	SCSI	0	3.50	HH	RLL				400	0	0	0			
TYPE 0663 MODEL H12	SCSI	1039.61	3.50	HH	RLL	AUTO	N/A	N/A	400	15	2051	66			
TYPE 0663 MODEL L08	SCSI	623.76	3.50	HH	RLL	AUTO	N/A	N/A	400	9	2051	66			
TYPE 0663 MODEL L11	SCSI	900.99	3.50	HH	RLL	AUTO	N/A	N/A	400	13	2051	66			
TYPE 0663 MODEL L12	SCSI	1039.61	3.50	HH	RLL	AUTO	N/A	N/A	880	15	2051	66			
TYPE 0664 CSH/ESH	SCSI	4000	5.25	FH	RLL	AUTO	N/A	N/A	375	2	2857	0			
TYPE 0664 MODEL M1H (50-PIN)	SCSI-2 F	2000	3.50	HH		AUTO	N/A	N/A		6	2857	0			
TYPE 0664 MODEL M1H (68-PIN)	SCSI-2 FW	2000	3.50	HH		AUTO	N/A	N/A		6	2857	0			
TYPE 0664 MODEL N1H (50-PIN)	SCSI-2 F	2000	3.50	HH		AUTO	N/A	N/A		6	2857	0			
TYPE 0664 MODEL N1H (68-PIN)	SCSI-2 FW	2000	3.50	HH		AUTO	N/A	N/A		6	2857	0			
TYPE 0665 MODEL 38	ST-506/412	31.9	5.25	FH	MFM	AUTO	N/A	N/A	0	5	733	17			
TYPE 0665 MODEL 53	ST-506/412	44.66	5.25	FH	MFM	AUTO	N/A	N/A	0	7	733	17			

(continues)

Table D.11   IBM CORPORATION Continued

MODEL	INT	CAP	FF	HGT	CODE	LZ	WP	RWC	MTBF	PHDS	PCYL	PSPT	LHDS	LCYL	LSPT
TYPE 0667 MODEL 61	ESDI-10MHZ	52.14	5.25	FH	RLL	AUTO	N/A	N/A	0	5	582	35			
TYPE 0667 MODEL 85	ESDI-10MHZ	73	5.25	FH	RLL	AUTO	N/A	N/A	0	7	582	64			
TYPE 0669 MODEL 61	ESDI-10MHZ	48.42	5.25	FH	RLL	AUTO	N/A	N/A	0	5	582	35			
TYPE 0669 MODEL 85	ESDI-10MHZ	67.79	5.25	FH	RLL	AUTO	N/A	N/A	0	7	582	64			
TYPE 0671 MODEL S11	SCSI	234.38	5.25	FH	RLL	AUTO	N/A	N/A	0	11	1224	34			
TYPE 0671 MODEL S15	SCSI	319.61	5.25	FH	RLL	AUTO	N/A	N/A	0	15	1224	34			
TYPE 0681 MODEL 500	SCSI	476.26	5.25	FH	RLL	AUTO	N/A	N/A	150	11	1458	58			
TYPE 0681 MODEL1000	SCSI	865.93	5.25	FH	RLL	AUTO	N/A	N/A	150	20	1458	58			
ULTRASTAR 2ES (50-PIN)	U-SCSI	0	3.50	3H		AUTO	N/A	N/A		0	0	0			
ULTRASTAR 2ES (68-PIN)	U-SCSI W	0	3.50	3H		AUTO	N/A	N/A		0	0	0			
ULTRASTAR 2ES (80-PIN)	U-SCSI W	2160	3.50	3H		AUTO	N/A	N/A		0	0	0			
ULTRASTAR 2XP (50 PIN)	SCSI-2 F	4550	3.50	3H	PRML	AUTO	N/A	N/A		0	0	0			
ULTRASTAR 2XP (68-PIN)	SCSI-2 FW	4550	3.50	3H	PRML	AUTO	N/A	N/A		0	0	0			
ULTRASTAR 2XP (80-PIN)	U-SCSI	4550	3.50	3H	PRML	AUTO	N/A	N/A		0	0	0			
ULTRASTAR ES (50-PIN)	U-SCSI	2160	3.50	3H		AUTO	N/A	N/A	800	0	0	0	5		
ULTRASTAR ES (68-PIN)	U-SCSI W	2160	3.50	3H		AUTO	N/A	N/A	800	0	0	0	5		
ULTRASTAR ES (80-PIN)	U-SCSI W	0	3.50	3H		AUTO	N/A	N/A	800	0	0	0	5		
WD-12	ST-506/412	10	5.25	FH	MFM		296	296	0	4	306	17			
WD-2120	MCA	127.28	3.50	3H	RLL	AUTO	N/A	N/A	150	4	1243	50			
WD-240	MCA	43.65	2.50	4H	RLL	AUTO	N/A	N/A	150	2	1122	38			
WD-25	ST-506/412	20	5.25	FH	MFM		296	296	0	0	0	17			
WD-3158	MCA	120.58	3.50	FH	RLL	AUTO	N/A	N/A	45	8	920	32			
WD-3160	MCA	163.09	3.50	HH	RLL	AUTO	N/A	N/A	110	8	1021	39			
WD-380	MCA	81.54	3.50	HH	RLL	AUTO	N/A	N/A	110	4	1021	39			
WD-387	MCA	60.81	3.50	HH	RLL	AUTO	N/A	N/A	45	4	928	32			
WD-L40	MCA	41.45	3.50	HH	RLL	AUTO	N/A	N/A	90	2	1038	39			
WD-L40S	MCA	41.45	3.50	HH	RLL	AUTO	N/A	N/A	90	2	1038	39			

MODEL	INT	CAP	FF	HGT	CODE	LZ	WP	RWC	MTBF	PHDS	PCYL	PSPT	LHDS	LCYL	LSPT
WDA-2120	IDE(AT)	126.51	3.50	3H	RLL 1	AUTO	N/A	N/A	150	4	1243	50	15	969	17
WDA-240	IDE(AT)	43.1	2.50	4H	RLL 1	AUTO	N/A	N/A	150	2	1122	38	8	619	17
WDA-260	IDE(AT)	63.64	3.50	3H	RLL	AUTO	N/A	N/A	150	2	1243	50			
WDA-280	IDE(AT)	86.08	2.50	3H	RLL 1	AUTO	N/A	N/A	150	4	1122	38	10	989	17
WDA-3160	IDE(AT)	81.54	3.50	HH	RLL	AUTO	N/A	N/A	110	4	1021	39			
WDA-380	IDE(AT)	81.54	3.50	HH	RLL	AUTO	N/A	N/A	110	4	1021	39			
WDA-L160	IDE(AT)	171.29	3.50	3H	RLL 1	AUTO	N/A	N/A	150	4	1923	44	10	984	34
WDA-L40	IDE(AT)	41.53	3.50	3H	RLL 2	AUTO	N/A	N/A	90	2	1040	39			
WDA-L42	IDE(AT)	42.61	3.50	3H	RLL 2	AUTO	N/A	N/A	90	2	1067	39			
WDA-L80	IDE(AT)	85.64	3.50	3H	RLL 1	AUTO	N/A	N/A	150	2	1923	44	10	984	17
WDA-S260	IDE(AT)	63.3	3.50	4H	RLL 1	AUTO	N/A	N/A	150	2	1243	50	8	909	17
WDS-240	SCSI-2	43.65	2.50	5H	RLL	AUTO	N/A	N/A	150	2	1122	38			
WDS-280	SCSI-2	87	2.50	5H		AUTO	N/A	N/A		4	1122	38			
WDS-3100	SCSI-2	108.27	3.50	4H	RLL	AUTO	N/A	N/A	150	2	2009	0			
WDS-3160	SCSI-2	163.09	3.50	HH	RLL	AUTO	N/A	N/A	110	8	1021	39			
WDS-3200	SCSI-2	216.53	3.50	4H	RLL	AUTO	N/A	N/A	150	4	2009	0			
WDS-380	SCSI-2	81.54	3.50	HH	RLL	AUTO	N/A	N/A	110	4	1021	39			
WDS-L160	SCSI	0	3.50	5H		AUTO	N/A	N/A	150	2	0	112			
WDS-L40	SCSI-2	41.45	3.50	FH	RLL	AUTO	N/A	N/A	90	2	1038	39			
WDS-L42	SCSI-2	42.57	3.50	3H	RLL 1	AUTO	N/A	N/A	80	2	1066	39			
WDS-L80	SCSI	0	3.50	5H		AUTO	N/A	N/A	150	2	0	112			

Table D.12   MAXTOR CORPORATION

MODEL	INT	CAP	FF	HGT	CODE	LZ	WP	RWC	MTBF	PHDS	PCYL	PSPT	LHDS	LCYL	LSPT
250837	IDE(44PIN)	837	2.50	5H	RLL 1	AUTO	N/A	N/A	300	5	3196	0	16	1621	63
250840	IDE(AT)	840	2.50	5H	RLL 1	AUTO	N/A	N/A	300	5	3232	0			
25084A	IDE(AT)	84	2.50	3H	RLL	AUTO	N/A	N/A	150	0	0	0	16	569	18
251005	IDE(44PIN)	11005	2.50	5H	RLL 1	AUTO	N/A	N/A	300	6	3196	0	16	1945	63
251010	IDE(AT)	1010	2.50	5H	RLL 1	AUTO	N/A	N/A	300	6	3232	0			
25125S	SCSI	128.2	2.50	4H	RLL 1	AUTO	N/A	N/A	150	4	1092	0			
25128A	IDE(AT)	128.2	2.50	4H	RLL 1	AUTO	N/A	N/A	150	4	1092	0	14	1024	17
251340	IDE(44PIN)	1340	2.50	5H	RLL 1	AUTO	N/A	N/A	300	8	3196	0	16	2594	63
251350	IDE(AT)	1350	2.50	5H	RLL 1	AUTO	N/A	N/A	300	8	3232	0			
25252A	IDE(AT)	252	2.50	3H	RLL	AUTO	N/A	N/A	150	0	0	0	16	569	54
25252S	SCSI	252	2.50	4H	U	AUTO	N/A	N/A	0	6	1418	0			
2585A	IDE(AT)	85.41	2.50	4H	RLL 1	AUTO	N/A	N/A	150	4	1092	0	10	981	17
2585S	SCSI	85.41	2.50	4H	RLL 1	AUTO	N/A	N/A	150	4	1092	0			
7040A	IDE(AT)	43.13	3.50	3H	RLL 1	AUTO	N/A	N/A	150	2	1170	36	5	981	17

(continues)

Table D.12 MAXTOR CORPORATION Continued

MODEL	INT	CAP	FF	HGT	CODE	LZ	WP	RWC	MTBF	PHDS	PCYL	PSPT	LHDS	LCYL	LSPT
7040A (VER. 2)	IDE(AT)	41	3.50	FH		AUTO	N/A	N/A	150	4	1170	1			
7040S	SCSI	42.57	3.50	3H	RLL 1	AUTO	N/A	N/A	40	2	1155	36			
7060A	IDE(AT)	65.2	3.50	3H	RLL 1	AUTO	N/A	N/A	150	2	1516	42	7	1024	17
7060S	SCSI	64.42	3.50	3H	RLL 1	AUTO	N/A	N/A	150	2	1498	42			
7080A	IDE(AT)	85.15	3.50	3H	RLL 1	AUTO	N/A	N/A	150	4	1155	36	10	981	17
7080A (VER. 2)	IDE(AT)	82	3.50	FH		AUTO	N/A	N/A	150	4	1170	36			
7080S	SCSI	85.15	3.50	3H	RLL 1	AUTO	N/A	N/A	150	4	1155	36			
71000A	IDE(AT)	1002	3.50	3H	RLL 1	AUTO	N/A	N/A	300	3	0	0			
71050A	IDE(AT)	1050	3.50	3H	U	AUTO	N/A	N/A	0	0	0	0	16	2045	63
71084A	IDE(AT)	1	3.50	4H	RLL 1	AUTO	N/A	N/A	300	4	3	0	16	2,105	63
71084AP	IDE(AT)	1	3.50	4H	RLL 1	AUTO	N/A	N/A	300	4	3	0	16	2,105	63
7120A	IDE(AT)	130.4	3.50	3H	RLL 1	AUTO	N/A	N/A	150	4	1516	42	6	771	55
7120S	SCSI	128.85	3.50	3H	RLL 1	AUTO	N/A	N/A	150	4	1498	42			
71260A	IDE(AT)	1260	3.50	3H	U	AUTO	N/A	N/A	0	0	0	0	16	2448	63
71260AP	IDE(AT)	1260	3.50	3H	U	AUTO	N/A	N/A	0	0	0	0	16	2448	63
7131A	IDE(AT)	130	3.50	3H	RLL 1	AUTO	N/A	N/A	150	0	0	0	8	1002	32
71336A	IDE(AT)	1336	3.50	3H	RLL 1	AUTO	N/A	N/A	300	4	4702	0	16	2595	63
71336AP	IDE(AT)	1336	3.50	3H	RLL 1	AUTO	N/A	N/A	300	4	4702	0	16	2595	63
71350A	IDE(AT)	1350	3.50	3H	RLL 1	AUTO	N/A	N/A	300	0	0	0	16	2624	63
71350AP	IDE(AT)	1350	3.50	3H	RLL 1	AUTO	N/A	N/A	300	0	0	0	16	2624	63
7135AV	IDE(AT)	135	3.50	HH	U		N/A	N/A	0	0	0	0	13	966	21
71626A	IDE(AT)	1626	3.50	3H	RLL 1	AUTO	N/A	N/A	300	6	3721	0	16	3158	63
71626AP	IDE(AT)	1	3.50	3H	RLL 1	AUTO	N/A	N/A	300	6	3	0	16	3158	63
71670A	IDE(AT)	1670	3.50	3H	RLL 1	AUTO	N/A	N/A	300	5	4702	0	16	3244	63
71670AP	IDE(AT)	1670	3.50	3H	RLL 1	AUTO	N/A	N/A	300	5	4702	0	16	3244	63
71687A		0								0	0	0			
71687AP		0								0	0	0			
7170A	IDE(AT)	170	3.50	3H	RLL 1	AUTO	N/A	N/A	150	0	0	0	15	866	26
7171A	IDE(AT)	171	3.50	3H	RLL 1	AUTO	N/A	N/A	150	0	0	0	15	866	26
72004A	IDE(AT)	2004	3.50	3H	RLL 1	AUTO	N/A	N/A	300	6	4702	0	16	3893	63
72004AP	IDE(AT)	2004	3.50	3H	RLL 1	AUTO	N/A	N/A	300	6	4702	0	16	3893	63
72025AP	IDE(AT)	2025	3.50	3H	RLL 1	AUTO	N/A	N/A	300	0	0	0	16	3936	63
7213A	IDE(AT)	212.78	3.50	3H	RLL 1	AUTO	N/A	N/A	150	4	1690	0	16	683	38
7213S	SCSI	212.78	3.50	3H	RLL 1	AUTO	N/A	N/A	150	4	1690	0			
7245A	IDE(AT)	245.57	3.50	3H	RLL 1	AUTO	N/A	N/A	150	4	1944	0	16	967	31
7245S	SCSI	245	3.50	3H	RLL 1	AUTO	N/A	N/A	150	4	1944	0			
72577AP	IDE(AT)	2577	3.50	3H	RLL 1	AUTO	N/A	N/A	300	0	0	0	16	4996	63
72700AP	IDE(AT)	2700	3.50	3H	RLL 1	AUTO	N/A	N/A	300	0	0	0	16	5248	63

MODEL	INT	CAP	FF	HGT	CODE	LZ	WP	RWC	MTBF	PHDS	PCYL	PSPT	LHDS	LCYL	LSPT
7270AV	IDE(AT)	270	3.50	HH	U		N/A	N/A	0	0	0	0	11	959	50
7270S	SCSI	270	3.50	3H	RLL 1	AUTO	N/A	N/A	300	4	1629	0			
7273A	IDE(AT)	275.39	3.50	3H	RLL 1	AUTO	N/A	N/A	150	2	2771	0	16	967	31
7273A (NEWER VER)	IDE(AT)	273	3.50	3H	RLL 1	AUTO	N/A	N/A	300	2	2793	0	16	1012	33
7290A	IDE(AT)	290	3.50	HH	RLL 1	AUTO	N/A	N/A	150	0	0	0	9	998	63
7290S	SCSI	290	3.50	3H	RLL 1	AUTO	N/A	N/A	0	4	1765	0			
7345A	IDE(AT)	345	3.50	3H	RLL 1	AUTO	N/A	N/A	150	4	0	0	15	790	57
7345S	SCSI	345		—	RLL 1	AUTO	N/A	N/A	0	4	2219	0			
7405A	IDE(AT)	405	3.50	3H	U	AUTO	N/A	N/A	150	0	0	0	16	989	50
7405AV	IDE(AT)	405	3.50	HH	U		N/A	N/A	0	0	0	0	16	989	50
7420AV	IDE(AT)	420	3.50	HH	U		N/A	N/A	0	0	0	0	16	986	52
7425AV	IDE(AT)	425	3.50	3H	U	AUTO	N/A	N/A	0	0	0	0	16	1002	52
7540A	IDE(AT)	528.4	3.50	3H	RLL 1	AUTO	N/A	N/A	150	4	2771	0	16	1024	63
7540AV	IDE(AT)	540	3.50	HH	U		N/A	N/A	0	0	0	0	16	1046	63
7541A	IDE(AT)	541	3.50	4H	RLL 1	AUTO	N/A	N/A	300	2	3	0	16	1,052	63
7541AP	IDE(AT)	541	3.50	4H	RLL 1	AUTO	N/A	N/A	300	2	3	0	16	1,052	63
7546A	IDE(AT)	528.48	3.50	3H	RLL 1	AUTO	N/A	N/A	150	4	2771	0	16	1024	63
7546A (NEWER VER)	IDE(AT)	547	3.50	3H	RLL 1	AUTO	N/A	N/A	300	4	2793	0	16	1060	63
7668A	IDE(AT)	668	3.50	3H	RLL 1	AUTO	N/A	N/A	300	2	4702	0	16	1297	63
7668AP	IDE(AT)	668	3.50	3H	RLL 1	AUTO	N/A	N/A	300	2	4702	0	16	1297	63
7850AV	IDE(AT)	850	3.50	3H	U	AUTO	N/A	N/A	0	0	0	0	16	1648	63
8050S	SCSI	50	3.50	HH	RLL 2	AUTO	N/A	N/A	30	4	809	26			
8051A	IDE(AT)	42.72	3.50	HH	RLL 2	AUTO	N/A	N/A	150	4	745	28	4	745	28
8051S	SCSI	44.9	3.50	HH	RLL 2	AUTO	N/A	N/A	150	4	783	0			
80875A	IDE(AT)	875	3.50	3H		AUTO	N/A	N/A		0	0	0	16	1700	63
80875A2	IDE(AT)	875	3.50			AUTO	N/A	N/A	0	0	0	0			
81080A3	IDE(AT)	1080	3.50			AUTO	N/A	N/A	0	0	0	0			
81081A2	IDE(AT)	1081	3.50	3H						0	0	0	16	2100	63
81275A3	IDE(AT)	1275	3.50			AUTO	N/A	N/A	0	0	0	0			
81280A	IDE(AT)	213	2.50		U					0	0	0	16	684	38
81280A2	IDE(AT)	1280	3.50	3H		AUTO	N/A	N/A		0	0	0	16	2481	63
81312A	IDE(AT)	1312	3.50	3H		AUTO	N/A	N/A		0	0	0	16	2548	63
81312A3	IDE(AT)	1312	3.50			AUTO	N/A	N/A	0	0	0	0			
81620A3	IDE(AT)	1620	3.50	3H						0	0	0	16	3250	63
81630A4	IDE(AT)	1630	3.50			AUTO	N/A	N/A	150	0	0	0			
81750A	IDE(AT)	1750	3.50	3H		AUTO	N/A	N/A		0	0	0	16	3400	63
81750A2	IDE(AT)	1750	3.50			AUTO	N/A	N/A	0	0	0	0			

(continues)

Table D.12 MAXTOR CORPORATION Continued

MODEL	INT	CAP	FF	HGT	CODE	LZ	WP	RWC	MTBF	PHDS	PCYL	PSPT	LHDS	LCYL	LSPT
81750A4	IDE(AT)	1750	3.50			AUTO	N/A	N/A	0	0	0	0			
81750D2	IDE(AT)	1750	3.50			AUTO	N/A	N/A	0	0	0	0			
82100A4	IDE(AT)	2100	3.50	3H						0	0	0	16	4092	63
82160D2	IDE(AT)	2160	3.50			AUTO	N/A	N/A	0	0	0	0			
82187A	IDE(AT)	2187	3.50	3H		AUTO	N/A	N/A		0	0	0	16	4248	63
82187A5	IDE(AT)	2187	3.50			AUTO	N/A	N/A	0	0	0	0			
82400A4	IDE(AT)	2400	3.50		RLL 8	AUTO	N/A	N/A	0	0	0	0			
82559A4	IDE(AT)	2559	3.50		RLL 8	AUTO	N/A	N/A	0	0	0	0			
82560A	IDE(AT)	2560	3.50	3H	RLL					0	0	0	16	4962	63
82560A3	IDE(AT)	2560	3.50			AUTO	N/A	N/A	0	0	0	0			
82560A4	IDE(AT)	2560	3.50	3H						0	0	0	16	4962	63
82560D3	IDE(AT)	3240	3.50			AUTO	N/A	N/A	0	0	0	0			
82577A6	IDE(AT)	2577	3.50			AUTO	N/A	N/A	0	0	0	0			
82580A5	IDE(AT)	2580	3.50	3H						0	0	0	16	5004	63
82625A	IDE(AT)	2625	3.50	3H		AUTO	N/A	N/A		0	0	0	16	5100	63
82625A6	IDE(AT)	2625	3.50			AUTO	N/A	N/A	0	0	0	0			
83062A	IDE(AT)	3062	3.50	3H		AUTO	N/A	N/A		0	0	0	16	5948	63
83062A7	IDE(AT)	3062	3.50			AUTO	N/A	N/A	0	0	0	0			
83200A5	IDE(AT)	3200	3.50			AUTO	N/A	N/A	0	0	0	0			
83200A6	IDE(AT)	3200	3.50			AUTO	N/A	N/A	0	0	0	0			
83200A8	IDE(AT)	3200	3.50			AUTO	N/A	N/A	0	0	0	0			
83201A6	IDE(AT)	3201	3.50	3H						0	0	0	16	6218	63
83202A6	IDE(AT)	3202	3.50			AUTO	N/A	N/A	0	0	0	0			
83209A5	IDE(AT)	3209	3.50			AUTO	N/A	N/A	0	0	0	0			
83240A4	IDE(AT)	3240	3.50		RLL 8	AUTO	N/A	N/A	0	0	0	0			
83240D3	IDE(AT)	3240	3.50			AUTO	N/A	N/A	0	0	0	0			
83240D4	IDE(AT)	3240	3.50			AUTO	N/A	N/A	0	0	0	0			
83500A	IDE(AT)	3500	3.50	3H		AUTO	N/A	N/A	0	0	0	0	16	6800	63
83500A4	IDE(AT)	3500	3.50			AUTO	N/A	N/A	0	0	0	0			
83500A8	IDE(AT)	3500	3.50			AUTO	N/A	N/A	0	0	0	0			
83500D4	IDE(AT)	3500	3.50			AUTO	N/A	N/A	0	0	0	0			
83840A	IDE(AT)	3840	3.50	3H	RLL					0	0	0	16	7441	63
83840A6	IDE(AT)	3840	3.50	3H						0	0	0	16	7443	63
84000A6	IDE(AT)	4000	3.50	3H						0	0	0	16	7763	63
84004A8	IDE(AT)	4004	3.50			AUTO	N/A	N/A	0	0	0	0			
84200A8	IDE(AT)	4200	3.50			AUTO	N/A	N/A	0	0	0	0			
84320A5	IDE(AT)	4320	3.50			AUTO	N/A	N/A	0	0	0	0			

MODEL	INT	CAP	FF	HGT	CODE	LZ	WP	RWC	MTBF	PHDS	PCYL	PSPT	LHDS	LCYL	LSPT
84320A8	IDE(AT)	4320	3.50	3H						0	0	0	16	8400	63
84320D4	IDE(AT)	4320	3.50			AUTO	N/A	N/A	0	0	0	0			
84320D5	IDE(AT)	4320	3.50			AUTO	N/A	N/A	0	0	0	0			
85120A	IDE(AT)	5120	3.50	3H	RLL					0	0	0	16	9924	63
85120A6	IDE(AT)	5120	3.50			AUTO	N/A	N/A	0	0	0	0			
85120A8	IDE(AT)	5120	3.50	3H						0	0	0	16	9924	63
85121A8	IDE(AT)	5121	3.50			AUTO	N/A	N/A	0	0	0	0			
85250D6	IDE(AT)	5250	3.50			AUTO	N/A	N/A	0	0	0	0			
86480A8	IDE(AT)	6480	3.50			AUTO	N/A	N/A	0	0	0	0			
86480D6	IDE(AT)	6480	3.50			AUTO	N/A	N/A	0	0	0	0			
86480D8	IDE(AT)	6480	3.50			AUTO	N/A	N/A	0	0	0	0			
87000A8	IDE(AT)	700	3.50			AUTO	N/A	N/A	0	0	0	0			
87000D8	IDE(AT)	7000	3.50			AUTO	N/A	N/A	0	0	0	0			
88400D8	IDE(AT)	8400	3.50			AUTO	N/A	N/A	0	0	0	0			
EXT-4175	ESDI-10MHZ	149.15	5.25	FH					20	7	1224	34			
EXT-4280	ESDI-10MHZ	149.1	5.25	FH					20	11	1224	34			
EXT-4380	ESDI-10MHZ	319.61	5.25	FH	RLL	AUTO	N/A	N/A	20	15	1224	34			
LXT-100S	SCSI	93.07	3.50	HH	RLL 1	AUTO	N/A	N/A	150	8	733	31			
LXT-200A	IDE(AT)	207	3.50	HH	RLL 1	AUTO	N/A	N/A	150	7	1320	0	15	816	32
LXT-200S OPTION A	SCSI	207	3.50	HH	RLL 2	AUTO	N/A	N/A	150	7	1320	0			
LXT-200S OPTION B	SCSI	207	3.50	HH	RLL 2	AUTO	N/A	N/A	150	7	1320	0			
LXT-213A	IDE(AT)	212	3.50	HH	RLL 1	AUTO	N/A	N/A	150	7	1320	0	16	683	38
LXT-213S OPTION A	SCSI	212	3.50	HH	RLL 1	AUTO	N/A	N/A	150	7	1320	0			
LXT-213S OPTION B	SCSI	212	3.50	HH	RLL 1	AUTO	N/A	N/A	150	7	1320	0			
LXT-340A	IDE(AT)	340	3.50	HH	RLL 2	AUTO	N/A	N/A	150	7	1560	0	16	654	63
LXT-340S OPTION A	SCSI	340	3.50	HH	RLL 2	AUTO	N/A	N/A	150	7	1560	0			
LXT-340S OPTION B	SCSI	340	3.50	HH	RLL 2	AUTO	N/A	N/A	150	7	1560	0			
LXT-437A	IDE(AT)	437	3.50	HH	RLL 2	AUTO	N/A	N/A	150	9	1560	0	16	842	63
LXT-437S OPTION A	SCSI	437	3.50	HH	RLL 2	AUTO	N/A	N/A	150	9	1560	0			
LXT-437S OPTION B	SCSI	437	3.50	HH	RLL 2	AUTO	N/A	N/A	150	9	1560	0			
LXT-50S	SCSI	46.53	3.50	HH	RLL 1	AUTO	N/A	N/A	40	4	733	31			
LXT-535A	IDE(AT)	528.48	3.50	HH	RLL 2	AUTO	N/A	N/A	150	11	1560	0	16	1024	63

(continues)

Table D.12   MAXTOR CORPORATION Continued

MODEL	INT	CAP	FF	HGT	CODE	LZ	WP	RWC	MTBF	PHDS	PCYL	PSPT	LHDS	LCYL	LSPT
LXT-535S OPTION A	SCSI	535	3.50	HH	RLL 2	AUTO	N/A	N/A	150	11	1560	0			
LXT-535S OPTION B	SCSI	535	3.50	HH	RLL 2	AUTO	N/A	N/A	150	11	1560	0			
MX9217SDN	SCSI-2 D	2170	3.50	3H	PRML	AUTO	N/A	N/A	800	9	3703	0			
MX9217SDW	SCSI-2 WD	2170	3.50	3H	PRML	AUTO	N/A	N/A	800	9	3703	0			
MX9217SSN	SCSI-2	2170	3.50	3H	PRML	AUTO	N/A	N/A	800	9	3703	0			
MX9217SSW	SCSI SCA	2170	3.50	3H	PRML	AUTO	N/A	N/A	800	9	3703	0			
MXT-1240S	SCSI-2	1240	3.50	3H	RLL 1	AUTO	N/A	N/A	300	0	0	0			
MXT-540A	IDE(AT)	528.48	3.50	3H	RLL 1	AUTO	N/A	N/A	300	0	0	0	16	1024	63
MXT-540AL	IDE(AT)	528.5	3.50	3H	RLL 1	AUTO	N/A	N/A	300	7	2234	0	16	1024	63
MXT-540SL	SCSI-2	540	3.50	3H	RLL 1	AUTO	N/A	N/A	300	0	0	0			
PANTHER P0-12S	SCSI-2	1051	5.25	FH	RLL	AUTO	N/A	N/A	100	15	1795	0			
PANTHER P1-08E	ESDI-24MHZ	696.4	5.25	FH	RLL	AUTO	N/A	N/A	100	9	1778	85			
PANTHER P1-08S	SCSI-2	696.4	5.25	FH	RLL	AUTO	N/A	N/A	100	9	1778	85			
PANTHER P1-12E	ESDI-24MHZ	1051.43	5.25	FH	AUTO	N/A	N/A	100K	0	15	1778	77			
PANTHER P1-12S	SCSI-2	1005.48	5.25	FH	RLL	AUTO	N/A	N/A	100	19	1216	85			
PANTHER P1-13E	ESDI-24MHZ	1160.67	5.25	FH	AUTO	N/A	N/A	N/A	100	15	1778	85			
PANTHER P1-16E	ESDI-24MHZ	1331.82	5.25	FH	RLL	AUTO	N/A	N/A	100	19	1778	77			
PANTHER P1-17E	ESDI-24MHZ	1470.19	5.25	FH	RLL	AUTO	N/A	N/A	100	19	1778	85			
PANTHER P1-17S	SCSI-2	1470.19	5.25	FH	RLL	AUTO	N/A	N/A	100	19	1778	85			
RXT-800 SERIES	SCSI	0		—	RLL				0	0	0	0			
XT 8800E	ESDI-10MHZ	694.68	5.25	FH	RLL 1	AUTO	N/A	N/A	150	15	1274	71			
XT-1050	ST-506/412	39.25	5.25	FH	MFM				150	5	902	17			
XT-1065	ST-506/412	55.93	5.25	FH	MFM		919	919	150	7	918	17			
XT-1085	ST-506/412	71.3	5.25	FH	MFM		N/A	N/A	150	8	1024	17			
XT-1105	ST-506/412	87.89	5.25	FH	MFM		919	919	150	11	918	17			
XT-1120R	ST-506/412	104.85	5.25	FH	RLL 2		N/A	N/A	70	8	1024	25			
XT-1140	ST-506/412	119.85	5.25	FH	MFM		N/A	N/A	150	15	918	17			
XT-1240R	ST-506/412	196.6	5.25	FH	RLL 2		N/A	N/A	150	15	1024	25			
XT-2085	ST-506/412	74.57	5.25	FH	MFM		1,225	1,225	150	7	1224	17			
XT-2140	ST-506/412	117.19	5.25	FH	MFM		1,225	1,225	150	11	1224	17			
XT-2190	ST-506/412	159.8	5.25	FH	MFM		N/A	N/A	150	15	1224	17			

MODEL	INT	CAP	FF	HGT	CODE	LZ	WP	RWC	MTBF	PHDS	PCYL	PSPT	LHDS	LCYL	LSPT
XT-3170 NON-SHROUDE	SCSI	141	5.25	FH	RLL	AUTO	N/A	N/A	20	9	1224	25			
XT-3170 SHROUDED	SCSI	141	5.25	FH	RLL	AUTO	N/A	N/A	20	9	1224	25			
XT-3280 NON-SHROUDE	SCSI	235	5.25	FH	RLL	AUTO	N/A	N/A	20	15	1224	25			
XT-3280 SHROUDED	SCSI	235	5.25	FH	RLL	AUTO	N/A	N/A	20	15	1224	25			
XT-3380	SCSI	319.61	5.25	FH	RLL	AUTO	N/A	N/A	20	15	1224	34			
XT-4170E	ESDI-10MHZ	153.53	5.25	FH	RLL 1	AUTO	N/A	N/A	30	7	1224	36			
XT-4170SPCB REV. 3	SCSI	157.92	5.25	FH	RLL 1	AUTO	N/A	N/A	150	7	1224	36			
XT-4170S PCB REV. 1	SCSI	157.92	5.25	FH	RLL 1	AUTO	N/A	N/A	150	7	1224	36			
XT-4230E	ESDI-10MHZ	197.4	5.25	FH	RLL 1	AUTO	N/A	N/A	150	9	1224	36			
XT-4280E	ESDI-10MHZ	241.27	5.25	FH	RLL	AUTO	N/A	N/A	30	11	1224	35			
XT-4280S PCB REV. 3	SCSI	248.16	5.25	FH	RLL	AUTO	N/A	N/A	30	11	1224	36			
XT-4280S PCB REV. 1	SCSI	248.16	5.25	FH	RLL	AUTO	N/A	N/A	30	11	1224	36			
XT-4380E	ESDI-10MHZ	329.01	5.25	FH	RLL 1	AUTO	N/A	N/A	30	15	1224	36			
XT-4380EF	ESDI-10MHZ	329.01	5.25	FH	RLL 1	AUTO	N/A	N/A	30	15	1224	36			
XT-4380F PCB REV.3	SCSI	338.41	5.25	FH	RLL 1	AUTO	N/A	N/A	150	15	1224	36			
XT-4380S PCB REV. 3	SCSI	338.41	5.25	FH	RLL 1	AUTO	N/A	N/A	150	15	1224	36			
XT-4380S PCB REV. 1	SCSI	338.41	5.25	FH	RLL 1	AUTO	N/A	N/A	150	15	1224	36			
XT-8380DS	SCSI	360	5.25	FH	U	AUTO	N/A	N/A	150	8	1632	0			
XT-8380E VER. 1	ESDI-15MHZ	360.97	5.25	FH	RLL 1	AUTO	N/A	N/A	150	8	1632	54			
XT-8380E VER. 2	ESDI-15MHZ	360.97	5.25	FH	RLL 1	AUTO	N/A	N/A	150	8	1632	54			
XT-8380E VER. 3	ESDI-15MHZ	360.97	5.25	FH	RLL 1	AUTO	N/A	N/A	150	8	1632	54			
XT-8380E VER. 4	ESDI-15MHZ	360.97	5.25	FH	RLL 1	AUTO	N/A	N/A	150	8	1632	54			
XT-8380E VER. 5	ESDI-15MHZ	360.97	5.25	FH	RLL 1	AUTO	N/A	N/A	150	8	1632	54			
XT-8380E VER. 6	ESDI-15MHZ	360.97	5.25	FH	RLL 1	AUTO	N/A	N/A	150	8	1632	54			
XT-8380EH VER. 1	ESDI-15MHZ	360.97	5.25	FH	RLL 1	AUTO	N/A	N/A	150	8	1632	54			
XT-8380EH VER. 2	ESDI-15MHZ	360.97	5.25	FH	RLL 1	AUTO	N/A	N/A	150	8	1632	54			
XT-8380EH VER. 3	ESDI-15MHZ	360.97	5.25	FH	RLL 1	AUTO	N/A	N/A	150	8	1632	54			
XT-8380EH VER. 4	ESDI-15MHZ	360.97	5.25	FH	RLL 1	AUTO	N/A	N/A	150	8	1632	54			
XT-8380EH VER. 5	ESDI-15MHZ	360.97	5.25	FH	RLL 1	AUTO	N/A	N/A	150	8	1632	54			

(continues)

Table D.12   MAXTOR CORPORATION Continued

MODEL	INT	CAP	FF	HGT	CODE	LZ	WP	RWC	MTBF	PHDS	PCYL	PSPT	LHDS	LCYL	LSPT
XT-8380EH VER. 6	ESDI-15MHZ	360.97	5.25	FH	RLL 1	AUTO	N/A	N/A	150	8	1632	54			
XT-8380S	SCSI	360.97	5.25	FH	RLL 1	AUTO	N/A	N/A	150	8	1632	54			
XT-8380SH	SCSI	360.3	5.25	FH	RLL 1	AUTO	N/A	N/A	150	8	1632	54			
XT-8610E VER. 1	ESDI-15MHZ	541.45	5.25	FH	RLL 1	AUTO	N/A	N/A	150	12	1632	54			
XT-8610E VER. 2	ESDI-15MHZ	541.45	5.25	FH	RLL 1	AUTO	N/A	N/A	150	12	1632	54			
XT-8610E VER. 3	ESDI-15MHZ	541.45	5.25	FH	RLL 1	AUTO	N/A	N/A	150	12	1632	54			
XT-8610E VER. 4	ESDI-15MHZ	541.45	5.25	FH	RLL 1	AUTO	N/A	N/A	150	12	1632	54			
XT-8610E VER. 5	ESDI-15MHZ	541.45	5.25	FH	RLL 1	AUTO	N/A	N/A	150	12	1632	54			
XT-8610E VER. 6	ESDI-15MHZ	541.45	5.25	FH	RLL 1	AUTO	N/A	N/A	150	12	1632	54			
XT-8702S	SCSI	616.68	5.25	FH	RLL 1	AUTO	N/A	N/A	150	15	1487	54			
XT-8760DS	SCSI	676	5.25	FH	U	AUTO	N/A	N/A	150	15	1632	0			
XT-8760E VER. 1	ESDI-15MHZ	676.82	5.25	FH	RLL 1	AUTO	N/A	N/A	150	15	1632	54			
XT-8760E VER. 2	ESDI-15MHZ	676.82	5.25	FH	RLL 1	AUTO	N/A	N/A	150	15	1632	54			
XT-8760E VER. 3	ESDI-15MHZ	676.82	5.25	FH	RLL 1	AUTO	N/A	N/A	150	15	1632	54			
XT-8760E VER. 4	ESDI-15MHZ	676.82	5.25	FH	RLL 1	AUTO	N/A	N/A	150	15	1632	54			
XT-8760E VER. 5	ESDI-15MHZ	676.82	5.25	FH	RLL 1	AUTO	N/A	N/A	150	15	1632	54			
XT-8760E VER. 6	ESDI-15MHZ	676.82	5.25	FH	RLL 1	AUTO	N/A	N/A	150	15	1632	54			
XT-8760EH VER. 1	ESDI-15MHZ	676.82	5.25	FH	RLL 1	AUTO	N/A	N/A	150	15	1632	54			
XT-8760EH VER. 2	ESDI-15MHZ	676.82	5.25	FH	RLL 1	AUTO	N/A	N/A	150	15	1632	54			
XT-8760EH VER. 3	ESDI-15MHZ	676.82	5.25	FH	RLL 1	AUTO	N/A	N/A	150	15	1632	54			
XT-8760EH VER. 4	ESDI-15MHZ	676.82	5.25	FH	RLL 1	AUTO	N/A	N/A	150	15	1632	54			
XT-8760EH VER. 5	ESDI-15MHZ	676.82	5.25	FH	RLL 1	AUTO	N/A	N/A	150	15	1632	54			
XT-8760EH VER. 6	ESDI-15MHZ	676.82	5.25	FH	RLL 1	AUTO	N/A	N/A	150	15	1632	54			
XT-8760S	SCSI	676.82	5.25	FH	RLL 1	AUTO	N/A	N/A	150	15	1632	54			
XT-8760SH	SCSI	675.6	5.25	FH	RLL 1	AUTO	N/A	N/A	150	15	1632	54			
XT-8800E	ESDI-24MHZ	694	5.25	FH	RLL 1	AUTO	N/A	N/A	150	15	1274	71			
XT81000E	ESDI-24MHZ	889.89	5.25	FH	RLL 1	AUTO	N/A	N/A	150	15	1632	71			

Table D.13   QUANTUM CORPORATION

MODEL	INT	CAP	FF	HGT	CODE	LZ	WP	RWC	MTBF	PHDS	PCYL	PSPT	LHDS	LCYL	LSPT
ATLAS II XP32181S	U-SCSI	2180	3.50	3H	RLL 1	AUTO	N/A	N/A	1000	6	5952	0			
ATLAS II XP 32181SCA	SCSI SCA	2180	3.50	3H	RLL 1	AUTO	N/A	N/A	1000	6	5952	0			
ATLAS II XP 32181W	U-SCSI W	2180	3.50	3H	RLL 1	AUTO	N/A	N/A	1000	6	5952	0			

MODEL	INT	CAP	FF	HGT	CODE	LZ	WP	RWC	MTBF	PHDS	PCYL	PSPT	LHDS	LCYL	LSPT
ATLAS II XP 32181WD	U-SCSI WD	2180	3.50	3H	RLL 1	AUTO	N/A	N/A	1000	6	5952	0			
ATLAS II XP32275D		0								0	0	0			
ATLAS II XP34361S	U-SCSI	4360	3.50	3H	RLL 1	AUTO	N/A	N/A	1000	10	5952	0			
ATLAS II XP 34361SCA	SCSI SCA	4360	3.50	3H	RLL 1	AUTO	N/A	N/A	1000	10	5952	0			
ATLAS II XP34361W	U-SCSI W	4360	3.50	3H	RLL 1	AUTO	N/A	N/A	1000	10	5952	0			
ATLAS II XP34361WD	U-SCSI WD	4360	3.50	3H	RLL 1	AUTO	N/A	N/A	1000	10	5952	0			
ATLAS II XP34550D		0								0	0	0			
ATLAS II XP39100D		0								0	0	0			
ATLAS II XP 39100SCA	SCSI SCA	8678	3.50	FH	RLL 1	AUTO	N/A	N/A	1000	20	5952	0			
ATLAS XP31070S	SCSI-2 F	1075	3.50	3H	RLL 1	AUTO	N/A	N/A	800	5	3832	0			
ATLAS XP31070SCA	SCSI SCA	1075	3.50	3H	UNIDEN					5	3832	0			
ATLAS XP31070W	SCSI-2 FW	1075	3.50	3H	RLL 1	AUTO	N/A	N/A	800	5	3832	0			
ATLAS XP31070WD	SCSI-2 FWD	1075	3.50	3H	RLL 1	AUTO	N/A	N/A	800	5	3832	0			
ATLAS XP32150S	SCSI-2 F	2150	3.50	3H	RLL 1	AUTO	N/A	N/A	800	10	3832	0			
ATLAS XP32150W	SCSI-2 FW	2150	3.50	3H	RLL 1	AUTO	N/A	N/A	800	10	3832	0			
ATLAS XP32150WD	SCSI-2 FWD	2150	3.50	3H	RLL 1	AUTO	N/A	N/A	800	10	3832	0			
ATLAS XP34300S	SCSI-2 F	4300	3.50	HH	RLL 1	AUTO	N/A	N/A	800	20	3832	0			
ATLAS XP34300W	SCSI-2 FW	4300	3.50	HH	RLL 1	AUTO	N/A	N/A	800	20	3832	0			
ATLAS XP34300WD	SCSI-2 FWD	4300	3.50	HH	RLL 1	AUTO	N/A	N/A	800	20	3832	0			
BIGFOOT 1.2AT	IDE(AT)	1280	5.25	4H	PRML	AUTO	N/A	N/A	300	0	0	0	16	2492	63
BIGFOOT 1275	IDE(AT)	1275	5.25	4H	PRML	2492	N/A	N/A		2	5738	0	16	2492	63
BIGFOOT 1275AT	IDE(AT)	1275	5.25	4H	PRML	2492	N/A	N/A		2	5738	0	16	2492	63
BIGFOOT 2.5AT	IDE(AT)	2500	5.25	4H	PRML	AUTO	N/A	N/A	300	0	0	0	16	4994	63
BIGFOOT 2550	IDE(AT)	2500	5.25	4H	PRML	4994	N/A	N/A		4	5738	0	16	4994	63
BIGFOOT 2550AT	IDE(AT)	2500	5.25	4H	PRML	4994	N/A	N/A		4	5738	0	16	4994	63
BIGFOOT CY 2.1AT	IDE(AT)	170.8	3.50	5	UNIDEN	AUTO	N/A	N/A	250	16	4092	63			
BIGFOOT CY 4.3AT	IDE(AT)	4300	3.50	5	UNIDEN	AUTO	N/A	N/A	250	15	8960	63			
BIGFOOT CY 6.4AT	IDE(AT)	6400	3.50	5	UNIDEN	AUTO	N/A	N/A	250	15	13446	63			
CAPELLA VP31110	SCSI-2 F	1108	3.50	3H	RLL 1	AUTO	N/A	N/A	800	4	4165	0			
CAPELLA VP31110S	SCSI-2 F	0	3.50	HH	RLL 1	AUTO	N/A	N/A	300	0	0	0			
CAPELLA VP31110W	SCSI-2 FW	1108	3.50	3H	RLL 1	AUTO	N/A	N/A	800	4	4165	0			
CAPELLA VP31110WD	SCSI-2 FWD	1108	3.50	3H	RLL 1	AUTO	N/A	N/A	800	4	4165	0			
CAPELLA VP32210	SCSI-2 F	2216	3.50	3H	RLL 1	AUTO	N/A	N/A	800	8	4165	0			
CAPELLA VP32210S	SCSI-2 F	0	3.50	HH	RLL 1				300	0	0	0			
CAPELLA VP32210W	SCSI-2 FW	2216	3.50	3H	RLL 1	AUTO	N/A	N/A	800	8	4165	0			
CAPELLA VP32210WD	SCSI-2 FWD	2216	3.50	3H	RLL 1	AUTO	N/A	N/A	800	8	4165	0			

(continues)

Table D.13 QUANTUM CORPORATION Continued

MODEL	INT	CAP	FF	HGT	CODE	LZ	WP	RWC	MTBF	PHDS	PCYL	PSPT	LHDS	LCYL	LSPT
DAYTONA 127AT	IDE(AT)	127	2.50	3H	RLL 1	AUTO	N/A	N/A	350	0	0	0	9	677	41
DAYTONA 127S	SCSI	127	2.50	5H	RLL 1	AUTO	N/A	N/A	350	2	0	0			
DAYTONA 170AT	IDE(AT)	170	2.50	3H	RLL 1	AUTO	N/A	N/A	350	0	0	0	10	538	62
DAYTONA 170S	SCSI	170	2.50	5H	RLL 1	AUTO	N/A	N/A	350	3	0	0			
DAYTONA 256AT	IDE(AT)	256	2.50	3H	RLL 1	AUTO	N/A	N/A	350	0	0	0	11	723	63
DAYTONA 256S	SCSI	256	2.50	5H	RLL 1	AUTO	N/A	N/A	350	4	0	0			
DAYTONA 341AT	IDE(AT)	341	2.50	3H	RLL 1	AUTO	N/A	N/A	350	0	0	0	15	1011	44
DAYTONA 341S	SCSI	341	2.50	4H	RLL 1	AUTO	N/A	N/A	350	6	0	0			
DAYTONA 514AT	IDE(AT)	514	2.50	3H	RLL 1	AUTO	N/A	N/A	350	0	0	0	16	997	63
DAYTONA 514S	SCSI	514	2.50	4H	RLL 1	AUTO	N/A	N/A	350	8	0	0			
DSP3053L	SCSI-2 W	535	3.50	3H	RLL 1	AUTO	N/A	N/A	500	4	3117	0			
DSP3053LD	SCSI-2 D	535	3.50	3H	RLL 1	AUTO	N/A	N/A	500	4	3117	0			
DSP3085	SCSI-2	852	3.50	HH	NONE	AUTO	N/A	N/A	0	14	0	57			
DSP3105	SCSI-2	1050	3.50	HH	NONE	AUTO	N/A	N/A	250	14	0	57			
DSP3105D	SCSI-2	1050	3.50	HH	NONE	AUTO	N/A	N/A	250	14	0	57			
DSP3107L	SCSI-2 D	1070	3.50	3H	RLL 1	AUTO	N/A	N/A	500	8	3117	0			
DSP3107LD	SCSI-2 D	1070	3.50	3H	RLL 1	AUTO	N/A	N/A	500	8	3117	0			
DSP3133L	SCSI-2	1338	3.50	3H	RLL 1	AUTO	N/A	N/A	500	10	3117	0			
DSP3133LD	SCSI-2 D	1338	3.50	3H	RLL 1	AUTO	N/A	N/A	500	10	3117	0			
DSP3160	SCSI-2	1600	3.50	3H	RLL 1	AUTO	N/A	N/A	350	16	2599	0			
DSP3210	SCSI-2	2148	3.50	3H	RLL 1	AUTO	N/A	N/A	500	16	3045	0			
EMPIRE 1080S	U-SCSI	1232	3.50	HH	RLL 1	AUTO	N/A	N/A	500	8	2874	0			
EMPIRE 1400S	U-SCSI	1400	3.50	HH	PRML	AUTO	N/A	N/A	500	8	3115	0			
EMPIRE 1440S	U-SCSI	1440	3.50	HH	RLL 1	AUTO	N/A	N/A	500	8	0	0			
EMPIRE 2100S	U-SCSI	2100	3.50	HH	PRML	AUTO	N/A	N/A	500	12	3115	0			
EMPIRE 2160S	U-SCSI	2160	3.50	HH	RLL 1	AUTO	N/A	N/A	500	12	0	0			
EMPIRE 540S	U-SCSI	540	3.50	HH	RLL 1	AUTO	N/A	N/A	500	4	2874	0			
EPS 510	SCSI-2 F	107	5.25	FH	UNIDEN					0	0	0			
EPS 530	SCSI-2 F	267	5.25	FH	UNIDEN					0	0	0			
EPS 540	SCSI-2 F	428	5.25	FH	UNIDEN					0	0	0			
EPS 580	SCSI-2 F	856	5.25	FH	UNIDEN					0	0	0			
EUROPA 1080AT	IDE(AT)	1.08	2.50	4H	PRML	AUTO	N/A	N/A	350	8	2	0	15	2,352	60
EUROPA 540AT	IDE(AT)	540	2.50	5H	PRML	AUTO	N/A	N/A	350	4	2	0	15	1,176	60
EUROPA 810AT	IDE(AT)	810	2.50	4H	PRML	AUTO	N/A	N/A	350	6	2	0	15	1,764	60
FIREBALL 1080AT	IDE(AT)	1089	3.50	3H	PRML	2112	N/A	N/A	500	4	3835	0	16	2112	63
FIREBALL 1080S	U-SCSI	1092.7	3.50	3H	PRML	AUTO	N/A	N/A	500	4	3835	0			
FIREBALL 1280AT	IDE(AT)	1282	3.50	3H	PRML	AUTO	N/A	N/A	500	4	4142	0	16	2484	63
FIREBALL 1280S	U-SCSI	1282	3.50	3H	PRML	AUTO	N/A	N/A	500	4	4142	0			

MODEL	INT	CAP	FF	HGT	CODE	LZ	WP	RWC	MTBF	PHDS	PCYL	PSPT	LHDS	LCYL	LSPT
FIREBALL 540AT	IDE(AT)	544	3.50	3H	PRML	1056	N/A	N/A	500	2	3835	0	16	1056	63
FIREBALL 540S	U-SCSI	545.4	3.50	3H	PRML	AUTO	N/A	N/A	500	2	3835	0			
FIREBALL 640AT	IDE(AT)	642	3.50	3H	PRML	AUTO	N/A	N/A	500	2	4142	0	16	1244	63
FIREBALL 640S	SCSI-2	852	3.50	3H	RLL 1	AUTO	N/A	N/A	300	4	3653	0	16	1647	63
FIREBALL ST 2.1S	U-SCSI	2111	3.50	0					0	6	820	17			
FIREBALL ST 3.2AT	U-SCSI	3228	3.50	0					0	16	6256	63			
FIREBALL ST 3.2S	U-SCSI	3228	3.50	0					0	16	6256	63			
FIREBALL ST 4.3AT	U-SCSI	4310	3.50	0					0	9	14848	63			
FIREBALL ST 4.3S	U-SCSI	4310	3.50	0					0	9	14848	63			
FIREBALL ST 6.4AT	U-SCSI	6448	3.50	0					0	15	13328	63			
FIREBALL ST 6.4S	U-SCSI	6448	3.50	0					0	15	13328	63			
FIREBALL TM 1.0AT	IDE(AT)	1080	3.50	3H	PRML	AUTO	N/A	N/A	400	2	6825	0			
FIREBALL TM 1.0S	U-SCSI	1082	3.50	3H		AUTO	N/A	N/A		0	0	0			
FIREBALL TM 2.1AT	IDE(AT)	2168	3.50	3H	PRML	AUTO	N/A	N/A	400	4	6825	0			
FIREBALL TM 2.1S	U-SCSI	2168	3.50	3H		AUTO	N/A	N/A		0	0	0			
FIREBALL TM 2.5AT		0								0	0	0			
FIREBALL TM 3.2AT	IDE(AT)	3254	3.50	3H	PRML	AUTO	N/A	N/A	400	6	6825	0			
FIREBALL TM 3.2S	U-SCSI	3254	3.50	3H		AUTO	N/A	N/A		0	0	0			
FIREBALL TM 3.8AT		0								0	0	0			
GODRIVE 120AT	IDE(AT)	126.62	2.50	3H	RLL 1	AUTO	N/A	N/A	150	4	1097	0	13	731	26
GODRIVE 120S	SCSI	126.62	2.50	3H	RLL 1	AUTO	N/A	N/A	150	4	1097	0			
GODRIVE 40AT	IDE(AT)	41.15	2.50	3H	RLL 1	AUTO	N/A	N/A	80	2	957	42	6	820	17
GODRIVE 40S	SCSI	42.9	2.50	3H	RLL 1	AUTO	N/A	N/A	80	2	870	0			
GODRIVE 60AT	IDE(AT)	63.03	2.50	3H	RLL 1	AUTO	N/A	N/A	150	2	1097	0	7	1024	17
GODRIVE 60S	SCSI	63	2.50	5H	RLL 1	AUTO	N/A	N/A	150	2	0	0			
GODRIVE 80AT	IDE(AT)	82.31	2.50	3H	RLL 1	AUTO	N/A	N/A	80	4	957	42	9	1024	17
GODRIVE 80S	SCSI	86.3	2.50	3H	RLL 1	AUTO	N/A	N/A	80	4	870	0			
GODRIVE GLS 127AT	IDE(AT)	127.9	2.50	3H	RLL 1	AUTO	N/A	N/A	350	3	1395	0	9	677	41
GODRIVE GLS 127S	SCSI	127.91	2.50	3H	RLL 1	AUTO	N/A	N/A	350	3	1395	0			
GODRIVE GLS 170AT	IDE(AT)	170.78	2.50	3H	RLL 1	AUTO	N/A	N/A	350	4	1395	0	10	538	62
GODRIVE GLS 170S	SCSI	170.78	2.50	3H	RLL 1	AUTO	N/A	N/A	350	4	1395	0			
GODRIVE GLS 256AT	IDE(AT)	256.53	2.50	3H	RLL 1	AUTO	N/A	N/A	350	6	1395	0	11	723	63
GODRIVE GLS 256S	SCSI	256.53	2.50	3H	RLL 1	AUTO	N/A	N/A	350	6	1395	0			
GODRIVE GLS 85AT	IDE(AT)	85.02	2.50	3H	RLL 1	AUTO	N/A	N/A	350	2	1395	0	10	722	23
GODRIVE GLS 85S	SCSI	85.03	2.50	3H	RLL 1	AUTO	N/A	N/A	350	2	1395	0			
GODRIVE GRS 160AT	IDE(AT)	169.87	2.50	3H	RLL 1	AUTO	N/A	N/A	150	4	1376	0	9	1024	36
GODRIVE GRS 160S	SCSI-2	168.16	2.50	3H	RLL 1	AUTO	N/A	N/A	150	4	1376	0			
GODRIVE GRS 80AT	IDE(AT)	84.08	2.50	3H	RLL 1	AUTO	N/A	N/A	150	2	1376	0	5	966	34

(continues)

Table D.13 QUANTUM CORPORATION Continued

MODEL	INT	CAP	FF	HGT	CODE	LZ	WP	RWC	MTBF	PHDS	PCYL	PSPT	LHDS	LCYL	LSPT
GODRIVE GRS 80S	SCSI-2	84.1	2.50	3H	RLL 1	AUTO	N/A	N/A	150	2	1376	0			
GRAND PRIX XP32151S	SCSI	2152	3.50	HH	UNIDEN	AUTO	N/A	N/A	800	10	0	0			
GRAND PRIX XP32151SCA	SCSI	3215	3.50	HH	UNIDEN	AUTO	N/A	N/A		0	0	0			
GRAND PRIX XP34301S	SCSI	4306	3.50	HH	UNIDEN	AUTO	N/A	N/A	800	20	0	0			
GRAND PRIX XP34301SCA	SCSI	3430	3.50	HH	UNIDEN	AUTO	N/A	N/A		0	0	0			
LIGHTNING 365AT	IDE(AT)	365.7	3.50	HH	RLL 1	AUTO	N/A	N/A	300	0	0	0	12	976	61
LIGHTNING 365S	SCSI-2	366.5	3.50	HH	RLL 1	AUTO	N/A	N/A	300	2	0	0			
LIGHTNING 540AT	IDE(AT)	541.3	3.50	HH	RLL 1	AUTO	N/A	N/A	300	0	0	0	16	1120	59
LIGHTNING 540S	SCSI-2	550.7	3.50	HH	RLL 1	AUTO	N/A	N/A	300	2	0	0			
LIGHTNING 730AT	IDE(AT)	730.8	3.50	HH	RLL 1	AUTO	N/A	N/A	300	0	0	0	16	1416	63
LIGHTNING 730S	SCSI-2	733.1	3.50	HH	RLL 1	AUTO	N/A	N/A	300	4	0	0			
MAVERICK 270AT	IDE(AT)	270.66	3.50	3H	RLL 1	944	N/A	N/A	300	2	2740	0	14	944	40
MAVERICK 270S	SCSI	270.7	3.50	3H	RLL 1	AUTO	N/A	N/A	300	2	0	0			
MAVERICK 540AT	IDE(AT)	541.32	3.50	3H	RLL 1	1120	N/A	N/A	300	4	2740	0	16	1048	63
MAVERICK 540S	SCSI	541.5	3.50	3H	RLL 1	AUTO	N/A	N/A	300	4	0	0			
PIONEER SG 1080AT	IDE(AT)	1000	3.50	3H					300	0	0	0			
PIONEER SG 2110AT	IDE(AT)	2100	3.50	3H					300	0	0	0			
PRODRIVE 1050S	SCSI	1054.71	3.50	HH	RLL 1	AUTO	N/A	N/A	150	12	2448	0			
PRODRIVE 105AT	IDE(AT)	105.24	3.50	HH	RLL 2	AUTO	N/A	N/A	60	4	1219	0	16	755	17
PRODRIVE 105S	SCSI	104.99	3.50	HH	RLL 2	AUTO	N/A	N/A	50	6	1019	0			
PRODRIVE 1080S	U-SCSI	1232	3.50	HH	RLL 1	AUTO	N/A	N/A	500	8	2874	0			
PRODRIVE 120AT	IDE(AT)	120.04	3.50	HH	RLL 1	AUTO	N/A	N/A	50	5	1123	0	9	814	32
PRODRIVE 120S	SCSI	120.04	3.50	HH	RLL 1	AUTO	N/A	N/A	50	5	1123	0			
PRODRIVE 1225S	SCSI	1230.5	3.50	HH	RLL 1	AUTO	N/A	N/A	150	14	2448	0			
PRODRIVE 160AT	IDE(AT)	168.39	3.50	HH	RLL 1	AUTO	N/A	N/A	80	4	839	0			
PRODRIVE 170AT	IDE(AT)	168.52	3.50	HH	RLL 1	AUTO	N/A	N/A	50	7	1123	0	10	968	34
PRODRIVE 170S	SCSI	169.52	3.50	HH	RLL 1	AUTO	N/A	N/A	50	7	1123	0			
PRODRIVE 1800S	SCSI-2	1800	3.50	HH	RLL 1	AUTO	N/A	N/A	350	14	2959	0			
PRODRIVE 210AT	IDE(AT)	209.19	3.50	HH	RLL 1	AUTO	N/A	N/A	50	7	1156	0	13	873	36
PRODRIVE 210S	SCSI	209.19	3.50	HH	RLL 1	AUTO	N/A	N/A	50	7	1156	0			
PRODRIVE 40AT	IDE(AT)	42.27	3.50	HH	RLL 2	AUTO	N/A	N/A	50	3	834	0	5	968	17
PRODRIVE 40S	SCSI	42.27	3.50	HH	RLL 2	AUTO	N/A	N/A	50	3	834	0			
PRODRIVE 425	IDE(AT)	426.57	3.50	HH	RLL 1	AUTO	N/A	N/A	150	9	1512	0	16	1021	51
PRODRIVE 425AT	IDE(AT)	426	3.50	HH	RLL 1	N/A	N/A	N/A	150	9	1520	44	16	1021	51
PRODRIVE 425IAT	IDE(AT)	426.57	3.50	HH	RLL 1	AUTO	N/A	N/A	150	9	1512	0	16	1021	51

MODEL	INT	CAP	FF	HGT	CODE	LZ	WP	RWC	MTBF	PHDS	PCYL	PSPT	LHDS	LCYL	LSPT
PRODRIVE 425IS	SCSI	426.57	3.50	HH	RLL 1	AUTO	N/A	N/A	150	9	1512	0			
PRODRIVE 425S	SCSI	426.57	3.50	HH	RLL 1	AUTO	N/A	N/A	150	9	1512	0			
PRODRIVE 525S REV. 1	SCSI-2	525	3.50	3H	RLL 1	AUTO	N/A	N/A	350	6	2448	0			
PRODRIVE 525S REV. 2	SCSI-2	525	3.50	3H	RLL 1	AUTO	N/A	N/A	350	6	2448	0			
PRODRIVE 52S	SCSI	52.42	3.50	HH	RLL 2	AUTO	N/A	N/A	60	2	1219	0			
PRODRIVE 700S	SCSI	703.14	3.50	HH	RLL 1	AUTO	N/A	N/A	150	8	2448	0			
PRODRIVE 80AT	IDE(AT)	84.54	3.50	HH	RLL 2	AUTO	N/A	N/A	50	6	834	0	10	965	17
PRODRIVE 80S	SCSI	84.54	3.50	HH	RLL 2	AUTO	N/A	N/A	50	6	834	0			
PRODRIVE ELS 127AT	IDE(AT)	127.98	3.50	3H	RLL 1	AUTO	N/A	N/A	250	2	1536	0	16	919	17
PRODRIVE ELS 127S	SCSI	127.98	3.50	3H	RLL 1	AUTO	N/A	N/A	250	2	1536	0			
PRODRIVE ELS 170AT	IDE(AT)	170.81	3.50	3H	RLL 1	AUTO	N/A	N/A	250	4	1536	0	15	1011	22
PRODRIVE ELS 170S	SCSI	170.81	3.50	3H	RLL 1	AUTO	N/A	N/A	250	4	1536	0			
PRODRIVE ELS 42AT	IDE(AT)	42.12	3.50	3H	RLL 2	AUTO	N/A	N/A	250	1	1536	0	5	968	17
PRODRIVE ELS 42S	SCSI	42.12	3.50	3H	RLL 2	AUTO	N/A	N/A	250	1	1536	0			
PRODRIVE ELS 85AT	IDE(AT)	85.03	3.50	3H	RLL 2	AUTO	N/A	N/A	250	2	1536	0	10	977	17
PRODRIVE ELS 85S	SCSI	85.03	3.50	3H	RLL 2	AUTO	N/A	N/A	250	2	1536	0			
PRODRIVE LPS 105AT	IDE(AT)	104.85	3.50	3H	RLL 2	AUTO	N/A	N/A	60	4	1219	0	16	755	17
PRODRIVE LPS 105S	SCSI	104.85	3.50	3H	RLL 2	AUTO	N/A	N/A	60	4	1219	0			
PRODRIVE LPS 120AT	IDE(AT)	122.24	3.50	3H	RLL 2	AUTO	N/A	N/A	250	2	1800	0	5	901	53
PRODRIVE LPS 120S	SCSI	122	3.50	3H	RLL 1	AUTO	N/A	N/A	250	2	1800	0			
PRODRIVE LPS 127AT	IDE(AT)	127.9	3.50	3H	RLL	AUTO	N/A	N/A	300	0	0	0	16	919	17
PRODRIVE LPS 127S	SCSI-2	128.31	3.50	3H	RLL 1	AUTO	N/A	N/A	300	2	1745	0			
PRODRIVE LPS 170AT	IDE(AT)	426.57	3.50	HH	RLL 1	AUTO	N/A	N/A	150	9	1520	0	16	1021	51
PRODRIVE LPS 170S	SCSI-2	171.65	3.50	3H	RLL 1	AUTO	N/A	N/A	300	2	2337	0			
PRODRIVE LPS 210AT	IDE(AT)	211	3.50	3H	RLL 1	AUTO	N/A	N/A	300	2	0	0	15	723	38
PRODRIVE LPS 240AT	IDE(AT)	245.42	3.50	3H	RLL 1	AUTO	N/A	N/A	250	4	1800	0	13	723	51
PRODRIVE LPS 240S	SCSI	245	3.50	3H	RLL 1	AUTO	N/A	N/A	250	4	1800	0			
PRODRIVE LPS 270AT	IDE(AT)	270.66	3.50	3H	RLL 1	944	N/A	N/A	300	2	2740	0	14	944	40
PRODRIVE LPS 270S	SCSI-2	270.66	3.50	3H	RLL 1	AUTO	N/A	N/A	300	2	2740	0			
PRODRIVE LPS 340AT	IDE(AT)	340	3.50	3H	RLL 1	AUTO	N/A	N/A	250	4	1800	0	15	1011	44
PRODRIVE LPS 340S	SCSI-2	342.63	3.50	3H	RLL 1	AUTO	N/A	N/A	300	4	2337	0			
PRODRIVE LPS 420AT	IDE(AT)	421.9	3.50	3H	RLL	AUTO	N/A	N/A	300	0	0	0	16	1021	51
PRODRIVE LPS 525AT	IDE(AT)	524.86	3.50	HH	RLL 1	AUTO	N/A	N/A	250	6	2448	0	16	1017	63
PRODRIVE LPS 525S	SCSI-2	525	3.50	HH	RLL 1	AUTO	N/A	N/A	250	6	0	0			
PRODRIVE LPS 52AT	IDE(AT)	52.42	3.50	3H	RLL 2	AUTO	N/A	N/A	60	2	1219	0	8	751	17
PRODRIVE LPS 52S	SCSI	52.42	3.50	3H	RLL 2	AUTO	N/A	N/A	60	2	1219	0			
PRODRIVE LPS 540AT	IDE(AT)	541.32	3.50	3H	RLL 1	1120	N/A	N/A	300	4	2740	0	16	1048	63

(continues)

Table D.13 QUANTUM CORPORATION Continued

MODEL	INT	CAP	FF	HGT	CODE	LZ	WP	RWC	MTBF	PHDS	PCYL	PSPT	LHDS	LCYL	LSPT
PRODRIVE LPS 540S	SCSI-2	541.33	3.50	3H	RLL 1	AUTO	N/A	N/A	300	4	2740	0			
PRODRIVE LPS 80AT	IDE(AT)	85	3.50	3H	RLL 2	AUTO	N/A	N/A	60	0	0	0	16	611	17
PRODRIVE LPS 80S	SCSI	85	3.50	3H	RLL 2	AUTO	N/A	N/A	60	4	0	0			
Q-160	SCSI	200	5.25	HH	RLL 1	AUTO	N/A	N/A	0	12	1800	0			
Q-2010	SA1000	16.77	8.00	FH	MFM		256	256	12	2	512	32			
Q-2020	SA1000	33.55	8.00	FH	MFM		256	256	12	4	512	32			
Q-2030	SA1000	50.33	8.00	FH	MFM		256	256	12	6	512	32			
Q-2040	SA1000	67.1	8.00	FH	MFM		256	256	12	8	512	32			
Q-2080	SA1000	134.41	8.00	FH	MFM		256	256	8	7	1172	32			
Q-250	SCSI	53.93	5.25	HH	RLL 1	AUTO	256	256	25	4	823	32			
Q-280	SCSI	80.9	5.25	HH	RLL 1	AUTO	256	256	25	6	823	32			
Q-510	ST-506/412	8.91	5.25	HH	MFM		256	256	0	2	512	17			
Q-520	ST-506/412	17.82	5.25	HH	MFM		256	256	0	4	512	17			
Q-540	ST-506/412	35.65	5.25	FH	MFM		256	256	15	8	512	17			
SATURN VP31080	SCSI-2 F	1085	3.50	3H	UNIDEN	N/A	N/A	N/A	800	0	0	0		3432	
SATURN VP31080S	SCSI-2	1080	3.50	3H	RLL 1					5	0	0			
SATURN VP32170	SCSI-2 F	2170	3.50	3H	UNIDEN	N/A	N/A	N/A	800	0	0	0		3432	
SATURN VP32170S	SCSI-2	2170	3.50	3H	RLL 1	AUTO	N/A	N/A		0	0	0			
SIROCCO 1700AT	IDE(AT)	1700	3.50	3H	UNIDEN	AUTO	N/A	N/A	400	4	0	0	16	3309	63
SIROCCO 2550AT	IDE(AT)	2250	3.50	3H	UNIDEN	AUTO	N/A	N/A	400	6	0	0	16	4969	63
TRAILBLAZER 420AT	IDE(AT)	421.97	3.50	3H	RLL 1	AUTO	N/A	N/A	300	2	3653	0	16	1010	51
TRAILBLAZER 420S	SCSI-2	425	3.50	3H	RLL 1	AUTO	N/A	N/A	300	2	3653	0	16	1010	51
TRAILBLAZER 635AT	IDE(AT)	636.86	3.50	3H	RLL 1	AUTO	N/A	N/A	300	3	3653	0	16	1234	63
TRAILBLAZER 840S	SCSI-2	852	3.50	3H	RLL 1	AUTO	N/A	N/A	300	3	3653	0	16	1647	63
TRAILBLAZER 850AT	IDE(AT)	850	3.50	3H	RLL 1	AUTO	N/A	N/A	300	4	3653	0	16	1647	63
TRAILBLAZER 850S	SCSI-2	852	3.50	3H	RLL 1	AUTO	N/A	N/A	300	4	3653	0	16	1647	63
VIKING 2.2S	U-SCSI	2275	3.50	6						0	0	0			
VIKING 2.2SCA	U-SCSI W	2275	3.50	6						0	0	0			
VIKING 4.5S	U-SCSI	2275	3.50	6						0	0	0			
VIKING 4.5SCA	U-SCSI W	4550	3.50	6						0	0	0			

Table D.14 SEAGATE TECHNOLOGY, INC.

MODEL	INT	CAP	FF	HGT	CODE	LZ	WP	RWC	MTBF	PHDS	PCYL	PSPT	LHDS	LCYL	LSPT
BARRACUDA 1 (VER. 1)	SCSI-2	1690	3.50	HH	RLL 1	AUTO	N/A	N/A	500	15	2706	0			
BARRACUDA 1 (VER. 2)	SCSI-2 W	0	3.50	HH	RLL 1	AUTO	N/A	N/A	500	15	2706	0			
BARRACUDA 2 (VER. 1)		0	3.50	HH	RLL 1	AUTO	N/A	N/A	500	0	0	0			

MODEL	INT	CAP	FF	HGT	CODE	LZ	WP	RWC	MTBF	PHDS	PCYL	PSPT	LHDS	LCYL	LSPT
BARRACUDA 2 (VER. 2)	SCSI-2	0	3.50	HH	RLL 1	AUTO	N/A	N/A	500	0	0	0			
BARRACUDA 2 (VER. 3)	SCSI-2 W	2139	3.50	HH	RLL 1	AUTO	N/A	N/A	500	19	2707	0			
BARRACUDA 2LP (VER. 1)	SCSI-2 F	0	3.50	3H	RLL 1	AUTO	N/A	N/A	800	5	3711	0			
BARRACUDA 2LP (VER. 2)	SCSI-2 F	0	3.50	3H	RLL 1	AUTO	N/A	N/A	800	5	3711	0			
BARRACUDA 2LP (VER. 3)	SCSI-2 F	0	3.50	3H	RLL 1	AUTO	N/A	N/A	800	5	3711	0			
BARRACUDA 2LP (VER. 4)	SCSI-2 F	0	3.50	3H	RLL 1	AUTO	N/A	N/A	800	5	3711	0			
BARRACUDA 4 (VER. 1)		0	3.50	HH	RLL 1	AUTO	N/A	N/A	800	0	0	0			
BARRACUDA 4 (VER. 2)	SCSI-2 W	4297	3.50	HH	RLL 1	AUTO	N/A	N/A	800	21	3711	0			
BARRACUDA 4LP (VER. 1)	U-SCSI	0	3.50	3H	RLL	AUTO	N/A	N/A	1000	5	5167	0			
BARRACUDA 4LP (VER. 2)	U-SCSI	0	3.50	3H	RLL	AUTO	N/A	N/A	1000	5	5167	0			
BARRACUDA 9 (VER. 1)	U-SCSI	9100	3.50	HH	PRML	AUTO	N/A	N/A	1000	20	5273	0			
BARRACUDA 9 (VER. 2)	U-SCSI W	9100	3.50	HH	PRML	AUTO	N/A	N/A	1000	20	5273	0			
CHEETAH 4LP (VER. 1)	U-SCSI	4550	3.50	3H	UNIDEN	AUTO	N/A	N/A	300	6	0	0	16	1016	63
CHEETAH 4LP (VER. 2)	U-SCSI W	4550	3.50	3H	UNIDEN	AUTO	N/A	N/A		8	6526	0			
CHEETAH 9 (VER. 1)	U-SCSI	9100	3.50	HH		AUTO	N/A	N/A		16	6526	0			
CHEETAH 9 (VER. 2)	U-SCSI W	9100	3.50	HH		AUTO	N/A	N/A		16	6526	0			
DECATHLON 1080	IDE(AT)	1083.8	3.50	3H	RLL 1	AUTO	N/A	N/A	300	4	4834	0	16	2100	63
DECATHLON 540	IDE(AT)	540.1	3.50	3H	RLL 1	AUTO	N/A	N/A	300	2	4834	0	16	1050	63
DECATHLON 545 (VER. 1)	SCSI-2	545.29	3.50	3H	RLL 1	AUTO	N/A	N/A	0	4	3420	77			
DECATHLON 545 (VER. 2)	IDE(AT)	545.51	3.50	3H	RLL 1	AUTO	N/A	N/A	300	4	3420	0	16	1057	63
DECATHLON 850 (VER. 1)	IDE(AT)	854.7	3.50	3H	RLL 1	AUTO	N/A	N/A	500	4	0	0	32	828	63
DECATHLON 850 (VER. 2)	IDE(AT)	854.7	3.50	4H	RLL 1	AUTO	N/A	N/A	500	4	0	0	32	828	63
ELITE 23 (VER. 1)	U-SCSI	23400	5.25	FH	UNIDEN	AUTO	N/A	N/A		28	6880	0			
ELITE 23 (VER. 2)	U-SCSI W	23400	5.25	FH	UNIDEN	AUTO	N/A	N/A		28	6880	0			
ELITE 9 (VER. 1)		9080	5.25	FH	RLL 1	AUTO	N/A	N/A	500	27	4925	0			
ELITE 9 (VER. 2)	SCSI-2 W	9090	5.25	FH	RLL 1	AUTO			500	27	4925	0			
HAWK 1		0	3.50	HH	RLL 1	AUTO	N/A	N/A	200	0	0	0			

(continues)

Table D.14 SEAGATE TECHNOLOGY, INC. Continued

MODEL	INT	CAP	FF	HGT	CODE	LZ	WP	RWC	MTBF	PHDS	PCYL	PSPT	LHDS	LCYL	LSPT
HAWK 1LP (VER. 1)	SCSI-2 FW	0	3.50	3H	RLL 1	AUTO	N/A	N/A	500	9	2700	84			
HAWK 1LP (VER. 2)	SCSI-2	1052.4	3.50	3H	RLL 1	AUTO	N/A	N/A	200	9	2700	0			
HAWK 1LP (VER. 3)	SCSI-2 F	0	3.50	3H	RLL 1	AUTO	N/A	N/A	500	5	2700	78			
HAWK 2 (VER. 1)		0	3.50	HH	RLL 1	AUTO	N/A	N/A	500	0	0	0			
HAWK 2 (VER. 2)	SCSI-2 W	0	3.50	HH	RLL 1	AUTO	N/A	N/A	500	19	2626	0			
HAWK 2 (VER. 3)	SCSI-2 FW	1430	3.50	HH	RLL 1	AUTO	N/A	N/A	500	13	2626	0			
HAWK 2 (VER. 4)	SCSI-2 FW	1430	3.50	HH	RLL 1	AUTO	N/A	N/A	500	13	2626	0			
HAWK 2LP (VER. 1)	SCSI-2 F	0	3.50	3H	RLL 1	AUTO	N/A	N/A	800	5	3992	103			
HAWK 2LP (VER. 2)	SCSI-2 W	0	3.50	3H	RLL	AUTO	N/A	N/A	800	5	3992	0			
HAWK 2LP (VER. 3)	SCSI-2	1700	3.50	3H	RLL	AUTO	N/A	N/A	0	0	0	0			
HAWK 2LP (VER. 4)	SCSI-2	1700	3.50	3H	RLL	AUTO	N/A	N/A	0	0	0	0			
HAWK 2XL (VER. 1)	SCSI-2 F	0	3.50	3H	RLL	AUTO	N/A	N/A	800	4	4569	0			
HAWK 2XL (VER. 2)	SCSI-2 FW	0	3.50	3H	RLL	AUTO	N/A	N/A	800	4	4569	0			
HAWK 4 (VER. 1)	SCSI-2 FW	0	3.50	3H	RLL 1	AUTO	N/A	N/A	800	19	3992	110			
HAWK 4 (VER. 2)	SCSI-2 F	0	3.50	HH	RLL 1	AUTO	N/A	N/A	800	19	3992	110			
MARATHON 130SL	IDE(44PIN)	131.07	2.50	4H	RLL 1	AUTO	N/A	N/A	300	2	0	0	13	419	47
MARATHON 170SL	IDE(44PIN)	171.63	2.50	4H	RLL 1	AUTO	N/A	N/A	300	4	0	0	16	873	24
MARATHON 210SL	IDE(44PIN)	210.43	2.50	4H	RLL 1	AUTO	N/A	N/A	300	4	0	0	8	988	52
MARATHON 260SL	IDE(44PIN)	262.19	2.50	4H	RLL 1	AUTO	N/A	N/A	300	4	0	0	15	569	60
MARATHON 340	IDE(AT)	341.44	2.50	4H	RLL 1	AUTO	N/A	N/A	300	6	0	0	14	934	51
MARATHON 420SL	IDE(44PIN)	420.8	2.50	5H	RLL 1	AUTO	N/A	N/A	300	4	0	0	16	988	53
MARATHON 455	IDE(AT)	455.29	2.50	4H	RLL 1	AUTO	N/A	N/A	300	6	0	0	16	942	59
MARATHON 520	IDE(44PIN)	524.35	2.50	4H	RLL 1	AUTO	N/A	N/A	300	6	0	0	16	1016	63
MARATHON 810	IDE(44PIN)	810	2.50	5H	RLL 1	AUTO	N/A	N/A	300	8	0	0	16	1571	63
MEDALIST 1012	IDE(AT)	1012	3.50	3H		AUTO	N/A	N/A		0	0	0	16	2098	63
MEDALIST 1080 (VER. 1)	IDE(AT)	1083.2	3.50	3H	RLL 1	AUTO	N/A	N/A	300	6	0	0	16	2099	63
MEDALIST 1080 (VER. 2)	IDE(AT)	1088	3.50	3H	RLL 1	AUTO	N/A	N/A	300	6	0	0	16	2099	63
MEDALIST 1080SL	IDE(AT)	1083.8	3.50	3H	RLL 1	AUTO	N/A	N/A	300	4	4834	0	16	2100	63
MEDALIST 1270	IDE(AT)	1282.8	3.50	3H	RLL 1	AUTO	N/A	N/A	300	0	0	0	16	2485	63
MEDALIST 1270SL	IDE(AT)	1282.4	3.50	4H	RLL 1	AUTO	N/A	AUTO	300	4	5414	0	16	2485	63
MEDALIST 1276	IDE(AT)	1275	3.50			AUTO	N/A	N/A	300	0	0	0	16	2482	63
MEDALIST 1640	IDE(AT)	1625.7	3.50	3H	RLL 1	AUTO	N/A	N/A	500	6	4834	0	16	3150	63
MEDALIST 1720	IDE(AT)	1705	3.50			AUTO	N/A	N/A		0	0	0	16	3305	68
MEDALIST 1722	IDE(AT)	1722	3.50	3H		AUTO	N/A	N/A		0	0	0	16	3303	63
MEDALIST 210XE	IDE(AT)	213.9	3.50	3H	RLL 1	AUTO	N/A	N/A	300	2	0	0	12	1024	34
MEDALIST 2122	IDE(AT)	212.2	3.50	2		AUTO	N/A	N/A		0	0	0	64	1023	63

MODEL	INT	CAP	FF	HGT	CODE	LZ	WP	RWC	MTBF	PHDS	PCYL	PSPT	LHDS	LCYL	LSPT
MEDALIST 2140	IDE(AT)	2113.4	3.50	3H	RLL 1	AUTO	N/A	N/A	500	8	4726	0	16	4095	63
MEDALIST 270 XE (VER. 1)	IDE(AT)	272.7	3.50	3H	RLL 1	AUTO	N/A	N/A	300	2	0	0	14	761	50
MEDALIST 270 XE (VER. 2)	IDE(AT)	272.74	3.50	3H	RLL 1	AUTO	N/A	N/A	300	4	0	0	14	761	50
MEDALIST 3232	IDE(AT)	3232	3.50	3H		AUTO	N/A	N/A		0	0	0	16	6253	63
MEDALIST 340XE	IDE(AT)	341.31	3.50	3H	RLL 1	AUTO	N/A	N/A	300	4	0	0	14	768	62
MEDALIST 425XE	IDE(AT)	428.1	3.50	3H	RLL 1	AUTO	N/A	N/A	300	4	0	0	15	899	62
MEDALIST 4342	IDE(AT)	4342	3.50	3H		AUTO	N/A	N/A		0	0	0	15	8894	63
MEDALIST 455	IDE(AT)	452.41	3.50	3H	RLL 2	AUTO	N/A	N/A	150	5	1691	0	14	1018	62
MEDALIST 540	IDE(AT)	528.48	3.50	3H	RLL 2	AUTO	N/A	N/A	200	5	0	0	16	1024	63
MEDALIST 540SL	IDE(AT)	540.1	3.50	3H	RLL 1	AUTO	N/A	N/A	300	2	4834	0	16	1050	63
MEDALIST 545XE	IDE(AT)	545	3.50	3H	RLL 1	AUTO	N/A	N/A	300	0	0	0	16	1057	63
MEDALIST 630XE	IDE(AT)	631.1	3.50	3H	RLL 1	AUTO	N/A	N/A	300	4	0	0	16	1223	63
MEDALIST 636	IDE(AT)	635	3.50		UNIDEN	AUTO	N/A	N/A	300	0	0	0	16	1241	63
MEDALIST 720	IDE(AT)	722.02	3.50	3H	RLL 1	AUTO	N/A	N/A	300	4	0	0	16	1399	63
MEDALIST 850	IDE(AT)	852	3.50			AUTO	N/A	N/A		0	0	0	16	1652	68
MEDALIST 850SL	IDE(AT)	854.7	3.50	4H	RLL 1	AUTO	N/A	AUTO	300	4	4834	0	16	1656	63
MEDALIST PRO 2160	IDE(AT)	810	3.50		UNIDEN	AUTO	N/A	N/A		8	0	0	16	4095	63
MEDALIST PRO 2520	IDE(AT)	810	3.50		UNIDEN	AUTO	N/A	N/A		8	0	0	16	4970	63
MEDALIST PRO 6450	IDE(AT)	6400	3.50	3H		AUTO	N/A	N/A		0	0	0	15	13328	63
MEDALIST PRO 6451	IDE(AT)	6400	3.50	3H		AUTO	N/A	N/A		0	0	0	15	13328	63
ST1057A	IDE(AT)	53.47	3.50	HH	RLL	AUTO	N/A	N/A	150	6	1024	17	6	1024	17
ST1057N	SCSI-2	49.09	3.50	HH	RLL 2	AUTO	N/A	N/A	150	3	940	34			
ST1090A	IDE(AT)	79.58	3.50	HH	RLL 2	AUTO	N/A	N/A	150	5	1072	29	16	335	29
ST1090N	SCSI	79.28	3.50	HH	RLL 2	AUTO	N/A	N/A	150	5	1068	29			
ST1096N	SCSI	84.42	3.50	HH	RLL 2	AUTO	N/A	N/A	150	7	906	26			
ST1100	ST-506/412	83.97	3.50	HH	MFM	AUTO	1,073	1,073	150	9	1072	17			
ST1102A	IDE(AT)	89.12	3.50	HH	RLL	AUTO	N/A	N/A	50	10	1024	17	10	1024	17
ST1102N	SCSI-2	83.99	3.50	HH	RLL	AUTO	N/A	N/A	50	5	965	0			
ST1106R	ST-506/412	91.04	3.50	HH	RLL 2		978	978	50	7	977	26			
ST1111A	IDE(AT)	98.79	3.50	HH	RLL 2	AUTO	N/A	N/A	70	5	1072	36	10	536	36
ST1111E	ESDi-10MHZ	98.79	3.50	HH	RLL 2	AUTO	N/A	N/A	150	5	1072	36			
ST1111N	SCSI	98.42	3.50	HH	RLL 2	AUTO	N/A	N/A	70	5	1068	36			
ST11200N	SCSI-2	1054	3.50	HH	RLL 1	AUTO	N/A	N/A	200	15	1872	0			
ST11200NC	SCSI SCA	1050	3.50	HH	RLL 1	AUTO	N/A	N/A	200	15	1877	0			
ST11200ND	SCSI-2 D	1050	3.50	HH	RLL 1	AUTO	N/A	N/A	200	15	1877	0			
ST11201N	SCSI-2	1050	3.50	HH	RLL 1	AUTO	N/A	N/A	200	15	1877	0			
ST11201ND	SCSI-2 D	1050	3.50	HH	RLL 1	AUTO	N/A	N/A	500	15	1877	0			

(continues)

Table D.14 SEAGATE TECHNOLOGY, INC. Continued

MODEL	INT	CAP	FF	HGT	CODE	LZ	WP	RWC	MTBF	PHDS	PCYL	PSPT	LHDS	LCYL	LSPT
ST1126A	IDE(AT)	111.41	3.50	HH	RLL 2	AUTO	N/A	N/A	150	7	1072	29	16	469	29
ST1126N	SCSI	111	3.50	HH	RLL 2	AUTO	N/A	N/A	150	7	1068	29			
ST1133A	IDE(AT)	117.22	3.50	HH	RLL 2	AUTO	N/A	N/A	150	5	1272	36	10	636	36
ST1133N	SCSI-2	116.85	3.50	HH	RLL 2	AUTO	N/A	N/A	150	5	1268	36			
ST1144A	IDE(AT)	130.69	3.50	HH	RLL	AUTO	N/A	N/A	150	7	0	0	15	1001	17
ST1144N	SCSI-2	125	3.50	HH	RLL	AUTO	N/A	N/A	50	7	0	0			
ST1150R	ST-506/412	128.43	3.50	HH	RLL 2	AUTO	300	1,073	150	9	1072	26			
ST1156A	IDE(AT)	138.31	3.50	HH	RLL 2	AUTO	N/A	N/A	150	7	1072	36	14	536	36
ST1156E	ESDI-10MHZ	138.31	3.50	HH	RLL 2	AUTO	N/A	N/A	70	7	1072	36			
ST1156N	SCSI	137.79	3.50	HH	RLL 2	AUTO	N/A	N/A	70	7	1068	36			
ST1156NS	SCSI-2	137.79	3.50	HH	RLL 2	AUTO	N/A	N/A	70	7	1068	36			
ST1162A	IDE(AT)	143.25	3.50	HH	RLL 2	AUTO	N/A	N/A	150	9	1072	29	16	603	29
ST1162N	SCSI	142.71	3.50	HH	RLL 2	AUTO	N/A	N/A	70	9	1068	29			
ST11700N	SCSI-2	1430	3.50	HH	RLL 1	AUTO	N/A	N/A	500	13	2626	0			
ST11700ND	SCSI-2 D	1430	3.50	HH	RLL 1	AUTO	N/A	N/A	500	13	2626	0			
ST1186A	IDE(AT)	164.11	3.50	HH	RLL 2	AUTO	N/A	N/A	150	7	1272	36	14	636	36
ST1186N	SCSI-2	163.6	3.50	HH	RLL 2	AUTO	N/A	N/A	150	7	1268	36			
ST11900N	SCSI-2	1700	3.50	HH	RLL 1	AUTO	N/A	N/A	500	15	2621	0			
ST11900NC	SCSI SCA	1700	3.50	HH	RLL 1	AUTO	N/A	N/A	500	15	2621	0			
ST11900ND	SCSI-2	1700	3.50	HH	RLL 1	AUTO	N/A	N/A	500	15	2621	0			
ST11900W	SCSI-2 FW	1430	3.50	HH	RLL 1	AUTO	N/A	N/A	500	13	2626	0			
ST11900WC	SCSI-2 FW	1700	3.50	HH	RLL 1	AUTO	N/A	N/A	500	15	2621	83			
ST11900WD	SCSI-2 FW	1430	3.50	HH	RLL 1	AUTO	N/A	N/A	500	13	2626	0			
ST11950N	SCSI-2	1690	3.50	HH	RLL 1	AUTO	N/A	N/A	500	15	2706	0			
ST11950ND	SCSI-2	1690	3.50	HH	RLL 1	AUTO	N/A	N/A	500	15	2706	0			
ST11950W	SCSI-2 W	1690	3.50	HH	RLL 1	AUTO	N/A	N/A	500	15	2706	0			
ST11950WD	SCSI-2 WD	1690	3.50	HH	RLL 1	AUTO	N/A	N/A	500	15	2706	0			
ST1201A	IDE(AT)	177.83	3.50	HH	RLL 2	AUTO	N/A	N/A	150	9	1072	36	12	804	36
ST1201E	ESDI-10MHZ	177.83	3.50	HH	RLL 2	AUTO	N/A	N/A	150	9	1072	36			
ST1201N	SCSI	177.16	3.50	HH	RLL 2	AUTO	N/A	N/A	150	9	1068	36			
ST1201NS	SCSI-2	177.16	3.50	HH	RLL 2	AUTO	N/A	N/A	150	9	1068	36			
ST1239A	IDE(AT)	211	3.50	HH	RLL 2	AUTO	N/A	N/A	150	9	1272	0	14	814	36
ST1239A (SHROUDED)	IDE(AT)	211	3.50	HH	RLL 2	AUTO	N/A	N/A	150	9	1272	0	12	954	36
ST1239N	SCSI-2	210.34	3.50	HH	RLL 2	AUTO	N/A	N/A	150	9	1268	36			
ST124	ST-506/412	21.41	3.50	HH	MFM	670	616	616	150	4	615	17			
ST12400N	SCSI-2	2148	3.50	HH	RLL 1	AUTO	N/A	N/A	500	19	2621	0			
ST12400NC	SCSI SCA	2100	3.50	HH	RLL 1	AUTO	N/A	N/A	500	19	2626	0			

MODEL	INT	CAP	FF	HGT	CODE	LZ	WP	RWC	MTBF	PHDS	PCYL	PSPT	LHDS	LCYL	LSPT
ST12400ND	SCSI-2 D	2148	3.50	HH	RLL 1	AUTO	N/A	N/A	500	19	2621	0			
ST12400W	SCSI-2 W	21	3.50	HH	RLL 1	AUTO	N/A	N/A	500	19	2626	0			
ST12400WC	SCSI-2 W	2148	3.50	HH	RLL 1	AUTO	N/A	N/A	500	19	2621	0			
ST12400WD	SCSI-2 WD	21	3.50	HH	RLL 1	AUTO	N/A	N/A	500	19	2626	0			
ST12401N	SCSI-2	21	3.50	HH	RLL 1	AUTO	N/A	N/A	500	19	2626	0			
ST12401ND	SCSI-2 D	21	3.50	HH	RLL 1	AUTO	N/A	N/A	500	19	2626	0			
ST12450W	SCSI-2 FW	2134	3.50	HH	RLL 1	AUTO	N/A	N/A	500	18	2710	0			
ST12450WD	SCSI-2 FW	2134	3.50	HH	RLL 1	AUTO	N/A	N/A	500	18	2710	0			
ST125	ST-506/412	21.41	3.50	HH	MFM	AUTO	616	616	150	4	615	17			
ST125-1	ST-506/412	21.41	3.50	HH	MFM	AUTO	616	616	150	4	615	17			
ST12550N	SCSI-2	2139	3.50	HH	RLL 1	AUTO	N/A	N/A	500	19	2707	0			
ST12550ND	SCSI-2	2139	3.50	HH	RLL 1	AUTO	N/A	N/A	500	19	2707	0			
ST12550W	SCSI-2 W	2139	3.50	HH	RLL 1	AUTO	N/A	N/A	500	19	2707	0			
ST12550WD	SCSI-2 WD	2139	3.50	HH	RLL 1	AUTO	N/A	N/A	500	19	2707	0			
ST12551N	SCSI-2	2100	3.50	HH	RLL 1	AUTO	N/A	N/A	500	19	2756	0			
ST12551ND	SCSI-2 D	2100	3.50	HH	RLL 1	AUTO	N/A	N/A	500	19	2756	0			
ST125A (10-PIN VER.)	IDE(AT)	21.51	3.50	HH	RLL 2	AUTO	N/A	N/A	70	4	404	26	4	404	26
ST125A (6-PIN VER.)	IDE(AT)	21.51	3.50	HH	RLL 2	AUTO	N/A	N/A	70	4	404	26	4	404	26
ST125A-1 (10-PIN VER.)	IDE(AT)	21.51	3.50	HH	RLL 2	AUTO	N/A	N/A	70	4	404	26	4	404	26
ST125A-1 (6-PIN VER.)	IDE(AT)	21.51	3.50	HH	RLL 2	AUTO	N/A	N/A	70	4	404	26	4	404	26
ST125N	SCSI	21.67	3.50	HH	RLL 2	AUTO	N/A	N/A	70	4	407	26			
ST125N-1	SCSI	21.67	3.50	HH	RLL 2	AUTO	N/A	N/A	70	4	407	26			
ST125R	ST-506/412	21.51	3.50	HH	RLL 2	404	N/A	N/A	150	4	404	26			
ST1274A	IDE(AT)	21.67	3.50	HH	RLL 2	AUTO	N/A	N/A	70	4	407	26	4	407	26
ST137R	ST-506/412	32.74	3.50	HH	RLL 2	AUTO			70	4	615	26			
ST138	ST-506/412	32.11	3.50	HH	MFM	AUTO	616	616	150	6	615	17			
ST138-1	ST-506/412	32.11	3.50	HH	MFM	AUTO	616	616	150	6	615	17			
ST138A (10-PIN VER.)	IDE(AT)	32.16	3.50	HH	RLL 2	AUTO	N/A	N/A	150	4	604	26	4	604	26
ST138A (6-PIN VER.)	IDE(AT)	32.16	3.50	HH	RLL 2	AUTO	N/A	N/A	150	4	604	26	4	604	26
ST138A-1 (10-PIN VER.)	IDE(AT)	32.16	3.50	HH	RLL 2	AUTO	N/A	N/A	150	4	604	26	4	604	26
ST138A-1 (6-PIN VER.)	IDE(AT)	32.16	3.50	HH	RLL 2	AUTO	N/A	N/A	150	4	604	26	4	604	26
ST138N	SCSI	32.74	3.50	HH	RLL 2	AUTO	N/A	N/A	150	4	615	26			
ST138N-1	SCSI	32.74	3.50	HH	RLL 2	AUTO	N/A	N/A	150	4	615	26			

(continues)

Table D.14 SEAGATE TECHNOLOGY, INC. Continued

MODEL	INT	CAP	FF	HGT	CODE	LZ	WP	RWC	MTBF	PHDS	PCYL	PSPT	LHDS	LCYL	LSPT
ST138R	ST-506/412	32.74	3.50	HH	RLL 2	AUTO	616	616	150	4	615	26			
ST138R-1	ST-506/412	32.74	3.50	HH	RLL 2	AUTO	616	616	150	4	615	26			
ST1400A (J6-4 PINS)	IDE(AT)	331	3.50	HH	RLL	AUTO	N/A	N/A	150	7	1478	0	12	1018	53
ST1400A (J6-6 PINS)	IDE(AT)	331	3.50	HH	RLL	AUTO	N/A	N/A	150	7	1478	0	12	1018	53
ST1400N	SCSI-2	331	3.50	HH	RLL	AUTO	N/A	N/A	150	7	1476	0			
ST1401A (J6-4 PINS)	IDE(AT)	340	3.50	HH	RLL	AUTO	N/A	N/A	150	9	1100	0	15	726	61
ST1401A (J6-6 PINS)	IDE(AT)	340	3.50	HH	RLL	AUTO	N/A	N/A	150	9	1100	0	15	726	61
ST1401N	SCSI-2	340	3.50	HH	RLL	AUTO	N/A	N/A	150	9	1100	0			
ST14207N	SCSI-2 FW	4295	3.50	3H	RLL 1	AUTO	N/A	N/A	999	20	3924	96			
ST14207W	SCSI-2 FW	4295	3.50	3H	RLL 1	AUTO	N/A	N/A	999	20	3924	96			
ST14207WC	SCSI-2 FW	4295	3.50	3H	RLL 1	AUTO	N/A	N/A	999	20	3924	96			
ST1480A (J6-4 PINS)	IDE(AT)	426	3.50	HH	RLL	AUTO	N/A	N/A	150	9	1478	0	15	895	62
ST1480A (J6-6 PINS)	IDE(AT)	426	3.50	HH	RLL	AUTO	N/A	N/A	150	9	1478	0	15	895	62
ST1480N	SCSI-2	426	3.50	HH	RLL	AUTO	N/A	N/A	150	9	1476	0			
ST1480NV	SCSI-2	426	3.50	HH	RLL 1	AUTO	N/A	N/A	150	9	1478	0			
ST1481N	SCSI-2	426	3.50	HH	RLL	AUTO	N/A	N/A	150	9	1476	0			
ST151	ST-506/412	42.51	3.50	HH	MFM	AUTO	978	978	150	5	977	17			
ST15150DC	SCSI-2 FW	4294	3.50	HH	RLL 1	AUTO	N/A	N/A	800	21	3711	0			
ST15150N	SCSI-2 W	4297	3.50	HH	RLL 1	AUTO	N/A	N/A	800	21	3711	0			
ST15150ND	SCSI-2 W	4294	3.50	HH	RLL 1	AUTO	N/A	N/A	800	21	3711	0			
ST15150W	SCSI-2 FW	4294	3.50	HH	RLL 1	AUTO	N/A	N/A	800	21	3711	0			
ST15150WC	SCSI-2 FW	4294	3.50	HH	RLL 1	AUTO	N/A	N/A	800	21	3711	0			
ST15150WD	SCSI-2 FW	4294	3.50	HH	RLL 1	AUTO	N/A	N/A	800	21	3711	0			
ST15230DC	SCSI SCA	4	3.50	HH	UNIDEN	AUTO	N/A	N/A	800	19	3992	0			
ST15230N	SCSI-2 F	4294	3.50	HH	RLL 1	AUTO	N/A	N/A	800	19	3992	110			
ST15230NC	SCSI-2 F	4294	3.50	HH	RLL 1	AUTO	N/A	N/A	800	19	3992	110			
ST15230ND	SCSI-2 F	4596	3.50	HH	RLL 1	AUTO	N/A	N/A	800	19	3992	110			
ST15230W	SCSI-2 FW	4294	3.50	3H	RLL 1	AUTO	N/A	N/A	800	19	3992	110			
ST15230WC	SCSI-2 FW	4294	3.50	3H	RLL 1	AUTO	N/A	N/A	800	19	3992	110			
ST15230WD	SCSI-2 FW	4294	3.50	HH	RLL 1	AUTO	N/A	N/A	800	19	3992	0			
ST157A (10-PIN VER.)	IDE(AT)	44.72	3.50	HH	RLL 2	AUTO	N/A	N/A	150	6	560	26	6	560	26
ST157A (6-PIN VER.)	IDE(AT)	44.72	3.50	HH	RLL 2	AUTO	N/A	N/A	150	6	560	26	6	560	26
ST157A-1 (10-PIN VER.)	IDE(AT)	44.72	3.50	HH	RLL 2	AUTO	N/A	N/A	150	6	560	26	6	560	26
ST157A-1 (6-PIN VER.)	IDE(AT)	44.72	3.50	HH	RLL 2	AUTO	N/A	N/A	150	6	560	26	6	560	26
ST157N	SCSI	48.96	3.50	HH	RLL 2	AUTO	N/A	N/A	150	6	613	26			
ST157N-1	SCSI	48.96	3.50	HH	RLL 2	AUTO	N/A	N/A	150	6	613	26			

MODEL	INT	CAP	FF	HGT	CODE	LZ	WP	RWC	MTBF	PHDS	PCYL	PSPT	LHDS	LCYL	LSPT
ST157R	ST-506/412	49.12	3.50	HH	RLL 2	AUTO	616	616	150	6	615	26			
ST157R-1	ST-506/412	49.12	3.50	HH	RLL 2	AUTO	616	616	150	6	615	26			
ST1581N	SCSI-2	525	3.50	HH	RLL	AUTO	N/A	N/A	150	9	1476	0			
ST177N	SCSI	61.3	3.50	HH	RLL 2	AUTO	N/A	N/A	150	5	921	26			
ST1830N	SCSI-2 F	702	3.50	HH	RLL	AUTO	N/A	N/A	0	0	0	0			
ST19101DC	U-SCSI D	9100	3.50	HH		AUTO	N/A	N/A		16	6526	0			
ST19101N	U-SCSI	9100	3.50	HH		AUTO	N/A	N/A		16	6526	0			
ST19101W	U-SCSI W	9100	3.50	HH		AUTO	N/A	N/A		16	6526	0			
ST19101WC	U-SCSI W	9100	3.50	HH		AUTO	N/A	N/A		16	6526	0			
ST19101WD	U-SCSI WD	9100	3.50	HH		AUTO	N/A	N/A		16	6526	0			
ST19171DC	U-SCSI D	9100	3.50	HH	PRML	AUTO	N/A	N/A	1000	20	5273	0			
ST19171N	U-SCSI	9100	3.50	HH	PRML	AUTO	N/A	N/A	1000	20	5273	0			
ST19171W	U-SCSI W	9100	3.50	HH	PRML	AUTO	N/A	N/A	1000	20	5273	0			
ST19171WC	U-SCSI W	9100	3.50	HH	PRML	AUTO	N/A	N/A	1000	20	5273	0			
ST19171WD	U-SCSI WD	9100	3.50	HH	PRML	AUTO	N/A	N/A	1000	20	5273	0			
ST1950N	SCSI-2 F	803	3.50	HH	RLL	AUTO	N/A	N/A	0	13	1575	0			
ST1980N	SCSI-2	860	3.50	HH	RLL 1	AUTO	N/A	N/A	200	13	1730	0			
ST1980NC	SCSI SCA	860	3.50	HH	RLL 1	AUTO	N/A	N/A	200	13	1730	0			
ST1980ND	SCSI-2 D	860	3.50	HH	RLL 1	AUTO	N/A	N/A	200	13	1730	0			
ST206	ST-506/412	5.32	5.25	HH	MFM		128	307	0	2	306	17			
ST2106E	ESDI-10MHZ	94.37	5.25	HH	RLL 2	AUTO	N/A	N/A	100	5	1024	36			
ST2106N	SCSI	94.18	5.25	HH	RLL 2	AUTO	N/A	N/A	100	5	1022	36			
ST2106NM	SCSI	94.18	5.25	HH	RLL 2	AUTO	N/A	N/A	100	5	1022	36			
ST212 (VER. 1)	ST-506/412	10.65	5.25	HH	MFM	319	128	307	11	4	306	17			
ST212 (VER. 2)	ST-506/412	10.65	5.25	HH	MFM	319	128	307	11	4	306	17			
ST212 (VER. 3)	ST-506/412	10.65	5.25	HH	MFM	319	128	307	11	4	306	17			
ST2125N	SCSI	107	5.25	HH	RLL	AUTO	N/A	N/A	100	3	1544	0			
ST2125NM	SCSI	107	5.25	HH	RLL	AUTO	N/A	N/A	100	3	1544	0			
ST2125NV	SCSI	107	5.25	HH	RLL	AUTO	N/A	N/A	100	3	1544	0			
ST213	ST-506/412	10.7	5.25	HH	MFM	670	300	N/A	20	2	615	17			
ST2182E	ESDI-15MHZ	160.69	5.25	HH	RLL 2	AUTO	N/A	N/A	100	4	1453	54			
ST2209N	SCSI	183	5.25	HH	RLL	AUTO	N/A	N/A	100	5	1544	0			
ST2209NM	SCSI	183	5.25	HH	RLL	AUTO	N/A	N/A	100	5	1544	0			
ST2209NV	SCSI	183	5.25	HH	RLL	AUTO	N/A	N/A	100	5	1544	0			
ST224N	SCSI	21.41	5.25	HH	RLL 2	AUTO	N/A	N/A	100	4	615	17			
ST225	ST-506/412	21.41	5.25	HH	MFM	670	300	N/A	100	4	615	17			
ST225N	SCSI	21.41	5.25	HH	RLL	670	N/A	N/A	100	4	615	17			
ST225R	ST-506/412	21.17	5.25	HH	RLL 2	667			100	2	667	31			

(continues)

Table D.14 SEAGATE TECHNOLOGY, INC. Continued

MODEL	INT	CAP	FF	HGT	CODE	LZ	WP	RWC	MTBF	PHDS	PCYL	PSPT	LHDS	LCYL	LSPT
ST2274A	IDE(AT)	241.5	5.25	HH	RLL 2	AUTO	N/A	N/A	100	5	1747	54	10	873	54
ST238	ST-506/412	32.74	5.25	HH	RLL 2	615			100	4	615	26			
ST2383A	IDE(AT)	338.1	5.25	HH	RLL 2	AUTO	N/A	N/A	100	7	1747	54	14	873	54
ST2383E	ESDI-15MHZ	338.1	5.25	HH	RLL 2	AUTO	N/A	N/A	100	7	1747	54			
ST2383N	SCSI	332	5.25	HH	RLL	AUTO	N/A	N/A	100	7	1261	0			
ST2383NM	SCSI	332	5.25	HH	RLL	AUTO	N/A	N/A	100	7	1261	0			
ST238R	ST-506/412	32.74	5.25	HH	RLL 2	615			100	4	615	26			
ST2502N	SCSI	442	5.25	HH	RLL	AUTO	N/A	N/A	100	7	1755	0			
ST2502NM	SCSI	442	5.25	HH	RLL	AUTO	N/A	N/A	100	7	1755	0			
ST2502NV	SCSI	442	5.25	HH	RLL	AUTO	N/A	N/A	100	7	1755	0			
ST250N	SCSI	42.34	5.25	HH	RLL 2	AUTO	N/A	N/A	100	4	667	31			
ST250R	ST-506/412	42.34	5.25	HH	RLL 2	670			100	4	667	31			
ST251	ST-506/412	42.82	5.25	HH	MFM	AUTO			100	6	820	17			
ST251-1	ST-506/412	42.82	5.25	HH	MFM	AUTO	821	821	100	6	820	17			
ST251N	SCSI	43.66	5.25	HH	RLL 2	AUTO	N/A	N/A	70	4	820	26			
ST251N-1	SCSI	43.86	5.25	HH	RLL 2	AUTO	N/A	N/A	70	4	630	34			
ST251R	ST-506/412	43.66	5.25	HH	RLL 2				100	4	820	26			
ST252	ST-506/412	42.82	5.25	HH	MFM	AUTO			100	6	820	17			
ST253	ST-506/412	43.04	5.25	HH	MFM	AUTO			40	5	989	17			
ST274A	IDE(AT)	63.09	5.25	HH	RLL 2	AUTO	N/A	N/A	40	5	948	26	5	948	26
ST277N	SCSI	65.49	5.25	HH	RLL 2	AUTO	N/A	N/A	70	6	820	26			
ST277N-1	SCSI	65.59	5.25	HH	RLL 2	AUTO	N/A	N/A	70	6	628	34			
ST277R	ST-506/412	65.49	5.25	HH	RLL 2	AUTO			70	6	820	26			
ST277R-1	ST-506/412	65.49	5.25	HH	RLL 2	AUTO			70	6	820	26			
ST278R	ST-506/412	65.49	5.25	HH	RLL 2	AUTO			70	6	820	26			
ST279R	ST-506/412	65.82	5.25	HH	RLL 2	AUTO			40	5	989	26			
ST280A	IDE(AT)	71.33	5.25	HH	RLL 2	AUTO	N/A	N/A	40	5	1032	27	10	516	27
ST296N	SCSI	85.64	5.25	HH	RLL 2	AUTO	N/A	N/A	70	6	820	34			
ST3025A	IDE(AT)	21.51	3.50	3H	RLL 2	AUTO	N/A	N/A	50	1	1616	26	2	808	26
ST3025N	SCSI-2	21.51	3.50	3H	RLL 2	AUTO	N/A	N/A	50	1	1616	26			
ST3051A	IDE(AT)	43.1	3.50	3H	RLL 2	AUTO	N/A	N/A	150	0	0	0	6	820	17
ST3057N	SCSI-2	49.09	3.50	3H	RLL 2	AUTO	N/A	N/A	50	3	940	34			
ST3096A	IDE(AT)	89.12	3.50	3H	RLL 2	AUTO	N/A	N/A	50	10	1024	17	10	1024	17
ST3096N	SCSI-2	89.12	3.50	3H	RLL 2	AUTO	N/A	N/A	50	10	1024	17			
ST31012A	IDE(AT)	1012	3.50	3H		AUTO	N/A	N/A		0	0	0	16	2098	63
ST31051N	SCSI-2 F	1050	3.50	3H	RLL	AUTO	N/A	N/A	800	4	4569	0			
ST31051W	SCSI-2 FW	1050	3.50	3H	RLL	AUTO	N/A	N/A	800	4	4569	0			
ST31051WC	SCSI SCA	1050	3.50	4H	RLL	AUTO	N/A	N/A	800	4	4569	0			

MODEL	INT	CAP	FF	HGT	CODE	LZ	WP	RWC	MTBF	PHDS	PCYL	PSPT	LHDS	LCYL	LSPT
ST31055N	U-SCSI	1060	3.50	3H	RLL	AUTO	N/A	N/A	800	4	4176	0			
ST31055W	U-SCSI	1060	3.50	3H	RLL	AUTO	N/A	N/A	800	4	4176	123			
ST31055WC	U-SCSI	1060	3.50	3H	RLL	AUTO	N/A	N/A	800	4	4176	0			
ST31080N	SCSI-2 F	0	3.50	3H	RLL 1	AUTO	N/A	N/A	500	0	0	0			
ST31081A	IDE(AT)	1080	3.50	3H	RLL 1	2097	N/A	N/A	300	4	3924	0	16	2097	63
ST31200N	SCSI-2	0	3.50	3H	RLL 1	AUTO	N/A	N/A	200	9	2700	0			
ST31200NC	SCSI SCA	1052	3.50	3H	RLL 1	AUTO	N/A	N/A	500	9	2700	84			
ST31200ND	SCSI-2	1052.4	3.50	3H	RLL 1	AUTO	N/A	N/A	200	9	2700	0			
ST31200W	SCSI-2 FW	1052	3.50	3H	RLL 1	AUTO	N/A	N/A	500	9	2700	84			
ST31200WC	SCSI-2 FW	1052	3.50	3H	RLL 1	AUTO	N/A	N/A	500	9	2700	84			
ST31200WD	SCSI-2 FW	1052	3.50	3H	RLL 1	AUTO	N/A	N/A	500	9	2700	84			
ST3120A	IDE(AT)	106.9	3.50	3H	RLL 2	AUTO	N/A	N/A	150	0	0	0	12	1024	17
ST31220A	IDE(AT)	1083.2	3.50	3H	RLL 1	AUTO	N/A	N/A	300	6	0	0	16	2099	63
ST31220A (VER. 2)	IDE(AT)	1088	3.50	3H	RLL 1	AUTO	N/A	N/A	300	6	0	0	16	2099	63
ST31230DC	SCSI-2 WD	1060	3.50	3H	UNIDEN	AUTO	N/A	N/A	800	5	3992	0			
ST31230N	SCSI-2 F	1060	3.50	3H	RLL 1	AUTO	N/A	N/A	800	5	3992	103			
ST31230NC	SCSI SCA	1060	3.50	3H	RLL 1	AUTO	N/A	N/A	800	5	3992	103	5	3992	103
ST31230ND	SCSI-2 D	1060	3.50	3H	RLL 1	AUTO	N/A	N/A	800	5	3992	103			
ST31230W	SCSI-2 W	1060	3.50	3H	RLL	AUTO	N/A	N/A	800	5	3992	0			
ST31230WC	SCSI-2 FW	1060	3.50	3H	RLL 1	AUTO	N/A	N/A	800	5	3992	0			
ST31230WD	SCSI-2 FW	1060	3.50	3H	RLL	AUTO	N/A	N/A	800	5	3992	0			
ST31231N	SCSI-2 F	1060	3.50	3H	RLL 1	AUTO	N/A	N/A	800	5	3992	103			
ST3123A	IDE(AT)	106.6	3.50	3H	RLL 1	AUTO	N/A	N/A	250	0	0	0	12	1024	17
ST31250DC	SCSI SCA	1020.9	3.50	3H	RLL 1	AUTO	N/A	N/A	800	5	3711	0			
ST31250N	SCSI-2 F	1020.9	3.50	3H	RLL 1	AUTO	N/A	N/A	800	5	3711	0			
ST31250ND	SCSI-2 F	1020.9	3.50	3H	RLL 1	AUTO	N/A	N/A	800	5	3711	0			
ST31250W	SCSI-2 F	1020.9	3.50	3H	RLL 1	AUTO	N/A	N/A	800	5	3711	0			
ST31250WC	SCSI SCA	1020.9	3.50	3H	RLL 1	AUTO	N/A	N/A	800	5	3711	0			
ST31250WD	SCSI-2 F	1020.9	3.50	3H	RLL 1	AUTO	N/A	N/A	800	5	3711	0			
ST31270A	IDE(AT)	1282.8	3.50	3H	RLL 1	AUTO	N/A	N/A	300	0	0	0	16	2485	63
ST31274A	IDE(AT)	1278	3.50	3H	RLL 1	2480	N/A	N/A	300	6	2479	0	16	2479	63
ST31275A	IDE(AT)	1278	3.50	3H	RLL 1	2479	N/A	N/A	250	0	0	0	16	2479	63
ST31276A	IDE(AT)	1275	3.50			AUTO	N/A	N/A	300	0	0	0	16	2482	63
ST3144A	IDE(AT)	130.69	3.50	3H	RLL 2	AUTO	N/A	N/A	150	3	0	0	15	1001	17
ST3145A	IDE(AT)	130.2	3.50	3H	RLL 1	AUTO	N/A	N/A	250	2	0	0	15	1001	17
ST31621A	IDE(AT)	1620	3.50	3H		3146	N/A	N/A	300	6	3924	0	16	3146	63
ST31640A	IDE(AT)	1625.7	3.50	3H	RLL 1	AUTO	N/A	N/A	500	6	4834	0	16	3150	63
ST31720A	IDE(AT)	1705	3.50			AUTO	N/A	N/A		0	0	0	16	3305	68

(continues)

Table D.14 SEAGATE TECHNOLOGY, INC. Continued

MODEL	INT	CAP	FF	HGT	CODE	LZ	WP	RWC	MTBF	PHDS	PCYL	PSPT	LHDS	LCYL	LSPT
ST31722A	IDE(AT)	1722	3.50	3H		AUTO	N/A	N/A		0	0	0	16	3303	63
ST31930N	SCSI-2	1700	3.50	3H	RLL	AUTO	N/A	N/A	0	0	0	0			
ST31930ND	SCSI-2	1700	3.50	3H	RLL	AUTO	N/A	N/A	0	0	0	0			
ST3195A	IDE(AT)	170.77	3.50	3H	RLL 2	AUTO	N/A	N/A	150	4	0	0	10	981	34
ST32105N	SCSI-2 F	2147	3.50	3H	UNIDEN	N/A	N/A	AUTO	999	10	3892	0			
ST32105W	SCSI-2 FW	2147	3.50	3H	UNIDEN	N/A	N/A	AUTO	999	10	3892	0			
ST32107N	SCSI-2 FW	2110	3.50	3H	RLL 1	AUTO	N/A	N/A	999	10	3924	91			
ST32107W	SCSI-2 FW	2110	3.50	3H	RLL 1	AUTO	N/A	N/A	999	10	3924	91			
ST32107WC	SCSI-2 FW	2110	3.50	3H	RLL 1	AUTO	N/A	N/A	999	10	3924	91			
ST32122A	IDE(AT)	2122	3.50	3H		AUTO	N/A	N/A		0	0	0	16	4092	63
ST32140A	IDE(AT)	2113.4	3.50	3H	RLL 1	AUTO	N/A	N/A	500	8	4726	0	16	4095	63
ST32151N	SCSI-2 F	2147	3.50	3H	RLL	AUTO	N/A	N/A	800	8	4569	0			
ST32151W	SCSI-2 FW	2147	3.50	3H	RLL	AUTO	N/A	N/A	800	8	4569	0			
ST32151WC	SCSI SCA	2147	3.50	4H	RLL	AUTO	N/A	N/A	800	8	4569	0			
ST32155N	U-SCSI	2148	3.50	3H	RLL	AUTO	N/A	N/A	800	8	4176	0			
ST32155W	U-SCSI	2148	3.50	3H	RLL	AUTO	N/A	N/A	800	8	4176	125			
ST32155WC	SCSI-2 W	2148	3.50	3H	RLL	AUTO	N/A	N/A	800	8	4176	0			
ST32161A	IDE(AT)	2147	3.50	3H	RLL 1	AUTO	N/A	N/A	500	8	4474	0	16	4095	63
ST32171DC	U-SCSI D	2150	3.50	3H	RLL	AUTO	N/A	N/A	1000	5	5167	0			
ST32171N	U-SCSI	2150	3.50	3H	RLL	AUTO	N/A	N/A	1000	5	5167	0			
ST32171ND	U-SCSI D	2150	3.50	3H	RLL	AUTO	N/A	N/A	1000	5	5167	0			
ST32171W	U-SCSI	2150	3.50	3H	RLL	AUTO	N/A	N/A	1000	5	5167	0			
ST32171WC	U-SCSI W	2150	3.50	3H	RLL	AUTO	N/A	N/A	1000	5	5167	0			
ST32171WD	U-SCSI	2150	3.50	3H	RLL	AUTO	N/A	N/A	1000	5	5167	0			
ST32430DC	SCSI SCA	2140	3.50	3H	UNIDEN	AUTO	N/A	N/A	800	9	3992	0			
ST32430N	SCSI-2 F	2140	3.50	3H	RLL 1	AUTO	N/A	N/A	800	9	3992	116			
ST32430NC	SCSI SCA	2140	3.50	3H	RLL 1	AUTO	N/A	N/A	800	9	3992	116			
ST32430ND	SCSI-2 D	2140	3.50	3H	RLL 1	AUTO	N/A	N/A	800	9	3992	116			
ST32430W	SCSI-2 FW	2140	3.50	3H	RLL 1	AUTO	N/A	N/A	800	9	3892	0			
ST32430WC	SCSI-2 W	2140	3.50	3H	RLL 1	AUTO	N/A	N/A	800	9	3992	116			
ST32430WD	SCSI-2 FW	2140	3.50	3H	RLL 1	AUTO	N/A	N/A	800	9	3992	0			
ST3243A	IDE(AT)	213.9	3.50	3H	RLL 2	AUTO	N/A	N/A	150	4	0	0	12	1024	34
ST3250A	IDE(AT)	213.9	3.50	3H	RLL 1	AUTO	N/A	N/A	300	2	0	0	12	1024	34
ST32550DC	SCSI SCA	2147.8	3.50	3H	RLL 1	AUTO	N/A	N/A	800	11	3510	0			
ST32550N	SCSI-2 F	2147.8	3.50	3H	RLL 1	AUTO	N/A	N/A	800	11	3510	0			
ST32550ND	SCSI-2 F	2147.8	3.50	3H	RLL 1	AUTO	N/A	N/A	800	11	3510	0			
ST32550W	SCSI-2 F	2147.8	3.50	3H	RLL 1	AUTO	N/A	N/A	800	11	3510	0			
ST32550WC	SCSI SCA	2147.8	3.50	3H	RLL 1	AUTO	N/A	N/A	800	11	3510	0			

MODEL	INT	CAP	FF	HGT	CODE	LZ	WP	RWC	MTBF	PHDS	PCYL	PSPT	LHDS	LCYL	LSPT
ST32550WD	SCSI-2 F	2147.8	3.50	3H	RLL 1	AUTO	N/A	N/A	800	11	3510	0			
ST325A\X (12-PIN VER.)	IDE(XT/AT)	21.41	3.50	3H	RLL 2	AUTO	N/A	N/A	150	2	697	30	2	697	30
ST325A\X (18-PIN VER.)	IDE(XT/AT)	21.41	3.50	3H	RLL 2	AUTO	N/A	N/A	150	2	697	30	2	697	30
ST325N	SCSI	21.41	3.50	3H	RLL 2	AUTO	N/A	N/A	50	2	697	30			
ST3270A	IDE(AT)	270.9	3.50	3H	RLL 1	AUTO	N/A	N/A	250	4	0	0	16	525	63
ST3283A	IDE(AT)	245.36	3.50	3H	RLL 2	AUTO	N/A	N/A	150	5	1691	0	14	978	35
ST3283N PCB <260035	SCSI	245.36	3.50	3H	RLL 2	AUTO	N/A	N/A	150	5	1691	0			
ST3283N PCB >260035	SCSI	245.36	3.50	3H	RLL 2	AUTO	N/A	N/A	150	5	1691	0			
ST3285N	SCSI-2 F	248.62	3.50	3H	RLL 1	AUTO	N/A	N/A	250	3	1689	0			
ST3290A	IDE(AT)	261.38	3.50	3H	RLL 1	AUTO	N/A	N/A	150	4	1691	0	15	1001	34
ST3291A	IDE(AT)	272.74	3.50	3H	RLL 1	AUTO	N/A	N/A	300	4	0	0	14	761	50
ST3295A	IDE(AT)	272.7	3.50	3H	RLL 1	AUTO	N/A	N/A	300	2	0	0	14	761	50
ST33232A	IDE(AT)	3232	3.50	3H		AUTO	N/A	N/A		0	0	0	16	6253	63
ST3385A	IDE(AT)	340	3.50	3H	RLL 2	AUTO	N/A	N/A	150	5	1691	0	14	768	62
ST3390A	IDE(AT)	341.3	3.50	3H	RLL 2	AUTO	N/A	N/A	250	3	2676	0	14	768	62
ST3390N	SCSI-2	344.3	3.50	3H	RLL 2	AUTO	N/A	N/A	250	3	2676	0			
ST3391A	IDE(AT)	341.31	3.50	3H	RLL 1	AUTO	N/A	N/A	300	4	0	0	14	768	62
ST3423A	IDE(AT)	426	3.50	3H	RLL 1	863	N/A	N/A	300	2	862	0	16	826	63
ST3425A	IDE(AT)	425	3.50	3H	RLL 1	AUTO	N/A	N/A	250	2	0	0	16	826	63
ST34342A	IDE(AT)	4342	3.50	3H		AUTO	N/A	N/A		0	0	0	15	8894	63
ST34371DC	U-SCSI D	4350	3.50	3H	RLL	AUTO	N/A	N/A	1000	10	5167	0			
ST34371N	U-SCSI	4350	3.50	3H	RLL	AUTO	N/A	N/A	1000	10	5167	0			
ST34371ND	U-SCSI D	4350	3.50	3H	RLL	AUTO	N/A	N/A	1000	10	5167	0			
ST34371W	U-SCSI	4350	3.50	3H	RLL	AUTO	N/A	N/A	1000	10	5167	0			
ST34371WC	U-SCSI W	4350	3.50	3H	RLL	AUTO	N/A	N/A	1000	10	5167	0			
ST34371WD	U-SCSI	4350	3.50	3H	RLL	AUTO	N/A	N/A	1000	10	5167	0			
ST34501DC	U-SCSI D	4550	3.50	3H	UNIDEN	AUTO	N/A	N/A		8	6526	0			
ST34501N	U-SCSI	4550	3.50	3H	UNIDEN	AUTO	N/A	N/A	300	6	0	0	16	1016	63
ST34501W	U-SCSI W	4550	3.50	3H	UNIDEN	AUTO	N/A	N/A		8	6526	0			
ST34501WC	U-SCSI W	4550	3.50	3H	UNIDEN	AUTO	N/A	N/A		8	6526	0			
ST34501WD	U-SCSI WD	4550	3.50	3H	UNIDEN	AUTO	N/A	N/A		8	6526	0			
ST3491A	!DE(AT)	428.1	3.50	3H	RLL 1	AUTO	N/A	N/A	300	4	0	0	15	899	62
ST3500A	IDE(AT)	426.16	3.50	3H	RLL 1	AUTO	N/A	N/A	200	7	1874	0	15	895	62
ST3500N	SCSI-2	426	3.50	3H	RLL 1	AUTO	N/A	N/A	200	7	1872	0			
ST351A\X (12-PIN VER.)	IDE(XT/AT)	42.82	3.50	3H	RLL 2	AUTO	N/A	N/A	150	6	820	17	6	820	17

(continues)

Table D.14 SEAGATE TECHNOLOGY, INC. Continued

MODEL	INT	CAP	FF	HGT	CODE	LZ	WP	RWC	MTBF	PHDS	PCYL	PSPT	LHDS	LCYL	LSPT
ST351A\X (18-PIN VER.)	IDE(XT/AT)	42.82	3.50	3H	RLL 2	AUTO	N/A	N/A	150	6	820	17	6	820	17
ST352	IDE(XT/AT)	42.82	3.50	3H	RLL 2	AUTO	N/A	N/A	150	6	820	17			
ST3541A	IDE(AT)	540	3.50	3H	RLL 1	1045	N/A	N/A	300	2	3924	0	16	1048	63
ST3543A	IDE(AT)	540	3.50	3H	RLL 1	AUTO	N/A	N/A	250	4	0	0	16	1050	63
ST3550A	IDE(AT)	452.41	3.50	3H	RLL 2	AUTO	N/A	N/A	150	5	1691	0	14	1018	62
ST3550N	SCSI-2	456.48	3.50	3H	RLL 1	AUTO	N/A	N/A	200	5	2128	0			
ST3600A (VER. A)	IDE(AT)	528.48	3.50	3H	RLL 1	AUTO	N/A	N/A	200	7	1874	0	16	1024	63
ST3600A (VER. B)	IDE(AT)	528.48	3.50	3H	RLL 1	AUTO	N/A	N/A	200	7	1874	0	16	1024	63
ST3600N	SCSI-2	525	3.50	3H	RLL 1	AUTO	N/A	N/A	200	7	1872	0			
ST3600ND	SCSI-2 D	525	3.50	3H	RLL 1	AUTO	N/A	N/A	200	7	1872	0			
ST3610N	SCSI-2	535	3.50	3H	RLL 1	AUTO	N/A	N/A	200	7	1872	0			
ST3610NC	SCSI SCA	570	3.50	3H	RLL 1	AUTO	N/A	N/A	0	7	1872	0			
ST3610ND	SCSI-2 D	535	3.50	3H	RLL 1	AUTO	N/A	N/A	200	7	1872	0			
ST3620N	SCSI-2 F	545.9	3.50	3H	RLL 1	AUTO	N/A	N/A	500	5	2700	78			
ST3620NC	SCSI SCA	545.9	3.50	3H	RLL 1	AUTO	N/A	N/A	500	5	2700	78			
ST3620ND	SCSI-2 D	545.9	3.50	3H	RLL 1	AUTO	N/A	N/A	500	5	2700	78			
ST3620W	SCSI-2 W	545.9	3.50	3H	RLL 1	AUTO	NA	N/A	400	0	0	0			
ST3630A	IDE(AT)	631.1	3.50	3H	RLL 1	AUTO	N/A	N/A	300	4	0	0	16	1223	63
ST3636A	IDE(AT)	635	3.50		UNIDEN	AUTO	N/A	N/A	300	0	0	0	16	1241	63
ST36450A	IDE(AT)	6400	3.50	3H		AUTO	N/A	N/A		0	0	0	15	13328	63
ST36451A	IDE(AT)	6400	3.50	3H		AUTO	N/A	N/A		0	0	0	15	13328	63
ST3655A	IDE(AT)	528.48	3.50	3H	RLL 2	AUTO	N/A	N/A	200	5	0	0	16	1024	63
ST3655N	SCSI-2	545.48	3.50	3H	RLL 1	AUTO	N/A	N/A	200	5	2676	79			
ST3660A	IDE(AT)	545	3.50	3H	RLL 1	AUTO	N/A	N/A	300	0	0	0	16	1057	63
ST3780A	IDE(AT)	722.02	3.50	3H	RLL 1	AUTO	N/A	N/A	300	4	0	0	16	1399	63
ST3852A	IDE(AT)	852	3.50			AUTO	N/A	N/A		0	0	0	16	1652	68
ST3853A	IDE(AT)	850	3.50	3H	RLL 1	N/A	N/A	N/A	250	4	3640	0	16	1652	63
ST4026	ST-506/412	21.41	5.25	FH	MFM	AUTO	307	616	15	4	615	17			
ST4038	ST-506/412	31.9	5.25	FH	MFM	AUTO	734	734	25	5	733	17			
ST4038M	ST-506/412	31.9	5.25	FH	MFM	AUTO	734	734	25	5	733	17			
ST4051	ST-506/412	42.51	5.25	FH	MFM	AUTO	978	978	40	5	977	17			
ST4053	ST-506/412	44.56	5.25	FH	MFM	AUTO	1,024	1,024	40	5	1024	17			
ST406	ST-506/412	5.32	5.25	FH	MFM	319	128	307	11	2	306	17			
ST4077N	SCSI	68.15	5.25	FH	RLL 2	AUTO	N/A	N/A	0	5	1024	26			
ST4077R	ST-506/412	68.15	5.25	FH	RLL 2		1,025	1,025	0	5	1024	26			
ST4085	ST-506/412	71.3	5.25	FH	MFM	AUTO	1,025	1,025	40	8	1024	17			
ST4086	ST-506/412	72.46	5.25	FH	MFM	AUTO	926	926	40	9	925	17			

MODEL	INT	CAP	FF	HGT	CODE	LZ	WP	RWC	MTBF	PHDS	PCYL	PSPT	LHDS	LCYL	LSPT
ST4096	ST-506/412	80.21	5.25	FH	MFM	AUTO	1,025	1,025	40	9	1024	17			
ST4096N	SCSI	80.21	5.25	FH	RLL	AUTO	N/A	N/A	40	9	1024	17			
ST4097	ST-506/412	80.21	5.25	FH	MFM	AUTO	1,024	1,024	40	9	1024	17			
ST410800N	SCSI-2 W	9090	5.25	FH	RLL 1	AUTO			500	27	4925	0			
ST410800ND	SCSI-2	9080	5.25	FH	RLL 1	AUTO	N/A	N/A	500	27	4925	0			
ST410800W	SCSI-2 FW	9090	5.25	FH	RLL 1	AUTO	N/A	N/A	500	27	4925	0			
ST410800WD	SCSI-2 FW	9090	5.25	FH	RLL 1	AUTO	N/A	N/A	500	27	4925	0			
ST412	ST-506/412	10.65	5.25	FH	MFM	319	128	307	11	4	306	17			
ST41200N	SCSI	1037	5.25	FH	RLL 1	AUTO	N/A	N/A	150	15	1931	0			
ST41200ND	SCSI	1037	5.25	FH	RLL 1	AUTO	N/A	N/A	150	15	1931	0			
ST41200NM	SCSI	1037	5.25	FH	RLL 1	AUTO	N/A	N/A	150	15	1931	0			
ST41200NV	SCSI	1037	5.25	FH	RLL 1	AUTO	N/A	N/A	150	15	1931	0			
ST4135R	ST-506/412	115.01	5.25	FH	RLL 2	AUTO	128	1,025	40	9	960	26			
ST4144N	SCSI	122.68	5.25	FH	RLL 2	1023	N/A	N/A	0	9	1024	26			
ST4144R	ST-506/412	122.68	5.25	FH	RLL 2	AUTO	1,025	1,025	40	9	1024	26			
ST41520N	SCSI-2	370	5.25	FH	RLL 2	AUTO	N/A	N/A	150	17	2101	0			
ST41520ND	SCSI-2 D	1370	5.25	FH	RLL 2	AUTO	N/A	N/A	150	17	2101	0			
ST41600N	SCSI-2	1370	5.25	FH	RLL 2	AUTO	N/A	N/A	150	17	2101	0			
ST41600ND	SCSI-2 D	1370	5.25	FH	RLL 2	AUTO	N/A	N/A	150	17	2101	0			
ST41601N	SCSI-2	1370	5.25	FH	RLL 2	AUTO	N/A	N/A	150	17	2101	0			
ST41601ND	SCSI-2	1370	5.25	FH	RLL 2	AUTO	N/A	N/A	150	17	2101	0			
ST41650N	SCSI-2	1415	5.25	FH	RLL 1	AUTO	N/A	N/A	150	15	2107	0			
ST41650ND	SCSI-2 D	1415	5.25	FH	RLL 1	AUTO	N/A	N/A	150	15	2107	0			
ST41651N	SCSI-2	1415	5.25	FH	RLL 1	AUTO	N/A	N/A	150	15	2107	0			
ST41651ND	SCSI-2 D	1415	5.25	FH	RLL 1	AUTO	N/A	N/A	150	15	2107	0			
ST4182E	ESDI-10MHZ	151.81	5.25	FH	RLL 2	AUTO	N/A	N/A	100	9	969	34			
ST4182N (2X7 PIN VER.)	SCSI	160.74	5.25	FH	RLL 2	AUTO	N/A	N/A	100	9	969	36			
ST4182N (3X5 PIN VER.)	SCSI	160.74	5.25	FH	RLL 2	AUTO	N/A	N/A	100	9	969	36			
ST4182NM (2X7 PIN VER.)	SCSI	160.74	5.25	FH	RLL 2	AUTO	N/A	N/A	100	9	969	36			
ST419	ST-506/412	15.98	5.25	FH	MFM		128	307	11	6	306	17			
ST4192E	ESDI-10MHZ	169.13	5.25	FH	RLL 2	AUTO	N/A	N/A	20	8	1147	36			
ST4192N	SCSI	169.13	5.25	FH	RLL 2	AUTO	N/A	N/A	20	8	1147	36			
ST42000N	SCSI-2	1792	5.25	FH	RLL 2	AUTO	N/A	N/A	150	16	2627	0			
ST42000ND	SCSI-2 D	1792	5.25	FH	RLL 2	AUTO	N/A	N/A	150	16	2627	0			
ST42100N	SCSI-2	1900	5.25	FH	RLL 2	AUTO	N/A	N/A	150	16	2627	0			
ST42101N	SCSI-2	1900	5.25	FH	RLL 2	AUTO	N/A	N/A	150	16	2627	0			

(continues)

Table D.14 SEAGATE TECHNOLOGY, INC. Continued

MODEL	INT	CAP	FF	HGT	CODE	LZ	WP	RWC	MTBF	PHDS	PCYL	PSPT	LHDS	LCYL	LSPT
ST423451N	U-SCSI	23400	5.25	FH	UNIDEN	AUTO	N/A	N/A		28	6880	0			
ST423451W	U-SCSI W	23400	5.25	FH	UNIDEN	AUTO	N/A	N/A		28	6880	0			
ST423451WD	U-SCSI WD	23400	5.25	FH	UNIDEN	AUTO	N/A	N/A		28	6880	0			
ST42400N	SCSI-2	2129	5.25	FH	RLL 2	AUTO	N/A	N/A	150	19	2627	0			
ST42400ND	SCSI-2	2129	5.25	FH	RLL 2	AUTO	N/A	N/A	150	19	2627	0			
ST425	ST-506/412	21.3	5.25	FH	MFM		128	307	0	8	306	17			
ST43400N	SCSI-2	2912	5.25	FH	RLL 1	AUTO	N/A	N/A	150	21	2738	0			
ST43400ND	SCSI-2 D	2912	5.25	FH	RLL 1	AUTO	N/A	N/A	150	21	2738	0			
ST43401N	SCSI-2 FW	2912	5.25	FH	RLL 1	AUTO	N/A	N/A	150	21	2738	0			
ST43401ND	SCSI-2 FW	2912	5.25	FH	RLL 1	AUTO	N/A	N/A	150	21	2738	0			
ST43402ND	SCSI-2 FWD	2912	5.25	FH	RLL 1	AUTO	N/A	N/A	150	21	2738	0			
ST4350N	SCSI	307	5.25	FH	RLL	AUTO	N/A	N/A	100	9	1412	0			
ST4350NM	SCSI	307	5.25	FH	RLL	AUTO	N/A	N/A	100	9	1412	0			
ST4376N	SCSI	330	5.25	FH	RLL	AUTO	N/A	N/A	100	9	1541	0			
ST4376NM	SCSI	330	5.25	FH	RLL	AUTO	N/A	N/A	100	9	1541	0			
ST4376NV	SCSI	330	5.25	FH	RLL	AUTO	N/A	N/A	100	9	1541	0			
ST4383E	ESDI-10MHZ	319.54	5.25	FH	RLL 2	AUTO	N/A	N/A	100	13	1412	34			
ST4384E	ESDI-10MHZ	319.61	5.25	FH	RLL 2	AUTO	N/A	N/A	100	15	1224	34			
ST4385N	SCSI	337	5.25	FH	RLL	AUTO	N/A	N/A	100	15	791	0			
ST4385NM	SCSI	337	5.25	FH	RLL	AUTO	N/A	N/A	100	15	791	0			
ST4385NV	SCSI	337	5.25	FH	RLL	AUTO	N/A	N/A	100	15	791	0			
ST4442E	ESDI-10MHZ	368.7	5.25	FH	RLL 2	AUTO	N/A	N/A	100	15	1412	34			
ST4702N	SCSI	613	5.25	FH	RLL	AUTO	N/A	N/A	100	15	1546	0			
ST4702NM	SCSI	613	5.25	FH	RLL	AUTO	N/A	N/A	100	15	1546	0			
ST4766E	ST-506/412	664.28	5.25	FH	RLL 1	AUTO	N/A	N/A	150	15	1632	53			
ST4766N	SCSI	676.82	5.25	FH	RLL 2	AUTO	N/A	N/A	150	15	1632	54			
ST4766NM	SCSI	676.82	5.25	FH	RLL 2	AUTO	N/A	N/A	150	15	1632	54			
ST4766NV	SCSI	676.82	5.25	FH	RLL 2	AUTO	N/A	N/A	150	15	1632	54			
ST4767ES	ESDI-15MHZ	676.89	5.25	FH	RLL 1	AUTO	N/A	N/A	150	15	1399	63			
ST4767N	SCSI-2	666.5	5.25	FH	RLL 1	AUTO	N/A	N/A	150	15	1356	64			
ST4767ND	SCSI-2	666.5	5.25	FH	RLL 1	AUTO	N/A	N/A	150	15	1356	64			
ST4767NM	SCSI-2	666.5	5.25	FH	RLL 1	AUTO	N/A	RWC	150	15	1356	64			
ST4767NV	SCSI-2	666.5	5.25	FH	RLL 1	AUTO	N/A	N/A	150	15	1356	64			
ST4769ES	ESDI-15MHZ	631.72	5.25	FH	RLL 1	AUTO	N/A	N/A	150	15	1552	53			
ST506	ST-506/412	5.32	5.25	FH	MFM	157	128	128	11	4	153	17			
ST51080A	IDE(AT)	1083.8	3.50	3H	RLL 1	AUTO	N/A	N/A	300	4	4834	0	16	2100	63
ST51080N	SCSI-2 F	1080.23	3.50	4H	RLL 1	AUTO	N/A	N/A	300	4	4826	0			
ST51270A	IDE(AT)	1282.4	3.50	4H	RLL 1	AUTO	N/A	AUTO	300	4	5414	0	16	2485	63

MODEL	INT	CAP	FF	HGT	CODE	LZ	WP	RWC	MTBF	PHDS	PCYL	PSPT	LHDS	LCYL	LSPT
ST52160A	IDE(AT)	810	3.50		UNIDEN	AUTO	N/A	N/A		8	0	0	16	4095	63
ST52520A	IDE(AT)	810	3.50		UNIDEN	AUTO	N/A	N/A		8	0	0	16	4970	63
ST5540A	IDE(AT)	540.1	3.50	3H	RLL 1	AUTO	N/A	N/A	300	2	4834	0	16	1050	63
ST5660A	IDE(AT)	545.51	3.50	3H	RLL 1	AUTO	N/A	N/A	300	4	3420	0	16	1057	63
ST5660N	SCSI-2	545.29	3.50	3H	RLL 1	AUTO	N/A	N/A	0	4	3420	77			
ST5660NC	SCSI SCA	545.29	3.50	3H	RLL 1	AUTO	N/A	N/A	300	4	3002	0			
ST5850A (VER. 1)	IDE(AT)	854.7	3.50	3H	RLL 1	AUTO	N/A	N/A	500	4	0	0	32	828	63
ST5850A (VER. 2)	IDE(AT)	854.7	3.50	4H	RLL 1	AUTO	N/A	N/A	500	4	0	0	32	828	63
ST5851A	IDE(AT)	854.7	3.50	4H	RLL 1	AUTO	N/A	AUTO	300	4	4834	0	16	1656	63
ST7050P	PCM	42	1.80	4H	RLL 1	AUTO	N/A	N/A	250	2	0	0			
ST706	ST-506/412	5.32	5.25	FH	MFM		128	307	0	2	306	17			
ST81236N	SCSI	1056	8.00	FH	RLL 2	AUTO	N/A	N/A	150	15	1635	0			
ST81236N VER. 1	SCSI	1000	8.00	FH	RLL 2				0	15	1371	0		1381	
ST81236N VER. 2	SCSI	1000	8.00	FH	RLL 2				0	15	1371	0		1381	
ST81236N VER. 3	SCSI	1000	8.00	FH	RLL 2				0	15	1371	0		1381	
ST81236ND VER. 1	SCSI D	1000	8.00	FH	RLL 2				0	15	1371	0		1381	
ST81236ND VER. 2	SCSI D	1000	8.00	FH	RLL 2				0	15	1371	0		1381	
ST81236ND VER. 3	SCSI D	1000	8.00	FH	RLL 2				0	15	1371	0		1381	
ST82500N	SCSI	2140	8.00	FH	RLL 2	AUTO	N/A	N/A	150	19	2611	0			
ST8741N VER. 1	SCSI	608	8.00	FH	RLL 2				0	15	1371	0		1381	
ST8741N VER. 2	SCSI	608	8.00	FH	RLL 2				0	15	1371	0		1381	
ST8741N VER. 3	SCSI	608	8.00	FH	RLL 2				0	15	1371	0		1381	
ST8741ND VER. 1	SCSI D	608	8.00	FH	RLL 2				0	15	1371	0		1381	
ST8741ND VER. 2	SCSI D	608	8.00	FH	RLL 2				0	15	1371	0		1381	
ST8741ND VER. 3	SCSI D	608	8.00	FH	RLL 2				0	15	1371	0		1381	
ST8851N	SCSI	727	8.00	FH	RLL 2	AUTO	N/A	N/A	100	15	1381	0			
ST8851N VER. 1	SCSI	693	8.00	FH	RLL 2				0	15	1371	0		1381	
ST8851N VER. 2	SCSI	693	8.00	FH	RLL 2				0	15	1371	0		1381	
ST8851N VER. 3	SCSI	693	8.00	FH	RLL 2				0	15	1371	0		1381	
ST8851ND VER. 1	SCSI D	693	8.00	FH	RLL 2				0	15	1371	0		1381	
ST8851ND VER. 2	SCSI D	693	8.00	FH	RLL 2				0	15	1371	0		1381	
ST8851ND VER. 3	SCSI D	693	8.00	FH	RLL 2				0	15	1371	0		1381	
ST9051A	IDE(44PIN)	42.86	2.50	4H	RLL 2	AUTO	N/A	N/A	150	4	654	32	6	820	17
ST9052A	IDE(44PIN)	42.6	2.50	4H	RLL 2	AUTO	N/A	N/A	150	0	0	0	5	980	17
ST9077A	IDE(44PIN)	64.05	2.50	4H	RLL 2	AUTO	N/A	N/A	150	4	802	39	11	669	17
ST9080A	IDE(44PIN)	64	2.50	4H	RLL 2	AUTO	N/A	N/A	150	0	0	0	4	823	38

(continues)

Table D.14   SEAGATE TECHNOLOGY, INC. Continued

MODEL	INT	CAP	FF	HGT	CODE	LZ	WP	RWC	MTBF	PHDS	PCYL	PSPT	LHDS	LCYL	LSPT
ST9096A	IDE(44PIN)	85.3	2.50	4H	RLL 2	AUTO	N/A	N/A	50	0	0	0	10	980	17
ST9100A	IDE(44PIN)	85.8	2.50	5H	RLL 1	AUTO	N/A	N/A	300	0	0	0	14	748	16
ST9100AG	IDE(44PIN)	85.3	2.50	3H	RLL 1	AUTO	N/A	N/A	150	0	0	0	14	748	16
ST9140AG	IDE(44PIN)	127.94	2.50	4H	RLL 1	AUTO	N/A	N/A	300	4	0	0	15	980	17
ST9144A	IDE(44PIN)	130.69	2.50	4H	RLL 2	AUTO	N/A	N/A	150	3	0	0	15	980	17
ST9145A	IDE(44PIN)	127.94	2.50	4H	RLL 1	AUTO	N/A	N/A	300	4	1463	0	15	980	17
ST9145AG	IDE(44PIN)	127.94	2.50	4H	RLL 1	AUTO	N/A	N/A	300	4	1463	0	15	980	17
ST9150AG	IDE(44PIN)	131.07	2.50	4H	RLL 1	AUTO	N/A	N/A	300	2	0	0	13	419	47
ST9190AG	IDE(44PIN)	171.63	2.50	4H	RLL 1	AUTO	N/A	N/A	300	4	0	0	16	873	24
ST9235A	IDE(AT)	209.7	3.50	4H	RLL 2	AUTO	N/A	N/A	150	0	0	0	13	985	32
ST9235AG	IDE(44PIN)	209.7	2.50	4H	RLL 2	AUTO	N/A	N/A	150	0	0	0	13	985	32
ST9235N	SCSI	209	2.50	4H	RLL 2	AUTO	N/A	N/A	150	0	0	0			
ST9240A	IDE(44PIN)	210.43	2.50	4H	RLL 1	AUTO	N/A	N/A	300	4	0	0	8	988	52
ST9240AG	IDE(44PIN)	210.43	2.50	4H	RLL 1	AUTO	N/A	N/A	300	4	0	0	8	988	52
ST9295AG	IDE(44PIN)	261	2.50	4H	RLL 2	AUTO	N/A	N/A	150	0	0	0			
ST9295N	SCSI	250.6	2.50	4H	RLL 2	AUTO	N/A	N/A	150	0	0	0			
ST9300AG	IDE(44PIN)	262.19	2.50	4H	RLL 1	AUTO	N/A	N/A	300	4	0	0	15	569	60
ST9352A	IDE(AT)	350	2.50	FH	RLL 1	905	N/A	N/A	300	4	2225	0	12	905	63
ST9385AG	IDE(AT)	341.44	2.50	4H	RLL 1	AUTO	N/A	N/A	300	6	0	0	14	934	51
ST9420A	IDE(44PIN)	420.8	2.50	5H	RLL 1	AUTO	N/A	N/A	300	4	0	0	16	988	52
ST9420AG	IDE(44PIN)	420.8	2.50	5H	RLL 1	AUTO	N/A	N/A	300	4	0	0	16	988	53
ST9422A	IDE(AT)	422	2.50	5H	RLL 1	818	N/A	N/A	300	4	2393	0	16	818	63
ST9550AG	IDE(AT)	455.29	2.50	4H	RLL 1	AUTO	N/A	N/A	300	6	0	0	16	942	59
ST9655AG	IDE(44PIN)	524.35	2.50	4H	RLL 1	AUTO	N/A	N/A	300	6	0	0	16	1016	63
ST9816AG	IDE(44PIN)	810	2.50	5H	RLL 1	AUTO	N/A	N/A	300	8	0	0	16	1571	63

Table D.15   TOSHIBA

MODEL	INT	CAP	FF	HGT	CODE	LZ	WP	RWC	MTBF	PHDS	PCYL	PSPT	LHDS	LCYL	LSPT
HDD 2214	IDE(44PIN)	86.03	2.50	4H	RLL 2	AUTO	N/A	N/A	80	0	0	0	10	988	17
HDD 2216	IDE(AT)	130.09	2.50	4H	RLL 2	934	N/A	N/A		0	0	0			
HDD 2238	IDE(44PIN)	213	2.50	4H	RLL	AUTO	N/A	N/A	150	4	1560	0	16	684	38
HDD 2324	IDE(AT)	86	2.50	3H	RLL	AUTO	N/A	N/A	150	2	1501	56	10	988	17
HDD 2326	IDE(AT)	126	2.50		RLL	AUTO	N/A	N/A		2	0	0	8	812	38
HDD 2336	IDE(AT)	131	2.50		RLL	AUTO	N/A	N/A		2	0	0	16	842	38
HDD 2339	IDE(AT)	262	2.50			AUTO	N/A	N/A		0	0	0	16	842	38
HDD 2412	IDE(44PIN)	340	2.50	4H	RLL 1	AUTO	N/A	N/A	150	6	1830	0	14	969	49
HDD 2414	IDE(44PIN)	524	2.50	4H	RLL 1	AUTO	N/A	N/A	150	8	1920	0	16	1016	63

MODEL	INT	CAP	FF	HGT	CODE	LZ	WP	RWC	MTBF	PHDS	PCYL	PSPT	LHDS	LCYL	LSPT
HDD 2416		704	2.50	5H	RLL 1	1365	N/A	N/A	300	0	0	0	16	1365	63
HDD 2417		810	2.50	5H	RLL 1	1571	N/A	N/A	300	0	0	0	16	1571	63
HDD 2434		528	2.50	5H	RLL 1	1023	N/A	N/A	300	0	0	0	16	1023	63
HDD 2512	IDE(44PIN)	352	2.50	5H	RLL 1	AUTO	N/A	N/A	300	0	0	0	16	682	63
HDD 2514	IDE(44PIN)	543	2.50	5H	RLL 1	AUTO	N/A	N/A	300	0	0	0			
HDD 2517	IDE(44PIN)	810	2.50	4H	RLL 1	1579	N/A	N/A	300	0	0	0	16	1579	63
HDD 2612		1.35	2.50	5H	RLL 1	AUTO	N/A	N/A	300	10	2920	0			
HDD 2616	IDE(AT)	2.16	2.50	4H	RLL	AUTO	N/A	N/A	300	10	3650	0			
HDD 2619	IDE(44PIN)	3300	2.50	3					300	0	0	0	16	6409	63
HDD 2632	IDE(AT)	1080	2.50	4H		AUTO	N/A	N/A	300	8	0	0	16	2633	63
HDD 2634	IDE(AT)	1080	2.50	4H		AUTO	N/A	N/A	300	10	0	0	16	3294	63
HDD 2710	IDE(AT)	1080	2.50	4H		AUTO	N/A	N/A	300	3	0	0	16	2100	63
HDD 2712	IDE(44PIN)	1350	2.50	3					300	0	0	0	16	2800	63
HDD 2714	IDE(44PIN)	1440	2.50	3					300	0	0	0	16	2800	63
HDD 2716	IDE(AT)	2160	2.50	4H		AUTO	N/A	N/A	300	3	0	0	16	4200	63
HDD 2731	IDE(AT)	1080	2.50	4H		AUTO	N/A	N/A	300	3	0	0	16	2100	63
MK-1002	IDE(AT)	1080	2.50	4H		AUTO	N/A	N/A	300	6	0	0	16	2100	63
MK-1034FC	IDE(AT)	107.42	3.50	3H	RLL 2	AUTO	N/A	N/A	40	4	1345	39	8	664	39
MK-1122FC	IDE(AT)	43.01	2.50	4H	RLL 2	AUTO	N/A	N/A	80	2	977	43	5	988	17
MK-1301MAV	IDE(AT)	1.35	2.50	5H	UNIDEN	AUTO		128	300	6	3650	0			
MK-1302	IDE(AT)	1700	2.50	4H		AUTO	N/A	N/A	300	4	0	0	16	2633	63
MK-134FA	ST-506/412	44.66	3.50	HH	MFM		512	N/A	30	7	733	17			
MK-134FA(R)	ST-506/412	68.3	3.50	HH	RLL 2				30	7	733	26			
MK-1422FCV	IDE(AT)	86	2.50	3H	RLL	AUTO	N/A	N/A	150	2	1501	56	10	988	17
MK-153FA	ESDI-10MHZ	74.36	5.25	FH	RLL 2	AUTO	N/A	N/A	30	5	830	35			
MK-153FA-I	ESDI-10MHZ	74.36	5.25	FH	RLL 2	AUTO	N/A	N/A	30	5	830	35			
MK-154FA	ESDI-10MHZ	104.11	5.25	FH	RLL 2	AUTO	N/A	N/A	30	7	830	35			
MK-154FA-I	ESDI-10MHZ	104.11	5.25	FH	RLL 2	AUTO	N/A	N/A	30	7	830	35			
MK-154FB	ESDI-10MHZ	104.11	5.25	FH	RLL 2	AUTO	N/A	N/A	30	7	830	35			
MK-156FA	ESDI-10MHZ	148.73	5.25	FH	RLL 2	AUTO	N/A	N/A	30	10	830	35			
MK-156FB	ESDI-10MHZ	148.73	5.25	FH	RLL 2	AUTO	N/A	N/A	30	10	830	35			
MK-1824FCV	IDE(44PIN)	352	2.50	5H	RLL 1	682	N/A	N/A	300	0	0	0	16	682	63
MK-1924FCV	IDE(44PIN)	543	2.50	5H	RLL 1	1053	N/A	N/A	300	0	0	0	16	1053	63
MK-1926FCV	IDE(44PIN)	810	2.50	5H	RLL 1	1579	N/A	N/A	300	0	0	0	16	1579	63
MK-2024FC	IDE(AT)	86.03	2.50	4H	RLL 2	AUTO	N/A	N/A	80	4	977	43	10	988	17
MK-2124FC	IDE(AT)	130.09	2.50	4H	RLL 2	934	N/A	N/A	80	4	1155	55	16	934	17
MK-2224FB	SCSI	213	2.50	4H	RLL 1		N/A	N/A		4	1560	0	16	684	38
MK-2224FC	IDE(AT)	213	2.50	3H	RLL	AUTO	N/A	N/A	150	4	1560	0	16	684	38

(continues)

Table D.15   TOSHIBA Continued

MODEL	INT	CAP	FF	HGT	CODE	LZ	WP	RWC	MTBF	PHDS	PCYL	PSPT	LHDS	LCYL	LSPT
MK-2326FB	SCSI	340	2.50	4H	RLL 1		N/A	N/A		6	1830	0	14	969	49
MK-2326FC	IDE(44PIN)	340.34	2.50	4H	RLL 1	AUTO	N/A	N/A	150	6	1830	0	14	969	49
MK-232FB	SCSI	45.42	3.50	HH	RLL 2	AUTO	N/A	N/A	30	3	845	35			
MK-232FBS	SCSI	45.42	3.50	HH	RLL 2	AUTO	N/A	N/A	30	3	845	35			
MK-232FC	IDE(AT)	45.42	3.50	HH	RLL 2	AUTO	N/A	N/A	30	3	845	35			
MK-232FCH	IDE(AT)	0	2.50	4H	RLL 1	AUTO	N/A	N/A	150	14	969	49			
MK-233FB	SCSI	75.71	3.50	HH	RLL 2	AUTO	N/A	N/A	30	5	845	35			
MK-234FB	SCSI	105.99	3.50	HH	RLL 2	AUTO	N/A	N/A	30	7	845	35			
MK-234FBS	SCSI	105.99	3.50	HH	RLL 2	AUTO	N/A	N/A	30	7	845	35			
MK-234FC	IDE(AT)	110.44	3.50	HH	RLL 2	AUTO	N/A	N/A	30	7	856	36	7	845	35
MK-234FCF	IDE(AT)	0	2.50	4H	RLL 1				150	0	0	0	14	969	49
MK-234FCH	IDE(AT)	107.37	3.50	HH	RLL 2	AUTO	N/A	N/A	30	7	856	35			
MK-234FCH-I	IDE(AT)	107.37	3.50	HH	RLL 2	AUTO	N/A	N/A	30	7	856	35			
MK-2428FB	SCSI	524	2.50	4H	RLL 1		N/A	N/A		8	1920	0	16	1016	63
MK-2428FC	IDE(44PIN)	524.35	2.50	4H	RLL 1	AUTO	N/A	N/A	150	8	1920	0	16	1016	63
MK-250FB	SCSI	219.34	5.25	FH	RLL 2	AUTO	N/A	N/A	30	10	1224	35			
MK-2526FB	SCSI-2	528	2.50	5H						6	2050	0			104
MK-2526FC	IDE(44PIN)	528	2.50	5H	RLL 1	1023	N/A	N/A	300	0	0	0	16	1023	63
MK-2528FC	IDE(44PIN)	704	2.50	5H	RLL 1	1365	N/A	N/A	300	0	0	0	16	1365	63
MK-253FA	ESDI-15MHZ	162.8	5.25	FH	RLL 1	AUTO	N/A	N/A	30	5	1223	52			
MK-254FA	ESDI-15MHZ	227.92	5.25	FH	RLL 1	AUTO	N/A	N/A	30	7	1223	52			
MK-256FA	ESDI-15MHZ	325.61	5.25	FH	RLL 1	AUTO	N/A	N/A	30	10	1223	52			
MK-2628FB	SCSI-2	811	2.50	5H						8	2360	0			104
MK-2628FC	IDE(44PIN)	810	2.50	5H	RLL 1	1571	N/A	N/A	300	0	0	0	16	1571	63
MK-2720	IDE(AT)	1035	2.50		UNIDEN	AUTO	N/A	N/A	250	0	0	0			
MK-355FA	ESDI-15MHZ	405.65	5.25	FH	RLL 2	AUTO	N/A	N/A	30	9	1661	53			
MK-355FB	SCSI-2	405.65	5.25	FH	RLL 2	AUTO	N/A	N/A	30	9	1661	53			
MK-358FA	ESDI-15MHZ	676.09	5.25	FH	RLL 2	AUTO	N/A	N/A	30	9	1661	53			
MK-358FB	SCSI-2	676.09	5.25	FH	RLL 2	AUTO	N/A	N/A	30	15	1661	53			
MK-438FB ASSY. 0605	SCSI-2	877	3.50	HH	RLL 1	AUTO	N/A	N/A	200	15	1692	0			
MK-438FB ASSY. 0817	SCSI-2	900	3.50	HH	RLL 1	AUTO	N/A	N/A	200	11	1980	0			
MK-438FB ASSY. 0834	SCSI-2	877	5.25	FH	RLL 1	AUTO	N/A	N/A	200	11	1980	35			
MK-537FB	SCSI-2	1064	3.50	HH	RLL 1	AUTO	N/A	N/A	200	13	1980	0			
MK-538FB	SCSI-2	1228	3.50	HH	RLL 1	AUTO	N/A	N/A	200	15	1980	0			
MK-53FA	ST-506/412	36.12	5.25	FH	MFM	830	512		20	5	830	17			
MK-53FB	ST-506/412	36.12	5.25	FH	MFM		512	830	20	5	830	17			

MODEL	INT	CAP	FF	HGT	CODE	LZ	WP	RWC	MTBF	PHDS	PCYL	PSPT	LHDS	LCYL	LSPT
MK-53FB(M)	ST-506/412	36.12	5.25	FH	MFM		512	830	20	5	830	17			
MK-53FB(R)	ST-506/412	36.12	5.25	FH	RLL		512	830	20	5	830	17			
MK-53FB-I	ST-506/412	36.12	5.25	FH	MFM		512	830	20	5	830	17			
MK-54FA(M)	ST-506/412	50.57	5.25	FH	MFM	830	512		20	7	830	17			
MK-54FB(M)	ST-506/412	50.57	5.25	FH	MFM	830	512	830	20	7	830	17			
MK-54FB-I	ST-506/412	50.57	5.25	FH	MFM	830	512	830	20	7	830	17			
MK-56FA(M)	ST-506/412	72.24	5.25	FH	MFM		831	831	20	10	830	17			
MK-56FA(R)	ST-506/412	110.48	5.25	FH	RLL 2	830	512		20	10	830	26			
MK-56FB(M)	ST-506/412	72.24	5.25	FH	MFM	830	512	830	20	10	830	17			
MK-56FB(R)	ST-506/412	110.48	5.25	FH	RLL 2		831	831	20	10	830	26			
MK-56FB-I	ST-506/412	72.24	5.25	FH	MFM	830	512	830	20	10	830	17			
MK-72PC	ST-506/412	72.24	5.25	FH	MFM				20	10	830	17			
MK-72PCR	ST-506/412	110.48	5.25	FH	RLL 2				20	10	830	26			
MKM-0351E	ST-506/412	36.12	5.25	FH	MFM	830	512	830	20	5	830	17			
MKM-0351J	ST-506/412	36.12	5.25	FH	MFM	830	512	830	20	5	830	17			
MKM-0352E	ST-506/412	50.57	5.25	FH	MFM	830	512		20	7	830	17			
MKM-0352J	ST-506/412	50.57	5.25	FH	MFM	830	512		20	7	830	17			
MKM-0353E	ST-506/412	72.24	5.25	FH	MFM	830	512	830	20	10	830	17			
MKM-0353J	ST-506/412	72.24	5.25	FH	MFM	830	512	830	20	10	830	17			
MKM-0363A	ESDI-10MHZ	74.36	5.25	FH	RLL 2	AUTO	N/A	N/A	30	5	830	35			
MKM-0363J	ESDI-10MHZ	74.36	5.25	FH	RLL 2	AUTO	N/A	N/A	30	5	830	35			
MKM-0364A	ESDI-10MHZ	104.11	5.25	FH	RLL 2	AUTO	N/A	N/A	30	7	830	35			
MKM-0364J	ESDI-10MHZ	104.11	5.25	FH	RLL 2	AUTO	N/A	N/A	30	7	830	35			
MKM-0381E	ST-506/412	36.12	5.25	FH	MFM		512	830	20	5	830	17			
MKM-0381J	ST-506/412	36.12	5.25	FH	MFM	830	512	830	20	5	830	17			
MKM-0382E	ST-506/412	50.57	5.25	FH	MFM	830	512		20	7	830	17			
MKM-0382J	ST-506/412	50.57	5.25	FH	MFM	830	512		20	7	830	17			
MKM-0383E	ST-506/412	72.24	5.25	FH	MFM	830	512	830	20	10	830	17			
MKM-0383J	ST-506/412	72.24	5.25	FH	MFM	830	512	830	20	10	830	17			

Table D.16 WESTERN DIGITAL CORPORATION

MODEL	INT	CAP	FF	HGT	CODE	LZ	WP	RWC	MTBF	PHDS	PCYL	PSPT	LHDS	LCYL	LSPT
PHD1000	IDE(AT)	1083	3.50	5H					300	0	0	0			
WD-262	ST-506/412	20	5.25	HH	MFM	663			20	4	615	17			
WD-344R	ST-506/412	41.63	3.50	HH	RLL		783	783	0	4	782	26			
WD-362	ST-506/412	20	3.50	HH	MFM	663			20	4	615	17			
WD-382R	ST-506/412	20.81	3.50	HH	RLL 2		783	783	0	2	782	26			
WD-383R	ST-506/412	32.74	3.50	HH	RLL 2		616	616	0	4	615	26			

(continues)

Table D.16 WESTERN DIGITAL CORPORATION Continued

MODEL	INT	CAP	FF	HGT	CODE	LZ	WP	RWC	MTBF	PHDS	PCYL	PSPT	LHDS	LCYL	LSPT
WD-384R	ST-506/412	41.63	3.50	HH	RLL 2		783	783	0	4	782	26			
WD-544R	ST-506/412	41.63	3.50	HH	RLL 2		783	783	0	4	782	26			
WD-562-5	ST-506/412	21.41	3.50	HH	MFM				40	4	615	17			
WD-582R	ST-506/412	20.81	3.50	HH	RLL 2		783	783	0	2	782	26			
WD-583R	ST-506/412	32.74	3.50	HH	RLL 2		616	616	0	4	615	26			
WD-584R	ST-506/412	41.63	3.50	HH	RLL 2		783	783	0	4	782	26			
WD-MI130-44	MCA	31.08	3.50	3H	RLL 2	AUTO	N/A	N/A	45	2	920	33			
WD-MI130-72	MCA	30.4	3.50	3H	RLL 2	AUTO	N/A	N/A	45	2	928	32			
WD-MI260-72	MCA	63.61	3.50	3H	RLL 2	AUTO	N/A	N/A	45	6	767	27			
WD-MI4120-72	MCA	125.03	3.50	3H	RLL 2	AUTO	N/A	N/A	45	8	925	33			
WD-TM262R	ST-506/412	20.81	3.50	HH	RLL 2		783	783	0	2	782	26			
WD-TM364	ST-506/412	41.63	3.50	HH	RLL 2		783	783	0	4	782	26			
WD93024-A	IDE(AT)	21.62	3.50	HH	RLL 2	862	N/A	N/A	40	2	782	27	4	615	17
WD93024-X	IDE(XT)	21.62	3.50	HH	RLL 2	862	N/A	N/A	50	2	782	27			
WD93028-AD	IDE(AT)	21.62	3.50	HH	RLL 2	862	N/A	N/A	40	2	782	27	4	615	17
WD93028-X	IDE(XT)	21.62	3.50	HH	RLL 2	862	N/A	N/A	40	2	782	27			
WD93034-X	IDE(XT)	32.43	3.50	HH	RLL 2	862	N/A	N/A	50	3	782	27			
WD93038-X	IDE(XT)	32.43	3.50	HH	RLL 2	862	N/A	N/A	40	3	782	27			
WD93044-A	IDE(AT)	43.24	3.50	HH	RLL 2	862	N/A	N/A	40	4	782	27	5	977	17
WD93044-X	IDE(XT)	43.24	3.50	HH	RLL 2	862	N/A	N/A	50	4	782	27			
WD93048-AD	IDE(AT)	43.24	3.50	HH	RLL 2	862	N/A	N/A	40	4	782	27			
WD93048-X	IDE(XT)	43.24	3.50	HH	RLL 2	862	N/A	N/A	40	4	782	27			
WD95024-A	IDE(AT)	21.62	3.50	HH	RLL 2	862	N/A	N/A	40	2	782	27	4	615	17
WD95028-AD	IDE(AT)	21.62	3.50	HH	RLL 2	862	N/A	N/A	40	2	782	27			
WD95028-X	IDE(XT)	21.62	3.50	HH	RLL 2	862	N/A	N/A	40	2	782	27			
WD95038-X	IDE(XT)	32.43	3.50	HH	RLL 2	862	N/A	N/A	40	3	782	27			
WD95044-A	IDE(AT)	43.24	3.50	HH	RLL 2	862	N/A	N/A	40	4	782	27	5	977	17
WD95048-AD	IDE(AT)	43.24	3.50	HH	RLL 2	862	N/A	N/A	40	4	782	27	5	977	17
WD95048-X	IDE(XT)	43.24	3.50	HH	RLL 2	862	N/A	N/A	40	4	782	27			
WDAB130	IDE(44PIN)	31.9	2.50	4H	RLL 2	AUTO	N/A	N/A	50	2	1020	0	4	916	17
WDAB140	IDE(44PIN)	42.7	2.50	5H	RLL 2	AUTO	N/A	N/A	0	2	1390	0	5	980	17
WDAC11200	IDE(AT)	1281.9	3.50	3H	UNIDEN					0	0	0			
WDAC11200 (10-PIN)	IDE(AT)	1281.9	3.50	3H	UNIDEN					0	0	0			
WDAC1170	IDE(AT)	170.64	3.50	3H	RLL 2	AUTO	N/A	N/A	100	2	2233	0	6	1010	55
WDAC1210	IDE(AT)	212	3.50	3H	RLL 2	AUTO	N/A	N/A	100	0	0	0	12	989	35
WDAC1270	IDE(AT)	270.4	3.50	3H	RLL 2	AUTO	N/A	N/A	250	2	2233	0	12	917	48
WDAC1365	IDE(AT)	365.4	3.50	3H	RLL 1	AUTO	N/A	N/A	250	0	0	0	16	708	63

MODEL	INT	CAP	FF	HGT	CODE	LZ	WP	RWC	MTBF	PHDS	PCYL	PSPT	LHDS	LCYL	LSPT
WDAC140	IDE(AT)	42.65	3.50	3H	RLL 2	AUTO	N/A	N/A	50	2	1082	39	5	980	17
WDAC1425	IDE(AT)	426.8	3.50	3H	RLL 1	AUTO	N/A	N/A	250	0	0	0	16	827	63
WDAC160	IDE(AT)	63.2	3.50	3H	RLL 2	AUTO	N/A	N/A	100	2	1349	0	7	1024	17
WDAC21000	IDE(AT)	1083.8	3.50	3H	UNIDEN	AUTO	N/A	N/A	300	4	0	0	16	2100	63
WDAC21000 (10-PIN)	IDE(AT)	1083.8	3.50	3H	UNIDEN					0	0	0			
WDAC2120	IDE(AT)	126.4	3.50	3H	RLL 2	AUTO	N/A	N/A	100	4	1349	0	8	872	35
WDAC21200	IDE(AT)	1281.9	3.50	3H	PRML	AUTO	N/A	N/A	300	4	0	0	16	2484	63
WDAC21200 (10-PIN)	IDE(AT)	1281.9	3.50	3H	UNIDEN					0	0	0			
WDAC21600	IDE(AT)	1624.6	3.50	3H	PRML	AUTO	N/A	N/A	300	4	0	0	16	3148	63
WDAC21600 (10-PIN)	IDE(AT)	1624.6	3.50	3H	UNIDEN					0	0	0			
WDAC2170	IDE(AT)	170.6	3.50	3H	RLL 2	AUTO	N/A	N/A	100	4	1584	0	6	1010	55
WDAC2200	IDE(AT)	212.67	3.50	3H	RLL 2	AUTO	N/A	N/A	100	4	1971	0	12	989	35
WDAC22000	IDE(AT)	2000.3	3.50	3H	UNIDEN					0	0	0			
WDAC22000 (10-PIN)	IDE(AT)	2000.3	3.50	3H	UNIDEN					0	0	0			
WDAC22100	IDE(AT)	2111.8	3.50	3H	UNIDEN					0	0	0			
WDAC22100 (10-PIN)	IDE(AT)	2111.8	3.50	3H	UNIDEN					0	0	0			
WDAC2250	IDE(AT)	256	3.50	3H	RLL 2	AUTO	N/A	N/A	100	3	2233	0	9	1010	55
WDAC22500	IDE(AT)	2559.8	3.50	3H	UNIDEN					0	0	0			
WDAC22500 (10-PIN)	IDE(AT)	2559.8	3.50	3H	UNIDEN					0	0	0			
WDAC2340	IDE(AT)	341.29	3.50	3H	RLL 2	AUTO	N/A	N/A	100	4	2233	0	12	1010	55
WDAC2420	IDE(AT)	425.3	3.50	3H	RLL 2	AUTO	N/A	N/A	100	0	0	0	15	989	56
WDAC2540	IDE(AT)	540.86	3.50	3H	RLL 2	AUTO	N/A	N/A	100	0	0	0	16	1048	63
WDAC2540 (10-PIN)	IDE(AT)	540.8	3.50	3H	UNIDEN	AUTO	N/A	N/A		0	0	0			
WDAC2635	IDE(AT)	639.9	3.50	3H	RLL 1	AUTO	N/A	N/A	250	0	0	0	16	1240	63
WDAC2635 (10-PIN)	IDE(AT)	639.9	3.50	3H	UNIDEN	AUTO	N/A	N/A		0	0	0			
WDAC2700	IDE(AT)	696.6	3.50	3H	RLL 2	AUTO	N/A	N/A	100	0	0	0	16	1416	63
WDAC2700 (10-PIN)	IDE(AT)	730.8	3.50	3H	UNIDEN					0	0	0			
WDAC280	IDE(AT)	85.29	3.50	3H	RLL 2	AUTO	N/A	N/A	50	4	1082	39	10	980	17
WDAC2850	IDE(AT)	853.6	3.50	3H	RLL 1	AUTO	N/A	N/A	250	0	0	0	16	1654	63
WDAC2850 (10-PIN)	IDE(AT)	853.6	3.50	3H	UNIDEN					0	0	0			
WDAC31000	IDE(AT)	1084	3.50	3H	RLL 2	AUTO	N/A	N/A	250	6	0	0	16	2100	63

(continues)

Table D.16 WESTERN DIGITAL CORPORATION Continued

MODEL	INT	CAP	FF	HGT	CODE	LZ	WP	RWC	MTBF	PHDS	PCYL	PSPT	LHDS	LCYL	LSPT
WDAC31000 (10-PIN)	IDE(AT)	1083.8	3.50	3H	UNIDEN					0	0	0			
WDAC31200	IDE(AT)	1222.6	3.50	3H	RLL 2	AUTO	N/A	N/A	0	0	0	0	16	2484	63
WDAC31200 (10-PIN)	IDE(AT)	1281.9	3.50	3H	UNIDEN					0	0	0			
WDAC31600	IDE(AT)	1549	3.50	3H	RLL 2	AUTO	N/A	N/A	250	0	0	0	16	3148	63
WDAC31600 (10-PIN)	IDE(AT)	1624.6	3.50	3H	UNIDEN					0	0	0			
WDAC32100	IDE(AT)	2111.8	3.50	3H	PRML	AUTO	N/A	N/A	300	5	0	0	16	4092	63
WDAC32100 (10-PIN)	IDE(AT)	2111.8	3.50	3H	UNIDEN					0	0	0			
WDAC32500	IDE(XT)	2559.8	3.50	3H	PRML	AUTO	N/A	N/A	300	6	0	0	16	4960	63
WDAC32500 (10-PIN)	IDE(AT)	2559.8	3.50	3H	UNIDEN					0	0	0			
WDAC33100	IDE(AT)	3166	3.50	3H	UNIDEN	AUTO	N/A	N/A	300	6	0	0	16	6136	63
WDAC33100 (10-PIN)	IDE(AT)	3166.7	3.50	3H	UNIDEN					0	0	0			
WDAC33200	IDE(AT)	3249.3	3.50	3H	UNIDEN					0	0	0			
WDAC33200 (10-PIN)	IDE(AT)	3249.3	3.50	3H	UNIDEN					0	0	0			
WDAC34000	IDE(AT)	1083	3.50	3H		AUTO	N/A	N/A	350	0	0	0	16	7752	63
WDAC34000 (10-PIN)	IDE(AT)	4000.7	3.50	3H	UNIDEN					0	0	0			
WDAH260	IDE(44PIN)	63.25	2.50	4H	RLL 2	AUTO	N/A	N/A	50	4	1020	0	7	1024	17
WDAH280	IDE(44PIN)	85.57	2.50	4H	RLL 2	AUTO	N/A	N/A	50	4	1390	0	10	980	17
WDAL1100	IDE(44PIN)	100.06	2.50	4H	RLL 1	AUTO	N/A	N/A	100	2	1900	0	6	958	34
WDAL2120	IDE(AT)	126.4	2.50	3H	RLL 2	AUTO	N/A	N/A	100	4	1349	0	8	872	35
WDAL2170	IDE(AT)	170.6	2.50	3H	RLL 2	AUTO	N/A	N/A	100	4	1584	0	6	1010	55
WDAL2200	IDE(44PIN)	200.12	2.50	4H	RLL 1	AUTO	N/A	N/A	100	2	1900	0	12	958	34
WDAL2540	IDE(44PIN)	540.8	2.50	5H	UNIDEN	AUTO	N/A	N/A	300	4	0	0	16	1048	63
WDAP105 PIRANHA	IDE(AT)	104	3.50	HH	RLL 2	AUTO	N/A	N/A	50	4	0	0			
WDAP4200 PIRANHA	IDE(AT)	214.95	3.50	HH	RLL 2	AUTO	N/A	N/A	86	8	1280	41	12	987	35
WDCU140	PCM	42.65	2.50	4H	RLL 1	AUTO	N/A	N/A	255	2	1050	0	5	980	17
WDE2170 (50-PIN)	U-SCSI	2170	3.50	3H		AUTO	N/A	N/A	1000	0	0	0			
WDE2170 (68-PIN)	U-SCSI W	2170	3.50	3H		AUTO	N/A	N/A	1000	0	0	0			
WDE2170 (80-PIN)	U-SCSI W	2170	3.50	3H		AUTO	N/A	N/A	1000	0	0	0			
WDE4360 (50-PIN)	U-SCSI	4360	3.50	3H		AUTO	N/A	N/A	1000	0	0	0			

MODEL	INT	CAP	FF	HGT	CODE	LZ	WP	RWC	MTBF	PHDS	PCYL	PSPT	LHDS	LCYL	LSPT
WDE4360 (68-PIN)	U-SCSI W	4360	3.50	3H		AUTO	N/A	N/A	1000	0	0	0			
WDE4360 (80-PIN)	U-SCSI W	4360	3.50	3H		AUTO	N/A	N/A	1000	0	0	0			
WDSC8320	SCSI-2	326.51	3.50	HH	RLL 1	AUTO	N/A	N/A	150	14	949	48			
WDSC8400	SCSI-2	412.53	3.50	HH	RLL 1	AUTO	N/A	N/A	150	14	1199	48			
WDSP105 PIRANHA	SCSI	104	3.50	HH	RLL 2	AUTO	N/A	N/A	50	4	0	0			
WDSP2100 PIRANHA	SCSI-2	106.21	3.50	HH	RLL 2	AUTO	N/A	N/A	50	4	1265	41			
WDSP4200 REV. 1	SCSI	209.71	3.50	HH	RLL 2	AUTO	N/A	N/A	86	8	1280	40			
WDSP4200 REV. 2	SCSI	209.71	3.50	3H	RLL 2	AUTO	N/A	N/A	86	8	1280	40			
WDUC140	PCM	42.65	5.25	FH	RLL 2	AUTO	N/A	N/A	50	2	1050	0			

If the logical parameters for your IDE hard drive are not listed in Tables D.10–D.16 and the actual physical drive parameters are not legal for the BIOS, use Table D.17* to configure an IDE hard drive as a user-definable drive type in your BIOS (typically type 46 or 47). In the table, look up your drive capacity in column one and enter the specifications into the host system's user-definable drive type section.

This table is valid only when used with IDE-type hard drives.

Table D.17   IDE Quick Reference Chart

CAP	HDS	SPT	CYL	CAP	HDS	SPT	CYL	CAP	HDS	SPT	CYL
20	4	17	574	37	5	17	850	54	7	17	886
21	4	17	603	38	5	17	873	55	7	17	902
22	4	17	631	39	5	17	896	56	7	17	919
23	4	17	660	40	5	17	919	57	7	17	935
24	4	17	689	41	5	17	942	58	7	17	951
25	4	17	718	42	5	17	965	59	7	17	968
26	4	17	746	43	5	17	988	60	7	17	984
27	4	17	775	44	5	17	1011	61	7	17	1001
28	4	17	804	45	6	17	861	62	7	17	1017
29	4	17	832	46	6	17	880	63	8	17	904
30	4	17	861	47	6	17	899	64	8	17	919
31	4	17	890	48	6	17	919	65	8	17	933
32	4	17	919	49	6	17	938	66	8	17	947
33	4	17	947	50	6	17	957	67	8	17	962
34	4	17	976	51	6	17	976	68	8	17	976
35	4	17	1005	52	6	17	995	69	8	17	990
36	5	17	827	53	6	17	1014	70	8	17	1005

(continues)

* *Table D.17 is reprinted from* The Micro House PC Hardware Library, *Copyright © Que Corporation and Micro House International, Inc. 1988.*

Table D.17	IDE Quick Reference Chart Continued										
CAP	**HDS**	**SPT**	**CYL**	**CAP**	**HDS**	**SPT**	**CYL**	**CAP**	**HDS**	**SPT**	**CYL**
71	8	17	1019	228	14	33	963	267	16	33	987
72	9	17	919	229	14	33	968	268	16	33	991
73	9	17	931	230	14	33	972	269	16	33	995
74	9	17	944	231	14	33	976	270	16	33	998
75	9	17	957	232	14	33	980	271	16	33	1002
76	9	17	970	233	14	33	985	272	16	33	1006
77	9	17	982	234	14	33	989	273	16	33	1009
78	9	17	995	235	14	33	993	274	16	33	1013
79	9	17	1008	236	14	33	997	275	16	33	1017
80	9	17	1021	237	14	33	1001	276	16	33	1020
81	10	17	930	238	14	33	1006	277	16	33	1024
82	10	17	942	239	14	33	1010	278	9	63	957
83	10	17	953	240	14	33	1014	279	9	63	961
84	10	17	965	241	14	33	1018	280	9	63	964
85	10	17	976	242	14	33	1023	281	9	63	967
86	10	17	988	243	15	33	958	282	9	63	971
87	10	17	999	244	15	33	962	283	9	63	974
88	10	17	1011	245	15	33	966	284	9	63	978
89	10	17	1022	246	15	33	970	285	9	63	981
90	11	17	940	247	15	33	974	286	9	63	985
91	11	17	950	248	15	33	978	287	9	63	988
92	11	17	960	249	15	33	982	288	9	63	992
93	11	17	971	250	15	33	986	289	9	63	995
94	11	17	981	251	15	33	990	290	9	63	998
95	11	17	992	252	15	33	994	291	9	63	1002
96	11	17	1002	253	15	33	998	292	9	63	1005
97	11	17	1013	254	15	33	1002	293	9	63	1009
98	11	17	1023	255	15	33	1006	294	9	63	1012
99	12	17	947	256	15	33	1010	295	9	63	1016
100	12	17	957	257	15	33	1014	296	9	63	1019
101	12	17	966	258	15	33	1017	297	9	63	1023
102	12	17	976	259	15	33	1021	298	10	63	923
103	12	17	986	260	16	33	961	299	10	63	926
104	12	17	995	261	16	33	965	300	10	63	930
105	12	17	1005	262	16	33	969	301	10	63	933
106	12	17	1014	263	16	33	972	302	10	63	936
107	12	17	1024	264	16	33	976	303	10	63	939
108	13	17	954	265	16	33	980	304	10	63	942
109	13	17	963	266	16	33	983	305	10	63	945

CAP	HDS	SPT	CYL	CAP	HDS	SPT	CYL	CAP	HDS	SPT	CYL
110	13	17	972	149	9	33	979	189	11	33	1016
111	13	17	980	150	9	33	986	190	11	33	1022
112	13	17	989	151	9	33	993	191	12	33	942
113	13	17	998	152	9	33	999	192	12	33	946
114	13	17	1007	153	9	33	1006	193	12	33	951
115	13	17	1016	154	9	33	1012	194	12	33	956
116	14	17	951	155	9	33	1019	195	12	33	961
117	14	17	960	156	10	33	923	196	12	33	966
118	14	17	968	157	10	33	929	197	12	33	971
119	14	17	976	158	10	33	935	198	12	33	976
120	14	17	984	159	10	33	941	199	12	33	981
121	14	17	992	160	10	33	946	200	12	33	986
122	14	17	1001	161	10	33	952	201	12	33	991
123	14	17	1009	162	10	33	958	202	12	33	996
124	14	17	1017	163	10	33	964	203	12	33	1001
125	15	17	957	164	10	33	970	204	12	33	1006
126	15	17	965	166	10	33	982	205	12	33	1011
127	15	17	972	167	10	33	988	206	12	33	1016
128	15	17	980	168	10	33	994	207	12	33	1020
129	15	17	988	169	10	33	1000	208	13	33	946
130	15	17	995	170	10	33	1006	209	13	33	951
131	15	17	1003	171	10	33	1012	210	13	33	956
132	15	17	1011	172	10	33	1017	211	13	33	960
133	15	17	1018	173	10	33	1023	212	13	33	965
134	16	17	962	174	11	33	936	213	13	33	969
135	16	17	969	175	11	33	941	214	13	33	974
136	16	17	976	176	11	33	946	215	13	33	978
137	16	17	983	177	11	33	952	216	13	33	983
138	16	17	990	178	11	33	957	217	13	33	987
139	16	17	998	179	11	33	963	218	13	33	992
140	16	17	1005	180	11	33	968	219	13	33	997
141	16	17	1012	181	11	33	973	220	13	33	1001
142	16	17	1019	182	11	33	979	221	13	33	1006
143	9	33	940	183	11	33	984	222	13	33	1010
144	9	33	946	184	11	33	990	223	13	33	1015
145	9	33	953	185	11	33	995	224	13	33	1019
146	9	33	960	186	11	33	1000	225	13	33	1024
147	9	33	966	187	11	33	1006	226	14	33	955
148	9	33	973	188	11	33	1011	227	14	33	959

(continues)

Table D.17   IDE Quick Reference Chart Continued

CAP	HDS	SPT	CYL	CAP	HDS	SPT	CYL	CAP	HDS	SPT	CYL
306	10	63	948	388	12	63	1002	428	13	63	1020
307	10	63	951	389	12	63	1004	427	13	63	1018
308	10	63	954	390	12	63	1007	427	13	63	1018
309	10	63	957	391	12	63	1010	428	13	63	1020
310	10	63	961	392	12	63	1012	429	13	63	1023
311	10	63	964	393	12	63	1015	430	14	63	952
312	10	63	967	394	12	63	1017	431	14	63	954
313	10	63	970	395	12	63	1020	432	14	63	956
314	10	63	973	396	12	63	1023	433	14	63	958
315	10	63	976	397	13	63	946	434	14	63	961
316	10	63	979	398	13	63	949	435	14	63	963
317	10	63	982	399	13	63	951	436	14	63	965
318	10	63	985	400	13	63	953	437	14	63	967
362	11	63	1020	401	13	63	956	438	14	63	969
363	11	63	1023	402	13	63	958	439	14	63	972
364	12	63	940	403	13	63	961	440	14	63	974
365	12	63	942	404	13	63	963	441	14	63	976
366	12	63	945	405	13	63	965	442	14	63	978
367	12	63	948	406	13	63	968	443	14	63	980
368	12	63	950	407	13	63	970	444	14	63	983
369	12	63	953	408	13	63	972	445	14	63	985
370	12	63	955	409	13	63	975	446	14	63	987
371	12	63	958	410	13	63	977	447	14	63	989
372	12	63	961	411	13	63	980	448	14	63	992
373	12	63	963	412	13	63	982	449	14	63	994
374	12	63	966	413	13	63	984	450	14	63	996
375	12	63	968	414	13	63	987	451	14	63	998
376	12	63	971	415	13	63	989	452	14	63	1000
377	12	63	973	416	13	63	992	453	14	63	1003
378	12	63	976	417	13	63	994	454	14	63	1005
379	12	63	979	418	13	63	996	455	14	63	1007
380	12	63	981	419	13	63	999	456	14	63	1009
381	12	63	984	420	13	63	1001	457	14	63	1011
382	12	63	986	421	13	63	1003	458	14	63	1014
383	12	63	989	422	13	63	1006	459	14	63	1016
384	12	63	992	423	13	63	1008	460	14	63	1018
385	12	63	994	424	13	63	1011	461	14	63	1020
386	12	63	997	425	13	63	1013	462	14	63	1023
387	12	63	999	427	13	63	1018	463	15	63	956

CAP	HDS	SPT	CYL	CAP	HDS	SPT	CYL	CAP	HDS	SPT	CYL
464	15	63	958	486	15	63	1004	508	16	63	984
465	15	63	961	487	15	63	1006	509	16	63	986
466	15	63	963	488	15	63	1008	510	16	63	988
467	15	63	965	489	15	63	1010	511	16	63	990
468	15	63	967	490	15	63	1012	512	16	63	992
469	15	63	969	491	15	63	1014	513	16	63	994
470	15	63	971	492	15	63	1016	514	16	63	995
471	15	63	973	493	15	63	1018	515	16	63	997
472	15	63	975	494	15	63	1020	516	16	63	999
473	15	63	977	495	15	63	1023	517	16	63	1001
474	15	63	979	496	16	63	960	518	16	63	1003
475	15	63	981	497	16	63	962	519	16	63	1005
476	15	63	983	498	16	63	964	520	16	63	1007
477	15	63	985	499	16	63	966	521	16	63	1009
478	15	63	987	500	16	63	968	522	16	63	1011
479	15	63	989	501	16	63	970	523	16	63	1013
480	15	63	992	502	16	63	972	524	16	63	1015
481	15	63	994	503	16	63	974	525	16	63	1017
482	15	63	996	504	16	63	976	526	16	63	1019
483	15	63	998	505	16	63	978	527	16	63	1021
484	15	63	1000	506	16	63	980	528	16	63	1023
485	15	63	1002	507	16	63	982				

The parameters provided are calculated *not to exceed* the formatted capacity specified. For example:

> The parameters' list for 130Ms, 15HDS×995CYL×17SPT×512BPS = 129,907,200 bytes.

If you know the exact capacity of the drive, you may increase the cylinder count to achieve maximum capacity. For example:

> If the drive's capacity is 130.76M, you could increase the cylinder count to 1001 for a capacity of 130,690,560 bytes, forfeiting only about 7K.

You'll notice that the largest drive available with 17 sectors is 142M. You can still use a drive with a higher capacity by increasing the sectors, such as the 143 to 528M drives shown previously.

ROM BIOS Hard Drive Parameters

The following explains the column headings used in Tables D.18–D.22:

> Type = Drive type number

> Cylinders = Total number of cylinders

Heads = Total number of heads

WPC = Write precompensation starting cylinder

65535 = No write precompensation
0 = Write precompensation on all cylinders

Ctrl = Control byte, with values according to the following table.

Bit Number	Hex	Meaning
Bit 0	01h	Not used (XT = drive step rate)
Bit 1	02h	Not used (XT = drive step rate)
Bit 2	04h	Not used (XT = drive step rate)
Bit 3	08h	More than eight heads
Bit 4	10h	Not used (XT = embedded servo drive)
Bit 5	20h	OEM defect map at (cylinders + 1)
Bit 6	40h	Disable ECC retries
Bit 7	80h	Disable disk access retries

LZ = Landing-zone cylinder for head parking

S/T = Number of sectors per track

Meg = Drive capacity in megabytes

M = Drive capacity in millions of bytes

Table D.18 IBM AT and PS/2 BIOS Hard Disk Table

Type	Cylinders	Heads	WPC	Ctrl	LZ	S/T	Meg	M
1	306	4	128	00h	305	17	10.16	10.65
2	615	4	300	00h	615	17	20.42	21.41
3	615	6	300	00h	615	17	30.63	32.12
4	940	8	512	00h	940	17	62.42	65.45
5	940	6	512	00h	940	17	46.82	49.09
6	615	4	65535	00h	615	17	20.42	21.41
7	462	8	256	00h	511	17	30.68	32.17
8	733	5	65535	00h	733	17	30.42	31.90
9	900	15	65535	08h	901	17	112.06	117.50
10	820	3	65535	00h	820	17	20.42	21.41
11	855	5	65535	00h	855	17	35.49	37.21
12	855	7	65535	00h	855	17	49.68	52.09
13	306	8	128	00h	319	17	20.32	21.31
14	733	7	65535	00h	733	17	42.59	44.66
15	0	0	0	00h	0	0	0	0
16	612	4	0	00h	663	17	20.32	21.31

Type	Cylinders	Heads	WPC	Ctrl	LZ	S/T	Meg	M
17	977	5	300	00h	977	17	40.55	42.52
18	977	7	65535	00h	977	17	56.77	59.53
19	1024	7	512	00h	1023	17	59.50	62.39
20	733	5	300	00h	732	17	30.42	31.90
21	733	7	300	00h	732	17	42.59	44.66
22	733	5	300	00h	733	17	30.42	31.90
23	306	4	0	00h	336	17	10.16	10.65
24	612	4	305	00h	663	17	20.32	21.31
25	306	4	65535	00h	340	17	10.16	10.65
26	612	4	65535	00h	670	17	20.32	21.31
27	698	7	300	20h	732	17	40.56	42.53
28	976	5	488	20h	977	17	40.51	42.48
29	306	4	0	00h	340	17	10.16	10.65
30	611	4	306	20h	663	17	20.29	21.27
31	732	7	300	20h	732	17	42.53	44.60
32	1023	5	65535	20h	1023	17	42.46	44.52
33	614	4	65535	20h	663	25	29.98	31.44
34	775	2	65535	20h	900	27	20.43	21.43
35	921	2	65535	20h	1000	33	29.68	31.12
36	402	4	65535	20h	460	26	20.41	21.41
37	580	6	65535	20h	640	26	44.18	46.33
38	845	2	65535	20h	1023	36	29.71	31.15
39	769	3	65535	20h	1023	36	40.55	42.52
40	531	4	65535	20h	532	39	40.45	42.41
41	577	2	65535	20h	1023	36	20.29	21.27
42	654	2	65535	20h	674	32	20.44	21.43
43	923	5	65535	20h	1023	36	81.12	85.06
44	531	8	65535	20h	532	39	80.89	84.82
45	0	0	0	00h	0	0	0.00	0.00
46	0	0	0	00h	0	0	0.00	0.00
47	0	0	0	00h	0	0	0.00	0.00

The landing zone (LZ) and sectors per track (S/T) fields are not used in the 10M (original) controller and contain 00h values for each entry.

Table entry 15 is reserved to act as a pointer to indicate that the type is greater than 15. Older IBM systems do not have every entry in this table. The maximum usable type number varies for each particular ROM version.

Most IBM PS/2 systems were supplied with hard disk drives that have the defect map written as data on the cylinder one cylinder beyond the highest reported cylinder. This special data is read by the IBM PS/2 Advanced Diagnostics low-level format program.

This process automates the entry of the defect list and eliminates the chance of human error, as long as you use only the IBM PS/2 Advanced Diagnostics for hard disk low-level formatting.

This type of table does not apply to IBM ESDI or SCSI hard disk controllers, host adapters, and drives. Because the ESDI and SCSI controllers or host adapters query the drive directly for the required parameters, no table-entry selection is necessary. Note, however, that the table for the ST-506/412 drives can still be found currently in the ROM BIOS of most of the PS/2 systems, even if the model came standard with an ESDI or SCSI disk subsystem.

Table D.19 shows the Compaq motherboard ROM BIOS hard disk parameters for the Compaq Deskpro 386.

Table D.19	Compaq Deskpro 386 Hard Disk Table							
Type	Cylinders	Heads	WPC	Ctrl	LZ	S/T	Meg	M
1	306	4	128	00h	305	17	10.16	10.65
2	615	4	128	00h	638	17	20.42	21.41
3	615	6	128	00h	615	17	30.63	32.12
4	1024	8	512	00h	1023	17	68.00	71.30
5	940	6	512	00h	939	17	46.82	49.09
6	697	5	128	00h	696	17	28.93	30.33
7	462	8	256	00h	511	17	30.68	32.17
8	925	5	128	00h	924	17	38.39	40.26
9	900	15	65535	08h	899	17	112.06	117.50
10	980	5	65535	00h	980	17	40.67	42.65
11	925	7	128	00h	924	17	53.75	56.36
12	925	9	128	08h	924	17	69.10	72.46
13	612	8	256	00h	611	17	40.64	42.61
14	980	4	128	00h	980	17	32.54	34.12
15	0	0	0	00h	0	0	0	0
16	612	4	0	00h	612	17	20.32	21.31
17	980	5	128	00h	980	17	40.67	42.65
18	966	6	128	00h	966	17	48.11	50.45
19	1023	8	65535	00h	1023	17	67.93	71.23
20	733	5	256	00h	732	17	30.42	31.90
21	733	7	256	00h	732	17	42.59	44.66
22	805	6	65535	00h	805	17	40.09	42.04
23	924	8	65535	00h	924	17	61.36	64.34
24	966	14	65535	08h	966	17	112.26	117.71
25	966	16	65535	08h	966	17	128.30	134.53
26	1023	14	65535	08h	1023	17	118.88	124.66

Type	Cylinders	Heads	WPC	Ctrl	LZ	S/T	Meg	M
27	966	10	65535	08h	966	17	80.19	84.08
28	748	16	65535	08h	748	17	99.34	104.17
29	805	6	65535	00h	805	26	61.32	64.30
30	615	4	128	00h	615	25	30.03	31.49
31	615	8	128	00h	615	25	60.06	62.98
32	905	9	128	08h	905	25	99.43	104.26
33	748	8	65535	00h	748	34	99.34	104.17
34	966	7	65535	00h	966	34	112.26	117.71
35	966	8	65535	00h	966	34	128.30	134.53
36	966	9	65535	08h	966	34	144.33	151.35
37	966	5	65535	00h	966	34	80.19	84.08
38	611	16	65535	08h	611	63	300.73	315.33
39	1023	11	65535	08h	1023	33	181.32	190.13
40	1023	15	65535	08h	1023	34	254.75	267.13
41	1023	15	65535	08h	1023	33	247.26	259.27
42	1023	16	65535	08h	1023	63	503.51	527.97
43	805	4	65535	00h	805	26	40.88	42.86
44	805	2	65535	00h	805	26	20.44	21.43
45	748	8	65535	00h	748	33	96.42	101.11
46	748	6	65535	00h	748	33	72.32	75.83
47	966	5	128	00h	966	25	58.96	61.82

Table D.20 shows the AMI ROM BIOS (286 BIOS version 04/30/89) hard disk parameters.

Table D.20	AMI ROM BIOS (286 BIOS Version 04/30/89) Hard Disk Table							
Type	**Cylinders**	**Heads**	**WPC**	**Ctrl**	**LZ**	**S/T**	**Meg**	**M**
1	306	4	128	00h	305	17	10.16	10.65
2	615	4	300	00h	615	17	20.42	21.41
3	615	6	300	00h	615	17	30.63	32.12
4	940	8	512	00h	940	17	62.42	65.45
5	940	6	512	00h	940	17	46.82	49.09
6	615	4	65535	00h	615	17	20.42	21.41
7	462	8	256	00h	511	17	30.68	32.17
8	733	5	65535	00h	733	17	30.42	31.90
9	900	15	65535	08h	901	17	112.06	117.50
10	820	3	65535	00h	820	17	20.42	21.41
11	855	5	65535	00h	855	17	35.49	37.21
12	855	7	65535	00h	855	17	49.68	52.09
13	306	8	128	00h	319	17	20.32	21.31

(continues)

Type	Cylinders	Heads	WPC	Ctrl	LZ	S/T	Meg	M

Table D.20   AMI ROM BIOS (286 BIOS Version 04/30/89) Hard Disk Table Continued

Type	Cylinders	Heads	WPC	Ctrl	LZ	S/T	Meg	M
14	733	7	65535	00h	733	17	42.59	44.66
15	0	0	0	00h	0	0	0	0
16	612	4	0	00h	663	17	20.32	21.31
17	977	5	300	00h	977	17	40.55	42.52
18	977	7	65535	00h	977	17	56.77	59.53
19	1024	7	512	00h	1023	17	59.50	62.39
20	733	5	300	00h	732	17	30.42	31.90
21	733	7	300	00h	732	17	42.59	44.66
22	733	5	300	00h	733	17	30.42	31.90
23	306	4	0	00h	336	17	10.16	10.65
24	925	7	0	00h	925	17	53.75	56.36
25	925	9	65535	08h	925	17	69.10	72.46
26	754	7	526	00h	754	17	43.81	45.94
27	754	11	65535	08h	754	17	68.85	72.19
28	699	7	256	00h	699	17	40.62	42.59
29	823	10	65535	08h	823	17	68.32	71.63
30	918	7	874	00h	918	17	53.34	55.93
31	1024	11	65535	08h	1024	17	93.50	98.04
32	1024	15	65535	08h	1024	17	127.50	133.69
33	1024	5	1024	00h	1024	17	42.50	44.56
34	612	2	128	00h	612	17	10.16	10.65
35	1024	9	65535	08h	1024	17	76.50	80.22
36	1024	8	512	00h	1024	17	68.00	71.30
37	615	8	128	00h	615	17	40.84	42.82
38	987	3	805	00h	987	17	24.58	25.77
39	987	7	805	00h	987	17	57.35	60.14
40	820	6	820	00h	820	17	40.84	42.82
41	977	5	815	00h	977	17	40.55	42.52
42	981	5	811	00h	981	17	40.72	42.69
43	830	7	512	00h	830	17	48.23	50.57
44	830	10	65535	08h	830	17	68.90	72.24
45	917	15	65535	08h	918	17	114.18	119.72
46	1224	15	65535	08h	1223	17	152.40	159.81
47	0	0	0	00h	0	0	0.00	0.00

Table D.21 shows the Award ROM BIOS (286 BIOS version 04/30/89) (Modular 286, 386SX, and 386 BIOS version 3.05) hard disk parameters.

Table D.21   Award ROM BIOS Version 3.05 Hard Disk Table

Type	Cylinders	Heads	WPC	Ctrl	LZ	S/T	Meg	M
1	306	4	128	00h	305	17	10.16	10.65
2	615	4	300	00h	615	17	20.42	21.41
3	615	6	300	00h	615	17	30.63	32.12
4	940	8	512	00h	940	17	62.42	65.45
5	940	6	512	00h	940	17	46.82	49.09
6	615	4	65535	00h	615	17	20.42	21.41
7	462	8	256	00h	511	17	30.68	32.17
8	733	5	65535	00h	733	17	30.42	31.90
9	900	15	65535	08h	901	17	112.06	117.50
10	820	3	65535	00h	820	17	20.42	21.41
11	855	5	65535	00h	855	17	35.49	37.21
12	855	7	65535	00h	855	17	49.68	52.09
13	306	8	128	00h	319	17	20.32	21.31
14	733	7	65535	00h	733	17	42.59	44.66
15	0	0	0	00h	0	0	0	0
16	612	4	0	00h	663	17	20.32	21.31
17	977	5	300	00h	977	17	40.55	42.52
18	977	7	65535	00h	977	17	56.77	59.53
19	1024	7	512	00h	1023	17	59.50	62.39
20	733	5	300	00h	732	17	30.42	31.90
21	733	7	300	00h	732	17	42.59	44.66
22	733	5	300	00h	733	17	30.42	31.90
23	306	4	0	00h	336	17	10.16	10.65
24	977	5	65535	00h	976	17	40.55	42.52
25	1024	9	65535	08h	1023	17	76.50	80.22
26	1224	7	65535	00h	1223	17	71.12	74.58
27	1224	11	65535	08h	1223	17	111.76	117.19
28	1224	15	65535	08h	1223	17	152.40	159.81
29	1024	8	65535	00h	1023	17	68.00	71.30
30	1024	11	65535	08h	1023	17	93.50	98.04
31	918	11	65535	08h	1023	17	83.82	87.89
32	925	9	65535	08h	926	17	69.10	72.46
33	1024	10	65535	08h	1023	17	85.00	89.13
34	1024	12	65535	08h	1023	17	102.00	106.95
35	1024	13	65535	08h	1023	17	110.50	115.87
36	1024	14	65535	08h	1023	17	119.00	124.78
37	1024	2	65535	00h	1023	17	17.00	17.83
38	1024	16	65535	08h	1023	17	136.00	142.61

(continues)

Type	Cylinders	Heads	WPC	Ctrl	LZ	S/T	Meg	M
Table D.21 Award ROM BIOS Version 3.05 Hard Disk Table Continued								
39	918	15	65535	08h	1023	17	114.30	119.85
40	820	6	65535	00h	820	17	40.84	42.82
41	1024	5	65535	00h	1023	17	42.50	44.56
42	1024	5	65535	00h	1023	26	65.00	68.16
43	809	6	65535	00h	808	17	40.29	42.25
44	820	6	65535	00h	819	26	62.46	65.50
45	776	8	65535	00h	775	33	100.03	104.89
46	0	0	0	00h	0	0	0.00	0.00
47	0	0	0	00h	0	0	0.00	0.00

Table D.22 shows the Phoenix 286 ROM BIOS (80286 ROM BIOS version 3.01, dated 11/01/86) hard disk parameters.

Type	Cylinders	Heads	WPC	Ctrl	LZ	S/T	Meg	M
Table D.22 Phoenix 286 (80286 ROM BIOS Version 3.01) Hard Disk Table								
1	306	4	128	00h	305	17	10.16	10.65
2	615	4	300	00h	638	17	20.42	21.41
3	615	6	300	00h	615	17	30.63	32.12
4	940	8	512	00h	940	17	62.42	65.45
5	940	6	512	00h	940	17	46.82	49.09
6	615	4	65535	00h	615	17	20.42	21.41
7	462	8	256	00h	511	17	30.68	32.17
8	733	5	65535	00h	733	17	30.42	31.90
9	900	15	65535	08h	901	17	112.06	117.50
10	820	3	65535	00h	820	17	20.42	21.41
11	855	5	65535	00h	855	17	35.49	37.21
12	855	7	65535	00h	855	17	49.68	52.09
13	306	8	128	00h	319	17	20.32	21.31
14	733	7	65535	00h	733	17	42.59	44.66
15	0	0	0	00h	0	0	0.00	0.00
16	612	4	0	00h	633	17	20.32	21.31
17	977	5	300	00h	977	17	40.55	42.52
18	977	7	65535	00h	977	17	56.77	59.53
19	1024	7	512	00h	1023	17	59.50	62.39
20	733	5	300	00h	732	17	30.42	31.90
21	733	7	300	00h	733	17	42.59	44.66
22	733	5	300	00h	733	17	30.42	31.90
23	0	0	0	00h	0	0	0.00	0.00
24	0	0	0	00h	0	0	0.00	0.00

Type	Cylinders	Heads	WPC	Ctrl	LZ	S/T	Meg	M
25	0	0	0	00h	0	0	0.00	0.00
26	0	0	0	00h	0	0	0.00	0.00
27	0	0	0	00h	0	0	0.00	0.00
28	0	0	0	00h	0	0	0.00	0.00
29	0	0	0	00h	0	0	0.00	0.00
30	0	0	0	00h	0	0	0.00	0.00
31	0	0	0	00h	0	0	0.00	0.00
32	0	0	0	00h	0	0	0.00	0.00
33	0	0	0	00h	0	0	0.00	0.00
34	0	0	0	00h	0	0	0.00	0.00
35	0	0	0	00h	0	0	0.00	0.00
36	1024	5	512	00h	1024	17	42.50	44.56
37	830	10	65535	08h	830	17	68.90	72.24
38	823	10	256	08h	824	17	68.32	71.63
39	615	4	128	00h	664	17	20.42	21.41
40	615	8	128	00h	664	17	40.84	42.82
41	917	15	65535	08h	918	17	114.18	119.72
42	1023	15	65535	08h	1024	17	127.38	133.56
43	823	10	512	08h	823	17	68.32	71.63
44	820	6	65535	00h	820	17	40.84	42.82
45	1024	8	65535	00h	1024	17	68.00	71.30
46	925	9	65535	08h	925	17	69.10	72.46
47	1024	5	65535	00h	1024	17	42.50	44.56

DOS Command Reference

Even if the systems you support, upgrade, and repair are all running the latest version of Windows, you will inevitably find yourself occasionally troubleshooting these systems from the DOS command line. With that in mind, I have included this brief DOS command reference to aid you when you are at the command line.*

DOS Commands Found in DOS 6.22, Windows 95, and Windows 98

Windows 95 and Windows 98 both still include DOS commands. The version of DOS with Windows 95 is called 7.0 and the version with Windows 98 is called 7.1. For the most part, DOS 7.x commands are just a subset of the commands found in DOS 6.22. However, DOS 7.x does have a few new features not found in DOS 6.x, so the new DOS is not the same as the old DOS. Here's a partial list of improvements:

- You can start Windows programs from the DOS prompt and even from within batch files.

- The new DOS includes support for long file names.

* This DOS command reference is based substantially on material found in Paul McFedries' Windows 98 Unleashed Professional Reference Edition, copyright © 1998 Sams Publishing, all rights reserved. Used with permission.

- Reduced reliance on real-mode drivers means that more conventional memory is available for DOS programs.

- Each DOS program can have its own settings and environment (CONFIG.SYS and AUTOEXEC.BAT). These are controlled via property sheets, so there's no need to create program information files (PIFs) from scratch for each program.

- You can run DOS programs in MS-DOS mode if they need full access to the computer's resources.

- The DOS session window has a toolbar for easy access to common features.

- You can access shared network folders via the command prompt.

- Most DOS commands are now native Windows 98 commands.

Windows 98 is, for the most part, the operating system on your machine. Yes, it comes with some real-mode components (such as IO.SYS) that are DOS-like, but they really just handle a few chores until Windows 98 can get itself into protected mode. After Windows 98 is running, however, "DOS" is just two things:

- COMMAND.COM, which provides the DOS prompt and a collection of internal DOS commands (such as COPY and DIR)

- A few external DOS commands, such as FORMAT.COM and XCOPY.EXE

For Windows 95 (and, so, Windows 98), Microsoft enhanced some of these commands, dropped other commands, and made a few of the dropped commands available on the CD-ROM.

Table D.23 lists the internal DOS commands available within the DOS 6.22, Windows 95, and Windows 98 versions of COMMAND.COM.

Table D.23   The Windows 98 Internal DOS Commands

Command	Description
BREAK	Sets or clears extended Ctrl+C checking.
CD	Changes to a different directory or, if run without parameters, displays the name of the current directory.
CHCP	Displays the number of the active character set (code page). You can also use this command to change the active character set for all devices that support character-set switching.
CHDIR	Takes the same action as the CD command.
CLS	Clears the screen.
COPY	Copies one or more files to the location you specify.
CTTY	Changes the terminal device used to control the computer.
DATE	Displays or sets the current date.
DEL	Deletes the files you specify.
DIR	Displays a list of the files and subfolders that exist in the current or specified folder.

Command	Description
ERASE	Deletes the files you specify.
EXIT	Quits COMMAND.COM and returns to the program that started the command interpreter, if one exists.
LH	Loads a program into upper memory.
LOADHIGH	Takes the same action as the LH command.
LOCK	Enables direct disk access.
MD	Creates a folder or subfolder.
MKDIR	Takes the same action as the MD command.
PATH	Specifies which folders Windows 98 should search for executable files.
PROMPT	Changes the appearance of the command prompt.
RD	Deletes a folder.
REN	Changes the name of the specified file or files.
RENAME	Takes the same action as the REN command.
RMDIR	Takes the same action as the RD command.
SET	Displays, sets, or removes environment variables.
TIME	Displays or sets the current time.
TYPE	Displays the contents of the specified text file.
UNLOCK	Disables direct disk access.
VER	Displays the operating system version number.
VERIFY	Directs the operating system to verify that files are written correctly to a disk and displays the status of verification.
VOL	Displays the volume label and serial number for a disk.

The DOS external commands are located in the COMMAND subfolder of the main Windows 95/98 folder. Table D.24 lists the external DOS commands that ship with Windows 95/98.

Table D.24 The Windows 98 External DOS Commands

Command	Description
ATTRIB.EXE	Displays or changes the attributes of the specified files.
CHKDSK.EXE	Checks a disk for (and optionally repairs) lost and cross-linked clusters. ScanDisk does a better job at finding and repairing these errors.
CHOICE.COM	Used in batch files to present the user with a list of options.
COMMAND.COM	Starts a new instance of the command interpreter. This file is usually found in the root directory of the boot drive.
CSCRIPT.EXE	(Windows 98 only) Runs Windows Scripting Host scripts.
CVT.EXE	(Windows 95 OSR 2 and Windows 98 only) Converts FAT drives to FAT32.
DEBUG.EXE	Tests and edits executable files.
DELTREE.EXE	Deletes a folder and all its files and subfolders.
DISKCOPY.COM	Makes an exact copy of a floppy disk.

(continues)

Table D.24 The Windows 98 External DOS Commands Continued

Command	Description
DOSKEY.COM	A memory-resident program that recalls commands, edits previous command lines, and runs macros.
EDIT.COM	Starts a text editor you can use to create and edit ASCII text files.
EXTRACT.EXE	(Windows 95/98 only) Extracts files from a compressed cabinet (CAB) file.
FC.EXE	Compares two files and displays the differences between them.
FDISK.EXE	Starts the FDISK utility.
FIND.EXE	Searches files for a specified text string.
FORMAT.COM	Formats a disk.
IEXTRACT.EXE	Extracts a file from an Internet Explorer backup information (DAT) file.
KEYB.COM	Configures a keyboard for a specific language.
LABEL.EXE	Creates or modifies the volume label of a disk.
MEM.EXE	Displays the amount of used and free memory on the computer.
MODE.COM	Configures a printer, serial port, or display adapter; sets the keyboard repeat rate; redirects printer output from a parallel port to a serial port; prepares, selects, refreshes, or displays the numbers of the character sets (code pages) for parallel printers or the keyboard and screen; and displays the status of all the devices installed on the computer.
MORE.COM	Pauses command output to display one screen at a time.
MOVE.EXE	Moves files and renames folders.
MSCDEX.EXE	Loads the real-mode CD-ROM driver.
NLSFUNC.EXE	Loads country-specific information for national language support.
SCANDISK.EXE	The real-mode version of ScanDisk.
SCANREG.EXE	(Windows 98 only) Scans the Registry for damage.
SORT.EXE	Reads input, sorts data, and writes the results to the screen, a file, or another device.
START.EXE	Enables you to set various parameters for running Windows programs from the DOS prompt.
SUBST.EXE	Substitutes a drive letter for a path name.
SYS.COM	Creates a bootable disk by copying Windows 98's system files and COMMAND.COM to the disk.
XCOPY.EXE	The extended copy command.
XCOPY32.EXE	(Windows 95 and Windows 98 only) The 32-bit version of XCOPY.

DOS 6.22 Commands Not Installed by Windows 95/98 but Available on the CD-ROM

Microsoft deleted quite a few DOS commands when it put together the Windows 98 package. Most of these commands were either obsolete (such as EGA.SYS) or dangerous (such as RECOVER). Three of these commands, however, can be found on the Windows 98 CD-ROM in the \TOOLS\OLDMSDOS\ folder. I've summarized them in Table D.25.

Table D.25	Old DOS Commands Available on the Windows 98 CD-ROM
Command	**Description**
HELP.COM	Displays descriptions, syntax, and examples for all DOS commands. HELP.HLP is also available.
MSD.EXE	Runs the Microsoft Diagnostics program used to gather system information for troubleshooting. Superseded by the System Information utility in Windows 98.
QBASIC.EXE	The programming environment for creating QBASIC applications. QBASIC.HLP is also available.

Table D.26 lists commands that were available in the Windows 95 CD-ROM in the \OTHER\OLDMSDOS folder. These were commands that were available in DOS 6.22 but were not installed by Windows 95 because they are obsolete.

Table D.26	Old DOS Commands Available on the Windows 95 CD-ROM
Command	**Description**
APPEND.EXE	Establishes a DOS search path for data files.
CHKSTATE.SYS	A device driver used by MemMaker to optimize memory use. You cannot use this driver.
EXPAND.EXE	Extracts a file from compressed format on the DOS distribution disks to a usable uncompressed form.
GRAPHICS.COM	Enables the Print Screen key to print the contents of a graphics screen on a suitable printer.
HELP.COM	Launches a full screen online help utility for the DOS commands.
INTERLNK.EXE	Client device driver for an InterLnk network.
INTERSVR.EXE	Server device driver for an InterLnk network.
LOADFIX.COM	Forces a program to load into the second 64K of memory.
MEMMAKER.EXE	Utility for optimizing memory usage by device drivers and other programs loaded by CONFIG.SYS and AUTOEXEC.BAT.
MSD.EXE	Runs the Microsoft Diagnostics program used to gather system information for troubleshooting.
PRINT.EXE	Print spooler for ASCII text files.
QBASIC.EXE	Starts the Microsoft QuickBASIC development environment, a program for writing and running BASIC language programs.
REPLACE.EXE	Replaces or adds files to a subdirectory.
RESTORE.EXE	Restores files created by the BACKUP program from one disk to another.
SIZER.EXE	A program used by MemMaker to optimize memory use. You cannot use this program.
TREE.EXE	Displays the subdirectory stricture of a disk.
UNDELETE.EXE	Undeletes a file or group of files.

DOS 6.22 Commands Not Available in Windows 95 or Windows 98

Finally, Table D.27 is a list of DOS 6.22 commands that are gone for good and won't be found in either Windows 95 or Windows 98.

Table D.27   DOS 6.22

Command	Description
ASSIGN	In DOS 2–5, attached an alias drive letter to an existing drive. Replaced by SUBST in DOS 6 and later.
BACKUP	A utility to back up files from a hard disk to a series of floppy disks. Replaced by MSBACKUP in DOS 6 and with the GUI version of Backup for Windows 95 and Windows 98.
COMP	Compares two sets of disk files of the same name and same length. Included in DOS 1–5 but only on supplemental disk in DOS 6.
DOSSHELL	In DOS 4–6, a full screen menu driven shell for the DOS command line. Included only on the supplemental disk for DOS 6.2.
EDLIN	In DOS 1–5, edits an ASCII file, replaced by EDIT. Only on supplemental disk in DOS 6.
FASTHELP	Returns the same help information as including the /? switch with a DOS command.
FASTOPEN	A utility that sped up the process of opening files in DOS.
GRAFTABL	A DOS 3–5 utility for loading tables of additional character sets for CGA adapters. Only on the supplemental disk in DOS 6.
JOIN	In DOS 3.1–5, connects one drive to a subdirectory of another. Only on the supplemental disk in DOS 6.
MIRROR	In DOS 5, records information about the FAT, the root directory, and optionally the partition table which can be used by UNFORMAT and UNDELETE. Only on the supplemental disk in DOS 6.
MSAV	Microsoft Anti-Virus for Windows 3.x.
MSBACKUP	Microsoft Backup for Windows 3.x.
POWER	Controls use of APM in laptop systems and other APM-enabled systems.
RECOVER	A file recovery utility with DOS 2–5 that was not distributed with DOS 6 or later. Not recommended for use with any version.
SETVER	DOS version control program that reports a different DOS version number to programs requiring a specific version of DOS to run.
SHARE	File sharing and locking capabilities for DOS.
SMARTMON	SMARTDrive monitoring and configuration program for Windows 3.x.
UNFORMAT	Recovers a disk that was accidentally formatted. Note that using the /U switch with the FORMAT command will prevent the UNFORMAT command from being able to recover the disk.
VSAFE	A memory resident utility that warns you of virus-like activity.

List of
Acronyms

A

AAD (Analog Alignment Diskette)
Accelerated Graphics Port (AGP)
Acer Laboratories, Inc. (ALI)
ACPI (Advanced Configuration and Power Interface)
Adaptive Differential Pulse Code Modulation (ADPCM)
ADCs (analog-to-digital converters)
ADPCM (Adaptive Differential Pulse Code Modulation)
Advanced Configuration and Power Interface (ACPI)
Advanced Micro Devices (AMD)
Advanced Power Management (APM) standard
Advanced Programmable Interrupt Controller (APIC)
Advanced Run Length Limited (ARLL)
Advanced SCSI Programming Interface (ASPI)
AGC (Automatic Gain Control)
AGP (Accelerated Graphics Port)
ALI (Acer Laboratories Inc.)
AMD (Advanced Micro Devices)
analog-to-digital-converters (ADCs)
AAD (Analog Alignment Diskette)
APIC (Advanced Programmable Interrupt Controller)
APM (Advanced Power Management) standard
ARLL (Advanced Run Length Limited)
ASPI (Advanced SCSI Programming Interface)
AT Attachment Packet Interface (ATAPI)
ATAPI (AT Attachment Packet Interface)
Automatic Gain Control (AGC)

B

BASIC (Beginners All-Purpose Symbolic Instruction)
Basic Input Output System (BIOS)
Basic Rate Interface (BRI)

BBSs (bulletin board systems)
Beginners All-purpose Symbolic Instruction Code (BASIC)
BiCMOS (Bipolar Complementary Metal Oxide Semiconductor)
BIOS (Basic Input Output System)
BPI (bits per inch)
bps (bits per second)
Branch Target Buffer (BTB)
BRI (Basic Rate Interface)
BSRAMs (Burst Static RAMs)
BTB (Branch Target Buffer)
bulletin board systems (BBSs)
Burst Static RAMs (BSRAMs)

C

Cable Select (CSEL) signals
Cache On A Stick (COAST)
CACP (Central Arbitration Control Point)
CAM ATA (Common Access Method AT Attachment) interface
Canadian Standards Agency (CSA)
Card Edge Low Profile (CELP)
cathode ray tubes (CRTs)
CAV (Constant Angular Velocity)
CBT (Computer-Based Training)
Consultative Committee on International Telephone and Telegraph (CCITT)
CD-R (CD-Recordable)
CD-RW (CD-Rewritable)
CELP (Card Edge Low Profile)
Central Arbitration Control Point (CACP)
Central Processing Units (CPUs)
CGA (Color Graphics Adapter)
characters per second (cps)
CHS (Cylinder Head Sector)

CISC (Complex Instruction Set Computer)
CLKMUL (Clock Multiplier)
CLV (Constant Linear Velocity)
CMOS (Complementary Metal Oxide
  Semiconductor)
CMOS RAM (Complimentary Metal-Oxide
  Semiconductor)
COAST (Cache On A Stick)
Color Graphics Adapter (CGA)
color super-twist nematic (CSTN)
Common Access Method AT Attachment
  (CAM ATA) interface
Compact Video Coded (CVC)
Complex Instruction Set Computer (CISC)
Complimentary Metal-Oxide Semiconductor
  (CMOS)
CompuCom Speed Protocol (CSP)
Computer-Based Training (CBT)
Constant Angular Velocity (CAV)
Constant Linear Velocity (CLV)
Consultative Committee on International
  Telephone and Telegraph (CCITT)
CP/M (Control Program for Microprocessors)
cps (characters per second)
CPUs (Central Processing Units)
CRC (cyclic redundancy check)
CRTs (cathode ray tubes)
CSA (Canadian Standards Agency)
CSEL (Cable Select) signals
CSP (CompuCom Speed Protocol)
CSTN (color super-twist nematic)
CVC (Compact Video Coded)
cyclic redundancy check (CRC)
Cylinder Head Sector (CHS)

D

DAC (Digital to Analog Converter)
DASP signals (Drive Active/Slave Present)
DAT (digital audio tape)
db (decibels)
DBB (dynamic bass boost)
DBR (DOS Boot Record)
DCC (Direct Cable Connection)
DDD (Digital Diagnostic Diskette)
DDMs (Digital Multi-Meters)
DDR (Double Data Rate)
decibels (db)
Desktop Management Interface (DMI)
Desktop Video (DTV)
device-independent bitmap (DIB)
DIB (Dual Independent Bus)
digital audio tape (DAT)
Digital Diagnostic Diskette (DDD)
digital linear tape (DLT)

Digital Mulit-Meter (DMM)
Digital Signal Processors (DSPs)
Digital to Analog Converter (DAC)
Digital Versatile Disc (DVD)
Digital Volt Ohm Meters (DVOMs)
Digital-to-Analog Converter (RAMDAC)
DIME (DIrect Memory Execute)
DIMMs (Dual Inline Memory Modules)
DIN (Deutsche Industrie Norm)
DIP (Dual Inline Package) chips
Direct Cable Connection (DCC)
Direct Memory Access (DMA)
DIrect Memory Execute (DIME)
DIS (dynamic impedance stabilization)
Disk Operating System (DOS)
Display Power-Management Signaling (DPMS)
DLT (digital linear tape)
DMA (Direct Memory Access)
DMI (Desktop Management Interface)
DMM (Digital Multi-Meter)
DOS (Disk Operating System)
DOS Boot Record (DBR)
dots per inch (dpi)
Double Data Rate (DDR)
double-layer super-twist nematic (DSTN)
dpi (dots per inch)
DPMS (Display Power-Management Signaling)
Drive Active/Slave Present (DASP)
DSPs (Digital Signal Processors)
DSTN (double-layer super-twist nematic)
DTV (Desktop Video boards)
Dual Independent Bus (DIB)
Dual Inline Memory Modules (DIMMs)
DVD (Digital Versatile Disc)
DVOM (Digital Multi-Meters)
dynamic bass boost (DBB)
dynamic impedance stabilization (DIS)

E

ECC (Error Correcting Code)
ECHS (Extended Cylinder Head Sector)
ECP (Enhanced Capabilities Ports)
EDC (Error Detection Code)
EDO (Extended Data Out)
EDO DRAM (Extended Data Out DRAM)
EDO memory (Extended Data Out)
EEPROM (Electrically Erasable Programmable
  Read Only Memory)
EGA (Enhanced Graphics Adapter)
EISA (Extended Industry Standard Architecture)
Electrically Erasable Programmable Read Only
  Memory (EEPROM)
electrostatic discharge (ESD)

ELF (extremely low frequency)
EMS (Expanded Memory Specification)
encoder/decoder (endec)
endec (encoder/decoder)
Enhanced Capabilities Ports (ECP)
Enhanced Graphics Adapter (EGA)
Enhanced Parallel Ports (EPP)
Enhanced Serial Ports (ESP)
Enhanced Small Device Interface (ESDI)
EPIC (Explicitly Parallel Instruction
    Computing)
EPP (Enhanced Parallel Ports)
EPROM (Erasable Programmable Read Only
    Memory)
Erasable Programmable Read Only Memory
    (EPROM)
Error Correcting Code (ECC)
Error Detection Code (EDC)
ESD (electrostatic discharge)
ESDI (Enhanced Small Device Interface)
ESP (Enhanced Serial Ports)
Explicitly Parallel Instruction Computing (EPIC)
Extended Cylinder Head Sector (ECHS)
Extended Data Out (EDO)
Extended Data Out DRAM (EDO DRAM)
Extended Data Out memory (EDO memory)
eXtended Graphics Array (XGA)
Extended Industry Standard Architecture (EISA)

F

Failures in Time (FIT)
Fast Page-Mode RAM (FPM RAM)
FAT (File Allocation Table)
FCC (Federal Communications Commission)
FDDI (fiber distributed data interface)
FDIV (Floating Point Divide)
Federal Communications Commission (FCC)
fiber distributed data interface (FDDI)
FIFO (first in/first out)
File Allocation Table (FAT)
first in/first out (FIFO)
FIT (Failures in Time)
Floating Point Divide (FDIV)
Floating Point Units (FPUs)
FM (Frequency Modulation)
FPM DRAM (Fast Page-Mode RAM)
FPUs (Floating Point Units)
Frequency Modulation (FM)
frequency-shift keying (FSK)
FSK (frequency-shift keying)

G

Gb (Gigabit)
GB (Gigabyte)
GUI (Graphical User Interface)

H

HAL (hardware abstraction layer)
hard error rates (HERS)
hardware abstraction layer (HAL)
HDAs (Head Disk Assemblies)
Hercules Graphics Card (HGC)
HERS (hard error rates)
Hertz (Hz)
HGC (Hercules Graphics Card)
high performance addressing (HPA)
High-Level Formatting (HLF)
High-Resolution Diagnostic Diskette (HRD)
HLF (High-Level Formatting)
HMA (High Memory Area)
HPA (high performance addressing)
HRD (High-Resolution Diagnostic Diskette)
Hz (Hertz)

I-J

iCOMP (Intel Comparative Microprocessor
    Performance)
ICs (integrated circuits)
IDE (Integrated Drive Electronics)
IDE/ATAPI (Integrated Drive Electronics/AT
    Attachment)
IDT (Integrated Device Technology)
IML (Initial Microcode Load)
Industry Standard Architecture (ISA)
Infrared Data (IrDA)
Initial Microcode Load (IML)
integrated circuits (ICs)
Integrated Device Technology (IDT)
Integrated Drive Electronics (IDE)
Integrated Drive Electronics/AT Attachment Packet
Integrated Peripherals Controller (IPC)
Integrated Services Digital Network (ISDN)
Intel Comparative Microprocessor Performance
    (iCOMP)
International Organization for Standardization (ISO)
interrupt requests (IRQs)
IPC (Integrated Peripherals Controller)
IPL (Initial Program Load) ROM
IrDA (Infrared Data)
IRQs (Interrupt Requests)

ISA (Industry Standard Architecture)
ISDN (Integrated Services Digital Network)
ISO (International Organization for
   Standardization)

JPEG (Joint Photographic Experts Group)

K-L

Kb (Kilobit)
KB (Kilobyte)
landing zone (LZ)
LANs (local area networks)
LAPM (Link Access Procedure for Modems)
LBA (Logical Block Addressing)
LCDs (liquid crystal displays)
LEDs (Light Emitting Diodes)
LIF (Low Insertion Force)
Light Emitting Diodes (LEDs)
LIM (Lotus Intel Microsoft)
Link Access Procedure for Modems (LAPM)
liquid crystal displays (LCDs)
LLC (Logical Link Control)
LLF (Low-Level Formatting)
local area networks (LANs)
Logical Block Addressing (LBA)
Logical Link Control (LLC)
Lotus Intel Microsoft (LIM)
Low Insertion Force (LIF)
Low-Level Formatting (LLF)
LZ (landing zone)

M

MAC (Media Access Control)
Master Boot Record (MBR)
Master Boot Sector (MBS)
Master File Table (MFT)
Mb (Megabit)
MB (Megabyte)
Mbps (megabits per second)
MBR (Master Boot Record)
MBS (Master Boot Sector)
MCA (Micro Channel Architecture)
MCGA (MultiColor Graphics Array)
MCM (Multi-Chip Module)
MDA (Monochrome Display Adapter)
MDRAM (Multibank DRAM)
Mean Time Between Failures (MTBF)
Media Access Control (MAC)
Megabit (Mb)
megabits per second (Mbps)
Megabyte (MB)
Memory Management Unit (MMU)
Metal-In-Gap (MIG)

metal-oxide varistors (MOVs)
MFM (Modified Frequency Modulation)
MFT (Master File Table)
MHZ (Megahertz)
Micro Channel Architecture (MCA bus)
Microcom Networking Protocol (MNP)
Microsoft CD-ROM Extensions (MSCDEX)
Microsoft Diagnostics (MSD)
Microsoft Video for Windows (VFW)
MIDI (Musical Instrument Digital Interface)
MIG (Metal-In-Gap)
MMU (Memory Management Unit)
MMX (MultiMedia eXtension)
MNP (Microcom Networking Protocol)
modem (modulator/demodulator)
Modified Frequency Modulation (MFM)
modulator/demodulator (modem)
Monochrome Display Adapter (MDA)
Motion Pictures Expert Group (MPEG)
MOVs (metal-oxide varistors)
MPC (Multimedia PC)
MPEG (Motion Pictures Expert Group)
MPS (Multi-Processor Specification)
MSCDEX (Microsoft CD-ROM Extensions)
MSD (Microsoft Diagnostics)
MTBF (Mean Time Between Failures)
Multi-Chip Module (MCM)
Multi-Processor Specification (MPS)
Multibank DRAM (MDRAM)
MultiColor Graphics Array (MCGA)
MultiMedia eXtension (MMX)
Multimedia PC (MPC)
Musical Instrument Digital Interface (MIDI)

N

National Television System Committee (NTSC)
NDP (numeric data processor)
NFAS (Non-Facility Associated Signaling)
NMI (non-maskable interrupt)
Non-Facility Associated Signaling (NFAS)
Non-Volatile RAM (NVRAM)
NTSC (National Television System Committee)
numeric data processor (NDP)
NVRAM (Non-Volatile RAM)

O

Object Linking and Embedding (OLE)
OEM Service Release (OSR)
OEMs (Original Equipment Manufacturers)
OLE (Object Linking and Embedding)
One Time Programmable (OTP)
Open Systems Interconnection (OSI)

Original Equipment Manufacturers (OEMs)
OSI (Open Systems Interconnection)
OSR (OEM Service Release)
OTP (One Time Programmable)

P

Page Description Language (PDL)
pages per minute (ppm)
PAL (Phase Alternate Line)
PARD (Periodic and Random Deviation)
Partial-Response, Maximum-Likelihood (PRML)
PCI (Peripheral Component Interconnect)
PCI ISA IDE Xcelerator (PIIX) chips
PCL (Printer Control Language)
PDL (Page Description Language)
Periodic and Random Deviation (PARD)
Peripheral Component Interconnect (PCI)
PGA (Pin Grid Array)
PGA (Professional Graphics Adapter)
Phase Alternate Line (PAL)
phase-shift keying (PSK)
PIIX chips (PCI ISA IDE Xcelerator)
Pin Grid Array (PGA)
PJL (Printer Job Language)
Plastic Quad Flat Pack (PQFQ)
PnP (Plug and Play)
POST (Power On Self Test)
PostScript Printer Descriptions (PPDs)
Power On Self-Test (POST)
power supply unit (PSU)
Power-On Self Test (POST)
PPDs (PostScript Printer Descriptions)
PPI (Programmable Peripheral Interface)
ppm (pages per minute)
PQFP (Plastic Quad Flat Pack)
PRI (Primary Rate Interface)
Printer Control Language (PCL)
Printer Job Language (PJL)
PRML (Partial-Response Maximum-Likelihood)
Professional Graphics Adapter (PGA)
PROM (Programmable ROM)
PSK (phase-shift keying)
PSTN (Public Switched Telephone Network)
PSU (power supply unit)
Public Switched Telephone Network (PSTN)

Q-R

QAM (quadrature-amplitude modulation)
QIC (Quarter-Inch Committee)
radio-frequency interference (RFI)
RAID (Redundant Array of Inexpensive Disks)
RAM (Random Access Memory)

RAMDAC (Digital-to-Analog Converter)
raster output scanner (ROS)
RDRAM (Rambus Dynamic RAM)
Read Only Memory (ROM)
Real Time Clock (RTC)
Reduced Instruction Set Computer (RISC)
Redundant Array of Inexpensive Disks (RAID)
RET (Resolution Enhancement Technology)
RFI (radio-frequency interference)
RIMMs (Rambus Inline Memory Modules)
RISC (Reduced Instruction Set Computer)
RLL (Run Length Limited)-
ROM (Read Only Memory)
room-temperature vulcanizing (RTV)
ROS (raster output scanner)
RTC (Real Time Clock)
RTV (room-temperature vulcanizing)
Run Length Limited (RLL)

S

SBIC (SCSI Bus Adapter Chip)
SDL (Shielded Data Link)
SDRAM (Synchronous Dynamic RAM)
SEC (Single Edge Cartridge)
SECAM (SEquential Couleur Avec Memoire)
SERS (soft error rates)
SEUs (single event upsets)
SGRAM (Synchronous Graphics DRAM)
Shielded Data Link (SDL)
shielded twisted pair (STP)
Silicon Integrated Systems (SIS)
SIMD (Single Instruction Multiple Data)
SIMMs (Single Inline Memory Modules)
Single Edge Cartridge (SEC)
single event upsets (SEUS)
Single Inline Memory Modules (SIMMs)
Single Inline Pin Package (SIPP)
Single Instruction Multiple Data (SIMD)
SIPPs (Single Inline Pin Package)
SIS (Silicon Integrated Systems)
Small Quad Flat Pack (SQFQ)
SMI (System Management Interrupt)
SMM (System Management Mode)
soft error rates (SERS)
SPGA (Staggered Pin Grid Array)
Spindle Synchronization (SPSYNC) signals
SPS (Standby Power Supplies)
SPSYNC (Spindle Synchronization) signals
SQFP (Small Quad Flat Pack)
SRAM (Static RAM)
Staggered Pin Grid Array (SPGA)
Standby Power Supplies (SPS)
STP (shielded twisted pair)
SVGA (Super VGA)

Synchronous Dynamic RAM (SDRAM)
Synchronous Graphics DRAM (SGRAM)
System Management Interrupt (SMI)
System Management Mode (SMM)

T

TAB (tape automated bonding)
tape automated bonding (TAB)
tape carrier packaging (TCP)
Tb (Terabit)
TB (Terabyte)
TCP (tape carrier packaging)
TCQAM (trellis coded quadrature amplitude
  modulation)
Terabit (Tb)
Terabyte (TB)
TFT (thin-film transistors)
THD (Total Harmonic Distortion)
thin-film transistors (TFT)
TLB (Translation Lookaside Buffer)
Total Harmonic Distortion (THD)
TPI (tracks per inch)
Translation Lookaside Buffer (TLB)
trellis coded quadrature amplitude modulation
  (TCQAM)

U

UART (Universal Asynchronous Receiver/
  Transmitter)
UL (Underwriters Labratories, Inc.)
Ultra VGA (UVGA)
UMA (Upper Memory Area)
UMB (Upper Memory Block)
Underwriters Laboratories Inc. (UL)
Uninterruptable Power Supplies (UPS)
Universal Asynchronous Receive/Transmitter
  (UART)
Universal Peripheral Interface (UPI)
Universal Serial Bus (USB)
unshielded twisted pair (UTP)
UPI (Universal Peripheral Interface)
Upper Memory Area (UMA)
Upper Memory Block (UMB)
UPS (Uninterruptable Power Supplies)

USB (Universal Serial Bus)
UTP (unshielded twisted pair)
UVGA (Ultra VGA)

V

VAFC (VESA Advanced Feature Connector)
Very Large Scale Integration (VLSI)
Very Long Instruction Words (VLIW)
very low frequency (VLF)
VESA (Video Electronics Standards Association)
VESA Advanced Feature Connector (VAFC)
VESA Media Channel (VMC)
VFAT (Virtual File Allocation Table)
VFC (Video Feature Connector)
VFW (Microsoft Video for Windows)
VGA (Video Graphics Array)
VID (Voltage Identification)
Video Electronics Standards Association (VESA)
Video Graphics Array (VGA)
video RAM (VRAM)
Virtual File Allocation Table (VFAT)
VLF (very low frequency)
VLIW (Very Long Instruction Words)
VLSI (Very Large Scale Integration)
VMC (VESA Media Channel)
Voltage Identifications (VID)
Voltage Reduction Technology (VRT)
Voltage Regulator Module (VRM)
Volume of Table of Contents (VTOC)
VRAM (video RAM)
VRM (Voltage Regulator Module)
VRT (Voltage Reduction Technology)
VTOC (Volume Table of Contents)

W-Z

what you see is what you get (WYSIWYG)
Window RAM (WRAM)
WORM (write once/read many)
WRAM (Window RAM)
WYSIWYG (what you see is what you get)

XGA (eXtended Graphics Array)
XMS (extended memory specification)

ZIF (Zero Insertion Force)

Index of Manufacturers

Index

T

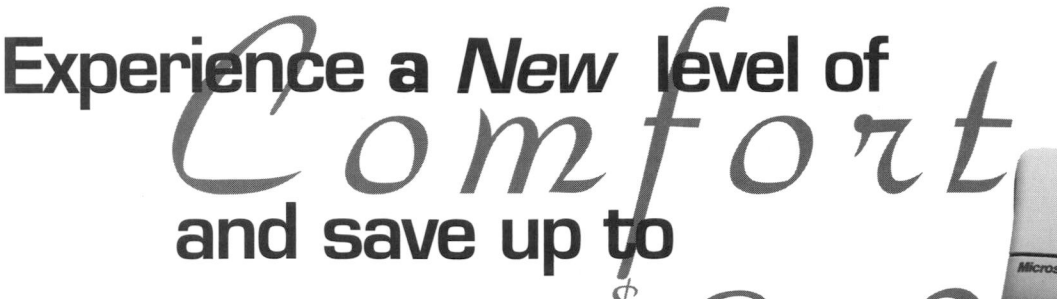

Experience a *New* level of *Comfort*
and save up to $20

Designed for your comfort.

The split, gently sloped shape of the Microsoft® Natural® Keyboard Elite encourages a natural hand position.

o The Natural Keyboard Elite's smaller footprint saves valuable desk space.

o The USB adapter allows you to use your keyboard with the latest PC technology.

o Most people adapt to the Natural Keyboard Elite within a few hours. The 30-day retail money-back guarantee allows you to take it home and try it risk free!

Comfortable and precis

The Microsoft® IntelliMouse® Pro is the more efficient way to work.

o Shaped for superior comfort. The ergonomic design supports your ha and helps keep your wrist and hand aligned in their natural position.

o Rubber sides for a better grip.

o Work more efficiently with the whe for scrolling. It's a fast and easy wa to move through your documents o the Web. Or, work hands free with AutoScroll.

*The zoom function works in Microsoft Office 97-compati applications. For a complete list, please visit http://microsoft.com/mouse/

---

1. Print the following information:

First name   Last name

Address (sorry, no P.O. Boxes)

City   State/Province   Zip/Postal Code

(   )
(Area code) Phone number

Name of store where purchased   City   State/Province

2. Enclose ALL of the following as proofs of purchase*:

(a) a copy of the original sales receipt for Microsoft IntelliMouse Pro pointing device and/or the Microsoft Natural Keyboard Elite (with the date and store where acquired clearly identified)

(b) AND the box top with product name and bar code from the Microsoft IntelliMouse Pro and/or the Microsoft Natural Keyboard Elite clearly identified.

3. Send proofs of purchase and completed coupon to:

IntelliMouse Pro & Natural Keyboard Elite
$10 US Currency Promotion
497-99-504
P.O. Box 2819
Ridgely, MD 21681

*If you have questions about this offer, call (800) 62 4445 (8:30A.M. to 5:30 P.M. eastern time, except ho days). No rebate will be authorized over the phon Please allow 6 to 8 weeks for delivery of your rebate(Limit one $10U.S. currency rebate per household p one Microsoft IntelliMouse Pro and/or one Micros Natural Keyboard elite only. Offer good only in the United States and the District of Columbia and Cana only. Not valid in U.S. territories including Puerto Ric the U.S. Virgin Islands or Guam. Offer Expires Febr ary 28, 1999. Coupon must be received by Micros by March 15, 1999. Only original coupons will be a cepted. Offer not valid in conjunction with any oth Microsoft rebate offer. Offer not valid if Micros IntelliMouse Pro or Microsoft Natural Keyboard El acquired directly from Microsoft. Rebate offer not va toward academic product versions or products suppli by a computer manufacturer (OEM). Cash redemption value 1/100 of 1 cent.

© 1998 Microsoft Corporation. All rights reserve Microsoft, IntelliMouse and Natural are either registe trademarks or trademarks of Microsoft Corporatio the U.S. and/or other countries.

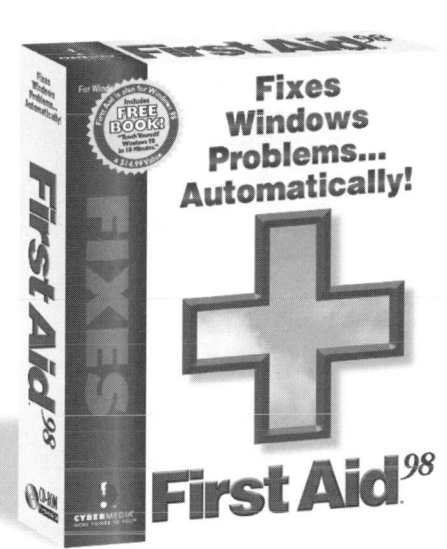

Incredible Pictures.
Incredible Choices.

KODAK Digital Cameras

• A range of megapixel digital cameras offering outstanding image quality, full of features and bundled with everything you need to get started right away • KODAK Picture Easy Software, the fast, easy way to download, view and print your pictures (included with all KODAK Digital Cameras)

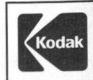

GET THE BEST QUALITY DIGITAL PICTURES– GUARANTEED!

Stock Up

on Lexar Media's High Performance Digital Film™ and *new* Digital Film Readers™

FREE overnight shipping*!

HUGE discounts**!

CompactFlash™   SmartMedia™

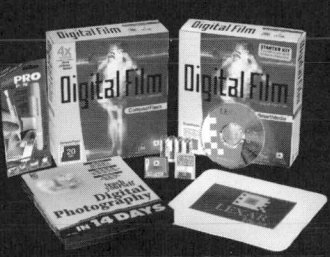

Film Packs:

20% savings on all:

- ▸ 4MB, 16MB *SmartMedia* Film Packs
- ▸ 16MB, 32MB *CompactFlash* Film Packs

Regular prices start at $29.99

Starter Kits:

20% savings on all:

- ▸ 4MB, 16MB *SmartMedia* Starter Kits
- ▸ 16MB, 32MB *CompactFlash* Starter Kits

Regular prices start at $59.99

Starter Kits include over $300 of **FREE** accessories:

- · $40, 385-page "Teach Yourself Digital Photography" Book
- · $200 worth of CD-Rom Software to manipulate, manage, and distribute your digital photographs
- · "My First Photo" Mouse Pad, Kodak PHOTOLIFE™ Camera Batteries, LENSPEN®

Digital Film Readers:

$20 off with the purchase of any:

- ▸ *CompactFlash* or *SmartMedia* Starter Kit
- ▸ *CompactFlash* or *SmartMedia* Film Pack

Regular prices start at $89.99

Call now to order:

ph: **800-789-9418*** or **408-848-3853**   fax: **408-848-5784**

*US and Canada Only   **US Dollars

Source Code **1MCPLXR**
Offer Expires 3/1/99

LEXAR *Media*

www.digitalfilm.com

Award-Winning Supra modems deliver 112K Internet access today!

FREE INFOPEDIA CD-ROM with purchase ($29.95 VALUE)

Enter our Sweepstakes at www.diamondmm.com/shotgun

Get 112K Today!

The SupraSonic II integrates two powerful 56K modems on one board utilizing two analog phone lines for speeds up to 112K. High-performance SupraExpress 56 modems provide a complete data/fax and voicemail solution. The SupraMax 56 is an extremely affordable 56K data/fax modem for a reliable Internet connection. These modems support the 56K ITU Standard (V.90), K56flex Technology and Diamond's Shotgun(tm) Technology for Internet connections up to 112K!. Shotgun Technology features manual controls, bandwidth on demand and voice-priority. For more information call 1-800-468-5846 or visit our web site at www.diamondmm.com/shotgun

V.90

* Limited offer, for details and redemption form, visit Diamond's web site at www.diamondmm.com/infopedia

This modem is designed with the 56K specifications released by the ITU in February/March 1998. The actual standard will not be fully-approved until the ITU voting procedure (projected for September, 1998.) SupraExpress and Supra PC Card are trademarks of Diamond Multimedia Systems Inc. Rockwell and associated logo are trademarks of Rockwell International. Though this modem is capable of 56 Kbps download performance, line impairments, public telephone infrastructure and other external technological factors currently prevent maximum 56 Kbps connections.

1-800-468-5846

Mike Meyers
A+ CERTIFICATION EXPERT

The A+ certification program was established by the Computing Technology Industry Association (CompTIA) and is sponsored by many of the largest PC vendors in the industry, including IBM, Hewlett-Packard, Apple and COMPAQ. The purpose of this certification is to set a standard for those working as technicians, help desk and support staff in the personal computer industry .

A+ certification has become one of the most sought-after industry credentials. Many employers require their technicians to become A+ certified. These companies notice an increase in customer satisfaction, improved hiring capabilities and better retention of employees. Certified professionals increase their marketability and their earning potential.

An A+ certificate shows that the applicant possess the knowledge and skills essential to be a successful computer service technician. To become certified, a candidate must pass two test modules--the "Core," and either a DOS/Win or Macintosh module. The two-part exam covers hardware and software technologies and is not related to any vendor-specific products.

*All company names/products are trademarks of their respective holders.

$649⁰⁰

A+ Certification Bundle
(6 Videos, Course Book and MasterExam)

A+ Certification at Your Fingertips.

Training for A+ Certification Exams

LearnKey offers a complete traing program to help you prepare for the A+ Certification Exam. The A+ course includes six videos, a course book and MasterExam Test Prep Software. The videos provide a step by step visual approach which allows you to sit back and absorb the information, techniques and procedures. Course books provide important supplemental references to the video training, and expound upon critical exam topics. The MasterExam CD-ROM includes 600 sample exam questions.

For more information:
Phone: (435) 674-9733
Fax: (435) 674-9734
Internet: www.learnkey.com

The Computing Technology Industry Association and A+ are registered trademarks. All rights reserved. "Computer Service Quality That You Can Trust." "A+ Certification Program is an industry-wide, vendor-neutral program developed and sponsored by the Computing Technology Industry Association."

1.800.865.0165

Source Code #802

Proud member of
COMPUTING
technology
INDUSTRY
association

Learn From The Experts ™

Upgrading and Repairing PCs
Quick Reference
Second Edition

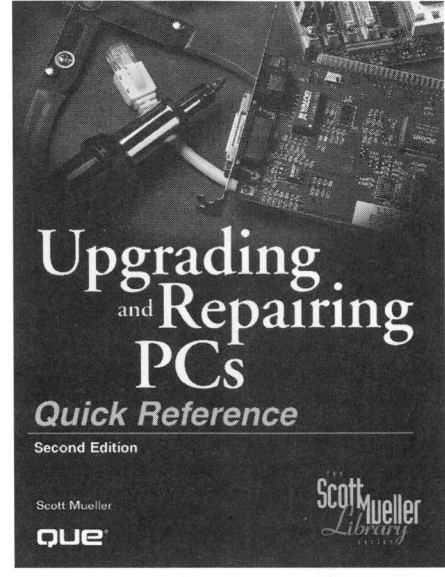

0-7897-1669-0
Pub Date 5/15/98
$19.99 US/$28.95 CAN

The best of the best– all the essential reference tables and configuration settings without the bulk for the full version of *Upgrading and Repairing PCs*. Just a few of the many improvements for readers are

Hundreds of Tables: This edition includes tables and charts on everything from BIOS settings, to monitor sizing, to jumper settings for corner peripherals IDE Drives to SCSI data-transfer rates and more!

Troubleshooting and Error-Code Coverage: IBM and AMI Bios Audio Post Codes Nonfatal System Board Errors Personal Computer Error Codes.

Top 100 Vendor Reference: The top 100 vendors including addresses, phone numbers, and URLs.

Originating out of the best-selling PC hardware book ever– *Upgrading and Repairing PCs* (1.5 million units sold worldwide).

The essential tables and data! Covering memory, IRQ and BIOS tables, drive controller specifications, error code listings, configurations and settings, and more.

The necessary reference material without the bulk. This edition provides the reader with the necessary accurate tables and settings for repairing hardware and the convenience of scale for portability.

201 W. 103rd Street, Indianapolis, Indiana
Orders: 1-800-428-5331   **FAX:** 1-800-835-3202   **Customer Service:** 1-800-858-7674

MICRO HOUSE
PC Hardware Library

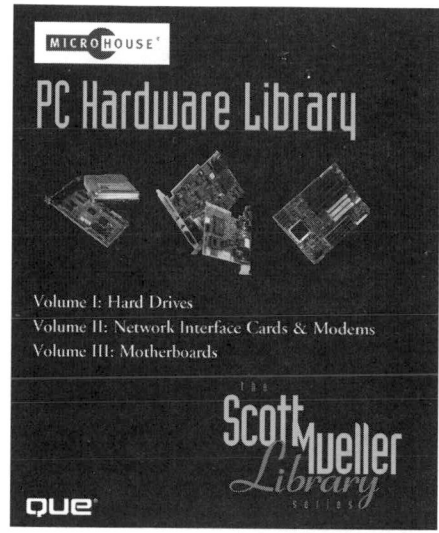

Part of the new Scott Mueller Library series, the *Micro House PC Hardware Library* is the most complete documentation of PC hardware available anywhere. This three volume set includes the following components: *Volume I: Hard Disks, Volume II: Network Interface Cards and Modems, Volume III: Motherboards*. Each of these components begins with a thorough explanation of the relevant hardware and settings that will be detailed in the reference material that follows. The bulk of the book (over 400 pages for each book) consists of the tables, diagrams, and functions of the specific pieces of hardware.

> Set-up specifications for over 4000 drives and drive controller cards.

> Set-up and configuration information for over 500 modems, network cards, and other communication devices such as ISDN terminal adapters.

0-7897-1662-3
Pub Date 6/17/98
$99.99 US/$142.95 CAN

Specifications and settings for over 200 motherboards from Intel and major vendors. The CD-ROM included with the kit includes all the specifications from the printed books in the powerful support source search and retrieval database.

Also included on the CD-ROM is Micro House's Image Cast LE hard disk imaging utility along with other useful hardware set-up and configuration utilities

---

201 W. 103rd Street, Indianapolis, Indiana
Orders: 1-800-428-5331   **FAX:** 1-800-835-3202   **Customer Service:** 1-800-858-7674

MICRO HOUSE

Computer Dictionary

This book is a complete reference on the terms and acronyms relating to computers, hardware, software, programming, data communications, and more. The reader is provided detailed explanations about each acronym rather than short often empty standard dictionary definitions. Because the technology is often somewhat complex, the explanation associated with it must be as detailed and accurate as possible. This encyclopedia gives the reader cross references to additional material in the text which will further explain a term or the technology. Readers are often directed to websites for additional information. This is the one-stop resource for anyone trying be learn what a term/acronym in the computer technology area means.

A complete reference on computer and software terms in the information technology arena

This Encyclopedia has detailed descriptions and explanations about the acronym defined that satisfy the reader's quest for knowledge/explanation

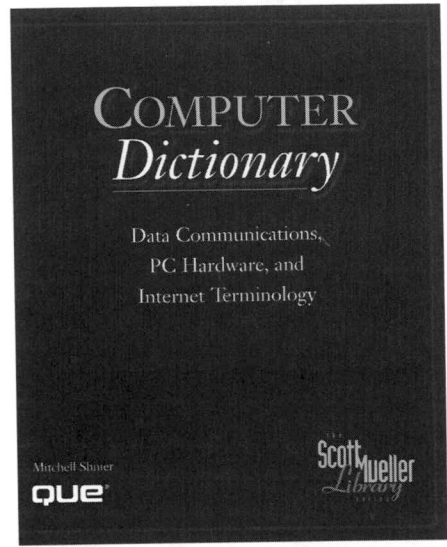

0-7897-1670-4
Pub Date 5/20/98
$19.99 US/$28.95 CAN

The acronyms and terms defined have definitions/explanations that span one or more pages where necessary rather than just one small paragraph (often found in Dictionaries) that leaves the reader "still hungry". This title is the complete dictionary/reference for anyone exposed to computers and computer technology

201 W. 103rd Street, Indianapolis, Indiana
Orders: 1-800-428-5331 **FAX:** 1-800-835-3202 **Customer Service:** 1-800-858-7674

pgrading and Repairing PCs, nth Anniversary Edition

Scott Muller

nk you for making *Upgrading and Repairing PCs* by Scott Muller the best-selling PC hardware ir book ever. Please help us tailor the content of the next edition to best fit your needs by taking a minutes to complete and return this self-addressed form.

Does your job involve upgrading, repairing, building, or troubleshooting PCs on a regular basis?
❏ Yes   ❏ No

Why did you buy this book?
❏ Professional use   ❏ Personal use

Where did you buy this book?
❏ Bookstore   ❏ Computer Store   ❏ Consumer Electronics Store   ❏ Department Store
❏ Office Club   ❏ Warehouse Club   ❏ Direct from Publisher   ❏ Mail Order
❏ Internet Site   ❏ Other _____

Are you A+ certified?
❏ Yes   ❏ No

f you answered "No" to question 2, do you plan to become A+ certified in the next 6 months?
❏ Yes   ❏ No

What types of processors are in the computers that you currently use, upgrade, repair, build, or troubleshoot?
❏ Pentium II/Celeron/Zeon   ❏ Mobile Pentium II   ❏ Pentium Pro
❏ Pentium/Pentium MMX   ❏ Mobile Pentium   ❏ 486
❏ 386   ❏ AMD K6 II   ❏ AMD K6
❏ AMD K5   ❏ Cyrix Media GX   ❏ Cyrix 6x86/6x86MX
❏ Other _____

What type of bus slots are in use in the systems that you currently use, upgrade, repair, build, or troubleshoot?
❏ AGP   ❏ PCI   ❏ VL-Bus   ❏ EISA
❏ MCA   ❏ 16-bit ISA   ❏ 8-bit ISA

What types of removable magnetic media drives are currently in use in the systems that you use, upgrade, epair, build, or troubleshoot?
❏ 360K 5 1/4" floppy   ❏ 1.2M 5 1/4" floppy   ❏ 720K 3 1/2" floppy
❏ 1.44M 3 1/2" floppy   ❏ 2.88M floppy   ❏ 21M floptical
❏ LS-120 (120M)   ❏ Zip   ❏ Jazz
❏ Syquest or other optical   ❏ Sparq   ❏ Other _____

What type of hard drive interfaces are currently in use in the systems that you use, upgrade, repair, build, r troubleshoot?
❏ ST-506/412   ❏ ESDI   ❏ IDE   ❏ SCSI

10. **What operating systems are currently in use in the systems that you use, upgrade, repair, build, or troubleshoot?**
- ❏ MS DOS 5 or earlier DOS versions
- ❏ MS DOS 6.x
- ❏ Windows 95
- ❏ Windows 9
- ❏ Windows NT 3.5x
- ❏ Windows NT 4
- ❏ Other _____

11. **What troubleshooting, diagnostic, or configuration software do you use to upgrade, repair, build, or troubleshoot PCs?**
- ❏ Norton Utilities
- ❏ Checkit
- ❏ MicroScope
- ❏ Ghost
- ❏ Disk Manager
- ❏ Tools provided with operating system (MSD,
- ❏ Other (please specify product name) _____ Windows 9x Control Panel, Windows 98 System Informa

12. **What hardware or tools do you use to upgrade, repair, build, or troubleshoot PCs?**
- ❏ POST card
- ❏ memory tester
- ❏ Loopback connectors (wrap plugs)
- ❏ Logic probe
- ❏ Digital multi-meter
- ❏ Other (please specify) _____

13. **Please list any upgrading, repairing, troubleshooting, or hardware configuration topics that are not covered this book that you would like to see covered or topics that are covered that should be covered in more detail differently.**

14. **What other books in the Scott Mueller Library do you plan on purchasing in the next six months?**
- ❏ Micro House PC Hardware Library
- ❏ Phil Croucher's BIOS Companion
- ❏ Computer Dictiona
- ❏ Upgrading and Repairing Networks
- ❏ Upgrading and Repairing PCs Quick Reference Second Edition

15. **If you have any additional overall comments about *Upgrading and Repairing PCs* or Scott Mueller, please li them here.**

Please print your name and sign here if you give Macmillan Computer Publishing permission to use your comm in marketing, sales, or promotional material related to this book.

Print Name

Signature

FOLD HERE AND TAPE TO

Ilᵐᵖᵉ┃ᵖᵉᵐᵐᵖᵉ┃

Upgrading 10th Anniversary
Macmillan Computer Publishing
201 West 103rd Street
Indianapolis, IN 46290